Schroeder's Collectible
TOYS
Antique to Modern
Price Guide

Eighth Edition

Edited by Sharon and Bob Huxford

COLLECTOR BOOKS
A Division of Schroeder Publishing Co., Inc.

The current values in this book should be used only as a guide. They are not intended to set prices, which vary from one section of the country to another. Auction prices as well as dealer prices vary greatly and are affected by condition as well as demand. Neither the editors nor the publisher assumes responsibility for any losses that might be incurred as a result of consulting this guide.

On The Cover:

Front: Lehman Halloh tin windup motorcycle, 8" x 7", 1930s, $3,500.00 – 4,000.00. Brumberger two-story contemporary dollhouse, 20" x 24", 1970, $60.00. Chein Krazy Kat, wood jointed, 7", 1920s, $1,250.00. Tippco VW Coca-Cola Truck, German, 9", 1950s, $1,000.00. Dakin Practical Pig, 7½", $45.00. Comet Curtiss Tiger Shark model plane, 13½", $175.00.

Back: Dick Tracy Detective Set, 1930s, #119, EX (VG box), $125.00. Freezy Sliddle Liddle Kiddle, $65.00. Fisher-Price Katy Kackler wooden pull-toy, $225.00.

Editorial Staff:

Editors: Sharon and Bob Huxford
Research and Editorial Assistants: Michael Drollinger, Donna Newnum, Loretta Suiters
Cover Design: Beth Summers
Layout: Terri Hunter and Beth Ray

Searching For A Publisher?

We are always looking for people knowledgeable within their fields. If you feel that there is a real need for a book on your collectible subject and have a large comprehensive collection, contact Collector Books.

COLLECTOR BOOKS
P.O. Box 3009
Paducah, Kentucky 42002-3009
www.collectorbooks.com

Introduction

Isn't it interesting how things change? The nineties saw an incredible surge of interest in toy collecting. Prices soared, toy shows were held nationwide with record attendances, new trade papers and magazines hit the stands one after another, and it was 'good.' Suddenly, everyone became computer literate, and somebody flipped the switch. The result? Change!

There's no denying that the antiques and collectibles market in general has been profoundly affected by the Internet, eBay in particular. With the number of eBay listings ever increasing, it is a given that the supply and demand balance has been affected; that needs no discussion. And 'pickers' are no more; suddenly everyone is a dealer. The toy they found at Saturday's garage sale goes on eBay first thing Monday morning, with a reserve usually well under 'book,' since at garage sale prices, they generally invest very little money in their purchases. Unless it is an especially collectible item that results in an active bidding war, it will do well to bring 75% of the established value. Good for the buyer; good for the seller.

We spent some time talking with our advisors this year, and they were very vocal and extremely insightful in their observations of today's vacillating market. Bob Armstrong (our puzzles expert) gives a scenario relative to his field, but one that typifies all areas of collecting: "Essentially, eBay has cut out the middle man, making it easy for anyone who finds old puzzles and other collectibles in a relative's home or at a yard sale to list the items themselves. The result has been to reduce the inventories of most dealers, putting many out of business, while encouraging a flood of collectibles onto the market, overwhelming it, and killing prices of many items. The days of other dealers and pickers offering me batches of puzzles at moderate prices are over; now they sell them themselves."

Dan Iannotti (our modern banks advisor) explains his reason for lowering banks prices this year: "The primary reason is the (result) of the Internet, primarily eBay auctions. This current phenomenon illustrates the forces at work which bring to the entire globe a 'giant worldwide flea market economy' — with the added excitement of individual auction bidding. The collectible landscape has changed forever."

As a result, the market is constantly changing. Where we saw our values drop dramatically in this edition were for toys of recent vintage, still generally readily available — fast-food toys, action figures, etc. Even mid-century battery-ops were affected by about 25%. But had the prices of some toys become unreasonably high? Probably. As one advisor says, eBay has served to "wake people up to realistic values."

And though values of some toys have softened, in other areas they have remained stable, and in some cases, gains were made. Quality tin toys, pressed steel, dolls, good Christmas and Halloween items, better character collectibles, vintage GI Joes, Transformers — good merchandise in general — at the very least held their own.

Even if (as some say) investors have all but disappeared from the scene, the true collector is alive and well, still buying for all the right reasons, the most important of which is personal enjoyment. To quote from Joel Cohen, of Cohen Books and Collectibles (our Disney specialist): "Like the art world, like the book world, things go in and out of favor. In my opinion, 'good stuff' will always be in favor. Prices might drop and prices will rise, but these things will always be wanted by the collector. Gloom in the market? Maybe for the weekend seller. Maybe for the investor that purchased what he considered a rare find only to learn today that he can quickly locate many of the same item at a lower price than he paid only a couple of years ago. Hurray for the collector! This is the first time in history that anyone can do a search — at home! — for an item that years ago he could not locate even after making many phone calls, traveling to numerous antique shows and flea markets, searching the classifieds, and going to auctions. (If he did locate the item) he would most likely purchase it at whatever price."

Regarding the plight of the toy dealer, he goes on to say: "I believe that even though the Internet has opened up the world to the collector, allowing him to buy and sell to other collectors, bypassing the dealer, there is still a place for the 'true dealer' in this world of antiques and collectibles — the dealer who participates in his business full time. He cannot be just a weekend warrior. He must be able to buy, sell, and appraise full time. He must be an expert in his field of endeavor. He must build up a reputation. He must be willing not to expect to double his money but rather to make a reasonable profit on his items. Though many have dropped out of the market, there will still be room for those with the stated qualifications."

There's no doubt that the number of toy shows being held is down all across the country, as is attendance, simply due to the fact that it is more convenient for both buyer and seller to stay at home and deal via the Internet. No booth expenses, no days lost to travel, no food or lodging expenses — just the comfort of home. Many dealers now have their own websites; others choose to sell their merchandise through online auctions. This has affected trade papers as well, through loss of advertising.

Where do these changes point? Is all doom and gloom? Pamela Apkarian-Russell, author of several books and our advisor on Halloween, offered an interesting observation. She believes the market is self-perpetuating in that during peak time when strong activity results in very high prices, new collectors are essentially discouraged from becoming involved. When prices are high, young families attend shows in fewer numbers, and children (the next generation of collectors) are seldom exposed to the fun and adventure of finding an inexpensive toy they can afford to purchase within the limits of their allowances. The peak passes, due in part to the lack of involvement on the part of new collectors. Prices drop, and once again, the younger collector finds he can afford to become interested. Off goes the family to the toy show, children buy the snow domes and action figures, and a new wave of interest is created.

Yes, change is interesting. Just about the time we were convinced to discount all else, now it seems, there is noticible change in eBay. Perhaps it is not going to be the know-all, be-all dominator of the marketplace after all. Perhaps its influence is waning, cooling to some degree, not as strong as we assumed it would always be. It can be fickle. Though the numbers of posted items continue to climb, sellers find that some things are not sellable after all, even on eBay. Recent studies cite dropping prices over the past year, due in part to shipping charges that are passed on to the buyer (many including the cost of handling and packing material), items that have been fraudulently represented (often by sellers who simply are not knowledgeable about their merchandise), buyers that too often do not follow through with their end of the bargain, and simply put, more supply than there is demand.

Complicated enough without factoring in the state of the economy, isn't it? Though, of course, we must. Some of our advisors felt that in truth the Internet was not the fly in the ointment, the economy was. But no matter the equation, the prime and basic element that guarantees the viability of the collectible toy market is the eternal resiliency of the toy collector and their love of the toys of their youth. There are no words to describe the thrill of finding the same sparking, walking, gun-firing Japanese robot you first found under the Christmas tree thirty years ago.

So perhaps after the toy boom explosion, the dust will simply settle, the chaff will winnow away, and as so many of our advisors feel, the elements of value will remain. And we'll be into the next phase, which no doubt will also be full of change.

With such a market to deal with, this edition has been particularly difficult to edit. Some of our advisors are comfortable with accepting online auction results as a market barometer, others are not. Our viewpoint tends to lean toward regarding them as an additional source of good information but one that requires some study and research to interpret. With the help of many qualified people, our purpose with this book is to offer the best, most inclusive learning tool possible to prepare. We try very hard not to omit categories where we find even a minor amount of market activity — being collectors ourselves, we know how frustrating it can be when you are unable to find any information on an item in question. You will find that we have represented toys of all kinds, from the nineteenth century up to today.

Our concept is unique. Though we designed the book first and foremost to be a price guide, we wanted to make it a buying/selling guide as well. So we took many of our descriptions and values from the websites and toys for sale lists of dealers and collectors around the country. In each of those listings we included a dealer's code, so that if you were looking for the particular toy that S5 (for example) had to offer, you'd be able to match his code with his name and address in the Dealers' Codes section and simply drop him a line or call him to see if it were still available. Our experiment has been very successful. Feedback indicates that many of our sellers do very well, making productive contacts with collectors who not only purchase items from them on their initial call but leave requests for other merchandise they are looking for as well.

Each edition contains about 24,000 listings, but even at that we realize that when it comes to the toy market, that only began to scratch the surface. Our intent is to provide our readers with fresh information, issue after issue. The few categories that are repeated in their entirety in succeeding editions generally are those that were already complete or as nearly complete as we or our advisors could make them. But even those are checked to make sure that values are still current and our information up to date.

Some of our values are auction results; you'll be able to recognize these by the 'A' at the end of the description line. The listings that have neither the 'A' code or the dealer code mentioned above were either sent to us by collectors who specialize in those specific types of toys or were originally dealer coded but altered at the suggestion of an advisor who felt that the stated price might be far enough outside the average market price range to be misleading (in which case, the dealer's code was removed). The bottom line is that there are two factors that determine selling price: the attitude of the individual collector (how strongly he desires to own) and the motivation of the dealer (does he need to turn over his merchandise quickly to replenish and freshen his stock, or can he wait for the most opportune time to turn it over for maximum profit). Where you buy affects prices as well. One of our advisors used this simple analogy: while a soda might cost you $2.50 at the ball park, you can buy the same thing for 39¢ at the corner 7 – 11. So all we (or anyone) can offer is whatever facts and information we can compile, and ask simply that you arrive at your own evaluations based on the data we've provided, adapted to your personal buying/selling arena.

We hope you enjoy our book and that you'll be able to learn by using it. We don't presume to present it as the last word on toys or their values — there are many specialized books by authors who are able to devote an entire publication to one subject, covering it from 'A' to 'Z,' and when we're aware that such a text book exists, we'll recommend it in our narratives. If you have suggestions that you think will improve our format, let us hear from you — we value your input. Until next time — happy hunting! May you find that mint-in-the-box #1 Barbie or, if you prefer, that rare mechanical bank that has managed to so far elude you. But even if you never do, we wish you much enjoyment, a treasure now and then, and new friends along the way.

— The Editors

Advisory Board

The editors and staff take this opportunity to express our sincere gratitude and appreciation to each person who has contributed their time and knowledge to help us. We've found toys to be *by far* the largest, most involved field of collecting we've ever tried to analyze, but we will have to admit, it's great fun! We've been editing general price guides for twenty years now, and before ever attempting the first one, we realized there was only one way we would presume to publish such a guide — and that would be to first enlist the help of knowledgeable collectors around the country who specialized in specific areas. We now have more than one hundred toy advisors, and we're still looking for help in several areas. Generally, the advisors are listed following each category's narrative, so if we have mentioned no one and you feel that you are qualified to advise us, have the time, and would be willing to help us out with that subject, please contact us. We'd love to have you on our advisory board. (We want to stress that even if an advisor is credited in a category narrative, that person is in no way responsible for errors — those are our responsibility.) Even if we currently list an advisor for your subject, contact us so that we'll have your name on file should that person need to be replaced. This of course happens from time to time due to changing interests or because they find they no longer have the time.

While some advisors sent us listings and prices, others provided background information and photographs, checked printouts, or simply answered our questions. All are listed below. Each name is followed by their code, see the section called *Dealer and Collector Codes* for an explanation of how these are used in the listings.

Matt and Lisa Adams (A7)	Bill Campbell (C10)	Larry DeAngelo (D3)
Geneva Addy (A5)	Candelaine (Candace Gunther) (G16)	Doug Dezso
Diane Albert (T6)	Casey's Collectible Corner (C1)	Dawn Diaz (P2)
Sally and Stan Alekna (A1)	Brad Cassity (C13)	Donna and Ron Donnelly (D7)
Pamela E. Apkarian-Russell (H9)	Mark Chase (C2)	George Downs (D8)
Bob Armstrong (A4)	Ken Clee (C3)	Larry Doucet (D11)
Richard Belyski (B1)	Joel Cohen (C12)	Marcia Fanta (M15)
Larry Blodget (B2)	Cotswold Collectibles (C6)	Paul Fink (F3)
Bojo (B3)	Marilyn Cooper (C9)	Steve Fisch (F7)
Scott Bruce (B14)	Cynthia's Country Store (C14)	Mike and Kurt Fredericks (F4)
Felicia Browell	Rosalind Cranor (C15)	Fun House Toy Co. (F5)
Jim Buskirk (B6)	Marl Davidson (D2)	Lee Garmon

Bill Hamburg (H1)
George Hardy (H3)
Joan and Jerry Harnish (H4)
Amy Hopper
Tim Hunter (H13)
Dan Iannotti (I3)
Kerry and Judy Irvin (K5)
Terri Ivers (I2)
Ed Janey (J2)
Keith and Donna Kaonis (K6)
David Kolodny-Nagy (K2)
Trina and Randy Kubeck (K1)
Tom Lastrapes (L4)
Kathy and Don Lewis (L6)
Val and Mark Macaluso (M1)
Helen L. McCale (M12)
John McKenna (M2)
Nancy McMichael (M18)
Michael and Polly McQuillen (M11)
Lucky Meisenheimer (M3)

Steven Meltzer (M9)
Bruce Middleton (M20)
Gary Mosholder (G1)
Judith Mosholder (M7)
Peter Muldavin (M21)
Natural Way/Russian Toy Co. (N1)
Roger Nazeley (N4)
Dawn Diaz (P2)
Diane Patalano (P8)
Pat Peterson (P1)
The Phoenix Toy Soldier Co. (P11)
Pat and Bill Poe (P10)
Gary Pollastro (P5)
Judy Posner (P6)
Michael Paquin (P12)
John Rammacher (S5)
Jim Rash (R3)
Robert Reeves (R4)
Charlie Reynolds (R5)
David Riddle (R6)

Cindy Sabulis (S14)
Brian Semling (Brian's Toys) (S8)
Scott Smiles (S10)
Carole and Richard Smyth (S22)
Steve Stephenson (S25)
Bill Stillman (S6)
Nate Stoller (S7)
Mark and Lynda Suozzi (S24)
Toy Scouts, Inc. (Bill Bruegman) (T2)
Richard Trautwein (T3)
Marcie and Bob Tubbs (T5)
Judy and Art Turner (H8)
Marci Van Ausdall (V2)
James Watson (W8)
Randy Welch (W4)
Dan Wells (W1)
Larry White (W7)
Mary Young (Y2)
Henri Yunes (Y1)

How to Use This Book

Concept. Our design for this book is two-fold. Primarily it is a market report compiled from many sources, meant to be studied and digested by our readers, who can then better arrive at their own conclusion regarding prices. Were you to ask ten active toy dealers for their opinion as to the value of a specific toy, you would no doubt get ten different answers, and who's to say which is correct? Quite simply, there are too many variables to consider. Where you buy is critical. Condition is certainly subjective, prices vary from one area of the country to another, and probably the most important factor is how badly you want to add the item in question to your collection or at what price you're willing to sell. So use this as a guide along with your own observations.

The second function of this book is to put buyers in touch with sellers who deal in the type of toys they want to purchase. We contact dealers allover the country, asking them to send us their 'for sale' lists and permission to use them as sources for some of our listings, which we code so as to identify the dealer from whose inventory list the price and description are taken. Even though by publication much of their merchandise will have been sold since we entered our data early last spring, many of them tell us that they often get similar or even the same items in over and over, so if you see something listed you're interested in buying, don't hesitate to call any of them. Remember, though, they're not tied down to the price quoted in the book, since their asking price is many times influenced by what they've had to pay to restock their shelves.

Toys are listed by name. Every effort has been made to list a toy by the name as it appears on the original box. There have been very few exceptions made, and then only if the collector-given name is more recognizable. For instance, if we listed 'To-Night Amos 'n Andy in Person' (as the name appears on the box lid), very few would recognize the toy as the Amos 'n Andy Walkers. But these exceptions are few.

Descriptions and sizes may vary. When we were entering data, we often found the same toy had sold through more than one auction gallery or was listed in several dealer lists. So the same toy will often be described in various ways, but we left descriptions just as we found them, since there is usually something to be gleaned from each variation. We chose to leave duplicate lines in when various conditions were represented so that you could better understand the impact of condition on value. Depending on the source and who was doing the measuring, we found that the size of a given toy might vary by an inch or more. Not having the toy to measure ourselves, we had to leave dimensions just as they were given in auction catalogs or dealer lists.

Lines are coded as to source. Each line that represents an auction-realized price will be coded 'A' at the end, just before the price. Other letter/number codes identify the dealer who sent us that information. These codes are explained later on. Additional sources of like merchandise will be noted under the narratives. These are dealers whose lists arrived at our office too late to be included in the lines themselves.

As we said before, collectors have various viewpoints regarding auction results. You will have to decide for yourself. Some feel they're too high to be used to establish prices while others prefer them to 'asking' prices that can sometimes be speculative. But for the most part, auction prices were not far out of line with accepted values. Many times, compared to the general market place, toys in less-than-excellent condition actually sold under 'book.' Because the average auction-consigned toy is in especially good condition and many times even retains its original box, it will naturally bring higher prices than the norm. And auctions often offer the harder-to-find, more unusual items. Unless you take these factors into consideration, prices may seem high, when in reality, they may not be at all. Prices may be driven up by high reserves, but not all galleries have reserves. Whatever your view, you'll be able to recognize and consider the source of the values we quote and factor that into your personal evaluation.

Categories that have priority. Obviously there are thousands of toys that would work as well in one category as they would in another, depending on the preference of the collector. For instance, a Mary Poppins game would appeal to a games collector just as readily as it would to someone who bought character-related toys of all kinds. The same would be true of many other types of toys. We tried to make our decisions sensibly and keep our sorts simple. But to avoid sending our character advisors such huge printouts, we felt that it would be best to pull out specific items and genres to create specific categories, thereby reducing the size of the character category itself. We'll guide you to those specialized categories with cross-references and 'See Also' notations. If all else fails, refer to the index. It's as detailed as we know how to make it.

Price Ranges. Once in awhile, you'll find a listing that gives a price range. These result from our having found varying prices for the same item. We've taken a mid-range — less than the highest, a little over the lowest — if the original range was too wide to really be helpful. If the range is still coded 'A' for auction, all that were averaged were auction-realized prices.

Condition, how it affects value, how to judge it. The importance of condition can't be stressed enough. Unless a toy is exceptionally rare, it must be very good or better to really have much collector value. But here's where the problem comes in: though each step downward on the grading scale drastically decreases a toy's value, as the old saying goes, 'beauty is in the eye of the beholder.' What is acceptable wear and damage to one individual may be regarded by another as entirely too degrading. Criteria used to judge condition even varies from one auction company to the next, so we had to attempt to sort them all out and arrive at some sort of standardization. Please be sure to read and comprehend what the description is telling you about condition; otherwise you can easily be misled. Auction galleries often describe missing parts, repairs and paint touch-ups, summing up overall appearance in the condition code. When losses and repairs were noted in the catalog, we noted them as well. Remember that a toy even in mint restored condition is never worth as much as one in mint original condition. And even though a toy may be rated 'otherwise EX' after losses and repairs are noted, it won't be worth as much as one with original paint and parts in excellent condition. Keep this in mind when you use our listings to evaluate your holdings.

These are the conditions codes we have used throughout the book and their definitions as we have applied them:

M — mint. Unplayed with, brand new, flawless.
NM — near mint. Appears brand new except on very close inspection.
EX — excellent. Has minimal wear, very minor chips and rubs, a few light scratches.
VG — very good. Played with, loss of gloss, noticeable problems, several scratches.
G — good. Some rust, considerable wear and paint loss, well used.
P — poor. Generally unacceptable except for a filler.

Because we do not use a three-level pricing structure as many of you are used to and may prefer, we offer this table to help you arrive at values for toys in conditions other than those that we give you. If you know the value of a toy in excellent condition and would like to find an approximate value for it in near mint condition, for instance, just run your finger down the column under 'EX' until you find the approximate price we've listed (or one that easily factors into it), then over to the column headed 'NM.' We'll just go to $100.00, but other values will be easy to figure by addition or multiplication.

G	VG	EX	NM	M
40/50%	55/65%	70/80%	85/90%	100%
5.00	6.00	7.50	9.00	10.00
7.50	9.00	11.00	12.50	15.00
10.00	12.00	15.00	18.00	20.00
12.00	15.00	18.00	22.00	25.00
14.00	18.00	22.50	26.00	30.00
18.00	25.00	30.00	35.00	40.00
22.50	30.00	37.50	45.00	50.00
27.00	35.00	45.00	52.00	60.00
32.00	42.00	52.00	62.00	70.00
34.00	45.00	55.00	65.00	75.00
35.00	48.00	60.00	70.00	80.00
40.00	55.00	68.00	80.00	90.00
45.00	60.00	75.00	90.00	100.00

Condition and value of original boxes and packaging. When no box or packaging is referred to in the line or in the narrative, assume that the quoted price is for the toy only. Please read the narratives! In some categories (Corgi, for instance), all values are given for items mint and in original boxes. Conditions for boxes (etc.) are in parenthesis immediately following the condition code for the toy itself. In fact, any information within parenthesis at that point in the line will refer to packaging. Collector interest in boxes began several years ago, and today many people will pay very high prices for them, depending on scarcity, desirability, and condition. The more colorful, graphically pleasing boxes are favored, and those with images of well-known characters are especially sought-after. Just how valuable is a box? Again, this is very subjective to the individual. We asked this question to several top collectors around the country, and the answers they gave us ranged from 20% to 100% above mint-no-box prices.

Listing of Standard Abbreviations

These abbreviations have been used throughout this book in order to provide you with the most detailed descriptions possible in the limited space available. No periods are used after initials or abbreviations. When two dimensions are given, height is noted first. When only one measurement is given, it will be the greater — height if the toy is vertical, length if it is horizontal. (Remember that in the case of duplicate listings representing various conditions, we found that sizes often varied as much as an inch or more.)

al	aluminum
Am	American
att	attributed to
bl	blue
blk	black
brn	brown
bsk	bisque
cb	cardboard
CI	cast iron
compo	composition
dbl	double
dk	dark
dtd	dated
emb	embossed
EX	excellent
F	fine
fr	frame, framed
ft, ftd	feet, foot, footed
G	good
gr	green
hdl	handle, handled
hdw	hardware
illus	illustrated, illustration
inscr	inscribed
jtd	jointed
L	long, length
litho	lithographed
lt	light, lightly
M	mint
MBP	mint in bubble pack
mc	multicolored
MIB	mint in box
MIP	mint in package
mk	marked
MOC	mint on card
MOT	mint on tree
NM	near mint
NP	nickel plated
NRFB	never removed from box
NRFP	never removed from package
orig	original
o/w	otherwise
P	poor
pk	pink
pkg	package
pnt	paint, painted
pr	pair
prof	professional
rfn	refinished
rnd	round
rpl	replaced
rpr	repaired
rpt	repainted
rstr	restored
sz	size
turq	turquoise
unmk	unmarked
VG	very good
W	with, width, wingspan
wht	white
wm	white metal
w/	with
w/up	windup
yel	yellow

Action Figures

You will find a wide range of asking prices from dealer to dealer, and under the influence of e-Bay buying, prices have softened to a great extent. Be critical of condition! Original packaging is extremely important. In fact, when it comes to the recent issues, loose, played-with examples are seldom worth more than a few dollars. Remember, if no box is mentioned, values are for loose (unpackaged) dolls. When no size is given, assume figures are 3¾" or standard size for the line in question.

For more information we recommend *Collectible Action Figures, 2nd Edition*, by Paris and Susan Manos (Collector Books).

Advisors: George Downs (D8); Robert Reeves (R4), Best of the West.

Other Sources: B3, F5, I2, J2, M15.

See also Character, TV, and Movie Collectibles; Dolls, Celebrity; GI Joe; Star Trek; Star Wars.

A-Team, accessory, Headquarters Set, NRFB.....................$30.00
Advanced Dungeons & Dragons, figure, War Duke or Strongheart, 3¾", MOC, ea.....................$20.00
Adventures of Indiana Jones, accessory, Arabian Horse, Kenner, complete, M.....................$65.00
Adventures of Indiana Jones, accessory, Desert Convoy Truck, Kenner, MIB.....................$70.00
Adventures of Indiana Jones, accessory, Map Room, Kenner, MIB (sealed).....................$110.00
Adventures of Indiana Jones, accessory, Mola Ram, Kenner, MOC.....................$70.00
Adventures of Indiana Jones, figure, Cairo Swordsman, Kenner, 3¾", MOC.....................$30.00
Adventures of Indiana Jones, figure, Indiana Jones, Kenner, 3¾", MOC.....................$200.00
Adventures of Indiana Jones, figure, Toht, Kenner, 3¾", MOC.....................$30.00

Adventures of Indiana Jones, playset, Raiders of the Lost Ark, Well of the Souls, Kenner, 1982, MIB, from $100.00 to $125.00. (Photo courtesy June Moon)

Batgirl, figure, Ideal, 1967, bendable, 12", MIB, T2, from $1,250 to.....................**$1,750.00**

Batman, accessory, Switch 'N Go playset, Mattel, 1966, complete, VG (VG box).....................$250.00
Battlestar Galactica, figure, Colonial Scarab or Cylon Raider, Mattel, M (NM Canadian box), ea.....................$60.00
Battlestar Galactica, figure, Colonial Scarab, Mattel, 12", MIB (sealed).....................$45.00
Battlestar Galactica, figure, Cylon Raider, Mattel, remote control, 12", MIB (sealed).....................$195.00
Battlestar Galactica, figure, Cylon Raider, Mattel, remote control, 12", complete, M.....................$80.00
Battlestar Galactica, figure, Imperious Leader or Ovion, Mattel, 3¾", complete, MOC, ea from $10 to.....................$15.00
Battlestar Galactica, figure set, Cylon Centurian & Colonial Warrior, Mattel, 12", MIB.....................$125.00
Best of the West, accessory, Circle X Ranch, Marx, MIB, from $135 to.....................$160.00
Best of the West, accessory, Jeep & Horse Trailer, Marx, MIB.....................$150.00
Best of the West, accessory, Johnny West Covered Wagon, Marx, complete, EX (EX box), from $90 to.....................$135.00
Best of the West, accessory, Travel Case, Marx, NM.....................$30.00
Best of the West, figure, Bill Buck, Marx, complete, M (EX box), from $450 to.....................$590.00
Best of the West, figure, Captain Maddox, Marx, complete, NM (EX Fort Apache Fighters box).....................$115.00
Best of the West, figure, Captain Maddox, Marx, missing few accessories, VG.....................$45.00
Best of the West, figure, Chief Cherokee, Marx, complete, NM (NM box).....................$160.00
Best of the West, figure, Fighting Eagle, Marx, complete, NM.....................$150.00
Best of the West, figure, General Custer, Marx, complete, NM (VG Fort Apache Fighters box).....................$65.00
Best of the West, figure, Geronimo, Marx, missing few accessories, EX.....................$40.00
Best of the West, figure, Geronimo, Marx, missing few accessories, EX (VG box).....................$65.00
Best of the West, figure, Jaimie West, Marx, complete, NM (EX box).....................$75.00
Best of the West, figure, Jaimie West, Marx, missing few accessories, EX.....................$30.00
Best of the West, figure, Jane West, Marx/Canadian issue, missing few accessories, EX (EX box).....................$60.00
Best of the West, figure, Janice West, complete, NM (EX box).....................$45.00
Best of the West, figure, Janice West, Marx, no accessories, EX.....................$10.00
Best of the West, figure, Jay West, Marx, complete, NMIB.........$70.00
Best of the West, figure, Jed Gibson, Marx, complete, NMIB..$315.00
Best of the West, figure, Johnny West, Marx, complete, EX.......$45.00
Best of the West, figure, Johnny West, Marx, later version w/quick-draw arm, complete, NM.....................$40.00
Best of the West, figure, Josie West, Marx, MIB.....................$50.00
Best of the West, figure, Princess Wildflower, Marx, complete, NM.....................$60.00
Best of the West, figure, Princess Wildflower, Marx, complete, NMIB.....................$135.00
Best of the West, figure, Sam Cobra, Marx, complete, M.$60.00

Best of the West, figure, Sam Cobra, Marx, later version w/quick-draw grip, MIB $40.00

Best of the West, figure, Sam Cobra, Marx, missing few accessories, EX..$30.00

Best of the West, figure, Sam Cobra, Marx, missing few accessories, NM (EX box)................................$110.00

Best of the West, figure, Sheriff Garrett, Marx, complete, NM (VG box)..$175.00

Best of the West, figure, Sheriff Garrett, Marx, missing few accessories, NM $70.00

Best of the West, figure, Zeb Zachary, Marx, complete, EX (EX box), minimum value $135.00

Best of the West, figure set, Jane West & Flame, Marx, missing few accessories, EX (EX box) $165.00

Best of the West, figure set, Johnny West & Thunderbolt, Marx, missing few accessories, VG (VG box) $90.00

Best of the West, horse, Comanche, Marx, complete, EX (EX Fort Apache Fighters box) $110.00

Best of the West, horse, Flame, Marx, palomino, complete, EX (EX box) $110.00

Best of the West, horse, Flame, Marx, palomino, no accessories, EX..$30.00

Best of the West, horse, Pancho, Marx, palomino w/brn tack, complete, NM..$45.00

Best of the West, horse, Pancho, Marx, sorrel w/blk tack, complete, EX (EX box)..................................$75.00

Best of the West, horse, Pancho, Marx, sorrel w/blk tack, complete, NM..$45.00

Best of the West, horse, Thunderbolt, Marx, bay, no accessories, NM..$30.00

Best of the West, horse, Thunderbolt, Marx, blk, no accessories, VG $25.00

Best of the West, horse, Thunderbolt, Marx, blk w/blk tack, complete, NM, from $45 to $60.00

Best of the West, horse, Thunderbolt, Marx, cream colored, complete, EX (EX box)..............................$45.00

Best of the West, horse, Thunderbolt, Marx, palomino, NM (EX box), from $100.00 to $125.00.

Big Jim, accessory, Action Set, Mattel, several variations, MIB, ea $20.00

Big Jim, accessory, Jungle Truck, Mattel, M $45.00

Big Jim, accessory, Kung Fu Studio, Mattel, MIB..............$75.00

Big Jim, accessory, Motocross Honda, complete, NM.......$20.00

Big Jim, accessory, Rescue Rig, Mattel, complete, M $35.00

Big Jim, accessory, Safari Hut, Mattel, complete, NM......$20.00

Big Jim, accessory, Sea Rescue set, Mattel, complete, NM..$15.00

Big Jim, accessory, Sky Commander Jet, Mattel, MIB $50.00

Big Jim, accessory, Sports Camper w/Boat, Mattel, MIB...$45.00

Big Jim, figure, any character, Mattel, complete, EX, ea from $20 to $25.00

Big Jim, figure, Baron Fangg, English/Italian, Mattel, MIB, from $20.00 to $30.00.

Big Jim, figure, Big Jeff, #7316, NRFB..............................$50.00

Bionic Woman, accessory, Carriage House, Kenner, 1977, for 12" dolls, MIB, from $180 to $225.00

Bionic Woman, accessory, Dome House, Kenner, 1976, MIB $50.00

Bionic Woman, figure, Fembot, Kenner, 1977, 12", MIB..$160.00

Black Hole, figure, Alex Durant, Charles Pizer, Hans Reinhardt or Harry Booth, Mego, 12", MIB, ea from $45 to $65.00

Black Hole, figure, Dan Holland, 1979, 8", MIB $22.00

Black Hole, figure, Hans Reinhardt, Mego, MOC............$25.00

Black Hole, figure, Maximillian, Mego, MOC..................$35.00

Black Hole, figure, Old Bob, Mego, rare, MOC..............$215.00

Black Hole, figure, Sentry, Mego, MOC $40.00

Black Hole, figure, Vincent, Mego, MOC........................$50.00

Blackstar, accessory, Battle Set, MIP $50.00

Blackstar, figure, Vizir, MOC...$25.00

Blackstar, figure, White Knight, MOC.............................$30.00

Bonanza, figure, Ben, Little Joe, Hoss or Outlaw, Am Character, 8", ea from $180 to $225.00

Buck Rogers, figure, any character, Mego, 12", MIB.........$65.00

Buck Rogers, figure, any character, Mego, 3¾", MOC, ea ..$20.00

Buddy Charlie, figure, Buddy, Marx, 12", rare, MIB $125.00

Captain Action, accessory, Action Cave, Ideal, M.........$100.00

Captain Action, accessory, Anti-Gravitational Power Pack, Ideal, complete, MIB..$180.00

Captain Action, accessory, Aquaman outfit, Ideal, complete, MIB, from $450 to $540.00

Captain Action, accessory, Buck Rogers outfit, Ideal, complete, M..$95.00

Captain Action, accessory, Directional Communicator, Ideal, 1966, MIB, T2 ....$200.00

Captain Action, accessory, Green Hornet outfit, Ideal, complete, MIB, from $1,800 to...................................$2,700.00

Captain Action, accessory, Inter-Galactic Jet Mortar, Ideal, complete, MIB $180.00

Captain Action, accessory, Jet Mortar, Ideal, MIB $100.00

Captain Action, accessory, Lone Ranger outfit, Ideal, complete, NM..$200.00

Captain Action, accessory, Lone Ranger outfit, Ideal, complete, MIB, from $720 to $900.00

Captain Action, accessory, Parachute Pack, Ideal, complete, NM..$65.00

Captain Action, accessory, Silver Streak Amphibian Car, Ideal, 1967, MIB, from $1,500 to.............................$2,500.00

Captain Action, accessory, Silver Streak Garage, Ideal/Sears, 24", NM, from $590 to $675.00

Captain Action, accessory, Steve Canyon outfit, Ideal, complete, NM, from $360 to.......................................$450.00

Captain Action, accessory, Survival Kit, Ideal, 1966, MIB, T2 ....$175.00

Captain Action, accessory, Weapons Arsenal, Ideal, MIB, from $200 to..$250.00

Captain Action, carrying case, opens to reveal headquarters, vinyl, Ideal, EX $75.00

Captain Action, figure, Action Boy, Ideal, 12", complete, EX..$360.00

Captain Action, figure, Captain Action, Ideal, 1967, complete, NMIB..$250.00

Captain Action, figure, Captain America, Ideal, 12", complete, M...$200.00

Captain Action, figure, Mera, Ideal, complete, rare, MIB...$400.00

Captain Action, figure, Phantom, Ideal, 1966, 12", MIB $175.00

Captain Action, figure, Robin, Ideal, 8½", complete, M..$225.00

Captain Action, figure, Steve Canyon, Ideal, 12", MIB.$215.00

Captain Action, figure, Super Girl, Ideal, complete, rare, MIB..$375.00

Captain Action, figure, Superman w/dog, Ideal, 1966-68, 12", M $150.00

Captain Planet & the Planeteers, figure, Commander Clash, Tiger/Kenner, MOC...$12.00

CHiPs, accessory, motorcycle, Mego, MIB.........................$50.00

CHiPs, figure set, Jon, Ponch & Sarge, Mego, 8", MOC..$45.00

Clash of the Titans, figure, Pegasus, MIB (sealed) $40.00

Cops, figure, Bullet Proof, Hasbro, 1988, M $7.00

Dragon Heart, figure, Draco, Medusa or Razorthorn, MOC, ea...$12.00

Dragon Heart, figure, Electronic Draco, MIB (sealed)......$55.00

Dragon Heart, figure set, Draco w/Bowen or Evil Griffin Dragon w/King, MIB (sealed), ea $15.00

Dukes of Hazzard, figure, Bo Duke, Mego, complete, M ...$30.00

Dukes of Hazzard, figure, Boss Hogg, Mego, complete, MOC...$22.00

Dungeons & Dragons, figure, Strongheart, Warduke or Zarak, MOC, ea...$20.00

Eagle Force, figure, Captain, Turk, Beta Man or Savitar, Mego, 1981, ea..$10.00

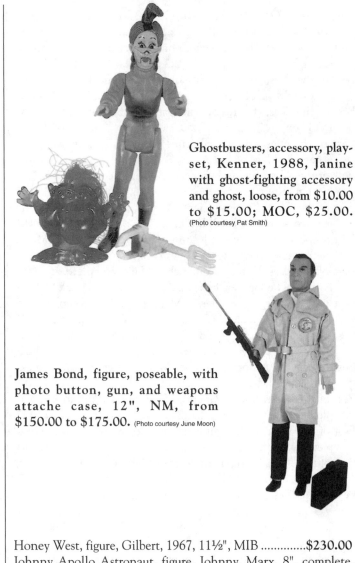

Ghostbusters, accessory, play-set, Kenner, 1988, Janine with ghost-fighting accessory and ghost, loose, from $10.00 to $15.00; MOC, $25.00.
(Photo courtesy Pat Smith)

James Bond, figure, poseable, with photo button, gun, and weapons attache case, 12", NM, from $150.00 to $175.00. (Photo courtesy June Moon)

Honey West, figure, Gilbert, 1967, 11½", MIB $230.00

Johnny Apollo Astronaut, figure, Johnny, Marx, 8", complete, MIB..$40.00

Knights & Vikings, figure, Gold Knight or Silver Knight, Marx, 1960s, MIB, ea $50.00

Knights & Vikings, horse, Gold Knight or Silver Knight, Marx, 1960s, M, complete..$30.00

Lone Ranger Rides Again, accessory, Prairie Wagon, Gabriel, MIB..$40.00

Lone Ranger Rides Again, accessory, Tribal Teepee, Gabriel, MIB..$35.00

Lone Ranger Rides Again, figure, any character, Gabriel, 9", MIB, H4, ea $50.00

Lost in Space, figure, Don West, Trendmasters, 8", MIB..$40.00

Lost in Space, figure, Judy Robinson, Trendmasters, 8", MIB $35.00

Lost in Space, figure, Tybo the Carrot Man, Trendmasters, 8", MIB $45.00

Lost in Space, figure, Will Robinson, Trendmasters, 8", MIB $40.00

Love Boat, accessory, Love Boat, Multi-Toys, 1983, MIB, from $50 to $60.00

M*A*S*H, accessory, Jeep w/Hawkeye, TriStar, 1981, MIB..$30.00

M*A*S*H, accessory, Military Base, TriStar International, complete, NMIB...$40.00

M*A*S*H, figure, any character, TriStar, 1981, 3¾", MOC, ea...$20.00

M*A*S*H, figure, Father Mulcahy, Mego, 3¾", MOC, from $15 to...$20.00

M*A*S*H, figure, Hot Lips, Mego, 3¾", MOC.............$20.00

Major Matt Mason, accessory, Astro Trac, Mattel, 1966, MIB...$100.00

Major Matt Mason, accessory, Jet Pak, Mattel, complete, EX...$10.00

Major Matt Mason, accessory, Mattel's Man in Space Talking Command Console, EX, $94.00. (Photo courtesy June Moon)

Major Matt Mason, accessory, Rocket Launch Pack, Mattel, complete, EX.......................................$20.00

Major Matt Mason, accessory, Satellite Locker, Mattel, 1967, EX..$30.00

Major Matt Mason, accessory, Space Crawler Action Set w/figure, Mattel, MIB.....................................$100.00

Major Matt Mason, accessory, Space Station, Mattel, 1966, MIB..$200.00

Major Matt Mason, figure, Callisto, Mattel, 1968, 6", MOC...$200.00

Major Matt Mason, figure, Doug Davis, Mattel, w/helmet, EX..$60.00

Major Matt Mason, figure, Jeff Long, Mattel, w/helmet, VG..$75.00

Major Matt Mason, figure, Matt Mason on glider w/talking backpack, Mattel, 1967, MIB..................................$450.00

Man From UNCLE, figure, Illya Kuryakin, Gilbert, 12", MIB.$100.00

Man From UNCLE, figure, Napoleon Solo, Gilbert, 12", complete, M..$60.00

Marvel Super Heroes, accessory, Batcave, Mego, MIB....$200.00

Marvel Super Heroes, figure, Aquaman, Mego, 8", complete, M...$125.00

Marvel Super Heroes, figure, Batman, Mego, 8", complete, M...$150.00

Marvel Super Heroes, figure, Batman, Mego, 8", MIB....$225.00

Marvel Super Heroes, figure, Captain America, Mego, 8", 1974, complete, M..$60.00

Marvel Super Heroes, figure, Catwoman, Mego, 8", MIB (sealed), from $300 to..$350.00

Marvel Super Heroes, figure, Falcon, Mego, 8", MIB (sealed)...$190.00

Marvel Super Heroes, figure, Green Arrow, Mego, 8", complete, M...$125.00

Marvel Super Heroes, figure, Green Goblin, Mego, complete, NM...$120.00

Marvel Super Heroes, figure, Green Goblin, Mego, 8", MIB....$350.00

Marvel Super Heroes, figure, Human Torch, Mego, 8", EX.........$40.00

Marvel Super Heroes, figure, Human Torch, Mego, 8", MIB....$180.00

Marvel Super Heroes, figure, Incredible Hulk, Just for Toys, M in package, $8.00.

Marvel Super Heroes, figure, Incredible Hulk, Mego, 8", MOC...$60.00

Marvel Super Heroes, figure, Iron Man, Mego, 8", complete, M...$65.00

Marvel Super Heroes, figure, Iron Man, Mego, 8", MIB.$150.00

Marvel Super Heroes, figure, Mr Fantastic, Mego, MOC (Canadian)..$60.00

Marvel Super Heroes, figure, Mr Mxyzptlk, Mego, 8", complete, M...$30.00

Marvel Super Heroes, figure, Mr Mxyzptlk, Mego, 8", MIB..$60.00

Marvel Super Heroes, figure, Penguin, Mego, 8", complete, M...$30.00

Marvel Super Heroes, figure, Penguin, Mego, 8", MIB.....$90.00

Marvel Super Heroes, figure, Riddler, Mego, 8", complete, M...$125.00

Marvel Super Heroes, figure, Riddler, Mego, 8", MIB....$200.00

Marvel Super Heroes, figure, Robin, Mego, 8", MIB........$90.00

Marvel Super Heroes, figure, Shazam!, Mego, 8", complete, M...$80.00

Marvel Super Heroes, figure, Spider-Man, Mego, 8", MIB..$60.00

Marvel Super Heroes, figure, Supergirl, Mego, 8", complete, M...$140.00

Marvel Super Heroes, figure, Superman, Mego, MIB (Japanese)..$450.00

Marvel Super Heroes, figure, Superman, Mego, 8", complete, M...$70.00

Marvel Super Heroes, figure, Superman, Mego, 8", MOC..$145.00

Marvel Super Heroes, figure, Thing, Mego, complete, M.$80.00

Marvel Super Heroes, figure, Thor, Mego, MIB.............$235.00

Marvel Super Heroes, figure, Thor, Mego, 8", complete, M..$95.00

Marvel Super Heroes, figure, Wonder Woman, Mego, 8", complete, M...$100.00

Marvel Super Heroes, figure set, Fantastic Four, Mr Fantastic, Thing, Human Torch, Invisible Girl, Mego, 8", MOC...$225.00

Marvel's X-Men X-Force, figure, G.W. Bridge, Toy Bizz #4955, jointed vinyl with molded-on clothes, 1992, M, $6.50. (Photo courtesy Myla Perkins)

Masters of the Universe, figure, any character except Hurricane Hordack or Flying Fists He-Man, MOC, ea from $15 to $20.00

Masters of the Universe, figure, Flying Fists He-Man, MOC...$40.00

Masters of the Universe, figure, Hurricane Hordak, complete, M..$25.00

Masters of the Universe, figure, Megator or Tytus, Mattel, MIB (sealed), ea...$325.00

Micronauts, accessory, Astro Station, EXIB.....................$50.00

Micronauts, accessory, Hydrocopter, MIB (sealed) $80.00

Micronauts, figure, Alphatron, Mego, MIB.....................$30.00

Micronauts, figure, Andromeda, Mego, MIB $50.00

Micronauts, figure, Antron, Mego, NRFB $100.00

Micronauts, figure, Baron Karza, Mego, MIB...................$75.00

Micronauts, figure, Betatron, Mego, MIB $25.00

Micronauts, figure, Blizzard, Mego, MIB $60.00

Micronauts, figure, Emperor, Mego, MIB......................$265.00

Micronauts, figure, Galactic Defender, Mego, MOC........$80.00

Micronauts, figure, Megas, Mego, NRFB..........................$60.00

Micronauts, figure, Microtron, Mego, complete, M $25.00

Micronauts, figure, Oberon, Mego, MIB $35.00

Micronauts, figure, Pegasus, gr version, Mego, MOC, from $40 to $50.00

Official Scout High Adventure, accessory, camping set, Kenner, complete, M..$25.00

Official Scout High Adventure, accessory, first-aid equipment, Kenner, complete, M $25.00

Official Scout High Adventure, accessory, observation tower, Kenner, complete, M $25.00

Official Scout High Adventure, figure, Bill Scout, Kenner, mail-in, rare, complete, M $45.00

Official Scout High Adventure, figure, Bob Scout, Kenner, MIB...$30.00

Official Scout High Adventure, figure, Craig Cub Scout, Kenner, MIB...$30.00

Official Scout High Adventure, figure, Dave Cub Scout, Kenner, MIB...$30.00

Official Scout High Adventure, figure, Steve Scout, Kenner, complete, M..$25.00

Official World's Greatest Super Heroes, accessory, Amazing Spider Car, EX..$15.00

Official World's Greatest Super Heroes, accessory, Amazing Spider Car, MIB..$50.00

Official World's Greatest Super Heroes, accessory, Batcopter, Mego, NM (NM box)..............................$175.00

Official World's Greatest Super Heroes, figure, Aquaman, Mego, 8", EX..$45.00

Official World's Greatest Super Heroes, figure, Aquaman, Mego, 8", M (NM box) $175.00

Official World's Greatest Super Heroes, figure, Batman, Bend'n Flex, Mego, 5", NMOC......................$50.00

Official World's Greatest Super Heroes, figure, Batman, Mego, 12", MIB..$75.00

Official World's Greatest Super Heroes, figure, Captain America, Mego, 8", EX $50.00

Official World's Greatest Super Heroes, figure, Falcon, Mego, 8", M (EX+ box) $85.00

Official World's Greatest Super Heroes, figure, Green Goblin, Mego, 8", EX..$125.00

Official World's Greatest Super Heroes, figure, Human Torch, Mego, 8", MOC..$50.00

Official World's Greatest Super Heroes, figure, Incredible Hulk, Mego, 8", MIB $100.00

Official World's Greatest Super Heroes, figure, Joker, Mego, 8", complete, M $55.00

Official World's Greatest Super Heroes, figure, Mr Mxyzptlk, Mego, 8", MOC (sealed) $175.00

Official World's Greatest Super Heroes, figure, Mr Mxyzptlk (smiling version), Mego, 8", EX $45.00

Official World's Greatest Super Heroes, figure, Penguin, Mego, 8", MOC (sealed) $125.00

Official World's Greatest Super Heroes, figure, Riddler, First Fighting, Mego, 8", M..................................$150.00

Official World's Greatest Super Heroes, figure, Riddler, Mego, 8", complete, NM $95.00

Official World's Greatest Super Heroes, figure, Robin, First Fighting, Mego, 8", M..................................$125.00

Official World's Greatest Super Heroes, figure, Shazam, Mego, 8", EX..$50.00

Official World's Greatest Super Heroes, figure, Spider-Man, Mego, 8", EX..$35.00

Official World's Greatest Super Heroes, figure, Spider-Man, Bend'n Flex, Mego, MOC $75.00

Official World's Greatest Super Heroes, figure, Spider-Man, Mego, 12", NRFB..$80.00

Official World's Greatest Super Heroes, figure, Supergirl, Bend'n Flex, Mego, MOC (sealed)....................$150.00

Official World's Greatest Super Heroes, figure, Superman, Bend'n Flex, Mego, MOC (sealed) $150.00

Official World's Greatest Super Heroes, figure, Tarzan, Mego, 8", EX...$45.00

Planet of the Apes, accessory, Forbidden Zone Trap, Mego, MIB (sealed) $265.00

Planet of the Apes, figure, Alan Verdon, Mego, 8", MOC..$130.00

Planet of the Apes, figure, Astronaut, Mego, 8", M..........$65.00

Planet of the Apes, figure, Cornelius, Mego, complete, 8", M...$50.00

Planet of the Apes, figure, Dr Zaius, Mego, complete, 8",
    M..**$50.00**

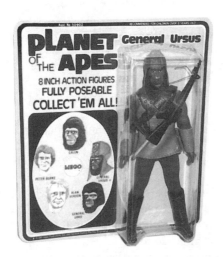

Planet of the Apes, figure, General Ursus, Mego, MOC, $350.00.

(Photo courtesy Jerry Harnish)

Planet of the Apes, figure, Peter Burke, Mego, 8", MOC...**$110.00**
Planet of the Apes, figure, Soldier Ape, Mego, complete, 8",
    M..**$55.00**
Planet of the Apes, figure, Soldier Ape, Mego, 8", MOC ...**$350.00**
Power Lords, figure, any character, MOC, ea from $20 to .**$30.00**
Rambo, accessory, .50 Caliber Machine Gun, Coleco, MIB
    (sealed) **$8.00**
Rambo, accessory, Weapons Pak, Coleco, 1985, MOC **$10.00**
Rapid Deployment Force, figure, any character, Time Products,
    1992, 12", MIB, ea **$12.00**
Robotech, accessory, Bioroid Hovercraft, MIB **$15.00**
Robotech, figure, Corg, Matchbox, MOC.........................**$12.50**
Robotech, figure, Dana Sterling, Matchbox, MOC..........**$15.00**
Robotech, figure, Lisa Hayes, Matchbox, MOC **$15.00**
Robotech, figure, Max Sterling, Matchbox, MOC **$15.00**
Robotech, figure, Miriya, Matchbox, purple version, MOC .**$15.00**
Robotech, figure, Miriya, Matchbox, red version, MOC..**$15.00**
Robotech, figure, Rick Hunter, Matchbox, MOC **$17.50**
Robotech, figure, Rook Bartley, Matchbox, MOC............**$17.50**
Ronin Warriors, figure, any character, MOC, ea from $10
    to **$15.00**
Rookies, accessory, Action Accessories Set, 1976, MIB ...**$20.00**
Rookies, accessory, police car, 1975, diecast, MOC..........**$10.00**
Six Million Dollar Man, accessory, Turbo Moto, Clipper, 1977,
    MIB **$60.00**
Six Million Dollar Man, accessory, Venus Space Probe, Kenner,
    1976, NRFB..**$700.00**
Six Million Dollar Man, figure, Oscar Goldman, Kenner, 12",
    MIB **$85.00**
Skeleton Warriors, figure, any character, MOC, ea from $8
    to **$10.00**
Space: 1999, figure, Dr Russell, Mattel, 1975, MOC........**$20.00**
Space: 1999, figure, Professor Bergman, Mattel, 1975, MOC...**$20.00**
Stargate, accessory, Winged Glider, MIB (sealed).............**$25.00**
Stargate, figure, any character, MOC, ea from $6 to.........**$10.00**
Starriors, figure, Backfire, MIB (sealed) **$20.00**
Starriors, figure, Speed Drill, loose, EX **$10.00**
Starriors, figure, Vultor, MIB..**$25.00**
Starriors, figure set, Deadeye & Cricket, MIB...................**$25.00**

Starsky & Hutch, figure, any character other than Starsky &
    Hutch, Mego, 1976, 2nd issue, MOC, ea from $20 to.**$30.00**
Starsky & Hutch, figure, Dobey, Mego, complete, 8", M..**$25.00**
Starsky & Hutch, figure, Huggy Bear, Mego, MOC..........**$35.00**
Starsky & Hutch, figure, Starsky or Hutch, Mego, 1975, 1st
    issue, MOC, ea from $25 to.......................................**$35.00**
Starsky & Hutch, figure, Starsky or Hutch, Mego, 1976, 2nd
    issue, MOC, ea from $25 to.......................................**$35.00**

Stony Smith, figure, Battling Soldier, Marx, complete, NM in NM box, $185.00.

Super Pirates, figure, Black Beard, Mego, complete, 8", M....**$35.00**
Super Powers, accessory, Batmobile, Kenner, 1985, MIB **$100.00**
Super Powers, figure, Aquaman, Kenner, complete, NM..**$15.00**
Super Powers, figure, Batman, Kenner, MOC, from $40 to...**$50.00**
Super Powers, figure, Brainiac, Kenner, MOC.................**$20.00**

Super Powers, figures, Cyborg, Kenner, 1986, MOC, from $150.00 to $200.00; Samurai, Kenner, 1986, MOC, $45.00.
(Photo courtesy June Moon)

Super Powers, figure, Cyclotron, Kenner, complete, M **$25.00**
Super Powers, figure, Darkseid, Kenner, MOC **$15.00**
Super Powers, figure, Dr Fate, Kenner, complete, NM **$20.00**
Super Powers, figure, Firestorm, Kenner, MOC
    (unpunched)...**$25.00**
Super Powers, figure, Golden Pharaoh, Kenner, MOC.....**$30.00**
Super Powers, figure, Green Arrow, Kenner, MOC
    (unpunched)...**$25.00**
Super Powers, figure, Hawkman, Kenner, MOC
    (unpunched)...**$25.00**

Super Powers, figure, Lex Luthor, Kenner, MOC..............$15.00

Super Powers, figure, Mantis, Kenner, complete w/ID card & comic book, NM.......................................$20.00

Super Powers, figure, Mr Freeze, Kenner, complete, NM..$10.00

Super Powers, figure, Orion, Kenner, MOC (unpunched)..$30.00

Super Powers, figure, Penguin, Kenner, complete w/ID card & comic book, NM.......................................$20.00

Super Powers, figure, Red Tornado, Kenner, MOC..........$45.00

Super Powers, figure, Riddler, Kenner, MOC (unpunched Mexican Super Amigos).....................................$110.00

Super Powers, figure, Steppenwolf, Kenner, complete w/ID card & comic book, NM...............................$15.00

Super Powers, figure, Superman, Kenner, MOC (unpunched)..$40.00

Superman, accessory, Justice League of America playset, Multiple/Canada, 1967, complete, EX (EX box), T2, from $200 to...$250.00

SWAT, accessory, Air Assault, 1975, MOC.....................$10.00

SWAT, accessory, Rescue Parachute, 1976, MOC............$10.00

SWAT, accessory, truck, 1975, diecast, MOC.................$10.00

Thundercats, figure, any character, LJN, MOC, ea from $25 to...$35.00

Thundercats, figure, any character other than Stinger or Driller, LJN, MOC, ea from $20 to.......................$30.00

Thundercats, figure set, Cheetara w/Wilykit, LJN, EX.....$20.00

Waltons, figure set, Johnboy & Mary Ellen, Mom & Pop or Grandma & Grandpa, Mego, 1974, 8", MIB, ea........$35.00

Wizard of Oz, accessory, Wizard of Oz & His Emerald City, Mego, complete, MIB...............................$250.00

Wizard of Oz, figure, any character except Scarecrow or Wicked Witch, Mego, 8", MOC, ea.......................$35.00

Wizard of Oz, figure, Scarecrow or Wicked Witch, Mego, 8", MOC, ea...$45.00

Wizard of Oz, playset, 50th Anniversary Poseable Collection, Multi-Toys Corp, 1989, MIB, $25.00.

Wonder Woman, figure, Nubia, Mego, 1976, 12", MIB, T2, from $75 to.......................................$100.00

Wonder Woman, figure, Queen Hippolyte, Mego, 1976, 12", MIB, T2, from $75 to...............................$100.00

Wonder Woman, figure, Steve Trevor, Mego, 1976, 12", EX (EX box)...$75.00

Wonder Woman, figure, Wonder Woman, Mego, 1976, 12", MIB, T2, from $100 to............................$125.00

World Championship Wrestling, figure, Butch Reed, Galoob, 5", M...$10.00

World Wrestling Federation, figure, Bam Bam Bigelow, LJN, MOC, from $35 to...................................$50.00

World Wrestling Federation, figure, British Bulldog, Hasbro, MOC, from $10 to.......................................$12.00

World Wrestling Federation, figure, Honky Tonk Man, Hasbro, MOC...$10.00

World Wrestling Federation, figure, Honky Tonk Man, LJN, MOC, from $35 to.......................................$40.00

World Wrestling Federation, figure, Hulk Hogan, wht shirt, LJN, MOC...$30.00

World Wrestling Federation, figure, Jimmy Hart, LJN, MOC, from $15 to.......................................$20.00

World Wrestling Federation, figure, Nasty Boys, Hasbro, MOC, from $25 to.......................................$35.00

World Wrestling Federation, figure, Rick Martel, Hasbro, MOC...$20.00

World Wrestling Federation, figure, Rick Rude, Hasbro, MOC...$25.00

World Wrestling Federation, figure, Typhoon, Hasbro, MOC...$15.00

World Wrestling Federation, figure, Vince McMan, LJN, MOC...$25.00

Activity Sets

Activity sets that were once enjoyed by so many as children — the Silly Putty, the Creepy Crawlers, and those Mr. Potato Heads — are finding their way back to some of those same kids, now grown up, more or less, and especially the earlier editions are carrying pretty respectable price tags when they can be found complete or reasonably so. The first Thingmaker/Creepy Crawlers (Mattel, 1964) in very good but played-with condition will sell for about $65.00 to $75.00.

Advisor: Bill Bruegman (T2).

See also Character, TV, and Movie Collectibles; Coloring, Activity, and Paint Books; Disney; Playsets; and other specific categories.

Conjuring Set, Berwich/England, complete, EX (EX box), A, $50.00.

Abascus Tinker, Toy Tinkers, 1929-30, NMIB...............**$100.00**

Colorforms, 1950, 1st issue, complete w/100 geometric shapes, unused, rare, MIB, T2...**$80.00**

Cooky Cucumber w/Her Friend Mr Potato Head, Hasbro, 1966, complete, EX (EX box)...**$50.00**

Crazy Clay Characters, Fisher-Price Arts & Crafts, 1981-83, MIB, C13 ....**$30.00**

Creative Clips, Fisher-Price Arts & Crafts, 1983 – 84, MOC, C13, $25.00. (Photo courtesy Brad Cassity)

Creeple Peeple Thingmaker, Mattel, 1965, complete, MIB ..**$100.00**

Creeple Peeple Thingmaker Pak, EX, T2.........................**$50.00**

Creepy Crawlers, collectors case, Mattel, 1964, litho vinyl w/metal clasp, 12x9", rare, EX....................................**$65.00**

Drawing Teacher, Milton Bradley, complete, EX (EX box) **$100.00**

Easy-Bake Dual-Temp Oven Baking Toy, Kenner, 1983, complete, M, $25.00.

Easy-Bake Oven, Kenner, 1960s, complete, MIB, from $75 to **$100.00**

Easy-Wash Dishwasher, Kenner, 1967, MIB, from $55 to ...**$65.00**

Electric Service Station, T Cohn, complete, NM (VG box) **$225.00**

Famous American Cartoonists Art Series & Coloring Kit, Gem Color, 1954, few pcs missing, EX (VG box)...............**$40.00**

FBI Jr Finger Print Set, Nasta, complete, MIB................**$100.00**

Federal Agent Finger Print Outfit, Transogram, 1938, complete, NM (EX box), A **$100.00**

Fireball XL5, Magic Wand, 1963, complete, EX (EX box)....**$75.00**

Fort Comanche, T Cohn, complete, EX (EX box) **$475.00**

Fort Laramie, Ideal #4876, 1957, complete, VG (VG box), A ...**$500.00**

Girl's World Thingmaker, Mattel, 1968, complete, NMIB ..**$50.00**

Great Foodini Magic Set, Pressman/RC Cox Corp, 1951, complete, rare, EX (EX box) **$125.00**

Grocery Store, Coleman, 1950, cb store complete w/counter, scale & advertising boxes, EX (EX box), A **$125.00**

Gun Emplacement Assault Set, Airfix, complete, EX (EX box)..**$50.00**

Harbor Police Cruiser, MPC #565, complete, EX (EX box) ..**$100.00**

Harvey-Toon Tinkle Toy Stuffies, Saalfield, 1960, complete, EX (EX box), T2...**$50.00**

Harvey-Toon TV Flannel Funnies, Saalfield, 1960, complete, EX (EX box), T2...**$65.00**

Hasko Mystic Board, Haskelite Mfg, 1950s, complete, NM (VG box)..**$65.00**

Johnny Seven One Man Army, Topper, 1960s, complete, NM (EX box)...**$250.00**

Jumpin' Mr Potato Head, Hasbro, 1966, few pcs missing, scarce, VG (VG box), M17...**$125.00**

Krazy Ikes, Whitman, 1964, complete, EX (EX canister), T2 ...**$25.00**

Lab Technician Set for Girls, Gilbert #13120, 1950s, complete, EX (EX box) **$150.00**

Little Lace-Ups, Fisher-Price Arts & Crafts, 1981-85, bear, horse or bunny, MIP, C13, ea **$5.00**

Little Mother's Pastry Set, Pressman, 1930s, complete, NM (EX box), A, from $40 to..**$50.00**

Little Skipper Toy Boat Fleet, Transogram, 1950, complete, NMIB, A...**$200.00**

Magic Kit of Tricks & Puzzles, Transogram, 1960s, complete, EX (EX box) **$55.00**

Magic Set, Adams, complete, NM (NM box), A, $100.00.

Mandrake the Magician Magic Kit, Transogram, 1949, complete, NMIB, from $150 to...**$200.00**

Matchbox Service Station, #MG-1, complete, NM (NM box), A **$50.00**

McDonaldland Playset, Remco, 1976, complete, NM (NM box)..**$195.00**

Mini Monster Play Case, Remco, 1980, complete, MIP (sealed) **$35.00**

Missiles to the Moon Playset, MPC, Deluxe issue, complete, NMIB..$350.00

Monster Machine, Gabriel, 1970, complete, EX (EX box) ..$85.00

Motorized Monster Maker, Topper, 1960s, complete, EX (EX box)..$100.00

Mr & Mrs Potato Head Funny Face Combination Kit, Hasbro, 1950s, complete, EX (EX box), M17.......................$100.00

Mr Potato Head on the Moon, Hassenfeld, 1968, MIB, from $175 to..$250.00

Mr Potato Head Plus His Friend Donald Duck, Hasbro, 1970, complete, scarce, EX (EX box), M17 ....$100.00

Mr Space Head, Bell Toy, 1952, scarce, complete, NMIB, from $75 to..$100.00

My Mixer, Gilbert, complete, MIB, from $40.00 to $50.00.

Mysto Magic Exhibition Set, Gilbert, 1920s, EX (EX box) ...$450.00

Mysto Magic Exhibition Set, Gilbert, 1938, complete, EX (EX box)..$200.00

Old West Playset, Ideal, complete, EX (EX box), from $50 to ...$75.00

Operation X-500 Playset, Deluxe Reading, 1960s, complete, NM (EX box) $335.00

Panama Canal Playset, Renwal #273, complete, EX (EX box)..$300.00

Post Office, Wolverine #183, 1930s, litho tin, complete, NMIB $250.00

Printer's Kit, Fisher-Price Arts & Crafts, 1981-84, MIB, C13..$15.00

Scotty's Diner, T Cohn, litho tin, complete, NM..........$275.00

See 'N Say Talking Picture Puzzle w/Spellums, Mattel, 1969, complete, MIB, L6..$125.00

Sgt Rock Vs the Bad Guys Playset, Remco, 1982, complete, NMIB, J6..$85.00

Simple Stitch Quilting, Fisher-Price Arts & Crafts, 1984-85, MIB, C13 ....$6.00

Smoky Joe Sheriff Office, Halpern, 1955, complete, MIB, A ..$575.00

Sneaky Pete's Magic Show, Remco, 1960s, complete, NMIB ..$150.00

Super Adventure Colorforms, 1974, features Batman, Robin, Superman, etc, complete, EX (EX box), T2..............$35.00

Suzy Homemaker Grill, Topper, 1960s, MIB....................$65.00

Tammy Needlepoint & Frame Set, Hasbro, 1960s, complete, MIP, S14..$45.00

Tammy's Weaving Loom, Hasbro, 1963, complete, NMIB, S14, from $40 to..$50.00

Terrytoon Fun Kit, Milton Bradley, 1958, complete, NMIB, T2..$75.00

Thingmaker Fun Flowers, Mattel, complete, EX..............$35.00

Tinker Beads No. 2 and No. 1 jars with beads, etc., No. 1: from $10.00 to $25.00; No. 2: from $15.00 to $30.00. (Photo courtesy Craig Strange)

Tinker Fish, Toy Tinkers, 1927, complete, EX (worn box)....$50.00

Tinker Spots, Toy Tinkers, late 1930s, EX (EX box).........$60.00

Tinkerprints, Toy Tinkers, 1938, complete, EX (EX box).....$60.00

Tinkertoy Beginners Set, Playskool, 1980s, complete, EX (EX container) $20.00

Tinkertoy Big Builder Set, Playskool, 1980s, complete, EX (EX container) $20.00

Tinkertoy Count 'N Stack, Spalding, 1967, complete, EX $25.00

Tinkertoy Super Set, Playskool, 1980s, complete, EX (EX container) $25.00

Water Wiggle, Wham-O, EX (EX box)..........................$150.00

Weaving Loom Project, pillow, Fisher-Price Arts & Crafts, 1983 – 85, MIB, C-13, $5.00. (Photo courtesy Brad Cassity)

Weebles Circus, Hasbro/Romper Room, MIB..................$25.00

Weebles Marina, Hasbro/Romper Room, complete, EX (EX box)..$60.00

Weebles Playground, Hasbro/Romper Room, complete, MIB, J6..$45.00

Weebles Tumblin' Funhouse, Hasbro/Romper Room, complete, NM...$30.00

Winko Magic Set, Pressman/Marvel Screen Ent, 1953, complete, EX (EX box), from $75 to.............................$100.00

Advertising

The assortment of advertising memorabilia geared toward children is vast — plush and cloth dolls, banks, games, puzzles, trucks, radios, watches, and much, much more. And considering the popularity of advertising memorabilia in general, when you add to it the crossover interest from the realm of toys, you have a real winning combination! Just remember to check for condition very carefully; signs of play wear are common. Think twice about investing much money in soiled items, especially cloth or plush dolls. (Stains are often impossible to remove.)

For more information we recommend *Advertising Character Collectibles* by Warren Dotz; *Cracker Jack Toys* and *Cracker Jack, the Unauthorized Guide to Advertising* both by Larry White; *Pepsi-Cola Collectibles, Vols I, II,* and *III,* by Bill Vehling and Michael Hunt.

Advisors: Michael Paquin (P12), Jim Rash (R3), advertising dolls; Larry White (W7), Cracker Jack.

See also Bubble Bath Containers; Cereal Boxes and Premiums; Character, TV, and Movie Collectibles; Dakins; Disney; Fast-Food Collectibles; Halloween Costumes; Pin-Back Buttons; Premiums; Radios; Telephones; Western; and other specific categories.

A&P Super Markets, truck, Marx, pressed steel, red & silver w/plastic mesh rear door, 19", NMIB, A $600.00

Abercrombie & Fitch, yo-yo, Tom Kuhn, 1980s, wood w/laser carved seal, tournament shape, NM $40.00

AC Spark Plug, doll, Sparky the Horse, Ideal, 1960s, inflatable vinyl w/logo, 25x15" L, EX.....................................$100.00

AC Spark Plugs, doll, AC man w/1 arm extended & other hand on hip, wht & gr w/AC on chest, gr hat, 6", EXIB..$160.00

Aero Mayflower Transit Co, truck, Linemar, litho tin, friction, MIB...$350.00

Alka-Seltzer, bank, Speedy figure, vinyl, 5½", EX, minimum value...$200.00

Alka-Seltzer, charm, Speedy, 1960s, flasher image, glass covered w/frame & mirrored back, 1x1", EX $65.00

Alka-Seltzer, doll, Speedy, 1960, vinyl, 8", EX, from $500 to $700.00

Allied Van Lines, truck, Smith-Miller, pressed steel, orange w/blk & wht lettering, 38", NMIB, A..................$1,100.00

Aunt Jemima, Breakfast Bear, bl plush w/chef's hat, apron & bandana, 13", M $175.00

Aunt Jemima, doll, Diana, 1940-50 premium, stuffed oilcloth, 8½", EX, P6 ....$150.00

Aunt Jemima, doll, Uncle Mose, 1940s-50s, stuffed oilcloth, 12"..$95.00

Aunt Jemima, doll, 1940s-1950s, stuffed oilcloth, 11", EX...$95.00

Bazooka Bubble Gum, doll, Bazooka Joe, stuffed cloth, 1973, EX $20.00

Bean Bag Bunch, doll, w/tag, Kellogg's, MIP......................$9.00

Betty Crocker, doll, Kenner, 1974, stuffed cloth, 13", VG, M15..$20.00

BF Goodrich Tires, yo-yo, 1970s, sculpted plastic tire shape w/emb seal, NM $10.00

Big Boy, bank, figure, wearing red & wht checked overalls, 1973, plastic, 9"..$20.00

Big Boy, bank, figure holding hamburger, ceramic..........$500.00

Big Boy, bank, figure w/ or w/o hamburger, vinyl, M, ea...$25.00

Big Boy, comic book, Adventures of Big Boy, #1 ....$250.00

Big Boy, comic book, Adventures of Big Boy, #2-#5, ea .$150.00

Big Boy, comic book, Adventures of Big Boy, #6-#10, ea...$100.00

Big Boy, comic book, Adventures of Big Boy, #11-#100, ea.....$50.00

Big Boy, comic book, Adventures of Big Boy, #101-#250, ea...$20.00

Big Boy, doll, Dakin, complete w/hamburger & shoes....$150.00

Big Boy, figure, Bob on yel surfboard w/bl wave underneath, 1990, PVC, 3" $10.00

Big Boy, kite, Big Boy image on paper, M $100.00

Big Boy, nodder, 1965, papier-mache figure $800.00

Big Boy, yo-yo, 1960s, wood w/die-stamp seal, NM $28.00

Blue Bonnet Margarine, doll, Blue Bonnet Sue, 1980s, stuffed cloth w/yel yarn hair, NM, minimum value $20.00

Borden, bank, Beauregard, Irwin, 1950s, red plastic figure, 5", EX $65.00

Borden, Elsie's Funbook Cut-Out Toys & Games, 1940s, EX, P6 ....$65.00

Borden, figure, Elsie the Cow, PVC, 3½", M, from $10 to..$20.00

Borden, game, Elsie the Cow, Junior Edition, complete, EXIB..$125.00

Borden, hand puppet, Elsie's baby, vinyl w/cloth body, EX...$75.00

Borden, push-button puppet, Elsie the Cow, wood, EX ..$125.00

Bosco Chocolate, doll, Bosco the Clown, vinyl, NM $45.00

Brach's Peppermint, wristwatch, 1980s, MIB, I1..............$15.00

Allied Van Lines, tin friction-powered truck, MIB, $325.00.
(Photo courtesy Dunbar Gallery)

Buster Brown Treasure Hunt Game shoe box, 1930s, unused, from $50.00 to $75.00. (Photo courtesy Dunbar Gallery)

Buster Brown Shoes, doll, Buster Brown, 1974, stuffed cloth, 14", NM $40.00

Buster Brown Shoes, kite, 1940s, NM..............................$40.00

Buster Brown Shoes, yo-yo, late 1960s, litho tin, several color variations, NM..$30.00

Butterfinger Candy Bar, Butterfinger Bear, 1987, stuffed plush, 15", M...$22.50

Calgon Soap, ring, M, C10......................................$150.00

Camels, card game, 48 cards, 6 dice, score pad & pencil, features Joe Camel, M..$35.00

Camels, dart board, arched top, Joe Camel holding dart on 2-part front (opens), unused, 27x20", M.....................$250.00

Campbell's Soups, coloring book, A Story of Soup, shows kids in Prehistoric dress, 1977, EX $26.00

Campbell's Soups, comic book, Captain America & Campbell Kids, 1980, promotional, M...$24.00

Campbell's Soups, doll, Campbell girl, Ideal, 1955, rubber & vinyl w/cloth outfit, 8", EX, minimum value $125.00

Campbell's Soups, doll, Campbell girl as cheerleader, 1967, vinyl, 8", EX...$75.00

Campbell's Soups, doll, Home Shopper, 1995, in pirate clothes, comes in lg soup-can box, 10", EX $79.00

Campbell's Soups, doll kit, Boy & Girl Scottish Dolls, Douglas Co, 1979, ea..$35.00

Campbell's Soups, dolls, Campbell Kids, vinyl, 1970s, 9", MIB, pr...$125.00

Campbell's Soups, dolls, Campbell Kids, 1970s, rag-type, MIB, pr..$75.00

Campbell's Soups, dolls, Campbells Kids, ca 1972, vinyl, (soup label premium), unmk, 10", ea from $30 to $45.00

Campbell's Soups, dolls, Colonial boy & girl (Paul Revere & Betsy Ross replicas), 1976 premiums, 10", M, ea from $45 to..$65.00

Campbell's Soups, figurine, Soup's On, girl w/bowl of soup, Campbell Kids Historical Series, ca 1983, 4" $40.00

Campbell's Soups, game, The Campbell Kids Shopping Game, Parker Bros, 1955, scarce, NMIB................................$65.00

Campbell's Soups, kaleidoscope, 1981, replica of alphabet soup can, 4¾x2½" dia...$40.00

Campbell's Soups, play-kit, w/yo-yo, paddle ball & trick book, Duncan, 1963, MIP $40.00

Campbell's Soups, puzzle, jigsaw; All Aboard, Jaymar Mfg, 28 pcs, 1986, VG $25.00

Campbell's Soups, sled, Souper Slider, 1986, roll-up vinyl w/logo & Kid graphics, mail-in offer, Canada.......................$10.00

Campbell's Soups, wristwatch, Campbell Kids, 1982, 4 different, MIB, I1, ea $75.00

Canada Dry, truck, Buddy L, 1960s, 2-tone gr, w/slide-up side ramp door & 5 cases, 9½", NM...............................$150.00

Cap'n Crunch, bank, 1973, figural, pnt plastic, VG $65.00

Cap'n Crunch, bank, 1984, treasure chest, bl plastic, NM .$5.00

Cap'n Crunch, Cap'n Crunch Cruiser, 1987, plastic, EX .$10.00

Cap'n Crunch, coloring book, Whitman, 1968, VG $20.00

Cap'n Crunch, comic book, Center of the Earth, 1987, 8 pgs, EX $10.00

Cap'n Crunch, doll, Quaker Oats Co, 1990, plush, 18"....$20.00

Cap'n Crunch, figure, Smog Master, 1986, silver plastic robot, 1½", NM...$5.00

Cap'n Crunch, figure, Soggie, 1986, nearly clear plastic, 1½", EX $5.00

Cap'n Crunch, figure, 1986, bl plastic, 1½", VG $5.00

Cap'n Crunch, handkerchief, wht w/4 colorful scenes, 8x8", EX $50.00

Cap'n Crunch, kaleidoscope, 1965, cardboard, 7", EX $35.00

Cap'n Crunch, puzzle, Fisher-Price, 8 figures, wooden, 8½x12"..$38.00

Cap'n Crunch, ring, plastic figure, NM............................$100.00

Cap'n Crunch, treasure chest, tan w/Cap'n & skull & cross-bones, 5 gold coins, lock & treasure map inside, EX..$75.00

Cheer, doll, Cheer Girl, Proctor & Gamble, 1960, plastic w/cloth clothes, 10", NM...$20.00

Cheetos, doll, Chester Cheetah, stuffed plush, 18", EX....$20.00

Cherry 7-Up, wristwatch, 1980s, M, I1 ....$15.00

Chevrolet, mask, 1940, smiling moon-faced man w/See the New 1940... lettered on top hat, cb, NM............................$65.00

Chevrolet, wristwatch, 1927, salesman's award, EX, I1 ..$400.00

Chips Ahoy, figure, Nabisco, 1990s, rubber, 5", M............$20.00

Chiquita Bananas, doll, Chiquita Banana girl, 1974, mail-in pre-mium, stuffed cloth, NM, minimum value.................$40.00

Chrysler, figure, Mr Fleet, 1970s, vinyl, all-wht version, 10", VG, from $150 to $250.00

Chucky Cheese Pizza, bank, vinyl Chucky Cheese figure, 7", EX $10.00

Coca-Cola, bank, Line-mar Toys, cooler style, poured beverage into cup (included) as coin was inserted, 9¾", EX, from $300.00 to $500.00.

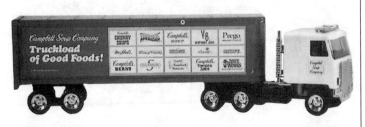

Campbell's Soups, truck, metal with decaled sides, copyright 1985, 19" long, VG, $200.00.

Coca-Cola, bear, plug in & he takes a sip of Coke & grunts, plush w/plastic bottle, 15", EX, A...............................$40.00

Coca-Cola, boomerang, 1950s, EX $35.00

Coca-Cola, car, Ford Taxi, Taiyo, litho tin, friction, 9", MIB $400.00

Coca-Cola, car, Taiyo, 1960s, tin, red & wht w/logo, friction, 10½", EX..$250.00

Coca-Cola, dispenser, Linemar, 1950s, insert coin & Coke dispenses into cup, tin, battery-op, 9½", NM (EX box) ..$950.00

Coca-Cola, doll, Frozen Coca-Cola mascot, 1960s, stuffed cloth, NM..$150.00

Coca-Cola, game, Steps to Health, 1938, complete, 26x11", NM, M2, $150.00.

Coca-Cola, jigsaw puzzle, pictures several Coca-Cola items, 2,000 pcs, EX (EX box) $60.00

Coca-Cola, jigsaw puzzle, Teenage Party, NMIB.............$100.00

Coca-Cola, kite, Am Flyer, 1930s, bottle at end, EX......$400.00

Coca-Cola, pocket radio, Leader Wave, M $15.00

Coca-Cola, truck, Barclay #690, 1950s, diecast metal, yel w/fishtail ad panel down center of stepped bed, 2", M $175.00

Coca-Cola, truck, Buddy L #5536, 1955, pressed steel, yel 3-tier, 8 red & yel cases, metal hand truck, 14½", MIB $350.00

Coca-Cola, truck, Buddy L #5646, 1957-58, pressed steel, yel 2-tier, straight bumper, blk-walls, complete, MIB $500.00

Coca-Cola, truck, Cragstan Tiny Giant, 1950s-60s, tin w/plastic cab, red w/yel litho bed, friction, 4", EX $150.00

Coca-Cola, truck, Hubley, 1950s, metal, red Chevy w/compartments in bed, Drink..., 4½", NM $750.00

Coca-Cola, truck, Lincoln Toy, 1950s, pressed steel, red, 12 wooden blocks, 16", NMIB $850.00

Coca-Cola, truck, Marx, plastic, yel w/blk tires, complete w/cases & bottles, 10", M (NM box), A $450.00

Coca-Cola, truck, Marx, 1950-54, plastic, red & yel Chevy w/enclosed bed & top ad panel, 11", EX $800.00

Coca-Cola, truck, Marx, 1956-57, litho tin w/Sprite Boy logo, 17", NMIB $625.00

Coca-Cola, truck, Marx #91, early 1950s, pressed steel, gray & yel stake bed w/Sprite Boy logo, 20", MIB..............$750.00

Coca-Cola, truck, Pyro Plastic Corp, 1950s, yel w/red lettering & blk tires, 5½", MIP..$150.00

Coca-Cola, truck, Rosko, 1950s, tin, yel w/4 rows of litho bottles, Sign of Good Taste logo on back, friction, 8", MIB...$750.00

Coca-Cola, truck, Sanyo, 1950s, tin, yel & wht w/red logo & detail, battery-op, 12½", EX (EX box mk Route Truck), A $700.00

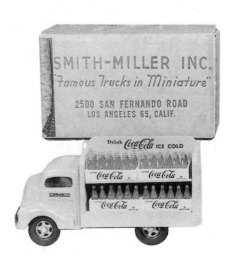

Coca-Cola, truck, Smith-Miller, pressed steel, yellow with two-panel open bed, complete with plastic cases, 13", NM (NM box), A, $2,400.00.

Coca-Cola, truck, Taiyo, Big Wheel Van, plastic & tin, advances w/non-fall action, battery-op, 10", EX (EX box), A...$125.00

Coca-Cola, whistle, 1930, tin, red & yel w/Drink Coca-Cola logo, VG $125.00

Coca-Cola, whistle, 1950, plastic, Merry Christmas...Memphis Tenn, EX $25.00

Coca-Cola, yo-yo, Duncan Imperial, 1980s, plastic w/imprint seal, tournament shape, NM....................................$15.00

Coca-Cola, yo-yo, Russell, 1960s, wood w/pnt seal, tournament shape, NM $120.00

Coca-Cola, yo-yo, Russell, 1977, Enjoy Coca-Cola, plastic w/molded seal, slim-line shape, MIP $28.00

Colonel Sanders, see Kentucky Fried Chicken

Cracker Jack, airplane, tin, orange w/blk & red circles.....$45.00

Cracker Jack, airplane, tin, yel & gr, NM......................$55.00

Cracker Jack, animal charms, lion, rabbit, camel, fox, horse, etc, pot metal, various colors, unmk, ea $5.00

Cracker Jack, banjo, litho tin $47.00

Cracker Jack, dog figure, plastic, $9.50; Smitty badge, plastic, $42.00; put-together clown, plastic, $8.00; plate, plastic, $5.50; coin, plastic, $5.00. (Photo courtesy Larry White)

Cracker Jack, circus animals, litho tin, 5 different, ea **$135.00**

Cracker Jack, dexterity puzzle, Gee Cracker Jack Is Good, NM.**$125.00**

Cracker Jack, figure, skunk, squirrel, fish, etc, plastic, 1950s, EX, ea..**$10.00**

Cracker Jack, garage, litho tin, NM....................................**$80.00**

Cracker Jack, Halloween mask, paper, orange, blk & red, 5 different, ea **$22.00**

Cracker Jack, Indian headdress, Me For Cracker Jack **$230.00**

Cracker Jack, pin, Pied Piper, metal **$65.00**

Cracker Jack, pin-back button, celluloid w/mirror back, NM.**$125.00**

Cracker Jack, puzzle, Last Round-Up, paper, red & gr, 1940, EX **$30.00**

Cracker Jack, sled, metal w/silver finish **$18.00**

Cracker Jack, Zodiac coin, plastic, various colors, ea..........**$8.00**

Crayola Crayons, doll, Crayola Bear, stuffed plush, various colors, Graphics International, 1986, 6", NM, ea...........**$10.00**

Curad Band-Aids, figure, Taped Crusader, Kendall-Futuro, 1975, vinyl, 7½", NM, from $25 to **$30.00**

Curtiss, tractor trailer, Buddy L, pressed steel, rear drop gate, 1950s, 29", EX, A, $635.00.

Dan Dee Potato Chips, yo-yo, 1960s, wood w/gold-leaf stamped seal, 3-pc, NM..**$12.00**

Del Monte, bank, Big Top Bonanza Clown, plastic, 1985, 7", M, from $10 to...**$15.00**

Del Monte, doll, Country Yumkin, Fruits or Veggies, stuffed plush, 1980s, 8" & 11", M, ea from $10 to **$15.00**

Del Monte, doll, Shoo Shoo Scarecrow, 1983, stuffed plush, NM...**$15.00**

Diaparene, figure, Diaparene Baby, 1980s, vinyl, orig diaper, M, from $50 to...**$75.00**

Dole Pineapple, yo-yo, 1980s, plastic w/paper seal, NM **$6.00**

Dow Brands, bank, Scrubbing Bubble, mail-in premium, 4¾", from $20 to...**$22.00**

Dr Pepper, dart game, 1943, EX...**$300.00**

Dunkin' Donuts, doll, Dunkin' Munchkin, stuffed cloth, 15", EX, from $15 to..**$20.00**

Dunkin' Donuts, wristwatch, 1999, M, I1 ....**$10.00**

Dutch Boy Paints, coloring book, WDP, 1957 premium, unused, EX..**$20.00**

Eggo Waffles, wristwatch, 1990, Eggosaurus, M, I1 ....**$15.00**

Elsie the Cow, See Borden

Energizer Batteries, doll, Energizer Bunny, plush, battery-op, 24", M..**$45.00**

Energizer Batteries, squeeze light, Energizer Bunny figure, MIP (sealed)...**$8.00**

Ernie the Keebler Elf, See Keebler

Eskimo Pie, doll, Eskimo Pie Boy, Chase Bag Co, 1964-74, stuffed cloth, 15", EX, from $15 to **$20.00**

Esso, Happy bank, plastic, 7x3", NM, A, $95.00.

Fanta, yo-yo, Russell, 1980s, Fanta Galaxy 200, plastic w/wood axle, imprint seal, MIP **$12.00**

Firestone Tire Service, truck, Buddy L, pressed steel, bl, orange & yel, 28", rare, EX **$2,400.00**

Fisk Tires, bank, Fisk Tire Boy, 1970s, plaster, all-wht yawning figure standing w/tire & holding candle, 8½", NM .**$130.00**

Florida Oranges, bank, Orange Bird, 1974, vinyl, MIP.....**$40.00**

Frito Lay, eraser, Frito Bandito figure, 1960s, various colors, 1½", NM, ea from $30 to **$40.00**

Gerber, boxcar, Bachmann, 1978, bl, HO scale, 6", MIB, G8 .**$95.00**

Gerber, doll, Arrow Rubber & Plastic & Co, 1965, premium, w/diaper & bib, MIB, from $55 to **$65.00**

Gerber, dolls, boy & girl, Atlanta Novelty, 1985, squeak vinyl, 8", EX, ea...**$20.00**

Gerber, frisbee, Safety Comes in Cans..., lettering around image of baby, bl & wht, EX...**$8.00**

Gerber, squeaker dolls, boy & girl, Atlanta Novelty, 1985, vinyl, 8", EX, G8, ea **$20.00**

Gerber, truck, Nylint, 1978, GMC 18-wheeler, pressed steel, 21½", M, $85.00. (Photo courtesy Joan Grubaugh)

Goodyear Tires, wristwatch, 1970s, revolving disk, G, I1 .**$50.00**

Gordon's Farm Products, truck, MSK, 1950s, tin, wht van-type w/2 bottle carriers on top, friction, 6½", NMIB **$250.00**

Green Giant, bank, Little Sprout, compo, plays Valley of the Green Giant, 8½" **$50.00**

Green Giant, doll, ca 1975, vinyl, 9", EX.....................**$85.00**

Green Giant, doll, cloth, 1966, 16", M (in orig mailer), from $25 to **$35.00**

Green Giant, doll, Jolly Green Giant, 1960s, stuffed cloth, 12", NM, from $15 to **$20.00**

Green Giant, doll, Little Sprout, talker, MIP...................**$55.00**

Green Giant, doll, Little Sprout, 1970s, inflatable vinyl, 24", MIP, from $35 to **$65.00**

Green Giant, doll, Little Sprout, 1970s, plush w/felt hat & clothes, from $20 to **$30.00**

Green Giant, doll, Little Sprout, 1970s-90s, vinyl, 6½", EX, from $10 to................................**$20.00**

Green Giant, doll, Little Sprout, 1974, stuffed cloth, 10½", NM **$15.00**

Green Giant, jump rope, Little Sprout hdls, MIP **$20.00**

Green Giant, kite, late 1960s, plastic, mail-in premium, 42x48", unused, M.....................................**$30.00**

Green Giant, puzzle, Planting Time in the Valley, 1981, 1,000 pcs in can, EX **$15.00**

Green Giant, truck, Nylint, Green Giant Corn tractor-trailer, 21", VG **$55.00**

Green Giant, truck, Tonka, Green Giant tractor-trailer, 1951, M, from $150 to........................**$200.00**

Green Giant, truck, Tonka, pressed steel, rubber tires, 24", G, A, $165.00.

Gulf, service station, 1947 premium, complete w/cb station, tin trucks & gas pumps, MIB, A **$575.00**

Gulf Gasoline, yo-yo, 1960s, wood w/pnt seal, 3-pc, NM ...**$22.00**

Hamburger Helper, doll, Helping Hand, plush glove-like figure w/facial features on palm, 14", M **$10.00**

Hawaiian Punch, game, Mattel, 1978, complete, EX (EX box).....................................**$30.00**

Hawaiian Punch, wristwatch, Punchy, 1970s, red strap, digital, VG, I1 ....**$50.00**

Hawaiian Punch, yo-yo, Imperial Toy, 1996, plastic butterfly shape w/image of Punchy, MIB..................**$6.00**

Heinz 57, truck, Metalcraft, 1920s, gr w/wht stake bed, 12", G+, A...**$1,300.00**

Hershey's Chocolate, yo-yo, Humphrey, Hershey's Chocolate World sticker, NM **$5.00**

Hess Gasoline & Fuel Oils, truck, 1970s, plastic & tin, MIB...**$50.00**

Hess Premium Diesel, truck, plastic, gr & wht w/gr & red lettering, 16", NMIB, A **$750.00**

Hood's Sarsaparilla, jigsaw puzzle, 2-sided, Rainy Day/Hood's Balloon Puzzle, 10x15", NM, A..................**$75.00**

Howard Johnson's, truck, Marx, 1950, plastic, wht w/decals, 9½", MIB, A **$225.00**

Icee, bank, Icee Bear w/drink in front of him, rubber, 7", EX **$30.00**

Jack Frost, doll, Jack Frost, stuffed cloth, 17", M..............**$50.00**

Jell-O, hand puppet, Sweet Tooth Sam, General Mills, 1960s, gr vinyl head w/1 long fang & blk top hat, EX+ **$85.00**

Jell-O, puppet, Mr Wiggle, 1966, red vinyl, M **$150.00**

Jif Peanut Butter, periscope, 1950s, features Jifaroo the Kangaroo, yel cb, 20", EX **$25.00**

Joe Camel, See Camels

Johnson's Baby Powder, Joan Palooka doll, vinylite plastic head, latex body, molded hair, c 1952/Ham Fisher/Ideal Doll on head, 14", all original, minimum value, $85.00. (Photo courtesy Judith Izen)

Jordache, doll, Jeans Man, Mego, 12", MIB **$30.00**

Keebler, bank, Keebler Elf figure, ceramic, lg, NM, S21 ...**$60.00**

Keebler, bank, Keebler Elf figure, ceramic, sm, NM, S21 .**$25.00**

Keebler, truck, Nylint, 1986, MIB, P12 ....**$85.00**

Keebler, wristwatch, Ernie the Keebler Elf, 1970s, G, I1 ..**$50.00**

Kentucky Fried Chicken, bank, figural Colonel Sanders, dtd 1977, plastic, 7½" **$12.50**

Kentucky Fried Chicken, bank, figural Colonel Sanders, mk Marquart Corp, 1972, plastic, red w/blk tie, 10" **$27.50**

Kentucky Fried Chicken, bank, Run Starling Plastics LTD, figural Colonel Sanders on rnd base w/cane, 13", NM ..**$35.00**

Kentucky Fried Chicken, camera, Colonel Sanders, Japan premium, 3x4", MIB **$35.00**

Kentucky Fried Chicken, coloring book, Favorite Chicken Stores, 1960s, EX **$25.00**

Kentucky Fried Chicken, hand puppet, 1960s, Colonel Sanders in wht suit, plastic, EX.............................**$20.00**

Kentucky Fried Chicken, nodder, Colonel Sanders, mk Charl-sprod Japan, 1960s, bsk, 7½", M, from $100 to........$125.00

Kentucky Fried Chicken, nodder, Colonel Sanders, Tops Enterprises, ca 1967, papier-mache, 7½", MIB.................$150.00

Kentucky Fried Chicken, nodder, Colonel Sanders, 1960s, pnt compo, 7", EX...$75.00

Kentucky Fried Chicken, playset, Let's Play at KY Fried Chicken, Child Guidance, 1970s, EX (EX box) $140.00

Kist Beverages, yo-yo, Duncan, 1950s, wood w/gold leaf stamped seal, tournament shape, 3-pc, NM $16.00

Kodak, doll, Colorkins, ca 1990, stuffed, 8" to 10", ea......$20.00

Kool-Aid, bank, 1970, Kool-Aid man pitcher on yel base, plastic, 7", NM...$60.00

Kool-Aid, snow-cone machine, 1984, plastic, w/packet of Kool-Aid, unused, MIB (sealed)....................................$50.00

Kool-Aid, wristwatch, Goofy Grape, 1976, G, I1 ....$200.00

Kool-Aid, yo-yo, Duncan, 1980s, plastic w/imprint seal, tournament shape, NM $5.00

Kraft Macaroni & Cheese, wristwatch, 1980s, M, I1 ....$10.00

Kroger Food Express, truck, Metalcraft, pressed steel, orange w/wht disk wheels, 12", VG, A $600.00

Lee Jeans, doll, Buddy Lee as train engineer in Lee overalls, bl shirt & bl & wht striped hat mk Lee, 13", EX $180.00

Lifesavers, yo-yo, 1960s, wood Lifesaver shape w/pnt seal, NM...$45.00

Little Caesar's Pizza, doll, Pizza Pizza Man, 1990, plush, holding pizza slice, EX...$5.00

Lysol, doll, Lysol Kid, Trudy Corp, 1986, stuffed cloth w/yel hair, NM, minimum value $30.00

M&M, bean bag toys, M&M shape, red, gr, bl or yel, 6", ea....$5.00

M&M, bean bag toys, peanut shape, golfer or witch, 6", ea ..$10.00

M&M, bear, stuffed plush w/cloth M&M shirt, orig tag, M, minimum value $10.00

M&M, calculator, yel w/different color M&M Keys, MIB, P10...$10.00

M&M, dispenser, M&M shape, 1991, brn, sm $5.00

M&M, dispenser, 1995, M&M Fun Machine, M, $12.00.

M&M, dispenser, M&M shape, 1991, holding bouquet of flowers, yel, sm $2.00

M&M, dispenser, M&M shape, 1991, red, lg....................$10.00

M&M, dispenser, peanut shape, orange, gr, or yel, sm, ea...$2.00

M&M, dispenser, peanut shape, 1991, brn, sm...................$2.00

M&M, dispenser, peanut shape, 1995, football player, lg .$20.00

M&M, dispenser, peanut shape, 1995, yel, lg....................$10.00

M&M, dispenser, peanut shape, 1997, basketball player ..$15.00

M&M, dispenser, spaceship shape w/M symbol, press button to dispense candy, battery-op, red, yel, or bl, MOC, ea...$8.00

M&M, doll, M&M shape, plush, 4½" $5.00

M&M, doll, M&M shape, plush, 8"...................................$5.00

M&M, doll, M&M shape, plush, 12"................................$10.00

M&M, Easy Bake Set, w/M&M stencil & spoon, MIB.....$12.00

M&M, figure, peanut shape, bendable arms & legs, bl or yel, 7", ea...$15.00

M&M, wristwatch, 1980s, several variations, M, I1, ea....$25.00

Mack Trucks, doll, Mack Bulldog, stuffed plush, NM $40.00

Meow Mix, figure, vinyl cat, EX.....................................$35.00

Michelin, costume, Mr Bib, nylon & metal w/yel sash, EX ...$900.00

Michelin, dice game, wht plastic container w/3-D Mr Bib holds 8 dice w/blk letters & bl Mr Bib figures, 3½x2½", M......$85.00

Michelin, doll, Mr Bib standing & holding baby wearing bl bib w/Michelin in emb letters, rubber, 7".......................$125.00

Michelin, figure, Mr Bib, plastic, 12", NM.......................$75.00

Michelin, figure, Mr Bib on motorcycle, plastic, EX $110.00

Michelin, figure, Mr Bib w/hands at waist, 1950s, gr glaze, ceramic, made in Holland, 12½" $500.00

Michelin, nodder, Mr Bib, attaches to dashboard, 2 styles, ea...$18.00

Michelin, puzzle, Mr Bib on motorcycle, put together to form figure, MIP $55.00

Michelin, ramp walker, Mr Bib w/up, MIB.......................$25.00

Michelin, yo-yo, Mr Bib in blk outline on wht, EX $10.00

Mobil, yo-yo, Duncan, 1960s, plastic w/hot stamped seal, metal string slot, tournament shape, NM.............................$15.00

Mobilgas, truck, Cragstan, ½-cab, litho tin, friction, EX (EX box)...$225.00

Mobilgas, truck, Smith-Miller, pressed steel, red w/wht lettering & logo, 36", NMIB, A...$1,000.00

Mobiloil, truck & pup trailer, Smith-Miller, pressed steel, red w/wht decals, blk rubber tires, 36", EX, A................$850.00

Mott's Apple Juice, doll, Apple of My Eye Bear, stuffed plush, 1988, M...$15.00

Mountain Dew, yo-yo, Imperial, 1990s, sculpted plastic bottle cap w/paper seal, MIP $5.00

Mr Bubble, figure, Mr Bubble Tub Pal, Airwick Industries, 1990, pk vinyl, 8", NM...$25.00

Nestle Chocolate, doll, Chocolate Man, Chase Bag Co, 1970, stuffed cloth, 15", EX...$20.00

Nestle Chocolate, doll, Chocolate Man, 1969, plastic w/cloth clothes, 12½", NM $50.00

Nestle Quik, doll, Quik Bunny, plush, 1980s mail-in, M, P12...$35.00

Nestle Quik, figure, Quik Bunny, bendable, 6", EX $10.00

Northern Toilet Paper, doll, 1980s, stuffed cloth w/vinyl head, rooted hair, several variations, NM, ea from $25 to...$35.00

Orange-Crush, truck, London Toy/Canada, diecast, w/up, 6", scarce, VG, A $125.00

Oreo Cookies, wristwatch, 1998, M, I1 ....$50.00

Oreo Cookies, yo-yo, 1980s, plastic cookie shape w/emb seal, metal axle, NM $8.00

Oscar Mayer, bank, Weinermobile, 1988, plastic, 10", M ..$25.00

Oscar Mayer, pedal car, Weinermobile, 1994-95, 2 different, P12, ea from $250 to................$350.00

Oscar Mayer, remote control car, Weinermobile, 1994-95, MIB, P12, from $100 to $200.00

Oscar Mayer, ring, Little Oscar, 1970s, red & yel plastic, EX ..$5.00

Pepsi-Cola, kite, 1960s, features Mary Poppins, EX........$125.00

Pepsi-Cola, Santa doll, Animal Fair Inc, stuffed plush w/fur beard, logo on belt buckle, 20", NM $55.00

Pepsi-Cola, truck, Barclay, 1950s, metal, 2", M $155.00

Pepsi-Cola, truck, Buddy L, 1943, van-type, Buy...Sparkling Satisfying decal, 16", EX................$500.00

Pepsi-Cola, truck, Marx, 1940s, plastic, NMIB..............$450.00

Pepsi-Cola, truck, Ny-Lint, pressed steel, red & bl w/wht open-sided body, 3 cases of Pepsi, 16", MIB................$775.00

Pepsi-Cola, yo-yo, Duncan Beginner, 1950s, wood w/die-stamped seal, tournament shape, NM $30.00

Peters Weatherbird Shoes, yo-yo, Alox, 1950s, wood w/decal seal, NM................$30.00

PF Flyers, ring, EX, C10 ....$80.00

Phillips 66, tanker truck, metal, Ralstoy 3 Made in USA, 7¾", VG, $125.00.

Pillsbury, bank, Poppin' Fresh, 1980s, mail-in premium, ceramic, M, P12................$35.00

Pillsbury, beanie, Poppin' Fresh, 2 different styles, M, P12, ea from $10 to................$20.00

Pillsbury, decals, Poppin' Fresh, set of 18, MIP, P12..........$10.00

Pillsbury, doll, Poppin' Fresh, Mattel, stuffed cloth, pull-string talker, Mattel, 16", NM................$100.00

Pillsbury, doll, Poppin' Fresh, 1970s, stuffed cloth, 14", VG..$15.00

Pillsbury, doll, Poppin' Fresh, 1972, stuffed cloth, 11", EX $20.00

Pillsbury, doll, Poppin' Fresh, 1972, stuffed cloth, 11", EX, from $15 to $20.00

Pillsbury, doll, Poppin' Fresh, 1982, stuffed plush, M, from $40 to $50.00

Pillsbury, doll, Poppin' Fresh, 1982, stuffed plush, scarce, EX...$30.00

Pillsbury, figure, Grandmommer, 1974, vinyl, 5", M, from $75 to................$95.00

Pillsbury, figure, Grandpopper, 1974, vinyl, 5¼", M, from $75 to................$95.00

Pillsbury, figure, Poppie Fresh, vinyl, M $20.00

Pillsbury, figure, Poppin' Fresh, cold-cast porcelain, set of 4 various poses, 5", MIB................$60.00

Pillsbury, figure, Poppin' Fresh & Poppie, vinyl, on stands as a set, M, pr, from $35 to $40.00

Pillsbury, finger puppet, Ben Bun (girl), Popper (boy), Poppin' Fresh or Poppie Fresh, vinyl, 1974, ea................$25.00

Pillsbury, finger puppet, Biscuit (cat) or Flapjack (dog), 1974, vinyl, ea................$35.00

Pillsbury, finger puppets, Poppin' Fresh & Pals, set of 3, rare, MIB, P12................$235.00

Pillsbury, gumball machine, Poppin' Fresh, w/5-lbs of gum, MIB..$125.00

Pillsbury, magnet set, Poppin' Fresh & Poppie, 1970s premium, plastic, scarce, MIP, P12 ....$35.00

Pillsbury, wristwatch, 1996, Doughboy, talker, M, I1 ....$15.00

Planters, bank, Mr Peanut figure, 1950s-70s, clear plastic, EX, from $90 to $125.00

Planters, beach ball, 1970s, yel w/image of Mr Peanut in bl, 13½" dia, EX................$10.00

Planters, charm bracelet, 1941, 6 plastic charms on brass-colored chain, VG $50.00

Planters, costume, Mr Peanut, 1970s, cloth w/plastic mask, 2-pc, NMIB................$75.00

Planters, dart board, 1980s, wood case w/Planters lettered in yel above Mr Peanut on hinged doors, EX................$25.00

Planters, dish set, child's, Melmac, 1970s, 3-pcs, MIB......$20.00

Planters, doll, Mr Peanut, Chase Bag, 1967, cloth, 21", EX ..$40.00

Planters, doll, Mr Peanut, Chase Bag, 1970, cloth, 18", NM ...$25.00

Planters, doll, Mr Peanut, 1930s, wood w/yel body, blk arms, legs & shoes, bl hat, 9", EX $200.00

Planters, frisbee, wht plastic w/Heritage logo, M $15.00

Planters, Mr Peanut Peanut Butter Maker, 1970s, 12", MIB....$65.00

Planters, nodder, Mr Peanut, Lego, papier-mache, NM..$150.00

Planters, puppet, Mr Peanut, 1942, rubber, tan w/blk hat & monocle, 6", EX, from $750 to................$1,000.00

Planters, radio backpack, Munch 'N Go, 1991, EX, from $35 to................$40.00

Planters, train set, 1988, battery-op, MIB $50.00

Planters, truck, Mr Peanut's Peanut Wagon, Pyro, yel & red, 5", NM, from $350 to................$450.00

Planters, vendor's costume, Mr Peanut, life-size, EX, from $800 to................$900.00

Planters, wristwatch, Mr Peanut, 1966, yel face, VG, I1 ..$50.00

Planters, wristwatch, Mr Peanut, 1967, yel face w/date window, VG, I1 ....$50.00

Planters, wristwatch, Mr Peanut, 1975, bl face, mechanical, EX, I1 ....$50.00

Planters, yo-yo, Mr Peanut, Humphrey, 1976, NM..........$12.00

Poll Parrot Shoes, figures, Bride & Groom, Sonsco, celluloid, 4", EX, M15 ....$65.00

Poll Parrot Shoes, ring, 1950s, brass w/emb parrot, EX.....$65.00

Poppin' Fresh, see Pillsbury

Raid, doll, Raid Bug, 1980s, plush, 5 different styles, M, P12, ea from $50 to $125.00

Raid Bug Spray, wristwatch, Raid Bug, 1970s, revolving disk, EX, I1 ....$150.00

Ralston Purina, figure, Magic Pup, 1951, plastic w/pnt features cloth ears, w/ring that moves Pup's mouth, 3", NM...$100.00

Red Goose Shoes, bank, 1920s, red-pnt CI, 9", EX $135.00

Red Goose Shoes, ring, Secret Compartment, w/photo, glow-in-the-dark, NM, C10 ....$150.00

Red Goose Shoes, Tuck-A-Tab Theatre Play Kit, 1950s premium, complete, unpunched, NM $50.00

Red Goose Shoes, wristwatch, 1960s, G, I1 ....$130.00

Red Goose Shoes, yo-yo, Duncan, 1950s, wood w/gold leaf stamped seal, tournament shape, NM $45.00

Reddy Kilowatt, coloring book, PA Electric Co (PENELEC), 1960s, 14x10½", G $20.00

Reddy Kilowatt, figure, lg head, red & wht plastic on blk outlet switch-plate base, MCMLXI, 6", minimum value ...$150.00

Reddy Kilowatt, figure, sm head, hands & ft, red & wht plastic, on base (harder to find than lg-head version), 6", EX......$200.00

Reddy Kilowatt, figure, 1930s, hard rubber, 3" $8.00

Reddy Kilowatt, wristwatch, 1930s, VG, I1 ....$250.00

Reese's, doll, Reese's Bear, 1989, in Reese's T-shirt, NM+ $10.00

Ritz Crackers, wristwatch, 1971, MIB, I1 ....$200.00

Salamander Shoes, figures, vinyl, sm, set of 6, M, P12 ...$125.00

Sambo's restaurant, Family Funbook/Fun, Games & Puzzles/Featuring JY & the Tiger Kids, 1978, EX $32.00

Sears, truck, Linemar, 1950s, tin, bl & orange, friction, 13", M (EX box), A $400.00

Seven-Up, car, Taiyo, 1960s, litho tin w/logo, friction, 10½", NMIB...$235.00

Seven-Up, figure, Spot, Commonwealth Toy & Novelty, 1988, plush & felt w/suction cups on hands, 6", MIB..........$10.00

Seven-Up, Fresh-Up Freddie, Canadian, stuffed cloth w/rubber head, 15", EX $75.00

Seven-Up, music box, can shape, plays Love Story, NM, J2..$50.00

Seven-Up, yo-yo, Duncan, 1950s, wood w/die-stamped seal, tournament shape, NM...$45.00

Shell, truck, Smith-Miller, pressed steel, red & yel w/blk rubber tires, 20", MIB, A $850.00

Shell Fuel Oils, truck, Buddy L, yel & red, handlebars extend from hood, emb spoke wheels, 28½", EX, A $6,000.00

Shoney's, bank, Shoney's bear, vinyl, M, P12....................$20.00

Sinclair, truck, Marx, litho tin, 18½", VG, A, $375.00.

Smokey Bear, bank, ceramic, wht w/gold details, EX........$60.00

Smokey Bear, bank, US Pat Off A-478, Norcrest, ceramic figure, from $275 to $300.00

Smokey Bear, coloring book, Whitman #1987, 1969, Smokey & friends on cover, unused, M..$45.00

Smokey Bear, doll, inflatable vinyl, MIP.......................$245.00

Smokey Bear, doll, 50th Anniversary, 12", MIB $30.00

Smokey Bear, figurine, ceramic, holding remnants of burned tree, mk A-19, M $55.00

Smokey Bear, game, Smokey Bear Puts Out the Fires Pinball, Gordy, MOC..$15.00

Smokey Bear, magic slate, Watkins-Strathmore, 1969, EX ..$85.00

Snickers Candy Bar, wristwatch, 1990s, revolving sundial, NM, I1 ....$35.00

Sprite, doll, Lucky Lymon, 1990s, talker, vinyl, 7½", M...$25.00

Sprite, yo-yo, Russell, 1984, Sprite Super, plastic w/wood axle, imprint seal, MIP...$12.00

Squirt, figure, Squirt Boy, 1961, vinyl, 18", very rare, M...$200.00

Standard, truck, Tonka, pressed steel w/plastic tanker, blk rubber tires, 28", VG, A..$800.00

Standard Oil, truck, Japan, litho tin, friction, 8½", EX (VG box), A..$200.00

Standard Oil, truck, Metalcraft, pressed steel, red w/wht stake bed, blk rubber tires, electric headlights, 12", NM, A $1,800.00

Stanley Powerlock, wristwatch, 1980s, M, I1 ....$45.00

Star-Kist Tuna, bank, Charlie Tuna, Japan, ceramic figure, 10", MIB, A7..$35.00

Star-Kist Tuna, doll, Charlie Tuna, Mattel, 1969, stuffed cloth w/pull-string talker, says 11 phrases, 14", NM, L6......$85.00

Star-Kist Tuna, doll, 2-tone bl Charlie Tuna w/pk hat & glasses, vinyl, mk, 7"...$65.00

Star-Kist Tuna, figure, Charlie Tuna, 1973, vinyl, arms up (rare version), 7½", (M, $125), MIB $200.00

Star-Kist Tuna, figure, Charlie Tuna, 1973, vinyl w/bl Star-Kist on pk hat, 7", EX, from $50 to................................$60.00

Star-Kist Tuna, wristwatch, Charlie Tuna, 1971, facing left, VG, I1 ....$50.00

Star-Kist Tuna, wristwatch, Charlie Tuna, 1973, facing right, VG, I1 ....$50.00

Star-Kist Tuna, wristwatch, Charlie Tuna, 1986, 25th Anniversary, MIB, I1 ....$25.00

Sun-Maid Raisins, van, gas-powered, early style w/brass grille & headlights, 72", M..$700.00

Sunbeam Bread, doll, Little Miss Sunbeam, Eegee, 1959, vinyl w/rooted hair, cotton dress w/wht apron, 1959, 17", NM.$50.00

Sunbeam Bread, yo-yo, 1980s, plastic w/paper sticker seal, NM $4.00

Sunshine Animal Crackers, elephant, 1930s, stuffed cloth, EX, minimum value $85.00

Sunshine Biscuits, truck, Metalcraft, yel w/blk rubber tires, electric headlights, NMIB, A $4,300.00

Swiss Miss Chocolate, doll, Swiss Miss, stuffed cloth w/vinyl face & yel yarn hair, EX, minimum value.........................$25.00

Swiss Miss Chocolate, wristwatch, 1981, EX, I1 ....$50.00

Tango Orange Drink, figure, Tango Voodoo, British premium, vinyl, MIB, P12..$45.00

Tastee Freeze, doll, Miss Tastee Freeze, 1950s, hard plastic, 7", NM...$20.00

Tastee Freeze, yo-yo, 1970s, wood w/die-stamp seal, NM....$15.00

Texaco, doll, Texaco Cheerleader, 1973, 11", NRFB, from $100 to...$125.00

Texaco, fire engine, Buddy L, 24", EX (VG box), A.......$550.00

Texaco, gumball machine, 1970s, pump shape, plastic & metal, 21", MIB, from $125 to...$150.00

Texaco, Service Station, steel w/plastic accessories, MIB (sealed)..$350.00

Texaco, truck, Buddy L, 1950s, pressed steel, red w/wht decal, blk rubber tires, 24", EX, A $200.00

Texaco, truck, Buddy L, 1960s, pressed steel, red w/wht grille, MIB..$375.00

Texaco, Fire Chief hat, plastic w/battery-operated speaker, Brown & Bigelow, 8x13", EX, $75.00.

Texaco, truck, Smith-Miller, pressed steel, red tractor-trailer w/wht lettering & star logo, 31", rare, NM, A......$1,300.00

Tropicana Orange Juice, doll, Tropic-Ana, 1997, stuffed cloth, 17", NM $35.00

Tupperware, doll, 1988, stuffs into satin Tupperware bowl, 13", M, M15 ....$25.00

Tyson Chicken, doll, Chicken Quick, stuffed cloth, 13", VG ...$15.00

Victor Toy Oats, yo-yo, tin w/paper seal, coaster shape w/riveted disk axle, NM..$45.00

Vlastic Pickles, doll, Stork, Trudy Toys, 1989, wht fur w/glasses & bow tie, 1989, 22", NM $30.00

Walgreens, truck, Marx, metal, wht w/bl detail, blk tires, rear door opens, 20", G, A $300.00

Welch's Grape Juice, wristwatch, 1989, M, I1...................$20.00

Whirlpool, yo-yo, Duncan, 1950s, wood w/die-stamped seal, tournament shape, NM..$30.00

Wilkins Coffee, hand puppet, Wontkins, 1958, pnt rubber, 7", scarce, EX..$100.00

Wrigley's Spearmint Chewing Gum, truck, Buddy L, 1930s, pressed steel, gr w/colorful decals, 24", VG, A.........$475.00

Advertising Signs, Ads, and Displays

A common advertising ploy used as far back as the late 1900s and still effective today is to catch the eye of the potential consumer with illustrations of well-known celebrities or popular fictional characters. Nowadays, with the intense passion character-collectibles buffs pour into their hobby, searching for these advertising items is a natural extension of their enthusiasm, adding even more diversity to an already multi-faceted collecting field.

Carson & Barnes Wild Animal Circus, poster, paper, 33x42", EX, A $50.00

Disney Roll A Toys, electric display, litho tin on wood base, various characters spin etc, Fun on Wheels, 18x12", EX .$550.00

Green Hornet Signal Ray Flashlight, store display, Colorforms, 1966, cb, EX, from $100 to.......................................$200.00

Howdy Doody Fudge Bar, tin sign, 1980s repro by AAA Sign Co $20.00

Howdy Doody Royal Gelatin, cb sign, diecut image, rare, 30x40", VG..$450.00

Kellogg's Corn Flakes, display, 1930s-40s, nursery rhyme & cereal box graphics, paper litho, 10x4", NM..............$50.00

Keystone Steam Shovels & Trucks, orig artwork, mixed media on brd, fr, 20x14", G..............................$5,500.00

Pillsbury Doughboy, styrofoam display of Poppin' Fresh, 54" in metal stand, G, $285.00.

Popeye in airplane, 1940s, Merchant's Display & Novelty Co, pnt wood w/compo figure, 24" W, NM....................$950.00

Puffed Rice/Gabby Hayes, banner, 1951, Quaker Oats, Prospector Hat offer, 21"...$250.00

Raggedy Ann & Andy by Knickerbocker, paper sign, Who Will Capture..., c 1977 KTC, from $12 to $15.00

Ringling Bros & Barnum & Bailey Circus, poster, paper, fr, 43x28½", EX, A $175.00

Roy Rogers & Dale Evans for Kool-Aid, sign, Got Your Kool-Aid Yet... above faces, diecut cb, 17x17", NM, A ...$350.00

RPM Motor Oil, Mickey Mouse on tin display sign, Walt Disney Copyright 1939, 23½", G, A, $800.00.

Schwinn Lightweight Bicycles, poster, Ride a... w/image of young couple on bicycles, fr, 39½x24", EX, A $400.00

Slinky, store display, 1950s, wood w/decals, electrical w/slinky on moving paddle, 17x16", EX.....................................$225.00

Smokey Bear US Forest Service, sign, 1956, brush-burning scene & Use Care in Burning Brush..., litho cb, 17x14", NM $40.00

Tarzan Tablets, Composition Books & Note Book Fillers, Birmingham Paper, 1930s, cb, 14x10", NM, A................$185.00

Tinkertoy Oil Well, motorized company display pc $350.00

Toots & Casper, poster, 1927, image & ...For Kids of All Ages, 24x18", VG, A $125.00

Woody Woodpecker, clock display, 1959 Walter Lantz, die-cut w/base & easel back, 20x14", EX+ $465.00

Aeronautical

Toy manufacturers seemed to take the cautious approach toward testing the waters with aeronautical toys, and it was well into the second decade of the twentieth century before some of the European toy makers took the initiative. The earlier models were bulky and basically inert, but by the '50s, Japanese manufacturers were turning out battery-operated replicas with wonderful details that advanced with whirling motors and flashing lights.

See also Battery-Operated Toys; Cast Iron, Airplanes; Gasoline-Powered Toys; Model Kits; Robots and Space Toys; Windups, Friction, and Other Mechanicals.

Aeroplane, CK, w/up, aluminized tin w/celluloid prop, 8" W, NM (NM box), A $650.00

Air Service, American Flyer, sheet metal, single prop, brass cockpit, clockwork mechanism, rubber tires, 24", EX, A, $3,000.00.

Air Transport Service Car Ferry, Germany, 1950s, friction, litho tin, 13½" W, NM (NM box) $265.00

Airplane, Wyandotte, 1940s, single-prop, bl & red w/wooden wheels, 9" W, EX+ $150.00

Akron Blimp, Steelcraft, 1920s, pressed steel, 25" L, VG, A ...$1,200.00

American Airlines Boeing 707 Astrojet, Y, battery-op, several actions, litho tin, 22" L, EX (EX box), A $650.00

American Airlines DC-7, Linemar, 1950s, battery-op, litho tin, 19" W, NM $400.00

American Airlines DC-7, Linemar, 1950s, friction, 4-prop, litho tin, 15" W, EX, A $500.00

American Airlines Electra, Linemar, 1950s, 4-prop, litho tin, 19½" W, NM $200.00

American Airlines Electra Jet, TN, 4-prop, battery-op, litho tin & plastic, 17" W, NM (EX box), A $300.00

B-50 Super Fortress, Japan, 1950s, 4-prop, friction, litho tin, 15" W, NM $435.00

B-58 Hustler Jet, Marx, 1950s, battery-op, litho tin, 12" W, rare, NM, minimum value $900.00

Boeing Airplane, Kingsbury, single-prop, clockwork, yel- & red-pnt pressed steel, 12" W, VG, A $650.00

Boeing Plane, Kingsbury, single-prop, clockwork, yel- & red-pnt pressed steel, 12" W, G, A $300.00

Boeing Stratocruiser, Japan, 4-prop, friction, litho tin, 20" W, G, A $275.00

Boeing 727 Jetliner, Y, 1960s, battery-op, litho tin, 16" W, EX $285.00

Boeing 737 Jetliner, TN, 1960s, battery-op, litho tin, 10½" W, EX $200.00

Bristol Bulldog T-360, S&E, battery-op, litho tin, 14½" W, EX $325.00

Bristol Jet 188, Marx, 1960s, battery-op, tin & plastic, 9" W, EX $185.00

Cabin Plane, Kingsbury, single-prop, clockwork, gr-pnt pressed steel, 8" W, VG, A $350.00

Capitol Airlines Viscount, Japan, 1950s, 4-prop, litho tin, battery-op, remote control, 14" W, NM $195.00

Capitol Airlines Viscount 321, Linemar, 1950s, battery-op, litho tin, 14" W, NM $325.00

Chicago Zeppelin, Strauss, clockwork, litho tin, 10" L, EX, A $250.00

Comet Jetliner, Japan, 1950s, 4-prop, friction, litho tin, 15" W, NM $185.00

Cragstan Skymaster, mk Cessna, friction, litho tin, 11" W, NM (EX box), A $225.00

Cragstan Vertol 1107 Helicopter, 1950s, battery-op, litho tin, 13½" L, NM $250.00

Eastern Airlines, Japan, 1950s, 4-prop, litho tin, friction, 12" W, EX $95.00

FA-059 Fighter Plane, TN, 1950s, battery-op, litho tin, 13" W, NM $350.00

Flying Tiger Cargo Plane, TN, 4-prop, litho tin, 15" L, EX (EX box) $485.00

Fokker Tri-Wing Model, stick and sheet construction, EX details, 40" long, EX, A, $360.00.

Ford Trimotor Plane, TN, friction, litho tin w/plastic props, 14½" W, rare, NM (EX box), A $475.00

Grumman F9F-8 Navy Jet, Alps, 1950s, friction, litho tin w/plastic cockpit cover, 9½" W, EX, A $175.00

Hillclimber Biplane, single-prop, friction, orange-pnt pressed steel, 16" L, EX, A $500.00

Japan Airlines DC-8 Model, four-prop, cast aluminum, cream and silver with red details, 36" long, EX, A, from $500.00 to $600.00. (Photo courtesy Noel Barrett)

Keystone Airmail Plane, double doors, axle clicker, nickel prop, 24", VG+, A, $1,300.00; Turner Airmail Plane, single-engine, Northwest Airway decals, 23", VG, A, $750.00.

KLM Stratocruiser, TN, 1950s, battery-op, litho tin, 14" W, EX $300.00

Lockheed Constellation, 1950s, friction, 4-prop, diecast w/plastic props, 8" W, NM, A..$225.00

Lockheed Starfire Jet, M, friction, litho tin, advances w/sparks, 8" W, NM (EX box), A $200.00

Lufthansa Jet, Gama, 1960s, battery-op, litho tin, 18½" W, EX $225.00

Northwest Airlines DC-7, Asahi, 4-prop, battery-op, litho tin, 19" W, EX (EX box), A $650.00

Northwest DC-6 Airliner, ATC, 1950s, battery-op, litho tin, 19" W, rare, EX...$400.00

NWA Orient Airlines, Japan, 1950s, 4-prop, litho tin, friction, 11½" W, NM $100.00

Pan Am Boeing Vertol 107 Sky Taxi, Haji, 1970s, battery-op, 13" L, NM...$250.00

Pan American World Airways DC-7, TN, 1950s, 4-prop, battery-op, litho tin, 19" W, EX $275.00

Passenger Plane, single-prop, blk- & orange-pnt pressed steel w/wooden tires, 18" W, EX, A....................................$450.00

Right Plane, Schiebles, single-prop, pressed steel w/paper litho image of pilot & passengers, 27½" W, EX, A...........$650.00

Silver Eagle, 2-prop, w/up, aluminum w/red lettering, 13" W, VG, A...$125.00

Spirit of St Louis Airplane Tower, litho tin tower w/2 tin airplanes, 18" tower, VG, A...$750.00

Stratoliner Skycruiser, Marx, 4-prop, friction, litho tin, 19" W, NM (VG box), A $350.00

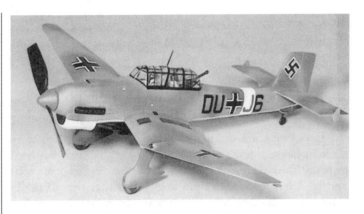

Stuka Dive Bomber Model, balsa and silk span, rubber-band powered, two figures, 33x26", EX, A, $165.00.

Training Plane, single-prop, w/up, silver w/pilot in red helmet, 4" W, NM (EX box), A...$100.00

Transatlantic Monoplane, Kingsbury, clockwork, pressed steel, 10" W, VG, A $300.00

Transport Plane, Buddy L, 4-prop, wht w/bl wings, 27" W, VG, A $275.00

TWA DC-7C Airliner, Yonezawa, 1960s, battery-op, litho tin, 23" W, rare, EX $400.00

TWA DC-9 Airliner, TM, 1960s, battery-op, litho tin, 14" W, EX $275.00

United Airlines Mainline Stratocruiser, Linemar, 1950s, 4-prop, friction, litho tin, 13" W, EX+ $150.00

United DC-7 Mainliner, Yonezawa, 1950s, battery-op, litho tin, 14" W, rare, EX $400.00

US Airmail Bi-Wing Plane, Kingsbury, clockwork, orange- & bl-pnt pressed steel, CI pilot, 12" W, VG, A...............$300.00

US Army Helicopter N-41312, Alps, 1960s, battery-op, tin & plastic, 12" L, EX $165.00

US Army Plane, Marx, w/up, 2-prop, litho tin, 18" W, EX, A...$200.00

US Mail Plane, Steelcraft, 3-prop, blk- & orange-pnt pressed steel, 22" L, VG, A $650.00

US Mail Plane, Steelcraft, 3-prop, red- & yel-pnt pressed steel, 24" L, VG, A $650.00

US Navy 7F7 Biplane, Cragstan, 1950s, battery-op, litho tin, 11½" W, EX..$400.00

USAF C-120 Pack Plane, Japan, 2-prop, friction, litho tin, 15" W, G, A...$125.00

USAF Convair B-36, Yonezawa, 6-prop, friction, litho tin, 26" W, EX, A $385.00

USAF Helicopter, TN, friction, litho tin, 10" L, NM (EX box), A $85.00

USAF Military Air Transport Service Jet w/Escorts, Japan, friction, 2 planes attached to rods, litho tin, 12" L, NM, A........$300.00

USAF Military Airlift Command Jet, TN, 1960s, battery-op, litho tin, 14" W, EX $265.00

USAF Sabre Jet Fighter, ASC, friction, litho tin, 9" L, NM (EX box), A..$250.00

USAF Strato Jet, TN, 1950s, battery-op, litho tin, 14" W, NM...$250.00

USAF XF-160 Jet, TN, battery-op, litho tin, bump-&-go action w/lights & sound, 11" L, rare, EX, A...................$200.00

XF-160 Jet, Japan, battery-op, litho tin, bump-&-go action w/lights & sound, 10½" L, NM, A $200.00

Automobiles and Other Vehicle Replicas

Listed here are the model vehicles (most of which were made in Japan during the 1950s and 1960s) that were designed to realistically represent the muscle cars, station wagons, convertibles, budget models, and luxury cars that were actually being shown concurrently on showroom floors and dealers' lots all over the country. Most were made of tin, many were friction powered, some were battery operated. In our descriptions, all are tin unless noted otherwise.

When at all possible, we've listed the toys by the names assigned to them by the manufacturer, just as they appear on the original boxes. Because of this, you'll find some of the same models listed by slightly different names. All vehicles are painted or painted and lithographed tin unless noted.

Advisor: Kerry and Judy Irvin (K5).

See also Promotional Cars; specific manufacturers.

Bentley Touring Car, Minic, clockwork, red & blk w/chrome detail, 5", NMIB, A $375.00
BMW Convertible, Shuco #2002/Germany, w/up, wht, 5½", EX $50.00
Bonneville Salt-Flats Special #12, Mattel, friction, gold w/Mobilgas decals, NM (NM box).........................$300.00
Buick, Ichiko, 1960, friction, cream & red w/chrome detail, 6½", M...$450.00
Buick, MSK, friction & battery-op, red w/chrome detail, 6½", NMIB..$100.00
Cadillac, Alps, 1952, friction, blk 2-door w/chrome detail, red interior, 11", NMIB $675.00
Cadillac, Bandai, 1959, friction, cream w/chrome detail, 11", NM, A $170.00
Cadillac, Bandai, 1959, friction, lt bl w/chrome detail, 11", NM, A $300.00
Cadillac, Bandai, 1959, Model Auto Series, gold w/chrome detail, MIB..$265.00
Cadillac, Bandai, 1960, friction, bl w/chrome detail, 11½", M $200.00
Cadillac, Japan, 1954, friction, red w/blk top & chrome detail, 10", MIB, A $565.00
Cadillac, Marusan, 1953, friction, gray w/chrome detail, wht-wall tires, 12½", NM, A $640.00
Cadillac Coupe DeVille, Asahitoy, 1965, friction, red w/chrome detail, 17", EX (EX box), A $1,650.00
Cadillac Old Timer Convertible, Bandai, 1933, friction, red w/chrome detail, side-mounted spare, 8", NM (EX box), A $170.00
Cadillac Sedan, Bandai, 1964, friction, gold w/chrome detail, 2-tone bl interior, 17", NM (EX box), A....................$900.00
Cadillac Sedan, Marusan, 1950, battery-op, cream w/dk gr top & chrome detail, 11", MIB..............................$1,900.00
Chevrolet, Marusan, 1954, friction, beige w/blk roof, striped interior, 11", EX..$600.00

Chevrolet, Linemar, tin, painted gray with black roof, chrome trim, rubber tires, friction, 11¼", NMIB, A, $1,300.00.

Chevrolet Convertible w/U-Haul Trailer, friction, red w/chrome detail, 12", EX (EX box), A.....................................$150.00
Chevrolet Corvair Sedan, NGS, friction, red w/chrome detail, 8", NM (NM box) $150.00
Chevy Corvette, Bandai, 1965, friction, cream, 8", EX..$120.00
Chevy Corvette Convertible, Y, 1960, friction, red w/chrome detail, 8", NM, A..$150.00
Chrysler Airflow Sedan, Cor-Cor, w/up w/battery-op headlights, dk gray w/chrome detail, 16", NM, A $975.00
Chrysler Imperial, Bandai, 1961, friction, red w/blk top, chrome detail, plastic taillights, 8", NM (NM box)..............$210.00
Chrysler Sedan, Yonezawa, 1953, friction, red w/chrome detail, 10", rare, NM, A..$300.00
Citroen, Bandai, friction, gray & lt gr w/chrome detail, 12", NM, A..$265.00
Citroen DS-19, Bandai, 1950, friction, gr w/cream top, chrome detail, 8", NM, A...$270.00

Citroen Sedan, Bandai, tin with gray and light green paint, friction, 12", EX, A, $350.00.

Corvette Sting Ray, Bandai, 1964, friction, bl w/chrome detail, Sting Ray decal on hood, 8", NM, A $100.00
DeSoto, Asahi, friction, red w/chrome detail, 8", EX (EX box mk New DeSoto) $140.00
Dodge Streamline Sedan, 1958, battery-op, cream w/chrome detail, 9", NM (EX box), A...$190.00
Edsel, TY, 1958, friction, red & cream w/chrome detail, 7½", EX, A..$75.00
Electro Matic 7500 Convertible, Distler, battery-op, red w/chrome detail, 10", NM (NM box), A.................$375.00

Falcon and Trailer, Bandai, 1962, tin, red and black with red and white trailer, friction, 17", VG, A, $175.00.

Ferrari Coupe, Bandai, tin with dark gray and red paint, friction, 11", EX, A, $350.00.

Fiat Convertible, Usagai, friction, lt metallic bl w/chrome detail, 6", NM (EX box) $140.00

Firebird III, Cragstan/Alps, 1950s, 11½", EX $375.00

Ford Convertible, Haji, 1956, friction, red & cream w/chrome detail, 12", rare, NM, A $1,875.00

Ford Crown Victoria, Yonezawa, 1956, friction, wht & red w/bl roof, chrome detail, 12", MIB $1,125.00

Ford Fairlane, SAN, 1956, friction, scarce chrome version, 13", EX (G box) $570.00

Ford Fairlane Ranch Wagon, Bandai, 1950s, friction, lt gr & wht w/chrome detail, 11½", NM (EX box), A $675.00

Ford Fairlane 500 Skyliner, Cragstan, friction, red w/wht top that slides into trunk, chrome detail, 11", NMIB, A $300.00

Ford Lincoln & House Trailer, Miller Ironson, yel & bl car w/removable top, silver & bl trailer, 40", NM (EX box), A $1,800.00

Ford Mustang, Taiyo, 1960s, friction, bl w/chrome detail, 9½", NM (NM box) $75.00

Ford Mustang 2+2, 1960s, friction, bl, 14", MIB $120.00

Ford Sedan, Marusan, 1956, friction w/battery-op headlights, bl & wht w/chrome detail, 13", rare, NM, A $6,000.00

Ford Skyliner, TN, 1958, battery-op, red w/chrome detail, detractable roof, NMIB $225.00

Ford Thunderbird, Bandai, 1958, friction, red w/blk sliding door sunroof, chrome detail, 2-tone bl interior, 8", NM, A .$100.00

Ford Thunderbird, Bandai, 1959, friction, yel w/gr top & chrome detail, 8", NM, A $140.00

Ford Thunderbird, Bandai, 1962, friction, bl w/blk top & chrome detail, 11", M, A $300.00

Ford Thunderbird, Ichiko, 1969, friction, lime gr w/chrome detail, 10½", EX (EX box), A $300.00

Ford Thunderbird, Japan, 1956, friction, bl w/gr see-through roof, chrome detail, 11", NM, A $340.00

Ford Thunderbird Convertible, Japan, 1964, friction, red w/wht retractable roof, chrome detail, 15", EX (EX box), A $340.00

Ford 1957, Ichiko, tin, pale green and white two-door hardtop, friction, 10", EX (EX box), A, $500.00.

Ford 2-Door Hardtop, Ichiko, 1957, friction, bl & wht w/chrome detail, 9½", VG+ $225.00

House Trailer & Station Wagon, SSS Toys, friction, red car, wht trailer w/red detail, MIB $170.00

Isetta, Bandai, 1950s, friction, red & cream, 6½", MIB..$360.00

Isetta, Bandai, 1950s, friction, 2-tone gr, 6½", NMIB $320.00

Jaguar, MT, 1950s, friction, red w/blk top, chrome detail, 7½", MIB $190.00

Jaguar Coupe, Bandai, friction, red w/chrome detail, blk top, 9", NM (EX box)... $510.00

Jaguar E-Type, TT, friction, red w/chrome detail, 11", NM (NM box)... $360.00

Jaguar E-Type Convertible, Europe, friction, blk w/chrome detail, Cordatic tires, 10", EX (EX box) $60.00

Lincoln Continental Mark III, Bandai, 1958, friction, red w/gold top, 11½", NM (NM box), A................................. $525.00

Lincoln Convertible Continental Mark III, tin, light green with skirts, friction, 11½", EX (VG box), A, $450.00.

Mercedes Benz 219 Convertible, Bandai, friction, metallic bl w/chrome detail, litho interior, 8", NM, A $120.00

Mercedes Benz 230 SL Convertible, TN, 1960, friction, metallic bl w/chrome detail, retractable roof, 9½", NMIB, A.......$150.00

Mercedes Benz 300 SE, Ichiko, friction, red w/chrome detail, 27", NMIB, A $150.00

Mercedes Benz 300SE, Made in Japan, tin with lithographed interior, plastic tires and steering wheel, friction, 7", NMIB, $100.00.

Mercedes Sedan 219, Bandai, friction, bl w/chrome detail, 8", MIB...$190.00

Mercedes 220 S, Schuco, w/up, red w/wht top & chrome detail, 5", EX (VG box)...$100.00

Mercedes 300 SL Gullwing Coupe, Marklin, 1955, w/up, chrome, steerable front end, 13", MIB....................$245.00

Mercury, 1953, Rock Valley Toy Co./Japan, tin, battery-operated with forward and reverse, litho interior, 9½", NMIB, A, $350.00.

MG Magnette Mark III Convertible, Japan, friction, 8", EX (EX box)...$245.00

New Cunningham C-6R Convertible, Irco, friction, bl & wht w/chrome detail, 8", NM (EX box) $340.00

Oldsmobile Convertible, Y, 1952, friction, red w/chrome detail, 10", EX (EX box)...$375.00

Packard Hawk Convertible, Schuco, 1957, battery-op, 10½", EX (VG box)..$675.00

Packard Sedan, Alps, friction, red w/chrome detail, 16½", EX $2,250.00

Packard Sedan, Alps, 1953, friction, blk w/chrome detail, 16", EX (EX box), A...$5,400.00

Packard Sedan, Daiya, 1950s, friction, red & cream w/chrome detail, 9", EX (EX box), A.......................................$245.00

Packard 52, Japan, friction, red w/bright bl tires, chrome detail, 7", EX (EX box) $110.00

Plymouth Convertible, 1959, friction, red w/wht tail fins, chrome detail, 11", EX...$450.00

Plymouth Station Wagon, Bandai, 1958, friction, bl & cream w/chrome detail, 8½", rare, EX, A $200.00

Plymouth Valiant Sedan, Bandai, 1963, friction, metallic gr w/chrome detail, 8", VG (VG box), A.....................$75.00

Pontiac Deluxe Sedan, Asahitoy, friction, red & wht w/chrome detail, family lithoed in windows, 10", rare, NMIB .$575.00

Porsche, Bandai, battery-op, cream w/chrome detail, features opening doors, w/driver, 10", NM (EX box) $150.00

Porsche Sedan, Joustra, friction, red w/passengers lithoed in windows, blk rubber tires, 8", EX (EX box) $100.00

Rambler Sedan, Y, 1950s, friction, brn w/wht top, working wipers, 8", M...$55.00

Renault, Rossignol, w/up, red, bl & cream w/tin balloon tires, 8½", VG $190.00

Rolls Royce Sedan, Minic, clockwork, red & blk w/chrome detail, 5", NMIB, A $340.00

Rolls Royce Silver Cloud Convertible, Bandai, friction, metallic bl w/blk top, chrome detail, 12", NM (EX box), A .$600.00

Rolls-Royce Silver Cloud Sedan, Bandai, tin, friction, green and cream, EX+ (EX box), A, $550.00.

Shasta Travel Trailer, Fleet Line, 1950s, wht & yel w/plastic windows, 11½", scarce, NM (EX box) $300.00

Station Wagon, Joustra, friction, red w/cream top, chrome detail, 8", EX (EX box), A.......................................$120.00

Streamline Sports Roadster Convertible, Minic, clockwork, gr w/chrome detail, 5", NMIB, A $340.00

Toyota 2000 GT, Ichiko, 1960s, friction, red w/chrome detail, 16", VG, A...$230.00

Vauxhall Cabriolet, Minic, clockwork, bl & blk w/chrome detail, 5", NMIB, A $270.00

Vauxhall Town Coupe, Minic, clockwork, gr & blk w/chrome detail, 5", NMIB, A $240.00

Volkswagen, Bandai, 1963, friction, bl w/chrome detail, 8", NM (EX box) $120.00

Volkswagen, Taiyo, battery-op, red w/chrome detail, 10", EX (EX box), A $75.00

Volkswagen Convertible, Japan, friction, bl w/cream top, red plastic seats, lighted piston action, 9½", EX (EX box) $100.00

Volkswagen w/Camper, Bandai, battery-op, cream w/see-through trunk, silver trailer, 16", NM (EX box), A $565.00

Volvo Amazon Sedan, Bandai, friction, gr w/wht top, chrome detail, 8¼", EX+ $240.00

Banks

The impact of condition on the value of a bank cannot be overrated. Cast iron banks in near-mint condition with very little paint wear and all original parts are seldom found and might bring twice as much (if the bank is especially rare, up to five times as much) as one in average, very-good original condition with no restoration and no repairs. Overpainting and replacement parts (even screws) have a very negative effect on value. Mechanicals dominate the market, and some of the hard-to-find banks in outstanding, near-mint condition may exceed $20,000.00! (Here's a few examples: Girl Skipping Rope, Calamity, and Mikado.) Modern mechanical banks are also emerging on the collectibles market, including Book of Knowledge and James D. Capron, which are reproductions with full inscriptions stating that the piece is a replica of the original. Still banks are widely collected as well, with more than 3,000 varieties having been documented. Beware of unmarked modern reproductions. All of the banks listed below are cast iron unless noted otherwise.

For more information we recommend *The Dictionary of Still Banks* by Long and Pitman; *The Penny Bank Book* by Moore; *The Bank Book* by Norman; and *Penny Lane* by Davidson. For information on porcelain and ceramic banks we recommend *Collector's Guide to Banks* by Beverly and Jim Mangus and *Ceramic Coin Banks* by Tom and Loretta Stoddard. For information on glass banks Collector Books offers *Collector's Guide to Glass Banks* by Charles V. Reynolds.

Advisors: Bill Bertoia, mechanicals; Dan Iannotti (I3), modern mechanicals; and Diane Patalano (P8).

See also Advertising; Battery-Operated; Character, TV, and Movie Collectibles; Disney; Diecast Collector Banks; Political; Reynolds Banks; Robots, Miscellaneous; Rock 'n Roll; and other specific categories.

MECHANICAL BANKS

Afghanistan Bank, Mechanical Novelty Works, EX, A...$4,950.00

Always Did 'Spise a Mule (Boy on Bench), J&E Stevens, G, A $750.00

Always Did 'Spise a Mule (Jockey), J&E Stevens, G-, A..$500.00

Artillery Bank, Book of Knowledge, NM, I3 ....$295.00

Artillery Bank, J&E Stevens, EX+, A........................$2,000.00

Artillery Bank, J&E Stevens, VG, A $800.00

Auto, John Wright, limited edition of 250, NM, I3 ....$600.00

Bad Accident, J&E Stevens, VG, A $2,100.00

Bad Accident, James Capron, M, I3 ....$795.00

Bear & Tree Stump, gold, EX, D10 ....$875.00

Betsy Ross, Davidson/Imswiller, bl or yel dress, M, I3, ea...$875.00

Bill E Grin, pnt aluminum, EX......................................$325.00

Bobby Riggs & Billy Jean King, John Wright, limited edition of 250, scarce, M, I3...$795.00

Bowler's Strike, Richards/Wilton, scarce, NM, I3...........$595.00

Boy on Trapeze, Book of Knowledge, M, $495.00.
(Photo courtesy Dan Ianotti)

Boy on Trapeze, J Barton & Smith, VG, A..................$1,750.00

Boy Robbing Bird's Nest, J&E Stevens, NM, A $6,100.00

Boy Scout Camp, J&E Stevens, VG+, A.....................$6,900.00

Boy Stealing Watermelon, Kyser & Rex, VG, A.........$1,650.00

Bread Winner's Bank, J&E Stevens, EX, A $14,300.00

Bulldog, J&E Stevens, EX, $1,100.00. (Photo courtesy Dunbar Gallery)

Butting Buffalo, Book of Knowledge, M, I3 ....$350.00

Butting Goat, Judd Mfg, G, A $450.00

Cabin, Book of Knowledge, NM, I3 ....$325.00

Cabin, J&E Stevens, NM, A...$1,100.00

Calamity, J&E Stevens, VG, A....................................$12,100.00

Cat & Mouse, Book of Knowledge, NM, I3 ....$325.00

Cat and Mouse (cat balancing), J&E Stevens, Pat. 1891, EX, $4,000.00. (Photo courtesy Dunbar Gallery)

Eagle and Eaglets, gray base, J&E Stevens, EX, $1,540.00. (Photo courtesy Dunbar Gallery)

Cat Boat, Richards/Wilton, NM, I3	$695.00
Chief Big Moon, J&E Stevens, EX+, D10	$4,400.00
Chief Big Moon, J&E Stevens, G-, A	$800.00
Chinaman Reclining, J&E Stevens, VG, A	$2,200.00
Circus Ticket Collector, Judd, EX, A	$475.00
Clown on Globe, J&E Stevens, EX+ (EX wooden box), A	$7,700.00
Clown on Globe, James Capron, M, I3	$775.00
Columbian Magic Savings, Introduction Co, ca 1892, G, A	$450.00
Console TV, litho tin, EX	$100.00
Cow (Kicking), Book of Knowledge, NM, I3	$315.00
Creedmoor Bank, J&E Stevens, G, A	$400.00
Creedmoor Bank, J&E Stevens, VG, from $500 to	$650.00
Darktown Battery, J&E Stevens, VG, A	$3,500.00
Dentist Bank, Book of Knowledge, EX, I3	$175.00

Eagle & Eaglets, J&E Stevens, VG, A	$825.00
Elephant, James Capron, M, I3	$250.00
Elephant, John Wright, NM, I3	$175.00
Elephant (Jumbo on Wheels), J&E Stevens, VG, A	$550.00
Elephant & Three Clowns, J&E Stevens, NM, A	$4,200.00
Elephant w/Howdah (Man Pops Out), Enterprise Mfg, VG, A	$350.00
Ferris Wheel, Hubley, EX	$5,000.00
Football, John Harper, EX, A	$2,400.00

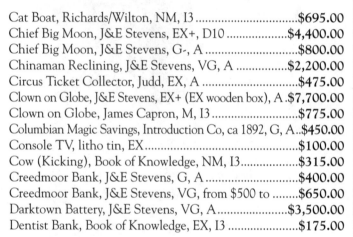

Dentist, J&E Stevens, 1880 – 1890, 9½", EX+, $18,000.00. (Photo courtesy Dunbar Gallery)

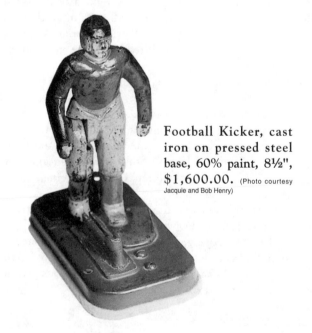

Football Kicker, cast iron on pressed steel base, 60% paint, 8½", $1,600.00. (Photo courtesy Jacquie and Bob Henry)

Dog on Turntable, Judd, G, A	$350.00
Eagle & Eaglets, Book of Knowledge, M, I3	$450.00
Eagle & Eaglets, J&E Stevens, NM, A	$3,300.00

Frog (Two Frogs), J&E Stevens, VG, A	$1,000.00
Frog (Two Frogs), James Capron, NM, I3	$625.00
Frog on Round Base, J&E Stevens, VG, A	$550.00
Frog on Stump, 4" base, VG, A	$600.00
Girl in Victorian Chair, WS Reed, rpt, A	$1,550.00
Girl Skipping Rope, J&E Stevens, VG, A	$14,300.00
Hall's Excelsior, J&E Stevens, VG+, A	$350.00
Hall's Excelsior, rpl teller, G, A	$200.00

Harold Lloyd, Germany, tin, EX, A $1,100.00
Hen & Chick, J&E Stevens, EX $3,200.00
Home Bank, Judd, NM, D10.....................................$2,200.00
Hoopla, John Harper, EX, A.......................................$250.00
Horse Race, J&E Stevens, straight base, VG+, A $6,600.00
Humpty Dumpty, Book of Knowledge, M, I3 ....$325.00
Humpty Dumpty, Shepard Hardware, VG, from $800 to...$1,000.00
Indian Shooting Bear, J&E Stevens, rpl feathers, VG, A..$1,600.00
John Deere Anvil, diecast, MIB, I3 ....$125.00
Jolly N, High Hat; red coat, wht collar, G, A $230.00
Jolly N, High Hat; wht top hat, G, A $260.00

Jonah and the Whale, Shepard Hardware, Pat. 1890, EX, $4,400.00. (Photo courtesy Dunbar Gallery)

Jonah & the Whale, Shepard Hardware, VG, A.........$2,200.00
Leap Frog, Book of Knowledge, NM, I3 ....$335.00
Leap Frog, Shepard Hardware, G, A $1,500.00

Leap Frog, Shepard Hardware, VG, from $1,800.00 to $2,200.00. (Photo courtesy Dunbar Gallery)

Lighthouse, unknown Am maker, EX, A.....................$4,100.00
Lion & Monkeys, James Capron, M, I3 ....$875.00
Lion & Monkeys, Kyser & Rex, VG+, A.......................$950.00
Little Joe, John Harper, VG, A $225.00
Lucky Wheel Money Box, litho tin, EX, A....................$150.00
Magic Bank, J&E Stevens, VG, A $1,600.00
Magic Bank, James Capron, MIB, I3................................$650.00
Magician, Book of Knowledge, MIB, I3 ....$325.00

Magician, J&E Stevens, VG, A $3,800.00
Mammy & Child, Kyser & Rex, EX..............................$8,500.00
Man w/Mustache & Top Hat, litho tin, NM, A $275.00
Mason, Shepard Hardware, EX+, A.............................$6,600.00
Merry-Go-Round, Kyser & Rex, 4⅝", VG, A $400.00
Milking Cow, Book of Knowledge, NM, I3....................$295.00
Minstrel, Saalheimer & Strauss, litho tin, EX, A $385.00
Monkey, Hubley, bl base, rare, NM, A..........................$4,600.00
Monkey, James Capron, MIB, I3 ....$395.00
Monkey & Coconut, J&E Stevens, VG, A $2,700.00
Monkey w/Tray, litho tin, EX, A $200.00
Motor Bank, Kyser & Rex, VG....................................$3,450.00
Mule Entering Barn, J&E Stevens, G, A $600.00
Mule Entering Barn, James Capron, NM, I3..................$495.00
Multiplying Bank, J&E Stevens, VG, A.......................$1,300.00
Organ Bank (Boy & Girl), Book of Knowledge, NM, I3 ..$375.00
Organ Bank (Boy & Girl), Kyser & Rex, G, from $600 to....$800.00
Organ Bank (Cat & Dog), Kyser & Rex, EX+, A $3,500.00
Owl (Turns Head), Book of Knowledge, NM, I3 ....$250.00
Owl (Turns Head), J&E Stevens, brn w/yel eyes, EX, D10....$700.00
Paddy & the Pig, Book of Knowledge, NM, I3 ....$375.00
Paddy & the Pig, J&E Stevens, G, A $600.00
Pay Phone, J&E Stevens, NP, EX, A............................$700.00
Penny Pineapple, Richards/Wilton, commemorates Hawaii 50th
    state, G, A $200.00
Penny Pineapple, Richards/Wilton, commemorates Hawaii 50th
    state, NM, I3 ....$450.00
Picture Gallery, Shepard Hardware, VG, A.................$9,900.00
Pig in Highchair, J&E Stevens, EX, A $775.00
Pistol, Kyser & Rex, rpl trap, G, A................................$275.00
Professor Pug Frog, J&E Stevens, VG, A $6,050.00
Professor Pug Frog, James Capron, M, I3 ....$850.00
Punch & Judy, Book of Knowledge, NM, I3 ....$325.00
Punch & Judy, Shepard Hardware, EX, from $2,800 to ...$3,100.00
Punch & Judy, Shepard Hardware, G-, A $750.00
Rabbit in Cabbage, Kilgore, VG, from $400 to..............$500.00
Rabbit Standing, Lockwood Mfg, sm, EX, A $2,100.00
Race Course, James Capron, NM, I3.............................$575.00
Reagan O'Neill, Miley's, bronze finish, scarce, NM, I3 ..$550.00
Rooster, Kyser & Rex, NM, D10..................................$1,100.00
Saluting Sailor (No Verse), Germany, litho tin, EX, A ..$2,400.00
Saluting Sailor (w/Verse), Germany, litho tin, VG, A...$1,300.00

Santa Claus, Shepard Hardware, Pat. 1889, EX, $2,500.00. (Photo courtesy Dunbar Gallery)

Santa at Chimney, Shepard Hardware, 6", VG, A $1,400.00
Scotchman, Saalheimer & Strauss, EX, A $770.00
Speaking Dog, Shepard Hardware, red dress & base, NM,
A $10,450.00
Squirrel & Tree Stump, Mechanical Novelty Works, VG,
A $350.00
Stump Speaker, Shepard Hardware, EX, D10 ....$2,100.00
Sweet Thrift Vending Bank, Beverly Novelty, litho tin, EX,
A $225.00
Tammany, Book of Knowledge, NMIB, I3 ....$325.00
Tammany (Brown Pants), J&E Stevens, EX, A $1,000.00
Tammany (Gray Pants), J&E Stevens, VG, A $550.00
Teddy & the Bear, Book of Knowledge, NM, I3 ....$300.00
Teddy & the Bear, J&E Stevens, VG, A $1,600.00
Tid Bits Vending Bank, Lehmann, litho tin, G, A $3,100.00
Toad on Stump (Chartreuse), J&E Stevens, G, A $400.00
Treasure Chest (Musical), Black Faith Mfg, EX, A $500.00
Trick Dog, Hubley, bl base, VG, A $500.00
Trick Dog, James Capron, NM, I3 ....$400.00
Trick Pony, Book of Knowledge, NM, I3 ....$350.00

Uncle Remus, Kyser & Rex, Pat. 1891, EX, $2,800.00.
(Photo courtesy Dunbar Gallery)

Trick Pony, Shepard Hardware, Pat. 1885, NM, $4,100.00.
(Photo courtesy Dunbar Gallery)

William Tell, J&E Stevens, NM, $3,100.00.
(Photo courtesy Dunbar Gallery)

Uncle Bugs, Warner Bros, M, I3 ....$195.00
Uncle Remus, Book of Knowledge, M, I3 ....$375.00
Uncle Remus, Kyser & Rex, VG+, A $2,100.00
Uncle Sam, Richards/Wilton, scarce, rear trap, NM, I3 .$450.00
Uncle Sam, Shepard Hardware, VG, A $1,600.00
United States Bank, J&E Stevens, VG, A $850.00
US & Spain, Book of Knowledge, M, I3 ....$335.00
Vending Bank (Performing Bears), Germany, litho tin, EX+,
A $1,200.00
Vending Bank (Pinball), Germany, litho tin, VG, A $750.00
Washington at Rappahannock, John Wright, scarce, NM,
I3 ....$550.00
William Tell, Book of Knowledge, NM, I3 ....$325.00
World's Fair, Book of Knowledge, mc version, NM, I3 ...$450.00
Zoo Bank, Kyser & Rex, VG, A $825.00

World's Fair, J&E Stevens, Pat. 1893, EX, $1,200.00.
(Photo courtesy Dunbar Gallery)

REGISTERING BANKS

Bank of America, cash register shape, litho tin, 4", EX,
A...$50.00
Captain Marvel Magic Dime Saver, litho tin, EX, A......$300.00

Davy Crockett Frontier Dime Bank, litho tin, EX, A.....$400.00
Dime Coin Barrel, pnt CI, 4", EX $165.00
Dime Register Trunk, CI, 4", EX, A $225.00
Dopey Dime Register, WDE, 1938, litho tin, NM $350.00
Five Coin Economy Bank, cash register shape, litho tin, 4", EX,
    A $40.00
Jackie Robinson Daily Dime Register, litho tin, EX, A ..$600.00

Keep 'Em Smiling Dime Register, lithographed tin, EX, A, $375.00; Keep 'Em Rolling Dime Register, lithographed tin, EX, A, $450.00; Keep 'Em Flying Dime Register, lithographed tin, EX, A, $400.00. (Photo courtesy Henry Pierce)

Mickey Mouse Dime Register, WDE, 1939, litho tin, EX,
    A $300.00
Popeye Daily Quarter, litho tin, NM, from $150 to........$200.00
Prince Valiant Dime Register, litho tin, EX, A $250.00
Provident Four Coin Bank, cash register shape, litho tin, 5", EX,
    A $35.00
Prudential Dime Savings, NP CI, 7¼", EX, A $150.00
Select-O-Matic Juke Box, litho tin, 4½", NM, A $85.00
Snow White & the Seven Dwarfs Dime Register, WDE, 1938,
    litho tin, NM $350.00

Snow White Dime Register, lithographed tin, EX, A, $165.00; Little Orphan Annie Dime Register, lithographed tin, EX, A, $375.00; Superman Dime Register, lithographed tin, EX, A, $275.00. (Photo courtesy Henry Pierce)

Three Coin Commonwealth Bank, cash register shape, litho tin,
    4", EX $35.00
Three Coin Thrift Bank, cash register shape, litho tin, 5", EX,
    A $60.00
Thrifty Elf Dime Register, litho tin, 2½" sq $175.00
Uncle Sam's Dime Register, cash register shape, litho tin, 3", EX,
    A $45.00
Uncle Sam's Nickel Register, cash register shape, litho tin, 3",
    EX, A $35.00

STILL BANKS

$100,000 Money Bag, 3½", NM.....................................$375.00
Alamo, Alamo Iron Works, 2¾x3½", VG, A...............$325.00
Andy Gump Seated on Stump, Arcade, 4½", EX, A ..$1,750.00
Apple, Kyser & Rex, reddish-yel, 5", EX, A...................$900.00
Armored Car, AC Williams, red w/gold disk wheels, 6", EX,
    A $2,600.00
Automobile (Green Cab Co), Arcade, gr, blk & wht, open win-
    dows, disk wheels, w/driver, 8¼", EX, A...............$1,300.00
Automobile (Red Top Cab Co), Arcade, red, wht & blk, screened
    rear windows, disk wheels, w/driver, 7¾", EX, A $935.00
Bailey's Centennial Money Bank 1876, JS Semon, NP base, 4",
    VG, A $200.00
Bank Building (Alliance Savings & Loan), wht metal, 2½",
    EX $100.00
Bank Building (Banker's Trust), wht metal, 6½", M.........$50.00
Bank Building (Caisse), brass, 5", NM $65.00
Bank Building (Century of Progress), Arcade, wht w/bl roof, 7"
    L, NM, A $2,200.00
Bank Building (Clock), Hubley, silver w/gold trim, 6", EX,
    A $550.00
Bank Building (Columbia), Kenton, silver w/gold highlights, 7",
    EX, A $550.00
Bank Building (Columbia), Kenton, wht, 6", VG, A $500.00
Bank Building (Cook County Federal Savings), wht metal, 4",
    EX $85.00
Bank Building (County Bank), Harper, japanned, 4", EX,
    A $300.00
Bank Building (Crown), J&E Stevens, gray w/red trim, brn roof
    w/gold highlights, 3½", EX, A...............................$350.00
Bank Building (Double Doors), AC Williams, blk w/red roof &
    gold trim, 5", EX, A $500.00
Bank Building (Eagle on Cupola), US, copper finish, 9¾", EX+,
    A $7,700.00
Bank Building (Home Savings), yel, 3½", VG, A $225.00
Bank Building (Olympic Savings), wht metal, 3½", NM ..$100.00
Bank Building (Pointed Finial), brass, arched pane windows
    above door & on ea side, 7", EX, A..........................$500.00
Bank Building (Pullman Bank & Trust Co), wht metal, 4½",
    EX $25.00
Bank Building (Tacoma Park), silver, 4", EX, A..........$1,700.00
Bank Building (1876), 3", NM $50.00
Bank Building w/Horse Atop (Savings Bank), wht metal, 6",
    NM...$125.00
Baseball Mascot Standing on Ball (Am League), Hubley, 5", EX,
    A $1,500.00
Baseball on Three Bats, Hubley, EX.............................$1,650.00
Battleship Maine, Grey Iron, bl w/gold detail, 5", EX $325.00
Battleship Maine, J&E Stevens, wht, 10", NM, A $10,400.00
Battleship Oregon, J&E Stevens, gray w/gold & red trim, 6", EX,
    A $650.00
Bean Pot, red w/NP top & wire hdl, 3" dia, VG, A $250.00
Bear Stealing Honey from Beehive, Sydenham & McOustra, 7",
    EX, A $250.00
Bear Stealing Pig, gold, 5½", scarce, NM, A $1,400.00
Bear w/Honey Pot, Hubley, 6½", NM $225.00
Beehive, J Harper, 4", EX+, A.......................................$525.00

Billy Bounce (Give Billy a Penny), Hubley, silver w/red trim, 4¾", VG, A $385.00

Bird Cage, CI & tin, 3⅞", VG $100.00

Black Man's Head (Two-Faced), AC Williams, gold hat, 4", NM, A $350.00

Boat (Battleship Maine), Grey Iron, japanned w/gold highlights, 4½", EX, A $200.00

Boat (Battleship Maine), Grey Iron, silver, 4½", G, A..$100.00

Boat (Contributions for the Royal National Lifeboat Institution), rpt, 15", A $300.00

Boat (Side-Wheeler), emb Made in Canada, gold w/red trim, 7½", EX, A $550.00

Boat (When My Fortune Ship Comes In), brn, 5⅜", G, A..$500.00

Bomb, chalkware, 7½", VG, A......................................$50.00

Boy Scout, AC Williams, 1910 – 1934, 5⅞", EX, $200.00. (Photo courtesy Dunbar Gallery)

Bulova Watch, wht metal, 3", NM $85.00

Buster Brown & Tige, AC Williams, bl w/red scarf, 5½", NM, A...$550.00

Buster Brown & Tige, AC Williams, gold w/red trim, 5½", NM $350.00

Cadet Officer Hat, Hubley, bl w/gold trim, 5¾", VG, A..$1,000.00

Caisse Building w/Bird on Cupola, brass, 6", EX, A........$600.00

Camel Kneeling w/Backpack, Kyser & Rex, japanned, 2½", EX+, A...$550.00

Camel w/Saddle, AC Williams, gold, 7¼", VG, A.........$225.00

Campbell Kids, AC Williams, gold, 4", EX, A................$300.00

Captain Kidd Beside Tree, US, 5½", G...........................$300.00

Cat (Feed the Kitty), lead, 5", EX $75.00

Cat on Tub, 4⅛", G $150.00

Cat w/Ball, AC Williams, 5½", EX, A............................$350.00

Church, Germany, 1890, gr-pnt tin w/red roof, 4", G, A..$200.00

Church (West Side Presbyterian), gr, 4", VG, from $300 to....$400.00

Church (1882), Kyser & Rex, japanned w/red finial, lattice window cutouts, 6", VG, A...$300.00

Church on Base, litho tin, 6", NM, A............................$210.00

Church w/Steeple, litho tin, 3", NM...............................$225.00

Clock (Time Is Money), HC Hart, tin face w/CI top & base, paper insert & dial, 5", NM, A....................................$225.00

Columbia Tower, Grey Iron, japanned, 6½", EX, A.......$950.00

Conch Shell (Shell Out), J&E Stevens, wht, 4¾", EX, A..$600.00

Cottage (Two-Story), litho tin, 2", EX, A......................$225.00

Cottage on Scalloped Base, litho tin, 2", NM, A............$200.00

Cottage w/Side Porch, gold w/bl roof, 3", NM...............$150.00

Cow, red, 5", VG, A..$125.00

Cow (Holstein), Arcade, 4½" L, NM, A.........................$715.00

Cow on Base, NP brass, 4¼", EX...................................$325.00

Cupola, J&E Stevens, wht w/red & bl trim, 3¼", EX, A..$375.00

Dignity & Impudence, litho tin book-shape, 7", EX........$55.00

Dirigible, AC Williams, silver, 6½", NM, A...................$225.00

Dog (Basset Hound), blk, 3", rare color, G, A.............$1,050.00

Dog (Basset Hound), gold, 3", EX $300.00

Dog (Bulldog Seated), emb Made in Canada, gold, 4", VG, A $175.00

Dog (Cocker Spaniel), 6", EX, A $110.00

Dog (Fido), Hubley, wht w/blk ears, red collar, 5", EX, A $100.00

Dog (I Hear a Call), AC Williams, blk, 5½x7¾", VG...$100.00

Dog (Lost Dog), US, 5", EX, A $400.00

Dog (Puppo on Pillow), Hubley, blk & wht, 6", EX+, A..$225.00

Dog (Scottie Seated), blk, 3", EX, A..............................$200.00

Dog (Spaniel w/Pack), blk w/gold detail, 5½", NM........$100.00

Dog (Spitz), Grey Iron, brn, 4¼", VG, A $275.00

Dog (St Bernard w/Package), AC Williams, 7", EX $225.00

Dog (Terrier), wht w/brn spots & red collar, 5", EX, A..$225.00

Dog on Ball, brass, 3", EX, A...$60.00

Dog w/Victrola, Germany, lead w/tin Victrola, 4¼", VG, A....$475.00

Dolphin (Boy in Boat), US, gold, 4½", EX+, A $825.00

Donkey, AC Williams, gray w/brn saddle, 6", NM, A $400.00

Doughboy, 6", VG, A $250.00

Duck in Top Hat on Tub, Hubley, 5½", EX+, A.............$165.00

Dutch Boy on Barrel, Hubley, red, yel & bl w/tan barrel, 5½", EX+, A...$125.00

Dutch Girl, Grey Iron, gold, 6½", VG, A......................$385.00

Eagle w/Shield, 4", scarce, VG, from $900 to $950.00

Eiffel Tower, Sydenham & McOustra, ca 1908, japanned w/gold trim, 9", VG, A...$850.00

Elephant in Circus Clothes, NM, D10............................$350.00

Elephant on Wheels, AC Williams, gold w/red spoke wheels, 4", NM, A $500.00

Elephant w/Blanket Standing on Tub, silver & red, 5", EX, A $225.00

Elephant w/Trunk Down & Curled Under, Arcade, gr, decal on side, 4½", EX+, A..$385.00

Elk, AC Williams, gold, 9½", NM, A $300.00

Eureka Stove, bl-pnt tin w/silver front, 5", NM.............$110.00

Federal Washing Machine, litho tin, 4¼", NM $200.00

Fidelity Trust Vault w/Lord Fauntleroy, J Barton Smith, NM, D10 ....$850.00

Fobrux Furnace, tin & CI, 5½", EX $175.00

Football Player, AC Williams, gold, 6", EX+, A............$500.00

Foxy Grandpa, Hubley, 5½", VG, A..............................$325.00

Gas Pump, Arcade, red w/gold globe, emb gallon meter w/hand-crank dial, 5½", VG, A $650.00

GE Refrigerator, cream, 4", VG, A................................$200.00

Geisha Girl Seated on Pillow Playing Instrument, Hubley, 7", VG, A $350.00

General Sheridan on Horse, Arcade, 6", VG, A............$310.00

George V Royal, Chamberlain & Hill, japanned, 5¼", NM, A $310.00

German Grenade, tin, 3½", EX, A....................................$250.00

German Helmet, tin, 2½", EX...$165.00

Gingerbread House, litho tin, 4", EX, A $55.00

Globe Furnace, lead, 5", NM, A.....................................$200.00

Globe on Arc, Grey Iron, red, 5¼", EX, A....................$400.00

Globe on Arc, Grey Iron, red, 5¼", G, A.....................$185.00

Globe Savings Fund Building, Kyser & Rex, japanned, 7", EX+, A..$4,400.00

Golliwog, John Harper, 6", EX, A $600.00

Grandfather Clock, Germany, litho tin w/visible balances, 7", EX+, A $550.00

Gunboat, Kenton, silver w/red highlights, 8½", scarce, M, A...$2,200.00

Happy Days Barrel, litho tin, w/1933 Chicago sticker, 4", EX..$45.00

Hat (Shriner's Fez), brass finish, 2¾", EX, A $225.00

Home Bank, HL Judd, brown finish, 1895, EX, A, $415.00; Old South Church, paper label on tower, original paint, EX, A, $3,575.00; Independence Hall, Enterprise, Pat. Sept. 14, 1875, EX, A, $660.00.

Horse (Beauty), Arcade, EX...$150.00

Horse (My Pet), Arcade, 4", NM, A $250.00

Horse Prancing on Base, AC Williams, glossy blk w/wht hooves, 7½", NM, A...$265.00

Horse Rearing on Pebbled Base, emb Made in Canada, copper finish, blk base, 7", EX...........................$225.00

Horse w/Blanket on Tub, blk w/red saddle, 5", NM, A...$300.00

Horse w/Front Legs on Tub, AC Williams, gold, 6", EX, A...$125.00

Humpty Dumpty, Shepard Hardware, VG, A $825.00

Ice Box (Kelvinator), Arcade, wht, 4", NMIB, A $2,000.00

Indian Lady, diecast w/pnt, Souvenir of VA, 3¼", VG, A ..$175.00

Indian w/Tomahawk, Hubley, brn, 6", G, A $150.00

Indian w/Tomahawk, Hubley, brn w/red & gold highlights, 6", NM, A...$450.00

Infantry Helmet, tin, 3", EX $125.00

Joe Socko, Straits Corp, litho tin, EX+, A.....................$250.00

Jolly Joe Clown, Saalheimer & Strauss, G, A $450.00

King Midas, Hubley, flesh & yel, 4½", NM+, A..........$1,650.00

Lamb (Feed My Sheep), lead, 3" L, NM, A $250.00

Lamb in Stride, Grey Iron, japanned, 5½", NM, A.......$225.00

Lamb Standing, gold, 4¼", EX, A $265.00

Liberty Bell Hat, litho tin, 2", EX, A..............................$95.00

Lincoln Memorial, wht metal, 6", NM, A........................$75.00

Lindberg Bust, lead, 5½", NM, A....................................$115.00

Lindberg Bust, wht metal, 6½", NM, A...........................$55.00

Lion on Tub, AC Williams, gold, bl & red, 5½", NM, A $200.00

Litchfield Cathedral, Chamberlain & Hill, ca 1908, japanned, 6½", EX, A...$300.00

Little Red Riding Hood Safe, Harper, 5", scarce, VG, A ..$3,500.00

Log Cabin, Kyser & Rex, red, 2½", EX, A.......................$350.00

Log Cabin, litho tin, 3", NM..$225.00

Magic Chef Stove, Save w/Magic Chef, wht-pnt metal, 3½", EX...$200.00

Mailbox (US Airmail), red w/bl & wht detail, 6½", EX, A..$500.00

Mailbox (US Mail w/Eagle), Kenton, gr w/gold highlights, 4", EX, A...$200.00

Main Street Trolley w/People, gold, 3", NM..................$225.00

Mammy w/Hands on Hips, Hubley, red & wht dress w/bl head scarf, 5", VG, A..$100.00

Mammy w/Spoon, AC Williams, 6", VG, A....................$175.00

Marietta Silo, gold, 5½", EX, A.......................................$625.00

Master Simpson, litho tin book-shape, 7", EX, A $50.00

Mermaid (Girl in Boat), US, gold, 4½", VG, A..............$650.00

New Deal Roosevelt, bust figure on base, silver, 5", EX, A...$165.00

Old Doc Yak Conversion, Arcade, wht, red & blk, 4¼", EX, A $650.00

Oriental Camel, US, blk w/gr rocking base, 4", EX, A ...$935.00

Oseola County Courthouse, wht metal, 5½", EX $50.00

Owl, Vindex, orange & wht, 4", VG, A...........................$150.00

Owl (Be Wise & Save Money), AC Williams, gold w/red trim, 5", EX, from $150 to $200.00

Palace, blk, 7", EX, A...$450.00

Palace, Ives, ca 1885, japanned & hand-pnt w/gold trim, 7½x8x5", EX, minimum value..............................$2,000.00

Pelican, Hubley, wht w/yel bill & gr base, 4¾", NM, A..$875.00

Pig (A Christmas Roast), blk, 3¼", VG, A......................$200.00

Pioneer Train of the Mohawk & Hudson Railroad, Van Cyten Mfg, lead, 7" L, EX, A $200.00

Pirates, litho tin book-shape, 6", EX, A $50.00

Policeman w/Club (Mulligan), AC Williams, bl, Englebry the Clothier stamped on back, 6", G, A......................$350.00

Possum, Arcade, metallic gold, 4½", G, A......................$500.00

Post Office, litho tin, tower shape w/peaked roof & graphics of children & postal worker, 7", EX, A..................$325.00

Punch & Judy Theater, litho tin, 3", NM, A $65.00

Rabbit, wht, 4½", VG, A...$125.00

Rabbit Begging, gold w/red eyes, 5", EX, A $150.00

Rabbit Lying Down, gold, 5" L, NM, A..........................$600.00

Radio (Crosley), Kenton, red w/gold highlights, 5", EX, A $850.00

Radio (Floor Model w/Combination Lock), Kenton, gr-pnt pressed steel w/NP front, 4½", G, A $200.00

Radio (GE), Arcade, gr, 4", G, A $250.00

Radio (Majestic Floor Model), Arcade, NP, 4½", EX, A ..$500.00

Radio (Templetone Floor Model), Kenton, red w/gold trim, 4", NM, A...$550.00

Reindeer, gr, 6", EX, A...$175.00

Reindeer, AC Williams, bronze paint, 1910 – 35, 9½", EX, $265.00.

Rhinoceros, Arcade, blk w/gold horn & pnt features, 5", G, A $300.00

Rhinoceros, Arcade, gold, 5" L, VG+, A $300.00

Roly Poly Monkey, litho tin, 6", M $500.00

Rooster, Arcade, blk w/red highlights, wht eyes, 4½", NM, A $275.00

Rumplestiltskin, US, gold w/red hat, 6", EX, A $350.00

Safe (American Globe), 5", NM, A $175.00

Safe (Animal), gold, 3", NM, A $185.00

Safe (Arabian), Kyser & Rex, japanned, 4½", EX, A.....$175.00

Safe (Bank of Commerce), Kenton, 6¾", VG, A $250.00

Safe (Boom), 3½", NM $100.00

Safe (Broadway Saving Bank), litho tin, 4", EX.............$75.00

Safe (Champion), red w/bl front & gold dial, 4⅛", NM ...$150.00

Safe (Chicago & New York), Kenton Hardware, 2 combination locks, 6", EX, A...$350.00

Safe (Child's Safe Fire Proof), litho tin, 5½", NM, A $115.00

Safe (Child's Safe), red-pnt tin, 4", EX, A $50.00

Safe (Daisy), 3½", NM, A $75.00

Safe (Fidelity Trust), Henry C Hart, blk w/gold trim, brass lock, paper litho labels on sides, 8½", VG, A $275.00

Safe (Fidelity), Kyser & Rex, emb dog on front, gr w/gold trim, 3½", EX, A $250.00

Safe (Filitup Savings Bank), litho tin, 4", NM, A $85.00

Safe (Harper Stork), blk w/gold stork, 6", NM, A.......$1,500.00

Safe (IXL), bl w/gr front, 3", EX, A $125.00

Safe (Jewel), J&E Stevens, NP, 7", VG, A $250.00

Safe (Liberty Head Dime), 3", EX, A $250.00

Safe (Mascot), litho tin, 4", NM, A $55.00

Safe (Moon & Star), blk w/gold trim, 5½", VG, A $110.00

Safe (My Secret Safe), red-pnt tin, 5", EX, A $40.00

Safe (National), Kyser & Rex, gold w/floral design, mc trim, beveled bottom, 4½", VG, A $125.00

Safe (Pet Safe), gold, 4½", NM, A $350.00

Safe (Roller), Kyser & Rex, 1882, japanned, 3½", EX+, A $165.00

Safe (Save Your Pennies), 3½", NM, A $100.00

Safe (Savings Bank), Kenton, silver w/emb filigree door, 4½", VG+, A $125.00

Safe (Security Safe Deposit), Ives, blk w/gold trim, brass dial, 8¼", VG, A $135.00

Safe (Sport), Kyser & Rex, japanned w/gold trim, depicts man feeding dog, 3", EX, A $55.00

Safe (State), red w/gold door, 4⅛", EX, A........................$75.00

Safe (Sun Dial Bank), litho tin, 4", NM, A $95.00

Safe (Thrift Bank), Champion, red w/bl door, NP combination lock, 4", EX, A...$200.00

Safe (Time), EM Rouch/USA, NP, dbl front doors w/emb eagle & stars on back plate, 7", EX, from $450 to............$500.00

Safe (Union), NP, 3¼", VG, A $95.00

Safe (White City Puzzle Safe No 12), 5", NM, A...........$150.00

Safe (White City Puzzle Safe No 326), 4", EX, A.............$85.00

Safe (White City Puzzle Safe No 357), gold, 3", NM, A ..$475.00

Safe (Young America), Kyser & Rex, japanned w/gold trim, bicyclist on front, 4½", EX+, A $225.00

Safe (8-Point Star), 7", NM, A $650.00

Sailor Saluting, Hubley, silver w/bl scarf, 5", NM, A......$300.00

Santa Holding Tree, Wing, red suit & wht beard, gold bears, tree & trim, 6", NM, A $2,850.00

Santa Standing w/Toys, US, ceramic, reddish brn, 6¾", EX, A $275.00

Save & Smile Money Box, England, blk w/red hat brim, wht eyes, 4", NM, A $700.00

Scout Bank, litho tin cylinder, 3", M $425.00

Seal on Rock, Arcade, blk, 3½", NM, A $350.00

Sears Tower, wht metal, 7½", NM, A...............................$45.00

Second National Bank Money Tree, wht metal, 8½", NM, A $50.00

Sharecropper, mk Made in Canada, blk w/gold trim, 5½", VG, A $300.00

Sharp Shooter, litho tin book shape, 6", NM, A $175.00

Shell, brass, 5", NM, A $175.00

Singer Sewing Machine, Germany, wood-look table w/Singer label, 5x4½", NM (VG box), A $1,000.00

Skyscraper (Six Finials), AC Williams, silver w/gold trim, 6½", EX+, A $550.00

Squirrel w/Nut, US, gold, 4", scarce, NM, A $825.00

State Bank, Kenton, japanned w/bronze trim, 3", VG, A ..$250.00

State Bank, Kenton, japanned w/bronze trim, 7", VG, A ...$465.00

State Bank, Kenton, japanned w/bronze trim, 9", EX+, A ..$800.00

State Bank, Kenton, japanned w/gold & bronze trim, 5½", EX, A $350.00

Statue of Liberty, worn paint, 6¼", G, $50.00; Mutt and Jeff, old paint, 5", VG, $170.00; Baseball Player, old paint, 5¾", G, $130.00; Mulligan, paint chips, 5¾", G, $90.00; Middy Bank, old paint, 5¼", VG, $100.00.

Statue of Liberty, gold, 6", EX, A $85.00
Statue of Liberty, Kenton, silver, 10", EX, A $400.00
Stove (Gas Stove), Bernstein, CI w/tin sides, blk, 5½", NM, A.$225.00
Stove (Gem Abendroth Bros NY), 4¾", NM, A............$100.00
Stove (Hot Point Electric), Arcade, wht w/gray trim, 6", VG, A...$525.00
Stove (Parlor), Schneider & Trenkamp, red inserts simulate fire, 6¼", EX, A $265.00
Stove (Roper), wht-pnt CI & tin, 4", EX, A $165.00
Tally-Ho, Chamberlain & Hill, 4½", NM, A $250.00
Teapot, wood & tin w/floral design, 3", EX, A.................$55.00
Teddy Bear, Arcade, blk, 2½", VG, A.............................$175.00
Telephone (Baby Bell), Kantor, blk-pnt tin w/image of children stenciled in gold, 10", EX+, A...............................$350.00
Temple Bar, England, 4", VG, A $525.00
Three Wise Monkeys, AC Williams, gold, 3½", EX, A..$225.00
Throne, mk ER II 1953, gold detail, 8", NM, A................$50.00
Tower Bank, Kyser & Rex, japanned w/red roof & highlights, 6½", EX, A $1,200.00
Tower Bank, Kyser & Rex, red, brn, gold & bl, 9¼", EX+, A .$9,300.00
Town Hall, Kyser & Rex, wht w/paper litho clock face, 4¾", EX, A..$1,400.00
Trolley, japanned, 4½", NM, A $500.00
Turkey, AC Williams, 3½", G, A $100.00
Two Kids, Harper, blk w/silver tree trunk, gr base, 4½", EX, A..$1,400.00
Uncle Sam Hat, litho tin, 3", EX, A $50.00
US Treasury Building, Grey Iron, wht w/red roof & trim, sheet metal base, 3¾", EX+, A..............................$450.00
Victory Ship, chalkware, 4", NMIB, A $100.00
Villa, Kyser & Rex, japanned w/gold roof, 5", NM, A...$3,100.00
Villa w/Brick Facade & Bay Window, Sydenham & McOustra, japanned, 4", EX+, A $1,500.00
Washington Monument, AC Williams, gold, 6⅛", VG, A.....$250.00
Weary Willie (Seated Hobo), Germany, litho tin, 5", EX, A..$225.00
Westminster Abbey, England, japanned, 6", EX, A........$165.00
Westward Ho, litho tin book shape, 6", EX......................$50.00
Whale of a Bank, blk w/wht lettering, 3", EX $50.00
Windmill, litho tin, 4", EX $35.00
Winston Churchill Bust, compo & wood, 4", EX, A $35.00
Wisconsin Begga/r Boy, gold, 7", EX $100.00
Wise Pig, Hubley, EX, D10...$150.00
World's Fair Administration Building, wht w/red roof, gold dome, 6", rpl door, A $325.00

Barbie Doll and Friends

No one could argue the fact that vintage Barbies dolls are holding their own as one of the hottest areas of toy collecting on today's market. Barbie doll was first introduced in 1959, and since then her face has changed three times. She's been blond and brunette; her hair has been restyled over and over, and it's varied in length from above her shoulders to the tips of her toes. She's worn high-fashion designer clothing and pedal pushers. She's been everything from an astronaut to a veterinarian, and no matter what her changing lifestyle required, Mattel (her 'maker') has provided it for her.

Though even Barbie doll items from recent years are bought and sold with fervor, those made before 1970 are the most sought after. You'll need to do a lot of studying and comparisons to learn to distinguish one Barbie doll from another, but it will pay off in terms of making wise investments. There are several books available; we recommend them all: *The Wonder of Barbie* and *The World of Barbie Dolls* by Paris and Susan Manos; *The Story of Barbie, Second Edition*, by Kitturah B. Westenhouser; *Barbie Doll Fashion, Vol. 1, 1959 – 1967*, and *Barbie Doll Fashion, Vol. II, 1968 – 1974*, by Sarah Sink Eames; *Barbie Exclusives*, *Books I* and *II*, by Margo Rana; *A Decade of Barbie Dolls and Collectibles, 1981 – 1991*, by Beth Summers; *The Barbie Doll Boom, 1986 – 1995, Collector's Encyclopedia of Barbie Doll Exclusives and More* and *Thirty Years of Mattel Fashion Dolls*, all by by J. Michael Augustyniak; *The Barbie Years, 1959 to 1996, Fourth Edition*, by Patrick C. Olds; *Skipper, Barbie's Little Sister*, by Scott Arend, Karla Holzerland, and Trina Kent; and *Collector's Guide to Barbie Doll Vinyl Cases* by Connie Craig Kaplan (all published by Collector Books).

Remember that unless the box is mentioned in the line (orig box, MIB, MIP, NRFB, etc.), values are given for loose items. As a general rule, a mint-in-the-box doll is worth twice as much (or there about) as one mint, no box. The same doll, played with and in only good condition, is worth half as much (or even less). Never-removed-from-box examples sell at a premium.

Advisor: Marl Davidson (D2).

Dolls

Allan, 1963, pnt red hair, straight legs, MIB, D2, from $125 to...$145.00
Barbie, #1, 1958-59, blond or brunette hair, MIB, D2, ea from $5,000 to...$6,500.00
Barbie, #2, 1959, blond or brunette hair, MIB, D2, ea from $5,000 to...$6,000.00
Barbie, #3, 1960, blond hair (extra long), orig swimsuit, NM, D2..$1,100.00
Barbie, #3, 1960, blond or brunette hair, orig swimsuit, NM, D2, ea...$950.00
Barbie, #4, 1960, blond or brunette hair, orig swimsuit, M, D2, ea from $450 to..$500.00
Barbie, #5, 1961, blond hair, MIB, D2, from $550 to $650.00
Barbie, #5, 1961, red hair, orig swimsuit, NM, D2 ....$375.00
Barbie, #6, blond hair, orig swimsuit, EX, D2 ....$250.00

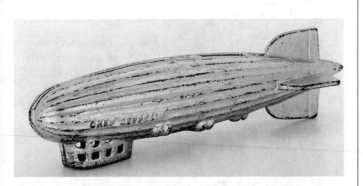

Zeppelin, AC Williams, silver paint, 6½", EX, 250.00.

Barbie, #6, brunette hair, MIB, D2, from $525 to **$600.00**
Barbie, American Beauty Queen, 1991, NRFB.................**$35.00**
Barbie, American Girl, 1964, blond, brn, or brunette hair, NRFB, ea **$1,500.00**

Barbie, American Girl, 1964, brunette, replica swimsuit, M (orig box), $900.00; NRFB: $1,500.00.
(Photo courtesy McMasters Auctions)

Barbie, American Girl, 1964, platinum cheek-length hair, orig swimsuit, NM, D2..**$650.00**
Barbie, American Girl, 1964, red hair, replica swimsuit, NM, D2 ....**$600.00**
Barbie, Amethyst Aura, 1997, Bob Mackie, NRFB **$115.00**
Barbie, Angel of Joy, 1998, Timeless Sentiments, NRFB..**$55.00**
Barbie, Antique Rose, 1996, FAO Schwarz, NRFB........**$195.00**
Barbie, Army, 1989, American Beauty Collection, NRFB...**$40.00**
Barbie, Beauty Secrets, 1980, Pretty Reflections, MIB **$85.00**
Barbie, Blue Elegance, 1992, Hills, MIB **$40.00**
Barbie, Blue Rhapsody, 1991, Service Merchandise, NRFB ..**$165.00**
Barbie, Brazilian, 1989, Dolls of the World, NRFB, D2....**$75.00**
Barbie, Bubble-Cut, 1961, blond, brunette or red hair, orig swimsuit, NM, D2, ea **$200.00**
Barbie, Bubble-Cut, 1962, blond or brunette hair, NRFB, ea **$400.00**
Barbie, Bubble-Cut w/side part, 1962-64, red hair, orig swimsuit, NM, D2...**$500.00**
Barbie, Calvin Klein, 1996, Bloomingdales, NRFB, D2 ...**$65.00**
Barbie, Canadian, 1988, Dolls of the World, NRFB **$60.00**
Barbie, Chinese, 1993, Dolls of the World, NRFB, D2.....**$50.00**
Barbie, Circus Star, 1995, FAO Schwarz, MIB..................**$95.00**
Barbie, City Shopper, 1996, Macy's, MIB.........................**$75.00**
Barbie, City Style, 1993, Classique Collection, NRFB...**$125.00**
Barbie, Coca-Cola Soda Fountain Sweetheart, 1996, NRFB, D2 ....**$300.00**
Barbie, Color-Magic, 1966, blond or brunette hair, orig swimsuit hair band & belt, NM, D2, ea **$750.00**
Barbie, Cool Looks, 1990, Toys R Us, MIB......................**$25.00**
Barbie, Country & Western Star, 1994, Wal-Mart, NRFB...**$30.00**
Barbie, Country Looks, 1993, Ames, MIB **$25.00**
Barbie, Cute 'N Cool, 1991, Target, MIB.........................**$30.00**
Barbie, Czechslovakian, 1991, Dolls of the World, NRFB ..**$100.00**

Barbie, Diamond Dazzle, 1997, Bob Mackie, NRFB.......**$135.00**
Barbie, Disney, 1990, Children's Palace, MIB..................**$45.00**

Barbie, Disney Fun, 1992, MIB, $50.00.
(Photo courtesy Margo Rana)

Barbie, Dorothy (Wizard of Oz), 1994, Hollywood Legends Series, NRFB **$350.00**
Barbie, Dramatic New Living, 1970, brunette hair, NRFB...**$250.00**
Barbie, Dramatic New Living, 1970, red hair, orig swimsuit & cover-up, NM, D2...**$175.00**
Barbie, Dream Date, 1983, MIB **$45.00**
Barbie, Dream Princess, 1992, Sears Exclusive, NRFB **$40.00**
Barbie, Dreamtime, 1982, NRFB......................................**$25.00**
Barbie, Egyptian Queen, 1994, Great Eras, NRFB..........**$125.00**
Barbie, Eliza Dolittle, 1996, Hollywood Legends Series, pk dress, NRFB **$85.00**
Barbie, Elizabethan, 1994, Great Eras, MIB, D2 ....**$50.00**
Barbie, Emerald Elegance, 1994, Toys R Us, MIB.............**$35.00**
Barbie, Empress Bride, 1992, Bob Mackie, NRFB..........**$850.00**
Barbie, English, 1992, Dolls of the World, NRFB.............**$65.00**
Barbie, Evening Elegance, 1990, JC Penney Exclusive, MIB..**$55.00**

Barbie, Fashion Queen, 1963, painted brunette hair, NRFB, $450.00.
(Photo courtesy McMasters Doll Auction)

Barbie, Evening Majesty, 1997, JC Penney Exclusive, NRFB.$40.00
Barbie, Fancy Frills, 1992, NRFB $40.00
Barbie, Fantastica, 1992, Wholesale Clubs, NRFB $60.00
Barbie, Fantasy Goddess of Asia, 1998, Bob Mackie, NRFB, D2 ....$175.00
Barbie, Flapper, 1993, Great Eras, NRFB $225.00
Barbie, Flight Time, 1990, NRFB $35.00
Barbie, Flower Seller (My Fair Lady), 1995, Hollywood Legend Series, NRFB, D2 ....$70.00
Barbie, Free Moving, 1974, NRFB $165.00
Barbie, Gift Giving, 1986, NRFB $35.00
Barbie, Glinda, 1995, Hollywood Legend Series, NRFB, D2..$85.00
Barbie, Gold Jubilee, 1994, NRFB $625.00
Barbie, Gold Medal Skater, 1976, MIB $85.00
Barbie, Great Shape, 1984, MIB.....................................$25.00
Barbie, Grecian Goddess, 1996, Great Eras, NRFB $55.00
Barbie, Greek, 1986, Dolls of the World, MIB.................$75.00

Barbie, Growing Pretty hair, 1971, M (EX box), A, $220.00.
(Photo courtesy McMasters Doll Auction)

Barbie, Hair Fair, 1967, NRFB $250.00
Barbie, Hawaiian Superstar, 1977, MIB $110.00
Barbie, Holiday, 1988, NRFB, D2, minimum value.....$1,000.00
Barbie, Holiday, 1989, NRFB, D2 ....$250.00
Barbie, Holiday, 1990, NRFB, D2 ....$250.00
Barbie, Holiday, 1991, NRFB, D2 ....$250.00
Barbie, Holiday, 1992, NRFB, D2 ....$150.00
Barbie, Holiday, 1993, NRFB, D2 ....$200.00
Barbie, Holiday, 1994, NRFB, D2 ....$175.00
Barbie, Holiday, 1995, NRFB, D2...................................$75.00
Barbie, Holiday, 1996, NRFB, D2...................................$50.00
Barbie, Holiday, 1997, NRFB, D2...................................$35.00
Barbie, International Travel, 1995, Wessco, MIB $50.00
Barbie, Irish, 1984, Dolls of the World, NRFB $125.00
Barbie, Italian, 1980, Dolls of the World, NRFB............$185.00

Barbie, Jewel Essence, 1996, Bob Mackie, NRFB, D2 ....$150.00
Barbie, Korean, 1988, Dolls of the World, NRFB $60.00
Barbie, Little Bo Peep, 1996, Children's Collector Series, NRFB...$115.00
Barbie, Live Action, 1971, blond hair, NRFB.................$165.00
Barbie, Loving You, 1984, MIB $40.00
Barbie, Madame Du, 1997, Bob Mackie, NRFB $250.00
Barbie, Magic Curl (Black), 1982, MIB $35.00
Barbie, Malibu, 1978, MIB $55.00
Barbie, Marilyn Monroe, 1997, Hollywood Legends Series, pk, red, or wht dress, MIB, ea $50.00
Barbie, Masquerade Ball, 1993, Bob Mackie, NRFB.......$400.00
Barbie, Midnight Gala, 1995, Classique Collection, NRFB..$75.00
Barbie, Montgomery Ward Anniversary, 1972, NRFB ...$750.00
Barbie, Moon Goddess, 1996, Bob Mackie, NRFB, D2 ..$175.00
Barbie, Music Lovin,' 1986, NRFB.................................$50.00
Barbie, My Size, 1993, MIB $175.00
Barbie, My Size Bride, 1994, MIB $175.00
Barbie, Native American, 1994, Dolls of the World, NRFB, D2 ....$55.00
Barbie, Navy, 1991, Stars 'n Stripes, NRFB $35.00
Barbie, New Living, 1969, blond hair, NRFB $200.00
Barbie, Nigerian, 1990, Dolls of the World, NRFB...........$60.00
Barbie, Night Dazzle, 1994, JC Penney Exclusive, NRFB.$55.00
Barbie, Norwegian, 1996, Dolls of the World, NRFB $75.00
Barbie, Olympic Skating Star, 1987, NRFB $50.00
Barbie, Oreo Fun, 1997, NRFB, D2................................$35.00
Barbie, Oriental, 1981, Dolls of the World, NRFB.........$150.00
Barbie, Oscar de la Renta, 1998, Bloomingdale's, NRFB..$80.00
Barbie, Paint & Dazzle, 1993, NRFB..............................$25.00
Barbie, Parisian, 1980s, Dolls of the World, NRFB $150.00
Barbie, Party Lace, 1989, Hills, NRFB $35.00

Barbie, Party Perfect, 1992, MIB, $50.00. (Photo courtesy Margo Rana)

Barbie, Patriot, 1995, American Stories Collection, NRFB..$35.00
Barbie, Peach Pretty, 1989, K-Mart, MIB........................$35.00
Barbie, Peaches 'N Cream, 1985, MIB $35.00
Barbie, Phantom of the Opera, 1998, FAO Schwarz, NRFB ..$150.00
Barbie, Pink & Pretty, 1982, MIB...................................$60.00

Barbie, Pink Ice, 1996, Toys R Us, MIB $95.00
Barbie, Pink Jubilee, 1987, Wal-Mart 25th Anniversary, NRFB $55.00
Barbie, Pretty in Purple, 1992, K-Mart, MIB $25.00
Barbie, Puerto Rican, 1996, Dolls of the World, NRFB, D2 .$35.00
Barbie, Queen of Hearts, 1994, Bob Mackie, NRFB, D2 ..$325.00
Barbie, Quick Curl Miss America, 1972, orig outfit, EX, D2 ...$75.00
Barbie, Quick Curl Miss America, 1976, MIB $125.00
Barbie, Radiant in Red, 1992, Toys R Us, MIB $50.00
Barbie, Rapunzel, 1995, Children's Collector Series, NRFB .$45.00
Barbie, Regal Reflections, 1992, Spiegel, MIB................$250.00
Barbie, Royal, 1980, Dolls of the World, NRFB $185.00
Barbie, Royal Invitation, 1993, Spiegel, NRFB $85.00
Barbie, Russian, 1988, Dolls of the World, NRFB, D2......$50.00
Barbie, Sapphire Dreams, 1995, Toys R Us, NRFB...........$80.00
Barbie, Sara Lee, 1993, MIB..$65.00
Barbie, Satin Nights, 1992, Service Merchandise, NRFB.$75.00
Barbie, Show 'N Ride, 1988, Toys R Us, NRFB................$40.00
Barbie, Silver Screen, 1994, FAO Schwarz, NRFB.........$200.00
Barbie, Skating Star, 1988, Sears Exclusive, NRFB $65.00
Barbie, Snow Princess, 1994, Enchanted Seasons Collection, NRFB..$160.00

Barbie, Sun Lovin' Malibu, 1979, MIB $50.00
Barbie, Super Talk, 1994, NRFB......................................$50.00
Barbie, Superstar, 1977, MIB...$110.00
Barbie, Swan Lake Ballerina, 1991, NRFB, D2 ....$200.00
Barbie, Swan Queen, 1997, Classic Ballet Series, NRFB..$30.00

Barbie, Swirl Ponytail #6, 1964, original red swimsuit, NRFB, $650.00.
(Photo courtesy McMasters Doll Auction)

Barbie, Swirl Ponytail, 1964, blond or brunette hair, orig swimsuit, M, D2, ea from $400 to....................................$500.00
Barbie, Swirl Ponytail, 1964, platinum hair, NRFB.....$1,300.00
Barbie, Talking, 1968, blond, brunette, or red hair, NRFB, ea...$400.00
Barbie, Talking, 1970, blond, brunette, or red hair, NRFB..$300.00
Barbie, Tango, 1991, Bob Mackie, NRFB $500.00
Barbie, Thailand, 1998, Dolls of the World, NRFB, D2 ...$25.00
Barbie, Theatre Elegance, 1994, Spiegel, NRFB.............$175.00
Barbie, Twinkle Lights, 1993, NRFB...............................$50.00
Barbie, Twirly Curls, 1983, MIB $45.00

Barbie, Southern Belle, 1991, MIB, $40.00.
(Photo courtesy Margo Rana)

Barbie, Spanish, 1983, Dolls of the World, NRFB..........$110.00
Barbie, Sparkle Eyes (Black), 1992, NRFB $40.00
Barbie, Sparkling Splendor, 1993, Service Merchandise, MIB...$50.00
Barbie, Spring Bouquet, 1995, Enchanted Seasons, NRFB ..$115.00
Barbie, Standard, 1967, brunette hair, straight legs, NRFB..$600.00
Barbie, Standard, 1967, red hair, straight legs, NRFB .$1,100.00
Barbie, Standard, 1970, blond hair, replica swimsuit, NM, D2 ....$325.00
Barbie, Star Dream, 1987, Sears Exclusive, MIB.............$50.00
Barbie, Star Lily Bride, 1995, Wedding Flower Collection, NRFB..$275.00
Barbie, Style Magic (Black), 1988, NRFB........................$30.00

Barbie, Winter Fantasy, 1990, FAO Schwarz exclusive, MIB, $175.00. (Photo courtesy Margo Rana)

Barbie, Twist 'N Turn, 1966, blond hair, MIB, D2 ....$600.00

Barbie, Twist 'N Turn, 1966, brunette hair, orig swimsuit, NM, D2 ....$275.00

Barbie, Twist 'N Turn, 1967, blond or cinnamon hair, orig swimsuit, NM, D2, ea $250.00

Barbie, Twist 'N Turn, 1968, blond hair, MIB, D2 ....$700.00

Barbie, Twist 'N Turn, 1969, lt brn flipped-up hair, NRFB, D2 ....$900.00

Barbie, Twist 'N Turn, 1971, brunette hair, NRFB $500.00

Barbie, Uptown Chic, 1994, Classique Collection, NRFB .$75.00

Barbie, Walk Lively, 1972, blond hair, NRFB.................$200.00

Barbie, Winter Fantasy, 1990, FAO Schwarz, NRFB, D2 ..$200.00

Barbie, Winter Royale, Pace Club, 1993, NRFB...............$75.00

Brad, Talking, 1971, MIB, $250.00. (Photo courtesy McMasters Doll Auction)

Cara, Ballerina, 1976, MIB...$75.00

Cara, Free Movin', 1975, NRFB..$125.00

Casey, Twist 'N Turn, 1968, blond or brunette hair, NRFB ...$350.00

Chris, 1967, blond hair, orig outfit, NM, D2 ....$125.00

Chris, 1974, auburn hair, orig outfit & shoes, EX, D2 ......$75.00

Christie, All American, 1991, MIB....................................$25.00

Christie, Beauty Secrets, 1980, MIB.................................$60.00

Christie, Fashion Photo, 1978, MIB.................................$95.00

Christie, Golden Dream, 1980, MIB $50.00

Christie, Kissing, 1979, MIB...$65.00

Christie, Lights 'N Lace, 1991, NRFB...............................$30.00

Christie, Pink & Pretty, 1982, NRFB................................$35.00

Christie, Pretty Reflections, 1979, NRFB $85.00

Christie, Sunsational Malibu, 1982, NRFB.......................$30.00

Christie, Superstar, 1977, MIB $95.00

Christie, Talking, 1969, brunette hair, NRFB...................$250.00

Christie, Twist 'N Turn, 1968, red hair, orig swimsuit, NM, D2 ....$250.00

Francie, Busy, 1972, NRFB...$425.00

Francie, Growin' Pretty Hair, 1970, orig outfit, NM, D2 ..$150.00

Francie, Malibu (Japanese), dk brn hair w/side part, orig swimsuit, NM, D2..$2,200.00

Francie, Twist 'N Turn, 1966, blond hair, orig swimsuit, NM, D2 ....$350.00

Francie, Twist 'N Turn, 1966, brunette hair, orig swimsuit, EX, D2 ....$150.00

Francie, 30th Anniversary, 1996, NRFB $65.00

Ginger, Growing Up, 1977, MIB......................................$95.00

Jamie, New & Wonderful Walking, blond hair, orig outfit, EX, D2 ....$225.00

Kelley, Quick Curl, 1972, NRFB, D2 ....$175.00

Ken, Air Force, 1994, Stars 'N Stripes, NRFB $30.00

Ken, Army, 1993, Stars 'N Stripes, NRFB.........................$35.00

Ken, Beach Blast, 1989, NRFB...$25.00

Ken, Bendable Legs, 1965, painted brunette hair, MIB, $350.00. (Photo courtesy McMasters Doll Auction)

Ken, Benetton, 1991, NRFB..$60.00

Ken, Busy, 1972, NRFB $175.00

Ken, California Dream, 1988, NRFB $30.00

Ken, Crystal, 1984, NRFB..$40.00

Ken, Dream Date, 1983, NRFB...$30.00

Ken, Fashion Jeans, 1982, MIB...$35.00

Ken, Gold Medal Skier, 1975, NRFB.................................$100.00

Ken, Hawaiian, 1979, MIB $45.00

Ken, Henry Higgins, 1996, Hollywood Legends Series, NRFB $65.00

Ken, Ice Capades, 1990, NRFB...$40.00

Ken, Live Action, 1971, NRFB...$100.00

Ken, Marine Corps, 1992, Stars 'N Stripes, NRFB $40.00

Ken, Party Time, 1977, NRFB...$35.00

Ken, Rappin' Rockin,' 1992, MIB $25.00

Ken, Rhett Butler, 1994, Hollywood Legend Series, NRFB, D2..$75.00

Ken, Sea Holiday, 1993, FAO Schwarz, NRFB.................$40.00

Ken, Sport & Shave, 1980, MIB $40.00

Ken, Sun Charm, 1989, MIB...$25.00

Ken, Sun Lovin' Malibu, 1979, NRFB...............................$35.00

Ken, Superstar, 1977, MIB..$95.00

Ken, Tin Man, 1995, Hollywood Legends Series, NRFB, D2 ..$60.00

Ken, Totally Hair, 1991, NRFB, D2 ....$50.00

Ken, Walk Lively, 1972, MIB $150.00
Ken, Western, 1982, MIB $35.00
Ken, 1961, flocked blond or brunette hair, straight legs, MIB, D2, ea from $150 to $200.00
Ken, 1962, pnt blond or brunette hair, NRFB, ea..........$175.00
Ken, 1965, pnt blond hair, bendable legs, NRFB............$650.00
Ken, 1965, pnt blond hair, orig outfit & shoes, bendable legs, M, D2 ....$225.00

Midge, 1963, straight legs, blond hair, EX/NM, $150.00; wearing Barbie in Switzerland, 1964, $200.00. (Photo courtesy McMasters Doll Auction)

Midge, Cool Times, 1989, NRFB.....................................$30.00
Midge, Earring Magic, 1993, NRFB $30.00
Midge, Japanese, brunette hair, straight legs, orig swimsuit, rare, NM, D2 ....$1,250.00
Midge, Ski Fun, 1991, Toys R Us, MIB $30.00
Midge, Winter Sports, 1995, Toys R Us, MIB..................$40.00
Midge, 1963, blond or red hair, bendable legs, MIB, D2, ea ..$500.00
Midge, 30th Anniversary, 1992, porcelain, MIB, D2......$175.00
Nikki, Animal Lovin', 1989, NRFB $30.00
PJ, Deluxe Quick Curl, 1976, MIB $65.00
PJ, Fashion Photo, 1978, MIB $95.00
PJ, Free Moving, 1976, MIB $85.00
PJ, Gold Medal Gymnast, 1975, NRFB...........................$120.00
PJ, Live Action, 1971, orig outfit, M, D2......................$150.00
PJ, Malibu, 1978, MIB $55.00
PJ, New & Groovy Talking, 1969, orig swimsuit, beads & glasses, NM, D2..$150.00
PJ, Sun Lovin' Malibu, 1979, MIB $50.00
PJ, Sunsational Malibu, 1982, MIB.................................$40.00
PJ, Talking, 1970, orig outfit & beads, M, D2, from $175 to...$250.00
Ricky, 1965, orig outfit & shoes, NM, D2 ....$75.00
Scott, Skipper's boyfriend, 1980, MIB............................$55.00
Skipper, Deluxe Quick Curl, 1975, NRFB $125.00
Skipper, Dramatic New Living, 1970, orig swimsuit, NM, D2..$50.00
Skipper, Dream Date, 1990, NRFB..................................$25.00
Skipper, Growing Up, 1976, MIB....................................$100.00
Skipper, Hollywood Hair, 1993, NRFB $30.00
Skipper, Homecoming Queen, 1989, NRFB $35.00

Skipper, Music Lovin', 1985, NRFB................................$65.00
Skipper, Pepsi Spirit, 1989, NRFB..................................$70.00
Skipper, Sunsational Malibu, 1982, MIB $40.00
Skipper, Super Teen, 1980, NRFB...................................$35.00
Skipper, Totally Hair, 1991, NRFB..................................$30.00
Skipper, Twist 'N Turn, 1969, blond banana curls, MIB, D2 ....$400.00
Skipper, Twist 'N Turn, 1969, brn hair, w/certificate of authenticity, MIB, D2...$550.00
Skipper, Western, 1982, NRFB...$40.00
Skipper, Workout Teen Fun, 1988, NRFB........................$30.00
Skipper, 1965, blond or red hair, bendable legs, MIB, D2, ea from $350 to..$400.00
Skipper, 30th Anniversary, 1994, porcelain, NRFB........$165.00
Skooter, 1963, brunette hair, orig swimsuit & bows, MIB, D2 ....$175.00
Skooter, 1965, blond hair, bendable legs, MIB, D2.........$225.00

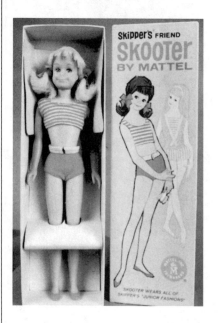

Skooter, 1965, blond hair, straight legs, MIB, $225.00. (Photo courtesy McMasters Doll Auction)

Stacey, Talking, blond or red hair, orig swimsuit, NM, D2, ea from $250 to $350.00
Stacey, Twist 'N Turn, 1968, blond hair, NRFB, D2 ....$900.00
Stacey, Twist 'N Turn, 1968, red hair, orig swimsuit, NM, D2 .$350.00
Steffie, Walk Lively, 1968, orig outfit & scarf, NM, D2 .$175.00
Teresa, All American, 1991, MIB.....................................$25.00
Teresa, California Dream, 1988, MIB $30.00
Teresa, Country Western Star, 1994, NRFB.....................$30.00
Teresa, Rappin' Rockin', 1992, NRFB.............................$45.00
Tutti, Night Night Sleep Tight, 1966, NRFB $275.00
Tutti, 1966, brunette hair, orig outfit, NM, D2 ....$85.00
Tutti, 1974, blond hair, orig outfit, EX, D2 ....$60.00
Whitney, Nurse, 1987, NRFB...$80.00
Whitney, Style Magic, 1989, NRFB $35.00

CASES

Barbie, Francie, Casey & Tutti, hard plastic, EX, from $50 to...$75.00
Barbie, Stacey, Francie & Skipper, pk hard plastic, rare, NM, from $75 to $100.00

Barbie, 1961, red vinyl, Barbie pictured in 4 different outfits, EX, from $30 to...$40.00

Barbie, 1963, pk vinyl, Bubble-Cut Barbie wearing Solo in the Spotlight, rare, NM, from $75 to....................$85.00

Barbie, 1967, vinyl, Barbie wearing All That Jazz surrounded by flowers, from $30 to $40.00

Barbie & Ken, 1963, blk vinyl, Barbie wearing Party Date & Ken wearing Saturday Night Date, EX, D2..............$65.00

Barbie & Midge, pk vinyl, Barbie wearing Rain Coat & Midge wearing Sorority Meeting, NM, from $45 to.............$55.00

Barbie & Stacey, 1967, vinyl, NM, from $65 to...............$75.00

Barbie & Stacey Sleep 'N Keep, 1960s, vinyl, several color variations, EX, ea from $55 to $65.00

Barbie Goes Travelin', vinyl, rare, NM $100.00

Barbie on Madison Avenue, FAO Schwarz, 1992, blk background, pk hdl, M $40.00

Circus Star Barbie, FAO Schwarz, 1995, M $25.00

Fashion Queen Barbie, 1963, red vinyl, w/mirror & wig stand, EX, D2 ....$100.00

Francie & Casey, vinyl, Francie wearing Groovy Get-Up & Casey wearing Iced Blue, rare, from $65 to $75.00

Midge, 1963, bl vinyl, Midge wearing Movie Date, rare, NM, from $100 to $125.00

Miss Barbie, 1963, wht vinyl, w/orig wig, wig stand & mirror, rare, EX, D2 ....$150.00

Skooter, 1965, bl vinyl, Skooter wearing Country Picnic & chasing butterflies, rare, from $125 to..............................$175.00

Tutti Play Case, bl or pk vinyl w/various scenes, EX, ea from $30 to $40.00

Tutti, orange vinyl with plastic handle and closure, 1974, NM, $150.00.

CLOTHING AND ACCESSORIES

Aboard Ship, Barbie, #1631, 1965, NRFB $450.00

All About Plaid, Barbie, #3433, 1971-72, complete, M .$200.00

All American Girl, Barbie, #3337, 1972, complete, M.....$75.00

All Over Felt, Skipper, #3476, NRFB, D2 ....$150.00

All the Trimmings Fashion Pak, Barbie & Stacey, #0050, 1970 , MOC..$75.00

Altogether Elegant, Francie, #1242, 1970, NRFB $200.00

Arabian Nights, Ken, #0774, 1964, NRFB $200.00

Barbie Fashion Classics, K-Mart, 1986, several different, MIP, ea $15.00

Barbie in Switzerland, #822, 1964, NRFB.....................$250.00

Beach Beat Fashion Pak, Ken & Brad, 1972, MOC $125.00

Beach Peachy, Skipper, #1938, 1967, NRFB..................$150.00

Beautiful Bride, Barbie, #1698, complete, M, D2 ....$900.00

Big Business (Ken), #1434, 1970, NRFP, $200.00. (Photo courtesy Sarah Sink Eames)

Birthday Beauties, Tutti, #3617, 1968, NRFB.................$165.00

Black Magic Ensemble, Barbie, #1609, 1964, NRFB $400.00

Blue Royalty, Barbie, #1469, 1970, MIB $250.00

Bold Gold, Ken, #1436, 1970, NRFB $75.00

Breakfast At 7, Ken, #1428, 1969-70, complete, M........$200.00

Bridal Beauty, Francie, #3288, 1972, complete, M $500.00

Brunch Time, Barbie, #1628, complete, NM, D2 ....$125.00

Busy Morning, Barbie, #956, 1963, NRFB $225.00

Caribbean Cruise, Barbie, #1687, 1967, NRFB $225.00

Casual All-Stars, Ken, #1436, 1970, NRFB $50.00

Chilly Chums, Skipper, #1973, 1969-70, MIB................$225.00

Cinderella, Barbie, #872, complete, NM, D2 ....$150.00

City Sophisticate, Barbie, #2671, 1979, NRFB................$25.00

Combination (Francie and Casey), #1234, NRFB, $295.00. (Photo courtesy McMasters Doll Auction)

Clam Diggers, Francie, #1258, 1966, NRFB $185.00
Cloud 9, Barbie, #1489, 1969-70, complete, M $200.00
Clowning Around, Tutti, #3606, 1967, NRFB................$195.00
Confetti Cutie, Skipper, #1952, 1968, NRFB $250.00
Cool-It! Fashion Pak, Francie & Casey, 1968, MIP $50.00
Corduroy Cape, Francie & Casey, #1764, 1970-71, MIB..$150.00
Country Club Dance, Barbie, #1627, 1965, NRFB.........$400.00
Culotte-Wot?, Francie & Casey, #1214, 1968-69, MIB..$300.00
Curtain's Up, Barbie, #4811, 1984, NRFB $15.00
Daisy Crazy, Skipper, #1732, 1970, complete, M $150.00
Dance Party, Francie, #1257, complete, M, D2................$150.00
Dancing Doll, Barbie, #1626, 1965, NRFB.....................$475.00
Denims for Fun, Ken, #3376, 1972, complete, M $75.00
Dream Team, Barbie, #3427, 1971-72, MIB....................$175.00
Dream Wrap, Barbie, #1476, 1969-70, complete, M $150.00
Dream-Ins, Barbie, #1867, 1969, NRFB..........................$125.00
Dream-Ins, Skipper, #3293, 1972, MIB............................$175.00
Dreamy Duo, Francie, #3450, 1971-72 & 1974, complete,
    M $175.00
Dressed in Velvet, Skipper, #3477, 1971, NRFB.............$125.00
Enchanted Evening, Barbie, #983, complete, EX, D2 ..$195.00
Evening Elegance, Barbie, #1414, 1980, NRFB $20.00
Evening In, Barbie, #3406, 1971, NRFB.........................$150.00
Evening Splendour, Barbie, #961, 1959, NRFB.............$275.00
Fab City, Barbie, #1874, 1969, complete, M $300.00
Fancy-Dancy, Barbie, #1858, 1968, NRFB.....................$200.00
Fashion Luncheon, Barbie, #1656, complete, EX, D2 ....$450.00
Finishing Touches Fashion Pak, Barbie & Stacey, 1969,
    NRFP..$150.00
Firelights, Barbie, #1481, 1969-70, MIB $175.00
First Things First, Francie, #1252, 1966, NRFB.............$115.00
Flats 'N Heels Fashion Pak, Barbie & Stacey, 1969, MOC ..$75.00
Floating In, Francie & Casey, #1207, 1968-69, MIB $200.00
Flying Colors, Barbie, #3492, 1972, complete, M...........$300.00
Foot Lights Fashion Pak, Barbie & Stacey, #0040, 1970,
    MOC...$75.00
Formal Occasion, Barbie, #1697, 1967, NRFB $500.00
Fraternity Dance, Barbie, #1638, complete, M, D2 ....$400.00
Fringe Benefits, Barbie, #3401, 1971, NRFB.................$100.00
Frosty Fur, Francie, #3455, 1971-72 & 1974, complete, M ..$150.00
Fun Flakes, Barbie, #3412, 1971-72, complete, M...........$175.00
Fun Fur, Barbie, #3434, 1971, NRFB $200.00
Fun on Ice, Ken, #791, 1963, NRFB $125.00
Fun Runners, Skipper & Fluff, #3372, 1972, MIP.............$50.00
Fun Shine, Barbie, #3480, 1972, complete, M................$250.00
Fur Out, Francie, #1262, complete, M, D2 ....$400.00
Furry-Go-Round, Francie, #1294, Sears Exclusive, 1967,
    NRFB...$500.00
Galaxy A Go-Go, Barbie, #2742, 1986, NRFB................$30.00
Garden Tea Party, Barbie, #1606, 1964, NRFB.............$200.00
Get-Ups 'N Go Candy Striper, Francie, #7709, 1973, MIP...$100.00
Get-Ups 'N Go Doctor Ken, #7705, 1973, MIP $75.00
Get-Ups 'N Go Flower Girl, Skipper, #7847, 1974-76, MIP..$100.00
Get-Ups 'N Go Ice Skater, Francie, #7845, 1974-75, MIP....$75.00
Get-Ups 'N Go Indian Print Separates, Barbie, #7241, 1975,
    NRFP $35.00
Get-Ups 'N Go Pink & Pretty Ballet, Skipper, #7714, 1973-74,
    MIP $75.00

Get-Ups 'N Go, Skipper, #7715, 1973, NRFP, $75.00.

Get-Ups 'N Go Tennis Gear, Ken, #7837, 1974-75, MIP ...$75.00
Get-Ups 'N Go United Airlines Pilot, Ken, #7707, 1973-75,
    MIP $75.00
Glo-Go, Barbie, #1865, 1969, complete, M $200.00
Glowin' Gold, Barbie, #3354, 1972, complete, M $50.00
Goin' Sleddin', Skipper, #3475, 1971, NRFB.................$75.00
Gold 'N Glamour, Barbie, #1647, complete, M, D2 ....$800.00
Golden Evening, Barbie, #1610, 1964, NRFB $275.00
Golden Glory, Barbie, #1645, complete, M, D2 ....$250.00
Goldswingers, Barbie, #1494, 1969-70, complete, M $250.00
Golf Gear Fashion Pak, Ken & Brad, 1971, MIP.............$75.00
Golfing Greats, Barbie, #3413, 1971, NRFB..................$200.00
Gypsy Spirit, Barbie, #1458, 1970, MIB.........................$175.00
Happy Go Pink, Barbie, #1868, 1969, NRFB.................$200.00
Hearts 'N Flowers, Skipper, #1945, 1967, NRFB $300.00
Hiking Holiday, Ken, #1412, 1965, NRFB.....................$250.00
Hip Knits, Francie, #1265, 1966, NRFB $225.00
Hot Togs, Barbie, #1063, NRFB, D2.........................$1,300.00
Hurray for Leather, Barbie, #1477, 1969, NRFB.............$75.00
Ice Cream 'N Cake, Skipper, #1970, 1969-70, MIB $200.00
Ice Skatin', Skipper, #3470, 1971-72, MIB....................$150.00
In Blooms, Barbie, #3424, 1971, NRFB $90.00
In-Print, Francie, #1288, 1967, NRFB $150.00
Jeepers Creepers, Skipper, #1966, 1969, NRFB $125.00
Junior Prom, Barbie, #1614, 1965, NRFB $575.00
Ken Fashion Classics, K-Mart, 1986, several different, MIP,
    ea $15.00
Ken in Mexico, #0778, 1964, NRFB.............................$175.00
King Arthur, Ken, #773, NRFB, D2..............................$400.00
Knit Hit, Barbie, #1804, 1968, complete, M..................$75.00
Knitting Pretty, Barbie, #957, 1963, bl, NRFB $350.00
Lace Caper, Barbie, #1791, 1970, NRFB........................$125.00
Lemon Kick, Barbie, #1465, 1970, complete, M............$200.00
Let's Explore, Ricky, #1506, 1966, NRFB......................$135.00
Light 'N Lazy, Barbie, #3339, 1972, MIB $75.00
Little Bow Pink, Barbie, #1483, 1969-70, complete, M..$150.00
Little Miss Midi, Skipper, #3468, 1971, NRFB...............$70.00
Little Red Riding Hood, Barbie, #880, complete, M,
    D2 ....$300.00
Long on Leather, Francie, #1769, 1970, NRFB..............$155.00

Long 'N Short of It, #3478, 1971 – 72, complete, NRFB, $175.00 (shown loose). (Photo courtesy Sarah Sink Eames)

Loop Scoop, Barbie, #1454, 1970, complete, M $150.00
Lovely Sleep-Ins, Barbie, #1463, 1970, NRFB...............$100.00
Matinee Fashion, Barbie, #1640, complete, M, D2 ....$500.00
Maxi 'N Midi, Barbie, #1799, 1970, complete, M $300.00
Merry-Go-Rounders, Francie, #1230, NRFB, D2 ....$375.00
Midi Bouquet, Francie, #3446, 1971, NRFB...................$125.00
Midi Magic, Barbie, #1869, 1969, NRFB......................$175.00
Mood Matchers, Barbie, #1792, complete, NM, D2 ....$75.00
Morning Workout Fashion Pak, Ken, 1964, NRFP...........$50.00
Movie Groovie, Barbie, #1866, 1969, NRFB..................$125.00
Mr Astronaut, Ken, #1415, 1965, NRFB $725.00
Nifty Knickers, Skipper, #3291, 1972, MIB $175.00
Night Lighter, Barbie, #3423, 1971, NRFB....................$175.00
On the Go Fashion Pak, Barbie, 1964, NRFP...................$85.00
Orange Blossom, Barbie, #987, 1961, NRFB $225.00
Orange Blossom, Midge, #987, 1967, NRFB....................$75.00
Orange Zip, Francie, #1548, Sears Exclusive, 1968, NRFB .$475.00
Patio Party, Barbie, #1692, 1967, NRFB $350.00
Pazam!, Francie & Casey, #1213, 1968-69, MIB.............$300.00
Peach Plush, Francie, #3461, 1971, NRFB......................$250.00
Peachy Fleecy, Barbie, #915, complete, NM, D2 ....$100.00
Pert Skirt Fashion Pak, Barbie, 1966, NRFP...................$150.00
Pink Lightning, Francie & Casey, #1231, 1969-70, MIB ..$250.00
Pink Moonbeams, Barbie, #1694, 1967, NRFB $300.00
Pink Power, Francie & Casey, #1762, 1970-71, MIB......$150.00
Play It Cool, Ken, #1433, 1970, NRFB...........................$100.00
Pleasantly Peasanty, Barbie, #3360, 1972, complete, M .$100.00
Pleat-Neat Fashion Pak, Francie, 1967, NRFP $100.00
Plush Pony, Barbie, #1873, 1969, complete, M...............$250.00
Poodles Doodles Put-Ons & Pets, Barbie, #1061, 1972, MIB...$350.00
Popover, Skipper, #1943, 1967, NRFB............................$175.00
Posie Party, Skipper, #1955, 1965, complete, M $200.00
Pretty Frilly, Francie, #3366, 1972, MIB $200.00
Purple Pleasers, Barbie, #3483, 1972, complete, M $175.00
Quick Shift, Francie, #1266, 1966, NRFB $200.00
Rain or Shine, Barbie, #2788, 1979, NRFB $20.00
Rainbow Wraps, Barbie, #1796, complete, NM, D2 ....$135.00
Real Sporty, Skipper, #1961, 1968, NRFB $200.00
Reception Line, Barbie, #1654, 1966, NRFB..................$600.00
Rik Rak Rah, Skipper, #1733, 1970, complete, M..........$150.00
Rolla-Scoot, Skipper, 1940, 1967, NRFB.......................$150.00

Romantic Ruffles, Barbie, #1871, complete, M, D2........$150.00
Royal Velvet, Barbie, #3215, 1972, NRFB.....................$500.00
Satin Happenin', Francie, #1237, 1970, NRFB.................$75.00
Saturday Matinee, Barbie, #1615, complete, M, D2 ....$600.00
Scene Stealers, Barbie, #1845, 1968, complete, M $250.00
School's Cool, Skipper, #1976, 1969-70, MIB $200.00
Sea Scene, Ken, #1449, 1971, NRFB $60.00
Sea-Shore Shorties, Tutti & Chris, #3614, 1968-69, complete,
    M..$125.00
Shape-Ups, Barbie, #1782, 1970-71, MIB......................$175.00
Shimmering Magic, Barbie, #1664, complete, M, D2.....$900.00
Shoe Parade Fashion Pak, Skipper, 1965, NRFP..............$45.00
Silver Serenade, Barbie, #3419, 1971-72, complete, MIB...$300.00
Silver Sparkle, Barbie, #1885, 1969, MIP $200.00
Simply Super, Francie, #3277, 1972, complete, M..........$175.00
Skating Fun, Skipper, #1908, NRFB, D2 ....$175.00
Ski Champion, Ken, #798, 1963, NRFB $100.00
Ski Queen, Barbie, #948, 1963, NRFB...........................$200.00
Skimmy Stripes, Skipper, #1956, 1968, MIB $200.00
Slacks 'N Cap Young Teen Fashion Pak, Francie, 1970-71,
    MIP $75.00
Slightly Summery Fashion Pak, Francie, 1968, NRFP......$95.00
Slumber Party Fashion Pak, Skipper & Fluff, 1971, MIP..$65.00
Snap Dash, Barbie, #1824, 1968, complete, M $200.00
Snooze News, Francie & Casey, #1226, 1969, complete, M ..$150.00
Snug Fuzz, Barbie, #1813, 1968-69, complete, M $250.00
Some Shoes Fashion Pak, Skipper & Fluff, 1971, MOC...$65.00
Somethin' Else, Francie & Casey, #1219, 1969-70, complete,
    M...$150.00

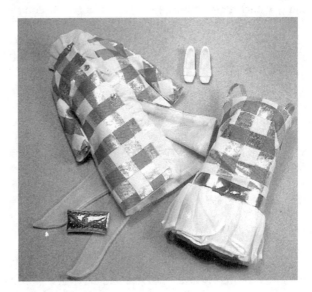

Sparkle Squares, #1814, 1968 – 1969, complete, M, $300.00. (Photo courtesy Sarah Sink Eames)

Special Date, Ken, #1401, complete, NM, D2 ....$85.00
Sporty Shorty Fashion Pak, Skipper & Fluff, 1971, MOC ..$65.00
Stripes Are Happenin', Stacey, #1544, 1968, NRFB.........$75.00
Student Teacher, Barbie, #1622, 1965, complete, M, D2...$250.00
Studio Tour, Barbie, #1690, 1967, NRFB......................$275.00
Summer Job, Ken, #1422, 1966, NRFB..........................$450.00
Summer Number, Francie, #3454, 1971-72 & 1974, MIB .$175.00

Summer Slacks Fashion Pak, Skipper, 1970, MIP............$75.00
Sun Fun Fashion Pak, Ken & Brad, 1971, MIP.................$75.00
Super Snoozers, Skipper & Fluff, #3371, 1972, NRFB......$55.00
Sweet 'N Swinging, Francie, #1283, complete, NM, D2 $300.00
Sweetheart Satin, Barbie, #3361, 1972, complete, M.....$250.00
Swinging Easy, Barbie, #955, 1963, NRFB.......................$200.00
Tangerine Scene, Barbie, #1451, 1970, NRFB.................$75.00
Tea Party, Skipper, #1924, 1966, NRFB...........................$250.00
Team Ups, Barbie, #1855, 1968-69, complete, M...........$150.00
Teeter Timers, Skipper, #3467, 1971-72, complete, M ..$175.00
Tennis Time, Francie & Casey, #1221, 1969-70, MIB......$150.00
Tenterrific, Francie & Casey, #1211, 1968-69, complete, M...$250.00
Terrific Twosome Fashion Pak, Barbie & Stacey, 1969, MIP.....$75.00
Totally Terrific, Francie, #3280, 1972, MIP $225.00
Town Turtle, Ken, #1430, 1969-70, complete, M $200.00
Trail Blazer, Barbie, #1846, 1968, NRFB........................$250.00
Trim Twosome, Skipper, #1960, 1968, complete, M.......$200.00
Twinkle Togs, Barbie, #1854, 1968-69, complete, M......$150.00
Two for the Ball, Francie, #1232, MOC, D2 ....$225.00
Two-Way Tiger, Barbie, #3402, 1971-72, complete, M...$150.00
Undertones Fashion Pak, Skipper, 1970, MIP.................$75.00
Vacation Time, Barbie, #1623, 1965, NRFB...................$200.00
Velvet Blush, Skipper, #1737, 1970, NRFB $100.00
Velvet Venture, Barbie, #1488, 1969-70, complete, M...$250.00
Victorian Wedding, Francie & Casey, #1233, 1969-70,
     MIB...$300.00
VIP Scene, Ken, #1473, 1971, NRFB................................$75.00
Waltz in Velvet, Francie & Casey, #1768, 1970, NRFB .$225.00
Way Out West, Ken & Brad, #1720, 1972, MIB.............$175.00
Wedding Whirl, Francie, #1244, 1970-71 & 1974, complete,
     M..$275.00
Wedding Wonder, Barbie, #1849, 1968, NRFB $350.00
Weekenders, Barbie, #1815, Sears Exclusive, 1967, NRFB..$900.00
Western Wild Young Teen Fashion Pak, Francie, 1970-71,
     MIP $75.00
White Is Right Fashion Pak, Ken, 1964, NRFP $40.00
Wild 'N Wintery, Barbie, #3416, complete, M, D2.........$300.00
Wild 'N Wooly, Francie & Casey, #1218, 1968, MIB $300.00
Wild Things, Barbie, #3439, 1971-72, complete, M.......$200.00
Wild' N Wonderful, Barbie, #1856, 1968-69, MIB.........$200.00
With-It Whites, Francie, #3448, 1971, NRFB.................$125.00
Yachtsman, Ken, #789, complete, NM, D2....................$225.00

FURNITURE, ROOMS, HOUSES, AND SHOPS

Action Sewing Center, 1972, MIB...................................$50.00
Barbie & Ken Little Theatre, 1964, complete, NMIB....$600.00
Barbie & Skipper Deluxe Dream House, Sears Exclusive, 1965,
     MIB, minimum value $175.00
Barbie & Skipper School, 1965, rare, MIB $500.00
Barbie & the Beat Dance Cafe, 1990, MIB.....................$35.00
Barbie & the Rockers Dance Cafe, 1987, MIB $50.00
Barbie & the Rockers Hot Rockin' Stage, 1987, MIB $40.00
Barbie Baby-Sitting Room, Canada, MIB......................$100.00
Barbie Beauty Boutique, 1976, MIB $40.00
Barbie Café, JC Penney Exclusive, 1993, MIB.................$45.00
Barbie Café Today, 1971, MIB..$400.00
Barbie Cookin' Fun Kitchen, MIB $50.00

**Barbie Dance Club Dancetime Shop, #4840, 1989, M,
from $25.00 to $35.00.** (Photo courtesy Beth Summers)

Barbie Deluxe Family House, 1966, complete, VG, D2..$135.00
Barbie Dream Armoire, 1980, NRFB $35.00
Barbie Dream Bath Chest & Commode, 1980, lt pk, MIB .$25.00
Barbie Dream Bed & Nightstand, 1984, pk, MIB.........$25.00
Barbie Dream Dining Center, 1984, MIB........................$25.00
Barbie Dream Glow Vanity, 1986, MIB...........................$20.00
Barbie Dream House, 1961, 1st edition, complete, NM, D2 ...$150.00
Barbie Dream House Bedroom, 1981, MIB $6.00
Barbie Dream House Kitchen Set, 1981, MIB....................$6.00
Barbie Dream Luxury Bathtub, 1984, pk, MIB................$20.00
Barbie Dream Store Makeup Department, 1983, MIB......$40.00
Barbie Fashion Salon, Sears Exclusive, 1964, MIB........$225.00
Barbie Fashion Wraps Boutique, 1989, MIB $35.00
Barbie Glamour Home, 1985, MIB $125.00
Barbie Lively Livin' Room, MIB.......................................$50.00
Barbie Mountain Ski Cabin, Sears Exclusive, MIB...........$50.00
Barbie Playhouse Pavillion, Europe, MIB........................$75.00
Barbie Teen Dream Bedroom, MIB $50.00
Barbie Unique Boutique, Sears Exclusive, 1971, MIB....$185.00
Barbie Vanity & Shower, Sears Exclusive, 1975, MIB......$50.00

**Barbie Wash & Watch Dishwasher, #2232, 1991,
NRFB, from $20.00 to $25.00.** (Photo courtesy Beth Summers)

Barbie's Apartment, 1975, MIB.......................................$140.00
Barbie's Room-Fulls Country Kitchen, 1974, MIB............$50.00
Barbie's Room-Fulls Firelight Living Room, 1974, MIB.$100.00
California Dream Barbie Hot Dog Stand, 1988, NRFB....$50.00
Cool Tops Skipper T-Shirt Shop, 1989, complete, MIB ...$25.00
Francie & Casey Housemates, 1966, complete, NM, D2 ..$200.00

Town & Country Market, 1971, MIB $135.00
Tutti Playhouse, 1966, M...$100.00
Workout Center, 1985, MIB..$30.00
World of Barbie House, 1966, MIB...............................$175.00

Francie and Casey Studio House, #1026 (doll not included), M, $100.00. (Photo courtesy Paris and Susan Manos)

Superstar Barbie Piano Concert, #7314, 1989, NRFB, $40.00. (Photo courtesy Beth Summers)

Francie House, 1966, complete, M....................................$150.00
Go-Together Chair, Ottoman & End Table, MIB...........$100.00
Go-Together Chaise Lounge, MIB $75.00
Go-Together Couch, 1964, MIB...$30.00
Go-Together Dining Room, Barbie & Skipper, 1965, MIB...$50.00
Go-Together Lawn Swing & Planter, 1964, complete, MIB, D2 ..$150.00
Go-Together Living Room, Barbie & Skipper, 1965, MIB....$60.00
Ice Capades Skating Rink, 1989, MIB $70.00
Jamie's Penthouse, Sears Exclusive, 1971, MIB $475.00
Living Pretty Cooking Center, 1988, MIB........................$25.00
Living Pretty Refrigerator/Freezer, 1988, MIB..................$30.00
Magical Mansion, 1989, MIB..$125.00
Movietime Prop Shop, 1989, MIB.....................................$50.00
Party Garden Playhouse, 1994, MIB $275.00
Pink Sparkles Armoire, 1990, NRFB...............................$25.00
Pink Sparkles Starlight Bed, 1990, MIB...........................$30.00
Skipper Dream Room, 1964, MIB...................................$300.00
Skipper's Deluxe Dream House, Sears Exclusive, 1966, MIB...$500.00
Superstar Barbie Beauty Salon, 1977, MIB $55.00
Superstar Barbie Photo Studio, Sears Exclusive, 1977, MIB ...$45.00
Surprise House, 1972, MIB...$100.00
Susy Goose, Barbie & Midge Queen Size Chifferobe, NM ..$100.00
Susy Goose, Ken Wardrobe, M..$50.00
Susy Goose, Skipper's Jeweled Bed, 1965, MIB $150.00
Susy Goose, Skipper's Jeweled Vanity, Sears Exclusive, 1965, NRFB..$200.00
Susy Goose Canopy Bed, 1962, MIB...............................$150.00
Susy Goose Chifferobe, 1964, MIB $275.00
Susy Goose Mod A Go-Go Bedroom, 1966, NRFB $2,300.00
Susy Goose Queen Size Bed, Sears Exclusive, 1963, NRFB...$200.00
Susy Goose Vanity, 1963, EX, D2....................................$35.00
Susy Goose Wardrobe, 1962, EX, D2 ....$35.00

Gift Sets

Army Barbie & Ken, 1993, Stars 'N Stripes, MIB $60.00
Ballerina Barbie on Tour, 1976, MIB $175.00
Barbie & Her Horse Dancer, Canada, MIB.......................$75.00
Barbie & Ken Campin' Out, 1983, MIB $75.00

Barbie & Ken Little Theatre Gift Set, 1964, MIB, $3,000.00; NRFB, $6,000.00.

Barbie Beautiful Blues, Sears Exclusive, 1967, MIB $3,000.00
Barbie Loves Elvis, 1996, NRFB, D2 ....$75.00
Barbie Snap 'N Play Deluxe Gift Set, JC Penney Exclusive, 1992, MIB $40.00
Barbie Travel in Style, Sears Exclusive, 1968, MIB.....$1,500.00

Barbie Denim Blues, 1989, NRFB, $65.00. (Stephanie Deutsch)

Barbie's 'Round the Clock Gift Set, 1964, MIB.............$700.00
Barbie's Olympic Ski Village, MIB $75.00
Barbie's Sparkling Pink Gift Set, 1963, MIB...................$600.00
Barbie's Wedding Party, 1964, MIB.................................$700.00
Beauty Secrets Barbie Pretty Reflections, 1980, NRFB ..$100.00
Birthday Fun at McDonald's, 1994, NRFB......................$75.00
Bright & Breezy Skipper, Sears Exclusive, 1969, NRFB .$975.00
Dance Magic Barbie & Ken, 1990, NRFB........................$50.00
Dance Sensation Barbie, 1985, MIB $35.00
Dolls of the World II, 1995, NRFB $100.00
Dramatic New Living Skipper Very Best Velvet, Sears Exclusive,
    1970-71, NRFB $1,500.00
Francie & Her Swingin' Separates, Sears Exclusive, 1966,
    MIB..$600.00
Golden Dreams Glamorous Nights, 1980, NRFB $100.00
Golden Groove Barbie, Sears Exclusive, 1969, NRFB...$2,000.00
Halloween Party Barbie & Ken, Target, 1998, NRFB, D2 ..$65.00
Happy Birthday Barbie, 1985, NRFB $50.00
Happy Meal Stacie & Whitney, JC Penney Exclusive, 1994,
    MIB..$30.00
Ken Red, White & Wild, Sears Exclusive, 1970, NRFB...$525.00

Live Action PJ Fashion 'N Motion, Sears Exclusive, 1971-72,
    NRFB..$1,500.00
Living Barbie Action Accents, Sears Exclusive, 1970, MIB..$450.00
Loving You Barbie, 1984, MIB $75.00
Malibu Barbie Beach Party, M (M case)...........................$75.00
Malibu Barbie Fashion Combo, 1978, NRFB...................$80.00
Malibu Ken Surf's Up, Sears Exclusive, 1971, NMIB.....$350.00
New Talking Barbie Dinner Dazzle Set, Sears Exclusive, 1968,
    MIB..$1,500.00
Night Night Sleep Tight Tutti, NRFB, D2....................$300.00
Pretty Pairs Nan 'N Fran, 1970, NRFB $250.00
Skipper Bright 'N Breezy, Sears Exclusive, 1969, MIB...$2,000.00
Skipper Party Time, 1964, NRFB..................................$500.00
Stacey & Butterfly Pony, 1993, NRFB $30.00
Stacey Nite Lighting, Sears Exclusive, 1969, NRFB ...$2,000.00
Stacey Stripes Are Happening, Sears Exclusive, 1968, MIB..$1,500.00

Sun Sensation Barbie Spray & Play Fun, 1992, MIB, $60.00.
(Photo courtesy Margo Rana)

Superstar Barbie & Ken, 1978, MIB...............................$175.00
Superstar Barbie Fashion Change-Abouts, 1978, NRFB ..$95.00
Superstar Barbie in the Spotlight, 1977, MIB.................$125.00
Talking Barbie Golden Groove Set, Sears Exclusive, 1969,
    MIB..$1,500.00

**Malibu Ken Surf's Up, blond painted hair, 1971, NRFB,
$550.00.** (Photo courtesy McMasters Doll Auction)

Tennis Stars Barbie & Ken, 1986, NRFB, from $60.00 to $75.00.
(Photo courtesy Beth Summers)

Talking Barbie Mad About Plaid, Sears Exclusive, 1970, NRFB..$1,200.00
Talking Barbie Perfectly Plaid, Sears Exclusive, 1971, MIB...$500.00
Travelin' Sisters, 1995, NRFB...$70.00
Tutti & Todd Sundae Treat, 1966, NRFB $500.00

Walking Jamie Furry Friends, Sears Exclusive, 1970, M (NM Box), $1,550.00.

Walking Jamie Strollin' in Style, NRFB $450.00
Wedding Party Midge, 1990, NRFB..............................$150.00

VEHICLES

Allan's Roadster, 1964, aqua, MIB $500.00
ATC Cycle, Sears Exclusive, 1972, MIB...........................$65.00
Austin Healy, Irwin, 1962, red & wht, very rare, NRFB, D2..$3,500.00
Barbie & Ken Dune Buggy, Irwin, 1970, pk, MIB...........$250.00
Barbie & the Rockers Hot Rockin' Van, 1987, MIB.........$60.00
Barbie Silver 'Vette, MIB...$30.00
Barbie Travelin' Trailer, MIB $40.00
Beach Buggy for Skipper, Irwin, 1964, rare, MIB, minimum value...$500.00
Beach Bus, 1974, MIB..$45.00

Dune Buggy, 1970, MIB, $150.00. (Photo courtesy McMasters Doll Auction)

California Dream Beach Taxi, 1988, MIB.........................$35.00
Ken's Classy Corvette, 1976, yel, MIB $75.00
Ken's Dream 'Vette, 1981, dk bl, MIB...........................$100.00
Ken's Hot Rod, Sears Exclusive, 1964, red, MIB $900.00
Snowmobile, Montgomery Ward, 1972, MIB $65.00
Sports Plane, Sears Exclusive, 1964, MIB...................$3,600.00
Star 'Vette, 1977, red, MIB..$100.00
Starlight Motorhome, 1994, MIB....................................$45.00

Sunsailer (catamaran), #9106, 1975, NRFB, $55.00. (Photo courtesy Sibyl DeWein and Joan Ashabraner)

Western Star Traveler Motorhome, 1982, MIB $50.00
1957 Belair Chevy, 1989, 1st edition, aqua, MIB $150.00
1957 Belair Chevy, 1990, 2nd edition, pk, MIB $125.00

MISCELLANEOUS

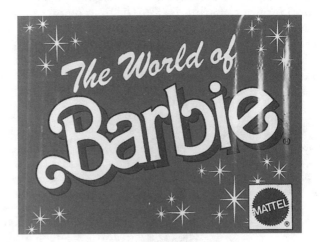

Banner, Barbie logo on pink vinyl, 1988, 48x62", M, $35.00.
(Photo courtesy Beth Summers)

Barbie & Francie Color Magic Fashion Set, complete, MIB...$275.00
Barbie & Ken Sew Magic Add-Ons, 1973-74, complete, MIB..$55.00
Barbie & Me Dress-Up Set, MIB....................................$100.00

Barbie & the Rockers, purse, vinyl, w/comb & cologne, M .$15.00
Barbie Beautiful Hair Vanity Set, 1994, MIB....................$10.00
Barbie Beauty Kit, 1961, complete, M $125.00
Barbie Cutlery Set, Sears Exclusive, 1962, MIP...............$50.00
Barbie Dough Dessert Maker, 1994, complete, MIB.........$40.00
Barbie Electric Drawing Set, 1970, complete, MIB $75.00
Barbie Electronic Drawing Set, Sears Exclusive, 1963, MIB...$200.00
Barbie Ge-Tar, 1965, M $325.00
Barbie Magic Plastic Molding Machine, 1994, MIB.........$25.00
Barbie Make-Up Case, 1963, NM...................................$25.00
Barbie Play Jewelry Set, MIP...$125.00
Barbie Pretty-Up Time Perfume Pretty Bath, 1964, complete,
     M..$150.00
Barbie Sew Magic Fashion Set, 1973-75, complete, MIB ..$100.00
Barbie Shrinky Dinks, 1979, MIB $30.00
Barbie Snaps 'N Scraps Scrapbook, several color variations, rare,
     ea from $200 to...$250.00
Barbie Young Travelers Play Kit, Sears Exclusive, 1964,
     MIB $75.00
Barbie's Miss America Beauty Center, Sears Exclusive, 1974,
     MIB $95.00
Bicycle, Camp Barbie, 1985, 16", NM............................$85.00
Book, Barbie's Fashion Success, Random House, 1962, hard-
     cover, w/dust jacket, NM, D2 ....$50.00
Book, Happy Go Lucky Skipper, 1963, Random House, hard-
     cover, EX $35.00
Book, Target's 30th Anniversary Barbie Keep Sake, 1989, hard-
     cover, EX $20.00
Book, World of Barbie, Random House, hardcover, EX....$15.00
Booklet, World of Barbie Fashion, 1968, M, D2 ....$10.00
Christie Quick Curl Beauty Center, Sears Exclusive, 1982,
     MIB...$35.00
Coloring Book, Ballerina Barbie, 1977, unused, EX............$8.00
Coloring Book, Barbie & Ken, 1963, unused, NM $50.00
Embroidery Set, Barbie, Ken & Midge, 1963, complete, MIB...$100.00
Embroidery Set, Barbie & Ken, 1962, complete, rare,
     NMIB, D2 ....$150.00
Francie & Barbie Electric Drawing Set, 1965, complete,
     MIB $150.00
Game, Barbie Queen of the Prom, Mattel, 1962, MIB $80.00
Game, Barbie 35th Anniversary, Golden, 1994, MIB.......$60.00

Ornament, Holiday Barbie, Hallmark, 1993, 1st edition,
     MIB...$75.00
Ornament, Holiday Barbie, Hallmark, 1994, 2nd edition,
     MIB...$35.00
Paper Dolls, Angel Face Barbie, Golden #1982-45, 1983, uncut,
     M...$20.00
Paper Dolls, Ballerina Barbie, Whitman #1993-1, 1977, uncut,
     M...$30.00
Paper Dolls, Barbie, Midge & Skipper, Whitman #4793, 1964,
     MIB...$80.00
Paper Dolls, Barbie, Whitman #4601, 1963, uncut, M.....$85.00
Paper Dolls, Barbie & Ken, Whitman #4797, 1963, MIB..$120.00
Paper Dolls, Barbie & Skipper Campsite at Lucky Lake, Whit-
     man #1836-31, 1980, M, uncut $25.00
Paper Dolls, Barbie Country Camper, Whitman #1990, 1973,
     uncut, M..$30.00
Paper Dolls, Malibu Skipper, Whitman #1945-2, 1973, uncut,
     M...$25.00

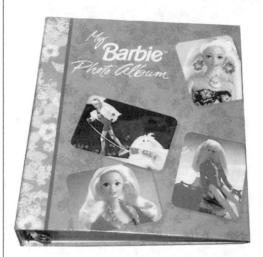

Photo Album, Hallmark, M, $10.00. (Photo courtesy Patrick C. Olds)

Plate, High Fashion Barbie, Solo in the Spotlight, Danbury Mint, 1960, M, $43.00. (Photo courtesy Beth Summers)

Jigsaw puzzle, Crystal Barbie doll and Ken doll, Western Publishing #4609-43, 1987, NRFB, $8.00. (Photo courtesy Beth Summers)

Puzzle, jigsaw; Barbie & Ken, Whitman, 1963, 100 pcs,
     MIB...$40.00
Puzzle, jigsaw; Nostalgic Barbie, Am Publishing, 1989, 550 pcs,
     MIB...$25.00
Puzzle, jigsaw; Skipper & Skooter, 1965, 100 pcs, MIB $30.00
Quick Curl Miss America Beauty Center, Sears Exclusive, 1975,
     MIB...$75.00

Tea Set, Barbie, Chilton Globe, 1989, china, 16 pcs, NRFB ...$30.00
Tea Set, Barbie, Sears Exclusive, 1962, 42 pcs, MIB.......$200.00
Tea Set, Barbie 25th Anniversary, 1984, complete, M ...$150.00
Umbrella, Barbie, 1962, several variations, EX, ea $65.00
Wagon, Camp Barbie, 1995, 34", EX.................................$50.00
Wristwatch, Barbie & Ken, Bradley, 1963, MIB.............$200.00
Wristwatch, Swirl Ponytail Barbie, 1964, bl or yel band, MIB,
    ea $400.00
Wristwatch, 30th Anniversary, 1989, MIB $80.00
Yo-yo, Spectra Star, plastic w/paper sticker, MIP $5.00

Battery-Operated Toys

From the standpoint of being visually entertaining, nothing can compare with the battery-operated toy. Most (probably as much as 95%) were made in Japan from the '40s through the '60s, though some were distributed by American companies — Marx, Ideal, and Daisy, for instance — who often sold them under their own names. So even if they're marked, sometimes it's just about impossible to identify the actual manufacturer. Though batteries had been used to power trains and provide simple illumination in earlier toys, the Japanese toys could smoke, walk, talk, drink, play instruments, blow soap bubbles, and do just about anything else humanly possible to dream up and engineer. Generally, the more antics the toy performs, the more collectible it is. Rarity is important as well, but first and foremost to consider is condition. Because of their complex mechanisms, many will no longer work. Children often stopped them in mid-cycle, rubber hoses and bellows aged and cracked, and leaking batteries caused them to corrode, so very few have survived to the present intact and in good enough condition to interest a collector. Though it's sometimes possible to have them repaired, unless you can buy them cheap enough to allow for the extra expense involved, it is probably better to wait on a better example. Original boxes are a definite plus in assessing the value of a battery-op and can sometimes be counted on to add from 30% to 50% (and up), depending on the box's condition, of course, as well as the toy's age and rarity.

We have made every attempt to list these toys by the name as it appears on the original box. Some will sound very similar. Many toys were reissued with only minor changes and subsequently renamed. Battery toys in general are down in price — except for the rare ones. Now might be a good time to buy them because they probably will come back in stronger demand as so many other toys have always done. For more information we recommend *Collecting Toys* by Richard O'Brien (Books Americana) and *Collecting Battery Toys* by Don Hultzman (Collector Books).

Advisors: Tom Lastrapes (L4); Judy and Kerry Irvin (K5).
See also Aeronautical; Automobiles and Other Vehicle Replicas; Boats; Marx; Robots and Space Toys.

ABC Toyland Express, MT, 1950s, 4 actions, litho tin, 14½",
    NM...$125.00
Accordion Player Hobo w/Monkey, Alps, seated hobo plays
    accordion while monkey plays cymbals, MIB, L4, from $500
    to $575.00

Accordion Bear, Alps Co., 1950s, five actions with remote microphone, 11", MIB, $975.00. (Photo courtesy Don Hultzman)

Acrobat Cycle, Sunny Brand (Taiwan), 1970s, 4 actions, mostly
    plastic, 9", NM...$65.00
Aerial Ropeway, TN, 1950s, tin, 5", EX (EX box), L4, from $125
    to $165.00
Airport Saucer, MT, 1960s, 4 actions, litho tin, 8" dia, NM....$140.00
Amtrak Locomotive, ST, 1960s, litho tin, 16", EX.........$100.00
Animal Train, MIB, L4, from $225 to.............................$300.00
Annie Tugboat, Y, 1950s, 4 actions, litho tin, 12½",
    NM $140.00
Antique Gooney Car, Alps, 1960s, several actions, litho tin
    w/vinyl-headed figure, 9", EX..............................$120.00
Army Radio Jeep, Linemar, 1950s, several actions, litho tin
    w/full-figure driver, 7", EX.................................$150.00
Arthur A-Go-Go Drummer, Alps, 1960s, several actions, 10",
    M, L4, from $425 to..$475.00
Automatic Tollgate w/Plymouth Valiant, Sears, 1955, several actions, litho tin, 16x17" base, NMIB, L4, from
    $325 to...$375.00
B-Z Rabbit, MT, 1950s, 4 actions, litho tin, 7" L, EX.....$100.00
Ball Playing Bear, 1940s, several actions, litho tin & celluloid,
    10½", rare, NM..$675.00
Balloon Blowing Monkey, Alps, 1950s, several actions, litho tin,
    11½", NM..$125.00
Balloon Bunny, rare, MIB, L4...$250.00
Bambi, see Walking Bambi
Barber Bear, TN, barber clips & combs hair w/several actions,
    tin & plush, 10", MIB, L4...................................$695.00
Barber Bear, TN, 1950s, barber clips & combs hair w/several
    actions, tin & plush, 10", VG (VG box), L4 ....$395.00
Barney Bear the Drummer Boy, Alps/Cragstan, 1950s, plush
    & tin w/cloth clothes, remote control, 11", MIB, L4,
    $200 to $250.00
Bartender, TN, 1960s, several actions, litho tin & vinyl w/cloth
    clothes, 11½", MIB...$65.00
Batman Car, Taiwan, 1970, w/Batman & Robin figures, bump-
    &-go action w/lights & sound, 10", rare, NM, A.....$265.00
Batman Flying Batplane, Remco, 1966, performs aerial stunts,
    plastic, remote control, 12", EX (EX box), T2, from $100
    to $125.00

Batmobile, Gama, tin, flashes lights, fires rockets, 12", NMIB, A, $1,500.00.

Batmobile w/Fire Lighted Engine, ASC, 1970s, 3 actions, litho tin, 11", rare, EX $475.00

Beauty Parlor Bears w/Lighted Dryer Stand, S&E, 1950s, several actions, litho tin & plush, 9½", rare, EX (EX box), A..$825.00

Big Dipper, Technofix, 1960s, 3 cars travel track, litho tin, 21" L, EX $150.00

Big Ring Circus Truck, MT, lithographed tin, NM, A, $175.00.

Big Top Champ Circus Clown, Alps, 1960s, 3 actions, 14", NMIB, L4, from $120 to........................$150.00

Big Wheel Ice Cream Truck, Taiyo, 1970s, 3 actions, 10", EX $100.00

Bimbo the Drumming Clown, Alps/Cragstan, 1950s, several actions, litho tin, 9", rare, MIB, L4, from $600 to ...$675.00

Bingo the Clown, TN, 1950s, 3 actions, 13", rare, NM, L4, from $400 to..$475.00

Blacksmith Bear, A1, 1950s, several actions, litho tin & plush w/cloth clothes, 10", NM (EX box), A $245.00

Blinky the Clown, Amico, 1950s, advances & plays xylophone, light-up eyes, remote control, 10", MIB, L4, from $550 to...$650.00

Blushing Gunfighter, Y, 1960s, several actions, litho tin w/cloth shirt, 11", NM (NM box), A...............$250.00

Bowling Bank, MB Daniel, 1960s, several actions, 10", EX (EX box), L4, from $100 to.............................$125.00

Brave Eagle, TN, 1950s, several actions, litho tin, 11", EX ..$140.00

Bruno Accordion Bear, Y, rocks back & forth & plays accordion, eyes light, remote control, 10", MIB, from $275 to .$325.00

Bruno the Walking Bear, rare, MIB, L4, from $300 to....$375.00

Bubble Blowing Boil Over Car, MT, 1950s, 3 actions, litho tin, 10", EX...$140.00

Bubble Blowing Dog, M, L4, from $225 to $275.00

Bubble Blowing Monkey, Alps, complete w/bubble solution, NMIB, A..$175.00

Bubble Blowing Road Roller, MIB, L4, from $200 to $250.00

Bubble Washing Bear, Y, several actions, litho tin, 8", MIB, L4..$440.00

Bubbling Bull (Wild West Rodeo), Linemar, 1950, several actions, litho tin, MIB, L4, from $300 to.................$375.00

Bulldog Tank, Remco, 1960s, 22", EX (EX box)............$150.00

Bunny the Magician, Alps, 1950s, several actions, litho tin & plush w/cloth clothes, 14½", EX (EX box) $400.00

Busy Housekeeper Bunny, Alps, 1950s, several actions, litho tin, 10", EX..$185.00

Busy Secretary, Linemar, 1950s, several actions, 7½", MIB ...$300.00

Butterfly w/Flapping Wings, Linemar, 1950s, 3 actions, litho tin, 10" W, EX.......................................$100.00

Buttons the Pup, EX, L4, $200 to...................................$250.00

Calypso Joe, Linemar, Black man advances & plays drum w/several actions, tin, rubber & cloth, remote control, 10", EX, A..$340.00

Cannon Truck, Ny-Lint, tin, 23", EX (G box), A $140.00

Cappy the Happy Baggage Porter, Alps, 1960s, several actions, litho tin, 12", MIB, L4, from $300 to......................$375.00

Captain Blushwell, Y, 1960s, several actions, tin & vinyl w/cloth clothes, 11", VG $65.00

Captain Hook, Marusan, 1950s, 3 actions, 11", scarce, EX, L4, minimum value..$750.00

Captain Kidd Pirate Ship, Yonezawa, 1960s, several actions, litho tin, 13", rare, EX, L4........................$300.00

Captain Kidd Pirate Ship, Yonezawa, 1960s, several actions, litho tin, 13", rare, MIB, L4...................................$400.00

Champion Weight Lifter, monkey lifts barbells, plastic w/cloth clothes, 10", EX (G box), A...........................$100.00

Chap the Obedient Dog, Rosko, 1960s, 3 actions, MIB, L4, from $200 to...$250.00

Charlie the Funny Clown, Alps, 1960s, 3 actions, litho tin, 9", NMIB, L4, from $300 to..........................$350.00

Chee Chee Chihuahua, Mego, 1960s, several actions, 8", EX...$50.00

Chimp & Pup Rail Car, Cragstan, 1950s, several actions, 9", rare, EX $140.00

Chimp w/Xylophone, Y, 1970s, w/4 records & hammer, 12" L, EX...$100.00

Chippy the Chipmunk, Alps, 1950s, several actions, MIB, L4, from $175 to...$225.00

Cindy the Meowing Cat, Tomiyama, 1950s, 4 actions, 12", EX..$75.00

Circus Clown Car Galaxie 500, Rico, litho tin, 19", EX, L4, from $600 to $650.00

Circus Elephant, TN, balances ball on trunk & umbrella spins by stream of air, tin & plush, 8", NM (EX box), A..$135.00

Circus Fire Engine, MT, 1960s, 4 actions, litho tin & plastic, 11", EX...$200.00

Circus Queen Seal, Japan, 1950s, swivels & balances ball on nose, litho tin, 11", rare, NM (EX box) $325.00

Circus Queen Seal, Playthings, rare, MIB, L4................$375.00

Clancy the Great, Ideal, 1960s, 3 actions, MIB, L4........$285.00

Clever Typist Miss Bear, TN, 1950s, several actions, litho tin & plush, 7½", rare, EX (EX box), L4, from $1,200...$1,500.00

Climbing Clown, rare, EX, L4.....................$1,650.00

Clown Bumper Car, 1961, bump-&-go action w/lights & sound, litho tin, 10", NM, A.....................$150.00

Clown Candy Vending Machine, rare, NMIB, L4, from $1,000 to.....................$1,200.00

Clown Magician, Alps, 1950s, several actions, litho tin & vinyl w/cloth clothes, 12", MIB, L4 ....$375.00

Clown on Unicycle, MT, 1960s, 3 actions, litho tin, 10½", rare, EX.....................$350.00

Clucking Clara, CK, litho tin, MIB, L4, from $175 to ...$225.00

Cock-A-Doodle Doo Rooster, Mikuni, 1950s, several actions, litho tin, 8", VG, L4 ....$50.00

College Jalopy, Linemar, advances w/lights & sound, litho tin w/4 figures, remote control, 9½", EX (EX box) $340.00

Comic Choo Choo, Cragstan, 1960s, 3 actions, 10", EX..$65.00

Crackers the Talking Plush Parrot, Mattel, MIB.............$340.00

Cragstan Beep Beep Greyhound Bus, 1950s, 3 actions, litho tin, EX $170.00

Cragstan Crapshooter, Y, 1950s, several actions, mixed materials, 9", MIB, A $175.00

Cragstan Galloping Cowboy, litho tin, MIB, L4, from $225 to.$275.00

Cragstan Jumping Princess Poodle, NGS, 1950s, several actions, litho tin, 9", EX.....................$65.00

Cragstan One-Arm Bandit, Y, 1960s, 3 actions, 6", NMIB, L4, from $200 to $250.00

Cragstan Playboy, 1960s, several actions, litho tin, 13", NMIB, L4, from $225 to $275.00

Cragstan Rolling Honey Bear, rare, MIB, L4, from $475 to...$575.00

Cragstan Roulette Man, litho tin w/cloth clothes, EX (EX box), L4, from $275 to $325.00

Cragstan Shaking Antique Car, litho tin, 10", EX (EX box), A.....................$60.00

Cragstan Telly Bear, S&E, 1950s, several actions, litho tin & plush w/cloth clothes, 9", MIB, L4, from $475 to....$550.00

Cragstan Telly Bear, S&E, 1950s, several actions, litho tin & plush w/cloth clothes, 9", NM.....................$325.00

Cragstan Yo-Yo Clown, 1960s, 3 actions, 9", NM, L4 ....$250.00

Cycling Daddy, Bandai, 1960s, several actions, litho tin, 10", NM, L4, from $100 to $125.00

Cyclist Clown, Alps, 1950s, several actions, litho tin w/cloth clothes, 9", EX $300.00

Cyclist Clown, K, 1950s, several actions, litho tin w/cloth clothes, remote control, 7", EX, from $325 to $375.00

Daisy the Jolly Drumming Duck, Alps, 1950s, drum mk Cragstan Melody Band, litho tin & plush, MIB, L4, from $325 to $375.00

Dalmatian One-Man Band, Alps, 1950s, plays drum & cymbals, 9", VG.....................$100.00

Dancing Dan w/His Mystery Mike, Bell Prod, 1950s, litho tin, 13½", EX.....................$150.00

Dancing Merry Chimp, CK, several actions, litho tin & plush w/cloth clothes, 11", MIB, L4, from $200 to............$250.00

Dandy the Happy Drumming Pup, Cragstan/Alps, 1950s, litho tin & plush, NM, L4, from $150 to.....................$175.00

Dashee the Derby Hat Dachshund, Mego Corp., four actions, 1971, complete with plastic Derby, remote control, MIB, $80.00. (Photo courtesy Don Hultzman)

Dennis the Menace Xylophone Player, Rosko, 1950s, plays London Bridge, 9", MIB, L4, from $325 to.....................$375.00

Dentist Bear, S&E, 1950s, several actions, litho tin & plush w/cloth clothes, 9", NM, L4, from $400 to $475.00

Desert Patrol Jeep, MT, 1960s, several actions, litho tin, 11", EX $140.00

Dilly Dalmatian, Cragstan, 1950s, several actions, 9½", EX..$100.00

Dip-ie the Whale, SH, 1950s, 3 actions, litho tin, 13", EX....$190.00

Donald Duck Acrobat, Linemar, flips over highbar, celluloid, 9", NM (NM box mk Disney Acrobat), A $375.00

Donald Duck Locomotive, MT, 1970, several actions, tin & plastic, 9", M, L4.....................$325.00

Donny the Smiling Bulldog, Tomiyama, 1961, 3 actions, 8½", NMIB, L4, from $145 to.....................$175.00

Doxie the Dog, Linemar, 1950s, several actions, 9", EX ...$50.00

Dozo the Steaming Clown, Rosko, 1960s, litho tin w/cloth clothes, 10", MIB, L4, from $500 to.....................$575.00

Drinking Dog w/Lighted Eyes, Y, 1950s, 4 actions, 9", EX..$140.00

Drinking Sheriff, NM, L4, from $75 to $100.00

Drumming Bunny, Alps, 1960s, MIB, L4, from $100 to .$125.00

Drumming Target Bear, EX, L4, from $225 to................$275.00

Dual-Lite Marine Speedster, GW, 1950s, mostly wood, 12", EX $100.00

Electric Vibraphone, TN, 1950s, 3 actions, litho tin, 5½", EX $110.00

Electro Special Racer, Yonezawa, 1950s, 3 actions, litho tin, 10", rare, EX $375.00

Electro Toy Fire Engine, TN, 1950s, MIB, L4, from $145 to...$175.00

Electro Toy Sand Loader, TN, 1950s, MIB, L4, from $175 to ...$225.00

Excalibur Car, Bandai, 1960s, 3 actions, litho tin, 10", EX ..$125.00

Farm Truck, TN, bump-&-go w/lighted pistons & several other actions, litho tin, 9", NM (EX box), A $300.00

Father Bear Reading & Drinking in His Old Rocking Chair, MT, 1950s, tin & plush w/cloth clothes, 9½", rare, NMIB, A $340.00

FBI Godfather Car, Bandai, 1970s, 3 actions, 10", EX......$65.00

Feeding Bird Watcher, Linemar, 1950s, several actions, litho tin & plush, 9", EX $245.00

Ferris Wheel Truck, TPS, 1960s, several actions, litho tin & plastic, 7", EX $115.00

Fido the Xylophone Player, Alps, 1950s, several actions, litho tin & plush, 9", MIB, L4..$375.00

Fire Command Car, TN, 1950s, several actions, litho tin, EX..$260.00

Fire Truck, Hess/Hong Kong, plastic, 11", M (VG box), A, $325.00.

Firefly Bug, TN, 1950s, 3 actions, litho tin, EX $100.00

Fishing Polar Bear, Alps, bear pulls fish out of pond, throws it in basket & squeals, plush & tin, 10", EX (EX box), A..$190.00

Flexie the Pocket Monkey, Alps, 1960s, 3 actions, 12", EX...$115.00

Flintstone Paddy Wagon, Remco, 1960s, mostly plastic, 18", EX $115.00

Flipper the Spouting Dolphin, Bandai, MIB, L4, from $100 to...$125.00

Flippy the Only Roller Skating Monkey That Skis, Alps, 1950s, 3 actions, 12", rare, MIB, L4, from $550 to.............$650.00

Frankenstein, Poynter Products, 1970s, several actions, plastic w/cloth clothes, 12", EX $100.00

Frankie the Roller Skating Monkey, Alps, 1950s, 3 actions, remote control, 12", EX (EX box), A.......................$115.00

Fred Flintstone's Bedrock Band, Alps, Fred plays drums & cymbals, litho tin & vinyl w/cloth clothes, 9", EX, A....$300.00

Fruit Juice Counter, Japan, waitress mixes juice w/several actions, litho tin, EX (EX box converts into store), A $210.00

Fumbling Pussy, MT, 1970s, 3 actions, 10" L, EX..............$65.00

Funland Cup Ride, Sonsco, 1960s, kids spin around in cups, NMIB, L4, from $200 to...$250.00

GM Coach, Yonezawa, 1950s, bump-&-go, push button on top & stewardess appears in doorway, litho tin, 16", NMIB, A...$600.00

Gomora Monster, Bullmark, 1960s, several actions, complete w/plastic missiles, 8", EX $225.00

Grand-Pa Car, Y, 1950s, 4 actions, litho tin, 9", EX $75.00

Grand-Pa Panda Bear, MT, sits in rocking chair & eats popcorn, eyes light, tin & plush, 9", EX (EX box), A.............$265.00

Greyhound Bus, KKK, 1950s, litho tin, 7", EX $140.00

Growling Tiger Trophy Plaque, Cragstan, 1950s, 3 actions, 10", EX, L4, from $150 to...$200.00

Happy 'N Sad Magic Face Clown, Yonezawa, 1960s, plays accordion as facial expressions change, 10", EX (EX box), A..$115.00

Happy Band Trio, MT, 1970s, dog, rabbit & bear play instruments on litho tin stage, 11", MIB, L4, from $550 to..........$600.00

Happy Dog Family, MIB, L4, from $100 to.................$1,125.00

Happy Fiddler Clown, Alps, 1950s, several actions, litho tin w/cloth clothes, 9½", MIB, L4, from $475 to $575.00

Happy Fiddler Clown, Alps, 1950s, several actions, litho tin w/cloth clothes, 9½", NM $340.00

Happy Miner, Bandai, 1960s, litho tin, rare, MIB, from $900 to $1,100.00

Happy Plane, TPS, 1960s, 3 actions, litho tin, 9" L, EX.$115.00

Happy Santa One-Man Band, Alps, several actions, 9", MIB, l4, from $250 to $300.00

Happy the Clown Puppet Show, Y, 1960s, 3 actions, litho tin & vinyl w/cloth clothes, 10", NM (NM box), L4, from $450 to..$500.00

Happy Tractor, Daiya, 1960s, 4 actions, 8", EX...............$65.00

Hasty Chimp, Y, 1960s, several actions, 9", MIB, L4, from $100 to $125.00

Hess Fire Truck, Hong Kong, red plastic, 11", MIB, A ...$245.00

High Jinks at the Circus, Alps, clown w/performing monkey, several actions, MIB, L4, from $325 to $400.00

Hi-Power Dozer, TN, lithographed tin, seated driver, chromed grille, 11", NMIB, A, $150.00.

Honda Big Rider Motorcycle #34, litho tin, 10", EX (worn box), A $75.00

Hooty the Happy Owl, Alps, 1960s, several actions, 9", MIB, L4, from $140 to $185.00

Hopping Pup w/Cart, Alps, 1950s, 3 actions, 9", MIB, L4, from $100 to...$125.00

Howdy Doody World Touring Car, rare, EX, from $700 to ..$800.00

Hungry Baby Bear, Y, 1950s, mama bear feeds baby w/several actions, tin & plush w/cloth clothes, 9½", EX (EX box), A $140.00

Hungry Cat, Linemar, cat reaches in fishbowl w/several actions, tin & plush, 9", EX (VG box), A $375.00

Hungry Hound Dog, Y, 1950s, several actions, 9½", EX...$285.00

Hungry Sheep, MT, 1950s, 3 actions, 9", EX $150.00

Ice Cream Eating Bear, MT, 1950s, lifts spoon to mouth, tin & plush, 9½", scarce, NM, L4, from $425 to $475.00

Indian Joe, Alps, advances & plays drum, litho tin, NMIB..$100.00

Jack 'N Jill Action Rail Car, Hong Kong, 1960s, 3 actions, mostly plastic, EX $100.00

Japanese Monster, rare, NM, L4, from $425 to $475.00

Jocko the Drinking Monkey, Linemar, 1950s, several actions, 11", VG, L4..$75.00

Jolly Bambino the Eating Monkey, Alps, 1950s, eats candy w/several actions, litho tin & plush, 9", NM $475.00

Jolly Bambino the Eating Monkey, Alps, 1950s, eats candy w/several actions, litho tin & plush, 9", MIB, L4 ....$750.00

Jolly Bear w/Robin, MT, several actions, litho tin & plush w/cloth clothes, 9½", rare, NM (NM box), A.........$640.00

Jolly Daddy Smoking Elephant, Marusan, 1950s, 4 actions, tin & plush w/cloth clothes, 9", VG $125.00

Jolly Peanut Vendor, TN, 1950s, bear pushes peanut cart w/several actions, litho tin & plush, 8", NMIB, L4, from $500 to .$575.00

Jolly Plane, TPS, bump-&-go w/spinning prop & moving pistons, tin & plastic, 7½", NM (EX box), A $110.00

Jolly Santa on Snow, Alps, 1950s, 12", MIB, L4, from $350 to..$400.00

Josie the Walking Cow, Daiya, 1950s, several actions, plush over tin, NM, L4, from $125 to..$150.00

Jungle Jumbo, B-C Toy Co., six actions, 1950s, MIB, $600.00. (Photo courtesy Don Hultzman)

Jungle Trio, Linemar, 1950s, elephant plays flute & monkey plays drum & cymbals, tin & vinyl, 8", MIB, minimum value...$900.00

Junior Phone, Modern Toys, 1950s, 2 plastic phones, NM (NM fold-out display box)..$50.00

Kiddie Trolley, MT, 1960s, advances w/lights & ringing bell, tin & plastic, 8", EX $75.00

King Size Volkswagen, tin, 15", MIB, L4, from $325 to $375.00

Lady Pup Tending Her Garden, Cragstan, 1950s, several actions, litho tin w/cloth clothes, 8", MIB, from $385 to $445.00

Lady Pup Tending Her Garden, Cragstan, 1950s, several actions, litho tin w/cloth clothes, 8", EX...............................$250.00

Laffin' Head Indian Squaw, M, L4, from $120 to............$150.00

Laughing Skull, MIB, L4, from $225 to $275.00

Lite-It-Up-Ford, Ichiko, 1950s, 7½", EX $170.00

Lite-O-Wheel Go Kart, Rosko, 1950s, 3 actions, MIB...$225.00

Little Indian, TN, 1960s, 3 actions, 9", EX....................$125.00

Loop Plane, MT, advances w/gun sound & lights, litho tin w/compo figure, remote control, 9" W, NM (EX box), A.............$225.00

Loop-the-Loop Monkey, TN, 1960s, 10", EX....................$75.00

Lookout Louie, Linemar Co., 1950s, 6½", M (VG box), $175.00.

Lotus Hi-Speed Racer #12, Japan, 1960s, tin, 12", NM (NM box)...$120.00

Lotus Hi-Speed Racer #19, Japan, 1960s, litho tin, NMIB .$115.00

Lucky Car, Marusan, rare, NM, L4, from $325 to...........$375.00

Lucky Cement Mixer, MT, 1960s, several actions, 12", MIB, L4, from $265 to $325.00

M-48 Army Tank, TN, advances w/bump-&-go action as gun fires, litho tin, 8", MIB, A $75.00

M-99 Army Tank, MT, forward & reverse action w/lights & sound, tin w/plastic treads, 18", NM (EX box), A..$140.00

Magic Action Bulldozer, TN, 1950s, 3 actions, 9½", MIB, L4, from $200 to $250.00

Magic Snowman, Santa Creations, 1950s, several actions, complete w/broom, pipe & ball, 11", EX $115.00

Major Tooty, Alps, 1960s, drum major plays drum, 14", MIB, L4, from $225 to $275.00

Make-Up Bear, MT, 1960s, sits in chair w/mirror & puts on make-up, tin & plush, 9", scarce, NM, L4, minimum value $600.00

Mambo the Jolly Drumming Elephant, Alps, 1950s, plays drum & cymbals, tin & plush, 9½", MIB, from $300 to ...$350.00

Man From UNCLE Talking Patrol Car, Rico, 1960s, litho tin, 19", EX (EX box)..$340.00

Marshall Wild Bill, Y, advances & fires gun w/lights & sound, litho tin w/cloth clothes, remote control, 12", NMIB $325.00

Marvelous Locomotive, TN, 1950s, 4 actions, litho tin, EX $125.00

Mary's Little Lamb, Alps, 1950s, 3 actions, 10½", EX....$150.00

Maxwell Coffee-Loving Bear, TN, 1960s, pours cup of coffee w/several actions, mixed materials, 10", MIB, L4, from $250 to...$300.00

Mentor Wizard, Hasbro, MIB, L4, from $120 to.............$150.00

Merry-Go-Round Truck, TN, 1950s, several actions, litho tin, 11", rare, NM..$375.00

Metropolitan Line Trolley, rare, EX, L4, from $200 to ...$250.00

Mickey Acrobat, Linemar, flips over highbar, celluloid, 9", rare, NM (EX box mk Disney Acrobat), A......................$375.00

Mickey Mouse Flying Saucer, MT, MIB, L4, from $200 to...$250.00

Mickey Mouse Locomotive, MT, 1960s, several actions, litho tin & plastic, 9", EX $225.00

Mickey Mouse Loop the Loop, Illco, MIB, L4, from $150 to..$200.00

Mickey Mouse Sand Buggy, MT, 1960s, several actions, litho tin & plastic, 11", EX $225.00

Mickey Mouse Tow Truck, Andy Gard, 1960s, remote control, 7½", NMIB $475.00

Mickey Mouse Trolley, MT, 1960s, 3 actions, litho tin, EX ...$225.00

Mickey the Magician, Linemar, raises wand, lifts hat & chick appears, litho tin, 10½", scarce, NM (EX box) $1,800.00

Microphone Dancer, National Co, Black man attached to lamp-post dances wildly, voice activated, 12", EX, A $170.00

Mighty Kong, MIB, from $525 to $600.00

Mimi Poodle w/Bone, Nomura, plush over tin, EX (EX box), A.................................$150.00

Mischievous Monkey, MT, monkey scoots up & down tree in front of doghouse, litho tin, 13", EX (EX box), A ..$225.00

Mobile Loudspeaker, 1960s, plastic, 22", NM (NM box) .$60.00

Monkee Mobile, Aoshin, 1967, 12", NMIB.................$525.00

Monkey Locomotive, litho tin, M, L4, from $100 to......$125.00

Monkey on Scooter, rare, NM, from $425 to $475.00

Monkey the Shoe Maker, TN, 1950s, 3 actions, 9", rare, NM ..$475.00

Mother Bear, MT, sits in rocking chair & knits, eyes light, tin & plush, 9", NM (EX box), A $115.00

Mother Goose, Yonezawa, litho tin, MIB, L4, from $200 to ...$250.00

Mr Al E Gator, rare, MIB, L4 ....$400.00

Mr McClean Car Wash, JC Penney catalog item, 1960s, MIB.................................$75.00

Mr Strong Pup the Mighty Weightlifter, K, 1950s, several actions, 9", EX (EX box) $265.00

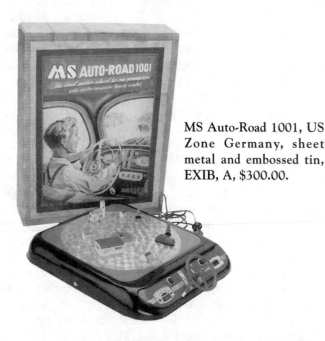

MS Auto-Road 1001, US Zone Germany, sheet metal and embossed tin, EXIB, A, $300.00.

Mumbo Jumbo Hawaiian Drummer, Alps, 1960s, 3 actions, litho tin & vinyl, 10", MIB, L4, from $250 to $300.00

Mumbo Jumbo Hawaiian Drummer, Alps, 1960s, 3 actions, litho tin & vinyl, 10", EX.................................$150.00

Music Hall, Linemar, 1950s, several actions, litho tin, EX..$200.00

Musical Bear, Linemar, 1950s, plays drum, horn & cymbals, litho tin, 10", rare, NM $475.00

Musical Bulldog, Marusan, 1950s, plays piano, litho tin & plush w/cloth clothes, 8½", rare, VG, A $700.00

Musical Car, Asahitoy, 1950s, advances & plays There's No Place Like Home, 9", EX $225.00

Musical Comic Jumping Jeep, Alps, several actions, 12", M, L4, from $150 to $175.00

Musical Dancing Sweethearts, KO, 1950s, litho tin, 10", rare, NM.................................$300.00

Musical Ford, 1955, MIB, from $475 to $535.00

Musical Ice Cream Truck, Bandai, 1960s, several actions, litho tin & plastic, 10½", EX.................................$225.00

Musical Jackal, Linemar, 1950s, several actions, litho tin, 10", extremely rare, NM, minimum value $750.00

Musical Marching Bear, Alps, 1950s, beats drum & blows horn, tin & plush w/cloth pants, 11", MIB, from $550 to .$600.00

Musical Monkey Melody Train, MIB, L4, from $225 to .$275.00

Musical Showboat, Gakken, 1960s, litho tin & plastic, 13", EX $190.00

Musical Vegetable Truck, Bandai, 1960s, several actions, litho tin, 10½", MIB, L4, from $250 to $300.00

My Fair Dancer, MIB, L4, from $225 to $275.00

New Adventures of Clown, TN, NMIB, L4, from $600 to..$650.00

New Service Car (World News), TPS, 3 actions, litho tin, 9½", EX $300.00

New Silver Mountain Express, MT, 1960s, 3 actions, 16", EX $65.00

Ol' Sleepy Head Rip, Y, 1950s, several actions, 9½", EX ...$225.00

Old Fashioned Hot Rod w/Driver, Bandai, 1960s, 4 actions, 6½", NM.................................$190.00

Oldtimer Train Set, Cragstan, 1950s, MIB $225.00

Open Sleigh w/Eskimo & Huskies, MT, 1950s, 4 actions, litho tin, 16" L, rare, NM $525.00

Overland Express Locomotive, Masudaya, litho tin, EX (EX box), A.................................$140.00

Overland Stage Coach, M-T Co., 1950s, four actions, two plastic horses, MIB, $300.00. (Photo courtesy Don Hultzman)

Pat the Dog, NGS, 1950s, several actions, 9½", MIB, L4, from $140 to.................................$175.00

Pat the Roaring Elephant, Y, 1950s, 4 actions, litho tin, 9", EX .$225.00

Pee Pee Puppy, TN, 1960s, several actions, plush over tin, 9", NMIB.................................$150.00

Peppermint Twist Doll, Haji, 1950s, litho tin, 12", NM ..**$225.00**

Peppy Puppy, Rosko, plush over tin, remote control, 8", EX (G box), A..**$115.00**

Peppy the Purky Pup, Japan, 1958, plush & tin, remote control, EX (EX box) **$140.00**

Periscope Firing Range, Cragstan, tin, MIB.....................**$190.00**

Pete the Policeman, Bandai, litho tin, M, L4, from $100 to..**$125.00**

Picnic Bunny, Alps, 1950s, pours juice in cup & drinks w/realistic action, tin & plush, 11", MIB, A **$190.00**

Piggy Cook, Y, 1950s, several actions, litho tin & vinyl w/cloth clothes, 9½", MIB......................................**$275.00**

Piggy Cook, Y, 1950s, several actions, litho tin & vinyl w/cloth clothes, 9½", EX.....................................**$210.00**

Pilot Electro Boat, TN, litho tin, 11", NM (EX box), A...**$170.00**

Pinky the Juggling Clown, Alps, juggles a lighted ball, blows whistle, balls twirl on rod, 10", NM, L4, from $200 to........**$250.00**

Pipie the Whale, Alps, 1950s, litho tin, 12", rare, EX.........**$225.00**

Pistol Pete, SAN, advances, stops & fires gun w/lights, sound & smoke, litho tin & cloth, remote control, 11", NMIB.**$360.00**

Playful Puppy w/Caterpillar, MT, 4 actions, litho tin, 5", EX...**$150.00**

Playland Train, Gakken, 1970s, w/7 figures, 3 actions, mostly plastic, 7½" dia, NM................................**$40.00**

Pluto Acrobat, Linemar, flips over highbar, celluloid, 9", NM (EX box mk Disney Acrobat), MIB, L4 ....**$675.00**

Police Auto Cycle, Bandai, 1960s, several actions, litho tin w/plastic figure, remote control, 11½", M **$250.00**

Police Jeep, Rosko, litho tin, 13", MIB, from $500 to **$550.00**

Police Patrol Auto-Tricycle, TN, lithographed tin, 9½", MIB, A, $695.00.

Popcorn Eating Panda, MT, 1950s, several actions, EX, L4, from $140 to..**$175.00**

Popcorn Vendor, S&E, 1960s, bear pushes cart as popcorn pops, 7", EX..**$300.00**

Popcorn Vendor, TN, 1950s, duck pushes cart as popcorn pops, 8", EX..**$300.00**

Popeye, see also Smoking Popeye

Popeye in Rowboat, Linemar, litho tin, remote control, 10½", extremely rare, NM (EX box), A.........................**$4,875.00**

Poverty Pup Bank, Poynter/Alabe, 1966, 6", MIB, L4, from $60 to **$75.00**

Princess the Begging Poodle, Alps, 1950s, several actions, 8", EX **$65.00**

Puffy Morris, Y, 1960s, smokes real cigarette, 10", MIB, L4 ....**$285.00**

Puzzled Puppy, MT, 1950s, several actions, 5", EX..........**$150.00**

Rabbits & the Carriage, S&E, 1950s, several actions, litho tin & plush, 8" L, rare, EX......................................**$225.00**

Radar Jeep, Cragstan, military jeep w/searchlight & 2 figures, tin, 11", NMIB, A..**$100.00**

Radicon Boat, MT, radio controlled, rare, MIB, minimum value **$700.00**

Radicon Oldsmobile, MT, NMIB, from $600 to **$700.00**

Raggedy Ann & Andy Play Along Xylophone, Azrak/Hamway Inc, 1978, metal & plastic, w/4 records & song book, NMIB..**$30.00**

Rambling Ladybug, MT, 1960s, litho tin, 8", EX **$100.00**

RCA-NBC Mobile Color TV Truck, Cragstan, 1950s, forward & reverse action w/circus scene on lighted screen, 9", MIB, A **$675.00**

Roaring Gorilla Shooting Gallery, MT, 1950s, 3 actions, litho tin & plastic, 9½", EX (EX box) **$340.00**

Rock 'N Roll Monkey, Alps, brn pants, plays guitar w/several actions, 12", NM, A................................**$115.00**

Rock 'N Roll Monkey, Alps, orange pants, plays guitar w/several actions, 12", EX (EX box), A **$210.00**

Roll-Over Rover, Mego, 1970s, 3 actions, 9", EX **$65.00**

Rooster, Mikuni, advances w/sound, litho tin, 7", EX (EX box), A **$60.00**

Sam the Shaving Man, Plaything Toys, 1960s, several actions, litho tin & vinyl w/cloth clothes, 11½", EX (EX box) **$265.00**

Santa Claus on Reindeer Sleigh, MT, 1950s, several actions, litho tin & plastic, 17", rare, EX (EX box) **$695.00**

Santa Copter, MT, 1950s, 3 actions, 8½", VG.................**$75.00**

Santa on Monorail, rare, MIB, L4, from $600 to **$650.00**

Sea Bear #7 Racing Boat, Bandai, 1950s, 10", EX **$100.00**

Searchlight Jeep, TN, 1950s, 3 actions, 8", EX..............**$140.00**

Serpent Charmer, Linemar, 1950s, several actions, 7", extremely rare, NM, minimum value.......................................**$750.00**

Shaggy the Friendly Pup, Alps, 1960s, 3 actions, 8", EX ..**$65.00**

Shoeshine Joe w/Lighted Pipe, TN, 1950s, several actions, litho tin & plush, 11", EX **$215.00**

Shooting Cowboys in Barrel, very rare, EX, from $700 to..**$850.00**

Singing Bird in Cage, TN, 1950s, several actions, NM, L4..**$75.00**

Siren Patrol Motorcycle, MT, 1960s, several actions, litho tin, 12", rare, MIB, L4.......................................**$675.00**

Slalom Game, TN, steering wheel guides skier, litho tin, 11" base, EX (EX box), A **$150.00**

Sleeping Baby Bear, Linemar, mixed materials, bear yawns and cries, 9", NMIB, $475.00.

Slurpy Pup, TN, 1960s, several actions, litho tin & plush, 6½", MIB, L4, from $100 to..$125.00

Smokey Bear Jeep, MT, 1950s, bump-&-go w/flashing light & siren, litho tin w/full figure, 10", rare, MIB, L4 ....$1,000.00

Smokey Bill, MIB, L4 ....$190.00

Smoking Pop Locomotive, SAN, 1950s, 4 actions, 10½", EX..$110.00

Smoking Popeye, Linemar, King Features Syndicate, lithographed tin, NM (EX box), A, $1,900.00.

Smoky (sic) Bear, Marusan, several actions, litho tin & plush, EX (EX box), A $225.00

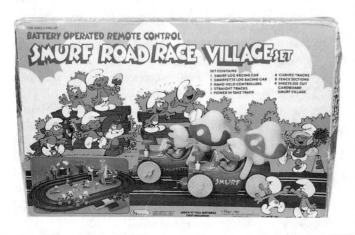

Smurf Road Race Village Set, Talbot Toys, remote control, 1983, EXIB, $65.00.

Snapping Alligator, S&E, litho tin, EX (EX box), A $100.00

Snappy the Happy Bubble Blowing Dragon, TN, 1960s, several actions, litho tin, 30", scarce, NM, minimum value ..$3,000.00

Sneezing Bear, Linemar, 1950s, several actions, litho tin & plush, 9", MIB...$475.00

Snoopy & His Flyin' Doghouse, Mattel Preschool, 1974, MIB, from $150 to $150.00

Snowman, MIB, L4, from $225 to...................................$275.00

Spanking Bear, Linemar, 1950s, mama spanks baby w/several other actions, litho tin & plush, 9", EX, L4, from $200 to...$250.00

Speed King Racer, Y, 1960s, 3 actions, 12½", EX...........$110.00

Steamroller, Yonezawa, 1950s, advances w/smoking action, litho tin, 12½", NM (VG box) $290.00

Stunt Plane, TPS, 1960s, 3 actions, litho tin, 10½" W, MIB, L4, from $225 to $275.00

Sunday Driver, MT, 1950s, 4 actions, detachable driver, 10", EX...$110.00

Super Susie, Linemar, 1950s, bear pushes groceries on conveyor belt w/several other actions, tin & plush, 8", NMIB..$800.00

Swan the Queen of the Water, litho tin, MIB, L4, from $300 to..$375.00

Swimming Duck, Bandai, 1950s, several actions, litho tin, 8", EX...$140.00

Swimming Fish, litho tin, rare, NMIB, L4, from $225 to..$275.00

Swimming Snoopy, Concept 2000/Determined, 1970s, NMIB...$35.00

Switchboard Operator, Linemar, 1950s, several actions, litho tin & vinyl, 7½", rare, NM $525.00

Talking Trixie, Alps, 1950s, 4 actions, 6½", EX...............$65.00

Tarzan, SAN, 1966, advances & emits Tarzan yell, plastic w/loin-cloth, remote control, 13", rare, NM (NM box), A .$825.00

Teddy Bear Swing, Yonezawa, performs flips on bar, litho tin & plush, 13", MIB, from $525 to................................$575.00

Teddy-Go-Kart, Alps, four actions, 1960s, 10½", MIB, from $225.00 to $275.00. (Photo courtesy Don Hultzman)

Teddy the Artist, Yonezawa, 1950s, simulates drawing, complete w/9 templates, EX (EX box), A $340.00

Teddy the Champ Boxer, Y, 1950s, several actions, 9", MIB...$435.00

Teddy the Manager, see Cragstan Telly Bear

Telephone Bear, TN, sits at desk & answers phone w/several actions, tin & plush, 7", EX (EX box), A.................$300.00

Telephone Rabbit, MT, rocks & talks on telephone w/moving mouth, litho tin & plush, 10", MIB, L4, from $200 to..$250.00

Terry the Wonder Dog w/Lighted Eyes, Linemar, 1960s, 3 actions, 9", VG...$38.00

Thunder Jet Boat, MIB, L4, from $300 to......................$375.00

Tinkling Trolley, MT, 1950s, several actions, litho tin, 10½", MIB, L4, from $150 to..$200.00

Tom & Jerry Choo Choo, MT, 1960s, several actions, litho tin, 10", NM...$190.00

Tom & Jerry Comic Car, MT, Tom drives as Jerry spins on stick of dynamite, tin w/vinyl figures, 11", M (EX box), A $435.00

Tom & Jerry Formula Racing Car, MT, 1960s, 3 actions, litho tin, 11", EX..$140.00

Tom & Jerry Highway Patrol, MT, 1960s, 3 actions, 8", VG..$100.00

Topo Gigio Xylophone Player, TN, 1960s, 3 actions, litho tin, 10½", scarce, MIB, miminum value......................$1,000.00

Traffic Policeman, A1, 1950s, several actions, litho tin, 6x6" base, rare, EX $375.00

Traveler Bear, K, three actions, 1950s, 8", MIB, $495.00.

Tric-Cycling Clown, MT, pedals unicycle & holds lighted balls, litho tin & vinyl w/cloth clothes, 11", NMIB, $400 to $500.00

Tricky Doghouse, Y, 1960s, several actions, litho tin, MIB, L4, from $225 to $275.00

Tricky Doodle Duck, Remco, 1968, advances w/whistle, quacks & bill moves, plastic, MIB...$200.00

Trumpet Playing Monkey, Alps, 1950s, 4 actions, 9", M...$265.00

Tumbling Clown, Remco, EX, L4, from $100 to.............$125.00

Tumbling Monkey, MIB, L4, from $100 to $125.00

Turn-O-Matic Gun Jeep, TN, 1960s, 10", MIB, L4, from $200 to...$250.00

Twin Racing Cars, Alps, 1950s, litho tin w/coupling rod, MIB, L4 ....$675.00

Union Mountain Monorail, TN, 1950s, MIB, L4, from $175 to...$225.00

VIP Busy Boss Bear, S&E, 1950s, several actions, 8", NM (NM box)...$340.00

VIP Busy Boss Bear, S&E, 1950s, several actions, 8", VG, A $225.00

Waddles Family Car, Y, 1960s, MIB, L4, from $135 to...$175.00

Walking Bambi, Linemar, 1950s, several actions, litho tin, 9", scarce, MIB, from $550 to $650.00

Walking Cat, Linemar, 1950s, 3 actions, 6", EX $65.00

Walking Esso Tiger, litho tin, NM, L4 ....$375.00

Walking Gorilla, rare, NM, L4, from $650 to $750.00

Walking Knight in Armour, MT, 1950s, several actions, rare, NMIB, L4 ....$3,000.00

Walt Disney's Tomorrowland Rocket Ride, Wen-Mac, 1960, 29", rare, EX $300.00

Walt Disney's Tomorrowland Space Wheel, Wen-Mac, 1960s, 28", rare, EX...$300.00

Waltzing Matilda, TN, rare, MIB, L4, from $800 to.......$900.00

Water Spouting Whale w/Flopping Tail, KKS, 1950s, 13", EX.$150.00

Weeping Skeleton, rare, MIB, L4, from $300 to $375.00

Western Choo Choo, Masudaya, litho tin, EX (G box), A...$60.00

Whirlybird Helicopter, Remco, 1960s, 3 actions, 25", NMIB, L4, from $200 to $250.00

Wild West Rodeo, see Bubbling Bull

Willie the Walking Car, Y, 1960s, several actions, 8½", MIB, L4, from $265 to $325.00

Windy the Juggling Elephant, TN, 1950s, litho tin, 10½", MIB, L4, from $265 to $325.00

Winston the Barking Bulldog, Tomiyama, 1950s, 3 actions, 10", NM...$120.00

Wonderland Locomotive, Bandai, 1960s, 3 actions, 9", EX ..$65.00

Worried Mother Duck & Baby, TN, 1950s, 3 actions, litho tin, 11", MIB, L4, from $175 to $225.00

Xylophone Bear, Linemar, walking version, rare, MIB, L4, from $475 to...$575.00

Yo-Yo Clown, see Cragstan Yo-Yo Clown

Yo-Yo Monkey, YM, 1960s, 12", EX $150.00

Yummy-Yum Kitten w/Fish, Linemar, 1950s, several actions, 9", rare, NM $375.00

Zoom Boat F-570, K, 1950s, forward & reverse action, litho tin, remote control, 10", EX (EX box), A.......................$170.00

Beanie Babies

Who can account for this latest flash in collecting that some liken to the rush for Cabbage Patch dolls we saw many years ago! The appeal of these stuffed creatures is disarming to both children and adults, and excited collectors are eager to scoop up each new-found treasure. There is much to be learned about Beanie Babies. For instance, there are different swing and tush tag styles and these indicate year of issue:

#1, Swing tag: single heart-shaped tag; comes on Beanies with tush tags dated 1993.

#2, Swing tag: heart-shaped; folded, with information inside; narrow letters; comes on Beanies with tush tags dated 1993.

#1 Swing tag

#2 Swing tag

#3 Swing tag

#6 Zodiac variation Swing tag

#4 Swing tag

#6 Holiday variation Swing tag

#5 Swing tag

#8 Swing tag

#6 Swing tag

#3, Swing tag: heart-shaped; folded, with information inside; wider letters; comes on Beanies with tush tags dated 1993 and 1995.

#4, Swing tag: heart-shaped; folded, with information inside; wider lettering with no gold outline around the 'ty'; yellow star on front; first tag to include a poem and birth date; comes on Beanies with tush tags dated 1993, 1995, and 1996.

#5, Swing tag: heart-shaped; folded, with information inside; different font on front and inside; birth month spelled out, no style numbers, website listed; comes on Beanies with tush tags dated 1993, 1995, 1996, 1997, 1998, and 1999.

#6, Swing tag: features holographic star with '2000' across star; inside: Ty, Inc., Ty Canada, Ty Europe, and Ty Japan; birthdate, website address, and poem in smaller font than #5; new safety precaution on back, smaller font, and UPC; comes on Beanies with tush tags dated 2000.

Variations on #6 Swing tags: The twelve Zodiac Beanie Babies, released in September 2000, have all the characteristics of the sixth generation swing tag, with the exception of the word 'Zodiac' on the front of the swing tag, which replaces the star and 2000. The interiors of the three Holiday Beanie Babies' tags, released in October 2000, have blue backgrounds, and white snowflakes.

#7, Swing tag: identical to #6 hang tag except 'Beanies' is written across the holographic star instead of '2000.' This tag appears in UK Beanie Babies (photo not available); comes on Beanies with tush tags dated 2000.

#8, Swing tag: shows a ¼" holographic star with the word 'Beanie' above and 'Baby' below in fine yellow print. Inside information identical to #6 swing tag; comes on Beanies with tush tags dated 2000 and 2001.

Prices are for toys with swing tags in mint or near-mint condition. For Beanies with a #1, #2, or #3 tag, add $30.00 to $50.00 to the prices suggested below. Style numbers are the last four digits in the UPC code located on the back of the Beanie's swing tag.

Advisor: Amy Hopper.

Key:
R = Retired   BBOC = Beanie Babies Official Club

#1 Bear, red w/#1 on chest, issued only to Ty sales reps, 253 made, R, minimum value **$5,000.00**

Addison the bear, given to ticketholders at Chicago Cubs vs. Arizona Diamondbacks baseball game at Wrigley Field, May 20, 2001, R, from $20 to **$75.00**

Ally the Alligator, #4032, R, from $30 to **$40.00**

Almond the Bear, #4246, R, from $5 to **$10.00**

Amber the Cat, #4243, R, gold tabby, from $5 to **$10.00**

Ants the Anteater, #4195, R, from $5 to **$10.00**

Ariel, Fund Raising Bear for the Elizabeth Glaser Pediatric AIDS Foundation, #4288, from $10 to **$15.00**

Aruba the Angelfish, #4314, R, from $7 to........................**$10.00**

Aurora the Polar Bear, #4271, R, from $7 to.....................**$10.00**

Baldy the Eagle, #4074, R, from $10 to $20.00

Bananas the Orangutan, #4316, R, from $7 to.................$10.00

Batty the Bat, #4035, pk, R, from $5 to.............................$10.00

Batty the Bat, #4035, tie-dyed, R, from $5 to $15.00

B B the Birthday Bear, #4253, from $10 to $15.00

Beak the Kiwi Bird, #4211, R, from $5 to $10.00

Bernie the St Bernard, #4109, R, from $5 to....................$15.00

Bessie the Cow, #4009, brn, R, from $30 to $45.00

Billionaire Bear (1998), brn, dollar sign on chest, issued only to Ty employees, R, minimum value $950.00

Billionaire 2 the bear (1999), purple, issued only to Ty employees, R, minimum value..$1,400.00

Billionaire 3 the bear (2000), orange, issued only to Ty employees, R, minimum value..$1,100.00

Blackie the Bear, #4011, R, from $10 to............................$20.00

Blizzard the Tiger, #4163, wht, R, from $10 to $15.00

Bones the Dog, #4001, brn, R, from $10 to.......................$15.00

Bongo the Monkey, #4067, brn, R, from $30 to...............$50.00

Bongo the Monkey, #4067, 2nd issue w/tan tail, R, from $5 to $15.00

Britannia the Bear, #4601, Ty UK exclusive, R, minimum value..$50.00

Bronty the Brontosaurus, #4085, bl, R, minimum value.$400.00

Brownie the Bear, #4010, w/swing tag, R, minimum value..$2,000.00

Bruno the Terrier, #4183, R, from $5 to $10.00

Bubbles the Fish, #4078, yellow and black, retired, minimum value $45.00. (Photo courtesy Amy Hopper)

Buckingham the Bear, #4603, UK exclusive, R, minimum value.$65.00

Bucky the Beaver, #4016, R, from $10 to.........................$15.00

Bumble the Bee, #4045, R, minimum value.....................$275.00

Bushy the Lion, #4285, R, from $7 to $10.00

Butch the Bull Terrier, #4227, R, from $5 to.....................$10.00

Buzzie the Bee, #4354, from $7 to $10.00

Buzzy the Buzzard, #4308, R, from $7 to...........................$10.00

Canyon the Cougar, #4212, R, from $5 to $10.00

Cashew the Bear, #4292, br, R, from $7 to.......................$10.00

Cassie the Collie, #4340, from $7 to $10.00

Caw the Crow, #4071, R, from $275 to.............................$325.00

Cheeks the Baboon, #4250, R, from $5 to........................$10.00

Cheery the Sunshine Bear, #4359, from $7 to $10.00

Cheezer the Mouse, #4301, R, from $7 to.........................$10.00

Chilly the Polar Bear, #4012, R, minimum value $900.00

China the Panda, #4315, R, from $7 to.............................$10.00

Chinook the Bear, #4604, Ty Canada exclusive, R, from $40 to...$60.00

Chip the Calico Cat, #4121, R, from $5 to $10.00

Chipper the Chipmunk, #4259, R, from $5 to $10.00

Chocolate the Moose, #4015, R, from $5 to $15.00

Chops the Lamb, #4019, R, from $60..................................$80.00

Cinders the Bear, #4295, R, blk, from $7 to $10.00

Classy the Bear, 'The People's Beanie,' determined by voting on the Ty Internet website, April 2001, from $10 to $20.00

Claude the Crab, #4083, tie-dyed, R, from $5 to $15.00

Clubby the Bear, Beanie Babies Official Club exclusive, mail-order only, blue, retired, from $15.00 to $25.00. (Photo courtesy Amy Hopper)

Clubby II the Bear, BBOC exclusive, purple, R, from $10 to $20.00

Clubby III the Bear, BBOC exclusive, (mail-order or Internet order only) brn, R, from $10 to $20.00

Congo the Gorilla, #4160, R, from $5 to $15.00

Coral the Fish, #4079, tie-dyed, R, minimum value $60.00

Crunch the Shark, #4130, R, from $5 to...........................$10.00

Cubbie the Bear, #4010, brn, R, from $15 to $25.00

Curly the Bear, #4052, brn, R, from $10 to $15.00

Daisy the Cow, #4006, blk & wht, R, from $10 to $15.00

Dart the Blue Dart Frog, #4352, from $7 to $10.00

Dearest the Bear, #4350, peach, R, from $7 to $15.00

Derby the Horse, #4008, 1st issue, R, fine yarn mane & tail, minimum value $1,500.00

Derby the Horse, #4008, 2nd issue, R, brn, coarse mane & tail, from $10 to...$20.00

Derby the Horse, #4008, 3rd issue, R, brn w/wht star on forehead, from $5 to..$10.00

Derby the Horse, #4008, 4th issue, R, brn w/wht star on forehead, fur mane & tail, from $5 to...............................$10.00

Digger the Crab, #4027, 1st issue, orange, R, minimum value $350.00

Digger the Crab, #4027, 2nd issue, red, R, minimum value .$50.00

Dinky the Dodo Bird, #4341, from $7 to............................$10.00

Dizzy the Dalmatian, #4365, from $7 to $10.00

Doby the Doberman, #4110, R, from $5 to $15.00

Doodle the Rooster, #4171, tie-dyed, R, from $10 to........$20.00

Dotty the Dalmatian, #4100, R, from $5 to $10.00

Early the Robin, #4190, R, from $5 to.............................$10.00

Ears the Rabbit, #4018, brn, R, from $10 to....................$20.00

Echo the Dolphin, #4180, R, from $10 to $15.00

Eggbert the Baby Chick, #4232, R, from $5 to................$10.00

Eggs the Bear, #4337, pk, Easter bear, R, from $10 to $15.00

Erin the Bear, #4186, gr, R, from $10 to $15.00

Eucalyptus the Koala, #4240, R, from $5 to $10.00

Ewey the Lamb, #4219, R, from $5 to $10.00

Fetch the Golden Retriever, #4189, R, from $10 to..........$20.00

Fetcher the Chocolate Lab, #4298, R, from $7 to $10.00

Flash the Dolphin, #4021, R, minimum value $50.00

Flashy the Peacock, #4339, R, from $7 to $10.00

Fleece the Lamb, #4125, R, wht w/cream face, from $5 to...$10.00

Fleecie the Lamb, #4279, R, purple ribbon, from $5 to $10.00

Flip the Cat, #4012, wht, R, from $15 to $25.00

Flitter the Butterfly, #4255, R, from $5 to $10.00

Float the Butterfly, #4343, R, from $7 to $10.00

Floppity the Bunny, #4118, lilac, R, from $10 to $20.00

Flutter the Butterfly, #4043, R, tie-dyed, minimum value..$375.00

Fortune the Panda Bear, #4196, R, from $5 to $15.00

Freckles the Leopard, #4066, R, from $5 to......................$15.00

Frigid the Penguin, #4270, R, from $5 to $10.00

Frills the Hornbill Bird, #4367, R, from $7 to...................$10.00

Fuzz the Bear, #4237, R, from $10 to $20.00

Garcia the Bear, #4051, tie-dyed, R, from $85 to $110.00

Germania the German Bear, #4236, German exclusive, R, minimum value...$30.00

Gigi the Poodle, #4191, R, from $5 to.............................$15.00

Glory the Bear, #4188, R, from $15 to $25.00

Glow the Lightning Bug, #4283, R, from $7 to.................$10.00

Goatee the Mountain Goat, #4235, R, from $5 to............$10.00

Gobbles the Turkey, #4034, R, from $5 to.........................$10.00

Goldie the Goldfish, #4023, R, from $20 to......................$35.00

Goochy the Jellyfish, #4230, R, from $5 to.......................$10.00

Grace the Praying Bunny, #4274, R, from $7 to $10.00

Gracie the Swan, #4126, R, from $10 to $15.00

Groovy the Bear, #4256, R, from $10 to $15.00

Grunt the Razorback Pig, #4092, red, R, minimum value .$65.00

Hairy the Spider, #4336, R, from $10 to $20.00

Halo the Angel Bear, #4208, R, from $10 to.....................$15.00

Halo II the Angel Bear, #4269, R, from $10 to $15.00

Happy the Hippo, #4061, gray, R, minimum value $285.00

Happy the Hippo, #4061, lavender, R, from $10 to............$20.00

Hero the Bear, #4351, brn, R, with necktie, from $10 to..$20.00

Hippie the Bunny, #4218, tie-dyed, R, from $10 to $15.00

Hippity the Bunny, #4119, mint gr, R, from $10 to $20.00

Hissy the Snake, #4185, R, from $5 to $10.00

Honks the Goose, #4258, R, from $5 to $10.00

Hoot the Owl, #4073, R, from $20 to $30.00

Hope the Praying Bear, #4213, R, from $5 to...................$10.00

Hopper the Bunny, #4342, R, from $7 to $10.00

Hoppity the Bunny, #4117, pk, R, from $10 to $20.00

Hornsly the Triceratops, #4345, from $7 to.......................$10.00

Howl the Wolf, #4310, R, from $7 to...............................$10.00

Huggy the Bear, #4306, R, from $7 to $10.00

Humphrey the Camel, #4060, R, minimum value $800.00

Iggy the Iguana, #4038, all issues, R, from $5 to $15.00

Inch the Worm, #4044, R, felt antenna, from $65 to $80.00

Inch the Worm, #4044, R, yarn antenna, from $10 to......$20.00

India the Tiger, #4291, R, from $7 to...............................$10.00

Inky the Octopus, #4028, 1st issue, tan, no mouth, R, minimum value...$400.00

Inky the Octopus, #4028, 2nd issue, tan, w/mouth, R, minimum value...$375.00

Inky the Octopus, #4028, 3rd issue, pk, R, from $10 to $20.00

Issy the Bear, #4404, R, from $10 to $15.00

Issy the Bear, #4404, Four Seasons Hotel exclusive, New York, R, minimum value $300.00

Jabber the Parrot, #4197, R, from $5 to............................$10.00

Jake the Mallard Duck, #4199, R, from $5 to...................$10.00

Jester the clownfish, #4349, from $7 to $10.00

Jolly the Walrus, #4082, R, from $5 to $15.00

Kaleidoscope the Cat, #4348, R, from $7 to $10.00

Kicks the Soccer Bear, #4229, R, from $10 to $15.00

Kiwi the Toucan, #4070, R, minimum value.....................$65.00

Knuckles the Pig, #4247, R, from $5 to............................$10.00

Kooky the Cat, #4357, R, from $7 to $10.00

Kuku the Cockatoo, #4192, R, from $5 to $10.00

Legs the Frog, #4020, retired, from $10.00 to $20.00.
(Photo courtesy Amy Hopper)

Lucky the Ladybug, all three versions retired, #4040, left to right: third issue, with approximately 11 spots, from $10.00 to $20.00; second issue, with 21 spots, minimum value $275.00; first issue, with seven felt spots, minimum value $125.00. (Photo courtesy Amy Hopper)

Lefty the Donkey, #4057, R, bl-gray, w/American flag, minimum value...$130.00

Lefty 2000, the Donkey, #4290, red, wht & bl, R, from $7 to...$15.00

Libearty the Bear, #4057, wht, w/American flag, R, minimum value $225.00

Lips the Fish, #4254, R, from $5 to $10.00

Lizzy the Lizard, #4033, tie-dyed, R, minimum value $350.00

Lizzy the Lizard, #4033, bl, R, from $15 to $25.00

Loosy the Candian Goose, #4206, R, from $5 to $10.00

Luke the Lab Puppy, #4214, R, from $5 to $10.00

Lurkey the Turkey, #4309, R, from $7 to.........................$10.00

Mac the Cardinal, #4225, R, from $5 to.........................$10.00

Magic the Dragon, #4088, R, from $20 to.........................$35.00

Manny the Manatee, #4081, R, minimum value $85.00

Maple the Bear, #4600, R, Ty Canada exclusive, minimum value...$40.00

Mellow the Bear, #4344, tie-dyed, R, from $10 to $15.00

Mel the Koala Bear, #4162, R, from $5 to.........................$10.00

Midnight the Black Panther, #4355, from $7 to $10.00

Millennium the Bear, #4226, R, from $10 to $15.00

Mooch the Spider Monkey, #4224, R, from $5 to............$10.00

Morrie the Eel, #4282, R, from $7 to.................................$10.00

Mrs the Bride Bear, #4364, from $10 to $15.00

Mr the Groom Bear, #4363, from $10 to.........................$15.00

Mystic the Unicorn, #4007, 1st issue, R, soft fine mane & tail, minimum value...$175.00

Mystic the Unicorn, #4007, 2nd issue, R, coarse yarn mane & brn horn, from $10 to $15.00

Mystic the Unicorn, #4007, 3rd issue, R, iridescent horn, from $7 to $15.00

Mystic the Unicorn, #4007, 4th issue, R, iridiscent horn, rainbow fur mane & tail, from $7 to $15.00

Nana the Monkey, #4067, R, 1st issue of Bongo, minimum value $2,000.00

Nanook the Husky Dog, #4104, R, from $5 to..................$10.00

Nectar the Hummingbird, #4361, R, from $7 to..............$10.00

Neon the Sea Horse, #4239, R, from $5 to $10.00

Nibbler the Rabbit, #4216, cream, R, from $5 to..............$10.00

Nibbly the Rabbit, #4217, brn, R, from $5 to $10.00

Nipponia the Bear, R, Japan exclusive, minimum value ..$75.00

Nip the Cat, #4003, 1st issue, gold w/wht tummy and face, R, minimum value...$300.00

Nip the Cat, #4003, 2nd issue, all gold, R, minimum value .$325.00

Nip the Cat, #4003, 3rd issue, gold w/wht paws, R, from $20 to..$25.00

Nuts the Squirrel, #4114, R, from $5 to $15.00

Oats the Horse, #4305, R, from $7 to.................................$10.00

Osito the Mexican Bear, #4244, US exclusive, R, from $10 to...$20.00

Patriot the Bear, #4360, red, wht & bl, R, from $7 to.................$15.00

Patti the Platypus, #4025, 1st issue, maroon, R, minimum value...$285.00

Patti the Platypus, #4025, 2nd issue, purple, R, from $10 to .$20.00

Paul the Walrus, #4248, R, from $5 to $10.00

Peace the Bear, #4053, tie-dyed w/ Peace sign, R, from $10 to .$20.00

Peanut the Elephant, #4062, lt bl, R, from $5 to $10.00

Peanut the Elephant, #4062, royal bl (manufacturing mistake), R, minimum value...$2,000.00

Pecan the Bear, #4251, R, from $5 to.................................$10.00

Peekaboo the Turtle, #4303, R, from $7 to $10.00

Peking the Panda Bear, #4013, R, minimum value.........$850.00

Pellet the Hamster, #4313, R, from $7 to.........................$10.00

Periwinkle the e-Beanie Bear, #4400, bl, R, from $10 to ..$20.00

Pinchers the Lobster, #4026, R, from $10 to $20.00

Pinky the Flamingo, #4072, retired, from $5.00 to $10.00. (Photo courtesy Amy Hopper)

Niles the Camel, #4284, retired, from $7.00 to $10.00.
(Photo courtesy Amy Hopper)

Pouch the Kangaroo, #4161, retired, from $5.00 to $10.00.
(Photo courtesy Amy Hopper)

Poseidon the Whale Shark, #4356, R, from $7 to **$10.00**

Pounce the Cat, #4122, brn, R, from $5 to **$10.00**

Prance the Cat, #4123, gray w/stripes, R, from $5 to........**$10.00**

Prickles the Hedgehog, #4220, R, from $5 to....................**$10.00**

Princess the Bear, #4300, commemorating Diana, Princess of Wales, purple, R, PVC pellets, from $35 to **$40.00**

Princess the Bear, #4300, commemorating Diana, Princess of Wales, purple, R, PE pellets, from $10 to **$15.00**

Prince the Bullfrog, #4312, R, from $7 to **$10.00**

Puffer the Puffin, #4181, R, from $5 to **$10.00**

Pugsly the Pug Dog, #4106, R, from $5 to.......................**$15.00**

Pumkin' the Pumpkin, #4205, R, from $10 to..................**$20.00**

Punchers the Lobster, #4026, R, 1st issue of Pinchers, minimum value **$1,950.00**

Purr the Kitten, #4346, R, from $7 to **$10.00**

Quackers the Duck, #4024, R, 1st issue, no wings, minimum value **$800.00**

Quackers the Duck, #4024, R, w/wings, from $10 to **$20.00**

Radar the Bat, #4091, R, minimum value **$70.00**

Rainbow the Chameleon, #4037, all versions, R, from $5 to .**$15.00**

Regal the King Charles Spaniel, #4358, from $7 to..........**$10.00**

Rex the Tyrannosaurus, #4086, R, minimum value **$300.00**

Righty the Elephant, #4085, gray, R, w/American flag, minimum value...**$130.00**

Righty 2000 the Elephant, #4289, red, wht & bl, R, from $7 to **$15.00**

Ringo the Raccoon, #4014, R, from $10 to......................**$15.00**

Roam the Buffalo, #4209, R, from $5 to...........................**$10.00**

Roary the Lion, #4069, R, from $5 to................................**$15.00**

Rocket the Bluejay, #4202, R, from $5 to.........................**$10.00**

Rover the Dog, #4101, red, R, from $10 to **$20.00**

Roxie the Reindeer, #4334, blk nose, R, from $7 to **$10.00**

Roxie the Reindeer, #4334, red nose, R, from $10 to **$20.00**

Rufus the Dog, #4280, R, from $7 to **$10.00**

Runner the Mustelidae, #4304, R, from $7 to...................**$10.00**

Sakura the Bear, Japan exclusive, R, minimum value **$90.00**

Sammy the Bear, #4215, tie-dyed, R, from $5 to...............**$15.00**

Santa, #4203, R, from $20 to...**$30.00**

Sarge the German Shepard, #4277, R, from $7 to **$10.00**

Scaly the Lizard, #4263, R, from $5 to **$10.00**

Scat the Cat, #4231, R, from $5 to...................................**$10.00**

Schweetheart the Orangutan, #4252, R, from $5 to.........**$10.00**

Scoop the Pelican, #4107, R, from $5 to..........................**$10.00**

Scorch the Dragon, #4210, R, from $5 to **$10.00**

Scottie the Scottish Terrier, #4102, R, from $10 to **$20.00**

Scurry the Beetle, #4281, R, from $7 to **$10.00**

Seamore the Seal, #4029, wht, R, minimum value **$60.00**

Seaweed the Otter, #4080, brn, R, from $10 to................**$20.00**

Shamrock the Bear, #4338, R, from $10 to **$20.00**

Sheets the Ghost, #4260, R, from $7 to **$15.00**

Signature Bear (1999), #4228, R, from $10 to **$20.00**

Signature Bear (2000), #4266, R, from $10 to **$20.00**

Silver the Cat, #4242, gray, R, from $5 to **$10.00**

Slayer the Frilled Dragon, #4307, R, from $7 to **$10.00**

Slippery the Seal, #4222, gray, R, from $5 to **$10.00**

Slither the Snake, #4031, R, minimum value.................**$650.00**

Slowpoke the Sloth, #4261, R, from $5 to **$10.00**

Sly the Fox, #4115, 1st issue, all brn, R, minimum value .**$85.00**

Sly the Fox, #4115, brn w/wht belly, R, from $10 to **$20.00**

Smart the Graduation owl (2001), #4353, R, from $7 to .**$10.00**

Smooch the Bear, #4335, R, from $10 to **$20.00**

Smoochy the Frog, #4039, R, from $5 to...........................**$10.00**

Sneaky the Leopard, #4278, R, from $7 to **$10.00**

Sniffer the Beagle, #4299, R, from $7 to **$10.00**

Snip the Siamese Cat, #4120, R, from $5 to **$15.00**

Snort the Bull, #4002, red w/cream feet, R, from $10 to ..**$15.00**

Snowball the Snowman, #4201, R, from $20 to **$25.00**

Snowgirl the Snowgirl, #4333, R, from $10 to...................**$15.00**

Spangle the Bear, #4245, bl face, R, from $10 to **$20.00**

Spangle the Bear, #4245, pk face, R, from $10 to **$20.00**

Spangle the Bear, #4245, wht face, R, from $10 to **$15.00**

Sparky the Dalmatian, #4100, R, minimum value **$65.00**

Speckles the e-Beanie Bear, brn, exclusive to Ty Trade on the official Ty internet website, from $10 to **$20.00**

Speedy the Turtle, #4030, R, from $15 to **$25.00**

Spike the Rhinoceros, #4060, R, from $5 to.....................**$10.00**

Spinner the Spider, #4036, R, from $5 to..........................**$10.00**

Splash the Whale, #4022, R, minimum value....................**$60.00**

Spooky the Ghost, #4090, R, from $25 to **$35.00**

Spot the Dog, #4000, 1st issue, no spot on back, R, minimum value..**$750.00**

Spot the Dog, #4000, 2nd issue, blk spot on back, R, from $25 to **$40.00**

Springy the Bunny, #4272, lavender, R, from $7 to **$10.00**

Spunky the Cocker Spaniel, #4184, R, from $5 to...........**$15.00**

Squealer the Pig, #4005, R, from $10 to...........................**$15.00**

Squirmy the Worm, #4302, R, from $5 to **$10.00**

Steg the Stegosaurus, #4087, retired, minimum value, $325.00. (Photo courtesy Amy Hopper)

Stilts the Stork, #4221, R, from $5 to **$10.00**

Stinger the Scorpion, #4193, R, from $5 to **$10.00**

Sting the Stingray, #4077, tie-dyed, R, minimum value ...**$60.00**

Stinky the Skunk, #4017, R, from $5 to...........................**$15.00**

Stretch the Ostrich, #4182, R, from $5 to........................**$10.00**

Stripes the Tiger, #4065, 1st issue, gold w/thin stripes, R, minimum value **$245.00**

Stripes the Tiger, #4065, 2nd issue, caramel color w/wide stripes, R, from $10 to..**$20.00**

Strut the Rooster, #4171, R, from $10 to **$15.00**

Sunny the e-Beanie Bear, yel-orange, R, from $10 to **$20.00**

Swampy the Alligator, #4273, R, from $7 to.....................$10.00
Swirly the Snail, #4249, R, from $5 to $10.00
Swoop the Pterodactyl, #4268, R, from $7 to $10.00
Tabasco the Bull, #4002, R, minimum value.....................$70.00
Tank the Armadillo, #4031, 1st issue, 7 lines & no shell, R, minimum value $150.00
Tank the Armadillo, #4031, 2nd issue, 9 lines & no shell, R, minimum value...$200.00
Tank the Armadillo, #4031, 3rd issue, w/shell, R, minimum value $75.00
Teddy Bear, #4050, brn, new face, R, from $45 to............$65.00
Teddy Bear, #4050, brn, old face, R, minimum value $850.00
Teddy Bear, #4052, cranberry, new face, R, minimum value...$850.00
Teddy Bear, #4052, cranberry, old face, R, minimum value ..$850.00
Teddy Bear, #4057, jade, new face, R, minimum value...$850.00
Teddy Bear, #4057, jade, old face, R, minimum value $850.00
Teddy Bear, #4056, magenta, new face, R, minimum value .$850.00
Teddy Bear, #4056, magenta, old face, R, minimum value..$850.00
Teddy Bear, #4051, teal, new face, R, minimum value ...$850.00
Teddy Bear, #4051, teal, old face, R, minimum value.....$850.00
Teddy Bear, #4055, violet, new face, R, minimum value .$850.00
Teddy Bear, #4055, violet, old face, R, minimum value..$850.00
Thank You Bear, given to Ty authorized retailers to display in their stores, R, from $225 to...$400.00
The Beginning Bear, #4267, w/silver stars, R, from $10 to $20.00
The End Bear, #4265, blk, R, from $10 to.........................$20.00
Tiny the Chihuahua, #4234, R, from $5 to.......................$10.00
Tiptoe the Mouse, #4241, R, from $5 to...........................$10.00
Tracker the Basset Hound, #4198, R, from $5 to..............$10.00
Trap the Mouse, #4042, R, minimum value $350.00
Tricks the Dog, #4311, R, from $7 to $10.00
Trumpet the Elephant, #4276, R, from $7 to $10.00
Tuffy the Terrier, #4108, R, from $5 to.............................$15.00
Tusk the Walrus, #4076, R, minimum value $65.00
Twigs the Giraffe, #4068, R, from $10 to $15.00
Ty Employee Christmas Bear (1997), violet, R, new face, minimum value $1,500.00
Ty 2K the Bear, #4262, R, from $10 to $20.00
Unity the Bear, #4606, Ty Europe exclusive, from $20 to.$60.00
USA the American Bear, #4287, R, from $7 to $15.00
Valentina the Bear, #4233, fuchsia w/wht heart, R, from $10 to $20.00
Valentino the Bear, #4058, wht w/red heart, R, from $10 to ..$20.00
Velvet the Panther, #4064, R, from $15 to.......................$25.00
Waddle the Penguin, #4075, R, from $10 to $15.00
Wallace the Bear, #4264, R, from $10 to...........................$15.00
Waves the Whale, #4084, R, from $5 to $15.00
Web the Spider, #4041, blk, R, minimum value.............$385.00
Weenie the Dachshund, #4013, R, from $10 to................$20.00
Whiskers the Terrier, #4317, R, from $7 to......................$10.00
Whisper the Deer, #4187, R, from $5 to $10.00
Wiggly the Octopus, #4275, R, from $7 to........................$10.00
Wise the Graduation Owl (1998), #4187, R, from $10 to $15.00
Wiser the Graduation Owl (1999), #4238, R, from $10 to ..$15.00
Wisest the Graduation Owl (2000), #4286, R, from $5 to..$15.00
Wrinkles the Bulldog, #4103, R, from $5 to.....................$10.00
Zero the Penguin, #4207, R, from $10 to $20.00
Ziggy the Zebra, #4063, R, from $10 to............................$20.00

Zip the Cat, #4004, 1st issue, blk w/wht face and tummy, R, minimum value $250.00
Zip the Cat, #4004, 2nd issue, all blk, R, minimum value .$585.00
Zip the Cat, #4004, 3rd issue, blk w/wht paws, R, from $10 to .$20.00
Zodiac: Dog #4326, R, from $7 to.....................................$10.00

Zodiac: Dragon #4322, retired, from $7.00 to $10.00.
(Photo courtesy Amy Hopper)

Zodiac: Goat #4329, R, from $7 to $10.00
Zodiac: Horse #4324, R, from $7 to...................................$10.00
Zodiac: Monkey #4328, R, from $7 to.................................$10.00
Zodiac: Ox #4319, R, from $7 to...$10.00
Zodiac: Pig #4327, R, from $7 to..$10.00
Zodiac: Rabbit #4321, R, from $7 to...................................$10.00
Zodiac: Rat #4318, R, from $7 to..$10.00
Zodiac: Rooster #4325, R, from $7 to $10.00
Zodiac: Snake #4323, R, from $7 to $10.00
Zodiac: Tiger #4320, R, from $7 to.....................................$10.00
1997 Holiday Teddy, #4200, R, from $20 to.......................$30.00
1998 Holiday Teddy, #4204, R, from $20 to.......................$30.00
1999 Holiday Teddy, #4257, R, from $10 to.......................$20.00
2000 Holiday Teddy, #4332, R, from $7 to.........................$15.00

BEANIE BUDDIES

This line is of special interest to Beanie Babies collectors, since these animals are larger versions of the Beanie Babies. Like Beanie Babies, Beanie Buddies are periodically retired, and the listings will indicate this. Again, production of these animals in ongoing, so these listings may not include all of those produced during the year 2001.

Amber the Cat, #9341, R, from $10 to $15.00
Ariel the Bear, #9409, from $10 to....................................$15.00
Baldy the Eagle, #9408, R, from $10 to $20.00
Bananas the Orangutan, #9402, R, from $10 to...............$15.00
Batty the Bat, #9379, blk, from $55 to $70.00
Batty the Bat, #9378, pk, from $10 to $15.00
BB the Bear, #9398, from $15 to $20.00
Beak the Kiwi, #9301, R, from $15 to $25.00
Bones the Dog, #9377, from $10 to $15.00
Bongo the Monkey, #9312, R, from $10 to $15.00

Britannia the Bear, #9601, UK exclusive, R, from $70 to $85.00

Bronty the Brontosaurus, #9353, R, from $10 to..............$15.00

Bubbles the Fish, #9323, R, from $10 to $15.00

Buckingham the Bear, #9607, UK exclusive, from $50 to .$70.00

Bushy the Lion, #9382, from $10 to...............................$15.00

Cardinal the Cardinal, #9395, R, from $10 to $15.00

Cassie the Collie, #9405, R, from $10 to $15.00

Chilly the Polar Bear, #9317, R, from $10 to..................$20.00

Chip the Cat, #9318, calico, R, from $10 to $15.00

Chocolate the Moose, #9349, R, from $10 to $15.00

Chops the Lamb, #9394, R, from $15 to $20.00

Clubby the Bear, #9990, Babies Official Club Gold member exclusive (mail-order only), R, from $20 to..............$30.00

Clubby II the Bear, #9991, Beanie Babies Official Club Platinum member exclusive (mail-order only), R, from $10 to.$20.00

Clubby III the Bear, #9993, Beanie Babies Official Club exclusive, Internet and mail order only, R, from $10 to $20.00

Congo the Gorilla, #9361, R, from $10 to $15.00

Coral the Fish, #9381, from $10 to................................$15.00

Digger the Crab, #9351, R, orange, from $10 to $15.00

Digger the Crab, #9351, tie-dyed, R, from $25 to $40.00

Dotty the Dalmatian, #9364, R, from $10 to $20.00

Dotty the Dalmatian, lg, #9051, from $30 to $45.00

Dotty the Dalmatian, x-lg, #9052, from $45 to..................$65.00

Dragon the Dragon, #9365, R, from $10 to.....................$15.00

Ears the Rabbit, #9388, from $10 to..............................$20.00

Ears the Rabbit, lg, #9046, R, from $30 to $45.00

Ears the Rabbit, x-lg, #9047, R, from $50 to...................$65.00

Employee Bear, #9373, purple, from $10 to......................$20.00

Erin the Irish Bear, #9309, R, from $10 to $20.00

Eucalyptus the Koala, #9363, R, from $10 to $15.00

Fetch the Golden Retriever, #9338, R, from $10 to.........$15.00

Flip the Cat, #9359, R, from $10 to................................$15.00

Flippity the Bunny, #9358, bl, R, from $10 to.................$15.00

Flitter the Butterfly, #9384, from $10 to.........................$15.00

Floppity the Bunny, #9390, lilac, R, from $15 to $20.00

Fuzz the Bear, #9328, R, from $10 to $15.00

Fuzz the Bear, lg, #9040, R, from $20 to $40.00

Germania the Bear, #9063, German exclusive, R, from $65 to $80.00

Glory the Bear, #9410, R, from $10 to $15.00

Gobbles the Turkey, #9333, R, from $10 to.....................$15.00

Goochy the Jellyfish, #9362, R, from $10 to $15.00

Grace the Praying Bunny, #9389, R, from $10 to $20.00

Groovy the Bear, #9345, tie-dyed, R, from $10 to $20.00

Halo the Angel Bear, #9337, R, from $10 to $20.00

Halo II the Angel Bear, #9386, R, from $10 to $20.00

Happy the Hippo, #9375, lavender, from $10 to...............$15.00

Hippie the Bunny, #9357, tie-dyed, R, from $10 to $15.00

Hippie the Bunny, lg, #9039, tie-dyed, R, from $25 to $35.00

Hippie the Bunny, x-lg, #9038, tie-dyed, R, from $45 to.......$60.00

Hippity the Bunny, #9324, R, mint gr, from $10 to $15.00

Hope the Praying Bear, #9327, R, from $10 to.................$15.00

Hornsly the Triceratops, #9407, from $10 to....................$15.00

Humphrey the Camel, #9307, R, from $10 to $20.00

Inch the Worm, #9331, R, from $10 to $15.00

India the Tiger, #9406, from $10 to $15.00

Inky the Octopus, #9404, R, from $10 to........................$25.00

Jabber the Parrot, #9326, R, from $10 to........................$15.00

Jake the Mallard Duck, #9304, R, from $10 to.................$15.00

Kicks the Soccer Bear, #9343, R, from $10 to.................$15.00

Lefty the Donkey, #9370, gray, R, from $10 to.................$15.00

Libearty the Bear, #9371, R, from $10 to........................$20.00

Libearty the Bear, lg, #9371, R, from $30 to $45.00

Libearty the Bear, x-lg, #9042, R, from $50 to.................$65.00

Lips the Fish, #9355, from $10 to...................................$15.00

Lizzy the Lizard, #9366, tie-dyed, R, from $10 to............$15.00

Lucky the Ladybug, #9354, R, from $10 to $15.00

Maple the Bear, #9600, Ty Canada exclusive, R, from $40 to...$75.00

Millennium the Bear, #9325, R, from $10 to $20.00

Mystic the Unicorn, #9396, from $10 to..........................$15.00

Nanook the Husky, #9350, R, from $10 to.......................$15.00

Oats the Horse, #9392, R, from $10 to............................$15.00

Osito the Mexican Bear, #9344, R, from $10 to..............$15.00

Patti the Platypus, #9320, R, from $10 to $15.00

Peace the Bear, #9335, R, from $10 to............................$20.00

Peace the Bear, #9335, pastel, R, from $15 to $20.00

Peace the Bear, jumbo, #9035, from $95 to.....................$115.00

Peace the Bear, lg, #9037, R, from $30 to $45.00

Peace the Bear, x-lg, #9036, from $50 to.........................$70.00

Peanut the Elephant, #9300, lt bl, R, from $15 to $25.00

Peanut the Elephant, #9300, royal bl, R, from $10 to.......$15.00

Peking the Panda, #9310, R, from $10 to........................$15.00

Pinky the Flamingo, #9316, R, from $10 to $15.00

Pouch the Kangaroo, #9380, from $10 to.........................$15.00

Prince the Frog, #9401, from $10 to...............................$15.00

Princess the Bear, #9329, R, from $10 to........................$20.00

Pumkin' the Pumpkin, #9332, R, from $10 to...................$20.00

Quackers the Duck, #9302, no wings, R, from $120 to......$145.00

Quackers the Duck, #9302, R, from $10 to.......................$15.00

Rainbow the Chameleon, #9367, from $10 to....................$15.00

Rex the Tyrannosaurus, #9368, R, from $10 to.................$15.00

Righty the Elephant, #9369, R, from $10 to.....................$15.00

Roam the Buffalo, #9378, wht, from $10 to $15.00

Rover the Dog, #9305, R, from $10 to.............................$15.00

Rufus the Dog, #9393, from $10 to.................................$15.00

Sakura the Bear, #9608, Japanese exclusive, R, from $30 to .$40.00

Santa the Santa Claus, #9385, R, from $15 to $20.00

Schweetheart the Orangutan, #9330, R, from $10 to..........$15.00

Schweetheart the Orangutan, jumbo, #9045, from $90 to....$110.00

Schweetheart the Orangutan, lg, #9343, from $25 to.......$40.00

Schweetheart the Orangutan, x-lg, #9044, from $45 to.......$55.00

Silver the Cat, #9340, R, from $10 to $15.00

Slither the Snake, #9339, R, from $10 to.........................$15.00

Smoochy the Frog, #9315, R, from $10 to.........................$15.00

Sneaky the Leopard, #9376, from $10 to..........................$15.00

Snort the Bull, #9311, R, from $10 to..............................$15.00

Snowboy the Snowboy, #9342, R, from $15 to $20.00

Spangle the Bear, #9336, R, from $10 to $20.00

Speedy the Turtle, #9358, R, from $10 to.........................$15.00

Spinner the Spider, #9334, R, from $10 to........................$15.00

Spunky the Cocker Spaniel, #9400, R, from $10 to..........$20.00

Squealer the Pig, #9313, R, from $10 to...........................$15.00

Steg the Stegosaurus, #9383, R, from $10 to....................$15.00

Stretch the Ostrich, #9303, R, from $10 to.......................**$15.00**
Swoop the Pterodactyl, #9391, from $10 to......................**$15.00**
Teddy the Bear, #9306, cranberry, R, from $10 to.............**$20.00**
Teddy the Old Face Bear, #9372, from $10 to....................**$20.00**
The Beginning Bear, #9399, R, from $10 to......................**$25.00**
Tracker the Basset Hound, #9319, R, from $10 to **$15.00**
Trumpet the Elephant, #9403, from $10 to.......................**$15.00**
Twigs the Giraffe, #9308, R, from $75 to **$115.00**
Ty 2K the Bear, #9346, R, from $15 to **$25.00**
Valentina the Bear, #9397, R, from $10 to.......................**$25.00**
Valentina the Bear, jumbo, #9050, R, from $85 to **$120.00**
Valentina the Bear, lg, #9048, R, from $35 to...................**$55.00**
Valentina the Bear, x-lg #9049, R, from $50 to................**$70.00**
Valentino the Bear, #9347, R, from $10 to........................**$20.00**
Waddle the Penguin, #9314, R, from $10 to......................**$15.00**
Wallace the Bear, #9387, R, from $10 to..........................**$20.00**
Weenie the Dachshund, #9356, R, from $10 to.................**$15.00**
White Tiger the Tiger, #9374, from $10 to.......................**$15.00**
Zip the Cat, #9360, R, from $10 to **$15.00**
2000 Signature Bear, #9348, R, from $15 to **$20.00**

McDonald's Happy Meal Teenie Beanie Babies

The Teenie Beanie Babies debuted in April 1997 at McDonald's restaurants across the country. The result was the most successful Happy Meal promotion in the history of McDonald's. The toys were quickly snatched up by collectors, causing the promotion to last only one week instead of the planned five-week period. To date there have been four Teenie Beanie promotions, one annually in 1997, 1998, 1999, and 2000.

1997, Chocolate the Moose, Chops the Lamb, Patti the Platpus, or Pinky the Flamingo, ea from $12 to.......................**$15.00**
1997, Goldie the Goldfish, Seamore the Seal, Snort the Bull, or Speedy the Turtle, ea from $10 to **$12.00**
1997, Lizz the Lizard or Quacks the Duck, ea from $8 to..**$10.00**
1998, Bones the Dog, Peanut the Elephant, or Waddle the Penguin, ea from $3 to...**$6.00**
1998, Bongo the Monkey or Doby the Doberman, ea from $8 to...**$10.00**
1998, Happy the Hippo, Inch the Worm, Mel the Koala, Pinchers the Lobster, or Scoop the Pelican, ea from $3 to....**$5.00**
1998, Twigs the Giraffe or Zip the Cat, ea from $6 to.........**$8.00**
1999, Ants the Anteater, Freckles the Leopard, Smoochy the Frog, or Spunky the Cocker Spaniel, ea from $2 to **$4.00**
1999, Claude the Crab, Rocket the Bluejay, Iggy the Iguana, or Strut the Rooster, ea from $2 to **$4.00**
1999, Nuts the Squirrel, Stretchy the Ostrich, Nook the Husky, or Chip the Cat, ea from $2 to **$4.00**
2000, At the Zoo: Tusk the Walrus, Blizz the Tiger, Schweetheart the Orangutan, or Spike the Rhinoceros, ea from $2 to **$4.00**
2000, Garden Bunch: Spinner the Spider, Bumble the Bee, Flitter the Butterfly, or Lucky the Ladybug, ea from $2 to **$4.00**
2000, Under the Sea: Coral the Fish, Sting the Stingray, Goochy the Jellyfish, or Neon the Sea Horse, ea from $2 to **$4.00**

International Bears and Superstars

These were offered at McDonald's as separate purchases, specially packaged for collectors, and not included in Happy Meals.

1999, Britannia the British Bear, from $4 to **$6.00**
1999, Erin the Irish Bear, from $4 to **$6.00**
1999, Glory the American Bear, from $4 to **$6.00**
1999, Maple the Canadian Bear, from $4 to......................**$6.00**
2000, Bronty, Rex, or Steg, Dinosaurs, from $3 to **$6.00**
2000, Bushy the Lion, Springy the Bunny, mystery items, ea from $2 to...**$5.00**
2000, Chilly the Polar Bear, Humphrey the Camel, Peanut the Royal Blue Elephant, or The End Bear, ea from $3 to .**$6.00**
2000, Election/American Trio, Lefty the Blue-Gray Donkey or Righty the Gray Elephant, ea from $3 to **$6.00**
2000, Election/American Trio, Libearty the Bear from $3 to .**$7.00**
2000, Germania the German Bear, Osito the Mexican Bear, or Spangle the American Bear, ea from $4 to...................**$6.00**
2000, Millennium the Bear, offered only on 6/13/2000, benefit for Ronald McDonald House Charities, from $5 to...**$10.00**

Bicycles, Motorbikes, and Tricycles

The most interesting of the vintage bicycles are those made from the '20s into the '60s, though a few even later models are collectible as well. Some from the '50s were very futuristic and styled with sweeping Art Deco lines; others had wonderful features such as built-in radios and brake lights, and some were decked out with saddlebags and holsters to appeal to fans of Hoppy, Gene, and many other western heroes. Watch for reproductions.

Condition is everything when evaluating bicycles, and one worth $2,500.00 in excellent or better condition might be worth as little as $50.00 in unrestored, poor condition. But here are a few values to suggest a range.

Advisor: Richard Trautwein (T3).

Note: A girl's bicycle does not command the price as a boy's bicycle in the same model. The value could be from ⅓ to ½ less than a boy's.

Alenax Model 2500, boy's, 1985, red w/blk seat, lever drive, VG, from $300 to **$500.00**
Bendix Firestone, boy's, maroon w/cream seat, rstr, A....**$200.00**
Columbia Airrider, boy's, 1940-41, red w/cream detail, w/horn tank, headlight & rear book rack, EX, A **$800.00**
Columbia All Bright High-Wheeler, Pat July 1885, chrome-plated, VG, A..**$2,700.00**
Columbia Cyclone 60, girl's, bl & wht w/balloon tires, G, from $75 to..**$100.00**
Columbia High-Wheeler, early, handlebars mk Standard Columbia Made by Pope..., VG, A **$2,100.00**
Columbia Model 40, boy's, 1890s, blk w/early style hammock seat, rstr, A..**$650.00**
Columbia Model 60, girl's, ca 1896, chainless, orig front plunger brake, G-, A...**$400.00**
Columbia Model 200, boy's, dbl-sprung pneumatic safety, triple leaf spring front fork, solar head lamp, rare, EX, A.**$1,900.00**

Columbia Playbike, boy's, 1970s-80s, red w/blk seat, 3-speed, VG, A $125.00

Columbia RX5, boy's, 50th Anniversary replica, gr & cream, EX, from $200 to $400.00

Columbia Superb, boy's, 1941, cream & maroon, w/headlight & rear carrier, True Test Deluxe wht-wall tires, VG, A...$525.00

Columbia 3-Star Deluxe Diamond Jubilee, girl's, 1952, 75th Anniversary model, lime gr & blk, G, from $300 to..$400.00

Crawford Pneumatic Safety, lady's, ca 1898, manufactured in Hagerstown MD, wooden fender, chain guard, needs restoration, from $100.00 to $150.00.

Crescent Pneumatic Safety, girl's, 1901, G, A $225.00

Elgin Special, girl's, 1939, dk bl w/wht stripes, w/headlight, tank, rack/skirt guards, Allstate tires, EX, A, $400 to.......$600.00

Elliot Hickory Model C, girl's, 1892, rstr, A $5,700.00

Evinrude Imperial Stream Flow, boy's, 1937, red w/blk seat, w/speedometer, horn & lock, rare, EX, from $9,500 to $11,000.00

Gendron No 7, boy's, 1892, split frame, rstr, A $2,500.00

Huffy American Thunderbird, boy's, 1960s, gold & chrome, G, from $75 to $100.00

Huffy BMX, boy's, 1970s, red w/blk detail & seat, VG, from $100 to..$150.00

Indian Pneumatic Safety, girl's, 1920s, bl & red 2-speed, Messenger seat, chrome stepped fenders, G, A $650.00

Iver Johnson Pneumatic Safety, girl's, ca 1897, wooden chain guard & rims, G, A....................................$200.00

J.C. Higgins, boy's, Wonderide Spring Fork, EX restored, from $800.00 to $900.00.

JC Higgins Flow Motion, girl's, 1948, bl & wht, G, from $100 to..$150.00

JC Higgins Murray, boy's, 1948, blk w/balloon tires, rstr, from $150 to...$200.00

JC Higgins Spring Fork, girl's, 1950s, gr & cream w/gold pinstripes, rstr, A..$150.00

Mead Ranger Pneumatic Safety, boy's, 1915, VG, from $500 to..$700.00

Monarch Middle Weight, girl's, 1948, bl & wht, w/True Tension twin spring fork, horn tank & rear carrier, VG, A...$150.00

Monarch Silver King Model M1, boy's, 1938, EX, A $600.00

Monarch Silver King Super 5-Bar, boy's, maroon w/blk & gold accents, w/tank horn & luggage rack, 1939, 72", prof rstr, A..$2,500.00

Pierce Chainless Pneumatic Safety, girl's, cushion frame w/front & rear suspension, Christy saddle, scarce, G, A ...$2,000.00

Raleigh 'Chopper,' boy's, purple with red, 1970s, EX, from $150.00 to $200.00.

Raleigh Superb, girl's, 1960s, gr & wht Sturmy Archer 3-speed, Brooks saddle, G, from $75 to $100.00

Roadmaster Supreme, boy's, 1937, yel w/maroon detail, All American head badge, illuminated rear rack, NM, A.........$5,600.00

Ross Polo Bike Jr Convertible, boy's, bl w/wht detail, chrome fenders, balloon tires, VG, from $100 to...................$150.00

Schwinn American, boy's, 1960, red & wht Bendix 2-speed, Cadet speedometer, G, from $75 to $100.00

Schwinn B-6, boy's, blk & red, w/springer fork, tank horn & luggage rack, battery-op headlight, 69", rstr, A $2,900.00

Schwinn Bantam, girl's, 1960, bl & wht w/chrome fenders, West Wind wht-wall tires, G, A $75.00

Schwinn BF Goodrich Challenger DX, boy's, 1940, red w/cream detail, w/horn tank, Delta headlight, etc, EX, A $500.00

Schwinn Collegiate 3, boy's, 1972, bl & silver, M, from $50 to $75.00

Schwinn Grey Ghost Stingray, boy's, silver 5-speed w/suspended banana seat, rear brakes, 1971, 54", rstr, A $650.00

Schwinn Hollywood Model BA307, girl's, 1936-37, w/hanging tank, locking fork w/key & Delta headlight, rstr, A...$450.00

Schwinn Lady's Standard Model BC308, red & blk w/ACE head badge, VG, from $100 to $200.00

Schwinn Green Phantom, boy's, balloon tires, springer front end, luggage rack, horn tank, Bendex rear brake, 68", partial restoration, EX+, $1,200.00.

Schwinn Mark IV Jaguar, boy's, 1960s, bl & chrome w/West Wind tires, VG, A.................................$2,900.00
Schwinn Model B, girl's, bl & wht, w/spring fork & fender headlight, VG, A.................................$250.00
Schwinn Panther, boy's, burgundy, w/springer fork, Delta Rocket Ray headlight & luggage rack w/light, 1952, 72", rstr, A.................................$2,200.00
Schwinn Standard Autocycle, boy's, 1937-38, blk w/wht detail, Arnold Schwinn Autocycle head badge, rstr, A......$950.00
Schwinn Streamline Aero Cycle, boy's, 1934, red & aluminum, Delta gangway pancake horn, rstr, A...................$3,700.00
Schwinn Town & Country Tandem, 1952, gr w/blk seats & child carrier, EX, from $400 to.........................$500.00

Sears Free Spirit, boy's, with tank, 1960s, 20", EX original, from $100.00 to $150.00.

Schwinn Whizzer US Army, boy's, mk 1945 F4322, w/front drum brake, headlight & springer fork, 70", rstr, A..........$3,300.00
Sears Spaceliner, boy's, 1960s, chrome w/red carrier, G, from $100 to.................................$150.00
Shelby Flyer Airflow, boy's, 1938, Bendix front brake, rear carrier, EX, A.................................$1,100.00
Shelby Speedline Airflow, girl's, 1939, red & blk, VG, from $1,800 to.................................$2,000.00

Standard Columbia by Pope Mfg. Co., early high-wheeler, leather seat, saddle bag, hand brake, rubber tires, 59", G, A, $2,100.00.

Swiss Army, dated 1943, two parcel bags, rear wheel and lock key, leather tool pouch with tools, air pump, bell, generator, and license plate, G, from $800.00 to $1,200.00.

Swiss Army, boy's, 1941, w/2 parcel bags, leather pouch w/tools, air pump, bell & generator, VG, from $700 to $1,000.00
Victor Highwheel, down-swept handlebars w/pear grips, pedals mk Overman Wheel Co, gray tires, EX, A...........$4,200.00
Ward's Hawthorn, boy's, 1940s, red & wht w/balloon tires, rear carrier w/side running lights, G, A.........................$275.00
Western Flyer Buzz Bike 2+1, boy's, 1960-70, bl & chrome w/wheelie bar, G, A.................................$475.00
Western Flyer Cruiser, boy's, prewar, red & wht, G-, A..$100.00
Wolff American Pneumatic Safety, girl's, red w/All Bright frame, fancy chain guard, G, A.............................$325.00

MOTORBIKES

Honda Passport Scooter, 1981, yel & cream w/maroon seat, EX, A.................................$500.00
Indian Motorcycle, Citan, 1940s-50s, blk & cream w/Indian Motorcycle logo, rstr.................................$4,200.00
Monarch Super-Twin, ca 1949, blk w/red-orange trim, chrome fender headlight, rear-wheel kickstand, EX.........$3,200.00
Spaceliner, Sears, girl's, bl-gr w/chrome fenders, wht seat & grips, electric light & horn, wht-walls, 67", EX.......$200.00

Whizzer Sportsman, w/windshield & spring seat, rear carrier, wht-walls, 20", rstr, from $3,600 to $4,000.00

TRICYCLES

American National, orange & cream w/chrome handlebar, wheels & pedal arms, 30x37", rstr, A $300.00

Canterpony Riding Horse, Deeks Engineering Corp, 1930, pnt wood & aluminum w/glass eyes, 40", VG.................$400.00

Donaldson Jockey Cycle, scooter-type handlebars, rubber tires, 24½x37", rpt...$850.00

Early American, CI w/wooden seat & handlebars, VG, A..$575.00

Early American, 1875-85, natural wood w/allover pin-striping, VG, A $750.00

Early American, 1875-85, red-pnt wood w/pin-stripes, fabric seat w/fringe, VG, A $1,400.00

Gendron Pioneer, red, no fenders, 19½", wide-spoked front wheel, G...$375.00

Horse Velocipede, 1890, cvd wooden horse w/CI head, hand crank drive, G, A..$700.00

Horse Velocipede, 1890-1910, wooden horse w/leather saddle, rare, G, A..$550.00

Taylor, 2-tone bl w/chrome handlebar, spoke wheels & pedal arms, blk streamlined rubber handle grips, 30x21", rstr, A...$350.00

Tricycle, painted iron, spoke wheels, flat leather seat, wooden grip handle bars, solid rubber tire front wheels, VG, A, $420.00.

Black Americana

Black subjects were commonly depicted in children's toys as long ago as the late 1870s. Among the most widely collected today are the fine windup toys made both here and in Germany. Early cloth and later composition and vinyl dolls are favorites of many; others enjoy ceramic figurines. Many factors enter into evaluating Black Americana, especially in regard to the hand-made dolls and toys, since quality is subjective to individual standards. Because of this you may find wide ranges in dealers' asking prices. In order to better understand this field of collecting, we recommend *Black Collectibles Sold in America* by P.J. Gibbs.

Advisor: Judy Posner (P6).

See also Banks; Battery-Operated Toys; Schoenhut; Windups, Friction, and Other Mechanicals.

Accordion, Black couple on 1 side, watermelons on the other, metal & paper, 5", EX, A...$125.00

Bank, boy in alligator's mouth, ceramic, 6" L, A $100.00

Bank, golliwog, ceramic, English mark on bottom with Pottery Co. and registration number, EX-, 5¼x4x3", A, $350.00.

Bank, golliwog, pnt wood w/mink hair, long wht coat w/stand-up collar, Germany, 1920s, 5", EX.................................$185.00

Bike Bobber, golliwog mounted on spring, eyes move, 5", MOC, A $50.00

Book, Funny Little Darkies, McLoughlin Bros, 1876, hardcover, NM, A $600.00

Book, Little Alexander, by Besse Schiff, Wartburg Press, 1955, hardcover, 30 pgs, EX, P6 ....$95.00

Book, Little Brown Koko Has Fun, Blanche Seale Hunt, American Colortype publisher, 1945, $85.00. (Photo courtesy P.J. Gibbs)

Book, Polly & Her Dollys, by Ajo, Blackie & Son Ltd, 1933, hardcover, 20 pgs, EX, P6 ....$125.00

Book, Ten Little Colored Boys, 1942, hardcover, diecut heads on ea pg, scarce, NM, A $250.00

Book, Ten Little Niggers, Agatha Christie, 1939, softcover, EX, A $75.00

Book, Ten Little Pickaninnies, Faultless Starch, 1890s, softcover, rare, NM, A $100.00

Book, Three Golliwogs Wiggie, Waggie & Wollie, by Enid Blyton, 1956, softcover, EX, A $50.00

Book, Tiger Island, 1930s, hardcover, NM, A.................$100.00

Candy Container, porter pushing trunk, cb, 1930s, EX+, A ...$125.00

Cap Gun, Little Black Sambo, japanned CI, Pat 1887/90, 4½", EX, A $675.00

Coloring Book, Little Brown Koko, illus by Dorothy Wadstaff, 1941, 22 pgs, unused, EX $125.00

Dexterity Puzzle, boy on ostrich, unmk, 1930s, EX...........$75.00

Dexterity Puzzle, Sambo, bl plastic head figure w/exaggerated features, Fun Inc, 1950s, MIP, P6 ....$65.00

Dice Toy, depress plunger & man's head & dice spin, plastic, Alco/Britain, 2" dia, NM, A $50.00

Diecut Set, minstrels w/various instruments, 1880s, set of 6, uncut, rare, NM, A $100.00

Doll, baby, bsk/compo, sleep eyes, open mouth w/2 lower teeth, jtd w/bent legs, mk AM Germany 351/8K, 1900-20s, 20", EX $700.00

Doll, girl, bsk/compo, blk hair wig, open mouth w/4 upper teeth, sleep eyes, ball-jtd, Simon & Halbig, 1900-20s, 17", EX...........$650.00

Doll, girl, hard plastic, synthetic rooted hair, jtd at shoulders & hips, Beatrice Wright, ca 1967, 18", EX...................$275.00

Doll, girl, stuffed cloth w/pnt eyes & mouth, stiff arms & legs, orig sunsuit outfit, 1930-50, 6½", EX.......................$100.00

Doll, golliwog, hand-knit yarn w/felt features, red & wht striped jeans & bl jacket, 1930s, 17", EX, P6.......................$150.00

Doll, golliwog, stuffed cloth w/orange shirt & red pants, plush hair, 12", EX, P6.......................$65.00

Doll, My Lovely Topsy, dk brn skin tone w/blk pigtails, side-glance eyes, 1940s, 5", MIP, P6..................$60.00

Doll, pickaninny, 1950s, inflatable plastic w/flasher eyes, yel skirt & hair bow, 10", EX, P6.......................$35.00

Doll, topsy-turvy, blk/wht, stuffed w/papier-mache heads, jtd compo arms, human hair, glass eyes, early, 8¼", EX...$425.00

Doll, topsy-turvy, Topsy & Little Eva, stuffed cotton w/embroidered features, 1920s, 11½", VG, P6.......................$125.00

Doll Kit, Mammy, 1930s, complete, rare, unused, MIB, A..$165.00

Figure, bsk, boy & girl lying on stomachs, Austria, 1880s, 5", NM, pr $275.00

Figure, bsk, boy w/goose, Austria, 1880s, 4½", rare, EX+, A ...$150.00

Figure, bsk, minstrel playing banjo on throne, Austria, 1880s, 5½", rare, NM, A $200.00

Figure, bsk, shoeshine boy shining woman's shoe, It's a Shame to Take the Money, 1880s, 4", M, A...........................$225.00

Figure, bsk, Snowflake, movable eyes, Oscar Hitt/Germany, 2½", rare, NM, A $100.00

Figure, ceramic, boy playing accordion, Royal Dux, 1853, 7", NM, A $150.00

Figure, ceramic, dog biting boy's pants, Japan, prewar, 3", EX, A $75.00

Figure, chalkware, 3 boys behind fence eating watermelon, 16" L, rare, NM, A $200.00

Figure, lead, alligator biting boy's pants, Japan, prewar, 4" L, VG+, A.......................$100.00

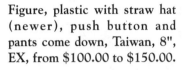
Figure, plastic with straw hat (newer), push button and pants come down, Taiwan, 8", EX, from $100.00 to $150.00.

Figure, wood, dancer w/articulated arms & legs, litho features, 1920s, 16", EX, A $150.00

Figure, wood, minstrel on platform, mechanical, 1900s, 16" oblong platform, NM.......................$175.00

Figure, wood, 3 naked babies sitting on watermelon, early 1900s, 12" L, NM, A $250.00

Figure Set, bsk, choir boys, 22k gold trim, Japan, set of 4, 5", NM, A $200.00

Finger Toy, Black man's face w/hat & bow tie, pull-tab eyes, mouth opens & closes, teeth drop down, cb, 1890s, 5", NM, A $75.00

Game, Amos 'N Andy Card Party, Davis, 1930s, few pcs missing, EX (VG box), A $125.00

Game, Atta Boy, Parker Bros, 1880s, complete, rare, EX (EX box), A.......................$550.00

Game, Bean-Em, All-Fair, 1931, complete, NMIB, from $300 to.......................$350.00

Game, Bobs Y'r Uncle, England, 1935, complete, NM (worn box), A $75.00

Game, Cake Walk, Parker Bros, 1920, complete, NMIB, from $350 to.......................$400.00

Game, Chuckler's, Rosebud, 1931, complete, NMIB, A...$200.00

Game, Coon Hunt, Parker Bros, 1920, complete, NMIB .$400.00

Game, Darkie Pellet Target, 1890s, VG+, A $125.00

Game, Funny Zulu Target, Knickerbocker, 14", NM, A....$200.00

Game, Jolly Darkie Target, Milton Bradley, 1880s, missing balls, EX (VG box), A.......................$285.00

Game, Little Black Sambo, Cadaco-Ellis, 1945, complete, NMIB, A.......................$200.00

Game, Noddy's Ring Toss, England, 1960s, complete, EX (EX box), A.......................$125.00

Game, Sambo Target, Wyandotte, 1920s, complete, 23", EX, A.......................$125.00

Game, Snake Eyes, Selchow & Righter, 1939, complete, EX (EX box), A.......................$150.00

Game, Snake Eyes, Selchow & Righter, 1941, complete, NMIB, A.......................$100.00

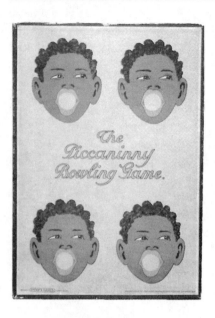

Game, The Piccaninny Bowling Game, Spears, 1928, $425.00. (Photo courtesy P.J. Gibbs)

Game, Watch on de Rind, All-Fair, 1931, complete, rare, NMIB, A $425.00
Game, White-Eyed Coon, Spears, 1890s, complete, NM (G+ box), A $150.00
Hand Toy, clown w/hammer hits golliwog, litho tin, 4", EX, A $150.00
Jack-in-the-Box, golliwog, Germany, 1950s, 7", EX $250.00
Jack-in-the-Box, Munchie Melon, Marx, 1960s, 8", NM, A $150.00
Mask, minstrel, muslin, 1890s, VG, A $100.00
Music Box, litho tin w/image of golliwog, baby & puppy, crank hdl, Gesch, 1915, 5", EX, A $200.00

Nodder, papier-mache with felt and cotton outfit, clockwork, paint cracked on face, some flaking, ca 1900, 24", $1,200.00.

Noisemaker, litho tin w/man in dancing pose, 1940s, EX, P6 ....$50.00
Pinball Machine, Black Sambo, metal & glass, Northwestern Prod, 1920s, 23", EX, A $225.00

Playette Moving Theatre, w/Little Black Sambo book & assorted cutouts, litho paper, EX (EX box) $225.00
Pull Toy, Sambo & donkey on wheeled platform, pnt wood, Hustler Toys, early 1900s, 12", EX, A $175.00

Puppet marionette, boy, wood with clothing (soiled and tattered), paint loss, damage to fingers, 15", VG, A, $85.00.

Puppet, marionette, Jambo the Jiver, jtd wood w/cloth clothes, fiber hair, Talent Products, 1948, 14", VG $225.00
Puppet, marionette, minstrel strumming banjo, wood w/cloth clothes, Pelham, 13", MIB, A $225.00
Puzzle, fr-tray; Tea For Two, cook being scared by bears, 1920s, complete, NMIB, P6 ....$150.00
Puzzle, jigsaw; Boogy Man, complete, NMIB, A $75.00
Puzzle, jigsaw; Dark Town Fancy Ball, 1880s, very rare, EX ...$275.00
Puzzle, jigsaw; My Old Kentucky Home, Viking, 1920, complete, EX (EX box), A $100.00
Puzzle, Pick the Pickannies, Ullman, 1907, opens to 16x10", rare, NM, A $175.00
Stacking Blocks, features Sambo & Tiger, 1940s, set of 5, P6 .$125.00
Tea Set, porcelain w/golliwog graphics by Florence Upton, ca 1904, 5 pcs, NM $250.00
Ventriloquist Doll, papier-mache & wood w/stuffed arms & legs, in bowler hat, Hamilton, 35", VG $850.00

Boats

Though some commercially made boats date as far back as the late 1800s, they were produced on a much larger scale during WWI and the decade that followed and again during the years that spanned WWII. Some were scaled-down models of battleships measuring nearly three feet in length. While a few were actually seaworthy, many were designed with small wheels to be pulled along the carpet or out of doors on dry land. Others were motor-driven windups, and later a few were even battery operated. Some of the larger manufacturers were Bing (Germany), Dent (Pennsylvania), Orkin Craft (California), Liberty Playthings (New York), and Arnold (West Germany).

Advisor: Richard Trautwein (T3).

See also Cast Iron, Boats; Battery-Operated Toys; Tootsietoys; Windups, Friction, and Other Mechanicals; and other specific manufacturers.

Aircraft Carrier, Cragston, friction, helicoptor rises off deck, two tin jets included, 9½", EX+ (EX box), A, $200.00.

Aircraft Carrier, Marx, battery-op, tin, advances as jets on deck go up & down, NM (EX box), A $450.00

Aircraft Carrier, Y, friction, litho tin, 5 jets attached to deck, 4 deck guns & 2 side guns, 11", NMIB, A $275.00

Aircraft Carrier Saratoga 60, Bandai, friction, litho tin w/10 plastic planes, 14", VG, A $150.00

Baby L Speedboat, Lindstrom, w/up, litho tin, w/driver, 11", VG, A, from $400 to $500.00

Battleship, Orkin, clockwork, pressed steel & wood, 4 2-gun turrets, twin funnels & cage masts, EX, from $850 to ..$1,200.00

Battleship, Orkin, 1920s, clockwork, pressed steel, rstr deck, 31", A...$1,000.00

Battleship B2, Orkin, pressed steel, gray, red & cream w/Orkin Fleet decal, 37", EX, A $3,800.00

Battleship Columbia, Hess, clockwork, pnt tin w/diecast components, 8", EX, A $400.00

Battleship Destroyer D2, Orkin, 1920s, clockwork, pressed steel, gr & cream, 24", VG, A $1,100.00

Battleship New York, Marklin, hand-painted tin, steam powered, EX details, 35", restored, A, $1,650.00.

Battleship Marcella, Orkin, w/up, pressed steel, gray & gr, 19", VG, A $650.00

Battleship Nevada, Orkin, 1920s, clockwork, pressed steel, gray & gr, 22", VG, A $1,200.00

Battleship New York, paper litho on wood, 29", EX, A..$900.00

Battleship 57, Bandai, friction, litho tin, moving turrets, 14", EX, A $150.00

Blue Comet Motorboat, pnt wood w/metal fittings & plastic windshield, battery-op Evinrude motor, 16½", EX, A..........$400.00

Brigantine sailboat, believed to be French, tin with detailed rigging and embossed decoration, late 1800s, 34½x45x8", VG/EX, A, $660.00.

Cabin Cruiser, Marusan, friction, tin, brn, wht & red, 12", VG, A $150.00

Cabin Cruiser, Ohio Art, w/up, litho tin, 14½", NMIB, from $125 to $160.00

Cabin Cruiser, Orkin, clockwork, pnt steel w/glassine windows, detailed cockpit w/enunciator, 30", EX.................$1,400.00

Cabin Cruiser, Orkin, clockwork, pressed steel & wood, blk, cream & red, 31", EX, A $1,700.00

Caribbean Luxury Liner, Marx, friction, litho tin, 15", NM, A $100.00

Cruise Ship US Marcella, Orkin, clockwork, pressed steel w/diecast components, dk gray, working motor, 18", EX...$950.00

Diving Submarine, Wolverine, 1940s, pnt tin, bl & wht, railed top, 2 brass cannons, 13", NM (EX box) $300.00

Dreadnaught Flotilla, Hess, clockwork, litho tin, w/5 sm boats on wire armature, 6", EX, from $700 to $900.00

Dreadnaught US New Mexico, Orkin, clockwork, pressed steel, dk gray, working motor, 25", EX.............................$1,400.00

Fire Boat No 3500, Modern Toys, battery-op, litho tin, 15", VG, A $150.00

Flyer Speedboat, Lindstrom, w/up, litho tin, w/driver, 15", EX, A $165.00

Gunboat, Stroud, clockwork, pnt tin, wht & gray w/red detail, w/turret, swivel gun & 2 side guns, 13½", EX, A .$2,100.00

Harbor Patrol B-390 Gunboat, Bandai, 1950s, battery-op, litho tin, 9", EX $150.00

Lackawanna Railroad Ferryboat, CK, clockwork, litho tin, rnd pilot house, 1 stack, 10", NM, A $300.00

Motorboat, Lindstrom, clockwork, litho tin, w/driver, 12", G, A $275.00

Motorboat, Orkin, clockwork, pressed steel, maroon & wht w/red hull, 30", EX $3,500.00

Nautilus Submarine, Sutcliffe, clockwork, tin, 10", EX (EX box), A $250.00

Neptune Tugboat, Masudaya, battery-op, litho tin, EX (EX box), A $175.00

Ocean Liner, Arnold, w/up, pnt tin, red & bl w/wht upper deck, 2 masts & stacks, 2 tiers of lifeboats, 13½", EX $1,000.00

Ocean Liner, Bing, clockwork, pressed steel, red, wht & bl, 3 stacks & 2 masts, 2 railed decks, 16", EX.............$1,900.00

Ocean Liner, Dayton, friction, pressed steel w/wood funnels & masts, 4 lifeboats, rpt, 13", EX, A............................$200.00

Ocean Liner, painted and lithographed tin, clockwork, 7x11", EX (EX box with colorful lithographed label), A, $1,300.00.

Ocean Liner Chicago, Ives, clockwork, pnt tin, red, wht & bl, 10½", EX, A $900.00

Ocean Liner Grace, MT, 1950s, battery-op, litho tin, 15", NM .$350.00

Ocean Liner Libertania, Liberty Playthings, clockwork, tin w/wood hull & decks, twin funnels, 27", EX, A.......$700.00

Patrol Boat 272B, Orkin, w/up, pressed steel, red, wht & bl, 16", VG, A $450.00

Phantom Raider Ship, Ideal, battery-op, plastic, 27½", VG, A $100.00

Pirate Ship, Modern Toys, battery-op, litho tin, bump-&-go action w/sound, 14", EX (G+ box), A......................$200.00

Pond Yacht Sea Spray, Jackrim Mfg, pnt wood, blk & red, full rigging, 34", EX, from $500 to $600.00

Queen of the Sea Ocean Liner, MT, 1950s, battery-op, pnt tin, red, wht & bl, 21½", EX (EX box) $600.00

Racing Skull, Bing, w/up, litho tin, single rower, 8", EX, A...$1,375.00

Revenue Cutter No 76, Orkin, 1920s, pressed steel, cream & gr, 24", EX, A $900.00

Rowboat, Japan, clockwork, litho tin, w/full-figure, 8", EX, A $600.00

Scull with coxwain, German, lithographed tin, eight-man crew, each with oars, clockwork mechanism, disc wheels, 27" long, M, A, $28,600.00.

Side-Wheeler Great Swanee, TN, friction, litho tin, 10", EX (EX box) $200.00

Silver Mariner Cargo Liner, Bandai, battery-op, litho tin, 16", rare, NM (EX box) $400.00

Speedboat, Kellermann, clockwork, pnt & stained wood, driver w/bsk head, 24", EX..$1,200.00

Speedboat, Lindstrom, clockwork, litho tin, orange & bl, w/driver, 7", EX, A..$100.00

Speedboat, Lindstrom, w/up, litho tin, w/driver, 12½", VG, A $250.00

Speedboat, Lionel, w/up, tin, cream & red, rpl driver & passenger, 17", VG, A $450.00

Speedboat, Orkin, clockwork, pressed steel, cream, gr & red, w/driver, 22", EX, A $1,300.00

Speedboat, Orkin, clockwork, wood & masonite w/diecast components, complete w/figure & ski sled, 23", NMIB, A..$2,800.00

Speedboat, Orkin, 1920s, clockwork, pressed steel, brn, cream & red, twin cockpit, 31", VG, A $1,200.00

Speedboat Baby L, mk USA, w/up, litho tin, w/driver, 11", VG, A $300.00

Speedboat Blue Comet, KO, 1950s, battery-op, mostly wood, 14½", EX...$200.00

Speedboat Flying Yankee, Jackrim Mfg, model 66, clockwork, wood hull, 22", EX, A...$300.00

Speedboat 44, Lionel, clockwork, litho tin w/diecast components, w/driver & display stand, 16", EX (EX box)............$1,200.00

SSN 25 Submarine, Marusan, flywheel mechanism, pnt tin, gr & red, 10", EX, A...$125.00

Steamboat King, Ives, blk & red hull, single funnel, 10½", VG $400.00

Submarine, Wolverine, w/up, tin, bl & wht, 13", VG, A...$125.00

Thunder Jet Speedboat, litho tin, battery-op, MIB, L4 ..$275.00

Torpedo boat, Gebruder Bing, hand-painted tin, steam powered, four masts, rails, three swivel cannons, 27½" L, M, A, $3,080.00.

Torpedo Boat, Linemar, battery-op, remote control, tin, 11", NM (G box), A...$175.00

Torpedo Boat PT-107, Linemar, 1950s, battery-op, litho tin, 11½", EX...$225.00

Tugboat, SAN, multicolored tinplate, battery-operated, smoking action, 12", EX (torn box), A, $200.00.

Tugboat Neptune, MT, 1950s, battery-op, litho tin, 15", EX...$185.00

US Ocean Liner, battery-op, pnt tin, red, wht & bl, 18½", EX, A...$450.00

US Ocean Liner, Linemar, 1950s, battery-op, pnt tin, red, wht & bl, 14", NM...$400.00

USS Cruise Ship, Marusan, friction, litho tin, 16", EX, A..$300.00

Vesuvius Cruiser, Bliss, paper litho on wood, w/bridge, turret, masts & tunnel, 21", EX, A...$700.00

Woodette Coast Guard Rowboat, pressed steel w/jtd wood figure, 12", EX, A...$75.00

Zoom Prop Motorboat, TET, battery-op, pnt tin, bl & red, 14", EX (EX box), A...$250.00

Books

Books have always captured and fired the imagination of children, and today books from every era are being collected. No longer is it just the beautifully illustrated Victorian examples or first editions of books written by well-known children's authors, but more modern books as well.

One of the first classics to achieve unprecedented success was *The Wizard of Oz* by author L. Frank Baum — such success, in fact, that far from his original intentions, it became a series. Even after Baum's death, other authors wrote Oz books until the 1960s, for a total of more than forty different titles. Other early authors were Beatrix Potter, Kate Greenaway, Palmer Cox (who invented the Brownies), and Johnny Gruelle (creator of Raggedy Ann and Andy). All were accomplished illustrators as well.

Everyone remembers a special series of books they grew up with, the Hardy Boys, Nancy Drew Mysteries, Tarzan — there were countless others. And though these are becoming very collectible today, there were many editions of each, and most are very easy to find. Generally the last few in any series will be most difficult to locate, since fewer were printed than the earlier stories which were likely to have been reprinted many times. As is true of any type of book, first editions or the earliest printing will have more collector value. For more information on series books as well as others, we recommend *Collector's Guide to Children's Books, 1850 – 1950, Volume I, II, and III*, by Diane McClure Jones and Rosemary Jones (Collector Books).

Big Little Books came along in 1933 and until edged out by the comic-book format in the mid-1950s, sold in huge volumes, first for a dime and never more than 20¢ a copy. They were printed by Whitman, Saalfield, Goldsmith, Van Wiseman, Lynn, and World Syndicate, and all stuck to Whitman's original layout — thick hand-sized sagas of adventure, the right-hand page with an exciting cartoon, well illustrated and contrived so as to bring the text on the left alive. The first hero to be immortalized in this arena was Dick Tracy, but many more were to follow. Some of the more collectible today feature well-known characters like G-Men, Tarzan, Flash Gordon, Little Orphan Annie, Mickey Mouse, and Western heroes by the dozens. (Note: At the present time, the market for these books is fairly stable — values for common titles are actually dropping. Only the rare, character-related titles are increasing.) For more information we recommend *Big Little Books* by Larry Jacobs (Collector Books).

Little Golden Books were first published in 1942 by Western Publishing Co. Inc. The earliest had spines of blue paper that were later replaced with gold foil. Until the 1970s the books were numbered from 1 to 600, while later books had no numerical order. The most valuable are those with dust jackets from the early '40s or books with paper dolls and activities. The three primary series of books are Regular (1 – 600), Disney (1 – 140), and Activity (1 – 52). Books with the blue or gold paper spine (not foil) often sell at $8.00 to $15.00. Dust jackets alone are worth $20.00 and up in good condition. Paper doll books are generally valued at about $30.00 to $35.00, and stories about TV Western heroes at $12.00 to $18.00. First editions of the 25¢ and 29¢ cover-price books can be identified by a code (either on the title page or the last page); '1/A' indicates a first edition while a 'number/Z' will refer to the twenty-sixth printing. Condition is important but subjective to personal standards. For more information we recommend *Collecting Little Golden Books, Vols I and II*, by Steve Santi The second edition also includes information on Wonder and Elf books. For further study we recommend *Whitman Juvenile Books* by David and Virginia Brown (Collector Books).

Advisors: Ron and Donna Donnelly (D7), Big Little Books; Joel Cohen (C12), Disney Pop-Up Books.

See also Black Americana; Coloring, Activity, and Paint Books; Rock 'N Roll; and other specific categories.

BIG LITTLE BOOKS

Ace Drummond, Whitman #1177, EX, 1935....................$18.00

Andy Panda & Tiny Tom, Whitman #1425, NM.............$40.00

Arizona Kid, On The Bandit Trail, Whitman #1192, EX ...$20.00

Believe It or Not by Ripley, Whitman #760, EX...............$25.00

Big Chief Wahoo & the Magic Lamp, Whitman #1483, NM $45.00

Blondie, Fun For All!, Whitman #1463, NM, $45.00.
(Photo courtesy Larry Jacobs)

Bonanza, The Bubble Gum Kid, Whitman #2002, 1967, EX............$12.00

Brenda Star & the Masked Impostor, Whitman #1427, NM $45.00

Bringing Up Father, Whitman #1133, NM............$60.00

Buck Jones in the Fighting Rangers, Whitman #1188, EX .$35.00

Buck Rogers War w/the Planet Venus, Whitman #1437, 1938, NM............$100.00

Bugs Bunny All Pictures Comics, Whitman #1435, EX, 1944 ....$35.00

Charlie Chan, Whitman #1478, EX, 1939............$35.00

Clyde Beatty Daredevil Lion & Tiger Tamer, Whitman #1410, NM, 1939............$45.00

Desert Eagle & the Hidden Fortress, Whitman #1431, NM, 1941 ....$40.00

Dick Tracy & the Mad Killer, Whitman #1436, NM, 1947 ..$55.00

Dick Tracy Out West, Whitman #723, NM, 1933..........$165.00

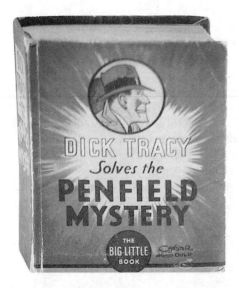

Dick Tracy Solves the Penfield Mystery, VG+, $40.00.

Don Winslow Navy Intelligence Ace, Whitman #1418, EX, 1942 ....$35.00

Donald Duck in Volcano Valley, Whitman #1457, NM, 1949............$95.00

Eddie Cantor in An Hour w/You, Whitman, #774, NM, 1934............$75.00

Ellery Queen, The Master Detective, Whitman #1472, NM, 1942 ....$60.00

Felix the Cat, Whitman #1439, NM, 1943............$90.00

Fighting Heroes Battle of Freedom, Whitman #1401, NM, 1943............$35.00

Flash Gordon & the Power Men of Mongo, Whitman #1469, NM, 1943............$100.00

Flash Gordon & the Witch Queen of Mongo, Whitman #1190, NM............$110.00

Flash Gordon in the Ice World of Mongo, Whitman #1443, 1942, EX............$45.00

G-Men & the Gun Runners, Whitman #1469, NM............$30.00

Gang Busters in Action, Whitman #1451, 1938, NM......$35.00

Gene Autry & the Land Grab Mystery, Whitman #1430, 1948, NM............$40.00

George O'Brien & the Hooded Riders, Whitman #1457, NM $40.00

Houdini's Big Little Book of Magic, Whitman #715, 1927, 1933, NM............$60.00

Huckleberry Finn, Whitman #1422, EX $35.00

Inspector Wade Solves the Mystery of Red Aces, Whitman #1448, NM............$40.00

Invisible Scarlet O'Neil Versus The King of the Slums, Whitman #1406, NM............$45.00

Jack Armstrong & the Ivory Treasure, Whitman #1435, NM............$35.00

Jackie Cooper Movie Star of Skippy & Sooky, Whitman #714, NM............$45.00

Lone Ranger & the Secret Killer, Whitman #1431, EX ...$45.00

Lone Ranger & the Vanishing Herd, Whitman #1196, NM..$65.00

Og Son of Fire, Whitman #1115, NM............$35.00

Peggy Brown & the Mystery Basket, Whitman #1411, NM..$35.00

Red Ryder & the Outlaw of Painted Valley, Whitman #1475, NM............$50.00

Shadow & the Living Death, Whitman #1430, 1940, NM............$200.00

Smilin' Jack & the Stratosphere Ascent, Whitman #1152, 1937, EX............$35.00

Snow White and the Seven Dwarfs, c Walt Disney Enterprises, 1938, from $50.00 to $75.00. (Photo courtesy David Longest)

Tarzan in the Land of the Giant Apes, Whitman #1467, 1949, EX..$45.00

Tarzan Lord of the Jungle, Whitman #1407, NM, **$45.00.** (Photo courtesy Larry Jacobs)

Tarzan the Fearless, Whitman #769, 1934, NM.............$100.00
Tom Mix & Tony Jr on Terror Trail, Whitman #762, , 1934, NM $70.00
Wimpy the Hamburger Eater, Whitman #1458, 1938, VG..$35.00
Zane Grey's Tex Thorne Comes Out of the West, Whitman #1440, EX...$20.00
Zip Sauders King of the Speedway, Whitman #1465, EX .$25.00

DELL FAST ACTION BOOKS BY WHITMAN

Adventures of Charlie McCarthy & Edger Bergen, 1938, NM...$85.00
Andy Panda, #531, 1943, NM......................................$75.00
Bugs Bunny & the Secret of Storm Island, 1942, NM $75.00
Captain Marvel, 1941, NM $225.00
Dan Dunn Secret Operative 48 & the Zeppelin of Doom, 1938, NM...$120.00
Dick Tracy & the Blackmailers, 1939, NM.....................$150.00
Dick Tracy & the Chain of Evidence, 1938, NM $175.00
Dick Tracy & the Maroon Mask Gang, 1938, EX.............$95.00
Dick Tracy Detective & Federal Agent, 1936, NM........$200.00

Donald Duck and The Ducklings, EX, **$95.00.** (Photo courtesy Larry Jacobs)

Donald Duck Out of Luck, 1940, NM......................$165.00
Donald Duck Takes It on the Chin, 1941, NM $165.00
Dumbo the Flying Elephant, 1944, NM..........................$125.00
Flash Gordon & the Ape Men of Mor, 1942, NM..........$200.00
Flash Gordon Vs the Emperor of Mongo, 1936, EX..........$85.00
G-Man on Lightning Island, 1936, NM.............................$85.00
Gang Busters & Guns of Law, 1940, NM.......................$100.00

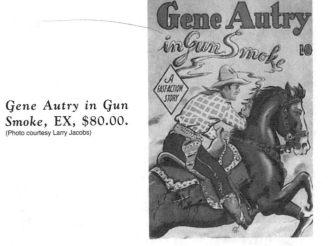

Gene Autry in Gun Smoke, EX, **$80.00.** (Photo courtesy Larry Jacobs)

Katzenjammer Kids, NM...$90.00
Little Orphan Annie Under the Big Top, NM $140.00
Lone Ranger & the Lost Valley w/Silver & Tonto, NM ...$90.00
Mickey Mouse & Pluto, NM $90.00
Mickey Mouse the Sheriff of Nugget Gulch, NM...........$175.00
Mickey Mouse w/Goofy & Mickey's Nephews, rare, NM ..$225.00
Pinocchio & Jiminy Cricket, NM $100.00
Red Ryder Brings Law to Devil's Hole, NM....................$80.00
Smilin' Jack & the Border Bandits, EX $60.00
Tailspin Tommy & the Airliner Mystery, NM $100.00
Tailspin Tommy in Flying Aces, NM $100.00
Tarzan the Avenger, rare, NM......................................$200.00
Terry & the Pirates & the Mystery Ship, NM...............$130.00
Tom Mix in the Riding Avenger, NM.............................$90.00
Zane Grey's King of the Royal Mounted Policing the Frozen North, NM...$75.00

LITTLE GOLDEN BOOKS

A Day on the Farm, #407, D edition, VG, K3 ....$10.00
Annie Oakley & the Rustlers, #22125, A edition, NM....$20.00
Baby Dear, #466, C edition, EX, K3 ....$20.00
Baby's Day Out, #113-01, A edition, EX, K3 ....$15.00
Bambi, 1948, A edition, EX, M8 ....$20.00
Bambi Friends of the Forest, #101-59, A edition, EX, K3 ..$4.00
Beauty & the Beast — Teapot's Tale, #104-70, A edition, EX, K3 ....$5.00
Big Bird's Day on the Farm, #200-50, C edition, EX, K3 ....$5.00
Biskitts Double Trouble, #111-49, A edition, EX, K3 ....$8.00
Bozo & the Hide 'N Seek Elephant, #598, D edition, EX, K3...$6.00
Bozo the Clown, #446, C edition, EX, K3 ....$8.00
Brave Cowboy Bill, #93, B edition, no puzzle, EX, K3 ......$15.00

Buck Rogers & the Children of Hopetown, #500, A edition, VG, K3 ....$8.00

Bugs Bunny Pioneer, #111-66, A edition, EX, K3 ....$6.00

The Bunny Book, A edition, #215, EX, $6.00.

Bunny's Magic Tricks, #441, A edition, EX, K3 ....$25.00

Captain Kangaroo, #421, D edition, VG, K3 ....$6.00

Charmin' Chatty, 1960s, A edition, NM $20.00

Chipmunk's ABC, #512, A edition, VG, K3 ....$10.00

Christmas Tree That Grew, #458-1, A edition, EX, K3 ......$6.00

Cinderella, #D13, A edition, G, K3 ....$8.00

Cinderella's Friends, #D115, F edition, VG, K3................$14.00

Color Kittens, #86, A edition, VG, K3 ....$22.00

Cookie Monster & the Cookie Tree, #159, C edition, EX, K3.$6.00

Corky, #486, A edition, VG, K3...$12.00

Dale Evans & the Lost Gold Mine, #213, A edition, EX, K3 ..$25.00

Davy Crockett, #D45, C edition, G+, K3 ....$6.00

Davy Crockett King of the Wild Frontier, 1955, A edition, EX, M8...$12.00

Donald Duck & Santa Claus, #D27, C edition (C is a 1st), EX, K3...$20.00

Donald Duck in America on Parade, #D131, B edition, VG, K3...$10.00

Exploring Space, #342, A edition, EX, K3 ....$14.00

Fire Engines, #310-88, Fisher-Price A edition, EX, K3 .....$12.00

Fozzie's Funnies, #111-87, A edition, EX, K3 ....$5.00

Friendly Book, #199, A edition, EX, K3............................$12.00

Funny Bunny, #304-59, A edition, EX, K3.........................$8.00

Golden Egg Book, #456, B edition, G, K3............................$4.00

Hansel & Gretel, #17, D edition, VG, K3 ....$14.00

Happy Birthday, #384, B edition, EX, K3.........................$20.00

Happy Little Whale, #393, A edition, VG, K3.................$12.00

Heidi, #258, C edition, EX, K3..$5.00

Howdy Doody & Santa Claus, #237, A edition, EX $30.00

Jungle Book, #D120, A edition, VG, K3...........................$15.00

Little Brown Bear, #304-60, A edition, EX, K3..................$6.00

Little Pee Wee the Circus Dog, #52, G edition, VG, K3 ....$4.00

Little Red Riding Hood, #307-59, C edition, EX, K3 ....$4.00

Little Trapper, #79, A edition, EX, K3 ....$16.00

Ludwig Von Drake, #D98, A edition, G, K3 ....$18.00

Mary Poppins, #D113, A edition, EX, K3 ....$12.00

Mickey Mouse Heads for the Sky, #100-60, A edition, EX, K3..$4.00

Mickey Mouse Picnic, #D15, A edition, EX, K3...............$25.00

Mother Goose, #4, B edition, EX, K3................................$20.00

Mr Frumble's Coffee Shop Disaster, #208-67, A edition, EX, K3..$5.00

Mrs Brisby & the Magic Stone, #110-38, B edition, EX, K3 ..$2.00

My Dolly & Me, #418, A edition, VG, K3 ....$50.00

My Own Grandpa, #208-56, A edition, EX, K3..................$5.00

New Friends for the Saggy Baggy Elephant, #131, B edition, VG, K3..$5.00

New Puppy, #370, A edition, VG, K3 ....$12.00

Noah's Ark, #109, A edition, VG, K3...............................$10.00

Noah's Ark, 1952, A edition, EX, M8...............................$12.00

Noises & Mr Flibberty-Jib, #29, F edition, VG, K3 ....$22.00

Old Mother Hubbard, #300-42, J edition, EX, K3 ....$2.00

Old Yeller, #D65, D edition (D is a 1st), VG, K3...............$8.00

Oscar's New Neighbor, #109-67, A edition, EX, K3 ....$5.00

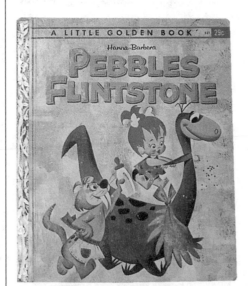

Pebbles Flintstone, Hanna-Barbera, 1960s, from $12.00 to $20.00. (Photo courtesy David Longest)

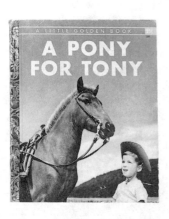

The Giant with the Three Golden Hairs, #219, 1955, EX, $12.00; A Pony for Tony, #220, 1955, EX, $9.00.

Pepper Plays Nurse, #555, A edition, EX $10.00

Peter & the Wolf, #D5, A edition, EX, K3 ....$30.00

Peter Pan & the Pirates, #D73, B edition, EX, K3 ....$10.00

Peter Potamus, #556, A edition, EX, K3 ....$22.00

Pinocchio, #D8, G edition, EX, K3 ....$12.00

Porky Pig & Bugs Bunny Just Like Magic, #146, D edition, EX, K3..$5.00

Quints Cleanup, #107-72, A edition, EX, K3 ....$6.00

Raggedy Ann & Andy Help Santa Claus, #156, A edition, EX, K3 ....$6.00

Right's Animal Farm, #200-46, A edition, EX, K3..............$8.00

Rin-Tin-Tin & the Outlaw, #304, A edition, VG, K3 ......$16.00

Robin Hood & the Daring Mouse, #D128, B edition, EX, K3 .$8.00

Robotman & Friends at School, #110-58, A edition, VG, K3 .$6.00

Rocky & His Friends, #408, A edition, EX, K3................$22.00

Ronald McDonald & the Tale of the Talking Plant, #111-50, B edition, EX, K3 ....$10.00

Saggy Baggy Elephant, #36, G edition, VG, K3................$12.00

Santa's Toy Shop, 1950, A edition, EX, M8....................$12.00

Shazam!, #110-36, B edition, EX, K3 ....$5.00

Shy Little Kitten, #23, F edition, EX, K3........................$14.00

Swiss Family Robinson, #D95, A edition, G+, K3............$12.00

This Is My Family, #312-02, A edition, 50th Anniversary, EX, K3..$10.00

Three Billy Goats Gruff, #173, A edition, EX, K3............$22.00

Thumbelina, #153, A edition, VG, K3 ....$15.00

Tiny Toon Adventures Lost in the Fun House, #111-68, A edition, EX, K3 ....$6.00

Tom & Jerry Meet Little Quack, #181, B edition, EX, K3 ..$5.00

Tom & Jerry's Party, #235, E edition, EX............................$8.00

Tom & Jerry's Photo Finish, #124, A edition, VG, K3 .....$28.00

Tom Thumb, #353, A edition, G, K3 ....$8.00

Tortoise & the Hare, #207-56, Fisher-Price A edition, EX, K3..$8.00

Tweety & Sylvester in Birds of a Feather, #110-78, A edition, EX, K3 ....$5.00

Twelve Days of Christmas, #526, A edition, EX, K3.........$12.00

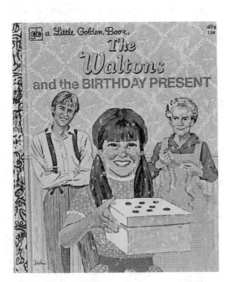

The Waltons and the Birthday Present, Golden Press, 1975, from $10.00 to $15.00.

Where's Woodstock, #111-63, A edition, EX, K3............$10.00

Wiggles, #166, B edition, VG, K3 ....$30.00

Willie Found a Wallet, #205-56, C edition, EX, K3............$6.00

Wonderful School, #582, C edition, EX, K3 ....$4.00

Woody Woodpecker Takes a Trip, #445, C edition, EX, K3 ....$5.00

POP-UP & MOVABLE BOOKS

Adventures & Surprises w/Raggedy Ann & Andy, Hallmark, 1974, movable pgs, NM, from $25 to $30.00

Adventures of Oz, Derrydale, 1991, 1st edition, 3 pop-ups, 6 pgs, EX, K3 ....$10.00

Ann of Green Gables — A Big Imagination, 1993, 12 pop-ups, 6 movable, EX, K3 ....$10.00

Buck Rogers, Pleasure Books, 1934, EX $600.00

Buck Rogers Strange Adventures in the Spider-Ship, Blue Ribbon, 1935, 3 pop-ups, M..$350.00

Child's Garden of Verses, Dutton, 1991, 1st edition, 5 pop-ups, 3 movable, 14 pgs, EX, K3 ....$15.00

Christmas Time w/Snoopy & His Friends, Hallmark, 1978, NM..$45.00

Cinderella, Blue Ribbon, 1933, 4 pop-ups, NM..............$425.00

Dick Tracy Capture of Boris Arson, 1935, 3 pop-ups, NM ..$375.00

Disney's Aladdin, 1993, 1st edition, 4 pop-ups, 12 movable, M, K3 ....$12.00

Emerald City, Derrydale, 1991, 1st edition, 3 pop-ups, EX, K3 ....$10.00

Flying Nun, 1982, 5 pop-ups, 10 pgs, EX, K3 ....$6.00

Goldilocks & the Three Bears, Blue Ribbon Press, 1934, 3 pop-ups, EX $50.00

Hocus Pocus, 1991, 1 pop-up, 11 movable, 14 pgs, EX, K3 ..$15.00

Hopalong Cassidy & Lucky, EX, J2............................$100.00

Hopalong Cassidy Lends a Helping Hand, Bonnie Books, 1950, 2 pop-ups, EX, A..$75.00

Huckleberry Hound & the Dog Cat, Modern, 1974, 4 pop-ups, EX..$15.00

Jack & the Giant Killer, by Harold Lentz, Blue Ribbon, 1932, 3 pop-ups, EX..$325.00

Jack in the Beanstalk, 1944, 5 pop-ups, w/dust jacket, EX, K3 ...$50.00

Little Orphan Annie and Jumbo, the Circus Elephant, three pop-ups, Blue Ribbon Books, EX, $250.00 (M, $350.00).
(Photo courtesy David Longest)

Little Red Riding Hood, Blue Ribbon, 1933, 1 pop-up, NM ...$150.00

Mickey Hop-La! Une Partie de Polo, Hachette, 1930s, 3 pop-ups, NM, C12 ....$500.00

Mickey Mouse Waddle Book, Blue Ribbon, 1934, M..$3,500.00

Mother Goose, Blue Ribbon, 3 pop-ups, NM $250.00

Peter Rabbit, Blue Ribbon, 1934, 1 pop-up, NM............$350.00

Pinocchio, Blue Ribbon, 1933, 4 pop-ups, w/dust jacket, EX...$400.00

Pop-Up Mickey Mouse, Blue Ribbon, 1930s, 3 pop-ups, EX ...$250.00

Pop-Up Minnie Mouse, Blue Ribbon, 1930s, 3 pop-ups, EX ...$250.00

Rudolph the Red-Nosed Reindeer, by Robert L May, 1950, 5 pop-ups, NM $35.00

Silly Symphonies, Babes in the Woods, King Neptune, Blue Ribbon, four pop-ups, 1933, EX with dust jackets, $1,500.00.
(Photo courtesy Joel Coehn)

Sleeping Beauty, Blue Ribbon, 1934, 1 pop-up, NM $150.00

Teenage Mutant Ninja Turtles, Random House, EX, from $10 to..$15.00

Terry & the Pirates, Blue Ribbon, 1935, 3 pop-ups, EX..$200.00

Tim Tyler in the Jungle, Blue Ribbon, 1935, 3 pop-ups, NM $325.00

Wizard of Oz Waddle Book, Blue Ribbon, 1934, scarce, NM $250.00

TELL-A-TALE BY WHITMAN

A Farm of My Own, Big Tell-a-Tale, #2420, 1967, VG, K3 ...$10.00

A Fuzzy Pet, #2671, 1959, fuzzy cover & pgs, EX $10.00

Amy's Long Night, #2512, 1970, EX $5.00

Animal ABC, #887, 1949, VG, K3 ....$24.00

Bambi, #2548, 1972, EX, K3..$5.00

Bedtime Book, #2559, 1963, VG, K3 ....$6.00

Benji the Detective, #2640, 1978, VG, K3 ....$8.00

Bugs Bunny Hangs Around, #2410, 1957, VG, K3 ....$6.00

Bugs Bunny's Chimney Adventure, Top Top Tale, #2464, 1963, VG, K3 ....$8.00

Cinderella, #2552, 1954, EX, K3 ....$8.00

Columbus the Exploring Burro, #826, 1951, EX, K3..........$5.00

Daniel's New Friend, #2560, 1968, EX, K3 ....$5.00

Donald Duck on Tom Sawyer Island, #2455-31, 1960, EX, K3 ....$5.00

Flintstones at the Circus, #2552, 1963, VG, K3 ....$12.00

Gingerbread Man, #2590, 1958, VG, K3 ....$5.00

Gingerbread Man, Top Top Tale, #2472, 1960, EX, K3 ......$8.00

Gumby & Gumby's Pal Pokey to the Rescue, #2552, 1969, VG, K3...$12.00

Hippety Hop Around the Block, #2616, 1953, VG, K3 ...$12.00

Hooray for Lassie, #2414, 1964, VG, K3 ....$6.00

Huffin Puff Express, #2421-2, 1974, EX, K3 ....$5.00

I Like To Be Little, #2615, 1976, VG, K3 ....$5.00

Jetsons Birthday Surprise, Top Top Tale, #2484, 1963, EX, K3 ....$20.00

Johnny Appleseed, #808, 1949, EX, K3 ....$18.00

Lady, #2552, 1954, EX, K3..$8.00

Lassie & Her Kittens, #2503, 1956, VG, K3 ....$8.00

Little Folks in Mother Goose, #2471, Top Top Tale, #2471, EX, K3..$5.00

Little Joe's Puppy, #2622, 1957, EX, K3 ....$12.00

Little Red Riding Hood, #2670, 1960, fuzzy cover & pgs, EX, K3..$10.00

Loopy de Loop Odd Jobber, #2611, 1964, VG, K3............$20.00

Magic Zoo, #2474-32, 1972, EX, K3....................................$5.00

Mary Poppins, #2606, 1964, EX, K3................................$8.00

Mickey Mouse & the Mouseketeers, #2454-35, 1977, EX, K3..$5.00

Mother Goose, #2638, 1958, EX, K3................................$6.00

Mr Grabbit, #2526, 1952, EX, K3................................$8.00

Mr Mogg's Dogs, #2652, 1954, fuzzy cover & pgs, EX, K3...$14.00

My Color Game, Big Tell-a-Tale, #2436, 1966, EX, K3....$10.00

My Little Book of Pets, #2413-5, 1972, VG, K3 ....$6.00

Patrick & the Duckling, Top Top Tale Fuzzy-Wuzzy Book, #2456, 1963, EX, K3..$10.00

Peter Potamus Meets the Black Knight, #2567, 1965, EX, K3..$8.00

Petunia, Top Top Tale, #2482, 1948, VG, K3 ....$16.00

Pink Panther Rides Again, #2403-1, 1976, EX, K3.............$6.00

Princess & the Pea, #2610, 1961, VG, K3..........................$4.00

Road Runner & the Bird Watchers, #2509, 1968, EX, K3..$5.00

Roundabout Train, #2436, 1958, VG, K3..........................$6.00

Roy Rogers & the Sure 'Nough Cowpoke, #80115, 1952, VG, K3..$25.00

Slowpoke at the Circus, #2457, 1973, EX, K3...................$8.00

Sneezer, #854, 1945, w/dust jacket, EX, K3...................$30.00

Speckles & His Triplets, #874, 1949, VG, K3 ....$15.00

Story of Christmas, Big Tell-a-Tale, #2446, 1965, VG, K3....$5.00

Surprise for Howdy Doody, #2573, 1950, EX, K3.............$28.00

Tag Along Shadow, #2601, 1959, VG, K3 ....$12.00

Tip-Top Tree House, #2555, 1969, EX, K3 ....$8.00

Tom Tucker & Dickie-Bird, Big Tell-a-Tale, #2412, 1965, VG, K3..$8.00

Tommy & Timmy, #2656, 1951, fuzzy pgs & cover, EX, K3....$12.00

Tortoise & the Hare, Top Top Tale, #2455, 1963, fuzzy cover & pgs, EX, K3..$15.00

Tuffy the Tugboat, Top Top Tale, #2481, 1947, EX, K3 ......$8.00

Tweety & Sylvester, #2452-35, 1978, EX, K3....................$5.00

Wacky Witch Royal Birthday, #2546, 1971, EX, K3.........$10.00

Winnie the Pooh, #2526, 1974, EX, K3................................$4.00

Woody Woodpecker Shoots the Works, #2618, 1955, VG, K3..$10.00

Yippee Kiyi & Whoa Boy, #2514, 1954, EX, K3................$5.00

Yogi Bear Takes a Vacation, Big Tell-a-Tale, #2406, 1965, VG, K3..$10.00

101 Dalmatians, #2622, 1962, EX, K3................................$5.00

WHITMAN MISCELLANEOUS

A Parade for Chatty Baby, 1960s, hardcover, NM $15.00

Alice in Wonderland, 1970, hardcover, EX..........................$5.00

Annette & the Mystery at Moonstone Bay, 1962, hardcover, EX $25.00

Beautiful Joe, 1955, hardcover, EX $6.00

Bedknobs & Broomsticks, 1971, hardcover, EX..............$12.00

Betty Grable & the House of Cobwebs, 1947, hardcover, EX ...**$25.00**
Bewitched, The Opposite Uncle, 1970, hardcover, EX **$35.00**
Big Valley, 1966, hardcover, EX...**$25.00**
Bobbsey Twins in the Country, 1953, hardcover, EX **$6.00**
Brenda Starr Girl Reporter, 1943, hardcover, EX.............**$30.00**
Cheyenne & the Lost Gold of Lion Park, 1958, hardcover, EX...**$18.00**
Circus Boy Under the Big Top, 1957, hardcover, EX........**$25.00**
Diamond Cave Mystery, 1956, hardcover, EX.....................**$6.00**
Dick Tracy Meets the Night Crawler, 1945, hardcover, EX ..**$25.00**
Donna Parker at Cherrydale, 1957, hardcover, EX **$8.00**
Dr Kildare Assigned to Trouble, 1963, hardcover, EX **$12.00**
F Troop, The Great Indian Uprising, 1967, hardcover, EX **$25.00**
Five Little Peppers & How They Grew, 1955, hardcover, EX **$6.00**
Flipper, Mystery of the Black Schooner, 1966, hardcover, EX...**$15.00**
Garrisons Gorillas & the Fear Formula, 1968, hardcover, EX ...**$20.00**
Gene Autry & the Badmen of Broken Arrow, 1951, hardcover, EX...**$15.00**
Gilligan's Island, 1966, hardcover, VG, N2 ....**$25.00**
Ginny Gordon & the Broadcast Mystery, 1956, hardcover, EX...**$8.00**
Gunsmoke Showdown on Front Street, 1969, hardcover, EX...**$15.00**
Have Gun Will Travel, 1959, hardcover, EX **$25.00**
Heidi Grows Up, 1971, hardcover, EX **$4.00**
Ironside, 1969, hardcover, EX..**$15.00**
Janet Lennon & the Angels, 1963, hardcover, EX............**$15.00**

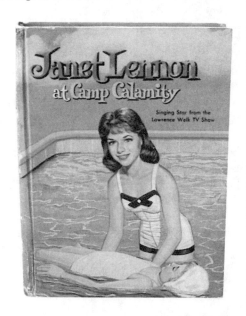

Janet Lennon at Camp Calamity, Barlow Meyer, illustrated authorized TV edition, Whitman #1539, 1962, EX, **$15.00.** (Photo courtesy David and Virginia Brown)

Land of the Giants — Flight of Fear, 1969, hardcover, EX..**$300.00**
Lassie Treasure Hunter, 1960, hardcover, EX **$14.00**
Leave It to Beaver, 1962, hardcover, EX **$40.00**
Man From UNCLE, 1967, hardcover, EX **$18.00**
Meg & the Disappearing Diamonds, 1967, hardcover, EX..**$8.00**
Mickey Mouse Crusoe, 1936, softcover, VG, M8.............**$50.00**
Mickey Mouse Has a Busy Day, 1938, softcover, EX **$75.00**
Mission Impossible, 1970, hardcover, EX **$20.00**
Munsters, 1965, hardcover, EX, N2 ....**$30.00**
Munsters Last Resort, 1966, hardcover, EX **$25.00**

Outdoor Girls at Cedar Ridge, 1931, hardcover, EX.........**$16.00**
Patty Duke & Mystery Mansion, 1964, hardcover, NM, from $10 to **$15.00**
Pee-Wee Harris on the Trail, 1922, hardcover, w/dust jacket, EX **$12.00**
Pinocchio — A Tale of the Puppet, 1967, hardcover, EX...**$5.00**
Polly in New York, 1922, hardcover, w/dust jacket, VG...**$15.00**
Real McCoys & Danger at the Ranch, 1961, hardcover, EX ...**$25.00**
Rebecca of Sunnybrook Farm, 1960, hardcover, EX **$6.00**
Red Ryder & the Secret of Lucky Mine, 1947, hardcover, EX...**$20.00**
Restless Gun, 1959, hardcover, EX, N2............................**$35.00**
Rin Tin Tin & Call to Danger, 1957, hardcover, EX **$18.00**
Robin Kane Mystery in the Clouds, 1971, hardcover, EX...**$8.00**
Roy Rogers & Dale Evans — River of Peril, 1957, hardcover, EX...**$25.00**
Roy Rogers & the Enchanted Canyon, 1954, hardcover, EX ..**$25.00**
Shirley Temple & the Spirit of Dragonwood, 1945, hardcover, w/dust jacket, EX **$25.00**
Silver Seven, 1972, hardcover, EX **$5.00**
Sylvia Sanders & the Tangled Web, 1946, hardcover, VG ..**$16.00**
Tammy Adventure in Squaw Valley, 1964, hardcover, EX, S14...**$10.00**
Tarzan & the Lost Safari, 1957, hardcover, EX **$12.00**

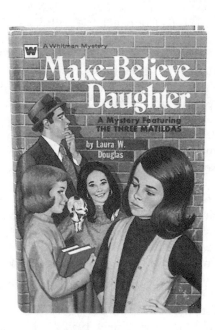

Three Matildas, Make-Believe Daughter, Laura W. Douglas, Whitman #1502, 1972, EX, **$4.00.**

Tillie the Toiler & the Masquerading Duchess, 1943, hardcover, w/dust jacket, EX **$25.00**
Trixie Belden & the Black Jacket Mystery, 1961, hardcover, EX **$12.00**
Voyage to the Bottom of the Sea, 1965, hardcover, EX **$25.00**
Walt Disney's Spin & Marty — Trouble at Triple-R, 1958, hardcover, EX **$25.00**
Walt Disney's Story of Clarabelle the Cow, WDE, 1938, hardcover, EX **$45.00**
Waltons Penny Sale, 1975, hardcover, NM **$15.00**
Winnie Winkle, 1946, hardcover, w/dust jacket, EX **$28.00**
Wonderful Wizard of Oz, 1970, hardcover, EX.................**$5.00**
Zane Gray's Last Trail, 1954, hardcover, EX......................**$10.00**

WONDER BOOKS

A Visit to the Hospital, #690, 1958, VG, K3 ....$5.00

Baby Animal Friends, #608, 1976, VG, K3 ....$8.00

Baby Elephant, #541, 1950, EX, K3 ....$10.00

Baby Huey, #787, 1975, VG, K3.....................................$25.00

Baby Susan's Chickens, #546, 1951, EX, K3 ....$10.00

Bewitched, 1965, NM, from $25 to $30.00

Black Beauty, #595, 1973, VG, K3 ....$8.00

Brave Little Steam Shovel, #555, 1951, EX, K3................$8.00

Buzzy the Funny Crow, #821, 1963, EX, K3 ....$15.00

Casper & Wendy Adventures, #855, 1969, VG, K3 ....$10.00

Christmas Is Coming, #593, 1952, EX, K3 ....$10.00

Cinderella, #640, 1954, EX, K3 ....$10.00

Cow in the Silo, #534, 1950, EX, K3 ....$20.00

Donkey Who Wanted To Be Wise, #771, 1961, EX, K3 .....$4.00

Favorite Nursery Tales, #1504, 1953, sculptured cover, EX,
K3 ....$10.00

Gandy Goose, #695, 1957, EX, K3 ....$10.00

Hans Christian Andersen's Fairy Tales, #599, 1952, EX, K3 ..$8.00

Hector Heathcote & the Knights, #840, 1965, EX, K3 ....$25.00

Heidi, #532, 1950, EX, K3 ....$10.00

How Peter Cottontail Got His Name, #668, 1957, VG, K3..$8.00

It's a Secret, #540, 1950, EX, K3 ....$10.00

Let's Go to School, #691, 1954, EX, K3 ....$10.00

Little Peter Cottontail, #641, 1956, EX, K3 ....$8.00

Magic Bus, #516, 1948, VG, K3 ....$10.00

Make-Believe Parade, #520, 1949, VG, K3.....................$18.00

Mother Goose, #501, 1946, VG, K3 ....$8.00

Night Before Christmas, #858, 1974, EX, K3 ....$5.00

Pecos Bill, #767, 1961, EX, K3 ....$12.00

Peter Rabbit, #513, 1947, VG, K3...................................$10.00

Polly's Christmas Present, #819, 1953, VG, K3 ....$12.00

Puppy Who Found a Boy, #561, 1951, VG, K3 ....$10.00

Romper Room Book of Happy Animals, #687R, 1957, VG,
K3 ....$8.00

Romper Room Book of Manners, #763, 1977, VG, K3.......$5.00

Shy Little Horse, #1509, 1947, sculptured cover, EX, K3 .$15.00

Sleeping Beauty, #635, 1956, VG, K3 ....$5.00

Sonny the Bunny, #591, 1952, EX, K3 ....$6.00

Three Little Pigs/Little Red Riding Hood, #609, 1974, EX,
K3...$15.00

Traveling Twins, #596, 1953, EX, K3...............................$8.00

Tutu the Little Fawn, #836, 1964, VG, K3 ....$5.00

Who Lives Here?, #669, 1958, EX, K3 ....$8.00

Why the Bear Has a Short Tail, #508, 1946, EX, K3 ....$10.00

Wonder Book of Bible Stories, #577, 1951, VG, K3.........$15.00

Wonder Book of Finger Plays & Action Rhymes, #627, 1955,
VG, K3 ....$10.00

Yogi Bear Mosquito Flying Day, #924, 1976, EX, K3...........$5.00

10 Rabbits, #648, EX, K3 ....$8.00

MISCELLANEOUS

A Child's Garden of Verses, by Robert Louis Stevenson, Saalfield, 1929, softcover, EX $65.00

A New Home for Snowball, Eager Reader, 1st edition, EX,
K3..$5.00

Adventures of Raggedy Ann, by Johnny Gruelle, hardcover, EX,
from $15 to...$20.00

Aladdin & the Wonderful Lamp, McLouglin Bros, Little Color
Classics, 1940, EX, K3 ....$20.00

Alexander Kitten, Jr Elf/Rand McNally, 1959, VG, K3 ......$8.00

Amazing Spider-Man, Lancer, 1966, softcover, NM, T2 ..$30.00

Angel Child, Elf/Rand McNally, 1946, EX, K3................$12.00

Away in a Manger, Happy Day Books, 1985, EX, K3 ....$5.00

Babes in Toyland, Big Golden, 2nd edition, hardcover, EX,
K3 ....$22.00

Baby's Own Mother Goose, Jr Elf/Rand McNally, 1969, VG,
K3 ....$6.00

Bambi, Disney/Heath, 1944, hardcover, NM, M8.............$75.00

Birds We Know, Grosset & Dunlap, My Easy To Read True
Book, 1954, hardcover, w/dust jacket, EX, K3 ....$20.00

Blaze and Thunderbolt, C.W. Anderson, illustrated by author, MacMillan, 1955, stated first printing, illustrated paper boards, black and white illustrations by author, VG in worn dust jacket, $60.00. (Photo courtesy Marvelous Books)

Blondie's Family, Treasure Books, 1954, by Chic Young, EX,
K3...$25.00

Bobby Bear's Busy Day, Saalfield, 1952, hardcover, EX, K3...$15.00

Bobby Snoozes, Pied Piper, 1945, hardcover, VG, K3.......$15.00

Boo & the Flying Flews, Eager Reader, 1st edition, EX, K3...$10.00

Brownie the Little Bear Who Liked People, McLoughlin Bros,
Little Color Classics, 1939, VG, K3 ....$20.00

Charlie Brown Christmas, World/Signet, 1965, hardcover,
NM..$20.00

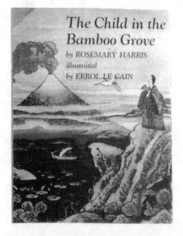

The Child in the Bamboo Grove, Rosemary Harris, Faber & Faber Limited, 1972 first edition, pictorial boards, NM, $65.00. (Photo courtesy Marvelous Books)

Choo-Choo the Little Switch Engine, Elf/Rand McNally, 1954, VG, K3...$10.00

Clampetts of Beverly Hills, Avon, 1964, softcover, NM, from $15 to...$20.00

Complete Story of Walt Disney's Snow White & the Seven Dwarfs, Grosset & Dunlap/WDE, 1937, hardcover, EX $125.00

Cowboy Eddie, Elf/Rand McNally, 1950, VG, K3.............$8.00

David & Goliath, Happy Day Books, 1990, EX, K3............$5.00

David & Nancy's Train Ride, Jr Elf/Rand McNally, 1946, EX, K3...$15.00

Dolls of Other Lands, Miss Frances Ding Dong School, EX, K3...$15.00

Donald Duck & His Ups & Downs, WDE, 1930s, hardcover, EX $100.00

Donald Duck & the Hidden Gold, Sandpiper, 1951, hardcover, EX, K3 ....$30.00

Dr Seuss, Sneetches & Other Stories, 1961, 1st edition, hardcover, NM $75.00

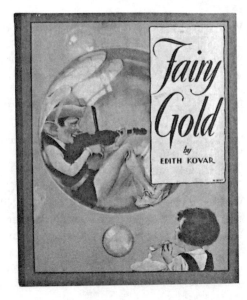

Fairy Gold and Other Stories, Edith Kovar, Roy Best color illustrations, Whitman, 1931, EX, $60.00. (Photo courtesy Marvelous Books)

Flash Gordon, Treasure Books, 1956, EX, K3....................$15.00

Flintstones, Big Golden, 1st edition, hardcover, EX, K3...$25.00

G-Man's Son, by W Robinson, Goldsmith Publishing, 1936, hardcover, w/dust jacket, EX $30.00

Gene Autry & the Red Shirt, Sandpiper, 1951, hardcover, EX, K3...$30.00

God Is Good, Jr Elf/Rand McNally, 1955, EX, K3..............$5.00

Golden Happy Birthday, Big Golden, 1st edition, VG, K3 ..$20.00

Goody Two Shoes, Samuel Lowe, 1944, softcover, EX, K3 ..$10.00

Grimms Fairy Tales, Sturdibilt Books, 1948, EX, K3 ....$12.00

Hardy Boys & Nancy Drew Meet Dracula, Grosset & Dunlap, 1978, hardcover, NM...$20.00

He's Your Dog Charlie Brown, World/Signet, 1968, hardcover, NM...$15.00

Heidi's Children, Golden Illustrated Classics, 1967, hardcover, EX, K3..$10.00

Here Comes the Train, Sunny Books, 1970, softcover, EX, K3...$6.00

Hey Diddle Diddle, Elf/Rand McNally, 1961, EX, K3.........$5.00

House That Jack Built, Elf/Rand McNally, 1956, EX, K3 ...$5.00

Humpty Dumpty & Other Nursery Rhymes, Jr Elf/Rand McNally, 1952, VG, K3 ....$5.00

Jack & the Beanstalk, McLoughlin Bros, Little Color Classics, 1938, G, K3..$10.00

Johnny the Fireman, Elf/Rand McNally, 1954, VG, K3 ...$12.00

Josie & the Pussycats Bag Factory Detour, Rand McNally, 1971, hardcover, NM...$15.00

Kankie Kangaroo...Who Couldn't Hop, Roselle Ross, Maxton, Bracker textual illustrations, cover by Paul Kaloda, 1945, VG, $65.00. (Photo courtesy Marvelous Books)

Kittens & Puppies, Rand McNally Giant, 1960, EX, K3 ..$18.00

Lassie Finds a Way, Big Golden, 1st edition, hardcover, EX, K3...$18.00

Let's Take a Trip, Bonnie Books, 1955, EX, K3 ....$35.00

Little Bo Peep, Jr Elf/Rand McNally, 1966, VG, K3 ....$5.00

Little Bobo & His Blue Jacket, Elf/Rand McNally, 1953, EX, K3...$8.00

Little Pig's Picnic & Other Stories, Disney/Heath, 1939, hardcover, NM, M8...$75.00

Little Red Riding Hood & the Big Bad Wolf, David McKay, 1934, softcover, rare, VG, M8 ....$50.00

Little Red Riding Hood & the Big Bad Wolf, McKay, 1934, hardcover, NM...$65.00

Little Swiss Guard, Bruce Publishing, 1955, EX, K3.........$15.00

Lone Ranger & the Silver Bullet, by Fran Striker, Grosset & Dunlap, 1948, hardcover, w/dust jacket, NM.............$35.00

Lucinda the Little Donkey, Elf/Rand McNally, 1952, EX, K3 ..$6.00

Mickey Fait Du Camping, Hachette of France, 1933, hardcover, G+, M8 ....$60.00

Mickey Mouse Fire Brigade, WD, 1930s, hardcover, VG .$75.00

Mickey Mouse in Giantland, David McKay, 1930s, hardcover, EX $100.00

Mickey Mouse Movie Stories, 1931, hardcover, EX $200.00

Mickey Mouse Stories, Dean & Son Ltd, 1952, hardcover, VG, M8...$85.00

Mostly Happy Henrietta, Hawthorne, 1973, hardcover, NM...$20.00

Mother Goose, Bonnie Books, 1951, EX, K3 ....$20.00

Mother Goose, by Eulalie Osgood Grover, Volland, 1915, 1st edition, cloth cover w/pasted-on illus, NM $200.00

Mother Goose, Elf/Rand McNally, 1955, EX, K3..............$10.00

Mr Flop Ears, Jr Elf/Rand McNally, 1969, G, K3 ....$12.00

Muggins Takes Off, Elf/Rand McNally, 1964, EX, K3.......$12.00

My Elephant Book, Big Golden, 1st edition, hardcover, EX, K3..$30.00

My Prayer Book, Rand McNally Giant, 1974, VG, K3.....$10.00

New Baby, Golden, by Ruth & Harold Shane, 1948, 1st edition, cloth cover, EX $65.00

Old Mother Hubbard, Elf/Rand McNally, 1958, EX, K3.....$5.00

One Tiny Baby, Happy Day Books, 1992, EX, K3 ....$6.00

Pandora, Sunny Books, 1968, illus by Erika Weihs, softcover, EX, K3..$10.00

Peek In, Miss Frances Ding Dong School, VG, K3 ....$12.00

Peppy the Lonely Little Puppy, Elf/Rand McNally, 1958, EX, K3..$15.00

Peter Pig & His Airplane Trip, McLoughlin Bros, Little Color Classics, 1943, VG, K3 ....$15.00

Pinocchio, Disney/Heath, 1940, hardcover, NM, M8.......$75.00

Poky Little Puppy & the Patchwork Blanket, Big Golden, 2nd edition, EX, K3 ....$10.00

Prayers for Little Children, Jr Elf/Rand McNally, 1944, EX, K3..$10.00

Prince Valiant in the Days of King Arthur, Treasure Books, 1950s, hardcover, EX, T2..$25.00

Princess Pat the Paddle Boat, Jolly, VG, K3......................$10.00

Puppy Dog Tales, Random House, 1964, hardcover, EX, K3 ...$10.00

Puss in Boots, Samuel Lowe, 1944, softcover, EX, K3.......$10.00

Raggedy Ann & Andy & the Camel w/the Wrinkled Knees, by Johnny Gruelle, PF Volland, 1924, hardcover, EX, from $75 to $85.00

Raggedy Ann & Andy's Sunny Stories, by Johnny Gruelle, 1974, hardcover, EX, from $25 to................................$30.00

Raggedy Ann & the Paper Dragon, by Johnny Gruelle, 1972, hardcover, EX, from $25 to.......................................$30.00

Raggedy Ann's Lucky Pennies, by Johnny Gruelle, MA Donohue, 1932, hardcover, EX, from $40 to.......................$45.00

Rusty the Pup Who Wanted Wings, McLoughlin Bros, Little Color Classics, 1939, VG, K3....................................$15.00

Seven Wonderful Cats, Elf/Rand McNally, 1956, EX, K3...$12.00

Simpsons Fun in the Sun, Harper Perennial, softcover, M, K1..$15.00

Snoopy & the Red Baron, HRW, 1966, hardcover, NM ...$10.00

Snow White & the Seven Dwarfs, Treasure Books, 1955, EX, K3..$8.00

Snow White & the Seven Dwarfs, WDE, 1937, hardcover, EX $85.00

Songs of the Gilded Age, Big Golden, 1st edition, hardcover, torn dust jacket, EX, K3..$55.00

Sounds We Hear, Grosset & Dunlap, My Easy To Read True Book, 1955, hardcover, w/dust jacket, EX, K3 ....$20.00

Spoodles, Jolly, 1952, EX, K3...$8.00

Squeeze Please & Hear Me Say Bow Wow, Bonnie Books, 1955, EX, K3..$40.00

Squirrel Twins, Elf/Rand McNally, 1961, VG, K3..............$5.00

Story of Jesus, Jr Elf/Rand McNally, 1936, EX, K3...........$15.00

Storybook for Little Tots, Elf/Rand McNally, EX, K3 ....$10.00

Superman at Fifty, Octavia Press, 1987, hardcover, M......$25.00

Tammy & Pepper, Big Golden, 1st edition, hardcover, EX, K3..$40.00

Tarzan & the Desert Rescue, Superscope, 1977, EX, K3...$15.00

Tenggren's Pirates, Ships & Sailors, Big Golden, 1st edition, hardcover, EX, K3...$30.00

Three Little Ducks, Jr Elf/Rand McNally, 1945, VG, K3....$5.00

Tom Thumb, Elf/Rand McNally, 1959, EX, K3..................$8.00

Tubby the Tuba, Treasure Books, 1950s, EX.....................$20.00

Volksy the Little Yellow Car, Elf/Rand McNally, 1965, NM, K3..$22.00

Walt Disney's Mickey Mouse Birthday, Big Golden, 1st edition, hardcover, EX, K3..$30.00

Walt Disney's Story of Mickey Mouse, 1930s, hardcover, EX ...$50.00

Walt Disney's Version of Pinocchio, Random House/WDP, 1939, hardcover, EX...$75.00

Water Babies' Circus & Other Stories, Disney/Heath, 1940, hardcover, NM...$75.00

Wild Animals & Their Babies, Giant Golden, 1971, hardcover, EX, K3..$30.00

Wild Babies, Jr Elf/Rand McNally, 1971, VG, K3...............$4.00

Willie Woodchuck, Bonnie Books, 1954, EX, K3.............$30.00

Wonderful Plane Ride, Elf/Rand McNally, 1949, EX, K3 ...$15.00

Yogi Bear, Big Golden, 1st edition, hardcover, VG, K3 ....$15.00

You're a Good Man Charlie Brown, Random House, 1967, hardcover, NM $15.00

10 Animal Stories, Pied Piper, 1946, hardcover, w/dust jacket, EX, K3..$30.00

Breyer

Breyer collecting seems to be growing in popularity, and though the horses dominate the market, the company also made dogs, cats, farm animals, wildlife figures, dolls, and tack and accessories such as barns for their models. They've been in continuous production since the '50s, all strikingly beautiful and lifelike in both modeling and color. Earlier models were glossy, but since 1968 a matt finish has been used, though glossy and semiglossy colors are now being re-introduced, especially in special runs. (A special run of Family Arabians was done in the glossy finish in 1988.)

One of the hardest things for any model collector is to determine the value of his or her collection. The values listed below are for models in excellent to near mint condition. This means no rubs, no scratches, no chipped paint, and no breaks — nothing that cannot be cleaned off with a rag and little effort. A

Stories From Uncle Remus, Joel Chandler Harris, Saalfield, 1934, color pictorial boards, original A.B. Frost illustrations, NM in dust jacket, $125.00. (Photo courtesy Marvelous Books)

model which has been altered in any way, including having the paint touched up, is considered a customized model and has an altogether different set of values than one in the original finish. The models listed herein are completely original. For More information we recommend *Breyer Animal Collector's Guide, First* and *Second Edition,* by Felicia Browell.

Advisor: Felicia Browell.

CLASSIC SCALE MODELS

Andalusian Foal (Proud Mare & Newborn Foal), apricot dun, 1993 ....$10.00
Andalusian Mare (Sears), alabaster, 1984 ....$20.00
Andalusian Stallion, bay pinto w/blk points, 1998 ....$11.00
Arabian Foal, chestnut, 1973-82 ....$13.00
Arabian Foal (Desert Arabian Family), red bay, 1992-94 .$10.00
Arabian Mare (Classic Arabian Family), chestnut, 1973-91 ..$15.00
Arabian Stallion (Desert Arabian Family), red bay w/blk points, 1992-94 ....$15.00
Black Beauty (King of the Wind Set), bay w/blk points, 1990-93 ....$15.00
Black Stallion (Black Stallion Returns Set), blk, 1983-93 ..$15.00
Bucking Bronco, blk, 1966-73 & 1975-76 ....$42.00
Cutting Horse, bay w/blk points, 1997-99 (w/out calf).....$22.00

Fighting Mesteno, buckskin with black points, 1994 – 97, $25.00. (Photo courtesy Felicia Browell)

Duchess (Black Beauty Family), bay w/blk points, 1980-93 ..$15.00
Ginger (Toys R Us/Sweet Memories), brn appaloosa, 1997 ...$20.00
Hobo, buckskin, from Hobo Gift Set, 1975-81 (horse only) ..$45.00
Hobo (Hobo Gift Set), buckskin, 1975-81 ....$60.00
Jet Run (Trakehner Family), dk red chestnut w/star, 1992-94 ....$15.00
Johar (Toys R Us/Drinkers of the Wind), rose gray, 1993 ....$18.00
Keen (Equestrian Team Gift Set), chestnut, 1980-93 ....$15.00
Kelso (Jeremy), brn, 1993-94 ....$20.00
Kelso (Sears/Draw Horses w/Sam Savitt), bay w/blk points, full set, 1992 ....$40.00
Lipizzan Stallion, alabaster, 1975-80 ....$35.00
Lipizzan Stallion (Toys R Us/Unicorn III), blk w/gold accents, 1997 ....$35.00
Man O'War, red chestnut, 1975-90 ....$20.00

Man O'War (Apache), gray w/darker gray points, w/ribbon, 1995-96 ....$15.00
Merrylegs (Black Beauty Family), dapple gray, 1980-93 ...$15.00
Mesteno, dk buckskin w/dk brn points, 1992-98 ....$15.00

Might Tango (US Equestrian Team Set), 1980 – 91, dapple gray, $15.00. (Photo courtesy Carol Karbowiak Gilbert)

Mustang Foal (JC Penney/Breyer Mustang Family), grulla, 1992 ....$12.00
Mustang Mare (Mustang Family), chestnut pinto, 1976-90 ..$15.00
Mustang Stallion (Mustang Family), sorrel, 1976-90 ....$15.00
Mustang Stallion (Three Piece Family Gift Set), grulla pinto, 1998-2000 ....$35.00
Pegasus (Lipizzan Stallion), alabaster (no trim color), 1984-87 ....$50.00
Polo Pony, bay w/blk points, 1976-82 ....$40.00
Quarter Horse Foal (Montgomery Ward/Appaloosa Family), blk w/hind blanket, 1982 ....$18.00
Quarter Horse Foal (Quarter Horse Family), lt bay w/blk points, 1974-93 ....$12.00
Quarter Horse Mare (Three Piece Family Gift Set), dk chestnut, 1998-2000 ....$15.00
Quarter Horse Stallion (Sears/Collector's Edition Appaloosa Family), chestnut blanket, 1986 ....$20.00
Rearing Stallion, bay w/blk points, 1965-80 ....$25.00
Rearing Stallion (Promises), dk bay pinto, 1994-95 ....$15.00
Reflections Mesteno, buckskin w/blk points, 1996 ....$15.00
Ruffian, dun w/blk points, from Glory & Plank Jump Gift Set, 1995-96 (horse only) $18.00
Ruffian (Glory & Plank Jump Gift Set), dun w/blk points, 1995-96 ....$30.00
Ruffian (Lula), bay w/blk points, 1991-92 ....$18.00
Scamper (Barrel Racer), bay w/blk points, 1998 ....$20.00
Silky Sullivan, brn w/darker mane & tail, 1975-90 ....$18.00
Silky Sullivan (T-Bone), flea-bit gray, 1991-92 ....$15.00
Swamps (Black Silk), blk, 1997 ....$15.00
Swamps (Hawk), blk, 1991 ....$18.00
Terrang, dk brn, 1975-90 ....$20.00
Wahoo King, chestnut pinto, from Legendary Roping Horse & Calf Gift Set, 1999-current (horse only) $25.00

Wahoo King (Legendary Roping Horse & Calf Gift Set), chestnut pinto, 1999-current $35.00

STABLEMATE SCALE

Arabian Mare, bay, 1975-88..............................$9.00
Arabian Mare, gray, 1996-97 ....$4.00
Arabian Stallion, bay, 1975-88........................$10.00
Arabian Stallion (Sears/Stablemate Assortment III), blk, 1991 ....$9.00
Citation, bay, 1975-81.....................................$8.00
Draft Horse, dapple gray, 1989-94....................$9.00
Draft Horse, sorrel, 1976-81.............................$8.00
Morgan Stallion (Sears/Stablemate Assortment IV), blk blanket appaloosa, 1993...........................$7.00
Native Dancer, gray, 1976-94............................$7.00
Quarter Horse Stallion, palomino, 1976-88 ......$9.00
Saddlebred, blk, 1989-90.................................$13.00
Seabiscuit, bay, 1976-90...................................$9.00
Thoroughbred Mare, blk, 1975-88....................$8.00

TRADITIONAL SCALE

Action Stock Horse Foal (Cricket), brn bay, 1995-96......$18.00
Adios (Best Tango Quarter Horse), shaded bay, 1997.......$30.00

Adios, Clayton Quarter Horse, dappled palomino, 1995 – 96, $25.00. (Photo courtesy Carol Karbowiak Gilbert)

Adios (Rough & Ready Quarter Horse), dk reddish points, 1993-95 ....$32.00
Appaloosa Performance Horse (Chief of Fourmile), blk blanket, 1999 ....$30.00
Appaloosa Performance Horse (Stallion, JC Penney), gray blanket, ca 1984...$55.00
Balking Mule, matt liver chestnut, 1968-71 ....$100.00
Belgian, chestnut, 1965-80 ....$40.00
Black Beauty, diamond-shaped star, various stockings, 1979-88...$32.00
Black Beauty (Dream Weaver), sorrel, limited edition, 1991..$35.00
Black Beauty (Fade to Grey), dk dappled gray, 1989-90 ...$35.00

Black Stallion (Sapphire, Toys R Us/Medallion Series), buckskin, 1996..$40.00
Buckshot Famous Spanish Barb, chestnut pinto, 1988-89 ..$32.00
Cantering Welsh Pony, bay, blk points, yel ribbons, 1971-73 ....$110.00

Cantering Welsh Pony, chestnut, no ribbons, 1979 – 81, $50.00. (Photo courtesy Carol Karbowiak Gilbert)

Cantering Welsh Pony (Plain Pixie), red roan, 1992-93 ..$28.00
Cantering Welsh Pony (QVC Parade of Breeds), bay roan, 1995 ....$40.00
Clydesdale Foal, chestnut, 1969-89 ....$18.00
Clydesdale Foal (Satin Star), dk chestnut w/wht mane, 1994-95 ....$20.00
Clydesdale Mare, lt bay w/blk mane & tail, 1990-91 ......$30.00
Clydesdale Mare (JC Penney/Clydesdale Family), red bay, 1982-84 ....$50.00
Clydesdale Mare (Northumberland Flowergirl), bay w/blk points, 1999-current $30.00
Clydesdale Stallion, bay w/blk mane & tail, alternating wht & red bobs, red tail ribbon, ca 1972-89 ....$32.00
Clydesdale Stallion, glossy bay w/blk mane & tail, gold ribbons, ca 1958-63 ....$175.00
Clydesdale Stallion (Sears/Horses Great & Small Set), bl roan w/shaded body, yel & bl bobs, yel tail ribbon, 1992 ...$40.00
El Pastor Paso Fino, bay w/blk points, 1974-81 ....$35.00
Family Arabian Foal, bay w/blk points, 1989-90..............$16.00
Family Arabian Foal, glossy gray appaloosa w/blk points, 1963-67 ....$20.00
Family Arabian Foal (JC Penney), lt chestnut, 1983.......$25.00
Family Arabian Mare, bay w/blk points, 1967-74 ....$25.00
Family Arabian Mare, liver chestnut, 1988..................$32.00
Family Arabian Mare, woodgrain, 1963-67..................$65.00
Family Arabian Mare (Sears/Spirit of the Wind Set), dapple gray w/blk points, 1991.................................$40.00
Family Arabian Stallion, glossy palomino, 1961-66.........$20.00
Family Arabian Stallion (Sears/Arabian Horses of the World Set), alabaster w/blk points, 1991-92 ....$32.00
Family Arabian Stallion (Toys R Us/Medallion Series/No Doubt), red roan, 1997 ....$30.00
Fighting Stallion, bay, 1961-87........................$30.00
Fighting Stallion, glossy charcoal w/wht mane, tail, stockings, 1961-71 ....$120.00

Fighting Stallion, glossy Florentine w/wht points, 1963-65...$1,000.00

Fighting Stallion (Chaparral), buckskin pinto, limited edition, 1992 ....$40.00

Five-Gaiter, Wedgwood w/wht points, blk & bl ribbons, 1964-65...$1,000.00

Five-Gaiter (American Saddlebred), dapple gray, blk & red ribbons, 1987-88...$65.00

Five-Gaiter (JC Penney/Gaited Breeds of America), bay pinto, gold-on-wht ribbons, 1996 ....$35.00

Foundation Stallion, blk, no markings, 1977-87.............$25.00

Foundation Stallion (Azteca), dapple gray, 1980-87.........$35.00

Foundation Stallion (Fugir Cacador Lusitano Stallion), buckskin, limited edition, 1993................................$35.00

Foundation Stallion (JC Penney/Traditional Western Horse Collector Set), semigloss charcoal, 1987.........................$60.00

Friesian (Sears Wish Book/Dashing Dan), palomino, 1998 ....$40.00

Fury Prancer, glossy blk pinto w/wht mane & blk tail w/wht tip, blk saddle, no rider, 1954-63 ....$100.00

Fury Prancer, glossy blk pinto w/wht mane & blk tail w/wht tip, blk saddle, w/rider, 1954-63 ....$190.00

Fury Prancer, woodgrain, 1958-62.........................$350.00

Galiceno, bay w/blk points, 1978-82 ....$35.00

Gem Twist Champion Show Jumper, alabaster, red ribbons, 1993-95 ....$35.00

Grazing Foal, palomino, 1964-81 ....$28.00

Grazing Mare (Sears/Mare & Foal Set), blanket appaloosa w/blk points, 1989-90 ....$35.00

Haflinger (Horses International), sorrel w/gray or brn mane & tail, 1984-85 ....$32.00

Halla (JC Penney/International Equestrian Collector's Set), flea-bit gray, 1989...$40.00

Hanoverian, dk bay w/blk points, 1980-84................$35.00

Hanoverian (Your Horse Source), red chestnut, 1987....$100.00

Indian Pony, alabaster, red hand print on left haunch, bl square on left neck, 1970-71................................$200.00

Indian Pony, dk bay appaloosa w/blk points, 1973-85.......$35.00

Indian Pony (JC Penney/English Horse Collector's Set), red dun, 1988 ....$45.00

John Henry (JC Penney/Cowboy Pride Three Piece Horse Set, bay roan, 1998..$25.00

Jumping Horse (Sears), seal brn w/blk points, 1982-83 ....$80.00

Justin Morgan (Tri-Mi Boot Scootin' Boogie), blk spotted blaze, high wht stockings, 1996-97.............................$30.00

Khemosabi, red bay w/blk points, 1990-95....................$28.00

Lady Phase, chestnut, from Lynn Anderson's Gift Set, 1976-85, (horse only)..$40.00

Lady Phase (Breezing Dixie Appaloosa Mare), dk bay w/wht blanket, limited edition, 1988 ....$65.00

Lady Phase (Lynn Anderson's Gift Set), chestnut, 1976-85 ....$65.00

Legionario III, alabaster $30.00

Lying Down Foal, buckskin, 1969-73 ....$30.00

Lying Down Foal (JC Penney/Serenity Set), buckskin (yellowish), 1995 ....$20.00

Lying Down Unicorn (Toys R Us), glossy blk or wht, 1997, ea...$25.00

Lying Foal, 1969 – 84, black blanket appaloosa, $30.00. (Photo courtesy Carol Karbowiak Gilbert)

Man O'War, red chestnut, 1969-95 ....$25.00

Man O'War (General Lee's Horse Traveller), 1998-99.....$30.00

Midnight Sun Tennessee Walker, blk, wht (Xs) on red braids, 1972-87...$32.00

Midnight Sun Tennessee Walker, red bay w/blk points, red-on-wht braids, 1988-89 ....$35.00

Misty of Choncoteague, palomino pinto, 1972-current....$14.00

Morgan, bay, bald face, 1965-71 ....$55.00

Morgan, bay, w/star, 1965-71 ....$120.00

Morganglanz, chestnut, 1980-87 ....$28.00

Mustang Semi-Rearing, buckskin w/blk points, 1961-86..$30.00

Mustang Semi-Rearing, glossy charcoal w/wht mane & tail, 1961-70...$140.00

Mustang Semi-Rearing (American Mustang), sorrel, 1987-89 ....$42.00

Mustang Semi-Rearing (JC Penney/Wild Horses of America Set), semigloss blk w/left fore sock, 1993 ....$40.00

Nursing Foal (JC Penney/Frisky Foals Set), 1992, palomino pinto, 1992...$25.00

Nursing Foal (Sears/Pinto Mare & Suckling Foal Set), bay pinto, 1982-83 ....$28.00

Old Timer, alabaster (w/hat), 1966-76 ....$50.00

Old Timer (Montgomery Ward), alabaster (w/hat w/yel band), 1983 ....$55.00

Pacer, Dan Patch, red bay w/blk points, 1990 ....$45.00

Pacer (Aldens), blk, 1982...............................$110.00

Phar Lap (Galloping Thoroughbred), dk bay, 1989-90.....$28.00

Phar Lap (Toys R Us/Dustin), buckskin, 1995 ....$32.00

Pony of the Americas, bay/chestnut appaloosa, 1979-84..$28.00

Pony of the Americas (Country Store/Three Piece Horse Set), blk leopard appaloosa w/blk points, 1990-91 ....$38.00

Proud Arabian Foal, glossy alabaster, 1956-60 ....$28.00

Proud Arabian Foal, rose gray w/gray points, 1989-90......$25.00

Proud Arabian Mare, glossy alabaster, 1956-60 ....$125.00

Proud Arabian Mare, mahogany bay w/blk points, 1972-80..$40.00

Proud Arabian Mare (Sears/Arabian Mare & Foal Set), red bay pinto w/blk points, left hind sock, 1988.............$50.00

Proud Arabian Stallion (Black Horse Ranch), red bay w/blk points, 1987 ....$70.00

Proud Arabian Stallion (JC Penney/Arabian Stallion w/English Tack Set), bay w/blk points w/tack, 1983-84 ....$80.00
Proud Arabian Stallion (Sundown), sorrel, 1995-96 ....$30.00
Quarter Horse Gelding, buckskin w/blk points, 1961-80..$45.00
Quarter Horse Gelding (JC Penney/Traditional Horse Set), 1990...$42.00
Quarter Horse Yearling, liver chestnut, 1970-80..............$35.00

Quarter Horse Yearling, sandy bay blanket appaloosa, 1971 – 88, $40.00. (Photo courtesy Carol Karbowiak Gilbert)

Quarter Horse Yearling (Presentation Collection w/base), palomino, 1972-73...$150.00
Racehorse (Just About Horses/Phantom), dapple gray, blk halter, 1997 ....$50.00
Roemer (Toys R Us/Sandstone), lt bay, 1998.....................$40.00
Rugged Lark (Sears/Quiet Foxhunters Set), dapple gray, 1992 ....$35.00
Running Foal, glossy Florentine w/wht points, 1963-65.$700.00
Running Foal, smoke w/wht points, 1963-70.....................$32.00
Running Foal (Sears/Running Horse Family Set), bay w/blk points, 1984 ....$35.00
Running Mare, alabaster, 1961-72.....................................$60.00
Running Mare, woodgrain, 1963-65.................................$150.00
Running Mare (Sears/Running Horse Family Set), bay w/blk points, 1984 ....$50.00
Running Mare (Wild Diamond), bay w/blk points, 1994-95..$30.00
Running Stallion, blk appaloosa, 1968-81 ....$40.00
Running Stallion (Black Horse Ranch), dk chestnut, 1989 ..$110.00
Saddlebred Weanling (Just About Horses), sorrel, 1984...$150.00
San Domingo, chestnut pinto, 1978-87 ....$35.00
Scratching Foal, red roan w/chestnut points, 1970-73......$75.00
Sea Star Chincoteague Foal, buckskin, 1992-93...............$15.00
Secretariat (Sears/Race Horse Set), glossy chestnut, 1990..$35.00
Sham (Arabian Stallion & Frisky Foal I), dapple bay w/blk points, 1994 ....$35.00
Sherman Morgan Prancing, blk, 1991-92 ....$55.00
Shetland Pony, bay w/blk points, 1973-88 ....$20.00
Shire, honey sorrel, 1972-76 & 1978-80 ....$55.00
Shire (Riegseckers), palomino, 1985...............................$125.00

Sham, 1984 – 88, red bay, $45.00. (Photo courtesy Carol Karbowiak Gilbert)

Stock Horse Foal (American Buckskin), blk points, 1987-88...$20.00
Stock Horse Foal (Phantom Wings), brn or blk blanket appaloosa, 1979-82 ....$15.00
Stock Horse Mare (Paint Horse), dk chestnut pinto, 1989-90...$25.00
Stock Horse Mare (Sorrel Quarter Horse), sorrel, 1982-86..$28.00
Stock Horse Stallion (JC Penney/Brown & White Pinto), bay pinto, 1984...$40.00
Stock Horse Stallion (Tobiano Pinto), blk, 1981-88 ....$28.00
Stormy (Marguerite Henry's Stormy), chestnut pinto, 1977-current...$10.00
Stud Spider (Blanket Appaloosa), chestnut, 1990-91 ......$35.00
Stud Spider (Sears/Appaloosa-American Classic Set), bl roan semi-leopard appaloosa $45.00
Thoroughbred Mare (JC Penney Pride & Joy), lt chestnut, 1996 ....$32.00
Touch of Class, bay w/blk points, 1986-88 ....$30.00
Trakehner, bay w/blk points, brand on left thigh, 1979-84...$40.00
Western Horse, glossy blk pinto, w/orig saddle, 1954-76 ..$45.00
Western Horse, glossy blk pinto, w/out saddle, 1954-76...$25.00
Western Horse (Black Beauty), glossy blk w/gold accents, blk snap-girth saddle, 1956-60................................$75.00
Western Pony, palomino, w/out saddle, 1968-73 ....$20.00
Western Pony, palomino, w/saddle, 1968-73.....................$28.00
Western Prancing Horse, smoke, 1961-76.........................$30.00

OTHER ANIMALS

Black Angus Bull (standing), blk, 1978-current $20.00
Boxer, tan/fawn, 1958-74...$35.00
Buffalo, brn, 1965-91 ....$35.00
Cow (Holstein), blk & wht, 1972-89 ....$25.00
Elephant, battleship gray, w/boy......................................$100.00
Elephant, battleship gray, w/out boy.................................$65.00
Jasper the Market Hog, wht & gray, 1974-2000................$10.00
Kitten, gray-point Siamese, 1966-71 ....$50.00
Moose, med brn, 1966-96 ....$25.00
Pronghorn Antelope, 1971-76...$65.00
Rin Tin Tin, brn, 1958-66 ....$40.00

St Bernard, 1972-80..$40.00
Texas Longhorn Bull, sorrel, 1961-89................$25.00
Texas Longhorn Bull, woodgrain, 1963-66 .....$150.00

Bubble Bath Containers

Since back in the 1960s when the Colgate-Palmolive Company produced the first Soaky, hundreds of different characters and variations have been marketed, bought on demand of the kids who saw these characters day to day on TV by parents willing to try anything that might make bathtime more appealing. Purex made their Bubble Club characters, and Avon and others followed suit. Most Soaky bottles came with detachable heads made of brittle plastic which cracked easily. Purex bottles were made of a softer plastic but tended to loose their paint.

Rising interest in US bubble bath containers has created a collector market for those made in foreign countries, i.e., UK, Canada, Italy, Germany and Japan. Licensing in other countries creates completely different designs and many characters that are never issued here. Foreign containers are generally larger and are modeled in great detail, reminiscent of the bottles that were made in the US in the '60s. Prices may seem high, considering that some of these are of fairly recent manufacture, but this is due to their limited availability and the costs associated with obtaining them in the United States. We believe these prices are realistic, though many have been reported much higher. Rule of thumb: pay what you feel comfortable with — after all, it's meant to be fun. And remember, value is affected to a great extent by condition. Unless noted otherwise, our values are for examples in near-mint condition. Bottles in very good condition are worth only about 60% to 65% of these prices. For slip-over styles, add 100% if the bottle is present.

Advisors: Matt and Lisa Adams (A7).

Alvin (Chipmunks), Colgate-Palmolive, red sweater w/wht A, w/puppet, neck tag & contents, M, A7......................$50.00
Alvin (Chipmunks), Colgate-Palmolive, wht sweater w/blk A, cap head, NM, A7 ....$30.00
Alvin (Chipmunks), DuCair Bioescence, holding microphone, w/contents, M, A7...$25.00
Anastasia, Kid Care, 1997, NM...$8.00
Astroniks Robot, DuCair Bioescence, gold buck-toothed robot on red base, EX+, A7...$15.00
Atom Ant, Purex, 1965, NM $70.00
Augie Doggie, Purex, orange w/gr shirt, orig tag, EX, A7 ..$45.00
Baba Looey, Purex, 1960s, brn w/bl scarf & gr hat, NM, A7 ..$35.00
Baba Looey, Roclar (Purex), 1977, NM $15.00
Baloo Bear, Colgate-Palmolive, 1966, NM, A7 ....$40.00
Bambi, Colgate-Palmolive, sitting & smiling, NM, A7....$25.00
Bamm-Bamm, Purex, blk or gr suspenders, NM, A7, ea ..$35.00
Barney, Kid Care, 1994, yel hat & puppy slippers, NM.......$8.00
Barney Rubble, Milvern (Purex), bl outfit w/yel accents, NM, A7 ....$35.00
Barney Rubble, Roclar (Purex), brn outfit w/yel accents, MIB, A7 ....$25.00
Batman, Colgate-Palmolive, 1966, NM, A7.....................$75.00

Batman, Kid Care, 1995, bl & gray w/yel belt, M, A7 ......$10.00
Batmobile, Avon, 1978, bl & silver w/decals, EX, A7 ......$20.00
Bear, Tubby Time, 1960s, NM $45.00

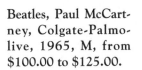

Beatles, Paul McCartney, Colgate-Palmolive, 1965, M, from $100.00 to $125.00.

Beauty & the Beast, Cosrich, orig tag, M, A7, ea from $5 to ..$8.00
Betty Bubbles, Lander, 1960s, NM $15.00
Big Bad Wolf, Tubby Time, cap head, EX, A7 ....$35.00
Biker Mice From Mars, Grosvenor/England, 1994, NM ...$30.00
Bobo Bubbles, Lander, 1950s, NM $30.00
Bozo the Clown, Colgate-Palmolive, 1960s, NM, A7 ......$30.00
Bozo the Clown, Step Riley, cap head, EX, A7.................$30.00
Broom Hilda, Lander, 1977, EX, A7...................................$30.00
Brutus (Popeye), Colgate-Palmolive, 1965, red shorts w/red & wht striped shirt, EX, A7 ....$40.00
Bugs Bunny, Colgate-Palmolive, gray, wht & orange w/cap ears, EX, A7 ....$30.00
Bugs Bunny, Colgate-Palmolive, lt bl & wht, NM, A7.....$25.00
Bugs Bunny, Kid Care, in swim trunks w/surfboard, M, A7...$8.00
Bullwinkle, Colgate-Palmolive, several color variations, NM, A7, ea..$45.00
Bullwinkle, Fuller Brush, 1970s, NM $60.00
Butterfly Princess Barbie, Kid Care, orig tag, M, A7..........$5.00
Care Bear, AGC, 1984, NM $10.00
Casper the Ghost, Colgate-Palmolive, wht w/lavender & bl accents, EX, A7 ....$30.00
Cecil (Beany & Cecil), Purex, 1962, NM.........................$25.00
Cement Truck, Colgate-Palmolive, bl & gray w/movable wheels, EX+, A7 ....$35.00
Charlie Brown, Avon, red baseball outfit, NM, A7 ....$20.00
Cinderella, Colgate-Palmolive, 1960s, movable arms, NM, A7..$35.00
Creature From the Black Lagoon, Colgate-Palmolive, 1960s, NM, A7 ....$125.00
Darth Vader, Omni, 1981, NM...$20.00
Deputy Dawg, Colgate-Palmolive, 1960s, gray, yel & bl w/cap hat, VG (VG box), A7...$30.00
Dick Tracy, Colgate-Palmolive, 1965, NM, A7 ....$50.00
Dino & Pebbles, Cosrich, 1994, NM..................................$15.00

Donald Duck, Colgate-Palmolive, 1960s, M, $30.00.
(Photo courtesy Greg Moore and Joe Pizzo)

Dopey, Colgate-Palmolive, 1960s, purple, yel & red, NM, A7 ....$25.00
Dum Dum, Purex, 1964, wht w/pk accents, rare, EX, A7....$100.00
El Cabong, Knickerbocker (Purex), blk, yel & wht, rare, G+, A7 ....$50.00
Elmer Fudd, Colgate-Palmolive, 1960s, hunting outfit, NM, A7 ....$30.00
Elmo, Kid Care, 1997, NM...$10.00
Ernie (Sesame Street), Minnetonka, holding rubber duckie, orig tag, M, A7 ....$8.00
ET, Avon, 1984, NM...$15.00
Felix the Cat, Colgate-Palmolive, 1960s, bl, red or blk, EX, A7 ....$30.00
Fozzie Bear, Muppet Treasure Island, Calgon, 1996, NM..$10.00
Frankenstein, Colgate-Palmolive, 1963, NM....................$95.00
Fred Flintstone, Milvern (Purex), 1960s, red outfit w/blk accents, EX+, A7 ....$30.00
Garfield, Kid Care, lying in tub, NM, A7 ....$10.00
Genie (Aladdin), Cosrich, M, A7 ....$5.00
GI Joe (Drill Instructor), DuCair Bioescence, 1980s, NM.$15.00
Goofy, Colgate-Palmolive, 1960s, red, wht & blk w/cap head, NM, A7..$20.00
Gravel Truck, Colgate-Palmolive, 1960s, orange & gray w/movable wheels, EX, A7................................$35.00
Gumby, M&L Creative Packaging, 1987, NM.................$30.00
Harriet Hippo, Merle Norman, in party hat, NM, A7......$10.00
Holly Hobbie, Benjamin Ansehl, 1980s, several variations, M, ea..$15.00
Huckleberry Hound, Knickerbocker (Purex), bank, red & blk, orig neck tag, 15", M, A7 ....$60.00
Huckleberry Hound, Secol, 1960s, bl w/yel bow tie, rare, EX, A7..$100.00
Huckleberry Hound & Yogi Bear, Milvern (Purex), 1960s, MIB (sealed), A7 ....$75.00
Hunchback of Notre Dame, Kid Care, in robe w/sceptor, M, A7..$5.00

Incredible Hulk, Benjamin Ansehl, standing on rock, M, A7...$25.00
Jasmine (Aladdin), Cosrich, w/bird or mirror, orig tag, M, A7, ea $6.00

Jiminy Cricket, Colgate-Palmolive, 1960s, yellow and red jacket, EX+, $30.00.
(Photo courtesy Greg Moore and Joe Pizzo)

Kermit the Frog, Calgon, Treasure Island outfit, w/tag, M, A7 ....$8.00
King Louie (Jungle Book), Colgate-Palmolive, slip over, 1960s, NM...$15.00
Lamb Chop (Shari Lewis), Kid Care, holding duck, w/tag, M, A7..$8.00
Lippy the Lion, Purex, 1962, purple vest, rare, EX, A7 ....$35.00
Little Mermaid, Kid Care, 1991, tail up, NM...................$10.00
Little Orphan Annie, Lander, 1977, NM, A7, from $25 to....$30.00
Lucy (Peanuts), Avon, 1970, red dress w/top hat, MIB, A7 ...$20.00
Mad Hatter, Avon, 1970, bronze w/pk hat & clock, EX, A7..$20.00
Magilla Gorilla, Purex, 1960s, NM...................................$35.00
Marvin the Martian, Warner Bros, 1996, NM $15.00
Mickey Mouse, Avon, 1969, MIB, A7.............................$30.00

Mr Magoo, Colgate-Palmolive, 1960s, M, $35.00.

Mickey Mouse, Colgate-Palmolive, red shirt & wht pants, cap head, NM, A7...$30.00

Mickey Mouse as Band Leader, Colgate-Palmolive, 1960s, NM...$30.00

Mighty Mouse, Colgate-Palmolive, yel & red, lg head, EX, A7...$25.00

Miss Piggy, Muppet Treasure Island, Calgon, 1996 ....$10.00

Morocco Mole, Purex, 1966, rare, EX, A7 ....$100.00

Mr Do Bee, Manon Freres, 1960s, w/sticker, rare, NM, A7..$75.00

Mr Jinks w/Pixie & Dixie, Purex, w/contents, MIB, A7 ...$40.00

Mr Magoo, Colgate-Palmolive, 1960s, red or bl outfit, EX, A7, ea...$25.00

Mr Robottle, Avon, 1971, MIB, A7 ....$20.00

Mummy, Colgate-Palmolive, 1960s, NM, A7.................$100.00

Oil Truck, Colgate-Palmolive, gr & gray w/movable wheels, VG, A7...$35.00

Pebbles & Dino, Cosrich, Pebbles on Dino's back, M, A7..$6.00

Pebbles Flintstone, Purex, 1960s, several color variations, EX, A7, ea...$35.00

Peter Potamus, Purex, 1960s, purple w/wht or yel shirt, w/contents & orig tag, M, A7, ea...$25.00

Pinocchio, Colgate-Palmolive, 1960s, red & wht or solid brn or red, M, A7, ea...$25.00

Pluto, Colgate-Palmolive, 1960s, orange w/cap head, NM, A7...$25.00

Popeye, Colgate-Palmolive, 1967, wht w/bl accents, w/contents, NMIB, A7...$50.00

Popeye, Colgate-Palmolive, 1977, bl w/wht accents, NM, A7...$35.00

Porky Pig, Colgate-Palmolive, 1960s, red or bl tuxedo, EX+, A7, ea...$25.00

Power Rangers, Kid Care, 1994, any character, M, A7, ea..$8.00

Punkin Puss, Purex, 1966, M, $50.00.

Quick Draw McGraw, Purex, 1960s, several variations, NM, A7, ea...$30.00

Race Car, Tidy Toys, several variations w/movable wheels, NMIB, A7, ea..$40.00

Raggedy Ann, Lander, 1960s, NM $65.00

Rainbow Brite, Hallmark, 1995, NM $10.00

Red Power Ranger, Centura (Canada), 1994 ....$20.00

Ricochet Rabbit, Purex, movable arms, VG, A7 ....$35.00

Robin, Colgate-Palmolive, 1966, EX, A7 ....$75.00

Robocop, Cosway, 1990, NM $15.00

Schoolhouse, Avon, 1968, red, MIB, A7 ....$15.00

Schroeder, Avon, 1970, MIB, A7.....................................$25.00

Secret Squirrel, Purex, 1966, rare, VG, A7 ....$45.00

Simba, Kid Care, M, A7..$6.00

Simon (Chipmunks), Colgate-Palmolive, 1960s, 3 color variations, w/tag & puppet, M, A7, ea................................$50.00

Skeletor (Masters of the Universe), DuCair Bioescence, NM, A7...$15.00

Smokey Bear, Colgate-Palmolive, 1960s, NM, A7 ....$25.00

Snaggle Puss, Purex, 1960s, pk w/gr hat, NM, A7 ....$50.00

Snoopy & Woodstock, Avon, 1974, on red skis, MIB, A7...$20.00

Snoopy as Flying Ace, Avon, 1969, MIB, A7 ....$20.00

Snoopy as Flying Ace on Doghouse, Minnetonka, M, A7..$10.00

Snoopy as Joe Cool, Minnetonka, 1996, NM $10.00

Snoopy in Tub of Bubbles, Avon, 1971, MIB, A7............$20.00

Snow White, Colgate-Palmolive, 1960s, bank, bl & yel, VG, A7...$25.00

Snow White, Colgate-Palmolive, 1960s, movable arms, NM..$35.00

Snow White, 1993, M, $10.00. (Photo courtesy Greg Moore and Joe Rizzo)

Speedy Gonzales, Colgate-Palmolive, 1960s, EX, A7.......$30.00

Spider-Man, Benjamin Ansehl, orig tag, M, A7 ....$25.00

Splash Down Space Capsule, Avon, 1970, MIB, A7 ....$20.00

Spouty Whale, Roclar (Purex), bl, orig card, M, A7 ....$25.00

Squiddly Diddly, Purex, 1960s, purple w/pk shirt, rare, NM, A7...$75.00

Superman, Avon, 1978, complete w/cape, MIB, A7.........$40.00

Sylvester & Tweety, DuCair Bioescence, 1988, Sylvester holding Tweety, M, from $10 to..$15.00

Sylvester & Tweey, Minnetonka, Tweety standing on Sylvester's head, M, A7..$8.00

Superman, Colgate-Palmolive, 1965, EX, $50.00.

Sylvester the Cat w/Microphone, Colgate-Palmolive, 1960s, EX, A7 ....$30.00

Tasmanian Devil in Inner Tube, Kid Care, 1992, EX, A7...$8.00

Teenage Mutant Ninja Turtles, Kid Care, 1990, any character, M, A7, ea...$8.00

Tennessee Tuxedo, Colgate-Palmolive, 1965, w/ice-cream cone, NM, A7...$30.00

Tex Hex (Brave Starr), DuCair Bioescence, w/tag, M, A7 .$15.00

Theodore (Chipmunks), Colgate-Palmolive, wht w/bl T or gr w/red sweater & gr T, w/tag & puppet, M, A7, ea......$50.00

Three Little Pigs, Tubby Time, 1960s, any character, rare, M, A7, ea...$40.00

Thumper, Colgate-Palmolive, 1960s, EX, A7 ....$25.00

Tic Toc Tiger, Avon, orange w/yel hands & hat, M, A7 ...$15.00

Tic Toc Turtle, Avon, 1968, gr w/yel face & pk hands, MIB, A7 ....$20.00

Tommy (Rugrats), Kid Care, 1977, NM $8.00

Top Cat, Colgate-Palmolive, 1963, yel w/bl or red shirt, EX, A7, ea...$30.00

Touche Turtle, Purex, lying on stomach, gr w/pk accents, EX, A7...$30.00

Touche Turtle, Purex, standing, NM, A7 ....$40.00

Tweety on Cage, Colgate-Palmolive, NM, A7..................$30.00

Wally Gator, Purex, 1963, rare, VG, A7 ....$35.00

Watering Can, Avon, 1962, yel w/flowers, NM, A7 ....$15.00

Wendy the Witch, Colgate-Palmolive, 1960s, NM, A7 ...$30.00

Whitey the Whale, Avon, 1959, EX, A7 ....$15.00

Winkie Blink Clock, Avon, 1975, yel w/bl hands & hat, MIB, A7 ....$15.00

Winnie the Pooh, Johnson & Johnson, 1997, NM $6.00

Winsome Witch, Purex, 1965, rare, NM, A7...................$30.00

Wolfman, Colgate-Palmolive, 1963, red pants, NM, A7 ...$100.00

Woodsy Owl, Lander, early 1970s, EX...........................$35.00

Woody Woodpecker, Colgate-Palmolive, 1977, NM.......$45.00

Yaaky Doodle Duck, Roclar (Purex), w/contents & neck card, M, A7...$25.00

Yoda (Star Wars), Omni, 1981, NM $20.00

Yogi Bear, Milvern (Purex), brn, rare, NM, A7 ....$50.00

Yogi Bear, Purex, powder/bank, gr hat & yel tie, NM, A7 ..$30.00

101 Dalmatians, Kid Care, red & blk doghouse w/2 pups, M, A7 .$5.00

FOREIGN

Action Man (Night Creeper), Rosedew Ltd/UK, 1994, topper, silver gun, w/suction cups, M, A7 ....$15.00

Action Man (Space Commando), Rosedew Ltd/UK, 1994, bl & gray combat uniform, M, A7 ....$35.00

Aladdin, Grosvenor/UK, 1994, flying on carpet w/girl & monkey, M, A7..$30.00

Alf, PE/Germany, 1980s, NM, A7....................................$40.00

Alice in Wonderland, Aidee International Ltd/UK, 1993, NM, A7 ....$35.00

Alice in Wonderland, Aidee/England, 1993, NM $35.00

Aliens, Grosvenor/UK, 1993, topper, M, A7 ....$25.00

Ariel (Little Mermaid), Damascar/Italy, 1995, sitting on purple rock, NM, A7..$35.00

Asterix, Euromark/Switzerland, 1992, wing-headed man w/yel mustache, M, A7, from $50 to...................................$75.00

Baloo (Jungle Book), Boots/England, 1965, NM $70.00

Barbie, Grosvenor/UK, 1994, wht & pk striped/heart dress, holding rose, M, A7..$30.00

Barney Rubble, Damascar/Italy, 1995, wearing Water Buffalo hat, w/bowling ball, M, A7.......................................$35.00

Bart Simpson, Grosvenor, 1991, w/wht towel & soap, NM, A7 ....$35.00

Bashful, Grumpy & Happy, Grosvenor/UK, 1994, topper, M, A7 ....$15.00

Batman, Grosvenor/UK, 1992, gray suit & blk cape, NM, A7 ....$35.00

Batman (Animated), Damascar/Italy, 1995, NM, A7.......$35.00

Batmobile (Batman Forever), Prelude/UK, 1995, blk w/silver wheels, body lifts for bottle, NM, A7 ....$35.00

Beano (Dennis the Menace), Rosedew/UK, 1990, red & blk striped outfit, blk curly hair, NM, A7......................$35.00

Bear (Forever Friends), Grosvenor/UK, 1995, in wooden tub w/bubbles, NM, A7...$30.00

Beast (Beauty & the Beast), Centura/Canada, 1993, topper, hand under chin, M, A7..$15.00

Beast (Beauty & the Beast), Prelude/UK, 1994, movable arms, comes apart at waist, NM, A7................................$35.00

Belle (Beauty & the Beast), Prelude/UK, 1994, yel gown, w/hands crossed & head tilted back, NM, A7 ....$35.00

Benjamin Bunny (Beatrix Potter), Grosvenor/UK/Canada, 1991, topper, holding bag & onion, red & gr hat, M, A7....$30.00

Big Bird, Grosvenor/UK, 1995, topper, sitting in bubbles w/teddy bear, M, A7 ....$15.00

Big Breakfast Teapot, Euromark/England, 1994, NM $25.00

Boo Boo Bear, Damascar/Italy, M, A7 ....$35.00

Bubba Saurus, Belvedere/Canada, 1995, bank, pk dinosaur, M, A7 ....$15.00

Bubbasaurus, Belvedere/Canada, 1990s, NM $10.00

Bugs Bunny, Centura/Canada, 1994, in purple robe holding carrot, NM, A7...$30.00

Bugs Bunny, Prelude/UK, 1995, cloth hand puppet, slips over bottle, M, A7..$35.00

California Raisin, Belvedere/Canada, 1994, bank, holding microphone, w/sunglasses, NM, A7 ....$15.00

Captain Scarlet (Thunderbirds), Euromark/UK, 1993, kneeling, red & blk outfit, NM, A7 ....$35.00

Casper the Ghost, Damascar/Italy, 1995, sitting on pumpkin, glow-in-the-dark, M, A7 ....$35.00

Casper's Friends, Damascar/Italy, 1995, 3 ghosts sitting on trunk, NM, A7...........................$35.00

Cinderella, Damascar/Italy, 1994, gray & wht gown, NM, A7 ....$35.00

Cindy Bear, Damascar/Italy, 1995, sitting on purple rock, NM, $35.00. (Photo courtesy Matt and Lisa Adams)

Cookie Monster, Jim Henson/PI/UK, 1995, bl w/wht cloth towel, NM, A7...........................$30.00

Daffy Duck, Prelude/England, 1995, NM $35.00

Daffy Duck, Prelude/UK, 1994, wearing shark suit, M, A7 ...$35.00

Daffy Duck, Prelude/UK, 1995, cloth hand puppet, slips over bottle, M, A7 ....$35.00

Darth Vader, Grosvenor/UK, 1995, holding light saber, movable arm, M, A7 ....$35.00

Dewey Duck (Donald's Nephew), Rosedew/UK, 1994, bl outfit & hat, M, A7 ....$35.00

Dino (Flintstones), Rosedew/UK, 1993, M, A7................$35.00

Dino (Flintstones), Rosedew/UK, 1993, topper, NM, A7...$20.00

Doc & Dopey, Grosvenor/UK, 1994, topper, NM, A7......$15.00

Doctor Who, DMS Toiletries/UK, 1987, bl phone booth bottle, MIB, A7 ....$40.00

Doctor X (Action Man), Rosedew Ltd/UK, 1994, topper, bald man w/X on back of head, NM, A7 ....$15.00

Donald Duck, Centura/Canada, 1994, standing on red base, NM, A7...........................$30.00

Donald Duck, Grosvenor/England, 1997, NM...........................$25.00

Donald Duck (Mickey & Pals), Centura/Canada, 1995, Donald driving yel boat, NM, A7 ....$25.00

Dopey & Sneezy, Grosvenor/ UK, 1994, NM, A7 ....$35.00

Dot (Animaniacs), Prelude/UK, 1995, topper, girl w/yel flower in hair, NM, A7...........................$15.00

Ernie (Sesame Street), Grosvenor/UK, 1995, topper, in tub w/rubber duckie, NM, A7...........................$15.00

Fireman Sam, Rosedew/England, 1993, NM....................$30.00

Flipper Riding a Wave, Euromark/England, 1996, NM $25.00

Florence (Magic Roundabout), Grosvenor/UK, 1993, girl w/flower, orange & bl outfit, M, A7 ....$35.00

Forever Friends, Grosvenor/England, 1995, NM $20.00

Fred Flintstone, Damascar/Italy, 1994, w/golf club, NM, A7...$35.00

Fred Flintstone, Rosedew/UK, 1994, w/bowling ball, NM, A7 ....$35.00

Garfield, Grosvenor/England, 1981, NM $35.00

Genie (Aladdin), Centura/Canada, 1994, holding microphone, NM, A7...........................$25.00

Genie (Aladdin), Damascar/Italy, 1994, released from lamp, real hair, NM, A7 ....$35.00

Goofy, Centura/Canada, 1995, coming out of shower/tub, M, A7..$30.00

Hulk Hogan, Fulford/Canada, 1986, Hulkmania on shirt, NM...........................$20.00

James Bond (Roger Moore), BRB/England, 1970s, NM .$120.00

Jasmin (Aladdin), Damascar/Italy, 1994, in purple dress, head tilted, M, A7 ....$35.00

Jemima Puddleduck (Beatrix Potter), Grosvenor/UK, 1991, topper, bl bonnet, M, A7 ....$30.00

John Smith (Pocahontas), Centura/Canada, 1995, sitting on rock, opens at waist, NM, A7...........................$25.00

Joker (Batman), Prelude/UK, 1995, topper, NM, A7 ....$15.00

Jungle Land Boat, Top Care/Canada, 1995, NM $15.00

Little Mermaid, Prelude/UK, 1994, sitting on clear bubbles, NM, A7 ....$30.00

Magic Princess, Boots/England, 1996, NM $20.00

Magic School Bus (Teacher), Kid Care/Canada, 1995, purple & wht dress, dragon at base, NM, A7...........................$35.00

Mario (Mario Bros), Grosvenor/UK, 1992, red & bl outfit w/red hat, M, A7 ....$35.00

Mask (Jim Carey movie), Prelude/England, 1996, NM $30.00

Matchbox Dump Truck, Grosvenor/UK, 1995, yel, blk & red, cap on front, NM, A7...........................$30.00

Matchbox Indy Race Car, Grosvenor/UK, 1995, topper, red w/blk & wht checker flag, NM, A7...........................$15.00

Matchbox 4x4 Truck, Grosvenor/UK, 1995, topper, on big rock, NM, A7...........................$15.00

Mickey Mouse, Centura/Canada, 1994, NM $25.00

Mickey Mouse, Disney/Canada, 1994, pie-eyed, traditional outfit, M, A7 ....$35.00

Mickey Mouse, Prelude/UK, 1994, topper, pie-eyed, legs crossed, NM, A7...........................$15.00

Minnie Mouse, Disney World/UK, 1989, red dress, yel shoes, flower & umbrella, NM, A7...........................$35.00

Minnie Mouse, Prelude/UK, 1994, topper, pie-eyed, w/legs crossed, red skirt, NM, A7...........................$15.00

Minnie Mouse in Boat, Centura/Canada, 1995, NM........$15.00

Mr Blobby, Rosedew Ltd/UK, 1992, pk w/yel polka dots, gr bug eyes, M, A7 ....$35.00

Mr Men, UK, yel & orange hat, M, A7...........................$40.00

Nala (Lion King), Centura/Canada, 1994, sitting on pk base, M, A7...........................$30.00

Noddy, Grosvenor/UK, 1994, topper, sitting w/coffee cup, NM, A7 ....$15.00

Noddy, Noddy Enterprises/BBC/UK, 1994, red shirt & lt bl shorts, NM, A7...........................$35.00

Olive Oyl, Damascar/Italy, 1990s, NM.............................$45.00

Olive Oyl, Damascar/Italy, 1995, sitting w/hands clasped, NM, A7 ....$35.00

Oscar the Grouch, Grosvenor/UK, 1994, taking a bath in trash can w/I Hate Baths sign, NM, A7 ....$35.00

Paddington Bear, Coltsmore/England, 1992, NM.............$30.00

Paddington Bear, Grosvenor/UK, 1989, topper, EX (EX window box), A7...$20.00

Papa Smurf, IMPS Brussels/Germany, 1991, bl w/red pants & hat, M, A7 ....$40.00

Pebbles & Bamm-Bamm, Damascar/Italy, 1995, sitting on saber-tooth tiger, M, A7...$35.00

Percy (Thomas the Tank), Grosvenor/UK, 1994, topper, sitting on blk tracks & gray bricks, NM, A7 ....$15.00

Peter Rabbit, Grosvenor/UK/Canada, 1991, bl coat, NM, A7.$30.00

Piglet (Winnie the Pooh), Prelude/UK, topper, waving, M, A7 ....$20.00

Pingo Penguin, Grosvenor/UK, 1995, w/seal on sled, NM, A7 ....$30.00

Pocahontas, Grosvenor/UK, 1995, standing on rock in dive position, NM, A7...$35.00

Pocahontas, Grosvenor/UK, 1995, topper, in canoe w/raccoon, NM, A7..$15.00

Polly Pocket's Castle, Centura/Canada, 1995, NM...........$25.00

Popeye, Rosedew Ltd/UK, 1987, on black base holding spinach can, NM, $40.00.
(Photo courtesy Matt and Lisa Adams)

Postman Pat, Rosedew/UK, 1991, mailman w/lg brn mail bag, NM, A7...$35.00

Postman Pat's Cat on Mailbox, Rosedew/England, 1995, NM .$25.00

Pumba (Lion King), Prelude/England, 1995, NM.............$30.00

Pumba (Lion King), Prelude/UK, 1994, M, A7 ....$35.00

Robin, Damascar/Italy, 1995, squatting on eagle head statue, M, A7 ....$35.00

Rockin' Raisin, Belvedere/Canada, 1980s, NM.................$20.00

Rupert Bear, UK, 1995, topper, in yel airplane, M, A7.....$20.00

R2-D2, Cliro/England, 1978, NM $55.00

Scooby Doo, Damascar/Italy, 1995, brn, M, A7................$40.00

Scrappy Doo & Creature, Damascar/Italy, 1995, NM.......$35.00

Simba (Lion King), Prelude/UK, 1994, sitting on rock w/paw up, NM, A7...$35.00

Sleeping Beauty, Damascar/Italy, 1994, holding roses, NM, A7 ....$35.00

Sneezy & Sleepy, Grosvenor/UK, 1994, topper, NM, A7 ...$15.00

Snoopy & the Red Baron, Grosvenor/UK, red & blk heart goggles & red cloth scarf, NM, A7 ....$35.00

Snow White, Damascar/Italy, 1994, standing w/bluebird on hand, M, A7..$35.00

Snow White, Rosedew/UK, 1994, standing w/arms crossed, M, A7 ....$35.00

Space Precinct Monster, Euromark/UK, 1995, topper, bl, gr, or tan, NM, A7, ea...$15.00

Spider-Man, Euromark/UK, 1995, walking over trash can & tire, NM, A7...$35.00

Super Mario Brothers, Grosvenor/England, 1992, NM.....$35.00

Superman, Euromark/England, 1994, NM $35.00

Superman, Euromark/UK, 1994, flying pose, comes apart at waist, M, A7..$35.00

Superman, Euromark/UK, 1994, topper, kneeling, M, A7 ..$25.00

Sylvester, Prelude/UK, 1995, cloth hand puppet, slips over bottle, M, A7 ....$35.00

Tasmanian Devil, Prelude/UK, 1995, mouth wide open, movable arms, M, A7 ....$35.00

Thomas the Tank, Rosedew/UK, 1986, red & bl, NM, A7..$35.00

Tom & Jerry, Damascar/Italy, 1995, sitting in drum, NM, A7 .$35.00

Tom & Jerry, Damascar/Italy, 1995, sitting on Swiss cheese, M, A7 ....$35.00

Tweety Bird, Prelude/UK, 1995, bl robe & wht towel, NM, A7..$35.00

Two-Face (Batman), Prelude/UK, 1995, topper, NM, A7...$15.00

Uncle Bulgaria (Wombles), Euromark/UK, 1994, M, A7 ...$35.00

USS Enterprise (Star Trek), Euromark/England, 1994, NM...$30.00

Wallace & Gromit, Euromark/England, 1996, NM $30.00

Warrior Dude, Belvedere/Canada, 1990s, NM.................$15.00

Wile E Coyote, Prelude/UK, 1995, w/rocket backpack, NM, A7 ....$35.00

Wilma Flintstone, Damascar/Italy, 1993, standing on turtle shell, M, A7..$35.00

Winnie the Pooh, Boots/UK, blk base, M, A7 ....$35.00

Yakko (Animaniacs), Prelude/UK, 1995, topper, blk & wht w/red nose, NM, A7 ....$15.00

Yogi Bear, Damascar/Italy, 1994, standing on gr base w/purple grass, M, A7 ....$35.00

101 Dalmatians, Grosvenor/UK, 1994, father w/pup on head & 1 between legs, NM, A7 ....$35.00

101 Dalmatians, Grosvenor/UK, 1994, topper, pups on pillow w/red sunglasses, M, A7 ....$15.00

Buddy L

First produced in 1921, Buddy L toys have escalated in value over the past few years until now. Early models in good original condition (or restored, for that matter) often bring prices well into the four figures when they hit the auction block. The business was started by Fred Lundahl, founder of Moline Pressed Steel Co., who at first designed toys for his young son, Buddy. They were advertised as being 'Guaranteed Indestructible,' and indeed they were so sturdy and well built that they just about were. Until wartime caused a shortage, they were made of heavy-gauge pressed steel. Many were based on actual truck models; some were ride-ons, capable of supporting a grownup's weight. Fire trucks with hydraulically activated water towers and hoisting towers that actually worked kept little boys entertained for hours. After the war, the quality of Buddy Ls began to decline, and wood was used to some extent. Condition is everything. Remember that unless the work is done by a professional restorer, overpainting and amateur repairs do nothing to enhance the value of a toy in poor condition. Professional restorations may be expensive, but they may be viable alternatives when compared to the extremely high prices we're seeing today. In the listings that follow, toys are all pressed steel unless noted.

Advisors: Kerry and Judy Irvin (K5).

See also Advertising; Aeronautical; Boats; Catalogs; Character, TV, and Movie Collectibles.

CARS AND BUSSES

Army Combat Car, wood, gr w/cannon in bk, 15", VG, A $270.00

Bus, gr w/red & gold stripe, NP disk wheels w/2 side-mounted spares, 28", VG, A.................................$2,625.00

Flivver Coupe, blk w/aluminum spoke wheels, 11", prof rstr, A $300.00

Flivver Huckster, 1920s, blk w/aluminum wheels & red-pnt spokes, 14", rare, EX, A..$4,875.00

Ford Model T, #201B, EX $375.00

Greyhound Bus, No 755, bl & wht w/blk rubber tires, w/up w/battery-op taillight, 16", NMIB, A......................$750.00

Greyhound Bus, 1940s, wood, bl & wht w/logo, doors open, 18", EX, A $715.00

Motor Coach, 1920s, gr w/aluminum disk wheels & 2 side-mounted spares, door opens, 28½", EX, A $2,100.00

Motor Coach, 1920s, orange & blk w/aluminum disk wheels & 2 side-mounted spares, door opens, 30", EX, A $2,325.00

School Bus, 1920s, mk School District..., yel w/aluminum disk wheels & 2 side spares, opening door, 29", G, A..$1,275.00

Station Wagon, 1940s, wood w/metal grille, headlights & hubcaps, 18½", CG...$240.00

Woodie Station Wagon, wood, maroon w/simulated woodgrain finish, celluloid windows, 19", EX, A.......................$525.00

CONSTRUCTION

Aerial Tramway, NP, w/working crane, 34", rare, VG, A $2,325.00

Cement Mixer, gr w/drum & chute mounted on wheeled base, lever action, 11", NM, A...$340.00

Cement Mixer, 1920s, gray w/red decals, 18", VG, A.....$490.00

Derrick, red & blk w/rotating boom, 18", EX+, A..........$715.00

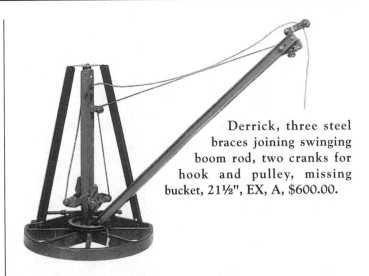

Derrick, three steel braces joining swinging boom rod, two cranks for hook and pulley, missing bucket, 21½", EX, A, $600.00.

Hoisting Tower, blk, 38", missing chutes, G, A $300.00

Hoisting Tower, gray w/3 telescopic chutes, 38", G, A ..$1,800.00

Hy-Way Maintenance Truck w/Cement Mixer, 1949, bl & yel w/red drum, blk rubber tires, complete w/ramp, EX, A.............$450.00

Mobile Power Digger, orange & yel w/red chassis, gr crane, 20", EX $190.00

Railway Steam Shovel, blk w/red corrugated roof, decal on side, 22½", EX, A $525.00

Road Roller, 1920s, gr & red, chain drive, 20", EX, A .$2,025.00

Steam Shovel, 1950s, bl w/orange roof & scoop, 20", G, A...$100.00

Traveling Bucket Loader, clamshell on movable base, blk frame w/cross supports on sides, 33x46", EX, A..............$1,650.00

Trench Digger, yellow and red, actually digs 1½" trench, scarce, 24", VG, $2,250.00.

FIREFIGHTING

Aerial Ladder Truck, wood, red w/blk tires, unpnt ladder, lever action elevates ladder, 19", VG, A..........................$270.00

Hook & Ladder Truck, 1920s, mk CFD, red w/aluminum disk wheels, removable boom & ladders, 29", VG, A $75.00

Hook & Ladder Truck, 1920s, red w/aluminum disk wheels & red hubs, w/tow boom, hose reel & 4 ladders, 26", VG, A..$975.00

Hydraulic Aerial Ladder Truck, 1920s, red w/aluminum disk wheels, NP ladder, 38", G, A.................$715.00
Hydraulic Water Tower Truck, #205D, 1930-31, red w/silver latticework tower, VG, A...................$1,875.00
Ladder Truck, 1920s, red w/aluminum disk wheels, NP ladders, 26", prof rstr, A.........................$525.00
Ladder Truck, 1930s, red w/2 yel ladders, blk rubber tires w/emb red spokes, electric headlights, 21", VG, A.............$340.00
Pumper Truck, mk CFD, 1920s, red w/aluminum disk wheels, NP boiler, 24", prof rstr, A...................$750.00
Pumper Truck, 1920, red w/aluminum disk wheels & red hubs, NP boiler & railed rear platform, orig pull cord, 23½", EX.........................$1,875.00

Pumper Truck, #205AB, 1930 – 31, EX, A, $1,000.00.

Water Tower Truck, rider, red w/NP tower, blk rubber tires w/red-pnt hubs, battery-op headlights, 45", scarce, VG, A...$2,070.00

OUTDOOR TRAINS

Boxcar, red, 21", prof rstr, A $270.00
Caboose, 1920s, red, opening doors at front & rear, 20", VG, A...$975.00
Cattle Car, 1920s, red, 21", EX, A...............................$490.00
Gondola, blk w/decals, 21", VG, A................................$490.00
Locomotive & Tender, 1920s, blk, 42", VG, A...........$2,700.00
Tank Car, red w/blk frame & straps, ladder on sides, filler caps on top, 15½", NM, A..........................$1,425.00
Tank Car, red w/blk frame & trucks, center ladder, 20", VG, A..$1,040.00
Tank Car, yel w/blk frame & trucks, center ladder, 19½", EX ..$1,125.00
Wrecking Crane, blk w/red corrugated roof, working swivel crane, 36", NM, A...$2,900.00

TRUCKS AND VANS

Army Supply Truck w/Cannon, 1950s, gr w/canvas cover, 22", NMIB, A...$225.00
Army Transport Truck & Trailer, wood, gr w/yel lettering, 28", VG, A..$150.00
Army Transport w/Cannon, spoke wheels, 27", EX, from $250 to...$270.00

Army Truck, original Army canvas, #506, 18", NM (EX box), A, $300.00.

Baggage Truck, 1927, blk cab w/yel stake bed, VG+.......$700.00
Big Show Circus Truck, #484, wood, 25½", EX..............$675.00

Coal Truck, 1920s, aluminum disk wheels, side chute, 26", professionally restored, A, $1,000.00.

Coal Truck, 1920s, blk w/blk rubber tires & emb red spokes, hopper body & opening chute, 26", NM, A.........$6,375.00
Daytona Racing Team Truck, #5463, lt bl & wht, 1964, NM (EX box)..$360.00
Dump Truck, blk open cab, aluminum disk wheels w/red-pnt hubs, crank-operated chain dump, orig pull string, 24", EX, A..$825.00
Dump Truck, 1920s, blk open cab w/red fr, aluminum disk wheels w/red hubs, A-fr rope lift dump, 25", G, A ..$375.00
Emergency Auto Wrecker, #3317, NM..........................$190.00
Excavator Truck w/Steam Shovel, 2-tone bl & gray truck w/orange steam shovel, 21", EX, A $675.00
Express Line Delivery Truck, 1930s, red & gr w/blk rubber tires & emb red spokes, removable roof, 24", NM, A......$600.00
Federal Van Lines Moving Truck, wood, bl & red w/wht lettering, blk wheels w/NP hubs, 21", VG $675.00
Flivver Huckster, blk w/aluminum spoke wheels, 14", scarce, G, A...$1,275.00
Flivver Pickup Truck, blk w/aluminum spoke wheels, 12", rstr, A...$300.00
Ford Model T Pickup, 1920s, blk w/aluminum tires & red-pnt spokes, 12", EX, A $825.00

Hy-Way Maintenance Truck w/Cement Mixer, yel & bl enclosed cab, yel & red mixer in flat bed, w/ramp, 10½", EX, A $450.00

Hy-Way Transport, #5263, red plastic cab, wht steel trailer w/MPS decals, 19", NMIB......................................$115.00

Hydraulic Dump Truck, 1950s, red & gray w/Deluxe decal on door, blk rubber tires w/fancy hubs, 20", EX, A $225.00

Hydraulic Missile Launcher, MIB...................................$525.00

Ice Delivery Truck, doorless cab, chained tailgate, canvas tarp, ice blocks, disc wheels, earliest of ice truck models, 26", VG, A, $1,700.00.

International Harvester Red Baby Dump Truck, rare version w/opening doors, 23", rstr, A $900.00

Junior City Dray Truck, bl w/yel stake bed, blk rubber tires w/red-pnt hubs, 24", G, A...$1,200.00

Junior City Dray Truck, blk w/yel stake body, red decal, blk rubber tires w/emb red spokes, 24", NM, A $1,875.00

Junior Tanker Truck, blk & gr w/blk rubber tires & emb red spokes, doors open, 25", VG, A $2,100.00

Mister Buddy Ice Cream Van, EX...................................$150.00

Moving Truck, wood, red & blk, opening rear door, 27", VG, A $245.00

One-Ton Flivver Truck, blk w/aluminum disk wheels & red-pnt spokes, 14½", rare, EX, A $3,300.00

Pickup w/Camper & Jeanie B Boat, 1950s, #5433-B, MIB .$190.00

Railway Express Truck, #763, 1950s, yel & gr w/Serve Ice Cream decal, 22", NMIB, A $1,500.00

Railway Express Truck, 1950s, gr w/decal of little girl writing letter to Santa, opening rear doors, 22", EX, A............$750.00

Sand Loader and Dump Truck, 1950s, EX/NM (EX box), A, $1,100.00.

Ranch Truck, 1950s, tan w/brn horse head decals on doors, wht-wall tires, 12½", VG, A $75.00

Red Baby Dump Truck, 1920s, doorless cab, spoke wheels, 24", EX, A $900.00

Sand & Gravel Truck, #202A, blk w/red frame & hubs, opening doors, old rpt, 26" L, EX $2,450.00

Stake Truck, 1920s, blk open cab w/red stakes, aluminum tires w/red-pnt spokes, 25", rstr, A $1,050.00

US Mail Truck, brn w/slide-off roof, 20½", NM, A $270.00

Wild Animal Circus Truck, 1960s, red w/wht-wall tires, complete w/animals, 26", VG, A $270.00

Wrecker, #358, 1940s, wood, gr & brn w/blk tires, 18", NMIB, A $490.00

Wrecker, open drivers seat, red and black with brass hand rails, aluminum wheels, decals, 18", EX, A, $3,000.00.

Wrecker, rider, red & wht w/emb spoke wheels, child's seat & hand-op crank in back, 32", NM, A $2,625.00

Wrecker, 1940s, wood, brn & gr w/Buddy L Wood Toys decals, 18", EX $170.00

Zoo-A-Rama Truck & Cage, complete w/plastic monkeys & polar bears, 20", NMIB, A $190.00

Miscellaneous

Buddy L Roundup, complete, MIB....................................$375.00

Cash Register, pressed steel, yel & red, complete w/play money, 9x10", M, A $270.00

Catapault Airplane and Hanger, red and yellow plane with 10" wingspan, 8x12" hanger, 1930s, EX, A, $1,000.00.

Savings & Recording Bank, litho tin, 5", EX, A $35.00

Tool Chest, wood, w/tray, apron & tool list (no tools), 23" L, EX, A $300.00

Transport Plane, cream, 4 props, 19½", EX.................$240.00
Wrench, blk w/red logo in center, 6" L, EX $180.00

Building Blocks and Construction Toys

Toy building sets were popular with children well before television worked its mesmerizing influence on young minds; in fact, some were made as early as the end of the eighteenth century. Important manufacturers include Milton Bradley, Joel Ellis, Charles M. Crandall, William S. Tower, W.S. Read, Ives Manufacturing Corporation, S.L. Hill, Frank Hornby (Meccano), A.C. Gilbert Brothers, The Toy Tinkers, Gebruder Bing, R. Bliss, S.F. Fischer, Carl Brandt Jr., and F. Ad. Richter (see Anchor Stone Building Sets by Richter). Whether made of wood, paper, metal, glass, or 'stone,' these toys are highly prized today for their profusion of historical, educational, artistic, and creative features.

Richter's Anchor (Union) Stone Building Blocks were the most popular building toy at the beginning of the twentieth century. As early as 1880, they were patented in both Germany and the USA. Though the company produced more than six hundred different sets, only their New Series is commonly found today (these are listed below). Their blocks remained popular until WWI, and Anchor sets were one of the first toys to achieve international 'brand name' acceptance. They were produced both as basic sets and supplement sets (identified by letters A, B, C, or D) which increased a basic set to a higher level. There were dozens of stone block competitors, though none were very successful. During WWI the trade name Anchor was lost to A.C. Gilbert (Connecticut) who produced Anchor blocks for a short time. Richter responded by using the new trade name 'Union' or 'Stone Building Blocks,' sets considered today to be Anchor blocks despite the lack of the Richter's Anchor trademark. The A.C. Gilbert Company also produced the famous erector sets which were made from about 1913 through the late 1950s.

Note: Values for Richter's blocks are for sets in very good condition; (+) at the end of the line indicates these sets are being reproduced today.

Advisors: Bill Bruegman (T2); George Hardy (H3), Anchor Stone Building Sets by Richter.

Auto-Dux 60 Constructor Set, for a Veritas, Borgward, and Volkswagen, EX, with parts and tools tied in box, A, $375.00.

American Logs, Halsam, complete, EX (EX box) $40.00
American Plastic Bricks, Halsam, 1950s, complete, EX (EX container) $35.00
American Skyline, Elgo, 1950s, complete, NM (VG box), T2..$35.00
Big Boy Tinkertoy, Spalding/Toy Tinkers, 1950s-60s, complete, EX (G container)...$45.00
Big Tinkertoy Construction Set for Little Hands, Questor, 1976, complete, EX (VG container) $25.00
Block City #B-500, Plastic City Block Inc, 1960, complete, EX (EX container), T2 ....$50.00
Building Bricks, Auburn Rubber, 1950s, complete, EX (EX container), T2...$40.00
Busy Mechanic Construction Kit, Renwal #375-198, complete, EX (EX box) $300.00
Construx Action Building System, Fisher-Price, #6331 Mobile Missiles, Military Series, complete, NMIB, from $50 to $75.00

Curtain Wall Builder No. 640, Toy Tinkers/Spalding, 1959 – 64, EX (EX container), $40.00. (Photo courtesy Craig Strange)

Dirigible Builder, Schoenhut, complete, assembles to 21", EX (EX box)...$1,000.00
Double Tinkertoy, Toy Tinkers, 1927, complete, EX (EX container) $40.00
Drawbridge Set, Renwal #155, complete, rare, EX (EX box) $250.00
Erector Set, Gilbert #3, complete, MIB $200.00
Erector Set, Gilbert #4, complete, VG (VG box)..........$125.00
Erector Set, Gilbert #5½, complete, MIB.....................$175.00
Erector Set, Gilbert #6½, complete, MIB.....................$165.00
Erector Set, Gilbert #7, complete, EX (EX wooden box)..$250.00
Erector Set, Gilbert #7½, complete, EX (EX wooden box) $350.00
Erector Set, Gilbert #8, complete, EX (EX wooden box)..$850.00
Erector Set, Gilbert #8½, complete, EX (EX wooden box) $950.00
Erector Truck, Gilbert A, complete, 27" assembled, VG (VG box), A...$250.00
Executive Tinkertoy, Spalding, 1966, complete, EX (EX container) $35.00
Falcon Building Lumber Set, complete, EX (EX wood box), A...$150.00

Fire Alarm Set, Hasbro, complete, NM (EX box), A $135.00
Giant Tinker, Toy Tinkers, 1926, complete, EX (EX box) $225.00
Girder & Panel Constructioneer Set #8, Kenner, complete, EX (EX box) $100.00
Girder & Panel Hydro-Dynamic Double Set #18, Kenner, complete, VG (VG box) $200.00
Girder & Panel Hydro-Dynamic Single Set #17, Kenner, complete, VG (VG box) $175.00
Girder & Panel International Airport, Kenner, 1977, complete, EX (EX box)...$40.00
Junior Tinkertoy, Spalding, 1963, complete, EX (EX container) $25.00
Major Tinkertoy, Spalding, 1964, complete, EX (EX container) $25.00
Mold Master Road Builder, Kenner, 1964, complete, NMIB, J2..$125.00
Motorized Tinkertoy, Toy Tinkers/Spalding, complete, EX (EX container) $60.00
Roadster Constructor, Meccano, complete, EX (EX box) ...$500.00
Special Tinkertoy w/Windlass Drive, Toy Tinkers, 1943, complete, EX (EX container) $35.00
Spirit of St Louis Airplanes, Metalcraft, builds over 250 airplanes, complete, VG (VG box), A $450.00
Super City Heliport Building Set, Ideal, 1968, complete, EX (EX vinyl case) $50.00
Super City Skyscraper Building Set, Ideal, 1960s, complete, EX (EX box) $75.00
Super City Town & Country, Ideal, complete, VG (VG box) $50.00
Teck Tinkertoy, Spalding, 1963, complete, EX (EX container) $25.00
Tinker Zoo No 717, Spalding, 1970, complete, EX (EX container) $15.00
Tinker Zoo No 737, Spalding, 1962-70, complete, EX (EX container) $25.00
Tinkerblox, Toy Tinkers, 1917-20, complete, EX (EX box) $60.00
Tinkertoy Design Blocks, Questor, complete, EX (EX container) $30.00
Tinkertoy Giant Engineer, Questor, complete, EX (EX container) $25.00
Tinkertoy Junior Architect, Questor, complete, EX (EX container) $25.00
Tinkertoy Little Designer, Questor, complete, EX (EX container)...$25.00
Tinkertoy Locomotive & Driver, Questor, complete, EX (EX container) $15.00
Tinkertoy Master Builder, Questor, complete, EX (EX container)...$25.00
Tinkertoy No 30040, Gabriel, complete, EX (EX container) ..$25.00
Tinkertoy No 30060, Gabriel, motorized, complete, EX (EX container) $35.00
Tinkertoy Panel Builder #600, Toy Tinkers/Spalding, 1958, complete, EX (EX container) $30.00
Tinkertoy Panel Builder #800, Toy Tinkers/Spalding, 1958, complete, EX (EX container) $40.00
Train Kit, Metalcraft, builds stock car, caboose & trucks, complete, EX (EX box) $300.00
Tru Model Erector Set, Gilbert #1, complete, EX (EX box) ..$200.00

Tinkertoy Safe Power Unit, battery-operated, #177, M, from $40.00 to $60.00. (Photo courtesy Craig Strange)

Wonder Builder Tinkertoy, Spalding, 1953-54, complete, EX (EX container) $30.00
Wood Airplane Kit, Fisher-Price Arts & Crafts, 1982-85, MIB, C13..$25.00

Wood Racer Kit, Fisher-Price Arts & Crafts, 1983 – 85, Indy racer with four wood wheels, two plastic spoilers and sheet of decals, MIB, $25.00. (Photo courtesy Brad Cassity)

Wood Sailboat Kit, Fisher-Price Arts & Crafts, 1982-85, MIB, C13..$25.00

ANCHOR STONE BUILDING SETS BY RICHTER

American House & Country Set #206, VG, H3.............$600.00
American House & Country Set #208, VG, H3.............$600.00
American House & Country Set #210, VG, H3.............$700.00
DS Set #E3, w/metal parts & roof stones, VG, H3 ....$80.00
DS Set #3A, w/metal parts & roof stones, VG, H3..........$80.00

DS Set #5, w/metal parts & roof stones, VG, H3 ....$150.00
DS Set #5A, w/metal parts & roof stones, VG, H3 ....$150.00
DS Set #7, w/metal parts & roof stones, VG, H3 ....$270.00
DS Set #7A, w/metal parts & roof stones, VG, H3 ....$200.00
DS Set #9A, w/metal parts & roof stones, VG, H3 ....$250.00
DS Set #11, w/metal parts & roof stones, VG, H3 ....$675.00
DS Set #11A, w/metal parts & roof stones, VG, H3 .....$300.00
DS Set #13A, w/metal parts & roof stones, VG, H3 .....$325.00
DS Set #15, w/metal parts & roof stones, VG, H3 ......$1,500.00
DS Set #15A, w/metal parts & roof stones, VG, H3 .....$475.00
DS Set #19A, w/metal parts & roof stones, VG, H3 .....$475.00
DS Set #21A, w/metal parts & roof stones, VG, H3 .....$975.00
DS Set #23A, w/metal parts & roof stones, VG, H3 .....$750.00
DS Set #25A, w/metal parts & roof stones, VG, H3 ...$1,500.00
DS Set #27, w/metal parts & roof stones, VG, H3 .....$6,000.00
DS Set #27B, w/metal parts & roof stones, VG, H3 ....$2,000.00
Fortress Set #402, VG, H3..$100.00
Fortress Set #402A, VG, H3 ....$130.00
Fortress Set #404, VG, H3...$250.00
Fortress Set #404A, VG, H3 ....$275.00
Fortress Set #406, VG, H3...$500.00
Fortress Set #406A, VG, H3 ....$400.00
Fortress Set #408, VG, H3...$1,000.00
Fortress Set #408A, VG, H3 ....$800.00
Fortress Set #410, VG, H3...$1,800.00
Fortress Set #410A, VG, H3 ....$1,000.00
Fortress Set #412A, VG, H3 ....$1,500.00
Fortress Set #414, VG, H3...$5,000.00
German House & Country Set #301, VG, H3................$500.00
German House & Country Set #301A, VG, H3 ....$500.00
German House & Country Set #303, VG, H3 ....$1,000.00
German House & Country Set #303A, VG, H3 ....$2,000.00
German House & Country Set #305, VG, H3 ....$3,000.00
GK-AF Great-Castle Set, VG, H3...............................$9,950.00
GK-NF Set #6, VG, H3 (+) $140.00
GK-NF Set #6A, VG, H3 (+) $160.00
GK-NF Set #8, VG, H3...$300.00
GK-NF Set #8A, VG, H3 (+) $180.00
GK-NF Set #10, VG, H3...$480.00
GK-NF Set #10A, VG, H3 (+) $200.00
GK-NF Set #12, VG, H3...$680.00
GK-NF Set #12A, VG, H3 (+) $250.00
GK-NF Set #14A, VG, H3...$250.00
GK-NF Set #16, VG, H3 ....$1,180.00
GK-NF Set #16A, VG, H3...$300.00
GK-NF Set #18A, VG, H3...$400.00
GK-NF Set #20, VG, H3 ....$2,000.00
GK-NF Set #20A, VG, H3...$500.00
GK-NF Set #22A, VG, H3...$500.00
GK-NF Set #24A, VG, H3...$600.00
GK-NF Set #26A, VG, H3...$1,000.00
GK-NF Set #28, VG, H3 ....$4,000.00
GK-NF Set #28A, VG, H3...$1,200.00
GK-NF Set #30A, VG, H3...$1,200.00
GK-NF Set #30A, VG, H3...$1,200.00
GK-NF Set #32B, VG, H3...$1,600.00
GK-NF Set #34, VG, H3 ....$7,000.00
KK-NF Set #5, VG, H3..$110.00

KK-NF Set #5A, VG, H3..$100.00
KK-NF Set #7, VG, H3...$200.00
KK-NF Set #7A, VG, H3..$115.00
KK-NF Set #9A, VG, H3..$120.00
KK-NF Set #11, VG, H3...$315.00
KK-NF Set #11A, VG, H3...$275.00
KK-NF Set #13A, VG, H3...$300.00
KK-NF Set #15A, VG, H3...$450.00
KK-NF Set #17A, VG, H3...$750.00
KK-NF Set #19A, VG, H3..$2,500.00
KK-NF Set #21, VG, H3..$4,500.00
Neue Reihe Set #102, VG, H3..$100.00
Neue Reihe Set #104, VG, H3..$150.00
Neue Reihe Set #106, VG, H3..$200.00
Neue Reihe Set #108, VG, H3..$300.00
Neue Reihe Set #110, VG, H3..$600.00
Neue Reihe Set #112, VG, H3.....................................$1,000.00
Neue Reihe Set #114, VG, H3.....................................$1,500.00
Neue Reihe Set #116, VG, H3.....................................$2,000.00

California Raisins

The California Raisins made their first TV commercials in the fall of 1986. The first four PVC figures were introduced in 1987, the same year Hardee's issued similar but smaller figures, and three 5½" Bendees became available on the retail market. In 1988 twenty-one more Raisins were made for retail as well as promotional efforts in grocery stores. Four were graduates identical to the original four characters except standing on yellow pedestals and wearing blue graduation caps with yellow tassels. Hardee's increased their line by six.

In 1989 they starred in two movies: *Meet the Raisins* and *The California Raisins — Sold Out*, and eight additional characters were joined in figurine production by five of their fruit and vegetable friends from the movies. Hardee's latest release was in 1991, when they added still four more. All Raisins issued for retail sales and promotions in 1987 and 1988 (including Hardee's) are dated with the year of production (usually on the bottom of one foot). Of those released for retail sales in 1989, only the Beach Scene characters are dated, and these are actually dated 1988. Hardee's 1991 series are also undated.

Advisors: Ken Clee (C3) and Larry DeAngelo (D3).
Other Sources: C11, W6.

Applause, Captain Toonz, w/bl boom box, yel glasses & sneakers, Hardee's Second Promotion, 1988, sm, M, from $1 to...$3.00
Applause, FF Strings, w/bl guitar & orange sneakers, Hardee's Second Promotion, 1988, sm, M, from $1 to $3.00
Applause, Michael Raisin, Special Edition, 1989, M........$15.00
Applause, Rollin' Rollo, w/roller skates, yel sneakers & hat mk H, Hardee's Second Promotion, 1988, sm, M, from $1 to...$3.00
Applause, SB Stuntz, w/yel skateboard & bl sneakers, Hardee's Second Promotion, 1988, sm, M, from $1 to $3.00
Applause, Trumpy Trunote, w/trumpet & bl sneakers, Hardee's Second Promotion, 1988, sm, M, from $1 to $3.00

Applause, Waves Weaver I, w/yel surfboard connected to foot, Hardee's Second Promotion, 1988, sm $3.00

Applause, Waves Weaver II, w/yel surfboard not connected to foot, Hardee's Second Promotion, 1988, sm, M $2.00

Applause-Claymation, Banana White, yellow dress, Meet the Raisins First Edition, 1989, M, $20.00. (Photo courtesy Larry DeAngelo)

Applause-Claymation, Lick Broccoli, gr & blk w/red & orange guitar, Meet the Raisins First Edition, 1989, M $20.00

Applause-Claymation, Rudy Bagaman, w/cigar, purple shirt & flipflops, Meet the Raisins First Edition, 1989, M......$20.00

CALRAB, Blue Surfboard, board connected to foot, Unknown Promotion, 1988, M..$35.00

CALRAB, Blue Surfboard, board in right hand, not connected to foot, Unknown Promotion, 1987, M, $50.00. (Photo courtesy Larry DeAngelo)

CALRAB, Christmas Issue, 1988, w/candy cane, M.........$12.00

CALRAB, Christmas Issue, 1988, w/red hat, M $12.00

CALRAB, Guitar, red guitar, First Commercial Issue, 1988, M..$8.00

CALRAB, Hands, left hand points up, right hand points down, Post Raisin Bran Issue, 1987, M $2.00

CALRAB, Hands, pointing up w/thumbs touching head, First Key Chains, 1987, M $5.00

CALRAB, Hands, pointing up w/thumbs touching head, Hardee's First Promotion, 1987, sm, M $3.00

CALRAB, Microphone, right hand in fist w/microphone in left, Post Raisin Bran Issue, 1987, M $2.00

CALRAB, Microphone, right hand points up w/microphone in left, Hardee's First Promotion, 1987, M.......................$3.00

CALRAB, Microphone, right hand points up w/microphone in left, First Key Chains, 1987, M.....................................$5.00

CALRAB, Saxophone, gold sax, no hat, First Key Chains, 1987, M $5.00

CALRAB, Saxophone, gold sax, no hat, Hardee's First Promotion, 1987, sm, M $3.00

CALRAB, Saxophone, inside of sax pnt red, Post Raisin Bran Issue, 1987, M $2.00

CALRAB, Singer, microphone in left hand not connected to face, First Commercial Issue, 1988, M........................$6.00

CALRAB, Sunglasses, index finger touching face, First Key Chains, 1987, M...$5.00

CALRAB, Sunglasses, index finger touching face, orange glasses, Hardee's First Promotion, 1987, M...................$3.00

CALRAB, Sunglasses, right hand points up, left hand points down, orange glasses, Post Raisin Bran Issue, 1987, M .$2.00

CALRAB, Sunglasses II, eyes not visible, aqua glasses & sneakers, First Commercial Issue, 1988, M............................$4.00

CALRAB, Sunglasses II, eyes visible, aqua glasses & sneakers, First Commercial Issue, 1988, M $35.00

CALRAB, Winky, hitchhiking pose & winking, First Commercial Issue, 1988, M...$6.00

CALRAB-Applause, AC, 'Gimme-5' pose, Meet the Raisins Second Edition, 1989, M..$225.00

CALRAB-Applause, Alotta Stile, purple boom box, Hardee's Fourth Promotion, 1991, sm, MIP (w/collector's card) ..$15.00

CALRAB-Applause, Anita Break, shopping w/Hardee's bags, Hardee's Fourth Promotion, 1991, sm, MIP (w/collector's card) $15.00

CALRAB-Applause, Bass Player, w/gray slippers, Second Commercial Issue, 1988, M $8.00

CALRAB-Applause, Benny, w/bowling ball & bag, Hardee's Fourth Promotion, 1991, sm, MIP (w/collector's card) $15.00

CALRAB-Applause, Boy in Beach Chair, orange glasses, brn base, Beach Theme Edition, 1988, M $20.00

CALRAB-Applause, Boy w/Surfboard, purple board, brn base, Beach Theme Edition, 1988, M $20.00

CALRAB-Applause, Boy w/Surfboard (not connected to foot), brn base, Beach Theme Edition, 1988, M..................$20.00

CALRAB-Applause, Cecil Tyme (Carrot), Meet the Raisins Second Promotion, 1989, M $250.00

CALRAB-Applause, Girl with Boom Box, purple glasses, green shoes, Beach Theme Edition, 1988, M, $20.00.

CALRAB-Applause, Drummer, Second Commercial Issue, 1988, M..$10.00

CALRAB-Applause, Girl with Tambourine, green shoes and bracelet, Beach Theme Edition, 1988, M, $15.00.

CALRAB-Applause, Girl w/Tambourine (Ms Delicious), yel shoes, Second Commercial Issue, 1988, M $15.00

CALRAB-Applause, Hip Band Guitarist (Hendrix), w/headband & yel guitar, Third Commercial Issue, 1988, M..........$30.00

CALRAB-Applause, Hip Band Guitarist (Hendrix), w/headband & yel guitar, Second Key Chains, 1988, sm, M...........$65.00

CALRAB-Applause, Hula Girl, yel shoes & bracelet, gr skirt, Beach Theme Edition, 1988, M $20.00

CALRAB-Applause, Lenny Lima Bean, purple suit, Meet the Raisins Second Promotion, 1989, M.........................$175.00

CALRAB-Applause, Microphone (female), yel shoes & bracelet, Third Commercial Issue, 1988, M...............$12.00

CALRAB-Applause, Microphone (female), yel shoes & bracelet, Second Key Chains, 1988, sm, M................$45.00

CALRAB-Applause, Microphone (male), left hand extended w/open palm, Second Key Chains, 1988, sm, M........$45.00

CALRAB-Applause, Mom, yel hair, pk apron, Meet the Raisins Second Promotion, 1989, M, from $150 to $200.00

CALRAB-Applause, Piano, bl piano, red hair, gr sneakers, Meet the Raisins First Edition, 1989, M..............................$35.00

CALRAB-Applause, Saxophone, blk beret, bl eyelids, Third Commercial Issue, 1988, M $15.00

CALRAB-Applause, Singer (female), reddish purple shoes & bracelet, Second Commercial Issue, 1988, M $12.00

CALRAB-Applause, Sunglasses, Graduate w/index fingers touching face or Sax Player, Graduate Key Chains, 1988, M, ea...$85.00

CALRAB-Applause, Valentine, boy holding heart, Special Lover's Edition, 1988, M...$8.00

CALRAB-Applause, Valentine, girl holding heart, Special Lover's Edition, 1988, M..$8.00

CALRAB-Claymation, Graduate on yel base, Post Raisin Bran, 1988, M, from $45 to..$65.00

CALRAB-Claymation, Sunglasses, Singer, Hands, Saxophone, Graduate on yel base, Post Raisin Bran, 1988, ea, from $45 to $65.00

MISCELLANEOUS

Activity Book, 5½x8½"...$20.00

Backpack, maroon & yel w/3 figures, 1987, EX, W6........$30.00

Balloon, lead singer, CTI Industries, 1988, EX, W6...........$8.00

Bank, cereal box w/lid, plastic, EX, W6, from $10 to $15.00

Bank, Sun Maid Raisin in orange sunglasses and sneakers stands beside box, marked 1987, CALRAB, 7½", from $20.00 to $25.00.

Baseball Cap, 1988, EX, W6...$5.00

Beach Towel, CALRAB, M...$35.00

Belly Bag, bl or yel nylon fabric w/Conga Line, 1988, EX, W6, ea..$25.00

Book, Birthday Boo Boo, 1988, EX, W6 ....$12.00

Book, Raisin the Roof, 1988, EX, W6..............................$12.00

Bookmark, various images, M, D3, ea................................$5.00

Bulletin Board, Singer & Conga Line or Beach Scene, 1988, MIP, W6, ea...$25.00

Chalkboard, Singer & Conga Line, Rose Art, 1988, MIP, W6 ....$25.00

Clay Factory, Rose Art, 1988, complete, MIB...................$40.00

Colorforms, MIB...$25.00

Coloring Book, California Raisins on Tour, Marvel, 1988, unused, EX $12.00

Crayon-By-Number Set, Rose Art, 1988, complete, MIB...$40.00

Cross-Stitch Pattern, Leaflet #1, #3, #4 or #6, 1988, M, W6, ea...$12.00

Doll, vinyl w/suction cups, 1987, lg version, EX, W6 ....$5.00

Doll, vinyl w/suction cups, 1987, sm version, EX, W6......$10.00

Door Knob Hanger, various images, 9x4", M, D3, ea..........$7.00

Figure, Imperial Toy, 1987, inflatable vinyl, 42", MIB, W6, from $40 to..$50.00

Game, California Raisin board game, Decipher Inc, 1987, MIB, from $15 to..$20.00

Key Chain, glasses & orange tennis shoes, metal, 1988, MOC, W6...$5.00

Official Fan Club Watch Set, MIP, P12 ....$30.00

Patch, Ice Capades w/Raisin Singer, felt, 1988, EX, W6.....$8.00

Picture Album, 1988, EX, W6...$25.00

Poster, Join the California Raisin Club, 1990, EX, W6 ....$12.00

Puffy Stick-On, 1987, EX, W6 ....$10.00

Punching Bag, Imperial Toys, 1987, inflatable, 36", MIB, W6..$60.00

Puppet, female figure w/yel or gr shoes, Bendy/Sutton Happenings, 1988, MIB, W6, ea $30.00

Puppet, male w/yel shoes & glasses, Bendy/Sutton Happenings, 1988, MIB, W6 ....$35.00

Puzzle, American Publishing, 1988, 500 pcs, MIB, W6 ....$20.00

Record, California Raisins Sing the Hit Songs, 78 rpm, Priority Records, 1987, EX (EX sleeve), W6............................$20.00

Record, I Heard It Through the Grapevine, 45 rpm, 1988, EX (EX picture sleeve) $20.00

Record, Rudolph the Red-Nosed Reindeer, 45 rpm, 1988, EX (EX picture sleeve) $25.00

Record, Signed, Sealed, Delivered, 45 rpm, 1989, EX (EX picture sleeve)..$20.00

Record, When a Man Loves a Woman, 45 rpm, 1989, EX (EX picture sleeve) $20.00

Sandwich Stage, Del Monte Fruit Snacks, MIB, from $50 to ..$75.00

School Kit, w/promotion ideas, activities, recipes, etc, 1988, M, W6 ....$30.00

School Kit, w/ruler, pencil sharpener, eraser & pencil holder, 1988, MOC...$30.00

Shoulder Bag, bl & orange w/dancing raisins, 1988, MOC, W6 ....$25.00

Sleeping Bag, purple, 1988, EX, W6...$40.00

Sticker Album, w/slide-o-scope, Diamond Publishing, 1988, M, W6 ....$15.00

Sunglasses, Raisin Hell, 8 different colors, M, D3, ea $8.00

Suspenders, I Heard It Through the Grapevine, yel, 1987, EX, W6, from $30 to...$35.00

Tambourine & Kazoo, Imperial Toy Corporation, 1987, MOC, P12/W6, from $35 to $35.00

Target Game, 1988, foam rubber, 12", EX $15.00

Tote Bag, yel w/Conga Line, 1987, EX, W6 ....$20.00

Umbrella, lady raisins on the beach, 1988, EX, W6 ....$45.00

Video, Meet the Raisins, 1988, MIP, W6 ....$25.00

Video, Raisins Sold Out, 1990, MIP, W6 ....$25.00

Watercolor-By-Number Set, Rose Art, complete, 1988, EX, W6 ....$30.00

Wind-up Toy, figure, boy's, 1987, MOC $5.00

Wind-up Toy, figure, girl's, 1987, MOC $15.00

Winross Truck, New America Highway Series, 1989, red Ford long-nose tandem axle w/dual stacks, M, D3, from $225 to $300.00

Candy Containers

As early as 1876, candy manufacturers used figural glass containers to package their candy. They found the idea so successful that they continued to use them until the 1960s. The major producers of these glass containers were Westmoreland, West Bros., Victory Glass, J.H. Millstein, J.C. Crosetti, L.E. Smith, and Jack and T.H. Stough. Some of the most collectible and sought after today are the character-related figurals such as Amos 'N Andy, Barney Google, Santa Claus, and Jackie Coogan, but there are other rare examples that have been known to command prices of well over $1,000.00. Some of these are Black Cat for Luck (that books for $1,800.00, even in worn

paint); Cat Winking, Stretched Neck ($3,800.00 to $4,200.00); Irish Hat ($3,500.00 to $4,00.00); and Car, Black and White Taxi ($1,000.00 to $1,200.00). There are many reproductions; know your dealer. For a listing of these reproductions, refer to *Schroeder's Antiques Price Guide.*

For more information we recommend *The Collector's Guide to Candy Containers,* written by Doug Dezso and Leon and Rose Poirier. The plate numbers in the following listings refer to this book. Also available is *Modern Candy Containers* by Jack Brush and William Miller. Both books are available from Collector Books.

For other types of candy containers, see Halloween; Pez Dispensers; Santa Claus.

Battleship on Waves, plate #100, from $150 to $200.00

Bear on Circus Tub, plate #2, from $400 to $600.00

Bottle, Dolly's Milk, plate #109, from $50 to $75.00

Bus, New York–San Francisco, plate #154, from $500 to..$600.00

Camel, plate #4, from $75 to..$100.00

Candlestick, plate #321, from $300 to $325.00

Cannon, 2-wheel mount #1, plate #384, from $350 to...$450.00

Car, miniature streamlined, plate #173, from $20 to $30.00

Cash Register, plate #420, from $500 to $600.00

Charlie Chaplin by Straight Barrel, plate #196, L.E. Smith Co., ca 1920, 4", from $450.00 to $600.00. (Photo courtesy Doug Dezso and Leon and Rose Poirier)

Chicken on Sagging Basket, plate #14, from $75 to $100.00

Circus Dog w/Hat, plate #21, from $20 to.........................$40.00

Clock, milk glass w/pnt scene, plate #483, from $300 to...$350.00

Dirigible, Mu-Mu, plate, #90, from $250 to $300.00

Fire Engine, Ladder Truck, plate #254, from $200 to......$275.00

Flapper, plate #203, from $80 to.....................................$120.00

Flossie Fisher's Chair, plate #300, from $600 to $800.00

Harmonica, Sweetone, plate #447, from $100 to...........$150.00

Helicopter, plate #91, metal propellor & cap, from $250 to ..$300.00

Kaleidoscope, plate #429, from $8,000 to................$10,000.00

Lamp, monkey shape, plate #338, from $500 to $550.00

Lantern, aluminum top & bottom, plate #343, from $50 to..$55.00

Lantern, JS Co, plate #367, from $20 to $30.00

Lantern K600, plate #355, from $20 to $25.00
Locomotive, Little 23, plate #496, from $100 to $125.00
Luggage, trunk w/rnd top, plate #378, milk glass, from $125 to...$150.00
Man on Motorcycle, plate #446, from $500 to $600.00
Nurser, Lynne Doll, plate #122, from $25 to $35.00
Oil Can, Independence Bell, plate #435, from $750 to..$900.00
P-38 Lightning Airplane, plate #82, from $200 to.........$250.00
Piano, plate #460, from $375 to $425.00
Porch Swing, plate #315, from $200 to $250.00
Pumpkin Head Policeman, plate #270, from $1,700 to ..$1,900.00
Rabbit Eating Carrot, plate #55, from $60 to....................$80.00
Rabbit Running on Log, plate #62, from $300 to $400.00
Scottish Terrier, plate #32, from $75 to...........................$100.00
Snowman w/Pipe, plate #290, from $10 to........................$15.00
Spark Plug, plate #211, from $100 to $150.00
Stutz Bear Cat Racer, plate #474, from $1,300 to........$1,600.00

Trojan Horse, plate #48, from $15 to..................................$20.00
Turkey Gobbler, plate #75, from $175 to $225.00
Uncle Sam by Barrel, plate #215, from $750 to $900.00
Village City Garage, plate #136, from $125 to................$150.00
Village Railroad Station, complete, plate #142, from $200 to...$250.00
Yellow Taxi, plate #184, from $1,200 to $1,400.00

Cast Iron

Realistically modeled and carefully detailed cast-iron toys enjoyed their heyday from about the turn of the century (some companies began production a little earlier) until about the 1940s when they were gradually edged out by lighter-weight toys that were less costly to produce and to ship. (Some of the cast irons were more than 20" in length and very heavy.) Many were vehicles faithfully patterned after actual models seen on city streets at the time. Horse-drawn carriages were phased out when motorized vehicles came into use.

Some of the larger manufacturers were Arcade (Illinois), who by the 1920s was recognized as a leader in the industry; Dent (Pennsylvania); Hubley (Pennsylvania); and Kenton (Ohio). In the 1940s Kenton came out with a few horse-drawn toys which are collectible in their own right but naturally much less valuable than the older ones. In addition to those already noted, there were many minor makers; you will see them mentioned in the listings.

For more detailed information on these companies, we recommend *Collecting Toys* by Richard O'Brien (Books Americana). Note: World record prices continue to climb for mint and mint-in-box examples which are generally found at most larger toy shows. Prices for rare toys can be absolutely breathtaking. However, prices for common toys are generally stable and have not changed much. Neary all of our listings have been gleaned from the large auction houses that specialize in toy sales. Prices realized at these auctions generally represent the higher end of value ranges.

Advisor: John McKenna (M2).

See also Banks; Dollhouse Furniture; Guns; Pull and Push Toys.

Tank, Two Cannons; plate #413, marked USA on each side, 4¼" long, from $40.00 to $50.00. (Photo courtesy Doug Dezso and Leon and Rose Poirier)

Tank, WWI, bl glass, plate #415, from $200 to...............$225.00
Telephone, glass receiver, plate #226, from $50 to...........$75.00
Telephone, Lynne style, raised dial, plate #231, from $50 to $60.00
Telephone, Redlich's Screw Top #2, plate #242, from $400 to..$450.00
Toonerville Trolley, plate #214, from $750 to..............$1,000.00

AIRPLANES

Windmill, T.G. Stough's; plate #538, marked Pat Mar 16th 1915 #47, 122 in circle, traces of paint, 3¼", from $350.00 to $400.00. (Photo courtesy Doug Dezso and Leon and Rose Poirier)

TAT, Kilgore, tri-motor, green with white wings and tail, some restoration to paint, 13½", A, $2,400.00; America, Hubley, tri-motor with dual pilots, 17", some restoration, A, $3,600.00.

Lockheed, Vindex, silver w/emb gold lettering, NP prop & wheels, salesman's sample, 10" W, NM, A $24,000.00

Lucky Boy, Dent, gr w/NP prop & disk wheels, 9½" W, NM, A $2,750.00
Monocoupe, Arcade, orange & blk w/NP prop, rubber tires, 9" L, EX, A $1,100.00

BOATS

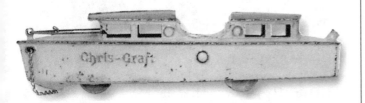

Chris-Craft, Kilgore, green and cream, 11", EX, A, $4,000.00.

Baby Speedboat, Hubley, turq, integral driver, 4", G, A....$125.00
City of New York Side-Wheeler, Wilkins, cream w/red trim, yel deck floor, 15", VG, A $1,500.00

New York Battleship, Dent, complete with all accessories, 20½", EX, A, $3,800.00.

New York Showboat, Dent, cream & yel w/bl detail, NP figure, 20½", EX, A $3,800.00
Side-Wheeler, Harris, cream w/red trim, 7", EX, A $600.00
Static Speedboat, Hubley, red, driver in wht w/red cap, 9", EX, A...$1,850.00

CHARACTER

Andy Gump car, Arcade, deluxe version, 7¼", EX, A, $4,000.00.

Andy Gump Car, Arcade, red & gr w/disk wheels, figure in suit & top hat, 7", VG, A $3,200.00
Chester Gump Cart, Arcade, figure in horse-drawn cart w/spoke wheels, 7½", G, A $150.00
Chester Gump Cart, Arcade, figure in horse-drawn cart w/spoke wheels, 7½", NM, A $1,400.00
Happy Hooligan Police Patrol, Kenton, yel w/red spoke wheels, w/2 figures & 2 blk horses, 19", VG, A.................$2,500.00

Popeye on Motorcycle, Hubley, 8⅜", EX, A, $3,500.00.

Popeye Spinach Wagon, Hubley, red w/blk rubber tires, mc figure, 6", VG, A...$750.00

CIRCUS ANIMALS AND ACCESSORIES

Overland Circus Band Wagon, Kenton, red, w/6 musicians, driver & 2 wht horses w/riders, 14", EX, A $500.00
Overland Circus Cage Truck, Kenton, red w/gold highlights, disk wheels w/yel hubs, 9", EX, A $900.00

Overland Circus Calliope, Kenton, red with yellow-painted spoke wheels, with driver and two white horses, 11", M (original box), A, $1,200.00.

Royal Circus Cage Wagon, Hubley, gray w/red spoke wheels, w/lions, driver & 2 horses, 16", VG, A $350.00
Royal Circus Cage Wagon, Hubley, red w/yel spoke wheels, w/lion, driver & 2 blk horses, 9", VG, A $375.00
Royal Circus Cage Wagon, Kenton, bl w/spoke wheels, w/bear & 2 blk horses, 12", EX, A...$375.00
Royal Circus Calliope, Hubley, bl w/gold highlights, red spoke wheels, w/driver & 2 wht horses, 9", EX, A $500.00

CONSTRUCTION

Huber Roller, Hubley, nickel wheels, original driver, bright paint, 8", EX, A, $400.00; Buckeye Ditch Digger, red and green, all original, 13", NM, A, $2,000.00.

Huber Road Roller, Army gr w/ornate NP spoke wheels, 7½", VG, A $975.00

McCormick Deering Thresher, gray w/red detail, spoke wheels, 10", G, A..$200.00

FARM TOYS
See also Horse-Drawn.

Allis-Chalmers Tractor & Dump Trailer, Arcade, orange w/blk rubber tires, integral driver, 13", NM, A...............$2,200.00

Ford Model 9N Tractor and Plow, 1939, Arcade, gray with red, 8¾", M, A, $4,000.00; Whitehead & Kales Wagon, red, eight removable stake sides, 6¾", MIB, A, $1,300.00.

Fordson Tractor, Arcade, gr w/red spoke wheels, NP driver, 6", VG, A $150.00

Fordson Tractor & Stake Wagon, Arcade, gray w/blk rubber tires, red wagon mk Whitehead & Kaels, NP driver, 13", VG, A $300.00

Fordson Tractor w/Scoop Cart, Arcade, gray w/red spoke wheels, NP driver, 14", VG, A $200.00

John Deere Model A Tractor, Arcade, gr w/silver highlights, bl rubber tires w/yel hubs, NP driver, 7½", MIB, A...$2,100.00

McCormick-Deering Thresher, Arcade, gray w/red trim & yel spoke wheels, 11½", EX...$675.00

McCormick-Deering Tractor, Arcade, gray w/gold trim & red spoke wheels, NP driver, 7½", EX.........................$625.00

Oliver Row Crop 70 Tractor, Arcade No 356, gr w/blk rubber tires, NP driver, 7", NMIB, A $1,800.00

Silver Arrow Sedan, Arcade, silver w/wht rubber tires, 7", VG, A $200.00

John Deere Harvester, Vindex, silver with green trim, 13½", EX, A, $4,150.00; Case Combine, Vindex, silver and red, cutter reel revolves, very rare, 12" long, recast motor and hopper, otherwise EX, A, $2,475.00.

FIREFIGHTING

Only motor vehicles are listed here; **see also Horse-Drawn.**

Ahrens Fox Fire Engine, Hubley, red with nickel-detailed engine, 11", NM, from $12,000.00 to $15,000.00.

Friendship Pumper, red w/gr detail, spoke wheels, 13", VG, A .$465.00

Ladder Truck, AC Williams, red w/NP spoke wheels, w/driver & fireman on rear, 7½", G, A.......................................$275.00

Ladder Truck, Kenton, red w/wht rubber tires, NP ladders & driver, 14", VG, A..$400.00

Pontiac Ladder Truck, Arcade, red w/NP grille, blk rubber tires w/wht hubs, 2 firemen, 8", NM, A........................$1,650.00

Pontiac Ladder Truck, Arcade, red w/yel ladders, wht rubber tires, integral driver, 10", VG, A $300.00

Pontiac Pumper Truck, Arcade, red w/NP grille, wht rubber tires, 2 integral firemen, 9", EX, A $450.00

Pumper Truck, AC Williams, red w/NP spoke wheels, integral firemen, 6", EX, A $150.00

Pumper Truck, Arcade, red w/silver-trimmed hoses & fire equipment, blk rubber tires, 6 firemen, NMIB, A.........$2,600.00

Pumper Truck, Hubley, red w/gold detail, blk rubber tires w/NP spokes, NP driver, 12½", VG, A $600.00

Pumper Truck, Kenton, red w/NP boiler, blk rubber tires w/red spokes, w/driver, 15", EX, A..................................$575.00

Pumper Truck, Kenton, red w/NP boiler, hose reel & driver, spoke wheels, 14½", missing rear fireman, VG, A...$850.00

HORSE-DRAWN AND OTHER ANIMALS

Arab Cart, gray w/red spoke wheels, w/figure & elephant, 7", VG, A $200.00

City Transfer Wagon, Kenton, steel canopy with paper litho-covered sides, red with yellow spoke wheels, 19½", VG/EX, A, $2,750.00.

City Truck Stake Wagon, yel w/spoke wheels, w/driver & 2 mules, 15", VG, A $600.00

Coal Cart, Ives, gray w/red spoke wheels, w/driver & blk donkey w/gold harness & saddle, 13", EX, A.......................$900.00

Daisy Cart, Ives, red w/yel spoke wheels, standing driver & single blk horse, 10", rare, NM, A $8,200.00

Donkey-Drawn Coal Cart, orange w/gr spoke wheels, Black driver, 13", VG, A...$300.00

Dray Wagon, Kenton, gr w/red spoke wheels, w/driver & 2 horses, 14", NM, A $200.00

Eagle Milk & Cream Wagon, Hubley, wht w/red spoke wheels, single blk horse, 12", EX, A.....................................$700.00

Elephant-Drawn Cart, Kenton, red w/gold spoke wheels, native driver, 7½", VG, A $250.00

Express Wagon, Kenton, gr w/red spoke wheels, 2 blk horses, w/driver, 15", EX, A...$250.00

Express Wagon, red w/yel spoke wheels, w/lady driver & single goat, 9", VG, A...$100.00

Farm Wagon, Kenton, yellow running gear, red wagon, and Black driver, 15", G, A, $275.00.

Fire Chief Wagon, Pratt & Letchworth, red w/spoke wheels, w/driver & single wht horse, 14", EX, A...............$3,100.00

Fire Ladder Wagon, Carpenter, red w/spoke wheels, 4 ladders & 2 firemen, 1 blk & 1 wht horse, 25", VG, A.........$1,600.00

Fire Patrol Wagon, Wilkins, wht w/spoke wheels, 7 firemen, 2 blk horses, VG, A....................................$685.00

Fire Pumper, Pratt & Letchworth, red spoke wheels w/NP boiler, 2 firemen, 1 blk & 1 wht horse, 17", VG, A.........$1,600.00

Grocery Wagon, Wilkins, red w/yel spoke wheels, w/driver & single blk horse, 13", VG, A....................................$900.00

Hansom Cab, bl w/yel spoke wheels, w/driver & single wht horse, 9", G, A...$100.00

Hansom Cab, Kenton, bl w/yel spoke wheels, w/driver & single wht horse, 11½", NM, A..................................$350.00

Hansom Cab, Kenton, bl w/yel spoke wheels, w/driver & single wht horse, 15", EX, A.....................................$350.00

Hose Reel Wagon, Ives, black with ornate gold-trimmed hose reel, 24", VG, A, $3,300.00.

Ice Wagon, Hubley, red w/spoke wheels, 1 blk & 1 wht horse, w/driver, 15", EX, A....................................$450.00

Industrial Cart, Wilkins, red w/yel spoke wheels, single blk horse, 12", VG, A.....................................$250.00

Log Wagon, Kenton, yel w/spoke wheels, driver seated on lg log, single blk horse w/silver mane & tail, 15", EX, A....$525.00

Plantation Cart, yel w/red spoke wheels, w/cotton bale, driver & blk oxen, 12", VG, A.......................................$525.00

Sand & Gravel Wagon, Kenton, gr w/spoke wheels, w/driver, 1 blk & 1 wht horse, 14", VG, A $250.00

Santa in Sleigh, Hubley, wht w/red detail, 2 reindeer, 17", VG, A $2,700.00

Stake Wagon, Arcade, w/driver, 1 blk & 1 wht horse, 12", VG, A $175.00

Sulky, Wilkins, red, w/jockey & blk horse, 8", VG, A....$300.00

Tally Ho Wagon, Carpenter, wht w/red trim & spoke wheels, rpl figures on roof, 4 blk horses, 28", VG, A $7,100.00

MOTOR VEHICLES

Note: Description lines for generic vehicles may simply begin with 'Bus,' 'Coupe,' or 'Motorcycle,' for example. But more busses will be listed as 'Coach Bus,' 'Coast To Coast,' 'Greyhound,' 'Interurban,' 'Mack,' or 'Public Service' (and there are other instances); coupes may be listed under 'Ford,' 'Packard,' or some other specific car company; and lines describing motorcycles might be also start 'Armored,' 'Excelsior-Henderson,' 'Delivery,' 'Policeman,' 'Harley-Davidson,' and so on. Look under 'Yellow Cab' or 'Checker Cab' and other cab companies for additional 'Taxi Cab' descriptions. We often gave any lettering or logo on the vehicle priority when we entered descriptions, so with this in mind, you should have a good idea where to look for your particular toy. Body styles (Double-Decker Bus, Cape-Top Roadster, etc.) were also given priority.

Auburn Coupe, Champion, red w/NP spoke wheels, 7", VG, A $300.00
Auto Express 548 Delivery Truck, Kenton, cream w/NP disk wheels & red hubs, w/driver, 9", VG, A $2,900.00

Auto Transport, tin carrier, 14", EX (one car G), A, $240.00.

Bell Telephone Truck, Hubley, gr w/wht rubber tires, complete w/accessories, 10", EX, A...$500.00
Bell Telephone Truck, Hubley, gr w/wht rubber tires, integral tires, complete w/accessories, 19", VG, A $1,200.00
Bell Telephone Truck, Hubley, gr w/wht rubber tires & red-pnt hubs, 5", EX, A $225.00
Borden's Milk Truck, Hubley, wht w/red lettering, wht rubber tires, 6", G-, A $275.00
Buick, Arcade, gr & blk w/wht rubber tires & mounted rear spare, 8½", EX, A $5,700.00
Bus, Arcade, red w/NP disk wheels, 6", VG, A..............$150.00

Bus, Kenton, rubber tires, 9", EX, A, $260.00.

Bus Line School Bus, Dent, orange rpt w/NP disk wheels, 8", EX, A $175.00
Car Carrier, AC Williams, red w/gr carrier, NP spoke wheels, w/3 Austin sedans, 12", VG, A $825.00
Car Carrier, gr w/repro red flat-bed trailer, wht rubber tires, w/2 Pontiacs, 14", G, A...$200.00
Chrysler Airflow, Hubley, tan w/wht rubber tires, NP grille & bumpers, 4½", G-, A $125.00
Chrysler Airflow Coupe, Dent, 2-tone bl w/orange fenders & NP grille, wht rubber tires, 6½", VG, A $2,200.00
City Ambulance, Arcade, cream w/blk rubber tires, 6", scarce, EX, A $575.00
Coast To Coast Bus, Dent, gray w/orange wheels, w/driver, 15", VG, A $300.00

Coast to Coast GMC Bus, Arcade, gr & cream w/blk rubber tires, NP front & rear, 9", VG, A $200.00
Crash Car, Hubley, orange w/wht rubber tires, integral driver, 4½", EX, D10..$250.00
Double-Decker Bus, Arcade, gr w/blk rubber tires, 3 NP passengers, 8", VG, A $250.00
Dump Truck, Hubley, red w/NP spoke wheels, integral driver, 9", EX, A $1,000.00
Express Truck, Jones & Bixler, yel w/red spoke wheels, w/driver, 16", VG, A $600.00
Faegol Bus, Arcade, gr w/NP tires, 8", EX, A $575.00
Ford Coupe, AC Williams, red w/NP spoke wheels, 6", G, A..$100.00
Gasoline Truck, Champion, bl & red rpt w/wht rubber tires, 7", G, A $125.00
Greyhound Lines, Arcade, bl & wht w/wht rubber tires, 9", EX (worn box), A...$950.00
Greyhound Lines Century of Progress, Chicago-1933, Arcade, bl & wht w/wht rubber tires, 11", G, A.......................$150.00
Harley-Davidson Civilian Motorcycle, Hubley, gr w/wht rubber tires & NP spokes, integral driver, 6½", NM, D10 ..$750.00

Harley-Davidson Civilian Motorcycle, Hubley, rubber-tired metal wheels, original driver, 8½" long, EX, A, $2,400.00.

Harley-Davidson Motorcycle w/Sidecar, Hubley, gr w/blk rubber tires & NP spokes, w/driver & passenger, 9", EX, A .$1,950.00
Harley-Davidson Parcel Post Delivery Cycle, Hubley, gr w/blk rubber tires & NP spokes, driver in bl, 9½", EX, A........$3,900.00
Harley-Davidson Police Motorcycle, Hubley, orange w/wht rubber tires & NP spokes, integral figure, 5", VG, A $400.00
Indian Motorcycle w/Sidecar, Hubley, red w/blk rubber tires & NP spokes, w/driver & passenger, 9", VG, A........$1,100.00
Indian Police Motorcycle w/Sidecar, Hubley, red w/blk rubber tires & NP spokes, w/driver & passenger, 9", EX, A $1,250.00
Indian Traffic Car, Hubley, red & bl w/wht rubber tires & NP spokes, integral driver, 9", EX, A.............................$800.00
International Dump Truck, Arcade, red w/gr dump, NP grille, blk rubber tires, 9", VG, A $400.00
International Dump Truck, Arcade, red w/NP dump, blk rubber tires, 11", VG, A $350.00
International Pickup, Arcade, yel w/blk rubber tires, 9½", prof rstr, A $300.00
International Stake Truck, Arcade, red w/blk rubber tires, 11", VG, A $300.00
Livestock Truck, Kilgore, bl & red w/NP disk wheels, 6", G, A $100.00

Mack Dump Truck, Arcade, logo on doors, with driver, 8¼", VG, A, $275.00.

Mack Dump Truck, Arcade, red w/wht rubber tires, NP driver, w/orig shovel, 12", VG, A $525.00

Mack Gasoline Truck, AC Williams, red w/NP spoke wheels, 7", VG, A $200.00

Mack Gasoline Truck, Arcade, bl w/NP spoke wheels, rpl tank, 13", EX, A $1,100.00

Mack Ice Truck, Arcade, bl w/wht rubber tires, integral driver, 7", G, A...$200.00

Mack Ice Truck, Arcade, red w/wht rubber tires, integral driver, 7", VG, A...$300.00

Mack Stake Truck w/Plow, Arcade, orange w/wht rubber tires, integral driver, 7", VG, A...$450.00

Mack Wrecker, Arcade, red w/gr boom, NP spoke wheels & driver, 13", VG, A...$1,300.00

Model A Weaver Wrecker, Arcade, red w/gr tow hook, NP spoke wheels, 7", EX, A.......................................$550.00

Motorcycle w/Sidecar, Hubley, olive gr w/blk rubber tires & NP spokes, w/driver & passenger, 9", VG, A $650.00

Motorcycle w/Sidecar, Hubley, red w/blk rubber tires & NP spokes, w/driver, 9", VG, A $600.00

Panel Van, Arcade, 2-tone bl w/yel stripe, wht rubber tires, NP driver, 9½", VG, A..$1,300.00

Parcel Post Delivery Cycle, Hubley, olive gr w/blk rubber tires & NP spokes, driver in bl, 9", EX, A.........................$2,600.00

Police Motorcycle, AC Williams, bl w/wht rubber tires, integral driver, 7", EX, A $525.00

Police Motorcycle, Champion, bl w/wht rubber tires, integral driver, 7", G, A $300.00

Police Motorcycle, rubber tires, 8½", VG, A, $950.00.

Police Motorcycle, Champion, gr w/wht rubber tires, integral driver, 7", G, A $400.00

Police Motorcycle, Champion, gr w/wht rubber tires, integral driver, 5", G-, A $150.00

Police Motorcycle w/Sidecar, Champion, bl w/red sidecar & wht rubber tires, integral driver, 4", VG, A.....................$175.00

Pontiac Sedan, Arcade, red w/NP grille, wht rubber tires, 6", VG, A...$150.00

Public Service Bus, Dent, orange with black roof, open-casted windows, repainted, 15", A, $1,000.00.

Racer, Champion, gr w/rpl wht rubber tires, integral driver, 8½", G, A...$385.00

Racer, Champion, red w/NP tires & driver, 8½", G, A ..$450.00

Racer, Hubley, gr w/wht rubber tires, electric headlight, integral driver, 6½", G-, A..$225.00

Racer, Hubley, orange boat-tail style w/wht rubber tires, integral driver, 6½", G, A...$350.00

Racer, Hubley, red w/wht rubber tires, integral driver, 6½", G, A $385.00

Racer #1, Hubley, red w/wht rubber tires, integral driver, 8", G, A $400.00

Racer #5, Hubley, silver w/blk rubber tires & NP spokes, integral driver, 10", EX, A...$1,100.00

Red Baby Dump Truck, Arcade, rpt w/rpl wht rubber tires, NP driver, 10½", EX, A..$350.00

Say It With Flowers Delivery Cycle, Hubley, red Harley-Davidson cycle, blue van, movable driver's head, very rare, 9½", VG, A, $28,600.00.

Sedan, Kenton, turq & blk w/disk wheels, rear spare mk Stop 1926, rare, EX, A $11,000.00

Stake Truck, AC Williams, bl w/wht rubber tires, 7", EX, D10 ....$275.00

Stake Truck, Arcade, red w/NP disk wheels, 7", G, A $150.00

Studebaker Dump Truck, Hubley, yel w/NP grille, blk rubber
tires, 7", VG, A...$150.00

Stutz Roadster, Kilgore, yel & bl w/NP disk wheels, grille,
bumpers, etc, 10", scarce, EX, A $2,100.00

Touring Car, Jones & Bixler, red w/yel spoke wheels, w/driver &
lady passenger, 9", G, A.......................................$200.00

**Traffic Car Motorcycle, Hubley, red Indian cycle
with nickeled motor, attached blue stake-sided body,
working clicker, 11½", M, A, $4,600.00.**

White Dump Truck, Arcade, red & blk w/wht rubber tires, NP
driver, EX, A $13,700.00

White Lammerts Moving Van, Arcade, dk gray w/NP tires &
driver, opening rear doors, 13½", rare, NM, A...$18,000.00

White Moving Van, Arcade, gr w/yel Union Supply Co decals,
wht rubber tires, 13½", rare, NMIB, A.............$28,000.00

Wrecker, Arcade, red & yel w/blk rubber tires, steel crane, 13",
MIB, A $1,900.00

Wrecker, Champion, bl w/wht rubber tires, 7", EX, A....$200.00

Wrecker, Champion, red w/wht rubber tires, NP crank & barrel,
8", NMIB, A...$1,500.00

Wrecker, Champion, red w/wht rubber tires, 8", VG, A..$150.00

Wrecker, Kenton, red w/yel tow hook, disk wheels w/yel hubs,
w/driver, 9", prof rstr, A $600.00

Yellow Cab, Arcade, yel w/blk rubber tires, w/driver & passenger,
8", NMIB, A...$2,400.00

**Yellow Coach Bus, Arcade, red with much gold trim, sten-
ciled Fifth Ave Bus on sides, 13½", missing two seats, otherwise M, A, $1,850.00.**

Catalogs

In any area of collecting, old catalogs are a wonderful source
for information. Toy collectors value buyers' catalogs, those from

toy fairs, and Christmas 'wish books.' Montgomery Ward issued
their first Christmas catalog in 1932, and Sears followed a year
later. When they can be found, these 'first editions' in excellent
condition are valued at a minimum of $200.00 each. Even later
issues may sell for upwards of $75.00, since it's those from the
'50s and '60s that contain the toys that are now so collectible.

Aurora, 1970, M, P3 ....$125.00
Beach's Toyland, 1953-54, VG+...............................$65.00
Black Beauty Bicycles, 1917, G, A $50.00
Blinn's Toy Comp, The Toy Yearbook, 1949-50, VG $105.00
Daisy Air Rifles, 1952, 39 pages, 3½x7½", VG $38.00
FAO Schwarz, Christmas 1941, EX............................$140.00
Gimbels, Christmas 1953, VG+ $42.00
Goodyear, 1955 Christmas Toys, VG $115.00
Growing Up w/Fisher-Price, 1980-85, EX, C13 ....$5.00

Hot Wheels
Collector's Cat-
alog, 1968, M,
$25.00.

Iver Johnson's Bicycle
Catalog, 1899, 8½" x 5",
EX, A, $160.00.

Hot Wheels, 1970 International Collector's Catalog, EX ...$35.00
Iver Johnson Bicycles, 1917, NM, A $75.00
JC Penney, 1964, 300 pages, VG $45.00
Jordan Marsh, Christmas 1967, 21 pages, VG+ $15.00
Lionel Trains, 1942, M $135.00
Lionel Trains, 1952, NM $100.00
Mattel, Cap Guns, 1959, EX+...................................$100.00
Mattel, 1966, VG+ $45.00
Mattel, 1971, 29 pages, NM $30.00
Mohr's Toys for Boys & Girls, 1928, NM, A $165.00

Parents' Guide to Fisher-Price Toys, 1960-69, EX, C13 ....**$25.00**
Railroading w/American Flyer, 1946, NM, A **$150.00**
Revell Hobby Kit, 1956, 31 pages, 8½x10¾", EX.............**$35.00**
Schoenhut, 1904, 7½x10", VG+......................................**$50.00**

Schoenhut's Humpty Dumpty Circus, 1918, VG, A, $150.00.

Sears, Christmas 1945, 209 pages, VG+............................**$45.00**
Sears, Christmas 1967, 600 pages, EX **$65.00**
Stover Bicycle Mfg Co, 1891, G, A...................................**$85.00**
Sutcliffe Co, 1920s, 144 pages, VG+..............................**$160.00**
Tinkertoys, 1927, EX..**$50.00**
Tinkertoys, 1931, EX..**$50.00**
Tinkertoys, 1935, EX..**$50.00**
Topper Toys, Johnny Eagle Toy Guns, 1965, VG+ **$25.00**
Ward's, Christmas 1967, 411 pages, Peanuts characters on cover, EX...**$50.00**
Weeden Toy Steam Engines, 1937, 20 pages, 6x9", EX **$32.00**

Cereal Boxes and Premiums

This is an area of collecting that attracts crossover interest from fans of advertising as well as character-related toys. What makes a cereal box interesting? Look for Batman, Huckleberry Hound, or a well-known sports figure like Larry Bird or Roger Maris on the front or back. Boxes don't have to be old to be collectible, but the basic law of supply and demand dictates that the older ones are going to be expensive! After all, who saved cereal boxes from 1910? By chance if Grandma did, the 1910 Corn Flakes box with a printed-on baseball game could get her $750.00. Unless you're not concerned with bugs, it will probably be best to empty the box and very carefully pull apart the glued flaps. Then you can store it flat. Be sure to save any prize that might have been packed inside.

Advisor: Larry Blodget (B2), Post Cereal cars.

General Mills Cheerios, 1940, Lone Ranger Frontier Town cutouts on back, NM **$250.00**
General Mills Cheerios, 1957, Disneyland Adventure story & picture to color on back, EX....................................**$100.00**

General Mills Cheerios, 1958, Wyatt Earp Marshal's Ring offer, EX **$125.00**
General Mills Corn Kix, 1955, Lone Ranger Branding Iron offer, EX **$250.00**
General Mills Kix, 1965, National Parks coloring book & stamp album offer, NM **$100.00**
General Mills Lucky Charms, 1968, free Glider inside, NM...**$150.00**
General Mills Twinkles, 1960-61, story w/Twinkles the Elephant on back, EX, T2....................................**$125.00**

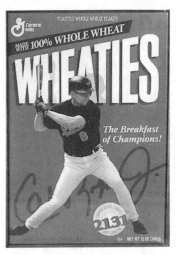

General Mills Wheaties, Cal Ripkens Jr., $10.00.

General Mills Wheaties, 1956, Mouseketeer record offer, EX **$100.00**
General Mills Wheaties, 1957, Champy & Mr Fox hand puppet offer on back, EX **$125.00**
General Mills Wheaties, 1960, features baseball player w/free comic books offer, NM **$125.00**
Kellogg's Corn Flakes, 1955, Superman belt & buckle offer, EX..**$250.00**
Kellogg's Corn Flakes, 1959, free Huckleberry Hound Toy Statue inside, NM **$150.00**
Kellogg's Corn Flakes, 1961, Huckleberry Hound Stampets Printing Set offer, EX.................................**$125.00**

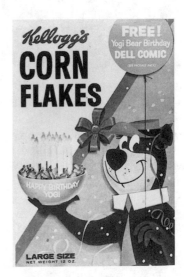

Kellogg's Corn Flakes, 1962, Yogi Bear Birthday Dell Comic, EX, $250.00. (Photo courtesy Scott Bruce)

Kellogg's Fruit Loops, 1967, Woody Woodpecker Swimmer offer, VG **$80.00**

Kellogg's Pep, 1952, Tom Corbett Space Cadet Radio-TV show, Your Space Cadet Heroes w/Dr Joan Dale on back, EX $450.00

Kellogg's Pep, 1952, Tom Corbett Space Goggles offer, NM, C10..$465.00

Kellogg's Rice Krispies, 1954, Howdy Doody & friends cut-out masks on back, EX....................................$350.00

Kellogg's Rice Krispies, 1955, Famous Jets of the World cutout on back, NM..$50.00

Kellogg's Rice Krispies, 1955, free PT Boat inside, Canada, NM..$75.00

Kellogg's Rice Krispies, 1955, Lady & the Tramp figures, EX .$125.00

Kellogg's Rice Krispies, 1958, Woody Woodpecker kazoo offer, EX $125.00

Kellogg's Stars, 1969, Banana Splits poster offer, EX $150.00

Kellogg's Sugar Corn Pops, 1952, Wild Bill Hickok's Famous Gun Series on back, EX.................................$150.00

Kellogg's Sugar Frosted Flakes, 1963, Tony the Tiger stuffed doll offer, NM $200.00

Kellogg's Sugar Pops, 1950s, Andy Devine as Jingles on front, Make 'Em Ourself Moccasins on back, EX................$75.00

Kellogg's Sugar Pops, 1957, features Andy Devine as Jingles & 45-pc Printing Set offer, EX $150.00

Kellogg's Sugar Pops, 1969, Dick Dastardly Vulture Squadron Membership offer, NM $250.00

Kellogg's Sugar Smacks, 1953, features Paul Jung circus clown, EX $300.00

Kellogg's Sugar Smacks, 1957, Smaxey the Seal, chance to win Admiral TV, EX, $150.00. (Photo courtesy Scott Bruce)

Kellogg's Sugar Smacks, 1960s, features Smaxey the Seal & free color-by-numbers cartoon, NM................................$125.00

Kellogg's Sugar Smacks, 1964, Quick Draw McGraw w/road race game on back, NM $300.00

Maltex Maypo Oat Cereal, 1956, lg image of Marky Maypo, NM $175.00

Nabisco Rice Honeys, 1950s, Rin-Tin-Tin on front, telegraph key offer, EX, C10...$175.00

Nabisco Rice Honeys, 1956, free Sky King Statuette inside, NM $100.00

Nabisco Rice Honeys, 1960, features Buffalo Bee & free Howdy Doody Action Ring inside, EX.............................$200.00

Nabisco Rice Honeys, 1965, features Buddy Bee, free Winnie the Pooh Breakfast Buddy inside, EX......................$110.00

Nabisco Rice Honeys, 1969, w/free Beatles rub-ons, NM ...$650.00

Nabisco Wheat Honeys, 1956, Buffalo Bee hummer toy on back, EX..$100.00

Nabisco Wheat Honeys, 1969, free Space Explorers inside, NM $100.00

Post Alpha Bits, 1963, features Jack E Leonard Postman & Cowboys & Indians set for 2 boxtops, NM....................$175.00

Post Alpha Bits, 1966, free Mystery Diver inside, NM...$100.00

Post Alpha-Bits, 1964, Lovable Truly Inflatable Toy offer, NM..$150.00

Post Corn Fetti, 1954, free Captain Jolly comic book, EX ..$150.00

Post Grape-Nuts Flakes, 1954, free Ford or Mercury car inside, EX $200.00

Post Raisin Bran, 1953, free Roy Rogers ring inside, EX ...$350.00

Post Raisin Bran, 1959, Fun-A-Rama Fury Game cutout on back, NM..$100.00

Post Sugar Coated Corn Flakes, 1961, features Cornelius w/paint brush & free Bugs Bunny Water Paint Book offer, NM...$125.00

Post Sugar Crisp, 1961, Looney Tunes character mask cutouts on back, EX $100.00

Post Sugar Rice Krinkles, 1955, free Flip-Top inside, EX..$45.00

Post Sugar Sparkled Rice Krinkles, 1964, features So-Hi & free Toy Boat inside, NM..$125.00

Post Toasties, 1950-51, Hopalong Cassidy Wild West Trading Card inside, NM..$400.00

Post Toasties, 1957, Mighty Mouse T-shirt, cape & playbook offer, NM $200.00

Post Toasties Corn Flakes, 1959, Linda Williams doll offer, EX $85.00

Quaker Cap'n Crunch, 1964, free Bo'Sun Whistle inside, EX..$125.00

Quaker Life, 1962, free finger puppets inside w/hand puppet offer on back, NM $100.00

Quaker Oats, Roy Rogers cup offer, NM, C10 ....$150.00

Quaker Puffed Rice, 1950, Sgt Preston Yukon Adventure cards, EX $150.00

Quaker Puffed Wheat, 1951, Gabby Hayes Western Gun Collection offer, EX..$200.00

Quaker Puffed Wheat, 1952, Gabby Hayes Scale-Model Building Kits offer on back, EX..$200.00

Quaker Quake, 1967, Cavern Helmet offer, NM...........$500.00

Ralston Purina Rice Chex, 1953, Space Patrol Magic Space Pictures inside w/Space Binoculars offer, EX $350.00

PREMIUMS

Sure, the kids liked the taste of the cereal too, but in families with more than one child there was more clamoring over the prize inside than there was over the last bowlfull! In addition to the 'freebies' included in the boxes, many other items were made available — rings, decoders, watches, games, books, etc. — often for just mailing in boxtops or coupons. If these premiums weren't free, their prices were minimal. Most of them were easily broken, and children had no qualms about throwing them away, so few survive to the present. Who would have ever thought those kids would be trying again in the '90s to get their hands on those very same prizes, and at considerable more trouble and expense. Note: Only premiums that specifically relate to cereal companies or their character logos are listed here. Other character-related premiums are listed in the Premiums category. If you need more information on Post cars, we recommend *Free Inside!, Scale Model Car!*, by our advisor Larry Blodget. Ordering information may be found in the Categories of Special Interest section in the Directory under Promotional Vehicles.

Apple Jack, mug w/hat lid, 1967, plastic, VG $50.00
Banana Splits, eraser, 1968, any character, NM, ea from $25 to...$30.00
Boo Berry, figure, vinyl, 8", EX, from $200 to $300.00
Buffalo Bee, hummer toy, Nabisco, 1956, cb cutout, 4", NM...$10.00
Buffalo Bee & Jolly Clown, bowl riders, Nabisco, 1961, plastic figures, NM, 2", ea $10.00
Bugs Bunny, Magic Paint Book, Kellogg's, 1961, EX.........$50.00
Cap'n Crunch, binoculars, 1975, bl plastic, MIP $15.00
Cap'n Crunch, Bo'Sun Whistle, Quaker, 1964, plastic, 3¼", NM..$15.00
Cap'n Crunch, compass, 1966, 8", EX...............................$45.00
Cap'n Crunch, kaleidoscope, 1964-65, cb, 7", EX $35.00
Cap'n Crunch, treasure chest bank, 1966, 6" L, EX.........$45.00
Cap'n Crunch, wiggle figures, 1969, 3 different, EX, ea....$50.00

Champy and Mr. Fox, hand puppets, 1957, cloth and vinyl, 7½", EX, $25.00. (Photo courtesy Scott Bruce)

Cocoa Puffs, train, 1959-61, litho tin, 12", NM..............$100.00
Cocoa Puffs, train station, General Mills, 1961, cb, 30", EX...$100.00
Count Chocula, figure, vinyl, 8", EX, from $200 to........$300.00
Count Chocula, ring, secret compartment, M, C10 ....$275.00
Dig-'em, secret decoder, MIP...$15.00
Frankenberry, figure, vinyl, 8", EX, from $200 to............$300.00
Frankenberry, ring, secret compartment, M, C10 ....$275.00
Honeycomb Kid, monster mitt, 1974, plastic w/red eyeball, M...$15.00
Honeycomb Kid, ring, 1966, 14-karat gold, EX $75.00
Huckleberry Hound, fun cards, 1959, several different, 3½", EX, ea...$10.00
Huckleberry Hound, Stampets Printing Set, Kellogg's, 1961, features 12 different characters, EX....................................$45.00
Huckleberry Hound & Pals, figures, Kellogg's, 1959, plastic w/interchangable bodies, 6 different, NM, ea from $15 to........$25.00
Lady & the Tramp, figures, Kellogg's, 1955, plastic, 2", M, ea from $15 to...$25.00

Marky Maypo, bank, 1960s, plastic, EX $100.00
Mystery Diver, Post, 1966, plastic figure, 2½", NM..........$25.00
National Parks Coloring Book & Stamps Album Starring Tennesse Tuxedo & Chumley the Walrus, General Mills, 1965, NM..$60.00
Paul Jung & Lou Jacobs, shuttle action toy, Kellogg's, 1953, 10", NM..$45.00
Post Vehicle, Ford Fairlane 500 Sunliner, Flame Red, F&F Mold, EX..$15.00
Post Vehicle, 1950 Ford Custom, orange, NM, B2 ....$75.00
Post Vehicle, 1951 Ford Custom, red, NM, B2 ....$175.00
Post Vehicle, 1954 Ford Crestline Fordor Sedan, Glacier Blue, F&F Mold, EX...$40.00
Post Vehicle, 1954 Ford Crestline Victoria, Goldenrod Yellow, NM, B2 ....$65.00
Post Vehicle, 1954 Ford Crestline Victoria, Sierra Brown, F&F Mold, EX..$25.00
Post Vehicle, 1954 Ford Customline, Cameo Coral, 2-door sedan, F&F Mold, EX $25.00

Post Vehicle, 1954 Ford Victoria, Sierra Brown, NM, B2, $25.00. (Photo courtesy Larry Blodget)

Post Vehicle, 1954 Mercury Monterey, Goldenrod Yellow, 4-door sedan, F&F Mold, EX $45.00
Post Vehicle, 1954 Mercury Monterey Sport Coupe, Torch Red, F&F Mold, EX $150.00
Post Vehicle, 1954 Mercury Monterey 4-door sedan, Glacier Blue, NM, B2...$65.00
Post Vehicle, 1954 Mercury Monterey 4-door sedan, Goldenrod Yellow, NM, B2..$55.00
Post Vehicle, 1954 Mercury Monterey 4-door sedan, lavender, NM, B2 ....$300.00
Post Vehicle, 1954 Mercury Monterey 4-door sedan, Torch Red, NM, B2 ....$65.00
Post Vehicle, 1954 Mercury XM/800, Cameo Coral, NM, B2 ..$45.00
Post Vehicle, 1954 Mercury XM/800, Empire Green, F&F Mold, EX..$35.00
Post Vehicle, 1954 Mercury XM/800, Glacier Blue, NM, B2 ....$40.00
Post Vehicle, 1955 Ford Customline Tudor Sedan, Buckskin Brown, F&F Mold, EX $15.00
Post Vehicle, 1955 Ford Thunderbird, Aquatone Blue, F&F Mold, EX..$25.00
Post Vehicle, 1956 Century Arabian Speed Boat, wht over yel, F&F Mold, EX...$10.00
Post Vehicle, 1957 Ford Country Sedan, Flame Red, NM, B2 ....$10.00

Post Vehicle, 1957 Ford Custom Fordor Sedan, Coral Sand, NM, B2 ....$45.00

Post Vehicle, 1957 Ford Custom 300 Tudor Sedan, Flame Red, NM, B2 ....$10.00

Post Vehicle, 1957 Ford Fairlane 500 Sunliner, Colonial White, NM, B2 ....$65.00

Post Vehicle, 1957 Ford Fairlane 500 Sunliner, Coral Sand, NM, B2 ....$45.00

Post Vehicle, 1957 Ford Fairlane 500 Sunliner, Cumberland Green, NM, B2 ....$65.00

Post Vehicle, 1957 Ford Fairlane 500 Sunliner, pale red, NM, B2 ....$75.00

Post Vehicle, 1957 Ford Fairlane 500 Town Victoria, Dresden Blue, NM, B2 ....$45.00

Post Vehicle, 1959 Ford Thunderbird Convertible, Starlet Blue, NM, B2 ....$10.00

Post Vehicle, 1966 Ford Mustang 2+2, Springtime Yellow, NM, B2..$10.00

Post Vehicle, 1966 Ford Mustang 2+2 GT, Arcadian Blue, F&F Mold, EX $10.00

Post Vehicle, 1967 Mercury Cougars, M in original mailer, each car: $10.00; original box: from $10.00 to $20.00. (Photo courtesy Pat Webb)

Quake, cavern helmet, 1967, plastic, 10", EX................$225.00

Quake, ring, friendship, 1966, bl plastic, EX...................$300.00

Quake, ring, world globe, 1966, red plastic, EX $400.00

Quangaroo, free-wheeler, 1964, plastic snap-together figure on wheels, EX...$50.00

Quisp, bank, 1960s, ceramic figure on base, NM $100.00

Quisp, doll, 1968, stuffed cloth, 11", EX $75.00

Quisp, propeller beanie, 1966, M, from $500 to $600.00

Quisp, ring, friendship, 1966, bl plastic, EX...................$600.00

Quisp, ring, meteorite, 1966, red & clear plastic, EX $200.00

Quisp, ring, space gun, 1966, red plastic, EX $200.00

Shari Lewis, finger puppets, Quaker, 1962, plastic, 4 different, 2", ea from $15 to..$25.00

Smaxey the Seal, action cutout, Kellogg's, 1959, 5", EX...$10.00

Snap, Crackle, Pop & Toucan Sam, parade drum, Kellogg's, 4x9" dia, EX..$5.00

Snap, Crackle or Pop, dolls, Kellogg's, Rushton, stuffed cloth bodies w/vinyl heads, 18", EX......................................$30.00

Snap, Crackle or Pop, dolls, Kellogg's, 1948, images stamped on cloth, uncut, set of 3, NM+.....................................$160.00

Snap, Crackle or Pop, hand puppets, Kellogg's, 1950s, cloth w/plastic heads, felt hands, set of 3, 8½", VG+ $75.00

Snap! Crackle! & Pop!, hand puppets, 1950, cloth & vinyl, 8", EX, ea..$75.00

Snap! Crackle! & Pop!, Magic Color Cards, 1933, cb, NM (NM envelope..$75.00

Snap! Crackle! & Pop!, ring, 1950s, rubber face w/brass band, changes expressions when you spin dial, EX............$175.00

Space Explorers, figures, Nabisco, 1969, plastic, 6 different, 2", ea from $2 to $5.00

Tony the Tiger, bank, Kellogg's, figural, 1968, orange, wht & blk plastic, 9¼", EX...$50.00

Tony the Tiger, doll, Kellogg's, 1970s, squeeze vinyl, Product People, NM+...$100.00

Tony the Tiger, doll, Kellogg's, 1973, stuffed cloth, 14", EX, from $20 to $25.00

Tony the Tiger, doll, Kellogg's, 1973, stuffed cloth, 14", EX ...$40.00

Tony the Tiger, doll, Kellogg's, 1991, plush, mail-in premium, 8" $8.00

Tony the Tiger, doll, 1954, inflatable vinyl, 45", EX.......$300.00

Tony the Tiger, wristwatch, Kellogg's, 1976, MIB, I1 .....$200.00

Toucan Sam, bicycle license plate, 1973, bl plastic, 3x6", EX...$10.00

Toucan Sam, decoder, MIP (sealed) $20.00

Toucan Sam, doll, Kellogg's, 1964, stuffed cloth, 8", EX...$30.00

Toucan Sam, doll, 1964, stuffed cloth, 8", EX..................$30.00

Trix, rocket, 1969, plastic, spring-fired, 3", EX................$25.00

Trix, wallet, w/flasher image of Trix rabbit & cereal box, M (sealed)...$15.00

Trix Rabbit, mug & bowl, General Mills, 1964, plastic, EX $100.00

Twinkles the Elephant, bank, 1960, red plastic, 9", EX ..$350.00

Twinkles the Elephant, sponge, 1960-61, 4", EX $25.00

Winnie the Pooh, Breakfast Buddies, Nabisco, 1965, plastic figures, 6 different, 2", ea from $5 to $15.00

Woody Woodpecker, kazoo, 1958, red plastic, 6½", EX ...$35.00

Woody Woodpecker, swimmer toy, Kellogg's, 1967, plastic, 7½", NM..$100.00

Yogi Bear & Huckleberry Hound, mug & bowl, Kellogg's, 1960, plastic, M $40.00

Yogi Bear & Huckleberry Hound, spoons, Kellogg's, 1960, metal, 6", ea from $10 to...$15.00

Zillyzoo Animals, figures, Post, 1963-64, plastic, 6 different, 1½" to 4", M, ea from $5 to...$15.00

Character and Promotional Drinking Glasses

Once given away by fast-food chains and gas stations, a few years ago you could find these at garage sales everywhere for a dime or even less. Then, when it became obvious to collectors that these glass giveaways were being replaced by plastic, as is always the case when we realize no more (of anything) will be forthcoming, we all decided we wanted them. Since many were character-related and part of a series, we felt the need to begin to organize these garage-sale castaways, building sets and completing series. Out of the thousands available, the better ones are those with super heroes, sports stars, old movie stars, Star Trek, and Disney and Walter Lantz cartoon characters. Pass up those whose colors are worn and faded. Unless another condition or material is indicated in the description, values are for glass tumblers in mint condition. Cups are plastic unless noted otherwise.

There are some terms used in our listings that may be confusing if you're not familiar with this collecting field. 'Brockway' style tumblers are thick and heavy, and they taper at the bottom. 'Federal' is thinner, and top and diameters are equal. For more information we recommend *Collectible Drinking Glasses, Identification and Values*, by Mark E. Chase and Michael J. Kelly (Collector Books) and *The Collector's Guide to Cartoon and Promotional Drinking Glasses* by John Hervey. See also Clubs, Newsletters, and Other Publications.

Advisor: Mark E. Chase (C2).

Other Sources: B3, C10, D9, J2, H11, I2, M8, P3, P6, P10, T2.

Al Capp, Dogpatch USA, ruby glass, oval portraits of Daisy or Li'l Abner, ea, from $25 to $30.00

Al Capp, Shmoos, USF, 1949, Federal, 3 different sizes (3½", 4¾", 5¼"), from $10 to $20.00

Al Capp, 1975, flat bottom, Daisy Mae, Li'l Abner, Mammy, Pappy, Sadie, ea, from $50 to...................................$70.00

Al Capp, 1975, ftd, Daisy Mae, Li'l Abner, Mammy, Pappy, Sadie, ea, from $40 to...$80.00

Al Capp, 1975, ftd, Joe Btsfplk, from $60 to.....................$90.00

Animal Crackers, Chicago Tribune/NY News Syndicate, 1978, Eugene, Gnu, Lana, Lyle Dodo, ea, from $7 to $10.00

Animal Crackers, Chicago Tribune/NY News Syndicate, 1978, Louis, scarce, from $25 to..$35.00

Annie Oakley, see Western Heroes

Apollo Series, Marathon Oil, Apollo 11, Apollo 12, Apollo 13, Apollo 14, ea, from $2 to...$4.00

Apollo Series, Marathon Oil, carafe, from $6 to..............$10.00

Aquaman, see Super Heroes

Arby's, Actor Series, 1979, 6 different, smoked-colored glass w/blk & wht images, silver trim, numbered, ea, from $5 to $7.00

Arby's, Bicentennial Cartoon Characters Series, 1976, 10 different, 5", ea, from $18 to $25.00

Arby's, Bicentennial Cartoon Characters Series, 1976, 10 different, 6", ea, from $20 to $30.00

Arby's, Gary Patterson Thought Factory Collector Series, 1982, 4 different cartoons of sporting scenes, ea, from $2 to .$4.00

Arby's, see also specific name or series

Arby's, Stained Glass Series, late 1970s, carafe, from $6 to...$8.00

Arby's, Stained Glass Series, late 1970s, 5" or 6", ea, from $2 to $4.00

Archies, Welch's, 1971 & 1973, many variations in ea series, ea, from $3 to..$5.00

Armour Peanut Butter, Transportation Series, 1950s, 8 different, ea, from $3 to $5.00

Avon, Christmas Issues, 1969-72, 4 different, ea, from $2 to...$5.00

Baby Huey & Related Characters, see Harvey Cartoon Characters

Batman & Related Characters, see Super Heroes

Battlestar Galactica, Universal Studios, 1979, 4 different, ea, from $7 to..$10.00

BC Ice Age, Arby's, 1981, 6 different, ea, from $3 to..........$5.00

Beatles, Dairy Queen/Canada, group photos & signatures in wht starburst, gold trim, ea, from $95 to $125.00

Beverly Hillbillies, CBS promotion, 1963, rare, NM......$200.00

Buffalo Bill, see Western Heroes or Wild West Series

Bugs Bunny & Related Characters, see Warner Bros

Bullwinkle, Rocky & Related Characters, see Warner Bros or PAT Ward

Burger Chef, Burger Chef & Jeff, Now We're Glassified!, from $15 to $25.00

Burger Chef, Endangered Species Collector's Series, 1978, Tiger, Orang-Utan, Panda, Bald Eagle, ea, from $5 to $7.00

Burger Chef, Friendly Monster Series, 1977, 6 different, ea, from $20 to $35.00

Burger Chef, Presidents & Patriots, 1975, 6 different, ea, from $7 to $10.00

Burger King, Collector Series, 1979, 5 different Burger King characters featuring Burger Thing, etc, ea, from $4 to.$6.00

Burger King, Dallas Cowboys, Dr Pepper, 6 different, ea, from $7 to $15.00

Burger King, Have It Your Way 1776-1976 Series, 1976, 4 different, ea, from $4 to...$6.00

Burger King, Mardi Gras, 1988, wht glass mug w/red & yellow logo, from $8 to...$10.00

Burger King, Mardi Gras, 1989, blk glass mug w/wht logo, from $8 to...$10.00

Burger King, Put a Smile in Your Tummy, features Burger King mascot, from $8 to $10.00

Burger King, see also specific name or series

Burger King, Where Kids Are King Series, pitcher, glass w/wht label featuring Burger King & phrase, from $35 to $40.00

Burger King, Where Kids Are King Series, set of 4 glasses matching pitcher above, ea, from $3 to $5.00

Calamity Jane, see Wild West Series

Captain America, see Super Heroes

Casper the Friendly Ghost & Related Characters, see Arby's Bicentennial or Harvey Cartoon Characters

Charles Dickens' A Christmas Carol, Subway, early 1980s, 4 different, ea, from $4 to...$6.00

Charlie McCarthy & Edgar Bergen, Libbey, 1930s, set of 8, M (EX illus display box) $600.00

Children's Classics, Libbey Glass Co, Alice in Wonderland, Gulliver's Travels, Tom Sawyer, from $10 to **$15.00**

Children's Classics, Libbey Glass Co, Moby Dick, Robin Hood, Three Musketeers, Treasure Island, ea, from $10 to...**$15.00**

Children's Classics, Libbey Glass Co, The Wizard of Oz, from $25 to **$30.00**

Chilly Willy, see Walter Lantz

Chipmunks, Hardee's (no logo on glass), 1985, Alvin, Simon, Theodore, Chipettes, ea, from $2 to.............................**$4.00**

Cinderella, Disney/Libbey, 1950s-60s, set of 8 ....**$120.00**

Cinderella, see also Disney Collector Series or Disney Film Classics

Clarabell, see Howdy Doody

Currier & Ives, Arby's, 1975-76, 4 different, titled, ea, from $3 to **$5.00**

Currier & Ives, Kraft Cheese, 1970s, Old Homestead in Winter, American Winter Scene, ea, from $1 to......................**$3.00**

Daffy Duck, see Warner Bros

Daisy Mae, see Al Capp

Dick Tracy, Domino's Pizza, M **$185.00**

Dick Tracy, 1940s, frosted, 8 different characters, 3" or 5", ea, from $50 to...**$75.00**

Dilly Dally, see Howdy Doody

Dinosaur Series, see Welch's

Disney, see also Wonderful World of Disney or specific characters

Disney, 1980s, juice set, carafe (chiller) w/4 8-oz tumblers, complete w/box, from $15 to................................**$20.00**

Disney Characters, 1936, Clarabelle, Donald, F Bunny, Horace, Mickey, Minnie, Pluto, 4¼" or 4¾", ea, from $30 to ...**$50.00**

Disney Characters, 1989, frosted juice, face images of Daisy, Donald, Mickey, Minnie, Scrooge, ea, from $5 to........**$8.00**

Disney Characters, 1990, frosted tumbler, face images of of Daisy, Donald, Goofy, Mickey, Minnie, Scrooge, from $5 to...**$8.00**

Disney Collector Series, Burger King, 1994, mc images on clear plastic, 8 different, MIB, ea.............................**$3.00**

Disney Film Classics, McDonald's/Coca-Cola/Canada, Cinderella, Fantasia, Peter Pan, Snow White & the Seven Dwarfs, ea..**$15.00**

Disney's All-Star Parade, 1939, 10 different, ea, from $40 to...**$75.00**

Domino's Pizza, Avoid the Noid, 1988, 4 different, ea........**$7.00**

Donald Duck, Donald Duck Cola, 1960s-70s, from $15 to .**$20.00**

Donald Duck or Daisy, see also Disney or Mickey Mouse (Happy Birthday)

Dudley Do-Right, see Arby's Bicentennial or PAT Ward

Dynomutt, see Hanna-Barbera

Elsie the Cow, Borden, Elsie & Family in 1976 Bicentennial parade, red, wht & bl graphics, from $5 to **$7.00**

Elsie the Cow, Borden, 1950s, wht head image on waisted style, from $15 to...**$20.00**

Elsie the Cow, Borden, 1960, yel daisy image, from $10 to .**$12.00**

Empire Strikes Back, see Star Wars Trilogy

ET, Army & Air Force Exchange Service, 1982, rnd bottom, 4 different mc images, ea, from $5 to **$10.00**

ET, Pepsi/MCA Home Video, 1988, 6 different, ea, from $15 to **$25.00**

ET, Pizza Hut, 1982, ftd, 4 different, from $2 to **$4.00**

Fantasia, see Disney Film Classics or Mickey Mouse (Through the Years)

Flintstone Kids, Pizza Hut, 1986, 4 different, ea, from $2 to...**$4.00**

Flintstones, see also Hanna-Barbera

Flintstones, Welch's, 1962 (6 different), 1963 (2 different), 1964 (6 different), ea, from $8 to **$12.00**

Ghostbusters II, Sunoco/Canada, 1989, 6 different, ea, from $5 to **$8.00**

Goonies, Godfather's Pizza/Warner Bros, 1985, 4 different, from $4 to **$8.00**

Great Muppet Caper, McDonald's, 1981, 4 different, 6", ea...**$2.00**

Green Arrow, see Super Heroes

Green Lantern, See Super Heroes

Gulf Oil Co, Gulf Collector Series, 1980s, 6 different featuring early company history, ea, from $3 to..........................**$5.00**

Hanna-Barbera, Pepsi, 1977, Dynomutt, Flintstones, Mumbly, Scooby, Yogi & Huck, ea, from $20 to **$35.00**

Hanna-Barbera, Pepsi, 1977, Josie and the Pussy Cats, from $20.00 to $35.00. (Photo courtesy Greg Davis and Bill Morgan)

Hanna-Barbera, 1960s, jam glasses featuring Cindy Bear, Flintstones, Huck, Quick Draw, Yogi Bear, rare, ea, from $75 to..**$110.00**

Happy Days, Dr Pepper, 1977, Fonzie, Joanie, Potsie, Ralph, Richie, from $8 to...**$12.00**

Happy Days, Dr Pepper/Pizza Hut, 1977, Fonzie or Richie, ea, from $10 to...**$15.00**

Happy Days, Dr Pepper/Pizza Hut, 1977, Joanie, Potsie, Ralph, ea, from $8 to **$12.00**

Harvey Cartoon Characters, Pepsi, 1970s, action pose, Baby Huey, Hot Stuff, Wendy, ea, from $8 to **$15.00**

Harvey Cartoon Characters, Pepsi, 1970s, static pose, Baby Huey, Casper, Hot Stuff, Wendy, ea, from $12 to **$20.00**

Harvey Cartoon Characters, Pepsi, 1970s, static pose, Richie Rich, from $15 to...**$25.00**

Harvey Cartoon Characters, Pepsi, 1970s, static pose, Sad Sack, scarce, from $25 to...**$35.00**

Harvey Cartoon Characters, see also Arby's Bicentennial Series

He-Man & Related Characters, see Masters of the Universe

Hersey's Chocolate, A Kiss for You, from $3 to **$5.00**

Holly Hobbie, American Greetings/Coca-Cola, 1980 Christmas, 4 different: Christmas Is..., Wrap Each..., etc, ea, $3 to......**$5.00**

Holly Hobbie, American Greetings/Coca-Cola, 1981 Christmas, 3 different: 'Tis the Season..., A Gift..., etc, ea, $2 to ..**$4.00**

Holly Hobbie, American Greetings/Coca-Cola, 1982 Christmas, 3 different: Wishing You..., Share in the Fun..., ea, from $2 to...**$4.00**

Honey, I Shrunk the Kids, McDonald's, 1989, plastic, 3 different, ea, from $1 to **$2.00**

Hopalong Cassidy, milk glass w/blk graphics, Breakfast Milk, Lunch Milk, Dinner Milk, ea, from $15 to **$20.00**

Hopalong Cassidy, milk glass w/red & blk graphics, 3 different, ea, from $20 to..**$25.00**

Hopalong Cassidy's Western Series, ea, from $25 to.........**$30.00**

Hot Dog Castle, Collector Series, 1977, Abilene Past, Abilene Present, Abilene Future, ea, from $6 to.......................**$8.00**

Hot Stuff, see Harvey Cartoon Characters or Arby's Bicentennial

Howard the Duck, see Super Heroes

Howdy Doody, Welch's/Kagran, 1950s, 6 different, emb bottom, ea, from $15 to...**$20.00**

Huckleberry Hound, see Hanna-Barbera

Incredible Hulk, see Super Heroes

Indiana Jones & the Temple of Doom, 7-Up (w/4 different sponsers), 1984, set of 4, from $8 to.....................................**$15.00**

Indiana Jones: The Last Crusade, wht plastic, 4 different, ea, from $2 to...**$4.00**

James Bond 007, 1985, 4 different, ea, from $10 to **$15.00**

Jewel Tea Jelly, Old Time Series, 1950s, 6 different, ea, from $12 to **$4.00**

Joe Btsfplk, see Al Capp

Joker, see Super Heroes

Jungle Book, Disney/Canada, 1966, 6 different, numbered, 5", ea, from $40 to...**$75.00**

Jungle Book, Disney/Canada, 1966, 6 different, numbered, 6½", ea, from $30 to...**$60.00**

Jungle Book, Disney/Pepsi, 1970s, Bagheera or Shere Kahn, unmk, ea, from $60 to...**$90.00**

Jungle Book, Disney/Pepsi, 1970s, Mowgli, unmk, from $40 to **$50.00**

Jungle Book, Disney/Pepsi, 1970s, Rama, unmk, from $50 to **$60.00**

Keebler Soft Batch Cookies, 1984, 4 different, ea, from $7 to **$10.00**

Kellogg's, 1977, Big Yella, Dig 'Em, Snap!, Crackle! & Pop!, Tony, Tony Jr, Toucan Sam, ea, from $7 to **$10.00**

King Kong, Coca-Cola/Dino De Laurentis Corp, 1976, from $5 to **$8.00**

Laurel & Hardy, see Arby's Actor Series

Leonardo TTV, see also Arby's Bicentennial Series

Leonardo TTV Collector Series, Pepsi, Underdog, Go-Go Gophers, Simon Bar Sinister, Sweet Polly, 6", ea, from $15 to **$25.00**

Leonardo TTV Collector Series, Pepsi, Underdog, Simon Bar Sinister, Sweet Polly, 5", ea, from $8 to.....................**$15.00**

Li'l Abner & Related Characters, see Al Capp

Little Rascals, see Arby's Actor Series

Lone Ranger, see Western Heroes

Mae West, see Arby's Actor Series

Mark Twain Country Series, Burger King, 1985, 4 different, ea, from $8 to...**$10.00**

Masters of the Universe, Mattel, 1983, He-Man, Man-at-Arms, Skeletor, Teels, ea, from $5 to **$10.00**

Masters of the Universe, Mattel, 1986, Battle Cat/He-Man, Man-at-Arms, Orko, Panthor/Sketetor, ea, from $3 to **$5.00**

McDonald's, Classic '50s, 1993, fountain shape, 4 different, sm distribution, ea, from $3 to **$5.00**

McDonald's, Hawaiians & Their Sea Series, 1980s, smoke-tinted glass w/wht graphics, 4 different, ea, from $6 to..........**$8.00**

McDonald's, McDonaldland Action Series, 1977, 6 different, ea **$5.00**

McDonald's, McDonaldland Collector Series, 1970s, 6 different, ea **$4.00**

McDonald's, McVote, 1986, 3 different, ea, from $4 to **$6.00**

McDonald's, mugs, ceramic, AM (w/circle & \ symbol) Warning: First Cup, Gone for the Morning, ea, from $3 to ..**$5.00**

McDonald's, mugs, smoked glass embossed w/4 different McDonald's characters, ca 1977, ea, from $8 to **$10.00**

McDonald's, Olympics, 1984, clear glass mugs w/painted-on graphics, 4 different featuring various events, ea, from $5 to **$7.00**

McDonald's, 1982 Knoxville World's Fair, Coca-Cola, flared tumbler, from $3 to **$5.00**

MGM Collector Series, Pepsi, 1975, Tom, Jerry, Barney, Droopy, Soike, Tuffy, ea, from $10 to.......................................**$15.00**

Mickey Mouse, Happy Birthday, Pepsi, 1978, Clarabelle & Horace, from $15 to...**$20.00**

Mickey Mouse, Happy Birthday, Pepsi, 1978, Daisy & Donald, from $12 to...**$15.00**

Mickey Mouse, Happy Birthday, Pepsi, 1978, Donald, Goofy, Mickey, Minnie, Pluto, Uncle Scrooge, ea, from $6 to ..**$10.00**

Mickey Mouse, Mickey's Christmas Carol, Coca-Cola, 1982, 3 different, ea **$10.00**

Mickey Mouse, see also Disney Characters

Mickey Mouse, Through the Years, K-Mart, glass mugs w/4 different images (1928, 1937, 1940, 1955), ea, from $3 to **$5.00**

Mickey Mouse, Through the Years, Sunoco/Canada, 1988, 6 different (1928, 1938, 1940, 1955, 1983, 1988), ea, from $6 to..**$10.00**

Mister Magoo, Polomar Jelly, many different variations & styles, ea, from $25 to **$35.00**

Morris the Cat, 9-Lives, ca late 1970s, 2 different, mail-in premium, ea, from $5 to..**$7.00**

NFL, Mobil Oil, helmets on colored bands, low, ftd bottom, Colts, Cowboys, Oilers, Steelers, ea, from $2 to...........**$4.00**

NFL, Mobil Oil, helmets on wht bands, low, flat bottom, Bills, Buccaneers, Eagles, Red Skins, Steelers, ea, from $3 to..**$5.00**

Norman Rockwell, Saturday Evening Post Series, Arby's, early 1980s, 6 different, numbered, ea, from $2 to................**$4.00**

Norman Rockwell, Saturday Evening Post Series, Country Time Lemonade, 4 different, w/authorized logo, ea, from $3 to..**$5.00**

Norman Rockwell, Saturday Evening Post Series, Country Time Lemonade, 4 different, no logo, ea, from $3 to **$5.00**

Norman Rockwell, Summer Series, Arby's, 1987, 4 different, tall, ea, from $3 to..**$5.00**

Norman Rockwell, Winter Series, Arby's/Pepsi, 1979, 4 different, short, ea, from $3 to..**$5.00**

Pac-Man, Arby's Collector Series, 1980, rocks glass, from $2 to....**$4.00**

Pac-Man, Bally Midway MFG/AAFES/Libbey, 1980, Shadow (Blinky), Bashful (Inky), Pokey (Clyde), Speedy (Pinky), ea, from $4 to **$6.00**

Pac-Man, Bally Midway Mfg/Libbey, 1982, 6" flare top, 5⅜" flare top or mug, from $2 to **$4.00**

PAT Ward, Collector Series, Holly Farms Restaurants, 1975, Boris, Bullwinkle, Natasha, Rocky, ea, from $30 to ...**$50.00**

PAT Ward, Pepsi, late 1970s, action pose, Bullwinkle w/balloons, Dudley in Canoe, Rocky in circus, 5", ea, from $10 to .**$15.00**

PAT Ward, Pepsi, late 1970s, static pose, Boris, Mr Peabody, Natasha, 5", ea, from $10 to **$15.00**

PAT Ward, Pepsi, late 1970s, static pose, Boris & Natasha, 6", from $20 to..**$25.00**

PAT Ward, Pepsi, late 1970s, static pose, Bullwinkle, brn lettering, no Pepsi logo, 6", from $20 to **$25.00**

PAT Ward, Pepsi, late 1970s, static pose, Bullwinkle, wht or blk lettering, 6", from $15 to **$20.00**

PAT Ward, Pepsi, late 1970s, static pose, Bullwinkle, 5", from $25 to **$30.00**

PAT Ward, Pepsi, late 1970s, static pose, Dudley Do-Right, blk lettering, 6", from $15 to **$20.00**

PAT Ward, Pepsi, late 1970s, static pose, Dudley Do-Right, red lettering, no Pepsi logo, 6", from $15 to.....................**$20.00**

PAT Ward, Pepsi, late 1970s, static pose, Dudley Do-Right, 5", from $15 to..**$20.00**

PAT Ward, Pepsi, late 1970s, static pose, Rocky, brn lettering, no Pepsi logo, 6", from $20 to..................................**$25.00**

PAT Ward, Pepsi, late 1970s, static pose, Rocky, wht or blk lettering, 6", from $15 to...**$20.00**

PAT Ward, Pepsi, late 1970s, static pose, Rocky, 5", from $20 to..**$25.00**

PAT Ward, Pepsi, late 1970s, static pose, Snidley Whiplash, wht or blk lettering, 6", from $15 to..................................**$20.00**

PAT Ward, Pepsi, late 1970s, static pose, Snidley Whiplash, 5", from $10 to..**$15.00**

PAT Ward, see also Arby's Bicentennial Series

Peanuts Characters, Dolly Madison Bakery, Snoopy for President, 4 different, ea, from $4 to **$6.00**

Peanuts Characters, Dolly Madison Bakery, Snoopy Sport Series, 4 different, ea, from $4 to **$6.00**

Peanuts Characters, ftd, Snoopy sitting on lemon or Snoopy sitting on lg red apple, ea, from $2 to...............................**$3.00**

Peanuts Characters, Kraft, 1988, Charlie Brown flying kite, Lucy on swing, Snoopy in pool, Snoopy on surfboard, ea.....**$2.00**

Peanuts Characters, McDonald's, 1983, Camp Snoopy, wht plastic w/Lucy or Snoopy, ea, from $5 to **$8.00**

Peanuts Characters, McDonald's, 1983, Camp Snoopy, 5 different, ea, from $1 to..**$2.00**

Peanuts Characters, milk glass mug, At Times Life Is Pure Joy (Snoopy & Woodstock dancing), from $3 to...............**$5.00**

Peanuts Characters, milk glass mug, Snoopy for President, 4 different, numbered & dated, ea, from $5 to **$8.00**

Peanuts Characters, milk glass mug, Snoopy in various poses, from $2 to..**$4.00**

Peanuts Characters, plastic, I Got It! I Got It!, I Have a Strange Team, Let's Break for Lunch!, ea, from $5 to **$8.00**

Penguin, see Super Heroes

Pepsi, Batgirl and Robin, 1977, $2,000.00. (Photo courtesy Collector Glass News)

Pepsi, Historical Advertising Posters, 1979, 4 different, blk & wht, ea, from $8 to..**$10.00**

Pepsi, Night Before Christmas, 1982-83, 4 different, ea, from $4 to **$6.00**

Pepsi, Twelve Days of Christmas, 1976, ea, from $1 to **$3.00**

Peter Pan, see Disney Film Classics

Pillsbury, Doughboy w/various musical instruments, 1991, mail-in premium, from $6 to..**$12.00**

Pinocchio, Dairy Promo/Libbey, 1938-40, 12 different, ea, from $15 to **$25.00**

Pinocchio, see also Disney Collector's Series or Wonderful World of Disney

Pluto, see Disney Characters

Pocahontas, Burger King, 1995, 4 different, MIB, ea **$3.00**

Popeye, Kollect-A-Set, Coca-Cola, 1975, Popeye, from $7 to..**$10.00**

Popeye, Kollect-A-Set, Cocoa-Cola, 1975, 6 different, any except Popeye, ea, from $5 to **$7.00**

Popeye, Pals, Popeye's Famous Fried Chicken, 1979, 4 different, ea, from $10 to **$20.00**

Popeye, 10th Anniversary Series, Popeye's Famous Fried Chicken/Pepsi, 1982, 4 different, ea, from $10 to......**$15.00**

Quick Draw, McGraw, see Hanna-Barbera

Rescuers, Pepsi, 1977, Brockway tumbler, Bernard, Bianca, Brutus & Nero, Evinrude, Orville, Penny, ea, from $8 to.........**$15.00**

Rescuers, Pepsi, 1977, Brockway tumbler, Madame Medusa or Rufus, ea, from $25 to...**$30.00**

Return of the Jedi, see Star Wars Trilogy

Richie Rich, see Harvey Cartoon Characters

Riddler, see Super Heroes

Ringling Bros Circus Clown Series, Pepsi, 1980s, 8 different, ea **$12.00**

Ringling Bros Circus Poster Series, Pepsi, 1980s, 6 different, ea **$20.00**

Road Runner & Related Characters, see Warner Bros

Robin, see Super Heroes

Rocky & Bullwinkle, see Arby's Bicentennial or PAT Ward

Roger Rabbit, McDonald's, 1988, plastic, ea, from $1 to **$3.00**

Roy Rogers Restaurant, 1883-1983 logo, from $5 to...........**$7.00**

Sad Sack, see Harvey Cartoon Characters

Sadie Hawkins, see Al Capp

Scooby Doo, see Hanna-Barbera

Shmoos, see Al Capp

Sleeping Beauty, American, late 1950s, 6 different, ea, from $15 to $20.00

Sleeping Beauty, Canadian, late 1950s, 12 different, ea, from $20 to $25.00

Smurfs, Hardee's, 1982 (8 different), 1983 (6 different), ea, from $1 to $3.00

Snidley Whiplash, see PAT Ward

Snoopy & Related Characters, see Peanuts Characters

Snow White & the Seven Dwarfs, Bosco, 1938, ea, from $25 to..$45.00

Snow White & the Seven Dwarfs, Libbey, 1930s, verses on back, various colors, 8 different, ea, from $15 to $25.00

Snow White & the Seven Dwarfs, see also Disney Collector's Series or Disney Film Classics

Star Trek, Dr Pepper, 1976, 4 different, ea, from $20 to ...$25.00

Star Trek, Dr Pepper, 1978, 4 different, ea, from $30 to ...$40.00

Star Trek II, The Search for Spock, Taco Bell, 1984, 4 different, ea, from $3 to $5.00

Star Trek: The Motion Pitcure, Coca-Cola, 1980, 3 different, ea, from $10 to..$15.00

Star Wars Trilogy: Empire Strikes Back, Burger King/Coca-Cola, 1980, 4 different, ea, from $7 to $10.00

Star Wars Trilogy: Return of the Jedi, Burger King/Coca-Cola, 1983, 4 different, ea, from $6 to $8.00

Star Wars Trilogy: Star Wars, Burger King/Coca-Cola, 1977, 4 different, ea, from $12 to $15.00

Sunday Funnies, 1976, Brenda Star, Gasoline Alley, Moon Mullins, Orphan Annie, Smilin' Jack, Terry & the Pirates, $8 to $15.00

Sunday Funnies, 1976, Broom Hilda, from $100 to........$150.00

Super Heroes, Marbel, 1978, Federal, flat bottom, Captain America, Hulk, Spider-Man, Thor, ea, from $100 to $150.00

Super Heroes, Marvel, 1978, Federal, flat bottom, Spider-Woman, from $175 to $250.00

Super Heroes, Marvel/7 Eleven, 1977, ftd, Amazing Spider-Man, from $30 to..$45.00

Super Heroes, Marvel/7 Eleven, 1977, ftd, Captain America, Fantastic Four, Howard the Duck, Thor, ea, from $20 to.....$35.00

Super Heroes, Marvel/7 Eleven, 1977, ftd, Incredible Hulk, from $25 to..$35.00

Super Heroes, Pepsi Super (Moon) Series/DC Comics, 1976, Green Arrow, from $20 to $30.00

Super Heroes, Pepsi Super (Moon) Series/DC Comics, 1976, Green Lantern, Joker, Penguin, Riddler, ea, from $35 to $50.00

Super Heroes, Pepsi Super (Moon) Series/DC Comics or NPP, 1976, Batgirl, Batman, Shazam!, ea, from $10 to......$15.00

Super Heroes, Pepsi Super (Moon) Series/NPP, 1976, Green Lantern, Joker, Penguin, Riddler, ea, from $20 to......$40.00

Superman, NPP/M Polanar & Son, 1964, 6 different, various colors, 4¼" or 5¾", ea, from $20 to............................$35.00

Sylvester the Cat, see Warner Bros

Tasmanian Devil, see Warner Bros

Tom & Jerry & Related Characters, see MGM Collector Series

Underdog & Related Characters, see Arby's Bicentennial or Leonardo TTV

Terrytoons, Sourpuss and Gandy Goose, from $350.00 to $400.00.
(Photo courtesy Collector Glass News)

Universal Monsters, Universal Studio, 1980, ftd, Creature, Dracula, Frankenstein, Mummy, Mutant, Wolfman, ea, from $100 to..$160.00

Urchins, Coca-Cola/American Greetings, 1976-78, baseball, bicycling, golf, skating, swimming, tennis, ea, from $3 to $5.00

Walter Lantz, Pepsi, 1970s, Chilly Willy or Wally Walrus, ea, from $35 to..$55.00

Walter Lantz, Pepsi, 1970s, Cuddles, from $60 to.............$80.00

Walter Lantz, Pepsi, 1970s, Mighty Mouse or Space Mouse, from $600.00 to $700.00 each.
(Photo courtesy Collector Glass News)

Walter Lantz, Pepsi, 1970s, Woody Woodpecker, from $10 to $20.00

Walter Lantz, Pepsi, 1970s-80s, Anty/Miranda, Chilly/Smelley, Cuddles/Oswald, Wally/Homer, ea, from $30 to........$40.00

Walter Lantz, Pepsi, 1970s-80s, Buzz Buzzard/Space Mouse, from $20 to $30.00

Walter Lantz, Pepsi, 1970s-80s, Woody Woodpecker/Knothead & Splinter, from $15 to $20.00

Walter Lantz, see also Arby's Bicentennial Series

Warner Bros, Arby's Adventure Series, 1988, ftd, Bugs, Daffy, Porky, Sylvester & Tweety, ea, from $35 to................$45.00

Warner Bros, Marriot's Great America, 1975, 12-oz, 6 different (Bugs & related characters), ea, from $25 to.............$30.00

Warner Bros, Marriott's Great America, 1989, Bugs, Porky, Sylvester, Taz, ea, from $5 to $10.00

Warner Bros, Pepsi, 1973, Brockway 12-oz tumbler, Bugs, Porky, Road Runner, Sylvester, Tweety, ea, from $10 to **$15.00**

Warner Bros, Pepsi, 1973, Federal 16-oz tumbler, Bugs Bunny, wht lettering, from $8 to **$12.00**

Warner Bros, Pepsi, 1973, Federal 16-oz tumbler, Cool Cat, blk lettering, from $10 to **$15.00**

Warner Bros, Pepsi, 1973, Federal 16-oz tumbler, Elmer Fudd, wht lettering, from $5 to **$8.00**

Warner Bros, Pepsi, 1973, Federal 16-oz tumbler, Henry Hawk, blk lettering, from $25 to **$40.00**

Warner Bros, Pepsi, 1973, Federal 16-oz tumbler, Speedy Gonzales, blk lettering, from $6 to **$10.00**

Warner Bros, Pepsi, 1973, wht plastic, 6 different, Bugs, Daffy, Porky, Road Runner, Sylvester, Tweety, ea, from $3 to..... **$5.00**

Warner Bros, Pepsi, 1976, Interaction, Beaky Buzzard & Cool Cat w/kite or Taz & Porky w/fishing pole, ea, from $8 to...... **$10.00**

Warner Bros, Pepsi, 1976, Interaction, Bugs & Yosemite w/cannon, Yosemite & Speedy Gonzales panning gold, ea, from $10 to **$15.00**

Warner Brothers, Pepsi, 1976, Interaction, Foghorn Leghorn and Henry Hawk; Foghorn Leghorn, from $5.00 to $10.00 each. (Photo courtesy David Longest)

Warner Bros, Pepsi, 1976, Interaction, others, ea, from $5 to ... **$10.00**

Warner Bros, Pepsi, 1979, Collector's Series, rnd bottom, Bugs, Daffy, Porky, Road Runner, Sylvester, Tweety, ea, from $7 to **$10.00**

Warner Bros, Welch's, 1974, action poses, 8 different, phrases around top, ea, from $2 to.. **$4.00**

Warner Bros, Welch's, 1976-77, 8 different, names around bottom, ea, from $5 to **$7.00**

WC Fields, see Arby's Actor Series

Welch's, Dinosaur Series, 1989, 4 different, ea.................... **$2.00**

Welch's see also Archies, Howdy Doody or Warner Bros

Wendy's, Clara Pella (Where's the Beef?) or Clara Pella (no phrase), ea, from $4 to **$6.00**

Wendy's, Cleveland Browns, Dr Pepper, 1981, 4 different, ea, from $5 to.. **$8.00**

Western Heroes, Annie Oakley, Buffalo Bill, Wild Bill Hickok, Wyatt Earp, ea, from $8 to.. **$12.00**

Western Heroes, Lone Ranger, from $10 to **$15.00**

Wild Bill Hickok, see Western Heroes

Wild West Series, Coca-Cola, Buffalo Bill, Calamity Jane, ea, from $10 to.. **$15.00**

Wile E Coyote, see Warner Bros

Winnie the Pooh, Sears/WDP, 1970s, 4 different, ea, from $15 to **$25.00**

Wizard of Id, Arby's, 1983, 6 different, ea, from $7 to **$10.00**

Wizard of Oz, Coca-Cola/Krystal, 1989, 50th Anniversary Series, 6 different, ea, from $10 to............................ **$15.00**

Wizard of Oz, see also Children's Classics

Wizard of Oz, Swift's, 1950s-60, fluted bottom, Emerald City or Flying Monkeys, ea, from $15 to **$20.00**

Wizard of Oz, Swift's, 1950s-60s, fluted bottom, Glinda, from $15 to **$25.00**

Wizard of Oz, Swift's, 1950s-60s, fluted bottom, Wicked Witch, from $35 to **$50.00**

Wonder Woman, see Super Heroes

Wonderful World of Disney, Pepsi, 1980s, Alice, Bambi, Lady & the Tramp, Pinocchio, Snow White, 101 Dalmatians, ea.. **$25.00**

Woody Woodpecker & Related Characters, see Arby's Bicentennial or Walter Lantz

Wyatt Earp, see Western Heroes

Yogi Bear, see Hanna-Barbera

Yosemite Sam, see Warner Bros

Ziggy, 7-Up Collector Series, 4 different, ea, from $4 to **$7.00**

7-11, New York Islanders, from $15.00 to $20.00 each.
(Photo courtesy Collector Glass News)

Character Bobbin' Heads

Frequently referred to as nodders, these papier-mache dolls reflect accurate likenesses of the characters they portray and have become popular collectibles. Made in Japan throughout the 1960s, they were sold as souvenirs at Disney, Universal Studios, and Six Flags amusement parks, and they were often available at roadside concessions as well. Papier-mache was was used until the mid-'70s when ceramic composition came into use. They were very susceptible to cracking and breaking, and it's difficult to find mint specimens — little wonder, since these nodders were commonly displayed on car dashboards!

Our values are for nodders in near-mint condition. To calculate values for examples in very-good condition, reduce our prices by 25% to 40%.

Advisors: Matt and Lisa Adams (A7).

Andy Griffith, 1992, ceramic, NM, J6 ....$75.00
Barney Fife, 1992, ceramic, NM, J6................................$75.00
Beetle Bailey, NM, A7, from $100 to $150.00
Bugs Bunny, NM, A7, from $100 to $175.00
Charlie Brown, Japan, ceramic w/gr baseball cap & mitt, NM, A7 ....$60.00
Charlie Brown, sq blk base, NM.....................................$95.00
Charlie Brown, 1970s, no base, sm, NM, A7 ....$45.00
China Man, Japan, 1960s, compo, NM, J6........................$65.00
Chinese Boy & Girl, 5½", NM, pr $65.00
Colonel Sanders, 2 different styles, NM, A7, ea from $100 to $125.00
Dagwood, 1950s, compo, Kiss Me on gr rnd base, 6", EX, A $150.00
Danny Kaye, kissing, NM, A7....................................$100.00
Danny Kaye & Girl, kissing, NM, A7, pr.....................$150.00
Dobie Gillis, NM, A7, from $250 to $300.00
Donald Duck, Walt Disney World, sq wht base, NM, A7...$75.00
Donald Duck, 1970s, rnd gr base, NM, A7 ....$75.00
Donny Osmond, wht jumpsuit w/microphone, NM, A7, from $100 to $150.00
Dr Ben Casey, NM, A7, from $100 to $125.00
Dr Kildare, 1960s, compo, rnd wht base, 7", EX $65.00
Dumbo, rnd red base, NM, A7 ....$100.00
Elmer Fudd, NM, A7, from $100 to $175.00
Foghorn Leghorn, NM, A7, from $100 to......................$175.00
Goofy, Disneyland, arms at side, sq wht base, NM, A7.....$75.00
Goofy, Walt Disney World, arms folded, sq wht base, NM, A7 ....$75.00
Hobo, Japan, 1960s, compo, NM, J6 ....$65.00
Linus, Japan, ceramic, baseball catcher w/gr cap, NM, A7...$60.00
Linus, Lego, sq blk base, NM, A7..................................$95.00
Little Audrey, NM, A7, from $100 to $150.00
Lt Fuzz (Beetle Bailey), NM, A7, from $100 to $150.00

Lucy (Peanuts), Japan, ceramic, gr baseball cap & bat, NM, A7 ....$60.00
Lucy (Peanuts), Lego, sq blk base, NM, A7 ....$95.00
Lucy (Peanuts), 1970s, no base, sm, NM, A7 ....$45.00
Mammy (Dogpatch USA), NM, A7 ....$75.00
Mary Poppins, Disneyland, 1960s, wood, w/umbrella & satchel, 5¾", M $95.00
Maynard Krebs (Dobie Gillis), hold bongos, NM, A7, from $250 to $350.00
Mickey Mouse, Disneyland, red, wht & bl outfit, sq wht base, NM, A7 ....$100.00
Mickey Mouse, Walt Disney World, bl & shirt & red pants, NM, A7 ....$75.00
Mickey Mouse, yel shirt & red pants, rnd gr base, NM, A7.....$75.00
Mr Peanut, moves at waist, w/cane, NM, A7, from $150 to..$200.00
New York World's Fair Boy & Girl, kissing, NM, A7 .....$125.00
Oodles the Duck (Bozo the Clown), NM, A7, from $150 to..$200.00
Pappy (Dogpatch USA), NM, A7................................$75.00
Peppermint Patti, Japan, ceramic, gr baseball cap & bat, NM, A7 ....$60.00

Phantom of the Opera and Wolfman, square bases, NM, $500.00 each (EX, $300.00 each). (Photo courtesy Matt and Lisa Adams)

Phantom of the Opera, Universal Studios of California, gr face, NM, A7 ....$150.00
Pig Pen (Peanuts), Lego, sq blk base, NM.........................$95.00
Pluto, 1970s, rnd gr base, NM, A7 ....$75.00
Porky Pig, NM, A7, from $100 to $175.00
Raggedy Andy, bank, mk A Penny Earned, NM, A7........$75.00
Roy Rogers, Japan, 1962, compo, sq gr base, 6½", M, from $150 to $200.00
Schroeder (Peanuts), Lego, sq blk base, NM....................$95.00
Sgt Snorkel (Beetle Bailey), NM, A7, from $100 to $150.00
Smokey the Bear, w/shovel, rnd base, NM, A7, from $125 to...$200.00
Smokey the Bear, w/shovel, sq base, NM, A7, from $125 to.....$200.00
Snoopy, as Flying Ace, 1970s, no base, NM, A7...............$45.00
Snoopy, as Joe Cool, 1970s, no base, sm, NM, A7...........$45.00
Snoopy, in Christmas outfit, 1970s, no base, sm, NM, A7..$45.00
Snoopy, Japan, ceramic, gr baseball cap & mitt, NM, A7...$60.00

Lucy, Snoopy, and Charlie Brown, Lego, NM, $95.00 each.
(Photo courtesy June Moon)

Snoopy, Lego, sq blk base, lg, NM, A7 ....$95.00
Space Boy, blk space suit & helmet, NM, A7 ....$75.00
Speedy Gonzales, NM, A7, from $100 to $175.00
Three Little Pigs, bl overalls & yel cap, rnd red base, NM, A7,
   ea..$100.00
Topo Gigio, standing w/apple, orange or pineapple, NM, A7,
   ea..$75.00
Topo Gigio, standing w/out fruit, NM, A7 ....$75.00
Tweety Bird, NM, A7, from $100 to $175.00
Wile E Coyote, NM, A7, from $100 to $175.00
Winnie the Pooh, 1970s, rnd gr base, NM, A7, from $100
   to $150.00
Wolfman, sq base, rare, NM, A7 ....$500.00
Woodstock, Japan, ceramic, w/bat, NM, A7 ....$60.00
Woodstock, 1970s, no base, sm, NM, A7 ....$45.00
Yosemite Sam, NM, A7, from $100 to $175.00
Zero (Beetle Bailey), NM, A7, from $100 to $150.00

Character Clocks and Watches

Clocks and watches whose dials depict favorite sports and TV stars have been manufactured with the kids in mind since the 1930s, when Ingersoll made a clock, a wristwatch, and a pocket watch featuring Mickey Mouse. The #1 Mickey wristwatch came in the now-famous orange box commonly known as the 'critter box,' illustrated with a variety of Disney characters. There is also a blue display box from the same time period. The watch itself featured a second hand with three revolving Mickey figures. It was available with either a metal or leather band. Babe Ruth stared on an Exacta Time watch in 1949, and the original box contained not only the watch but a baseball with a facsimile signature.

Collectors prize the boxes about as highly as they do the watches. Many were well illustrated and colorful, but most were promptly thrown away, so they're hard to find today. Be sure you buy only watches in very good condition. Rust, fading, scratches, or other signs of wear sharply devaluate a clock or a watch. Hundreds have been produced, and if you're going to collect them, you'll need to study *Comic Character Clocks and Watches* by Howard S. Brenner (Books Americana) for more information.

Note: Our values are typical of high retail. A watch in exceptional condition, especially an earlier model, may bring even more. Dealers (who will generally pay about half of book when they buy for resale) many times offer discounts on the more pricey items, and package deals involving more than one watch may sometimes be made for as much as a 15% discount.

Advisor: Bill Campbell (C10).

See also Advertising; other advertising related categories.

CLOCKS

Bart Simpson Alarm Clock, Wesco/UK, head image on face, yel
   plastic case, MIB, K1 ....$20.00
Batman, 1993, alarm 'voice' says 'Gotham City in trouble, Call for
   Batman,' Batlight shines on ceiling, battery-op, NM....$40.00
Bozo the Clown Alarm Clock, Larry Harmon/French, 1960s,
   Bozo's head moves, rare, EX, A $150.00

Dig 'Em Alarm Clock, 1979, NM..............................$35.00
Donald Duck Alarm Clock, Bayard, 1930s, Donald's hands keep
   time, bl-pnt metal case & base, 5" dia, NM, A........$250.00
Foghorn Leghorn & Henry Hawk, Foghorn w/bass drum, Henry
   w/trumpet, battery-op, 5x6x1½", M..........................$38.00
Fred Flintstone Alarm Clock, Germany, 1973, image & Yabba
   Dabba Doo! on face, Fred's hands keep time, dbl bell, M,
   A $125.00
Garfield, Sunbeam, eyes & tail move, battery-op, 7½x16",
   MIB $35.00
Mickey's Clockshop, Walt Disney, 1993, animated, musical,
   lights up, electric, MIB $60.00
Partridge Family Wall Clock, Time Setters, 1972, full-color
   photo image, 10" dia, NM, from $200 to $250.00
Pluto Desk Clock, Allied Mfg, 1948, plastic figure w/bones as
   hands, tongue moves & eyes roll, 9", rare, NM $200.00

Popeye Alarm Clock, King Features Syndicate, lithographed graphics on outside of case, M, $1,000.00 (EX, $500.00).
(Photo courtesy David Longest)

Road Runner, Seth Thomas, 1970, folding travel alarm, 3" dia
   when closed, MIB......................................$185.00
Simpsons Talking Radio Alarm Clock, Wesco/UK, Bart pouring
   beer in Homer's mouth, MIB, K1 ....$45.00
Simpsons Wall Clock, JPI, Simpson family on blk background,
   wht fr, 11x9", M, K1 ....$40.00
Smokey the Bear Alarm Clock, Bradley, 1950s, wht case, bl dbl
   bells, 7", NMIB, A $150.00
Snoopy Alarm Clock, Citizen, 1980s, Snoopy & Woodstock
   w/umbrellas, lt bl plastic case, dbl bell, 5" dia, NM ...$20.00
Snoopy Alarm Clock, Citizen, 1980s, Snoopy kicking soccer
   ball, pk plastic case, 3x3", MIB..............................$15.00
Snoopy Alarm Clock, Equity, Snoopy & Woodstock dancing in front
   of rainbow, wht metal case, 4x3", MIB, from $35 to $45.00
Snoopy Alarm Clock, Equity, Snoopy w/tennis racket &
   ball, wht metal casing w/silver trim, 4" dia, MIB, from
   $50 to $65.00
Snoopy Alarm Clock, Equity, 1980s, Snoopy w/baseball &
   bat, wht metal case w/silver trim, 4" dia, MIB, from
   $75 to $100.00
Snoopy Cuckoo Clock, Citizen, 1983, plastic house w/2-D figures
   of Snoopy & Woodstock, 16", M, from $175 to........$250.00

Snoopy Cuckoo Clock, Japan, 1983, Snoopy golfing, Woodstock is cuckoo bird, NM, from $175 to $250.00

Snoopy Pendulum Clock, Citizen, 1980s, Snoopy & Woodstock on face, plastic casing, 13", M, from $95 to $135.00

Mickey Mouse, Ingersoll for English market, pink celluloid face, second hand with tiny Mickey figures racing the dial, 1933, NM, $700.00.

Snow White Alarm Clock, Bayard Blanche Neige, 1960, 4½" diameter, NM, $300.00. (Photo courtesy Michael Stern)

Tweety & Sylvester, animated, talking, wireless remote for demo, battery-op, 9x22½", NM $170.00

Woody Woodpecker, 1950s, waving cowboy hat while riding horse, molded plastic, wind-up, 7x7", EX $105.00

Mickey Mouse, Ingersoll, 1934, Mickey in yel shorts, rare, NM, A $2,000.00

Popeye, Fossil, silver-tone w/matching chain, w/hand-pnt ceramic figure of Wimpy, M (in litho tin 'can' package) $75.00

Popeye, Ingersoll, 1935, Popeye surrounded by various characters between numbers, 2" dia, EX, A............................$850.00

Snoopy, Fossil, gold-tone, limited edition of 500, w/hand-decor red ceramic dog dish & orig paperwork, MIB $135.00

Woody Woodpecker Alarm Clark, Walter Lantz, 1st issue, Woody in chef's hat in front of Woody's Cafe tree, EX (EX box), $300.00.

Three Little Pigs, Ingersoll, 1935, wolf's eyes move and tick off seconds, NM (EX box), $2,500.00.

POCKET WATCHES

Bart Simpson, 1997, mfg for Marks & Spencer (English store), brushed steel, sports diver style, MIP.........................$70.00

Big Bad Wolf, EX, C10 ....$950.00

Buck Rogers, USA, 1935, colorful image of Buck & Wilma, emb space monster on back, 2" dia, EX, A $775.00

Buster Brown, 1928, EX, I1 ....$175.00

Buster Brown, 1960s, VG, I1 ....$75.00

WRISTWATCHES

Bart Simpson, Butterfinger Candy Bar premium, 1980s, M, I1 ....$20.00

Big Boy, 1970, Big Boy's hands keep time, EX, I1 ....$75.00

Blondie & Dagwood, rare, C10 ....$450.00

Boris & Natasha, Fossil, 1991, blk leather strap, in rnd blk bomb-shaped case, MIB..$80.00

Bugs Bunny & Gossamer, Armitrom JPO #0476, brn leather band, NM...$60.00

Buster Brown, 1970s, red costume, VG, I1 ....$75.00

Campbell Kids, 1982, 4 different, MIB, I1, ea..................$75.00

Campbell's Vegetable Soup, 1994, Campbell Kids, M, I1 .$50.00

Captain Midnight, Ovaltine premium, 1988, M, I1 ....$40.00

Cat in the Hat & Dr Seuss, sold at Universal Studios Island in Florida, M (red resin box w/Cat in the Hat on top) .**$165.00**

Charlie Tuna, 1971 and 1972 versions, Starkist premiums, EX, $65.00 each.

Charlie Tuna, 1973, facing right, VG, I1 ....**$50.00**
Charlie Tuna, 1986, 25th Anniversary, MIB, I1 ....**$25.00**
Cinderella, plastic figural, Disney, unused, M (VG+ box), from $465 to **$500.00**
Count Chocula, Booberry & Frankenberry, Lafayette Watch Co, MIB, I1..**$300.00**

Dick Tracy, 1940s, replaced band, EX, $75.00.

Dizzy Dean, 1933, Everbrite/Ingersoll, complete, all orig, scarce, M, C10 ....**$1,100.00**
Dracula, Fossil, 1990s w/figure, MIB, C10 ....**$265.00**
Ernie the Keebler Elf, 1970s, G, I1 ....**$50.00**
Farrah Fawcett, 1970s, photo image, lt bl band, NM, from $100 to **$125.00**
Felix the Cat, Fossil, style #8, w/polyresin Bag-O-Tricks bank, MIB **$75.00**
Flintstones, Fossil, 1993, M (lunch box-style case)...........**$45.00**
Frankenstein, 1995, glow-in-the-dark, MOC, C10..........**$25.00**
Gene Autry, New Haven, 1951, Gene holds gun that ticks off seconds, orig blk leather band, NM, A **$200.00**

Gene Autry, Wilane, 1948, bust image on face, orig brn leather band, NM (EX box), A **$350.00**
Goofy, Helbros, 1972, runs backwards, MIB, C10.......**$1,400.00**
Goofy Grape, 1976, G, I1 ....**$200.00**
Green Lantern, MIB, C10 ....**$85.00**

Howdy Doody, 1971, copyright NBC, EX, $25.00; 1950s moving-eye version, Bob Smith, EX, from $200.00 to $300.00.

Johnny Quest, Fossil, M (orig TV set-style box)..............**$45.00**
Man From Uncle, Bradley, 1960s, very rare w/box, MIB, C10..**$200.00**
Mary Marvel, 1948, extremely rare, EX (EX plastic box), C10..**$625.00**
Max Headroom, Coca-Cola, 1987, M, I1.......................**$10.00**
Mayor Daley, WWC, 1971, hands keep time, striped band, VG **$50.00**
Mickey Mouse, Bradley, Mickey's head moves back & forth, wind-up, NM **$55.00**

Mickey Mouse, Fossil, style #LI-1452, silver-tone case w/blk leather strap, w/vintage-style wooden pull toy train, MIB..$75.00

Mickey Mouse, Ingersoll, 1948, full-figure on rectangular face, orig red band, NM (EX box), A $325.00

Mickey Mouse, Kelton, MIB, C10 ....$700.00

Mr Magoo, Nutrasweet, 1995, M, I1 ....$30.00

Mr Peanut, 1966, yel face, VG, I1 ....$50.00

Mr Peanut, 1967, yel face w/date window, VG, I1 ....$50.00

Mr Peanut, 1975, bl face, digital, EX, I1 ....$50.00

Pepe Le Pew, Armitron, blk leather strap, plays I'm in the Mood for Love, lady's or youth sz, NM $35.00

Pink Panther, Fossil, 1998, deco-style tank case w/blk leather band, w/Pink Panther resin figure, M (litho tin pnt box) $105.00

Porky Pig, Ingraham, mid-1950s, MIB, C10 ....$600.00

Porky Pig, 1940s-50s, image on rectangular face, red vinyl band, EX, A $100.00

Punchy, 1970s, digital, red strap, VG, I1 ....$50.00

Raid Bug, 1970s, revolving disk, EX, I1 ....$150.00

Red Goose Shoes, 1960s, G, I1 ....$130.00

Ren & Stimpy, Powdered Toast, Bigtime Enterprises, 1992, MIP $40.00

Robin Hood, Bradley, 1956, Robin Hood w/bow & arrow on face, orig brn leather band, rare, NM, A $75.00

Rocky Jones Space Ranger, Ingraham, 1950s, MIB, C10 ..$750.00

Ronald McDonald, 1970s, MIB, I1...................................$50.00

Roy Rogers, metal bracelet band, MIB, C10 ....$450.00

Rudolph the Red Nose Reindeer, Montgomery Wards, 1939, red leather band, VG+...$45.00

Snow White, red cloth strap, Ingersoll, M (NM oval illus magic mirror box w/paperwork)..$325.00

Sonic the Hedgehog, Sega, 1994, MIP.............................$45.00

Spawn, Fossil, 1997, limited edition of 5,000, push-button light-up eyes, MIB $120.00

Superman, Dabbs, NM, C10 ....$100.00

Superman, 1940s – 50s, original band, nonworking, VG, $200.00.

Swiss Miss, 1981, EX, I1 ....$50.00

Tarzan, Bradley, MIB, C10..$60.00

Three Little Pigs & Big Bad Wolf, Ingersoll, 1934, MIB, C10, from $2,500 to...$3,000.00

Tinker Bell, bl face & bl band, sports watch, wings move, MIB $35.00

Tom Mix, 100th Anniversary, M, C10............................$275.00

Tony the Tiger, 1976, MIB, I1 ....$100.00

Toppie Elephant, 1950s, G, I1.......................................$100.00

Tweety, Armitron, silver & gold, tennis-bracelet style, 6 interchangeable watch faces, M (vinyl cloth-covered case) .$70.00

Twinkie the Brown Shoe Elf, 1920s, G, I1 ....$100.00

Winnie the Pooh, Ingersoll, lady's, MIP..........................$45.00

Wonder Woman, Dabbs, NM, C10 ....$125.00

Woody Woodpecker/Buzz Buzzard, Bradley, MIB............$110.00

Yogi Bear, Hanna-Barbera Productions, Swiss made, late 1950s-early 1960s, NM..$65.00

Zorro, US Time, 1955, Zorro in script on blk face, orig blk leather band, EX, A $75.00

Character, TV, and Movie Collectibles

To the baby boomers who grew up glued to the TV set and addicted to Saturday matinees, the faces they saw on the screen were as familiar to them as family. Just about any character you could name has been promoted through retail merchandising to some extent; depending on the popularity they attain, exposure may continue for weeks, months, even years. It's no wonder, then, that the secondary market abounds with these items or that there is such wide-spread collector interest. For more information, we recommend *Collector's Guide to TV Toys and Memorabilia, 1960s & 1970s, 2nd Edition* by Greg Davis and Bill Morgan; *Cartoon Toys and Collectibles Identification and Value Guide* by David Longest; *Peanuts Collectibles, Identification and Value Guide* by Andrea Podley and Derrick Bang; *Lone Ranger Collector's Reference and Value Guide* by Lee Felbinger; *Roy Rogers and Dale Evans Toys and Memorabilia* by P. Allan Coyle; and *Cartoon Friends of the Baby Boom Era* by Bill Bruegman.

Note: Though most characters are listed by their own names, some will be found under the title of the group, movie, comic strip, or dominate character they're commonly identified with. The Joker, for instance, will be found in the Batman listings.

Advisors: Lisa Adams (A7), Dr. Dolittle; Jerry and Joan Harnish (H4); Larry Doucet (D11), Dick Tracy; Ed Janey (J2); Trina and Randy Kubeck (K1), The Simpsons; TV Collector (T6); Casey's Collectible Corner (C1); Bill Stillman (S6), Wizard of Oz; Bill Bruegman (T2).

See also Action Figures; Battery-Operated; Books; Chein; Character Clocks and Watches; Coloring, Activity, and Paint Books; Dakins; Disney; Dolls, Celebrity; Fisher-Price; Games; Guns; Halloween Costumes; Lunch Boxes; Marx; Model Kits; Paper Dolls; Pin-Back Buttons; Plastic Figures; Playsets; Puppets; Puzzles; Ramp Walkers; Records; Toothbrush Holders; View-Master; Western; Windups, Friction, and Other Mechanicals.

Abbott & Costello, dolls, Ideal, 1984, Who's on First, 12", MIB, Y1 ....$100.00

Addams Family, figure, Lurch, Remco, 1964, vinyl w/cloth outfit, NM $65.00

Alien, movie viewer, Kenner, 1979, EX (EX box) $45.00

Alvin & the Chipmunks, squeeze toy, Alvin, Holland, 1964, rubber, EX $60.00

Amos & Andy, figures, Japan, prewar, bsk, 8" & 7", EX, pr ...$575.00

Andy Brown, sparkler, Germany, 1930s, push lever & eyes spark, tin, 7", NM $725.00

Andy Gump, doll, Bucherer, jtd metal & compo w/cloth clothes, 8", rare, VG...$400.00

Andy Panda, bank, litho-graphed tin, EX, $65.00.
(Photo courtesy David Longest)

Andy Panda, doll, stuffed felt w/velour outfit, orig tag, NM, T2, from $250 to $450.00

Annie, doll, Knickerbicker, 1982, 12", NRFB..................$25.00

Archies, doll, Archie, 1960s, stuffed cloth, 18", complete w/comic book, MIP..$75.00

Archies, stencil set, 1983, MOC $15.00

Astro Boy, bank, Japan, ceramic figure, 10", MIB, A7......$60.00

Baba Looey, bank, 1960s, plastic figure, 9", EX, N2..........$35.00

Baby Huey, figure, Alvimar, 1960s, inflatable vinyl w/bells inside, bl, wht & yel, 9", EX $25.00

Banana Splits, figure, Drooper Sutton, 1973, MIP............$80.00

Banana Splits, figure, Fleegle Sutton, 1973, MIP..............$80.00

Banana Splits, pillow, Fleegle or Snork, Kellogg's, 1960s, 10", minor fading o/w EX, ea $50.00

Barney Google, figure, mk 1944 KFS, wearing sailor suit, Syroco, scarce, NM, A1..$100.00

Barney Google & Spark Plug, pull toy, KFS, 1924, litho tin, 8", EX $850.00

Batman, bank, 1966, ceramic figure, EX $40.00

Batman, Batmobile pedal car, ca 1966, plastic, 34" long, EX, $575.00.

Batman, Batarang, Ideal, 1966, blk plastic, came w/utility belt, 8", NM $100.00

Batman, Batboat, 1973, inflatable vinyl, NM, from $35 to $45.00

Batman, Batcuffs, Ideal, 1966, came w/utility belt, 4", NM .$100.00

Batman, coins, Transogram, 1966, set of 20, MOC, T2...$50.00

Batman, Colorforms, 1966, few pcs missing, NMIB.........$40.00

Batman, figure, Robin, Fun Things/NPPI, 1966, rubber w/elastic string, 5", NM (EX card) $65.00

Batman, film, Adventures of Batman, Doom of the Rising Sun, Columbia, 1950s, 8mm, EX (EX box), T2 ....$50.00

Batman, flicker ring, plastic, NM $20.00

Batman, hat/mask, 1966, felt hat w/drop-down mask, Pow! patch on front, NM...$25.00

Batman, Hot-Line Batphone, Marx, 1966, red plastic w/decals, 8", NM (NM box), A $500.00

Batman, magic slate, Golden, 1989, MIP (sealed) $5.00

Batman, Official Batman Chute, NPPI, 1966, MOC $40.00

Batman, poncho & mask, 1976, MIP $35.00

Batman, poster, Ciro Art Corp, 1966, Batman & Robin swinging on rope in front of moon, glow-in-the-dark, 18x14", NM, T2..$50.00

Batman, Print Putty, 1966, MOC...................................$25.00

Batman, slippers, 1966, bl simulated leather boot-type w/colorful image, M, from $100 to $150.00

Batman, Stardust Touch of Velvet Art, Hasbro, 1966, complete, NMIB..$100.00

Batman, Super Top, 1977, MOC...................................$30.00

Batman, Switch 'N Go Playset, Mattel, 1966, complete, NMIB, T2, from $800 to $1,200.00

Batman, Thingmaker, Mattel, 1965, for rings or rubber stamps, EX..$35.00

Batman, yo-yo, Canada Games, 1990s, plastic w/imprint seal, tournament shape, MOC..$12.00

Batman & Robin, bank, Robin, Lego, 1966, ceramic, NM ..$65.00

Batman & Robin, pinball machine, Marx, 1966, litho tin & plastic, 21x10", EX, from $75 to............................$100.00

Batman & Robin, yo-yo, Duncan, 1978, plastic w/paper sticker eal, butterfly shape, MIP..$40.00

Batman & Wonder Woman, Etch-A-Sketch Action Pak, Ohio Art, 1981, MIP...$10.00

Batman Returns, mask, Penguin, Morris, 1992, latex, EX .$50.00

Battlestar Galactica, yo-yo, 1970s, plastic w/paper sticker seal, tournament shape, MIP...$16.00

Beaky Buzzard, bank, Beaky Buzzard standing beside barrel, pnt metal, 4", NM, A $85.00

Beany & Cecil, Beany-Copter, Mattel, 1960s, MOC $140.00

Beany & Cecil, Cecil & His Disguise Kit, Mattel, 1962, MIB (sealed) $125.00

Beany & Cecil, figural bowling game, comes w/10 Cecil figures (pins) & 2 balls, unused, EX+ (VG+ box)...............$225.00

Beany & Cecil, figure, talker, Mattel, 1961, NMIB........$245.00

Beany & Cecil, Skill Ball Game, tin litho w/mc graphics, 3 balls, Pressman, 1961, NMIB...............................$145.00

Beetle Bailey, doll, Presents, cloth w/vinyl head, orig tags, M...$25.00

Beetle Bailey, puffy stickers, Ja-Ru, 1983, MIP (sealed)....$20.00

Betty Boop, bank, Japan, ceramic figure, 7", MIB, A7......$45.00

Betty Boop, display, cb stand-up, life-sz, EX $30.00

Betty Boop, doll, compo & wood, orig decal, 12", EX $685.00

Betty Boop, doll, Fleischer Studios, 1930s, gr dress version, jtd wood & compo, 12", EX, A....................................$1,000.00

Betty Boop, doll, Ideal, jtd wood & compo, 12", rare, EX, A..$1,250.00

Betty Boop, figure, Jaymar, 1930s, jtd wood, 4¼", M......$100.00

Betty Boop, mask, Bimbo, celluloid, 6x6", NM $175.00

Betty Boop, tambourine, 1930s, litho tin, 6" dia, EX, A.$150.00

Betty Boop, transfers, Japan, 1935, set of 12, NMOC.......$25.00

Beverly Hillbillies, charm bracelet, 1960s, metal w/5 plastic photos, NM, from $50 to $75.00

Beverly Hillbillies, Magic Bubble Pipe, Kellogg's premium, 1960s, plastic corncob pipe, M, from $50 to $75.00

Beverly Hillbillies, slide-tile puzzle, 1960s, MOC............$60.00

Bewitched, doll, Samantha, Ideal, 1965, 12", rare, MIB..$600.00

Bewitched, Magic Doll Feeding Bottle, Amsco, 1965, MIB, from $300 to...$400.00

Bionic Woman, bank, Animals Plus Inc, 1976, plastic figure, 10", NM, from $30 to $40.00

Bionic Woman, Styling Boutique, Kenner, 1977, MIB, from $100 to...$125.00

Blippy, jack-in-the-box, Mattel, M, from $100 to...........$150.00

Bonzo, pull toy, Chein, litho tin, 7", NM.........................$400.00

Boo Boo, see Yogi Bear

Boob McNutt, cloth doll with original tag, felt hat, Star Company, 34", VG, A, $200.00. (Photo courtesy Noel Barrett)

Bozo the Clown, doll, Mattel, 1963, talker, 18", VG........$45.00

Bozo the Clown, sticker board, 1983, MIB.........................$15.00

Bozo the Clown, talking book, MIP (sealed) $55.00

Bozo the Clown, yo-yo, Roalex, 1960s, plastic w/paper sticker seal, tournament shape, NM.....................................$28.00

Brady Bunch, Dominoes, Larami, 1973, MOC, from $40 to..$50.00

Brady Bunch, Hex-A-Game, Larami, 1973, MOC, from $30 to $40.00

Brady Bunch, jump rope, Larami, 1973, MIP, from $50 to ..$75.00

Brady Bunch, Outdoor Fun Set, Larami, 1973, several different, MIB, ea from $40 to...$50.00

Brady Bunch, Pick 'N Play, Larami, 1973, MOC, from $50 to...$60.00

Breezy the Polar Bear, twistable stuffed doll, Hanna-Barbera/Ideal, 1964, 8", M, $115.00. (Photo courtesy Bill Bruegman, Toy Scouts)

Bringing Up Father, figure set, Borgfeldt, 1934, bsk, set of 3, M (EX box) $665.00

Buck Rogers, Chemical Laboratory, John F Dille, 1937, complete, EX (EX box), from $700 to $900.00

Buck Rogers, Midget Caster Set, 1934, extremely rare, VG (VG box)...$750.00

Bug Bunny, camera, 1976, EX (EX box), C10.................$140.00

Bugs Bunny, bank, Bugs Bunny standing beside barrel, pnt metal, 5½", NM, A...$50.00

Bugs Bunny, bank, Uncle Bugs, Great America, 1978, vinyl figure, EX $25.00

Bugs Bunny, Chatterchum, Mattel, 1976, 7", VG.............$30.00

Bugs Bunny, figure, WBC Inc, 1940s, litho tin figure on formed paws base, 9", scarce, G $65.00

Bugs Bunny, figure, 1988, bendable, 8", EX......................$20.00

Bugs Bunny, ring toss, Larami, 1981, MOC $15.00

Bullwinkle's Supermarket Game, Whitman, 1976, NM ...$30.00

Captain Action, flasher ring, Vari-Vue, 1967, several different, EX, ea...$35.00

Captain America, kite, Pressman, 1966, plastic w/full-color image, MIP, T2..$65.00

Captain America, Official Utility Belt, Remco, 1979, MIB $20.00

Captain America, playset, 1980s, complete w/shield, mask, handcuffs, keys & dart gun, MIP (sealed) $65.00

Captain America, ring, 1966, from gumball machine, rubber, NM..$50.00

Captain Kangaroo, Fun-Damental Activity Set, Lowe, 1977, NM (sealed)...$20.00

Casper the Ghost, baseball bat & ball set, inflatable vinyl, MOC..$15.00

Casper the Ghost, chalkboard, 12x18", MIP (sealed).......$40.00

Casper the Ghost, jack-in-the-box, Mattel, 1960, plays theme song, litho tin, EX, A..$75.00

Charlie McCarthy, doll, Effanbee, 1940, compo w/cloth clothes, complete w/monocle, 16", NM (EX box), A $950.00

Charlie McCarthy, doll, 1930w, compo, movable mouth, 13", EX..$250.00

Charlie McCarthy, Mazuma Phony Money, 1950s, MIP...$50.00

Charlie McCarthy, pencil sharpener, Bakelite, rnd, EX....$50.00

Charlie McCarthy, Radio Party, Chase & Sanborn premium, 1938, complete, NM (EX mailer), A..........................$75.00

Charlie's Angels, backpack, Travel Toys Inc, 1977, vinyl w/photo image, M, from $100 to.............................$150.00

Charlie's Angels, Beauty Hair Care Set, HG Toys, 1977, MIB, from $125 to $150.00

Charlie's Angels, Cosmetic Beauty Kit, HG Toys, 1977, MIB, from $100 to $125.00

Charlie's Angels, Paint-By-Numbers Set, Hasbro, 1978, unused, NMIB, from $50 to....................................$75.00

Charlie's Angels, playset, Toy Factory, 1977, MIB (sealed), from $100 to...$125.00

Charlie's Angels, Poster Art Kit, HG Toys, 1977, complete, NMIB, from $50 to..$75.00

Charlie's Angels, Rainy Day Set, Travel Toys Inc, 1977, MIB $175.00

Charlie's Angels, walkie-talkies, LJN, 1976, rare, NRFB, from $300 to...$350.00

Child's Play, doll, Chucky, Play by Play, 1992, 15", EX.....$25.00

CHiPs, .45 Magnum Target Set, Larami, 1983, MOC, from $30 to $40.00

CHiPs, bicycle siren, 1970s, EX, N2............................$25.00

CHiPs, bicycle siren, 1970s, M.....................................$30.00

CHiPs, bullhorn, Placo Toys, 1977, plastic, M, from $25 to..$35.00

CHiPs, camera, Fleetwood, 1978, MOC, from $40 to..........$50.00

CHiPs, Colorforms, 1981, MIB $25.00

CHiPs, Motorcycle Helmet Set, HG Toys, 1979, rare, MIB ...$100.00

Clarabelle, doll, Bend Me, soft foam, unused, 11½", NMIP...$100.00

Clarabelle, lollipop holder, diecut cb, 10", EX $55.00

Creature From the Black Lagoon, figure, Remco, 4", NM ..$40.00

Daffy Duck, bank, Daffy Duck standing beside barrel, pnt metal, 4¼", NM, A..$85.00

Dennis the Menace, doll, Dennis Play Products, 1957, vinyl w/cloth outfit, 13", NMIB $165.00

Dennis the Menace, doll, Joey, Presents, 1980s, cloth, EX...$25.00

Dennis the Menace, Stuff N' Lace Doll, Standard Toykraft, MIP, J6..$40.00

Dennis the Menace & Ruff, ornament set, 1977, MIB $20.00

Deputy Dawg, TV Lotto Game, Ideal, 1961, unused, NM (EX box)..$50.00

Dick Tracy, Candid Camera, Seymour/New York News, 1950s, complete w/instructions, EX (EX box), D11...........$100.00

Dick Tracy, Cartoon Kit, Colorforms, 1962, complete, EX (EX box)..$75.00

Dick Tracy, Crimestopper Set, John-Henry, 1930s, MOC, from $75 to...$100.00

Dick Tracy, doll, Breathless Mahoney, Playmates, 1990, plastic, bl dress, 19", NRFB...$60.00

Dick Tracy, figural barrette, Bonnie Braids, 1951, 1", NM+ (EX illus card) $33.00

Dick Tracy, figure, Bonnie Braids, Charmore, 1951, plastic, 1¼", NMOC...$50.00

Dick Tracy, figure, Dick Tracy, 1930s, pnt lead, EX $30.00

Dick Tracy, greeting cards, Norcross, 1960s, several styles w/neon backgrounds, NM, ea $20.00

Dick Tracy, jigsaw puzzle, 'Crime Does Not Pay' Club, orig box, NM..$50.00

Dick Tracy, Junior Detective Kit, Golden Press, 1962, complete, unused, NM, from $40 to......................................$50.00

Dick Tracy, magnifying glass, Larami, 1979, MOC..........$20.00

Dick Tracy, Sparkle Plenty Christmas Tree Lights, unused, M (VG+ cartoon illus box)...$115.00

Dick Tracy, TV Watch, Ja-Ru, NMOC.............................$20.00

Ding Dong School, Mr Bumps figure set, Barry Products, 1955, MIB...$60.00

Dixie Mouse, hand puppet, Knickerbocker, 1962, unused, NM+ (EX+ box)...$40.00

Dr Dolittle, bank, sea snail, 1971, AJ Renzi Plastic Corp, pk hard plastc, EX..$50.00

Dr Dolittle, bath toy, Fun Sponge, Amsco, NM $30.00

Dr Dolittle, Card Game, based on 1967 TV show, unused, NM+IB..$25.00

Dr Dolittle, cartoon kit, Colorforms #456, complete, EX (EX box)..$20.00

Dr Dolittle, doll, Mattel, 1967, w/Pushmi-Pullyu & Polynesia, 6", MIB..$90.00

Dr Dolittle, doll, Mattel, 1969, talker, 24", NMIB $150.00

Dr Dolittle, doll, Mattel #5349, talking, mute, otherwise NM $75.00

Dr Dolittle, hat, Jacobson, animal-skin print, NM (orig sticker)..$20.00

Dr Dolittle, Numbered Pencil Coloring Set, Hasbro #3633, M (sealed)..$30.00

Dr Dolittle, party cups, Hallmark, w/animals & their names, M (orig wrappers) $20.00

Dr Dolittle, periscope, Bar-Zim, NMIP $30.00

Dr Dolittle, periscope, Bar-Zim, w/characters pictured around sides, EX..$25.00

Dr Dolittle, press-out book, 1935, Whitman, in chair w/characters, NM...$25.00

Dr Dolittle, Stick-a-Story, Hasbro, NMIP.......................$25.00

Dr Kildare, telephone, Renzi, 1960s, plastic, NM............$50.00

Dr. Seuss, See 'N Say Talking Storybook, Mattel, 1970, NM, from $150.00 to $200.00. (Photo courtesy Martin and Carolyn Berens)

Dr Seuss, doll, Cat in the Hat, Coleco, 1983, stuffed plush, MIB, from $75 to $100.00

Dr Seuss, doll, Cat in the Hat, Mattel, 1970s, talker, NM ..$250.00

Dr Seuss, doll, Yertle the Turtle, Coleco, 1983, stuffed plush, EX $35.00

Dr Shrinker, Shrinking Machine, Harmony, 1977, MOC, from $35 to $45.00

Dr Who, yo-yo, 1970s, plastic w/paper sticker seal, butterfly shape, MIP $16.00

Dracula, doll, Hamilton Presents, 14", MIB......................$25.00

Dukes of Hazzard, bank, General Lee, AJ Renzi, plastic figure, 16", EX $15.00

Dukes of Hazzard, Colorforms, 1981, NM (NM box) $30.00

Dukes of Hazzard, ID Set, Grand Toy, MOC......................$10.00

Dukes of Hazzard, Speed Jumper Action Stunt Set, Knicker-bocker, VG (VG box) $20.00

Dukes of Hazzard, yo-yo, Duncan, 1980s, plastic w/chrome finish, imprint seal, butterfly shape, MIP......................$25.00

Eight Is Enough, fan club kit, Fan Club Images, 1979, complete, NM (NM folder), from $40 to...........................$50.00

Elmer Fudd, bank, Elmer standing beside barrel, pnt metal, 5½", NM, A...$85.00

Elvira, makeup kit, MOC, from $15 to $20.00

Emergency, fire helmet, Playco, 1975, plastic, EX+, A7...$30.00

Emmett Kelly Circus, Colorforms, 1960, complete, NMIB..$40.00

ET, doll, Showtime, 1982, plush, 8", NM $6.00

ET, pillow, bl or purple, EX, ea $20.00

ET, sponge ball, 1982, M..$6.00

E.T. Night Light, figure with glowing chest, MIB, $15.00.
(Photo courtesy Martin and Carolyn Berens)

Evel Knievel, bike flags, Schaper, 10x15", MIP $18.00

Family Affair, Buffy Fashion Wig, Amsco, 1971, MIB....$100.00

Family Affair, Cartoon Kit, Colorforms, 1970, complete, NMIB, from $40 to...$50.00

Family Affair, doll, Mrs. Beasley, talking, Mattel, 22", MIB, $695.00.
(Photo courtesy Marcia Fanta)

Family Affair, figure, Buffy & Mrs Beasley, 6", missing glasses o/w VG+ $50.00

Family Affair, wig, Buffy's, Amsco, 1971, brn or blond, MIB, ea $100.00

Fantasy Island, iron-ons, 1970s, several different, M, ea...$10.00

Felix the Cat, coin purse, vinyl head figure, MIP, C10 .....$10.00

Felix the Cat, dexterity puzzle, MIP, C10 ....$65.00

Felix the Cat, doll, 1982, stuffed plush, 14", NM.............$25.00

Felix the Cat, drum,1930s, litho tin, scarce, NM $200.00

Felix the Cat, figure, Germany, bsk, 1½", NM $350.00

Felix the Cat, figure, Schoenut, jtd wood, orig decals on chest & foot, 5½", rare, EX..$1,200.00

Felix the Cat, squeak toy, Germany, paper litho w/wood & paper squeaker, 6", EX $400.00

Felix the Cat, stencil set, Spears Bavaria by Pat Sullivan, complete, EX (EX box) $200.00

Flash Gordon, beanie w/fins & goggles, 1950s, NM $400.00

Flash Gordon, figure, chalkware, EX.............................$500.00

Flash Gordon, space outfit, Esquire Novelties, 1950s, complete, EX (EX box), from $300 to $400.00

Flintstones, Baby Pebbles vinyl doll and Cave House, 1964, 8", MIB, $275.00. (Photo courtesy Marcia Fanta)

Flintstones, bank, Barney figure, hard plastic, Homecraft, 1973, 9", NM+..$28.00

Flintstones, Fred and Barney banks, Homecraft, 14", 13", $30.00 each. (Photo courtesy Martin and Carolyn Berens)

Flintstones, bank, Pebbles in chair, 1973, vinyl, NM $20.00

Flintstones, bubble pipe, Bamm-Bamm, 1960s, 8", EX $20.00

Flintstones, coin purse, Barney, 1975, NM.......................$25.00

Flintstones, Color-By-Numbers, Pebbles & Bamm-Bamm, Transogram, 1963, NM+ (sealed box) $70.00

Flintstones, doll, Bamm-Bamm, Ideal, 1960s, plastic & vinyl w/cloth clothes, 16", MIB, from $150 to.................$200.00

Flintstones, doll, Pebbles, Ideal, 1967, plastic & vinyl w/cloth outfit, 12", MIB, from $150 to.................................$200.00

Flintstones, figure, any character, Just Toys, bendable, MOC, ea $10.00

Flintstones, figure, Dino, orange hard vinyl, 1960s, 18", EX+...$22.00

Flintstones, figure, Fred, 1960, vinyl, 12", NM $70.00

Flintstones, figures, Fred & Barney, rubber, Knickerbocker, 11", EX, pr $30.00

Flintstones, Great Big Punchout Book, Whitman, unpunched, 1961, 23x12", NM $62.00

Flintstones, lamp, Fred figural, vinyl, 11", NM $55.00

Flintstones, Quick Score Target, 1977, MOC.................$25.00

Flintstones, Shooting Gallery, w/up knock-down moving target game, Arco, 1976, complete, M (NM box)...............$70.00

Flintstones, squeeze toy, any character, Lanco, 1960s, NMIP, ea $135.00

Flintstones, Target Set, tin litho, Lido, 1965, NM (sealed 10x14" box)...$70.00

Flintstones, Tricky Walker, Barney, Jaymar, 1963, NM+ (VG+ box)...$40.00

Flintstones, xylophone, 1978, MOC $25.00

Flintstones, yo-yo, Fred, Festival, 1980, plastic w/paper insert seal, tournament shape w/view lens, NM..................$20.00

Flintstones, yo-yo, Fred & Pebbles, 1970s, litho tin, tournament shape, MIP $20.00

Flintstones, yo-yo, Pebbles, 1970s, litho tin w/image of Pebbles crawling, tournament shape, MIP $20.00

Flipper, Color-By-Number Set, Hasbro, 1966, complete, NMIB, from $50 to...$60.00

Flipper, doll, Knickerbocker, 1976, stuffed plush w/sailor hat, 17", EX $30.00

Flipper, magic slate, Whitman, 1967, cb w/lift-up erasable film sheet, NM $30.00

Flipper, Puncho Bag, Coleco, 1966, inflatable vinyl, MIP, from $50 to $75.00

Flipper, riding toy, Irwin, 1965, plastic figure w/red wheels & handles, NM, from $125 to $150.00

Flying Nun, Oil Painting-By-Numbers, Hasbro, 1967, complete, NMIB, from $75 to..$100.00

Foghorn Leghorn, stuffed plush toy, Warner Brothers, recent, from $12.00 to $18.00. (Photo courtesy David Longest)

Foghorn Leghorn, flicker ring, EX $40.00

Foodini, dexterity puzzle, Am Metal, 1950s, rare, NM ...$125.00

Frankenstein, flicker ring, flashes from Frankenstein to Phantom, M, C10 ....$35.00

Full House, doll, Jesse, Tiger, 1993, 11½", MIB, Y1 ....$40.00

Full House, doll, Michelle, talker, cloth & vinyl, 15", MIB ..$40.00

Garfield, doll, Mattel, 1983, talker, 10", EX.....................$60.00

Garfield, figure, Garfield as tennis player, ceramic, 4" $20.00

Garfield, necklace, Avon, MIB...$10.00

Garfield, slide-tile puzzle, MIP $5.00

Garfield, toothbush holder, United Features, 1978, plastic, $14.00.

Ghostbusters, yo-yo, Spectra Star, 1984, sculpted plastic, NM $5.00

Goldilocks, Storykins, Hasbro, 1967, MIP, from $75 to..$100.00

Good Times, doll, JJ, Shindana, 1975, cloth & vinyl, 15", MIB, Y1 ....$50.00

Green Hornet, charm bracelet, w/5 charms, NMOC $100.00

Green Hornet, Electric Drawing Set, Lakeside, 1966, complete, NMIB, T2 ....$250.00

Green Hornet, Follow the Colors Magic Rub-Off, Whitman, complete, EX (EX box), C10..$200.00

Green Hornet, movie viewer, 1966, MOC.......................$75.00

Green Hornet, Print Putty, Colorforms, 1966, MOC, T2 ...$75.00

Green Hornet, rub-ons, Hasbro, rare, MIB $425.00

Gumby and Pokey, figures, Lewco/Perma Toys, 12", 8½", from $15.00 to $20.00 each.

Green Hornet, slide-tile puzzle, Roalex, scarce, NMOC, A ..$285.00

Gremlins, Rub 'N Play Transfers, Colorforms, MIP $10.00

Gulliver's Travels, doll, King Little, Ideal, wood & compo, orig decal, 12", EX $575.00

Gumby & Pokey, Colorforms, 1988, MIB $10.00

Gumby & Pokey, figure, Pokey, Lakeside, 1965, bendable, MOC..$55.00

Gumby & Pokey, Gumby's Jeep, Lakeside, w/figures, VG, A $150.00

Gumby & Pokey, paint set, rare, NM...........................$200.00

Hanna Barbera, Break-A-Plate Carnival Pitch Game, Yogi, Huckleberry & Quick Draw, Transogram, 1961, NM (EX box)..$100.00

Happy Days, beanbag chair, Fonzie, 1970s, red & wht panels w/image of Fonz holding thumbs up, NM $125.00

Happy Days, Colorforms, Fonzie, unused, EX (EX box) ...$30.00

Happy Days, doll, Fonzie, Samet & Wells Inc, 1976, stuffed cloth, 16", NM...$30.00

Happy Days, Flip-A-Knot, 1977, MIP.............................$15.00

Happy Days, Fonz Bagatelle, Imperial, 1982, cartoon series, 10", NM..$15.00

Happy Days, Fonz Colorforms, 1976, complete, NMIB $20.00

Happy Days, Fonz Miracle Bubble Shooter, Imperial, 1981, MOC...$20.00

Happy Days, Fonz record player, Vanity Fair, 1976, NM, from $50 to $75.00

Happy Days, guitar, Fonzie, 1976, MIB (sealed) $75.00

Happy Days, Guitar 'N Mike Set, Gordy, 1983, plastic w/image of Joanie & Chachi, MOC, from $25 to $30.00

Happy Days, puffy stickers, Imperial, 1981, several variations, MIP, ea $10.00

Happy Hooligan, figure, Elastolin, minor pnt chips, 11", VG+..$68.00

Hardy Boys, dolls, Kenner, 1978, 12", NRFB, ea...............$50.00

Hardy Boys, Poster Pen Set, Craft House, 1977, MIP.......$45.00

Hardy Boys, Poster Put-Ons, Bi-Rite, 1977, 3 different styles, MIP, ea from $10 to $15.00

Hardy Boys, Shaun Cassidy phonograph, Vanity Fair, 1978, electric or battery-op version, NM, ea..............................$75.00

Harold Lloyd, doll, 1920s, stuffed cloth, mk Yours for Happiness-Harold Lloyd on bk, 12", EX $135.00

Harold Teen, ukelele, wood w/colorful decals, 21", EX.....$65.00

Home Alone, doll, Kevin, THQ, 1989, screams, MIB, Y1..$25.00

Hong Kong Phooey, pillow doll, 1977, 18", EX, N2 ....$45.00

Howdy Doodey, marionette, Flub-A-Dub, EX+ $295.00

Howdy Doody, Bee-Nee-Kit, 1950s, NMIB.....................$65.00

Howdy Doody, Clock-A-Doodle, 1950s, litho tin w/up, NMIB..$1,600.00

Howdy Doody, Color TV Set, complete w/5 rolls of film, NM (EX box) $100.00

Howdy Doody, Costume Playset, Princess Summerfall-Winterspring, Wonderland, 1950s, unused, NMIB $95.00

Howdy Doody, Costume Playset, Wonderland, 1950s, unused, NMIB...$95.00

Howdy Doody, cowboy figure, soft vinyl, NM+ (G illus cello case) $145.00

Howdy Doody, doll, Beehler, plastic w/cloth clothes, jaws move, 7", NM (NM box) $255.00

Howdy Doody, doll, hard plastic w/cloth clothes, lever action mouth & eyes, NM+ (VG+ box)............................$165.00

Howdy Doody, Electric Doodler, Harett-Gilmar, 1951, complete, EX (EX box)...$65.00

Howdy Doody, figural sand form set, Ideal, 1952, NM+ (EX box)..$80.00

Howdy Doody, figure, jtd cb, NMIP.................................$70.00

Howdy Doody, figure, Tee Vee, 1950s, Howdy w/microphone, plastic, push tab to make mouth move, 4", NM (EX box), A...$125.00

Howdy Doody, Flub-A-Dub's Flip-A-Ring Game, M (NM package)..$50.00

Howdy Doody, hand puppet, Zany Toys, 1952, NM (VG box)...$50.00

Howdy Doody, marionette, Mr Blister, NM.......................$265.00

Howdy Doody, night light, hard plastic cowboy figural on wood base, EX+...$100.00

Howdy Doody, paint set, Milton Bradley, complete, NM (NM box)..$200.00

Howdy Doody, Phono Doodle, Shuratone, 1950s, EX, from $250 to..$300.00

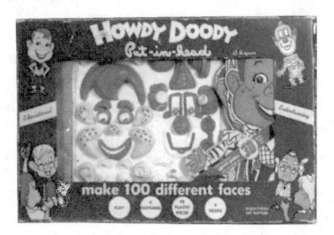

Howdy Doody, Put-In-Head Set, plastic pieces, clay to make one hundred different faces, M (VG box), $115.00. (Photo courtesy New England Auction House)

Howdy Doody, Ranch House Tool Box, Kagran, 1950s, metal, EX...$200.00

Howdy Doody, salt & pepper shakers, figural, pr, NMIB ..$95.00

Howdy Doody, Sand Forms, Ideal/Kagran, 1952, plastic, MOC, A...$125.00

Howdy Doody, squeak doll, Princess Summertime-Winterfall, vinyl, unused, NMIP...$90.00

Howdy Doody, squeak toy, 13", NM.................................$85.00

Howdy Doody, Uke, Emenee, plastic, 17", NM (EX box) $165.00

Howdy Doody, wall plaque, w/Santa, lighted, EX+ (VG box) $125.00

HR Pufnstuf, dolls, Cling & Clang, My Toy, 1970, stuffed cloth, 14", M, ea from $600 to..$700.00

Huckleberry Hound, charm bracelet, w/6 charms, 1959, NM (EX illus card) $36.00

Huckleberry Hound, Colorforms, 1960, unused, M (NM box)..$68.00

Huckleberry Hound, figural bank, 1960s, 10", NMIP.......$45.00

Huckleberry Hound, figural paddle ball, Mr Clean premium, 1960s, M (sealed bag) $28.00

Huckleberry Hound, Flip Show, 1961, EX (EX box) $40.00

Huckleberry Hound, gumball bank, Transogram, 1960, unused, NM (EX+ box) $55.00

Huckleberry Hound, Juggle Roll Skill Game, Transogram, unused, 1960, NM (VG box) $52.00

Huckleberry Hound, Pinball Game, Lido, 1964, 7½", NMOC $40.00

Huckleberry Hound, speedboat, Regal Toy, 1960s, plastic, 17", NM...$200.00

Huckleberry Hound, squeeze toy, vinyl, Dell, 1962, 7", NMIP $45.00

Huckleberry Hound, Tiddledy Winks Tennis Game, Milton Bradley, 1959, NM+ (NM sealed box)....................$30.00

Hugga Bunch, tray, 1984, litho metal, VG........................$10.00

Humpty Dumpty, bank, litho tin figure, 5", EX, A $50.00

Humpty Dumpty, bank, UK, 1970s, cast metal figure, 4½", NM, A7 ....$30.00

I Dream of Jeannie, Knitting & Embroidery Kit, Harmony, 1975, MOC...$35.00

I Dream of Jeannie, magic slate, Rand McNally, 1975, cartoon series, cb w/lift-up erasable film sheet, NM...............$45.00

I Dream of Jeannie, play suit, Ben Cooper, 1974, complete, NMIB, from $50 to..$60.00

In Living Color, doll, Homey the Clown, Acme, 1992, stuffed cloth, 24", MIB, from $25 to $35.00

Incredible Hulk, Crazy Foam, 1979, w/contents, VG+.....$25.00

Incredible Hulk, Hobbie Horse, 1978, VG $30.00

Incredible Hulk, Official Utility Belt, Remco, 1979, MIB..$20.00

Incredible Hulk, slide-tile puzzle, APC, 1977, MOC........$10.00

Incredible Hulk, Split Ring, 1977, inflatable vinyl, MIB..$20.00

Incredible Hulk, train set, 1979, NMIB $50.00

Incredible Hulk, wallet, 1976, vinyl, unused, NM $20.00

Incredible Hulk & Spider-Man, Shrinky Dinks, Skyline Toys, 1979, MIB (sealed) $15.00

Jack & the Beanstalk, bank, litho tin book shape, 6", NM, A...$60.00

James Bond, beach towel, Glidrose/Fon Prod Ltd, 1965, terrycloth w/red & blk image of Sean Connery, EX.....$100.00

James Bond, ID bracelet, Marvin Glass/Glidrose, 1965, 8", NM (NM box), A...$75.00

James Bond, wallet, mk Glidrose Productions, 1966, vinyl, NM...$80.00

James Bond 007, Electric Drawing Set, Lakeside, 1966, few pcs missing, EX (EX box) $125.00

Jerry Mahoney, bank, molded compo, 10", rare, EX.........$75.00

Jetsons, figure, any character, Just Toys, bendable, MOC, ea ...$10.00

Jetsons, Slate & Chalk Set, 1960s, unused, MIB...........$100.00

Joe Carioca, pencil sharpener, Plastic Novelties, 1940s, gr Bakelite w/decal, 1", EX...$50.00

Joe Palooka, bank/candy container, Little Max figural, 1940s, 4", M..$68.00

Josie & the Pussycats, Comic-Stiks, Deco Mfg, 1972, MOC..$40.00

Josie & the Pussycats, guitar, Larami, 1973, plastic, MOC, from $50 to..$75.00

Josie & the Pussycats, Pendant Jewelry Set, Larami, 1972, MOC...$30.00

Julia, Hospital Set, Transogram, 1970, complete, NMIB, from $75 to..$100.00

Jurassic Park, yo-yo, Spectra Star, 1993, plastic w/photo sticker seal, MIP...$12.00

Justice League of America, Paint-By-Number set, Hasbro, 1967, complete, EX (EX box), T2.....................................$150.00

Kaptain Kool & the Kongs, magic slate, Whitman, 1978, cb w/lift-up erasable film sheet, MOC, from $35 to.......$45.00

Kaptain Kool & the Kongs, Pencil-By-Numbers, Hasbro, 1977, unused, NMIB, from $40 to..$50.00

Kaptain Kool & the Kongs, Poster Art Kit, HG Toys, 1977, M, from $40 to...$50.00

Katzenjammer Kids, figures, Hans & Franz, 1930s, celluloid, rare, EX, pr...$375.00

King Kong, bank, plastic figural, 17", NM $35.00

King Leonardo, paint set, 8 color pictures, unused, 1960s, MIB...$50.00

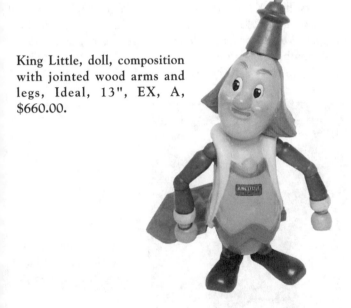

King Little, doll, composition with jointed wood arms and legs, Ideal, 13", EX, A, $660.00.

Knight Rider, kite, 1982, MIP (sealed) $25.00

Knight Rider, yo-yo, 1982, plastic w/paper sticker seal, butterfly shape, NM..$10.00

Krazy Kat, doll, stuffed velvet w/applied felt feet, orig red felt boots, 13", NM $1,000.00

Krazy Kat, figure, Chein, 1920s, jtd wood, 7", NM, D10 ..$250.00

Kung Fu, target set, Multiple, 1975, MOC, from $40 to...$50.00

Land Before Time, doll, Little Foot, JC Penney Exclusive, stuffed cloth, EX $35.00

Land of the Giants, Spaceship Spindrift, Remco, 1968, MIB ..$60.00

Land of the Lost, Moonbase Rocket, Larami, 1975, MOC, from $30 to...$40.00

Land of the Lost, Saucer Shooter, Larami, 1975, MIP, from $35 to..$45.00

Land of the Lost, Secret Look-Out, Larami, 1975, MIP, from $30 to..$40.00

Lassie, doll, Knickerbocker, stuffed cloth, 14" L, EX, C10..$150.00

Lassie Trick Trainer, Mousely Inc, 1956, complete, scarce, NM (EX box) $275.00

Laugh-In, flicker rings, set of 5, EX $20.00

Laurel & Hardy, windup figures, 1970, pnt plastic, 5" & 6", NM, J6, pr..$125.00

Laverne & Shirley, Bowling Game, Harmony, 1977, MOC, from $30 to...$40.00

Laverne & Shirley, dolls, Lenny & Squiggy, Mego, 1977, 12", NRFB, pr..$200.00

Laverne & Shirley, dolls, Mego, 1977, 12", NRFB, pr $125.00

Laverne & Shirley, Secretary Set, Harmony, 1977, MOC, from $25 to...$35.00

Li'l Abner, bank, Lil'Abner Can O' Coins, litho tin cylinder, 4½", EX..$30.00

Linus the Lion-Hearted, doll, Mattel, 1965, talker, 21", VG..$85.00

Linus the Lion-Hearted, jigsaw puzzle, 100 pcs, 1964, NM (VG+ box)..$22.00

Little Abner, flying saucer, bl vinyl w/mc Lil Abner decal insert, 1954, 9" dia, EX+...$45.00

Little Bo Peep, doll, Ideal, 1938, compo, sleep eyes, orig skirt & straw hat, 15½", EX...$165.00

Little Bo Peep, Storybook Small-Talk doll by Mattel, 1968, MIB..$125.00

Little House on the Prairie, Colorforms, 1978, MIB, from $40 to..$50.00

Little House on the Prairie, doll, Carrie, Knickerbocker, 1978, MIB..$35.00

Little House on the Prairie, tea set, Ohio Art, 1980, 26 pcs, MIB..$100.00

Little King, figure, Jaymar, 1939, walker, pnt wood, rubber band action, 4", EX...$85.00

Little Lulu & Tubby, figures, 1971, bsk, NM, C10, pr.....$125.00

Little Orphan Annie, bank, 1936, registering, litho tin, 3" dia, EX $450.00

Little Orphan Annie, figure, Sandy, Jaymar, 1930s, jtd wood, 4", M..$95.00

Little Orphan Annie, figure set, Annie, Daddy Warbucks & Sandy, Japan, bsk, 3½" & 1½", EX, A.....................$125.00

Little Orphan Annie, figure set, Annie, Harold Teen, Sandy & Lillums, Japan, prewar, bsk, M (EX box), A $400.00

Little Orphan Annie, Pastry Set, Transogram, 1930s, complete, NMIB, A...$100.00

Little Orphan Annie, pull toy, Annie sitting on 4-wheeled platform, wood, 10", EX+, A $350.00

Little Orphan Annie & Sandy, figure, copyright 1973, plaster, scarce, M, from $300 to.......................................$400.00

Little Red Riding Hood, bank, litho tin book shape, 6", NM ..$100.00

Little Red Riding Hood, tea set, early 1900s, litho tin w/various scenes from the story, 8 pcs, EX..............$375.00

Lost in Space, helmet & gun set, Remco, 1966, complete, NMIB $1,250.00

Lost in Space, tablet, 1960s, photo image of June Lockhart, unused, NM $25.00

Love Boat, playset, Multi-Toys, 1983, MIB, from $100 to...$125.00

Love Boat, puffy stickers, Imperial, 1982, several variations, MIP, ea..$10.00

Love Boat, Ship's Doctor Set, Fleetwood, 1979, MOC.....$25.00

Love Boat, Travel Stamp Set, Imperial, 1983, MOC........$20.00

Ludwig Von Drake, Do-It-Yourself Needlepoint, Hassenfeld, unused, MIB, A7..............................$35.00

M*A*S*H, canteen, Tristar, 1981, plastic, EX $10.00

M*A*S*H, dog tags, Tristar, 1981, MOC........................$10.00

M*A*S*H, Field Hospital Playset, Multiple, 1974, NM (VG box)..$50.00

Magilla Gorilla, doll, Nanco, 1990, stuffed plush, 7", NM..$15.00

Magilla Gorilla, Mixes Card Game, ED-U-Cards, unused, 1964, NM..$20.00

Magilla Gorilla, pull toy, rubber, Ideal, ca 1964, 9", NM..$55.00

Magnum PI, handcuffs, 1981, MOC $20.00

Man From Atlantis, Dip Dot Painting Kit, Kenner, 1977, NRFB..$130.00

Man From UNCLE, Secret Print Putty, Colorforms, NMOC ..$33.00

Mandrake the Magician, Magic Kit, Transogram, 1949, complete, NMIB, from $250 to..............$300.00

Marvel Super Heroes, light-up drawing desk, Lakeside, 1976, plastic, EX (EX box) $40.00

Marvel Super Heroes, notebook, Mead, 1970s, unused, M..$25.00

Mighty Mouse, magic slate, Lowe, 1950s, cb w/lift-up erasable film sheet, NM, T2 ....$50.00

Mighty Mouse, squeeze toy, 1950s, vinyl w/red felt cape, 10", rare, EX $55.00

Mod Squad, Instant Intercom, Larami, 1973, wht plastic walkie-talkies, MOC $50.00

Moon Mullins & Kayo, decal, Kayo Chocolate Drink, 1940s, unused, NM $30.00

Mork & Mindy, Dress-Up Set, Colorforms, 1979, MIB $25.00

Mork & Mindy, gumball machine, Mork from Ork, Hasbro, 1980, MIB, from $40 to $50.00

Mork & Mindy, Magic Show, Colorforms, 1980, MIB......$30.00

Mork & Mindy, Paint-By-Number set, Craft Master, 1979, complete, NMIB $25.00

Mork & Mindy, poster, Mork From Ork, 1970s, 36x24", EX ...$15.00

Mother Goose, dishes, Ideal, 1940s, plastic, 26 pcs, MIB..$150.00

Mr Magoo, doll, Ideal, 1961, stuffed cloth & vinyl, 16", EX .$75.00

Mr Smith, slide tile puzzle, 1983, MOC........................$20.00

Munsters, doll, Grandpa, Remco, 1964, 6", MIB...........$200.00

Munsters, doll, Herman, Presents, 1990, plush w/vinyl head, 12", MIB $35.00

Munsters, figure, Grandpa or Herman, Applause, 1991, MIP, ea..$40.00

Muppets, doll, Kermit the Frog, Fisher-Price, 1977-83, stuffed cloth, NM, C13 ....$10.00

Muppets, Miss Piggy Latch Hook Kit, MIB (sealed) $55.00

Mushmouth, pull toy, rubber, Ideal, ca 1964, 9", NM.......$55.00

Mutt & Jeff, figures, HC Fisher, celluloid, 4" & 5", VG, pr..$100.00

My Three Sons, Myrtle talking hand puppet, NM, $45.00.
(Photo courtesy Cindy Sabulis)

Miss America, Colorforms Dress-Up Set, 1972, complete in box with brochure, $32.00.

Nancy Drew, fan club kit, FCCA, 1978, complete, NM (NM folder)..$65.00

Nancy Drew, Mystery Pictures To Color, 1977, M............$15.00

New Zoo Revue, activity set, C'mon Be a Sport, Warren Paper Products, 1970s, complete, NMIB, from $25 to.........$35.00

New Zoo Revue, doll, any character, Rushton, 1970s, stuffed plush w/vinyl head, NM, from $30 to $40.00

New Zoo Revue, doll, Henrietta Hippo, stuffed cloth w/vinyl head, NM..$175.00

New Zoo Revue, figure, any character, Imperial, 1973, bendable, MIB, ea from $15 to..............................$20.00

New Zoo Revue, musical mobile, Young Designs, 1971, MIB, from $50 to.................$75.00

Oswald Rabbit, doll, Ideal, 1930s, stuffed cloth w/rubber hands & face, 21", rare, EX...................$200.00

Oswald Rabbit, magic slate, Saafield, 1962, EX...........$20.00

Pac-Man, w/up figures, Pac-Man & Ms Pac-Man, Tomy/Taiwan, plastic, 1¾", M, pr...................$10.00

Partridge Family, doll, Laurie, Remco, 1973, 16", rare, MIB..$250.00

Peanuts, bank, Peppermint Patty w/baseball bat, 1973, compo, 7½", M, from $50 to...................$60.00

Peanuts, bank, Snoopy in yel rain slicker & hat, 1979, ceramic, 5", M...................$25.00

Peanuts, bank, Snoopy on basketball, 1976, compo, 4½", M, from $20 to...................$25.00

Peanuts, bank, Woodstock, ceramic, 6", M...................$15.00

Peanuts, Colorforms, Hit the Ball Charlie Brown, MIB, from $15 to...................$20.00

Peanuts, Colorforms, Hold That Line Charlie Brown, MIB..$15.00

Peanuts, Colorforms, Lucy's Winter Carnival, MIB.........$25.00

Peanuts, Colorforms, Star Snoopy, MIB...................$25.00

Peanuts, Colorforms, What's on Sale Snoopy?, EX (EX box)..$25.00

Peanuts, Deluxe Peanuts Playset, Determined/Helm Toy, 1975, MIB, from $225 to...................$300.00

Peanuts, diary, Snoopy, Hallmark, 1990s, image & Happiness Is Having Secrets, M...................$10.00

Peanuts, doll, Charlie Brown, 1950s, vinyl, 9", VG.........$75.00

Peanuts, doll, Determined, 1968, stuffed plush, 18", NM, from $25 to...................$30.00

Peanuts, doll, Linus, Ideal, 1970s, stuffed cloth, 13½", MIB, from $40 to...................$50.00

Peanuts, doll, Lucy, Ideal, 1970s, stuffed cloth, 13½", MIB, from $40 to...................$50.00

Peanuts, doll, Peppermint Patty, Ideal, 1970s, stuffed cloth, 13½", MIB, from $40 to...................$50.00

Peanuts, doll, Snoopy, Ideal, stuffed cloth, 13½", MIB, from $50 to...................$60.00

Peanuts, doll, Snoopy as baseball player, 1984, PVC, 8½", NM, from $35 to...................$45.00

Peanuts, doll, Snoopy as chef, rag-type, 6", VG...............$10.00

Peanuts, doll, Snoopy w/rattle, plush, 9", MIP.................$10.00

Peanuts, drum, Chein, 1960s, litho tin, MIB, from $125 to...$175.00

Peanuts, Mattel-O-Phone, 1969, with extra talking records, MIB, $95.00. (Photo courtesy Tom Duncan)

Peanuts, figure, Charlie Brown w/stack of gifts, Applause, 1990, PVC, 2½", NM, from $15 to...................$20.00

Peanuts, figure, Snoopy as Joe Cool, 3", M...................$8.00

Peanuts, figure, Snoopy in rowboat, 4", M...................$10.00

Peanuts, jump rope, Snoopy, wht plastic...................$15.00

Peanuts, Paint & Pin Up, Saalfield, early 1970s, complete, NM (EX box), from $25 to...................$35.00

Peanuts, pencil sharpener, Snoopy fire truck, KFS, 1958, NM...................$15.00

Peanuts, Schroeder's Piano, Child Guidance, 1970s, MIB, from $75 to...................$100.00

Peanuts, See & Say, Snoopy Says, Mattel, VG...................$50.00

Peanuts, Snoopy Big 3 Fast Dry Paint-By-Number Set, Craft House, MIB...................$20.00

Peanuts, Snoopy Camping Set, Determined/Helm Toy, 1975, MIB, from $75 to...................$125.00

Peanuts, Snoopy Color 'N Recolor Mug Set, Avalon, 1980, MIB...................$30.00

Peanuts, Snoopy Felt Pen Picture Set, Craftmaster, 1979, complete, NMIB...................$15.00

Peanuts, Snoopy Ge-Tar, Mattel Preschool, 1972, plastic, MIB, from $50 to...................$75.00

Peanuts, Snoopy Mosaic Crushed Stone Craft Kit, Craftmaster, 1979, MIB...................$15.00

Peanuts, Snoopy Play Kitchen Set, Determined, 1985, litho tin, 12 pcs, MIB, from $100 to...................$150.00

Peanuts, Snoopy Playland, Aviva, 1979, complete, NMIB, from $75 to...................$100.00

Peanuts, Snoopy Sno-Cone Machine, Hasbro, 1979, MIB...................$25.00

Peanuts, Snoopy's Beagle Bugle, Child Guidance/Questor, 1970s, plastic, MIB, from $75 to...................$100.00

Peanuts, Snoopy's Good Grief Glider, Child Guidance, 1970s, MIB, from $35 to...................$50.00

Peanuts, Snoopy's Pound-A-Ball, Child Guidance, 1980, MIB, from $35 to...................$45.00

Peanuts, Super Cartoon Maker, Mattel, 1969, complete, EX (EX box), from $150 to...................$175.00

Peanuts, tea set, Chein, 1969, 12 pcs, MIB, from $200 to..$250.00

Peanuts, tea set, Snoopy, Chein, 1970, litho tin, 8 pcs, MIB, from $75 to...................$100.00

Peanuts, tea set, Snoopy, Coloroll, 1980s, ceramic w/image & I'm Allergic To Morning, w/teapot & 4 cups, M, from $125 to...................$175.00

Peanuts, telephone, Snoopy, Romper Room, 10", EX.......$25.00

Peanuts, top, Ohio Art, 1980s, red litho tin w/various characters & Snoopy & the Gang, MIB, from $20 to...................$25.00

Peanuts, yo-yo, Snoopy, Festival, 1970s, plastic w/view lens, paper seal w/image of Snoopy w/balloons, MIP.........$20.00

Peanuts, yo-yo, Woodstock, Festival, 1970s, plastic w/view lens, paper insert seal, NM...................$14.00

Pee Wee's Playhouse, Colorforms, 1988, MIB (sealed).....$20.00

Pee Wee's Playhouse, Playhouse Transfer Rub-Ons, Colorforms, MIP (sealed)...................$12.00

Pee Wee's Playhouse, Slap-Stix, Colorforms, MIB (sealed)...$12.00

Penelope Pitstop, Totum Bag, 1974, MOC...................$20.00

Pink Panther, bank, ceramic figure standing w/arms & legs crossed, blk or wht base, 7", MIB, ea...................$40.00

Pink Panther, doll, plush, 6", M..$10.00
Pink Panther, Silly Putty, Ja-Ru, 1980, MOC..................$10.00
Pink Panther, yo-yo, 1990s, plastic w/imprint seal, Humphrey
      shape, NM...$12.00
Pinky Lee, game, Who Am I?, 1955, unused, NMIB........$90.00
Pinky Lee, xylophone, Emenee, complete, NM (EX box),
      A..$200.00
Pippi Longstocking, doll, Horsman, vinyl w/cloth clothes,
      MIB...$65.00

Popeye, Dakin figure, M, $55.00. (Photo courtesy Martin and Carolyn Berens)

Planet of the Apes, General Ursus, bank, molded plastic, Apac Productions, 1967, 18", M, $25.00.

Popeye, Glow Putty, MOC $25.00
Popeye, harmonica, Popsicle premium, 1929, 4", rare, EX (EX
      box), A..$300.00
Popeye, lantern, pnt tin & glass figure, 11", EX.............$125.00
Popeye, pencil sharpener, Bakelite, figural, 1½", EX $85.00
Popeye, Pencil-By-Number Set, 1959, unused, MIB.........$35.00
Popeye, pennant, paper, Popeye & Wimpy eating hamburger
      around Christmas tree, 1946, 13x20", NM $265.00
Popeye, puffy magnet, EX $15.00
Popeye, pull toy, SS Popeye, paper litho on wood,
      NM+..$245.00
Popeye, slide-tile puzzle, 1960s, MOC............................$35.00
Popeye, somersault toy, wood & paper, 1930s, EX+.........$60.00
Popeye, squeak toy, Swee' Pea, 1930s, rubber, 6", VG $75.00
Porky Pig, bank, mk Japan, pnt bsk, bust figure, 5", EX $50.00
Porky Pig, bank, Porky Pig standing beside barrel, pnt metal,
      4½", NM, A..$85.00
Porky Pig, figure, 1930s, chalkware, 7", EX.....................$75.00
Punky Brewster, doll, Galoob, 1984, 18", NRFB..............$40.00
Quick Draw McGraw, bank, Baba Louey, figural, 9", EX+..$25.00
Raggedy Andy, bank, Japan, ceramic figure w/yarn hair, 14½",
      NM, from $20 to...$25.00
Raggedy Andy, doll, Georgene, 1938-45, stuffed cloth w/yarn
      hair, 19", NM, from $325 to....................................$350.00
Raggedy Andy, doll, inflatable vinyl, 12", M, from $30 to.$35.00
Raggedy Andy, doll, Knickerbocker, stuffed cloth w/yarn hair,
      40", NM, from $155 to $175.00
Raggedy Andy, Sew & Love, Colorforms, 1975, complete,
      MIB...$25.00
Raggedy Ann, bank, Pussy Willow Creations, 1981, sitting
      w/puppy, ceramic w/yarn hair, 6", NMIB, from $25 to..$30.00
Raggedy Ann, Busy Apron, Whitman, 1969, complete, MIP,
      from $30 to...$35.00
Raggedy Ann, coin purse, Hallmark, vinyl figure w/zipper clo-
      sure, NM, from $15 to $20.00
Raggedy Ann, cologne doll, Giftique, 1977, styrofoam doll
      w/cloth clothes & yarn hair over plastic bottle, NM.$20.00

Planet of the Apes, Mix 'N Mold Set, Burke, rare, MIB.$100.00
Popeye, bank, pnt ceramic, 7", EX $135.00
Popeye, bank, Popeye, Vandor, 1980, ceramic figure sitting on
      rope pile, 8", MIB...$45.00
Popeye, dexterity game, Popeye's Bingo, 1930s, tin & glass, 5x3",
      NM..$65.00
Popeye, dexterity puzzle, Intelligence Test, 1930s, 5x5", rare,
      NM, from $75 to...$100.00
Popeye, doll, Popeye, felt w/oilcloth hat, 20", rare, EX ..$385.00
Popeye, doll, Popeye, Japan, prewar, stuffed cloth, wooden pipe,
      paper shoes, 10", rare, NM, A $350.00
Popeye, doll, Popeye, Uneeda, 1979, stuffed cloth w/vinyl head
      & arms, 8", MIB, from $35 to....................................$45.00
Popeye, Dynamite Music Machine, Emerson, 2-speed record
      player w/3 45 rpm records, EX....................................$125.00
Popeye, figure, Popeye, Cameo, jtd rubber, 12½", from $75
      to...$100.00
Popeye, figure, Popeye, European, 1930s, celluloid, 3¾",
      NM, A...$150.00
Popeye, figure, Popeye, KFS, jtd wood, 6", EX+ $125.00
Popeye, figure, Popeye, plaster, 7", EX $165.00
Popeye, figure, Popeye, 1935, rubber, 7", NM, D10........$125.00
Popeye, figure, Popeye, 1940s, celluloid, 5", EX.............$125.00

Raggedy Ann, doll, Georgene, 1940s, cloth w/yarn hair, awake on 1 side, asleep on the other, 12½", NM, from $275 to $325.00

Raggedy Ann, doll, Georgene, 1946-63, stuffed cloth w/yarn hair, 15", NM, from $60 to $80.00

Raggedy Ann, doll, Georgene, 1946-63, stuffed cloth w/yarn hair, 22", NM, from $145 to...$165.00

Raggedy Ann, doll, inflatable vinyl, 14½", M, from $30 to..$35.00

Raggedy Ann, doll, Knickerbocker, stuffed cloth w/yarn hair, 40", NM, from $155 to $165.00

Raggedy Ann, doll, Knickerbocker, talker, cloth w/yarn hair, 19", NM, from $70 to $85.00

Raggedy Ann, doll, Knickerbocker, 1983, 12", EX $20.00

Raggedy Ann, Doll House, Colorforms, 1974, complete, MIB, from $25 to...$30.00

Raggedy Ann, Easy Needlepoint, Colorforms, 1990, complete, MIB $15.00

Raggedy Ann, Look Pretty Make-Up Purse, Giftique, 1975, plastic purse-type holder complete w/contents, M, from $20 to..$25.00

Raggedy Ann, pajama bag doll, Knickerbocker, 1960s, stuffed cloth w/yarn hair, 27", NM, from $75 to.....................$80.00

Raggedy Ann, Pop-Up Tea Party, Colorforms, complete, MIB, from $30 to...$40.00

Raggedy Ann, sewing cards, Colorforms, 1988, complete, MIB $15.00

Raggedy Ann, sink, Hasbro/Romper Room, 1978, plastic, 20x14½", complete, NMIB, from $50 to $65.00

Raggedy Ann, Surprise Package, Colorforms, 1975, complete, MIB $20.00

Raggedy Ann, Talking Telephone, 1980, plastic, battery-op, 9", M, from $40 to $55.00

Raggedy Ann, wall bag, Pussy Willow, 1981, vinyl w/4 pockets, MIP $25.00

Raggedy Ann, yo-yo, 1970s, plastic w/imprint seal, tournament shape, MIP $18.00

Raggedy Ann & Andy, ball, Ideal, 1974, inflatable vinyl, 20", MIP, from $30 to $35.00

Raggedy Ann & Andy, bank, Determined, 1971, sitting arm in arm, papier-mache, 6", NM, from $20 to $25.00

Raggedy Ann & Andy, camper, Buddy L, plastic & metal, 11", M, from $75 to..$100.00

Raggedy Ann & Andy, Color Poster Pack, OSP Publishing, 1993, MIP...$15.00

Raggedy Ann & Andy, cork board, Manton Cork Corp, diecut figures, 23", NM, ea from $25 to $30.00

Raggedy Ann & Andy, doll highchair, Roth Am Inc, wood, NMIB, from $35 to...$45.00

Raggedy Ann & Andy, dolls, Applause, 1986, musical, cloth w/yarn hair, head rotates when music plays, 7", ea from $50 to..$60.00

Raggedy Ann & Andy, dolls, Applause, 1992, 75th Anniversary edition, 19", M (M box), pr, from $160 to...............$175.00

Raggedy Ann & Andy, dolls, Nasco, 1973, plastic w/cloth clothes, yarn hair, 24", NM, ea from $35 to..............$40.00

Raggedy Ann & Andy, Fun & Learn Activity Calendar, 1990, 11x17", M $20.00

Raggedy Ann & Andy, Fun-Filled Playtime Box, Whitman, 1976, complete w/puzzles, coloring books, crayons, etc, NMIB..$30.00

Raggedy Ann & Andy, phonograph, Vanity Fair, 1974, NMIB, from $45 to...$55.00

Raggedy Ann & Andy, pinball game, Arco, 1978, plastic, 11", NM (VG box), from $25 to......................................$30.00

Raggedy Ann & Andy, Play-Pak, Colorforms, 1988, complete, MIB, from $15 to...$20.00

Raggedy Ann & Andy, playhouse cottage, 1980, complete w/wood furniture, NM, from $30 to $35.00

Raggedy Ann & Andy, Shrinky Dinks, 1976, complete, MIB, from $20 to...$25.00

Raggedy Ann & Andy, sleeping bag dolls, Applause, orig tags, 8", NM, ea from $20 to...$25.00

Raggedy Ann & Andy, tambourine, Kingsway, 1977, plastic, 6" dia, MIP, from $25 to $30.00

Raggedy Ann & Andy, tea set, Chein, 1972, litho metal, 9 pcs, MIB..$30.00

Raggedy Ann & Andy, toy wristwatch, Marx, 1975, MOC, from $50 to...$65.00

Raggedy Ann & Andy, watering can, Chein, 1973, litho metal, 9", NM, from $40 to $45.00

Raggedy Ann & Andy, yo-yo, 1997, made for Toy Fest, wood w/die stamp seal, tournament shape, NM $15.00

Raggedy Ann & Andy & Arthur, figure set, Janex, rubber & vinyl w/yarn hair, MIB...$30.00

Rainbow Brite, bank, vinyl figure, EX $10.00

Rainbow Brite, Color Cottage, MIB (sealed)...................$30.00

Rainbow Brite, doll, Twink Sprite, Spark Sprite or Lurky, 10", NMIB, ea $20.00

Rainbow Brite, figures, PVC, set of 5 ....$25.00

Rat Fink, decal, 1990, NM...$5.00

Reg'lar Fellas, doll, Jimmy, Bucherer, jtd metal & compo w/cloth clothes, 8", EX $385.00

Reg'lar Fellas, Microscope Set, complete, NMIB.............$275.00

Richie Rich, baseball bat & ball set, inflatable vinyl, MOC ..$15.00

Richochet Rabbit, pull toy, rubber, Ideal, ca 1964, 9", EX+....$50.00

Ripcord, Sky Diving Parachutist, 1950s, MOC................$30.00

Road Runner, Magic Cartoon Board, 1971, unused, M $25.00

RoboCop, pencil sharpener, MIP...$5.00

Rocky & Bullwinkle, Colorforms #146, unused, NM (EX box)..$85.00

Rocky & Bullwinkle, telescope, Larami, 1970s, MOC $25.00

Roger Rabbit, w/up, vinyl, Masudaya, 1987, M.................$33.00

Rookies, Action Accessory Set, 1976, MIB $25.00

Rookies, helmet, 1970s, plastic w/sticker on top, VG.......$15.00

Roy Rogers, frame-tray puzzle, Roy roping calf, 1952, 9½x12", MIP (sealed) $85.00

Roy Rogers, lantern, tin litho, 7½", NM.........................$90.00

Ruff & Ready, Spelling Game, unused, 1958, M.............$35.00

Saved by the Bell, doll, Tiger, 1992, 6 different, 11½", NRFB, Y1, ea $40.00

Scooby Doo, doll, stuffed plush, 16", EX $40.00

Sesame Street, doll, Ernie, stuffed cloth, 18", EX.............$20.00

Sesame Street, figure set, Applause, 1993, PVC, set of 8..$20.00

Sgt Rock, playset, Sgt Rock Vs the Bad Guys, Remco, 1981, complete, NMIB, T2 ....$25.00

Shari Lewis, Electric Drawing Set, 1962, complete, NMIB..$75.00

Shirley Temple, figure, chalkware, 12½", EX...................$275.00

Simpsons, activity album, Diamond, w/slide-o-scope, unused, NM, K1 ....$15.00

Simpsons, Activity Pack, Pancake Press, MIP (sealed), K1...$25.00

Simpsons, bank, Bart standing, Street Kids, PVC, 9", M, K1 ..$6.00

Simpsons, Bart Simpson Costume & Mask, Ben Cooper, fabric costume dress up w/mask, M (EX box), K1 ....$12.00

Simpsons, Book Marker, paper, picturing the family reading, 'Read, Man,' 6x¾", K1 ....$3.00

Simpsons, doll, any character, Dandee, rag-type, 11", NM, K1, ea...$18.00

Simpsons, doll, Bart, Dandee, rag-type, 17", NM, K1.......$15.00

Simpsons, doll, Bart, Dandee, soft vinyl, 10", MIB..........$15.00

Simpsons, doll, Bart, Dandee, stuffed cloth & vinyl, 10", NMIB, K1 ....$15.00

Simpsons, doll, Bart, Dandee, talker, stuffed cloth & vinyl, 18", MIB, K1 ....$75.00

Simpsons, doll, Bart, Vivid Imaginations, stuffed cloth w/vinyl head, 10", M, K1 ....$35.00

Simpsons, doll, Bubble Blowin' Lisa, Mattel, complete w/4-oz bottle of bubble solution, 10½", MIB, K1 ....$85.00

Simpsons, doll, Homer, Vivid Imaginations, stuffed cloth w/vinyl head, 11", M, K1 ....$35.00

Simpsons, Don't Have a Cow Game, Milton Bradley, dice game, MIB (sealed), K1...$30.00

Simpsons, Family Cut-Out, Starmakers Pub, full-body cb cut-out (no longer in sealed pkg, no stand), 17", K1 ....$2.00

Simpsons, figure, Bart, various poses, MIP, ea $4.00

Simpsons, figure, Lisa, Jesco, bendable, 3½", MOC, K1...$15.00

Simpsons, figure, Maggie, Jesco, bendable, 2", M, K1.......$15.00

Simpsons, figure, Marge, Jesco, bendable, 6", MOC, K1 ..$15.00

Simpsons, Fun Dough Model Maker, MIB, K1...................$45.00

Simpsons, Homer & Marge mylar balloon, M&D Balloons, silver, heart shaped, hugging, 'You Know I Love You,' 17", K1...$2.00

Simpsons, key chain, Bart, Street Kids, 3-D PVC figure on silver ring, M, K1 ....$3.00

Simpsons, Lisa Simpson Double Stamp Set, Jaru, MOC, K1 .$15.00

Simpsons, Marge Simpson Time & Money, Jaru, MOC, K1 ..$10.00

Simpsons, pajama bag, Bart, Dandee, stuffed cloth figure holding toothbrush & pillow, 24", M, K1 ....$40.00

Simpsons, pinball game, Jaru, plastic, MOC, K1................$5.00

Simpsons, pog, complete set of 50, M............................$15.00

Simpsons, Poster Street Signs, H&L Ent, Bart, 'Underachiever & Proud of It, Man,' flex plastic, 17x11", K1, ea $3.50

Simpsons, punch ball set, National Latex Products, MIP, K1 ......$5.00

Simpsons, Stamper Pak, Rubber Stampede, MIP (sealed), K1..$15.00

Simpsons, stickers, Simpsons in the Dark, Glow Zone (Australian), set of 8, MOC (sealed), K1................................$25.00

Simpsons, The Simpsons Study Kit, Pancake Press, pencil pouch, sharpener, 6" ruler, eraser, w/topper, M (sealed), K1 ...$15.00

Simpsons, The Simpsons Xmas Book, Harper Perennial, hardbound, 9¾x8¾", K1 ....$10.00

Simpsons, Trace 'N Color Drawing Set, Toymax, complete, NMIB, K1 ....$85.00

Simpsons, Write 'N Wipe, Rose Art, several variations, MIP (sealed), K1, ea $15.00

Simpsons, 3-D Chess Set, MIP (sealed), K1......................$35.00

Six Million Dollar Man, AM wrist radio, Illco, 1976, MIB, from $200 to $250.00

Six Million Dollar Man, bank, Animals Plus, 1976, plastic figure, 12", M $35.00

Six Million Dollar Man, Bionic Action Club Kit, Kenner, 1973, complete, M, from $50 to $75.00

Six Million Dollar Man, Paint-By-Number set, Craft Master, 1975, MIB, from $30 to $40.00

Six Million Dollar Man, Poster Put-Ons, Bi-Rite, 1978, MIP $15.00

Smokey Bear, Junior Forest Ranger Kit, US Dept of Agriculture, 1956-57, complete, NM $65.00

Smokey the Bear, doll, Ideal, 1960s, 13", EX...................$20.00

Smurfs, banner, Happy Smurfday, MIP............................$20.00

Smurfs, Colorforms, complete, EX (EX box)....................$35.00

Smurfs, sand bucket & shovel, plastic, EX $10.00

Smurfs, Smurfettes Amaze-ing Action Maze, EX.............$20.00

Sniffles, bank, Sniffles standing beside barrel, pnt metal, 5", NM, A $40.00

Snuffy Smith, figure set, Marx, 1950s, matt pk plastic, set of 4, NM..$65.00

Soupy Sales, figure, Remco, 1965, vinyl w/cloth clothes, EX...$35.00

Spider-Man, binder, Mead, 1970s, paper w/colorful image of several characters, NM $40.00

Spider-Man, doll, Amsco, 1976, stuffed cloth w/vinyl head, rooted hair, 8", EX, T2 ....$40.00

Spider-Man, Hippity-Hop, rubber, G $100.00

Spider-Man, Li'l Zips Buggy, 1970s, MOC.......................$55.00

Spider-Man, roller skates, 1970s, plastic, MIP (sealed).....$40.00

Spider-Man, Rub 'N Play Magic Transfer Set, Colorforms, 1978, complete, NMIB, T2, from $50 to................................$75.00

Spider-Man, Sharp Shooter, Larami, 1978, MIP, T2.........$50.00

Spider-Man, TV chair, Carlin Playthings, 1978, inflatable vinyl, MIB, T2, from $50 to...$75.00

Spider-Man, yo-yo, Duncan, 1980s, plastic w/flasher seal, slimline shape w/view lens, NM...$20.00

Starsky & Hutch, Handcuffs & Wallet Set, Fleetwood, 1976, 3 variations, MOC, ea from $25 to $35.00

Starsky & Hutch, iron-ons, 1970s, several different styles, MIP, ea from $20 to $25.00

Starsky & Hutch, Mini Target Set, Fleetwood, 1976, MOC, from $40 to...$50.00

Starsky and Hutch, Official Police Set, HG Toys, 1976, 15½x12", MIB, from $200.00 to $225.00.
(Photo courtesy Greg Davis and Bill Morgan)

Starsky & Hutch, Poster Art Kit, Board King, 1976, unused, MIB, from $50 to $75.00

Starsky & Hutch, 3-D viewer, Fleetwood, 1977, MIP, from $25 to $35.00

Super Friends, Magnetic Target, 1980, MOC $20.00

Super Powers, book & cassette, Earth Core, 1985, M.......$12.00

Superman, doll, Applause, 1988, 18", NM........................$25.00

Superman, doll, Ideal, jtd wood & compo w/cloth cape, 13", VG, A $600.00

Superman, figure, Multiple, 1967, plastic, 2", NM, T2, from $75 to $100.00

Superman, Fun Poncho, Ben Cooper, 1976, MIP (sealed)...$30.00

Superman, Horseshoe Set, complete, unused, NM+ (EX box...$125.00

Superman, kite, Hi-Flier, 1984, MIP $30.00

Superman, kite, Pressman, 1966, plastic w/full-color image, MIP, T2...$75.00

Superman, movie viewer, Acme, 1940, complete w/5 boxes of film, NMIB, T2, from $300 to.................................$400.00

Superman, playsuit, Ben Cooper/Superman Inc., 1940s – 50s, youth size, NM (EX box), A, $225.00.

Superman, Radio Quiz Master, 1948, EX (EX box), T2....$75.00

Superman, scrapbook, Saalfield, 1940, unused, NM, T2...$200.00

Superman, slide-tile puzzle, APC, 1977, MOC................$10.00

Superman, Sparkle Paints, 1966, w/5 pictures to pnt, NMIB..$65.00

Superman, Stardust Touch of Velvet Art, Hasbro, 1965, complete, EX (EX box), T2...$100.00

Superman, Tilt Track Marble Skill Game, Kohner, 1965, NM (EX box), T2...$100.00

Superman, yo-yo, Duncan, 1980s, plastic w/flasher seal, slimline shape w/view lens, NM......................................$20.00

Sylvester the Cat, roly poly, EX $25.00

Tasmanian Devil, doll, 1980, stuffed plush, 13" $15.00

Tasmanian Devil, yo-yo, 1980s, plastic light-up w/sticker seal, puck shape, MIP $10.00

Terminator, doll, Classic Plastic, 1992, 11½", EX+ $10.00

Thor, pillow, Marvel Comics, 1968, inflatable plastic, MIP, T2 ....$125.00

Three Stooges, Colorforms, few pcs missing o/w MIB $40.00

Three Stooges, flasher ring, Curly, Larry or Moe, EX, ea. ..$20.00

Tom & Jerry, Crayon-By-Number Set, Transogram, 1965, MIB (sealed)..$65.00

Tom & Jerry, figure, pnt plaster, 5", EX $85.00

Tom & Jerry, water pistols, Marx, 1960s, M.....................$65.00

Tom Corbett Space Cadet, 2-Way Phone Set, Rockhill, 1950, plastic, NM (G box), A...$125.00

Top Cat, figural bank, Transogram, 1962, 11", NM $45.00

Top Cat, viewer, Louis Marx, Hanna-Barbera, 1962, plastic house shape, eight color action scenes, NMIB, $95.00.

Topo Gigio, bank, Ross, ceramic, head shakes, 6½", MIB, A $150.00

Tweety Bird, lantern, Amico, 1950s, tin, battery-op, 5½", EX...$85.00

Uncle Wiggily, bank, Chein, litho tin, 5", EX, A $250.00

Uncle Wiggily, bank, Chein, litho tin, 5", M.................$400.00

Underdog, bank, 1972, plastic figure, 13", NM, T2 ....$40.00

Underdog, yo-yo, 1992, plastic w/paper sticker seal, tournament shape, MIP $18.00

Universal Monsters, charm, any character, M, C10, ea $10.00

Universal Monsters, Flicker Stickers, 1991, set of 6, MOC, C10 ....$15.00

Vincent Price, Transparent Watercolors, Sears, 1960s, complete, rare, EX (VG box) $85.00

Welcome Back Kotter, chalkboard, Board King, 1976, 18½x24½", NM...$50.00

Welcome Back Kotter, Classroom Brain Twister, Fleetwood, 1979, slide-tile puzzle shaped like calculator, MOC ..$35.00

Welcome Back Kotter, Colorforms, 1976, MIB.................$30.00

Welcome Back Kotter, guitar, Lapin, 1977, plastic, 18", MOC, from $75 to $100.00

Welcome Back Kotter, playset, Toy Factory, 1976, MIB (sealed), from $60 to...$80.00

Welcome Back Kotter, Poster Art Kit, Board King, 1976, MIP (sealed), from $35 to..$45.00

Welcome Back Kotter, record player, Peerless Vid-Tronic Corp, 1976, NM, from $50 to $75.00

Welcome Back Kotter, Sweathogs Bike, Mattel, 1976, MIB, from $75.00 to $100.00. (Photo courtesy Greg Davis and Bill Morgan)

Wizard of Oz, bank, Dorothy, Amart Imports, 1960s, hand-pnt, orig paper tag, 7", NMIB $825.00

Wizard of Oz, doll, Dorothy, Effanbee, 1984, Great Legends series, w/Toto & basket, 14½", MIB.........................$100.00

Wizard of Oz, doll, Dorothy, Multitoys, 1984, 50th Anniversary, rare, MIB..$100.00

Wizard of Oz, doll, Scarecrow, Ideal, 1939, cloth w/pnt mask face & yarn hair, 17", NM.......................................$800.00

Wizard of Oz, figure, Cowardly Lion, Multiple, 1960s, rubber, 6", EX...$55.00

Wizard of Oz, purse, zippered vinyl, Ice Capades (sold at arenas), 1950s, 7x5", NM, $60.00.

Wizard of Oz, magic kit, Fun Inc, 1967, complete, EX (EX box)...$75.00

Wizard of Oz, trinket box, ruby slippers, Presents, 1989, MIB $15.00

Wonder Woman, doll, 1979, inflatable vinyl, 24", MIP, A7..$30.00

Wonder Woman, figure, Ideal, 1966, pnt plastic, 4", EX ..$45.00

Wonder Woman, figure, inflatable vinyl, 24", MIP, A7....$25.00

Wonder Woman, tiaras, 1977, set of 5, MOC.................$20.00

Wonder Woman, yo-yo, Duncan, 1980s, plastic w/flasher seal, slimline shape w/view lens, MIP................................$30.00

Woody Woodpecker, bank, Imco, 1977, vinyl figure, 10½", MIP $150.00

Woody Woodpecker, film, 1960s, 8mm, NMIB $15.00

Woody Woodpecker, ring, 1970s, cloisonne, M................$15.00

Yogi Bear, bank, figural, 1960s, 10", NMIP $45.00

Yogi Bear, bank, plastic, 14", EX....................................$35.00

Yogi Bear, doll, Boo Boo, Knickerbocker, 1973, stuffed cloth, MIB (sealed) $35.00

Yogi Bear, doll, 1977, pillow-type w/bells inside, 15", EX .$20.00

Yogi Bear, guitar, crank-type, Mattel, 1961, EX $65.00

Yogi Bear, mug, 1961, pnt plastic, NM $20.00

Yogi Bear, riding stick, AJ Renzi, 1961, wood w/plastic head figure of Yogi, 34", EX..$55.00

Yogi Bear, roly poly, w/chimes, Transogram, 1962, 8", NMIP....$50.00

Yogi Bear, Score-A-Matic Ball Toss Game, Transogram, 1960, unused, NMIB $100.00

Yogi Bear, slippers, bl corduroy, 1962, unused, NMIB.......$70.00

Yogi Bear, yo-yo, 1970s, litho tin w/image of Yogi & Boo-Boo, tournament shape, NM...$10.00

Chein

Though the company was founded shortly after the turn of the century, this New Jersey-based manufacturer is probably best known for the toys it made during the '30s and '40s. Wind-up merry-go-rounds and Ferris wheels as well as many other carnival-type rides were made of beautifully lithographed tin even into the '50s, some in several variations. The company also made banks, a few of which were mechanical and some that were character-related. Mechanical, seaworthy cabin cruisers, space guns, sand toys, and some Disney toys as well were made by this giant company; they continued in production until 1979.

Advisor: Scott Smiles (S10).

See also Banks; Character, TV, and Movie Collectibles; Disney; Sand Toys.

WINDUPS, FRICTIONS, AND OTHER MECHANICALS

Aquaplane, 1939, advances w/spinning prop, 8½", NM...$350.00

Barnacle Bill, advances in waddling motion, 6", EX.......$300.00

Bass Drummer, 1930s, advances & plays drum, 9", NM .$400.00

Big Top Tent, 1961, spins & opens to reveal clown, tin w/plastic dome, 10", EX (EX box).......................................$200.00

Butterfly Sparkler, 1930, tin w/celluloid wings, 5", EX (EX box)...$225.00

Clown, 1930s, tin with celluloid punching bag, 8½", EX, A, $600.00.
(Photo courtesy Dunbar Gallery)

Penguin, advances in waddling motion, 4", NMIB........$125.00

Playland Merry-Go-Round, horses & swans circle w/bell sound, 10", EX..$450.00

Playland Whip, 4 cars w/bobbing head figures on rectangular base, litho tin, 20" L, NM (EX box)........................$900.00

Popeye Floor Puncher, litho tin figure hits celluloid ball on rectangular base, 7", NMIB.....................................$3,000.00

Popeye Heavy Hitter, 1932, figure rings strength meter bell, 12", rare, EX...$3,500.00

Popeye in Barrel, 1932, waddles back & forth in barrel, 7", NM, from $700 to $750.00

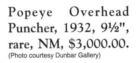

Popeye Overhead Puncher, 1932, 9½", rare, NM, $3,000.00.
(Photo courtesy Dunbar Gallery)

Drummer Boy, 1930s, NM, $250.00. (Photo courtesy Scott Smiles)

Popeye Shadow Boxer, advances in vibrating motion w/swinging arms, 7", rare, NM................................$1,600.00

Popeye the Drummer, advances & plays drum, litho tin, 7", VG...$1,200.00

Popeye Waddler, 1932, 6½", NM................................$1,300.00

Racer #52, tin w/wooden wheels, EX.............................$200.00

Racer #7, yel & orange boat-tail style, 19", missing windshield, G+...$500.00

Disneyland Ferris Wheel, spins w/bell sound, 17", EX....$500.00

Easter Bunny Delivery Cart, 1930s, rabbit rides cart w/sidecar, 9½", EX..$300.00

Fancy Groceries Truck, 6", EX......................................$350.00

Felix the Cat on Scooter, 7", EX $650.00

Fish, 1940s, advances as tail fin moves, NM $125.00

Hand-Standing Clown, 5", EX, from $100 to $125.00

Happy Hooligan, waddles side-to-side, 6", EX, A $400.00

Hercules Dump Truck, blk w/open bench seat, 18", VG, A ..$500.00

Hercules Ferris Wheel, spins w/ringing bells, 17", EX, from $300 to..$350.00

Junior Truck, mk 420 on doors, gr w/red tires, half-figure driver, 8", EX..$350.00

Musical Aero Swing, 4 gondolas spin around w/music, litho tin, 11", VG (VG box)....................................$650.00

Native on Turtle, 1930s, advances w/moving head, 8", NM ...$300.00

Navy Frog Man, litho tin w/plastic flippers, 12", NMOC ..$125.00

Pelican, waddles around, litho tin, 5", NM, A.................$150.00

Roller Coaster, 1930s, with two cars and bell, 19", NM (NM box), $300.00. (Photo courtesy Dunbar Gallery)

Santa Walker, advances in waddling motion w/gift in hand, 6",
  EX $550.00
Santa's Gnome, early mk, advances in waddling motion, 6",
  MIB..$300.00

Seaplane, 1930s, 9", EX, $250.00. (Photo courtesy Dunbar Gallery)

Ski Boy, advances on snow skis, 8", EX $275.00
Ski Boy, advances on snow skis, 8", G, A........................$150.00
Ski Ride, kids travel to top of ride, 19½", EX (EX box), from
  $900 to...$1,000.00
Skin Driver, swims w/realistic movement, litho tin, 11½", NM
  (NM box), A $200.00
Surf's Up, surfboard w/dog & surfer, litho tin & plastic, 10",
  NMOC..$100.00
US Army Soldier, 5", MOC $150.00
Yellow Taxi, early, mk Yellow Taxi Main 7570, 6", NMIB ...$400.00

Miscellaneous

Bank, church, litho tin, NM...$125.00
Bank, clown bust, litho tin, press lever & tongue pops out for
  coin, 5", EX, A..$100.00
Bank, clown bust, litho tin, 5", VG, A............................$75.00
Bank, elephant on drum, litho tin, EX...........................$100.00
Bank, monkey, litho tin, EX $125.00
Bank, Save for War Bonds & Stamps, blk-pnt shell-shape w/yel
  label, 6", NM $225.00
Bank, Save for War Bonds & Stamps, blk-pnt tin dome-shape
  w/yel label, 4½", NM, A $550.00
Bank, Uncle Wiggily, litho tin, M..................................$450.00
Bank, 1939 World's Fair, tin, 12", NM $275.00
Bank, 2nd National Duck Bank, litho tin w/image of Mickey,
  Minnie & Donald, NM $165.00
Cathedral Organ, turn crank & music plays, litho tin, 9½",
  NMIB, from $175 to...$200.00
Clown Roly Poly, 1930s, litho tin, scarce, NM $365.00
Easter Egg, take-apart w/lithoed scenes, 5", NM $75.00
Globe, litho tin, 10", NMIB..$125.00
Player Piano, electric, NM, L4 ....$325.00
Pull Toy, cat on 3-wheeled platform, litho tin, 7½", EX ...$500.00

Top, 1930s, litho tin w/various images of children's toys,
  NM $75.00
Top, 1970s, features Disney characters, litho tin w/plastic knob,
  6½", EX $50.00
Train Station, litho tin simulated brick building w/Grove Sta-
  tion sign, 6", EX...$75.00

Hercules Mack Crane Truck, 1930s, tin and pressed steel, 26", EX, from $800.00 to $1,000.00. (Photo courtesy Dunbar Gallery)

Chinese Tin Toys

China has produced toys for export since the 1920s, but most of their tin toys were made from the 1970s to the present. Collectors are buying them with an eye to the future, since right now, at least, they are relatively inexpensive.

Government-operated factories are located in various parts of China. They use various numbering systems to identify types of toys, for instance, ME (metal-electric — battery operated), MS (metal-spring — windup), MF (metal friction), and others. Most toys and boxes are marked, but some aren't; and since many of the toys are reproductions of earlier Japanese models, it is often difficult to tell the difference if no numbers can be found.

Prices vary greatly depending on age, condition, availability, and dealer knowledge of origin. Toys currently in production may be discontinued at any time and may often be as hard to find as the earlier toys. Records are so scarce that it is difficult to pinpoint the start of production, but at least some manufacture began in the 1970s and 1980s. If you have additional information (toy name and number; description as to size, color variations, actions, type, etc.; and current market), please contact our advisor. In the listings below, values are for new-in-the-box items.

Advisor: Steve Fisch (F7).

#ME021, police car, current, 16½x5x5", F7, from $55 to.....$125.00
#ME060, tank, remote control, 1970s, 7x4x4", F7, from $35 to..$75.00
#ME081, Lunar Explorer, 1970s, 12x6x4", F7, from $75 to..$125.00
#ME084, jet plane, current, 12½x13x5", F7, from $85 to $150.00
#ME086, Shanghai bus, battery-operated, 1970s-80s, approxi-
  mately 14", from $75 to $125.00

#ME087, jetliner, 1980s, 19x18x3", F7, from $55 to $125.00

#ME089, Universe car, 1970s, F7, from $85 to $150.00

#ME093, open-door trolley, discontinued, 10x5x4", F7, from $25 to $35.00

#ME095, fire chief car, current, 12½x5x5", F7, from $35 to...$75.00

#ME097, police car, 13x5x5", F7, from $35 to $75.00

#ME099, UFO spaceship, current, 8x8x5", F7, from $35 to..$75.00

#ME100, robot (resembles 1980s Star Strider), current, 12x4x6", F7, from $35 to $125.00

#ME102, spaceship, blows air, current, 13x5x4", F7, from $35 to $75.00

#ME104, locomotive, 15½x4x7", F7, from $35 to $75.00

#ME105, locomotive, 9½x5½x5½", F7, from $35 to $75.00

#ME379, dump truck, discontinued, 13x4x3", F7, from $25 to $35.00

#ME603, hen & chicken, battery-operated, 1980s, 12", from $50 to $75.00

#ME610, hen laying eggs, current, 7x4x6", F7, from $25 to..$50.00

#ME611, World Cup News Car, battery operated, multi-action, 1980s – 90s, from $75.00 to $150.00. (Photo courtesy Steve Fisch)

#ME614, automatic rifle, current, 23x2x8", F7, from $25 to.................$35.00

#ME630, Photo car, older version, 12½x5x5", F7, from $35 to $125.00

#ME677, Shanghai convertible, 1970s, 12x5x3", F7, from $60 to $100.00

#ME679, dump truck, discontinued, 13x4x3", F7, from $25 to.................$50.00

#ME742, walking camel, from $25.00 to $50.00. (Photo courtesy Steve Fisch)

#ME699, fire chief car, 10x5x2", from $25 to.................$50.00

#ME756, anti-aircraft armored tank, F7, from $35 to.......$75.00

#ME767, Universe boat, 1970s, 10x5x6", F7, from $75 to..$150.00

#ME767, Universe boat, 1990s, 10x5x6", F7, from $35 to..$75.00

**#ME770, Mr. Duck, 9",
from $25.00 to $50.00.**
(Photo courtesy Steve Fisch)

#ME774, tank, remote control, 1970s, 9x4x3", F7, from $45 to $75.00

#ME777, Universe Televiboat, 15x4x7", F7, from $35 to ...$75.00

#ME782, locomotive, 1970s-80s, battery-op, 10x4x7", F7, from $35 to $75.00

#ME809, anti-aircraft armoured car, 1970s, 12x6x6", F7, from $75 to.................$100.00

#ME821, Cicada, 1970s, 10x4x4", F7, from $50 to.........$125.00

#ME824, patrol car, 1970s, 11x4x3½", F7, from $35 to....$75.00

#ME842, camel, discontinued, 10x4x7", F7, from $35 to .$50.00

#ME884, police car, VW bus style, current, 11½x5x5", F7, from $35 to $75.00

#ME895, fire engine, 1970, 10x4x4", F7, from $50 to $85.00

#ME956, Sparking Tank, friction, 1980s-90s, 7", from $25 to $35.00

#ME972, open-door police car, 9½x4x4", F7, from $35 to.................$100.00

#ME984, jet plane, 13x14x4½", F7, from $35 to $75.00

#MF032, Eastwind Sedan, 6x2x2", F7, from $8 to............$15.00

#MF033, pickup truck, 6x2x2", F7, from $8 to $15.00

#MF044, sedan, Nissan style, 9x3½x3", F7, from $10 to ..$25.00

#MF046, Sparking Carbine, 18x5x1", F7, from $20 to $35.00

#MF052, sedan, 8x3x2", F7, from $15 to...........................$25.00

#MF083, sedan, 6x2x2", F7, from $8 to..........................$15.00

#MF107, airplane, 6x6x2", F7, from $20 to......................$35.00

#MF111, ambulance, 8x3x3", F7, from $15 to $20.00

#MF127, Highway patrol car, 9½x4x3", F7, from $20 to..$50.00

#MF132, ambulance, 1980s, 10x4x4", F7, from $15 to.....$35.00

#MF134, tourist bus, 6x2x3", F7, from $15 to $25.00

#MF135, red flag convertible, F7, from $35 to $75.00

#MF136, double-decker train, current, 8x2x3", F7, from $15 to $20.00

#MF146, Volkswagen, 5x2x2", F7, from $10 to.................$20.00

#MF151, Shanghai pickup, 1970s, 12x4x4", F7, from $50 to $100.00

#MF154, tractor, 1970s, 5x3x4", F7, from $25 to.............$50.00

#MF162, motorcycle, 6x2x4", F7, from $15 to..................$35.00

#MF163, fire truck, 6x2x3", F7, from $35 to....................$75.00

#MF164, construction truck, 1970s, 7x3x5", F7, from $35 to..$75.00

#MF164, Volkswagen, 4x2x3", F7, from $10 to................$15.00

#MF170, train, 10x2x4", F7, from $15 to.........................$25.00

#MF171, convertible, 5x2x2", F7, from $8 to $15.00

#MF183, emergency truck, friction, 1980s, 8", from $20 to ..$35.00

#MF184, coach bus, 12½x4x4", F7, from $15 to..............$30.00

#MF185, double-decker bus, current, 11x5x3", F7, from $15 to...$25.00

#MF193, soft-cover truck, 1970s, 11x3x4", F7, from $50 to..$75.00

#MF201, oil tanker, 1970s, 14x4x4", F7, from $15 to.......$25.00

#MF203, sedan, 10½x4x2½", F7, from $25 to..................$50.00

#MF206, panda truck, 6x3x2", F7, from $10 to................$20.00

#MF216, airplane, discontinued, 9x9x3", F7, from $15 to ..$35.00

#MF234, sedan, 6x2x2", F7, from $15 to.........................$25.00

#MF239, tiger truck, 10x3x4", F7, from $15 to................$30.00

#MF240, passenger jet, 13x11x4", F7, from $30 to...........$35.00

#MF249, flying boat, 1970s, 6x6x2", F7, from $35 to.......$75.00

#MF254, Mercedes Sedan, 8x4x3", F7, from $15 to $25.00

#MF274, tank, 1970s, 3x2x2", F7, from $8 to..................$15.00

#MF294, Mercedes Sedan, friction, 7x3x2", F7, from $12 to .$20.00

#MF298, traveling car, 8½x4x3½", F7, from $15 to.........$25.00

#MF304, race car, discontinued, 10x4x3", F7, from $15 to ..$35.00

#MF309, sedan, 9x2x3½", F7, from $20 to......................$35.00

#MF310, Corvette, 3x2x3", F7, from $10 to.....................$15.00

#MF316, 1953 Corvette, current, F7, from $20 to............$50.00

#MF317, Corvette convertible, current, 10x4x3", F4, from $20 to...$50.00

#MF320, Mercedes sedan, current, 7x3x2", F7, from $10 to .$20.00

#MF321, Buick convertible, current, 11x4x3", F7, from $20 to...$50.00

#MF322, Buick sedan, current, 11x4x3", F7, from $20 to.$50.00

#MF326, Mercedes, gull-wing sedan, 9", from $15.00 to $25.00. (Photo courtesy Steve Fisch)

#MF329, 1956, Corvette convertible, current, 10x4x4", F7, from $20 to...$50.00

#MF330, Cadillac Sedan, current, 11x4x3", F7, from $15 to ..$35.00

#MF339, 1956 Corvette, current, 10x4x4", F7, from $20 to .$50.00

#MF340, Cadillac convertible, current 11x4x3", F7, from $20 to...$50.00

#MF341, convertible, 12x4x3", F7, from $20 to $50.00

#MF342, sedan, 12x4x3", F7, from $20 to........................$50.00

#MF712, locomotive, current, 7x2x3", F7, from $10 to....$15.00

#MF713, taxi, 5x2x2", F7, from $8 to...............................$15.00

#MF714, fire chief car, 5x2x2", F7, from $8 to.................$15.00

#MF716, ambulance, 1970s, 8x3x3", F7, from $15 to.......$30.00

#MF717, dump truck, discontinued, 10x3x5", F7, from $15 to $35.00

#MF718, ladder truck, 10", from $15.00 to $35.00.
(Photo courtesy Steve Fisch)

#MF721, light tank, 6x3x3", F7, from $15 to....................$20.00

#MF722, jeep, current, 6x3x3", F7, from $15 to...............$20.00

#MF731, station wagon, 5x2x2", F7, from $8 to...............$15.00

#MF735, rocket racer, current, 7x3x3", F7, from $15 to...$35.00

#MF742, flying boat, current, 13x4x4", F7, from $15 to...$35.00

#MF743, Karmann Ghia sedan, 10x3x4", F7, from $15 t o...$45.00

#MF753, sports car, 8x3x2", F7, from $15 to....................$25.00

#MF782, circus truck, 9x3x4", F7, from $15 to.................$25.00

#MF787, Lucky open car, 8x3x2", F7, from $15 to $25.00

#MF798, patrol car, 8x3x3", F7, from $15 to....................$25.00

#MF800, race car #5, 6x2x2", F7, from $10 to $20.00

#MF804, locomotive, 16x3x5", F7, from $15 to...............$25.00

#MF832, ambulance, 5x2x2", F7, from $8 to $15.00

#MF844, double-decker bus, current, 8x4x3", F7, from $15 to $20.00

#MF851, space gun, 1970s, 10x2x6", F7, from $45 to.......$75.00

#MF893, animal van, 6x2x3", F7, from $15 to..................$20.00

#MF900, police car, 6x3x2", F7, from $8 to $15.00

#MF910, airport limo bus, 15x4x5", F7, from $20 to $35.00

#MF923, torpedo boat, 8x3x3", F7, from $15 to $25.00

#MF951, fighter jet, 1970s, 5x4x2", F7, from $15 to.........$20.00

#MF956, sparking tank, 8x4x3", F7, from $15 to..............$20.00

#MF957, ambulance helicopter, 7½x2x4", F7, from $15 to ..$35.00

#MF958, poultry truck, F7, from $15 to $20.00

#MF959, jeep, discontinued, 9x4x4", F7, from $15 to $20.00

#MF974, circus truck, 6x2x4", F7, from $15 to.................$20.00

#MF985, fowl transporter, 12x3x4", F7, from $25 to $50.00

#MF993, mini car, 5x2x2", F7, from $8 to........................$15.00

#MF998, sedan, 5x2x2", F7, from $8 to............................$15.00

#MF989, Noisy Locomotive, from $25.00 to $50.00.
(Photo courtesy Steve Fisch)

#MS002, jumping frog, current, 2x2x2", F7, from $8 to ...**$15.00**
#MS006, pecking chicken, 1970s, 2x1x1", F7, from $8 to.**$15.00**
#MS011, roll-over plane, 3x4x2", F7, from $10 to............**$20.00**
#MS014, single-bar exerciser, 1970s, 7x6x6", F7, from $25
    to **$50.00**
#MS057, horse & rider, 1970s, 6x2x5", F7, from $20 to...**$35.00**
#MS058, old-fashion car, current, 3x3x4", F7, from $15 to...**$20.00**
#MS082, jumping frog, current, 2x2x2", F7, from $8 to ...**$15.00**
#MS083, jumping rabbit, current, 3x3x2", F7, from $8 to ..**$15.00**
#MS085, xylophone girl, 7x3x9", F7, from $20 to **$35.00**
#MS107, jumping Bambi, current, 5½x6", F7, from $15 to ..**$20.00**
#MS134, sparking jet, F7, from $15 to **$30.00**
#MS141, koi, w/up, 1980s-90s, 8", from $15 to................**$35.00**
#MS166, crawling baby, vinyl head, current, 5x4x5", F7, from
    $15 to **$20.00**
#MS405, jumping zebra, current, 5x2x4", F7, from $10 to..**$20.00**
#MS565, drumming panda/wheel, current, 5x3x5", F7, from $10
    to **$20.00**
#MS568, sparrow, current, 5x2x2", F7, from $10 to..........**$15.00**
#MS569, oriole, current, 5x2x2", F7, from $10 to **$15.00**
#MS575, bear w/ camera, battery-operated & w/up, 1980s, from
    $35 to **$50.00**
#MS575, bear w/flash camera, 6x3x4", F7, from $35 to....**$50.00**
#MS702, motorcycle, current, 7x4x5", F7, from $15 to....**$35.00**
#MS704, bird music cart, 1970s, 3x2x5", F7, from $15 to .**$25.00**
#MS709, motorcycle w/sidecar, current, 7x4x5", F7, from $15
    to..**$35.00**
#MS710, tricycle, current, 5x3x5", F7, from $15 to..........**$20.00**
#MS713, washing machine, 3x3x5", F7, from $15 to **$20.00**
#MS765, drummer, 5x3x6", F7, from $15 to **$25.00**
#MS827, sedan, steering, 1970s, 9x3x3", F7, from $50 to...**$75.00**
#MS858, girl on goose, older style, 5x3x3", F7, from $25 to..**$50.00**
#MS858, girl on goose, 5x3x3", F7, from $15 to **$25.00**
#PMS102, rolling cart, current, 3x2x1", F7, from $15 to..**$20.00**
#PMS105, jumping dog, current, 3x2x6", F7, from $15 to.**$25.00**
#PMS106, jumping parrot, current, 3x2x6", F7, from $15 to...**$25.00**
#PMS108, duck family, current, 10x2x3", F7, from $15 to....**$25.00**
#PMS113, Fu dog, current, 4x2x3", F7, from $15 to........**$25.00**
#PMS119, woodpecker, current, 3x2x6", F7, from $15 to..**$25.00**
#PMS210, clown riding bike, current, 4x2x5", F7, from $15 to ..**$25.00**
#PMS212, elephant on bike, current, 6x3x8", F7, from $15 to...**$30.00**
#PMS213, duck on bike, current, 6x3x8", F7, from $15 to.........**$35.00**
#PMS214, lady bug family, current, 13x3x1", F7, from $15 to **$25.00**

#PMS215, crocodile, 9x3x1", F7, from $15 to **$20.00**
#PMS217, jumping rabbit, current, 3x2x6", F7, from $15 to..**$25.00**
#PMS218, penguin, current, 3x2x6", F7, from $15 to **$30.00**

Coloring, Activity, and Paint Books

Coloring and activity books from the early years of the twentieth century are scarce indeed and when found can be expensive if they are tied into another collectibles field such as Black Americana or advertising; but the ones most in demand are those that represent familiar movie and TV stars of the '50s and '60s. Condition plays a very important part in assessing worth, and though hard to find, unused examples are the ones that bring top dollar — in fact, as much as 50% to 75% more than one even partially used.

Advisor: Diane Albert (T6).

Adventures of Electro-Man, coloring book, Lowe, 1967, unused,
    NM, T2 ....**$20.00**
Alice in Wonderland, paint book, Whitman, 1951, unused,
    EX **$50.00**
Andy Griffith Show, coloring book, Saalfield, 1960s, several pgs
    colored, VG+ **$25.00**
Andy Panda, paint book, Whitman, 1944, several pgs colored,
    EX..**$40.00**
Annette, coloring book, WDP, 1964, unused, EX.............**$15.00**
Atom Ant, coloring book, Watkins-Strathmore, 1967, few pgs
    colored, EX..**$10.00**
Baba Louie, coloring book, Watkins-Strathmore, 1960, unused,
    EX, T2 ....**$15.00**
Bambi, paint book, Whitman/WDP, 1941-42, unused, EX ...**$55.00**
Banana Splits, coloring book, Whitman, 1969, unused, EX..**$25.00**
Batman w/Robin the Boy Wonder, dot-to-dot & coloring book,
    Vasquez Bros, 1967, unused, NM, from $50 to...........**$75.00**
Beatles, coloring book, Saalfield, unused, EX, B3 ....**$125.00**
Betty Grable, paint book, Whitman, 1947, unused, EX ...**$55.00**

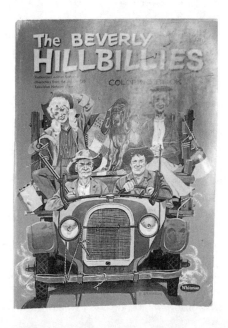

Beverly Hill-
billies, coloring
book, Whit-
man #1137,
unused, EX,
$30.00.

Bewitched Fun & Activity Book, Treasure Books #8908, 1965, unused, NM, from $25 ....$20.00

Bionic Woman Fun Coloring Book, Treasure Books, 1976, unused, NM, from $15 to...$20.00

Black Hole, coloring book, Whitman, 1979, unused, EX .$12.00

Blue Fairy Story Paint Book, Whitman, 1939, unused, EX ...$50.00

Bobbsey Twins, coloring book, Whitman, 1954, unused, VG...$25.00

Brady Bunch, coloring book, Whitman, 1973, unused, EX, from $25 to $35.00

Brady Bunch, sticker book, Whitman, 1973, unused, NM, from $50 to $75.00

Brave Little Taylor, paint & coloring book, Whitman, 1938, several pgs colored, VG, M8.....................................$75.00

Buffy & Jody, coloring book, Whitman, 1969, unused, NM..$25.00

Bullwinkle, coloring book, General Mills premium, 1963, unused, EX $30.00

Buzz Corry, coloring book, Ralston Purina, 1953, few pgs colored, scarce, EX..$75.00

Captain America, coloring book, Whitman, 1966, unused, EX, T2...$50.00

Captain Kangaroo's Treasure House, punch-out book, Whitman, 1959, unpunched, NM......................................$65.00

Casper & Nightmare, coloring book, Saalfield, 1964, unused, EX, T2 ....$20.00

Charlotte's Web, coloring book, Whitman, 1971, 2 pgs colored out of 64, EX $15.00

Charlie Chaplin, coloring book, Saalfield, 1941, unused, M..$50.00

Charlie McCarthy, paint book, Whitman, 1938, few pgs pnt, EX $50.00

Charlie's Angels, coloring book, Stafford Pemberton, 1978, unused, M, from $75 to $100.00

Chatty Baby, coloring book, Whitman, 1960s, unused, NM..$25.00

Cinderella, paint book, Whitman, 1950, unused, EX $30.00

Dennis the Menace, coloring book, Whitman, 1961, few pgs colored, NM...$20.00

Dick Tracy, coloring book, Saalfield, 1946, unused, EX....$45.00

Dick Van Dyke, coloring book, Saalfield, 1963, unused, EX...$40.00

Donald Duck Army Paint Book, Whitman, 1942, unused, EX...$45.00

Donna Reed, coloring book, Saalfield, 1964, unused, NM .$30.00

Donny & Marie, sticker book, Whitman, 1977, unused, NM...$20.00

Doris Day, coloring & cut-out book, Whitman, 1953, few pgs used, 15x11", EX...$215.00

Doris Day, coloring book, Whitman, 1955, unused, EX....$35.00

Dudley Do-Right Comes to the Rescue, coloring book, Saalfield, 1969, unused, M..$35.00

Dumbo the Elephant, coloring book, 1972, unused, M, N2..$25.00

Elizabeth Taylor, coloring book, Whitman, 1954, few pgs colored, EX $40.00

Fantastic Four vs Frightful Four, coloring book, Marvel, 1983, unused, NM..$8.00

Fat Albert & the Cosby Kids, coloring book, Whitman, 1973, unused, EX $8.00

Figaro & Cleo Story Paint Book, Whitman, 1940, unused, NM, M8...$75.00

Flash Gordon, paint book, Whitman, 1936, unused, EX ..$55.00

Flintstones, coloring book, Charlton, 1971, unused, EX, from $10 to $15.00

Flipper Paintless Paint Book, Whitman, 1964, unused, NM..$25.00

George of the Jungle, coloring book, Whitman, 1968, unused, EX, T2 ....$30.00

Geppetto Story Paint Book, Whitman/WDP, 1939, unused, EX $50.00

Gilligan's Island, coloring book, Whitman, 1965, unused, EX $45.00

Gloria Jean, coloring book, Saalfield, 1941, few pgs colored, VG $30.00

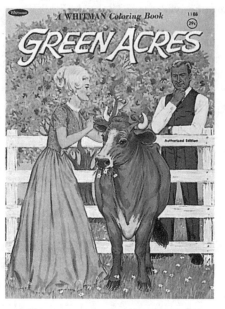

Green Acres, coloring book, Whitman, 1967, unused, M, from $30.00. (Photo courtesy Greg Davis and Bill Morgan)

Green Hornet, coloring book, Whitman, 1966, unused, NM, T2...$60.00

Grizzly Adams, activity book, Rand McNally, 1978, unused, NM..$20.00

Gulliver's Travels, coloring book, Saalfield, 1939, several pgs colored, VG+...$45.00

Gumps, The; paint book, unused, Art Co, 1931, 15½x11", EX+...$89.00

Gunsmoke, coloring book, Whitman, 1959, few pgs colored, EX $25.00

Hardy Boys Mystery Mazes, Tempo, 1977, unused, NM ...$10.00

Hayley Mills in Search of the Castaways, coloring book, Whitman, 1962, EX $25.00

Heckle & Jeckle, coloring book, Treasure Books, 1957, unused, EX, T2 ....$15.00

Hopalong Cassidy, coloring book, Lowe, 1950, unused, NM $75.00

How To Draw Super Heroes, sketchbook & coloring book, Golden, 1983, unused, EX $25.00

Howdy Doody, coloring book, Whitman, 1952, pgs slightly yel, VG...$15.00

HR Pufnstuf, coloring book, Whitman, 1970, unused, M.$35.00

Huckleberry Hound, coloring book, Whitman, 1959, few pgs colored, EX..$15.00

Humpty Dumpty, coloring book, Lowe, 1950s, unused, NM, T2...$10.00

I Love Lucy (Lucille Ball, Desi Arnez, Little Ricky), coloring book, Dell, 1955, unused, NM, A $75.00

J Worthington Foulfellow & Gideon Story Paint Book, Whitman, 1940, unused, NM, M8..............$75.00

Jeanette MacDonald Costume Parade, paint book, Merrill, 1941, unused, EX $30.00

Jiminy Cricket Story Paint Book, Whitman, 1940, unused, NM, M8..............$75.00

John Wayne, coloring book, Saalfield, 1951, few pgs colored, rare, EX $85.00

Johnny Quest, paint book, Hanna-Barbera, 1994, unused, EX $12.00

Julia, coloring book, Saalfield, 1969, unused, NM $25.00

Land of the Lost, coloring book, Western, 1975, unused, NM $25.00

Leave It to Beaver, coloring book, Saalfield, 1958, unused, NM $65.00

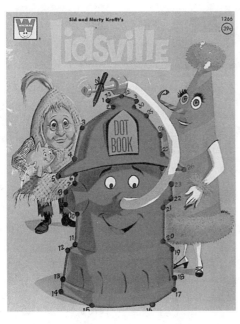

Lidsville Dot Book, Whitman, 1973, NM, $20.00. (Photo courtesy Greg Davis and Bill Morgan)

Little Lulu & Tubby Tom, paint book, 1946, unused, VG, T2 ....$40.00

Little Orphan Annie, coloring book, Artcraft, 1974, unused, NM..............$20.00

Lone Ranger, coloring book, Whitman, 1951, unused, EX $65.00

Lucille Ball & Desi Arnez, coloring book, Whitman, 1953, unused, EX $100.00

Man From UNCLE, coloring book, Whitman, 1967, unused, NM..............$40.00

Marty Mouse, coloring/activity book, Waldman, 1964, few pgs used, EX $20.00

Marvel Super Heroes Super Activity Book, Marvel, 1983, unused, EX $8.00

Mickey & Donald, paint book, Whitman, 1949, unused, EX, M8..............$45.00

Mickey Rooney, paint book, Merrill, 1940, unused, NM..$35.00

Mighty Hercules, sticker book, Lowe, 1963, unused, EX, T2 ....$25.00

Mighty Mouse, sticker book, Whitman, 1967, unused, NM, T2 ....$50.00

Moon Mullins Crayon & Paint Book, McLoughlin Bros, 1932, unused, EX $65.00

Mrs Beasley, coloring book, Whitman, 1970, unused, NM ...$25.00

Munsters, sticker book, Whitman, 1965, unused, M $75.00

My Favorite Martian, coloring book, Whitman, unused, EX...$35.00

Nanny & the Professor, coloring book, Saalfield, 1971, unused, NM $20.00

New Zoo Revue, coloring book, Saalfield, 1974, unused, NM $10.00

Old Yeller, coloring book, Whitman, 1957, unused, NM .$35.00

Oliver, sticker book, 1968, unused, M..............$30.00

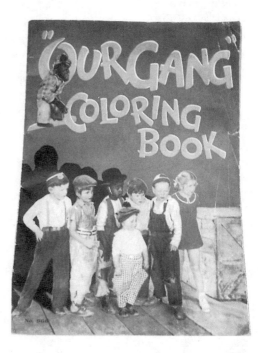

Our Gang Coloring Book, 1933, c Hall Roach Studios, Saalfield, unused, EX, $20.00. (Photo courtesy David Longest)

Parade of Comics, sticker book, Saalfield, 1968, unused, NM..............$50.00

Partridge Family, dot-to-dot book, World Distributors, 1972, unused, NM $30.00

Peanuts Pictures To Color, Saalfield, 1960, unused, NM, from $25 to $30.00

Peanuts Pictures To Color, Saalfield Authorized Edition, 1953, unused, VG, T2, from $50 to..............$75.00

Peanuts Trace & Color, Saalfield, 1960s, set of 5, unused, MIB, from $25 to..............$35.00

Pebbles & Bamm-Bamm, coloring book, Charlton, 1971, unused, EX $20.00

Pebbles & Bamm-Bamm, coloring book, Whitman, 1964, unused, NM, J2 ....$30.00

Pepper at School, sticker book, Whitman, 1966, unused, EX, S14 ....$20.00

Peppermint Patty, coloring book, Artcraft, 1972, unused, NM..$12.00

Peter Pan, coloring book, Whitman, 1952, unused, VG...$25.00

Pinocchio Story Paint Book, Whitman, 1940, few pgs colored, VG, M8..............$45.00

Pluto & the Lost Bone, coloring book, 1981, few pgs colored, EX, N2 ....$10.00

Popeye, coloring book, Samuel Lowe, 1961, unused, EX..$20.00

Popeye, Great Big Paint & Crayon Book, 100+ pictures, McLoughlin Bros, 1935, unused, 10x12", NM........$165.00

Popeye, paint book, Whitman, 1937, unused, EX, A........$75.00

Porky Pig, coloring book, Leon Schlesinger, 1930s, unused, EX, from $150 to $175.00

Quick Draw McGraw, coloring book, Whitman, few pgs colored, EX..$25.00

Raggedy Ann, sticker book, Whitman, 1962, unused, NM, from $25 to $30.00

Raggedy Ann & Andy, activity book, Whitman, unused, NM..$15.00

Raggedy Ann & Andy See-a-Word, Whitman, 1981, unused, NM, from $15 to $20.00

Raggedy Ann's Trace 'N Rub, Random House, 1987, EX....$15.00

Rin-Tin-Tin, coloring book, Whitman, 1955, unused, EX...$30.00

Rita Hayworth Dancing Star, coloring book, Merrill, 1942, unused, EX $50.00

Roger Ramjet, coloring book, Whitman, 1966, unused, NM, T2...$40.00

Roy Rogers & Dale Evans Ranch Tales, coloring book, Whitman, 1953, several pgs colored, EX $30.00

Scooby Doo's All Star Laugh-A-Lympics, coloring book, Rand McNally, 1978, EX...$15.00

Shirley Temple A Great Big Book To Color, Saalfield, 1936, oversized, unused, VG $55.00

Shirley Temple Crosses the Country, coloring book, Saalfield, 1939, unused, EX $75.00

Sigmund & the Sea Monsters, coloring book, Saalfield, 1974, unused, NM $25.00

Six Million Dollar Man, coloring book, Saalfield, 1976, unused, M...$15.00

Snoopy & Woodstock, coloring book, Allan Publishers Inc, 1982, unused, NM...$8.00

Snow White & the Seven Dwarfs, paint book, Whitman/WDE, 1938, unused, EX $75.00

Sonic the Hedgehog Paint & Marker Book, Golden Book, 1993, unused, EX $15.00

Space Angel, coloring book, Saafield, 1963, unused, EX..$35.00

Space Ghost, coloring book, Whitman, 1965, unused, NM, T2..$30.00

Steve Canyon, coloring book, Saalfield, 1952, oversized, unused, NM...$50.00

Sticker Fun w/Batman, Watkins-Strathmore, 1966, unused, NM, T2, from $50 to $75.00

Straight Arrow, coloring book, Stephens, 1949, few pgs colored, EX...$30.00

Superboy, coloring book, Whitman, 1967, unused, NM, T2..$50.00

Superman, coloring book, Saalfield, 1947, oversized, unused, NM, T2, from $150 to $200.00

Superman, coloring book, Whitman, 1965, unused, EX, T2..$30.00

Tammy & Her Friends, cut-out coloring book, Whitman, 1965, unused, EX, S14 ....$20.00

Tammy's Vacation, coloring book, Watkins-Strathmore, 1960s, unused, EX, S14 ....$20.00

Tarzan, punch-out book, Whitman, 1967, unpunched, NM..$45.00

Tennesse Tuxedo, coloring book, Whitman, 1975, 60 unused pgs, EX $15.00

Terry & the Pirates, coloring book, Saalfield, 1946, unused, NM, T2, from $50 to $75.00

That Girl, coloring book, Artcraft, 1968, unused, NM.....$25.00

Three Little Pigs, cut-out coloring book, Pocket Books, 1953, unused, EX $35.00

Thunderbirds, coloring book, Whitman, 1968, unused, EX, T2..$30.00

Tinker Toy, paint book, Whitman, 1939, unused, NM $40.00

Tiny Chatty Baby & Tiny Chatty Brother, sticker book, Whitman, 1960s, unused, NM $50.00

Tiny Chatty Twins, coloring book w/cut-out dolls, Whitman, Authorized Edition, 1960s, unused, NM...................$40.00

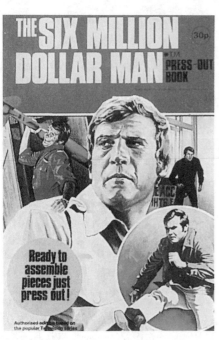

Six Million Dollar Man Press-Out Book, Stafford Pemberton, 1977, Made in United Kingdom, M, from $50.00 to $75.00. (Photo courtesy Greg Davis and Bill Morgan)

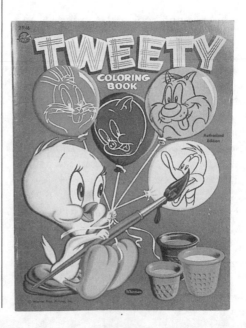

Tweety Coloring Book, Warner Brothers, Whitman, M, from $25.00 to $45.00. (Photo courtesy David Longest)

Sleeping Beauty Magic Forest, coloring book, Watkins-Strathmore, 1959, several pgs colored, NM $25.00

Smitty Color Book, McLoughlin Bros, 1931, unused, EX.$35.00

Tom Terrific w/Mighty Manfred the Wonder Dog, Treasure Books, 1957, unused, EX $25.00

Uncle Martin the Martian, coloring book, Golden Press, 1964, few pgs colored, EX+.............................$35.00

Underdog, coloring book, Whitman, 1965, unused, VG, T2 ..$20.00

Underdog, sticker book, Whitman, 1973, unused, NM, T2....$15.00

Universal City Studio, coloring book, Saalfield, 1964, few pgs colored, VG $30.00

Walt Disney, paint book, Whitman, 1938, unused, EX ..$100.00

Walt Disney's Magic Forest, coloring book, Watkins-Strathmore, 1959, few pgs colored, EX, T2 ....$15.00

Walt Disney's Pinocchio Paint Book, Giant Paper Back Coloring Book, Whitman, 1939, unused, EX, from $100.00 to $140.00. (Photo courtesy David Longest)

Waltons, coloring book, Whitman, 1975, unused, NM $25.00

Welcome Back Kotter, coloring book, Whitman, 1977, unused, NM $8.00

Welcome Back Kotter, Sticker Fun book, Whitman, 1977, M, $15.00. (Photo courtesy Greg Davis and Bill Morgan)

Winky Dink's Coloring Dot Book, Whitman, 1955, several pgs colored, EX.............................$30.00

Winnie the Pooh & Friends, punch-out book, Golden, 1983, unpunched, NM.............................$15.00

Wizard of Oz, coloring book, Whitman, 1962, unused, EX, T2.............................$25.00

Yogi Bear & the Great Green Giant, coloring book, Modern Promotions, 1976, unused, EX.............................$20.00

101 Dalmatians, coloring book, Whitman, 1960, unused, EX.............................$25.00

Comic Books

For more than a half a century, kids of America raced to the bookstand as soon as the new comics came in for the month and for 10¢ an issue kept up on the adventures of their favorite super heroes, cowboys, space explorers, and cartoon characters. By far most were eventually discarded — after they were traded one friend to another, stacked on closet shelves, and finally confiscated by mom. Discount the survivors that were torn or otherwise damaged over the years and those about the mundane, and of those remaining, some could be quite valuable. In fact, first editions of high-grade comics books or those showcasing the first appearance of a major character often bring $500.00 and more. Rarity, age, and quality of the artwork are prime factors in determining value, and condition is critical. If you want to seriously collect comic books, you'll need to refer to a good comic book price guide such as Overstreet's.

Advisor: Bill Bruegman (T2).

Other Sources: A3, P3, K1 (for Simpson's Comics).

See also Advertising; Disney; Premiums.

Adventures of Mighty Mouse, St John #2, 1952, EX $55.00

Alice Cooper, Tales From the Inside, Marvel Premier #50, 1979, VG+ $25.00

Andy Panda, Dell Four-Color #280, 1950, EX.............$25.00

Archie Comics, Archie Publications #4, 1943, VG........$325.00

Amazing Spider-Man, Marvel Comics #14, 1964, NM, $1,000.00. (Photo courtesy Bill Bruegman)

Avengers, Marvel #1, 1963, EX.............................$500.00

Batman & Robin Battle Mutiny in the Big House, DC Comics
    #46, 1948, scarce, EX.................................$150.00

Beany & Cecil, Dell #2, 1962, rare, EX.............................$25.00

Beatles Summer Love, #47, EX, B3 ....$50.00

Beatles Yellow Submarine, Gold Key, 1968, w/poster, NM, from
    $150 to...$200.00

Beverly Hillbillies, Dell #5, NM, from $75 to.................$100.00

Bewitched, Dell #2, 1965, NM, from $40 to $50.00

Bonanza, Dell #210, 1962, EX............................$125.00

Brady Bunch, Dell #2, 1970, NM $50.00

Bugaloos, Charlton #1, 1972, NM, from $20 to................$30.00

Bugs Bunny Halloween Parade, Dell Giant #1, EX $100.00

Captain Marvel, Fawcett #132, 1951, VG $20.00

Captain Marvel Jr, Master Comics #73, 1946, G $30.00

Captain Midnight, Dell #37, EX $85.00

Christmas in Disneyland, Dell #1, NM $95.00

Cindy, Marvel #38, 1950, EX..............................$20.00

Crazy, Marvel #1, 1972, NM................................$25.00

Have Gun Will Travel, Dell Four-Color #983, 1959, G, $8.00. (Photo courtesy Bill Bruegman)

Daredevil, Marvel Comics #1, 1964, G, $150.00. (Photo courtesy Bill Bruegman)

Dark Shadows, Gold Key #15, 1972, EX $15.00

Dick Tracy, Dell #4, NM, D11..............................$100.00

Dick Tracy Monthly, Dell #18, EX $35.00

Earthworm Jim, Marvel #1, 1995, NM.........................$25.00

Elmer Fudd, Dell #689, NM..................................$25.00

Fairy Tale Parade, Dell #3, 1943, VG+..........................$35.00

Family Affair, Gold Key #1, 1970, NM $40.00

Fantastic Four, Marvel #48, 1966, VG $25.00

Flintstones, Bedrock Bedlam, Dell Giant #48, 1961, NM..$450.00

Gene Autry, Dell #51, VG..................................$20.00

Green Hornet, Dell #496, 1953, EX..........................$35.00

Hawkman, DC Comics #1, 1964, NM, T2 ....$500.00

Hogan's Heroes, Dell #8, 1967, EX..........................$40.00

Howdy Doody, Dell #4, 1950, EX...........................$40.00

Howdy Doody, Dell #15, 1952, EX..........................$25.00

Human Torch Battling the Submariners, #8, 1942, NM, T2 ..$2,500.00

Hunchback of Notre Dame, Dell #854, 1957, EX.............$40.00

I Love Lucy, Dell #29, 1960, VG+.................................$35.00

Incredible Hulk, Marvel #102, EX..................................$75.00

Iron Man, Dell #10, NM..................................$25.00

Jetsons, Gold Key #35, EX................................$15.00

Josie & the Pussycats, Archie Comics #6, 1964, NM $20.00

Journey Into Mystery, Marvel #91, 1963, VG $25.00

Justice League of America, Dell #6, VG..........................$50.00

Kiss, Marvel #1, 1977, EX.................................$40.00

Krofft Supershow, Gold Key #1, 1976, NM..................$15.00

Lad the Dog, Dell Movie Classic #1303, 1961, VG+........$55.00

Lawman, Dell #8, 1961, VG+..............................$40.00

Leave It to Beaver, Dell Silver Age Classic #999, 1959,
    VG+ $55.00

Lil' Abner, Dell #61, 1947, NM $195.00

Lone Ranger, Dell #1, 1948, VG..........................$100.00

Lone Ranger, Dell #161, 1960, NM..........................$75.00

Looney Tunes & Merry Melodies, Dell #34, 1944, EX......$35.00

Man From UNCLE, Dell #8, VG $15.00

Marge's Little Lulu & Tubby at Summer Camp, Dell Giant #2,
    1958, VG+ $35.00

Marge's Little Lulu, Dell Four-Color #115, 1946, VG+ ..$150.00

Marvel Family Battles the Hissing Horror, Marvel #74, 1952,
    VG $25.00

Maverick, Dell #980, EX....................................$40.00

Mickey Mouse & the Beanstalk, Dell Four-Color #157, 1947,
    EX $60.00

Mickey Mouse & the Mystery Sea Monster, Wheaties premium,
    1950, NM...$15.00

Munsters, Dell #4, EX....................................$15.00

My Favorite Martian, Dell #3, EX $30.00

Nanny & the Professor, Dell #1, 1970, NM $25.00

Old Ironside w/Johnny Tremain, Dell #874, 1957, EX $15.00

Outlaws of the West, Dell #15, VG..........................$15.00

Peanuts, Gold Key #1, M $25.00

Playful Little Audrey, Dell #1, EX..........................$110.00

Raggedy Ann & Andy, Dell #452, 1952, NM, from $25 to..$30.00

Raggedy Ann & Andy, Gold Key #2, 1972, NM $25.00

Rawhide, Dell #1160, 1960, VG+..........................$30.00

Regards from Captain Wonder, Kid Komics #1, 1943, NM, from $2,500 to..$3,000.00

Roy Rogers & Trigger, Dell #124, 1958, EX $35.00

Scooby Doo, Marvel #1, 1977, M..$25.00

Sheena Queen of the Jungle, Jumbo Comics #140, 1950, VG..$30.00

Silly Symphonies, Dell #7, NM..$75.00

Silver Surfer, Marvel #4, 1969, VG $65.00

Simpsons, Bongo Comic Group #8, NM, K1 ....$4.00

Six Million Dollar Man, Charlton #1, 1976, NM.............$15.00

Smilin' Jack, Dell #149, 1947, NM $75.00

Space Ghost, Dell #1, NM $250.00

Spider-Man, Marvel #1, Gold Edition, NM...................$375.00

Spider-Man, Marvel #43, 1966, VG $35.00

Star Trek, Gold Key, 1968, M...$150.00

Star Trek, Gold Key, 1977, NM, $20.00.

Star Wars, Marvel #1, 1977, M...$45.00

Superboy, Dell #89, VG $60.00

Superman, DC Comics #1, 1939, NM, minimum value ..$10,000.00

Superman's Girlfriend Lois Lane, Dell #13, NM, $100.00.

Tales of Suspense, Marvel Silver Age #46, 1964, VG+ $25.00

Tales To Astonish, Marvel #22, 1961, VG $35.00

Tarzan, Dell #27, 1951, EX $35.00

Tarzan, Dell Silver Age #28, EX...$40.00

Terry & the Pirates, Dell #6, 1936, oversized, NM $150.00

Tessie the Typist, Marvel #21, 1949, VG $25.00

Three Stooges, Dell #1170, 1961, VG................................$30.00

Tom & Jerry Summer Fun, Dell Giant #1, VG $35.00

Tom Mix, Fawcett #2, VG..$110.00

Top Cat, Gold Key #5, 1963, NM $30.00

Transformers, Marvel #78, 1991, EX+ $40.00

Turok, Dell #10, 1958, VG $45.00

Tweety & Sylvester, Dell #11, NM......................................$20.00

Two-Gun Kid, Marvel Comics, 1964, NM, T2 ....$20.00

Ultimate Spider-Man, Dynamic Forces, Marvel #1, NMIP..$75.00

Uncle Remus & His Tales of Brer Rabbit, Dell Four-Color #129, 1946, EX..$55.00

Uncle Scrooge, Dell #386, 1952, VG $75.00

Walt Disney's Donald Duck Lost in the Andes, Dell #223, 1949, EX $175.00

Walt Disney's Zorro, Dell #15, 1961, VG..........................$45.00

Western Roundup, Dell #2, 1953, VG $40.00

Wonder Woman, Dell #34, G...$30.00

Wyatt Earp, Dell #860, NM..$75.00

X-Men, Marvel #13, 1965, EX...$30.00

77 Sunset Strip, Dell #1066, 1960, EX+...........................$30.00

Corgi

Corgi vehicles are among the favorites of the diecast collectors; they've been made in Great Britain since 1956, and they're still in production today. They were well detailed and ruggedly built to last. Some of the most expensive Corgi's on today's collector market are the character-related vehicles, for instance, James Bond (there are several variations), Batman, and Man From UNCLE.

Values are for mint-in-the-box or mint-in-package examples. Other Sources: G2, L1, N3, W1.

#50, Massey-Ferguson 50B Tractor $50.00

#50, Massey-Ferguson 65 Tractor $110.00

#51, Massey-Ferguson Tipper Trailer $25.00

#53, Massey-Ferguson Tractor Shovel $100.00

#54, Fordson Half-Track Tractor $160.00

#54, Massey-Ferguson Tractor Shovel $50.00

#55, David Brown Tractor $50.00

#55, Fordson Major Tractor $100.00

#56, Plough $25.00

#57, Massey-Ferguson Tractor & Fork...............................$110.00

#58, Beast Carrier $40.00

#60, Fordson Power Major Tractor $100.00

#61, Four-Furrow Plough $20.00

#62, Ford Tipper Trailer $20.00

#64, Conveyor on Jeep..$75.00

#66, Massey-Ferguson Tractor..$85.00

#67, Ford Super Major Tractor $90.00

#69, Massey-Ferguson Tractor Shovel $100.00
#71, Fordson Disc Harrow $20.00
#72, Ford 5000 Tractor & Trencher $130.00
#73, Massey-Ferguson Tractor & Saw $125.00
#74, Ford 5000 Tractor & Scoop $100.00
#100, Dropside Trailer..$20.00
#101, Platform Tractor $20.00
#102, Pony Trailer $25.00
#104, Dolphin Cabin Cruiser $30.00
#107, Batboat & Trailer $125.00
#112, Rice Horse Box $45.00
#150, Surtees TS9 ....$40.00
#150, Vanwall, regular $70.00
#151, Lotus XI, regular $80.00
#151, McLaren Yardley M19A $30.00
#152, BRM Racer $80.00
#152, Ferrari 312 B2 ....$35.00
#153, Bluebird Record Car $125.00
#153, Team Surtees $35.00
#154, Ferrari Formula I $50.00
#154, Lotus John Player $45.00
#154, Lotus Texaco Special $45.00
#155, Shadow FI Racer $40.00
#156, Shadow FI, Graham Hill..$40.00
#158, Lotus Climax $50.00
#158, Tyrrell-Ford Elf $40.00
#159, Cooper Maserati..$50.00
#159, Indianapolis Racer $45.00
#160, Hesketh Racer $45.00
#161, Elf-Tyrrell Project 34..$50.00
#161, Santa Pod Commuter..$45.00
#162, Quartermaster Dragster $40.00
#162, Tyrell P34 Racer...$40.00
#163, Santa Pod Dragster...$50.00
#164, Wild Honey Dragster $50.00
#165, Adams Bros Dragster...$40.00
#166, Ford Mustang $45.00
#167, USA Racing Buggy $35.00
#169, Starfighter Jet Dragster $40.00
#170, John Wolfe's Dragster...$40.00
#190, Lotus John Player Special $60.00
#191, McLaren Texaco-Marlboro $65.00
#200, BMC Mini 1000...$50.00
#200, Ford Consul, dual colors $200.00
#200, Ford Consul, solid colors $175.00
#200m, Ford Consul, w/motor $200.00
#201, Austin Cambridge..$160.00
#201, Saint's Volvo $150.00
#201m, Austin Cambridge, w/motor $200.00
#202, Morris Cowley..$150.00
#202, Renault R16 ....$40.00
#202m, Morris Cowley, w/motor $175.00
#203, Detomaso Mangust $40.00
#203, Vauxhall Velox, dual colors...................................$200.00
#203, Vauxhall Velox, solid colors $175.00
#203, Vauxhall Velox, w/motor, dual colors......................$300.00
#203, Vauxhall Velox, w/motor, red or yel.......................$200.00
#204, Morris Mini-Minor, bl $200.00

#204, Rover 90, colors other than wht & red $175.00
#204, Rover 90, wht & red, 2-tone $300.00
#204m, Rover 90, w/motor..$200.00
#205, Riley Pathfinder, bl $175.00
#205, Riley Pathfinder, red $130.00
#205m, Riley Pathfinder, w/motor, bl...............................$175.00
#205m, Riley Pathfinder, w/motor, red.............................$225.00
#206, Hillman Husky, metallic bl & silver........................$175.00
#206, Hillman Husky Estate, metallic bl & silver, 2-tone ..$175.00
#206, Hillman Husky Estate, solid colors.........................$130.00
#206m, Hillman Husky Estate, w/motor $175.00
#207, Standard Vanguard $125.00
#207m, Standard Vanguard, w/motor $175.00
#208, Jaguar 2.4 Saloon $140.00
#208m, Jaguar 2.4 Saloon, w/motor $180.00
#208s, Jaguar 2.4 Saloon, w/suspension...........................$135.00
#209, Riley Police Car $120.00
#210, Citroen DS19...$90.00
#210s, Citroen DS19, w/suspension $100.00
#211, Studebaker Golden Hawk $125.00
#211m, Studebaker Golden Hawk, w/motor......................$175.00
#211s, Studebaker Golden Hawk, plated, w/suspension .$125.00
#213, Jaguar Fire Chief $150.00
#213s, Jaguar Fire Chief, w/suspension............................$200.00
#214, Ford Thunderbird $125.00
#214m, Ford Thunderbird, w/motor.................................$300.00
#214s, Ford Thunderbird, w/suspension...........................$100.00
#215, Ford Thunderbird Sport..$125.00
#215s, Ford Thunderbird Sport, w/suspension $100.00
#216, Austin A-40, red & blk $175.00
#216, Austin A-40, 2-tone bl $100.00
#216m, Austin A-40, w/motor $300.00
#217, Fiat 1800 ....$80.00
#218, Austin Martin DB4...$110.00

#219, Plymouth Sports Suburban, 1959, $95.00.
(From the collection of Al Rapp)

#220, Chevrolet Impala $80.00
#221, Chevrolet Impala Cab $110.00
#222, Renault Floride $90.00
#223, Chevrolet Police $110.00
#224, Bentley Continental $100.00
#225, Austin 7, red $100.00
#225, Austin 7, yel...$300.00
#226, Morris Mini-Minor $100.00

#227, Mini-Cooper Rally...$275.00
#228, Volvo P-1800 ....$80.00
#229, Chevrolet Corvair...$70.00
#230, Mercedes Benz 222, red $75.00
#231, Triumph Herald $100.00
#232, Fiat 2100 ....$75.00
#233, Heinkel Trojan $90.00
#234, Ford Consul Classic $85.00
#235, Oldsmobile Super 88...$75.00
#236, Motor School, right-hand drive..............................$90.00

#237, Oldsmobile Sheriff Car, 1962, $100.00; #443, Plymouth U.S. Mail Van, 1963, $110.00. (From the collection of Al Rapp)

#238, Jaguar MK10, metallic gr or silver $190.00
#238, Jaguar MK10, metallic red or bl............................$125.00
#239, VW Karman Ghia..$90.00
#240, Fiat 500 Jolly...$145.00
#241, Chrysler Ghia...$80.00
#242, Fiat 600 Jolly...$175.00
#245, Buick Riviera...$95.00
#246, Chrysler Imperial, metallic turq $250.00
#246, Chrysler Imperial, red $110.00
#247, Mercedes Benz 600 Pullman $75.00

#248, Chevy Impala, 1965, $80.00; #486, Chevy Kennel Service, 1967, $100.00; #480, Taxi Cab, 1965, $80.00. (From the collection of Al Rapp)

#249, Morris Mini-Cooper, wicker $130.00
#251, Hillman Imp $100.00
#252, Rover 2000, metallic bl..$80.00
#252, Rover 2000, metallic maroon $165.00
#253, Mercedes Benz 220SE $90.00
#255, Motor School, left-hand drive $225.00
#258, Saint's Volvo P1800 ....$165.00
#259, Citroen Le Dandy, bl $180.00
#259, Citroen Le Dandy, maroon $120.00
#259, Penguin Mobile...$50.00
#261, James Bond's Aston Martin DB5..........................$235.00
#261, Spiderbuggy..$100.00
#262, Capt Marvel's Porsche $65.00

#256, Volkswagen 1200 East Africa Safari, with rhino, 1965, $200.00. (From the collection of Al Rapp)

#260, Renault R16, 1969, $45.00; #109, Pennyburn Workman's Trailer, 1968, $50.00. (From the collection of Al Rapp)

#262, Lincoln Continental Limo, bl $180.00
#262, Lincoln Continental Limo, gold $100.00
#263, Rambler Marlin $75.00
#264, Incredible Hulk $75.00
#264, Oldsmobile Toronado $85.00
#265, Supermobile $65.00
#266, Chitty-Chitty Bang-Bang, orig............................$350.00
#266, Chitty-Chitty Bang-Bang, replica $125.00
#266, Superbike $60.00
#267, Batmobile, red 'Bat'-hubs $400.00
#267, Batmobile, w/red whizzwheels $500.00
#267, Batmobile, w/whizzwheels $140.00

#268A, Black Beauty (Green Hornet), 1967, $300.00. (From the collection of Al Rapp)

#268, Batman's Bat Bike	$70.00
#269, James Bond's Lotus	$100.00
#270, James Bond's Aston Martin, w/tire slashers, 1/43 scale	$250.00
#270, James Bond's Aston Martin, w/whizzwheels, 1/43 scale	$120.00
#271, Ghia Mangusta De Tomaso	$65.00
#271, James Bond's Aston Martin	$90.00
#272, James Bond's Citroen 2CV	$60.00
#273, Honda Driving School	$40.00
#273, Rolls Royce Silver Shadow	$100.00
#274, Bentley Mulliner	$80.00
#275, Mini Metro, colors other than gold	$25.00
#275, Mini Metro, gold	$75.00
#275, Rover 2000 TC, gr	$75.00
#275, Rover 2000 TC, wht	$160.00
#275, Royal Wedding Mini Metro	$25.00
#276, Oldsmobile Toronado, metallic red	$70.00
#276, Triumph Acclaim	$20.00
#277, Monkeemobile	$300.00
#277, Triumph Driving School	$25.00
#279, Rolls Royce Corniche	$30.00
#280, Rolls Royce Silver Shadow, colors other than silver	$50.00
#280, Rolls Royce Silver Shadow, silver	$80.00
#281, Metro Datapost	$20.00
#281, Rover 2000 TC	$150.00
#282, Mini Cooper Rally Car	$90.00
#283, DAF City Car	$40.00
#284, Citroen SM	$45.00
#285, Mercedes Benz 240D	$25.00
#286, Jaguar XJ12C	$45.00
#287, Citroen Dyane	$25.00
#288, Minissima	$20.00
#289, VW Polo	$25.00
#290, Kojak's Buick, no hat	$125.00
#290, Kojak's Buick, w/hat	$75.00
#291, AMC Pacer	$20.00
#291, Mercedes Benz 240 Rally	$35.00
#292, Starsky & Hutch Ford Torino	$85.00
#293, Renault 5TS	$20.00
#294, Renault Alpine	$20.00
#298, Magnum PI's Ferrari	$50.00
#299, Ford Sierra 2.3 Ghia	$20.00
#300, Austin Healey, red or cream	$150.00
#300, Austin Healey Sports Car, bl	$300.00
#300, Chevrolet Corvette	$100.00
#300, Ferrari Daytona	$25.00
#301, Iso Grifo 7 Litre	$60.00
#301, Lotus Elite	$25.00
#301, Triumph TR2 Sports Car	$150.00
#302, Hillman Hunter Rally, kangaroo	$130.00
#302, MGA Sports Car	$140.00
#302, VW Polo	$20.00
#303, Mercedes Benz 300SL	$100.00
#303, Porsche 924	$20.00
#303, Roger Clark's Ford Capri	$75.00
#303s, Mercedes Benz 300SL, w/suspension	$100.00
#304, Chevrolet SS350 Camaro	$65.00
#304, Mercedes Benz 300SL, yel & red	$100.00
#304s, Mercedes Benz 300SL, w/suspension	$100.00

#305, Mini Marcos GT 850	$65.00
#305, Triumph TR3	$145.00
#306, Fiat X1/9	$30.00
#306, Morris Marina	$65.00
#307, Jaguar E Type	$125.00
#307, Renault	$20.00
#308, BMW M1 Racer, gold plated	$110.00
#308, BMW M1 Racer, yel	$25.00
#308, Monte Carlo Mini	$100.00
#309, Aston Martin DB4	$125.00
#309, Aston Martin DB4, w/spoked hubs	$175.00
#309, VW Turbo	$20.00
#310, Chevrolet Corvette, bronze	$165.00
#310, Chevrolet Corvette, red or silver	$65.00
#310, Porsche 924	$20.00
#311, Ford Capri, orange	$125.00
#311, Ford Capri, red	$80.00
#311, Ford Capri, w/gold hubs	$150.00
#312, Ford Capri S	$35.00
#312, Jaguar E Type	$100.00
#312, Marcos Mantis	$50.00
#313, Ford Cortina, bronze or bl	$100.00
#313, Ford Cortina, yel	$300.00
#314, Ferrari Berlinetta Le Mans	$65.00
#314, Supercat Jaguar	$30.00
#315, Lotus Elite	$35.00
#315, Simca Sports Car, metallic bl	$190.00
#315, Simca Sports Car, silver	$65.00
#316, Ford GT 70	$50.00
#316, NSU Sports Prinz	$90.00
#317, Mini Cooper Monte Carlo	$200.00
#318, Jaguar XJS	$25.00
#318, Lotus Elan, copper	$300.00
#318, Lotus Elan, metallic bl	$110.00
#318, Lotus Elan, wht	$250.00
#319, Jaguar XJS	$35.00
#319, Lamborghini P400 GT Miura	$35.00
#319, Lotus Elan, gr or yel	$140.00
#319, Lotus Elan, red or bl	$100.00
#320, Saint's Jaguar XJS	$85.00
#321, Monte Carlo Mini Cooper, 1965	$300.00
#321, Monte Carlo Mini Cooper, 1966, w/autographs	$600.00
#321, Porsche 924, metallic gr	$70.00
#321, Porsche 924, red	$25.00
#322, Rover Monte Carlo	$180.00
#323, Citroen DS19 Monte Carlo	$180.00
#323, Ferrari Daytona 365 GTB4	$25.00
#324, Marcos Volvo 1800 GT	$70.00
#325, Chevrolet Caprice	$65.00
#325, Ford Mustang Competition	$80.00
#326, Chevrolet Police Car	$40.00
#327, Chevrolet Caprice Cab	$40.00
#327, MGB GT	$130.00
#328, Hillman Imp Monte Carlo	$125.00
#329, Ford Mustang Rally	$50.00
#329, Opel Senator, bl or bronze	$40.00
#329, Opel Senator, silver	$50.00
#330, Porsche Carrera 6, wht & bl	$120.00

#330, Porsche Carrera 6, wht & red $60.00
#331, Ford Capri Rally...............................$90.00
#332, Lancia Fulvia Sport, red or bl $60.00
#332, Lancia Fulvia Sport, yel & blk $125.00
#332, Opel, Doctor's Car $50.00
#334, Ford Escort $20.00
#334, Mini Magnifique $90.00
#335, Jaguar 4.2 Litre E Type $125.00

#336, James Bond Toyota 2000 GT, 1967, $365.00.
(From the collection of Al Rapp)

#337, Chevrolet Stingray...........................$65.00
#338, Chevrolet SS350 Camaro $75.00
#338, Rover 3500 ....$30.00
#339, Rover 3500 Police Car $30.00
#339, 1967 Mini Cooper Monte Carlo, w/roof rack ...$300.00
#340, Rover Triplex $25.00
#340, 1967 Sunbeam IMP Monte Carlo $135.00
#341, Chevrolet Caprice Racer $25.00
#341, Mini Marcos GT850 ....$60.00
#342, Lamborghini P400 GT Miura $60.00
#342, Professionals Ford Capri.....................$80.00
#342, Professionals Ford Capri, w/chrome bumpers...$100.00
#343, Pontiac Firebird.............................$55.00
#344, Ferrari 206 Dino Sport.......................$70.00
#345, Honda Prelude $25.00
#345, MGC GT, orange...............................$300.00
#345, MGC GT, yel $125.00
#346, Citroen 2 CV $20.00
#347, Chevrolet Astro 1 ....$50.00
#348, Flower Power Mustang Stock Car $140.00
#348, Pop Art Mustang Stock Car $140.00
#348, Vegas Ford Thunderbird $85.00
#349, Pop Art Morris Mini, minimum value $1,500.00
#350, Thunderbird Guided Missile $125.00
#351, RAF Land Rover...............................$80.00
#352, RAF Vanguard Staff Car.......................$100.00
#353, Road Scanner.................................$60.00
#354, Commer Military Ambulance $110.00
#355, Commer Military Police $135.00
#356, VW Personnel Carrier $135.00
#357, Land Rover Weapons Carrier $180.00
#358, Oldsmobile Staff Car $125.00
#359, Commer Army Field Kitchen....................$165.00
#370, Ford Cobra Mustang $25.00
#371, Porsche Carrera..............................$40.00
#373, Peugeot 505..................................$25.00
#373, VW Police Car, Polizei $150.00
#374, Jaguar 4.2 Litre E Type $90.00

#374, Jaguar 5.3 Litre.............................$70.00
#375, Toyota 2000 GT...............................$75.00
#376, Chevrolet Stingray Stock Car $50.00
#377, Marcos 3 Litre, wht & gray...................$100.00
#377, Marcos 3 Litre, yel or bl $60.00
#378, Ferrari 308 GT $25.00
#378, MGC GT $140.00
#380, Alfa Romeo P33 ....$45.00
#380, Beach Buggy $40.00
#381, Renault Turbo $20.00
#382, Lotus Elite $25.00
#382, Porsche Targa 911S $50.00
#383, VW 1200, red or orange $70.00
#383, VW 1200, Swiss PTT $130.00
#383, VW 1200, yel ADAC $200.00
#384, Adams Bros Probe 15 ....$50.00
#384, Renault 11 GTL, cream $20.00
#384, Renault 11 GTL, maroon $40.00
#384, VW 1200 Rally $70.00
#385, Porsche 917 ....$40.00
#386, Bertone Runabout $50.00
#387, Chevrolet Corvette Stingray $100.00
#388, Mercedes Benz C111 ....$40.00
#389, Reliant Bond Bug 700, gr $100.00
#389, Reliant Bond Bug 700 ES, orange $60.00
#391, James Bond 007 Ford Mustang $250.00
#392, Bertone Shake Buggy $40.00
#393, Mercedes Benz 350 SL, metallic gr............$100.00
#393, Mercedes Benz 350 SL, wht or bl $65.00
#394, Datsun 240Z, East African Safari $45.00
#396, Datsun 240Z, US Rally $45.00
#397, Can Am Porsche Audi..........................$35.00
#400, VW Driving School, bl $65.00
#400, VW Driving School, red.......................$140.00
#401, VW 1200 ....$60.00
#402, Ford Cortina GXL, wht w/red stripe...........$80.00
#402, Ford Cortina GXL Police, wht $50.00
#402, Ford Cortina GXL Polizei $150.00
#403, Bedford Daily Express $150.00
#403, Thwaites Dumper..............................$45.00
#403m, Bedford KLG Plugs, w/motor..................$230.00
#404, Bedford Dormobile, cream, maroon & turq $110.00
#404, Bedford Dormobile, yel & 2-tone bl...........$200.00
#404, Bedford Dormobile, yel w/bl roof $125.00
#404m, Bedford Dormobile, w/motor..................$160.00
#405, Bedford Utilicon Fire Department, gr $160.00
#405, Bedford Utilicon Fire Department, red $200.00
#405, Chevrolet Superior Ambulance.................$40.00
#405, Ford Milk Float $25.00
#405m, Bedford Utilicon Fire Tender, w/motor $225.00
#406, Land Rover...................................$80.00
#406, Mercedes Ambulance $35.00
#406, Mercedes Benz Unimog $50.00
#407, Karrier Mobile Grocers.......................$150.00
#408, Bedford AA Road Service $150.00
#409, Allis Chalmers Fork Lift $30.00
#409, Forward Control Jeep $50.00
#409, Mercedes Dumper $50.00

#411, Karrier Lucozade Van......................................$160.00
#411, Mercedes 240D, orange...............................$80.00
#411, Mercedes 240D Taxi, cream or blk $65.00
#411, Mercedes 240D Taxi, orange w/blk roof $35.00
#412, Bedford Ambulance, split windscreen.............$130.00
#412, Bedford Ambulance, 1-pc windscreen..........$250.00
#412, Mercedes Police Car, Police.......................$50.00
#412, Mercedes Police Car, Polizei.....................$40.00
#413, Karrier Bantam Butcher Shop $150.00
#413, Mazda Maintenence Truck $50.00
#413s, Karrier Bantam Butcher Shop, w/suspension.......$200.00
#414, Bedford Military Ambulance.........................$120.00
#414, Coastguard Jaguar $45.00
#415, Mazda Camper $50.00
#416, Buick Police Car $40.00
#416, Radio Rescue Rover, bl..............................$125.00
#416, Radio Rescue Rover, yel.............................$400.00
#416s, Radio Rescue Rover, w/suspension, bl $100.00
#416s, Radio Rescue Rover, w/suspension, yel............$425.00
#417 Land Rover Breakdown $110.00
#417s, Land Rover Breakdown, w/suspension $85.00
#418, Austin Taxi, w/whizzwheels $50.00
#419, Ford Zephyr, Rijks Politie $350.00
#419, Ford Zephyr Politie $300.00
#419, Jeep...$30.00
#420, Airbourne Caravan......................................$100.00
#421, Bedford Evening Standard.............................$200.00
#422, Bedford Van, Corgi Toys, bl w/yel roof......$500.00
#422, Bedford Van, Corgi Toys, yel w/bl roof..........$200.00
#422, Riot Police Wagon.......................................$45.00
#423, Rough Rider Van...$45.00
#424, Ford Zephyr Estate Car $85.00
#424, Security Van...$30.00
#425, London Taxi...$25.00
#426, Chipperfield's Circus Booking Office $300.00
#426, Pinder's Circus Booking Office $50.00
#428, Mister Softee's Ice Cream Van $200.00
#428, Renault Police Car.......................................$25.00
#429, Jaguar Police Car...$40.00
#430, Bermuda Taxi, metallic bl & red $400.00
#430, Bermuda Taxi, wht.....................................$125.00
#430, Porsche 924 Polizei $30.00
#431, VW Pickup, metallic gold $300.00
#431, VW Pickup, yel..$100.00
#432, Vanatic Van $30.00
#433, VW Delivery Van $100.00
#434, Charlie's Angels Van...................................$50.00
#434, VW Kombi..$100.00
#435, Karrier Dairy Van...$125.00
#435, Superman Van...$50.00
#436, Citroen Safari $100.00
#436, Spider Van...$50.00
#437, Cadillac Ambulance $100.00
#437, Coca-Cola Van..$50.00
#438, Land Rover, gr..$60.00
#438, Land Rover, Lepra.......................................$400.00
#439, Chevrolet Fire Chief.....................................$100.00
#440, Ford Consul Cortina Super Estate Car, w/golfer & caddie .$160.00

#440, Ford Consul Cortina Super Estate Car, w/golfer & caddy $160.00
#440, Mazda Pickup $30.00
#441, Jeep...$25.00
#441, VW Toblerone Van.......................................$135.00
#445, Plymouth Sports Suburban $90.00
#447, Walls Ice Cream Van $275.00
#448, Police Mini Van, w/dog & handler................$200.00
#448, Renegade Jeep $20.00
#450, Austin Mini Van..$100.00
#450, Austin Mini Van, w/pnt grille $160.00
#450, Peugeot Taxi..$25.00
#452, Commer Lorry...$130.00
#453, Commer Walls Van......................................$200.00
#454, Commer Platform Lorry.................................$130.00
#455, Karrier Bantam 2-Ton...................................$120.00
#456, ERF Dropside Lorry $110.00
#457, ERF Platform Lorry $100.00
#457, Talbot Matra Rancho, gr or red $25.00
#457, Talbot Matra Rancho, wht or orange $45.00
#458, ERF Tipper Dumper $85.00
#459, ERF Moorhouse Van $375.00
#459, Raygo Road Roller $40.00
#460, ERF Cement Tipper $90.00
#461, Police Vigilant Range Rover, Police.............$35.00
#461, Police Viligant Range Rover, Politie $80.00
#462, Commer Van, Co-op $125.00
#462, Commer Van, Hammonds $170.00
#463, Commer Ambulance $100.00
#464, Commer Police Van, City Police, minimum value .$300.00
#464, Commer Police Van, County Police, bl $110.00
#464, Commer Police Van, Police, bl....................$100.00
#464, Commer Police Van, Police, gr....................$750.00
#464, Commer Police Van, Rijks Politie, bl, minimum value..$300.00
#465, Commer Pickup Truck $65.00
#466, Commer Milk Float, Co-op $170.00
#466, Commer Milk Float, wht $70.00
#467, London Routemaster Bus.............................$75.00
#468, London Transport Routemaster, Church's Shoes, red....$200.00
#468, London Transport Routemaster, Design Centre, red $250.00
#468, London Transport Routemaster, Gamages, red $200.00
#468, London Transport Routemaster Bus, Corgi Toys, brn, gr or cream $1,000.00
#468, London Transport Routemaster Bus, Corgi Toys, red...$100.00
#468, London Transport Routemaster Bus, Madame Tussand's, red $200.00
#468, London Transport Routemaster Bus, Outspan, red .$60.00
#470, Disneyland Bus..$40.00
#470, Forward Control Jeep...................................$60.00
#470, Greenline Bus $20.00
#471, Silver Jubilee Bus $40.00
#471, Smith's-Karrier Mobile Canteen $140.00
#471, Woolworth Silver Jubilee Bus.....................$40.00
#472, Public Address Land Rover $150.00
#474, Ford Musical Walls Ice Cream Van $250.00
#475, Citroen Ski Safari $150.00
#477, Land Rover Breakdown, w/whizzwheels $60.00
#478, Forward Control Jeep, Tower Wagon $75.00

#479, Mobile Camera Van.................................$150.00
#480, Chevrolet Police Car.............................$80.00
#481, Chevrolet Police Patrol Car................$125.00
#482, Chevrolet Fire Chief Car.....................$100.00
#482, Range Rover Ambulance.......................$50.00
#483, Dodge Tipper.......................................$50.00
#483, Police Range Rover, Belgian................$75.00
#484, AMC Pacer Rescue...............................$30.00
#484, AMC Pacer Secours..............................$50.00
#484, Livestock Transporter $60.00
#484, Mini Countryman Surfer, w/silver grille..............$175.00
#485, Mini Countryman Surfer, w/unpnt grille $225.00
#487, Chipperfield's Circus Parade..............$200.00
#489, VW Police Car......................................$30.00
#490, Touring Caravan $25.00
#490, VW Breakdown Truck $95.00
#491, Ford Escort Estate $100.00
#492, VW Police Car, Politie.........................$275.00
#492, VW Police Car, Polizei..........................$80.00
#492, VW Police Car, w/gr mudguards.........$300.00
#493, Mazda Pickup.......................................$35.00
#494, Bedford Tipper, red & silver................$175.00
#494, Bedford Tipper, red & yel......................$80.00
#495, Opel Open Truck $20.00
#497, Man From UNCLE, wht, minimum value $600.00

#497, Man from UNCLE Gun Firing Thrush-Buster,
$300.00. (From the collection of Al Rapp)

#499, Citroen, 1968 Olympics $175.00
#500, US Army Rover.....................................$400.00
#503, Chipperfield's Circus Giraffe Transporter..............$125.00
#506, Sunbeam Imp Police.............................$125.00
#508, Holiday Minibus $110.00
#509, Porsche Police Car, Polizei....................$80.00
#509, Porsche Police Car, Ritjks Politie.........$150.00
#510, Citroen Tour De France.......................$125.00
#511, Chipperfield's Circus Poodle Pickup $600.00
#513, Alpine Rescue Car................................$350.00
#647, Buck Rogers' Starfighter $75.00
#648, Space Shuttle $50.00
#649, James Bond's Space Shuttle..................$80.00
#650, BOAC Concorde, all others (no gold logo on tail)..$30.00
#650, BOAC Concorde, gold logo on tail......$100.00
#651, Air France Concorde, all others (no gold tail design)...$50.00
#651, Air France Concorde, gold tail design..................$140.00

#651, Japan Air Line Concorde $400.00
#653, Air Canada Concorde $325.00
#681, Stunt Bike..$250.00
#700, Motorway Ambulance $20.00
#701, Intercity Minibus $20.00
#703, Breakdown Truck $20.00
#703, Hi Speed Fire Engine $20.00
#801, Ford Thunderbird..................................$25.00

#801, Noddy's Car (back of box shown), $450.00.
(From the collection of Al Rapp)

#802, Mercedes Benz 300 Sl $25.00
#802, Popeye's Paddle Wagon $550.00
#803, Beatle's Yellow Submarine...................$550.00
#803, Jaguar XK120 ....$20.00
#804, Jaguar XK120 Rally...............................$20.00
#804, Jaguar XK120 Rally, w/spats..................$50.00
#804, Noddy's Car, Noddy only.....................$275.00
#804, Noddy's Car, w/Mr Tubby....................$350.00
#805, Hardy Boy's Rolls Royce $300.00
#805, Mercedes Benz 300 SC $20.00
#806, Lunar Bug..$150.00
#806, Mercedes Benz 300 SC $20.00
#807, Dougal's Car...$300.00
#808, Basil Brush's Car...............................$22,500.00
#809, Dick Dastardly's Racer.........................$150.00
#810, Ford Thunderbird..................................$25.00
#811, James Bond's Moon Buggy...................$500.00
#831, Mercedes Benz 300 SL $25.00
#851, Magic Roundabout Train.....................$350.00
#852, Magic Roundabout Carousel $800.00
#853, Magic Roundabout Playground...........$1,500.00
#859, Mr McHenry's Trike.............................$250.00
#900, German Tank $50.00
#901, British Centurion $50.00
#902, American Tank $50.00
#903, British Chieftain Tank...........................$50.00
#904, King Tiger Tank.....................................$50.00
#905, SU100 Tank Destroyer...........................$50.00

#906, Saladin Armoured Car $50.00
#907, German Rocket Launcher $75.00
#908, French Recovery Tank $75.00
#909, Quad Gun Tank, Trailer & Field Gun.....................$60.00
#920, Bell Helicopter $30.00
#921, Hughes Helicopter $30.00
#922, Sikorsky Helicopter..$30.00
#923, Sikorsky Helicopter Military $30.00
#925, Batcopter $75.00
#926, Stromberg Helicopter $75.00
#927, Chopper Squad Helicopter $60.00
#928, Spidercopter $90.00
#929, Daily Planet Helicopter $65.00
#930, DAAX Helicopter..$60.00
#931, Jet Police Helicopter..$50.00

CLASSICS

Daimler 38HP, #9021, red w/4 figures, MIB $35.00
Lionel City Bus Lines, #743, MIB $40.00

Mack Search and Rescue Truck, #C906/4, $28.00.

Morris Minor, 40th Anniversary of the British Toy Retailers,
    #764, M (EX box) $65.00
Petroleum Corporation, #5709, MIB..................................$25.00
St Mary's County Mack CF Pumper, #52004, MIB...........$30.00
1915 Ford Model T, #901, M (EX box) $30.00

CORGITRONICS

#1001, Corgitronics Firestreak..$80.00
#1002, Corgitronics Landtrain $50.00
#1003, Ford Torino $30.00
#1004, Corgitronics Beep Beep Bus....................................$40.00
#1005, Police Land Rover..$30.00
#1006, Roadshow, Radio..$50.00
#1007, Land Rover & Compressor $50.00
#1008, Chevrolet Fire Chief..$40.00
#1009, Maestro MG1600 ....$50.00
#1011, Firestreak $40.00

EXPLORATION MODELS

#2022, Scanotron..$60.00

#2023, Rocketron..$60.00
#2024, Lasertron $60.00
#2025, Magnetron..$60.00

GIFT SETS

#1, Carrimore Transporter, $850.00.

#1, Car Transporter Set $850.00
#1, Ford Sierra & Caravan..$40.00
#1, Ford 500 Tractor & Beast Trailer...............................$160.00
#2, Land Rover & Pony Trailer $180.00
#2, Unimog Dumper $150.00
#3, Batmobile & Batboat, w/'Bat'-hubs...........................$400.00
#3, Batmobile & Batboat, w/whizzwheels $210.00
#3, RAF Land Rover & Missile $250.00
#4, Country Farm Set...$75.00
#4, RAF Land Rover & Missile $500.00

#5, Agricultural Gift Set, five vehicles, animals, and figure, 1967, $300.00. (From the collection of Al Rapp)

#5, Country Farm Set, w/no hay...$90.00
#5, Racing Car Set...$300.00

#6, Rocket Age Set	$1,000.00
#6, VW Transporter & Cooper Maserati	$175.00
#7, Daktari Set	$150.00
#7, Tractor & Trailer Set	$130.00
#8, Combine Harvester Set	$400.00
#8, Lions of Longleat	$200.00
#9, Corporal Missile & Launcher	$600.00
#9, Tractor w/Shovel & Trailer	$200.00
#10, Centurion Tank & Transporter	$140.00
#10, Jeep & Motorcycle Trailer	$40.00
#10, Rambler Marlin, w/kayaks	$210.00
#11, ERF Truck & Trailer	$200.00
#11, London Set, no Policeman	$135.00
#11, London Set, w/Policeman	$600.00
#12, Chipperfield's Circus Crane Truck & Cage	$300.00
#12, Glider Set	$80.00
#12, Grand Prix Set	$450.00
#13, Fordson Tractor & Plough	$150.00
#13, Peugeot Tour De France	$90.00
#13, Renault Tour De France	$150.00
#14, Giant Daktari Set	$500.00
#14, Tower Wagon	$100.00
#15, Land Rover & Horsebox	$100.00
#15, Silvertone Set	$1,800.00
#16, Ecurie Ecosse Set	$500.00
#17, Land Rover & Ferrari	$200.00
#17, Military Set	$85.00
#18, Emergency Set	$80.00
#18, Fordson Tractor & Plough	$125.00
#19, Chipperfield's Circus Rover & Elephant Trailer	$325.00
#19, Emergency Set	$80.00
#19, Flying Club Set	$85.00
#20, Car Transporter Set, minimum value	$900.00
#20, Emergency Set	$70.00
#20, Golden Guinea Set	$300.00
#21, Chipperfield's Circus Crane & Trailer, minimum value	$1,600.00
#21, ERF Milk Truck & Trailer	$350.00
#21, Superman Set	$250.00
#22, James Bond Set	$265.00
#23, Chipperfield's Circus Set, w/Booking Office	$1,000.00
#23, Spiderman Set	$200.00
#24, Constructor Set	$150.00
#24, Mercedes & Caravan	$50.00
#25, Mantra Rancho & Trailer	$50.00
#25, Shell or BP Garage Set, minimum value	$1,600.00
#25, VW Transporter & Cooper Masarati	$160.00
#26, Beach Bug Set	$50.00
#26, Matra Rancho & Racer	$75.00
#27, Priestman Shovel Set	$195.00
#28, Mazda Pickup & Dinghy, w/trailer	$60.00
#28, Transporter Set	$800.00
#29, Ferrari Racing Set	$80.00
#29, Jeep & Horsebox	$40.00
#29, Tractor & Trailer	$140.00
#30, Grand Prix Set	$285.00
#30, Pinder's Circus Rover & Trailer	$135.00
#31, Buick Riviera & Boat	$225.00
#31, Safari Set	$100.00

#32, Lotus Racing Set	$110.00
#32, Tractor & Trailer	$170.00
#33, Fordson Tractor & Carrier	$150.00
#35, Chopper Squad	$60.00
#35, London Set	$175.00
#36, Tarzan Set	$250.00
#36, Tornado Set	$250.00
#37, Fiat & Boat	$60.00
#37, Lotus Racing Team	$500.00
#38, Jaguar & Powerboat	$75.00
#38, Mini Camping Set	$100.00
#38, Monte Carlo Set	$600.00
#40, Avengers, red & wht vehicles	$650.00

#40, Batman Set, $275.00.

#41, Ford Transporter Set	$850.00
#41, Silver Jubilee State Landau	$40.00
#42, Agricultural Set	$80.00
#43, Silo & Conveyor	$65.00
#44, Police Rover Set	$65.00
#45, All Winners Set	$800.00
#45, Royal Canadian Mounted Police	$85.00
#46, All Winners Set	$600.00
#46, Super Karts	$30.00
#47, Ford Tractor & Conveyor	$195.00
#47, Ford 5000 Tractor & Conveyor	$195.00
#47, Pony Club Set	$50.00
#48, Ford Transporter Set	$600.00
#48, Jean Richards' Circus Set	$200.00
#48, Scammell Transport Set	$900.00
#49, Flying Club Set	$50.00

HUSKIES

Huskies were marketed exclusively through the Woolworth stores from 1965 to 1969. In 1970, Corgi Juniors were introduced. Both lines were sold in blister packs. Models produced up to 1975 (as dated on the package) are valued from $15.00 to $30.00 (MIP), except for the character-related examples listed below.

#1001A, James Bond's Aston Martin, Husky on base	$200.00
#1001B, James Bond Aston Martin, Junior on base	$175.00
#1002A, Batmobile, Husky on base	$200.00
#1003A, Bat Boat, Husky on base	$125.00
#1003B, Bat Boat, Junior on base	$85.00
#1004A, Monkeemobile, Husky on base	$200.00
#1004B, Monkeemobile, Junior on base	$175.00
#1005A, UNCLE Car, Husky on base	$175.00

#1005B, UNCLE Car, Junior on base $1,500.00
#1006A, Chitty-Chitty Bang-Bang, Husky on base........$200.00
#1006B, Chitty-Chitty Bang-Bang, Junior on base $175.00
#1007, Ironside Police Van..$140.00
#1008, Popeye Paddle Wagon $200.00
#1011, James Bond Bobsleigh....................................$300.00
#1012, Spectre Bobsleigh..$300.00
#1013, Tom's Go-Kart...$75.00
#1014, Jerry's Banger..$75.00
#1017, Ford Holmes Wrecker....................................$175.00
#3008, Crime Busters Gift Set, scarce.......................$800.00

#3005, Corgi Junior Leisuretime, A, $120.00.

Major Packs

#1100, Carrimore Low Loader, red cab $140.00
#1100, Carrimore Low Loader, yel cab.....................$225.00
#1100, Mack Truck $900.01
#1101, Carrimore Car Transporter, bl cab.................$250.00
#1101, Carrimore Car Transporter, red cab...............$135.00
#1101, Hydrolic Crane $50.00
#1102, Crane Fruehauf Dumper $65.00
#1102, Euclid Tractor, gr..$150.00
#1102, Euclid Tractor, yel...$200.00
#1103, Airport Crash Truck......................................$85.00
#1103, Euclid Crawler Tractor..................................$125.00
#1104, Machinery Carrier $150.00
#1104, Racehorse Transporter $125.00
#1105, Berliet Racehorse Transporter $60.00
#1106, Decca Mobile Radar Van...............................$170.00
#1107, Berliet Container Truck.................................$60.00
#1107, Euclid Tractor & Dozer, orange $300.00
#1107, Euclid Tractor & Dozer, red...........................$375.00
#1108, Bristol Bloodhound & Launching Ramp.............$125.00
#1108, Michelin Container Truck...............................$50.00
#1109, Bristol Bloodhound & Loading Trolley.............$130.00
#1109, Michelin Truck $50.00
#1110, JCB Crawler Loader $60.00
#1110, Mobilgas Tanker $300.00
#1111, Massey-Ferguson Harvester $150.00
#1112, Corporal Missile on Launching Ramp.............$160.00
#1112, David Brown Combine...................................$120.00
#1113, Corporal Erector & Missile.............................$375.00
#1113, Hyster $50.00

#1113, Hyster Sealink...$135.00
#1115, Bloodhound Missile.......................................$110.00
#1116, Bloodhound Missile Platform.........................$100.00
#1116, Refuse Lorry $30.00
#1117, Bloodhound Missile Trolley............................$65.00
#1117, Faun Street Sweeper $30.00
#1118, Airport Emergency Tender $70.00
#1118, International Truck, Dutch Army.....................$300.00
#1118, International Truck, gr $150.00
#1118, International Truck, US Army..........................$275.00
#1119, HDL Hovercraft..$100.00
#1120, Midland Coach..$220.00

#1121, Chipperfield's Circus Crane, $250.00.

#1121, Corgimatic Ford Tipper.................................$50.00
#1123, Chipperfield's Circus Animal Cage....................$140.00
#1124, Corporal Missile Launching Ramp.......................$80.00
#1126, Ecurie Ecosse Transporter $200.00
#1126, Simon Snorkel Dennis Fire Engine.....................$60.00
#1127, Simon Snorkel Bedford Fire Engine..................$110.00

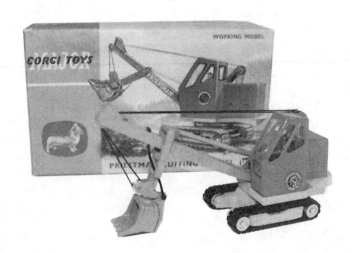

#1128, Priestman Cub Shovel, $75.00. (From the collection of Al Rapp)

#1129, Mercedes Truck...$25.00
#1129, Milk Tanker $275.00

#1130, Chipperfield's Circus Horse Transporter $275.00
#1130, Mercedes Tanker, Corgi.................................$25.00
#1131, Carrimore Machinery Carrier.......................$135.00
#1131, Mercedes Refrigerated Van...........................$20.00
#1132, Carrimore Low Loader.................................$250.00
#1132, Scania Truck..$20.00
#1133, Troop Transporter.......................................$250.00

#1134, Army Fuel Tanker, $400.00.

#1135, Heavy Equipment Transporter.......................$435.00
#1137, Ford Tilt Cab w/Trailer...............................$125.00
#1138, Carrimore Car Transporter, Corgi..................$150.00
#1140, Bedford Mobilgas Tanker.............................$300.00
#1140, Ford Transit Wrecker....................................$25.00
#1141, Milk Tanker..$300.00
#1142, Holmes Wrecker...$150.00
#1143, American LaFrance Rescue Truck...................$125.00
#1144, Berliet Wrecker...$80.00
#1144, Chipperfield's Circus Crane Truck..................$600.00
#1145, Mercedes Unimog Dumper............................$50.00
#1146, Tri-Deck Transporter..................................$185.00
#1147, Ferrymaster Truck.......................................$130.00
#1148, Carrimore Car Transporter...........................$160.00
#1150, Mercedes Unimog Snowplough......................$60.00
#1151, Scammell Co-op Set....................................$350.00
#1151, Scammell Co-op Truck.................................$250.00
#1152, Mack Truck, Esso Tanker..............................$85.00
#1152, Mack Truck, Exxon Tanker...........................$140.00
#1153, Priestman Boom Crane.................................$80.00
#1154, Priestman Crane..$100.00
#1154, Tower Crane...$75.00
#1155, Skyscraper Tower Crane................................$60.00
#1156, Volvo Cement Mixer....................................$60.00
#1157, Ford Esso Tanker..$50.00
#1158, Ford Exxon Tanker.......................................$75.00
#1159, Ford Car Transporter....................................$85.00
#1160, Ford Gulf Tanker...$55.00
#1161, Ford Aral Tanker...$85.00
#1163, Circus Cannon Truck....................................$70.00
#1164, Dolphinarium..$145.00
#1169, Ford Guiness Tanker....................................$85.00
#1170, Ford Car Transporter....................................$70.00

Dakins

Dakin has been an importer of stuffed toys as far back as 1955, but it wasn't until 1959 that the name of this San Francisco-based company actually appeared on the toy labels. They produced three distinct lines: Dream Pets (1960 – early 1970s), Dream Dolls (1965 – mid-1970s), and licensed characters and advertising figures, starting in 1968. Of them all, the latter series was the most popular and the one that holds most interest for collectors. Originally there were seven Warner Brothers characters. Each was made with a hard plastic body and a soft vinyl head, and all were under 10" tall. All in all, more than fifty cartoon characters were produced, some with several variations. Advertising figures were made as well. Some were extensions of the three already existing lines; others were completely original.

Goofy Grams was a series featuring many of their character figures mounted on a base lettered with a 'goofy' message. They also utilized some of their large stock characters as banks in a series called Cash Catchers. A second bank series consisted of Warner Brothers characters molded in a squatting position and therefore smaller. Other figures made by Dakin include squeeze toys, PVCs, and water squirters.

Advisor: Jim Rash (R3).

Alice in Wonderland, w/Alice, Mad Hatter & White Rabbit,
    artist Faith Wick, 18", MIB.......................................$150.00
Baby Puss, Hanna-Barbera, 1971, NM, R3....................$100.00
Bambi, Disney, 1960s, MIP, R3....................................$35.00
Bamm-Bamm, Hanna-Barbera, w/club, 1970, EX, R3......$30.00
Barney Rubble, Hanna-Barbera, 1970, EX, R3................$40.00
Benji, 1978, plush, EX...$10.00
Bozo the Clown, Larry Harmon, 1974, EX, R3...............$35.00
Bugs Bunny, Warner Bros, 1971, MIP, R3.....................$30.00
Bugs Bunny, Warner Bros, 1976, MIB (TV Cartoon Theater
    box)..$40.00
Bugs Bunny, Warner Bros, 1978, MIP (Fun Farm bag).....$20.00
Bullwinkle, Jay Ward, 1976, MIB (TV Cartoon Theater box),
    R3...$60.00
Cool Cat, Warner Bros, w/beret, 1970, EX+, R3.............$30.00
Daffy Duck, Warner Bros, 1968, EX, R3.......................$30.00
Daffy Duck, Warner Bros, 1976, MIB (TV Cartoon Theater
    box)..$40.00
Deputy Dawg, Terrytoons, 1977, EX, R3.......................$50.00
Dewey Duck, Disney, straight or bent legs, EX, R3..........$30.00
Dino Dinosaur, Hanna-Barbera, 1970, EX, R3...............$40.00
Donald Duck, Disney, 1960s, straight or bent legs, EX, R3.$20.00
Donald Duck, Disney, 1960s, straight or bent legs, NMIP.$30.00
Dream Pets, Bull Dog, cloth, EX.................................$10.00
Dream Pets, Hawaiian Hound, cloth, w/surfboard & orig tag,
    EX...$15.00
Dream Pets, Kangaroo, cloth, w/camera, wearing beret, EX..$10.00
Dream Pets, Midnight Mouse, cloth, orig tag, EX............$15.00
Dudley Do-Right, Jay Ward, 1976, MIB (TV Cartoon Theater
    box), R3...$75.00
Dumbo, Disney, 1960s, cloth collar, MIB, R3.................$25.00
Elmer Fudd, Warner Bros, 1968, hunting outfit w/rifle, EX, R3.$125.00

Elmer Fudd, Warner Bros, 1968, in tuxedo, EX, $30.00.

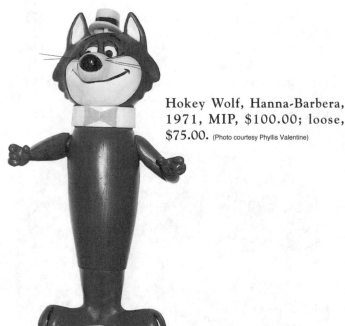

Hokey Wolf, Hanna-Barbera, 1971, MIP, $100.00; loose, $75.00. (Photo courtesy Phyllis Valentine)

Elmer Fudd, Warner Bros, 1978, MIP (Fun Farm bag), R3 ..**$60.00**
Foghorn Leghorn, Warner Bros, 1970, EX+, R3 ....**$75.00**
Fred Flintstone, Hanna-Barbera, 1970, EX, R3.................**$40.00**

Louie Duck, Disney, straight or bent legs, EX, R3.............**$30.00**
Merlin the Magic Mouse, Warner Bros, 1970, EX+ **$25.00**
Mickey Mouse, Disney, cloth clothes, EX, R3...................**$20.00**
Mighty Mouse, Terrytoons, 1978, mk Fun Farm, EX, R3 ..**$100.00**
Minnie Mouse, Disney, 1960s, cloth clothes, EX, R3 ....**$20.00**
Monkey on a Barrel, bank, 1971, EX, R3 ....**$25.00**
Olive Oyl, King Features, 1974, cloth clothes, MIP, R3 ...**$50.00**
Olive Oyl, King Features, 1976, MIB (TV Cartoon Theater box), R3 ....**$40.00**
Oliver Hardy, Larry Harmon, 1974, EX+, R3...................**$30.00**
Opus, 1982, cloth, w/tag, EX **$20.00**
Pebbles Flintstone, Hanna-Barbera, 1970, EX, R3............**$35.00**
Pepe Le Peu, Warner Bros, 1971, EX.................................**$55.00**
Pink Panther, Mirisch-Freleng, 1971, EX+, R3................**$50.00**
Pink Panther, Mirisch-Freleng, 1976, MIB (TV Cartoon Theater box), R3 ....**$50.00**
Pinocchio, Disney, 1960s, EX **$20.00**
Popeye, King Features, 1974, cloth clothes, MIP, R3........**$50.00**

Garfield, 1981, 6½", EX, $10.00.

Goofy, Disney, cloth clothes, EX **$20.00**
Goofy Gram, Bull, I'm Mad About You, EX, R3 ....**$25.00**
Goofy Gram, Dog, Congratulations Dumm-Dumm, EX, R3..**$25.00**
Goofy Gram, Frog, Happy Birthday, EX, R3 ....**$25.00**
Goofy Gram, Kangaroo, World's Greatest Mom, EX, R3..**$25.00**
Goofy Gram, Pepe Le Peu, You're a Real Stinker, 1971, EX...**$40.00**
Goofy Gram, Tiger, To a Great Guy, EX, R3.....................**$25.00**
Hoppy Hopperroo, Hanna-Barbera, 1971, EX+, R3 ....**$75.00**
Huckleberry Hound, Hanna-Barbera, 1970, EX+, R3 ......**$60.00**
Huey Duck, Disney, straight or bent legs, EX, R3 ....**$30.00**
Jack-in-the-Box, bank, 1971, EX, R3 ....**$25.00**
Lion in Cage, bank, 1971, EX, R3.....................................**$25.00**

Road Runner, Warner Bros, 1976, MIB, $45.00.

Popeye, King Features, 1976, MIB (TV Cartoon Theater box), R3 ....$50.00
Porky Pig, Warner Bros, 1968, EX, R3 ....$30.00
Porky Pig, Warner Bros, 1976, MIB (TV Cartoon Theater box), R3 ....$40.00
Practical Pig, EX $45.00
Ren & Stimpy, water squirters, Nickelodeon, 1993, EX, R3 ..$10.00
Road Runner, Warner Bros, 1968, EX, R3 ....$30.00
Rocky Squirrel, Jay Ward, 1976, MIB (TV Cartoon Theater box) $60.00
Scooby Doo, Hanna-Barbera, 1980, EX, R3......................$75.00
Scrappy Doo, Hanna-Barbera, 1982, EX, R3 ....$75.00
Seal on Box, bank, 1971, EX, R3.....................................$25.00
Second Banana, Warner Bros, 1970, EX, R3.....................$35.00
Snagglepuss, 1971, EX $100.00
Speedy Gonzales, Warner Bros, M...................................$35.00
Speedy Gonzales, Warner Bros, MIB (TV Cartoon Theater box), R3 ....$50.00
Stan Laurel, Larry Harmon, 1974, EX+, R3 ....$30.00
Sylvester, Warner Bros, 1968, EX, R3 ....$20.00

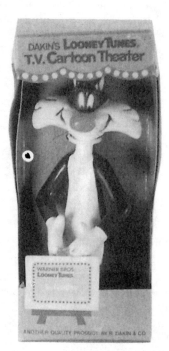

Sylvester, Warner Bros, 1976, MIB (cartoon theatre box), $40.00.

Sylvester, Warner Bros, 1978, MIP (Fun Farm bag), R3 ...$20.00
Tasmanian Devil, Warner Bros, 1978, rare, NM.............$300.00
Tiger in Cage, bank, 1971, EX, R3 ....$25.00
Top Banana, Warner Bros, NM, C17 ....$25.00
Tweety Bird, Warner Bros, 1976, MIB (TV Cartoon Theater box), R3 ....$40.00
Underdog, Jay Ward, 1976, MIB (TV Cartoon Theater box), R3 ....$150.00
Wile E Coyote, Warner Bros, 1968, MIB, R3...................$30.00
Wile E Coyote, Warner Bros, 1976, MIB (TV Cartoon Theater box), R3 ....$40.00
Yogi Bear, Hanna-Barbera, 1970, EX, R3 ....$60.00
Yosemite Sam, Warner Bros, 1968, MIB $40.00
Yosemite Sam, Warner Bros, 1976, MIP (Fun Farm bag), R3 ....$40.00

ADVERTISING

Bay View Bank, 1976, EX+, R3 ....$30.00
Bob's Big Boy, 1974, w/hamburger, EX+, R3 ....$150.00
Buddig Bull, Buggig Meats, 1970s, cloth, EX $20.00
Cocker Spaniel, Crocker National Bank, 1979, cloth, 12", VG $20.00
Diaperene Baby, Sterling Drug Co, 1980, EX, R3 ....$40.00
Freddie Fast Gas Attendant, 1976, M, P12 ....$75.00
Glamour Kitty, 1977, complete w/crown, EX, R3 ....$200.00
Hobo Joe, bank, Hobo Joe's Restaurant, EX.....................$60.00
Kernal Renk, American Seeds, 1970, rare, EX+, R3 ......$300.00
Li'l Miss Just Rite, 1965, EX+, R3 ....$60.00
Miss Liberty Bell, 1975, MIP, R3 ....$60.00
Quasar Robot, bank, 1975, NM, R3.................................$125.00
Sambo's Boy, 1974, vinyl, EX+, R3 ....$80.00
Sambo's Tiger, 1974, vinyl, EX+, R3 ....$125.00
Smokey the Bear, 1976, M...$25.00
St Bernard, Christian Bros Candy, 1982, cloth, VG $20.00
Woodsy Owl, 1974, MIP, R3...$60.00

Diecast

Diecast replicas of cars, trucks, planes, trains, etc., represent a huge corner of today's collector market, and their manufacturers see to it that there is no shortage. Back in the 1920s, Tootsietoy had the market virtually by themselves, but one by one other companies had a go at it, some with more success than others. Among them were the American companies of Barclay, Hubley, and Manoil, all of whom are much better known for other types of toys. After the war, Metal Masters, Smith-Miller, and Doepke Ohlsson-Rice (among others) tried the market with varying degrees of success. Some companies were phased out over the years, while many more entered the market with fervor. Today it's those fondly remembered models from the '50s and '60s that many collectors yearn to own. Solido produced well-modeled, detailed little cars; some had dome lights that actually came on when the doors were opened. Politoy's were cleanly molded with good detailing and finishes. Mebetoys, an Italian company that has been bought out by Mattel, produced several; and some of the finest come from Brooklyn.

In 1968 the Topper Toy Company introduced its line of low-friction, high-speed Johnny Lightning cars to be in direct competition with Mattel's Hot Wheels. To gain attention, Topper sponsored Al Unser's winning race car, the 'Johnny Lightning,' in the 1970 Indianapolis 500. Despite the popularity of their cars, the Topper Toy Company went out of business in 1971. Today the Johnny Lightnings are highly sought after, and a new company, Playing Mantis, is reproducing many of the original designs as well as several models that never made it into regular production.

If you're interested in Majorette Toys, we recommend *Collecting Majorette Toys* by Dana Johnson; ordering information is given with Dana's listing under Diecast, in the section called Categories of Special Interest in the back of the book. Dana is also the author of *Collector's Guide to Diecast Toys & Scale Mod-*

els, Second Edition, published by Collector Books.

Values are for examples in mint condition and in the original packaging.

Advisor: Dan Wells (W1).

Other Sources: N3, S5.

See also Corgi; Dinky; Diecast Collector Banks; Farm Toys; Hot Wheels; Matchbox; Tekno; Tootsietoys.

Ahi, Buick..$16.00
Ahi, Chevrolet Impala...$16.00
Ahi, Dodge Military Radar Truck.......................$12.00
Ahi, Ferrari 500 Formula 2 ....$25.00
Ahi, Maserati Racer...$16.00
Ahi, Porsche 356A...$16.00
Ahi, Rolls Royce Silver Wraith...........................$20.00
Ahi, Volkswagen 1200..$20.00
Ahi, 1903 Cadillac...$12.00
Ahi, 1914 Stutz Bearcat......................................$12.00
Ahi, 1915 Ford Model T.......................................$12.00

American Highway Legends, Dixie Beer Peterbilt 260 Tandem Trailer Truck, M, $35.00. (Photo courtesy Dana Johnson)

Anker, Alfa Romeo 1300.....................................$18.00
Anker, Renault Rodeo Jeep $18.00
Asahi Model Pet, Datsun Bluebird.....................$125.00
Asahi Model Pet, Honda S800 Coupe $100.00
Asahi Model Pet, Mitsubishi Galant GTO............$50.00
Asahi Model Pet, Toyota Crown...........................$125.00
Asahi Model Pet, Toyota Masterline Ambulance...........$225.00
Asahi Model Pet, Yamaha Police Motorcycle..................$30.00
Auto Pilen, Chevrolet Astro I...............................$45.00
Auto Pilen, Ford Mark II $45.00
Auto Pilen, Mercedes Taxi $45.00
Bandai, Mitsubishi Galant $5.00
Bandai, Nissan Ambulance...................................$5.00
Bandai, Porsche 930, silver $16.00
Bang, Ferrari 250 GTO Prova, red $25.00
Bang, Ford AC Cobra Spyder Stradale, red or blk, ea.......$25.00
Bang, Ford Mk II Le Mans, bl or blk, ea $22.00
Bang, Mercedes-Benz 300SL Gullwing Coupe, silver or blk,
  ea $25.00
Barclay, Ambulance, #50 ....$50.00
Barclay, Chrysler Imperial Coupe, #39 ....$25.00
Barclay, Searchlight Truck....................................$150.00
Barclay, Taxi, #318...$25.00
Barclay, Wrecker, #403, 2-pc $70.00
Barlux, Fiat Ambulance $30.00
Barlux, Garbage Truck $16.00
Barlux, Lotus Turbine $10.00

Barlux, Road Roller...$16.00
BBR, Alfa Romeo 6C 2500 MM Fangio, maroon..........$185.00
BBR, 1939 Alfa Romeo 2900 Berlinetta.........................$150.00
BBR, 1954 Ferrari 250 Europea Cabriolet Pininfarina....$150.00
BBR, 1984 Ferrari 288 GTO.................................$160.00
BBR, 1993 Ferrari 348 Cabriolet.........................$160.00
BBR, 1993 Porsche 911 Carrera $185.00
Bburago, Alfa Romeo 75 Polizia, M, from $15 to.............$20.00
Bburago, Audi Quattro, from $5 to $10.00
Bburago, Dump Truck, 1500 series, M.........................$25.00
Bburago, Lumber Truck, 1500 series, M $25.00
Bburago, Peugeot 205 Safari, from $15 to $20.00
Bburago, Porsche 924 Turbo, 4800 series, from $3 to.........$5.00
Bburago, 1954 Mercedes-Benz 300SL, 3000 series, from $20
  to $30.00
Bburago, 1957 Chevrolet Corvette, 3700 series, from $25
  to $30.00
Bburago, 1957 Ferrari 250 Testa Rossa, 3000 series, from
  $20 to $30.00
Bburago, 1984 Ferrari GTO, 3500 series, from $25 to $30.00
Bburago, 1990 Lamborghini Diablo, 3000 series, from $20 to .$30.00
Benbros, American Ford Convertible $15.00
Benbros, Army Scout Car.....................................$15.00
Benbros, Bedford Compressor Truck $25.00
Best Toys of Kansas, Oil Transport Trailer #102, 7" $30.00
Best Toys of Kansas, Racer #76, 4" $30.00
Best Toys of Kansas, Sedan #95, 2-door, 3½" $30.00
Best-Box of Holland, Ford Model T Coupe $20.00
Best-Box of Holland, Ford Model T Pickup $20.00
Best-Box of Holland, Mercedes-Benz 250 SE Coupe $20.00
Box Model, Ferrari 250 GT, gold-plated...........................$40.00
Box Model, 1959 Ferrari 250 GT Tour de France, wht.....$22.00
Box Model, 1966 Ferrari 275 GTB Spyder, blk w/wire
  wheels...$18.00
Brumm, 1903 Fiat S 61 ....$20.00
Brumm, 1931 Alfa Romeo 2300 ....$20.00
Brumm, 1952 Porsche 356 Targa Florio, 1990 limited edi-
  tion..$35.00
Brumm, 1957 Maserati 250F Muso Corto $20.00
Brumm, 1958 Vanwall F1, 1987 limited edition $35.00
Budgie, Crane Truck, red w/bl crane, 4" $20.00
Budgie, Rolls Royce Silver Cloud, from $30 to...............$40.00
Chad Valley, Commer Fire Engine $175.00
Chad Valley, Double-Decker Bus $250.00
Charbens, Ambulance $65.00
Charbens, Ferrari Racer.......................................$100.00
Charbens, 1906 Rolls Royce Silver Ghost, Old Crock series .$20.00
Charbens, 1907 Ford Model T, Old Crock series, bl $20.00
Con-Cor, Ferrari Testarossa..................................$8.00
Con-Cor, Mercedes-Benz 300E.............................$5.00
Conquest, 1954 Oldsmobile Starfire 98 Convertible, top down,
  2-tone..$190.00
Conquest, 1954 Pontiac Star Chief Convertible, top down ..$200.00
Conquest, 1960 Plymouth Fury $210.00
Conrad, Mercedes-Benz 206 Van $35.00
Conrad, Volkswagen Polo C $10.00
Dalia-Solido, Fiat Abarth 1000, orange, silver or tan, ea..$100.00
Dalia-Solido, Jaguar D Le Mans, red, gr or bl, ea $100.00

Dalia-Solido, Mercedes-Benz 190SL Roadster, copper, silver or wht, ea $100.00

Dalia-Solido, Porsche F2, silver & red $125.00

Dalia-Tekno, Ford Mustang Convertible........$50.00

Dalia-Tekno, Lincoln Continental $65.00

Dalia-Tekno, Oldsmobile Toronado $50.00

Danbury Mint, 1938 Rolls Royce Phantom III, maroon & blk, from $85 to $125.00

Danbury Mint, 1940 Ford Deluxe Coupe, red & beige, from $85 to........$125.00

Danbury Mint, 1953 Buick Skylark Convertible, 2-tone bl, from $85 to........$125.00

Danbury Mint, 1953 Chevrolet 3100 Pickup, gr, from $85 to........$125.00

Diapet, Corvette, #G76 ....$75.00

Diapet, Datsun Leopard 4-Door Sedan, #G2 ....$20.00

Diapet, Lexus Coupe, #SV22........$30.00

Diapet, Nissan Silvia Coupe, #G37........$20.00

Diapet, Toyota Crown Taxi, #P63 ....$20.00

Dugu, 1907 Fiat Grand Prix, 1964........$55.00

Dugu, 1934 Rolls Royce Silver Ghost, top up or down, 1969, ea $120.00

Durham Classics, 1938 Lincoln Zephyr Coupe, blk........$100.00

Durham Classics, 1941 Ford Coupe $100.00

Edil, Fiat 850, 1966, from $50 to $75.00

Edil, Mercedes-Benz 250SE, from $50 to $75.00

Efsi, Commer Ambulance........$15.00

Efsi, Ford Model T Sedan $10.00

Efsi, Porsche 911 S $15.00

Eligor, 1932 Ford Roadster, baby bl $25.00

Eligor, 1960 Jaguar Mk 1 ....$25.00

Enchanted, 1953 Kaiser Manhattan........$85.00

Enchanted, 1958 Ford Edsel Convertible........$115.00

Enchanted, 1960 Ford Thunderbird $85.00

Enchantment Land Coach Builders, 1947 Chrysler Durham Continental Hardtop........$110.00

Enchantment Land Coach Builders, 1951 Ford Victoria Hardtop $100.00

Enchantment Land Coach Builders, 1955 Chrysler Convertible........$120.00

Enchantment Land Coach Builders, 1968 Pontiac Convertible........$100.00

Ertl, 1967 Corvette L-71 Roadster, Sunfire Yellow $40.00

Ertl, 1969 Camaro Z-28, red & wht........$30.00

Ertl, 1970 Boss 302 Mustang, yel w/blk accents $30.00

Ertl, 1996 Pontiac Trans Am Coupe, metallic red $25.00

France Jouets, Ambulance Truck, 1959........$75.00

France Jouets, Dump Truck, 1962........$75.00

France Jouets, Police Jeep, 1965 ....$65.00

Franklin Mint, 1911 Rolls Royce Tourer, cream & brn, from $85 to........$125.00

Franklin Mint, 1915 Stutz Bearcat, yel, from $85 to $125.00

Franklin Mint, 1932 Ford Deuce Coupe, blk & beige, from $85 to........$125.00

Franklin Mint, 1949 Buick Skylark Convertible, yel & red, from $85 to........$125.00

Franklin Mint, 1955 Chevrolet Bel Air Police Chief #67, blk & wht, from $85 to $125.00

Franklin Mint, 1955 Chevrolet Corvette, metallic bl & beige, from $85 to........$125.00

Franklin Mint, 1958 Ford Thunderbird, from $55 to........$70.00

Franklin Mint, 1963 Cadillac Eldorado, from $55 to........$70.00

Gama, Henschel Wrecker, #31, 1969 ....$25.00

Gama, Opel Corsa........$15.00

Goodee, 1953 Ford Police Sedan, 3" $28.00

Goodee, 1953 Lincoln Capri Hardtop, 3" $15.00

Goodee, 1954 DeSoto Station Wagon, 6" $25.00

Goodee, 1954 Ford C600 Oil Truck, 3"........$28.00

Goodee, 1955 Ford Fuel Truck, 6" $25.00

Guisval, Audi Quattro Coupe $15.00

Guisval, Porsche 959........$15.00

Guisval, 1979 Chevrolet Camaro........$15.00

Hubley, Army Air Combat Squadron & Hangar, 1947, complete w/5 planes, EX (EX box converts to hangar), A $600.00

Hubley, Bell Telephone Truck, complete w/accessories, MIB, A........$150.00

Hubley, Chrysler Airflow, 5"........$85.00

Hubley, Jaguar, 7½"........$190.00

Hubley, Log Truck, complete w/lumber, G, A........$55.00

Hubley, Poultry Truck, #497, three plastic crates and poultry, 10", EX (VG box), $195.00.

Hubley Convertible, #465, rubber wheels, 7", MIB, $125.00.

Hubley Kiddie Toys, Dump Truck #510 ....$250.00

Hubley Kiddie Toys, Hook & Ladder Truck, EX (EX box)...$250.00

Hubley Kiddie Toys, Racer #457, 6½" $55.00

Hubley Kiddie Toys, Transport Truck, complete w/4 cars, 13", A........$400.00

Hubley Mighty-Metal, Tow Truck, A........$125.00

Jane Francis, Pickup Truck, 5" $25.00
Jane Francis, Tow Truck, 5" $35.00
Joal, Chrysler 150..$25.00
Joal, Mercedes-Benz 350SL Coupe $16.00
Joal, Renault R10..$25.00
Johnny Lightning, Custom Big Rig, 1971, from $40 to $50.00

Johnny Lightning, Custom GTO, $5.00. (Photo courtesy Dana Johnson)

Johnny Lightning, Custom XKE, doors open, 1969........$125.00
Johnny Ligntning, Custom T-Bird, 1969, from $75 to....$100.00
Jouef, Ferrari 330 P4 Spyder $20.00
Jouef, Ford Mustang GT Convertible, red, teal or yel, 1994,
     ea...$25.00
Jouef, Honda NS-X, gray $20.00
JRD, Citroen 2C Sedan, 1958 ....$75.00
JRD, Peugeot 404 Sedan, 1962 ....$60.00
Kansas Toy & Novelty, Austin Bantam Sedanette, #58, 2"...$35.00
Kansas Toy & Novelty, Buick Roadster w/Rumble Seat, #54,
     2" $20.00
Kansas Toy & Novelty, Chevrolet Sedan, 2"..............$40.00
Kansas Toy & Novelty, Sedan Limousine, 3" $60.00
Kiddie Car Classics, 1950 Murray Torpedo, 6" $50.00
Kiddie Car Classics, 1956 Garton Hot Rod Racer, 5½"....$55.00
Kiddie Car Classics, 1962 Murray Super Deluxe Fire Truck,
     7½" $55.00
Kirk, Chevrolet Monza GT $60.00
Kirk, Toyota 2000 GT..$65.00
Lansing Slik-Toys, Fire Truck, #9606, 6" $35.00
Lansing Slik-Toys, Pickup Truck, #9601, 7" $40.00
Lansing Slik-Toys, Wrecker, #9617, 5"...................$30.00
Lansing Slik-Toys, 4-Door Sedan, #9604, 6" $35.00
Lledo, Chevrolet Van, 1986................................$10.00
Lledo, Delivery Van, 1983 ....$10.00
Lledo, Ford Model A Touring Car, top up, 1985..........$10.00
Lledo, Ford Model T Tanker, 1984 ....$10.00
Lledo, Rolls Royce Silver Ghost Tourer, 1987 ....$10.00
Lledo, 1942 Dodge Truck, 1988..........................$10.00
Londontoy, Beverage Truck, 4"...........................$25.00
Londontoy, City Bus, 6".....................................$30.00
Lone Star, Cadillac Coupe de Ville, wht & bl..............$95.00
Lone Star, Dodge Dart Phoenix, metallic bl $95.00
Maisto, 1955 Mercedes-Benz 300S Convertible, custom air-
     brushed, from $35 to....................................$40.00
Maisto, 1966 Mercedes-Benz 280SE, wht, from $25 to.....$30.00

Maisto, 1989 Porsche 911 Speedster, red, from $25 to......$30.00
Maisto, 1995 Ferrari F50 Barchetta, yel, from $25 to........$30.00

Maisto, Porsche Boxster, #31814, black or silver, M, $25.00.
(Photo courtesy Dana Johnson)

Majorette, Citroen Maserati SM $10.00
Majorette, Ferrari Formula 1 Racer, chromed $15.00
Majorette, Fiat 127, lime gr $8.00
Majorette, Jeep 4x4 w/Motorcycle Trailer.....................$15.00
Majorette, Lotus F1 Racer $10.00
Majorette, Magic Circus Truck, red & yel w/blk base $10.00
Majorette, Mercedes-Benz 280SE........................$10.00
Majorette, Mercedes-Benz 300SL Gullwing.....................$5.00
Majorette, Pontiac Firebird Turbo $5.00
Mandarin, Honda 9 Coupe $5.00
Mandarin, Toyota Celica Mk 2 ....$5.00
Manoil, Convertible, 1945-55 ....$20.00
Manoil, Roadster, 1935-41................................$90.00
Manoil, Roadster, 1945-55, from $35 to...............$50.00
Manoil, Sedan, 1935-41....................................$90.00

**Master Caster, 1947 Ford, red with black rubber tires, 7",
underside aluminum plate replaced, A, $175.00.**

Mebetoys, BMW 320 Rally, 1980 ....$30.00
Mebetoys, Fiat 850, 1966..................................$30.00
Mebetoys, Ford GT Mk II, 1968.........................$40.00
Mebetoys, Land Rover Fire Truck, 1974....................$45.00
Mebetoys, Maserati Bora, 1973...........................$40.00
Mebetoys, Pontiac Firebird, 1983 ....$30.00
Mebetoys, Porsche Carrera 10, 1971 ....$40.00
Mebetoys, Porsche 917, 1971 ....$40.00
Mebetoys, Rolls Royce Silver Shadow, 1968...................$50.00
Mercury, Cadillac 62 Sedan, 1949.......................$150.00
Mercury, Farina, 1946......................................$100.00
Mercury, Ford GT 40, 1969 ....$55.00

Mercury, Ford Mustang, 1969 ....$55.00
Mercury, Harley-Davidson Electra..............................$40.00
Mercury, Porsche Carrera 6, 1967...............................$40.00
Mercury, Rembrandt Caravan, 1976 ....$25.00
Mercury, Studebaker Golden Hawk, 1957 ....$200.00
Midgetoys, Convertible, 1950s, bl, 5".........................$20.00
Midgetoys, Corvette, 1970s, gr, 2"................................$4.00
Midgetoys, Jeep, 1960s, red..$5.00
Midgetoys, Quarry Dump Truck $45.00
Midgetoys, Vanwall Formula 1 ....$45.00
Milton, Austin-Healey..$16.00
Milton, Ford Model T $25.00
Milton, Plymouth Suburban $36.00
Milton, Volkswagen 1200 ....$20.00
Mira, 1954 Chevrolet Convertible $25.00
Mira, 1955 Buick Century Hardtop, 2-tone $25.00
Mira, 1965 Ford Mustang Fastback $25.00
Morestone, AA Motorcycle w/Sidecar $30.00
Morestone, Austin-Healey 100......................................$30.00
Morestone, Volkswagen 1200 Sedan $35.00
Nicky Toys, Bentley S Coupe $30.00
Nicky Toys, Lincoln Continental $45.00
Nostalgic, Porsche 356 Coupe $65.00
Nostalgic, 1930 Ford Model A Pickup $60.00
Nostalgic, 1930 Ford Roadster, top down.....................$60.00
Nostalgic, 1934 LaSalle Coupe.....................................$65.00
Nostalgic, 1965 Ford Mustang 2+2, blk $60.00
NZG, CAT 245 Excavator $45.00
NZG, Kramer Tremo Utility Truck...............................$20.00
NZG, Porsche 968 Cabriolet $25.00
Playart, Chevrolet Blazer, Sears Roadmates #7242 ....$4.00
Playart, Dodge Challenger, Sears Roadmates #7178 ....$5.00
Quiralu, Mercedes-Benz 300SL, 1956, 2-tone $125.00
Quiralu, Renault Etoile Filante, 1958, w/decals............$100.00
Racing Champions, 1949 Buick Riviera, bl...................$6.00
Racing Champions, 1956 Ford Thunderbird, pk.........$6.00
Racing Champions, 1964 Chevy Impala, wht.............$6.00
Racing Champions, 1968 Ford Mustang, mint gr..........$6.00
Renwal, Ferrari Racer $160.00
Renwal, Ford Sedan $120.00
Renwal, Pontiac Convertible $120.00
Replicars, 1951 Ferrari 166M.......................................$60.00
Replicars, 1974 Triumph TR6 ....$60.00
Rextoys, 1935 Ford Woody Wagon $35.00
Rextoys, 1939 Cadillac Coupe De Ville $35.00
Rio, 1919 Fiat 501 Tourer, 1961 ....$25.00
Rio, 1937 Mercedes-Benz Cabriolet, 1966 ....$25.00
Rio, 1941 Lincoln Continental, 1969, top up or down, ea .$25.00
Sablon, BMW 1600 GT...$32.00
Sablon, Mercedes-Benz 200 ....$75.00
Sakura, Chevrolet Corvette Coupe $20.00
Sakura, Toyota Land Cruiser $20.00
Schabak, Audi 90 Quattro, 1984..................................$20.00
Schabak, Ford Sierra Police Car, 1988 ....$20.00
Schuco, Audi 80 LS, 1972 ....$25.00
Schuco, BMW 316, 1975..$25.00
Schuco, Krupp Cement Carrier, 5½" $60.00
Schuco, Mercedes-Benz Grand Prix, 1958, 2".............$50.00

Schuco, Mercedes-Benz 450SE, 1973............................$25.00
Siku, Ferrari Berlinetta, 1975-81 ....$15.00
Siku, Ford F500 Wrecker, 1965-73 ....$35.00
Siku, Ford T5 Mustang Mach 1, 1972-74 ....$20.00
Siku, Ford 12M, 1963 ....$35.00
Siku, Lamborghini Fire Truck, 1978............................$10.00
Siku, Opel Olympia, 1968-69 ....$60.00
Siku, Porsche 901, 1964-69 ....$35.00
Siku, Porsche 911 Rallye, 1986 ....$10.00
Siku, Volkswagen Bus, 1963-64 ....$40.00
Solido, 1934 Ford Roadster Convertible, top up or down, ea ..$30.00
Solido, 1936 Ford Pickup...$30.00
Solido, 1946 Chrysler Windsor, 1960s $20.00
Solido, 1957 Studebaker Silver Hawk, 1960s...............$20.00
Solido, 1961 Fiat Abarth, 1996 reissue.........................$20.00
Solido, 1962 Lola Climax V8 F1, 1994 reissue..............$20.00
Solido, 1964 Ford GT40 Le Mans $20.00
Solido, 1978 Peugeot 504 Coupe Rallye, 1995 reissue......$20.00

Solido, 1987 Bentley Continental, #1512, M, $15.00.
(Photo courtesy Dana Johnson)

Spot-On, Austin A40..$125.00
Spot-On, Ford Consul Classic $150.00
Spot-On, Ford Zodiac $125.00
Spot-On, Jaguar Mk 10..$175.00
Spot-On, MG Midget Mk II $175.00
Spot-On, Renault Floride Convertible $125.00
Superior, BMW Z1 Roadster $6.00
Superior, Ferrari 288 GTO Coupe $6.00
Superior, Porsche 959 Coupe $6.00
Tip Top Toy, Airflow, lg $40.00
Tip Top Toy, Airflow, sm $30.00
Tip Top Toy, Bus, 3" $40.00
Tip Top Toy, Stake Truck, 5" $55.00
Tomica, Cadillac Seville, #233-F45 ....$6.00
Tomica, Datsun 200SX, #235-6 ....$5.00
Tomica, Greyhound Bus Americruiser, #222-F49 ....$25.00
Tomica, Lotus Elite, #F47 ....$6.00
Tomica, Porsche 928, #204-F53 ....$5.00
Tomica, Rolls Royce Phantom VI, #110-F6 ....$6.00
Tomica, Super Bug Volkswagen, #195-F20....................$10.00
Tomica, Toyota Land Cruiser, #83-02 ....$10.00
Tomica, Winnebago Chieftain Motor Home, #92-F1 ....$15.00
Tri-Ang, Bentley Touring Car, 1938 ....$125.00
Tri-Ang, Breakdown Lorry Wrecker, 1936....................$200.00
Tri-Ang, Streamline Sports Car, 1935............................$125.00
Tri-Ang, Vauxhall Town Coupe, 1937 ....$125.00

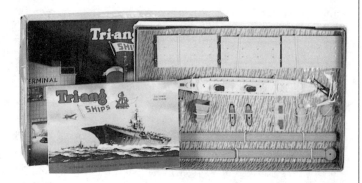

Tri-Ang Minic, SS United States, M892, complete, NMIB, $200.00.

Verem, Porsche Carrera, wht $20.00
Verem, Rolls Royce Silver Cloud, gold $20.00
Vilmer, Dodge Tow Truck, from $45 to $60.00
Vilmer, Ford Thames Cable Truck, from $45 to $60.00
Vilmer, Mercedes-Benz 220, 1957, from $45 to $60.00
Vitesse, 1947 Chrysler Windsor Sedan..............................$25.00
Vitesse, 1956 Triumph TR3 Convertible $25.00
Vitesse, 1959 Volkswagen 1200 w/Sunroof.....................$25.00
Vitesse, 1967 Porsche 911R...$25.00
Ziss, 1905 Mercedes-Benz Coupe, 1966...........................$25.00
Ziss, 1905 Mercedes-Benz Grand Prix, 1972 ....$25.00
Ziss, 1908 Opel Stadt-Coupe, 1963 ....$25.00
Ziss, 1969 Volkswagen Pickup Truck, 1970 ....$50.00
Ziss, 1971 Opel Commodore Coupe, 1971.......................$40.00

Diecast Collector Banks

Thousands of banks have been produced since Ertl made its first model in 1981, the 1913 Model T Parcel Post Mail Service #9647. The Ertl company was founded by Fred Ertl, Sr., in Dubuque, Iowa, back in the mid-1940s. Until they made their first diecast banks, most of what they made were farm tractors. Today they specialize in vehicles made to specification and carrying logos of companies as large as Texaco and as small as your hometown bank. The size of each 'run' is dictated by the client and can vary from a few hundred up to several thousand. Some clients will later add a serial number to the vehicle; this is not done by Ertl. Other numbers that appear on the base of each bank are a four-number dating code (the first three indicate the day of the year up to 365 and the fourth number is the last digit of the year, '5' for 1995, for instance). The stock number is shown only on the box, never on the bank, so it is extremely important that you keep them in their original boxes.

Other producers of these banks are Scale Models, incorporated in 1991, First Gear Inc., and Spec-Cast, whose founders at one time all worked for the Ertl company.

In the listings that follow, unless another condition is given, all values are for banks mint and in their original boxes. The symbol (#d) indicates a bank that was numbered by the client, not Ertl.

Advisors: Art and Judy Turner (H8).

Other Sources: S5.

Key: JLE — Joseph L. Ertl

ERTL

Babe Ruth, 1926 Mack Bulldog, #0906, 1992, MIB, $45.00.

Batman, Joker Van, MIP, $12.00.

American Airlines, DC-3 Airplane, #F312......................$45.00
Big A Auto Parts, 25th Anniversary, 1963 Corvette, #9280 ..$85.00
Big A Auto Parts, 30th Anniversary, 1963 Corvette, #9433 ..$50.00
Coca-Cola, Gamma Airplane, #B900 ....$35.00
Dama-Victor Reimz Gaskets & Seals, 1918 Ford, #19653 ..$18.00
Disney Safari Guide, 1938 Bantum, #20075 ....$65.00
Dr Pepper, DC-3 Airplane, #F482 ....$40.00

Ford, 1918 Ford Runabout, 1988, MIP, $24.00.

Football, Dallas Cowboys, Stearman Airplane, #F691......**$45.00**
Football, Washington Redskins, Bell Helicopter, no # **$25.00**
Goofy's Hayride, Tractor & Wagon, #18110 ....**$65.00**
Humble Oil Co, DC-3 Airplane, #F519...........................**$40.00**
IGA, Gamma Airplane, #F246...**$25.00**
JC Penney, Air Express Airplane, #B298 ....**$25.00**
Maryland State Police, Bell Helicopter, no #..................**$35.00**
Napa, Biplane, #K107...**$40.00**
New Hampshire State Police, Bell Helicopter, no # **$35.00**
Peanuts & Friends, School Bus, #H263............................**$75.00**
Penn State University, Blimp, #36054 ....**$40.00**
Penn State University, 1950 Divco Milk Truck, #20191 ..**$40.00**
Prairie Farms Milk, 1923 Chevrolet Van, #3558...............**$25.00**
Ringling Bros Circus, 1913 Ford, #9027..........................**$100.00**
Ringling Bros Circus, 1937 Ford Tractor Trailer, #9726....**$100.00**
Seven-Up, 1931 Hawkeye **$35.00**
Shell Oil Co, DC-3 Airplane, #F926 ....**$50.00**
Street Rod Series (Black & Silver), 1937 Chevy Cabriolet,
    #10059 ....**$25.00**

Texaco, 1925 Kenworth Stake Truck, #9, 1992, MIB, $28.00.

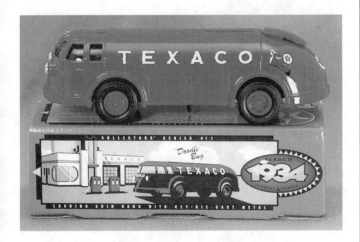

Texaco, 1934 Doodle Bug, #11, MIB, $25.00.

Texaco, #2, Gamma Airplane, #B223 ....**$40.00**
Texaco, Colwell Oil Co, 1953 Willys Stake Truck, #75513 ..**$45.00**
Texaco, Henry Ford Museum, 1939 Dodge Airflow, #K087 ..**$45.00**
True Value Hardware, #2, 1926 Mack Truck, #1362.......**$125.00**
True Value Hardware, #19, 1913 Ford, 2-pc, #19911 ....**$28.00**
United Airlines, Trimotor Airplane, #K057 ....**$50.00**

United States Army, Bell Helicopter, no #.........................**$35.00**
United Van Lines, 1917 Ford Model T **$35.00**
University of Florida, 1948 Fire Engine Pedal Car, #2289 ..**$45.00**
University of Tennessee, 1940 Gendron Pedal Car, #2319 ..**$45.00**

First Gear

Ace Hardware, 1953 White 3000, #18-2099 ....**$45.00**
Allegheny Coal Co, B-61 Mack Dump Truck, #19-1829..**$65.00**
Amoco, Mack B-61 Wrecker, #19-2501 ....**$55.00**
Armstrong Tires, Mack B-61 Tractor Trailer, #19-1465 ....**$120.00**
Atlantic Refining, 1951 Ford Tanker, #10-1290 ....**$40.00**
Atlas Van Lines Hydroplane, 1957 International, #19-1589..**$40.00**
Bare Truck Center, 1957 International Wrecker, #19-1457 ...**$45.00**
Bechtel Construction, B-61 Mack Dump Truck, #19-2033....**$55.00**
Bekins Van & Storage Co, Mack B-61 Wrecker, #19-1660....**$70.00**
Big Red Trucking, 1953 White 3000 Stake Truck, #19-2137....**$45.00**
Blue Diamond Co, B-61 Mack Dump Truck, #19-1834..**$150.00**
Boston Sand & Gravel, Mack B-61 Dump Truck, #19-
    2016..**$70.00**
Burlington Truck Lines, 1956 White Tractor Trailer, #18-
    1545..**$65.00**
Campbell's Family of Brands, 1957 International Box,
    #19-1313..**$40.00**
Campbell's 66 Express, B-61 Mack Dump Truck, #19-
    2154 ....**$150.00**
Carlisle Collector Events, Mack B-61 Tractor Trailer, #19-
    1781 ....**$55.00**
Chevrolet Motor Co, 1949 Chevrolet, #10-1328 ....**$32.00**
Chevron Gasoline, 1951 Ford Fuel Tanker, #10-1021 ......**$40.00**
Citgo, 1957 International Tanker, #29-1248....................**$60.00**
Coker Tire, 1951 Ford Stake Truck, #19-1249 ....**$75.00**
Cole's Express, Mack B-61 Tractor Trailer, #19-1826 ....**$85.00**
Colwell Power Wagon, 1949 Dodge Pickup, #18-2482.....**$50.00**
Custom Chrome, 25th Anniversary, 1952 GMC Box, #18-
    1361 ....**$85.00**
Daisy Air Rifles, Mack B-61 Tractor Trailer, #10-0123.....**$75.00**
Daisy Air Rifles, 1951 Ford Box, #10-0124 ....**$40.00**
Eastern Express, 1953 Ford Box, #19-1481......................**$45.00**
Eastwood, 1952 GMC Wrecker, #190109 ....**$70.00**
Erector (AC Gilbert), 1957 International Van, #19-0111 ..**$55.00**
Exxon Happy Motoring, 1960 Mack B-61 Tractor Trailer, #19-
    1708 ....**$85.00**
Fire Dept of New York, 1952 GM Stake Truck, #19-1205 ..**$65.00**
First Gear, 1959 International Lowboy, #19-0011............**$85.00**
Global Van Lines, 1957 International Moving Van, #19-
    1801 ....**$50.00**
Great Southern Trucking, 1952 GMC DGV, #19-1031....**$40.00**
Gulfpride, 1953 Ford F-100 Pickup, #19-1618.................**$45.00**
J Levy & Sons Moving & Storage, 1960 Mack B-61 Moving
    Van, #19-1971...**$50.00**
Kendall Racing Oil, 1952 GMC Fuel Tanker, #28-1083 ..**$40.00**
Lionel Trains, 1952 GMC DGV Eastwood, #19-0108 ......**$45.00**
Mack Excavating, Mack R Dump Trailer, #19-2500 ....**$70.00**
Magnolia Petroleum, 1951 Ford Stake Truck w/Barrels, #18-
    1056..**$70.00**
McLean Trucking Co, 1952 GMC DGV, #19-1009 ....**$90.00**
Michelin Tires, 1960 Mack B-61 Tractor Trailer, #19-1502 ...**$60.00**

Mobil Gas, IHC Fuel Tanker, #19-1405 ....$40.00
Model Garage, 1952 GMC Wrecker, #19-1143 ....$45.00
O'Doul's Oasis, 1952 GMC Insulated Van, #19-1352.......$40.00
Palumbo Brother Trucking, B-61 Mack Dump Truck, #19-1819 ....$225.00
Peach State Motorsports, 1949 Chevrolet, #19-1419 ....$35.00
Pennsylvania Railroad, Mack B-61 Tractor Trailer, #19-1435 ....$65.00

Pepsi Bottler's Truck, 1951 Ford, MIB, $50.00.

Pepsi-Cola, 1952 GMC Van, #19-1404.............................$40.00
Pepsi-Cola, 1953 Ford Pickup, #19-1582 ....$45.00
Pepsi-Cola, 1953 White 3000 Tanker, #19-2004 ....$65.00
Pepsi-Cola Big Shot, 1949 Chevrolet Panel Van, #29-1373 ..$50.00
Pepsi-Cola Cops, 1953 Ford DGV, #10-1351 ....$45.00
Phillips 66, 1951 Ford Fuel Tanker, #19-1034...................$45.00
Radio Flyer, 1960 Mack B-61 Tractor Trailer, Eastwood, #10-1346 ....$150.00
Railway Express, 1960 Mack B-61 Tractor Trailer, #19-1654 ....$50.00
Red Star Express, 1960 Mack B-61 Tractor Trailer, #19-1510...$70.00
Remington Arms Co, Mack B-61 Tractor Trailer, #10-1292.....$75.00
Remington I, Mallard, 1952 GMC Van, #10-1082 ....$28.00
Remington II, Rabbit, 1957 International Van, #10-1572..$28.00

Shell Aviation Fuel, 1957 International R-190 with fuel tanker, MIB, $40.00.

Roadrunner Express, 1951 Ford Van, #19-1108 ....$45.00
Roadway Express, 1953 Ford, #10-1379 ....$45.00
Rock Island Motor Transit, 1957 International R-190 .....$35.00
Rock-Ola Jukeboxes, 1955 Diamond T Van, #19-1987....$60.00
Rolling Thunder Cycles, 1951 Ford Box, #19-1141.........$38.00
Shell Oil Co, Dodge Powerwagon Fire, #19-2483.............$40.00
Shell Oil Co, Mack B-61 Tractor Trailer, #19-1392..........$95.00
Shell Oil Co, 1937 Chevrolet Wrecker, #19-2585............$50.00
Shell Oil Co, 1953 Ford Pickup, #19-1554 ....$40.00
Shell Oil Co, 1955 Diamond T Wrecker, #19-2025 ....$45.00
Shell Oil Co, 1957 IHC Fire Truck, #10-2172 ....$45.00
Smith & Wesson, Mack B-61 Tractor Trailer, #18-1219 ..$75.00
Smith & Wesson, 1952 GMC Stake Truck, #10-1326......$45.00
Standard Oil of CA, 1957 IHC Fuel Tanker, #29-1109....$80.00
Sunoco, 1951 Ford Fuel Tanker, #28-1055.......................$60.00
Sunshine Biscuits, Mack B-61 Tractor Trailer, #10-1472..$55.00
Sunshine Biscuits, 1957 International, #10-1473 ....$32.00
Texaco, 1949 Dodge PW Wrecker, #19-2475 ....$50.00
Texaco, 1953 Ford Tanker, #18-2175 ....$45.00
Texaco Fuel Chief, Mack B-61 Tractor Trailer, #19-2417...$80.00
Texaco Red Star, 1955 Diamond T Wrecker, #19-2427....$40.00
Texaco Star Enterprise, 1955 Diamond T Wrecker, #18-1941 ....$75.00
Tollway & Tunnel, 1957 IHC Wrecker, #19-1439............$55.00

True Value, 1951 Ford Delivery Truck, M, $40.00.

True Value Hardware, 1959 IHC Tractor Trailer, #19-2093 ...$50.00
Tydol Flying A, 1957 International Wrecker, #19-1707...$55.00
United Ice & Coal, B-61 Mack Dump Truck, #18-1850...$150.00
US Army Ambulance, 1949 Chevrolet, #19-1388 ....$35.00
Valley Asphalt, 1960 Mack B-61 Dump Truck, #19-1958 ..$60.00
Wayne Oil, 1951 Ford Fuel Tanker, #19-1015 ....$40.00
White Motor Co, 1953 White Stake Truck, #19-2084.....$55.00
Winchester, 1957 International Box, #18-1319 ....$60.00
Wolf's Head Motor Oil, 1951 Ford DGV, #19-1132 ....$35.00
Wonder Bread, 1949 Chevrolet, #19-1493 ....$32.00
Yellow Freight Lines, 1953 Ford DGV, #19-1432..............$45.00

SPEC-CAST

Allied Van Lines, Biplane, #37502.................................$55.00
Allis Chalmers, #1, Lockheed Vega, #35023....................$35.00
American Airlines, DC-3 Airplane, #45013....................$35.00

American Airlines, Lockheed Orion, #42511 .... $35.00
American Airlines, 1935 Ford Pickup, #13011 .... $25.00
Babe Ruth w/Santa, 1957 Ford Convertible, #56009 .... $40.00
Babe Ruth 60 Home Runs, 1936 Dodge Panel Van, #74002.. $40.00
Baby Duck, P-51 Mustang, #47034 .... $50.00
Bachmann Trains, Ford Trimotor Airplane, #49017 .... $35.00
Bad Boys of Bonneville, 1940 Ford Convertible, #427500... $20.00
Bad Boys of Bonneville, 1955 Chevy Convertible,
   #418000 .... $15.00
Baseball VII, New York Yankees, 1937 Ford Sedan, #173510... $30.00
Campbell's Soup, #1, Lockheed Vega, #35005 .... $40.00
Conoco Oil Co, Lockheed Vega, #35030 .... $45.00
Dairy Queen, Blimp, #36043 .... $25.00
Exxon, F4U Corsair, #47501 .... $75.00
Exxon Tiger Spirit, P-38 Lightning, #41007 .... $40.00
Football VII, Dallas Cowboys, 1937 Ford Sedan, #17103. $28.00
Football VIII, Baltimore Colts, 1937 Ford Sedan, #17119.. $28.00
Football VIII, New York Jets, 1937 Ford Sedan, #17125 .. $28.00
Football VIII, Washington Redskins, 1937 Ford Sedan,
   #17114 .... $28.00
Gentle Annie, P-38 Lightning, #41003 .... $40.00
Goodyear 50th Anniversary, Blimp, #36000 .... $50.00
Happy Jack's Go Buggy, P-38 Lightning, #41005 .... $40.00
Harley-Davidson, 1940 Ford Pickup, #97901 .... $20.00
Harley-Davidson, 1957 Dodge Pickup, #97901 .... $20.00
Harley-Davidson (Smith HD), 1955 Chevy Sedan, #99209 .. $25.00
Heinz '57, DC-3 Airplane, #45028 .... $40.00
Hot Wheels, Blimp, #36009 .... $35.00
Humble Oil, Twinbeech D-18, #48504 .... $40.00
JI Case, Hot Air Balloon, #ZJD761 .... $28.00
Lifesavers, Blimp, #36004 .... $50.00
Lionel, Biplane, #291000 .... $85.00
Pappy Boyington, P-40 Warhawk, #44006 .... $50.00
Penn State Nittany Lions, 1937 Ford Convertible, #16004 .. $35.00
Pennzoil, Biplane, #37550 .... $35.00
Pennzoil, Hot Air Balloon, #36033 .... $35.00
Pepsi-Cola, Ford Trimotor Airplane, #49014 .... $35.00
Pepsi-Cola, Lockheed Vega, #35036 .... $60.00
Phillips 66, DC-3 Airplane, #45009 .... $45.00
Phillips 66, Twinbeech D-18, #48505 .... $45.00
Planter Peanuts, Blimp, #36013 .... $25.00

Radio Flyer, Biplane, #313000 .... $40.00
Shell Oil Co, #4, Lockheed Orion, #42502 .... $45.00
Shell Oil Co, 1957 Chevy Convertible, #76019 .... $25.00
Signal Oil, Lockheed Vega, #35018 .... $35.00
State Farm Insurance, 1955 Chevy Convertible, #55050 . $50.00
Swiss Valley Farms, 1930s Steel Tanker, #38522 .... $45.00

Sunsweet, 1929 Ford, 75th Anniversary, #1012, 1992, M, $35.00.

Texaco, Model A Ford Pickup, Liberty Classics, MIB, $60.00.

Toy Farmer, Lockheed Vega, #35039 .... $40.00
TWA, Vega Plane, #35044 .... $45.00
University of Iowa Basketball, Blimp, #36044 .... $35.00
USAF Shangrila, P-51 Mustang, #47036 .... $50.00
USMC Ghost Rider, F4U Corsair, #47518 .... $50.00

Dinky

Dinky diecasts were made by Meccano (Britain) as early as 1933, but high on the list of many of today's collectors are those from the decades of the '50s and '60s. They made commercial vehicles, firefighting equipment, farm toys, and heavy equipment as well as classic cars that were the epitome of high style, such as the #157 Jaguar XK120, produced from the mid-'50s through the

Quaker State Racing, 1929 Ford, Liberty Classics, M, $25.00.

early '60s. Some Dinkys were made in France; since 1979 no toys have been produced in Great Britain. Values are for examples mint and in the original packaging unless noted otherwise.

See also Soldiers.

#14C, Coventry Climax Fork Lift Truck, EX (orig box), A, $135.00.

#100, Lady Penelope's Fab 1, luminous pk	$400.00
#100, Lady Penelope's Fab 1, pk	$250.00
#101, Sunbeam Alpine	$175.00
#101, Thunderbird II & IV, gr	$300.00
#101, Thunderbird II & IV, metallic gr	$400.00
#102, Joe's Car	$135.00
#102, MG Midget	$250.00
#104, Spectrum Pursuit Vehicle	$200.00
#105, Triumph TR2	$200.00
#106, Austin Atlantic, bl or blk	$150.00
#106, Austin Atlantic, pk	$350.00
#106, Prisoner Mini Moke	$260.00
#106, Thunderbird II & IV	$120.00
#107, Sunbeam Alpine	$150.00
#108, MG Midget	$200.00
#108, Sam's Car, gold, red or bl	$160.00
#108, Sam's Car, silver	$120.00
#109, Aston Healey 100	$160.00
#109, Gabriel Model T Ford	$150.00
#110, Aston Martin DB5	$110.00
#111, Cinderella's Coach	$50.00
#111, Triumph TR2	$160.00
#112, Austin Healey Sprite	$125.00
#112, Purdey's Triumph TR7	$75.00
#113, MGB	$110.00
#114, Triumph Spitfire, gray, gold or red	$125.00
#114, Triumph Spitfire, purple	$170.00
#115, Plymouth Fury	$125.00
#116, Volvo 1800S	$100.00
#117, Four Berth Caravan	$60.00
#120, Happy Cab	$60.00
#120, Jaguar E-Type	$110.00
#121, Goodwood Racing Gift Set	$2,000.00

#122, Touring Gift Set	$2,000.00
#122, Volvo 265 Estate Car	$50.00
#123, Mayfair Gift Set	$3,000.00
#123, Princess 2200 HL	$60.00
#124, Rolls Royce Phantom V	$80.00
#125, Fun A'Hoy Set	$250.00
#128, Mercedes Benz 600	$80.00
#129, MG Midget	$400.00
#129, VW 1200 Sedan	$80.00
#130, Ford Consul Corsair	$85.00
#131, Cadillac El Dorado	$150.00
#131, Jaguar E-Type, 2+2	$150.00
#132, Ford 40-RV	$60.00
#132, Packard Convertible	$165.00
#133, Cunningham C-5R	$130.00
#134, Triumph Vitesse	$100.00
#135, Triumph 2000	$100.00
#136, Vauxhall Viva	$80.00
#137, Plymouth Fury	$130.00
#138, Hillman Imp	$100.00
#139, Ford Cortina	$115.00
#139a, Hudson Commodore Sedan, dual colors	$350.00
#139a, Hudson Commodore Sedan, solid colors	$225.00
#139a, US Army Staff Car	$350.00
#140, Morris 1100	$80.00
#141, Vauxhall Victor	$80.00
#142, Jaguar Mark 10	$100.00
#143, Ford Capri	$100.00
#144, VW 1500	$100.00
#145, Singer Vogue	$100.00
#146, Daimler V8	$100.00
#147, Cadillac 62	$100.00
#148, Ford Fairlane, gr	$125.00
#148, Ford Fairlane, metallic gr	$225.00
#149, Citroen Dyane	$50.00
#149, Sports Car Gift Set	$1,800.00
#150, Rolls Royce Silver Wraith	$100.00
#151, Triumph 1800 Saloon	$150.00
#151, Vauxhall Victor 101	$100.00
#152, Rolls Royce Phantom V	$85.00
#153, Aston Martin	$100.00
#153, Standard Vanguard-Spats	$145.00
#154, Ford Taunus 17M	$85.00
#155, Ford Anglia	$120.00
#156, Mechanized Army Set	$5,000.00
#156, Rover 75, dual colors	$300.00

#157-G, Jaguar XK120, 1954, M, $150.00. (Photo courtesy Dana Johnson)

#156, Rover 75, solid colors.................................$150.00
#156, Saab 96...$100.00
#157, BMW 2000 Tilux..$100.00
#158, Riley..$140.00
#158, Rolls Royce Silver Shadow...........................$100.00
#159, Ford Cortina MKII.......................................$100.00
#159, Morris Oxford, dual colors..........................$300.00
#159, Morris Oxford, solid colors.........................$140.00
#160, Austin A30..$125.00
#160, Mercedes Benz 250 SE..................................$90.00
#161, Austin Somerset, dual colors......................$300.00
#161, Austin Somerset, solid colors.....................$150.00
#161, Ford Mustang...$100.00
#162, Ford Zephyr...$135.00
#162, Triumph 1300...$85.00
#163, Bristol 450 Coupe......................................$100.00
#163, VW 1600 TL, metallic bl.............................$150.00
#163, VW 1600 TL, red...$75.00
#164, Ford Zodiac MKIV, bronze...........................$200.00
#164, Ford Zodiac MKIV, silver............................$100.00
#164, Vauxhall Cresta..$125.00
#165, Ford Capri...$90.00
#165, Humber Hawk..$150.00
#166, Renault R16..$60.00
#166, Sunbeam Rapier...$135.00
#167, AC Acceca, all cream...................................$300.00
#167, AC Acceca, dual colors................................$140.00
#168, Ford Escort..$100.00
#168, Singer Gazelle..$140.00
#169, Fire Corsair...$100.00
#169, Studebaker Golden Hawk.............................$160.00
#170, Ford Fordor, dual colors.............................$300.00
#170, Ford Fordor, solid colors...........................$125.00
#170, Lincoln Continental....................................$120.00
#170m, Ford Fordor US Army Staff Car....................$350.00
#171, Austin 1800..$100.00
#171, Hudson Commodore, dual colors.....................$350.00
#172, Fiat 2300 Station Wagon...............................$75.00
#172, Studebaker Land Cruiser, dual colors...........$300.00
#172, Studebaker Land Cruiser, solid colors..........$165.00
#173, Nash Rambler...$110.00
#173, Pontiac Parisienne.......................................$85.00
#174, Mercury Cougar...$85.00
#175, Cadillac El Dorado......................................$100.00
#175, Hillman Minx..$140.00
#176, Austin A105, cream or gray...........................$150.00
#176, Austin A105, cream w/bl roof, or gray w/red roof.$250.00
#176, Austin A105, gray..$150.00
#176, NSU R80, metallic bl...................................$180.00
#176, NSU R80, metallic red....................................$80.00
#177, Opel Kapitan..$100.00
#178, Mini Clubman..$60.00
#178, Plymouth Plaza, bl w/wht roof......................$400.00
#178, Plymouth Plaza, pk, gr or 2-tone bl..............$150.00
#179, Opel Commodore...$70.00
#179, Studebaker President...................................$170.00
#180, Rover 3500 Sedan..$40.00
#181, Volkswagen, gr...$125.00

#181, VW..$100.00
#182, Porsche 356A Coupe, cream, red or bl.............$130.00
#182, Porsche 356A Coupe, dual colors...................$325.00
#183, Fiat 600..$100.00
#183, Morris Mini Minor.......................................$100.00
#184, Volvo 122S, red...$130.00
#184, Volvo 122S, wht...$375.00
#185, Alpha Romeo 1900...$125.00
#186, Mercedes Benz 200.......................................$100.00
#187, De Tomaso Mangusta 5000................................$75.00
#187, Volkswagen Karmann-Ghia Coupe......................$135.00
#188, Ford Berth Caravan.......................................$60.00
#188, Jensen FF..$75.00
#189, Lamborghini Marzal..$65.00
#189, Triumph Herald...$120.00
#191, Dodge Royal Sedan, cream w/bl flash...............$300.00
#191, Dodge Royal Sedan, cream w/brn flash, or gr w/blk
    flash...$170.00
#192, Desoto Fireflite..$165.00
#192, Range Rover...$50.00

#193, Rambler Cross Country, 1961, M, $95.00.
(Photo courtesy Dana Johnson)

#194, Bentley S Coupe..$130.00
#195, Range Rover Fire Chief..................................$60.00
#196, Holden Special Sedan....................................$75.00
#197, Austin Countryman, orange............................$325.00
#197, Morris Mini Traveller.................................$100.00
#197, Morris Mini Traveller, dk gr & brn...............$400.00
#197, Morris Mini Traveller, lime gr....................$300.00
#198, Rolls Royce Phantom V..................................$115.00
#199, Austin Countryman, bl.................................$115.00
#200, Matra 630..$75.00
#201, Plymouth Stock Car.......................................$75.00
#201, Racing Car Set..$750.00
#202, Customized Land Rover...................................$50.00
#202, Fiat Abarth 2000..$50.00
#203, Customized Range Rover..................................$50.00
#204, Ferrari..$55.00
#205, Talbot Labo, in bubble pkg...........................$325.00
#206, Customized Corvette Stingray.........................$70.00
#207, Triumph TR7...$50.00
#208, VW Porsche 914...$65.00
#210, Alfa Romeo 33..$65.00
#210, Vanwall, in bubble pkg................................$200.00
#211, Triumph TR7...$80.00
#213, Ford Capri...$75.00

#214, Hillman Imp Rally $100.00
#215, Ford GT Racing Car $70.00
#216, Ferrari Dino..$70.00
#217, Alfa Romeo Scarabo $50.00
#218, Lotus Europa $65.00
#219, Jaguar XJS Coupe $65.00
#220, Ferrari P5..$55.00
#221, Corvette Stingray..$60.00
#222, Hesketh Racing Car, dk bl............................$60.00
#222, Hesketh Racing Car, Olympus Camera.............$100.00
#223, McLaren M8A Can-Am..................................$50.00
#224, Mercedes Benz C111.....................................$55.00
#225, Lotus Formula 1 Racer...................................$55.00
#226, Ferrari 312/B2...$50.00
#227, Beach Bunny..$55.00
#228, Super Sprinter $60.00

#232, Alfa Romeo, 1952, EX, $90.00.

#236, Connaught Racer..$125.00
#237, Mercedes Benz Racer $125.00
#238, Jaguar Type-D Racer $140.00
#239, Vanwall Racer..$125.00
#240, Cooper Racer $70.00
#240, Dinky Way Gift Set $130.00
#241, Lotus Racer $80.00
#241, Silver Jubilee Taxi...$50.00
#242, Ferrari Racer..$85.00
#243, BRM Racer..$80.00
#243, Volvo Police Racer...$50.00
#244, Plymouth Police Racer...................................$50.00
#245, Superfast Gift Set...$225.00
#246, International Car Gift Set $235.00
#249, Racing Car Gift Set..$1,500.00
#249, Racing Car Gift Set, in bubble pkg..................$1,800.00
#250, Mini Cooper Police Car.................................$75.00
#251, USA Police Car, Pontiac $80.00
#252, RCMP Car, Pontiac.......................................$100.00
#254, Austin Taxi, yel...$120.00
#254, Police Range Rover..$65.00
#255, Ford Zodiac Police Car $80.00
#255, Mersey Tunnel Police Van..............................$100.00
#255, Police Mini Clubman.....................................$50.00
#256, Humber Hawk Police Car...............................$140.00
#257, Nash Rambler Candian Fire Chief Car................$100.00
#258, USA Police Car, Cadillac, Desoto, Dodge or Ford...$150.00
#259, Bedford Fire Engine $130.00
#260, Royal Mail Van..$160.00

#260, VW Deutsch Bundepost $185.00
#261, Ford Taunus Polizei $275.00
#261, Telephone Service Van....................................$150.00
#262, VW Swiss Post PTT Car, casting #129 ....$250.00
#262, VW Swiss Post PTT Car, casting #181, minimum value..$600.00
#263, Airport Fire Rescue Tender.............................$70.00
#263, Superior Criterion Ambulance........................$115.00
#264, RCMP Patrol Car, Cadillac.............................$175.00
#264, RCMP Patrol Car, Fairlane $135.00
#265, Plymouth Taxi..$170.00
#266, ERF Fire Tender $75.00
#266, ERF Fire Tender, Falck $100.00
#266, Plymouth Taxi, Metro Cab..............................$150.00
#267, Paramedic Truck..$75.00
#267, Superior Cadillac Ambulance..........................$100.00
#268, Range Rover Ambulance.................................$60.00
#268, Renault Dauphine Mini Cab $135.00
#269, Ford Transit Police Accident Unit $60.00
#269, Ford Transit Police Accident Unit, Faulk Zonen....$60.00
#269, Jaguar Motorway Police Car.............................$140.00
#270, AA Motorcycle Patrol $75.00
#270, Ford Panda Police Car $70.00
#271, Ford Transit Fire, Appliance $75.00
#271, Ford Transit Fire, Falck $150.00
#271, TS Motorcycle Patrol $265.00
#272, ANNB Motorcycle Patrol $300.00
#272, Police Accident Unit......................................$60.00
#273, RAC Patrol Mini Van......................................$165.00
#274, Ford Transit Ambulance $50.00
#275, Brink's Armoured Car, no bullion $75.00
#275, Brink's Armoured Car, w/gold bullion.................$200.00
#275, Brink's Armoured Car, w/Mexican bullion..........$1,000.00
#276, Airport Fire Tender...$100.00
#276, Ford Transit Ambulance $60.00
#277, Police Range Rover...$60.00
#277, Superior Criterion Ambulance.........................$115.00

#278, Plymouth Yellow Cab, $60.00.

#278, Vauxhall Victor Ambulance...............................$100.00
#279, Aveling Barford Diesel Roller............................$80.00
#280, Midland Mobile Bank......................................$140.00

#281, Fiat 2300 Pathe News Camera Car	$175.00
#281, Military Hovercraft	$65.00
#282, Austin 1800 Taxi	$85.00
#282, Land Rover Fire, Appliance	$60.00
#282, Land Rover Fire, Falck	$80.00
#283, BOAC Coach	$130.00
#283, Single-Decker Bus	$80.00
#284, London Austin Taxi	$70.00
#285, Merryweather Fire Engine	$80.00
#285, Merryweather Fire Engine, Falck	$150.00
#286, Ford Transit Fire, Falck	$160.00
#288, Superior Cadillac Ambulance	$85.00
#288, Superior Cadillac Ambulance, Falck	$150.00
#289, Routemaster Bus, Esso, purple	$750.00
#289, Routemaster Bus, Esso, red	$100.00
#289, Routemaster Bus, Festival of London Stores	$200.00
#289, Routemaster Bus, Madame Tussaud's	$150.00
#289, Routemaster Bus, Silver Jubilee	$40.00
#289, Routemaster Bus, Tern Shirts or Schwepps	$150.00
#290, Double-Decker Bus	$150.00
#290, SRN-6 Hovercraft	$60.00
#291, Atlantean City Bus	$70.00
#292, Atlantean City Bus, Regent or Ribble	$150.00
#293, Swiss Postal Bus	$60.00
#295, Atlantean City Bus, Yellow Pages	$70.00
#296, Duple Luxury Coach	$50.00
#296, Police Accident Unit	$100.00
#297, Silver Jubilee Bus, National or Woolworth	$60.00
#298, Emergency Services Gift Set, minimum value	$8,000.00
#299, Crash Squad Gift Set	$80.00
#299, Motorway Services Gift Set, minimum value	$700.00
#299, Post Office Services Gift Set, minimum value	$650.00
#300, London Scene Gift Set	$85.00
#302, Emergency Squad Gift Set	$100.00
#303, Commando Gift Set	$120.00
#304, Fire Rescue Gift Set	$120.00
#305, David Brown Tractor	$85.00
#308, Leyland 384 Tractor	$75.00
#309, Star Trek Gift Set	$150.00
#319, Week's Tipping Farm Trailer	$40.00
#320, Halesowen Harvest Trailer	$60.00
#321, Massey-Harris Manure Spreader	$60.00
#322, Disc Harrow	$50.00
#323, Triple Gang Mower	$50.00
#324, Hay Rake	$50.00
#325, David Brown Tractor & Harrow	$135.00
#340, Land Rover	$85.00
#341, Land Rover Trailer	$40.00
#342, Austin Mini Moke	$70.00
#342, Moto-Cart	$75.00
#344, Estate Car	$95.00
#344, Land Rover Pickup	$50.00
#350, Tony's Mini Moke	$150.00
#351, UFO Interceptor	$80.00
#352, Ed Straker's Car, red	$100.00
#352, Ed Straker's Car, yel or gold-plated	$140.00
#353, Shado 2 Mobile	$85.00
#354, Pink Panther	$60.00

#355, Lunar Roving Vehicle	$60.00
#357, Klingon Battle Cruiser	$80.00
#358, USS Enterprise	$80.00
#359, Eagle Transporter	$75.00
#360, Eagle Freighter	$75.00
#361, Galactic War Chariot	$75.00
#362, Trident Star Fighter	$75.00
#363, Cosmic Zygon Patroller, for Marks & Spencer	$70.00
#364, NASA Space Shuttle, w/booster	$100.00
#366, NASA Space Shuttle, w/no booster	$60.00
#367, Space Battle Cruiser	$80.00
#368, Zygon Marauder	$80.00
#370, Dragster Set	$70.00
#371, USS Enterprise, sm version	$60.00
#372, Klingon Battle Cruiser, sm version	$60.00
#380, Convoy Skip Truck	$30.00
#381, Convoy Farm Truck	$30.00
#382, Wheelbarrow	$25.00
#382 Convoy Dumper	$30.00
#383, Convoy NCL Truck	$40.00
#384, Convoy Fire Rescue Truck	$35.00
#384, Grass Cutter	$25.00
#384, Sack Truck	$25.00
#385, Convoy Royal Mail Truck	$40.00
#386, Lawn Mower	$100.00
#389, Med Artillery Tractor	$100.00
#390, Customized Transit Van	$50.00
#398, Farm Equipment Gift Set	$2,000.00
#399, Farm Tractor & Trailer Set	$200.00
#400, BEV Electric Truck	$70.00
#401, Coventry-Climax Fork Lift, orange	$70.00
#401, Coventry-Climax Fork Lift, red	$500.00

#402, Bedford Coca-Cola Truck, $250.00.

#404, Conveyancer Fork Lift	$50.00
#405, Universal Jeep	$50.00
#406, Commer Articulated Truck	$165.00
#407, Ford Transit	$60.00
#408, Big Ben Lorry, bl & yel, or bl & orange	$350.00
#408, Big Ben Lorry, maroon & fawn	$200.00

#408, Big Ben Lorry, pk & cream $2,000.00	#480, Bedford Van, Kodak...$160.00
#409, Bedford Articulated Lorry $175.00	#481, Bedford Van, Ovaltine..$160.00
#410, Bedford Van, Danish Post or Simpsons.................$125.00	#482, Bedford Van, Dinky Toys.......................................$175.00
#410, Bedford Van, MJ Hire, Marley or Collectors' Gazette...$60.00	#485, Ford Model T w/Santa Claus.................................$150.00
#410, Bedford Van, Royal Mail...$40.00	#486, Morris Oxford, Dinky Beats....................................$150.00
#411, Bedford Truck $140.00	#490, Electric Dairy Van, Express Dairy..........................$100.00
#412, Bedford Van AA...$60.00	#491, Electric Dairy Van, NCB or Job Dairies $150.00
#413, Austin Covered Wagon, lt & dk bl, or red & tan .$650.00	#492, Election Mini Van $350.00
#413, Austin Covered Wagon, maroon & cream, or med & lt	#492, Loudspeaker Van..$125.00
bl...$200.00	#500, Citroen 2-CV...$65.00
#413, Austin Covered Wagon, red & gray, or bl or cream ..$450.00	#501, Citroen Police, DS-19 ....$100.00
#414, Dodge Tipper, all colors other than Royal Blue $100.00	#501, Foden Diesel Eight-Wheel, 2nd cab.....................$525.00
#414, Dodge Tipper, Royal Blue $175.00	#501, Foden Diesel 8-Wheel, 2nd cab $600.00
#416, Ford Transit Van $50.00	#502, Foden Flat Truck, 1st or 2nd cab....................$1,000.00
#416, Ford Transit Van, 1,000,000 Transits....................$200.00	#503, Foden Flat Truck, 1st cab $1,200.00
#417, Ford Transit Van $50.00	#503, Foden Flat Truck, 2nd cab, bl & orange...............$400.00
#417, Leyland Comet Lorry...$175.00	#503, Foden Flat Truck, 2nd cab, bl & yel................$1,200.00
#419, Leyland Comet Cement Lorry.................................$250.00	#503, Foden Flat Truck, 2nd cab, 2-tone gr $3,000.00
#420, Leyland Forward Control Lorry $125.00	#504, Foden Tanker, red $800.00
#421, Hindle-Smart Electric Lorry $100.00	#504, Foden Tanker, 1st cab, 2-tone bl $500.00
#422, Thames Flat Truck, bright gr $200.00	#504, Foden Tanker, 2nd cab, red $600.00
#422, Thames Flat Truck, dk gr or red $100.00	#504, Foden Tanker, 2nd cab, 2-tone bl $3,500.00
#425, Bedford TK Coal Lorry $160.00	#505, Foden Flat Truck w/Chains, 1st cab $3,000.00
#428, Trailer, lg $50.00	#505, Foden Flat Truck w/Chains, 2nd cab..................$450.00
#429, Trailer $45.00	#505, Maserati 2000 ....$135.00
#430, Breakdown Lorry, red & gr $1,000.00	#506, Aston Martin $125.00
#430, Commer Breakdown Lorry, all colors other than tan &	#509, Fiat 850 ....$55.00
gr..$1,000.00	#510, Peugeot 204 ....$60.00
#430, Commer Breakdown Lorry, tan & gr.....................$175.00	#511, Guy 4-Ton Lorry, red, gr or brn $900.00
#430, Johnson Dumper $60.00	#511, Guy 4-Ton Lorry, 2-tone bl................................$350.00
#432, Foden Tipper $60.00	#512, Guy Flat Truck, all colors other than bl or red......$750.00
#432, Guy Warrior Flat Truck $400.00	#512, Guy Flat Truck, bl or red $400.00
#433, Guy Flat Truck w/Tailboard...................................$350.00	#512, Lesko Kart $125.00
#434, Bedford Crash Truck $125.00	#513, Guy Flat Truck w/Tailboard..................................$400.00
#435, Bedford TK Tipper, gray or yel cab $100.00	#514, Alfa Romeo Giulia..$85.00
#435, Bedford TK Tipper, wht, silver & bl.......................$250.00	#514, Guy Van, Lyons $2,000.00
#436, Atlas COPCO Compressor Lorry..............................$100.00	#514, Guy Van, Slumberland $600.00
#437, Muir Hill Loader $50.00	#514, Guy Van, Spratt's $600.00
#438, Ford D 800 Tipper, opening doors $50.00	#514, Guy Van, Weetabix..$3,500.00
#439, Ford D 800 Snow Plough & Tipper $85.00	#515, Ferrari 250 GT $135.00
#440, Mobilgas Tanker $175.00	#517, Renault R8 ....$95.00
#441, Petrol Tanker, Castrol..$175.00	#518, Renault 4L $50.00
#442, Land Rover Breakdown Crane $50.00	#519, Simca 100...$50.00
#442, Land Rover Breakdown Crane, Falck.....................$70.00	#520, Chrysler New Yorker...$225.00
#442, Petrol Tanker, Esso..$175.00	#521, Bedford Articulated Lorry $175.00
#443, Petrol Tanker, National Benzole $175.00	#522, Big Bedford Lorry, bl & yel...................................$350.00
#449, Chevrolet El Camino Pickup $120.00	#522, Big Bedford Lorry, maroon & fawn......................$200.00
#449, Johnson Road Sweeper $70.00	#522, Citroen DS-19 ....$225.00
#450, Bedford TK Box Van, Castrol..................................$150.00	#523, Simca 1500..$60.00
#451, Johnston Road Sweeper, opening doors $70.00	#524, Panhard 24-CT $75.00
#451, Trojan Van, Dunlop...$175.00	#524, Renault Dauphine..$145.00
#452, Trojan Van, Chivers...$175.00	#525, Peugeot 403-U $90.00
#454, Trojan Van Cydrax $175.00	#526, Mercedes-Benz 190-SL $180.00
#455, Trojan Van, Brooke Bond Tea $175.00	#527, Alfa Romeo 1900..$110.00
#470, Austin Van, Shell-BP $175.00	#529, Vespa 2-CV $125.00
#475, Ford Model T $100.00	#530, Citroen DS-23 ....$60.00
#476, Morris Oxford $100.00	#531, Leyland Comet Lorry, all colors other than bl or brn...$250.00
#477, Parsley's Car $100.00	#531, Leyland Comet Lorry, bl or brn $500.00

#531 Leyland Comet Lorry, orange and blue, $250.00.

#532, Bedford Comet Lorry w/Tailboard	$250.00
#532, Lincoln Premiere	$225.00
#533, Leyland Cement Wagon	$200.00
#533, Peugeot	$100.00
#534, BMW 1500	$90.00
#535, Citroen 2-CV	$60.00
#538, Buick Roadmaster	$300.00
#538, Renault 16-TX	$45.00
#539, Citroen ID-19	$11.00
#540, Opel Kadett	$65.00
#541, Simca Versailles	$130.00
#542, Simca Taxi	$125.00
#543, Renault Floride	$125.00
#545, De Soto Diplomat	$150.00
#546, Austin-Healey	$200.00
#548, Fiat 1800 Familiare	$100.00
#550, Chrysler Saratoga	$275.00
#551, Ford Taunus, Polizei	$175.00
#551, Rolls Royce	$285.00
#551, Trailer	$60.00
#552, Chevrolet Corvair	$120.00
#555, Fire Engine, w/extension ladder	$135.00
#555, Ford Thunderbird	$200.00
#556, Citroen Ambulance	$150.00
#558, Citroen	$95.00
#559, Ford Taunus	$95.00
#561, Blaw-Knox Bulldozer	$100.00
#561, Blaw-Knox Bulldozer, plastic	$500.00
#561, Citroen Van, Gervais	$225.00
#561, Renault Mail Car	$65.00
#562, Muir-Hill Dumper	$80.00
#563, Blaw-Knox Heavy Tractor	$120.00
#563, Estafette Pickup	$90.00
#564, Armagnac Caravan	$70.00
#564, Elevator Loader	$100.00
#566, Citroen Police Van	$130.00
#568, Ladder Truck	$150.00
#569, Dump Truck	$165.00
#570, Peugeot Van	$75.00

#571, Coles Mobile Crane	$140.00
#572, Dump Truck, Berliet	$140.00
#576, Panhard Tanker, Esso	$350.00
#577, Simca Van, Bailly	$200.00
#578, Simca Dump Truck	$165.00
#580, Dump Truck	$135.00
#581, Container Truck, Bailly	$200.00
#581, Horse Box, British Railway	$200.00
#581, Horse Box, Express Horse Van	$800.00
#582, Pullman Car Transporter	$160.00
#584, Covered Truck	$135.00
#585, Dumper	$135.00
#587, Citroen Van, Philips	$110.00
#589, Berliet Wrecker	$135.00
#590, City Road Signs Set	$70.00
#591, AEC Tanker, Shell	$225.00
#591, Country Road Signs Set	$70.00

#592, Esso Station, M (torn box), A, $160.00.

#593, Road Signs Set	$45.00
#595, Crane	$265.00
#595, Traffic Signs Set	$45.00
#597, Fork Lift	$80.00
#601, Austin Para Moke	$85.00
#602, Armoured Command Car	$50.00
#603, Army Personnel, box of 12	$125.00
#604, Land Rover Bomb Disposal Unit	$70.00
#609, 105mm Howitzer & Gun Crew	$50.00
#612, Commando Jeep	$50.00
#615, US Jeep & 105mm Howitzer	$60.00
#616, AEC Articulated Transporter & Tank	$110.00
#617, VW KDF w/Antitank Gun	$75.00
#618, AEC Articulated Transporter & Helicopter	$100.00
#619, Bren Gun Carrier & Antitank Gun	$65.00
#620, Berliet Missile Launcher	$140.00
#621, 3-Ton Army Wagon	$100.00
#622, Bren Gun Carrier	$50.00
#622, 10-Ton Army Truck	$140.00
#623, Army Covered Wagon	$80.00
#625, 6-Pounder Antitank Gun	$40.00

#626, Military Ambulance	$100.00
#640, Bedford Military Truck	$300.00
#641, Army 1-Ton Cargo Truck	$75.00
#642, RAF Pressure Refueller	$130.00
#643, Army Water Carrier	$110.00
#650, Light Tank	$160.00
#651, Centurion Tank	$120.00
#654, Mobile Gun	$50.00
#656, 88mm Gun	$50.00
#660, Tank Transporter	$130.00
#661, Recovery Tractor	$150.00
#662, Static 88mm Gun & Crew	$60.00
#665, Honest John Missile Erector	$175.00
#666, Missile Erector Vehicle w/Corporal Missile & Launching Platform	$350.00
#667, Armoured Patrol Car	$50.00
#667, Missile Servicing Platform Vehicle	$250.00
#668, Foden Army Truck	$50.00
#670, Armoured Car	$65.00
#671, MKI Corvette (boat)	$40.00
#671, Reconnaissance Car	$165.00
#672, OSA Missile Boat	$40.00
#673, Scout Car	$50.00
#674, Austin Champ, olive drab	$60.00
#674, Austin Champ, wht, UN version	$500.00
#674, Coast Guard Missile Launch	$45.00
#675, Motor Patrol Boat	$45.00
#676, Armoured Personnel Carrier	$80.00
#676, Daimler Armoured Car, w/speedwheels	$60.00
#677, Armoured Command Vehicle	$110.00
#677, Task Force Set	$100.00
#678, Air Sea Rescue	$60.00
#680, Ferret Armoured Car	$60.00
#681, DUKW	$60.00
#682, Stalwart Load Carrier	$60.00
#683, Chieftain Tank	$55.00
#686, 25-Pounder Field Gun	$40.00
#687, Convoy Army Truck	$25.00
#687, Trailer	$35.00
#688, Field Artillery Tractor	$60.00
#690, Mobile Antiaircraft Gun	$100.00
#690, Scorpion Tank	$50.00
#691, Striker Antitank Vehicle	$60.00
#692, Leopard Tank	$60.00
#692, 5.5 Med Gun	$60.00
#693, 7.2 Howitzer	$60.00
#694, Hanomag Tank Destroyer	$60.00
#695, Howitzer & Tractor	$250.00
#696, Leopard Antiaircraft Tank	$60.00
#697, 25-Pounder Field Gun Set	$150.00
#698, Tank Transporter & Tank	$230.00
#699, Leopard Recovery Tank	$70.00
#699, Military Gift Set	$400.00
#700, Spitfire MKII RAF Jubilee	$150.00
#701, Shetland Flying Boat	$650.00
#702, DH Comet Jet Airliner	$200.00
#704, Avro York Airliner	$175.00
#705, Viking Airliner	$100.00
#706, Vickers Viscount Airliner, Air France	$150.00
#708, Vickers Viscount Airliner, BEA	$150.00
#710, Beechcraft S35 Bonanza	$85.00
#712, US Army T-42A	$85.00
#715, Beechcraft C-55 Baron	$60.00
#715, Bristol 173 Helicopter	$85.00
#716, Westland Sikorsky Helicopter	$90.00
#717, Boeing 737	$85.00
#718, Hawker Hurricane	$85.00
#719, Spitfire MKII	$85.00
#721, Junkers Stuka	$80.00
#722, Hawker Harrier	$80.00
#723, Hawker Executive Jet	$60.00
#724, Sea King Helicopter	$75.00
#725, Phantom II	$100.00
#726, Messerschmitt, desert camouflage	$100.00
#726, Messerschmitt, gray & gr	$200.00
#727, US Air Force F-4 Phantom II	$300.00
#728, RAF Dominie	$80.00
#729, Multi-Role Combat Aircraft	$75.00
#730, US Navy Phantom	$100.00
#731, SEPECAT Jaguar	$80.00
#731, Twin-Engine Fighter	$60.00
#732, Bell Police Helicopter, M*A*S*H	$100.00
#732, Bell Police Helicopter, wht & bl	$60.00
#733, German Phantom II	$200.00
#733, Lockhead Shooting Star Fighter	$50.00
#734, Submarine Swift	$60.00
#735, Glouster Javelin	$60.00
#736, Bundesmarine Sea King	$90.00
#736, Hawker Hunter	$60.00
#737, P1B Lightning Fighter	$90.00
#738, DH110 Sea Vixen Fighter	$70.00
#739, Zero-Sen	$100.00
#741, Spitfire MKII	$100.00
#749, RAF Avro Vulcan Bomber	$3,500.00
#750, Call Telephone Box	$50.00
#751, Lawn Mower	$100.00
#752, Goods Yard Crane	$70.00
#752, Police Box	$50.00
#755, Standard Lamp, single arm	$30.00
#756, Standard Lamp, dbl arm	$30.00
#760, Pillar Box	$40.00
#766, British Road Signs, Country Set A	$100.00
#767, British Road Signs, Country Set B	$100.00
#768, British Road Signs, Town Set A	$100.00
#769, British Road Signs, Town B	$100.00
#770, Road Signs, set of 12	$150.00
#771, International Road Signs, set of 12	$160.00
#772, British Road Signs, set of 24	$200.00
#773, Traffic Signal	$30.00
#777, Belisha Beacon	$30.00
#781, Petrol Pumping Station, Esso	$100.00
#782, Petrol Pumping Station, Shell	$80.00
#784, Dinky Goods Train Set	$80.00
#785, Service Station	$200.00
#786, Tire Rack	$50.00
#787, Lighting Kit	$40.00

#796, Healy Sports Boat $65.00
#798, Express Passenger Train $170.00
#801, Mini USS Enterprise....................................$60.00
#802, Mini Klingon Cruiser...................................$60.00
#815, Panhard Armoured Tank $150.00
#817, AMX 13-Ton Tank $125.00
#822, M3 Half-Track...$150.00
#893, UNIC Pipe-Line Transporter.......................$275.00
#894, UNIC Boilot Car Transporter $275.00
#900, Building Site Gift Set...............................$1,500.00
#901, Guy 4-Ton Lorry, see #501
#902, Foden Flat Truck, see #502
#903, Foden Flat Truck w/Tailboard, see #503
#905, Foden Flat Truck w/Chains........................$450.00
#911, Guy 4-Ton Lorry, see #511
#912, Guy Flat Truck, see #512
#913, Guy Flat Truck w/Tailboard, see #513
#914, AEC Articulated Lorry $150.00
#915, AEC Flat Trailer $100.00
#917, Guy Van, Spratts......................................$350.00
#917, Mercedes Benz Truck & Trailer $120.00
#917, Mercedes Benz Truck & Trailer, Munsterland.......$300.00
#918, Guy Van, Ever Ready.................................$500.00
#919, Guy Van, Golden Shred.........................$1,000.00
#920, Guy Warrior Van, Heinz $3,000.00
#921, Bedford Articulated Lorry $175.00
#922, Big Bedford Lorry......................................$175.00
#923, Big Bedford Van, Heinz Baked Beans can & Heinz 57
    Varieties $600.00
#923, Big Bedford Van, Heinz Ketchup bottle............$2,000.00
#924, Aveling-Barford Dumper $110.00
#925, Leyland Dump Truck $235.00
#930, Bedford Pallet-Jekta Van, Dinky Toys $250.00
#931, Leyland Comet Lorry, colors other than bl & brn........$200.00
#931, Leyland Comet Lorry, bl & brn $500.00
#932, Leyland Comet Wagon w/Tailboard............$200.00
#933, Leyland Comet Wagon $200.00
#934, Leyland Octopus Wagon, colors other than bl & brn..$300.00
#934, Leyland Octopus Wagon, bl & yel $2,000.00
#936, Leyland 8-Wheel Test Chassis.....................$150.00
#940, Mercedes Benz Truck $85.00
#943, Leyland Octopus Tanker, Esso $300.00
#944, Shell-BP Fuel Tanker..................................$300.00
#944, Shell-BP Fuel Tanker, red wheels.................$500.00
#945, AEC Fuel Tanker, Esso $150.00
#945, AEC Fuel Tanker, Lucas $150.00
#948, Tractor-Trailer, McLean.............................$365.00
#949, Wayne School Bus.....................................$350.00
#950, Foden S20 Fuel Tanker, Burmah $100.00
#950, Foden S20 Fuel Tanker, Shell.....................$100.00
#951, Trailer...$50.00
#952, Vega Major Luxury Coach..........................$140.00
#954, Fire Station $300.00
#954, Vega Major Luxury Coach, no lights.............$130.00
#955, Fire Engine...$140.00
#956, Turntable Fire Escape, Bedford...................$125.00
#956, Turntable Fire Escape, Berliet.....................$225.00
#957, Fire Services Gift Set.................................$600.00

#953, Continental Touring Coach, $425.00.

#958, Snow Plough $260.00
#959, Foden Dump Truck.....................................$175.00
#960, Lorry-Mounted Concrete Mixer....................$125.00
#961, Blaw-Knox Bulldozer, see #561
#961, Vega Major Luxury Coach..........................$250.00
#962, Muir-Hill Dumper.......................................$80.00
#963, Blaw-Knox Heavy Tractor..........................$100.00
#963, Road Grader...$75.00
#964, Elevator Loader...$100.00
#965, Euclid Rear Dump Truck..............................$80.00
#965, Terex Dump Truck.....................................$275.00
#966, Marrel Multi-Bucket Unit............................$130.00
#967, BBC TV Mobile Control Room......................$250.00
#967, Muir-Hill Loader & Trencher........................$80.00
#968, BBC TV Roving Eye Vehicle.........................$260.00
#969, BBC TV Extending Mast Vehicle...................$275.00
#970, Jones Cantilever Crane $100.00
#971, Coles Mobile Crane....................................$145.00
#972, Coles 20-Ton Lorry, mounted crane, yel & blk.....$200.00

#972, Coles 20-Ton Lorry, mounted crane, yellow and
orange, $175.00.

#973, Eaton Yale Tractor Shovel $80.00
#973, Goods Yard Crane......................................$90.00
#974, AEC Hoyner Transporter $110.00

#975, Ruston Bucyrus Excavator $375.00
#976, Michigan Tractor Dozer $75.00
#977, Commercial Servicing Platform Vehicle..............$250.00
#977, Shovel Dozer $75.00
#978, Refuse Wagon $100.00
#979, Racehorse Transporter $400.00
#980, Coles Hydra Truck $85.00
#980, Horse Box, British Railways $200.00
#980, Horse Box Express $800.00
#984, Atlas Digger $85.00
#984, Car Carrier..$225.00
#985, Trailer for Car Carrier..$125.00
#986, Mighty Antar Low Loader w/Propeller $400.00
#987, ABC TV Control Room $375.00
#988, ABC TV Transmitter Van $375.00
#989, Car Carrier, Autotransporters $2,000.00
#990, Pullman Car Transporter w/4 Cars....................$2,500.00
#991, AEC Tanker, Shell Chemicals.............................$225.00
#992, Avro Vulcan Delta Wing Bomber.....................$3,000.00
#994, Loading Ramp for #992..$30.00
#997, Caravelle, Air France $300.00
#998, Bristol Britannia Canadian Pacific......................$300.00
#999, DH Comet Jet...$225.00

Disney

Through the magic of the silver screen, Walt Disney's characters have come to life, and it is virtually impossible to imagine a child growing up without the influence of his genius. As each classic film was introduced, toy manufacturers scurried to fill department store shelves with the dolls, games, battery-ops, and windups that carried the likeness of every member of its cast. Though today it is the toys of the 1930s and 1940s that are bringing exorbitant prices, later toys are certainly collectible as well, as you'll see in our listings. Even characters as recently introduced as Roger Rabbit already have their own cult following.

For more information we recommend *Character Toys and Collectibles, First* and *Second Series,* and *Antique & Collectible Toys, 1870 – 1950,* by David Longest; *Stern's Guide to Disney Collectibles* by Michael Stern (there are three in the series); *The Collector's Encyclopedia of Disneyana* by Michael Stern and David Longest; *Disneyana* by Cecil Munsey (Hawthorne Books, 1974); *Disneyana* by Robert Heide and John Gilman; *Walt Disney's Mickey Mouse Memorabilia* by Hillier and Shine (Abrams Inc., 1986); *Tomart's Disneyana Update Magazine;* and *Elmer's Price Guide to Toys* by Elmer Duellman (L-W Books).

Advisor: Joel J. Cohen (C12).

See also Battery-Operated; Books; Bubble Bath Containers; Character and Promotional Drinking Glasses; Character Clocks and Watches; Chein; Coloring, Activity, and Paint Books; Dakins; Fisher-Price; Games; Lunch Boxes; Marx; Paper Dolls; Pez Dispensers; Pin-Back Buttons; Plastic Figures; Puppets; Puzzles; Ramp Walkers; Records; Sand Toy; Toothbrush Holders; View-Master; Western; Windups, Friction, and Other Mechanicals.

Aladdin, bean bag, Jasmine, 10", M $12.00
Aladdin, figurine gift set, Mattel, 10 figures, MIB $12.00
Aladdin, game, Jasmine Magic Ring Game, 3-D board, EX ..$15.00
Alice in Wonderland, board game, Cadaco, 1984, complete, EXIB..$20.00
Alice in Wonderland, figure, Alice, Japan, 1970s, ceramic, 6", M, M8 ....$35.00
Alice in Wonderland, figure, Mouseketoys (sold only at Disney Parks), M (w/tag)..$20.00
Alice in Wonderland, Tea Time Dishes, Plasco, 1949, M (G box)..$40.00
Babes in Toyland, doll, Toyland Fairy Princess, Uneeda, all orig, 30", NM, from $75 to $95.00
Bambi, figure, Flower, Am Pottery, 1940s, 4½", M, M8....$65.00
Bambi, figure, Nicotoy (Belgium), stuffed polyester, 9", NM ...$20.00
Bambi, figure, Thumper, Am Pottery, 1940s, 4", M, M8..$65.00
Bambi, figure, Thumper's girlfriend, Am Pottery, 4", M, M8 ...$65.00
Bambi, figure, Thumper, pk plastic, Marx, mid-1950s, 2⅜" $75.00
Buzz Lightyear, figure, 12", MIB $115.00
Cinderella, bank, litho tin book-shape, 6", VG $30.00
Cinderella, doll, Storybook Small-Talk by Mattel, MIB, from $125 to...$175.00
Cinderella, figure, Mama Mouse, Shaw, 1950s, 3½", scarce, M, M8..$325.00
Cinderella, game, Walt Disney, 1960s, complete, EX $20.00
Cinderella, rubber stamp kit, Walt Disney, 10 foam-backed stamps w/purple ink pad, EXIB.............................$18.00
Davy Crockett, powder horn, Daisy #1810, MIB.............$70.00
Disney, bank, 2nd National Duck Bank, Chein, press Donald's tongue & coin disappears, litho tin, 6½", VG, A....$150.00
Disney, Disney's Adventureland Game, Parker Bros, 1956, MIB...$35.00

Disney, globe, attributed to Rand McNally, 1950s, $225.00. (Photo courtesy Joel Cohen)

Disney, Magic Erasable Pictures, Transogram, 1950s, unused, NMIB...$75.00
Disney, Movie Studio To Color & Erect, WDP, 1939, complete, EX (EX box) $250.00

Disney, top, Chein/WDP, 1950s, litho tin w/music notes & characters playing various instruments, EX........................$85.00

Disney, top, Mickey, Minnie, Baby Mickey, Baby Minnie, Donald Duck & Horace Horsecollar, 9" dia, VG............$150.00

Disney, Walt Disney Character Carousel, tin w/celluloid characters, Linemar, 7x6" dia, MIB.................................$3,500.00

Disney, Walt Disney's Television Playhouse, Marx/WDP, 1950s, complete, rare, NM (EX box), A............................$675.00

Disneyland, Haunted Mansion in Disneyland Secret Panel Box, 1960s, wood w/2 secret compartments, 3½x5½", EX, M8..$100.00

Disneyland, Melody Player, WDP, 1950s, litho tin, crank action, EX $200.00

Disneyland, Musical Map, Mattel, 1950s, opens up to 6-panel map w/5 uncut 78 rpm picture records, NM $85.00

Disneyland, pop gun, WDP, 1950s, litho tin, missing cork, 6", VG $40.00

Disneyland, Pop-Up Place Mat, 1950s-60s, paper litho, w/stand-up of ea park land, 14x11", EX $50.00

Disneyland, Safety Blocks, Halsam/WDE, complete, NMIP.$125.00

Disneyland, tea set, 1950s, litho tin w/yel border, 14 pcs, MIB, D10 ....$250.00

Disneyland, TV tray, 1950s, litho tin w/map of the park, 12½x17", rare, EX, M8.......................................$100.00

Disneyland, yo-yo, 1980s, plastic w/decal seal, butterfly shape, MIP $20.00

Donald Duck, bank, Scrooge McDuck ceramic figure, EX.$25.00

Donald Duck, doll, Knickerbocker, compo w/felt vest, 9", NM $1,200.00

Donald Duck, doll, Knickerbocker, 1930s, Donald as drum major, rare, NM......................................$1,600.00

Donald Duck, doll, Knickerbocker, 1930s, stuffed cloth, 12", NM..$400.00

Donald Duck, figure, Brio Sweden/WDP, 1949, jtd wood, 10", NM (EX box), A $600.00

Donald Duck, figure, Japan, 1930s, bsk, playing violin, 4", NM..$300.00

Donald Duck, figure, Japan, 1930s, bsk, riding tricycle, 3", EX $200.00

Donald Duck, figure, Japan, 1930s, bsk, 2", EX, M8 ....$50.00

Donald Duck, figure, 1930s, jtd celluloid, 3", rare, NM..$450.00

Donald Duck, figure, 1940s, chalkware, NM $45.00

Donald Duck, jack-in-the-box, Spear/WDP, 1940, compo w/cloth body, soft wood box, EX.........................$200.00

Donald Duck, Japan, 1930s, bsk, standing on scooter, 3½", NM $200.00

Donald Duck, Molding & Coloring Set, Model-Craft, complete, EX (EX box) $100.00

Donald Duck, Paint Box, Transogram/WDE, 1930s, red litho tin w/image of Donald & Mickey, NM $75.00

Donald Duck, projector, Stephens Products, 1950s, gray plastic, battery-op, 8", VG, M8...$50.00

Donald Duck, pull toy, NN Hill Brass, Donald pulls bell on axle between wheel, NM $450.00

Donald Duck, sweeper, Ohio Art/WDE, litho wood, EX..$125.00

Donald Duck, sweeper, WDP, 1940s, red litho tin w/wood hdl, EX $175.00

Donald Duck, telephone/bank, NN Hill Brass/WDE 1930s, EX $400.00

Donald Duck, tray, Casey Jr, 1961, VG, $22.00. (Photo courtesy June Moon)

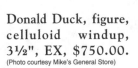

Donald Duck, figure, celluloid windup, 3½", EX, $750.00. (Photo courtesy Mike's General Store)

Dumbo, figurine, Goebel, 1950s, 5", $600.00. (Photo courtesy Joel Cohen)

Donald Duck, figure, Fun-E-Flex, Donald on sled, wood, NM.$1,500.00

Donald Duck, figure, Japan, 1930s, bsk, playing accordion, 4", NM..$300.00

Dumbo, trade card album, Spain, w/200 trade cards & storyline in Spanish, 13x10", EX, A..........................$125.00

Elmer the Elephant, doll, 1930s, stuffed plush w/cloth clothes, musical, EX $125.00

Ferdinand the Bull, bank, Crown Toy & Novelty/WDE, 1938, compo figure, NM..........................$125.00

Ferdinand the Bull, Cut-Outs, WDP, complete, unused, EX...$200.00

Ferdinand the Bull, figure, Japan, 1930s, bsk, 2", NM, M8........$50.00

Ferdinand the Bull, figure, Seiberling Rubber/WDE, EX..$75.00

Ferdinand the Bull, pull toy, NN Hill Brass/WDE, 1938, wood, NM..........................$300.00

Gideon, see Pinocchio

Goofy, car, Pippo Dingo Goofy, Burango #8005, Bugatti w/Goofy as driver, EXIB..........................$115.00

Goofy, doll, Schuco, 1950s, 14", EX, D10..........................$350.00

Goofy, figure, Japan, 1930s, bsk, 3½", EX..........................$135.00

Goofy, handcar, Lionel, 1995, Goofy pumps handcar while Pluto rides on front, AC/DC, MIB..........................$40.00

Goofy, Liberty Goofy, Disney Stores, plush, 13", M (w/M tag)..........................$25.00

Goofy, slippers, Disney Stores, sz 11½, EX..........................$50.00

Goofy, talker, Worlds of Wonder, mid-1980s, 24", EX....$120.00

Goofy, yo-yo, Festival, 1970s, plastic w/imprint seal, tournament shape, MIP..........................$25.00

Hunchback of Notre Dame, yo-yo, Spectra Star, 1996, plastic w/paper sticker seal, MIP..........................$5.00

Jiminy Cricket, see Pinocchio

Jungle Book, figure, Bagera Jiggler, Baloo Jiggler or Ziggy Jiggler, 1966, MOC, ea..........................$30.00

Lady & the Tramp, doll, Lady, Schuco, 1960s, mohair w/plastic google eyes, 8", NM..........................$250.00

Lady & the Tramp, doll, Tramp, Schuco, 1960s, mohair w/plastic google eyes, 8", NM..........................$250.00

Lady & the Tramp, figure, Lady, Hagen-Renaker, 1950s, porcelain, 1", M, M8..........................$35.00

Lady & the Tramp, figure, puppy, Hagen-Renaker, 1950s, porcelain, 1" L, M, M8..........................$50.00

Lady & the Tramp, figure set, Lady, Tramp & Beaver, Magic Memories, 1970s, bsk, 5½", M, M8..........................$60.00

Lady & the Tramp, pull toy, Lady, WDP, 1955, gr platform, NM..........................$125.00

Little Mermaid, yo-yo, Ariel, Spectra Star, 1989, plastic w/imprinted seal, MIP..........................$5.00

Ludwig Von Drake, figure set, Marx, 1960s, NMIB..........$95.00

Ludwig Von Drake, Needlepoint Set, Hasbro, 1961, complete, MIB (sealed)..........................$35.00

Ludwig Von Drake, squeeze toy, WDP, 1960s, vinyl, NM...$30.00

Mary Poppins, doll, Horsman, 1971, 1st edition, 12", MIB, Y1..........................$125.00

Mary Poppins, doll, Horsman, 1973, 2nd edition, 11", MIB, Y1..........................$75.00

Mary Poppins, figure, 1964 premium, figure shoots out of chimney, bl plastic, 4", scarce, MIP..........................$50.00

MGM Studios, yo-yo, 1990s, brass w/imprint seal, tournament shape, MIP..........................$12.00

Mickey Mouse, banjo, Noble & Cooley, NM..........................$400.00

Mickey Mouse, bank, Happynak, Post Office, litho tin, NM..$125.00

Mickey Mouse, bank, Mickey Mouse Post Office, litho tin, 6", NM..........................$65.00

Mickey Mouse, bank, suitcase shape w/image of Mickey, litho tin, 3", M..........................$750.00

Mickey Mouse, baton, compo head, WD label on bottom, VG..........................$300.00

Mickey Mouse, blackboard, Richmond School Furniture, mk WD, 1930s, EX..........................$200.00

Mickey Mouse, bow & arrow, WDE, 1930s, MOC..........$350.00

Mickey Mouse, Bubble Buster, Kilgore, 1930s, NP CI w/paper litho decal, complete w/Bubblets, 8", EX (EX box), A..........................$350.00

Mickey Mouse, car, Japan, celluloid, 10½", rare, EX, A, $2,850.00.

Mickey Mouse, doll, Dean's Rag, orig tag, 5", EX...........$500.00

Mickey Mouse, doll, Dean's Rag, 8", NM..........................$900.00

Mickey Mouse, doll, Knickerbocker, 1930s, as band leader, NM..........................$2,700.00

Mickey Mouse, doll, Knickerbocker, 1930s, compo w/jtd head & arms, NM..........................$1,500.00

Lady and the Tramp, platform toy with Lady, WDP, 1955, EX+, $125.00. (Photo courtesy David Longest and Michael Stern)

Mickey Mouse, doll, Knickerbocker, 1930s, stuffed cloth w/compo shoes, 21", NM $2,000.00

Mickey Mouse, doll, Steiff, stuffed cloth, orig chest tag, 7", NM $2,500.00

Mickey Mouse, doll, Steiff, stuffed plush, orig tags, 11", NM $3,000.00

Mickey Mouse, figure, celluloid, holding ball, VG $1,500.00

Mickey Mouse, figure, Fun-E-Flex by Ideal, 1930s, wood, w/decal, 5", scarce, EX $400.00

Mickey Mouse, figure, Germany, ceramic, w/cactus, NM, A..$75.00

Mickey Mouse, figure, Japan, 1930s, bsk, in bl nightshirt, 4", NM $150.00

Mickey Mouse, figure, Japan, 1930s, bsk, w/accordion, 4", M, M8 ....$175.00

Mickey Mouse, figure, Japan, 1930s, bsk, w/banjo, 5½", NM $500.00

Mickey Mouse, figure, Japan, 1930s, bsk, w/drum, 3½", EX, M8 ....$95.00

Mickey Mouse, figure, Japan, 1930s, bsk, w/French horn, 3½", EX, M8 ....$85.00

Mickey Mouse, figure, Japan, 1930s, bsk, w/saxophone, 3½", NM $175.00

Mickey Mouse, figure, Japan, 1930s, bsk, w/violin, 4", NM, M8 ....$175.00

Mickey Mouse, figure, Japan, 1930s, bsk, 2", EX, M8 ....$75.00

Mickey Mouse, figure, Japan, 1930s, bsk w/movable arms, standing on yel base, 9½", rare, NM $2,200.00

Mickey Mouse, figure, Rosenthal, ceramic, w/tuba, 3½", NM, A..$200.00

Mickey Mouse, figure set, celluloid, set of 5 w/various instruments, NM $900.00

Mickey Mouse, figure set, Japan, 1930s, bsk, dressed as baseball players, 3½", NM, set of 3 ....$950.00

Mickey Mouse, figure set, Japan, 1930s, celluloid, boxers, 8", VG, pr..$1,500.00

Mickey Mouse, flashlight, Usa Lite, litho tin, EX (G box)..$700.00

Mickey Mouse, Magic Movie Palette, WDE, 1930s, litho cb, 8x5", rare, EX..$125.00

Mickey Mouse, magic slate, WDE, 1930s, NM..............$100.00

Mickey Mouse, mask, Germany, hand-painted composition, adult size, label inside, G, A, $600.00.

Mickey Mouse, Minnie & Donald, bank, Chein, 2nd National Duck Bank, litho tin, EX....................................$165.00

Mickey Mouse, pail, litho tin, Ohio Art, WDE, 1930s, on island, 5", NM..$300.00

Mickey Mouse, pail, Ohio Art, WDE, 1930s, w/band, NM...$400.00

Mickey Mouse, pail, Ohio Art, 1930s, building sand castle, 8", NM..$550.00

Mickey Mouse, pencil sharpener, 1930s, celluloid figure, 2½", NM..$85.00

Mickey Mouse, Pluto & Minnie, figure set, Borgfeldt, 1930s, NM (NM box mk The Three Pals) $1,200.00

Mickey Mouse, Print Shop, Fulton Faultless Educational Toys/WDE, 1930s, complete, EX (EX box)..............$200.00

Mickey Mouse, pull toy, NN Hill Brass/WDE, 1930s, Mickey pulls wheel axle w/bell, EX....................................$500.00

Mickey Mouse, pull toy, on scooter, wood & celluloid, VG..$1,600.00

Mickey Mouse, rattle, celluloid w/bead-type hands & ears, NM $200.00

Mickey Mouse, saxophone, Czechoslovakia/WD, 1930s, gold w/decal, NM $400.00

Mickey Mouse, Soldier Set, Marks Bro, 1930s, cb figures w/wooden holders, NM $550.00

Mickey Mouse, sweeper, Ohio Art/WD, 1930s, litho tin & wood, NM..$300.00

Mickey Mouse, Talkie Jecktor, Movie Jecktor Co, 1935, complete, EX (EX box) $1,000.00

Mickey Mouse, Tinkersand Pictures, Toy Tinkers Inc, complete, EX (EX box) $150.00

Mickey Mouse, top, Borgfeldt/WDE, 1930s, litho tin w/characters playing various instruments, NM $350.00

Mickey Mouse, top, 1930s, litho tin w/image of Minnie chasing Mickey w/rolling pin, 8" dia, NM $350.00

Mickey Mouse, toy chest/children's seat, 1930s, wood, cb & cloth, 36" L, EX $350.00

Mickey Mouse, tray, Helpmate, litho tin, Ohio Art, 7½x5½", EX $155.00

Mickey Mouse, washing machine, Ohio Art, litho tin, rare, VG $650.00

Mickey Mouse, watering can, Ohio Art, litho tin w/image of Mickey watering flowers, 5", EX............................$250.00

Mickey Mouse, yo-yo, Billco, 1980s, plastic light-up w/decal seal, MIP $15.00

Mickey Mouse, yo-yo, Festival, 1970s, plastic w/imprint seal, tournament shape, MIP $20.00

Mickey Mouse & Donald Duck, drum, WDE, 1930s, tin w/paper insert, NM $400.00

Mickey Mouse & Donald Duck, figure, Japan, prewar, celluloid, Mickey & Donald in rowboat, 6", rare, EX, A $1,600.00

Mickey Mouse & Donald Duck, on fire truck, Sun Rubber, VG $85.00

Mickey Mouse & Goofy, teacup, litho tin, Ohio Art, 1932, 1⅛", EX..$55.00

Mickey Mouse & Minnie, figure set, Borgfeldt, 1930s, bsk, NM (NM box mk The Two Pals) $900.00

Mickey Mouse & Minnie, figures, 1933, celluloid figures on base, World's Fair Century of Progess label on bottom, NM, A $400.00

Mickey Mouse & Minnie, Magic Movie Palette, 1935 store giveaway, scarce, EX..$200.00

Mickey Mouse & Minnie, tambourine, Noble Cooley/WDE, NM..$300.00

Mickey Mouse & Minnie, tea set, Ohio Art/WD, 1930s, litho tin, 6 pcs, MIB..$600.00

Mickey Mouse & Minnie, yo-yo, Duncan, 1960s, paper insert seal, tournament shape, MIP $45.00

Mickey Mouse & Minnie (w/friends), cup & saucer, litho tin, Ohio Art, 1932, NM..$35.00

Mickey Mouse Club, Clubhouse, Hasbro/Romper Room, 1970s, MIB, J6..$125.00

Mickey Mouse Club, guitar, Mattel, 1955, 14" L, VG $75.00

Mickey Mouse Club, harmonica, 1960s, engraved on both sides, 5", NM..$35.00

Mickey Mouse Club, Jimmy Dodd, Admiral, 1950s, wood w/paper sticker seal, NM $100.00

Mickey Mouse Club, Magic Adder, 1950s, battery-op, NMIB $65.00

Mickey Mouse Club, magic slate, Jimmy Dodd, Strathmore, 1954, NM, M8 ....$45.00

Mickey Mouse Club, Magic Subtractor, Jacmar, 1950s, battery-op, EX (G box), M8..$55.00

Mickey Mouse Club, Newsreel, Mattel, 1950s, w/projector, screen, record & slides, NMIB $150.00

Mickey Mouse Club, newsreels, Mattel, 1955, 6", from $10.00 to $15.00 each.

Mickey Mouse Club, yo-yo, Duncan Imperial Jr, 1960s, plastic w/paper insert seal, tournament shape, MIP $55.00

Mickey Mouse Picture Printing Set, Fulton Specialty Co, 1930s, complete, NMIP $250.00

Minnie Mouse, doll, Knickerbocker, 1930s, Minnie dressed as cowgirl, VG $2,500.00

Minnie Mouse, doll, Steiff, stuffed cloth w/flower in hat, button in ear & chest tag, 8½", NM, A $2,500.00

Minnie Mouse, figure, Fun-E-Flex by Ideal, 1930s, wood, w/decal, 5", scarce, EX..$400.00

Mickey Mouse Club, card games, Russel Mfg. Co., complete, EX, $95.00.

Mickey Mouse, Donald Duck, Goofy, and Billy; Weebles, 1973, $12.00 each. (Photo courtesy June Moon)

Minnie Mouse, figure, Japan, 1930s, bsk, hands on hips, 2¾", EX, M8 ....$65.00

Minnie Mouse, figure, Japan, 1930s, bsk, in red nightshirt, 4", NM $150.00

Minnie Mouse, figure, Japan, 1930s, bsk, Minnie w/mandolin, 4", NM, M8 ....$150.00

Minnie Mouse, figure, Minnie on hobbyhorse, wood, VG ..$1,500.00

Minnie Mouse, roly poly, Minnie atop gr & red ball, celluloid, NM $1,200.00

Mouseketeers, doll, Horsman, 1960s, MIB......................$55.00

Nightmare Before Christmas, doll, Jack, JUN Planning, #N-232, w/Easter Bunny & Spooky, 12", MOC $35.00

Nightmare Before Christmas, doll, Jack in Coffin, JUN Planning, 16", M (NM box) $65.00

Nightmare Before Christmas, figure, Jack Skellington as Santa, Hasbro, 1993, MOC, $75.00.
(Photo courtesy June Moon)

Nightmare Before Christmas, figure, Lock, Shock & Barrel in bathtub, Applause, PVC, M $10.00

Nightmare Before Christmas, figure, Oogie Boogie, Applause, PVC, M $10.00

Nightmare Before Christmas, figure, Zero, Applause, PVC, M..$10.00

Nightmare Before Christmas figure set, Lock, Shock & Barrel, Hasbro, 1993, M (NM box)...................................$80.00

Peter Pan, figure, Tinkerbell, Goebel, 1950s, ceramic, 8½", M, A $150.00

Pinocchio, bank, Pinocchio Post Office, litho tin, 5", EX, A $65.00

Pinocchio, doll, Geppetto, Chad Valley, wood w/cloth clothes, orig tag, NM $1,250.00

Pinocchio, doll, Jiminy Cricket, Knickerbocker/WDP, 1939, compo w/felt clothes & hat, orig tag, 10", EX..........$600.00

Pinocchio, doll, Jiminy Cricket, 1930s, cloth w/molded velveteen head, hands & shoes, 15½", EX, A $800.00

Pinocchio, doll, Pinocchio, Crown Toy/WDE, jtd wood, orig tag, NM...$400.00

Pinocchio, doll, Pinocchio, Ideal, jtd wood, 19", NM $900.00

Pinocchio, doll, Pinocchio, Ideal/WDP, 1939, jtd wood & compo w/felt clothes, 11", EX (EX box) $400.00

Pinocchio, Figaro, jtd figure, compo, Knickerbocker, 1930s, 7½", EX $390.00

Pinocchio, figure, Geppetto, Multi-Products, 1940s, wood, 2½", EX, M8 ....$65.00

Pinocchio, figure, Geppetto, Multi-Products, 1940s, wood, 5½", EX, M8 ....$95.00

Pinocchio, figure, Gideon, Japan, 1940s, bsk, 3", EX, M8..$35.00

Pinocchio, figure, Pinocchio, Japan, 1940s, bsk, 3", EX, M8.....$75.00

Pinocchio, figure, Pinocchio, Japan, 1940s, bsk, 4", EX, M8...$100.00

Pinocchio, figure, Pinocchio, Japan, 1940s, porcelain, 3", EX, M8 ....$35.00

Pinocchio, figure, Pinocchio, Multi-Products, 1940s, wood, 2", EX, M8 ....$65.00

Pinocchio, figure, Pinocchio, 1940s, chalkware, NM $40.00

Pinocchio, pencil sharpener, Jiminy Cricket, WDE, 1930s, Bakelite, M..$75.00

Pinocchio, pull toy, Pinocchio Express #720, rides unicycle pulling cart, wooden w/lithoed decor, Fisher-Price, 1939, NM...$500.00

Pinocchio, tea set, Ohio Art, 1939, litho tin, 18 pcs, rare, NM $350.00

Pinocchio, xylophone, 1955, battery-op, 8½", NM........$250.00

Pluto, Disney's Remote Control Jumping Pluto, tin w/rubbber ears & tail, squeeze-hdl action, EX (VG box)..........$425.00

Pluto, figure, Japan, 1930s, sand-filled celluloid, 3", rare, NM, M8 ....$85.00

Pluto, figure, 1960s, inflatable vinyl, 9", MIP $50.00

Pluto, Peppy Puppet, Kohner Bros, MOC, $50.00.

Pluto the Pup, figure, Borgfeldt, jtd wood, orange w/felt ears, 6", EX (EX box), A $850.00

Pluto the Pup, figure, Fun-E-Flex by Ideal, 1930s, wood, lg, EX...$400.00

Pluto the Pup, figure, Fun-E-Flex by Ideal, 1930s, wood, sm, EX...$200.00

Pocahontas, yo-yo, Meeko, Spectra Star, sculpted plastic, MIP......$6.00

Scrooge McDuck, see Donald Duck

Sleeping Beauty, doll, Madame Alexander, 1957, Elise face, orig pk satin gown, rpl crown, 16", EX, M15......$300.00

Sleeping Beauty, figures, King & Queen, Hagen-Renaker, 1930s, 3", M, C12, ea......$525.00

Snow White & the Seven Dwarfs, bubble toy, Dopey, WDP, 1950s, plastic, 4", EX, M8......$25.00

Snow White and the Seven Dwarfs, bracelet, cloisonne on brass, 1940s, $1,500.00. (Photo courtesy Joel Cohen)

Snow White & the Seven Dwarfs, charms, Japan, 1930s, celluloid, set of 8, NM......$75.00

Snow White & the Seven Dwarfs, doll, Bashful, Knickerbocker, 1938, stuffed cloth, NM......$325.00

Snow White & the Seven Dwarfs, doll, Dopey, Chad Valley, 1930s, stuffed cloth w/felt clothes, orig tag, NM......$325.00

Snow White & the Seven Dwarfs, doll, Dopey, Knickerbocker, 1938, compo w/cloth clothes, orig tag, 9", NM......$325.00

Snow White & the Seven Dwarfs, doll, Grumpy, Knickerbocker, 1930s, compo w/felt clothes, EX......$325.00

Snow White & the Seven Dwarfs, doll, Happy, Chad Valley, 1930s, stuffed cloth w/felt clothes, 12", NM......$325.00

Snow White & the Seven Dwarfs, doll, Snow White, Reliable Toy/WDE, 1937, compo w/satin & velvet dress, 15", EX, A......$400.00

Snow White and the Seven Dwarfs, doll set, Knickerbocker, unplayed with/slight fading, otherwise MIB, $1,800.00. (Photo courtesy McMasters Doll Auctions)

Snow White & the Seven Dwarfs, doll, Sleepy, Knickerbocker, 1930s, compo w/felt clothes, EX......$325.00

Snow White & the Seven Dwarfs, doll, Snow White, Knickerbocker, 1930s, compo w/cloth dress, EX......$450.00

Snow White & the Seven Dwarfs, drum, Chein, litho tin, 11" dia, VG, A......$250.00

Snow White & the Seven Dwarfs, figure, Bashful, Shaw, 1950s, 2", M, M8......$125.00

Snow White & the Seven Dwarfs, figure, Doc, Japan, 1930s, bsk, 2", VG, M8......$35.00

Snow White & the Seven Dwarfs, figure, Dopey, Am Pottery, 1938, NM......$275.00

Snow White & the Seven Dwarfs, figure, Dopey, Hagen-Renaker, 1950s, porcelain, 1", M, M8......$100.00

Snow White & the Seven Dwarfs, figure, Grumpy, Hagen-Renaker, 1950s, porcelain, 1", M, M8......$100.00

Snow White & the Seven Dwarfs, figure, Happy, Shaw, 1950s, NM, M8......$115.00

Snow White & the Seven Dwarfs, figure, Sleepy, Japan, 1930s, bsk, movable arms, 4", EX, M8......$85.00

Snow White & the Seven Dwarfs, figure, Snow White, Hagen-Renaker, 1950s, porcelain, 2", M, M8......$150.00

Snow White & the Seven Dwarfs, figure set, Borgfeldt, 1939, bsk, set of 8, NM (EX box), A......$750.00

Snow White & the Seven Dwarfs, figure set, England, 1939, pottery-type material, dwarfs w/gardening tools, set of 8, NM......$350.00

Snow White & the Seven Dwarfs, figure set, Japan, prewar, bsk, ea dwarf w/different instrument, rare, set of 8, NM, A......$500.00

Snow White & the Seven Dwarfs, figure set, Leonardi, 1939, ceramic, extremely rare, set of 8, M, A......$2,100.00

Snow White & the Seven Dwarfs, pencil sharpener, Dopey, WDE/1930s, Bakelite, M......$75.00

Snow White & the Seven Dwarfs, pencil sharpener, Snow White, WDE, 1930s, Bakelite, M......$75.00

Snow White & the Seven Dwarfs, Safety Blocks, Halsam/WDE, set of 32, EX (EX box)......$250.00

Snow White & the Seven Dwarfs, Storykins, Hasbro, 1967, MIP, from $75 to......$100.00

Snow White & the Seven Dwarfs, tea set, Ohio Art/WDE, 1937, litho tin, 9 pcs, EX, from $300 to......$400.00

Snow White & the Seven Dwarfs, Tinkersand Pictures, Toy Tinkers/WDE, 1938, NMIB......$150.00

Snow White & the Seven Dwarfs, watering can, Ohio Art/WDE, 1930s, litho tin, 8", EX......$325.00

Snow White & the Seven Swarfs, tea set, Aluminum Goods, 10 pcs, NMIB......$375.00

Space Jam, yo-yo, Spectra Star, 1996, plastic w/photo seal of Michael Jordan & Bugs Bunny, MIP......$5.00

Three Little Pigs, figure, any character, Japan, 1930s, bsk, 3½", EX, M8, ea......$50.00

Three Little Pigs, figure set, Seiberling Rubber, rare, EX......$1,200.00

Three Little Pigs, tea set, WDE, 1930s, gr litho tin, 15 pcs, NM......$500.00

Three Little Pigs, wash tub, Ohio Art, 1930s, litho tin, EX......$125.00

Three Little Pigs, watering can, Ohio Art/WDE, 1930s, litho tin, NM......$275.00

Three Little Pigs, rubber figure, Seiberling, EX, from $350.00 to $400.00.
(Photo courtesy Michael Stern)

Three Little Pigs & the Big Bad Wolf, figure set, Japan, 1930s, bsk, EX $300.00

Thumper, see Bambi

Tinkerbell, see Peter Pan

Toy Story, bank, Alien, Sega, 11", M $30.00

Toy Story, doll, Woody, Think Way, talker, stuffed cloth w/vinyl head & hands, MIB $45.00

Toy Story, Woody, talker, 16", NRFB $60.00

Toy Story, yo-yo, Buzz Lightyear, Canada Games, 1995, plastic w/imprint seal, tournament shape, MIP $10.00

Who Framed Roger Rabbit, yo-yo, 1980s, plastic w/paper sticker seal, butterfly shape, MIP $18.00

Winnie the Pooh, doll, Pooh, Gund, 1964, soft felt plush, 6½", VG, M8 ....$30.00

Winnie the Pooh, doll, Pooh, Gund, 1990s, soft plush, 5½", M (NM box), M8 ....$30.00

Winnie the Pooh, jack-in-the-box, Mattel, litho tin w/cloth figure, EX, H8 ....$110.00

101 Dalmatians, ring set, MOC, C10................................$25.00

Dollhouse Furniture

Back in the '40s and '50s, little girls often spent hour after hour with their dollhouses, keeping house for their imaginary families, cooking on tiny stoves (that sometimes came with scaled-to-fit pots and pans), serving meals in lovely dining rooms, making beds, and rearranging furniture, most of which was plastic, much of which was made by Renwal, Ideal, Marx, Irwin, and Plasco. Jaydon made plastic furniture as well but sadly never marked it. Tootsietoy produced metal items, many in boxed sets.

Of all of these manufacturers, Renwal and Ideal are considered the most collectible. Renwal's furniture was usually detailed; some pieces had moving parts. Many were made in more than

one color, often brightened with decals. Besides the furniture, they made accessory items as well as 'dollhouse' dolls of the whole family. Ideal's Petite Princess line was packaged in sets with wonderful detail, accessorized down to the perfume bottles on the top of the vanity. Ideal furniture and parts are numbered, always with an 'I' prefix. Most Renwal pieces are also numbered.

Advisor: Judith Mosholder (M7).

Arcade, Roper gas stove, nickeled parts, removable black grill, 6", NMIB, A, $700.00; Boone kitchen cabinet, embossed silver-tone hinges, stenciled clock on front door, 8", NMIB, A, $950.00.

Acme/Thomas, carriage, bl w/bl top & wht wheels or bl w/pk top & wht wheels, M7, ea...$6.00

Acme/Thomas, chair, rocker; gr w/yel, yel w/gr, or yel w/red, M7, ea $4.00

Acme/Thomas, cradle, pk & bl w/molded storks & babies, M7, M7 ....$8.00

Acme/Thomas, doll, baby in diaper, w/bl or pk crocheted outfit, 1¼", M7, ea...$6.00

Acme/Thomas, doll, baby in diaper, 1¼", M7....................$3.00

Acme/Thomas, doll, baby in diaper, 1⅛", M7....................$2.00

Acme/Thomas, doll, baby in diaper, 2", M7.......................$4.00

Acme/Thomas, doll, baby sucking thumb; hard plastic, pk, M7 ....$3.00

Acme/Thomas, doll, Dutch boy or girl, flesh-colored, M7, ea..$5.00

Acme/Thomas, hammock, bl w/red supports or gr w/yellow supports, M7, ea $20.00

Acme/Thomas, seesaw, red w/yel horse heads, M7 ....$10.00

Acme/Thomas, shoofly, dk bl or red w/yel horse head, M7, ea...$18.00

Acme/Thomas, stroller, bl w/wht wheels, pk w/bl wheels, or pk w/wht wheels, M7, ea...$6.00

Acme/Thomas, swing, single, red w/gr swing & yel ropes, M7..$18.00

Allied/Pyro, buffet, aqua, M7..$8.00

Allied/Pyro, chair, barrel; aqua, M7.................................$5.00

Allied/Pyro, chair, dining room or kitchen; pk or red, M7, ea..$3.00

Allied/Pyro, chest of drawers, aqua, M7 ....$3.00

Allied/Pyro, cupboard, corner; aqua, M7..........................$8.00

Allied/Pyro, hutch, aqua or red, M7 ....$4.00

Allied/Pyro, lamp, table; bl w/orange shade, M7...............$18.00

Allied/Pyro, piano, blk w/wht keyboard, M7.....................$12.00

Allied/Pyro, radio, floor; yel, M7 ....$8.00

Allied/Pyro, refrigerator, ivory, M7 ....$4.00
Allied/Pyro, sofa, lt bl or aqua, M7, ea $5.00
Allied/Pyro, stove, pk or wht, M7..................................$4.00
Allied/Pyro, table, kitchen; wht, M7 ....$4.00
Allied/Pyro, toilet, wht w/red lid, M7 ....$8.00
Allied/Pyro, tub, lt bl, M7 ....$4.00
Allied/Pyro, vanity, aqua, bl or pk, M7, ea $4.00
Arcade, laundry set, yel-pnt CI, 4 pcs, EX, A $800.00
Arcade, tub, ivory, G pnt, M7 ....$125.00
Arco, table, end; peach, M7...$3.00
Ardee, chair, dining; red w/ivory, M7 ....$5.00

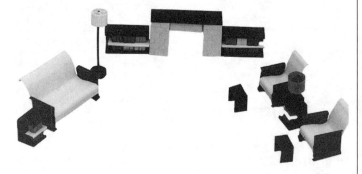

Ardee, living room pieces: couch, $15.00; chairs, $10.00; fireplace, $15.00; bookcases, from $8.00 to $12.00; floor lamp, $20.00; table lamp, $15.00; vanity stools, $5.00. (Photo courtesy Marcie Tubbs)

Babyland Nursery, any pc, bl or pk, M7, ea $5.00
Best, bunk bed or ladder, bl or pk, M7, ea $5.00
Best, doll, baby; pk, 3⅜", M7...$5.00
Best, doll, baby; sitting, 2", M7 ....$3.00
Best, doll, baby; standing, 2", M7 ....$4.00
Blue Box, bed, lt brn w/bl spread, M7............................$5.00
Blue Box, chair, dining; lt brn w/red seat, M7 ....$2.00
Blue Box, chest, 4-drawer, lt brn, M7 ....$4.00
Blue Box, piano, w/stool, M7..$15.00
Blue Box, table, dining; lt brn, M7 ....$5.00
Blue Box, vanity w/heart-shaped mirror, M7.......................$4.00
Cheerio, any hard plastic pc, M7, ea $4.00
Cheerio, any soft plastic pc, sm, M7, ea $2.00
Commonwealth, lamppost, w/street sign & mailbox, red, M7..$15.00
Commonwealth, lawn mower, red w/yel wheels & blk engine or gr w/yel wheels & blk engine, M7, ea...............$30.00
Commonwealth, rake, red or yel, M7, ea $4.00
Commonwealth, spade, pk, M7 ....$4.00
Commonwealth, water can, wht or red, M7, ea $6.00
Donna Lee, chair, kitchen; wht, M7 ....$5.00
Donna Lee, kitchen pcs, sink, stove, or table, wht, M7, ea.$6.00
Fisher-Price, armoire, wht, M7...$5.00
Fisher-Price, bathroom set, #253, M, C13 ....$6.00
Fisher-Price, chair, dining; brn w/tan seat, M7..................$2.00
Fisher-Price, chair, kitchen; wht w/yel, M7 ....$2.00
Fisher-Price, clock, grandfather; brn, M7........................$10.00
Fisher-Price, cradle, wht, M7 ....$5.00
Fisher-Price, dinette set, #251, M, C13 ....$4.00
Fisher-Price, dresser w/mirror, wht, M7 ....$5.00
Fisher-Price, refrigerator, wht w/yel, M7..........................$5.00

Fisher-Price, desk set, #261, 1980 – 83, M, $6.00.
(Photo courtesy Brad Cassity)

Fisher-Price, doll, boy #277, 1983 – 85, MOC, $2.50.
(Photo courtesy Brad Cassity)

Fisher-Price, rocker, #273, MOC, C13 ....$4.00
Fisher-Price, stove/hood unit, yel, M7 ....$5.00
French Provincial, refrigerator, sink/stove combo, toilet, or tub, ivory or pk, ½" scale, M7, ea $4.00
Ideal, bench, lawn; bl or red, M7, ea $18.00
Ideal, birdbath, highly marbleized ivory, M7...................$18.00
Ideal, buffet, dk brn or dk marbleized maroon, M7, ea......$10.00
Ideal, chair, bedroom; bl w/pk skirt, M7..........................$30.00
Ideal, chair, dining room; any 2-color or marbleized combination, M7, ea $10.00
Ideal, chair, kitchen; ivory w/bl seat or ivory w/red seat, M7, ea...$6.00
Ideal, chair, kitchen; wht w/red seat, M7 ....$15.00
Ideal, chair, lawn; wht, M7 ....$15.00
Ideal, chair, sq back, bl swirl w/brn or bright gr base or med gr w/brn base, M7, ea $15.00
Ideal, china closet; dk brn swirl or dk marbleized maroon, M7, ea $15.00
Ideal, cradle, bl or pk, M7, ea $45.00
Ideal, crib, bl w/decal, M7..$25.00
Ideal, doll, baby; pnt diaper, M7 ....$10.00
Ideal, fireplace, brn, M7..$35.00
Ideal, hamper, bl, M7..$6.00

Ideal, hamper, ivory, M7 ....$4.00

Ideal, highboy, dk marbleized maroon, M7.............$15.00

Ideal, highboy, ivory w/bl, M7 ....$18.00

Ideal, highchair, collapsible, bl or pk, M7, ea...........$25.00

Ideal, night stand, dk marbleized maroon, brn, M7, ea $6.00

Ideal, piano w/bench, dk marbleized brn, M7 ....$25.00

Ideal, piano w/bench, med marbleized brn w/decal & music
    sheet or caramel swirl, M7, ea........................$35.00

Ideal, playpen, pk w/bl bottom, M7 ....$35.00

Ideal, radio, floor; brn or dk marbleized maroon, M7, ea ..$10.00

Ideal, refrigerator, ivory w/blk, M7 ....$15.00

Ideal, sewing machine, dk marbleized brn or dk marbleized
    maroon, M7, ea......................................$20.00

Ideal, shopping cart, bl w/wht basket or red w/bl basket, M7,
    ea..$40.00

Ideal, sink, bathroom; bl w/yel, M7 ....$10.00

Ideal, sink, bathroom; ivory w/blk, M7 ....$8.00

Ideal, sofa, med bl swirl, med gr swirl, or orange-red swirl, all
    w/brn base, M7, ea...................................$22.00

Ideal, stool, vanity; ivory w/bl seat, M7 ....$6.00

Ideal, stove; ivory w/blk, M7...............................$15.00

Ideal, table, coffee; brn or dk marbleized maroon, M7, ea ...$10.00

Ideal, table, dining; dk marbleized maroon or brn swirl, M7,
    ea..$20.00

Ideal, table, kitchen; ivory, M7..........................$6.00

Ideal, table, kitchen; wht, M7 ....$20.00

Ideal, table, tilt-top; marbleized maroon, M7 ....$45.00

Ideal, television, dk marbleized maroon w/Mighty Mouse on
    screen, M7..$95.00

Ideal, tub, corner; bl w/yel, M7 ....$18.00

Ideal, tub, ivory w/blk, M7.............................$10.00

Ideal, vanity, ivory w/bl, M7 ....$18.00

Ideal Petite Princess, bed, #4416-4, pk, M7 ....$25.00

Ideal Petite Princess, bottle, wine; #4424-8, M7 ....$5.00

Ideal Petite Princess, buffet, #4419-8, complete, in orig box,
    M7..$25.00

Ideal Petite Princess, cabinet, #4418-0, in orig box, M7...$12.00

Ideal Petite Princess, candelabra, #4438-8, in orig box, M7..$22.00

Ideal Petite Princess, candelabra, #4439-6, in orig box, M7..$17.00

Ideal Petite Princess, chair, dressing table; #4417-2, pk, M ...$5.00

Ideal Petite Princess, chair, guest dining; #4414-9, M7.......$8.00

Ideal Petite Princess, chair, host dining; #4413-1, M7 ....$8.00

Ideal Petite Princess, chair, host dining; #4474-3, in orig box,
    M7..$17.00

Ideal Petite Princess, chair, hostess dining; #4415-6, M7....$8.00

Ideal Petite Princess, chair, salon drum; #4411-5, gold or gr, in
    orig box, M7, ea.....................................$17.00

Ideal Petite Princess, chair, salon wing; #4410-7, red, in orig box,
    M7..$15.00

Ideal Petite Princess, chair w/ottoman, #4412-3, in orig box,
    M7..$22.00

Ideal Petite Princess, clock, grandfather; #4423-0, M7.....$15.00

Ideal Petite Princess, clock and screen, #4423-0, in orig box,
    M7..$30.00

Ideal Petite Princess, dish rack, #4508-8, M7.............$10.00

Ideal Petite Princess, doll, Fantasy Family brother, #9710-5, M7..$18.00

Ideal Petite Princess, doll, Fantasy Family father, #97105-5,
    M7..$20.00

Ideal Petite Princess, Fantasy Family, MIB, $90.00.
(Photo courtesy Judith Mosholder)

Ideal Petite Princess, hamper, #4499-0, M7 ....$30.00

Ideal Petite Princess, hearthplace, Regency, #4422-2, w/acces-
    sories, no mirror, M7...............................$18.00

Ideal Petite Princess, piano, Royal Grand, #4425-5, in orig box,
    M7..$35.00

Ideal Petite Princess, planter, salon; #4440-4, in orig box,
    M7..$18.00

Ideal Petite Princess, range, #4507-0, no utensils, M7......$50.00

Ideal Petite Princess, table, dining room; #4421-4, M7 ....$15.00

Ideal Petite Princess, table, dressing; #4417-2, pk, no accessories,
    M7..$10.00

Ideal Petite Princess, table, kitchen; #4504-7, pk, no accessories,
    M7..$20.00

Ideal Petite Princess, table set, occasional; #4437-0, complete,
    M7..$25.00

Imagination, any pc, M7, ea $3.00

Irwin Interior Decorator, refrigerator, under-counter; yel, M7 ..$3.00

Irwin Interior Decorator, refrigerator, yel, M7 ....$5.00

Irwin Interior Decorator, shower curtain, lt gr, M7 ....$4.00

Irwin Interior Decorator, sink, yel w/orange, M7 ....$5.00

Irwin Interior Decorator, stove, yel w/chrome, M7 ....$5.00

Irwin Interior Decorator, toilet, lt gr, M7 ....$5.00

Irwin Interior Decorator, towels (2), lt gr, M7................$5.00

Irwin Interior Decorator, tub, lt gr, M7......................$5.00

Jaydon, buffet, reddish brn, M7............................$4.00

Jaydon, chair, dining; reddish-brn swirl, M7................$2.00

Jaydon, chair, living room; ivory w/brn or reddish-brn swirl, M7,
    ea..$15.00

Jaydon, chest of drawers, reddish-brn swirl, M7 ....$6.00

Jaydon, piano w/bench, reddish-brn swirl, M7................$12.00

Jaydon, sink, bathroom; ivory, M7..........................$10.00

Jaydon, sink, kitchen; ivory w/blk, M7......................$15.00

Kage, clock, table; walnut w/ivory shade, M7................$10.00

Kage, refrigerator, wht/w blk detail, M7 ....$8.00

Kilgore, rocking chair, bl, Fair pnt, M7 ....$50.00

Marx, accessory, board w/molded knife & bread, table radio or
    toaster, gray, M7, ea................................$4.00

Marx, accessory, bread box, red, M7 ....$4.00

Marx, accessory, pressure cooker or table radio, gold, M7,
    ea..$4.00

Marx, accessory set, 4-pc place setting, candelabra, telephone, etc, soft plastic, ivory, ½" scale, M7..................$5.00

Marx, bed, soft plastic, yel, ¾" scale, M7 ....$4.00

Marx, bench, vanity; soft plastic, yel, ¾" scale, M7 ....$3.00

Marx, buffet, hard plastic, dk brn, dk maroon swirl or med maroon swirl, ½" scale, M7, ea.....................................$3.00

Marx, buffet, hard plastic, w/molded fruit, tan, ½" scale, M7.$3.00

Marx, buffet, soft plastic, rust brn, ¾" scale, M7 ....$3.00

Marx, chair, armless; hard plastic, bright yel, ½" scale, M7..$3.00

Marx, chair, barrel; hard plastic, red, ½" scale, M7 ....$3.00

Marx, chair, bedroom; hard plastic, bright or lt yel, ¾" scale, M7, ea..$5.00

Marx, chair, boudoir; soft plastic, yel, ¾" scale, M7...........$3.00

Marx, chair, club (Florida Room); soft plastic, lt bl, ¾" scale, M7 ....$4.00

Marx, chair, dining room (w/or w/o arms); soft plastic, brn or dk brn, ¾" scale, M7, ea $3.00

Marx, chair, high back; hard plastic, bright yel or gr, ¾" scale, M7, ea..$5.00

Marx, chair, kitchen; hard plastic, ivory or wht, ½" scale, M7, ea...$3.00

Marx, chair, kitchen; soft plastic, ivory, ¾" scale, M7.........$3.00

Marx, chair, lawn; soft plastic, chartreuse, ¾" scale, M7, ea...$3.00

Marx, chair, living room; tufted, hard plastic, lt gr, ¾" scale, M7 ....$5.00

Marx, chair, living room; tufted, soft plastic, yel, ¾" scale, M7 ....$3.00

Marx, chest of drawers, hard plastic, bl or pk, ¾" scale, M7, ea $5.00

Marx, chest of drawers, soft plastic, pk, ¾" scale, M7, ea....$3.00

Marx, china cupboard, hard plastic, dk brn or dk maroon swirl, ½" scale, M7, ea...$3.00

Marx, counter w/molded phone & hot plate, hard plastic, marbleized ivory or wht, ½" scale, M7, ea $5.00

Marx, dining room set, hard plastic, table, buffet, china cupboard, 1 chair, med maroon swirl, ¾" scale, M7 ....$15.00

Marx, dining room set, soft plastic, table, buffet, hutch, 4 chairs, brn, ¾" scale, M7...$20.00

Marx, doll, baby w/arms up; flesh-colored or pk, M7, ea.....$4.00

Marx, doll, boy in diving position; M7...................................$4.00

Marx, doll, boy or girl in swinging position, pk, M7 ....$4.00

Marx, doll, boy or girl sitting, M7, ea $4.00

Marx, dresser, low; hard plastic, pk, ½" scale, M7................$3.00

Marx, hamper, hard plastic, bl, dk ivory, ivory, peach or pk, ¾" scale, M7, ea..$5.00

Marx, hassock, hard plastic, bright yel or lt yel, ¾" scale, M7, ea..$4.00

Marx, hassock, soft plastic, yel, ¾" scale, M7.......................$3.00

Marx, highboy, hard plastic, bright yel, ½" scale, M7 ....$3.00

Marx, highboy, soft plastic, yel, ¾" scale, M7 ....$3.00

Marx, hutch, hard plastic, med maroon swirl, ¾" scale, M7..$5.00

Marx, hutch, hard plastic, w/molded fruit, brn or tan, ½" scale, M7, ea..$3.00

Marx, hutch, soft plastic, brn or tan, ¾" scale, M7, ea........$3.00

Marx, milk bar, hard plastic, gr or red, ½" scale, M7, ea...$15.00

Marx, nightstand, hard plastic, bright yel or lt yel ½" scale, M7, ea..$3.00

Marx, nightstand, soft plastic, yel, ¾" scale, M7.................$3.00

Marx, piano w/bench, hard plastic, bright yel, ½" scale, M7..$15.00

Marx, playpen, hard plastic, peach or pk w/Donald Duck decal, ½" scale, M7, ea $8.00

Marx, playpen, soft plastic, pk, ¾" scale, M7 ....$3.00

Marx, privet hedge set, gr plastic, for ¾" dollhouses, 12-pc, M7..$150.00

Marx, refrigerator, hard plastic, wht, ½" scale, M7 ....$3.00

Marx, refrigerator, soft plastic, yel, ¾" scale, M7 ....$3.00

Marx, seesaw, hard plastic, bright yel w/emb Mickey Mouse, ¾" scale, M7 ....$10.00

Marx, sink, bathroom; hard plastic, bl, ¾" scale, M7..........$5.00

Marx, sink, dbl bowl, hard plastic, off wht, ½" scale, M7 ...$3.00

Marx, sink, dbl bowl, soft plastic, chartreuse or turq, ¾" scale, M7, ea..$3.00

Marx, sink, hard plastic, wht, ½" scale, M7 ....$3.00

Marx, sink, kitchen; soft plastic, lt ivory or soft yel, ¾" scale, M7, ea..$3.00

Marx, sink, utility; dbl bowl, hard plastic, wht, ¾" scale, M7..$5.00

Marx, sofa, game room; curved, hard plastic, red, ½" scale, M7.$15.00

Marx, sofa, soft plastic, yel or tan, ¾" scale, M7, ea...........$3.00

Marx, stove, hard plastic, dk ivory, ½" scale, M7 ....$3.00

Marx, stove, hard plastic, ivory or wht, ¾" scale, M7, ea....$5.00

Marx, stove, hard plastic, wht, ½" scale, M7.......................$3.00

Marx, stove, soft plastic, lt ivory, ¾" scale, M7 ea..............$3.00

Marx, table, coffee; curved, hard plastic, dk yel, ¾" scale, M7 ...$8.00

Marx, table, dining; hard plastic, med maroon swirl, ¾" scale, M7 ....$6.00

Marx, table, dining; soft plastic, brn or rust brn, ¾" scale, M7, ea..$3.00

Marx, table, kitchen; hard plastic, wht, ½" scale, M7.........$5.00

Marx, table, step-end; hard plastic, bl, ¾" scale, M7 ....$4.00

Marx, table, step-end; soft plastic, med bl, ¾" scale, M7 ....$3.00

Marx, table, umbrella; hard plastic, gr, no umbrella, ¾" scale, M7 ....$4.00

Marx, table, umbrella; hard plastic, red or yel, no umbrella, ½" scale, M7, ea...$3.00

Marx, table, umbrella; soft plastic, turq, no umbrella, ¾" scale, M7 ....$3.00

Marx, television, console; hard plastic, lt bl or lt gr, ½" scale, M7, ea..$3.00

Marx, television/phonograph, hard plastic, bl, lt bl, or bright yel, ¾" scale, M7, ea...$5.00

Marx, toilet, hard plastic, bl, dk ivory, ivory, peach, or pk, M7, ea...$5.00

Marx, toilet, hard plastic, bright yel, dk ivory, ivory, med bl, or wht, ½" scale, M7, ea...$3.00

Marx, toilet, hard plastic, peach, ¾" scale, M7 ....$5.00

Marx, tub, corner; hard plastic, bl, pk, or peach, ¾" scale, M7, ea...$5.00

Marx, tub, hard plastic, ivory or wht, ½" scale, ea $3.00

Marx, umbrella (for umbrella table), soft plastic, yel, ¾" scale, M7 ....$3.00

Marx, vanity, hard plastic, bright yel or soft yel, ¾" scale, M7, ea..$3.00

Marx, vanity, hard plastic, bright yel or tan, ½" scale, M7, ea $3.00

Marx, vanity, soft plastic, yel, ¾" scale, M7 ....$3.00

Marx, washer, front-load; hard plastic, wht, ¾" scale, M7..$6.00

Marx, washer, front-load; soft plastic, turq, ¾" scale, M7 ...$3.00

Marx Little Hostess, bench, vanity; ivory w/bright pk, M7.$4.00

Marx Little Hostess, chair, rocker; reddish-brn, M7 ....$12.00

Marx Little Hostess, chaise, ivory w/bright pk, M7...........$12.00

Marx Little Hostess, chest, block front, rust, M7 ....$12.00

Marx Little Hostess, clock, grandfather; red, M7 ....$18.00

Marx Little Hostess, fireplace, ivory, M7.........................$20.00

Marx Little Hostess, sofa, turq, M7 ....$15.00

Marx Little Hostess, table, gate-leg; rust, M7 ....$15.00

Marx Little Hostess, table, lowboy; red, M7 ....$12.00

Marx Little Hostess, table, tilt-top; blk, M7 ....$12.00

Marx Little Hostess, tub & shower, no curtain, M7..........$18.00

Marx Newlywed, bed, deep pk & bl, M7 ....$15.00

Marx Newlywed, sofa, mustard & red, M7 ....$15.00

Marx Newlywed, vanity, deep pk & bl, M7 ....$15.00

Mattel Littles, armoire, M7 ....$8.00

Mattel Littles, chair, living room; w/footstool & plant, in orig box, M7 ....$15.00

Mattel Littles, doll, Belinda; w/4 chairs & pop-up room setting, in orig box, M7 ....$25.00

Mattel Littles, doll, Hedy; w/sofa & pop-up room setting, in orig box, M7 ....$22.00

Mattel Littles, doll, Littles Family (Mr & Mrs Little & baby), in orig box, M7..$22.00

Mattel Littles, dresser w/lamp, in orig box, M7 ....$12.00

Mattel Littles, sofa, M7 ....$8.00

Mattel Littles, table, drop-leaf; w/cups & 4 plates, in orig box, M7 ....$15.00

Menasha, table, dining; wood w/reddish-walnut finish, 1930s, 1", M7..$25.00

Menasha, table, end; wood w/reddish-walnut finish, 1930s, 1", M7..$20.00

Miniaform, bed, bl spread, M7..$15.00

MPC, any pc, M7, ea..$3.00

Nancy Forbes, bathroom set: tub, sink, vanity w/mirror, medicine cabinet & scale, ivory, M7 ....$25.00

Nancy Forbes, bed; walnut, M7 ....$4.00

Nancy Forbes, cabinet, floor; walnut, M7 ....$4.00

Nancy Forbes, chair, kitchen; wht, M7...............................$2.00

Nancy Forbes, night stand, walnut, M7 ....$2.00

Plasco, bed, brn headboard w/yel spread, M7 ....$3.00

Plasco, bench, vanity; brn, dk brn, ivory, or pk, M7, ea......$3.00

Plasco, bird bath/fountain, ivory or dk ivory, M7, ea $12.00

Plasco, buffet, brn, marbleized reddish-brn, tan, or tan w/yel detail, M7, ea $4.00

Plasco, buffet, med maroon swirl or very dk maroon swirl, M7, ea $5.00

Plasco, chair, dining room; brn, M7....................................$3.00

Plasco, chair, dining room; tan w/striped seat cover, M7 ....$4.00

Plasco, chair, dining room; w/arms, brn or marbleized med brn, M7, ea...$3.00

Plasco, chair, kitchen; lt bl, med bl, royal bl, turq, or dk turq, M7, ea...$2.00

Plasco, chair, living room; no-base style, dk gr or yel, M7, ea.....$3.00

Plasco, chair, patio; bl w/dk ivory legs, bl w/ivory legs, M7, ea...$3.00

Plasco, chairs, kitchen; ivory, M7, ea..................................$3.00

Plasco, clock, grandfather; lt brn swirl w/cb face, M7 ....$15.00

Plasco, counter, kitchen; no-base style, pk, M7..................$3.00

Plasco, doll, baby; pk, M7 ....$25.00

Plasco, highboy, tan, M7 ....$8.00

Plasco, kitchen set (no-base style); table, refrigerator, sink & stove, pk, M7 ....$15.00

Plasco, nightstand, brn, marbleized med brn or tan, M7, ea..$3.00

Plasco, refrigerator, no-base style, pk, M7..........................$3.00

Plasco, refrigerator, wht w/bl base, M7 ....$5.00

Plasco, sink, bathroom; pk, M7...$4.00

Plasco, sink, kitchen; no-base style, lt gr w/rose trim, pk, or wht, ea $3.00

Plasco, sink, kitchen; no-base style, pk w/blk detail, M7 ....$4.00

Plasco, sofa, lt bl w/br base, M7 ....$15.00

Plasco, sofa, no-base style, dk teal, turq, dk turq, lt bl, M7, ea...$3.00

Plasco, stove, no-base style, lt gr w/rose trim or pk, M7, ea ...$3.00

Plasco, stove, wht w/bl base, M7 ....$5.00

Plasco, table, coffee; marbleized med brn, brn, or tan, M7, ea.$3.00

Plasco, table, coffee; tan w/leather-look top, M7...............$5.00

Plasco, table, dining room; w/4 chairs, dk brn, M7 ....$22.00

Plasco, table, kitchen; ivory or royal bl, M7, ea $5.00

Plasco, table, patio; bl w/dk ivory leg, sm, M7..................$4.00

Plasco, table, umbrella; bl w/dk ivory legs or bl w/ivory legs, no umbrella, M7, ea $5.00

Plasco, toilet, turq w/wht, M7..$8.00

Plasco, tub, pk, very pale pk, rose, or turq, M7, ea $4.00

Plasco, vanity, no-mirror style, pk, marbleized med brn, dk brn, red/brn, rose, tan, tan w/yel detail, M7, ea $5.00

Plasco, vanity, sq-mirror style, dk brn or pk, M7, ea...........$5.00

Reliable, bench, piano; brn, M7..$8.00

Reliable, chair, dining; rust, M7..$8.00

Reliable, chair, kitchen; ivory w/bl seat, M7 ....$8.00

Reliable, chair, living room; red w/rust base or bl w/rust base, M7, ea...$20.00

Reliable, doll, baby (jtd or sucking thumb), hard plastic, pk, 2¾", M7, ea..$20.00

Reliable, fireplace, rust, M7...$45.00

Reliable, piano, translucent or med gr, M7 ....$55.00

Reliable, radio, floor; rust, M7...$15.00

Reliable, stool, vanity; rust, M7 ....$8.00

Reliable, stove, ivory w/bl trim, M7 ....$20.00

Reliable, table, dining; rust, M7 ....$25.00

Reliable, table, kitchen; ivory, M7 ....$12.00

Reliable, tub, ivory w/bl trim, M7 ....$25.00

Renwal, baby bath, bl w/bunnies decal or pk w/bears decal, M7, ea...$15.00

Renwal, bench, piano/vanity; brn or lt brn swirl, M7, ea....$2.00

Renwal, bench, piano/vanity; lt gr, M7 ....$4.00

Renwal, broom, rnd style, metallic red hdl, M7.............$150.00

Renwal, buffet, nonopening drawer, brn, M7 ....$6.00

Renwal, buffet, opening drawer, red, M7 ....$20.00

Renwal, carpet sweeper, red w/bl hdl, 1 roller, M7............$30.00

Renwal, chair, barrel; bl w/brn base (stenciled) or red w/brn base, M7, ea $10.00

Renwal, chair, barrel; bl w/red base or ivory w/brn base, M7, ea $8.00

Renwal, chair, barrel; med bl w/ metallic red base, M7.......$9.00

Renwal, chair, club; bl w/brn base or bl w/red base, M7, ea...$8.00

Renwal, chair, club; dk gr w/brn base, M7.........................$10.00

Renwal, chair, club; ivory w/brn base, ivory w/red base, lt bl w/brn base, pk w/metallic red base, pk w/red base, M7, ea..........$8.00

Renwal, chair, rocker; yel w/red, M7 ....$8.00

Renwal, chair, teacher's; brn or bl, M7, ea $15.00

Renwal, china closet, opening door, ivory or reddish-brn w/stenciling, M7, ea $15.00

Renwal, clock, kitchen; ivory, M7 ....$20.00

Renwal, clock, mantel; ivory or red, M7, ea......................$10.00

Renwal, cradle, bl, no decal, doll insert, M7 ....$25.00

Renwal, cradle, bl, w/decal, M7..$35.00

Renwal, crib, nursery; ivory (John, Mary, Alice, Irene), matt pk (Peter) or pk (John, Mary, Peter), M7, ea $10.00

Renwal, crib, nursery; w/baby, blanket & cb insert, ivory (Alice), M7 ....$25.00

Renwal, desk, student; bl, red, or yel, M7, ea $12.00

Renwal, desk, teacher's; brn, M7 ....$20.00

Renwal, dining set, table w/4 chairs & china closet, reddish-brn w/ivory, M7 ....$32.00

Renwal, doll, baby, M7 ....$10.00

Renwal, doll, baby; chubby w/pnt diaper...........................$75.00

Renwal, doll, baby; plain, w/pnt diaper or w/pnt suit, M7, ea ..$10.00

Renwal, doll, father; metal rivets, bl suit, M7 ....$30.00

Renwal, doll, father; plastic rivets, all tan, M7 ....$25.00

Renwal, doll, mother; metal rivets, rose dress, M7...........$30.00

Renwal, doll, nurse or doctor, MIB, $150.00 each.
(Photo courtesy Judith Mosholder)

Renwal, doll, sister; plastic rivets, all tan, M7...................$25.00

Renwal, doll, sister; plastic rivets, yel dress, M7...............$22.00

Renwal, dust pan, red or yel, M7, ea...................................$10.00

Renwal, garbage can, red w/yel or yel w/red, M7, ea.........$15.00

Renwal, highchair, ivory, M7...$30.00

Renwal, insert, blanket or doll; M7, ea...............................$5.00

Renwal, ironing board w/iron, bl (pk & bl iron) or pk (pk & bl iron), M7, ea $25.00

Renwal, ironing board; bl or pk, M7, ea $7.00

Renwal, kiddie car, bl w/red & yel or yel w/red & bl, M7, ea...$55.00

Renwal, lamp, floor; brn or yel w/ivory shade, M7, ea......$20.00

Renwal, dresser with bench, $17.00; lamp, $10.00.

Renwal, lamp, table; caramel or metallic red w/ivory shade, M7, ea..$12.00

Renwal, lamp, table; highly marbleized brn w/ivory shade or brn w/wht or ivory shade, M7, ea.....................................$10.00

Renwal, piano, marbleized brn, M7.....................................$35.00

Renwal, playground seesaw, bl w/red & yel or yel w/red & bl, M7, ea $45.00

Renwal, playground slide, bl w/red steps or yel w/bl steps, M7, ea $22.00

Renwal, playpen, bl w/pk bottom or pk w/bl bottom, M7, ea $15.00

Renwal, radio, table; brn or red, M7, ea $15.00

Renwal, radio, table; metallic red, M7 ....$18.00

Renwal, radio phonograph, red, M7 ....$20.00

Renwal, refrigerator, nonopening door, wht (not ivory) w/blk, M7...$20.00

Renwal, scale, ivory or red, M7, ea......................................$10.00

Renwal, server, opening door or nonopening door, brn, ea ..$8.00

Renwal, server, opening drawer, brn or reddish brn w/stenciling, M7, ea $12.00

Renwal, server, opening drawer, red, M7............................$15.00

Renwal, sink, nonopening door, wht (not ivory) w/blk door, M7...$18.00

Renwal, sink, opening door, ivory w/red, M7.....................$18.00

Renwal, smoking stand, ivory w/red or red w/ivory, M7, ea $12.00

Renwal, stool, ivory w/red seat or red w/ivory seat, M7, ea $10.00

Renwal, stove, nonopening door, ivory w/blk or lt turq, M7, ea....$12.00

Renwal, stove, nonopening door, wht (not ivory) w/blk, M7 .....$18.00

Renwal, stove, opening door, ivory w/blk, M7 ....$15.00

Renwal, stove, opening door, ivory w/red, M7 ....$18.00

Renwal, table, cocktail; brn or reddish brn, M7, ea $10.00

Renwal, table, cocktail; red or metallic red, M7, ea.........$15.00

Renwal, table, dining; orange or reddish-orange, M7, ea..$15.00

Renwal, table, ivory or very deep ivory, M7, ea..................$5.00

Renwal, table, lamp; reddish brn, M7..................................$8.00

Renwal, telephone, red w/yel or yel w/red, M7, ea...........$22.00

Renwal, toydee, bl, matt bl or pk, M7, ea...........................$6.00

Renwal, toydee, bl w/Little Boy Blue decal, M7 ....$12.00

Renwal, tricycle, red w/bl seat & yel handlebar, M7.........$25.00

Renwal, tricycle, yel w/red seat & bl handlebar & wheels, M7 ..$25.00

Renwal, tub, nursery; ivory, M7......................................$10.00

Renwal, vacuum cleaner, yel w/red, good decal, M7.........$25.00

Renwal, washing machine, bl w/pk or pk w/bl, bear decal, M7, ea..$30.00

Strombecker, bathroom set, 6-pc, unfinished, metal hdls, w/orig boxes, sandpaper & instructions, 1936, ¾" scale, M7 ..$45.00

Strombecker, bed, pk, 1930s-40s, ¾" scale, M7, ea.............$8.00

Strombecker, bed, walnut, 1936, 1" scale, M7...................$18.00

Strombecker, bowl, silver or yel, ¾" scale, M7, ea $10.00

Strombecker, buffet, opening drawer, walnut, 1930s, 1" scale, M7...$30.00

Strombecker, chair, bedroom/dining; unfinished, 1930s, ¾" scale, M7...$6.00

Strombecker, chair, dining room; bl, 1930s, ¾" scale, M7..$6.00

Strombecker, chair, dining room; walnut, 1930s, 1" scale, M7...$30.00

Strombecker, chair, kitchen; red, ¾" scale, M7..................$6.00

Strombecker, chair, living room; aqua or red, 1940s-50s, ¾" scale, ea..$10.00

Strombecker, chair, living room; gr flocked, 1950s, ¾" scale, M7..$15.00

Strombecker, chair w/ottoman; lt brn flocked, 1" scale, M7..$25.00

Strombecker, clock, grandfather; red w/blk, bl w/blk or dk peach w/blk, ¾" scale, M7, ea..$15.00

Strombecker, lamp, floor; ivory shade, blk base, ¾" scale, M7 ...$15.00

Strombecker, lamp, floor; unfinished, ¾" scale, M7 ....$10.00

Strombecker, lamp, table; yel or gr w/ivory shade, ¾" scale, M7, ea..$15.00

Strombecker, living room set: sofa, chair, footstool, end/library tables, radio, grandfather clock & bench, 1" scale, M7.............$135.00

Strombecker, night stand, lt gr or pk, ¾" scale, M7, ea.......$6.00

Strombecker, night stand, walnut, 1936, 1" scale, M7 ......$15.00

Strombecker, piano, red, 1930s, ¾" scale, M7...................$18.00

Strombecker, radio, floor; walnut, 1930s, 1" scale, M7 .....$18.00

Strombecker, radio, floor; walnut w/etched detailing, ¾" scale, M7...$12.00

Strombecker, scale, bl or gr, ¾" scale, M7, ea $15.00

Strombecker, sink, bathroom; gr w/gold swirl, 1" scale, M7 ..$20.00

Strombecker, sink, ivory or aqua, ¾" scale, M7, ea.............$8.00

Strombecker, sofa, red (1930s-1940s-1950s), peach (1940s-1950s), aqua (1940s), unfinished (1930s), ¾" scale, M7, ea..$10.00

Strombecker, stove, ivory, ¾" scale, M7...........................$15.00

Strombecker, stove, kitchen; ivory w/blk, 1936, 1" scale, M7...$20.00

Strombecker, table, coffee; walnut, 1950s, 1" scale, M7 ...$12.00

Strombecker, table, dining room; bl, 1930s, ¾" scale, M7 ..$10.00

Strombecker, table, dining room; walnut, 1930s, 1" scale, M7...$20.00

Strombecker, table, living room; walnut, 1936, 1" scale, M7 ...$25.00

Strombecker, table, trestle; red, ¾" scale, M7 ....$8.00

Strombecker, table & 2 chairs, kitchen; red, 1936, 1" scale, M7...$35.00

Strombecker, toilet, ivory, ¾" scale, M7...........................$10.00

Strombecker, tub, aqua, bl, ivory, or unfinished, ¾" scale, M7, ea..$10.00

Strombecker, urn, gr or yel, ¾" scale, M7, ea....................$10.00

Strombecker, vanity & bench, walnut, 1936, 1" scale, M7 ..$30.00

Superior, any soft plastic pc, sm, M7, ea, from $1 to...........$2.00

Superior, bed, lt gr, turq, bright yel, or red, M7, ea..............$5.00

Superior, chair, dining room; bright bl or dk ivory, ¾" scale, M7, ea..$3.00

Superior, chair, kitchen; ivory, olive gr, pale yel, or wht, ¾" scale, M7, ea..$3.00

Superior, chair, living room; rnd back, aqua, bright yel, pale gr, or red, ¾" scale, M7, ea...$4.00

Superior, chair, living room; sq back, bl, brn, lt bl, lt pk, or ivory, ¾" scale, M7, ea...$4.00

Superior, chest of drawers, low, bright yel, dk ivory, med gr, pale gr, royal bl, bright bl, or red, ¾" scale, M7, ea..............$5.00

Superior, crib, rust brn or bright bl, ¾" scale, M7, ea..........$8.00

Superior, hutch, bright bl, bright yel, pk, or ivory, M7, ¾" scale, M7, ea..$5.00

Superior, potty chair, wht or bright bl, ¾" scale, M7, ea.....$8.00

Superior, refrigerator, wht, pearlized wht, ivory, med off-gr, or pale yel, ¾" scale, M7, ea..$5.00

Superior, sink, bathroom; med off-gr, ivory or wht, ¾" scale, M7, ea..$5.00

Superior, sink/stove combo, med off-gr, ivory, or wht, ¾" scale, M7, ea..$5.00

Superior, sofa, brn, pale gr, turq, or red, ¾" scale, M7, ea ...$5.00

Superior, stool, 4-legged, bl or turq, ¾" scale, M7, ea.........$2.00

Superior, table, coffee; pale gr or red, ¾" scale, M7, ea.......$8.00

Superior, table, dining; bright bl or bright yel, ¾" scale, M7, ea..$8.00

Superior, table & 2 chairs, kitchen; med off-gr, ¾" scale, M7, ea..$10.00

Superior, tub, bright yel, dk soft yel, lt gr, pale gr, or turq, ¾" scale, M7, ea..$5.00

Superior, vanity, bright yel, dk soft yel, lt yel, pale gr, or red, ¾" scale, M7, ea...$3.00

Superior, vanity stool, ivory or lt yel, ¾" scale, M7, ea.......$3.00

Superior, vanity w/mirror, red, ¾" scale, M7 ....$5.00

Tomy Smaller Homes, armoire, w/hangers, M7.................$15.00

Tomy Smaller Homes, bed, canopy; M7............................$15.00

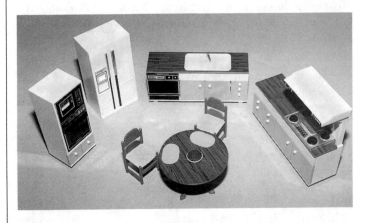

Tomy Smaller Homes, oven unit with microwave and cherry pie, $55.00; refrigerator, $15.00; sink/dishwasher with two racks, $15.00; stove/hood unit, $15.00; kitchen table, $8.00; kitchen chairs, $3.00 each. (Photo courtesy Judith Mosholder)

Tomy Smaller Homes, cabinet, bathroom; w/dbl-bowl sink, M7 ....$20.00
Tomy Smaller Homes, cabinet, stereo; M7 ....$15.00
Tomy Smaller Homes, cabinet, TV; high-wall, M7 ....$55.00
Tomy Smaller Homes, chest, nursery; 6 opening drawers, M7 ....$15.00
Tomy Smaller Homes, cushion, den; rust, M7 ....$3.00
Tomy Smaller Homes, mirror, bathroom; standing, M7....$15.00
Tomy Smaller Homes, planter, bathroom; no towels, M7 ...$10.00
Tomy Smaller Homes, range top w/hood unit, M7 ....$18.00
Tomy Smaller Homes, scale, bathroom; M7 ....$15.00
Tomy Smaller Homes, sink, kitchen; dbl bowl, w/dishwasher, no racks, M7 ....$8.00
Tomy Smaller Homes, sink, kitchen; dbl bowl, 1 rack, M7 ...$3.00
Tomy Smaller Homes, sofa, den; 2-pc, M7 ....$12.00
Tomy Smaller Homes, table, coffee; M7 ....$10.00
Tomy Smaller Homes, television, M7 ....$50.00
Tomy Smaller Homes, toilet, M7 ....$10.00
Tomy Smaller Homes, tub, bathroom;, M7 ....$15.00
Tomy Smaller Homes, vanity, M7 ....$15.00
Tomy Smaller Homes, vanity stool, M7 ....$6.00
Tootsietoy, cabinet, medicine; ivory, M7 ....$25.00
Tootsietoy, cabinet, medicine; lavender, M7 ....$15.00
Tootsietoy, chair, bedroom rocker; pk, M7 ....$18.00
Tootsietoy, chair, club; red flocked, M7 ....$20.00
Tootsietoy, chair, dining room; ivory, M7 ....$7.00
Tootsietoy, chair, living room; gold wicker-look w/cushion, M7 ....$18.00
Tootsietoy, chair, rocker; gold or ivory wicker-look w/cushion, M7, ea $22.00

Tootsietoy, dining room furniture set, MIB, A, $225.00; girl's bedroom set, MIB, A, $125.00; living room furniture set, MIB, A, $225.00.

Tootsietoy, lamp, floor; gold, M7 ....$40.00
Tootsietoy, lamp, table; bl, M7 ....$45.00
Tootsietoy, sofa, gold or ivory wicker-look w/cushion, M7, ea ...$25.00
Tootsietoy, table, living room; gold, M7 ....$20.00
Tootsietoy, telephone, gr, M7 ....$45.00
Tootsietoy, towel bar, ivory, M7 ....$20.00
Tootsietoy, tub, Little Lady Blue, hard plastic, 6", M7 ....$5.00
Tootsietoy, tub, Wannatoy, soft plastic, pk, ¾" scale, M7 ...$3.00
Wolverine, chair, club; pk or turq, M7, ea..........................$3.00
Wolverine, desk, turq or off-wht, M7, ea............................$3.00
Wolverine, dresser w/mirror, brn, M7 ....$3.00
Wolverine, highboy, brn or turq, M7, ea $3.00
Wolverine, refrigerator, wht, M7 ....$3.00
Wolverine, sink, bathroom; turq, M7 ....$3.00

Wolverine, sink/stove combo, lavender or wht, M7, ea $3.00
Wolverine, sofa, pk, M7 ....$3.00
Wolverine, table, coffee; brn, M7 ....$3.00
Wolverine, table, end; brn, M7...$3.00
Wolverine, television, brn, M7 ....$3.00
Wolverine, toilet, turq, M7 ....$3.00
Wolverine, tub, pk or turq, M7, ea $3.00
Young Decorator, buffet, dk marbleized maroon, M7 ....$25.00
Young Decorator, carpet sweeper, red w/bl hdl, no rollers, M7 ....$10.00
Young Decorator, carpet sweeper, red w/bl hdl, 2 rollers, M7 ....$30.00
Young Decorator, carpet sweeper, red w/yel, 2 rollers, M7...$30.00
Young Decorator, chair, dining room; dk marbleized maroon w/yel seats, M7, ea $12.00
Young Decorator, china closet, dk marbleized maroon, M7 ..$25.00
Young Decorator, crib, bl, M7 ....$45.00
Young Decorator, diaper pail, yel w/bl, M7 ....$25.00
Young Decorator, highchair, bl or pk, M7 ....$45.00
Young Decorator, lamp, floor; gr shade, M7 ....$60.00
Young Decorator, night stand, dk marbleized maroon, M7 ..$15.00
Young Decorator, playpen, pk, M7 ....$45.00
Young Decorator, refrigerator, wht, M7 ....$55.00
Young Decorator, sink, bathroom; yel w/bl, M7 ....$45.00
Young Decorator, sofa, 3 sections w/2 ends & curved center pc, gr, M7 ....$45.00
Young Decorator, sofa, 4 sections, rose, M7 ....$60.00
Young Decorator, stove, wht, M7 ....$55.00
Young Decorator, table, coffee; dk marbleized maroon, M7....$18.00
Young Decorator, table, dining; dk marbleized maroon, M7...$35.00
Young Decorator, television, M7 ....$75.00
Young Decorator, tub, corner; bl w/yel, M7......................$35.00

Dollhouses

Dollhouses were first made commercially in America in the late 1700s. A century later, Bliss and Schoenhut were making wonderful dollhouses that even yet occasionally turn up on the market, and many were being imported from Germany. During the '40s and '50s, American toy makers made a variety of cottages; today they're all collectible.

Advisors: Bob and Marcie Tubbs (T5).
Other Sources: M15.

Bliss, 1½-story w/attic, paper litho on wood, red slanted roof w/attic dormers, front porch w/steps, 20x18", G, A $1,800.00
Bliss, 2-room, 2-story, paper litho on wood, dbl front doors, steps, portico, lattice porch rail, 18x16x10", Fair, A $275.00
Bliss, 2-story, paper litho on wood, bl slanted roof, brick facade, sm porch, sm, EX $300.00
Bliss, 2-story, 2-room, litho paper on wood, front porch w/turned columns, celluloid windows, electric, 16½", EX, A .$1,700.00
Brumberger, 2-story comtemporary colonial w/5 rooms, wood compo w/plastic furniture, 1970, 20x24", MIB, T5....$60.00
English, 2-story, 2-room Tudor, electric, opening shutters, on sq base, 14x11x16", VG..$500.00

Fisher-Price, #250, 3-story w/5 rooms, spiral staircase, 1978-80, M, C13 ....$40.00

Fisher-Price, #280, three-story, lights up, MIB, $50.00.
(Photo courtesy Brad Cassity)

Marx, Little Red Schoolhouse, 1950s, with plastic furniture and figures, 16" x 7" x 8", $450.00. (Photo courtesy Bob and Marcie Tubbs)

German Blue Roof, paper litho over wood, 31" x 26", G, A, $1,600.00.

Ohio Art, Midget Manor, 1949, 8" x 3" x 5½", with furniture, MIB, $300.00. (Photo courtesy Bob and Marcie Tubbs)

Rich, 6-room bungalow, litho on fiberboard, Arts & Crafts style, 4 metal windows, flower boxes, 1930s, 33x21x16", VG..$200.00

German, bl roof, 3-story warehouse w/hoist, outfitted w/2-horse dray, barrels, boxes, etc, 22x11x9", VG $2,000.00

German, carriage house, pnt wood/litho paper, 2 stalls, office, carriage stall, hay loft, w/carriage, 25x36x17", VG, A..$1,700.00

German, 2-story, litho paper & pnt wod, window glass, electric, 27x24", VG $1,350.00

Gottschalk, 2-story, 2-room, litho paper on wood, Austrian villa, 31x27x19", losses/damage, otherwise EX, A.........$9,200.00

Gottschalk, 2-story, 2-room, litho paper on wood, Victorian, bl roof, turned details, glass windows, 27x18x14", EX, A $4,300.00

Jaylne, 2-story, 5-room, litho tin, gr siding over wht w/red bricks, purple roof, 4 windows, 18x14x7" $50.00

Marx, 2-story, 7-room, litho tin, 2nd-floor patio, breezeway-attached rec room, wht clapboard/mc stone, 38x14x8", VG $95.00

McLoughlin Bros, Dolly's Playhouse, folding 2-story w/2 rooms, paper litho on board, late 1800s, 21", EX (worn box), A...$400.00

Schoenut 'Daggle' two-story #5/50, 1923, wood and fiberboard, 28" x 26" x 24", VG, A, $1,800.00.

Schoenhut, 2-room bungalow, emb cardboard roof, electric, ea side opens, orig label, 17x17x15", EX, A $550.00

Superior, tin, MIB, $125.00.

T Cohn, 2-story, 6-room, litho tin, wht & red w/gr shutters, red roof, dbl patio, 28½x14x9½", VG $200.00
Unknown Maker, bungalow w/5 rooms, pnt wood w/glass windows, railed porch, lift-off roof, 27x24", EX............$900.00
Unknown Maker, Victorian Mansard roof mansion, on sq 49" lawn, attic, staircases, iron fence, wooden outhouse, 1890s, VG...$2,800.00
Unknown Maker, 2-story, wood w/faux bricks, gingerbread, window panels move, porch, staircase, 4 fireplaces, 35x34x24" $1,700.00

SHOPS AND SINGLE ROOMS

Bathroom, Marklin, 3-sided tin room, complete w/tub, sink & toilet, 7x14", VG, A..$950.00
Bathroom Set, Arcade #681, pedestal lavatory, corner bath, closet, bath stool & shower, NM $2,200.00

Bedroom Setting, attributed to Gerbruder Schneegas, Waltershausen, 1880s – 1900s, maple, 1" scale, in an S.S. Pierce wooden case, A, $650.00.

Corner Grocer, Wolverine, litho tin w/shelving, opens & includes many products, 12½x15½", G..................$350.00
Kitchen, Germany, wood, wallpapered throughout, tin stove, brickwork, assorted utensils, early, 12x22x13" VG, A..........$700.00

Country Store, wood with porcelain name plates on drawers, contemporary accessories, 14" x 13" x 28", EX, A, $700.00.

Kitchen, stained tin, dtd 1882, w/tin utensils, stenciled floor, 9½x14½", VG...$350.00
Kitchen, US, ca 1875, tin walls w/hanging pots & pans, floor stove, faux bricks, 18½x1x8½", VG $660.00
Laundry Set, Arcade #716, washing machine, wringer, dbl sinks, bench & chair, NM..$2,500.00
Little Red Schoolhouse, Remco, 1967, EX (orig box) $45.00
Newlyweds Bathroom, Marx #192, 1925, complete w/furniture, 3x5x3", NM, A...$225.00
Newlyweds Kitchen, Marx #190, 1925, complete w/furniture, 3x5x3", NM, EX, A..$225.00
Shop, German, pnt wood/papered, 16 drawers, light w/glass shade, many glass/pottery accessories, 16x29x10½", EX, A..$1,600.00

Dolls and Accessories

Obviously the field of dolls cannot be covered in a price guide such as this, but we wanted to touch on some of the later plastic dolls from the '50s and '60s, since so much of the collector interest today is centered on those decades. For in-depth information on dolls of all types, we recommend these lovely doll books, all of which are available from Collector Books: *Doll Values, Antique to Modern*, First – Fifth Editions, and *Modern Collectible Dolls*, Volume I – V, all by Patsy Moyer; *Madame Alexander Collector's Dolls Price Guide #26* and *Madame Alexander Store Exclusives and Limited Editions*, both by Linda Crowsey; *Collector's Guide to Ideal Dolls*, Second Edition, by Judith Izen; *Collector's Encyclopedia of Vogue Dolls* by Judith Izen and Carol Stover; *Collector's Encyclopedia of American Composition Dolls, 1900 – 1950*, by Ursula R. Mertz; *Effanbee Dolls* and *Collector's Encyclopedia of Madame Alexander Dolls, 1965 – 1990*, by Patricia Smith; and *Dolls of the 1960s and 1970s* by Cindy Sabulis. Other books are referenced in specific subcategories.

See also **Action Figures; Barbie and Friends; Character, TV, and Movie Collectibles; GI Joe;** and other specific categories.

BABY DOLLS

Remnants of baby dolls have been found in the artifacts of most primitive digs. Some are just sticks or stuffed leather or animal skins.

Baby dolls teach our young nurturing and caring. Mothering instincts stay with us — and aren't we lucky as doll collectors that we can keep 'mothering' even after the young have 'flown the nest.'

Baby dolls come in all sizes and mediums: vinyl, plastic, rubber, porcelain, cloth, etc. Almost everyone remembers some baby doll they had as a child. The return to childhood is such a great trip. Keep looking and you will find yours.

Advisor: Marcia Fanta (M15).

Baby Beans, Mattel, 1970, several variations, NM, ea from $15 to $20.00

Baby Colleen, Mattel, stuffed cloth & vinyl w/orig checked nightgown, 15", EX, from $40 to $50.00

Baby Crawl-Along, Remco, 1967, orig outfit, 20", EX, from $25 to $35.00

Baby Dear One, Vogue, 1961, cloth & vinyl, all orig, 25", NM, from $175 to $225.00

Baby Fun, Mattel, 1968, orig outfit, no accessories, 7", EX, from $25 to $30.00

Baby Luv, Eegee, cloth & vinyl, all orig, 14", EX, from $25 to $30.00

Baby Small-Walk, Mattel, 1968, MIB, from $55 to $65.00

Baby Snoozie, Ideal, 1965, re-dressed, EX, from $50 to $75.00

Belly Button Baby, Ideal, 1970, push belly button & she moves, all orig, EX, from $25 to $30.00

Busy Becky, Mattel/Montgomery Ward's Exclusive, 1972, MIB, from $65 to $75.00

Clapping doll by Ideal (claps when stomach is pressed), 15", EX, A, $200.00. (Photo courtesy McMasters Doll Auctions)

Dancerina, Mattel, 1968, battery-op, 24", MIB, from $75 to $125.00

Giggles, Ideal, 1967, plastic & vinyl, 18", MIB, from $125 to $200.00

Kissy, Ideal, 1960s, 22", MIB, from $100 to....................$125.00

My Fair Baby, Effanbee, 1960, vinyl, all orig, complete w/ID bracelet, 18", NM, from $45 to................................$65.00

Patchwork Kids, Ideal, 1976, several variations, 13", MIB, ea from $25 to..$35.00

Patti Playful, Ideal, 1970, 16", EX, from $25.00 to $35.00. (Photo courtesy Cindy Sabulis)

Peachy & Her Puppets, Mattel, 1972, MIB, from $35 to..$50.00

Penny Playpal, Ideal, 1959, re-dressed, 32", NM, from $300 to..$350.00

Pussy Cat, Madame Alexander, 1965, stuffed cloth & vinyl, 20", MIB, S14, from $150 to...$175.00

Rub-A-Dub Dolly, Ideal, 1973, vinyl, nude, EX...............$20.00

Saucy Walker, Ideal, all orig, 28", NM, from $150 to.....$225.00

Stoneage Baby (Pebbles Flintstone look-alike), Eegee, vinyl, 14", MIB, from $150 to...$175.00

Sweet April, Remco, 1971, 5½", complete, NM (NM case), from $25 to..$35.00

Swingy, Mattel, 1967, battery-op, MIB, from $75 to $100.00

Tearie Dearie, Ideal, 1964, all orig, complete w/highchair, EX, from $35 to..$45.00

Teenie Bopper, Horsman, 1969, 12", MIB, from $40 to....$50.00

Teeny Tiny Tear, American Character, vinyl, re-dressed, 12", EX, S14, from $25 to $30.00

Tiny Baby Pat-A-Burp, Mattel, 1965, vinyl, re-dressed, 14", EX, from $25 to..$30.00

Tiny Tears, American Character, Rock-A-Bye Eyes, 12", MIB, A, $350.00. (Photo courtesy McMasters Doll Auctions)

Toddler Thumbelina, Ideal, 1960s, complete w/walker, NMIB, from $75 to $100.00

Tumbling Tomboy, Remco, 1969, orig outfit, 17", EX, from $25 to $35.00

Victoria, in christening gown, $95.00. (Photo courtesy Marcia Fanta)

Wee Bonnie Baby, Allied Doll & Toy Corp, 1963, stuffed cloth & vinyl, 10", MIB, S14, from $30 to $40.00

BETSY McCALL

The tiny 8" Betsy McCall doll was manufactured by the American Character Doll Co. from 1957 through 1963. She was made from high-quality hard plastic with a bisque-like finish and hand-painted features. Betsy came in four hair colors — tosca, red, blond, and brunette. She had blue sleep eyes, molded lashes, a winsome smile, and a fully jointed body with bendable knees. On her back there is an identification circle which reads McCall Corp. The basic doll wore a sheer chemise, white taffeta panties, nylon socks, and Maryjane-style shoes, and could be purchased for $2.25.

There were two different materials used for tiny Betsy's hair. The first was a soft mohair sewn into fine mesh. Later the rubber skullcap was rooted with saran which was more suitable for washing and combing.

Betsy McCall had an extensive wardrobe with nearly one hundred outfits, each of which could be purchased separately. They were made from wonderful fabrics such as velvet, taffeta, felt, and even real mink. Each ensemble came with the appropriate footwear and was priced under $3.00. Since none of Betsy's clothing was tagged, it is often difficult to identify other than by its square snap closures (although these were used by other companies as well).

Betsy McCall is a highly collectible doll today but is still fairly easy to find at doll shows. Prices remain reasonable for this beautiful clothes horse and her many accessories. For further information we recommend *Betsy McCall, A Collector's Guide*, by Marci Van Ausdall.

Advisor: Marci Van Ausdall (V2).

See also Clubs, Newsletters, and Other Publications.

Doll, American Character, orig outfit, multi-jtd, 29", MIB..$250.00

Doll, American Character, Playtime outfit, 14", EX......$250.00

Doll, American Character, Town & Country outfit, 8", M..$175.00

Doll, Ideal, all orig, MIB, V2.....................................$225.00

Doll, orig outfit w/pk tissue & booklet, 8", MIB, V2, minimum value..$225.00

Doll, Starter Set, #9300, MIB, $275.00.
(Photo by Leslie Robinson/from the collection of Marci Van Ausdal)

Doll, TV Time #9153, all orig, complete w/TV, M, V2 ..$150.00

Doll, w/trunk & wardrobe, 14", M $500.00

Doll, wearing pk Prom Time formal, 8", EX, V2 ....$150.00

Doll, wearing 1958 pk ballerina outfit & slippers, EX, V2 ..$175.00

Doll, in cowgirl outfit, $350.00. (Photo by Leslie Robinson/from the collection of Marci Van Ausdal)

Everyday Calendar, Milton Bradley, EX (worn box)..........$25.00

Outfit, April Showers, complete, EX, V2.......................$45.00

Outfit, Bar-B-Que, MOC, V2.......................................$145.00

Outfit, Birthday Party, MOC, V2..................................$145.00

Outfit, fur stole & muff, MIB, V2..................................$225.00

Outfit, Prom Time Formal, bl, EX, V2 ....$50.00
Outfit, Sunday Best, 1957, complete, EX, V2 ....$125.00
Outfit, Zoo Time, complete, VG, V2 ....$65.00

BLYTHE BY KENNER

Blythe by Kenner is an 11" doll with a slender body and an extra large head. You can change her eye color by pulling a string in the back of her head. She came with different hair colors and had fashions, cases, and wigs that could be purchased separately. She was produced in the early 1970s which accounts for her 'groovy' wardrobe. In excellent condition, loose dolls are worth from $50.00 to $75.00.

Advisor: Dawn Diaz (P2).

Case, #33241, image of blond-haired doll wearing Pow-Wow
    Poncho, orange background, vinyl, EX, PS...............$50.00
Doll, blond hair, MIB, from $100 to................................$150.00
Doll, brunette, wearing Medieval Mood, EX, P2 ....$75.00
Doll, brunette hair, MIB, from $100 to $150.00
Doll, lt red hair, wearing Golden Goddess, EX, P2 ....$75.00
Doll, red hair, wearing Love 'N Lace, EX, P2 ....$75.00
Outfit, Aztec Arrival, complete, EX, P2............................$50.00
Outfit, Golden Goddess, NRFB, P2 ....$75.00
Outfit, Kozy Kape, complete EX, P2.................................$50.00
Outfit, Lounging Lovely, NRFB, P2 ....$75.00
Outfit, Love 'N Lace, NRFB, P2.......................................$75.00
Outfit, Pleasant Peasant, missing shoes, EX, P2 ....$40.00
Outfit, Pow-Wow Poncho, complete, EX, P2.....................$50.00
Wig, Lemon, complete w/instructions, M, P2 ....$75.00

CELEBRITY AND PERSONALITY DOLLS

Celebrity and character dolls have been widely collected for many years, but they've lately shown a significant increase in demand. Except for the rarer examples, most of these dolls are still fairly easy to find at doll shows, toy auctions, and flea markets, and the majority are priced under $100.00. These are the dolls that bring back memories of childhood TV shows, popular songs, favorite movies, and familiar characters. Mego, Mattel, Remco, and Hasbro are among the largest manufacturers.

Condition is a very important worth-assessing factor, and if the doll is still in the original box, so much the better! Should the box be unopened (NRFB), the value is further enhanced. Using mint as a standard, add 50% for the same doll mint in the box and 75% if it has never been taken out. On the other hand, dolls in only good or poorer condition drop at a rapid pace.

Advisor: Henri Yunes (Y1).

Abba, Matchbox, 1978, 4 different, 9", MIB, ea $85.00
Abbott & Costello (Who's on First), Ideal, 1984, 12", MIB,
    Y1...$100.00
Al Lewis (Grandpa Munster), Remco, 1964, 6", MIB $200.00
Alan Alda (Hawkeye from M*A*S*H), Woolworth, 1976, 9",
    MOC, Y1 ....$30.00
Alexandra Paul (Stephanie from Baywatch), Toy Island, 1997,
    11½", NRFB, Y1 ....$35.00
Andy Gibb, Ideal, 1979, 7½", NRFB $50.00

Angela Landsbury, 1970s, 7", MIB $55.00
Angie Dickinson (Police Woman), Horsman, 1976, 9", MIB...$60.00
Annissa Jones (Buffy from Family Affair), Mattel, 1967, talker,
    10" w/5" Mrs Beasley doll, MIB, Y1 ....$450.00
Annissa Jones (Buffy from Family Affair), Mattel, 1967, 6" w/3"
    Mrs Beasley doll, MIB $250.00
Audrey Hepburn (Breakfast at Tiffany's), Mattel, 1998, blk or pk
    outfit, 11½", MIB, Y1, ea $85.00
Barbara Eden (I Dream of Jeannie), Libby Majorette Doll Corp,
    1966, 20", rare, NM..$200.00
Barbara Eden (I Dream of Jeannie), outfit, Remco, 1977, several
    variations, for 6" dolls, MIP, ea..................................$45.00
Barbara Eden (I Dream of Jeannie), Remco, 1972, 6½",
    NRFB...$100.00
Beatles, Remco, 1964, ea member w/instrument, ea from $150
    to $200.00
Beverly Hills 90210, accessory, Peach Pit Snack Shop, Mattel,
    1992, complete, MIB...$100.00
Beverly Hills 90210, gift set, Mattel, 1991, w/Brandon, Dylan &
    Brenda, 11½", MIB, Y1 ....$150.00
Beverly Hills 90210, Mattel, 1991, 5 different, 11½", MIB, ea ..$65.00
Beverly Johnson, Real Models Collection, Matchbox, 1989,
    11½", NRFB...$55.00
Bobby Orr, Regal, 1975, 12", rare, MOC $800.00
Boy George, LJN, 1984, 11½", scarce, MIB.....................$135.00
Brooke Shields, LJN, 1982, 1st issue, 11½", NRFB $50.00
Brooke Shields, outfit, LJN, 1983, 12 different, MOC, Y1, ea.$25.00
Brooke Shields, LJN, 1983, 2nd issue, in swimsuit w/suntan
    body, 11½", rare, NRFB...$95.00
Brooke Shields, LJN, 1983, 3rd issue, Prom Party, 11½", rare,
    NRFB...$200.00
Captain & Tenille, Mego, 1970s, 12", MIB, ea $60.00

Carol Channing (Hello Dolly), Nasco Dolls, 1962, 11½", rare, MIB, $350.00.
(Photo courtesy Henri Yunes)

Charlie Chaplin, World Doll, 1989, 100th Anniversary, 11½",
    NRFB, Y1..$55.00
Cher, Mego, 1976, 1st issue, pk dress, 12", NRFB (orange box)..$70.00

Cher, Mego, 1977, 2nd issue, Growing Hair, 12", NRFB (photo on box)..$80.00

Cher, Mego, 1981, 3rd issue, red swimsuit, 12", rare, NRFB (photo on box)..$95.00

Cheryl Ladd (Kris from Charlie's Angels), Hasbro, 1977, jumpsuit & scarf, 8½", MOC..$40.00

Cheryl Ladd (Kris from Charlie's Angels), Mattel, 1978, 11½", NRFB...$80.00

Cheryl Tiegs, Real Models Collection, Matchbox, 1989, 11½", NRFB..$55.00

Christy Brinkley, Real Models Collection, Matchbox, 1989, 11½", NRFB..$55.00

Clark Gable (Rhett Butler), World Dolls, 1980, 1st edition, 12", NRFB...$65.00

Claudia Schiffer, Top Models Collection, Hasbro, 1995, 11½", rare, MIB...$100.00

David Hasselhoff (Mitch from Baywatch), Toy Island, 1997, 12", NRFB, Y1...$35.00

Debbie Boone, Mattel, 1978, 11", MIB, H4.....................$50.00

Deidra Hall (Marlena from Days of Our Lives), Mattel, 1999, 11½", NRFB, Y1..$85.00

Dennis Rodman (Bad As I Wanna Be), Street Players, 1995, 11½", MIB, Y1..$55.00

Dennis Rodman (Wedding Day), Street Players, 1995, 11½", MIB, Y1..$65.00

Desi Arnez (Ricky Ricardo), Applause, 1988, 17", MIB...$50.00

Desi Arnez (Ricky Ricardo), Hamilton Presents, 1991, 15½", MIB..$40.00

Diahann Carroll (Julia), Mattel, 1969, 1st edition, talker, gold & silver jumpsuit, straight hair, 11½", NRFB.............$200.00

Diahann Carroll (Julia), Mattel, 1969, 2-pc nurse uniform, 11½", NRFB..$200.00

Diahann Carroll (Julia), Mattel, 1970, 1-pc nurse uniform, 11½", NRFB, Y1...$200.00

Diahann Carroll (Julia), Mattel, 1971, 2nd edition, talker, gold & silver jumpsuit, Afro hair style, 11½", NRFB......$200.00

Diana Ross (of the Supremes), Ideal, 1969, 19", NRFB, $150.00.

Diana Ross, Mego, 1977, wht & silver dress, 12", NRFB..$125.00

Dick Clark, Juro, 1958, 24", MIB..................................$250.00

Dolly Parton, Eegee, 1980, 1st edition, red jumpsuit, 12", NRFB..$65.00

Dolly Parton, Eegee, 1987, 2nd edition, blk jumpsuit or cowgirl outfit, 11½", NRFB, ea...$50.00

Dolly Parton, Goldberger, 1996, red checked dress or long blk dress, 11½", NRFB, ea..$45.00

Dolly Parton, World Doll, 1987, red gown, 18", NRFB, M15..$100.00

Donna Douglas (Ellie Mae), 1964, jeans w/rope belt or yel dress, MIB, Y1, ea...$65.00

Donny & Marie, accessory, television stage set, Mattel, 1976, for 12" dolls, complete, MIB..$70.00

Donny & Marie, accessory, van, Lapin, 1978, MIB.........$70.00

Donny & Marie, gift set, Mattel, 1976, 11½", NRFB.....$125.00

Donny & Marie, outfit, Mattel/Sears Exclusive, 1977, several different, MIP, ea...$50.00

Dorothy Hamill, 1977, red olympic outfit w/medal, 11½", NRFB..$75.00

Dr J (Julius Erving), Shindana, Deluxe Set, 1977, w/outfits, 9½", MIB...$400.00

Dr J (Julius Erving), Shindana, 1977, w/basketball, 9½", MIB...$100.00

Drew Carey, Creation, 1998, 11½", NRFB, Y1...............$30.00

Elizabeth Montgomery (Samantha from Bewitched), Ideal, 1965, 12", rare, MIB..$600.00

Elizabeth Taylor (Bluebird), Horsman, 1976, w/3 outfits, 12", NRFB..$150.00

Elizabeth Taylor (Butterfield 8 or Cat on a Hot Tin Roof), Tristar, 1982, 11½", MIB, ea.......................................$125.00

Elizabeth Taylor (Father of the Bride, Butterfield 8, or Cat on a Hot Tin Roof), World Doll, 1989, 11½", MIB, ea.....$65.00

Elvis, Eugene, 1984, issued in 6 different outfits, 12", MIB, ea..$60.00

Elvis (Aloha Hawaii), World Doll, 1984, porcelain, wht jumpsuit, MIB...$200.00

Elvis (Burning Love), World Doll, 1984, 21", MIB.........$110.00

Elvis (Teen Idol, Jailhouse Rock or '68 Special), Hasbro, 1993, numbered edition, 12", MIB, ea................................$50.00

Farrah Fawcett (Jill from Charlie's Angels), Hasbro, 1977, jumpsuit & scarf, 8½", MOC..$40.00

Farrah Fawcett (Jill from Charlie's Angels), Mego, 1976, 1st edition, wht jumpsuit, 12", NRFB (photo on gr box).....$60.00

Farrah Fawcett (Jill from Charlie's Angels), Mego, 1981, lavender swimsuit, 12", rare, NRFB (photo on purple box)........$95.00

Flo-Jo, LJN, 1989, pk & bl athletic outfit w/bag, 11½", MIB...$85.00

Fran Dresher (Nanny), Street Players, 1995, 3 different outfits, talker, 11½", MIB..$55.00

Fred Gwynne (Herman Munster), Presents, 1990, plush w/vinyl head, 12", MIB...$35.00

Fred Gwynne (Herman Munster), Remco, 1964, MIB...$150.00

Grace Kelly (Swan or Mogambo), Tri-Star, 1982, 11½", MIB, ea..$125.00

Jaclyn Smith (Kelly from Charlie's Angels), Hasbro, 1977, jumpsuit & scarf, 8½", MOC..$40.00

Jaclyn Smith (Kelly from Charlie's Angels), Mego, 1978, bl dress, 12", rare, NRFB...$125.00

Jaleel White (Steve Urkel), Hasbro, 1991, cloth & vinyl, 17", MIB...$50.00

Jane Hathaway (Beverly Hillbillies), 1960s, 11½", MIB...$250.00

Jerry Springer, 1990s, 12", MIB $30.00

Jimmy Osmond, Mattel, 1978, 9", MIB.........................$75.00

Jimmy Walker (JJ from Good Times), Shindana, 1975, cloth & vinyl, 15", MIB, Y1 ....$50.00

Joe Namath, Mego, 1970, 11½", rare, MIB, $400.00. (Photo courtesy Henri Yunes)

John Stamos (Jesse from Full House), Tiger, 1993, 11½", MIB, Y1 ....$40.00

John Travolta (On Stage...Superstar), Chemtoy, 1977, 12", NRFB...$125.00

John Wayne, Effanbee, 1981, Great Legends series, Spirit of the West outfit, 17", MIB $125.00

John Wayne, Effanbee, 1982, Great Legends series, Guardian of the West outfit, 18", MIB...$125.00

Judy Garland (Wizard of Oz), Effanbee, 1984, Great Legends series, w/Toto & basket, 14½", MIB...........................$100.00

Judy Garland (Wizard of Oz), Multitoys, 1984, 50th Anniversary, rare, MIB...$100.00

Julie Andrews (Mary Poppins), Horsman, 1964, 1st edition, 12", MIB, Y1 ....$125.00

Julie Andrews (Mary Poppins), Horsman, 1973, 2nd edition, 11", MIB, Y1 ....$75.00

Karen Mulder, Top Models Collection, Hasbro, 1995, 11½", rare, MIB..$100.00

Kate Jackson (Sabrina from Charlie's Angels), Hasbro, 1977, jumpsuit & scarf, 8½", MOC $40.00

Kate Jackson (Sabrina from Charlie's Angels), Mattel, 1978, red & wht dress, 11½", NRFB $60.00

KISS, Mego, 1978, 4 different, 12", NRFB, ea.................$125.00

Kristy McNichol (Buddy from Family), Mattel, 1978, w/extra outfit, 9", MIB...$45.00

Kristy McNichol (Buddy from Family), Mego, 9½", MIB, Y1...$40.00

Laurel & Hardy, Knickerbocker, 1960s, cloth & vinyl, 9½", MIB, ea...$65.00

Laverne & Shirley, Mego, 1977, 12", NRFB, pr.............$125.00

Lenny & Squiggy, Mego, 1977, NRFB, pr.....................$200.00

Linda Carter (Wonder Woman), Mego, 1976, 1st issue, w/military uniform, rare, 12", MIB (photo on box) $85.00

Linda Evans (Krystle Carrington from Dynasty), 1980s, 19", MIB...$185.00

Lucille Ball (Lucy Ricardo), Mattel, Collector Edition, 1996, NRFB, minimum value...$75.00

Lucille Ball (Lucy Ricardo), 1952, cloth, 26", rare, NRFB, Y1..$800.00

Macaully Caulkin (Kevin from Home Alone), THQ Inc, 1989, screams, MIB, Y1...$25.00

Madonna (Breathless Mahoney), Applause, 1990, blk evening gown w/gold trim & heels, 10", MIB.........................$40.00

Madonna (Breathless Mahoney), Playmates, 1990, plastic, bl dress, 19", NRFB..$60.00

Mae West, Effanbee, 1982, Great Legends series, 18", MIB...$120.00

Marie Osmond, Mattel, 1976, 11", MIB..........................$60.00

Marie Osmond, Mattel, 1976, 30", MIB $115.00

Marilyn Monroe, DSI, 1993, issued in 6 different outfits, 11½", NRFB, ea...$60.00

Marilyn Monroe, Tristar, 1982, issued in 8 different outfits, 11½", NRFB, ea...$100.00

Mary Kate/Ashley Olsen (Michelle from Full House), cloth & vinyl, talker, 15", MIB $40.00

MC Hammer, Mattel, 1991, gold outfit w/boom box, 11½", MIB...$85.00

MC Hammer, Mattel, 1991, purple outfit, 11½", MIB.....$70.00

MC Hammer, outfit, Mattel, 1992, several different, MIP, ea..$15.00

Michael Jackson, LJN, 1984, Thriller outfit, 11½", NRFB ..$70.00

Michael Jackson (King of Pop Singing Doll), Streetlife, 1995, 11½", rare, MIB, Y1 ....$250.00

Mr T, Galoob, 1983, 1st edition, bib overalls, 12", MIB...$60.00

Mr T, Galoob, 1983, 2nd edition, talker, vest & jeans, 12", MIB...$75.00

Naomi Campbell, Top Models Collection, Hasbro, 1995, 11½", rare, MIB..$100.00

New Kids on the Block, accessory, Stage Set, 1990, MIB, Y1 ...$60.00

New Kids on the Block, 1990, 1st issue, Hangin' Loose, 5 different dolls, 12", MIB, ea $40.00

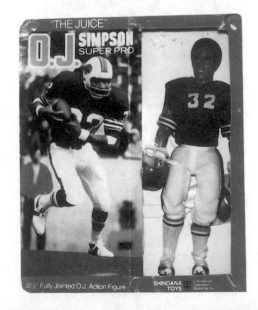

O.J. Simpson, Shindana, 1975, 9½", MIB, $250.00. (Photo courtesy Marcia Fanta)

New Kids on the Block, 1990, 2nd issue, In Concert, 5 different dolls, 12", MIB, ea..$50.00

OJ Simpson, Shindana, Deluxe Set, 1975, w/several outfits & accessories, 9½", MIB..$450.00

Pam Dawber (Mork & Mindy), Mattel, 1979, 8½", MIB .$50.00

Pamela Anderson Lee (CJ from Baywatch), Toy Island, 1997, 11½", NRFB, Y1 ....$35.00

Parker Stevenson (Frank from the Hardy Boys), Kenner, 1978, 12", NRFB...$50.00

Patty Duke (Patty Duke Show), Horsman, 1967, 12½", rare, NRFB...$400.00

Prince Charles, Goldberger, 1982, Military Wedding outfit, 12", NRFB...$250.00

Prince Charles, Goldberger, 1982, Palace Guard outfit, 12", rare, NRFB..$350.00

Prince Charles, Peggy Nesbit/England, 1984, wedding outfit, 8", MIB..$100.00

Prince William (baby), 1980s, 18", NMIB......................$250.00

Princess Charles & Princess Diana, Goldberger, 1982, wedding outfits, 12", rare, MIB...$600.00

Princess Diana, Danbury Mint, 1985, pk dress, 15", MIB ..$110.00

Princess Diana, Goldberger, 1982, silver dress, 11½", rare, NRFB...$350.00

Princess Diana, Goldberger, 1982, wedding gown, 11½", NRFB, Y1 ....$250.00

Princess Diana, Peggy Nesbit/England, 1984, wedding gown, 8", M..$100.00

Redd Fox, Shindana, 1977, cloth, talker, MIB..................$45.00

Rex Harrison (Dr Dolittle), accessory, Talking Puddleby Cottage, Mattel, 1968, vinyl, complete, M...................$130.00

Rex Harrison (Dr Dolittle), Mattel, 1967, w/Pushmi-Pullyu & Polynesia, 6", MIB $90.00

Rex Harrison (Dr Dolittle), Mattel, 1969, cloth & vinyl, talker, 24", MIB $130.00

Richard Taylor, 1990s, 11", MIB......................................$75.00

Robin Williams (Mork & Mindy), Mattel, 1979, w/space pak, 9", MIB...$45.00

Rosie O'Donnel, Mattel, 1998, 11½", NRFB, Y1 ....$50.00

Sally Ann Howes (Truly Scrumptious from Chitty-Chitty Bang-Bang), Mattel, 1969, pk dress, talker, 11½", MIB....$450.00

Sally Ann Howes (Truly Scrumptious from Chitty-Chitty Bang-Bang), Mattel, 1969, wht dress, 11½", MIB $400.00

Sally Field (Flying Nun), Hasbro, 1967, 5", MIB..............$80.00

Sally Field (Flying Nun), Hasbro, 1967, 12", MIB..........$200.00

Sarah Stimson (Little Miss Marker), Ideal, 1980, 12", MIB..$45.00

Saved by the Bell, Tiger, 1992, 6 different dolls, 11½", NRFB, Y1, ea...$40.00

Selena, Arm Enterprises, 1996, 11½", MIB $50.00

Shaun Cassidy (Joe from the Hardy Boys), Kenner, 1978, 12", NRFB..$50.00

Shirley Temple, Ideal, 1930s, flower print dress w/bl hair ribbon, 18", EX, from $700 to $800.00

Shirley Temple, Ideal, 1934, Stand Up & Cheer outfit, 15", EX..$700.00

Shirley Temple, Ideal, 1957, orig bl & pk flocked dress, 12", VG, M15..$150.00

Shirley Temple, Ideal, 1972, Stand Up & Cheer outfit, 16", MIB, M15 ....$160.00

Shirley Temple, Ideal, 1982, issued in 6 different outfits, 8", MIB, M15, ea...$60.00

Shirley Temple, Ideal, 1984, Glad Rags to Riches outfit, 16", rare, MIB, M15 ....$125.00

Shirley Temple (as Cinderella), Ideal, 1961, 15", scarce, NM, from $200 to $300.00

Sonny & Cher, Mego, 1975, 12", NM, ea $50.00

Sonny Bono, Mego, 1976, 12", NRFB (orange box).......$150.00

Soupy Sales, Sunshine Dolls, 1965, 6", NRFB...............$235.00

Spice Girls (Girl Power), Galoob, 1997, 1st issue, 5 different, 11½", NRFB, Y1, ea...$95.00

Spice Girls (On Tour), Galoob, 1997, 2nd issue, 5 different, 11½", NRFB, Y1, ea $65.00

Spice Girls (Superstar Spice Collection Gift Set), Galoob, 1998, 3rd issue, 11½", NRFB, Y1, ea $350.00

Susan Dey (Laurie from Partridge Family), Remco, 1973, 16", rare, MIB..$250.00

Susan Lucci (Erica Kane at the Ball), Mattel, 1998, 11½", NRFB, Y1..$85.00

Susan Lucci (Erica Kane at the Wedding), Mattel, 1999, 11½", NRFB, Y1..$85.00

Suzanne Somers (Chrissy from Three's Company), Mego, 1970s, 12½", MIB...$85.00

Sylvester Stallone (Over the Top), Lewco Toys, 1986, 20", NRFB..$35.00

Sylvester Stallone (Rocky), Phoenix Toys, 1983, 8", MOC..$45.00

Tatum O'Neal (International Velvet), Kenner, 1979, 11½", MIB $85.00

Twiggy, Mattel, 1967, 11½", rare, MIB $400.00

Twiggy, outfit, Mattel, 1968, several different, NRFB, ea from $100 to...$200.00

Vanilla Ice, THQ, 1991, issued in 3 different outfits, 12", NRFB, ea...$50.00

Vanna White, Pacific Media/Home Shopping Network, 1990, issued in 20 different outfits, 11½", NRFB, ea...........$50.00

Richard Chamberlain (Dr. Kildare), Bing Crosby Productions, 1962, MIB, rare, $450.00. (Photo courtesy Henry Yunes)

Vanna White, Totsy Toys, 1990, limited edition, wedding dress, MIB, rare, $125.00. (Photo courtesy Henri Yunes)

Vanna White, Totsy Toys, 1992, Mother's Day edition, w/baby, 11½", MIB, Y1..$100.00
Vanna White, Totsy Toys, 1992, special edition, silver, gold, or platinum dress, MIB, Y1, ea $125.00

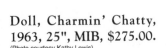

Vince Edwards (Ben Casey) Bing Crosby Productions, 1962, 12", MIB, rare, $400.00. (Photo courtesy Henri Yunes)

Vivian Leigh (Scarlett), World Dolls, 1980, 1st issue, 12", NRFB...$65.00
Wayne Gretzky, Mattel, 1982, The Great Gretzky/Le Magnifique, 11½", MIB..$150.00
Yvonne De Carlo (Lily Munster), Remco, 1964, MIB....$150.00

CHATTY CATHY

In their book, *Chatty Cathy Dolls, An Identification & Value Guide,* authorities Kathy and Don Lewis (L6) tell us that

Chatty Cathy (made by Mattel) has been the second most popular doll ever made. She was introduced in the 1960s and came as either a blond or a brunette. For five years, she sold very well. Much of her success can be attributed to the fact that Chatty Cathy talked. By pulling the string on her back, she could respond with eleven different phrases. During her five years of fame, Mattel added to the line with Chatty Baby, Tiny Chatty Baby and Tiny Chatty Brother (the twins), Charmin' Chatty, and finally Singing' Chatty. Charmin' Chatty had sixteen interchangeable records. Her voice box was activated in the same manner as the above-mentioned dolls, by means of a pull string located at the base of her neck. The line was brought back in 1969, smaller and with a restyled face, but it was not well received.

Advisors: Kathy and Don Lewis (L6).

Armoire, Chatty Cathy, L6 ....$175.00
Bedspread, Chatty Baby, twin-sz, L6 ....$400.00
Carrying Case, Chatty Baby, pk or bl, L6, ea $45.00
Carrying Case, Tiny Chatty Baby, pk or bl, L6, ea...........$35.00
Cover & Pillow Set, Tiny Chatty Cathy, L6 ....$75.00
Crib, Tiny Chatty Baby, MIB, L6 ....$300.00
Cut-Outs, Chatty Cathy, w/45 costumes & accessories, MIP, L6 ....$50.00
Doll, Black Chatty Baby, M, L6 ....$650.00
Doll, Black Chatty Baby, w/pigtails, M, L6.................$1,500.00
Doll, Black Chatty Cathy, 1962, pageboy-style hair, M, L6...$1,200.00
Doll, Black Tiny Chatty Baby, M, L6 ....$650.00

Doll, Charmin' Chatty, 1963, 25", MIB, $275.00. (Photo courtesy Kathy Lewis)

Doll, Chatty Baby, brunette hair, red pinafore over wht romper, orig tag, MIB, L6, ea..$250.00
Doll, Chatty Baby, early, brunette hair, brn eyes, M, L6..$160.00
Doll, Chatty Baby, early, ring around speaker, blond hair, bl eyes, M, L6 ....$250.00
Doll, Chatty Baby, open speaker, blond hair, bl eyes, M, L6 ....$250.00

Doll, Chatty Baby, open speaker, brunette hair, bl eyes, M, L6 ....$250.00

Doll, Chatty Baby, open speaker, brunette hair, brn eyes, M, L6 ....$375.00

Doll, Chatty Baby, unmk prototype, brunette hair, bl eyes, M, L6 ....$900.00

Doll, Chatty Cathy, brunette hair, brn eyes, M, L6 ....$375.00

Doll, Chatty Cathy, early, brunette hair, bl eyes, M, L6....$85.00

Doll, Chatty Cathy, later issue, open speaker, blond hair, bl eyes, M, L6 ....$750.00

Doll, Chatty Cathy, later issue, open speaker, brunette hair, bl eyes, M, L6...$750.00

Doll, Chatty Cathy, later issue, open speaker, brunette hair, brn eyes, M, L6...$850.00

Doll, Chatty Cathy, mid-year or transitional, brunette hair, brn eyes, M, L6...$650.00

Doll, Chatty Cathy, mid-year or transitional, brunette hair, bl eyes, M, L6...$650.00

Doll, Chatty Cathy, mid-year or transitional, open speaker, blond hair, bl eyes, M, L6 ....$600.00

Doll, Chatty Cathy, patent pending, brunette hair, bl eyes, M, L6 ....$750.00

Doll, Chatty Cathy, patent pending, cloth over speaker or ring around speaker, blond hair, bl eyes, M, L6, ea $750.00

Doll, Chatty Cathy, porcelain, 1980, MIB, L6...............$750.00

Doll, Chatty Cathy, reissue, blond hair, bl eyes, MIB, L6....$80.00

Doll, Chatty Cathy, soft face, w/pigtails, blond, brunette or auburn hair, M, L6, ea $550.00

Doll, Chatty Cathy, unmk prototype, brunette hair, brn eyes, M, L6...$1,000.00

Doll, Chatty Cathy, unmk prototype, cloth speaker, blond hair, M, L6 ....$900.00

Doll, Singin' Chatty, blond hair, M, L6 ....$250.00

Doll, Singin' Chatty, brunette hair, M, L6 ....$275.00

Doll, Tiny Chatty Baby, blond hair, bl eyes, M, L6.........$250.00

Doll, Tiny Chatty Baby, brunette hair, bl eyes, M, L6 ....$275.00

Doll, Tiny Chatty Baby, brunette hair, brn eyes, M, L6..$300.00

Doll, Tiny Chatty Twins, M, L6, ea..................................$250.00

Gift Set, Talking Charmin' Chatty Travels 'Round the World, complete, MIB, L6...$400.00

Jewelry Set, Chatty Cathy, MIP, L6..................................$150.00

Nursery Set, Chatty Baby, NRFB, L6 ....$200.00

Outfit, Charmin' Chatty, Cinderella, MIP, L6 ....$115.00

Outfit, Charmin' Chatty, Let's Go Shopping, MIP, L6 .....$85.00

Outfit, Charmin' Chatty, Let's Play Birthday Party, MIP, L6 ....$100.00

Outfit, Charmin' Chatty, Let's Play Nurse, MIP, L6..........$90.00

Outfit, Charmin' Chatty, Let's Play Pajama Party, MIP, L6....$100.00

Outfit, Charmin' Chatty, Let's Play Tea Party, MIP, L6.....$100.00

Outfit, Charmin' Chatty, Let's Play Together, MIP, L6.....$75.00

Outfit, Chatty Baby, Leotard Set, MIP, L6 ....$75.00

Outfit, Chatty Baby, Outdoors, MIP, L6 ....$75.00

Outfit, Chatty Baby, Overall set, pk or bl, MIP, L6, ea $65.00

Outfit, Chatty Baby, Party Pink, MIP, L6.........................$100.00

Outfit, Chatty Baby, Playsuit, MIP, L6 ....$45.00

Outfit, Chatty Baby, Sleeper set, MIP, L6 ....$55.00

Outfit, Chatty Cathy, Nursery School, MIP, L6..............$145.00

Outfit, Chatty Cathy, Party Coat, MIP, L6 ....$150.00

Outfit, Chatty Cathy, Party Dress, bl gingham, MIP, L6..$250.00

Outfit, Chatty Cathy, Pink Peppermint Stick, MIP, L6 ...$150.00

Outfit, Chatty Cathy, Playtime, MIP, L6 ....$145.00

Outfit, Chatty Cathy, Red Peppermint Stick (Candystripe), MIP, L6 ....$400.00

Outfit, Chatty Cathy, Sleepytime, MIP, L6.....................$125.00

Outfit, Chatty Cathy, Sunday Visit, MIP, L6 ....$200.00

Outfit, Chatty Cathy, Sunny Day, MIP, L6 ....$200.00

Outfit, Tiny Chatty Baby, Bye-Bye, MIP, L6 ....$65.00

Outfit, Tiny Chatty Baby, Dashin' Dots, MIP, L6 ....$175.00

Outfit, Tiny Chatty Baby, Fun Time, MIP, L6..................$140.00

Outfit, Tiny Chatty Baby, Night-Night, MIP, L6 ....$90.00

Outfit, Tiny Chatty Baby, Pink Frill, MIP, L6 ....$125.00

Outfit, Tiny Chatty Baby, Playtime, bl gingham, MIP, L6..$250.00

Pattern, Chatty Baby, uncut, L6 ....$18.50

Pattern, Chatty Cathy, uncut, L6 ....$18.50

Pencil Point Bed, Chatty Cathy, L6..................................$350.00

Play Hats, Charmin' Chatty, L6 ....$55.00

Play Table, Chatty Baby, L6 ....$175.00

Play Table, Chatty Baby, L6 ....$175.00

Stroll-a-Buggy, Chatty Baby, 9-way, complete, L6..........$300.00

Stroller, Chatty Baby, Walkin' Talk, L6 ....$500.00

Stroller, Chatty Cathy, 5-way, complete, L6 ....$225.00

Tea Cart, Chatty Cathy, w/2 trays, L6..............................$100.00

Teeter-Totter, Tiny Chatty Baby Twins, L6......................$500.00

TV Tray, Chatty Cathy, L6 ....$30.00

CRISSY AND HER FAMILY

Ideal's 18" Crissy doll with growing hair was very popular with little girls of the early 1970s. She was introduced in 1969 and continued to be sold throughout the 1970s, enjoying a relatively long market life for a doll. During the 1970s, many different versions of Crissy were made. Numerous friends followed her success, all with the growing hair feature like Crissy's. The other Ideal 'grow hair' dolls in the line included Velvet, Cinnamon, Tressy, Dina, Mia, Kerry, Brandi, and Cricket. Crissy is the easiest member in the line to find, followed by her cousin Velvet. The other members are not as common, but like Crissy and Velvet loose examples of these dolls frequently make their appearance at doll shows, flea markets, and even garage sales. Only those examples that are in excellent or better condition and wearing their original outfits and shoes should command book value. Values for the rare black versions of the dolls in the line are currently on the rise, as demand for them increases while the supply decreases.

Advisor: Cindy Sabulis (S14) author of *Dolls of the 1960s and 1970s.*

Baby Crissy, 1973-76, pk dress, EX $65.00

Baby Crissy, 1973-76, pk dress, MIB, M15 ....$125.00

Baby Crissy (Black); 1973-76, pk dress, EX.......................$80.00

Brandi (Black); 1972-73, orange swimsuit, EX $75.00

Cinnamon, Curly Ribbons (Black); 1974, EX...................$75.00

Cinnamon, Curly Ribbons; 1974, EX..............................$45.00

Cinnamon, Hairdoodler (Black); 1973, EX $75.00

Cinnamon, Hairdoodler; 1973, EX...................................$40.00

Crissy, Beautiful; 1969, orange lace dress, EX..................$40.00

Crissy, Country Fashion; 1982-83, EX $20.00
Crissy, Country Fashion; 1982-83, MIB, M15 ....$45.00
Crissy, Look Around; 1972, EX $40.00
Crissy, Magic Hair (Black); 1977, EX $100.00
Crissy, Magic Hair; 1977, EX $30.00
Crissy, Magic Hair; 1977, NRFB $100.00
Crissy, Movin' Groovin' (Black); 1971, EX $100.00

Crissy, Movin' Groovin' (Black); 1971, MIB, $150.00. (Photo courtesy Patsy Moyer/ Michele Lyons)

Crissy, Movin' Groovin'; 1971, EX $35.00
Crissy, Swirla Curla (Black); 1973, EX $100.00
Crissy, Swirla Curla; 1973, EX $35.00
Crissy, Twirly Beads; 1974, MIB, M15 ....$65.00
Dina, 1972-73, purple playsuit, EX $50.00
Kerry, 1971, gr romper, EX $55.00
Mia, 1971, turq romper, EX $50.00
Tara (Black); 1976, yel gingham outfit, MIB $95.00
Velvet, Beauty Braider; 1973, EX $35.00
Velvet, Look Around (Black); 1972, EX $100.00
Velvet, Look Around; 1972, EX $35.00
Velvet, Movin' Groovin'; 1971, EX $35.00
Velvet, Swirly Daisies; 1974, EX $35.00
Velvet, Swirly Daisies; 1974, MIB $65.00
Velvet, 1970, 1st issue, purple dress, EX $55.00
Velvet, 1982 reissue, EX...$30.00

DAWN

Dawn and her friends were made by Deluxe Topper, ca 1970s. They're becoming highly collectible, especially when mint in the box. Dawn was a 6" fashion doll, part of a series sold as the Dawn Model Agency. They were issued in boxes already dressed in clothes of the highest style, or you could buy additional outfits, many complete with matching shoes and accessories.

Advisor: Dawn Diaz (P2).

Dawn's Apartment, complete w/furniture $50.00
Doll, Dancing Angie, NRFB..$30.00
Doll, Dancing Dale, NRFB..$50.00

Doll, Dancing Dawn, NRFB, $30.00. (Photo courtesy Cindy Sabulis)

Doll, Dancing Gary, NRFB..$40.00
Doll, Dancing Glori, NRFB...$30.00
Doll, Dancing Jessica, NRFB..$30.00
Doll, Dancing Ron, NRFB...$40.00
Doll, Dancing Van, NRFB...$50.00
Doll, Daphne, Dawn Model Agency, gr & silver dress, NRFB...$75.00

Doll, Dawn Head to Toe, NRFB, from $75.00 to $100.00. (Photo courtesy Cindy Sabulis/Sharon Wendrow)

Doll, Dawn Majorette, NRFB...$75.00
Doll, Denise, NRFB $75.00
Doll, Dinah, NRFB $75.00

Doll, Gary, NRFB..$30.00
Doll, Jessica, NRFB...$30.00
Doll, Kip Majorette, NRFB...................................$45.00
Doll, Longlocks, NRFB..$30.00
Doll, Maureen, Dawn Model Agency, red & gold dress,
    NRFB..$75.00
Doll, Ron, NRFB...$30.00
Outfit, Bell Bottom Flounce, #0717, NRFB.....................$25.00

DOLLY DARLINGS BY HASBRO

Dolly Darlings by Hasbro are approximately 4" tall and have molded or rooted hair. The molded-hair dolls were sold in themed hatboxes with small accessories to match. The rooted-hair dolls were sold separately and came with a small brush and comb. There were four plastic playrooms that featured the rooted-hair dolls. Hasbro also produced the Flower Darling series which were 2" dolls in flower corsages. The Dolly Darlings and Flower Darlings were available in the mid to late 1960s.

Advisor: Dawn Diaz (P2).

Hipster, Sugar 'N Spice, and Casual, MIB and MOC, from $50.00 to $75.00 each. (Photo courtesy Paris Langford)

Cathy Goes to a Party, M (EX case), from $35 to.............$55.00
Flying Nun, MIB, from $75 to.......................................$125.00
Go-Team-Go, doll only, EX, from $25 to.....................$35.00
Hipster, doll only, EX, from $25 to...............................$35.00
John & His Pets, M (EX case), from $35 to....................$55.00
Lemon Drop, doll only, EX, from $30 to.......................$50.00
Powder Puff, doll only, EX, from $25 to........................$35.00
School Days, doll only, EX, from $25 to.........................$35.00
Sunny Day, doll only, from $30 to...............................$50.00
Susie Goes to School, M (EX case), from $35 to.............$55.00
Sweetheart, doll only, EX, from $25 to..........................$35.00
Teeny Bikini, doll only, EX, from $25 to.......................$35.00

FISHER-PRICE

Though this company is more famous for their ruggedly durable, lithographed wooden toys, they made dolls as well.

Many of the earlier dolls (circa mid-'70s) had stuffed cloth bodies and vinyl heads, hands, and feet. Some had battery-operated voice boxes. In 1981 they introduced Kermit the Frog and Miss Piggy and a line of clothing for both. For company history, see the Fisher-Price category. For more information, we recommend *Fisher-Price Toys*, by Brad Cassity, our advisor for this category.

See also Advertising; Character, TV, and Movie; Disney.

Audrey, #203, 1974-76, vinyl face & hands, cloth body, bl jeans remove, 13", EX...$25.00

Joey, #206, cloth and vinyl, 1975 – 76, M, $25.00.
(Photo courtesy Brad Cassity)

Mandy, #4009, 1985, Happy Birthday presentation, pk party dress, w/surprise gift for child, EX...............................$50.00
Mary, #200, 1974-77, vinyl face & hands, cloth body, rooted hair, apron & skirt remove, 13", EX.........................$25.00
Mikey, #240, 1979-80, removable baseball hat & jacket, 8" .$10.00
Miss Piggy, Dress-Up Muppet, #890, 1981-84, plush, removable evening gown, turban & gloves, EX.........................$12.00
My Friend Christie, #8120, 1990, short production run, EX, from $40 to...$75.00
My Friend Mandy, #211, 1979-81, flowered dress, EX......$20.00
Outfit, Aerobics, #4110, 1985, sweatshirt, mini skirt, headband, tights, leg warmers, sneakers & purse, EX.................$10.00
Outfit, Miss Piggy's Sailor Outfit, #891, 1981-82, jumpsuit & cap, EX..$12.00
Outfit, Springtime Party Dress Outfit & pattern, 1985, sweater, skirt, socks, sneakers, headband & 2 pompons, EX....$10.00
Outfit, Valentine Party Dress, #238, 1984-85, bl polka-dot bib dress, straw hat & red shoes, EX.............................$10.00

FLATSYS

Flatsy dolls were a product of the Ideal Novelty and Toy Company. They were produced from 1968 until 1970 in 2", 5", and 8" sizes. There was only one boy in the 5" line; all were dressed in '70s fashions, and not only clothing but accessory items such as bicycles were made as well.

In 1994 Justoys reissued Mini Flatsys. They were sold alone or with accessories such as bikes, rollerblades, and jet skis.

Advisor: Dawn Diaz (P2).

Ali Fashion Flatsy, NRFP, from $45 to $65.00
Baby Flatsy, no accessories, EX, from $10 to $15.00
Candy Mountain Flatsy & Her Car, MOC, from $50 to...$75.00
Casey Flatsy, MIB, from $50 to...$75.00

Dewie Flatsy, MIB, $60.00. (Photo courtesy Carolyn and Martin Berens)

Dewie Flatsy Locket, NRFP, from $25 to............................$35.00
Grandma Baker, Flatsyville series, complete, M, from $50 to ..$75.00
Gwen Fashion Flatsy, NRFP, from $45 to............................$65.00
Judy Flatsy, complete, NRFP, from $55 to $75.00
Kookie Flatsy, Flatsyville series, complete, M, from $50 to ..$75.00
Munch Time Flatsy, Mini Flatsy Collection, NRFP, from $50
        to...$85.00
Slumber Time Flatsy, Mini Flatsy Collection, NRFP, from $50
        to $85.00

GALOOB'S BABY FACE DOLLS

Galoob's Baby Face dolls were first available on the toy market in 1991. By the end of 1992 the short-lived dolls were already being discounted by toy stores. Although they were targeted as play dolls for children, it didn't take long for these adorable dolls to find their way into adult collectors' hearts. The most endearing quality of Baby Face dolls are their expressive faces. Sporting big eyes with long soft eyelashes, cute pug noses, and mouths that are puckered, pouting, smiling, or laughing, these dolls are delightful and fun. The 13" heavy vinyl Baby Face dolls are jointed at the shoulders, elbows, knees, and hips. Their jointed limbs allow for posing them in more positions than the average doll and adds to the fun of displaying or playing with them. Old store stock of Baby Face dolls was plentiful for several years, and since these dolls are still relatively new as collectibles, it isn't difficult to find never-removed-from-box examples.

Advisor: Cindy Sabulis (S14).

Activity Stroller, MIB, S14..$25.00
Asian Versions, NRFB, S14, from $65 to $80.00
Asian Versions, re-dressed, S14, from $20 to $25.00

Bathtub Babies, NRFB, from $40 to $50.00
Bathtub Babies, re-dressed, S14, from $15 to $20.00
Black Versions, NRFB, S14, from $60 to...........................$75.00
Black Versions, re-dressed, S14, from $20 to.....................$25.00
Hispanic Versions, NRFB, S14, from $85 to...................$125.00
Hispanic Versions, re-dressed, S14, from $25 to $40.00
Outfits, NRFB, S14, ea from $20 to $25.00

So Surprised Susie, complete with outfit, M, $25.00. (Photo courtesy Cindy Sabulis)

So Loving Laura and So Sweet Sandi, complete with outfits, M, $25.00 each. (Photo courtesy Cindy Sabulis)

White Versions, any other than So Silly Sally, NRFB, S14, from
        $50 to $75.00
White Versions, re-dressed, S14, from $15 to $20.00

GERBER BABIES

The first Gerber Baby dolls were manufactured in 1936. These dolls were made of cloth and produced by an unknown manufacturer. Since that time, six different companies working with leading artists, craftsmen, and designers have attempted to capture the charm of the winsome baby in Dorothy Hope

Smith's charcoal drawing of her friend's baby, Ann Turner (Cook). This drawing became known as the Gerber Baby and was adopted as the trademark of the Gerber Products Company, located in Fremont, Michigan. For further information see *Gerber Baby Dolls and Advertising Collectibles* by Joan S. Grubaugh.

Amsco, 1972-73, baby & feeding set, vinyl, complete, 14", NMIB...$85.00
Amsco, 1972-73 (Black), pk & wht rosebud sleeper, vinyl, 10", NM, from $60 to...$100.00

Amsco, 1972 – 73, pink and white rosebud sleeper, vinyl, 10", NM, from $45.00 to $55.00.
(Photo courtesy Joan S. Grubaugh)

Amsco, 1972-73, re-dressed, 14", M...............................$40.00
Arrow Rubber & Plastic Corp, 1965-67, pk & wht bib & diaper, 14", MIB, from $45 to....................................$60.00
Arrow Rubber & Plastic Corp, 1965-67, re-dressed, 14", EX .$45.00
Atlanta Novelty, Baby Drink & Wet (Black), 1979-81, 12", complete w/trunk & accessories, M.........................$100.00
Atlanta Novelty, 1978, 50th Anniversary, eyelet skirt & bib, stuffed cloth & vinyl, 17", NRFB, from $75 to..........$95.00
Atlanta Novelty, 1979, flowered bed jacket w/matching pillow & coverlet, 17", NRFB, from $75 to $95.00
Atlanta Novelty, 1979, snowsuit w/matching hood, 17", NRFB, from $75 to...$95.00
Atlanta Novelty, 1979-81, Baby Drink & Wet, 17", complete in trunk, M, from $75 to.....................................$85.00
Atlanta Novelty, 1979-81, w/'mama' voice, several different outfits, 17", NRFB, ea from $75 to...................................$85.00
Atlanta Novelty, 1979-81 (Black), bl or rose velour dress w/wht blouse, 17", M, ea from $75 to....................................$85.00
Atlanta Novelty, 1979-81 (Black), snowsuit w/matching hood, 17", NRFB, from $75 to..$85.00
Atlanta Novelty, 1979-81 (Black), w/'mama' voice, 17", NRFB, from $75 to..$85.00
Atlanta Novelty, 1981, limited edition, porcelain w/soft body, wht eyelet christening gown, 14", NRFB, from $275 to $350.00
Atlanta Novelty, 1984, rag doll, in pk or bl, 11½", EX.....$20.00

Atlanta Novelty, 1985, Bathtub Baby, vinyl, 12", MIB, from $70 to..$85.00
Lucky Ltd, 1989, Birthday Party Twins, 6", NRFB...........$40.00
Lucky Ltd, 1989, cloth & vinyl, wht christening gown, 16", EX...$40.00
Lucky Ltd, 1989-92, re-dressed, 14", EX.........................$25.00
Sun Rubber, 1955-58, orig nightgown, M.......................$175.00
Toy Biz, 1994-95, Potty Time Baby, vinyl, 15", NRFB......$25.00
Toy Biz, 1995, Food & Playtime Baby, MIB, from $25 to .$35.00
Toy Biz, 1996, Baby Care Set, MIB $25.00

HOLLY HOBBIE

Sometime around 1970 a young homemaker and mother, Holly Hobbie, approached the American Greeting Company with some charming country-styled drawings of children. Her concepts were well received by the company, and since that time over four hundred Holly Hobbie items have been produced, nearly all marked HH, H. Hobbie, or Holly Hobbie.

Advisor: Helen McCale (M12).

See also Clubs, Newsletters, and Other Publications.

Doll, Country Fun Holly Hobbie, 1989, 16", NRFB.........$20.00
Doll, Grandma Holly, Knickerbocker, cloth, 14", MIB.....$20.00
Doll, Grandma Holly, Knickerbocker, cloth, 24", MIB.....$25.00
Doll, Holly Hobbie, Heather, Amy, or Carrie, Knickerbocker, cloth, 6", MIB, ea...$5.00
Doll, Holly Hobbie, Heather, Amy, or Carrie, Knickerbocker, cloth, 9", MIB, ea...$10.00
Doll, Holly Hobbie, Heather, Amy, or Carrie, Knickerbocker, cloth, 16", MIB, ea...$20.00
Doll, Holly Hobbie, Heather, Amy, or Carrie, Knickerbocker, cloth, 27", MIB, ea...$25.00
Doll, Holly Hobbie, Heather, Amy, or Carrie, Knickerbocker, cloth, 33", MIB, ea...$35.00
Doll, Holly Hobbie, 1988, scented, clear ornament around neck, 18", NRFB...$30.00
Doll, Holly Hobbie, 25th Anniversary collector's edition, Meritus, 1994, 26", MIB, from $45 to $25.00
Doll, Holly Hobbie Bicentennial, Knickerbocker, cloth, 12", MIB..$25.00
Doll, Holly Hobbie Day 'N Night, Knickerbocker, cloth, 14", MIB..$15.00
Doll, Holly Hobbie Dream Along, Holly, Carrie, or Amy, Knickerbocker, cloth, 9", MIB, ea $10.00
Doll, Holly Hobbie Dream Along, Holly, Carrie, or Amy, Knickerbocker, cloth, 12", MIB, ea $15.00
Doll, Holly Hobbie Talker, cloth, 4 sayings, 16", MIB......$25.00
Doll, Little Girl Holly, Knickerbocker, 1980, cloth, 15", MIB..$20.00
Doll, Robby, Knickerbocker, cloth, 9", MIB....................$15.00
Doll, Robby, Knickerbocker, cloth, 16", MIB..................$20.00
Dollhouse, M $200.00
Sewing Machine, Durham, 1975, plastic & metal, battery-op, 5x9", EX...$25.00
Sing-A-Long Electric Parlor Player, Vanity Fair, 1970s, complete w/booklet, scarce, NMIB $45.00

JEM

The glamorous life of Jem mesmerized little girls who watched her Saturday morning cartoons, and she was a natural as a fashion doll. Hasbro saw the potential in 1985 when they introduced the Jem line of 12" dolls representing her, the rock stars from Jem's musical group, the Holograms, and other members of the cast, including the only boy, Rio, Jem's road manager and Jerrica's boyfriend. Each doll was posable, jointed at the waist, head, and wrists, so that they could be positioned at will with their musical instruments and other accessory items. Their clothing, their makeup, and their hairdos were wonderfully exotic, and their faces were beautifully modeled. The Jem line was discontinued in 1987 after being on the market for only two years.

Accessory, Jem Soundstage, Starlight House #14, EX, from $40 to $50.00

Accessory, speaker and dressing room, Hasbro, 1986, complete, NM, $95.00. (Photo courtesy June Moon)

Doll, Aja, 1st issue, nude, M...$15.00
Doll, Glitter 'N Gold Rio, nude, M.....................................$10.00
Doll, Kimber, 1st issue, nude, M..$10.00
Doll, Rio, 1st issue, nude, M...$10.00
Doll, Rock 'N Curl Jem, nude, M $7.00
Doll, Roxy, complete, 12½", MIB $40.00
Doll, Roxy, 1st issue, nude, M...$15.00
Doll, Shana, 1st issue, nude, M...$35.00
Doll, Stormer, complete, 12½", MIB....................................$40.00
Doll, Video, complete, 12½", MIB..$40.00
Outfit, Just Misbehavin', complete, M, minimum value...$45.00
Outfit, Let the Music Play, complete, M $20.00
Outfit, Music Is Magic, complete, M..................................$20.00
Outfit, Rhythm & Flash, complete, M $22.00
Outfit, Share a Little Bit, complete, M $55.00
Outfit, Sophisticated Lady, complete, M...........................$15.00
Outfit, We Can Change It, complete, M $75.00
Outfit, You Can't Catch Me, complete, M.........................$25.00

LIDDLE KIDDLES

From 1966 to 1971, Mattel produced Liddle Kiddle dolls and accessories, typical of the 'little kid next door.' They were made in sizes ranging from a tiny ¾" up to 4". They were all posable and had rooted hair that could be restyled. Eventually there were Animiddles and Zoolery Jewelry Kiddles, which were of course animals, and two other series that represented storybook and nursery-rhyme characters. There was a set of extraterrestrials, and lastly in 1979, Sweet Treets dolls were added to the assortment.

In the mid-1970s Mattel reissued Lucky Locket Kiddles. The dolls had names identical to the earlier lockets but were not of the same high quality.

In 1994 – 95 Tyco reissued Liddle Kiddles in strap-on, clip-on, Lovely Locket, Pretty Perfume, and baby bottle collections.

Loose dolls, if complete and with all their original accessories, are worth about 50% less than the same mint in the box. Dressed, loose dolls with no accessories are worth 75% less. For more information, refer to *Little Kiddles, Identification and Value Guide*, by Paris Langford (Collector Books).

Advisor: Dawn Diaz (P2).

Other Sources: S14.

Doll, Aja, blue hair, complete, M, $45.00. (Photo courtesy Lee Garmon)

Alice in Wonderliddle, complete, NM, $175.00. (Photo courtesy Cindy Sabulis)

Animiddles, NM, $40.00 each. (Photo courtesy Cindy Sabulis)

Aqua Funny Bunny, #3532, complete, EX $35.00
Aqua Funny Bunny, #3532, MIP...................................$100.00
Babe Biddle, #3505, complete, M..................................$50.00
Baby Din-Din, #3820, complete, M $75.00

Baby Liddle, 1969, rare, MOC, $750.00.
(Photo courtesy Tamela Storm and Debra Van Dyke)

Baby Rockaway, #3819, MIP $150.00
Beach Buggy, #5003, NM..$50.00
Beat-A-Diddle, #3510, MIP $500.00
Blue Funny Bunny, #3532, MIP $100.00

Chitty Chitty Bang Bang, #3597, 1968, MOC, $250.00.
(Photo courtesy Tamela Storm and Debra Van Dyke)

Calamity Jiddle, #3506, complete w/high saddle horse, M..$75.00
Chocolottie's House, #2501, MIP.......................................$40.00
Cinderriddle's Palace, #5068, plastic window version, M .$50.00
Cookin' Kiddle, #3846, complete, M $150.00
Dainty Deer, #3637, complete, M......................................$45.00
Florence Niddle, #3507, complete, M $75.00
Flower Charm Bracelet, #3747, MIP $50.00
Flower Pin Kiddle, #3741, MIP $50.00
Flower Ring Kiddle, #3744, MIP $50.00
Frosty Mint Kone, #3653, complete, M............................$60.00
Gardenia Kologne, #3710, MIP..$75.00

Greta Grape, #3728, 1968 – 69, M, $50.00.

Greta Griddle, #3508, complete, M $85.00
Heart Charm Bracelet Kiddle, #3747, MIP $50.00
Heart Pin Kiddle, #3741, MIP..$50.00
Heart Ring Kiddle, #3744, MIP $50.00
Henrietta Horseless Carriage, #3641, complete, M..........$60.00
Honeysuckle Kologne, #3704, MIP $75.00
Hot Dog Stand, #5002, M $25.00
Howard Biff Biddle, #3502, complete, M $75.00
Howard Biff Biddle, #3502, NRFB...................................$300.00
Jewelry Kiddles Treasure Box, #3735 & #5166, M, ea $40.00
Kampy Kiddle, #3753, complete, M $150.00
Kiddle & Kars Antique Fair Set, #3806, NRFB.............$300.00
Kiddle Komedy Theatre, #3592, EX $50.00
Kiddles Kologne Sweet Three Boutique, #3708, NRFB .$300.00
Kiddles Sweet Shop, #3807, NRFB.................................$300.00
King & Queen of Hearts, #3784, MIP............................$200.00
Kleo Kola, #3729, complete, M $50.00
Kola Kiddles Three-Pak, #3734, NRFB.........................$300.00
Lady Crimson, #A3840, NRFB $100.00
Lady Lavender, #A3840, NRFB $100.00
Laffy Lemon, #3732, MIP $85.00
Larky Locket, #3539, complete, EX.................................$25.00
Lenore Limousine, #3743, complete, M $60.00

Liddle Biddle Peep, #3544, 1967 – 68, M, $125.00.
(Photo courtesy Tamela Storm and Debra Van Dyke)

Liddle Diddle, #3503, complete, M $75.00
Liddle Kiddle Kottage, #3534, EX.................................$25.00
Liddle Kiddles Kabin, #3591, EX...................................$25.00
Liddle Kiddles Kastle, #3522, M $55.00
Liddle Kiddles Kolony, #3571, M $35.00
Liddle Kiddles Open House, #5167, MIB...................$40.00
Liddle Kiddles Pop-Up Boutique, #5170, M..................$30.00
Liddle Kiddles Pop-Up Playhouse, #3574, M $30.00
Liddle Kiddles Talking Townhouse, #5154, MIB $50.00

Liddle Kiddles Three-Story House, M, $35.00.

(Photo courtesy Martin and Carolyn Berens)

Liddle Lion Zoolery, #3661, complete, M $100.00
Liddle Red Riding Hiddle, #3546, complete, M $150.00
Lilac Locket, #3540, MIP $75.00
Limey Lou Spoonfuls, #2815, MIP $25.00
Lois Locket, #3541, complete, M $85.00
Lola Rocket, #3536, MIP..$75.00
Lolli-Grape, #3656, complete, M $60.00

Lolli-Lemon, #3657, MIP $75.00
Lolli-Mint, #3658, MIP $60.00
Lorelei Locket, #3717, MIP $75.00
Lorelei Locket, #3717, 1976 version, MIP $25.00
Lottie Locket, #3679, complete, M $35.00
Lou Locket, #3537, MIP $75.00
Luana Locket, #3680, complete, M $35.00
Luana Locket, #3680, Gold Rush version, MIP $85.00
Lucky Lion, #3635, complete, M $50.00
Lucky Locket Jewel Case, #3542, M..............................$150.00
Luscious Lime, #3733, glitter variation, complete, M.......$75.00
Luscouis Lime, #3733, complete, M $55.00
Luvvy Duvvy Kiddle, #3596, MIP $75.00
Millie Middle, #3509, complete, M $125.00
Miss Mouse, #3638, MIP..$95.00
Nappytime Baby, #3818, complete, M.............................$75.00
Nurse 'N Totsy Outfit, #LK7, MIP $25.00
Olivia Orange Kola Kiddle, #3730, MIP $80.00
Peter Pandiddle, #3547, NRFB......................................$300.00
Pink Funny Bunny, #3532, MIP $100.00

Playhouse Kiddles Bedroom, M (EX box), $300.00.
(Photo courtesy Tamela Storm and Debra Van Dyke)

Posies 'N Pink Skediddle Outfit, #3585, MIP $30.00
Rah Rah Skediddle, #3788, complete, M........................$135.00
Rapunzel & the Prince, #3783, MIP $200.00
Robin Hood & Maid Marion, #3785, MIP $200.00
Rolly Twiddle, #3519, complete, M................................$175.00
Romeo & Juliet, #3782, MIP..$200.00
Rosebud Kologne, #3702, MIP $75.00
Rosemary Roadster, #3642, complete, M $60.00
Santa Kiddle, #3595, MIP..$40.00
Shirley Skediddle, #3766, MIP.......................................$75.00
Shirley Strawberry, #3727, complete, M $50.00
Sizzly Friddle, #3513, complete, M $75.00
Sleep 'N Totsy Outfit, #LK5, MIP $25.00
Sleeping Biddle, #3527, complete, M..............................$100.00
Slipsy Sliddle, #3754, complete, M $125.00
Snap-Happy Bedroom, #5172, complete, M $15.00
Snap-Happy Furniture, #5171, MIP $30.00
Snap-Happy Living Room, #5173, NMIP $20.00

Snoopy Skediddleer & His Sopwith Camel, M $150.00
Suki Skediddle, #3767, complete, M.................................$25.00
Surfy Skediddle, #3517, complete, M...............................$75.00
Swingy Skediddle, #3789, MIP...$200.00
Teeter Time Baby, #3817, complete, M...........................$60.00
Teresa Touring Car, #3644, complete, M........................$60.00
Tessie Tractor, #3671, complete, NM.............................$150.00
Tiny Tiger, #3636, MIP..$100.00
Tracy Trikediddle, #3769, complete, M...........................$65.00
Trikey Triddle, #3515, complete, M $75.00
Vanilla Lilly, #2819, MIP..$25.00
Violet Kologne, #3713, MIP..$60.00
Windy Fliddle, #3514, complete, M $85.00

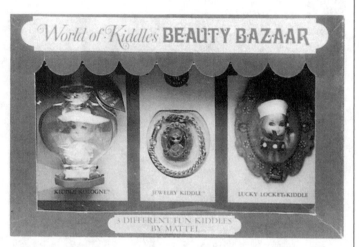

World of Kiddles Beauty Bazaar, #3586, NRFB, rare, $300.00. (Photo courtesy Paris Langford)

Zoolery Liddle Kiddle, loose, no chain, $100.00. (Photo courtesy Cindy Sabulis)

LITTLECHAP FAMILY

In 1964 Remco Industries created four fashion dolls that represented an upper-middle class American family. The Littlechaps family consisted of the father, Dr. John Littlechap, his wife, Lisa, and their two children, Judy and Libby. Their clothing and fashion accessories were made in Japan and are of the finest quality. Because these dolls are not as pretty as other fashion dolls of the era and their size and placement of arms and legs

made them awkward to dress, children had little interest in them at the time. This lack of interest during the 1960s has created shortages of them for collectors of today. Mint and complete outfits or outfits never removed from box are especially desirable to Littlechap collectors. Values listed for loose clothing are for ensembles complete with all their small accessories. If only the main pieces of the outfit are available, then the value could go down significantly.

Advisor: Cindy Sabulis (S14).

Dolls, Libby (back), Judy (front), EX (loose), from $15.00 to $20.00 each. (Photo courtesy Cindy Sabulis)

Dolls, John and Lisa, wearing tagged outfits, EX (loose), $25.00 each; complete outfits, EX, $30.00 each. (Photo courtesy Cindy Sabulis)

Carrying Case, EX, S14...$40.00
Doll, Doctor John, MIB, S14..$60.00
Doll, Judy, MIB, S14...$65.00
Doll, Libby, MIB, S14 ....$45.00
Doll, Lisa, MIB, S14..$60.00
Family Room, Bedroom or Doctor John's Office, EX, S14, ea..$125.00
Outfit, Doctor John, NRFB, S14, from $30 to $50.00
Outfit, Judy, complete, EX, S14, from $25 to $40.00

Outfit, Judy, NRFB, S14, from $35 to..............................$75.00
Outfit, Libby, complete, EX, S14, from $20 to.................$35.00
Outfit, Libby, NRFB, S14, from $35 to.........................$50.00
Outfit, Lisa, NRFB, S14, from $35 to.............................$75.00

Judy Littlechap Party Dress, NRFB, $65.00.
(Photo courtesy Cindy Sabulis)

MATTEL TALKING DOLLS

For more information refer to *Talking Toys of the 20th Century* by Kathy and Don Lewis (Collector Books).
Advisor: Kathy Lewis (L6).
See also Character, TV, and Movie Collectibles; Disney.

Mork with talking backpack, 1979, $25.00; activity book, $10.00. (Photo courtesy Cindy Sabulis)

Baby Cheryl, 1965, 16", MIB.................................$200.00
Baby Colleen, Sears Exclusive, 1965, 15½", MIB, L6 ....$100.00
Baby Drowsy, Black, 1968, 15", MIB, L6.....................$175.00
Baby First Step, 1967, MIB, L6 ....$225.00

Baby Flip-Flop, JC Penney Exclusive, 1970, MIB, L6.......$85.00
Baby See 'N Say, 1964, MIB, L6...............................$150.00
Baby Sing-A-Song, 1969, 16½", MIB, L6......................$150.00
Baby Small Talk, outfit, 1968, several different, MIP, ea ..$45.00
Baby Small Talk, 1968, MIB, L6 ....$125.00
Baby Whisper, 1968, 17½", MIB, L6.........................$200.00
Chatty Patty, 1980s, MIB, L6 ....$50.00
Cheerleader, 1970, several variations, MIB, L6, ea...........$75.00
Cynthia, M, S14..$45.00
Drowsy Sleeper-Keeper, 1966, MIB, L6.........................$125.00
Gramma & Grampa, 1968, MIB, L6, ea.........................$150.00
Hi Dottie, Black, 1972, complete w/telephone, NM, L6 ..$75.00
Little Sister Look 'N Say, Sears Exclusive, 18", M, L6....$150.00
Randi Reader, 1968, 19½", MIB, L6 ....$175.00
Sister Belle, 1961, MIB, L6..................................$300.00
Somersalty, 1970, MIB, L6 ....$200.00

Storybook Small Talk Snow White, MIB, from $125.00 to $175.00. (Photo courtesy Robin Englehart/ photo by Nancy Jean Mong)

Teachy Keen, Sears Exclusive, 1966, 16", MIB...............$125.00
Teachy Talk, 1970, MIB, L6 ....$50.00
Timey Tell, MIB, L6..$110.00

ROCKFLOWERS BY MATTEL

Rockflowers were introduced in the early 1970s as Mattel's answer to Topper's Dawn Dolls. Rockflowers are 6½" tall and have wire articulated bodies that came with mod sunglasses attached to their heads. There were four girls and one boy in the series with eighteen groovy outfits that could be purchased separately. Each doll came with their own 45 rpm record, and the clothing packages were also in the shape of a 45 rpm record.
Advisor: Dawn Diaz (P2).

Case, Rockflowers on Stage, vinyl, 3 compartments, NM...$15.00
Doll, Heather, NRFB, from $40 to $50.00
Doll, Iris, NRFB, from $40 to $50.00

Doll, Lilac, #1167, NRFB, from $35 to $50.00
Doll, Rosemary, #1168, NRFB...$50.00
Gift Set, Rockflowers in Concert, w/Heather, Lilac & Rosemary,
    NRFB...$100.00
Outfit, Jeans in Fringe, NRFP..$15.00

Doug, MIB, from $50.00 to $60.00.
(Photo courtesy Laura Coplen-Miller/Cindy Sabulis)

STRAWBERRY SHORTCAKE

It was around 1980 when Strawberry Shortcake came on the market with a bang. The line included everything to attract small girls — swimsuits, bed linens, blankets, anklets, underclothing, coats, shoes, sleeping bags, dolls and accessories, games, and many other delightful items. Strawberry Shortcake and her friends were short lived, lasting only until the middle of the decade.

    Advisor: Geneva Addy (A5).

Dollhouse, M, $150.00.
(Photo courtesy Geneva Addy)

Big Berry Trolley, 1982, EX...$40.00
Doll, Almond Tea, 6", MIB $25.00

Doll, Angel Cake, 6", MIB $25.00
Doll, Apple Dumpling, 6", MIB...$25.00
Doll, Apricot, 15", NM...$35.00
Doll, Baby Needs a Name, 15", NM.....................................$35.00
Doll, Berry Baby Orange Blossom, 6", MIB.........................$35.00
Doll, Butter Cookie, 6", MIB...$25.00
Doll, Cafe Ole, 6", MIB $35.00
Doll, Cherry Cuddler, 6", MIB...$25.00
Doll, Lime Chiffon, 6", MIB...$25.00
Doll, Mint Tulip, 6", MIB...$25.00
Doll, Raspberry Tart, 6", MIB..$25.00
Doll, Strawberry Shortcake, 12", NRFB $45.00
Doll, Strawberry Shortcake, 15", NM $35.00
Dollhouse Furniture, attic, 6-pc, rare, M.........................$150.00
Dollhouse Furniture, bathroom, 5-pc, rare, M $65.00
Dollhouse Furniture, bedroom, 7-pc, rare, M $90.00
Dollhouse Furniture, kitchen, 11-pc, rare, M..................$100.00
Dollhouse Furniture, living room, 6-pc, rare, M $85.00
Figure, Almond Tea w/Marza Panda, PVC, 1", MOC......$15.00
Figure, Cherry Cuddler w/Gooseberry, Strawberryland Minia-
    tures, MIP, from $15 to $20.00
Figure, Lemon Meringue w/Frappo, PVC, 1", MOC.........$15.00
Figure, Lime Chiffon w/balloons, PVC, 1", MOC $15.00
Figure, Merry Berry Worm, MIB..$35.00
Figure, Mint Tulip w/March Mallard, PVC, MOC $15.00
Figure, Purple Pieman w/Berry Bird, poseable, MIB..........$35.00
Figure, Raspberry Tart w/bowl of cherries, MOC..............$15.00
Figure, Sour Grapes w/Dregs, Strawberryland Miniatures, MIP,
    B5, from $15 to $20.00
Ice Skates, EX $35.00
Motorized Bicycle, EX...$95.00
Roller Skates, EX $35.00
Sleeping Bag, EX...$25.00
Storybook Play Case, M...$35.00
Stroller, Coleco, 1981, M...$85.00
Telephone, Strawberry Shortcake figure, battery-op, EX..$85.00

SUNSHINE FAMILY BY MATTEL

The Sunshine Family was produced and sold from 1974 to 1982. The first family consisted of the father, Steve, his wife, Steffie, and their daughter, Baby Sweets. In 1976 Mattel added The Happy Family (an African-American family consisting of mom, dad, and their two children). The line also included grandparents, playsets, vehicles, and a lot of other accessories that made them so much fun to play with. For more information we recommend *Thirty Years of Mattel Fashion Dolls* by Michael Augustynaik (Collector Books).

Camping Craft Kit, 1974, complete, MIP, minimum value...$35.00
Craft Store, 1976, complete, MIB, minimum value..........$70.00
Doll, Darlin', Honey Hill Bunch, 4", NM $10.00
Doll, Little Hon (Black, 1977, complete w/nursery set, MIB,
    minimum value..$35.00
Doll, Little Sweets, 1975, complete w/nursery set, MIB, mini-
    mum value...$35.00
Doll, New Baby, orig outfit, NM...$15.00
Doll, Sister, complete w/shoes, EX $20.00

Dolls, Steffie (missing apron) and Steve, from $15.00 to $20.00 each; Baby Sweets, from $5.00 to $10.00.
(Photo courtesy Cindy Sabulis)

Doll, Slugger, Honey Hill Bunch, 4", EX, from $5 to........**$10.00**
Doll & Craft Case, Sears Exclusive, 1977, vinyl, EX, minimum value..**$25.00**
Doll Set, Grandparents, 1976, MIB, minimum value.......**$60.00**
Doll Set, Happy Family (Black), 1975, MIB, minimum value..**$60.00**
Doll Set, Watch 'Em Grow Greenhouse, 1977, limited edition, complete w/3 dolls, craft kit & seeds, MIB, minimum value **$100.00**
Doll Set, 1976, Steve, Steffie & Baby Sweets, MIB, minimum value..**$65.00**
Family Farm, 1977, complete, rare, MIB, minimum value ..**$140.00**
Kitchen Craft Kit, 1974, complete, MIB, minimum value ..**$35.00**
Nursery Craft Kit, 1976, complete, MIP **$25.00**
Outfit, 1975, several variations, MIP, minimum value, ea...**$15.00**
Outfit, 1976, several variations, MIP, minimum value, ea...**$15.00**
Sunshine Family Home, 1974, 4 rooms, compete w/furniture, EX, minimum value..**$65.00**
Surrey Cycle, 1975, MIB, minimum value **$35.00**
Van w/Piggyback Shack, 1975, complete, MIB, minimum value **$50.00**

TAMMY

In 1962 the Ideal Novelty and Toy Company introduced their teenage Tammy doll. Slightly pudgy and not quite as sophisticated-looking as some of the teen fashion dolls on the market at the time, Tammy's innocent charm captivated consumers. Her extensive wardrobe and numerous accessories added to her popularity with children. Tammy had a car, a house, and her own catamaran. In addition, a large number of companies obtained licenses to issue products using the 'Tammy' name. Everything from paper dolls to nurse's kits were made with Tammy's image on them. Her success was not confined to the United States; she was also successful in Canada and several other European countries.

Interest in Tammy has risen quite a bit in the past few years according to Cindy Sabulis, co-author of *Tammy, the Ideal Teen* (Collector Books). Values have gone up and supply for quality mint-in-box items is going down. Loose, played-with dolls are still readily available and can be found for as low as $10.00 at doll shows. Values are given for mint-in-box dolls.

Advisor: Cindy Sabulis (S14).

Doll, Tammy's Mom, light or dark hair, EX, $45.00 each.
(Photo courtesy Cindy Sabulis)

Accessory Pak, #9179-3, w/plate of crackers, juice, glasses, sandals & newspaper, NRFP, S14....................................**$20.00**
Accessory Pak, #9183-80, w/camera, luggage case & airline ticket, NRFP, S14 ....**$15.00**
Accessory Pak, #9188-80, w/tennis racket, score book, ball & sneakers, NRFP, S14 ....**$15.00**
Accessory Pak, unknown #, w/frying pan, electric skillet & lids, NRFP, S14, from $45 to..**$50.00**
Case, Dodi, gr background, EX, S14....................................**$30.00**
Case, Misty, Dutch door-type, blk background, EX, S14 ..**$30.00**
Case, Misty, pk & wht background, EX, S14....................**$25.00**
Case, Misty & Tammy, hatbox style, EX, S14....................**$30.00**
Case, Pepper, gr or coral background, front snap closure, EX, S14, ea..**$15.00**
Case, Pepper, hatbox style, turq background, EX, S14......**$40.00**
Case, Pepper, yel or gr background, EX, S14, ea **$20.00**
Case, Pepper & Dodi, bl background, front opening, EX, S14..**$30.00**
Case, Pepper & Patti, Montgomery Ward's Exclusive, red background, EX, S14 ....**$50.00**
Case, Tammy Beau & Arrow, hatbox style, bl or red, EX, S14, ea **$40.00**
Case, Tammy Evening in Paris, bl, blk, or red background, EX, S14, ea..**$20.00**
Case, Tammy Model Miss, dbl trunk, red or blk, EX, S14, ea..**$25.00**
Case, Tammy Model Miss, hatbox style, bl or blk, EX, S14, ea..**$30.00**
Case, Tammy Model Miss, red or blk background, EX, S14, ea..**$25.00**

Case, Tammy Traveler, red or gr background, EX, S14, ea ...$45.00

Case Tammy & Her Friends, pk or gr background, EX, S14, ea...$30.00

Doll, Bud, MIB, S14, minimum value............................$600.00

Doll, Dodi, MIB, S14...$75.00

Doll, Glamour Misty the Miss Clairol Doll, MIB, S14 ...$150.00

Doll, Grown Up Tammy, MIB, S14...................................$85.00

Doll, Grown Up Tammy (Black), MIB, S14, minimum value...$300.00

Doll, Misty, MIB, S14..$100.00

Doll, Misty (Black), MIB, S14, minimum value $600.00

Doll, Patti, MIB, S14...$200.00

Doll, Pepper, 'carrot'-colored hair, MIB, S14 ....$75.00

Doll, Pepper, MIB, S14..$65.00

Doll, Pepper (Canadian version), MIB, S14 ....$75.00

Doll, Pepper (trimmer body & smaller face), MIB, S14....$75.00

Doll, Pos'n Dodi, M (decorated box), S14.......................$150.00

Doll, Pos'n Dodi, M (plain box), S14................................$75.00

Doll, Pos'n Misty & Her Telephone Booth, MIB, S14 ...$125.00

Doll, Pos'n Pepper, MIB, S14 ....$75.00

Doll, Pos'n Pete, MIB, S14...$125.00

Doll, Pos'n Salty, MIB, S14..$125.00

Doll, Pos'n Tammy & Her Telephone Booth, MIB, S14...$100.00

Doll, Pos'n Ted, MIB, S14..$100.00

Doll, Tammy, MIB, S14 ....$85.00

Doll, Tammy's Dad, MIB, S14 ....$65.00

Doll, Tammy's Mom, MIB, S14 ....$75.00

Doll, Ted, MIB, S14..$50.00

Outfit, Dad & Ted, bathrobe & slippers, #9457-3, NRFP, S14..$20.00

Outfit, Dad & Ted, blazer & slacks, #9477-1, NRFP, S14 ...$20.00

Outfit, Dad & Ted, cardigan sweater & high socks, #9462-3, NRFP, S14...$10.00

Outfit, Dad & Ted, pajamas & slippers, #9456-5, MIB, S14..$20.00

Outfit, Dad & Ted, sports car coat & cap, #9467-2, NRFP, S14..$20.00

Outfit, Dad & Ted, sweater, shorts & socks, #9476-3, MIP, S14..$25.00

Outfit, Pepper, After School, #9318-7, complete, M, S14 ..$25.00

Outfit, Pepper, Anchors Away, #9316-1, complete, M, S14...$30.00

Outfit, Pepper, Flower Girl, #9332-8, complete, M, S14 ..$45.00

Outfit, Pepper, Happy Holiday, #9317-9, complete, M, S14...$40.00

Outfit, Pepper, Miss Gadabout, #9331-0, MIP, S14 ....$50.00

Outfit, Pepper & Dodi, Light & Lacy, #9305-4, MIP, S14 ..$45.00

Outfit, Pepper & Dodi, Sun 'N Surf, #9321-1, MIP, S14..$50.00

Outfit, Tammy, Beach Party, #9056-3 or #9906-9, complete, M, S14 ....$45.00

Outfit, Tammy, Beau & Arrow, #9117-3 or #9925-9, complete, M, S14...$40.00

Outfit, Tammy, Career Girl, #9945-7, complete, M, S14 .$75.00

Outfit, Tammy, Cheerleader, #9131-4 or #9931-7, complete, M, S14, ea..$45.00

Outfit, Tammy, Cutie Coed, #9132-2 or 9932-5, complete, M, S14 ....$45.00

Outfit, Tammy, Fraternity Hop, #9137-1 or #9937-4, complete, M, S14...$50.00

Outfit, Tammy, Jet Set, #9155-3 or #9943-2, MIP, S14 ....$55.00

Outfit, Tammy, Knit Knack, #9094-4 or #9917-6, complete, M, S14, ea..$25.00

Outfit, Tammy, Opening Night, #9954-9, MIP, S14 ....$75.00

Outfit, Tammy, Pizza Party, #9115-7 or #9924-2, complete, M, S14...$30.00

Outfit, Tammy, Private Secretary, #9939-0, MIP, S14.......$75.00

Outfit, Tammy, Skate Date, #9177-7 or #9953-1, complete, M, S14...$45.00

Outfit, Tammy, Sorority Sweetheart, #9174-4 or #9950-7, complete, M, S14, ea...$50.00

Outfit, Tammy, Sweater Girl, #9135-5 or #9935-8, complete, M, S14...$40.00

Outfit, Tammy's Mom, Evening in Paris, #9421-9, complete, M, S14...$35.00

Outfit, Tammy's Mom, Lazy Days, #9418-5, MIP, S14......$25.00

Outfit, Tammy's Mom, Shopping Topping, #9419-3, complete, M, S14...$25.00

Pak clothing, #9220-5, w/skirt, belt, handkerchief, date book & hanger, MIP, S14..$30.00

Pak clothing, #9221-3, w/skirt, shoes & hanger, NRFP, S14...$20.00

Pak clothing, #9222-1, w/sleeveless blouse, necklace & hanger, NRFP, S14...$20.00

Pak clothing, #9224-7, w/pedal pushers, orange juice, newspaper & hanger, NRFP, S14..................................$25.00

Pak clothing, #9231-2, w/short sleeve blouse, red glasses & hanger, NRFP, S14..$15.00

Pak clothing, #9242-9, w/nightgown, sandals & 3 pcs of fruit, NRFP, S14..$25.00

Pak clothing, #9243-7, w/sheath dress, blk belt, shoes & hanger, NRFP, S14..$30.00
Pak clothing, #9244-5, w/sweater, scarf & hanger, NRFP, S14..$25.00
Pak clothing, #9345-2, w/afternoon dress & shoes, NRFP, S14..$25.00
Pepper's Jukebox, M, S14..$65.00
Pepper's Pony, MIB...$200.00
Pepper's Treehouse, MIB, S14..................................$150.00
Tammy & Ted Catamaran, MIB, S14.........................$200.00
Tammy Bubble Bath Set, NRFB, S14.........................$75.00
Tammy Dress-Up Kit, Colorforms, 1964, complete, MIB, S14..$30.00
Tammy Hair Dryer, sq or rnd case, NM, S14, ea.........$50.00
Tammy's Bed, Dress & Chair, MIB, S14......................$85.00
Tammy's Car, MIB, S14..$75.00

Tammy's Ideal House, EX, $100.00. (Photo courtesy Cindy Sabulis)

Tammy's Jukebox, M, S14...$50.00
Tammy's Magic Mirror Fashion Show, Winthrop-Atkins, NRFB, S14..$50.00

TRESSY

American Character's Tressy doll was produced in this country from 1963 to 1967. The unique feature of this 11½" fashion doll was that her hair 'grew' by pushing a button on her stomach. Tressy also had a little (9") sister named Cricket. Numerous fashions and accessories were produced for these two dolls. Never-removed-from-box Tressy and Cricket items are rare, so unless indicated, values listed are for loose, mint items. A never-removed-from-box item's worth is at least double its loose value.

Advisor: Cindy Sabulis (S14).

Apartment, M, S14...$150.00
Beauty Salon, M, S14...$125.00
Case, Cricket, M, S14..$30.00
Case, Tressy, M, S14..$30.00
Doll, Pre-Teen Tressy, M, S14....................................$60.00
Doll, Tressy, loose in original dress...........................$35.00
Doll, Tressy in Miss America Character outfit, NM, S14.$65.00
Doll, Tressy w/Magic Make-up Face, M, S14..............$25.00

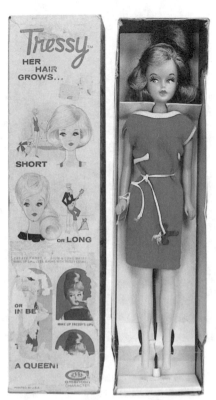

American Character Tressy, MIB, $100.00.
(Photo courtesy Cindy Sabulis)

Cricket doll and accessory set, NRFB, $200.00.
(Photo courtesy Cindy Sabulis)

Doll Clothes Pattern, M, S14......................................$10.00
Gift Pak w/Doll & Clothing, NRFB, S14, minimum value..$100.00
Hair Accessory Pak, NRFB, S14, ea............................$20.00
Hair Dryer, M, S14..$40.00
Hair or Cosmetic Accessory Kits, M, S14, minimum value, ea..$50.00
Millinery, M, S14..$150.00
Outfits, MOC, S14, ea, from $30 to...........................$40.00
Outfits, NRFB, S14, minimum value, ea.....................$65.00

Outfit, Cricket Just Pals, MOC, $40.00.
(Photo courtesy Cindy Sabulis)

UPSY DOWNSYS BY MATTEL

The Upsy Downsy dolls were made by Mattel during the late 1960s. They were small, 2½" to 3½", made of vinyl and plastic. Some of the group were 'Upsies' that walked on their feet, while others were 'Downsies' that walked or rode fantasy animals while upside-down.

Advisor: Dawn Diaz (P2).

Baby So-High, #3828, complete, M $50.00
Downy Dilly, #3832, complete, M.............................$50.00
Downy Dilly, #3832, NRFB $100.00
Flossy Glossy, #3827, doll & playland, EX $25.00
Funny Feeder, #3834, Gooey Chooey only, EX $25.00
Hairy Hurry Downsy Wizzer, #3838, complete, EX.........$100.00
Miss Information, #3831, NRFB $100.00
Mother What Now, #3829, complete, EX.......................$50.00
Pocus Hocus, #3820, complete, M..............................$50.00
Pudgy Fudgy, #3826, NRFB $100.00
Tickle Pinkle & Her Bugabout Car, MIB, from $75 to ...$100.00

Farm Toys

It's entirely probable that more toy tractors have been sold than real ones. They've been made to represent all makes and models, of plastic, cast iron, diecast metal, and even wood. They've been made in at least 1/16th scale, 1/32nd, 1/43rd, and 1/64th. If you buy a 1/16th-scale replica, that small piece of equipment would have to be sixteen times larger to equal the size of the real item. Limited editions (meaning that a specific number will be made and no more) and commemorative editions (made for special events) are usually very popular with collectors. Many models on the market today are being made by the Ertl company.

Advisor: John Rammacher (S5).
See also Cast Iron, Farm; Diecast.

Agco Allis 6670 Row Crop Tractor, Ertl, 1/64th scale, #1214, MIB, S5...$3.50
Agco Allis 6690 Tractor w/4-Post ROPS, Ertl, 1/64th scale, #1239, MIB, S5...$3.50
Agco R-52 Combine, Ertl, 1/64th scale, #1282, MIB, S5.$10.00
Allis Chalmers D-14 Tractor, Yoder, 1/16th scale, #15, M, from $150 to...$175.00
Allis Chalmers D-19 w/Loader, Ertl, 1/16th scale, #2030, MIB, S5 ....$40.00
Allis Chalmers WD 45 Precision #3, Ertl, 1/16th scale, #2252, MIB, S5...$110.00

Allis Chalmers Tractor, Ertl, 1/16th scale, MIB, $30.00.

C&J Systems Grain Cart, Ertl, 1/64th scale, #4432, MIB, S5 ....$5.00
C&J Systems Liquid Fertilizer Spreader, Ertl, 1/64th scale, #4433, MIB, S5...$5.00
Case Agriking 970 Tractor, Ertl, 1/16th scale, #4279, MIB, S5 ....$32.00
Case IH C-90, Ertl, 1998 Farm Show, 1/16th scale, #4601, MIB, S5 ....$60.00
Case IH Hay Rake, Ertl, 1/64th scale, #210, MIB, S5.........$3.00
Case IH Maxxum MX120, Ertl, 1997 Farm Show, 1/16th scale, #4487, MIB, S5...$45.00
Case IH Tractor w/End Loader, Ertl, 1/64th scale, #212, MIB, S5...$5.00
Case IH 1660 Combine, Ertl, 1/64th scale, #655, MIB, S5.$12.00
Case IH 2366 Axial-Flow Combine, Ertl, 1/64th scale, #4614, MIB, S5 ....$10.00
Case IH 2555 Cotton Express, Ertl, 1/64th scale, #4300, MIB, S5 ....$12.00
Case IH 5130 Row Crop, Ertl, 1991 Farm Show, 1/64th scale, #229, MIB, S5...$10.00
Case IH 7150 w/Duals, Ertl, 1/64th scale, #626, MIB, S5 ...$3.00
Case IH 7220 w/Loader, Ertl, 1/64th scale, #460, MIB, S5 .$5.00
Case IH 8312 Mower Conditioner, Ertl, 1/64th scale, #4362, MIB, S5 ....$4.00
Case IH 8920 Tractor w/Loader, Ertl, 1/64th scale, MIB, S5 ....$4.00

Case IH 9260 4-Wheel Drive, Ertl, 1993 Farm Show, 1/64th scale, #231, MIB, S5 ....$10.00

Case IH 946 Farm Tractor, Lone Star, M $20.00

Case L Tractor, Ertl, 150 Year Collector's Edition, 1/16th scale, #252, MIB, S5 ....$35.00

Case 1470 Traction King, Ertl, 1/64th scale, #4332, MIB, S5...$6.00

Case 400 Tractor, Yoder, 1/16th scale, #19, blk, M, from $250 to..$275.00

Case 400 Tractor, Yoder, 1/16th scale, #7, M, from $75 to ...$125.00

Case 580 E Tractor Loader, Conrad, 1/35th scale, M........$80.00

Case 65 HP Steam Engine Tractor, Ertl, 1/16th scale, #14024, MIB, S5 ....$50.00

Case 700 Tractor, Yoder, 1/16th scale, #9, 1986 Beaver Falls show, M, from $75 to $100.00

Case 90XT Skid Steer Loader, Ertl, 1/64th scale, #4216, MIB, S5...$25.00

Case 930 Precision #12, Ertl, 1/16th scale, #4284, MIB, S5 ..$110.00

Caterpillar Flotation Liquid Fertilizer Spreader, Ertl, 1/64th scale, #2324, MIB, S5 ....$5.00

Caterpillar Industrial Disc, Ertl, 1/64th scale, #2333, MIB, S5 ....$3.50

Caterpillar Road Grader, Ertl, Mighty Movers Construction, 1/64th scale, #1848, MIB, S5...........................$8.00

CIH 7150 Tractor w/Front-Wheel Assist, Ertl, 1992 Farm Show, 1/64th scale, #285, MIB, S5 ....$10.00

Claas Automatic Hay Loader, Siku, M..............................$25.00

Claas Jaguar 695 Combine, Siku, M.................................$30.00

Claas Jaguar 695 Forage Harvester, Siku, M....................$30.00

Cockshutt Tractor, Advanced Products USA, working steering and lift systems for draw bar, 8½", EX (VG+ box), A, $525.00.

Dalia-Solido, Porsche Carrera 6, yel & red, M, ea $75.00

Deutz Agroxtra Tractor w/Twin Rear Wheels, Siku, M $20.00

Deutz Allis Barge Wagon, Ertl, 1/64th scale, #2241, MIB, S5 ....$2.50

Deutz Allis Mixer Mill, Ertl, 1/64th scale, #2208, MIB, S5 .$2.50

Deutz Allis 7085 Tractor w/Loader, Ertl, 1/64th scale, #2233, MIB, S5 ....$4.00

Deutz Caterpillar Tractor, Schuco, 2", M $60.00

Deutz-Fahr Agrostar DX6.61 Turbo Tractor w/Tandem-Axle Trailer, Siku, M $30.00

Deutz-Fahr Agrostar 6.61 Turbo Tractor, Siku, 1/32nd scale, #2850, M...$20.00

Deutz-Fahr Agroxtra Tractor w/Front Mower, Siku, M.....$20.00

Deutz-Fahr DX6.31 Turbo Forestry Tractor, Siku, M $30.00

Deutz-Fahr M36.10 Corn Combine Harvester, Siku, M ...$50.00

Deutz-Fahr Round Baler, Siku, M....................................$15.00

Deutz-Fahr Top Liner Combine Harvester, Siku, 1/32nd scale, #4051, M...$50.00

Farm Set, Hubley Kiddie Toys, complete w/tractor, plow, spreader & cultipacker, MIB, A $250.00

Farm Set No 90, Hubley Kiddie Toys, complete w/tractor, wagon, plow & cultipacker, MIB, A $500.00

Farmall F-20 Precision Tractor, Ertl, 1/16th scale, #638, MIB, S5 ....$100.00

Farmall H Tractor, Ertl, 1/16th scale, #4441, MIB, S5......$25.00

Farmall Super M-T-A Tractor, Ertl, 1/16th scale, #445, MIB, S5 ....$20.00

Farmall 140 Tractor, Ertl, 1/16th scale, #4741, MIB, S5 ..$35.00

Farmall 300 Tractor, Ertl, 1/16th scale, #14000, MIB, S5 ..$25.00

Farmall 340 Crawler, Ertl, 1/16th scale, #4734, MIB, S5..$25.00

Farmall 350 Tractor, Ertl, 1/16th scale, #418, MIB, $25.00.

Farmall 806 Wide Front Tractor, Ertl, 1/16th scale, #4406, MIB, S5 ....$30.00

Ford F Tractor, Ertl, Collector's Edition, 1/16th scale, #872, MIB, S5 ....$45.00

Ford Foxfire 771 Tractor, Ertl, 1/16th scale, #3053, MIB, S5 ....$24.00

Ford New Holland Combine, Ertl, 1/64th scale, #815, MIB, S5 ....$15.00

Ford Pickup, Ertl, 50th Anniversary, #F019, MIB, S5 ......$22.00

Ford Precision Classic 2N, Ertl, 1/16th scale, #354, MIB, S5...$95.00

Ford Super Major 5000 Tractor, Ertl, 1/64th scale, #928, MIB, S5 ....$5.00

Ford TW-35 Tractor, Siku, M...$20.00

Ford TW-35 Tractor, Siku, 1/32nd scale, #2855, M **$20.00**

Ford 4000 Industrial Tractor, Ertl, 1/64th scale, #13506, MIB, S5...**$3.50**

Ford 5000 Tractor, Ertl, 1/64th scale, #3293, MIB, S5........**$4.00**

Ford 5640 w/Loader, Ertl, 1/64th scale, #334, MIB, S5.......**$4.00**

Ford 641 Workmaster w/Loader, 1/16th scale, MIB, S5..**$135.00**

Ford 7610 Farm Tractor, Lone Star, M **$20.00**

Ford 7740 Tractor w/Loader, Ertl, 1/64th scale, #387, MIB, S5...**$4.50**

Ford 8N Tractor, Ertl, 1/16th scale, #843, MIB, S5...........**$20.00**

Ford 8240 Tractor w/4-Wheel Drive, Ertl, 1/64th scale, #389, MIB, S5 ....**$4.00**

Ford 8340 w/4-Wheel Drive, Ertl, Collector's Edition, 1/16th scale, #877, MIB, S5...**$50.00**

Ford 8730 Tractor w/Loader, Ertl, 1/64th scale, #303, MIB, S5...**$4.50**

Ford 901 Power Master Tractor, Ertl, 1/64th scale, #927, MIB, S5 ....**$5.00**

Fordson Tractor, Chad Valley, 1/43rd scale, M...............**$175.00**

Genesis 8870 w/4-Wheel Drive, Ertl, 1/64th scale, #392, MIB, S5 ....**$4.00**

Hesston Mower Conditioner, Ertl, 1/64th scale, #2068, MIB, S5 ....**$3.50**

Hesston SL-30 Skid Steer Loader, Ertl, 1/64th scale, #2267, MIB, S5 ....**$4.50**

Hesston 8400 Self-Propelled Windrower, Ertl, 1/64th scale, #2261, MIB, S5 ....**$8.00**

IH Farmall Cub, Ertl, 1/16th scale, #653, MIB, S5 ....**$18.00**

IH T-340 Crawler w/Bullgrader, Ertl, 1/16th scale, #4380, MIB, S5 ....**$30.00**

IH 1586 Tractor w/Loader, Ertl, 1/16th scale, #416, MIB, S5 ....**$25.00**

IH 560 Gas Tractor, Ertl, 1/64th scale, #4830, MIB, S5......**$4.00**

IH 815 Combine, Ertl, 1/64th scale, #4354, MIB, S5 ....**$10.00**

International Harvester Combine, Replex, 1/43rd scale, M..**$50.00**

International Harvester 844 Farm Tractor, Replex, 1/43rd scale, M...**$45.00**

International 600 Diesel Tractor, Ertl, 1/16th scale, #282, MIB, S5 ....**$20.00**

John Deere Bulldozer, Ertl, Mighty Movers Construction, 1/64th scale, #568, MIB, S5 ....**$8.00**

John Deere C&J Liquid Fertilizer Spreader, Ertl, 1/64th scale, #5089, MIB, S5 ....**$4.50**

John Deere Compact Utility Tractor, Ertl, 1/16th scale, #581, MIB, S5...**$16.00**

John Deere CTS II Combine, Ertl, 1/64th scale, #5172, MIB, S5...**$10.00**

John Deere Dry Fertilizer Spreader, Ertl, 1/64th scale, #5184, MIB, S5 ....**$5.00**

John Deere Forage Harvester, Ertl, 1/64th scale, #566, MIB, S5 ....**$3.00**

John Deere Froehlich, Ertl, 1/16th scale, #15008, MIB, S5 .**$55.00**

John Deere G Tractor, Ertl, 1/16th scale, #5104, MIB, S5 ..**$25.00**

John Deere General Purpose Tractor, Ertl, Collector's Edition, MIB...**$75.00**

John Deere GP Wide Tread, Ertl, 1/16th scale, #5787, MIB, S5 ....**$26.00**

John Deere Grain Cart, Ertl, 1/64th scale, #5565, MIB, S5 ..**$5.00**

John Deere Excavator, Ertl, 1/64th scale, MIB, $7.50.

John Deere Gravity Wagon, Ertl, 1/64th scale, #5552, MIB, S5 ....**$3.00**

John Deere Hay Rake, Ertl, 1/64th scale, #5751, MIB, S5..**$3.50**

John Deere Model D Tractor, Kansas Toy & Novelty, 5", M ...**$75.00**

John Deere Model 150 Forage Blower, Ertl, 1/64th scale, #5728, MIB, S5 ....**$3.50**

John Deere Mower Conditioner, Ertl, 1/64th scale, #5657, MIB, S5 ....**$3.00**

John Deere Skid Steer Loader, Ertl, 1/16th scale, #569, MIB, S5 ....**$18.50**

John Deere Sprayer, Ertl, 1/64th scale, #5185, MIB, S5......**$5.00**

John Deere Tractor Factory Playset, Ertl, #5140, MIB, S5 ..**$32.00**

John Deere Utility Tractor w/Loader, Ertl, 1/16th scale, #517, MIB, S5 ....**$22.00**

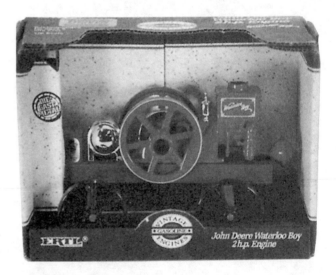

John Deere Waterloo Boy 2h.p. Engine, Ertl, 1992, MIB, $20.00.

John Deere Wheel Loader 744H, Ertl, Mighty Movers Construction, 1/50th scale, #5085, MIB, S5............................**$16.00**

John Deere 12-A Combine, Ertl, Collector's Edition, 1/16th scale, #5601, MIB, S5 ....**$45.00**

John Deere 1939 Model B Tractor, Ertl, Collector's Edition, 1/16th scale, #5822, MIB, S5 ....**$40.00**

John Deere 40 Crawler, Ertl, 1/16th scale, #5072, MIB, S5 ..**$26.00**

John Deere 4010 Diesel, Ertl, 1994 National Toy Show, 1/43rd scale, #5725, MIB, S5 ....$25.00

John Deere 4010 Tractor, Ertl, 1/16th scale, #5716, MIB, S5 ....$25.00

John Deere 430 Crawler, Ertl, 1/64th scale, #5616, MIB, S5 ....$4.00

John Deere 4700 Field Sprayer, Ertl, 1/64th scale, #5752, MIB, S5 ....$8.00

John Deere 5020 Tractor w/Disk, Ertl, 1/64th scale, #5198, MIB, S5 ....$7.50

John Deere 530 Tractor, Ertl, 1/64th scale, #5194, MIB, S5...$3.50

John Deere 6400 Tractor w/Loader, Ertl, 1/16th scale, #5916, MIB, S5 ....$38.00

John Deere 6410 Tractor w/Loader, Ertl, 1/64th scale, #5169, MIB, S5 ....$5.00

John Deere 720 Standard Tractor, Yoder, 1/16th scale, #39, M $100.00

John Deere 730 Standard Tractor, Yoder, 1/16th scale, #47, orange, M, from $150 to $175.00

John Deere 8200 Tractor, Ertl, 1/64th scale, #5064, MIB, S5 ....$4.00

John Deere 8400T Tractor, Ertl, 1/64th scale, #5051, MIB, S5 ....$6.50

John Deere 850C Crawler, Ertl, Mighty Movers Construction, 1/50th scale, #5261, MIB, S5 ....$15.00

John Deere 9400 4-Wheel Drive Tractor, Ertl, 1/64th scale, #5937, MIB, S5 ....$6.50

John Deere 9610 Combine, Ertl, 1/64th scale, #5809, MIB, S5 ....$10.00

John Deere 9976 Cotton Picker, Ertl, 1/64th scale, #5765, MIB, S5 ....$10.00

Landini Tractor, Mercury, 1961, M.....................$55.00

Manure Spreader, Chad Valley, M.....................$75.00

Massey-Ferguson Challenger Tractor, Ertl, 1/16th scale, #1103, MIB, S5 ....$25.00

Massey-Ferguson Farm Set, Mercury, 1960, M $55.00

Massey-Ferguson Farm Wagon, Mercury, 1960, M............$55.00

Massey-Ferguson Front End Loader, Siku, M $25.00

Massey-Ferguson Hay Baler, Mercury, 1960, M.................$55.00

Massey-Ferguson Tractor w/Hay Trailer, Siku, M.............$10.00

Massey-Ferguson Tractor w/Hay Trailer, Siku, 1/32nd scale, #2227, M...$10.00

Massey-Ferguson 3070 Tractor w/Front-Wheel Drive, Ertl, 1/64th scale, #1107, MIB, S5.........................$3.50

Massey-Ferguson 3120 Tractor w/Loader, Ertl, 1/64th scale, #1109, MIB, S5 ....$4.50

Massey-Ferguson 3140 Tractor w/Duals, Ertl, 1/64th scale, #1176, MIB, S5 ....$3.50

Massey-Ferguson 3140 Tractor w/Front-Wheel Drive, Ertl, 1/64th scale, #1107, MIB, S5.........................$3.50

Massey-Ferguson 50B Loader, Conrad, 1/35th scale, M....$75.00

Massey-Ferguson 699 Tractor w/Loader, Ertl, 1/64th scale, #1125, MIB, S5 ....$5.00

Massey-Ferguson 9400 Tractor, M $20.00

Massey-Ferguson 9400 Tractor, Siku, 1/32nd scale, #2868, M ..$20.00

Massey-Harris Challenger Tractor, Ertl, 1/43rd scale, #2511, MIB, S5 ....$6.00

Massey-Harris 44 Special Tractor, Ertl, 1/16th scale, #1115, MIB, S5 ....$20.00

McCormick-Deering #200 Spreader Precision, Ertl, 1/16th scale, #4201, MIB, S5................................$110.00

McCormick-Deering Farmall AV Tractor, Ertl, 1992 Lafayette Farm Toy Show Edition, 1 of 3,000, MIB..................$65.00

Michigan 380 Tractor Plow, Mercury, 1958, M.................$55.00

Minneapolis-Moline G-750 Tractor, Ertl, 1994 National Tractor Show, 1/16th scale, #4375, MIB, S5 ....$80.00

Minneapolis-Moline G-750 Tractor, Ertl, 1/43rd scale, #2291, MIB, S5 ....$6.00

New Holland Model 40 Forage Blower, Ertl, 1/64th scale, #343, MIB, S5 ....$3.50

New Holland Skid Loader, Ertl, 1/64th scale, #381, MIB, S5 ....$4.50

New Holland TX-34 Combine Harvester w/Corn Head, Joal, 1/42nd scale, #247, M.....................................$25.00

New Holland Wing Disk, Ertl, 1/64th scale, #3049, MIB, S5 .$4.00

New Holland 5635 Tractor, Siku, M $20.00

New Holland 8260 Tractor, Ertl, 1997 Farm Show, 1/43rd scale, #3050, MIB, S5 ....$22.00

New Holland 8560 Tractor, Ertl, 1/43rd scale, #3032, MIB, S5 ....$12.00

New Holland 8560 Tractor, Ertl, 1/43rd scale, #3032, MIB, S5 ....$12.00

Oliver Super 55 Tractor, Yoder, 1/16th scale, #5, M, from $250 to...$300.00

Oliver Super 77 Wide Front Precision #5 Tractor, Ertl, 1/16th scale, #2658, MIB, S5................................$110.00

Renault Tractor w/Front End Loader, Siku, M $12.00

Renault Tractor w/Rear Digger, Siku, 1/32nd scale, #3755, M...$30.00

Renault TX145-14 Tractor, Siku, M................................$20.00

Tractor & Harvester, Charbens, M...................................$75.00

Tractor Loader, Hubley, orange, 12", MIB, from $100 to ...$200.00

Fast-Food Collectibles

Fast-food collectibles are attracting a lot of attention right now — the hobby is fun and inexpensive (so far), and the little toys, games, buttons, and dolls originally meant for the kids are now being snatched up by adults who are much more likely to appreciate them. They were first included in kiddie meals in the late 1970s. They're often issued in series of up to eight or ten characters; the ones you'll want to watch for are Disney characters, popular kids' icons like Barbie dolls, Cabbage Patch Kids, My Little Pony, Star Trek, etc. But it's not just the toys that are collectible. So are the boxes, store signs and displays, and promotional items (like the Christmas items they once sold for 99¢). Supply dictates price. For instance, a test market box might be worth $20.00, a box from a regional promotion might be $10.00, while one from a national promotion could be virtually worthless.

Toys don't have to be old to be collectible, but if you can find them still in their original package, so much the better. Though there are exceptions, a loose toy is worth one half to two thirds the value of one mint in package. (The values given here are for MIP items unless noted otherwise.) For more information we recommend *McDonald's® Happy Meal® Toys — In the USA* and *McDonald's® Happy Meal® Toys — Around the World*, by Joyce and Terry Losonsky; *Tomart's Price Guide to Kid's Meal Collectibles (Non-McDonald's)* and *Kid's Meal Collectibles Update '94 – '95* by Ken Clee. Both authors are listed under Fast-Food Collectibles in the Categories of Special Interest section of this book. Also available is *McDonald's Collectibles, Second Edition*, by Gary Henriques and Audre DuVall (Collector Books).

Advisors: Bill and Pat Poe (P10); Scott Smiles (S10), Foreign.
Other Sources: C3, I2, K1 (Simpsons), M8.

ARBY'S

Babar's World Tour, finger puppets, 1990, ea........................$3.00
Babar's World Tour, pull-back racers, 1992, ea....................$3.00
Babar's World Tour, squirters, 1992, ea................................$2.00
Babar's World Tour, stampers, 1991, ea $3.00
Babar's World Tour, storybooks, 1991, ea.............................$3.00
Babar's World Tour, vehicles, 1990, ea $3.00
Little Miss, 1981, ea..$4.00
Looney Tunes Car Tunes, 1989, ea $3.00
Looney Tunes Characters, 1987, oval base, ea $5.00
Looney Tunes Characters, 1988, standing, ea $5.00
Looney Tunes Fun Fingers, 1989, ea.....................................$5.00

Mr. Men, $5.00 each.

Snow Domes, 1995, Yogi or Snagglepuss, ea $5.00
Winter Wonderland Crazy Cruisers, 1995, ea $4.00
Yogi Bear Fun Squirters, 1994, ea $4.00

BURGER KING

Action Figures, 1991, ea $3.00
Aladdin, 1992, ea..$3.00
Aladdin Hidden Treasures, 1994, ea....................................$2.00
Archies, 1991, 4 different, ea..$4.00
Beauty & the Beast, 1991, 4 different, ea $4.00
Beetlejuice, 1990, 6 different, ea..$2.00
Bone Age, 1989, 4 different, ea $5.00
Bonkers, 1993, 6 different, ea $3.00
Capitol Critters, 1992, 4 different, ea...................................$2.00
Captain Planet Flipover Star Cruisers, 1991, 4 different, ea...$2.00
Cool Stuff, 1995, 5 different, ea..$3.00
Crayola Christmas Bears, 1986, plush, 4 different colors, ea ..$5.00
Dino Crawlers, 1994, 5 different, ea $2.00
Gargoyles, 1995, 1st or 2nd set, ea......................................$3.00

Glo Force, 1996, 5 different, ea $3.00
Glow-in-the-Dark Glow Patrol, 1993, 4 different, ea $3.00
Glow-in-the-Dark Troll Patrol, 1993, 4 different, ea $3.00
Go-Go Gadgets, 1991, 4 different, ea....................................$3.00
Good Gobblin', 1989, 3 different, ea $3.00
Goofy & Max Adventures, 1995, any except yel runaway car, ea..$3.00
Goofy & Max Adventures, 1995, yel runaway car $2.00
Hunchback of Notre Dame, 1995, hand puppet, 4 different, ea..$10.00
Hunchback of Notre Dame, 1996, 8 different, ea $4.00
It's Magic, 1992, 4 different, ea...$2.00
Kid Transporters, 1990, 6 different, ea.................................$2.00
Life Savers Freaky Fellas, 1992, 4 different colors, ea..........$2.00
Lion King, 1994, 7 different, ea $3.00
Lion King, 1995, finger puppets, 6 different, ea $3.00
Little Mermaid, 1993, Urchin squirt gun, Flounder squirter, or Sebastian w/up, ea...$3.00
McGruff Cares for You, 1991, song book & tape set, 4 different, ea...$4.00
Mini Record Breakers, 1989, 6 different, ea $2.00
Mini Sports Games, 1993, 4 different, ea $3.00
Minnie Mouse, 1992 ....$2.00
Miss Daisy's Trolley w/Chip & Dale, 1993 ....$2.00
Nerfuls, 1989, 3 different, ea...$5.00
Nightmare Before Christmas, watches, set of 4, EX, H9...$20.00
Oliver & Co, 1996, 5 different, ea $3.00
Pinocchio Summer Inflatables, 1992, 5 different, ea...........$3.00
Pocahontas, 1995, 8 different, ea..$3.00
Pocahontas, 1996, finger puppets, 6 different, ea $3.00
Pranksters, 1994, 5 different, ea $3.00
Purrtenders, 1988, Free Wheeling Cheese Rider or Flip Top Car, ea $2.00
Purrtenders Sock-Ems, Christmas 1987, stuffed plush animals, 4 different, ea...$4.00
Rodney Reindeer & Friends, 1986, 4 different, ea $3.00
Silverhawks, 1987, pencil topper $5.00

Simpsons, 1990, $2.00 each.

Spacebase Racers, 1989, 4 different, ea $3.00
Sports All-Stars, 1994, 5 different, ea...................................$4.00

Super Powers, door shield $8.00
Super Powers, 1987, Aquaman tub toy................$6.00
Surprise Celebration Parade, 1992, 4 different, w/track, ea ...$6.00
Teenage Mutant Ninja Turtles Bike Gear, 1993, ea $3.00
Top Kids Wild Spinning Tops, 1994, 4 different, ea............$2.00
Toy Story, 1995, Action Wing Buzz......................$2.00
Toy Story, 1995, Rex Dinosaur, RC Racer, Mr Potato Head, or
     Army Recon Squadron, ea................................$2.00
Toy Story, 1995, Woody $3.00
Trak-Pak Golden Jr Classic Books, 1988, 4 different, ea $4.00
Water-Mates, 1991, any except Snaps/rowboat w/pk shirt or
     Wheels/hovercraft w/bl control panel, ea..................$2.00
Water-Mates, 1991, Snaps/rowboat w/pk shirt or Wheels/hover-
     craft w/bl control panel, ea $2.00
World Travel Adventure Kit, 1991, 4 different, ea $2.00
Z-Bots w/Pogs, 1994, 5 different, ea.......................$2.00

DAIRY QUEEN

Alvin & the Chipmunks Music Makers, 1994, 4 different, ea..$3.00
Baby's Day Out Books, 1994, 4 different, ea.........................$5.00
Bobby's World, 1994, 4 different, ea..................................$2.00
Dennis the Menace, 1994, 4 different, ea.............................$2.00
Radio Flyer, 1991, miniature wagon $3.00
Rock-A-Doodle, 1991, 6 different, ea.................................$5.00
Space Shuttle, 6 different, ea $2.00
Tom & Jerry, 1993, 4 different, ea......................................$3.00

DENNY'S

Adventure Seekers Activity Packet, 1993, ea $2.00
Dino-Makers, 5 different, ea $2.00
Flintstones Dino Racers, 1991, 3 different, ea $2.00
Flintstones Fun Squirters, 1991, 5 different, ea $2.00
Flintstones Glacier Gliders, 1990, Barney playing hockey,
     Bamm-Bamm on sled or Dino, ea.............................$2.00
Flintstones Plush Figures, 1989, Fred & Wilma or Barney &
     Betty, ea...$3.00
Flintstones Plush Figures, 1989, Pebbles & Bamm-Bamm,
     pr $5.00
Flintstones Rock 'N Rollers, 1991, Fred w/guitar or Barney
     w/saxophone, ea...$2.00
Flintstones Vehicles, 1990, 3 different, ea $2.00
Jetson's Go Back to School, 1992, 4 different, ea................$2.00
Jetson's Space Cards, 1992, 6 different, ea..........................$2.00
Jetson's Space-Age Puzzle Ornaments, 1992, ea..................$2.00

DOMINOS PIZZA

Avoid the Noid, 1988, 3 different, ea $2.00
Donnie Domino, 1989, 4" $3.00
Keep the Noid Out, 1987, 3 different, ea $3.00
Noid, 1989, bookmark $5.00

HARDEE'S

Apollo Spaceship, 1995, 3-pc set......................................$12.00
Balto, 1995, 6 different, ea..$2.00

Beach Bunnies, 1989, 4 different, ea $2.00
Bobby's World (At the Circus), 1996, 5 different, ea..........$2.00
Breakman's World, 1995, 4 different, ea.............................$2.00
Camp California, 1994, 4 different, ea $2.00
Dinobend Buddies, 1994, 4 different, ea.............................$2.00
Dinosaur in My Pocket, 1993, 4 different, ea $2.00
Eek! the Cat, 1995, 6 different, ea.....................................$2.00
Eureka Castle Stampers, 1994, 4 different, ea $2.00
Fender-Bender 500 Racers, 1990, 5 different, ea $2.00
Flintstones First 30 Years, 4 different, ea............................$2.00
Gremlin Adventures Read-Along Book & Record, 1984, 5 dif-
     ferent, ea...$3.00
Halloween Hideway, 1989, 4 different, ea $2.00
Homeward Bound II, 1996, 5 different, ea $2.00
Kazoo Crew Sailors, 1991, 4 different, ea $2.00
Marvel Super Heroes in Vehicles, 1990, 4 different, ea $2.00
Mickey's Christmas Carol, 1984, plush figures, 4 different,
     ea $3.00
Micro Super Soakers, 1994, 4 different, ea $2.00
Mouth Figurines, 1989, 4 different, ea................................$2.00
Muppets Christmas Carol, 1993, finger puppets, 4 different,
     ea $2.00
Nickelodeon School Tools, 1995, 6 different, ea..................$2.00
Nicktoons Cruisers, 1994, 8 different, ea.............................$2.00
Pound Puppies, 1986, plush, 4 different, ea.........................$2.00
Pound Puppies & Pur-R-Ries, 1987, plush, 5 different, ea ..$2.00
Shirt Tales, 1990, plush figures, 5 different, ea $2.00
Smurfs Funmeal Pack, 1990, 6 different, ea.........................$2.00
Speed Bunnies, 1994, 4 different, ea...................................$2.00
Swan Princess, 1994, 5 different, ea....................................$2.00
Tattoads, 1995, 4 different, ea..$2.00
Tune-A-Fish, 1994, 4 different, ea......................................$2.00
Waldo & Friends Holiday Ornaments, 1991, 3 different, ea ..$2.00
Waldo & Friends Straw Buddies, 1990, 4 different, ea........$2.00
Walt Disney Animated Film Classics, 1985, plush, 5 different,
     ea..$3.00
X-Men, 1995, 6 different, ea $2.00

JACK-IN-THE-BOX

Bendable Buddies, 1975, 4 different, ea..............................$5.00
Bendable Buddies, 1991, 5 different, ea..............................$2.00
Finger Puppets, 1994, 5 different, ea..................................$5.00
Garden Fun Seed Packages, 1994, 3 different, ea...............$3.00
Jack Pack Make-A-Scene, 1990, 3 different, ea $3.00
Star Trek the Next Generation, 1994, 6 different, ea $3.00

LONG JOHN SILVER'S

Berenstain Bears Books, 1995, 4 different, ea......................$2.00
Fish Car, 1989, 3 different, ea..$2.00
Free Willy II, 1995, 5 different, ea.....................................$2.00
I Love Dinosaurs, 1993, 4 different, ea $2.00
Map Activities, 1991, 3 different, ea $2.00
Once Upon A Forest, 1993, 2 different, ea $2.00
Sea Watchers, 1991, mini kaleidoscopes, 3 different, ea.....$2.00
Treasure Trolls, 1992, pencil toppers, 4 different, ea $2.00
Water Blasters, 1990, 4 different, ea $2.00

McDonald's

Airport, 1986, Fry Guy Flyer, Grimace Ace, or Birdie Bent Wing Blazer, ea...**$3.00**

Airport, 1986, Ronald McDonald seaplane........................**$5.00**

Airport, 1986, under age 3, Fry Guy Flyer (floater) **$3.00**

Aladdin & the King of Thieves, 1996, any except under age 3, ea **$2.00**

Amazing Wildlife, 1995, ea..**$2.00**

Animaniacs, 1995, any except under age 3, ea....................**$2.00**

Animaniacs, 1995, under age 3, ea **$2.00**

Babe, 1996, plush animals, 6 different, MIP, ea..................**$2.00**

Bambi, 1988, 4 different, ea...**$2.00**

Barbie/Hot Wheels, 1991, Barbie, any except under age 3, ea .**$2.00**

Barbie/Hot Wheels, 1991, Barbie, under age 3, Costume Ball or Wedding Day Midge **$3.00**

Barbie/Hot Wheels, 1991, Hot Wheels, ea **$2.00**

Barbie/Hot Wheels, 1993, Barbie, any except under age 3, ea...**$2.00**

Barbie/Hot Wheels, 1993, Barbie, under age 3, Rose Bride...**$2.00**

Barbie/Hot Wheels, 1993, Hot Wheels, any including under age 3, ea **$2.00**

Barbie/Hot Wheels, 1994, Real Hair Barbies, Butterfly Princess Teresa and Cool Country Barbie, $2.00 each.
(Photo courtesy Gary Henriques and Audre DuVall)

Barbie/Hot Wheels, 1994, Camp Teresa...............................**$3.00**

Barbie/Hot Wheels, 1995, Barbie, any including under age 3 except Black Lifeguard Barbie, ea..................................**$2.00**

Barbie/Hot Wheels, 1995, Hot Wheels, any including under age 3, ea **$2.00**

Barbie/Hot Wheels, 1996, Barbie, any except under age 3, ea ...**$2.00**

Barbie/Hot Wheels, 1996, Hot Wheels, under age 3, mini steering wheel **$2.00**

Barbie/Hot Wheels, 1997, Barbie, 5 different, ea **$2.00**

Barbie/Hot Wheels, 1997, Hot Wheels, 5 different, ea.......**$2.00**

Barbie/Hot Wheels, 1998, Barbie, 4 different, ea **$2.00**

Barbie/Hot Wheels, 1998, Hot Wheels, 4 different, ea.......**$2.00**

Barbie/Hot Wheels, 1999, Barbie, 8 different, ea **$2.00**

Barbie/Hot Wheels, 1999, Hot Wheels, 8 different, ea.......**$2.00**

Barbie/Hot Wheels, 1999-2000, Barbie, 10 different, ea.....**$2.00**

Barbie/Hot Wheels, 1999-2000, Hot Wheels, 10 different, ea...**$2.00**

Barbie/Mini Streex, 1991, Barbie, any except under age 3, ea..**$2.00**

Barbie/Mini Streex, 1992, Barbie, under age 3, Sparkle Eyes.....**$2.00**

Barbie/Mini Streex, 1992, Mini Streex, any including under age 3..**$2.00**

Barnyard (Old McDonald's Farm), 1986, 6 different, ea.....**$4.00**

Batman, 1992, 6 different, ea...**$2.00**

Batman (Animated), 1993, any including under age 3, ea .**$2.00**

Beanie Babies, see Beanie Babies category.........................**$.09**

Bedtime, 1989, drinking cup, M **$2.00**

Bedtime, 1989, Ronald, set of 4 ....**$3.00**

Bedtime, 1989, wash mitt, bl foam **$3.00**

Berenstain Bears, 1987, any except under age 3, ea **$3.00**

Berenstain Bears, 1987, under age 3, Mama or Papa w/paper punch-outs, ea...**$5.00**

Boats & Floats, 1987, Fry Kids raft or McNuggets lifeboat, w/separate sticker sheet, ea, from $5 to **$7.00**

Cabbage Patch Kids/Tonka Trucks, 1992, Cabbage Patch Kids, any except under age 3, ea...**$2.00**

Cabbage Patch Kids/Tonka Trucks, 1992, Tonka Trucks, under age 3, dump truck..**$2.00**

Changeables, 1987, 6 different, ea......................................**$2.00**

Chip 'N Dale Rescue Rangers, 1989, 4 different, ea............**$2.00**

Circus Parade, 1991, ea...**$2.00**

COSMc Crayola, 1988, under age 3, So Big, w/2 crayons & activity sheet...**$3.00**

Crayola Stencils, 1987, any including under age 3, ea........**$2.00**

Crazy Creatures w/Popoids, 1985, 4 different, ea **$3.00**

Dink the Little Dinosaur, 1990, Regional, 6 different, ea ...**$4.00**

Dinosaur Days, 1981, 6 different, ea **$2.00**

Disney Favorites, 1987, activity book, Sword & the Stone..**$3.00**

Disney Masterpiece Video Collection, 1996, under age 3, Dumbo...**$2.00**

Disney Masterpiece Video Collection, 1996, 8 different, ea...**$2.00**

Ducktails, 1987, ea...**$4.00**

Ducktails II, 1988, launch pad airport **$4.00**

Ducktails II, 1988, Scrooge McDuck in car or Huey, Louie & Dewey on surf ski, ea..**$4.00**

Ducktails II, 1988, Webby on tricycle **$4.00**

Funny Fry Friends, 1989, Matey, Gadzooks, and Tracker, from 2" to 2¾", $1.00 to $3.00 each. (Photo courtesy Gary Henriques and Audre Duvall)

Fast Mac II, 1985, wht squad car, pk cruiser, red sports car, or yel jeep, ea $2.00

Feeling Good, 1985, comb, Captain, red..................$2.00

Feeling Good, 1985, Fry Guy on duck $2.00

Feeling Good, 1985, mirror, Birdie $2.00

Feeling Good, 1985, soap dish, Grimace $2.00

Feeling Good, 1985, under age 3, Grimace in tub..............$2.00

Flintstone Kids, 1988, under age 3, Dino $8.00

Flintstone Kids, 1988, 4 different, ea..................$6.00

Friendly Skies, 1991, Ronald or Grimace, ea $3.00

Friendly Skies, 1994, United hangar w/Ronald in plane.....$3.00

Fun w/Food, 1989, ea $6.00

Funny Fry Friends, 1989, under age 3, Little Darling or Lil' Chief, ea $5.00

Ghostbusters, 1987, pencil case, Containment Chamber ...$3.00

Ghostbusters, 1987, pencil sharpener, ghost..................$2.00

Gravedale High, 1991, regional, 5 different, ea..................$3.00

Halloween (What Am I Going to Be), 1995, any except under age 3, ea $2.00

Halloween (What Am I Going to Be), 1995, under age 3, Grimace in pumpkin $3.00

Halloween McNuggets, 1993, any including under age 3, ea $2.00

Happy Birthday 15 Years, 1994, any except Tonka or Muppet babies, ea, from $3 to $2.00

Happy Birthday 15 years, 1994, Muppet Babies #11 train pc....$2.00

Happy Birthday 15 Years, 1994, Tonka train pc $4.00

Happy Pail, 1986, 5 different, ea..................$3.00

Hook, 1997, 4 different, ea $2.00

Jungle Book, 1989, 4 different, ea..................$2.00

Jungle Book, 1990, under age 3, Junior or Mowgli, ea $6.00

Lego Building Set, 1986, helicopter or airplane, ea..............$2.00

Lego Building Set, 1986, race car or tanker boat, ea..........$3.00

Lego Motion, 1989, any except under age 3, ea $3.00

Lego Motion, 1989, under age 3, Giddy Gator or Tuttle Turtle, ea..................$4.00

Little Gardener, 1989, Birdie shovel, Fry Kids planter, Grimace rake, or Ronald water can, ea $2.00

Little Golden Book, 1982, 5 different, ea $2.00

Little Mermaid, 1989, 4 different, ea..................$2.00

Littlest Pet Shop/Transformers, 1996, any including under age 3 ....$2.00

Looney Tunes Quack-Up Cars, 1993, 4 different, ea..........$2.00

Mac Tonight, 1988, any except under age 3, ea $3.00

Mac Tonight, 1988, under age 3, skateboard..................$4.00

Marvel Super Heroes, 1996, any including under age 3, ea...$3.00

McDino Changeables, 1991, any except under age 3, ea $2.00

McDino Changeables, 1991, under age 3, Bronto Cheeseburger or Small Fry Ceratops, ea..................$2.00

McDonald's Star Trek, 1979, from $5 to..................$6.00

McDonaldland Band, 1986, Fry Kid Trumpet, Pan Pipes, or Grimace Saxophone, ea $2.00

McDonaldland Band, 1986, Ronald harmonica..................$3.00

McDonaldland Dough, 1990, ea..................$3.00

McNugget Buddies, 1988, any except Corny w/red popcorn belt or Cowpoke w/scarf, ea $2.00

McNugget Buddies, 1988, Corny w/red popcorn belt or Cowpoke w/scarf, ea $4.00

Mickey & Friends Adventure at Disney World (Epcot Center), 1994, Chip in China or Dale in Morocco, ea..............$2.00

Mickey & Friends Adventure at Disney World (Epcot Center), 1994, any..................$2.00

Mickey's Birthdayland, 1988, any including under age 3, ea $2.00

Mix 'Em Up Monsters, 1989, Bibble, Corkle, Gropple, or Thugger, ea $2.00

Moveables, 1988, any except Ronald, ea..................$5.00

Moveables, 1988, Ronald, M $5.00

Muppet Treasure Island, 1996, tub toys, any including under age 3, ea $2.00

Muppet Workshop, 1995, ea..................$2.00

Mystery of the Lost Arches, 1992, Magic Lens Camera (recalled)..................$2.00

Mystery of the Lost Arches, 1992, micro-cassette/magnifyer, phone/periscope, or flashlight/telescope, ea $2.00

New Archies, 1988, 6 different, ea $6.00

New Food Changeables, 1989, any including under age 3, ea.$2.00

Oliver & Co, 1988, 4 different, ea..................$2.00

Peanuts, 1990, any except under age 3, ea..................$2.00

Peanuts, 1990, under age 3, Charlie Brown egg basket or Snoopy's potato sack, ea..................$3.00

Polly Pocket/Attack Pack, 1995, any including under age 3, ea..$2.00

Potato Heads, 1992, 8 different, ea..................$3.00

Power Rangers, 1995, any including under age 3, ea..........$2.00

Rescuers Down Under, 1990, any including under age 3, ea..$2.00

Runaway Robots, 1987, 6 different, ea $2.00

Safari Adventure, 1980, cookie molds, Ronald or Grimace, red or yel, ea..................$2.00

Safari Adventure, 1980, sponge, Ronald sitting cross-legged, M $3.00

School Days, 1984, eraser, Birdie or Grimace, M, ea $2.00

School Days, 1984, pencil or ruler, Grimace, Ronald, or Hamburglar, M, ea $2.00

Sea World of Texas, 1988, 4 different, M, ea..................$8.00

Snow White & the Seven Dwarfs, 1993, any including under age 3, ea..................$2.00

Space Jam, 1996, 8 different, ea..................$2.00

Space Rescue, 1995, any including under age 3, ea..............$2.00

Spider-Man, 1995, under age 3 ....$2.00

Sports Balls, 1990, ea $2.00

Stomper Mini 4x4, 1986, 15 different, M, ea $4.00

Super Looney Tunes, 1991, any including under age 3, ea..$2.00

Super Mario Bros, 1990, any including under age 3, ea $2.00

Tale Spin, 1990, any including under age 3, ea $2.00

Totally Toy Holiday, 1995, any including under age 3, ea...$2.00

Totally Toys, 1993, any including under age 3, ea..............$2.00

Turbo Macs, 1988, any including under age 3, M, ea $2.00

VR Troopers, 1996, any including under age 3, ea..............$2.00

Water Games, 1992, ea $2.00

Wild Friends, 1992, regional, any except under age 3, ea ...$2.00

Winter Worlds, 1983, ornament, any, M, eaea..................$3.00

Young Astronauts, 1992, any including under age 3, ea......$2.00

Zoo Face, 4 different, ea..................$2.00

101 Dalmatians, 1991, 4 different, ea $2.00

101 Dalmatians, 1996, snow dome ornaments, 4 different, ea $2.00

Young Astronauts, 1986, Apollo Command Module, $9.00. (Photo courtesy Gary Henriques and Audre DuVall)

PIZZA HUT

Air Garfield, 1993, kite or parachute, ea..............................$3.00
Beauty & the Beast, 1992, hand puppets, 4 different, ea $2.00
Brain Thaws, 1995, 4 different, ea.......................................$2.00
Eureeka's Castle, 1990, hand puppets, 3 different, ea..........$2.00
Land Before Time, 1988, hand puppet, any........................$2.00
Marvel Comics, 1994, 4 different, ea...................................$2.00
Mascot Misfits, 1995, 4 different, ea....................................$2.00
Pagemaster, 1994, 4 different, ea...$2.00
Squirt Toons, 1995, 5 different, ea.......................................$2.00
Universal Monsters, 1991, hologram cards, 3 different, ea .$2.00

SONIC

Airtoads, 6 different, ea..$2.00
All-Star Mini Baseballs, 1995, 5 different, ea.....................$2.00
Animal Straws, 1995, 4 different, ea $2.00
Bone-A-Fide Friends, 1994, 4 different, ea..........................$2.00
Brown Bag Bowlers, 1994, 4 different, ea $3.00
Brown Bag Buddies, 1989, 4 different, ea $3.00
Brown Bag Buddies, 1993, 3 different, ea $3.00
Creepy Strawlers, 1995, 4 different, ea $2.00
Flippin' Food, 1995, 3 different, ea $2.00
Food Train, 1995, set of 7 cars w/engine...........................$14.00
Go Wild Bills, 1995, 4 different, ea $2.00
Holiday Kids, 1994, 4 different, ea......................................$2.00
Monster Peepers, 1994, 4 different, ea................................$2.00
Shoe Biters, 1995, 4 different, ea $1.00
Squishers, 1995, 4 different, ea $2.00
Super Sonic Racers, 1995, 4 different, ea $2.00
Totem Pal Squirters, 1995, 4 different, ea..........................$2.00
Very Best Food, 1996, 4 different, ea $2.00
Wacky Sackers, 1994, set of 6...$4.00

SUBWAY

Battle Balls, 1995-96, 4 different, ea...................................$2.00
Bobby's World, 1995, 4 different, ea $2.00

Bump in the Night, 1995, 4 different, ea.............................$2.00
Cone Heads, 1993, 4 different, ea..$2.00
Explore Space, 1994, 4 different, ea.....................................$2.00
Hackeysack Balls, 1991, 4 different, ea................................$2.00
Hurricanes, 1994, 4 different, ea...$2.00
Inspector Gadget, 1994, 4 different, ea................................$2.00
Monkey Trouble, 1994, 5 different, ea.................................$2.00
Santa Claus, 1994, under age 3, Comet the Reindeer........$2.00
Save the Wildlife, 1995, 4 different, ea...............................$2.00
Tall Tale, 1995, any including under age 3, ea $2.00
Tom & Jerry, 1995, 4 different, ea.......................................$2.00

TACO BELL

Congo, 1995, watches, 3 different, ea...................................$3.00
Happy Talk Sprites, 1983, Spark, Twinkle, or Romeo, plush, ea $3.00
Hugga Bunch, 1984, Fluffer, Gigglet, or Tuggins, plush, ea.$3.00
Mask, 1995, It's Party Time switchplate or Milo w/mask, ea ..$3.00
Pebble & the Penguin, 1995, 3 different, ea........................$2.00
The Tick, 1995, finger puppet, Arthur Wall Climber or Thrakkorzog, ea..$2.00
The Tick, 1996, Arthur w/wings or Sewer Urchin, ea $2.00

TARGET MARKETS

Adventure Team Window Walkers, 1994-95, 4 different, ea ..$2.00
Muppet Twisters, 1994, 3 different, ea.................................$2.00
Olympic Sports Weiner Pack, 1996, figures, 4 different, ea .$2.00
Roll-O-Fun Coloring Kit, 1995, 3 different, ea $2.00
Targeteers, 1992, 5 different, ea $2.00
Targeteers, 1994, 5 different, rooted hair, ea $2.00

WENDY'S

Alf Tales, 1990, 6 different, ea...$2.00
All Dogs Go to Heaven, 1989, 6 different, ea.....................$2.00
Animalinks, 1995, 6 different, ea $2.00
Ballsasaurus, 1992, 4 different, ea $2.00
Cybercycles, 1994, 4 different, ea $2.00
Definitely Dinosaurs, 1988, 4 different, ea $2.00
Definitely Dinosaurs, 1989, 5 different, ea $2.00
Dino Games, 1993, 3 different, ea $2.00
Endangered Animal Games, 1993, any including under age 3, ea $2.00
Fast-Food Racers, 1990, 6 different, ea $2.00
Felix the Cat, 1990, plush figure...$2.00
Felix the Cat, 1990, Story Board, Zeotrope, Milk Cap set, or Ask Felix toy, ea $2.00
Felix the Cat, 1990, under age 3, rub-on set.......................$2.00
Furskins Bears, 1986, 4 different, plush, ea $3.00
Gear Up, 1992, handlebar streamers or back-off license plate, ea $2.00
Glo-Ahead, 1993, any including under age 3, ea $2.00
Glofriends, 1989, 9 different, ea $2.00
Gobots, 1986, Odd Ball/Monster...$3.00
Jetsons Space Vehicles, 1989, 6 different, ea $3.00
Jetsons: The Movie, 1990, 5 different, ea.............................$3.00

Jetsons, 1st series, 1989, $3.00.

Mega Wheels, 1995, any including under age 3, ea $2.00
Mighty Mouse, 1989, 6 different, ea $2.00
Potato Head II, 1988, 5 different, ea...................................$3.00
Speed Bumpers, 1992, any including under age 3, ea..........$2.00
Speed Writers, 1991, any including under age 3, ea.............$2.00
Tecno Cows, 1995, any including under age 3, ea...............$2.00
Too Cool! For School, 1992, bat pencil or pickel pen, ea...$2.00
Wacky Windups, 1991, 5 different, ea.................................$2.00
Weird Writers, 1991, 3 different, ea....................................$2.00
World of Teddy Ruxpin, 1987, 5 different, ea $2.00
World Wild Life, 1988, books, 4 different, ea......................$2.00
World Wild Life, 1988, plush figures, 4 different, ea...........$2.00
Write & Sniff, 1994, any including under age 3, ea.............$2.00
Yogi Bear & Friends, 1990, 6 different, ea...........................$2.00

WHITE CASTLE

Bow Biters, 1989, Blue Meany...$1.00
Camp White Castle, 1990, fork & spoon, ea.......................$2.00
Castle Dude Squirters, 1994, 3 different, ea $3.00
Castle Meal Friends, 1991, Wendell, Princess, or Woofleas,
    ea...$3.00
Castleburger Dudes, 1991, 4 different, ea $3.00
Castleburger Friends, 1989, 6 different, ea $3.00
Fat Albert & the Cosby Kids, 1990, 4 different, ea.............$5.00
Glow-in-the-Dark Monsters, 1992, 3 different, ea $3.00
Holiday Huggables, 1990, 3 different, ea............................$3.00
Super Balls, 1994, 3 different, ea $2.00

BOXES AND BAGS

Burger King, 1988, Trak-Pak, ea..$3.00
Burger King, 1989, Bone Age, Fairy Tales Cassette or Tricky
    Treaters, ea $2.00
Burger King, 1989, Critter Carton/Punch-Out Paper Masks,
    ea...$4.00
Hardee's, 1987, Little Golden Books, ea...............................$2.00
Hardee's, 1990, Days of Thunder, Fender Bender 500 Racers,
    Marvel Super Heroes, or Squirters, ea $2.00

Hardee's, 1993, Cruisin' Back to School or Muppets Christmas
    Carol, ea $2.00

McDonald's, 1979, Star Trek, from $4.00 to $5.00.

McDonald's, 1979, When Does a Monkey...., from $20.00 to $40.00.

McDonald's, 1987, Good Friends or Real Ghostbusters, ea...$2.00
McDonald's, 1988, Ducktails II, Fraggle Rock, Mac Tonight,
    McNugget Buddies, Oliver & Co, or Zoo Face, ea.......$2.00
McDonald's, 1989, Chip 'N Dale Rescue Rangers, Garfield, Lit-
    tle Mermaid, or Mickey's Birthdayland, ea...................$2.00
McDonald's, 1989, Raggedy Ann Schoolhouse...................$4.00
McDonald's, 1989, Rain or Shine (no toys produced to match
    boxes), ea $2.00
McDonald's, 1990, Beach Toy, Jungle Book, Peanuts, Rescuers
    Down Under, Super Mario, Tale Spin, or Valentine, ea..$2.00
McDonald's, 1990, Dink the Dinosaur $4.00
McDonald's, 1990, Fry Benders or Sportsballs, ea $3.00
McDonald's, 1991, Barbie/Hot Wheels, Gravedale High, Hook,
    Muppet Babies, Tiny Toons, or 101 Dalmatians, ea $2.00
McDonald's, 1992, Back to the Future, Crayon Squeeze Bottle,
    Wild Friends, or Yo-Yogi, ea $2.00
McDonald's, 1992, Barbie/Mini Streex, Batman, or Tiny Toon
    Adventures, ea $2.00

McDonald's, 1993, Batman, Dino Dinosaurs, Field Trip, Halloween McNugget Buddies, or Looney Tunes Quack-Up Cars, ea $2.00
McDonald's, 1993, Snow White & the Seven Dwarfs $2.00
McDonald's, 1994, Mickey & Friends Adventure at Disney World, 4 different Epcot scenes w/characters, ea $2.00
Wendy's, 1989, Wendy & the Good Stuff Gang, ea............$2.00
Wendy's, 1990, Fast Food Racers, Jetsons: The Movie, Micro Machines Super Sky Carrier, or Yogi Bear, ea $2.00
Wendy's, 1991, Rhyme Time, Weather Watch, or Wizard of Wonders, ea...$2.00
Wendy's, 1994, Carmen Sandiego Code Cracker, ea $2.00

FOREIGN

Burger King, Beauty & the Beast, 1992, set of 4, from $45 to..$50.00
Burger King, Cinderella, 1994, set of 3..............................$40.00
Burger King, Flintstones, 1994, set of 4 ....$35.00
Burger King, Snow White, 1995, set of 4 ....$20.00
Burger King, X-Men, 1996, set of 4 ....$20.00
Burger King (England), Peter Pan, set of 5........................$30.00
Burger King (England), Robin Hood, 1993, set of 5 ....$20.00
Burger King (England), Taz-Mania Crazies, 1994, set of 4 ..$20.00
Burger King (England), Tiny Toon Adventures, 1995, set of 4 ....$20.00
Burger King (England), Tom & Jerry, 1995, set of 4 ....$30.00
Kentucky Fried Chicken (Australia), Simpsons cups, plastic w/figural lids, set of 4, M...$25.00
Kentucky Fried Chicken (Australia), Simpsons water squirters, set of 4, K1 ....$15.00
McDonald's, Aristocrats, 1993, set of 4 ....$20.00
McDonald's, Dinosaurs, 1995, set of 4 ....$25.00
McDonald's, Disneyland Paris, 1996, set of 4, C1 ....$30.00
McDonald's (Australia), Aladdin, set of 4, C11................$20.00
McDonald's (Australia), Aladdin Straw Grippers, 1994, set of 4 ....$15.00
McDonald's (Australia), Bambi, set of 4, C11 ....$25.00
McDonald's (Australia), Batman Masks, 1992, 4 different, ea from $15 to..$20.00
McDonald's (Australia), Dark Wing Duck, 1994, set of 4...$20.00
McDonald's (Australia), McSports, 1995, set of 4 ....$20.00
McDonald's (Australia), Pocahontas finger puppets, 1995, set of 4 ....$25.00
McDonald's (Australia), Summer Fun Toys, 1995, set of 4 ..$15.00
McDonald's (Australia), Zoomballs, 1995, set of 4 ....$15.00
McDonald's (Canada), Fun w/Food, 1988, 4 different, ea...$5.00
McDonald's (Canada), Looney Tunes Characters, 1989, 4 different, ea $4.00
McDonald's (Canada), Mac Tonight Treat-of-the-Week, 1989, any except Mac Tonight decal, ea $3.00
McDonald's (Canada), Mac Tonight Treat-of-the-Week, 1989, decal $4.00
McDonald's (Canada), McDonaldland Cookies/Biscuits Trading Cards, 1980, ea..$4.00
McDonald's (Canada), Treat-of-the-Week, pencil holders, 1980/1986, ea...$3.00
McDonald's (England), Flubber, 1998, set of 4, C11 ....$15.00
McDonald's (England), Smurfs, 1997, set of 10 ....$50.00

McDonald's (European), Buckets of Fun, Beach, Picnic, Fun Fair, or Garden, 1986, ea..$6.00
McDonald's (European), Disneyland Paris, 1996, set of 4...$30.00
McDonald's (European), Euro Disney, 1992, set of 4 ....$30.00
McDonald's (European), Sticker Club, 1986-87, scented paper, ea $5.00
McDonald's (Germany), Smurfs, 1996, set of 10, MIP, C11...$60.00
McDonald's (Germany), Smurfs, 1998, set of 8 ....$45.00
McDonald's (Germany), Super Balls (Flummies), 1991, 5 different, ea $6.00
McDonald's (Guatemala), ornaments, Birdie, Grimage, Mayor, Hambuglar, or Ronald, 1984, ea $5.00
McDonald's (New Zealand), Disney Fun Riders, 1994, set of 4 ....$25.00
McDonald's (New Zealand), Mystery Riders, 1993, set of 4..$20.00
McDonald's (Panama), Back to the Future, 1992, 4 different, ea...$2.00
McDonald's (Panama), McDrive Thru Crew, 1990, any except Fries in Potato Speedster, ea from $10 to $12.00
McDonald's (Panama), McDrive Thru Crew, 1990, Fries in Potato Speedster, from $12 to..................................$15.00

MISCELLANEOUS

Burger Chef, yo-yo, 1972, plastic w/imprint seal of Burger Chef & Jeff, NM $12.00
Burger King, bear, 1986, Crayola Christmas, plush, 4 different, EX, ea from $8 to $10.00
Burger King, doll, Burger King, 1973, stuffed cloth, 16", NM..$25.00
Burger King, doll, Burger King, 1980, stuffed cloth, 18", EX....$20.00
Burger King, doll, Magic King, Knickerbocker, 1980, 20", MIB, M17..$50.00
Burger King, Star Wars card set, 1980, unused, NM, A....$25.00
Burger King, yo-yo, 1979, Yum Yum Burger King, plastic w/imprint seal, tournament shape, NM......................$8.00
Chuck E Cheese, doll, plush, 13", EX, from $15 to...........$20.00
Chuck E Cheese, yo-yo, EX $5.00
Dairy Queen, doll, Dairy Queen Kid, 1974, stuffed cloth, EX, minimum value $20.00
Dairy Queen, doll, Sweet Nell, Cheerleader, or Funfighter McDoom, 1974, stuffed cloth, EX, ea, minimum value .$20.00
Dominoes Pizza, yo-yo, Humphrey, Nobody Delivers Faster, plastic, NM $4.00
Dominos Pizza, doll, Noid, 1988, plush, 19", MIP.............$20.00
Hardee's, doll, Gilbert Giddy-Up, 1971, stuffed cloth, EX..$25.00
Hardee's, Pound Puppy, MIB, from $2 to.............................$3.00
Jack-in-the-Box, yo-yo, 1990s, plastic w/paper sticker seal, NM $3.00
Little Caesar's, doll, stuffed cloth, 6", H4 ....$5.00
McDonald's, backpack, 1980s, Ronald figure w/stuffed head, arms & feet, 22", NM, from $10 to..........................$15.00
McDonald's, backpack, 1983, colorful image of Ronald & Fry Guys on bl denim, NM, from $8 to $10.00
McDonald's, bank, Grimace, 1985, compo, NM, S21.......$15.00
McDonald's, bank, Ronald McDonald, ceramic bust figure, 7½", M..$15.00
McDonald's, bank, Ronald McDonald, plastic, NM, S21.$10.00
McDonald's, bank, Ronald's Singing Wastebasket, 1975, NM...$5.00

McDonald's, bop bag, Grimace, 1978, 8", MIP $6.00

McDonald's, calculator, Ronald McDonald, bl plastic, MIB ..$6.00

McDonald's, coloring book, McDonald's Circus, 1987, unused, EX, C11 ....$3.00

McDonald's, display, Bigfoot, 1987, M $25.00

McDonald's, display, Cabbage Patch/Tonka, 1994, NM, C11 ....$20.00

McDonald's, display, Duck Tales I, 1988, M...................$20.00

McDonald's, display, Funny Fry Friends, 1990, M.............$20.00

McDonald's, display, Lego Building Sets, 1989, M...........$20.00

McDonald's, display, Mickey's Birthdayland, 1988, plastic dome, NM, C11..$250.00

McDonald's, display, Sleeping Beauty, 1997, NM, C11 ....$20.00

McDonald's, display, 101 Dalmatians, 1992, w/plastic dome, M, C11...$2.00

McDonald's, doll, Big Mac, Remco, 1976, vinyl w/cloth clothes, knob in back for head movement, EX, from $10 to ...$25.00

McDonald's, doll, Captain Crook, Remco, 1976, vinyl w/cloth clothes, 6", EX, from $10 to..$25.00

McDonald's, doll, French Fries Critter, 1987, pillow-type, NM $10.00

McDonald's, doll, Fry Girl, 1987, stuffed cloth, 4", M $5.00

McDonald's, doll, Grimace, Remco, 1976, plush fleece, EX, from $10 to $25.00

McDonald's, doll, Hamburglar, 1980s, cloth & vinyl, 11", NM $15.00

McDonald's, doll, Mayor, 1970s, stuffed cloth, 15", NM ..$25.00

McDonald's, doll, McDonald's Girl, 1970s, stuffed cloth, NM, minimum value...$15.00

McDonald's, doll, Professor, Remco, 1976, vinyl w/cloth clothes, knob in back for head movement, 6", EX, from $10 to..$25.00

McDonald's, doll, Ronald McDonald, 1971, Chase Bag Co., 17", EX, $10.00.

McDonald's, doll, Ronald McDonald, Remco, 1976, vinyl w/cloth clothes, knob on back for head movement, EX, from $10 to..$25.00

McDonald's, frisbee, Ronald McDonald, 1980, wht plastic, 8", M...$2.00

McDonald's, game, McDonald's, Milton Bradley, 1975, MIB $25.00

McDonald's, game, McDonaldland Picnic, 1981, only 500 produced, M, C11..$50.00

McDonald's, game, Playland Funburst, Parker Bros, 1984, MIB $20.00

McDonald's, game, ring toss, 1978, M, C11 ....$4.00

McDonald's, game, tic-tac-toe, figural, EX, V1 ....$3.00

McDonald's, Happy Meal Magic Drink Fountain, Mattel, 1993, MIB $10.00

McDonald's, Happy Meal Magic Pie Maker, Mattel, 1993, MIB $5.00

McDonald's, kite, Kite Factory, 1980, wht plastic w/image of Ronald in hot air balloon, M.................................$8.00

McDonald's, music box, 1990, plays Silent Night & Jingle Bells, 2½x2½", MIB..$15.00

McDonald's, playset, McDonaldland, Remco, 1976, complete, MIB, from $100 to...$150.00

McDonald's, radio, 1985, 30th Anniversary edition, features early Burger Man, plastic, cylindrical, NM $35.00

McDonald's, record, Ronald McDonald & Friends, Casablanca, 1980, 45 rpm, EX (EX sleeve)..................................$8.00

McDonald's, record, Ronald McDonald All-Star Party, 33⅓ rpm, NM (NM cover) $10.00

McDonald's, records, Fisher-Price, 1985, $5.00 each.
(Photo courtesy Brad Cassity)

McDonald's, ring, Ronald McDonald, EX, C10 ....$8.00

McDonald's, sidewalk chalk in fries box, unused, M $2.00

McDonald's, slippers, Ronald McDonald, NM..................$10.00

McDonald's, translite, Bambi, 22x22", M, C11 ....$5.00

McDonald's, translite, Chip & Dale, 22x22", M, C11 ....$3.00

McDonald's, translite, Mac Tonight, M, C11....................$15.00

McDonald's, translite, Super Mario Bros 3, 14x14", M, C11..$5.00

McDonald's, translite, Tiny Toons Wacky Rollers, 14x14", M, C11 ....$5.00

McDonald's, yo-yo, Ronald McDonald, 1980s, plastic w/paper insert seal & view lens, NM $10.00

McDonald's, yo-yo, Ronald McDonald Championship, 1960s, plastic w/molded seal, NM.....................................$15.00

McDonald's, yo-yo, 1960s, wood w/gold leaf stamped seal, miniature, NM $20.00

Pizza Hut, kite, Garfield, MIP, B5 ....$5.00

Taco Bell, yo-yo, Humphrey, plastic, NM..........................$2.00

Wendy's, puzzle, Where's the Beef?, 1984, 551 pcs, EX, S13 ..$5.00

Fisher-Price

Fisher-Price toys are becoming one of the hottest new trends in the collector's marketplace today. In 1930 Herman Fisher, backed by Irving Price, Elbert Hubbard, and Helen Schelle, formed one of the most successful toy companies ever to exist. Located in East Aurora, New York, the company has seen many changes since then, the most notable being the changes in ownership. From 1930 to 1968, it was owned by the individuals mentioned previously and a few stockholders. In 1969 it became an aquisition of Quaker Oats, and in June of 1991 it became independently owned. In November of 1993, one of the biggest sell-outs in the toy industry took place: Fisher-Price became a division of Mattel.

There are a few things to keep in mind when collecting Fisher-Price toys. You should count on a little edge wear as well as some wear and fading to the paint. Unless noted otherwise, the prices in the listings are for toys in very good condition. Pull toys found in mint condition are truly rare and command a much higher value, especially if you find one with its original box. This also applies to playsets, but to command the higher prices, they must also be complete, with no chew/teeth marks or plastic fading, and with all pieces present. Another very important rule to remember is there are no standard colors for pieces that came with a playset. Fisher-Price often substituted a piece of a different color when they ran short. Please note that dates on the toys indicate their *copyright date and not the date they were manufactured.*

The company put much time and thought into designing their toys. They took care to operate by their five-point creed: to make toys with (1) intrinsic play value, (2) ingenuity, (3) strong construction, (4) good value for the money, and (5) action. Some of the most sought-after pull toys are those bearing the Walt Disney logo.

The ToyFest limited editions are a series of toys produced in conjunction with ToyFest, an annual weekend of festivities for young and old alike held in East Aurora, New York. It is sponsored by the 'Toy Town USA Museum' and is held every year in August. Fisher-Price produces a limited-edition toy for this event; these are listed at the end of this category. (For more information on ToyFest and the museum, write to Toy Town Museum, P.O. Box 238, East Aurora, NY 14052; see display ad this section.) For more information on Fisher-Price toys we recommend *Fisher-Price, A Historical Rarity Value Guide*, by John J. Murray and Bruce R. Fox; and *Fisher-Price Toys* by our advisor Brad Cassity.

Additional information may be obtained through the Fisher-Price Collectors' Club who publish a quarterly newsletter; their address may be found in their display ad (this section) and in the Directory under Clubs, Newsletters, and Other Publications.

Note: With the ever increasing influence of the Internet it is becoming harder and harder to establish book value. A toy can sell for 100% more than the book value or 75% less on the Internet. The prices we have listed here are derived from dealers' price lists, and toy shows and represent values for examples that show only a little edge and paint wear and minimal fading (VG).

Advisor: Brad Cassity (C13).
Other Sources: J2, J6, N2.

See also Building Blocks and Contstuction Toys; Catalogs; Character, TV, and Movie Collectibles; Dollhouse Furniture; Dollhouses; Dolls; Optical Toys; Puppets; and other specific categories.

#5 Bunny Cart, 1948-49, C13 ....$75.00
#6 Ducky Cart, 1948-49, C13..................................$75.00
#7 Doggy Racer, 1942-43, C13.................................$200.00
#7 Looky Fire Truck, 1950-53 & Easter 1954, C13.........$100.00
#8 Bouncy Racer, 1960-62, C13 ....$40.00
#10 Bunny Cart, 1940-42, C13..................................$75.00
#11 Ducky Cart, 1940-42, C13..................................$75.00
#12 Bunny Truck, 1941-42, C13.................................$75.00
#14 Ducky Daddles, 1941, C13 ....$85.00
#15 Bunny Cart, 1946-48, C13..................................$75.00
#16 Ducky Cart, 1946-48, C13..................................$75.00
#20 Animal Cutouts, 1942-46, duck, elephant, pony or Scotty dog, C13, ea $50.00
#28 Bunny Egg Cart, 1950, C13 ....$75.00
#50 Bunny Chick Tandem Cart, 1953-54, no number on toy, C13 ....$100.00
#51 Ducky Cart, 1950, C13....................................$75.00
#52 Rabbit Cart, 1950, C13....................................$75.00
#75 Baby Duck Tandem Cart, 1953-54, no number on toy, C13 ....$100.00
#100 Dr Doodle, 1931, C13....................................$700.00
#100 Dr Doodle, 1995, Fisher-Price limited edition of 5,000, 1st in series, C13 ....$125.00
#100 Musical Sweeper, 1950-52, plays Whistle While You Work, C13 ....$100.00
#101 Granny Doodle & Family, 1931-32, C13 ....$800.00
#102 Drummer Bear, 1931, C13..............................$700.00
#102 Drummer Bear, 1932-33, fatter & taller version, C13 ....$700.00
#103 Barky Puppy, 1931-33, C13 ....$700.00
#104 Looky Monk, 1931, C13..................................$700.00
#105 Bunny Scoot, 1931, C13..................................$700.00
#107 Music Box Clock Radio, 1971, plays Hickory Dickory Dock $5.00
#109 Lucky Monk, 1932-33, C13..............................$700.00
#110 Chubby Chief, 1932-33, C13............................$700.00
#110 Puppy Playhouse, 1978-80, C13 ....$10.00
#111 Play Family Merry-Go-Round, 1972-77, plays Skater's Waltz, w/4 figures, C13 ....$40.00
#112 Picture Disk Camera, 1968-71, w/5 picture disks, C13 ....$35.00
#114 Music Box TV, 1967-83, plays London Bridge & Row Row Row Your Boat, C13 ....$10.00
#114 Sesame Street Music Box TV, 1984-87, plays People in Your Neighborhood, C13.......................................$8.00
#117, Play Family Farm Barnyard, 1972-74, C13..............$25.00
#118 Tumble Tower Game, 1972-75, w/10 marbles, C13.....$10.00
#120 Cackling Hen, 1958-66, wht, C13 ....$40.00
#120 Gabby Goose, 1936-37 & Easter 1938, C13 ....$350.00
#121 Happy Hopper, 1969-76, C13............................$20.00
#122 Bouncing Buggy, 1974-79, 6 wheels, C13....................$5.00
#123 Cackling Hen, 1966-68, red litho, C13..................$40.00

#123 Roller Chime, 1953-60 & Easter 1961, C13 ....$50.00
#124 Roller Chime, 1961-62 & Easter 1963, C13 ....$35.00
#125 Music Box Iron, 1966, aqua w/yel hdl, C13 ....$45.00
#125 Music Box Iron, 1966-69, wht w/red hdl, C13 ....$40.00
#125 Uncle Timmy Turtle, 1956-58, red shell, C13 ....$100.00
#130 Wobbles, 1964-67, dog wobbles when pulled, C13 ....$40.00
#131 Milk Wagon, 1964-72, truck w/bottle carrier, C13.....$50.00
#131 Toy Wagon, 1951-54, C13......................................$225.00
#132 Dr Doodle, 1957-60, C13 ....$85.00
#132 Molly Moo Cow, 1972-78, C13 ....$25.00
#135 Play Family Animal Circus, 1974-76, complete, C13....$60.00
#136 Play Family Lacing Shoe, 1965-69, complete, C13 ...$60.00
#138 Jack-in-the-Box Puppet, 1970-73, C13 ....$30.00

#139 Tuggy Tooter, 1961 – 73, MIB, $40.00.
(Photo courtesy Brad Cassity)

#139 Tuggy Turtle, 1959-60 & Easter 1961, C13............$100.00
#140 Coaster Boy, 1941, C13..$700.00
#140 Katy Kackler, 1954-56 & Easter 1957, C13..............$85.00
#140 Katy Kackler, 1954-56 & Easter 1957, C13..............$85.00
#141 Snap-Quack, 1947-49, C13 ....$225.00
#142 Three Men in a Tub, 1970-73, w/bell, C13 ....$20.00
#142 Three Men in a Tub, 1974-75, w/flag, C13 ....$10.00
#145 Humpty Dump Truck, 1963-64 & Easter 1965, C13 ....$40.00
#145 Husky Dump Truck, 1961-62 & Easter 1963, C13 ....$45.00
#145 Musical Elephant, 1948-50, C13 ....$225.00
#146 Pull-A-Long Lacing Shoe, 1970-73, w/6 figures, C13 ...$60.00
#148 Ducky Daddles, 1942, C13 ....$225.00
#148 Jack & Jill TV Radio, 1959 & Easter 1960, wood & plastic,
    C13...$55.00
#149 Dog Cart Donald, 1936-37, C13 ....$700.00
#150 Barky Budd, 1934-35, C13 ....$600.00
#150 Pop-Up-Pal Chime Phone, 1968-78, C13.................$40.00
#150 Teddy Tooter, 1940-41, C13.................................$400.00
#150 Timmy Turtle, 1953-55 & Easter 1956, gr shell, C13..$100.00
#151 Goldilocks & the Three Bears Playhouse, 1967-71, C13.$60.00
#151 Happy Hippo, 1962-63, C13...................................$85.00
#152 Road Roller, 1934-35, C13 ....$700.00
#154 Pop Goes the Weasel TV-Radio, 1964-67, wood & plastic,
    C13...$25.00
#155 Jack & Jill TV Radio, 1968-70, wood & plastic, C13....$40.00

#155 Moo-oo Cow, 1958-61 & Easter 1962, C13 ....$85.00
#155 Skipper Sam, 1934, C13.......................................$850.00
#156 Baa-Baa Black Sheep TV-Radio, 1966-67, wood & plastic,
    C13...$50.00
#156 Circus Wagon, 1942-44, band leader in wagon,
    C13...$400.00
#156 Jiffy Dump Truck, 1971-73, squeeze bulb & dump moves,
    C13...$25.00
#158 Katie Kangaroo, 1976-77, squeeze bulb & she hops, C13..$25.00
#158 Little Boy Blue TV-Radio, 1967, wood & plastic, C13..$50.00
#159 Ten Little Indians TV-Radio, 1961-65 & Easter 1966,
    wood & plastic, C13 ....$20.00
#160 Donald & Donna Duck, 1937, C13 ....$700.00
#161 Creative Block Wagon, 1961-64, 18 building blocks & 6
    wooden dowels fit into pull-along wagon, C13 ....$75.00
#161 Looky Chug-Chug, 1949-52, C13 ....$250.00
#161 Old Woman Who Lived in a Shoe TV-Radio, 1968-70,
    wood & plastic w/see-through window on back, C13 ..$30.00
#162 Roly Poly Boats Chime Ball, 1967-69, C13 ....$10.00
#164 Chubby Cub, 1969-72, C13...................................$20.00
#164 Mother Goose, 1964-66, C13 ....$35.00
#165 Roly Poly Chime Ball, 1967-85, C13 ....$5.00
#166 Bucky Burro, 1955-57, C13 ....$250.00
#166 Farmer in the Dell TV-Radio, 1963-66, C13............$35.00
#166 Piggy Bank, 1981-82, pk plastic, C13 ....$15.00
#168 Magnetic Chug-Chug, 1964-69, C13 ....$50.00
#168 Snorky Fire Engine, 1960 & Easter 1961, gr litho, C13.$125.00
#169 Snorky Fire Engine, 1961 & Easter 1962, red litho,
    C13...$100.00
#170 American Airlines Flagship w/Tail Wing, 1941-42,
    C13..$1,000.00
#170 Change-A-Tune Carousel, 1981-83, music box w/crank
    hdl, 3 molded records & 3 figures, C13 ....$30.00
#171 Pull-Along Plane, 1981-88, C13..............................$5.00
#171 Toy Wagon, 1942-47, C13....................................$300.00
#172 Roly Raccoon, 1980-82, C13.................................$10.00
#175 Gold Star Stagecoach, 1954-55 & Easter 1956, C13 ....$250.00
#175 Kicking Donkey, 1937-38, C13 ....$450.00

#175 Winnie the Pooh TV-Radio, 1971-73, Sears only, C13 ..**$65.00**

#177 Donald Duck Xylophone, 1946-52, 2nd version w/'Donald Duck' on hat, C13 ....**$300.00**

#177 Oscar the Grouch, 1977-84, C13 ....**$20.00**

#178 What's in My Pocket Cloth Book, 1972-74, boy's version, C13..**$20.00**

#179 What's in My Pocket Cloth Book, 1972-74, girl's version, C13..**$20.00**

#180 Snoopy Sniffer, 1938-55, C13................................**$75.00**

#183 Play Family Fun Jet, 1970, 1st version, C13 ....**$25.00**

#185 Donald Duck Xylophone, 1938, mk WDE, C13 ....**$800.00**

#189 Looky Chug-Chug, 1958-60, C13 ....**$85.00**

#189 Pull-A-Tune Blue Bird Music Box, 1969-79, plays Children's Prayer, C13 ....**$8.00**

#190 Gabby Duck, 1939-40 & Easter 1941, C13............**$350.00**

#190 Molly Moo-Moo, 1956 & Easter 1957, C13 ....**$225.00**

#190 Pull-A-Tune Pony Music Box, 1969-72, plays Shubert's Cradle Song, C13 ....**$15.00**

#191 Golden Gulch Express, 1961 & Easter 1962, C13 ...**$100.00**

#192 Playland Express, 1962 & Easter 1963, C13 ....**$100.00**

#192 School Bus, 1965-69, new version of #990, C13....**$125.00**

#194 Push Pullet, 1971-72, C13 ....**$25.00**

#195 Peek-A-Boo Screen Music Box, 1965-68, plays Mary Had a Little Lamb, C13..**$30.00**

#195 Teddy Bear Parade, 1938, C13...............................**$600.00**

#196 Peek-A-Boo Screen Music Box, 1964, plays Hey Diddle Diddle, C13...**$50.00**

#198 Band Wagon, 1940-41, C13 ....**$350.00**

#201 Woodsy-Wee Circus, 1931-32, complete, C13 ......**$750.00**

#205 Walt Disney's Parade, WDE, 1936-41, C13, ea......**$250.00**

#205 Woodsy-Wee Zoo, 1931-32, C13 ....**$750.00**

#207 Walt Disney's Carnival, 1936-38, Mickey, Donald, Pluto or Elmer, complete, C13, ea..**$200.00**

#207 Woodsy-Wee Pets, 1931, complete w/goat, donkey, cow, pig & cart, C13 ....**$650.00**

#208 Donald Duck, 1936-38, C13..................................**$175.00**

#209 Woodsy-Wee Dog Show, 1932, complete w/5 dogs, C13 ....**$650.00**

#210 Pluto the Pup, 1936-38, C13 ....**$175.00**

#211 Elmer Elephant, 1936-38, C13 ....**$175.00**

#215 Fisher-Price Choo-Choo, 1955-57, engine w/3 cars, C13 ....**$85.00**

#225 Wheel Horse, 1935 & Easter 1936, C13 ....**$600.00**

#234 Nifty Station Wagon, 1960-62 & Easter 1963, removable roof, C13 ....**$250.00**

#237 Riding Horse, 1936, C13 ....**$600.00**

#250 Big Performing Circus, 1932-38, C13 ....**$950.00**

#300 Scoop Loader, 1975-77, C13...................................**$25.00**

#301 Bunny Basket Cart, 1957-59, C13..........................**$40.00**

#301 Shovel Digger, 1975-77, C13..................................**$25.00**

#302 Chick Basket Cart, 1957-59, C13 ....**$40.00**

#302 Husky Dump Truck, 1978-84, C13.........................**$20.00**

#303 Adventure People Emergency Rescue Truck, 1975-78, C13 ....**$15.00**

#303 Bunny Push Cart, 1957, C13 ....**$75.00**

#304 Adventure People Wild Safari Set, 1975-78, C13 ...**$55.00**

#304 Chick Basket Cart, 1960-64, C13 ....**$40.00**

#304 Running Bunny Cart, 1957, C13.............................**$75.00**

#305 Adventure People Air - Sea Rescue Copter, 1975 – 80, M, $15.00. (Photo courtesy Brad Cassity)

#305 Walking Duck Cart, 1957-64, C13..........................**$40.00**

#306 Adventure People Daredevil Sport Plane, C13..........**$8.00**

#306 Bizzy Bunny Cart, 1957-59, C13 ....**$40.00**

#307 Adventure People Wilderness Patrol, 1975-79, C13 ....**$30.00**

#307 Bouncing Bunny Cart, 1961-63 & Easter 1964, C13 ...**$40.00**

#309 Adventure People TV Action Team, 1977-78, C13 ....**$60.00**

#310 Adventure People Sea Explorer, 1975-80, C13........**$25.00**

#310 Mickey Mouse Puddle Jumper, 1953-55 & Easter 1956, C13 ....**$125.00**

#311 Bulldozer, 1976-77, C13..**$25.00**

#311 Husky Bulldozer, 1978-79, C13 ....**$20.00**

#312 Adventure People Northwoods Trail Blazer, 1977-82, C13 ....**$25.00**

#312 Running Bunny Cart, 1960-64, C13 ....**$45.00**

#313 Husky Roller Grader, 1978-80, C13 ....**$20.00**

#313 Roller Grader, 1977, C13...**$25.00**

#314 Husky Boom Crane, 1978-82, C13.........................**$25.00**

#314 Queen Buzzy Bee, 1956-58, C13............................**$40.00**

#315 Husky Cement Mixer, 1978-82, C13.......................**$30.00**

#316 Husky Tow Truck, 1978-80, C13............................**$15.00**

#317 Husky Construction Crew, 1978-80, C13 ....**$30.00**

#318 Adventure People Daredevil Sports Van, 1978-82, C13 ....**$30.00**

#319 Husky Hook & Ladder Truck, 1979-85, C13 ....**$25.00**

#320 Husky Race Car Rig, 1979-82, C13........................**$30.00**

#322 Adventure People Dune Buster, 1979-82, C13 ....**$15.00**

#325 Adventure People Alpha Probe, 1980-84, C13 ....**$25.00**

#325 Buzzy Bee, 1950-56, 1st version, yel & blk litho, wooden wheels & antenna tips, C13 ....**$40.00**

#326 Adventure People Alpha Star, 1983-84, C13 ....**$30.00**

#327 Husky Load Master Dump, 1984, C13 ....**$30.00**

#328 Husky Highway Dump Truck, 1980-84, C13 ....**$25.00**

#329 Husky Dozer Loader, 1980-84, C13........................**$15.00**

#331 Husky Farm Set, 1981-83, C13................................**$25.00**

#333 Butch the Pup, 1951-53 & Easter 1954, C13 ....**$75.00**

#334 Adventure People Sea Shark, 1981-84, C13............**$25.00**

#337 Husky Rescue Rig, 1982-83, C13............................**$25.00**

#338 Husky Power Tow Truck, 1982-84, C13 ....**$25.00**

#339 Husky Power & Light Service Rig, 1983-84, C13....$30.00
#344 Copter Rig, 1981-84, C13...$15.00
#345 Boat Rig, 1981-84, C13 ....$15.00
#345 Penelope the Performing Penguin, 1935, w/up, C13...$800.00
#347 Little People Indy Racer, 1983-90, C13 ....$8.00
#350 Adventure People Rescue Team, 1976-79, C13.......$18.00
#350 Go 'N Back Mule, 1931-33, w/up, C13 ....$900.00
#351 Adventure People Mountain Climbers, 1976-79, C13..$20.00
#352 Adventure People Construction Workers, 1976-79, C13...$20.00
#353 Adventure People Scuba Divers, 1976-81, C13.......$15.00
#355 Adventure People White Water Kayak, 1977-80, C13 ....$15.00
#355 Go 'N Back Bruno, 1931, C13 ....$800.00
#356 Adventure People Cycle Racing Team, 1977-81, C13 ..$10.00
#358 Adventure People Deep Sea Diver, 1980-84, C13 .....$15.00
#358 Donald Duck Back-Up, 1936, w/up, C13...............$800.00
#360 Adventure People Alpha Recon, 1982-84, C13 ......$15.00
#360 Go 'N Back Jumbo, 1931-34, w/up, C13 ....$900.00
#365 Puppy Back-up, 1932-36, w/up, C13 ....$800.00
#367 Adventure People Turbo Hawk, 1982-83, C13........$15.00
#368 Adventure People Alpha Interceptor, 1982-83, C13.....$15.00
#375 Adventure People Sky Surfer, 1978, C13 ....$25.00
#375 Bruno Back-Up, 1932, C13 ....$800.00
#377 Adventure People Astro Knight, 1979-80, C13.......$15.00
#400 Donald Duck Drum Major, 1946-48, C13..............$275.00
#400 Donald Duck Drum Major Cart, 1946 only, C13 .....$275.00
#400 Tailspin Tabby, 1931-38, rnd guitar, C13 ....$85.00
#401 Push Bunny Cart, 1942, C13...................................$225.00

#448 Mini Copter, 1971 – 84, MIB, $10.00. (Photo courtesy Brad Cassity)

#402 Duck Cart, 1943, C13..$200.00
#404 Bunny Egg Cart, 1949, C13.....................................$80.00
#405 Lofty Lizzy Pop-Up Kritter, 1931-33, C13..............$225.00
#406 Bunny Cart, 1950-53, C13 ....$50.00
#407 Chick Cart, 1950-53, C13..$50.00
#407 Dizzy Dino Pop-Up Kritter, 1931-32, C13 ....$225.00
#410 Stoopy Stork Pop-Up Kritter, 1931-32, C13..........$225.00
#415 Lop-Ear Looie Pop-Up Kritter, 1934, C13 ....$225.00
#415 Super Jet, 1952 & Easter 1953, C13......................$225.00
#420 Sunny Fish, 1955, C13 ....$225.00
#422 Jumbo Jitterbug Pop-Up Kritter, 1940, C13..........$225.00
#423 Jumping Jack Scarecrow, 1979, C13......................$10.00

#425 Donald Duck Pop-Up, 1938 & Easter 1939, C13.....$400.00

#433 Dizzy Donkey Pop-Up Kritter, 1939, C13 ....$125.00

#434 Ferdinand the Bull, 1939, C13 ....$600.00

#435 Happy Apple, 1979-84, short stem, C13 ....$3.00

#440 Goofy Gertie Pop-Up Kritter, 1935, C13................$225.00

#440 Pluto Pop-Up, 1936, mk WDP, C13.......................$100.00

#444 Fuzzy Fido, 1941-42, C13.....................................$225.00

#444 Puffy Engine, 1951-54, C13...................................$85.00

#444 Queen Buzzy Bee, 1959, red litho, C13 ....$40.00

#445 Hot Dog Wagon, 1940-41, C13..............................$250.00

#445 Nosey Pup, 1956-58 & Easter 1959, C13 ....$75.00

#447 Woofy Wagger, 1947-48, C13................................$85.00

#450 Donald Duck Choo-Choo, 1941, 8½", C13...........$400.00

#450 Donald Duck Choo-Choo, 1942-45 & Easter 1949, C13 ....$200.00

#450 Kiltie Dog, 1936, C13...$400.00

#450 Music Box Bear, 1981-83, plays Schubert's Cradle Song, C13 ....$10.00

#454 Donald Duck Drummer, 1949-50, C13 ....$300.00

#455 Tailspin Tabby Pop-Up Kritter, 1939-42, C13 ....$85.00

#456 Bunny & Container, 1939-40, C13.........................$225.00

#460 Dapper Donald Duck, 1936-37, no number on toy, C13..$600.00

#460 Movie Viewer, 1973-85, crank hdl, C13....................$8.00

#460 Suzie Seal, 1961-63 & Easter 1964, C13 ....$40.00

#461 Duck Cart, 1938-39, C13 ....$225.00

#462 Busy Bunny, 1937, C13..$200.00

#465 Teddy Choo-Choo, 1937, C13 ....$400.00

#466 Busy Bunny Cart, 1941-44, C13.............................$75.00

#469 Donald Cart, 1940, C13..$400.00

#469 Rooster Cart, 1938-40, C13 ....$400.00

#470 Tricky Tommy, 1936, C13 ....$350.00

#472 Jingle Giraffe, 1956, C13......................................$225.00

#472 Peter Bunny Cart, 1939-40, C13............................$225.00

#473 Merry Mutt, 1949-54 & Easter 1955, C13 ....$75.00

#474 Bunny Racer, 1942, C13.......................................$225.00

#476 Cookie Pig, 1966-70, C13......................................$50.00

#476 Mickey Mouse Drummer, 1941-45 & Easter 1946, C13 .$300.00

#476 Rooster Pop-Up Kritter, 1936, C13........................$350.00

#477 Dr Doodle, 1940-41, C13 ....$225.00

#478 Pudgy Pig, 1962-64 & Easter 1965, C13 ....$50.00

#479 Donald Duck & Nephews, 1941-42, C13 ....$400.00

#479 Peter Pig, 1959-61 & Easter 1962, C13...................$45.00

#480 Leo the Drummer, 1952 & Easter 1953, C13.........$225.00

#480 Teddy Station Wagon, 1942, C13 ....$225.00

#485 Mickey Mouse Choo-Choo, 1949-54, new litho version of #432, C13 ....$100.00

#488 Popeye Spinach Eater, 1939-40, C13 ....$600.00

#491 Boom-Boom Popeye, C13......................................$450.00

#494 Pinocchio, 1939-40, C13......................................$600.00

#495 Running Bunny Cart, 1941, C13 ....$225.00

#495 Sleepy Sue Turtle, 1962-63 & Easter 1964, C13 ......$45.00

#499 Kitty Bell, 1950-51, C13.......................................$125.00

#500 Donald Duck Cart, 1937, no number on toy, wheels not painted, C13 ....$700.00

#500 Donald Duck Cart, 1951-53, no baton, gr litho background, C13 ....$350.00

#500 Donald Duck Cart, 1953, w/baton, yel litho background, C13 ....$350.00

#500 Pick-Up & Peek Puzzle, 1972-86, C13 ....$10.00

#500 Pushy Pig, 1932-35, C13.......................................$500.00

#502 Action Bunny Cart, 1949, C13 ....$200.00

#503 Pick-Up & Peek Wood Puzzle, Occupations, 1972-76, C13...$10.00

#505 Bunny Drummer, 1946, bell on front, C13 ....$225.00

#506 Pick-Up and Peek Puzzle, Bear and Cubs, 1972 – 84, MIB, $10.00. (Photo courtesy Brad Cassity)

#507 Pushy Doodle, 1933, C13 ....$850.00

#508 Bunny Bell Drummer, 1949-53, C13 ....$85.00

#510 Pick-Up & Peek Wood Puzzle, Nursery Rhymes, 1972-81, C13...$15.00

#510 Strutter Donald Duck, 1941, C13 ....$250.00

#512 Bunny Drummer, 1942, C13..................................$225.00

#515 Pushy Pat, 1933-35, C13.......................................$550.00

#517 Choo-Choo Local, 1936, C13 ....$550.00

#517 Pick-Up & Piece Wood Puzzle, Animal Friends, 1977-84, C13...$10.00

#520 Bunny Bell Cart, 1941, C13 ....$225.00

#520 Pick-Up & Peek Puzzle, Three Little Pigs, 1979-84, C13..$15.00

#525 Cotton Tail Cart, 1940, C13 ....$350.00

#525 Pushy Elephant, 1934-35, C13 ....$550.00

#530 Mickey Mouse Band, 1935-36, C13 ....$800.00

#533 Thumper Bunny, 1942, C13 ....$500.00

#540 Granny Duck, 1939-40, C13 ....$225.00

#544 Donald Duck Cart, 1942-44, C13 ....$300.00

#549 Toy Lunch Kit, 1962-79, red w/barn litho, w/thermos, C13 ....$25.00

#550 Toy Lunch Kit, 1957, red, wht & gr plastic barn shape, no litho, C13 ....$40.00

#552 Basic Hardboard Puzzle, Nature, 1974-75, C13........$15.00

#563 Basic Hardboard Puzzle, Weather, 1975, C13 ....$10.00

#568 Basic Hardboard Puzzle, bear on log, C13 ....$10.00

#569 Basic Hardboard Puzzle, Airport, 1975, C13 ....$10.00

#600 Tailspin Tabby Pop-Up, 1947, C13.........................$250.00

#604 Bunny Bell Cart, 1954-55, C13..............................$100.00

#605 Donald Duck Cart, 1954-56, C13 ....$300.00

#605 Woodsey Major Goodgrub Mole & Book, 1981-82, 32 pgs, C13..$20.00

#606 Woodsey Bramble Beaver & Book, 1981-82, 32 pgs, C13..$20.00

#607 Woodsey Very Blue Bird & Book, 1981-82, 32 pgs, C13..$20.00

#615 Tow Truck, 1960-61 & Easter 1962, C13 ....$75.00

#616 Chuggy Pop-Up, 1955-56, C13 ....$100.00

#616 Patch Pony, 1963-64 & Easter 1965, C13 ....$50.00

#617 Prancy Pony, 1965-70, C13 ....$30.00

#621 Suzie Seal, 1965-66, ball on nose, C13....................$40.00

#623 Suzie Seal, 1964-65, umbrella on nose, C13 ....$55.00

#625 Playful Puppy, 1961-62 & Easter 1963, w/shoe, C13 ....$50.00

#628 Tug-A-Bug, 1975-77, C13..$5.00

#629 Fisher-Price Tractor, 1962-68, C13..........................$30.00

#630 Fire Truck, 1959-62, C13 ....$50.00

#634 Drummer Boy, 1967-69, C13 ....$50.00

#634 Tiny Teddy, 1955-57, C13..$75.00

#637 Milk Carrier, 1966-85, C13 ....$15.00

#640 Wiggily Woofer, 1957-58 & Easter 1958, C13 ....$85.00

#641 Toot Toot Engine, 1962-63 & Easter 1964, bl litho, C13..$60.00

#642 Bob-Along Bear, 1979-84, C13 ....$10.00

#642 Dinky Engine, 1959, blk litho, C13..........................$60.00

#642 Smokie Engine, 1960-61 & Easter 1962, blk litho, C13.$60.00

#649 Stake Truck, 1960-61 & Easter 1962, C13 ....$50.00

#653 Allie Gator, 1960-61 & Easter 1962, C13..............$100.00

#654 Tawny Tiger, 1962 & Easter 1963, C13..................$100.00

#656 Bossy Bell, 1960 & Easter 1961, w/bonnet, C13 ......$60.00

#656 Bossy Bell, 1961-63, no bonnet, new litho design, C13 .....$50.00

#657 Crazy Clown Fire Brigade, 1983-84, C13 ....$50.00

#658 Lady Bug, 1961-62 & Easter 1963, C13 ....$55.00

#659 Puzzle Puppy, 1976-81, C13....................................$10.00

#662 Merry Mousewife, 1962-64 & Easter 1965, C13 ......$50.00

#663 Play Family, 1966-70, blk dog, MIP, C13 ....$120.00

#663 Play Family, 1966-70, tan dog, MIP, C13 ....$170.00

#666 Creative Blocks, 1978-90, C13................................$10.00

#674 Sports Car, 1958-60, C13 ....$85.00

#677 Picnic Basket, 1975-79, C13....................................$30.00

#678 Kriss Kricket, 1955-57, C13 ....$100.00

#679 Little People Garage Squad, 1984-90, MIP, C13......$15.00

#684 Little Lamb, 1964-65, C13......................................$50.00

#685 Car & Boat, 1968-69, wood & plastic, 5 pcs, C13 ...$65.00

#686 Car & Camper, 1968-70, C13 ....$65.00

#686 Perky Pot, 1958-59 & Easter 1960, C13..................$50.00

#686 Play Family Car & Camper, 1968-70, MIB, C13 ...$130.00

#694 Suzie Seal, 1979-80, C13 ....$15.00

#695 Lady Bug, 1982-84, C13..$5.00

#695 Pinky Pig, 1956-57, wooden eyes, C13. ....$100.00

#695 Pinky Pig, 1958, litho eyes, C13............................$100.00

#698 Talky Parrot, 1963 & Easter 1964, C13..................$100.00

#700 Cowboy Chime, 1951-53, C13..............................$250.00

#700 Popeye, 1935, C13 ....$700.00

#700 Woofy Wowser, 1940 & Easter 1941, C13 ....$400.00

#703 Bunny Engine, 1954-56, C13 ....$100.00
#703 Popeye the Sailor, 1936, C13 ....$700.00
#705 Mini Snowmobile, 1971-73, C13 ....$45.00
#705 Popeye Cowboy, 1937, C13 ....$700.00
#710 Scotty Dog, 1933, C13 ....$550.00
#711 Cry Baby Bear, 1967-69, C13 ....$30.00
#711 Huckleberry Hound, 1961, Sears only, C13 ....$300.00
#711 Raggedy Ann & Andy, 1941, C13 ....$850.00
#711 Teddy Trucker, 1949-51, C13 ....$225.00
#712 Fred Flintstone Xylophone, 1962, Sears only, C13.....$250.00
#712 Johnny Jumbo, 1933-35, C13 ....$550.00
#712 Teddy Tooter, 1957-58 & Easter 1959, C13 ....$250.00
#714 Mickey Mouse Xylophone, 1963, Sears only, C13 ....$275.00
#715 Ducky Flip Flap, 1964-65, C13 ....$65.00
#717 Ducky Flip Flap, 1937-39, C13 ....$400.00
#718 Tow Truck & Car, 1969-70, wood & plastic, MIB, C13 ..$75.00
#719 Busy Bunny Cart, 1936-37, C13 ....$350.00
#719 Cuddly Cub, 1973-77, C13 ....$5.00
#720 Pinocchio Express, 1939-40, C13 ....$500.00
#721 Peter Bunny Engine, 1949-51, C13 ....$200.00
#722 Racing Bunny Cart, 1937, C13 ....$350.00
#722 Running Bunny, 1938-40, C13 ....$225.00
#723 Bouncing Bunny Cart, 1936, C13 ....$350.00
#724 Ding-Dong Ducky, 1949-50, C13 ....$225.00
#724 Jolly Jalopy, 1965, C13..$15.00
#725 Musical Mutt, 1935-36, C13 ....$350.00
#725 Play Family Bath/Utility Room Set, 1972, MIP, C13 ....$75.00
#726 Play Family Patio Set, 1970-73, MIP, C13 ....$75.00
#727 Bouncing Bunny Wheelbarrow, 1939, C13............$350.00
#728 Buddy Bullfrog, 1959-60, yel body w/red coat, C13....$75.00
#728 Pound & Saw Bench, 1966-67, C13.......................$25.00
#730 Racing Rowboat, 1952-53, C13 ....$200.00
#732 Happy Hauler, 1968-70, C13 ....$35.00
#732 Happy Whistlers, 1977-79, C13 ....$15.00
#733 Mickey Mouse Safety Patrol, 1956-57, C13...........$250.00
#734 Teddy Zilo, 1964, no coat, C13 ....$65.00
#734 Teddy Zilo, 1965-66, w/coat, C13 ....$45.00
#735 Juggling Jumbo, 1958-59, C13 ....$225.00
#736 Humpty Dumpty, 1972-79, plastic, C13 ....$4.00
#737 Galloping Horse & Wagon, 1948-49, C13.............$250.00
#737 Ziggy Zilo, 1958-59, C13 ....$75.00
#738 Dumbo Circus Racer, 1941 & Easter 1942, rubber arms,
    C13 ....$700.00
#738 Shaggy Zilo, 1960-61 & Easter 1962, C13 ....$75.00
#739 Poodle Zilo, 1962-63 & Easter 1964, C13...............$75.00
#740 Pushcart Pete, 1936-67, C13 ....$600.00
#741 Teddy Zilo, 1967, C13..$45.00
#741 Trotting Donald Duck, 1937, C13.........................$800.00
#742 Dashing Dobbin, 1938-40, C13 ....$350.00
#744 Doughboy Donald, 1942, C13 ....$600.00
#745 Elsie's Dairy Truck, 1948-49, w/2 bottles, C13.......$700.00
#746 Pocket Radio, 1977-78, It's a Small World, wood & plastic,
    C13...$25.00
#747 Chatter Telephone, 1962-67, wooden wheels, C13.....$30.00
#747 Talk-Back Telephone, 1961 & Easter 1962, C13 .....$75.00
#749 Egg Truck, 1947, C13 ....$225.00
#750 Hot Dog Wagon, 1938, C13 ....$400.00
#750 Space Blazer, 1953-54, C13 ....$400.00

#755 Jumbo Rolo, 1951-52, C13 ....$225.00
#756 Pocket Radio, 1973, 12 Days of Christmas, wood & plastic,
    C13...$25.00
#757 Howdy Bunny, 1939-40, C13 ....$350.00
#757 Humpty Dumpty, 1957 & Easter 1958, C13 ....$200.00
#757 Snappy-Quacky, 1950, C13 ....$225.00
#758 Pocket Radio, 1970-72, Mulberry Bush, wood & plastic,
    C13...$20.00
#758 Pony Chime, 1948-50, C13.................................$200.00
#758 Push-Along Clown, 1980-81, C13 ....$20.00
#759 Pocket Radio, 1969-73, Do-Re-Me, wood & plastic, C13..$20.00
#760 Peek-A-Boo Block, 1970-79, C13 ....$15.00
#760 Racing Ponies, 1936, C13...................................$350.00
#761 Play Family Nursery Set, 1973, C13 ....$30.00
#762 Pocket Radio, 1972-77, Raindrops, wood & plastic, C13 .$25.00
#763 Music Box, 1962, Farmer in the Dell, yel litho, C13 ....$50.00
#763 Pocket Radio, 1978, I Whistle a Happy Tune, wood &
    plastic, C13 ....$20.00
#764 Music Box, 1960-61 & Easter 1962, Farmer in the Dell, red
    litho, C13 ....$50.00
#764 Pocket Radio, 1975-76, My Name Is Michael, C13....$15.00
#765 Dandy Dobbin, 1941-44, C13 ....$200.00
#765 Talking Donald Duck, 1955-58, C13 ....$125.00
#766 Pocket Radio, 1968-70, Where Has My Little Dog Gone?,
    wood & plastic, C13 ....$25.00
#766 Pocket Radio, 1977-78, I'd Like To Teach the World To
    Sing, C13 ....$20.00
#767 Pocket Radio, 1977, Twinkle Twinkle Little Star, C13 .$25.00
#767 Tiny Ding-Dong, 1940, 6 wheels, C13 ....$400.00
#768 Pocket Radio, 1971-76, Happy Birthday, wood & plastic,
    C13...$15.00
#770 Doc & Dopey Dwarfs, 1938, C13.......................$1,000.00
#772 Pocket Radio, 1974-76, Jack & Jill, C13 ....$20.00
#773 Tip-Toe Turtle, 1962-77, vinyl tail, C13 ....$15.00
#775 Gabby Goofies, 1956-59 & Easter 1960, C13 ....$45.00
#775 Pocket Radio, 1967-68, Sing a Song of Six Pence, wood &
    plastic, C13 ....$25.00
#775 Pocket Radio, 1973-75, Pop Goes the Weasel, wood &
    plactic, C13..$20.00
#775 Teddy Drummer, 1936, C13 ....$675.00
#777 Pushy Bruno, 1933, C13 ....$725.00
#777 Squeaky the Clown, 1958-59, C13 ....$250.00
#778 Ice Cream Wagon, 1940 & Easter 1941, C13 ....$350.00
#778 Pocket Radio, 1967-68, Frere Jacques, wood & plastic,
    C13...$20.00
#779 Pocket Radio, 1976, Yankee Doodle, wood & plastic,
    C13...$20.00
#780 Jumbo Xylophone, 1937-38, C13 ....$275.00
#780 Snoopy Sniffer, 1955-57 & Easter 1958, C13 ....$75.00
#784 Mother Goose Music Chart, 1955-56 & Easter 1957,
    C13...$100.00
#785 Blackie Drummer, 1939, C13 ....$625.00
#785 Corn Popper, 1957-58, red base, C13 ....$75.00
#786 Perky Penguin, 1973-75, C13 ....$25.00
#788 Rock-A-Bye Bunny Cart, 1940-41, C13 ....$300.00
#789 Lift & Load Road Builders, 1978-82, C13...............$20.00
#791 Tote-A-Tune Music Box Radio, 1979, Let's Go Fly A Kite,
    plastic, C13 ....$10.00

#792 The Teddy Bear's Picnic Tote-A-Tune Radio, 1980 – 81, MIB, $10.00. (Photo courtesy Brad Cassity)

#793 Jolly Jumper, 1963-64 & Easter 1965, C13..............$50.00

#793 Tote-A-Tune Music Box, 1981, When You Wish Upon a Star, plastic, C13...$10.00

#794 Big Bill Pelican, 1961-63, w/cb fish, C13.................$85.00

#794 Tote-A-Tune Music Box, 1981-82, Over the Rainbow, plastic, C13...$5.00

#795 Micky Mouse Drummer, 1937, C13......................$700.00

#795 Musical Duck, 1952-54 & Easter 1955, C13..........$100.00

#795 Tote-A-Tune Music Box, 1984-91, Toyland, plastic, C13...$5.00

#798 Chatter Monk, 1957-58 & Easter 1959, C13..........$100.00

#798 Mickey Mouse Xylophone, 1939, w/hat, C13........$400.00

#798 Mickey Mouse Xylophone, 1942, no hat, C13.......$400.00

#799 Duckie Transport, 1937, C13.................................$400.00

#799 Quacky Family, 1940-42, C13................................$125.00

#800 Hot Diggety, 1934, w/up, C13...............................$800.00

#808 Pop'n Ring, 1956-58 & Easter 1959, C13................$85.00

#810 Hot Mammy, 1934, w/up, C13...............................$800.00

#810 Timber Toter, 1957 & Easter 1958, C13..................$85.00

#845 Farm Truck, 1954-55, C13.....................................$250.00

#870 Pull-A-Tune Xylophone, 1957-69, w/song book, C13....$35.00

#875, Looky Push Car, 1962-65 & Easter 1966, C13........$50.00

#900 Struttin' Donald Duck, 1939 & Easter 1940, C13...$650.00

#900 This Little Pig, 1956-58 & Easter 1959, C13...........$55.00

#902 Junior Circus, 1963-70, C13..................................$225.00

#904 Beginners Circus, 1965-68, C13..............................$60.00

#905 This Little Pig, 1959-62, C13..................................$30.00

#909 Play Family Rooms, 1972, Sears only, MIB, C13, from $300 to..$400.00

#910 Change-A-Tune Piano, 1969-72, Pop Goes the Weasel, This Old Man & The Muffin Man, C13....................$30.00

#915 Play Family Farm, 1968-79, 1st version w/masonite base, C13...$30.00

#923 Play Family School, 1971-78, 1st version, C13........$25.00

#926 Concrete Mixer, 1959-60 & Easter 1961, C13......$250.00

#928 Play Family Fire Station, 1980-82, C13...................$65.00

#929 Play Family Nursery School, 1978-79, C13..............$50.00

#931 Play Family Children's Hospital, 1976-78, C13.....$115.00

#931 Play Family Hospital, 1976-78, C13......................$115.00

(Photo courtesy Brad Cassity)

#932 Amusement Park, 1963-65, C13.............................$300.00

#932 Ferry Boat, 1979-80, C13..$45.00

#934 Play Family Western Town, 1982-84, C13...............$65.00

#935 Tool Box Work Bench, 1969-71, C13......................$25.00

#937 Play Family Sesame Street Clubhouse, 1977-79, C13...$70.00

#938 Play Family Sesame Street House, 1975-76, C13.....$75.00

#942 Play Family Lift & Load Depot, 1977-79, C13.........$50.00

#943 Lift & Load Railroad, 1978-79, C13........................$50.00

#944 Lift & Load Lumber Yard, 1979-81, C13.................$50.00

#945 Offshore Cargo Base, 1979-80, C13........................$65.00

#960 Woodsey's Log House, 1979-81, complete, C13.......$25.00

#961 Woodsey's Store, 1980 – 81, complete, M, $35.00.
(Photo courtesy Brad Cassity)

#962 Woodsey's Airport, 1980-81, complete, C13............$20.00

#969 Musical Ferris Wheel, 1966-72, 1st version w/4 wooden straight-body figures, C13.......................................$50.00

#972 Fisher-Price Cash Register, 1960-72, C13...............$50.00

#979 Dump Truckers Playset, 1965-67, C13....................$75.00

#982 Hot Rod Roadster, 1983-84, riding toy w/4-pc take-apart engine, C13...$45.00

#983 Safety School Bus, 1959, w/6 figures, Fisher-Price Club logo, C13 ....$250.00

#985 Play Family Houseboat, 1972-76, complete, C13 ....$45.00

#987 Creative Coaster, 1964-82, MIB, C13......................$50.00

#990 Play Family A-Frame, 1974-76, C13 ....$60.00

#991 Music Box Lacing Shoe, 1964-67, C13 ....$60.00

#991 Play Family Circus Train, 1973-78, w/gondola car, C13 ....$25.00

#991 Play Family Circus Train, 1979-86, no gondola car, C13 ....$15.00

#992 Play Family Car & Camper, 1980-84, C13..............$35.00

#993 Play Family Castle, 1974-77, 1st version, C13.......$100.00

#994 Play Family Camper, 1973-76, C13 ....$75.00

#996 Play Family Airport, 1972-76, 1st version w/bl airport & clear look-out tower, C13 ....$65.00

#997 Musical Tick-Tock Clock, 1962-63, C13 ....$40.00

#997 Play Family Village, 1973-77, C13 ....$75.00

#998 Music Box Teaching Clock, 1968-83, C13..............$40.00

#999 Huffy Puffy Train, 1958-62, C13 ....$80.00

#1005 Push Cone, 1937-38, C13......................................$400.00

#1006 Floor Train, 1934-38, C13 ....$600.00

#2155 McDonald's Happy Meal, 1989-90, C13 ....$15.00

#2352 Little People Construction Set, 1985, C13 ....$20.00

#2360 Little People Jetliner, 1986-88, C13......................$10.00

#2361 Little People Fire Truck, 1989-90, C13 ....$10.00

#2453 Little People Beauty Salon, 1990, C13..................$20.00

#2500 Little People Main Street, 1986-90, C13 ....$50.00

#2501 Little People Farm, 1986-89, C13 ....$20.00

#2502 Little People Airport, 1986 – 89, MIB, $15.00.
(Photo courtesy Brad Cassity)

#2504 Little People Garage, 1986, rare, C13 ....$55.00

#2524 Little People Cruise Boat, 1989-90, C13...............$20.00

#2525 Little People Playground, 1986-90, C13 ....$15.00

#2526 Little People Pool, 1986-88, C13 ....$15.00

#2550 Little People School, 1988-89, C13 ....$30.00

#2551 Little People Neighborhood, 1988-90, C13 ....$50.00

#2552 McDonald's Restaurant, 1990, 1st version, C13 ....$70.00

#2552 McDonald's Restaurant, 1991-92, 2nd version, same pcs as 1st version but lg-sz figures, C13 ....$50.00

#2580 Little People Little Mart, 1987-89, C13.................$20.00

#2581 Little People Express Train, 1987-90, C13 ....$15.00

#2582 Little People Floating Marina, 1988-90, C13........$15.00

#2712 Pick-Up & Peek Wood Puzzle, Haunted House, 1985-88, C13..$15.00

#2720 Pick-Up & Peek Wood Puzzle, Little Bo Peep, 1985-88, C13..$15.00

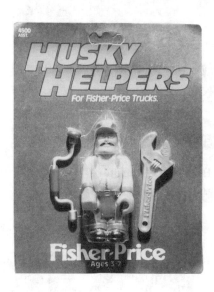

#4500 Husky Helper, 1985 – 86, MOC, $15.00. (Photo courtesy Brad Cassity)

#4520 Highway Dump Truck, 1985-86, C13.....................$20.00

#4521 Dozer Loader, 1985-86, C13 ....$15.00

#4523 Gravel Hauler, 1985-86, C13 ....$15.00

#4550 Chevy S-10 4x4, 1985, C13...................................$25.00

#4551 Pontiac Firebird, 1985, C13..................................$25.00

#4552 Jeep CJ-7 Renegade, 1985, C13............................$25.00

#4580 Power Tow, 1985-86, C13......................................$20.00

#4581 Power Dump Truck, 1985-86, C13 ....$20.00

#6145 Jingle Elephant, 1993, ToyFest limited edition of 5,000, C13 ....$150.00

#6464 Gran'Pa Frog, 1994 ToyFest limited edition of 5,000, C13 ....$60.00

#6550 Buzzy Bee, 1987, ToyFest limited edition of 5,000, C13 ....$120.00

#6558 Snoopy Sniffer, 1988, ToyFest limited edition of 3,000, C13 ....$550.00

#6575 Toot-Toot, 1989, ToyFest limited edition of 4,800, C13 ....$85.00

#6588 Snoopy Sniffer, 1990, Fisher-Price Commemorative limited edition of 3,500, Ponderosa pine, C13..............$150.00

#6590 Prancing Horses, 1990, Toy Fest limited edition of 5,000, MIB, $75.00. (Photo courtesy Brad Cassity)

#6592 Teddy Bear Parade, 1991, ToyFest limited edition of 5,000, C13..$75.00

#6593 Squeaky the Clown, 1995, ToyFest limited edition of 5,000, C13 ....$150.00

#6599 Molly Bell Cow, 1992, ToyFest limited edition of 5,000, C13 ....$150.00

#76880 Raggedy Ann & Andy, 1997, ToyFest limited edition of 5,000, C13 ....$150.00

#76594 Woodsy-Wee Zoo, 1996, Toy Fest limited edition of 5,000, MIB, $125.00. (Photo courtesy Brad Cassity)

Games

Early games (those from 1850 to 1910) are very often appreciated more for their wonderful lithographed boxes than their 'playability,' and you'll find collectors displaying them as they would any fine artwork. Many boxes and boards were designed by commercial artists of the day.

Though they were in a decline a few years ago, baby-boomer game prices have leveled off. Some science fiction and rare TV games are still in high demand. Games produced in the Art Deco era between the World Wars have gained in popularity — especially those with great design. Victorian games have become harder to find; their prices have also grown steadily. Condition and rarity are the factors that most influence game prices.

When you buy a game, check to see that all pieces are there. The games listed below are complete unless noted otherwise. For further information we recommend *Board Games of the '50s, '60s, and '70s* (L-W Book Sales). Note: In the listings that follow, assume that all are board games (unless specifically indicated card game, target game, bagatelle, etc.) and that each is complete as issued, unless missing components are mentioned.

Advisor: Paul Fink (F3).

See also Advertising; Black Americana; Barbie; California Raisins; Halloween; Political; Robots and Space Toys; Sporting Collectibles; Tops and Other Spinning Toys.

$10,000 Pyramid, Milton Bradley, 1972, EX (EX box) $15.00

$64,000 Dollar Question Jr Edition, Lowell, 1956, EXIB .$30.00

ABC Education, card game, Ed-U Cards, 1959, EX+ (EX box) $10.00

Adventures of Davy Crockett, Harett-Gilmar, 1955, EX (EX box) $75.00

Adventures of Lassie, Whiting, 1955, EX (EX box) $50.00

Adventures of Rin-Tin-Tin, Transogram, 1955, EX (EX box) $50.00

Adventures of Robin Hood, Bettye-B, 1956, EX (VG box) ..$65.00

Adventures of Superman, Milton Bradley, 1942, EX (EX box) $225.00

Alien, Kenner, 1979, EXIB...$50.00

All American Skittle Score-Ball, Aurora, 1974, EX (EX box) $35.00

Alvin & the Chipmunks Acorn Hunt, Hasbro, 1960, EX (EX box) $35.00

Amazing Dunninger Mind Reading Game, Hasbro, 1976, NM, $32.00. (Photo courtesy June Moon)

Amazing Spider-Man, Milton Bradley, 1966, EX (EX box) $250.00

Angela Cartwright's Buttons & Bows, Transogram, 1960, EXIB...$50.00

Annie Oakley, Game Gems/T Cohn, 1965, EX (EX box) ..$50.00

Aquanauts Underwater Adventure, Transogram, 1961, EX (EX box) $50.00

Archie Bunker Poker, Cadeaux, 1972, EX (EX container) ..$30.00

Astro Launch, Ohio Art, 1963, EXIB $75.00

Automobile Race, McLoughlin Bros, 1904, EX (EX box), A...$1,800.00

Babes in Toyland, Parker Bros, 1961, EX (EX box) $30.00

Baretta, Milton Bradley, 1976, EX (EX box).....................$20.00

Barnstormer, Marx, 1970, EX (EX box) $35.00

Bat Masterson, Lowell, 1958, VG (VG box) $40.00

Batman & Robin Marble Maze, Hasbro, 1966, EX (EX box) $100.00

Batman & Robin Pinball Machine, Marx, 1966, litho tin & plastic, 21x10", EX, from $75 to..............................$100.00

Batman & Robin Target, Hasbro, 1966, MIB $200.00

Batman Batarang Toss, Pressman, 1966, EX (EX box) ...$175.00

Batman Electronic Question & Answer, Lisbeth Whiting, 1966, EX (EX box)..$75.00

Batman Shooting Arcade, Marx, 1966, EX (EX box).....$250.00

Battleboard, Ideal, 1972, NMIB $30.00

Beach Head Invasion, Built-Rite, 1950s, EX (EX box).....$40.00

Beany & Cecil Jumping Dishonest John, Mattel, 1962, NMIB...$35.00

Beany & Cecil Ring Toss, Pressman, 1961, EX (EX box) .$50.00

Beatlemania, VG (VG box), B3 ....$40.00

Beverly Hillbillies, Standard Toykraft, 1963, NMIB.........$50.00

Black Hole Space Alert, Whitman, 1979, MIB $35.00

Blondie Hurry Scurry, Transogram, 1966, EX (EX box)....$40.00

Boots & Saddles, Gardner, 1958, EX (EX box).................$50.00

Bozo the Clown in Circus Land, Transogram, 1960s, EX (EX box)...$35.00

Brady Bunch, Whitman, 1973, MIB $100.00

Bruce Force & the Treasure of Shark Island, Ideal, 1963, EX (EX box)..$50.00

Buck Rogers, Game of the 25th Century A.D., Lutz & Sheinkman, c 1934 Slesinger, EX (EX box), A, $500.00.

Buffalo Bill Target Gallery, Airgam/Spain, 1970s, NMIB, P4 ....$35.00

Bugaloos, Milton Bradley, 1971, MIB, from $50 to...........$60.00

Bullwinkle Target & Ring Toss, Parks Plastics, 1961, EX (EX box)...$75.00

Burke's Law, target game, Transogram, 1964, EX (EX box) $45.00

Cabby, Selchow & Righter, 1950s, EX (EX box) $75.00

Camp Granada, Milton Bradley, 1965, EX (EX box)........$35.00

Camp Granada, Milton Bradley, 1965, MIB $45.00

Camp Runamuck, card game, Ideal, 1965, EX (EX box) ..$25.00

Candyland, Milton Bradley, 1962, VG (VG box), N2 .....$50.00

Captain America, Milton Bradley, 1966, MIB................$100.00

Captain Kangaroo TV Lotto, Ideal, 1961, EX (EX box)...$25.00

Captain Kangaroo's Tic Tagaroo, Milton Bradley, 1956, EX (EX box)...$40.00

Captain Kidd, Lowell, 1950s, EX (EX box).......................$50.00

Car 54 Where Are You?, Allison, 1963, EXIB................$175.00

Carl Hubbell Mechanical Baseball, Gotham, 1948, EX (EX box) $250.00

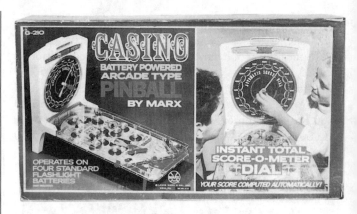

Casino Pinball, Marx, M (EX box), $95.00.
(Photo courtesy Martin and Carolyn Berens)

Casper the Ghost, card game, 1950s-60s, NM (NM box)...$15.00

Championship Baseball, Lansing, 1966, EX (EX box)......$35.00

Charlie 'N Me Robot, Topper, 1967, EX (EX box) $45.00

Chase Back, Milton Bradley, 1962, MIB (sealed) $15.00

CHiPs, Ideal, 1981, MIB, from $25 to................................$35.00

Chuck Conners Tin Can Alley Rifle Target, Ideal, 1976, EX+, A7 ....$50.00

Chutes Away, Gabriel, 1978, EX (EX box) $65.00

Cinderella, card game, Transogram, 1965, EX (EX box) ..$15.00

Cinderella, Milton Bradley, 1909, few pcs missing, EX (worn box)...$100.00

Cinderella, Parker Bros, 1964, EXIB $50.00

Clue, Parker Bros, 1949, orig issue, VG (VG box) $50.00

Cold Feet, Ideal, 1967, EX (EX box).................................$35.00

Conflict, Parker Bros, 1940s, 1st edition, EX (EX box), F3..$100.00

Cootie House, Schaper, 1966, EX (EX box).......................$35.00

Creature From the Black Lagoon, Hasbro, 1963, EX (EX box).$165.00

Crosby Derby, Fishlove, 1947, EX (EX box) $65.00

Crow Hunt, Parker Bros, 1930, VG (VG box) $65.00

Dancing Princess, Hasbro, 1964, EX (EX box) $35.00

Daniel Boone, card game, Transogram, 1964, EX (EX box)..$30.00

Dark Shadows, Milton Bradley, 1969, NMIB....................$40.00

Dark Shadows Mysterious Maze, Whitman, 1968, EX (EX box)...$65.00

Dating Game, Hasbro, 1967, EX (EX box) $30.00

Davy Crockett, card game, Ed-U Cards, 1955, EX (EX box) .$30.00

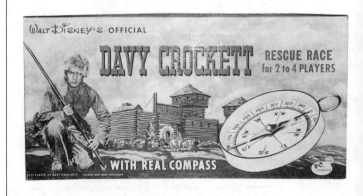

Davy Crockett Rescue Race, Gabriel, EX (EX box), from $55.00 to $75.00. (Photo courtesy Bill Bruegman, Toy Scouts)

Davy Crockett, Dart Gun Target Set, Knickerbocker, 1950s, complete, NRFB $75.00

Davy Crockett Adventures, Gabriel, 1955, NM (EX box) .$95.00

Davy Crockett Adventures, Gardner, 1950s, EX (EX box), from $65 to...$75.00

Davy Crockett Radar Action, Ewing, 1955, EX (EX box) ..$85.00

Deputy, Milton Bradley, 1960, EX (EX box) $65.00

Deputy Dawg, Milton Bradley, 1960, EX (EX box)...........$50.00

Dick Tracy Crimestopper, Ideal, 1963, NM (EX box), A .$75.00

Dick Tracy Sunday Funnies, Ideal, 1972, EX (EX box) $55.00

Dick Van Dyke, Standard Toykraft, 1964, EX (EX box $75.00

Disneyland Monorail, Parker Bros, 1950s, EX (EX box)...$50.00

Diver Dan Tug-O-War, Milton Bradley, 1961, EX (EX box) ...$50.00

Doctor Dolittle Marble Maze, Hasbro, 1967, EXIB $40.00

Dogfight, Milton Bradley, 1962, EX (EX box) $40.00

Don't Spill the Beans, Schaper, 1967, MIB (sealed)........$25.00

Donald Duck Ring Toss, Transogram, 1961, EX (EX box) ...$30.00

Donald Duck Wagon Train, 1977, NMIB $25.00

Donald Duck's Tiddley Winx, Jaymar/WDP, EX (EX box)....$75.00

Dracula, Hasbro, 1963, EX (EX box) $150.00

Dragnet, Transogram, 1955, NMIB $65.00

Dragnet Maze, Transogram, 1955, EX (EX box) $50.00

Dukes of Hazzard, Ideal, 1981, EXIB $25.00

Easy Money, Milton Bradley, 1936, EX (EX box) $30.00

Electric Baseball, Electric Game Co, 1940s, EX (EX box).$35.00

Electric Commin' Round the Mountain, Electric Game, 1954, EX (EX box)...$50.00

Electric Disneyland Tours Quiz, Jacmar, 1956, EX (EX box)...$60.00

Eliot Ness & the Untouchables, Transogram, 1961, EX (EX box)...$65.00

Ellsworth Elephant, Selchow & Righter, 1960, EX (EX box) ..$50.00

Elsie & Her Family, Selchow & Righter, 1941, EX (EX box) ..$50.00

Emergency, Milton Bradley, 1973, EXIB $22.00

Family Affair, Where's Mrs Beasley, Whitman, 1971, MIB, from $40 to...$50.00

Family Feud, Milton Bradley, 1984, 7th edition, VG (VG box) $10.00

Family Ties, Applestreet, 1986, EXIB..............................$30.00

Feeley Meeley, Milton Bradley, 1967, EX (EX box).........$30.00

Felix the Cat, target game, Lido, 1960, EX (EX box) $60.00

Fess Parker Target, Transogram, 1965, EX (EX box).........$55.00

Fess Parker Wilderness Trail, card game, Transogram, 1964, EX (EX box) $30.00

Fireball XL5, Milton Bradley, 1964, EX (EX box) $95.00

Flash Gordon Target, 1952, EX (EX box) $150.00

Flea Circus, Mattel, 1964, EX (EX box) $35.00

Flintstones, Milton Bradley, 1971, EX (EX box)...............$25.00

Flintstones Brake Ball, Whitman, 1962, EX (EX box) $85.00

Flintstones Mechanical Shooting Gallery, Marx, 1962, EX (EX box)...$225.00

Flintstones Pitch 'N Bowl, Transogram, 1961, EX (EX box) ..$55.00

Flintstones Stoneage, Transogram, 1961, EXIB $40.00

Flintstones Target Set, Lido, 1962, EX (EX box) $75.00

Flip-It 7-11, Aurora, 1973, EX (EX box)..........................$45.00

Flipper Flips, Mattel, 1965, EX (EX box) $55.00

Flying Nun, Milton Bradley, 1968, NMIB.......................$50.00

Flying the Beam, Parker Bros, EX (VG box), A...............$95.00

Fonz Hanging Out At Arnold's, card game, Milton Bradley, 1976, MIB $20.00

Fortune's Wheel, Parker Bros, 1903, EX (EX box), A $175.00

Frantic Frogs, Milton Bradley, 1965, EX (EX box)...........$30.00

Fugitive, Ideal, 1964, EX (EX box) $125.00

G-Men Clue Games, Whitman, EX (EX box) $85.00

Game of Mail Express or Accommodation, Milton Bradley, 1930s, EX (EX box), A..$200.00

Game of Politics, Parker Bros, 1952, VG (VG box) $40.00

Game of Snow White & the Seven Dwarfs, Milton Bradley/WDE, 1930s, NMIB..................................$100.00

Game of Steeplechase, McLoughlin Bros, 1889, EX (G box), A, $275.00.

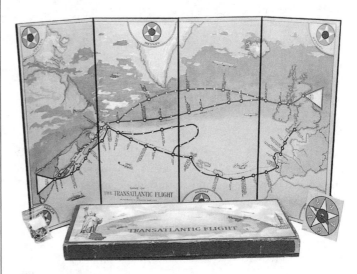

Game of the Transatlantic Flight, 1920s, box: 35" x 20", EX, $300.00. (Photo courtesy Dunbar Gallery)

Gang Busters, Whitman, 1939, EX (EX box), A $75.00

Gang Busters Target, Marx, NM (EX box), A $200.00

Garroway's Game of Possessions, Reco, 1955, EX (EX box)..$45.00

Get Smart Skittle Pool, Aurora, 1972, NM (EX box) $55.00

Giant Cootie, Schaper, 1950s, EX (EX box) $85.00

Gidget, Standard Toykraft, 1965, MIB, from $75 to.......$100.00

Gilligan's Island, Game Gems/T Cohn, 1965, EX (EX box) .$225.00
Gomer Pyle, Transogram, 1964, EX (EX box)....................$50.00
Goofy Finds His Marbles, Whitman, 1970s, EX (EX box) ..$25.00
Great Shakes Charlie Brown, Golden, 1988, MIB...........$12.00
Green Acres, Standard Toykraft, 1965, NMIB, from $100
    to...$125.00
Groucho's TV Quiz, Pressman, 1954, EXIB $75.00
Groucho's You Bet Your Life, Lowell, 1955, EX (EX box)...$95.00
Gulliver's Travels, card game, Paramount Pictures/England,
    1939, NM (VG box)..$75.00
Gunfight at OK Corral, Ideal, 1973, EX (EX box)............$45.00
Gunsmoke Target, Park Plastics, 1958, EX (EX box) $100.00
Gusher, Carrom, 1946, EX (EX box)................................$75.00
Happy Days, Parker Bros, 1976, EX (EX box)..................$20.00
Have Gun Will Travel, Parker Bros, 1959, EXIB $75.00
Hawaiian Eye, Lowell, 1963, EX (EX box)......................$85.00
Hearts, card game, Whitman, 1951, NM (EX box) $10.00
Hi-Ho Santa Claus, Whitman, 1962, EX (EX box)..........$35.00
High Dice, Bettye-B, 1956, EX (EX box)..........................$40.00
High Spirits w/Calvin & the Colonel, Milton Bradley, 1962, EX
    (EX box) $50.00
Hollywood Squares, Ideal, 1974, EX (EX box)................$25.00
Hoopla, Ideal, 1966, EX (EX box)...................................$40.00
Hopalong Cassidy, Milton Bradley, 1950, EX (EX box)....$85.00
Hopalong Cassidy, Milton Bradley, 1950, EX (EX box),
    P3 ....$125.00
Hopalong Cassidy Chinese Checkers, Milton Bradley, 1951, EX
    (EX box) $50.00
Hopalong Cassidy Pony Express Toss, Transogram, 1950, EX (EX
    box)...$100.00

Hopalong Cassidy Stagecoach Toss Game, Transogram/W Boyd, 1950, box: 18" x 25", contains illustrated board (shown on right), pegs and bean bags, complete, NM (EX box), A, $150.00.

Hoppity Hopper, Milton Bradley, 1964, EX (EX box) $45.00
Howdy Doody 3-Ring Circus, Harett-Gilmar, 1950, EX (EX
    box)...$60.00
Howdy Doody's Own Game, Parker Bros, 1949, EX (EX box)...$100.00
Huckleberry Hound Juggle Roll, Transogram, 1960, EX (EX
    box) $60.00
Huckleberry Hound Pop-A-Part Target, Knickerbocker, 1959,
    EX (VG box) $65.00
Huckleberry Hound Slits & Slots, Milton Bradley, 1959, EX (EX
    box)...$30.00
Huckleberry Hound Tumble Race, Transogram, 1961, EX (EX
    box)...$30.00

Hulla Baloo Electric Teen Game, Remco, 1965, rare, NM (EX
    box))...$75.00
Hunt for Red October, 1988, EXIB $30.00
I Dream of Jeannie, Milton Bradley, 1966, MIB, minimum
    value...$75.00

Indian Trail Game, ca 1920s, EX, $250.00. (Photo courtesy Dunbar Gallery)

Ipcress File, Milton Bradley, 1966, EX (EX box)...............$25.00
Ironside, Ideal, 1967, EX (EX box)..................................$95.00
Jack the Giant Killer, Lowell, 1950s, EX (EX box)...........$40.00
James Bond Secret Agent 007, Milton Bradley, 1960s, EX (EX
    box) $30.00
Jeanne Dixon's Game of Destiny, 1969, MIB (sealed) $20.00
Jetsons Fun Pad, Milton Bradley, 1963, EX (EX box).......$75.00
Jingle Dingle's Weather, Lowell, 1954, EX (EX box)........$40.00
Journey to the Unknown, Remco, 1968, EX (EX box).....$95.00
Kate Smith's Own Game America, Toy Creations, 1940s, EX
    (EX box) $50.00
King of the Cheese, Milton Bradley, 1959, EX (EX box)..$40.00

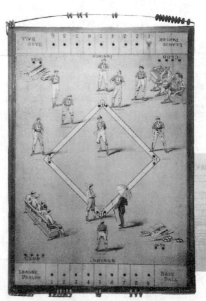

League Parlor Baseball, Bliss, c 1885, paper on wood, EX, A, $1,200.00.

KISS on Tour, EX (EX box), B3 ....$50.00
Knight Rider, Parker Bros, 1983, NM (EX box) $20.00
Knuckle Busters, Hasbro, 1967, EX (EX box) $55.00
Kreskin's ESP, Milton Bradley, EXIB $10.00
Kukla & Ollie, Parker Bros, 1962, EX (EX box) $30.00
Land of the Giants, Ideal, 1968, NM (NM box) $200.00
Land of the Lost, Milton Bradley, 1975, EX (EX box) $25.00
Lavern & Shirley, MIB (sealed)......................................$25.00
Leave It To Beaver Money Maker, Hasbro, 1959, EX (EX box)..$35.00
Let's Face It, Hasbro, 1955, EX (EX box) $30.00
Li'l Abner, Parker Bros, 1969, EX (EX box).....................$35.00
Limbo Legs, Milton Bradley, 1969, EX (EX box) $35.00
Little Orphan Annie Pursuit, Selchow & Righter, 1970s,
    MIB $20.00
Little Orphan Annie Rummy Cards, Whitman, 1937, NM (EX
    box), A..$65.00

Little Rascals Clubhouse Bingo, Gabriel & Sons, 1958, complete, scarce, NM (NM box), $100.00.

Liz Tyler Hollywood Starlet, Ideal, 1963, EX (EX box) $35.00
Lone Ranger & Tonto Spin To Win, Pressman, 1967, EX (EX
    box)..$35.00
Lone Ranger Double Target, Marx, 17", EX (EX box), A ..$200.00
Lone Ranger Horseshoe Set, Gardner, 1950s, NM (EX box),
    A...$165.00
Lone Ranger Target, Marx, 1946, NM (EX box), from $350
    to $400.00
Looney Tunes, Milton Bradley, 1968, EX (EX box) $50.00
Looney Tunes, Milton Bradley, 1968, VG (VG box)........$30.00
Lost Heir, Milton Bradley, 1905, EX (G box) $135.00
Lost in Space 3-D Game, Remco, 1966, EX (EX box) ...$225.00
Love Boat, Ungame, 1980, VG (VG box) $20.00
Lucky Star Gumball, Ideal, 1961, EX (EX box) $45.00
Ludwig Von Drake Cannoneers, Transogram, 1962, EX (EX
    box) $50.00
Ludwig Von Drake Wiggle-Waggle, Transogram, 1962, EX (EX
    box) $40.00
M*A*S*H, Milton Bradley, 1981, MIB $30.00
M*A*S*H Trivia, Golden, 1984, EX (EX box) $15.00
Magilla Gorilla, Ideal, 1964, NMIB $100.00
Magilla Gorilla Bowl & Toss, Ideal, 1964, EX (EX box)...$85.00
Magilla Gorilla Target Barrel, Ideal, 1964, EX (EX box) ..$85.00

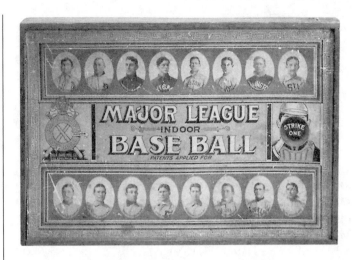

Major League Indoor Base Ball, Philadelphia Game Mfg. Co, oak case with photographs of Wagner, Cobb, and others, considerable wear, A, $1,700.00.

Major Matt Mason Space Exploration, Mattel, 1967, EX (EX
    box) $75.00
Man From UNCLE, target game, Marx, 1966, EX (EX box)..$300.00
Man From UNCLE Thrush Ray-Gun Affair, Ideal, 1965, EX (EX
    box)..$125.00
Marvel Super Heroes Card Game, Milton Bradley, 1978,
    MIB $40.00
Marvel Super Heroes Strategy, Milton Bradley, 1980, EX (EX
    box), T2 ....$35.00
Mary Hartman, Mary Hartman, Reiss, 1977, NM (EX box) ..$40.00
Mary Poppins, Milton Bradley, 1964, EX (EX box) $25.00
Melvin Pervis' G-Men Detective Game, Parker Bros, 1930s,
    NMIB..$175.00
Melvin the Moon Man, Remco, 1959, EX (EX box) $65.00
Men Into Space, Milton Bradley, 1960, EX (EX box).......$75.00
Mentor, Hasbro, 1961, EX (EX box) $40.00
Merry-Go-Round, card game, Milton Bradley, NM (G box),
    A $95.00
Miami Vice, Pepper Lane, 1984, EX (EX box).................$25.00
Mickey Mantle Big 6 Sports, Gardner, 1950s, VG (VG box)..$150.00
Mickey Mouse & Donald Duck Ski Jump Target, Am Toy
    Works/WDE, NM..$200.00
Mickey Mouse Bagatelle, Chad Valley/Mickey Mouse Ltd,
    1930s, EX, from $700 to $800.00
Mickey Mouse Bagatelle, Marx Bros, NM $700.00
Mickey Mouse Canasta Jr, Russell, 1950, EX (EX box) $40.00
Mickey Mouse Circus, Marks Bros, EX (EX box) $650.00
Mickey Mouse Club Game in Disneyland, Whitman, 1956, EX
    (EX box) $65.00
Mickey Mouse Club Tiddley Winks, Whitman, 1963, EX (EX
    box) $15.00
Mickey Mouse Pop Game, Marks Bros, 1930s, EX (EX box)..$650.00
Mickey Mouse Roll 'Em, Marks Bros, NM $600.00
Mickey Mouse Top Hat Target, Transogram, 1963, EX (EX
    box)...$50.00
Mighty Comics Super Hero, Transogram, 1966, EX (EX box)..$125.00
Mighty Hercules, Hasbro, 1963, NMIB $300.00
Mighty Mouse, Parker Bros, 1964, NMIB, T2..................$65.00

Mighty Mouse Presents the Game of Hide 'N Seek, Transogram, 1962, EX (EX box)..$55.00

Mighty Mouse Skill-Roll, Pressman, 1959, EX (EX box) .$65.00

Milton the Monster, Milton Bradley, 1966, NM (EX box) ..$30.00

Mission Impossible, Ideal, 1966, EX (EX box) $75.00

Monday Night Baseball, Aurora, 1973, EX (EX box) $35.00

Monopoly Deluxe, Parker Bros, 1964, EX (EX box) $45.00

Monster Old Maid, Milton Bradley, 1964, EX (EX box) ..$30.00

Monster Squad, Milton Bradley, 1977, NM (EX box) $30.00

Monstermania, Marx, 1977, MIB $30.00

Moon Tag, Parker Bros, 1957, EX (EX box).....................$85.00

Mr Brain, Jacmar, 1959, EX (EX box) $40.00

Mr Doodle's Dog, Selchow & Righter, 1948, EX (EX box)..$40.00

Mr Ed, Parker Bros, 1960s, EXIB..$65.00

Mr Machine, Ideal, 1961, EX (EX box) $75.00

Mr Magoo Visits the Zoo, Lowell, 1961, EX (EX box) $50.00

Murder She Wrote, Warren, VG (VG box)........................$20.00

Mushmouse & Punkin' Puss Feudin' Hillbillies Target, Ideal, 1964, EX (EX box) $125.00

My Favorite Martian, Transogram, 1963, VG (VG box)..$65.00

Mystery Date, Milton Bradley, 1965, EX (EX box).........$125.00

Nancy Drew Mystery, Parker Bros, 1957, EX (EX box) $90.00

New Adventures of Pinocchio, Lowell, 1960, EX (EX box) .$50.00

New Zoo Revue Bagatelle, Wolverine, 1970s, NM, from $50 to..$60.00

Newlywed Game, Hasbro, 1969, NMIB...............................$20.00

Nodding Nancy, Parker Bros, VG (VG box), A $85.00

Official Baseball, Milton Bradley, 1966, EX (EX box) $95.00

OK Telegraph, 1910, EX (VG box), A............................$300.00

Partridge Family, 1971, VG (VG box), N2 ....$35.00

Pathfinder, Milton Bradley, 1977, EX (EX box)...............$20.00

Peanuts Game of Charlie Brown & His Pals, Selchow & Righter, 1960, NMIB, from $45 to $55.00

Pebbles Flintstone Magnetic Fish Pond, Transogram, 1963, EX (EX box) $55.00

Peter Gunn, Lowell, 1965, EX (EX box) $75.00

Peter Pan, Transogram, 1953, EX (EX box) $40.00

Peter Potamus, Ideal, 1964, EX (EX box) $185.00

Peter Potamus Target Barrel, Ideal, 1964, EX (EX box)....$85.00

Peter Rabbit, Gabriel, 1946, EX (EX box) $75.00

Phantom of the Opera Mystery, Hasbro, 1963, EX (EX box)...$225.00

Pin the Nose on Pinocchio, Parker Bros, 1939, EX (EX box).$250.00

Pin the Tail on Mickey, Marks Bros, 1935, VG $100.00

Pink Panther, Milton Bradley, 1969, EX (EX box), N2 ....$50.00

Pinky Lee & the Runaway Frankfurters, Whiting, 1954, EX (EX box)..$60.00

Pirate Plunder, All-Fair, VG (VG box) $50.00

Pirates of the Caribbean, Parker Bros, 1967, EX (EX box)..$25.00

Pitfalls, A Pinocchio Marble Game, Whitman, 1940, EX (EX box)...$125.00

Planet of the Apes, Milton Bradley, 1974, MIB................$45.00

Poison Ivy, Ideal, 1969, VG (VG box)...............................$40.00

Pop-Za-Ball Target, Mattel, 1961, EX (EX box) $40.00

Popeye, card game, Whitman, 1937, EX (EX box), A $65.00

Popeye & His Pals, Ideal, 1963, EX (EX box)...................$50.00

Popeye Ball Toss, Transogram, 1966, EX (EX box) $65.00

Popeye Menu Bagatelle, Durable Toy & Novelty, 23", NM $350.00

Our Gang Tipple-Topple Game, All-Fair, c 1930, EX (EX box), A, $400.00. (Photo courtesy Buffalo Bay)

Outlaws, Transogram, 1961, EX (EX box)..........................$65.00

Overland Trail, Transogram, 1960, EXIB $65.00

Pac-Man, Milton Bradley, 1982, NMIB $15.00

Pan-American, Parker Bros, 1901, G (G box), F3.........$650.00

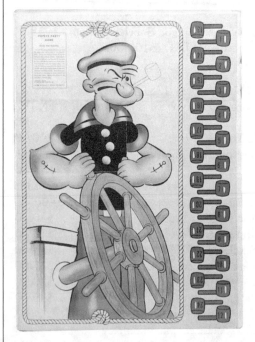

Popeye Party Game, uncut, 27" x 19", $75.00. (Photo courtesy Dunbar Gallery)

Popeye Pipe Toss, Rosebud Art, 1930s, EX (EX box) $60.00

Popeye Sliding Boards & Ladders, Built-Rite, 1958, EX (EX box)...$50.00

Popeye 3-Game Set for Boys & Girls, Built-Rite, 1956, EX (EX box)...$65.00

Prince Valiant, Transogram, 1955, EX (EX box)...............$45.00

Prince Valiant Crossbow Pistol, target game, Parva, 1948, EX (EX box), A $100.00

Pro League Basketball, Gotham, 1958, EX (EX box)........$75.00

Pro-Football, Milton Bradley, 1964, VG (VG box) $45.00

Psychic Base Ball Game, Parker Bros, 1935, EX, $300.00.
(Photo courtesy Dunbar Gallery)

PT Boat 109, Ideal, 1963, VG (G box) $35.00

Put the Tail on Ferdinand the Bull, Whitman/WDE, 1938, VG $125.00

Raggedy Ann, Milton Bradley, 1954, EX (EX box) $35.00

Raggedy Ann, Milton Bradley, 1974, EX (EX box) $20.00

Ramar of the Jungle Blow Gun Target, Gabriel, 1955, EX (EX box)..$85.00

Ramar of the Jungle Blow Gun Target, Gabriel Toys, 1955, NM $125.00

Rat Patrol Desert Combat, Transogram, 1966, NM (EX box) $125.00

Rawhide, Lowell, 1960, EX (EX box)..............................$85.00

Red Riding Hood w/Big Bad Wolf & Three Little Pigs, Parker Bros, 1930s, EX (EX box) $150.00

Red Ryder Pop-Um Shooting, target game, Daisy, 1950, EX (EX box), A...$200.00

Red Skelton's I Dood It, Zondine, 1947, EX (EX box) $85.00

Reddy-Clown 3-Ring Circus, Parker Bros, 1952, EX (EX box) $40.00

Rex Mars Space Target, Marx, 1950s, EX (EX box) $125.00

Ride the Surf, 1963, EX (EX box) $65.00

Rin-Tin-Tin, Transogram, EX (G box)..............................$25.00

Robinson Crusoe, Lowell, 1961, EX (EX box) $50.00

Rockets to the Moon Marble Game, Wolverine, EX (EX box), H8 ....$175.00

Rocky & His Friends, Milton Bradley, 1960, EX (EX box) ..$65.00

Rose-Petal Place, Parker Bros, 1984, NM (EX box) $25.00

Rosey the Robot, Transogram, 1962, EX (EX box)...........$85.00

Round the World, Milton Bradley, 1920, few pcs missing, EX (worn box)..$100.00

Ruff & Reddy at the Circus, Transogram, 1962, EX (EX box) $50.00

Sam Snead Tee Off, 1973, VG (VG box), A $35.00

Scooby Doo Where Are You?, Milton Bradley, 1973, EXIB..$30.00

Sea Hunt, Lowell, 1961, EX (EX box) $65.00

Seven Seas, Cadaco, 1960, EX (EX box) $35.00

Shari Lewis in Shariland, Transogram, 1959, EX (EX box)...$50.00

Sharpshooter, Cadaco, 1965, EX (EX box) $65.00

Shenanigans, Milton Bradley, 1964, EX (EX box)............$50.00

Sheriff of Dodge City, Parker Bros, 1966, EX (EX box), N2..$25.00

Sherlock Holmes' Murder on the Orient Express, Ideal, 1967, EX (EX box)..$50.00

Shooting Gallery, Wyandotte, 1940s, EX (EX box), A...$150.00

Show-Biz Game of the Stars, Lowell, 1956, EX (EX box)...$65.00

Silly Safari, Topper, 1966, EX (EX box) $50.00

Singing Bone, Hasbro, 1964, EX (EX box) $45.00

Sinking the Titantic, Ideal, 1976, EXIB $45.00

Six Million Dollar Man Bionic Crisis, card game, Parker Bros, 1976, MIB $20.00

Slap Trap, Ideal, 1967, EX (EX box) $30.00

Sleeping Beauty, Parker Bros, 1952, EX (EX box) $50.00

Smokey the Forest Fire Preventin' Bear, Ideal, 1961, EX (EX box) $45.00

Snagglepuss, Transogram, 1961, EX (EX box)..................$40.00

Snoopy, card game, Ideal, 1965, NM (EX box).................$25.00

Snoopy & His Pals Play Hockey, Determined/Munro Games, 1972, MIB, from $150 to $175.00

Snoopy & the Red Baron, Milton Bradley, 1970, EX (EX box) $35.00

Snoopy & the Red Baron, Milton Bradley, 1970, MIB.....$40.00

Snoopy Come Home, Milton Bradley, 1972, NMIB.........$20.00

Snoopy Dodgem, Parker Bros, 1970s, NMIB, from $35 to.$45.00

Snoopy Snack Attack, Gabriel, 1980, MIB.......................$25.00

Snoopy's Game of Tiddlywinks, Milton Bradley, 1980s, NMIB $10.00

Snow White & the Seven Dwarfs, card game, Pepys Games of London, 1930s, NMIB..$150.00

Snow White & the Seven Dwarfs, Parker Bros, 1938, EX (EX box)..$150.00

Snuffy Smith Time's a Wastin', Milton Bradley, 1963, EX (EX box) $35.00

Space Age, Parker Bros, 1953, EX (EX box) $75.00

Space Pilot, Cadaco, 1951, EXIB $75.00

Statue of Liberty Airplane Game, Bing, Germany, clockwork mechanism housed in airplane, 22" overall length, pristine, A, $3,400.00.

Space: 1999, Milton Bradley, 1976, VG (VG box)...........$30.00

Spider-Man, Milton Bradley, 1967, EX (EX box) $50.00

Spider-Man Web Spinning Action, Ideal, 1979, MIB (sealed) $125.00

Square Mile, Milton Bradley, 1962, EX (EX box)............$45.00

Starsky & Hutch Detective, Milton Bradley, 1976, MIB..$30.00

Starsky & Hutch Official Police Target Range, Arco, 1977, MIB, from $100 to $125.00

Starsky & Hutch Shoot-Out Target, Berwick, 1977, MIB, from $100 to...$125.00

Steve Canyon, Lowell, 1959, EX (EX box), T2 ....$60.00

Stingray Underwater Maze, Transogram, 1966, EX (EX box) ..$150.00

Stock Exchange, Milton Bradley, 1964, EX (EX box) $50.00

Sub Attack, Milton Bradley, 1965, EX (EX box) $35.00

Sunny Fox Fact Finder, Milton Bradley, 1962, EX (EX box) ...$30.00

Super Crow Shoot, Jaymar, 1958, EX (EX box) $40.00

Superman, card game, Whitman, 1966, NM (EX box) $50.00

Superman, Merry Mfg, 1965, NM (EX box), T2 ....$100.00

Superman Marble Maze, Hasbro, 1966, EX (EX box).......$75.00

Superman Match II, Ideal, 1978, MIB..............................$85.00

Surfside 6, Lowell, 1962, EX (EX box) $65.00

Sword in the Stone, Parker Bros, 1963, EX (EX box).......$30.00

Taffy's Baubles & Bangles, Transogram, 1966, EX (EX box)...$20.00

Talking Football, Mattel, 1971, EX (EX box) $100.00

Tarzan to the Rescue, Milton Bradley, 1977, NM (EX box)...$20.00

Tennesee Tuxedo, Transogram, 1963, EX (EX box)........$135.00

That Girl, Remco, 1969, EXIB...$70.00

Three Keys to Treasure Bagatelle, Marx, 1960, EX (EX box) ..$65.00

Three Little Pigs, card game, Russell, 1946, EX (EX box)...$20.00

Three Little Pigs, Einson-Freeman, 1930s, board only, EX...$65.00

Thunderball, Milton Bradley, 1965, EX (EX box) $50.00

Thunderbirds, Waddington, 1965, EX (EX box)...............$65.00

Tic-Tac Dough, Transogram, 1956, EX (EX box)..............$40.00

Tim Holt 2 Dart Games in 1, American Toy, 1949, NM (NM box), A...$225.00

Tin Can Alley, Ideal, 1976, EXIB....................................$50.00

Tiny Tim Game of Beautiful Things, Parker Bros, 1970, rare, EX (EX box) $75.00

To Tell the Truth, Lowell, 1957, EX (EX box) $40.00

Tom & Jerry, Parker Bros, 1948, EX (EX box) $50.00

Tom & Jerry Adventures in Blunderland, Transogram, 1965, EX (EX box) $40.00

Tom Mix Shooting Gallery, Parker Bros, 1930s, EX (EX box), A..$250.00

Top Cop, Cadaco, 1961, NM (NM box)..........................$45.00

Top Secret, National Games, 1956, EX (EX box)............$65.00

Toy Town, Milton Bradley, 1962, EX (EX box)...............$50.00

Tradewinds, Parker Bros, 1960, VG (VG box).................$75.00

Trapped, Bettye-B, 1956, EX (EX box) $40.00

Travels of Jamie McPheeters, Ideal, 1963, EX (EX box)...$45.00

Treasure Island, Harett-Gilmar, 1955, EX (EX box) $45.00

Truth or Consequences, Gabriel, 1955, EXIB $35.00

Twiggy, Milton Bradley, 1967, M (NM box), $50.00.
(Photo courtesy Cindy Sabulis)

Untouchables, target game, Marx, 1960, EX (EX box) ..$200.00

Virginian, Transogram, 1962, EX (EX box)......................$85.00

Voice of the Mummy, Milton Bradley, 1971, EX (EX box)....$150.00

Wagon Train, Milton Bradley, 1960, EX (EX box), from $35 to $50.00

Walt Disney's Adventureland, Parker Bros, 1956, EX (EX box)..$40.00

Walt Disney's Fantasyland, Parker Bros, 1950s, MIB........$50.00

Walt Disney's Tiddly Winks, Whitman, 1963, NMIB.......$10.00

Wanted Dead or Alive, Lowell, 1959, EXIB $75.00

Wanted Dead or Alive Target, Marx, 1959, EX (EX box)...$250.00

Wanted Dead or Alive Target, Marx, 1959, NM (G box), A ..$300.00

West Point Story, Transogram, 1961, EX (EX box) $50.00

Who's Afraid of the Big Bad Wolf, Marks Bros, board only, EX $65.00

Wide World Travel Game, Parker Bros, 1957, NMIB.......$35.00

Wild Bill Hickok & Jingles Pony Express, Built-Rite, 1956, EX (EX box) $50.00

Wild Bill Hickok & Jingles Pony Express, Built-Rite, 1958, NM (EX box), A $45.00

Wild Bill Hickok's Cavalry & the Indians, Built-Rite, 1958, NM (EX box), A $45.00

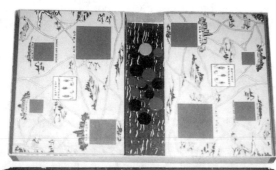

Tiddly Winks Barrage Game, Corey, c WWII, EX, $90.00.
(Photo courtesy Paul Fink)

Win, Place & Show, Milton Bradley, 1949, EX (EX box) ...$40.00

Winnie the Pooh Honey Tree, Ideal, 1966, EX (EX box) ...$40.00

Wolfman Mystery, Hasbro, 1963, EX (EX box) $150.00

Woody Owl's Give a Hoot, Whitman, 1976, NMIB........$40.00

Woody Woodpecker Ring Toss Game, 1958, MIB.........$100.00

Word of Word, Mattel, 1963, VG (VG box) $20.00

World's Fair, Milton Bradley, 1964, EX (EX box) $40.00

Wyatt Earp, Transogram, 1958, EX (EX box)....................$50.00

Yogi Bear & Huckleberry Hound Bowling Set, Transogram, 1960, EX (EX box)..$50.00

Yogi Bear Score-A-Matic Ball Toss, Transogram, EX (EX box) $65.00

You Don't Say, Milton Bradley, 1963, EXIB....................$20.00

Zorro, Whitman, 1965, NMIB.......................................$50.00

77 Sunset Strip, Lowell, 1960, NM (EX box) $50.00

Gasoline-Powered Toys

Two of the largest companies to manufacture gas-powered models are Cox and Wen-Mac. Since the late '50s they have been making faithfully detailed models of airplanes as well as some automobiles and boats. Condition of used models will vary greatly because of the nature of the miniature gas engine and damage resulting from the fuel that has been used. Because of this, 'new in box' gas toys command a premium.

Advisor: Richard Trautwein (T3).

Braemer Whirlwind #2, gr & wht, 1939, 18", NM $2,900.00

Bremer, Whirlwind Racer #8, louvered hood & belly pan, ca 1940, 18", EX..$2,300.00

Cameron Racer #4, red w/yel flame decals, 8", VG, A ...$275.00

Cessna UC 78 Bobcat (WWII era Bamboo Bomber), w/pilot, co-pilot & 2 passengers, 42x57½" W, EX $475.00

Cox AA Fuel Dragster, bl & red, 1968-70, M...............$125.00

Cox Baja Bug, yel & orange, 1968-73, M.........................$65.00

Cox Chopper, MIB $100.00

Cox E-Z Flyer Commanche, wht, NMIB $35.00

Cox Golden Bee, .49 engine, M......................................$30.00

Cox ME-109 Airplane, 1994, MIB (sealed).....................$100.00

Cox Mercedes Benz W196 Racer, red, 1963-65, EX $85.00

Cox Navy Helldiver, 2-tone bl, 1963-66, EX, from $65 to..$80.00

Cox P-51 Bendix Racer, red & yel, molded landing gear, 1963-64, EX, from $65 to..$80.00

Cox Pitts Special Biplane, wht, .20 engine, 1968, EX $50.00

Cox PT-19 Flight Trainer, yel & bl, EX............................$45.00

Cox RAF Spitfire, dk gr w/camouflage, 1966-69, EX, from $40 to..$50.00

Cox Ryan ST-3, w/pilot & co-pilot, wht & bl, .20 ignition power, M $65.00

Cox Sandblaster, brn & tan, 1968-72, M..........................$65.00

Cox Sky Raider, gray, EX (EX box) $85.00

Cox Skymaster, Sure Flyer Series, orange w/blk stickers, twin tail, 1976-79, EX...$50.00

Cox Snowmobile, silver, 1968, M $100.00

Cox Stealth Bomber, blk, 1987-89, EX $30.00

Cox Super Sabre F-100, wht or gray, .20 engine, 1958-63, EX, ea from $60 to...$80.00

Cox Super Stunter, 1974-79, EX, from $30 to $45.00

Cox Thimble Drome Comanche, metal w/plastic wings, .15 engine, 1960s, MIB..$75.00

Cox Thimble Drome Prop-Rod, yel & red, 12", EX (worn box), A $200.00

Cox Thimble Drome Prop-Rod, yel plastic w/metal chassis, EX, from $85 to $130.00

Cox Thunderbolt, E-Z Flyer Series, blk, w/muffler, 1993-95, M...$30.00

Cox UFO Flying Saucer, Wings Series, wht, 1990-91, M .$25.00

Curtiss Jenny WWI-era Plane, silk covered, 65" wingspan, 58" long, EX, A, $400.00.

Curtiss P-40D Tiger Shark, Comet Model Hobby Craft, Inc, plastic, 13½", MIB, from $95 to..............................$135.00

Dooling Bros F Racer, bl, cast magnesium body w/orig upper & lower hammertone finish, 1948, 16", EX.............$1,100.00

Dooling Bros F Series Racer #3, red, no engine, 1948, 16", EX...$1,000.00

Dooling Bros Frog Cabin Streamliner, cast aluminum, Super Cyclone engine, 1939, 16", EX, from $2,600 to ...$3,200.00

Dooling Bros Mercury Racer #59, aluminum w/some pnt detail, Hornet engine, ca 1940, 18½", VG, from $1,800 to .$2,300.00

Dooling Bros Racer #1, red flat-tail model w/Knoxville Champ logo, 19", EX...$850.00

Dooling Bros Racer #4, orange, articulated front end, McCoy engine, rstr, EX...$1,500.00

Dooling Bros Racer #5, red, 16", EX, A $950.00

Dooling Bros Racer #8, Atwood .60 Champion engine, 1939, 19", EX, from $1,500 to.......................................$1,800.00

Dreyer Special Racer #2, silver w/red seat, 18", NM, from $2,600 to..$2,800.00

England Special Racer #8, gr-pnt aluminum w/leather seats, centrifical clutch, ca 1948, 16", EX $825.00

Fairchild 22 Model Airplane, bl & cream, working shock absorbers in landing gear, 47" W, NM, A.................$300.00

Hiller-Comet #5, red, 1942, 19", EX..........................$1,800.00

Hot Rod Roadster, red, Hornet .60 engine, 15", EX....$1,200.00

McCoy Invader #41, red w/Ed Dowd's racing #300C, White Case .60 engine w/magneto, 1949, 18", EX $800.00

McCoy Invader #6, yel, McCoy .49 engine, 17", EX $800.00

McCoy Streamliner, gray, never drilled for engine, 17", NM...$475.00

Melcraft Racer, wht w/Champion tires, ignition engine, ca 1948, 16", EX...$475.00

Hiller T - Betz/Edmunds #19, Hiller .60 power, built by Butch Marx with Voit wheels and tires, 20", EX, A, $1,800.00; Salt Flats Hot Rod #1, cast aluminum, builder unknown, 19", EX, A, $650.00; So-Cal Bonneville Racer, by Randy Giovenale, Hornet .60 ignition engine, 16", EX, A, $2,600.00.

Miracle Power Special Racer #1, yel & blk w/red detail, Dooling engine, 17", EX..$1,600.00
Railton Champion Racer #12, red & yel, 17", NM, D10 ...$2,700.00
Reuhl Racer #39, Bakelite body, grille & seat, .49 McCoy engine, 1940, 17", EX..$2,200.00
Reuhl Racer #9, blk, McCoy White .60 engine, 1940, 17", EX...$2,000.00
Speed Demon #18, yel-pnt wood, Bunch .60 engine, 1937-38, 20", EX (EX box)..$5,700.00
Speedboat #37, orange-pnt wood, Apex Skylark engine, ca 1939, 37", EX...$1,400.00
Spit-Craft Speedboat, plastic, Royal Spitfire engine, 21", NMIB..$200.00
Testors Cosmic Wind, Spirit of '76, M $60.00
Testors OD P-51 Mustang, VG...$30.00
Testors Racer, wht Indy-style racer, w/driver, 1960s, MIB, A $185.00
Testors Sopwith Camel, Fly 'Em Series, NM.....................$35.00
Testors Sprite Indy Car, wht, 1966-68, M, from $75 to ..$100.00

Thimble Drome, solid rubber tires, Ray Co., Santa Ana, CA, minor paint loss, 8½", A, $200.00.

Wen-Mac '57 Chevy Racer, orange plastic w/decals, 12", VG...$160.00
Wen-Mac Aeromite, blk, Baby Spitfire engine, EX..........$60.00

Wen-Mac Albatross, Flying Wing Series, red, wht & bl, EX..$40.00
Wen-Mac Basic Trainer, red, bl, yel & blk w/chrome detail, 1962-64, EX $50.00
Wen-Mac Cutlass, bl, blk, & yel, 1958-60, EX $50.00
Wen-Mac Falcon, red, wht, & bl, 1963-64, EX................$45.00
Wen-Mac Giant P-40 Flying Tiger, wht, 1959-60, EX......$45.00
Wen-Mac Marine Corsair, red, ca 1960s, EX $40.00
Wen-Mac P-63 King Cobra, chrome, 1962-64, EX..........$50.00
Wen-Mac RAF Day Fighter, wht, 1963-64, EX $50.00
Wen-Mac SBD-5 Navy Dive Bomber, 1962-64, EX $50.00
Wen-Mac Turbojet, red & cream w/chrome detail, 1958-64, EX..$45.00
Wen-Mac Yellow Jacket Corsair, yel, 1959-64, EX $40.00

Woodette Tornado Racer, metal with rubber wheels; engineered and manufactured by Winzeler Mfg. & Tool Co., powered by Mot-Airette, 13", EX, A, $400.00.

GI Joe

GI Joe, the most famous action figure of them all, has been made in hundreds of variations since Hasbro introduced him in 1964. The first of these jointed figures was 12" tall; they can be identified today by the mark each carried on his back: GI Joe T.M. (trademark), Copyright 1964. They came with four different hair colors: blond, auburn, black, and brown, each with a scar on his right cheek. They were sold in four basic packages: Action Soldier, Action Sailor, Action Marine, and Action Pilot. A Black figure was also included in the line, and there were representatives of many nations as well — France, Germany, Japan, Russia, etc. These figures did not have scars and are more valuable. Talking GI Joes were issued in 1967 when the only female (the nurse) was introduced. Besides the figures, uniforms, vehicles, guns, and accessories of many varieties were produced. The Adventure Team series, made from 1970 to 1976, included Black Adventurer, Air Adventurer, Talking Astronaut, Sea Adventurer, Talking Team Commander, Land Adventurer, and several variations. Joe's hard plastic hands were replaced with kung fu grips, so that he could better grasp his weapons. Assorted playsets allowed young imaginations to run wild, and besides the doll-size items, there were wristwatches, foot lockers, toys, walkie-talkies, etc.

made for the kids themselves. Due to increased production costs, the large GI Joe was discontinued in 1976.

In 1982, Hasbro brought out the 'little' 3¾" GI Joe figures, each with its own descriptive name. Of the first series, some characters were produced with either a swivel or straight arm. Vehicles, weapons, and playsets were available, and some characters could only be had by redeeming flag points from the backs of packages. This small version proved to be the most successful action figure line ever made. Loose items are common; collectors value those still mint in the original packages at two to four times higher.

In 1993 Hasbro reintroduced the 12" line while retaining the 3¾" size. The highlights of the comeback are the thirtieth anniversary collection of six figures which are already selling in the collectors' market at well above retail ($29.00): Soldier, $100.00. Sailor, $125.00; Marine, $80.00; Pilot, $100.00; Black Soldier, $250.00; and Green Beret, $285.00.

Production of the 3¾" figures came to an end in December 1994. For more information we recommend *Collectible Male Action Figures* by Paris and Susan Manos (Collector Books); *Encyclopedia to GI Joe* and *The 30th Anniversary Salute to GI Joe* both by Vincent San Telmo; *Official Collector's Guide to Collecting and Completing, Official Guide to Completing 3¾" Series and Hall of Fame: Vol II,* and *Official Guide to GI Joe: '64 – '78,* all by James DeSimone. Note: All items are American issue unless indicated otherwise. (Action Man was made in England by Hasbro circa 1960 into the 1970s.)

Advisor: Cotswold Collectibles (C6).

Other Sources: D4, D8, J2, M15, T2.

See also Games; Lunch Boxes; Puzzles; Windups, Friction, and Other Mechanicals.

Key: A/M — Action Man

12" GI JOE FIGURES AND FIGURE SETS

Action Soldier, black hair, complete, EX (EX box), $300.00. (Photo courtesy McMaster's Doll Auctions)

Action Marine, complete, EX (G box), C6	$175.00
Action Marine, complete, MIB	$325.00
Action Marine, 30th Anniversary, 1994, NRFB	$80.00
Action Marine Dress Parade Set, #7710, complete, NMIB	$250.00
Action Marine Medic Set, #7719, complete, NMIB	$225.00
Action Pilot, complete, NM (EX+ box), C6	$400.00
Action Pilot, 30th Anniversary, 1994, NRFB	$100.00
Action Sailor, complete, VG (VG box), C6	$365.00
Action Sailor, 30th Anniversary, 1994, NRFB	$125.00
Action Soldier, 30th Anniversary, 1994, NRFB	$100.00
Adventure Team Aerial Recon, complete, EX, C6	$175.00
Adventure Team Air Adventurer, complete, EX, C6	$150.00
Adventure Team Air Adventurer, complete, NM (EX box), C6	$325.00
Adventure Team Black Adventurer, complete, NM (VG box), C6	$325.00
Adventure Team Eagle Eye Land Commander, moving eyes, MIP	$100.00
Adventure Team Land Adventurer, complete, EX (VG box), C6	$250.00
Adventure Team Man of Action, complete, VG (G box), C6	$200.00
Adventure Team Man of Action, orig outfit, no beard, EX	$150.00
Adventure Team Mike Power Atomic Man, MIP	$150.00
Adventure Team Sea Adventurer, complete, EX (VG box), C6	$250.00
Adventure Team Secret Mission to Spy Island, complete, EX, C6	$185.00
Adventure Team Smoke Jumper, complete, EX, C6	$175.00
Adventure Team Talking Astronaut, complete, EX (worn box), C6	$350.00
Adventure Team Talking Astronaut, complete, VG (VG repro box), C6	$300.00

Adventure Team Talking Commander, EX (VG box), $300.00. (Photo courtesy McMaster's Doll Auctions)

Air Cadet, complete, M	$550.00
American Revolution Minuteman, mail-in, MIB	$30.00

Annapolis Cadet, EX, C6 ....$435.00
Atomic Man, complete, NM $100.00
Australian Jungle Fighter, complete, EX, C6 ....$265.00
Australian Jungle Fighter, complete, NM $500.00
Black Action Soldier, complete, M $900.00
British Commando, complete, EX, C6 ....$400.00
Bullet Man, complete, NM $300.00
Canadian Mountie, A/M, complete, M $500.00
Combat Construction, complete, EX, C6 ....$450.00
Combat Engineer, complete, M $950.00
Construction Jack Hammer, complete, M $850.00
Crash Crew Fire Fighter, complete, NM $475.00
Danger of the Depths, complete, M $500.00
Deep Sea Diver, complete, NM, C6 ....$400.00
Fantastic Freefall, complete, NM $500.00
Fight for Survival w/Polar Explorer, complete, NMIB....$325.00
Fighter Pilot, complete, EX, C6 ....$425.00
German Stormtrooper, complete, VG, C6 ....$350.00
German Tanker, A/M, complete, M $425.00
Green Beret, complete, EX, C6 ....$250.00
Green Beret, complete, M $500.00
Hidden Missile Discover w/Spaceman, complete, NMIB ..$200.00
Hurricane Spotter, complete, NM $375.00
Japanese Imperial Soldier, complete, NM $400.00

Man of Action, Kung Fu hands, complete, MIB, $325.00.
(Photo courtesy Joseph Bourgeois)

Police State Trooper, complete, M $1,500.00
Red Devil, A/M, complete, M $500.00
Rescue Diver, complete, M $850.00
Royal Canadian Mounted Police, complete, NM, C6 ....$750.00
Russian Infantry Man, complete, MIB $2,700.00

Land Adventurer, hard hands, complete, EX (EX box), $265.00.
(Photo courtesy McMaster's Doll Auctions)

Landing Signal Officer, complete, M $475.00
Marine Beachhead Assault, complete, EX, C6 ....$250.00
Marine Demolition, complete, NM, C6 ....$300.00
Marine Jungle Fighter, complete, M $950.00
Marine Medic, complete, NM, C6 ....$325.00
Military Police, complete, M $500.00
Mountain Troops, complete, VG $165.00
Mouth of Doom w/Jungle Explorer, complete, NMIB $275.00
Navy Attack, rare version w/yel life jacket, complete, NM .$800.00

Sea Adventurer, hard hands, complete, EX (EX box), $265.00. (Photo courtesy Joseph Bourgeois)

Russian Soldier, complete, NM $550.00
SAS Underwater Attack, A/M, complete, NM.............$425.00
Scramble Pilot, complete, EX, C6.........................$350.00
Scramble Pilot, complete, NM $600.00
Secret Mission to Spy Island, mail-in, MIB.....................$40.00
Smoke Jumper, complete, M.................................$375.00
State Trooper, complete, EX, C6...........................$390.00
Talking Action Pilot, complete, M $650.00
Talking Action Sailor, complete, M $600.00
Tank Commander, complete, EX, C6.......................$525.00
Tank Commander, complete, M..............................$850.00
Underwater Explorer, A/M, complete, NM $425.00
West Point Cadet, complete, EX, C6.......................$265.00
World War I Aviator Ace, mail-in, MIB.........................$60.00

Accessories for 12" GI Joe

.45 Handgun, A/M, EX, C6 ....$5.00
Action Marine Communications Post Poncho Set, #7701,
    MIP $175.00
Adventure Team Aerial Recon, MIP $50.00
Adventure Team Crocodile, EX, C6 ....$15.00
Adventure Team Danger Ray Detection, MIP.................$75.00
Adventure Team Diving Helmet, EX, C6 ....$14.00
Adventure Team Emergency Rescue, MIP.....................$60.00

Adventure Team Flying Rescue Action Pack, MIB, $65.00.

Adventure Team Face Mask, red, EX, C6 ....$20.00
Adventure Team Flight Suit, orange, EX, C6 ....$25.00
Adventure Team Headquarters, complete, EX (worn box), C6 .$275.00
Adventure Team High Voltage Escape, MIP....................$50.00
Adventure Team Jettison to Safety, MIP.......................$75.00
Adventure Team Jumpsuit, mesh, EX, C6.......................$12.00
Adventure Team Snow Shoes, EX, C6............................$15.00
Adventure Team Training Tower, complete, EX.............$125.00
Adventure Team Volcano Jumper, MIP $50.00
Adventure Team White Tiger Hunt, complete, M (G box),
    C6 ....$225.00

Air Force Dress Tunic, VG, C6 ....$25.00
Air Force Dress Uniform, #7803, M (EX box) $1,450.00
Army Flag, EX, C6...$45.00
Astronaut Booties, EX, C6 ....$15.00
Astronaut Helmet, w/microphone & visor, EX, C6 ....$30.00
Binoculars, red, w/string, EX, C6..........................$14.00
British Helmet, EX, C6.....................................$18.00
Combat Field Jacket Set, #7501, MIP......................$100.00
Combat Field Pack, #7502, MIP $100.00
Communications Flag Set, #7704, complete, NM..........$125.00
Crash Crew Jacket, silver, EX, C6.........................$28.00
Deck Commander Set, #7621, MIP $125.00
Eight Ropes of Danger Underwater Diver Playset,
    MIB $200.00
Frogman Underwater Demolition Set, #7602, MIP........$175.00
Grenade Launcher, A/M, EX, C6 ....$15.00
Hidden Missile Discovery, complete, EX, C6................$225.00
Hunting Rifle, A/M, C6 ....$10.00
Ice Pick, A/M, EX, C6 ....$5.00
Japanese Helmet, EX, C6...................................$28.00
Life Guards Shoulder Pouch, A/M, EX, C6 ....$45.00
Marine Dress Parade Set, #7710, MIP.......................$175.00
Marine Medic Set, MIP.....................................$150.00

Military Police Set, #7521, MIB, from $1,000.00 to $1,200.00.

Mine Detector & Harness, VG, C6...........................$50.00
Navy Flag, EX, C6..$45.00
Rocket Firing Bazooka, MIP $70.00
Royal Canadian Mounted Police, #7910, M (EX pkg) ...$400.00
Russian Belt, A/M, EX, C6 ....$12.00
Russian Medal, A/M, EX, C6 ....$10.00
Russian Tunic, A/M, EX, C6 ....$35.00
Scramble Crash Helmet, #7810, MIP.........................$50.00
Scramble Parachute Pack, #7811, MIP $45.00

Scramble Pilot Jumper, EX, C6...........................$80.00
Scuba Top, A/M, EX, C6 ....$12.00
Snow Troops, complete, EX, C6.........................$200.00
Stretcher, wht, VG..$50.00
USAF Flag, EX, C6..$45.00

VEHICLES FOR 12" GI JOE

Action Pack Turbo Copter, MIB (sealed) $50.00
Adventure Team Avenger Pursuit Craft, M (VG box)....$125.00
Adventure Team Big Trapper, EX.................................$60.00
Adventure Team Helicopter, EX (worn box), C6...........$175.00
Adventure Team Sandstorm Jeep, gr, EX (EX box) $275.00
Adventure Team Sea Sled, bl, complete, EX, C6.............$75.00
Adventure Team Sea Wolf, M......................................$100.00
Adventure Team Turbo Swamp Craft, MIB...................$175.00
Adventure Team Underwater Explorer, EX $75.00
Amphibian Duck, M...$300.00
Blue Panther Navy Jet, complete, rare, M $600.00
British armored Car, Irwin, EX....................................$275.00
Carrier/Mine Sweeper, M $250.00
Desert Patrol Jeep w/.50 Caliber Machine Gun, #8030, M..$200.00

Devil of the Deep Set with Turbo Swamp Craft, 1974 – 75, MIB, $195.00.

Fire Engine, A/M, MIP $75.00
Five Star Jeep w/Trailer & Tripod, #7000, complete, NM...$200.00
Iron Knight Tank, EX, C6 ....$135.00
Jet Helicopter, complete, EX (EX box) $400.00
Official Jeep Combat Set, complete, EX (EX box) $425.00
Space Capsule, Sears Exclusive, complete, MIB.............$400.00
Team Vehicle, yel ATV, VG $55.00

3¾" GI JOE FIGURES

Ace, 1983, MIP..$25.00
Ace, 1983, w/accessories, NM $12.00
Aero-Viper, 1989, w/accessories, NM.....................$10.00
Airtight, 1985, w/accessories, EX $12.00

Alpine, 1985, complete, M, $5.00. (Photo courtesy Myla Perkins)

Annihilator, 1989, NMOC.................................$20.00
Annihilator, 1989, w/accessories, EX $10.00
Armadillo, 1988, w/accessories, NM $14.00
Astro Viper, 1988, NMOC.................................$24.00
AVAC, 1985, w/accessories, EX...........................$8.00
Backblast, 1988, NMOC $20.00
Barbecue, 1983-85, complete, EX........................$15.00
Barbecue, 1985, EX (EX card) $50.00
Baroness, 1984, EX (EX card) $200.00
Baroness, 1984, w/accessories, EX $45.00
Barricade, w/accessories, NM..............................$14.00
BAT, 1986, Canadian, NMOC (unpunched) $30.00
BAT, 1990, NMOC..$15.00

Bullet-Proof, 1992, complete, M, $7.00. (Photo courtesy Myla Perkins)

Bazooka, w/accessories, NM.................................$14.00
Bazooka, 1985, w/accessories, EX $10.00
Big Boa, 1987, NMOC $30.00
Blaster, 1987, w/accessories, NM $8.00
Blizzard, 1988, NMOC $18.00
Blocker, 1987, w/accessories, NM $8.00
Blocker, 1988, EX (EX card)...............................$45.00
Breaker, 1982, straight arm, VG (VG card) $85.00
Breaker, 1983, swivel-arm, EX (EX card) $85.00
Budo, 1988, EX (EX card) $20.00
Bullhorn, 1988, w/accessories, EX (EX card) $18.00
Buzzer, 1984, w/accessories, EX............................$8.00
Buzzer, 1985, MIP...$35.00
Charbroil, 1988, red eyes, MOC...........................$15.00
Chuckles, 1987, MOC $26.00
Cobra, 1982, straight arm, VG (VG card) $140.00
Cobra, 1982, w/accessories, NM $40.00
Cobra, 1983, swivel-arm, NMOC.........................$125.00
Cobra Commander, 1983, MIP $125.00
Cobra Commander, 1983, w/accessories, EX............$40.00
Cobra Commander, 1987, EX (EX card) $28.00
Cobra HISS Driver, 1983, w/accessories, EX $25.00
Cobra Officer, 1983, VG (VG card).......................$80.00
Cobra Soldier, 1983, MIP $60.00
Cobra Stinger Driver, 1982, complete, VG $15.00
Colonel Courage, 1992, complete, M......................$5.00
Crazylegs, 1987, EX (VG card).............................$10.00
Crimson Guard, 1984, w/accessories, EX $15.00
Crimson Guard Commander, w/accessories, NM.......$15.00
Croc Master, 1987, EX (EX card) $30.00
Cross Country, 1986, w/accessories, NM $8.00
Cutter, 1984, w/accessories, EX $10.00
D-Day, 1995, MOC...$8.00
D-Jay, 1989, w/accessories, NM $6.00
Deep-Six, 1989, MOC $25.00
Destro, 1983, w/accessories, VG $15.00
Dial-Tone, 1986, EX (EX card) $22.00
Doc, 1983, w/accessories, EX $15.00
Dojo, 1992, MOC...$10.00
Dr Mindbender, w/accessories, NM.......................$10.00
Dr Mindbender, 1986, EX (EX card) $20.00
Drop-Zone, 1986, w/accessories, NM $10.00
Duke, 1983, w/accessories, NM $20.00
Duke, 1985, NM $25.00
Eco War Cesspool, w/accessories, EX $10.00
Eco War Ozone, w/accessories, EX $10.00
Eels, 1985, MOC..$55.00
Falcon, 1987, w/accessories, EX $8.00
Ferret, 1988, w/accessories, EX $8.00
Firefly, 1984, w/accessories, EX.............................$50.00
Flint, 1985, EX (EX card) $45.00
Footloose, 1985, MOC $60.00
Frag Viper, 1989, MOC $15.00
Free Fall, 1990, NMOC.......................................$18.00
Fridge, 1986, MIP (factory bag)............................$30.00
Frostbite, 1985, w/accessories, NM.........................$12.00
General Hawk, 1992 mail-in, w/accessories, NM..........$6.00
Ghostrider, 1988, w/accessories, NM $12.00

Gnawgahyde, 1989, MOC $20.00
Grunt, 1982, straight arm, NMOC.........................$85.00
Grunt, 1982, w/accessories, EX.............................$22.00
Grunt, 1983, w/accessories, EX.............................$20.00
Gung-Ho, w/accessories, NM $12.00
Hardball, 1988, complete, M................................$12.00
Hawk, 1987, w/accessories, EX $15.00
Heat-Viper, 1989, EX (EX card)............................$15.00

Heavy Duty, 1990, complete, M, $6.00.
(Photo courtesy Myla Perkins)

Hydro-Viper, 1988, NMOC...................................$25.00
Iceberg, 1983-85, MOC.......................................$32.00
Iceberg, 1986, NMOC...$20.00
Iron Grenadier, 1988, MOC.................................$18.00
Joe Colton, 1994 mail-in, w/accessories, M...............$15.00
Lady Jaye, 1985, MOC...$75.00
Law & Order, 1986, VG (VG card) $30.00
Low-Light, 1986, NMOC......................................$25.00
Mainframe, 1986, MOC.......................................$32.00
Major Bludd, 1983, w/accessories & ID card, EX $15.00
Maverick, 1988, MOC..$30.00
Mega Marine Blast-Off, 1993, MOC.......................$18.00
Mega Marine Blast-Off, 1993, w/accessories, EX.........$8.00
Mega Marine Clutch, 1993, w/accessories, EX $8.00
Mega Marine Cyber-Viper, 1993, MOC...................$20.00
Mega Marine Cyber-Viper, 1993, w/accessories, EX.........$8.00
Mega Marine Mirage, 1993, MOC.........................$15.00
Mega Marine Mirage, 1993, w/accessories, EX $8.00
Mercer, 1987, w/accessories, NM...........................$8.00
Metal-Head, 1990, MOC $15.00
Monkeywrench, 1986, w/accessories, NM..................$6.00
Mutt & Junkyard, w/accessories, NM......................$12.00
Mutt & Junkyard, 1984, MOC...............................$50.00
Night Creeper, w/accessories, VG $12.00
Night Force Outback, 1988, w/accessories, EX $15.00

Ninja Force Banzai, w/accessories, EX................................$10.00
Ninja Force Bushido, Snake Eyes or Zartan, 1993, MOC, ea..$12.00
Ninja Force Bushido Shadow, w/accessories, EX..............$12.00
Ninja Force Dojo, w/accessories, EX $12.00
Ninja Force Nunchuk, w/accessories, EX $10.00
Ninja Force Storm Shadow, w/accessories, EX..................$12.00
Outback, 1987, MOC $18.00
Outback & Crazylegs, 1986, NMOC...................................$60.00
Psyche-Out, 1987, MOC $15.00
Psyche-Out, 1987, w/accessories, EX $6.00
Python Viper, 1988, NMOC $20.00
Quick Kick, 1985, MOC $35.00
Recoil, 1989, MOC..$15.00
Recondo, 1989, MOC...$40.00
Red Dog, 1987, w/accessories, NM $8.00
Repeater, 1988, EX (EX card)..$15.00
Ripper, 1984, w/accessories, NM $12.00
Ripper, 1985, w/accessories, EX $10.00
Road Pig, 1988, MOC $20.00
Road Pig, 1988, w/accessories & ID card, EX....................$10.00
Roadblock, 1985, EX (EX card)..$25.00
Roadblock, 1986, complete, NM...$12.00
Rock 'n Roll, 1982, EX (EX card) $100.00
Rock 'n Roll, 1982, w/accessories, NM $20.00
Rock 'N Roll, 1983, w/accessories, EX $18.00
Scarlett, 1982, straight arm, NMOC..................................$225.00
Scarlett, 1982, w/accessories, EX $24.00
Sci-Fi, 1986, w/accessories, EX $10.00
Sci-Fi, 1991, MOC $15.00
Scoop, 1989, MOC...$15.00
Sergeant Savage, 1995, MOC..$6.00
Shipwreck w/Parrot, 1985, MOC $70.00
Short-Fuze, 1982, straight arm, EX (EX card) $75.00
Skidmark, 1988, w/accessories, NM $10.00
Sky Patrol Drop Zone w/Parachute Pack, 1990, MOC.....$18.00
Slaughter's Renegades Mercer/Taurus/Red Dog, 1987, MOC ..$30.00
Slip Stream, 1986, w/accessories & ID card, EX $10.00
Snake Eyes, 1982, w/accessories, NM.................................$50.00
Snake Eyes, 1985, w/accessories, EX..................................$40.00
Snake Eyes, 1989, NMOC..$45.00
Sneak Peek, 1987, EX (EX card) $18.00
Snow Job, 1983, w/accessories, EX $18.00
Snow Serpent, 1985, MOC $50.00
Snow Storm, w/accessories, EX...$10.00
Spearhead & Max, 1988, EX (EX card) $25.00
Stalker, 1982, straight arm, EX (EX card) $85.00
Star Brigade Carcass, w/accessories, EX.............................$28.00
Star Brigade Cobra Commander, w/accessories, EX..........$15.00
Star Brigade Destro Armor, w/accessories, EX $15.00
Star Brigade Lobotomaxx, w/accessories, NM...................$20.00
Star Brigade Predacon, w/accessories, NM $25.00
Star Brigade Robo-Joe, prototype, w/accessories, EX $50.00
Steeler, 1983, MOC...$35.00
Storm Shadow, 1984, w/accessories, NM $40.00
Strato-Viper, 1986, w/accessories, EX $6.00
Street Fighter II Blanka, w/accessories, EX..........................$8.00
Street Fighter II Dhalsim, w/accessories, EX $8.00

Street Fighter II Ken Masters, w/accessories, EX................$8.00
Street Fighter II Sagat, w/accessories, EX $8.00

Stretcher, 1990, complete, M, $8.00.
(Photo courtesy Myla Perkins)

Sub-Zero, 1990, MOC..$15.00
TARGAT, 1989, MOC..$18.00
Taurus, 1987, w/accessories, EX $8.00
Techno-Viper, 1987, NMOC..$20.00
Tele-Viper, 1985, MOC..$42.00
Tele-Viper, 1989, MOC..$15.00
Thrasher, 1986, w/accessories, EX $6.00
Thunder, 1984, w/accessories, EX.......................................$10.00
Tiger Force Duke, 1988, w/accessories, EX $12.00
Tiger Force Tiger Shark, 1988, MOC..................................$18.00
Tomax & Xamot, 1985, w/accessories, NM.........................$30.00
Torch, 1985, MOC $35.00
Torpedo, 1983, complete, EX...$30.00
Torpedo, 1983, VG (VG card) $50.00
Toxo-Viper, 1988, MOC...$15.00
Toxo-Viper, 1988, w/accessories, EX....................................$6.00
Tripwire, 1983, w/accessories, EX $18.00
Tunnel Rat, 1987, MOC...$40.00
Tunnel Rat, 1987, VG (VG card) $25.00
Wet Suit, 1986, MOC $45.00
Wild Bill, 1992, MOC $14.00
Wild Weasel, 1984, w/accessories, EX.................................$16.00
Zandar, 1986, Canadian, NMOC...$25.00
Zap, 1982, straight arm, NMOC...$100.00
Zarana, 1986, EX (EX card)..$25.00
Zarana, 1986, w/earring, EX (EX card)...............................$85.00
Zartan, 1984, w/accessories, EX, H4...................................$35.00
Zartan w/Swamp Skier, 1984, MIB....................................$100.00

ACCESSORIES FOR 3¾" GI JOE

AGP w/Super Trooper Figure, 1988, complete, MIB $30.00

Ammo Dump Unit, 1985, EX (EX pkg) $20.00
Battle Gear Accessory Pack #1, 1983, MIP......................$16.00
Cobra Emperor w/Air Chariot, 1986, NRFB.....................$60.00
Cobra Overlord's Dictator Vehicle, w/Overlord figure, MIB..$25.00
Crusader Space Shuttle, 1988, NRFB.............................$175.00
Falcon Glider w/Grunt, complete, EX.............................$100.00
GI Joe Combat Infantry, Hasbro, NMIB...........................$75.00
Heavy Artillery Laser w/Grand Slam, 1982, NRFB........$110.00
Hovercraft, 1984 mail-in, MIP $40.00
Jet Pack Jump & Platform, 1982, MIP (Canadian)...........$50.00
Mauler MBT Tank, 1985, NRFB, H4................................$80.00
Missile Defense Unit, 1984, MIP...................................$20.00
Mobile Missile System, complete, EX $45.00
Motorized Battle Wagon, 1991, MIP..............................$35.00
Mountain Howitzer, 1984, w/accessories, EX $8.00
Phantom X-19 Stealth Fighter, 1988, MIB $70.00
Q-Force Battle Gear, Action Force, MIP $5.00
SAS Parachutist Attack, Action Force, MIP $35.00

Signal Flasher, battery-operated, MIB, $45.00.

Skyhawk, complete, EX (G box) $18.00
Special Force Battle Gear, Action Force, MIP $5.00
Tiger Cat w/Frostbite, 1988, complete, EX, H4.................$20.00
Transportable Tactical Battle Platform, 1985, complete, NM...$30.00

MISCELLANEOUS

Adventure Team Colorforms, complete, NMIB................$15.00
Astro Locker, complete, rare, NM.................................$100.00
Canteen, EX...$15.00
Combat Medic Doctor Kit, Hasbro, MIB.........................$55.00
Combat Watch, Gilbert, w/compass & sighting lenses, rare,
    MIB..$185.00
Flare Gun, EX $15.00
Game, Capture of Hill 79, Hasbro, 1969, EX (EX box)....$60.00
Game, Let's Go Joe, Hasbro, 1966, complete, EX (EX box)..$55.00
Game, Marine Paratroop, Hasbro, 1965, complete, EX (EX
    box)..$45.00

Game, Commando Attack, Milton Bradley #4516, Hasbro, 1985, M (VG box), $15.00.

Mess Kit, EX..$20.00
Official Foot Locker, complete, NM................................$65.00
Official Membership Pack, complete, unused, M $100.00
Walkie-Talkies, EX..$25.00

Guns

Until WWII, most cap guns were made of cast iron. Some from the 1930s were nickel-plated, had fancy plastic grips, and were designed with realistic details like revolving cylinders. After the war, a trend developed toward using cast metal, a less expensive material. These diecast guns were made for two decades, during which time the TV western was born. Kids were offered a dazzling array of weapons, endorsed by stars like the Lone Ranger, Gene, Roy, and Hoppy. Sales of space guns, made popular by Flash Gordon and Tom Corbett, kept pace with the robots coming in from Japan. Some of these early tin lithographed guns were fantastic futuristic styles that spat out rays of sparks when you pulled the trigger. But gradually the space race lost its fervor, westerns were phased out, and guns began to be looked upon with disfavor by the public in general and parents in particular. Since guns were meant to see a lot of action, most will show wear. Learn to be realistic when you assess condition; it's critical when evaluating the value of a gun.

    Advisor: Bill Hamburg (H1).
    Other Sources: C10, I2, H7.

Actoy Wells Fargo, nickel, 11", M $150.00
Blast-Away Cap Gun, Marx, plastic, 8", EX (EX box), A ...$75.00
Daisy Model 57 Soft Air Gun, 1980s, plastic & diecast, NMIP,
    P4 ....$75.00
Dent Mohican Cap Gun, 1930, CI, single shot, 6¼", EX.$60.00
Esquire/Actoy Shotgun Slade, 1960s, brn & blk plastic, rare, EX,
    P4 ....$200.00
Fanner 45 'Shootin' Shell,' Mattel, 11¼", EX $250.00
Halco Marshall, cylinder revolves, bullets, 10½", M $150.00
Hamilton Specialties Secret Agent Hideaway Pistol, diecast
    w/NP finish, bl plastic grips, VG (G box) $45.00

Auto-Magic Picture Pistol, with box of original films, 1938, 6x9", EX/NM, A, $125.00.

Hubley .36 Cap-Shooting Pistol, diecast w/blk plastic grips, complete w/bullets, 8", MIB, A $225.00

Hubley Army 45 Auto, dull gray finish, 6½", M...............$95.00

Hubley Atomic Disintegrator Cap Pistol, diecast w/red plastic grips, 7", VG, A $300.00

Hubley Atomic Disintegrator Cap Pistol No 270, 1954, diecast w/zinc finish, red plastic grips, 8", EX (EX box), P4...$425.00

Hubley Atomic Disintegrator Space Gun, diecast, 8", VG ..$425.00

Hubley Atta Boy Cap Gun, 1935, CI, single shot, 4", G-.$35.00

Hubley Champ Cap Gun, 1940, CI, star medallion, 5", EX $100.00

Hubley Colt .45, diecast, cylinder revolves, bullets, 14", VG ...$135.00

Hubley Cowboy, diecast, cylinder revolves, 12", M $165.00

Hubley Cowboy Cap Pistol No 275, 1950s, diecast w/NP finish, wht plastic steer grips, 12", G, P4...........................$100.00

Hubley Cowboy Repeating Cap Pistol, diecast w/wht plastic grips, 12", NM (G box), A $250.00

Hubley Eagle Cap Gun, 1935, CI, single shot, 8½", VG ..$100.00

Hubley Flintlock Cap Pistol No 280, 1954, diecast w/NP finish, brn swirl plastic stock, NMIB, P4................................$75.00

Hubley Flintlock Jr Cap Pistol, 1955, diecast w/NP finish, brn swirl plastic grips, 7½", NMIB, P4 ....$50.00

Hubley Gray Ghost, automatic, amber grips, 5", VG........$35.00

Hubley Miniature Frontier Single Action Six-Shooter, 1960, diecast w/NP finish, blk plastic grips, 4", MIB, P4.....$50.00

Hubley Miniature Remington .44, diecast w/NP finish, blk plastic grips, 4½", MIB, P4 ....$50.00

Hubley Mountie Repeating Cap Pistol No 251, diecast, 7", MOCC, A...$50.00

Hubley Pet, 1945-60, nickel, M...$5.00

Hubley Pioneer, nickel, amber grips, 10½", M...............$100.00

Hubley Pirate Cap Gun, 1940, CI, dbl bbl, 9⅜", M $125.00

Hubley Remington 36, cylinder revolves, bullets, 8¼", EX..$85.00

Hubley Scout Rifle, 1960, lever action, nickel, EX $125.00

Hubley Texan, cylinder revolves, gold finish, diecast, 9½", M $175.00

Hubley Texan Cap Pistol, 1950s, NP CI w/star logo, wht plastic steer grips, 9", VG, P4 ....$150.00

Hubley Tiny Tommy Machine Gun, plastic, 10", NMIB ..$50.00

Ideal Ray Gun Rifle, 1954, plastic, 25", VG, P4............$175.00

Ideal Space Water Ray Gun, 1960, translucent bl plastic w/glow-in-the-dark aliens on spaceship inside, 9½", NM, P4.......$125.00

Kenton Bull's Eye Cap Gun, 1940, CI, engraved, 6½", M .$125.00

Kenton Law Maker, nickel-plated finish, white plastic grips, 9", M (VG box), A, $250.00.

Kenton Wild West Cap Gun, 1920s, CI, single shot, 11½", rare, M...$225.00

Kilgore American Cap Gun, 1940s, CI, cylinder revolves, 9⅜", EX $350.00

Kilgore Big Bill Cap Gun, 1935, CI, 4⅞", M $35.00

Kilgore Big Horn Six-Shooter Cap Pistol, diecast w/NP finish, heavy scroll work, 7", NMIB, A $75.00

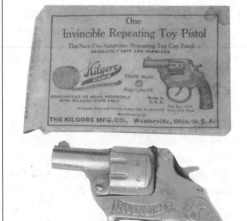

Kilgore Invincible, nickel-plated, 5½", G (G box), A, $75.00.

Kilgore Border Patrol Cap Gun, 1935, CI, automatic, 4½",
VG $65.00

Kilgore Bronco, diecast, cylinder revolves, 9¼", VG $75.00

Kilgore Buc-a-roo Single Shot Cap Pistol, 1950s, diecast w/brn
plastic grips, NMIB...$125.00

Kilgore Deputy Cap Pistol, purple-plated metal, emb bullet on
hdl, MOC, A $75.00

Kilgore Doughboy Cap Gun, 1920, CI, automatic, 4⅞", VG .$125.00

Kilgore Eagle, cylinder revolves, nickel, 8", M $75.00

Kilgore Fast-Draw Single Holster Set, 10" plastic gun, faux
leather holster w/studs & jewels, MIB, A...................$85.00

Kilgore Guard Cap Gun, 1935, CI, 6¼", EX...................$100.00

Kilgore Lasso 'Em Bill Cap Gun, 1930, CI, cylinder revolves, 9",
EX $200.00

Kilgore Lone Eagle Cap Gun, 1930, CI, cylinder revolves, 5¼",
EX $130.00

Kilgore Long Boy Cap Gun, 1920, CI, single shot, 11⅛",
VG $225.00

Kilgore Mountie, automatic, blk finish, 6", M $45.00

Kilgore Officer's Pistol Cap Gun, 1940s, CI, automatic, 6", rare,
M $200.00

Kilgore Presto Cap Gun, 1940, CI, automatic, 5⅛", VG..$65.00

Kilgore Six Shooter Cap Gun, 1940, CI, cylinder revolves, 6½",
VG $75.00

Kilgore Spitfire Cap Gun, 1940, CI, automatic, 4⅝", EX.$65.00

Kilgore Trooper Safety Cap Gun, 1925, repeater, 10¼", M..$95.00

KO Space Jet Friction Ray Gun, 1960s, litho tin w/gr plastic barrel, 9½", VG, P4 ....$55.00

KO Super Space Jet Gun, litho tin w/plastic barrel, 9½",
NMIB...$100.00

Leslie-Henry Champion, diecast, 9", VG.........................$75.00

Lone Star Tightrope Snub Nose, nickel, EX $65.00

Lonestar Pepperbox Derringer, 1965, diecast w/silver finish, 6",
rare, VG, P4 ....$65.00

Mac No 100 Machine Gun, pressed steel w/McDowal decal, 13",
EX, A $125.00

Maco USA Machine Gun, 1950s, plastic w/yel cb barrel, complete w/plastic tripod & bullets, 12", MIB, P4 ....$175.00

Marx Bullet Shooting Colt .45 Peacemaker Pistol, 1960s, bl
plastic w/simulated wood grips, M, P4......................$65.00

Marx Bullet Shooting Snub Nose Cap Pistol, 1960, diecast
w/blk-pnt finish, brn plastic grips, NM, P4 ....$75.00

**Marx Gung Ho Commando Outfit, 1963, complete,
unopened, EX+ (NM 34" x 9" x 18" box), A, $200.00.** (Photo
courtesy Bill Bruegman/Toy Scouts)

Marx Siren Signal Pistol, yel plastic, 6½", NM (G box),
A $100.00

Mattel Buckle Gun, derringer, diecast, 3", VG $50.00

Mattel Bullet-Loading Fanner-50 Cap Pistol, complete w/bullets,
MIB, A...$300.00

Mattel Fanner 50 Cap Pistol No 543, 1957, diecast w/chrome
finish, plastic stag grips, NM (NM box), P4 ....$275.00

Mattel Indian Scout Rifle, bullets, 30", M $200.00

Mattel Power-Jet Squad Gun, 1965, brn & blk plastic w/diecast
works, 30½", EX, P4 ....$85.00

Mattel Shootin' Shell Remington Derringer No 622, 1959, MIB,
P4 ....$100.00

Mattel Shootin' Shell, Winchester Carbine, 26", M $165.00

Mercury Plastics Martian Jet-Blast Bloon Gun, 1950s, red & yel
plastic, 9", VG, P4 ....$150.00

National Bunker Hill Cap Gun, 1925, CI, single shot, 5¼",
M $75.00

Nichols Dyna-Mite Derringer Cap Pistol, 1950s, diecast w/NP
finish, wht plastic grips, 3", MIB, P4 ....$75.00

Nichols Model 61, cylinder revolves, chrome finish, rare, M..$350.00

Nichols Spitfire Saddle Rifle & Holster, 1950s, diecast w/tan
plastic holster, 9", NM, P4...$55.00

**Nichols Stallion 32, nickel-plated finish, with belt clip and six
bullets, 9", M (EX box), A, $200.00.**

Nichols Stallion .38 Cap Pistol, 1955, diecast w/NP finish, wht
plastic grips, 9½", NM, P4...$125.00

Nichols Stallion 45 Mk II, cylinder revolves, gold, 12", rare,
EX $900.00

Nichols Tophand 250, diecast w/wht plastic grip, 10", MOC,
A $150.00

Nu-Age Smoke Ring Gun, 1950s, plastic Flash Gordon style, 9",
NMIB...$350.00

Ohio Art Astro Ray Signal Dart Gun, 1960s, red plastic w/wht
trim, 10", EX (EX box), P4..$250.00

Park Plastics Flying Saucer Gun, 1950s, plastic, complete, MIB,
A $150.00

Ranger Cosmic Ray Gun, red & bl plastic, 8", MIB, A ..$200.00

SAN Space Gun, 1950s, litho tin, friction, 3½", VG, P4.$65.00

Schmidt Buck 'N Bronc Deputy Cap Pistol, 1950, diecast w/NP
finish, metal grips w/copper finish, 8½", VG, P4.....$125.00

Schmidt Deputy BB Gun, copper grips, sm, 8½", EX $75.00

Stevens Big Scout Cap Gun, CI, single shot, 9¾", G-......$75.00

Stevens Colt Cap Gun, 1900, CI, single shot, 5½", EX....$50.00

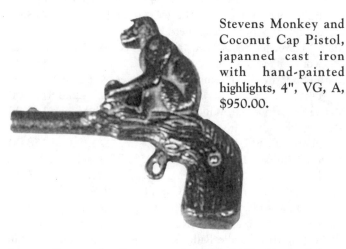

Stevens Monkey and Coconut Cap Pistol, japanned cast iron with hand-painted highlights, 4", VG, A, $950.00.

Stevens Peacemaker Repeating Cap Pistol, NP CI w/emb horse head on blk plastic grips, 9", EX (VG box), A.........$150.00

Stevens Sheriff, nickel-plated finish, highly embossed grips, 9½", MIB, A, $175.00; Stevens Peacemaker, nickel-plated finish, tenite grips, 8½", MIB, A, $175.00.

Stevens Spit Fire, nickel-plated finish, airplanes embossed on grips, 5", NM (G box), A, $225.00.

TN Quick Draw Rifle, 1960, litho tin, friction, 12½", EX, P4 ....$85.00

TN Space Control Gun, 1960, litho tin, friction, 4", VG, P4...$50.00

Tomy Shawnee Space Gun, 1950s, plastic, clicker action, 7", scarce, EX..$85.00

Topper Sixfinger Spy Gun, 1965, plastic, 3½", NMOC, P4...$85.00

Wesco Lugar Automatic, 1950s, hard plastic, complete w/10 pellets, 7", NMIB..$100.00

Wyandotte Water Pistol, 1940s, red-pnt pressed steel, 7", EX (G box), A...$50.00

CHARACTER

Agent Zero-M Camera Gun, Mattel, 1960s, machine gun converts into movie camera, 15", NM $95.00

Agent Zero-M Radio Rifle, Mattel, 1964, blk plastic w/diecast works, 22½", EX, P4.................................$165.00

Agent Zero-M Snap-Shot Pistol, Mattel, 1964, blk plastic w/diecast works, 7½", M, P4.............................$100.00

Agent Zero-W Fanner 50 Cap Pistol, Mattel, 1965, diecast w/blk-pnt finish, brn simulated wood grips, 11", NM, P4 ......$100.00

Agent Zero-W Shootin' Shell Buckle Gun, Mattel, 1965, diecast w/gold finish, NM, P4................................$125.00

Alan Ladd, Geo Schmidt, 10¼", EX...............................$275.00

Annie Oakley, Leslie-Henry, gold, 9", very rare.............$400.00

Batman Escape Gun, Lincoln International, 1966, red plastic w/decal, MOC, T2....................................$100.00

Billy the Kid Cap Gun, Mattel, 1950s, CI, single shot, 6¾", G-..$50.00

Bonanza, Leslie-Henry 44, cylinder revolves, 10¼", M..$175.00

Buck Rogers Pop Gun, Daisy, futuristic style, silver plastic, 10", VG, A..$100.00

Buck Rogers U-235 Atomic Pistol, Daisy, 1948, pressed steel w/bl finish, red spark windows, 10", rare, NMIB, P4..........$650.00

Buck Rogers Water Pistol, Daisy, yel & red litho tin w/brass works, 7", EX, A $250.00

Buck Rogers XZ-38 Disintegrator Pistol, Daisy, 1936, pressed steel w/copper finish, 9½", rare, NMIB, P4 ....$500.00

Buck Rogers XZ-44 Water Pistol, Daisy, 1936, litho pressed steel, 7½", NM, P4...$400.00

Buffalo Bill Cap Pistol, Stevens, cast iron with tenite grips, 8", M (EX box), A, $175.00.

Buffalo Bill Cap Gun, Kenton, 1930, CI, single shot, rare, 13½", VG $400.00

Buffalo BIll Cap Gun, Stevens, 1890s, CI, single shot, 11¾", G- $150.00

Captain Buck Flash Buzz Ray Gun, Remco, 1965, plastic, battery-op, 9", EX $100.00

Cisco Kid 100 Shot Repeater, Lone Star, 1960s, diecast w/silver finish, brn plastic grips, 9", NMIB..........................$100.00

Cowboy King Cap Gun, CI, MIB, C10 ....$365.00

Dale Evans, Geo Schmidt, jewels, 10¼", rare, VG $300.00

Davy Crockett, Flintlock Buffalo Rifle, Hubley, 25", EX ..$150.00

Dick Tracy Shoulder Holster Set, John Henry, 1950, complete, MIP, A..$85.00

Dick Tracy Siren Pistol, Marx, red finish, VG $75.00

Dick Tracy Sub-Machine Water Gun, Tops Plastic, EX (EX box)..$125.00

Dragnet Detective Special Repeating Revolver, Knickerbocker, blk-pnt diecast w/Badge 714 inlaid on grips, 6", NMIB..$75.00

Flash Gordon Click Ray Pistol, Marx, litho tin, 10", NM (NM box)..$250.00

G-Man Machine Gun, Marx, sparks and makes machine gun sound, wood stock handle, 24", EX, $325.00. (Photo courtesy Harry and Jody Whitworth)

G-Man Sparking Automatic Pistol, Marx, 1930s, steel w/decal, w/up, 4½", NM (NM box), A $200.00

Gene Autry Pistol, Leslie Henry, diecast, nickel-plated finish, 8", NM (EX box), A, $200.00.

Gene Autry Cap Gun, Kenton, 1940s, CI, dummy, 8⅜", rare, M, from $225 to $250.00

Gene Autry Cap Gun, Kenton, 1951, CI, 8⅜", rare, M.$250.00

Gene Autry Cap Pistol, Leslie-Henry, 1950s, diecast w/NP finish, wht plastic horse head grips, 9", EX, P4 ....$125.00

Gene Autry Repeating Cap Pistol, Kenton, CI, facsimile signature on red plastic grips, 8", EX (EX box), A...........$200.00

Hopalong Cassidy, Geo Schmidt, cameo grips, 9", EX....$250.00

Hopalong Cassidy, Wyandotte, nickel, 9", VG $175.00

Hopalong Cassidy Auto-Magic Projector Gun, 1950s, gray-pnt metal w/decals, 5", EX+ $65.00

Hopalong Cassidy Cap Pistol, diecast, 1955, 7½", VG, P4 ..$225.00

Hopalong Cassidy Zoomerang Gun, Tigrett Inc, 1950, red plastic, shoots coil of paper w/spring action, 9", NMIB.$175.00

James Bond 007 Multi-Buster Machine Gun, plastic, complete w/accessories, 19", scarce, EX (EX box) $350.00

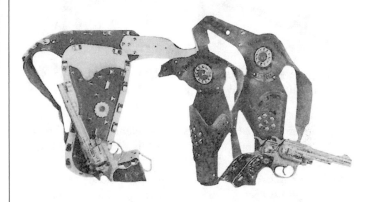

Kit Carson Cap Gun and Holster, umarked, 9", EX, $150.00; Wild Bill Hickok and Jingles Cap Guns and Holsters, Hubley, EX, $275.00.

Lone Ranger, Actoy, antique bronze, 10", VG...............$125.00

Lone Ranger, Kenton, 1940, nickel, 8¼", rare, M $325.00

Lone Ranger (Legend of), Gabriel, six-piece double holster set, NM (NM box), $75.00. (Photo courtesy Mike's General Store)

Lone Ranger Gun & Holster Set, Esquire, 1947, 2 Pony Boy guns, blk leather holster w/jewels & medallions, MIB $300.00

Marshal of the West Gun Set, Daisy, complete w/2 8" cap pistols, dbl-barrel shotgun, holster & ammunition, NMIB....**$125.00**

Pawnee Bill Cap Gun, Stevens, 1940, CI, 7⅝", VG.......**$175.00**

Popeye Pirate Pistol, Marx, 1935 King Features Synd, lithographed tin, 8", MIB, $250.00.

Range Rider Gun & Holster Set, Leslie-Henry, 1950s, complete w/2 diecast pistols & bullets, M (EX box)................**$350.00**

Red Ranger, Wyandotte, 7¾", VG **$45.00**

Red Ranger Clicker Pistol, Wyandotte, tin w/cattle head on grip, 6½", NM (G box), A **$100.00**

Red Ranger Jr Cap Pistol, Wyandotte, 1957, diecast w/silver finish, wht plastic horse head grips, 8", EX, P4 ....**$100.00**

Red Ryder Gun and Holster Set, Daisy, MIB, $250.00.

Roy Rogers, Geo Schmidt, copper grips, 10¼", EX **$225.00**

Roy Rogers, Leslie-Henry, gold, 9", EX **$225.00**

Smoky Joe Cap Pistol, Leslie-Henry, 1950s, diecast w/NP finish, translucent amber grips, 9", VG, P4..................**$100.00**

Starsky & Hutch Repeater Cap Gun, Fleetwood, 1976, MIP, from $40 to...**$50.00**

Starsky & Hutch Shoulder Holster Set, Lone Star, 1976, MOC...**$125.00**

Superman Daisy Cinematic Pistol, 1940s, M (EX box), $350.00. (Photo courtesy Dunbar Gallery)

Texas Ranger Gun & Holster Set, Leslie-Henry, 1950s, diecast w/wht grips, brn leather holster w/studs & jewels, NMIB............**$150.00**

Wagon Train Cap Pistol, Leslie-Henry, 1950s, diecast w/chrome finish, blk textured stag grips, 9", VG, P4 ....**$125.00**

Wild Bill Hickok Cap Pistol, Leslie-Henry, 1950s, diecast w/gold finish, wht plastic horse head grips, 9½", EX, P4.....**$175.00**

Wyatt Earp, Buntline Special, Actoy, 11", M **$150.00**

Wyatt Earp Buntline Special, 13½", NM (NM box), $300.00.

Wyatt Earp Cap Pistol, Kilgore, 1959, diecast w/NP finish, wht plastic horse head grips, 9", NM, P4 ....**$150.00**

Wyatt Earp Frontier Marshall Cap Guns & Holster, Actoy, complete w/2 9" cap guns & emb leather holster, NMIB, A **$450.00**

BB Guns

Values are suggested for BB guns that are in excellent condition. Advisor: Jim Buskirk.

Daisy '1,000 Shot Daisy,' lever action, wood stock, B6...**$400.00**

Daisy '500 Shot Daisy,' lever action, wood stock, B6......**$400.00**

Daisy Model A, break action, wood stock, B6 ....**$350.00**

Daisy Model B, lever action, wood stock, B6.................**$100.00**

Daisy, wire stock, break action, $800.00; top lever, $1,200.00. (Photo courtesy Jim Buskirk)

Daisy Model C, break action, wood stock, B6.................$300.00
Daisy Model H, lever action, wood stock, B6 ....$125.00
Daisy Model 1938B, 'Christmas Story/RED RYDER,' B6.$90.00
Daisy Model 21, 1968, dbl barrel, plastic stock, B6 ....$400.00
Daisy No 11, Model 29, lever action, wood stock, B6 ......$80.00
Daisy No 12, Model 29, lever action, wood stock, B6 ......$80.00
Daisy No 25, pump action, pistol-grip, wood stock, several variations, B6, ea $65.00
Daisy No 25, pump action, straight wood stock, several variations, B6, ea $75.00
Daisy No 30, lever action, wood stock, B6.......................$100.00
Daisy No 40, 'Military,' lever action, wood stock, B6 .....$250.00
Daisy No 40, 'Military,' w/bayonet, lever action, wood stock, B6 ....$500.00
Daisy No 100, Model 38, break action, wood stock, B6....$80.00
Daisy No 101, Model 33, lever action, wood stock, B6 ....$60.00
Daisy No 101, Model 36, lever action, wood stock, B6 ....$50.00
Daisy No 102, Model 36, lever action, wood stock, B6 ....$50.00
Daisy No 102, Model 36, lever action, wood stock, nickel finish, B6 ....$75.00
Daisy No 103, Model 33, 'Buzz Barton,' nickel finish, B6.$250.00
Daisy No 103, Model 33, lever action, wood stock, B6 ..$250.00
Daisy No 104, dbl barrel, wood stock, B6 ....$650.00
Daisy No 105, 'Junior Pump Gun,' wood stock, B6 ....$250.00
Daisy No 106, break action, wood stock, B6....................$40.00
Daisy No 107, 'Buck Jones Special,' pump action, wood stock, B6..$150.00
Daisy No 107, pump action, plastic stock, B6 ....$30.00
Daisy No 108, Model 39, 'Carbine,' lever action, wood stock, B6..$90.00
Daisy No 111, Model 40, 'Red Ryder,' aluminum lever, B6...$75.00
Daisy No 111, Model 40, 'Red Ryder,' iron lever, B6........$90.00
Daisy No 111, Model 40, 'Red Ryder,' plastic stock, B6 ...$50.00
Daisy No 140, 'Defender,' lever action, wood stock, B6 .$275.00
Daisy No 195, 'Buzz Barton,' lever action, wood stock, B6 .$100.00
Daisy No 195, Model 36, 'Buzz Barton,' lever action, wood stock, B6..$90.00
Daisy No 50, 'Golden Eagle,' lever action, blk wood stock, B6 ....$100.00
King Model 5533, lever action, wood stock, B6................$35.00
King Model 5536, lever action, wood stock, B6................$35.00
King No 1, break action, wood stock, B6........................$200.00
King No 2, break action, wood stock, B6 ....$65.00
King No 4, lever action, wood stock, B6.........................$250.00
King No 5, 'Pump Gun,' wood stock, B6.........................$150.00
King No 5, lever action, wood stock, B6.........................$200.00
King No 10, break action, wood stock, B6.........................$50.00
King No 17, break action, wood stock, B6.......................$175.00
King No 21, lever action, wood stock, B6 ....$65.00
King No 21, lever action, wood stock, B6.........................$65.00

King No 22, lever action, wood stock, B6 ....$70.00
King No 24, break action, wood stock, B6.......................$225.00
King No 24, lever action, wood stock, B6........................$75.00
King No 55, lever action, wood stock, B6........................$85.00
King No 2136, lever action, wood stock, B6.....................$40.00
King No 2236, lever action, wood stock, B6.....................$40.00
Markham/King 'Chicago,' break action, all wood, B6 ....$300.00
New King, repeater, break action, wood stock, B6..........$250.00
New King, single shot, break action, wood stock, B6 .....$225.00

Related Items and Accessories

Admiral Dewey Bomb, Grey Iron, 1900, CI, 1¾", VG...$250.00
Bullets, Daisy Soft Air Shot No 7170, 1980s, set of 100, MOC, P4..$5.00
Butting Match, Ives, 1885, CI, 5", EX...........................$450.00
Cannon, Kenton, 1900, CI, 4⅞", VG............................$300.00
Cap Bomb, bell, CI, 2", EX, A..$185.00
Cap Bomb, China man, CI, 2", EX, A $150.00
Cap Bomb, dog head, CI, 2", VG....................................$165.00
Cap Bomb, Yellow Kid, CI, 2", VG, A............................$150.00
Caps, Kilgore Bang Caps No 2502, 10 rolls per box, M, P4...$5.00
Caps, Kilgore Mammoth Disc Caps, 20 per box, M, P4......$5.00
Caps, Kilgore Round Caps No 514, 3 rolls per box, M, P4 .$4.00
Caps, Kilgore Stick-On Round Caps No 533, 3 rolls per box, M, P4..$4.00
Caps, Langston Super Nu-Matic Paper Buster Gun Ammunition, 3 rolls per box, M, P4 ....$5.00
Caps, Mattel Greenie Stick-M-Caps, 2 sheets of 60 per box, M, P4 ....$8.00
Caps, Nichols Stallion Round Caps, 100 per box, M, P4....$5.00
Caps, Nichols Tophand Round Caps, MIP, P4.................$15.00
Caps, Star Brand/M Backes Round Caps, 100 per box, M, P4 ....$5.00
Chinese Must Go, Ives, 1880, CI, 4¾", EX $450.00
Clown on Powder Keg, Ives, 1890s, CI, 3¾", VG $400.00
Devil's Head Bomb, Ives, 1880, CI, .22 blanks, 2¼", VG.$300.00
Dog's Head Bomb, Ives, 1880, CI, 2⅛", EX $265.00
George Washington Bomb, 1900, CI, 1¼", EX $300.00
Hobo Bomb, Ideal, 1890s, CI, 2", G- $100.00
Liberty Bell Bomb, 1876, CI, 2⅜", EX $200.00
Sea Serpent, Stevens, CI, figural, 3½", G-.....................$600.00

Halloween

Halloween is a uniquely American holiday melded from the traditions of superstitions brought to the new world from Germany and Scotland. St. Matrimony was reportedly the patron saint of this holiday, as it was at this time of the year when the harvest was safely in that betrothals and weddings took place. Most activity for the holiday focused on getting young eligible people married. Trick or Treat was a way of getting rid of bothersome younger siblings. Robert Burns, the poet of Scotland was a major influence on the folklore of the holiday. In this country today, Halloween is a holiday with little or no association with earlier religious rites of any group. It's an evening of fun, frolic, and fantasy filled with a lot of sugar and calories! For further information we recommend *Tastes & Smells of Halloween* (a cookbook, available from the author); *Collectible Halloween; Halloween: Decorations & Games;* and *More Halloween Collectibles,* by our advisor, Pamela E. Apkarian-Russell.

Advisor: Pamela E. Apkarian-Russell, The Halloween Queen (H9).

See also Halloween Costumes; Candy Containers (for glass examples).

Balancing Toy, pumpkin man, celluloid, EX $300.00
Book, Games for Halloween, by Mary E Blain, 1912, hardcover, 60 pgs, w/dust jacket, EX $45.00
Book, Peter Pumpkin in Wonderland, by Ida M Huntington, hardcover, EX $125.00
Book & Record Set, Georgie's Halloween, by Robert Bright, EX $25.00

Boxes, by folk artist Rich Connant, $40.00 each.
(Photo courtesy Pamela Apkarian-Russell)

Candy baskets, German, ca 1920s, 2½", EX, $125.00; and 9", EX, $300.00. (Photo courtesy Dunbar Gallery)

Candy Box, cb w/image of owl on branch, EX $45.00
Candy Box, diecut witch w/owl & blk cat on hat, EX, H9 .$45.00
Candy Container, baker, compo, NM, H9 ....$325.00

Candy Container, cat on rnd container, compo & cb, Germany, 2", EX $200.00
Candy Container, chauffeur w/pumpkin head, carrot arms & squash legs, compo, Germany, 5", NM, H9 ....$600.00
Candy Container, crying onion man w/wooden horn hat, crepe-paper bow tie, Germany, NM, H9 ....$350.00
Candy Container, devil head w/veggie body, compo, 6", EX, H9 ....$250.00
Candy Container, fisherman, compo, NM, H9 ....$400.00
Candy Container, Humpty Dumpty veggie man, compo, Germany, 5½", NM, H9 ....$600.00
Candy Container, jack-o'-lantern, cb w/crepe-paper ruffle, Germany, 5½", EX $250.00
Candy Container, jack-o'-lantern, cb w/paper insert, Germany, 5½", EX $200.00
Candy Container, jack-o'-lantern fisherman, compo, EX, H9 .$400.00
Candy Container, jack-o'-lantern man, pressed board head w/wire body & felt clothes, Germany, 11", EX $400.00
Candy Container, jack-o'-lantern pirate, compo, Germany, 4½", EX $350.00
Candy Container, jack-o'-lantern w/wiggling pickle nose, compo, EX $300.00
Candy Container, lemon-head girl, compo, Germany, EX ...$400.00
Candy Container, policeman, compo, NM, H9 ....$400.00
Candy Container, tree trunk, pressed cb, NM, H9 ....$150.00
Candy Container, veggie man & child, compo, Germany, 3½", EX $550.00
Candy Container, veggie trick-or-treater, compo, Germany, 5¼", NM, H9 ....$500.00
Candy Container, witch, crepe paper w/cb box, NM, H9 .$125.00
Candy Holder, cat pulling pumpkin coach, cb, dbl-sided, EX..$45.00

Cup, plastic Malibu sipper, removable glasses, $20.00.
(Photo courtesy Pamela Apkarian-Russell)

Coloring Book, furry blk cat on cover, Whitman, 1953, unused, EX+ $40.00

Decoration, cat, Beistle, ca 1930s, cb, thin jtd arms & legs, 27", VG $50.00

Decoration, Fat Cat, blk cat on pumpkin, spongy material w/magnet on bk, EX.................$5.00

Decoration, owl in top hat, movable arms, paper, EX, H9 ..$6.00

Decoration, owl on This Way sign, paper, EX.................$15.00

Decorations, String 'em Outs, Dennison, pumpkins, VG .$25.00

Diecut, devil face, Germany, 16", EX, H9.................$175.00

Diecut, witch & quarter moon, Germany, 1920s, 5" dia, NM.................$125.00

Doll, jack-o'-lantern man, movable cloth-covered arms & legs w/wooden hands & feet, 6¼", EX.................$1,200.00

Figure, donkey w/jack-o'-lantern in his mouth, hard plastic, EX $200.00

Figure, Humpty Dumpty pumpkin, compo w/felt arms & crepe-paper collar, EX.................$600.00

Figure, jack-o'-lantern boy holding parade stick w/pumpkin, compo, Germany, 3", EX, H9 ....$800.00

Figure, jack-o'-lantern lady, compo, Germany, 3", EX $325.00

Figure, jack-o'-lantern man playing accordion, compo, EX.................$75.00

Figure, owl, pulp, American, 1940s, 6½", NM.................$150.00

Figure, peasant woman w/vegetable body, compo w/crepe-paper scarf, NM, H9 ....$400.00

Figure, pumpkin w/accordion, plastic, 5", NM, A.............$85.00

Figure, scarecrow, celluloid, EX $200.00

Figure, veggie child dressed as clown, compo, H9...........$500.00

Figure, veggie man, jtd compo, 6", NM, H9.................$500.00

Figure, witch, pnt bsk, Japan, 1950s, 3", EX.................$40.00

Figure, witch holding blk cat, nodding head, hard plastic, 7", EX $150.00

Figure, witch holding blk cat, VC/USA, celluloid, 4½", VG $250.00

Finger Puppet, Kooky Spookys, glow-in-the-dark, several variations, MIP, ea $10.00

Game, Old Witch Brewsome Stunts, 1920s, complete, NMIB.................$45.00

Game, Witch-EE, Selchow & Righter, 1920s, complete, EX (EX box).................$150.00

Game, Zingo Halloween Fortune & Stunt, 1930s, EX (EX box), A $45.00

Games: Old Witch Brewsome Stunts, ca 1920s, 7½"x10", M, A, $35.00; Stunt Halloween Quiz Game, HE Luhrs, 1920s, 8½"x9½", EX, A, $35.00.

Hat, orange felt w/blk cat & jack-o'-lantern, EX, H9 ....$20.00

High Flyer Paddle Ball, China, MIP $5.00

Horn, jack-o'-lantern face, paper w/crepe-paper hair & dress, wooden mouthpc, NM, H9.................$20.00

Horn, pipe shape w/jack-o'-lantern face, pressed cb w/wooden nose, Germany, EX $145.00

Folk art by Jack Roads (from back cover of *Tastes & Smells of Halloween*), wood composition, papier-mache, and metal, $350.00. (Photo courtesy Pamela Apkarian-Russell)

Horns, carrot faces, German, 1920s, 6½" long, EX, $200.00 each. (Photo courtesy Dunbar Gallery)

Jack-o'-Lantern, cb, owl-type rings around eyes & pointed ears, Germany, NM, H9.................$300.00

Jack-o'-Lantern, compo, jack-o'-lantern head in tree, orig insert, Germany, 6", EX $700.00

Jack-o'-Lantern, compo, owl head atop jack-o'-lantern, Germany, EX, H9 ....$275.00

Jack-o'-Lantern, papier-mache, skull head, Germany, 1920s, rare, EX $750.00

Jack-o'-Lantern, pulp, smiling w/eyes crossed, pug nose, American, 1940s, 5", NM $150.00

Jack-o'-Lantern, soft plastic, battery-operated, Japan, 1950s, 4", MIB $65.00

Lantern, blk cat, papier-mache, 6", NM, D10 ....$350.00

Lantern, cat, orange, full figure, EX $500.00

Lantern, jack-o'-lantern, paper on wire frame, folds up, EX $25.00

Lantern, jack-o'-lantern man w/protruding tongue, cb & compo, 12", EX $2,500.00

Lantern, jack-o'-lantern w/accordion top, cb, Germany, EX, H9 ....$300.00

Lantern, singing jack-o'-lantern, papier-mache, several variations, EX, ea, from $100 to $175.00

Lantern, skull, papier-mache, w/toothy smile, mk 1911 in pencil on base, 4½", VG+ $400.00

Lantern, veggie goblin (full body), pulp, EX, H9 ....$400.00

Lantern, witch & owl on 4-panel lantern, cb & tissue paper, EX $65.00

Light bulb, Occupied Japan, milk glass with skull and crossbones, $45.00. (Photo courtesy Pamela E. Apkarian-Russell)

Lantern, witch by folk artist Ginny Betourne, composition and paper, $150.00. (Photo courtesy Pamela E. Apkarian-Russell)

Make A Model Haunted House Kit, paper, England, unused, EX, H9 ....$15.00

Noisemaker, blk cat, cb w/wooden hdl, Germany, 1920s, 6", EX $75.00

Noisemaker, frying pan shape w/blk cat face, tin, sm, EX, H9 ....$50.00

Noisemaker, jack-o'-lantern, litho tin w/plastic horn nose, EX $50.00

Noisemaker, pumpkin-head man on rachet, wood/papier-mache, very old, 6" figure, 7" long overall, EX $185.00

Noisemaker, ratchet-type w/jack-o'-lantern head, wood & pressed cb, Germany, EX $175.00

Noisemaker/Sparkler, jack-o'-lantern, tin, NMIB, H9 ......$50.00

Pan Knocker, litho tin w/apple dunking party scene, Chein, 1910, dbl-sided, 10", NM, A $300.00

Paper Doll Sheet from Magazine, Adventures of Polly & Peter Perkins, unused, EX, H9 ....$15.00

Paper Doll Sheet from Magazine, Betty Bonnet's Halloween Party, unused, EX, H9, from $15 to $25.00

Paper Doll Sheet from Magazine, Dolly Dingle's Halloween, complete, unused, EX, from $15 to $25.00

Party Kit, Beistle Co, 1923, thin cb decorations, VG (G box) $150.00

Saxophone, papier-mache, with black cat image, 20", NM, $150.00. (Photo courtesy Dunbar Gallery)

Party Set, Halloween Party Material Box, Whitman, complete, NMIB..$300.00

Pull Toy, scarecrow w/pumpkin head, hard plastic, vintage, 5½"...$100.00

Push-Button Puppet, jack-o'-lantern man standing on pumpkin, plastic, EX, H9..$35.00

Rattle, plastic witch head atop wooden hdl, 1950s, 8", EX, A...$40.00

Roly-Poly, jack-o'-lantern man w/hands on stomach, Schoenhut, 8", rare, NM, H9.....................................$2,500.00

Squeaker, smiling orange face, litho cb w/wooden squeaker device, Germany, 1920s, 2½" dia, NM.....................$50.00

Squeaker Toy, ca 1910, hand-painted cardboard jack-o'-lantern face, wooden arms and legs, original clothes; press stomach, he tips hat, 10" tall, EX, $1,200.00; holding composition parade lantern, $195.00.

Wind-up Jack-o'-lantern Dancing Clown Toy, German, 1920s, cardboard head, metal legs and feet, original felt clothes, rare, 10", NM, A, $1,400.00.

Squeeze Toy, Crying Pumpkin, mk Made in Boston USA, EX...$45.00

Tambourine, children playing w/lg pumpkin, litho tin, Chein, 1930s, 7" dia, NM..$100.00

Tambourine, laughing devil's face, tin, EX, H9.............$110.00

Tambourine, pumpkin face, ca 1920s, litho tin, VG+ $100.00

Tambourine, 2 blk cats & jack-o'-lantern, tin, EX, H9...$100.00

Target, wooden jack-o'-lantern, EX, H9........................$250.00

Yo-yo, jack-o'-lantern, tin, NM, H9................................$10.00

Yo-yo, litho tin w/images of skulls & crossbones, 1960s, MIP ...$10.00

Halloween Costumes

During the '50s and '60s Ben Cooper and Collegeville made Halloween costumes representing the popular TV and movie characters of the day. If you can find one in excellent to mint condition and still in its original box, some of the better ones can go for over $100.00. MAD's Alfred E. Neuman (Collegeville, 1959 – 60) usually carries an asking price of $150.00 to $175.00, and The Green Hornet (Ben Cooper, 1966), upwards of $200.00. Earlier handmade costumes are especially valuable if they are 'Dennison-Made.'

Advisor: Pamela E. Apkarian-Russell, The Halloween Queen (H9).

Bart Simpson, Ben Cooper (Canadian), MIB, K1 ....$12.00

Batgirl, mask only, Ben Cooper, 1977, NM, C10 ....$8.00

Batman, Ben Cooper, 1973, M (worn box), $75.00.

Beatles, any member, Ben Cooper, 1960s, MIB, ea.........$400.00

Big Bird, Ben Cooper, MIB...$20.00

Bigfoot, Collegeville, 1978, MIB, from $50 to $75.00

Bionic Woman, Ben Cooper, 1975, MIB, from $30 to......$40.00

Buffy & Mrs Beasley, Ben Cooper, 1970, MIB, ea.............$75.00
Captain American, Ben Cooper, 1967, NM, T2.............$100.00
Captain Stubing (Love Boat), Ben Cooper, 1978, complete,
    NMIB...$30.00
Casper the Ghost, Ben Cooper, 1961, complete, NMIB...$30.00
Charlie Brown, Collegeville, 1980s, MIB........................$15.00
Charlie Brown, Determined, 1970s, MIB.........................$25.00
Cowardly Lion (Wizard of Oz), 1989, NMIB...................$20.00
Cowboy in Africa, 1967, complete, EX............................$40.00
Creature From the Black Lagoon, 1973, MIB, C10.........$60.00
Daniel Boone, Ben Cooper, complete, EX.......................$65.00
Daredevil, Ben Cooper, 1966, complete, EX (EX box), T2..$100.00
David Cassidy, Kusan, 1973, complete, NMIB...............$200.00
Dick Dastardly, Ben Cooper, 1969, MIB.........................$45.00
Dick Tracy, Ben Cooper, 1967, complete, EX, T2............$50.00

Donald Duck, Collegeville, NMIB, $35.00.

Dr Doom, Ben Cooper, complete, rare, NMIB...............$125.00
Dracula, 1960s, complete, NM...$50.00
Ed Grimley, Collegeville, 1980s, MIB.............................$15.00
Flying Nun, Ben Cooper, 1967, complete, EX (EX box)..$75.00
Fonzie, Ben Cooper, 1976, complete, NMIB....................$35.00
Freddy Krueger, Don Post, 1986, mask only, latex, EX.....$30.00
Glow Worm, Ben Cooper, 1984, MIB...............................$20.00
Godzilla, Ben Cooper, 1978, complete, EX......................$85.00
Green Hornet, Ben Cooper, 1966, complete, EX (EX box), T2,
    from $200 to...$300.00
Green Lantern, Ben Cooper, 1967, complete, EX (EX box)..$50.00
Gumby, Collegeville, EX (G box)......................................$50.00
I Dream of Jeannie, Ben Cooper, 1965, MIB, from $125 to...$150.00
Iron Man, Ben Cooper, 1966, complete, EX (EX box), T2...$150.00
Jed Clampett, Ben Cooper, 1963, MIB, from $100 to.....$125.00
Jed Clampett, 1963, complete, NM (w/o box).................$50.00
Julia, Ben Cooper, 1960s, complete, NMIB, from $40 to..$50.00
Kung Fu, Ben Cooper, 1970s, complete, EX (VG box).....$25.00
Little Mermaid, MIP..$25.00
Little Red Riding Hood, Collegeville, complete, EX (EX box),
    C10..$50.00

Lucy (Peanuts), Collegeville, 1980s, MIB........................$15.00
Lucy (Peanuts), Determined, 1970s, MIB........................$25.00
Lurch (Adams Family), Ben Cooper, 1960s, complete,
    EXIB..$120.00
Man From UNCLE, Halco, complete, EX (EX box).........$75.00
Maverick, 1959, complete, EX...$50.00

Mickey Mouse, $150.00.

Micronauts, Ben Cooper, 1978, any character, MIB, ea.$125.00
Morticia (Addams Family), Ben Cooper, EX...................$75.00

Mr. Fantastic, Ben Cooper, 1967, MIB, $100.00.
(Photo courtesy Bill Bruegman)

Oscar the Grouch, Ben Cooper, MIB...............................$30.00
Phantom, Collegeville, 1956, complete, EX (EX box), T2.$150.00
Popeye, 1950s, complete, EX (EX box), from $75 to......$100.00

Raggedy Ann, Ben Cooper, TV-Comic series, 1973, MIB $40.00

Scarecrow (Wizard of Oz), 1989, complete, NMIB..........$20.00

Simpsons, any character, mask only, Ben Cooper (Canadian), M, K1, ea $10.00

Six Million Dollar Man, Berwick/United Kingdom, 1976, MIB, from $50 to...$75.00

Snoopy, Determined, 1970s, MIB.................................$25.00

Snow White, 1937, orig label reads WD Masquerade Costume & Mask, Fishbach-Spotlite, complete, EX, rare, A......$250.00

Space Ghost, Ben Cooper, 1965, complete, EX (EX box)...$75.00

Space Ghost, Ben Cooper, 1966, MIB, from $40 to.........$75.00

Spider-Woman, Ben Cooper, 1970s, complete, scarce, NM, (NM box)...$100.00

Starsky & Hutch, Collegeville, 1976, MIB, ea $50.00

Superman, Ben Cooper, 1950s, complete w/Superman's Buddy comic book, EX (EX box), A $225.00

SWAT, 1975, complete, EX (EX box) $35.00

Tarzan, Ben Cooper, 1975, complete, M (VG box) $95.00

Thor, mask only, Ben Cooper, 1967, NM, T2 ....$40.00

Tin Man, Ben Cooper, 1967, complete, EX (EX box) $125.00

Underdog, Ben Cooper, 1969, complete, EX (EX box), T2 ..$50.00

Wally Gator, 1960s, complete, EX (EX box)....................$50.00

Welcome Back Kotter, any character, Collegeville, 1976, MIB $35.00

Winky Dink, Halco, 1950s, complete, rare, NM..............$50.00

Witchiepoo, Collegeville, 1971, MIB.............................$50.00

Woodstock (Peanuts), Collegeville, 1980s, MIB $15.00

Zorro, Ben Cooper, 1955, complete, NM (EX box) $75.00

Zorro, Ben Cooper, 1981, complete, NMIB $40.00

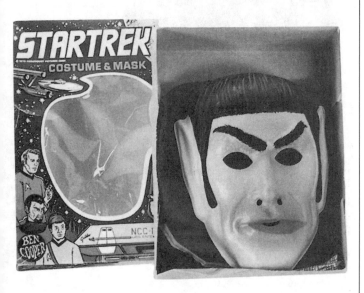

Spock, Ben Cooper, 1970s, complete, EX (EX box), $100.00.

Zorro, Spain/Walt Disney, Sgt. Garcia on lid, NM (EX box), A, $110.00.

Steve Austin, Ben Cooper, 1974, MIB, $25.00. (Photo courtesy Greg Davis and Bill Morgan)

Hartland Plastics, Inc.

Originally known as the Electro Forming Co., Hartland Plastics Ind. was founded in 1941 by Ed and Iola Walters. They first produced heels for military shoes, birdhouses, and ornamental wall decor. It wasn't until the late 1940s that Hartland produced their first horse and rider. Figures were hand painted with an eye for detail. The Western and Historic Horsemen, Miniature Western Series, Authentic Scale Model Horses, Famous Gunfighter Series, and the Hartland Sports Series of Famous Baseball Stars were a symbol of the fine workmanship of the '40s, '50s, and '60s. The plastic used was a virgin acetate. Paint was formulated by Bee Chemical Co., Chicago, Illinois, and Wolverine Finishes Corp., Grand Rapids, Michigan. Hartland figures are best known for their uncanny resemblance to the TV Western stars who portrayed characters like the Lone Ranger, Matt Dillon, and Roy Rogers.

Though in today's volatile marketplace, some categories of toys have taken a downward turn, Hartlands have remained strong. For more information we recommend *Hartland Horses and Riders* by Gail Fitch. See Also Clubs, Newsletters, and Other Publications.

Advisor: Judy and Kerry Irvin (K5).

See also Sporting Collectibles.

Alpine Ike, NM, K5..$150.00
Annie Oakley, NM, K5 ....$275.00
Bill Longley, NM, K5..$600.00
Brave Eagle, NM, K5 ....$200.00
Brave Eagle, NMIB, K5..$300.00
Bret Maverick, miniature series, NM, K5......................$75.00
Bret Maverick, NMIB, K5 ....$600.00
Bret Maverick, w/coffeedunn horse, NM, K5 ....$500.00
Bret Maverick, w/gray horse, rare, NM, K5...................$600.00
Buffalo Bill, NM, K5...$300.00
Bullet, NM, K5..$35.00
Bullet, w/tag, NM, K5...$100.00
Cactus Pete, NM, K5...$150.00
Champ Cowgirl, NM, K5 ....$150.00
Cheyenne, miniature series, NM, K5 ....$75.00
Cheyenne, w/tag, NM, K5...$190.00
Chief Thunderbird, rare shield, NM, K5......................$150.00
Cochise, NM, K5...$150.00
Commanche Kid, NM, K5 ....$150.00
Dale Evans, gr, NM, K5 ....$125.00
Dale Evans, purple, NM, K5..$250.00
Dale Evans, rare bl version, NM, K5 ....$500.00
Davy Crockett, NM, K5 ....$500.00
General Custer, NMIB, K5...$250.00
General Custer, repro flag, NM, K5 ....$150.00
General George Washington, NMIB, K5.......................$175.00
General Robert E Lee, NMIB, K5 ....$175.00
Gil Favor, prancing, NM, K5..$650.00
Gil Favor, semi-rearing, NM, K5 ....$550.00

Jim Bowie, w/tag, NM, K5..$250.00
Jim Hardy, NMIB, K5 ....$300.00

Jim Hardy, M, $250.00.
(Photo courtesy Pat Smith)

Jockey, NM, K5...$150.00
Jockey, repro crop, NM, K5..$100.00
Josh Randle, NM, K5...$650.00
Lone Ranger, champ, blk breast collar, NM, K5 ....$125.00
Lone Ranger, miniature series, NM, K5 ....$75.00

Hoby Gilman (Robert Culp), NM, $250.00.
(Photo courtesy Pat Smith)

Lone Ranger, NM, $150.00.
(Photo courtesy Shirley Bertrand)

Lone Ranger, rearing, NMIB, K5 ....$300.00
Matt Dillon, w/tag, NMIB, K5 ....$300.00
Paladin, NMIB, K5 ....$350.00
Rebel, miniature series, repro hat, NM, K5....................$100.00
Rebel, NMIB, K5..$1,200.00
Rifleman, miniature series, repro rifle, EX, K5 ....$75.00

Rifleman, all original, NMIB, $350.00. (Photo courtesy Kerry and Judy's Toys)

Ronald MacKenzie, NM, K5	$1,200.00
Roy Rogers, semi-rearing, NMIB, K5	$600.00
Roy Rogers, walking, NMIB, K5	$300.00
Seth Adams, NM, K5	$275.00
Sgt Lance O'Rourke, NMIB, K5	$300.00
Sgt Preston, repro flag, NM, K5	$650.00
Tom Jeffords, NM, K5	$175.00
Tonto, miniature series, NM, K5	$75.00
Tonto, NM, K5	$150.00
Tonto, rare semi-rearing, NM, K5	$650.00
Warpaint Thunderbird, w/shield, NMIB, K5	$350.00
Wyatt Eart, w/tag, NMIB, K5	$250.00

STANDING GUNFIGHTERS

Bat Masterson, NMIB, K5	$500.00
Bret Maverick, NM, K5	$150.00
Chris Colt, NM, K5	$150.00
Clay Holister, NM, K5	$225.00
Dan Troop, NM, K5	$500.00
Jim Hardy, NM, K5	$150.00
Johnny McKay, NM, K5	$800.00
Paladin, NM, K5	$400.00
Vint Bonner, w/tag, NMIB, K5	$650.00
Wyatt Earp, NM, K5	$150.00

Horses

Horse riding being the order of the day, many children of the nineteenth century had their own horses to ride indoors; some were wooden while others were stuffed, and many had glass eyes and real horsehair tails. There were several ways to construct these horses so as to achieve a galloping action. The most common types had rocker bases or were mounted with a spring on each leg.

Gliding Horse, cvd & pnt wood w/hair mane & tail, glass eyes, ears missing, 30x41", G $700.00
Gliding Horse, early 1900s, wood, dapple gray w/hair mane & tail, leather ears, red base w/yel & blk stripes, 39", EX, A $450.00
Platform Horse, cvd wood, blk w/red saddle & yel blanket, red platform w/CI spoke wheels, 30", EX.................$1,000.00

Platform Horse, wood with real horse hair mane and tail, restored saddle, otherwise original, 31" tall, G, A, $250.00.

Riding Horse, Gong Bell, 1955, wood w/metal legs & rubber wheels, 21½", EX, from $75 to................................$100.00
Riding Horse, Sebel Products, pressed steel, dapple gray w/red saddle & plaid blanket, 30", EX, A $450.00

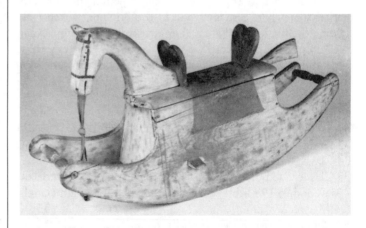

Rocking Horse, New England, early nineteenth century, painted wood, paint loss, minor damage, 25" x 51", A, $1,200.00.

Riding Horse, 1960s, wood, brn leather saddle w/straw stuffing, red leather bridle & breastpiece, 20x6x20", VG......**$425.00**

Rocking Horse, hide-covered w/leather saddle & tack, glass eyes, red base, 34", EX......................................**$550.00**

Rocking Horse, wood body w/2-part CI head & neck, metal rockers w/retractable wheels, leather saddle, 26x33", EX......................................**$1,265.00**

Hot Wheels

When they were introduced in 1968, Hot Wheels were an instant success. Sure, their racy style and flashy custom paint jobs were instant attention-getters, but what the kids loved most was the fact that they were fast! The fastest on the market! It's estimated that more than two billion Hot Wheels have been sold to date — every model with a little variation, keeping up with new trends in the big car industry. The line has included futuristic vehicles, muscle cars, trucks, hot rods, racers, and some military vehicles. A lot of these can still be found for very little, but if you want to buy the older models (collectors call them 'Red Lines' because of their red sidewall tires), it's going to cost you a little more, though many can still be found for under $25.00. By 1977, black-wall tires had become the standard and by 1978 'Red Lines' were no longer used.

A line of cars with Goodyear tires called Real Riders were made from 1983 until about 1987. (In 1983 the tires had gray hubs with white lettering; in 1984 the hubs were white.) California Customs were made in 1989 and 1990. These had the Real Rider tires, but they were not lettered 'Good Year' (and some had different wheels entirely).

Chopcycles are similar to Sizzlers in that they have rechargable batteries. The first series was issued in 1972 in these models: Mighty Zork, Blown Torch, Speed Steed, and Bruiser Cruiser. Generally speaking, these are valued at $35.00 (loose) to $75.00 (MIB). A second series issued in 1973 was made up of Ghost Rider, Rage Coach, Riptide, Sourkraut, and Triking Viking. This series is considerably harder to find and much more expensive today; expect to pay as much as $600.00 to $1,000.00 for a mint-in-package example.

Though recent re-releases have dampened the collector market somewhat, cars mint and in the original packages are holding their values and are still moving well. Near mint examples (no package) are worth about 50% to 60% less than those mint and still in their original package, excellent condition about 65% to 75% less.

Advisor: Steve Stephenson (S25).

'31 Doozie, 1977, red line, orange, M................................**$50.00**
'32 Ford Delivery, 1989, blk walls, yel, MIP....................**$22.50**
'34 Classic Caddy, 1986, blk walls, metalflake bl, NM+ **$3.00**
'35 Classic Caddy, metallic bl, MIP..................................**$8.00**
'40s Woodie, 1980, blk walls, orange w/ wood grain panels, MIP..**$35.00**
'57 Chevy, yel w/flame accents, MIP................................**$12.00**
'57 T-Bird, 1982, blk walls, metalflake red, M....................**$5.00**
'57 T-Bird, 1988, blk walls, wht, MIP..............................**$12.00**

'59 Caddy, metallic lavender w/wht interior, MIP..............**$6.00**
'65 Mustang Convertible, red w/tan interior, MIP **$8.00**
'80s Firebird, 1984, blk walls, blk MIP................................**$9.00**
'80s Firebird, 1988, blk walls, blk, M..................................**$5.00**
Alive '55 Chevrolet, 1974, red line, lt bl w/yel tampo, NM ..**$200.00**
Alive 55, 1973, red line, lt gr, EX....................................**$40.00**
Alive 55, 1976, red line, chrome, hood opens, M..............**$85.00**
Alive 55, 1977, red line, chrome, M **$40.00**
American Tipper, 1976, red line, red, M **$55.00**
American Tipper, 1977, blk walls, red, MIP......................**$45.00**
American Victory, speed machine, 1983, blk walls, gr, M...**$25.00**
AW Shoot, 1976, red line, olive, NM+ **$40.00**
Backwoods Bomb, 1975, red line, lt bl, NM+ **$58.00**
Baja Breaker, 1989, blk walls, blk MIP.............................**$12.50**
Baja Breaker Van, blk walls, Goodyear gray hubs, orange stripe on side, MIP...**$30.00**
Baja Bruiser, 1974, red line, orange, metal base, NM........**$50.00**
Beatnik Bandit, 1968, red line, bl w/wht interior, NM+...**$35.00**
Beatnik Bandit, 1968, red line, gr w/gr interior, NM+......**$30.00**
Beatnik Bandit, 1968, red line, ice bl w/blk interior, NM+..**$50.00**
Beatnik Bandit, 1968, red line, ice bl w/wht interior, NM..**$40.00**
Blown Camaro, 1989, blk walls, metalflake red, M...........**$20.00**
Blown Camaro Z-28, 1988, blk walls, turq, MIP..............**$12.00**
Boss Hoss, 1971, red line, bl w/wht interior, M...............**$190.00**

Boss Hoss, 1971, red line, chocolate brown, rare, MOC, $550.00.

Boss Hoss, 1971, red line, olive w/blk roof, NM **$160.00**
Brabham Repco F1, 1969, red line, aqua or bl, NM+ **$30.00**
Breakaway Bucket, 1974, red line, bl, M..........................**$100.00**
Bugeye, 1971, red line, red, NM+....................................**$50.00**
Bugeye, 1973, red line, pk, EX..**$75.00**
Bye Focal, 1971, red line, lt gr, M...................................**$265.00**
Bywayman, 1979, blk walls, lt bl, NM+ **$10.00**
Camaro Z-28, 1984, blk walls, metalflake red, MIP.........**$12.50**

Captain America Hot Bird, 1979, red, wht & bl, NM......$25.00
Carabo, 1970, red line, yel, NM+...............................$400.00
Cargoyle, 1986, blk walls, orange, M.............................$5.00
CAT Dump Truck, 1982, blk walls, yel, MIP $8.00
Chapparal 2G, 1969, red line, olive, M............................$80.00
Chapparal 2G, 1969, red line, yel, NM+..........................$45.00
Chevy Stocker, metalflake red, MIP................................$12.00
Chiefs Special, 1976, red line, red w/red bar, NM............$36.00
Classic '31 Ford Woody, 1969, red line, aqua, NM+.........$50.00
Classic '31 Ford Woody, 1969, red line, lt orange, NM+..$40.00
Classic '31 Ford Woody, 1969, red line, orange, M...........$50.00
Classic '31 Ford Woody, 1969, red line, red, M.................$40.00
Classic '31 Ford Woody, 1969, red line, yel, NM+............$45.00
Classic '32 Ford Vicky, 1968, red line, gold, NM+............$50.00
Classic '32 Ford Vicky, 1968, red line, olive, NM+...........$48.00
Classic '32 Ford Vicky, 1968, red line, orange w/wht interior,
    NM+ $48.00
Classic '32 Ford Vicky, 1968, red line, rose w/wht interior,
    NM+ $48.00
Classic '36 Ford Coupe, 1969, red line, aqua, NM+ $50.00
Classic '36 Ford Coupe, 1969, red line, purple, NM+.......$75.00
Classic '57 T-Bird, 1969, red line, aqua w/wht interior,
    NM+..$60.00
Classic '57 T-Bird, 1969, red line, gr w/brn interior, NM..$60.00
Classic Cord, 1971, red line, bl, NM+ $250.00
Classic Cord, 1971, red line, gr, NM-.............................$225.00
Classic Cord, 1971, red line, red, NM+ $310.00
Classic Nomad, 1970, red line, bl, M $85.00
Classic Nomad, 1970, red line, magenta, NM+ $125.00
Classic Nomad, 1970, red line, purple, NM+ $130.00
Classic Packard, 1983, blk walls, blk, MIP $20.00
Cockney Cab, 1971, red line, bl, NM+............................$100.00
Cockney Cab, 1971, red line, red, NM+...........................$75.00
Corvette Stingray, 1976, red line, chrome, NM+ $80.00
Corvette Stingray, 1982, blk walls, red, EX $5.00
Custom AMX, 1969, red line, bl, NM+ $85.00

Custom AMX, 1969, red line, magenta, NM+ $125.00
Custom AMX, 1969, red line, yel, NM+...........................$90.00
Custom Barracuda, 1968, red line, aqua, NM+ $85.00
Custom Barracuda, 1968, red line, purple w/wht interior, M ..$350.00
Custom Camaro, 1968, red line, chocolate brn, rare, NM ..$125.00
Custom Charger, 1969, red line, aqua, M $195.00
Custom Charger, 1969, red line, gold, M $175.00
Custom Charger, 1969, red line, purple, NM+ $250.00

Custom Charger, 1969, red line, red, MOC, $200.00.

Custom Charger, 1969, red line, yel, M $175.00
Custom Continental Mark III, 1969, red line, gold, NM+..$50.00
Custom Continental Mark III, 1969, red line, purple,
    NM+ $75.00
Custom Corvette, 1968, red line, gold w/wht interior, NM+ .$160.00
Custom Corvette, 1968, red line, red w/gold interior, NM+.....$130.00
Custom Corvette, 1968, red line, rose w/wht interior, NM+ ...$170.00
Custom Eldorado, 1968, red line, lt bl w/blk interior, NM+ $185.00
Custom Eldorado, 1968, red line, olive w/gold interior, NM+ ...$80.00
Custom Eldorado, 1968, red line, olive w/wht interior, NM+..$100.00
Custom Eldorado, 1968, red line, yel w/wht interior, NM+.....$70.00
Custom Firebird, 1968, red line, lt gr w/wht interior, NM+ .$170.00
Custom Firebird, 1968, red line, red w/brn interior, M...$100.00
Custom Fleetside, 1968, red line, bl, NM+ $165.00
Custom Fleetside, 1968, red line, lt purple, NM+.............$85.00
Custom Mustang, 1968, red line, brn, NM+ $150.00
Custom Mustang, 1968, red line, red w/red interior, NM+ ..$160.00
Custom T-Bird, 1968, red line, purple w/wht interior, NM+...$200.00
Custom Volkswagen, 1968, orange, NM+ $50.00
Custom Volkswagen, 1968, red line, bl, M......................$50.00
Custom Volkswagen, 1968, red line, ice bl, NM+ $145.00
Demon, 1970, red line, bl, NM+ $34.00
Demon, 1970, red line, olive w/wht interior, NM+ $75.00
Deora, 1968, red line, gold, NM+.................................$75.00
Double Header, 1973, red line, dk bl, NM+....................$155.00
Double Vision, 1973, red line, lt gr, NM+ $150.00

Custom AMX, 1969, red line, hot pink, MOC, A, $350.00.

Dumpin' A, 1983, blk walls, gray, M $27.00
Dune Daddy, 1973, red line, lt gr, NM+ $75.00
El Ray Special, 1974, red line, dk bl, NM+ $400.00
Emergency Squad, 1976, red line, red, M $35.00
Emergency Squad, 1982, blk walls, red, MIP $10.00

Evil Weevil, red line, red, NM, A, $50.00.

Ferarri 512P, 1973, red line, pk, NM+ $250.00
Ferrari Testarossa, 1987, blk walls, wht, M $4.50
Ferrari 312P, 1970, red line, pk, NM+ $100.00
Ferrari 312P, 1970, red line, red, M $45.00
Ferrari 512S, 1972, red line, gold, NM+ $140.00
Fiero 2M4, wht w/red, blk & yel accents, MIP $8.00
Fiero 2M4, 1985, blk walls, wht, MIP...............................$9.00
Fire Eater, 1977, red line, red, M $25.00
Firebird Funny Car, 1989, blk walls, yel, MIP $11.00
Flashfire, blk w/red interior, MIP.....................................$10.00
Ford Aerostar, purple w/chrome windows, MIP $5.00
Ford Dump Truck, 1982, blk walls, gr, NM+ $5.00
Ford J-Car, 1968, red line, magenta, NM+ $50.00
Ford J-Car, 1968, red line, wht, NM+ $55.00
Ford MK IV, 1969, red line, dk brn, M $35.00
Ford MK IV, 1969, red line, orange, NM+ $35.00
Formula Fever, 1983, blk walls, yel, MIP...........................$12.50
Formula PACK, 1978, blk walls, blk, EX+ $15.00
Formula 5000, 1976, red line, wht, NM+ $40.00
Funny Money, 1974, red line, plum, M $80.00
Grass Hopper, 1971, red line, lt gr, NM+ $50.00
Gremlin Grinder, 1975, red line, gr, NM+ $50.00
GT Racer, 1993, blk walls, metalflake silver, M $9.00
Gulch Stepper, 1987, blk walls, red, MIP $7.00
Gun Slinger, 1975, red line, lt olive, M...............................$55.00
Hairy Hauler, 1971, red line, lt gr, NM+ $30.00
Hairy Hauler, 1971, red line, magenta, NM+ $40.00
Heavy Chevy, 1970, red line, chrome w/gold interior, M .$85.00
Heavy Chevy, 1974, red line, yel, NM+..............................$110.00
Heavyweight Ambulance, 1970, red line, aqua, NM+ $55.00
Heavyweight Cement Mixer, 1970, red line, aqua, NM+ .$50.00
Heavyweight Dump Truck, 1970, red line, bl, M $60.00
Heavyweight Dump Truck, 1970, red line, wht, NM......$160.00
Heavyweight Moving Van, 1970, red line, gr/wht, NM+ .$70.00
Heavyweight Scooper, 1971, red line, bl, NM+ $100.00
Heavyweight Snorkle, 1971, red line, purple, NM+ $125.00

Heavyweight Tow Truck, 1970, red line, magenta, NM+ ...$65.00
Heavyweight Waste Wagon, 1971, red line, lt gr, M $120.00
Highway Robber, 1973, red line, red, NM+ $120.00
Hot Bird, 1979, blk walls, gold chrome, M.......................$20.00
Hot Heap, 1968, red line, gr w/wht interior, M................$45.00
Hot Heap, 1968, red line, magenta w/wht interior, M....$150.00
Hot Heap, 1968, red line, orange, NM+ $40.00
Ice T, 1971, red line, lt yel, M...$75.00
Ice T, 1973, red line, lt bl, NM+ $175.00
Indy Eagle, 1969, red line, aqua w/blk interior, NM+ $35.00
Indy Eagle, 1969, red line, gold chrome, NM+ $130.00
Inferno, 1976, red line, yel, M $55.00
Inside Story, 1980. blk walls, yel, MIP...............................$27.00
Jeep Scrambler, 1988, blk walls, metalflake red, MIP $16.00
Jet Threat, 1971, red line tires, metallic yel, M.................$75.00
Lamborghini Diablo, red, MIP..$5.00
Large Charge Mexican, 1985, blk walls, orange, M $40.00
Letter Getter, 1977, red line, wht, G+ $55.00
Light My Firebird, 1970, red line, red w/wht interior, NM+ ..$60.00
Lola GT-70, 1969, metallic pk, rare color, NM..............$150.00

Lola GT-70, 1969, red line, metallic brown, back lifted to show metal engine, M, $50.00. (Photo courtesy June Moon)

Lotus Turbine, 1969, red line, orange, NM+ $30.00
Mantis, 1970, red line, red w/wht interior, NM+ $35.00
McClaren M6A, 1969, red line, antifreeze, M $45.00
Mercedes Benz 280SL, 1969, red line, aqua w/brn interior, NM+ $40.00
Mercedes 380 SEL, 1982, blk walls, metalflake gray, MIP ..$8.00
Mercedes 540K, blk, MIP $15.00
Merceds Benz C111, 1972, red line, yel, NM+ $175.00
Mighty Maverick, 1970, red line, rose, NM+ $120.00
Minitrek, 1983, blk walls, wht, NM+................................$40.00
Mirada Stocker, 1982, blk walls, yel, MIP $15.00
Mod Quad, 1970, red line tires, metallic magenta, rare color, M..$100.00
Mongoose Funny Car, 1970, red line, red, NM+ $100.00
Mutt Mobile, 1971, red line, magenta, NM+ $160.00
Nissan 300ZX, yel w/red, wht & bl accents, MIP..............$8.00
Nitty Gritty Kitty, 1970, red line tires, metallic brn, NM ..$100.00
Odd Job, 1973, red line, lt yel, NM+ $200.00
Old Number 5, 1982, blk walls, red, NM+ $10.00
Omni 024, 1981, blk walls, gray, MIP...............................$8.00

Open Fire, 1972, red line, magenta, NM+ $175.00
Oshkosh Cement Mixer, red, wht & bl, MIP $5.00
P-911 Porsche, 1975, red line tires, yel w/bl & orange detail, NM $60.00
Packin' Pacer, 1980, blk walls, orange, MIP $30.00
Paramedic, 1977, blk walls, yel, NM+ $20.00
Peepin Bomb, 1970, red line, dk orange, NM+ $20.00
Peterbilt Dump Truck, red, MIP $8.00
Pit Crew Car, 1971, red line, wht w/gray interior, NM+...$140.00

Porsche 911, 1976, red line, Super Chromes series, M, $40.00. (Photo courtesy June Moon)

Porsche 917, 1970, red line, yel, NM+ $50.00
Porsche 959, 1988, blk walls, metalflake red, MIP............$10.00
Prowler, 1976, red line, chrome, M $60.00
Prowler, 1977, blk walls, chrome, NM- $35.00

Python, 1968, red line, metallic blue, based on *Car Craft Magazine's* 'Dream Car,' designed by Bill Cushenberry, M, $50.00. (Photo courtesy June Moon)

Python, 1968, red line, yel w/wht interior, NM+ $38.00
Radar Ranger, 1988, blk walls, metalflake silver, MIP $9.00
Rescue Ranger, 1988, blk walls, red, NM $4.00
Road Torch, 1987, blk walls, red, MIP $20.00
Rocket Bye Baby, 1971, red line, aqua, NM+ $85.00
Rolls Royce Phantom II, 1984, metallic bl, MIP.................$8.00
Sand Crab, 1970, red line, yel, NM+ $30.00
Seasider, 1970, red line, magenta, NM+ $110.00

Sheriff Patrol, 1988, blk walls, blk, MIP............................$10.00
Short Order, 1973, red line, dk bl, NM+............................$80.00
Side Kick, 1972, red line, magenta, NM+ $165.00

Side Kick, 1972, red line, metallic green, showing slide-out cockpit, M, $125.00. (Photo courtesy June Moon)

Silhouette, 1968, red line, lt gr, M $120.00
Six-Shooter, 1971, red line, magenta, EX $50.00
Six-Shooter, 1971, red line, magenta w/blk interior, NM+..$160.00
Snake, 1996, blk walls, wht, limited edition (10,000), M.$20.00
Sol-Aire CX4, 1989, blk walls, blk, MIP $6.00
Special Delivery, 1971, red line, lt bl, M $80.00
Split Window '63, 1983, blk walls, yel, NM+ $15.00
Spoiler Sport, 1980, blk walls, gr, MIP $16.00
Street Beast, wht & turq, MIP $5.00
Street Beast, 1988, blk walls, red, MIP $10.00
Super Cannon, 1985, blk walls, olive, MIP $7.00
T-Bird Stocker, wht & blk, #28 tampo, Ultra Hot Wheels, MIP $12.00
T-4-2, 1971, red line, magenta, EX....................................$50.00
Tall Rider, 1985, blk walls, gray, MIP $8.00
Thrill Drivers Torino, 1977, blk walls, wht, NM- $75.00
Thunderbird Stocker, 1984, blk walls, wht, MIP $35.00

Top Eliminator, 1974, red line, blue with orange, green, and yellow tampo, MOC, $175.00.

Tricar X8, 1982, blk walls, wht, MIP $7.00
Turbo Mustang, 1982, blk walls, red, MIP........................$10.00
Turbo Streak, red, unpainted spoiler, MIP........................$10.00
Turbo Streak, red w/ red spoiler, MIP $75.00
Turismo, 1981, blk walls, red, NM+ $7.00
Turismo, 1983, blk walls, yel, MIP..................................$10.00
Wind Splitter, 1984, blk walls, metallic bl, MIP $9.00

MISCELLANEOUS

Action City, 1969, complete, MIB, from $100 to $100.00
Button, Beatnik Bandit, metal, NM $8.00
Button, Classic '31 Ford Woody, metal, NM.......................$5.00
Button, Jet Threat, plastic, M...$10.00
Button, Short Order, plastic, M $6.00
Case, 12-car, 1969, yel w/red car on front, NM.................$30.00

Case, Rally; 12-car, red or blue, rare, M, from $20.00 to $35.00.

Case, 24-car, 1969, yel w/wht & bl cars on front, adjustable,
    EX $35.00
Case, 24-car, 1970s, Flying Colors, bl & wht, EX $25.00
Case, 48-car, 1969, yel, adjustable, NM $45.00

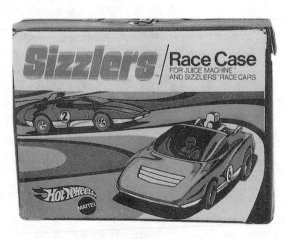

Case, Sizzlers; 1971, NM, from $25.00 to $30.00.

Catalog, Mattel, Spring 1970, M....................................$195.00
Chopcycles Rip Rider Set, MOC $120.00
Dual-Lane Rod Runner, 1970, MIB..................................$35.00
Dual-Lane Speedometer, 1970, wht & orange, EX $30.00
Farbs Human Race Set, 1972, MOC................................$150.00
Gran Toros, Chevy Astro II, 1970, gray, complete, NM ...$125.00
Gran Toros, Torpedo, 1970, MOC $275.00
Gran Toros Match Race Set, Italy, 1970, 1/43 scale, complete
    w/2 cars, MIB...$450.00
Hot Line Great Freight Set, complete, MIB, from $150 to ..$200.00
Hot Wheels Competition Pak, 1968, MIB (sealed)..........$16.00
Hot Wheels Dare Devil Loop, 1968, MIB (sealed) $20.00
Hot Wheels Dual-Lane Lap Counter, 1968, MIB $15.00
Hot Wheels Two-Way Super Charger, 1967, MIB $25.00
Mongoose & Snake Wild Wheelie Set, orig issue, complete,
    MIB...$500.00
Pop-Up Service Station, 1967, self-contained plastic w/pop-up
    service station, NM..$40.00
Revealers, Sol-Aire CX-4, 1993-94, several color variations,
    MIP, ea..$5.00
Sizzlers Fast Track Curve Pak, 1970, MIB $20.00
Sizzlers Fast Track Post Pak, 1970, MIB (sealed) $10.00

Sizzlers Mad Scatter Set, MIB, $60.00 plus price of car (varies). (Photo courtesy Mike's General Store)

Sizzlers Speed Brakes & Esses Pak, 1970, MIB (sealed) $25.00
Strip Action Set, 1969, MIB (sealed) $125.00
Super-Charger Sprint Set, complete, EX (EX box).........$225.00
Tune-Up Tower, 1970, MIB (contents sealed) $250.00
Yo-yo, 1990s, plastic tire shape w/imprint seal, MOC.........$8.00

Housewares

Back in the dark ages before women's lib and career-minded mothers, little girls emulated mommy's lifestyle, not realizing that by the time they grew up, total evolution would have taken place before their very eyes. They'd sew and bake, sweep, do laundry, and iron (gasp!), and imagine what fun it would be when *they* were big like mommy. Those little gadgets they played with are precious collectibles today, and any child-size houseware item is treasured, especially those from the '40s and '50s. If you're interested in learning about toy sewing machines, we recommend *Toy and Miniature Sewing Machines, Books I* and *II*, by Glenda Thomas (Collector Books).

CLEANING AND LAUNDRY

Cinderella Cleaning Set, Northstar Corp, 1947, MIB......**$95.00**
Cleaning Set, Little Homemaker, 1950s, litho metal, 4 pcs, MIP **$50.00**
Iron, Wolverine, 1960s, litho tin w/red plastic hdls, EX ...**$15.00**
Ironing Board, Sunnie Miss, Ohio Art, 1960s, tin, 20", VG .**$25.00**
My Merry Cleaning Closet, Merry, 1957, complete w/cleaning supplies, NMIB **$15.00**
Sad Iron, Dolly Dover, EX ....:.....................................**$50.00**

Washing Machine, Ertl, 1993, for the 100th year anniversary of the Maytag Company, $50.00. (Photo courtesy Nate Stoller)

Washing Machine, Hubley, 1920s, Maytag, made in red and blue, 7½", VG, $750.00. (Photo courtesy Nate Stoller)

Washing Machine, Pretty Maid, Marx, tin & plastic, EX **$150.00**

Washing Machine, Reliable Toy Co, 1950s, hand-crank wringer type, 8x5" dia, EX **$55.00**
Washing Machine, Thor, Arcade, yel-pnt CI w/NP parts, ftd, 5½", VG **$300.00**

COOKING

Bakeware Set, Betty Jane, McKee, nine pieces, MIB, from $100.00 to $125.00. (Photo courtesy Doris Lechler)

Cooking & Baking Set, Little Tikes, 34 pcs, EX **$30.00**
Cooking Set, Betsy Tapin, 42 pcs, metal, EX **$35.00**
Cooking Set, metal, 5 pcs, 1920s, EX.............................**$35.00**

Cooking Set, German, china and enameled utensils, recipe book in German, EX (VG box), A, $580.00.

Cookware Set, Germany, stainless steel, 22 pcs, EX $50.00

Stove, Acme, ornate CI w/7 range tops & 2 ovens, 11", EX, A $300.00

Stove, American w/ATF in shield mk on door, CI, 13x6x10½", EX..$85.00

Stove, Bonnie Glo on door, CI, comes w/1 cooking pot, 4¼x5", EX...$60.00

Stove, Crescent, CI w/oven, 5 range tops & shelves, 13½", EX, A $200.00

Stove, Crescent, CI w/2 side shelves, opening door & backdrop filigree, 4-ftd, 11", VG, A...$250.00

Stove, Crescent, CI w/2 side shelves & filigree backdrop, complete w/pots & kettles, 4-ftd, 8", VG, A $175.00

Stove, Daisy, pnt CI & steel, 9", VG, A............................$300.00

Stove, Eagle, CI w/bl-gray pnt, 3x5x4½", EX.................$100.00

Stove, Eagle by Hubley, NP CI, ornate panels, missing 1 lid, 5½x11x11", EX..$185.00

Stove, Fuchs, Germany, 1960s, tinplate & spirit-fired, w/frying pan, roasting tray & casserole dish, 6½x6½", NMIB.$55.00

Stove, Germany, tin w/2 ovens, 5 range tops, chimney & 2 pots, claw feet, 11", EX, A $200.00

Stove, Home, NP CI, w/chimney, 5 range tops, oven & 2 ledges, 15", EX, A..$250.00

Stove, Home by JE Stevens, 1900-1920s, removeable side panels, 11¾x10¾", w/bucket, shovel & pot lifter, EX...$175.00

Stove, Lady Junior by Metropolitan Mfg, 1950s, electric, missing cord o/w EX...$55.00

Stove, Lancaster by Hubley, CI, w/coal bucket, skillet, pot, plate lifter & shovel, 14x12¼", EX...................................$200.00

Stove, Lionel, porcelain & CI, cream & gr, 32x26", EX ...$600.00

Stove, Little Eva, CI, complete w/pipe, pots, pans & lids, 4 ftd, 8x13", VG, A..$575.00

Stove, Little Lady by Empire, 1950s, electric, wht w/red knobs & hdls, 6½x12½x11½", EX $50.00

Stove, Little Orphan Annie pictured on door, 1950s, electric, 3 doors & 2 burners, 5x9½x8½", EX $80.00

Stove, Little Tikes, complete w/baking, cooking utensils & food, 50 pcs, EX $55.00

Stove, mk EH, CI w/2 ovens, drawer, 2 graduated range tops & hot bin, brass rail, 9½", EX, A $375.00

Stove, Snow White, Wolverine, 10¾x11½", VG.............$30.00

Stove, Spark, CI w/interior grate sliding vents & opening door, 4-ftd, G, A...$125.00

Stove, Suzy Homemaker, tin, 12x12x19", EX $36.00

Stove, Toy Empire by Metal Ware Corp, electric, 15x14½", EX $200.00

Stove, Triumph, Kenton, NP CI w/ornate design, w/frying pans, kettles, etc, 15", EX, A $525.00

Stove, Wolverine, tin, 15¾", VG.....................................$38.00

Stove & sink, Step 2, plastic, comes w/31-pc set of dishes, EX $40.00

SEWING

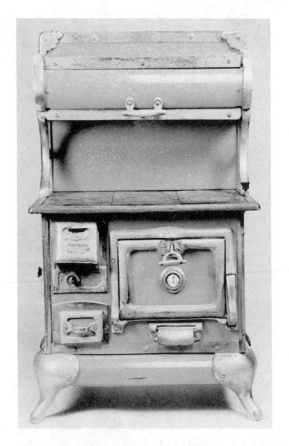

Stove, Karr Range Co., cast iron with blue enamel, nickeled doors, trim and pedestal feet, 21½", EX, A, $5,500.00.

Stove, Kenton, early 1900s, NP CI, wood burning, w/kettle, frying pan & shovel, EX $265.00

Sewing Machine, Casige Favorit, Germany, produced both before and after WWII, 7½" x 5¾" x 9⅝", NM, from $150.00 to $175.00. (Photo courtesy Glenda Thomas)

Sewing Machine, Jet Sew-O-Matic, Straco, mk Made in England, plastic & metal, 7x9", EX $65.00

Sewing Machine, Lindstrom, 1940s, litho metal w/wood hdl, 6x8", EX $50.00

Sewing Machine, Reliable, CI w/gilt decor, EX, A.........$275.00

Sewing Machine, Singer No 20, CI, EX, A $200.00
Sewing Machine, Singer Sewhandy No 20, 1940s, pressed steel
    & CI, MIB $100.00

Sewing Machine, Gabriela, VEB Piko, East Germany, 1980s, battery operated, 9" x 5½" x10", NM, from $75.00 to $95.00. (Photo courtesy Glenda Thomas)

TABLE SERVICE

Lemonade Set, Mirro, 1930s, service for 6 w/tray, MIB ..$125.00
Platter, Blue Willow, oval, 6", EX......................................$50.00
Tea Set, apple & pear motif, Ohio Art, 14 pcs, EX...........$90.00
Tea Set, Blue Willow, Ohio Art, litho tin, 21 pcs, EX....$145.00
Tea Set, Bunny Birthday, Ohio Art, late 1930s, litho tin, 7 pcs,
    M (VG box)...$365.00
Tea Set, Care Bears, 13 pcs, EX $65.00
Tea Set, children & ducks motif, Ohio Art, 1950s, litho tin, 14
    pcs, EX $80.00
Tea Set, Germany, wht porcelain w/Angel Kewpie dolls, service
    for 6, NM, A...$1,265.00
Tea Set, Ideal, 1950s, tin & plastic, service for 4, rare,
    MIB $165.00
Tea Set, Little American Maid, Akro Agate, MIB $350.00
Tea Set, Little Miss Homemaker, Plastic Art, 15 pcs, MIB ..$35.00
Tea Set, Mexican Boys, Ohio Art, 1940s, 7 pcs, EX $55.00
Tea Set, Mickey Mouse motif, Made in Japan w/Walt E Disney
    stamp, 17 pcs, NM..$260.00
Tea Set, Ohio Art, early 1930s, various scenes w/little girl at
    play, litho tin, 8 pcs, EX, from $200 to.....................$250.00
Tea Set, Ohio Art, 1920s, kittens w/ABC border, litho tin, 5 pcs,
    EX, from $300 to $350.00
Tea Set, Ohio Art, 1956, boy & girl in garden, litho tin, 15 pcs,
    MIB, from $100 to..$150.00
Tea Set, Puppies, Ohio Art, early 1940s, 30 pcs, VG+ ...$180.00
Tea Set, Victorian style characters, Ohio Art, 15 pcs, EX+ ...$180.00
Tea Set, wooden apple shape box w/7 pcs set inside, VG .$55.00

Teapot, Blue Willow, 3", M..$50.00
Tureen, Blue Willow, M..$65.00

Jack-in-the Boxes

Very early jack-in-the-box toys were often made of papier-mache and cloth, fragile material to withstand the everyday wear and tear to which they were subjected, so these vintage German examples are scarce today and very expensive. But even those from the '50s and '60s are collectible, especially when they represent well-known TV or storybook characters. Examples with lithographed space themes are popular as well.

See also Character, TV, and Movie Collectibles; Disney.

Boy, ca 1910, wood box w/image of children & St Bernard,
    compo figure w/cloth clothes, 8", EX $325.00
Castle Jester, Carnival, litho tin, VG, from $75 to........$100.00
Clown, Mattel, 1971, litho tin, EX...................................$50.00
Clown, Ohio Art, litho tin, VG, from $75 to.................$100.00
Clown, papier-mache w/paper-covered wood box, 4",
    EX $750.00
Jester, Lorraine Novelty, litho tin w/cloth figure, plays 'Pop Goes
    the Weasel,' NM..$50.00
Leprechaun, Germany, paper-covered wood box w/papier-mache
    & cloth figure, 3½", VG...$125.00
Man in Red Top Hat, Germany, paper-covered wood box, papier-
    mache figure w/gray hair, w/squeaker, 5", EX $450.00

Keystone

Though this Massachusetts company produced a variety of toys during their years of operation (ca 1920 – late 1950s), their pressed-steel vehicles are the most collectible, and that's what we've listed here. As a rule they were very large, with some of the riders being 30" in length.

Aerial Ladder Truck, 1920s, red w/blk rubber tires, NP ladder,
    32", prof rstr, A $950.00
Airmail Plane Y-288, rider, yel & red, 24" W, NM, A $600.00
American Railway Express Truck, blk w/screened-in body, alu-
    minum tires w/red-pnt hubs, 26", EX, A...............$1,800.00
American Railway Express Van, 1920s, blk doorless cab w/gr
    screened-in body, red chassis & hubcaps, 26", rstr, A .$700.00
Coast to Coast Bus, bl w/silver top, blk rubber tires w/bl-pnt
    hubs, 30", rstr, A..$2,750.00
Dump Truck, 1920s, blk doorless cab w/red chassis, aluminum
    disk wheels w/red hubcaps, 26", rstr, A $575.00
Fire Ladder Truck, 1920s, red w/Chemical Pump Engine decal,
    blk rubber tires, 29", EX, A...................................$4,600.00
Keystone Garage, complete w/plastic accessories, 15x26", EX,
    A..$150.00
Keystone Service Station, complete w/plastic vehicles, 12x22",
    VG, A..$150.00
Locomotive, rider, blk & red, 23", G, A.........................$225.00

Moving Van, blk doorless cab w/red body, blk rubber tires w/red-pnt hubs, 25", VG, A $1,700.00

Moving Van, 1920s, blk doorless cab w/red body, blk rubber tires w/red hubs, VG, A.............................$700.00

Packard Coast-to-Coast Bus, 1920s, bl w/blk rubber tires, top lifts open, 31", prof rstr, A.....................$2,800.00

Packard Coast-To-Coast Bus, 1920s, opening roof, working steering, 31½", EX, A, $8,000.00.

Packard Hook & Ladder Truck, w/rotating bell, extension ladder & 2 side ladders, 30", EX, A $550.00

Police Patrol Truck, blk w/screened-in body, blk rubber tires w/red-pnt hubs, 28", VG, A $935.00

Police Patrol Van, 1920s, blk doorless cab w/screened-in body, 29", VG, A................................$850.00

Pullman Railroad Car, rider, red & bl w/hinged roof, 24", EX, A $750.00

Railroad Wrecking Car, blk & gr w/blk rubber tires & red-pnt hubs, 20", rstr, A......................................$225.00

Road Roller, rider, 1920s, gray & red, 20", VG, A..........$450.00

Service Station, mk Keystone Garage, complete, 8x10", NM (EX box), A $300.00

Steam Shovel, 1920s, gray & red w/blk scoop & tires, 21", VG, A $150.00

Tank Department Truck, blk w/aluminum tires & red-pnt hubs, orig sprinkler & pull cord, 25", VG, A $1,700.00

Traffic Outfit, battery-op, complete, MIB, A $200.00

Truck Loader, khaki with red base and wheels, 20", EX, A, $300.00; Steam Shovel, gray with red roof and base, 20", NM, A, $400.00.

US Army Truck, 1920s, gr w/open bench seat, orig canvas cover, blk rubber tires, 26", G, A $450.00

US Mail Truck, 1920s, blk doorless cab w/gr screened-in body, blk rubber tires w/red hubcaps, 26", VG, A $650.00

US Mail Truck, 1920s, blk doorless cab w/gr screened-in body, blk rubber tires w/red hubcaps, 26", EX+, A.........$1,600.00

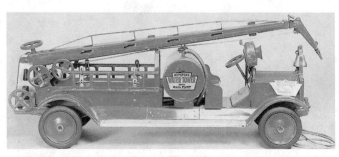

Water Pump Tower Truck, pump works by hand-lever action, two ladders, original string tag and pull cord, 30", NM, A, $2,600.00.

Water Tower Truck, 1920s, red w/blk rubber tires, 33", VG, A..$1,100.00

Wrecker, red open cab w/gr tow hook, blk rubber tires w/red hubs, 26", VG, A....................................$1,200.00

Lehmann

Lehmann toys were made in Germany as early as 1881. Early on they were sometimes animated by means of an inertia-generated flywheel; later, clockwork mechanisms were used. Some of their best-known turn-of-the-century toys were actually very racist and unflattering to certain ethnic groups. But the wonderful antics they perform and the imagination that went into their conception have made them and all the other Lehmann toys favorites with collectors today. Though the company faltered with the onset of WWI, they were quick to recover and during the war years produced some of their best toys, several of which were copied by their competitors. Business declined after WWI. Lehmann died in 1934, but the company continued for awhile under the direction of Lehmann's partner and cousin, Johannes Richter.

Advisor: Scott Smiles (S10).

See also Aeronautical; Banks.

Adam, porter pushing hand cart with large trunk, 8" x 7", NM (VG box), $1,500.00.

Acrobat, figure walks up & down slotted pole, VG $750.00

Adam the Porter, figure pushes trunk on cart, 8", NM ..$1,350.00

AHA Delivery Van, red & wht w/yel spoke wheels, 8", EX...$600.00

Ajax Acrobat, litho tin figure w/cloth costume performs somersaults, 9", VG..$1,100.00

Ajax Acrobat, litho tin figure w/cloth costume preforms somersaults, 9", NM...$1,800.00

Alabama Coon Jigger, 1910, Black man dances on stage, rare version w/checked pants, 10", EX $700.00

Alabama Coon Jigger, 1910, Black man dances on stage, rare version w/checked pants, 10", NMIB......................$900.00

ALSO Automobile, 1910, open auto w/full-figure driver, 4", VG, A $400.00

ALSO Automobile, 1910, open auto w/full-figure driver in red, 4", NM...$600.00

Anxious Bride, pnt & litho tin, 4½", NMIB..............$2,000.00

Autin Pedal Car, boy in pedal car, 4", NM (EX box mk American Boy) $1,300.00

Auto Post Delivery Van, red w/spoked wheels, driver in open cab, 5", EX...$1,200.00

Autobus #590, dbl-decker w/rear stairs, full-figure driver, 7", EX, A...$1,600.00

Autobus #590, dbl-decker w/rear steps, full-figure driver, 7", VG, A...$1,100.00

Autohutte & Galop Racer #1, NM............................$1,500.00

Captain of Kopenvil, soldier in long brn cloth coat, 7½", NM $2,700.00

Climbing Monkey, litho tin w/rough sprayed-on jacket, 8", NM (G box) $400.00

Crawling Beetle, Pat 1895, early version w/lt gr wings, 4½", NM $300.00

Crocodile, advances w/jaw movement, 9", NM (VG box) .$900.00

Dancing Sailor, litho tin w/cloth clothes, hat band stenciled HMS Dreadnaught, 7½", NM $1,200.00

DUO Rooster w/Rabbit on Egg, unmk, 7½", NM $1,700.00

Echo Motorcycle w/Driver, litho & hand-pnt tin, 8½", EX, A..$1,700.00

Echo Motorcycle w/Driver, litho & hand-pnt tin, 8½", NM (NM box)...$3,500.00

EHE & CO Truck, w/driver, 7", VG................................$500.00

EPL-1 Dirigible, litho tin w/celluloid props, 8", NM (EX box), A..$1,100.00

EPL-1 Dirigible, litho tin w/celluloid props, 8", VG (G box) .$750.00

EPL-11 Zeppelin, litho tin w/celluloid prop, 9½", EX.$1,000.00

Express Porter, 1910, porter pulls trunk on 2-wheeled cart, 6", NM...$800.00

Gala Sedan, bl & wht, rare, 12", VG $850.00

Galop Racer #1, w/driver, yel & bl stripe, 5½", NMIB, from $1,600 to..$1,700.00

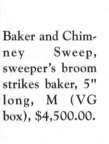

Baker and Chimney Sweep, sweeper's broom strikes baker, 5" long, M (VG box), $4,500.00.

Galop, zebra pulls cart driven by cowboy, 1954 reissue (determined by new color scheme), 7½", NM (EX box), from $500.00 to $650.00.

Balky Mule, 1910, clown bounces as cart advances, 8", EX, from $500 to..$600.00

Balky Mule, 1910, clown bounces as cart advances, 8", NM...$750.00

Berolina Convertible, bl w/red frame & brn cloth top, spoke wheels, w/driver, 7", NM.....................................$3,500.00

Boxer, 4 Chinese men mounted on base throw figure in cloth blanket, 5x5" base, rare, NM, from $5,500 to......$6,500.00

Bucking Bronco & Cowboy, brn horse, 6½", NM $900.00

Bucking Bronco & Cowboy, wht horse, 6½", EX $750.00

Buster Brown, seated in open auto, 4", NM.................$2,000.00

Going to the Fair, man pushing woman in promenade chair, 6", G...$1,300.00

Going to the Fair, man pushing woman in promenade chair, 6", NM..$3,000.00

Gustav the Miller, pull string & figure climbs shaft to mill, 18", NM...$500.00

Halloh Rider on Cycle, flywheel mechanism, 8", NM, D10..$2,400.00

Heavy Swell, litho tin figure w/cloth clothes & cane, 8½", G..$800.00

Heavy Swell, litho tin figure w/cloth clothes & cane, 8½", NM (VG box)..$3,300.00

IHI Meat Van, doorless cab w/opening cloth sides on body, w/driver, 6½", EX..................................$1,700.00

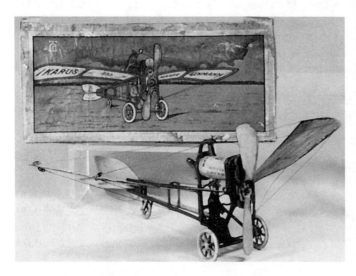

Ikarus Airplane, tin airplane with wire-supported paper wings, 10½" long, EXIB, A, $3,800.00.

ITO Sedan, w/driver, red w/blk top, spoke wheels, rpl flag, 6", VG..$600.00

Jonny, boy in sailor suit advances using pulley ropes, 6", EX (EX box)..$200.00

Jonny Lion, plastic, friction, 3", MIBN............................$50.00

Kadi, 2 Chinese men carrying tea set, 7", NM (EX box)..$4,000.00

Kadi, 2 Chinese men carrying tea set, 7", VG..............$1,200.00

Kamerun Ostrich Cart, Black boy on bench seat, 6", EX..$850.00

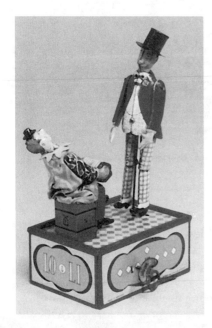

Lo and Li, dancer and seated accordion-playing clown, NM, $5,000.00.

Kimado Family, man pulls female passenger in rickshaw, hand-pnt & litho tin, 7", EX..........................$1,700.00

Lila Hansom Cab, w/driver, 2 lady passengers & dog, 5½", G..$1,000.00

Lila Hansom Cab, w/driver, 2 lady passengers & dog, 5½", NM (G box)..$2,200.00

Lo Lo Auto, gr & wht auto w/full-figure driver in red, 4", VG..$700.00

Lu Lu Delivery Van, gr & yel w/roof rack, spoke wheels, w/driver, 7", NM..................................$2,600.00

Mandarin, 2 Chinese men carrying sedan chair w/figure, 7", G..$1,600.00

Mandarin, 2 Chinese men carrying sedan chair w/figure, 7", NM (VG box), from $4,000 to..................$4,500.00

Masuyama, Pat 1913, coolie pulls Japanese lady w/parasol in 2-wheeled cart, 7", NM (G box), A..............$3,000.00

Masuyama, Pat 1913, coolie pulls Japanese lady w/parasol in 2-wheeled cart, 7", NM........................$2,500.00

Mensa Delivery Van, 3-wheeled vehicle w/driver, 5", EX..$2,200.00

Mice on Spiral Rod, 2 mice revolve around rod when turned upsidedown, EX..................................$250.00

Minstrel Man, 1906, flat tin, 7½", scarce, EX (EX envelpoe)..$800.00

Miss Blondin, tightrope walker, 10½", EX..................$3,000.00

Mixtum, Black man in 3-wheeled vehicle w/horn & lantern, rpl horn, 4½", EX..................................$1,300.00

Motor Car, driver in carriage w/spoke wheels, 5", EX (worn box)..$1,000.00

NA-OB Donkey Cart, driver in open cart, 6", EX..........$800.00

Nani Cart, plastic, friction, 3", MIB..........................$50.00

Naughty Boy, 1903, wht & bl auto, no figures, 5", VG, A..$200.00

Naughty Boy, 1903, wht & bl auto w/driver & boy facing ea other at center wheel, 5", NM........................$1,000.00

Naughty Boy, 1903, wht & bl auto w/driver & boy facing ea other at center wheel, 5", NM (VG box)............$2,100.00

New Century Cycle, man holding umbrella over driver in 3-wheeled vehicle, 5", NM, D10, from $850 to..........$900.00

Nu-Nu, Chinese man pulling tea chest, 4½", NM (partial box)..$1,300.00

OHO Cart, 1903, open auto w/driver, 4", G..................$400.00

Ostrich Cart (African), 6", EX..................................$600.00

Paak-Paak Quack-Quack Duck Cart, Pat 1903, mama pulls ducklings in 2-wheeled cart, 8", EX....................$500.00

Paddy & the Pig, Irishman riding pig, 5½", NM............$2,400.00

Panne Touring Car, gray & red w/spoke wheels, w/driver, 7", EX..$1,700.00

Performing Sea Lion, 7", NM (VG box)......................$450.00

Primus Roller Skater, boy skates w/realistic movement, 8½", rare, NM, from $6,500 to..........................$7,000.00

Rad Cycle, driver on 3-wheeled vehicle pulls lady in open carriage, NM..$2,500.00

Rigi Cable Car, complete w/rope & pulley, 4", EX (EX box)..$400.00

Royal Mail Van, driver in open cab w/overhang, spoke wheels, 7", NM..$2,000.00

Skirolf Cross Country Skier, advances on skis, 7", VG..$2,100.00

Snik-Snak, man walking 2 dogs, 8", EX (EX box)......$5,000.00

Stiller Berlin Truck, 1927, yel & blk w/spoke wheels, 6", rare, EX..$900.00

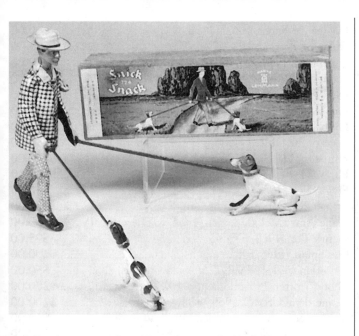

Snik-Snak, man walking two dogs, red checked suit version, 8" x 16", NMIB, $6,000.00.

Stubborn Donkey, clown bounces in cart as donkey advances, 8", NMIB $650.00

Tap-Tap Man w/Wheelbarrow, hand-pnt & litho tin, 6", NMIB $1,200.00

Terra Sedan, solid wheel version, red & blk, 10", EX ..$1,900.00

Titania Sedan, red & bl, electric headlights, 10", VG $600.00

Tom the Climbing Monkey, 1903, plain vest, hand-pnt face, 7½", MIB $400.00

Tom the Climbing Monkey, 1903, polka-dot vest, litho tin face, 7½", MIB $900.00

Tut-Tut, driver in open auto blowing horn, litho & hand-pnt tin, 6½", EX...$1,100.00

Tyras the Walking Dog, 6", NM $850.00

UHU Amphibious Car, 9", EX $650.00

Velleda Touring Car, driver in open auto w/folding seats, 10", G $1,000.00

Vineta Monorail, w/gyroscope stabilizer, 9½", EX $850.00

Waltzing Doll, hand-pnt tin w/celluloid head, cloth dress, advances on wheeled platform, 9", EX (worn box)..$1,800.00

Zig-Zag, 2 men in rocking chair w/lg wheels, 4", EX (EX box) $3,000.00

Zikra Dare Devil, driver in zebra cart, litho tin, 7", NM..$1,200.00

Zulu Ostrich Man, driver in ostrich-driven cart, 7", VG ..$650.00

Lunch Boxes

When the lunch box craze began in the mid-1980s, it was only the metal boxes that so quickly soared to sometimes astronomical prices. But today, even the plastic and vinyl ones are collectible. Though most lunch box dealers agree that with few exceptions, prices have become much more reasonable than they were at first, they're still holding their own and values seem to be stabilizing. So pick a genre and have fun. There are liter-

ally hundreds to choose from, and just as is true in other areas of character-related collectibles, the more desirable lunch boxes are those with easily recognized, well-known subjects — western heroes, TV, Disney and other cartoon characters, and famous entertainers. Thermoses are collectible as well. In our listings, values are just for the box unless a Thermos is mentioned in the description. If you'd like to learn more about them, we recommend *A Pictorial Price Guide to Metal Lunch Boxes and Thermoses* and a companion book *A Pictorial Price Guide to Vinyl and Plastic Lunch Boxes* by Larry Aikins and *Collector's Guide to Lunchboxes* by Carole Bess White and L.M. White (Collector Books). For more pricing information, Philip R. Norman (Norman's Olde Store) has prepared a listing of hundreds of boxes, Thermoses, and their variations. He is listed in the Categories of Special Interest under Lunch Boxes.

Advisor: Terri Ivers (I2).

Other Sources: C1, C10, J6, M15, T1, T2

METAL

A-Team, 1983, VG, N2 ....$20.00

Action Jackson, 1973, w/Thermos, A $175.00

Adam-12, 1972, VG $35.00

Addams Family, 1974, EX, $50.00.

America on Parade, 1975, VG, N2 ....$20.00

Animal Friends, 1975, EX, N2 ....$30.00

Annie, 1981, EX+, N2..$28.00

Astronauts, 1969, VG+, N2 ....$50.00

Atom Ant, 1966, G $40.00

Back in '76, 1975, EX, N2 ....$45.00

Batman & Robin, 1966, w/Thermos, NM, A $200.00

Battle of the Planets, 1979, EX, N2..............................$40.00

Battlestar Galactica, 1978, w/Thermos, EX, N2 ....$45.00

Beatles, 1965, bl, VG, B3 ....$200.00

Beatles, 1965, w/Thermos, NM, A...............................$600.00

Betsy Clark, 1975, beige, w/Thermos, EX, N2 ....$25.00

Beverly Hillbillies, 1963, w/Thermos, NM, A $200.00

Black Hole, 1979, EX, N2..$50.00

Bonanza, 1963, VG, N2..$85.00

Bond XX Secret Agent, 1966, EX, A $100.00
Bozo the Clown, 1963, dome top, EX, A $175.00
Bozo the Clown, 1963, dome top, w/Thermos, NM $250.00
Brady Bunch, 1970, w/Thermos, EX, A $125.00
Brave Eagle, 1957, w/Thermos, NM, A $400.00
Buccaneer, 1961, EX, A $185.00
Buck Rogers, 1979, EX, N2 ....$35.00

Bullwinkle and Rocky, 1962, blue background, NM, $600.00.

Cable Car, 1962, dome top, NM, A $125.00
Campbell Kids, 1975, NM, A $275.00
Captain Astro, 1966, NM, A $250.00
Captain Astro, 1966, VG $110.00
Care Bear Cousins, 1985, w/Thermos, EX, N2 ....$20.00
Cartoon Zoo Lunch Chest, 1962, EX, A $175.00
Casey Jones, 1960, dome top, w/Thermos, NM, A $400.00
Casey Jones, 1960, dome top, w/Thermos, VG $225.00
Chan Clan, 1973, blk rim, EX, N2 ....$50.00
Chavo, 1979, M, N2 ....$200.00
Chitty-Chitty Bang-Bang, 1968, VG+, N2 ....$75.00
Chuck Wagon, 1958, dome top, w/Thermos, NM, A $250.00
Clash of the Titans, 1980, VG, N2 ....$20.00
Colonel Ed McCauley Space Explorer, 1960, w/Thermos, NM,
    A $175.00
Cracker Jack, 1979, EX, N2 ....$50.00
Davy Crockett, 1955, gr rim, VG, N2 ....$75.00
Davy Crockett, 1955, w/Thermos, NM, A $225.00
Dick Tracy, 1967, VG $95.00
Dick Tracy, 1967, w/Thermos, NM, A $200.00
Disney Express, 1979, EX, N2 ....$20.00
Disney on Parade, 1970, VG, N2 ....$25.00
Disney World, 1976, w/Thermos, EX+, N2 ....$35.00
Double Deckers, 1970, EX, N2 ....$60.00
Dr Dolittle, 1967, w/Thermos, EX, N2 ....$95.00
Dr Seuss, 1970, VG+ $70.00
Dragon's Lair, 1983, EX, N2 ....$25.00
Duchess, 1960, w/Thermos, NM, N2 ....$125.00

Dudley Do-Right, 1962, bl rim, NM, A $1,000.00
Dukes of Hazzard, 1980, EX, N2 ....$35.00
Dynomutt, 1976, EX, N2 ....$50.00
Fall Guy, 1981, w/Thermos, NM, N2 ....$35.00
Family Affair, 1969, w/Thermos, EX $135.00
Fire House, 1959, w/Thermos, NM, A $425.00
Fireball X-L5, 1964, w/Thermos, NM, A $300.00
Flags of the United Nations, 1954, w/Thermos, NM, A .$250.00
Flintstones & Dino, 1962, w/Thermos, NM, A $250.00
Flipper, 1967, EX, N2 ....$100.00
Flying Nun, 1968, EX $60.00
Fraggle Rock, 1984, w/Thermos, EX, N2 ....$30.00
Gene Autry Melody Ranch, 1954, w/Thermos, NM, A .$500.00
Gentle Ben, 1968, EX, N2 ....$95.00
Get Smart, 1966, EX $200.00
Ghostland, 1977, EX, N2 ....$50.00
Globe-Trotter, 1959, dome top, EX, A $200.00
Gomer Pyle USMC, 1966, w/Thermos, EX, A $200.00
Goober & the Ghost Chasers, 1974, VG+, N2 ....$50.00
Goofy, 1984, EX+, N2 ....$30.00
Great Wild West, 1959, EX, N2 ....$375.00
Great Wild West, 1959, w/Thermos, NM, A $500.00
Green Hornet, 1967, w/Thermos, M, A $500.00
Gremlins, 1984, w/Thermos, M, N2 ....$40.00
Grizzly Adams, 1977, dome top, VG+, N2 ....$55.00
Guns of Will Sonnett, 1968, EX, N2 ....$100.00
Gun Smoke, 1959, EX $150.00
Hair Bear Bunch, 1971, EX, N2 ....$60.00
Hansel & Gretel, 1982, EX, N2 ....$100.00
Happy Days, 1976, VG $35.00
Heathcliff, 1982, EX, N2 ....$20.00
Hector Heathcote, 1964, w/Thermos, NM, A $200.00
Hee Haw, 1970, EX, N2 ....$70.00

Hogan's Heroes, 1966, dome top, VG, $150.00.

Hogan's Heroes, 1966, dome top, w/Thermos, EX, A $200.00
Home Town Airport, 1960, dome top, w/Thermos, NM, A..$750.00
Hopalong Cassidy, 1952, red w/sq decal, w/Thermos, EX, A.$285.00
How the West Was Won, 1978, w/Thermos, EX, N2 ....$55.00

HR Pufnstuf, 1970, w/Thermos, NM, A $185.00
Huckleberry Hound & Friends, 1961, VG, N2 ....$75.00
Incredible Hulk, 1978, EX, N2 ....$40.00
It's About Time, 1967, dome top, w/Thermos, NM, A...$350.00
James Bond 007, 1966, EX, A $250.00
Jet Patrol, 1957, w/Thermos, EX, A $200.00
Jetsons, 1963, dome top, EX $350.00
Jetsons, 1963, dome top, w/Thermos, NM, A $950.00
Jr Miss, 1973, attic scene, EX, N2 ....$25.00
Knight Rider, 1983, EX, N2 ....$35.00
Korg, 1974, EX, N2 ....$35.00
Krofft Supershow, 1976, VG, N2 ....$50.00
Lance Link Secret Chimp, 1971, NM, A $185.00
Land of the Giants, 1968, VG, N2 ....$75.00
Lassie, 1978, VG $35.00

Laugh-In, 1968, EX, $100.00.

Laugh-In, 1968, w/Thermos, EX, A $150.00
Lawman, 1961, EX+ $100.00
Lidsville, 1971, w/Thermos, from $100 to.....................$125.00
Little Dutch Miss, 1959, VG, N2 ....$75.00
Little House on the Prairie, 1978, w/Thermos, NM, from $75
    to..$100.00
Lone Ranger, 1954, VG, A...$100.00
Lone Ranger, 1980, VG, N2 ....$20.00
Loony Tunes, TV set version, 1959, w/Thermos, NM, A .$250.00
Lost in Space, 1967, dome top, w/Thermos, rare, NM, A.$600.00
Magic Kingdom, 1979, EX, N2....................................$25.00
Man From UNCLE, 1966, w/Thermos, EX....................$155.00
Marvel Super Heroes, 1976, EX....................................$45.00
Marvel Super Heroes, 1976, VG, N2 ....$25.00
Masters of the Universe, 1983, w/Thermos, M, N2 ....$40.00
Mickey Mouse Club, 1976, yel, EX, N2 ....$45.00
Mickey Mouse Club, 1977, red, VG, N2.........................$25.00
Mickey Mouse Lunch Kit, 1935, oval, w/pie tray & folding hdls,
    NM, A...$1,200.00
Miss America, 1972, w/Thermos, NM, A $150.00
Mod Tulip, 1962, dome top, EX, A $100.00

Monroes, 1967, EX, N2 ....$200.00
Mork & Mindy, 1979, VG+, N2...................................$30.00
Mr Merlin, 1981, VG, N2..$25.00
Munsters, 1965, w/Thermos, M, A $400.00
Munsters, 1965, w/Thermos, NM $250.00
Muppet Babies, 1985, EX, N2 ....$10.00
Muppets, 1979, VG, N2..$15.00
Nancy Drew, 1977, w/Thermos, NM, from $75 to..........$100.00
Nancy Drew Mysteries, 1977, VG, N2 ....$35.00
Pac Man, 1980, VG $20.00
Paladin, 1960, w/Thermos, NM, A $425.00
Partridge Family, 1971, w/Thermos, EX $50.00
Pathfinder, 1959, EX, N2...$400.00
Peanuts, 1973, EX, N2...$25.00
Pete's Dragon, 1978, EX..$45.00
Pigs in Space, 1978, EX, N2..$35.00
Pit Stop, 1968, EX+, N2..$175.00
Planet of the Apes, 1974, VG, N2 ....$60.00
Play Ball, 1969, w/Thermos, EX+ $35.00
Polly Pal, 1974, w/Thermos, EX, N2 ....$35.00
Popeye, 1962, w/Thermos, NM, A $400.00
Popeye, 1964, EX+ $100.00
Popples, 1986, w/Thermos, M, N2 ....$35.00

Porky's Lunch Wagon, 1959, dome top, EX, $400.00.

Raggedy Ann & Andy, 1973, w/Thermos, EX, N2 ....$40.00
Rambo, 1985, M, N2 ....$35.00
Return of the Jedi, 1983, VG, N2.................................$30.00
Road Runner, 1970, EX, A $75.00
Robin Hood, 1956, w/Thermos, EX, A $150.00
Ronald McDonald, 1982, w/Thermos, M, N2...................$40.00
Roy Rogers & Dale Evans Chow Wagon, 1958, dome top, EX,
    A..$175.00
Roy Rogers & Dale Evans Double R Bar Ranch, 1954, wood-
    grain rim, w/Thermos, NM, A $175.00
Scooby Doo, 1973, w/Thermos, NM, A.........................$175.00
Secret Agent T, 1968, VG, N2.....................................$60.00
Secret of Nimh, 1982, w/Thermos, M, N2 ....$40.00

Secret Wars, 1984, VG, N2 ....$15.00
Sesame Street, 1979, w/Thermos, EX, N2 ....$20.00
Six Million Dollar Man, 1974, w/Thermos, EX, N2 ....$55.00
Smokey Bear, 1975, NM, A $350.00
Snoopy, 1968, dome top, EX $65.00
Space Shuttle Orbiter Enterprise, 1977, VG, N2 ....$40.00
Space: 1999, 1974, G, N2 ....$25.00
Sport Goofy, 1983, VG $20.00
Sports Afield, 1957, EX, N2 ....$125.00
Star Trek, 1968, dome top w/Thermos, NM, A $900.00

Star Trek, 1979, EX+, $75.00.

Star Trek, 1979, VG, N2 ....$45.00
Steve Canyon, 1959, w/Thermos, NM, A $500.00
Strawberry Shortcake, 1980, w/Thermos, EX, N2 ....$25.00
Sunnie Miss, 1972, EX, N2 ....$45.00
Super Friends, 1976, w/Thermos, EX, N2 ....$50.00
Super Powers, 1983, VG+, N2 ....$25.00
Superman, 1967, VG $55.00
Superman, 1967, w/Thermos, NM, A $200.00
Superman, 1978, w/Thermos, EX $35.00
Tarzan, 1966, w/Thermos, NM, A $150.00
Three Little Pigs, 1982, EX, N2 ....$100.00
Thundercats, 1985, w/Thermos, EX, N2 ....$25.00
Tom Corbett Space Cadet, 1952, bl w/sq decal, w/Thermos, EX,
   A $175.00
Tom Corbett Space Cadet, 1952, red w/sq decal, w/Thermos,
   NM, A $250.00
Tom Corbett Space Cadet, 1954, w/Thermos, NM, A ...$425.00
Tony Tiger (Kellogg's Frosted Flakes), 1969, VG+ $150.00
Track King, 1975, NM, A $325.00
Transformers, 1986, w/Thermos, EX, N2 ....$25.00
UFO, 1973, VG, N2 ....$35.00
Underdog, 1974, wht rim, w/Thermos, NM, A $1,000.00
US Space Corps, 1961, w/Thermos, NM, A $275.00
Volkswagen Bus, 1960, dome top, w/Thermos, NM, A ..$850.00
Voyage to the Bottom of the Sea, 1967, w/Thermos, NM, A .$400.00
Wagon Train, 1964, VG, N2 ....$60.00

Wags 'N Whiskers, 1978, w/Thermos, EX, N2 ....$25.00
Wild Bill Hickok & Jingles, 1965, w/Thermos, NM $220.00

Wild Bill Hickok and Jingles, NM, $160.00.

Wild Frontier, 1977, EX $40.00
Wild Wild West, 1969, NM, A $200.00
Wonderful World of Disney, 1980, VG, N2 ....$10.00
Woody Woodpecker, 1972, w/Thermos, NM, A $200.00
World of Dr Seuss, 1970, w/Thermos, NM, A $200.00
Yankee Doodles, 1975, w/Thermos, G, N2 ....$20.00
Yellow Submarine, 1968, w/Thermos, NM, A $600.00
Zorro, 1958, VG $90.00

Zorro, 1958, EX, $145.00.

PLASTIC

American Gladiators, 1992, red, EX $9.00
Astrokids, 1988, w/Thermos, M, N2 ....$25.00

Barney & Baby Bop, 1992, w/Thermos, EX, N2 ....$8.00
Batman, 1982, bl, VG $5.00
Benji, 1974, EX, N2 ....$15.00
Cabbage Patch Kids, 1983, EX, N2 ....$9.00
Cabbage Patch Kids, 1983, yel, w/Thermos, EX $12.00
Casper the Ghost, 1996, w/Thermos, M, N2 ....$10.00
Chiclets Chewing Gum, 1987, w/Thermos, M, N2 ....$30.00
CHiPs, 1977, dome top, NM $30.00
Chuck E Cheese, 1996, w/Thermos, NM, N2 ....$15.00
Dick Tracy, 1990, w/Thermos, M, N2 ....$13.00
Disney School Bus, 1990, M, N2 ....$15.00
Dr Seuss, 1996, EX, N2 ....$15.00
Ewoks, 1983, EX, N2 ....$15.00
Flintstones, 1992, red, EX, N2 ....$10.00
Flintstones at the Zoo, 1989, w/Thermos, EX, N2 ....$20.00
Garfield, 1980s, w/Thermos, EX $15.00
Ghostbusters, 1986, purple, EX $20.00

Pink Panther and Sons, 1984, EX, $10.00.

Rap It Up, 1992, EX, N2 ....$15.00
Robot Man, 1984, EX, N2 ....$15.00
Rocky Roughneck, 1977, EX, N2 ....$20.00
Rover Dangerfield, 1990, w/Thermos, EX, N2 ....$20.00
Six Million Dollar Man, 1974, M $35.00
Smurfette, 1984, pk, EX $15.00
Smurfs, 1983, dome top, w/Thermos, EX, N2 ....$20.00
Snoopy & Woodstock, 1970, dome top, w/Thermos, EX, N2 .$25.00
Star Trek Next Generation, 1989, w/Thermos, M, N2 .....$20.00
Superman, 1980, EX+ $30.00
Superman, 1986, dome top, EX, N2 ....$25.00
SWAT, 1975, dome top, w/Thermos, EX, N2 ....$40.00
Teenage Mutant Ninja Turtles, 1990, purple, w/Thermos, M..$10.00
Tom & Jerry, 1992, w/Thermos, M, N2 ....$20.00
Voltron, 1984, bl, w/Thermos, NM $15.00
Winnie the Pooh, 1990, w/Thermos, M $25.00
101 Dalmatians, 1990, w/Thermos, EX $10.00

VINYL

Hammerman, 1991, with Thermos, NM, $30.00.
(Photo courtesy Joe Hilton and Greg Moore)

Holly Hobbie, 1989, w/Thermos, M, N2 ....$25.00
Hot Wheels, 1997, w/Thermos, M, N2 ....$20.00
Hulk Hogan, 1989, EX $10.00
Incredible Hulk, 1980, dome top, EX, N2 ....$40.00
Jabberjaw, 1977, NM, N2 ....$30.00
Jif Peanut Butter, 1980s, EX, N2 ....$20.00
Keebler Cookies, 1987, w/Thermos, M, N2 ....$30.00
Kermit the Frog, 1981, dome top, EX, N2 ....$25.00
Little Orphan Annie, 1973, dome top, w/Thermos, NM, N2 .$40.00
Looney Tunes, 1977, EX, N2 ....$10.00
Looney Tunes, 1988, purple, w/Thermos, VG $10.00
Lucy Luncheonette, 1981, dome top, EX, N2 ....$15.00
Mickey Mouse, 1988, head figure, w/Thermos, NM, N2 ..$25.00
Mickey Mouse & Donald Duck, 1984, w/Thermos, EX, N2 .$10.00
Mighty Mouse, 1979, EX+, N2 ....$20.00
Mr T, 1984, orange, w/Thermos, EX $20.00
Muppet Babies, 1986, pk, w/Thermos, EX, N2 ....$15.00
Nestle Quik, 1980, NM, N2 ....$25.00
New Kids on the Block, 1990, w/Thermos, EX, N2 ....$15.00
Nosey Bears, 1988, w/Thermos, EX, N2 ....$15.00
Pee Wee Herman, EX $15.00
Popeye, 1979, dome top, EX, N2 ....$30.00
Popeye & Sons, 1987, yel, 3-D, M $35.00

Bullwinkle, 1962, each with Thermos: with hot air balloon, NM, $450.00; Lunch Kit, NM, $285.00.

Airport Control Tower, 1972, EX $150.00
Alvin & the Chipmunks, 1963, w/Thermos, EX, A $150.00
Alvin & the Chipmunks, 1963, w/Thermos, M, A $270.00
Ballerina on Lily Pad, 1960s, EX, N2 ....$100.00

Banana Splits, 1969, w/Thermos, NM, A $450.00
Barbarino, 1977, brunch bag, NM, A............................$125.00
Barbie, 1972, pk, EX $35.00
Barbie & Francie, 1965, w/Thermos, NM, A.................$200.00
Barbie & Midge, 1965, w/Thermos, NM, A $200.00
Beany & Cecil, 1961, w/Thermos, NM, A $200.00
Beauty & the Beast, softie, w/Thermos, VG........................$8.00
Bobby Soxer, w/Thermos, NM, A $150.00
Bullwinkle, 1962, hot air balloon image, w/Thermos, NM, A $450.00
California Raisins, 1988, EX, N2.....................................$20.00
Captain Kangaroo, 1964, w/Thermos, EX.......................$150.00
Captain Kangaroo, 1964, w/Thermos, NM, A................$200.00
Casper the Fiendly Ghost, 1966, w/Thermos, NM, A $375.00
Charlie's Angels, 1977, brunch bag, EX, A.....................$125.00
Dawn, 1970, w/Thermos, EX...$175.00
Deputy Dawg, 1964, NM, from $300 to $325.00
Donny & Marie, 1977, w/Thermos, EX, N2 ....$110.00
Dream Boat, NM, A $125.00
Dudley Do-Right, 1972, railroad scene, w/Thermos, NM, A $475.00
Fess Parker Kaboodle Kit from the Daniel Boone TV Show, 1964, NM, A $165.00
Holly Hobbie, 1972, w/Thermos, EX, N2 ....$40.00
Junior Nurse, 1963, w/Thermos, EX, A...........................$120.00
Li'l Jodie, 1985, EX, N2 ....$50.00
Linus the Lion-Hearted, 1965, w/Thermos, NM, A $500.00
Lion in the Cart, 1985, EX, N2 ....$40.00
Lion in the Van, 1978, NM, N2 ....$60.00
Mardi Gras, 1971, floral, w/Thermos, EX, N2...................$60.00
Mary Poppins, 1973, VG, N2 ....$50.00
Monkees, 1967, w/Thermos, EX, A................................$325.00
Pac Man, 1980, EX, N2 ....$50.00
Peanuts, Snoopy at Mailbox, 1969, red, EX, N2 ....$60.00
Peanuts, 1965, w/Thermos, NM, A................................$150.00
Pepsi-Cola, 1980, yel, EX, N2 ....$50.00
Peter Pan, see Walt Disney's Peter Pan
Pink Panther, 1980, w/Thermos, EX, A $60.00
Ponytail Tid-Bit-Kit, 1959, w/Thermos, NM, A.............$100.00

Princess, 1963, yel, w/Thermos, EX................................$50.00
Pussycats, 1968, w/Thermos, NM, A.............................$125.00
Ringling Bros & Barnum & Bailey Circus, 1970, w/Thermos, NM, A $200.00
Roy Rogers, cream, w/Thermos, NM $350.00
Sabrina, 1972, NM, A $200.00
Sesame Street, 1980, yel gingham, EX, N2 ....$25.00
Shari Lewis, 1963, w/Thermos, EX, A...........................$125.00
Smokey Bear, w/Thermos, NM, A.................................$250.00
Soupy Sales, 1965, w/Thermos, NM, A $300.00
Speedy Turtle, 1978, drawstring closure, M, N2 ....$25.00
Strawberry Shortcake, 1980, checked design, VG $35.00
Tic Tac Toe, 1970s, EX, N2 ....$50.00
Tropicana Swim Club, 1980, EX, N2 ....$85.00
Twiggy, 1967, w/Thermos, EX, A $175.00

Walt Disney's Peter Pan, with Thermos, NM, $200.00.

Wizard in the Van, 1978, orange, VG+, N2.....................$50.00
Wonder Woman, 1977, yel background, w/Thermos, EX, A..$85.00
World of Barbie, 1971, pk, EX, N2 ....$35.00

Underdog, 1972, with Thermos, NM, $300.00.

World of Dr. Seuss, 1970, with Thermos, NM, $200.00.

Yogi Bear, 1961, w/Thermos, NM, A $200.00
Yosemite Sam/Bugs Bunny, w/Thermos, NM, A.............$400.00
Ziggy, 1979, EX, N2 ....$85.00

Yosemite Sam, EX, $235.00.

THERMOSES

ABC Wide World of Sports, 1976, metal, EX, N2 ....$35.00
Banana Splits, 1970s, metal, NM $185.00

Casper the Ghost, 1966, EX, $60.00.

Casper the Ghost, 1966, metal, NM, N2 ....$100.00
Chitty-Chitty Bang-Bang, 1968, metal, EX+, A7............$40.00
Clash of the Titans, 1980, plastic, NM...........................$10.00
Evil Knievel, 1974, plastic, VG+...................................$15.00
Flintstones, 1964, metal, EX, N2...................................$50.00
Flying Nun, 1968, metal, EX $60.00
Fonz, 1976, metal, M, N2 ....$50.00
Green Hornet, 1967, metal, EX.....................................$90.00
Heathcliff, 1982, plastic, EX...$10.00
Hopalong Cassidy, 1950, metal, EX, N2.........................$55.00
Junior Nurse, 1963, metal, EX $75.00
King Kong, 1977, plastic, EX, N2...................................$15.00
Kung Fu, 1974, plastic, EX..$15.00

Barbie, 1961, EX, $35.00.

Roy Rogers/Dale Evans Double R Bar Ranch, EX+, $60.00.

Bee Gees, 1978, plastic, M...$20.00
Beverly Hillbillies, 1963, metal, EX $50.00
Campbell's Soup, 1968, metal, EX, N2................................$60.00
Campus Queen, 1967, metal, EX..$25.00
Casey Jones, 1960, metal, EX, N2 ....$100.00

Little Dutch Miss, 1959, metal, EX $45.00
Mickey Mouse Club, 1976, plastic, EX............................$7.00
Partridge Family, 1973, plastic, M $45.00
Peanuts, 1966, metal, EX, N2...$25.00
Peter Pan, 1976, plastic, EX, N2.....................................$25.00
Punky Brewster, 1984, plastic, NM.................................$15.00
Rifleman, 1960, metal, EX..$125.00
Roy Rogers, metal, EX+, C10...$100.00
Sabrina, 1972, plastic, EX..$45.00
Secret Agent T, 1968, metal, EX, N2...............................$35.00
Street Hawk, 1984, plastic, EX, N2.................................$35.00
Superman, 1967, metal, EX, N2 ....$50.00
Tim Horton Donuts, 1970s, plastic, EX, N2....................$35.00
Waltons, 1973, plastic, EX..$22.00
Yogi Bear, 1963, metal, EX+, N2 ....$50.00

Marbles

Antique marbles are divided into several classifications: 1) Transparent Swirl (Solid Core, Latticinio Core, Divided Core, Ribbon Core, Lobed Core, and Coreless); 2) Lutz or Lutz-type (with bands having copper flecks which alternate with colored or clear bands); 3) Peppermint Swirl (made of red, white, and blue opaque glass); 4) Indian Swirl (black with multicolored surface swirls); 5) Banded Swirl (wide swirling bands on opaque or transparent glass); 6) Onionskin (having an overall mottled appearance due to its spotted, swirling lines or lobes: 7) End-of-Day (single pontil, allover spots, either two-colored or multicolored); 8) Clambroth (evenly spaced, swirled lines on opaque glass); 9) Mica (transparent color with mica flakes added); 10) Sulfide (nearly always clear, colored examples are rare, containing figures). Besides glass marbles, some were made of clay, pottery, china, steel, and even semiprecious stones.

Most machine-made marbles are still very reasonable, but some of the better examples may sell for $50.00 and up, depending on the colors that were used and how they are defined. Guineas (Christensen agates with small multicolored specks instead of swirls) sometimes go for as much as $200.00. Mt. Peltier comic character marbles often bring prices of $100.00 and more with Betty Boop, Moon Mullins, and Kayo being the rarest and most valuable.

From the nature of their use, mint-condition marbles are extremely rare and may be worth as much as three to five times more than one that is near-mint, while chipped and cracked marbles may be worth half or less. The same is true of one that has been polished, regardless of how successful the polishing was. If you'd like to learn more, Everett Grist has written three books on the subject that you will find helpful: *Antique and Collectible Marbles*, *Machine Made and Contemporary Marbles*, and *Everett Grist's Big Book of Marbles*. Also refer to *MCSA's Marble Identification and Price Guide*, recently re-written by Robert Block (Schiffer Publishing). See Clubs, Newsletters, and Other Publications for club information.

Advisors: Stanley A. and Robert S. Block (B8).

Artist-Made, swirls & ribbons, Harry Boyer, 1⅝", M........$50.00
Clambroth swirl, any color combination, ½" to ⅞", M, ea..$250.00

Akro Agate, Popeye on lid and carrying pouch, MIB, minimum value, $700.00. (Photo courtesy Everett Grist)

Comic, Andy Gump, Peltier Glass, M $125.00
Comic, Annie, Peltier Glass, M $150.00
Comic, Betty Boop, Peltier Glass, M.............................$200.00
Comic, Emma, Peltier Glass, M.......................................$75.00
Comic, Herbie, Peltier Glass, M......................................$150.00
Comic, Kayo, Peltier Glass, M $450.00
Comic, Koko, Peltier Glass, M..$125.00
Comic, Moon Mullins, Peltier Glass, M $300.00
Comic, Skeezix, Peltier Glass, M...................................$150.00
Comic, Smitty, Peltier Glass, M $125.00

Comic, Tom Mix, Peltier, minimum value, $500.00.
(Photo courtesy Everett Grist)

Divided Core Swirl, amethyst, 2 pk & bl on wht & 2 pk & gr on yel core bands, 2 wht & 2 yel outer bands, 1⅜", NM $120.00
Divided Core Swirl, yel, pk, gr & bl, 1⅝", NM $130.00
Divided Core Swirl, 2 wht strands & 2 yel strands, 1¾", EX ..$100.00
Divided Core Swirl, 3 bands w/yel center, flanked by gr, edged in red, 3 wht outer strands, ¾", NM+ $40.00

Divided Core Swirl, 3 pk & bl bands on wht inner core, 3 wht outer-layer strand, 1⅝", NM $130.00

End-of-Day, cloud, wht splotches w/bl, pk, gr & yel, pontil intact, 1⅝", NM $450.00

End-of-Day, onionskin, bl & pk skin w/opaque wht core, 1⅜", NM...$110.00

End-of-Day, onionskin, bl & pk skin w/opaque wht core, tiny chips, 1⅝", NM $185.00

End-of-Day, onionskin, clear base w/orange & some gr & wht, 1¼", NM $310.00

End-of-Day, onionskin, opaque yel core, gr skin, 1½", EX ..$140.00

End-of-Day, panelled onionskin, opaque wht core, left-twist, 2 pk & 2 gr panels, 2¼", NM $280.00

End-of-Day, panelled onionskin, opaque wht core, 2 bl & 2 pk panels, faceted pontil, 1⅞", NM $170.00

End-of-Day, 4-panelled onionskin, opaque wht core, 2 lt gr & 2 pk on yel panels, 2¼", NM $200.00

End-of-Day, 4-panelled onionskin, opaque wht core, 2 bl & 2 pk on yel panels, 1¾", NM+ $310.00

End-of-Day, 4-panelled onionskin, 2 bl on wht & 2 pk on yel panels, 1⅝", EX $120.00

Indian Swirl, Colonial Blue, 1¾"................................$1,750.00

Indian Swirl, Colonial Blue, ⅝" $85.00

Joseph Coat Swirl, bl base w/bl, red, yel & wht subsurface bands, ¾", NM+ $200.00

Latticinio Core, yellow core with red and blue outer bands, NM, ⅝", $25.00; NM, 1¾", $250.00. (Photo courtesy Brian Estepp/Everett Grist)

Latticinio Swirl, lt teal w/wht core, 2 pk & bl on wht & 2 pk & gr on wht outer layer bands, 1⅝", NM....................$210.00

Latticinio Swirl, orange core w/3 gray, gr & lt red & 3 dk purple, gray & lt red outer bands, 1¼", NM.....................$90.00

Latticinio Swirl, wht core w/2 bl & 2 gr bands all edged in yel & orange, 1¼", NM+ $120.00

Latticinio Swirl, wht core w/2 ea of pk on yel, pk on wht, bl on wht & gr on yel outer bands, 1¼", EX $75.00

Latticinio Swirl, yel core, red & blk outer bands, ⅝"........$25.00

Latticinio Swirl, yel core, red & blk outer bands, 1¾" ...$250.00

Latticinio Swirl, yel core, red & wht outer bands, ⅝" $25.00

Latticinio Swirl, yel core, red & wht outer bands, 1¾" ..$225.00

Latticnio Swirl, wht core, bl on wht, pk on wht & pk on yel outer layer bands, 2⅜", VG...................................$180.00

Machine-Made, pumpkin oxblood, Akro Agate, ⅝", rare, M $155.00

Machine-Made, World's Best Bloodies, Christensen Agate, boxed set of 25, 1¾", M, minimum value $600.00

Master Made Marbles, moss agates, in original box, NM (VG box), $225.00. (Photo courtesy Everett Grist/Jim and Louise O'Connell)

Peppermint Swirl, ½" to ⅞", M, ea $125.00

Peppermint Swirl w/Mica, ⅝", rare, M...........................$500.00

Peppermint Swirl w/Mica, 1¾", rare, M $3,500.00

Ribbon Core Swirl, naked dbl-ribbon core, 1 bl & pk on wht & 1 gr & pk on yel, ¾", NM+ $175.00

Ribbon Core Swirl w/Lutz, opaque emerald gr w/gold swirl, 1¾", M, minimum value..$1,000.00

Solid Core Swirl, opaque wht encased in transparent bl, outer layer is cage of wht strands, 2", NM $270.00

Solid Core Swirl, opaque wht w/pk, bl & gr bands in middle & 4 strands of yel on outer layer, 1¾", NM $130.00

Solid Core Swirl, red w/3 bl & 3 wht outer bands, ⅝", NM+ .$60.00

Solid Core Swirl, wht, gr, yel & red core, wht outer lines, 1¾" $350.00

Sulfide, alligator, 1¾", M...$200.00

Sulfide, angel, kneeling w/lyre, 1⅝", EX $210.00

Sulfide, baby in blanket, 1¾", M......................................$800.00

Sulfide, bear, 1¾", M..$200.00

Sulfide, buffalo, 1¾", M...$300.00

Sulfide, camel (1 hump), standing on mound of grass, 1½", NM $200.00

Sulfide, cherub, 1¾", M...$1,000.00

Sulfide, child w/hammer, 1¾", M....................................$600.00

Sulfide, child w/sailboat, 1¾", M $650.00

Sulfide, clown, 1¾", M...$1,000.00

Sulfide, crucifix, 1¾", M..................................$650.00
Sulfide, dog, bushy tail, 1¼", EX.......................$110.00

**Sulfide, dog with bird, wonderful detail, 1¾",
NM, $1,100.00.** (Photo courtesy Everett Grist)

Sulfide, duck, 1⅜", EX....................................$130.00
Sulfide, fish, 1⅝", EX......................................$180.00
Sulfide, goat, lt amethyst, 2", EX.....................$150.00
Sulfide, horse, grazing, 1⅝", NM....................$200.00
Sulfide, Jenny Lind, 1½", NM.........................$750.00
Sulfide, lion preparing to pounce, 1⅝", NM....................$180.00
Sulfide, lion standing on mound of grass, 2", NM...........$125.00
Sulfide, Little Boy Blue, 1¾", M $750.00
Sulfide, man (politician) standing by stump, 1¼", VG ..$450.00
Sulfide, man & woman sitting on ground while woman reads
    book, sm bubble, 1⅝", EX $420.00
Sulfide, man seated on potty, 1½", NM.....................$2,000.00
Sulfide, numeral #7, pnt gr, sm bubble, 1⅝", EX $975.00
Sulfide, owl, 1¾", M $350.00
Sulfide, parrot on perch, 1⅞", VG $140.00
Sulfide, peasant boy on stump w/legs crossed, 1½", NM ...$400.00
Sulfide, plaque of boy under tree w/goat about to jump on him,
    1⅞", EX..$350.00
Sulfide, pony running in field of grass, 1¾", M...............$200.00
Sulfide, Santa Claus, 1¾", M $1,300.00
Sulfide, sheep, honey amber, 2⅛", EX..................$900.00
Sulfide, Victorian boy in sailor's outfit kneeling w/pond sailboat,
    1⅞", EX..$260.00

Marx

Louis Marx founded his company in New York in the 1920s.
He was a genius not only at designing toys but also marketing
them. His business grew until it became one of the largest toy
companies ever to exist, eventually expanding to include several
factories in the United States as well as other countries. Marx
sold his company in the early 1970s; he died in 1982. Though
toys of every description were produced, collectors today admire
his mechanical toys above all others. For more information on
Marx battery-operated toys, refer to *Collector's Guide to Battery
Toys* by Don Hultzman.

Advisors: Scott Smiles (S10), windups; Tom Lastrapes (L4),
battery-ops.

**See also Advertising; Banks; Character, TV, and Movie
Collectibles; Dollhouse Furniture; Games; Guns; Plastic Figures; Playsets; and other categories. For toys made by Linemar (Marx's subsidiary in Japan), see Battery-Operated Toys;
Windups, Friction, and Other Mechanicals.**

BATTERY-OPERATED

Aircraft Carrier, 20", EX (EX box) $450.00
Alley the Roaring Stalking Alligator, 1960s, advances & roars, tin
    & plush, remote control, 17½", EX (EX box), A $450.00
Barking Boxer Dog, 1950s, 7", EX..................$100.00
Barking Spaniel Dog, 1950s, 7", EX $100.00
Barnyard Rooster, 1950s, several actions, 10", EX $125.00
Batcraft, 1966, advances w/lights & mystery action, plastic,
    NMIB, A..$375.00
Big Bruiser Highway Service Truck, 1960s, several actions, 23",
    EX $300.00
Big Parade, 1963, several actions, plastic, 15" L, NMIB.$200.00
Buttons w/Puppy w/a Brain, 1960s, several actions, tin & plush,
    12", MIB $475.00
Colonel Hap Hazard, 1968, several actions, 11", EX $700.00

**Frankenstein, advances and stops to pick up objects,
tin, remote control, 13", M (EX box), A, $3,600.00.**

Great Garloo, 1960s, several actions, mostly plastic, complete
    w/chain & medallion, 23", EX $400.00
Hootin' Hollow Haunted House, several actions, litho tin, 11",
    NMIB, A $1,700.00
Marx-A-Copter, 1961, remote control, complete w/figures &
    accessories, scarce, NM (NM box)...........................$250.00

Mickey Mouse Krazy Kar, advances w/erratic movement, plastic, 7", EX (EX box) $125.00

Mighty Kong, 1950s, several actions, plush over tin, remote control, 11", EX $300.00

Nutty Mad Indian, 1960s, rocks while beating drums, tongue moves & makes war whoop sounds, tin & vinyl, 12", MIB $275.00

Penny the Poodle, 1960, advances, barks & moves head, remote control, NM (EX box) $125.00

Race-A-Kart, 1960s, several actions, litho tin, 10½", EX .$150.00

Squawky the Parrot, tin & cloth, NMIB........................$575.00

VFD Emergency Truck, forward & reverse action, litho tin w/plastic extension ladder, 14", NMIB, A $500.00

Walking Esso Tiger, 1950s, several actions, tin & plush, remote control, 11½", EX $325.00

Whistling Spooky Kooky Tree, 1960s, bump-&-go w/several other actions, tin & plastic, 14", NM $975.00

PRESSED STEEL

Contractor's Dump Truck, 1940s, red w/yel scoop & red dump, 21", NM $250.00

Deluxe Auto Transport, 1940s, red & bl w/2 plastic cars, 22", VG, A $200.00

Deluxe Pickup Truck, 1950s, bl w/yel decal, battery-op headlights, 14", NM (EX box), A $950.00

Dump Truck, 1940s, gray & red w/coal-shoot door at rear, 20½", EX, A $265.00

Earth Hauler, 18", EX (EX box), A $100.00

Easter Truck, 1930s, turq, pk & yel w/chick & rabbit stamped on stake sides, 10", rare, NM $950.00

Whistling Spooky Kooky Tree (summer version), bump-and-go action, 14", NM (NM box), $1,300.00.

Farm Tractor, with rubber farmer, MIB, $300.00.
(Photo courtesy John Turney)

Fire Truck, rider, seat mounted on body, hand-crank siren, fire apparatus graphics on side, 31", MIB $225.00

Grocery Truck, 1940s, with stake-side body, 14", M (EX box), A, $350.00.

Yeti the Abominable Snowman, advances with several actions and grunts, tin, plush, and vinyl, 11", NMIB, A, $735.00.

Heavy Duty Dump Truck, orange & blk high side-extension body, MIB $300.00

Hauler and Stake Truck, pressed steel and plastic, MIB, $400.00. (Photo courtesy John Turney)

Hi-Way Express Truck, red & yel, mk New York...Chicago...San Francisco, 16", EX..............................$350.00

Jeep Truck w/Electric Headlights, 1939, Delivery Service decals on doors, battery-op headlights, 13", EX (G box), A.$400.00

Lazy Day Farms Stake Truck, bl w/litho tin bed, 18", NMIB, A..............................$400.00

Lumar Utility Service Truck, mk #18, gr w/yel detail, no accessories, 18½", VG, A..............................$100.00

Lumar Wrecker Service Truck, 16", EX..............................$200.00

Marine Corps Truck, gr w/canvas cover, complete w/2 plastic figures, 13", EX (EX box)..............................$300.00

Medical Corps Ambulance, gr, opening rear door, 12", VG+, A..............................$250.00

Motor Market Grocery Truck, 1940s, red w/bl stake body, 14", NM (G box), A..............................$300.00

Powerhouse Dump Truck, bl w/tan dump, 19", EX (EX box)..............................$250.00

US Army Truck & Searchlight Trailer, 1950s, gr w/canvas cover, 30", EX..............................$200.00

WINDUPS, FRICTIONS, AND OTHER MECHANICALS

Acrobatic Marvel, 1930s, monkey performs on rod attached to rocking base, litho tin, 13", NMIB..............................$300.00

American Railroad Express Truck, litho tin, 9½", EX....$400.00

Amos 'N Andy Fresh Air Taxi, 1920s, EX, $850.00.
(Photo courtesy Dunbar Gallery)

Amos 'N Andy Fresh Air Taxi, 1930, advances, stops & shakes, litho tin, 8", NM (EX box)..............................$1,300.00

Amos 'N Andy Walkers, figures advance & sway, litho tin, 11½", VG..............................$600.00

Animal Express, 1930s, 3 litho tin cars mk Bunny Express, complete w/track, 14½", scarce, MIB, A..............................$750.00

Army Command Car, 1950, litho tin, friction w/battery-op fender light, 20", NM (EX box), A..............................$500.00

Army Tank Corps No 12, 1920s, advances w/sparks, litho tin, 10", NM..............................$400.00

Astro, see Hopping Astro

Auto Mac the Automatic Wonder Truck Driver, plastic, 11½", VG, A..............................$150.00

Ballet Dancer, pull rod for action, litho tin, 6", VG (VG box)..............................$225.00

Barney Rubble, see Hopping Barney Rubble

Be-Bop Jigger, Black man dances on stage, litho tin & plastic, VG..............................$150.00

Bear Cyclist, 6", NM (EX box), $350.00.

Beat It! Komikal Kop, advances w/crazy action as driver's head spins, litho tin, 8½", VG, A..............................$450.00

Bedrock Express Train, 1962, litho tin, 12", NMIB........$250.00

Billy the Bird, see Hopping Billy the Bird

Blondie's Jalopy, 1935, bump-&-go action, litho tin, 16½", scarce, NM..............................$2,200.00

BO Plenty, 1939, advances while holding baby Sparkles, tips hat, litho tin, 8", MIB..............................$500.00

BO Plenty, 1939, advances while holding baby Sparkles, tips hat, litho tin, 8", NM, A..............................$350.00

Buck Rogers 25th Century Rocket Ship, 1927, advances w/sparks, litho tin, 12", EX..............................$900.00

Bunny Express, see Animal Express

Busy Bridge, cars navigate bridge from station to station, litho tin, 24" L, VG, A..............................$300.00

Busy Miners, 1930s, coal car travels from station house to mine entrance, litho tin, 17" base, MIB, A......................$450.00

Butter & Egg Man, 1930s, litho tin, 8", rare, EX, from $800 to..$900.00

Butterfly, 1930, advances w/flapping wings, litho tin w/celluloid wings, 5" W, NM (EX box), A $400.00

Cannonball Keller Mechanical Roadster w/Trailer, red litho tin w/bl plastic trailer, NMIB.......................................$350.00

Careful Johnnie, tin with plastic bobbing head, 6½", NMIB, A, $250.00.

Casey Jr Disneyland Express, litho tin & plastic, 12", NM (EX box), A...$225.00

Charleston Trio, 1921, jigger dances, boy plays violin & dog w/cane jumps atop cabin, litho tin, 10", VG, A $750.00

Charlie Chaplin Walker, litho tin w/CI shoes & cane, 8½", EX (EX box) $1,000.00

Charlie McCarthy, 1930s, waddles from side to side as mouth opens & closes, litho tin, 8½", NM (EX box) $750.00

Charlie McCarthy, 1930s, waddles side to side as mouth opens & closes, litho tin, 8½", EX, A.............................$350.00

Charlie McCarthy in His Benzine Buggy, 1938, advances in erratic pattern as Charlie's head spins, tin, 8", EX, A.............$575.00

City Coal Co Truck, mk Coal & Coke, dumping action, litho tin, 13½", NM..$850.00

Climbing Fireman, plastic & tin version, fireman climbs ladder, EX (EX box) $250.00

Coast Defense, 1924, plane circles above base w/several actions, litho tin, 9" dia base, MIB....................................$1,000.00

College Jalopy, advances w/crazy action, litho tin, 6", NMIB...$550.00

Construction Tractor, forward & reverse action, litho tin, 14", NM, A $250.00

Cowboy Rider, 1941, rearing horse vibrates around as cowboy spins lariat overhead & aims gun, NMIB.................$375.00

Cowboy Rider, over-head lariat, 7", EX (EX box), A, $300.00.

Dagwood Aeroplane, 1935, advances w/crazy action as Dagwood's head bobs, litho tin, 9", EX (EX box), A ..$1,100.00

Dagwood the Driver, 1935, advances w/crazy action as Dagwood's head spins, litho tin, 8", NM.....................$1,000.00

Dapper Dan Coon Jigger, 1910, Black man dances on stage, litho tin, 10", EX, from $800 to $850.00

Dare Devil Drone, car travels upwards in circles, litho tin & plastic, 9½" dia drone, EX.......................................$150.00

Dick Tracy Police Car, w/driver, advances w/siren sound, plastic, friction, 10", rare, NM (EX box), A.........................$350.00

Dick Tracy Police Station, car races out of garage, litho tin w/plastic station doors, station: 9", car: 8", NMIB, A........$1,100.00

Dick Tracy Sparkling Riot Car, advances w/siren sound, litho tin, 7", NM (EX box), A $425.00

Dick Tracy Squad Car, litho tin w/plastic figures, NM, from $300 to..$400.00

Dippy Dumper w/Popeye, advances & throws figure out, litho tin & celluloid, 8", VG, A.......................................$800.00

Dipsy-Doodle Bug Dodg'Em, 2 cars travel on base w/non-fall action, litho tin & plastic, 9½" base, NMIB............$450.00

Disney Parade Roadster, litho tin w/plastic figures, NMIB, A $850.00

Disney Turnover Tank, WDP/Mexico, 1950s, Goofy forces tank to turn over, litho tin, 4", rare, EX (EX box)........$1,000.00

Disneyland Jeep, litho tin, friction, 10", EX (EX box)....$275.00

Donald Duck Drummer, rocks back & forth while playing drum, litho tin, NMIB $700.00

Donald Duck Duet, 1946, Goofy dances on platform as Donald plays drum, litho tin, 10½", EX (G box), from $800 to..$950.00

Donald Duck Duet, 1946, Goofy dances on platform as Donald plays drum, litho tin, 10½", MIB.........................$1,200.00

Donald the Driver, WDP, advances & Donald waves, litho tin w/plastic figure, NM $500.00

Donald the Skier, 1960s, advances on snow skis, litho tin, NMIB..$450.00

Dopey Walker, 1938, advances & vibrates as eyes move up & down, litho tin, 8½", NM $500.00

Dora Dipsy Car, 1950s, advances as figure's head bobs, litho tin & plastic, 6", EX (EX box), A $250.00

Doughboy Tank, 1930, advances w/several actions as figure pops up from hatch, 9½", EX (EX box)..........................$750.00

Drive-Ur-Self Car, 1930s, litho tin, 14", G $150.00

Dum Dum & Touche Turtle, 1963, plastic, friction, 4", rare, MIB $200.00

Dump Truck, litho tin w/flat figure, 9½", EX..................$300.00

Falcon Sports Car, 1950, advances w/clicking engine, tin & plastic, friction, EX (G box), A..$400.00

Ferdinand the Bull, 1938, vibrates around w/spinning tail, litho tin, complete w/cloth flower & bee, 6", EX $400.00

Figaro, see Roll-Over Figaro

Fire Chief Car, litho tin w/blk rubber tires, 11", NM (NM box), A $400.00

Fire Chief Car, late 1940s, red plastic, siren, flashing roof light, 12", EX (EX box), A, $450.00; Police Car, 1940s, green plastic with tin litho images of policemen, 12", EX (EX box), A, $400.00.

Flintstone Log Car, 1977, Fred driving, plastic, friction, 5", MIB..$200.00

Flintstone Pals, Fred on Dino, litho tin & vinyl, 8½", NM, A $250.00

Flintstone Tricycle w/Dino, 1962, advances w/ringing bell, litho tin w/celluloid figure, 4", NM (NM box), from $700 to..$800.00

Flintstone Tricycle w/Wilma, 1962, advances w/ringing bell, litho tin w/celluloid figure, 4", NMIB, $500 to........$600.00

Flippo the Jumping Dog, 1930, does flips, litho tin, 4", NM (EX box), A..$250.00

Fred Flintstone, see Hopping Fred Flintstone

Funny Fire Fighters, Brutus drives vehicle w/Popeye on top of aerial ladder, litho tin & celluloid, 10", rare, NMIB...........$4,500.00

Funny Flivver, 1925, advances w/crazy action as driver's head spins, litho tin, 7½", EX, A $400.00

Funny Tiger, 1960s, tiger plays drum, litho tin, 6½", NMIB $200.00

George Jetson, see Hopping George Jetson

George the Drummer Boy, 1930s, moving eyes, litho tin, 9", NM..$350.00

George the Drummer Boy, 1930s, stationary eyes, litho tin, 9", NM..$250.00

Giant King Racer 711, w/driver, litho tin, 12", scarce, EX, A $500.00

Giant Reversing Tractor Truck, 14", NMIB, A, $300.00.

Golden Goose, 1930, advances & lays egg, litho tin, 9", EX, A $150.00

Goofy, see also Whirling Tail Goofy

Goofy the Walking Gardener, Goofy pushes cart, litho tin, 9x8", EX $350.00

Gorilla, advances in shackles & chains w/several actions, plush over tin, 8", M (EX box), A $475.00

Harold Lloyd Funny Face Walker, 1929, sways as facial expression changes, litho tin, 10", VG...............................$700.00

Hee-Haw the Balky Mule, 8½", EX (VG box), $350.00; Toytown Dairy Wagon, 9½", NM, $275.00. (Photo courtesy Jacquie and Bob Henry)

Hey Hey Chicken Snatcher, 1927, Black man carries chicken as dog bites his pants, litho tin, 8½", EX, A $1,200.00

Hi-Yo Silver the Lone Ranger, 1939, figure twirls lasso as horse vibrates around, litho tin, 8", EX (VG box) $600.00

Hi-Yo Silver the Lone Ranger, 1939, figure twirls lasso as horse vibrates around, litho tin, 8", VG (VG box), A $450.00

Honeymoon Express, 1940, litho tin, EX (EX box)........$225.00

Hopping Astro, litho tin, 4", EX $300.00

Hopping Barney Rubble, litho tin, 3", MIB, A $700.00

Hopping Billy the Bird, 1960s, litho tin, NMIB $100.00

Hopping Fred Flintstone, litho tin, 3", MIB, A $650.00

Hopping George Jetson, litho tin, 4", EX $350.00

Hy & Lo Karnival Kar, 2-tiered base w/swinging rods that catch & raise car, 7", MIB $500.00

Jetson Express, litho tin, 13", NMIB $450.00

Joe Penner & His Duck Goo Goo, 1934, advances w/shuffling feet & tips hat, litho tin, 8½", MIB $800.00

Joe Penner & His Duck Goo Goo, 1934, advances w/shuffling feet & tips hat, litho tin, 8½", VG, A $400.00

Jolly Joe Jeep, advances w/crazy action as driver's head spins, litho tin, 6", EX, A $200.00

Jumpin' Jeep, advances w/crazy action, litho tin, 6", EX, A ..$275.00

Jumpin' Jeep, advances w/crazy action, litho tin, 6", EX (EX box), A $300.00

Jumpin' Jeep, advances w/crazy action, litho tin, 6", VG, A $200.00

Kitty Cat, 1930, push tail for action, litho tin, 8", rare, NMIB $300.00

Leaping Lena, 1930s, rocks back & forth, litho tin w/colloquial sayings all over, 7", EX $300.00

Little Orphan Annie Skipping Rope, 1930s, litho tin, 6", EX, from $500 to $600.00

Little Orphan Annie's Dog Sandy, 1930s, advances w/book in mouth, litho tin, NM (G box) $475.00

Looping Plane, 1935, advances & performs flips, litho tin, 7½" W, EX (VG box), A $350.00

Mack Dump Truck, 1930s, w/driver, pnt tin, VG $400.00

Mars Planet Patrol Tank, 1950, litho tin, 9½", EX, A $385.00

Marvel Super Hero Tricycle, Thor peddles tricycle w/bell sound, litho tin, 4", MIB, A $650.00

Mary Poppins, 1964, whirls around, plastic, 8", NMIB ...$175.00

Merry Makers, 1930, 3 mice band members w/band leader atop piano, litho tin, w/marquee, 9½", EX $1,150.00

Merry Makers, 1930, 3 mice band members w/band leader atop piano, litho tin, w/marquee, 9½", VG, A $850.00

Mickey Mouse, see also Whirling Tail Mickey Mouse

Mickey Mouse Express, 1950s, Mickey flies over track w/Disneyville station in center, litho tin, 9" dia, NM $750.00

Mickey Mouse Express, 1950s, Mickey flies above track w/Disneyville station in center, litho tin, 9" dia, VG, A ..$500.00

Mickey Mouse Scooter, 1959, plastic, friction, 4", EX (EX box) $225.00

Mickey Mouse Train, litho tin, w/locomotive & 4 cars, 41", VG, A $1,100.00

Mickey the Driver, advances w/non-fall action, litho tin & plastic version, 7", NMIB $850.00

Mickey the Driver, advances w/non-fall action, litho tin version, 7", NMIB $950.00

Midget Climbing Fighting Tank, 1930s, advances w/sound, litho tin, 5", EX (worn box), A $300.00

Midget Special #2, 1930s, litho tin, 5", rare, NM $225.00

Military Tank E12, litho tin camouflage design w/rubber treads, 9½", VG, A $150.00

Milton Berle Car, advances w/crazy action as Milton's head spins, litho tin, 5½", VG, A $250.00

Monkey Cyclist, 1930s, circus monkey peddles tricycle, litho tin, lever action, 6", NM (EX box), A $225.00

Moon Creature, litho tin, EX, A $185.00

Moon Mullins & Kayo Handcar, 1930s, figures work handlebars, litho tin & steel, 6", complete w/track, NM (NM box) $1,200.00

Mortimer Snerd, 1939, sways as hat bounces up & down, litho tin, 8½", G, A $200.00

Mortimer Snerd Tricky Auto, 1939, advances w/crazy action as Mortimer's head spins, litho tin, 6½", NM, A $600.00

Motorcycle #3, policeman driver, advances w/siren sound, litho tin, 8", G $225.00

Mysterious Pluto, 1939, press tail for action, litho tin, NMIB ..$575.00

Mystic Motorcycle, advances w/non-fall action, litho tin, 4½", VG, A $175.00

New York Honeymoon Express, 1928, train travels track as plane flies above base w/skyscrapers, tin, 9" dia base, NMIB $1,000.00

Old Jalopy, mk Special Delivery Male, advances w/undulating motion, litho tin, 6½", NM, A $225.00

Old Mother Goose, 1930, litho tin, 9", EX (EX rare box) ..$900.00

Peter Rabbit Eccentric Car, advances as figure's head bobs, litho tin & plastic, 5½", NM (NM box) $500.00

Pinched, 1930, vehicle travels track under bridges w/several actions, litho tin, 10" sq base, G+, A $700.00

Pinched, 1930, vehicle travels track under bridges w/several actions, litho tin, 10" sq base, NM (EX box), A ..$1,400.00

Pinocchio, WDE, 1939, waddles back & forth w/2 buckets, litho tin, 9", NM $500.00

Pinocchio, WDE, 1939, waddles back & forth w/2 buckets, litho tin, 9", VG, A $300.00

Planet Patrol Space Tank, advances & figure pops out of turret, litho tin, 10", EX (EX box), A $350.00

Pluto, see also Roll-Over Pluto

Pluto, blows horn & shakes bells, plastic, 10", G, A $125.00

Pluto the Drum Major, 1940s, rocks & shakes bell, litho tin w/rubber tail & ears, NMIB $500.00

Police Car, advances w/siren sound, gr-pnt pressed steel w/yel lettering, 14", NM $600.00

Police Cycle with Side Car, EX/NM, A, $350.00.

Police Motorcycle, advances w/siren sound, litho tin, 8½", G, A..$250.00

Police Motorcycle, litho tin, 4½", VG, A.......................$200.00

Police Motorcycle, litho tin w/full-figure driver, 4", G, A..$125.00

Police Squad Motorcycle w/Sidecar, advances in circular motion w/lights & sound, litho tin, 8½", NMIB..................$550.00

Popeye, see also Walking Popeye

Popeye & Olive Oyl Jiggers, 1934, Olive plays accordion & sways as Popeye dances on roof, tin, 10", NM (NM box) .$2,000.00

Popeye Express, 1935, train travels under bridges as Popeye circles in plane above, litho tin, 10" dia, VG, A $1,200.00

Popeye Express w/Parrot, Popeye pushes wheelbarrow w/parrot in crate, litho tin, 8½", EX, A.....................................$650.00

Popeye the Pilot (Popeye Eccentric Airplane), 1930s, litho tin, 8", EX (EX box), A $1,500.00

Popeye the Pilot (Popeye Eccentric Airplane), 1930s, litho tin, 8", EX...$1,000.00

Popeye the Pilot (Popeye Eccentric Airplane), 1930s, litho tin, 8", VG, A...$850.00

Porky Pig, 1939, spins & twirls umbrella, litho tin, 8", VG..$350.00

Queen of the Campus Car, advances w/crazy action as girl's head spins, litho tin w/plastic figure, 6", EX, A $150.00

Racer #3, w/driver, litho tin w/balloon tires, 5", NM, A ...$150.00

Racer #3, w/driver, red-pnt tin, 12", VG $350.00

Racer #4, w/driver, litho tin w/balloon tires, 5", EX, A ..$125.00

Racer #5, 1930s, litho tin, friction, 5", NM $225.00

Racer #12, w/driver, litho tin, 16", VG $200.00

Racer #711, w/driver, litho tin, 13", VG, A.....................$300.00

Range Rider, cowboy on horse swings lasso on rocking base, litho tin, 11", NM (G box), A $750.00

Red Cap Porter, 1930, Black man advances w/2 bags, litho tin, 8", EX, A...$700.00

Red Cap Porter, 1930, Black man advances w/2 bags, litho tin, 8", VG...$500.00

Ring-A-Ling Circus, 1925, ringmaster w/elephant, lion & monkey, gr base, litho tin, 7" dia, VG, A.....................$1,500.00

Ring-A-Ling Circus, 1925, ringmaster w/elephant, lion & monkey, pk base, litho tin, 7" dia, VG, A.....................$2,000.00

Roadster, w/driver, litho tin w/side spare & rear luggage rack, 11", VG, A...$250.00

Roll-Over Figaro, 1939, advances & rolls over, litho tin, 9", NMIB...$350.00

Roll-Over Pluto, 1939, advances & rolls over, litho tin, 9", NM...$350.00

Rookie Pilot, 1938, advances as pilot's head moves back & forth, litho tin, 7", EX, from $600 to..................................$700.00

Royal Bus Lines Bus, litho tin, w/driver, 10", NM $400.00

Royal Van Co Moving Van, w/driver, mk We Haul Anything Anywhere, litho tin w/C-style cab, 9", VG.............$225.00

Sam the City Gardener, advances w/wheelbarrow, litho tin & plastic, complete w/garden tools, 8", NM (EX box), A......$275.00

Sam the City Gardener, advances w/wheelbarrow, litho tin & plastic, complete w/gardening tools, MIB, A...........$350.00

Sedan Coupe, 1951, tin & plastic, friction, 9", EX (EX box)..$185.00

Sheriff Sam Whoopie Car, advances w/crazy action as figure's head spins, litho tin & plastic, 6", NMIB $325.00

Siren Emergency Truck, 1950, litho tin, friction w/battery-op searchlight, 14", NM (EX box), A $475.00

Skybird Flyer, 1930s, 2 planes circle tower, litho tin, 10", NM (NM box), A $650.00

Smitty Scooter, boy advances on scooter w/realistic action, litho tin, 8", rare, VG..$1,300.00

Smokey Joe the Climbing Fireman, 1930s, fireman climbs ladder attached to base, 11½", EX (EX box), from $350 to..$450.00

Snoopy Gus Wild Fireman, 1927, travels in erratic pattern as fireman spins on ladder, tin, 8", rare, EX (EX box) $1,600.00

Sparkling Climbing Bulldozer, tin & pressed steel w/plastic figure, 10", EX (EX box)..$175.00

Sparkling Highboy Climbing Tractor, litho tin w/plastic blade & driver, rubber treads, 10", EX (EX box), A $200.00

Sparkling Hot Rod Racer, 1950, advances w/sparks, plastic, friction, 8", EX (EX box) $150.00

Sparkling Luxury Liner, 1949, litho tin & plastic, friction, 15", MIB...$300.00

Sparkling Motorcycle Soldier, 1936, advances w/sparking machine gun, litho tin, 8½", EX (VG box) $450.00

Speed Boy Delivery (Motorcycle Delivery), 1930s, litho tin, 10", EX (EX box) $550.00

Spic the Coon Drummer, Black man sits on drum & plays drum on rectangular platform, litho tin, 8", NMIB, A ..$2,400.00

Spider-Man Tricycle, 1967, litho tin w/vinyl figure, 4", NMIB...$200.00

Sportster Convertible, gr & cream, friction, 20", EX, A.$250.00

Staff Car, litho tin, battery-op light, 11½", EX, A..........$200.00

Stutz Roadster, w/driver, litho tin, 9", EX, A $400.00

Super Heroes Express Train, 1967, litho tin, 12", NMIB.$650.00

Superman Rollover Plane, silver version, Superman rolls plane over, litho tin, 6½", EX..$1,500.00

Tidy Tim the Clean-Up Man, mk Keep Your City Spic & Span, litho tin, 8", EX, A $500.00

Tiger Trike, 1960s, advances w/bell sound, litho tin & plush, EX (EX box), from $100 to $150.00

Tom Corbett Sparkling Spaceship, advances w/sparks, litho tin, 12", NM (NM box) $1,500.00

Toyland Dairy Wagon, 1930, litho tin, 9½", M (NM box), A..$625.00

Tricky Fire Chief Car, 1930, travels on base w/non-fall action, litho tin, 10x6" dia base, MIB $500.00

Tricky Taxi, advances & turns around at edge of table, litho tin, 4½", EX (EX box), A $275.00

Tricky Taxi, advances & turns around at edge of table, litho tin, 4½", G, A...$150.00

Uncle Wiggily Car, 1935, advances w/crazy action as driver's head spins, litho tin, 8", EX, A................................$700.00

Uncle Wiggily Car, 1935, advances w/crazy action as driver's head spins, litho tin, 8", NM (G box) $1,000.00

US Mail Aeroplane, 1930s, litho tin, 18½" W, NM (G box), A...$800.00

USA Army Truck, 1930, w/driver, gr-pnt tin w/canvas canopy, 10½", EX...$500.00

USA Army Truck, 1930, w/driver, tin, 10½", VG, A.....$250.00

Walking Owl, advances & chirps w/several actions, plush over tin, 8", EX (VG box) $150.00

Walking Popeye, King Features, 1935, carries 2 bags w/lithoed parrots, 8½", NMIB...$750.00

Walt Disney's Dumbo, 1941, jumps & somersaults, litho tin, 4", EX (G- box)...$475.00

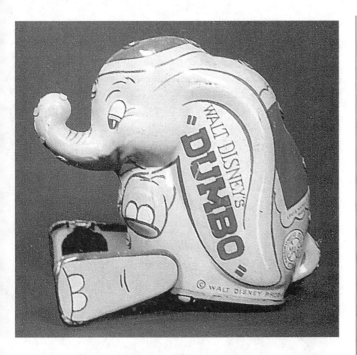

Walt Disney's Dumbo, tumbling action, EX, $375.00.
(Photo courtesy David Longest)

Walt Disney's Dumbo, 1941, jumps & somersaults, litho tin, 4",
    NM, A $425.00
Walt Disney's Mickey Mouse Meteor Train, WDP, litho tin,
    NM..$850.00
Walt Disney's Television Car, litho tin w/TV screen in roof, fric-
    tion, 7½", NM (EX box), A $525.00
Wee Scottie, 1930s, blk version, litho tin, 5", EX (EX box mk
    Running Scottie) $275.00
Whee-Whiz Auto Racer, 4 cars on rnd spinning platform, litho
    tin, 13" dia, rare, G (worn box), A $800.00
Whirling Tail Goofy, w/chipmunk biting his rear, plastic, 8",
    NMIB...$650.00
Whirling Tail Mickey Mouse, jumps around as tail spins, plastic
    w/wire tail, 7", NM (EX box), A $250.00
Whoopie Cowboy Car, advances w/crazy action as driver
    bounces in seat, litho tin, 8", EX, A.........................$350.00
Zippo the Climbing Monkey, litho tin, pull-string mechanism,
    10", VG...$225.00

MISCELLANEOUS

ACE Deluxe Hauler & Van Trailer, litho tin, complete w/cb
    advertising boxes, 21", EX (EX box) $350.00
Blue Bird Garage, litho tin, 7x12", EX (EX box mk Universal
    Gas Service Station) $300.00
Brightelite Filling Station, 1930, tin, complete, NM (EX box),
    A...$2,200.00
Cities Service Fix-All Wrecker, plastic, NMIB...............$300.00
Deluxe Delivery Truck, plastic w/tin bed, 12", NM (G box),
    A..$185.00
Fix-All Tractor, complete w/tools & accessories, NM (NM
    box) $100.00
Get Rich Quick Bank, 1930, litho tin w/image of bank build-
    ings, 4", NM (EX box), A..$175.00

Greyhound Bus Terminal, 1939, litho tin, complete w/buses,
    11x17", rare, EX (EX box), A $2,100.00
Grocery Truck, red w/bl stake bed, plastic & tin w/Motor
    Delivery Market decal, complete w/cb food containers,
    14", MIB $500.00
Gull Service Station, litho metal, complete, 11x17" base, rare,
    EX (G box), A..$1,600.00
Lumar Lines Deluxe Trailer-Truck, plastic cab w/tin trailer,
    wooden wheels, 14", EX (G box) $200.00
Marcrest Lines Hauler & Livestock Trailer, litho tin, complete
    w/plastic animals & fence, 17", EX (EX box), A $350.00
Marcrest Livestock Lines Cattle Truck, 1950, litho tin, complete
    w/15 rubber animals, EX (G box) $250.00

**Marine Corps Truck, lithographed tin with plastic marine
figures, MIB, $300.00.** (Photo courtesy John Turney)

Municipal Aeroplane Hanger, litho tin, complete w/accessories,
    3½x6", NM (G box) $1,400.00
Pathe Camera, 1930s, litho tin, crank action, 6", EX,
    A..$200.00
Roadside Rest Service Station, 1930s, litho tin, complete, 10
    x14" base, VG, A..$650.00
Roadside Rest Service Station, 1930s, litho tin, complete,
    10x14", EX...$800.00

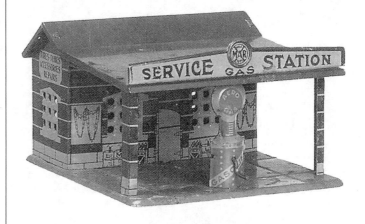

Service Station, 5½" x 6", EX, A, $400.00.

Sky-View Parking Garage, litho tin w/plastic vehicles, complete,
    15x26", EX, A..$150.00
Universal Airport, 1930s, mk Weather Bureau-Ticket
    Office, litho tin, complete w/2 airplanes, 7x12" base,
    NMIB, A $325.00

Matchbox

The Matchbox series of English and American-made autos, trucks, taxis, Pepsi-Cola trucks, steamrollers, Greyhound buses, etc., was very extensive. By the late 1970s, the company was cranking out more than five million cars every week, and while those days may be over, Matchbox still produces about seventy-five million vehicles on a yearly basis.

Introduced in 1953, the Matchbox Miniatures series has always been the mainstay of the company. There were seventy-five models in all but with enough variations to make collecting them a real challenge. Larger, more detailed models were introduced in 1957; this series, called Major Pack, was replaced a few years later by a similar line called King Size. To compete with Hot Wheels, Matchbox converted most models over to a line called SuperFast that sported thinner, low-friction axles and wheels. (These are much more readily available than the original 'regular wheels,' the last of which were made in 1969.) At about the same time, the King Size series became known as Speed Kings; in 1977 the line was reintroduced under the name Super Kings.

In the early '70s, Lesney started to put dates on the baseplates of their toy cars. The name 'Lesney' was coined from the first names of the company's founders. The last Matchboxes that carried the Lesney mark were made in 1982. Today many models can be bought for less than $10.00, though a few are priced much higher.

In 1988, to celebrate the company's 40th anniversary, Matchbox issued a limited set of five models that except for minor variations were exact replicas of the originals. These five were repackaged in 1991 and sold under the name Matchbox Originals. In 1993 a second series expanded the line of reproductions.

Another line that's become very popular is their Models of Yesteryear. These are slightly larger replicas of antique and vintage vehicles. Values of $20.00 to $60.00 for mint-in-box examples are average, though a few sell for even more.

Sky Busters are small-scale aircraft measuring an average of 3½" in length. They were introduced in 1973. Models currently being produced sell for about $4.00 each.

To learn more, we recommend *Matchbox Toys, 1947 – 1998*, by Dana Johnson; and a series of books by Charlie Mack: *Lesney's Matchbox Toys* (there are two: *Regular Wheel Years* and *Super Fast Years*) and *Universal Years*.

To determine values of examples in conditions other than given in our listings, based on MIB or MOC prices, deduct a minimum of 10% if the original container is missing, 30% if the condition is excellent, and as much as 70% for a toy graded only very good.

Key: LW — Laser Wheels (introduced in 1987)
       reg — regular wheels (Matchbox Miniatures)
       SF — SuperFast

1–75 SERIES

1-A, Diesel Road Roller, reg, 1953, lt gr, MIP, from $80 to....**$100.00**
1-C, Road Roller, reg, 1958, gr w/red metal wheels, MIP, from $50 to **$65.00**

1-F, Mercedes Benz Lorry, SF, 1969, metallic gold w/orange canopy, MIP, from $15 to..**$20.00**
2-A, Dumper, reg, 1953, gr metal wheels, MIP, from $125 to ..**$150.00**
2-D, Mercedes Trailer, reg, 1968, mint gr w/yel canopy, blk plastic wheels, MIP, from $10 to......................................**$12.00**
2-E, Mercedes Trailer, SF, 1969, metallic gold w/yel canopy, MIP, from $15 to..**$20.00**
3-B, Bedford Ton Tipper, red, 1961, maroon dumper, gray wheels, MIP, from $90 to..**$100.00**

4-B, Massey-Harris Tractor, 1957, no fenders, 1⅝", MIB, from $50.00 to $70.00. (Photo courtesy Dana Johnson)

4-D, Dodge Stake Truck, reg, 1967, bl-gr stakes, MIP, from $60 to **$75.00**
5-B, London Bus, reg, 1957, gray plastic wheels, MIP, from $65 to **$80.00**
5-F, Seafire Boat, reg, 1975, red deck w/wht hull, MIP **$8.00**

5-G, U.S. Mail Jeep, 1978, US Mail Tampo, MIB, from $4.00 to $6.00. (Photo courtesy Dana Johnson)

5-K, Nissan Fairlady Z, reg, 1981, red, MIP, from $12 to.....**$15.00**
6-A, 6-Wheel Quarry Truck, reg, 1955, gray plastic wheels, MIP, from $150 to **$200.00**

6-D, Ford Pickup, reg, 1968, wht grille, MIP, from $10 to **$12.00**

6-F, Mercedes Benz 350 SL Convertible, reg, 1973, orange w/blk roof, MIP, from $6 to..**$10.00**

7-A, Horse-Drawn Milk Cart, reg, 1955, orange w/silver bottles, metal wheels, MIP, from $100 to..........................**$125.00**

7-E, Hairy Hustler, reg, 1971, metallic orange-red w/purple windows, MIP, from $65 to..**$80.00**

8-A, Caterpillar Tractor, reg, 1955, lt yel w/red driver, no blade, MIP, from $80 to...**$100.00**

8-E, Ford Mustang Fastback, reg, 1966, orange, MIP, from $100 to...**$125.00**

8-H, DeTomaso Pantera, reg, 1975, wht w/bl base, MIP.....**$6.00**

9-C, Merryweather Marquis Fire Engine, reg, 1959, gold ladder, gray plastic wheels, MIP, from $30 to **$40.00**

9-E, AMX Javelin, reg, 1971, lime w/silver hood scoop, doors open, MIP **$12.00**

9-G, Fiat Arbarth, reg, 1984, wht w/blk interior, MIP, from $100 to...**$120.00**

10-B, Mechanical Horse & Trailer, reg, 1958, red cab w/tan trailer, gray plastic wheels, MIP, from $50 to.............**$60.00**

10-D, Leyland Pipe Truck, reg, 1966, wht grille, blk plastic wheels, w/6 pipes, MIP, from $12 to **$15.00**

11-A, Road Tanker, reg, 1955, dk yel w/metal wheels, MIP, from $75 to...**$100.00**

11-A, Road Tanker, reg, 1955, gr w/metal wheels, MIP, from $400 to...**$500.00**

11-C, Taylor Jumbo Crane, reg, 1965, yel weight box, MIP, from $15 to...**$20.00**

12-B, Land Rover, reg, 1959, olive gr w/blk plastic wheels, no roof or driver, MIP, from $25 to.................................**$30.00**

12-C, Safari Land Rover, reg, 1965, gold w/tan luggage, MIP, from $80 to **$100.00**

12-F, Big Bull Bulldozer, reg, 1975, orange rollers, MIP, from $4 to **$7.00**

12-N, Audi Avus, reg, 1995, silver chrome, MIP **$3.00**

13-A, Bedford Wrecker, reg, 1955, tan, MIP, from $45 to ..**$60.00**

13-F, Baja Dune Buggy, reg, 1971, bright gr w/flower label, MIP, from $175 to **$200.00**

13-F, Baja Dune Buggy, reg, 1971, metallic gr w/sunburst label, MIP, from $15 to **$20.00**

14-A, Daimler Ambulance, reg, 1956, MIP, from $50 to ..**$65.00**

14-C, Bedford Lomas Ambulance, reg, 1962, gray plastic wheels, MIP, from $100 to...**$125.00**

14-L, Corvette Convertible, reg, 1983, metallic silver w/red interior, MIP, from $3 to...**$5.00**

15-A, Prime Mover Truck Tractor, reg, 1956, orange w/plastic wheels, MIP, from $175 to...**$200.00**

15-A, Prime Mover Truck Tractor, reg, 1956, yel w/metal wheels, MIP, from $500 to...**$700.00**

15-D, Volkswagen 1500 Saloon, 1968, off-white w/137 decals on doors, M, from $10 to **$12.00**

15-G, Fork Lift Truck, reg, 1972, Lansing Bagnall decals, no steering wheel, MIP **$10.00**

16-B, Atlantic Trailer, reg, 1957, orange w/blk tow bar, gray plastic wheels, MIP, from $100 to.................................**$125.00**

16-D, Case Bulldozer, reg, 1969, blk treads, from $12 to ..**$15.00**

17-A, Bedford Matchbox Removal Van, reg, 1956, lt gr, MIP, from $60 to...**$75.00**

17-C, Hoveringham Tipper, reg, 1963, red cab w/orange tipper, MIP, from $15 to **$20.00**

17-H, AMX Pro Stocker, reg, 1983, metallic gray w/red & blk stripes, MIP, from $2 to **$5.00**

18-B, Caterpillar Dozer, reg, 1958, yel w/yel blade, no blade braces, MIP, from $55 to **$70.00**

18-E, Field Car, reg, 1969, gr wheel hubs, MIP, from $250 to **$300.00**

18-F, Field Car, SF, 1970, olive drab, MIP, from $40 to.....**$50.00**

18-F, Field Car, SF, 1970, wht, MIP, from $300 to **$400.00**

19-A, MG Midget Sports Car, reg, 1956, w/driver, MIP, from $50 to **$75.00**

19-C, Aston Martin Racing Car, reg, 1961, metallic gr w/52 decal, gray driver, MIP, from $40 to...........................**$50.00**

19-H, Peterbilt Cement Truck, reg, 1982, metallic gr w/orange barrel, Big Pete tampos, MIP, from $3 to **$5.00**

20-A, Stake Truck, reg, 1956, maroon w/silver grille & fuel tanks, gray plastic wheels, MIP, from $100 to **$125.00**

20-C, Chevrolet Impala Taxi, reg, 1965, orange w/ivory or red interior, blk wheels, MIP, ea from $20 to **$25.00**

20-C, Chevrolet Impala Taxi Cab, reg, 1965, orange w/ivory interior, gray wheels, MIP, from $250 to **$350.00**

20-G, Jeep 4x4, reg, blk w/wht roof, Laredo tampo, MIP, from $15 to **$20.00**

21-A, Bedford Duplé Long Distance Coach, reg, 1956, MIP, from $45 to..**$55.00**

21-C, Commer Milk Delivery Truck, reg, 1961, gray wheels, MIP, from $65 to...**$75.00**

14-L, Corvette Convertible, 1987, metallic purple with light orange interior, white accents, 3", MIB, $2.00. (Photo courtesy Dana Johnson)

21-G, Renault 5TL, 1978, white with Renault tampos, 2¾", MIB, from $7.00 to $10.00. (Photo courtesy Dana Johnson)

21-C, Commer Milk Delivery Truck, reg, 1961, silver wheels, MIP, from $25 to $35.00

21-F, Road Roller, red, 1973, yel w/metallic red rear wheels, MIP, from $15 to..$20.00

22-A, Vauxall Cresta Sedan, reg, 1956, red w/wht or cream roof, no windows, MIP, ea from $30 to $50.00

22-B, Vauxhall Cresta Sedan, reg, 1958, cream & turq w/gr windows, gray plastic wheels, MIP, from $350 to...........$400.00

22-B, Vauxhall Cresta Sedan, reg, 1958, gray & pk w/gr windows, gray plastic wheels, MIP, from $50 to $60.00

22-H, Toyota Mini Pickup Camper, reg, 1983, MIP, from $2 to $5.00

22-K, Opel Vectra/Chevrolet Cavalier GS, reg, 1990, gr, MIP, from $10 to..$12.00

23-A, Berkeley Cavalier Travel Trailer, reg, 1956, metallic gr, MIP, from $275 to $325.00

23-C, Trailer Caravan, reg, 1965, yel or pk, MIP, ea from $12 to...$16.00

23-E, Atlas Dump Truck, reg, 1975, red w/metallic silver dumper, MIP, from $6 to $10.00

24-A, Weatherhill Hydraulic Excavator, reg, 1956, yel w/metal wheels, MIP, from $80 to $100.00

24-C, Rolls Royce Silver Shadow, reg, 1967, metallic red w/chrome hubs, MIP, from $6 to $10.00

24-E, Team Matchbox Formula 1 Racer, reg, 1973, metallic bl w/wht driver, #1 label, MIP, from $275 to.............$325.00

24-E, Team Matchbox Formula 1 Racer, reg, 1973, orange w/yel driver, #44 label, MIP, from $35 to.......................$50.00

24-H, Datsun 280ZX 2+2, reg, 1983, wht w/red & bl Turbo 33 tampo, MIP $10.00

25-B, Volkswagen 1200 Sedan, reg, 1960, lt metallic bl w/gr windows, silver plastic windows, MIP, from $50 to $60.00

25-C, Bedford Petrol Tanker w/Tilt Cab, reg, 1964, yel cab, gray plastic wheels, MIP, from $140 to $160.00

25-E, Ford Cortina GT, SF, 1970, metallic bl, MIP, from $15 to...$20.00

25-G, Flat Car w/Container, reg, 1978, tan container w/United States Lines labels, MIP, from $10 to $12.00

25-L, Peugeot Quasar, SF, 1985, dk bl w/pk stripes, #9 tampo, MIP, from $4 to $6.00

26-A, Foden Ready-Mix Concrete Truck, reg, 1956, metal wheels, gold grille, MIP, from $65 to $85.00

26-B, Foden Ready-Mix Concrete Truck, reg, 1961, orange mixer, gray wheels, MIP, from $35 to $45.00

26-B, Foden Ready-Mix Concrete Truck, reg, 1961, orange mixer, silver wheels, MIP, from $130 to $150.00

26-C, GMC Tipper Truck, reg, 1968, MIP, from $6 to......$10.00

26-F, Site Dumper, reg, 1976, orange-red w/wht interior, MIP, from $30 to...$40.00

27-A, Bedford Low Loader, reg, 1956, lt bl w/dk bl trailer, MIP, from $625 to $800.00

27-A Bedford Low Loader, reg, 1956, dk gr w/tan trailer, MIP, from $35 to...$60.00

27-C, Cadillac Sixty Special, reg, 1960, metallic gray w/wht roof, MIP, from $35 to..$45.00

28-A, Bedford Compressor Truck, reg, 1956, MIP, from $35 to $55.00

28-D, Mack Dump Truck, reg, 1968, MIP, from $9 to.......$12.00

29-B, Austin A55 Cambridge, reg, 1961, 2-tone gr w/gray wheels, MIP, from $35 to $45.00

29-B, Austin A55 Cambridge, reg, 1961, 2-tone gr w/silver wheels, MIP, from $20 to $30.00

29-D, Fire Pumper, SF, 1970, no water gun, MIP, from $20 to..$25.00

30-A, Ford Perfect Sedan, reg, 1956, gray-brn or olive brn, MIP, ea from $35 to $50.00

30-A, Ford Perfect Sedan, reg, 1956, lt bl, MIP, from $35 to..$50.00

30-C, 8-Wheel Crane Truck, reg, 1965, mint gr, MIP, from $900 to..$1,000.00

30-E, Beach Buggy, reg, 1971, pk w/wht int, MIP, from $20 to..$35.00

30-I, Mercedes Benz 280GE G-Wagon, reg, 1984, red w/checkerboard pattern & wht roof, Rescue Unit tampo, MIP ...$5.00

31-A, Ford Customline Station Wagon, reg, 1957, yel w/gray plastic wheels, MIP, from $40 to............................$50.00

31-C, Lincoln Continental, reg, 1964, metallic bl w/blk plastic wheels, MIP, from $8 to $12.00

31-C, Lincoln Continental, reg, 1964, metallic lime gr w/blk plastic wheels, MIP, from $500 to $600.00

31-D, Lincoln Continental, SF, 1969, mint gr, MIP, from $1,800 to..$2,000.00

31-G, Mazda Savannah RX-7, reg, 1979, wht, no spoiler, MIP, from $3 to..$6.00

32-A, Jaguar XK140 Coupe, reg, 1957, red, MIP, from $75 to...$100.00

32-C, Leyland Petrol Tanker, reg, 1968, dk bl w/silver grille, Aral labels, MIP, from $40 to.................................$50.00

32-E, Maserati Bora, reg, 1972, gold, MIP, from $12 to $18.00

33-B, Ford Zephyr 6 Mk III Sedan, reg, 1963, blk plastic wheels, MIP, from $60 to..$70.00

33-B, Ford Zephyr 6 Mk III Sedan, reg, 1963, gray or silver plastic wheels, MIP, ea from $35 to $40.00

33-E, Datsun 126X, reg, 1973, yel w/orange base, MIP, from $8 to..$12.00

34-A, Volkswagen Matchbox Express Van, reg, 1957, bl w/blk plastic wheels, MIP, from $125 to $150.00

34-A, Volkswagen Matchbox Express Van, reg, 1957, bl w/gray plastic wheels, MIP, from $55 to............................$65.00

34-E, Formula 1 Racing Car, reg, 1971, bl, MIP, from $12 to...$15.00

34-G, Chevy Pro Stocker, reg, 1981, wht, from $12 to.....$16.00

35-A, Marshall Horse Box Truck, reg, 1957, red & brn w/blk plastic wheels, MIP, from $125 to $150.00

35-A, Marshall Horse Box Truck, reg, 1957, red & brn w/gray plastic wheels, MIP, from $40 to............................$50.00

35-C, Merryweather Fire Engine, SF, 1969, metallic red, from $10 to..$15.00

35-J, Pontiac Stock Car, reg, 1993, yel w/Seaside 15 tampo, MIP $4.00

36-A, Austin A50 Sedan, reg, 1957, metal or plastic wheels, MIP, ea from $35 to $45.00

36-C, Opel Diplomat, reg, 1966, metallic gold w/gray motor, MIP $10.00

36-F, Formula 5000, reg, 1975, wht w/Texaco on hood, MIP, from $250 to $300.00

37-C, Coca-Cola Lorry, reg, 1960, blk base, silver plastic wheels, even load, MIP, from $125 to $150.00

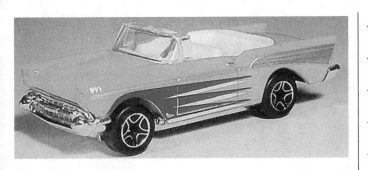

36-H, '57 Chevy Bel Air Convertible, 1998, baby blue with pink and white accents, MIB, from $1.00 to $2.00. (Photo courtesy Dana Johnson)

37-E, Dodge Cattle Truck, SF, 1970, silver-gray box, MIP, from $20 to $25.00

37-G, Atlas Skip Truck, reg, 1976, orange w/red skip, MIP, from $75 to $100.00

38-A, Karrier Refuse Truck, reg, 1957, dk gray w/metal or plastic wheels, MIP, ea from $30 to $40.00

38-A, Karrier Refuse Truck, reg, 1957, gray-brn w/metal wheels, MIP, from $100 to.............................$125.00

38-B, Vauxhall Victor Estate Car, reg, 1963, yel w/gr interior, silver plastic wheels, MIP, from $35 to.....................$40.00

38-C, Honda Motorcycle & Trailer, reg, 1967, orange w/Honda decals, MIP, from $30 to $35.00

38-D, Honda Motorcycle & Trailer, SF, 1970, purple w/yel trailer, MIP, from $15 to $20.00

38-E, Stingeroo Cycle, reg, 1973, purple w/chrome handlebars, MIP, from $300 to...$350.00

38-H, Ford Model A Truck, reg, 1982, bl w/Kellogg's labels, MIP, from $8 to..$10.00

39-A, Ford Zodiac Convertible, reg, 1957, pk w/tan interior & base, metal wheels, MIP, from $100 to $125.00

39-A, Ford Zodiac Convertible, reg, 1957, pk w/turq interior & base, gray plastic wheels, MIP, from $45 to $60.00

39-C, Ford Tractor, reg, 1967, yel & bl, from $10 to.........$12.00

39-E, Rolls Royce Silver Shadow II, reg, 1979, metallic silver-gray, red or tan, MIP, ea $6.00

39-G, BMW 323i Cabriolet, reg, 1985, wht w/BMW/323i tampos, MIP, from $10 to......................................$12.00

40-A, Bedford Tipper Truck, reg, 1957, red w/tan dumper, gray plastic wheels, MIP, from $30 to........................$45.00

40-B, Leyland Royal Tiger Coach, reg, 1961, metallic bl w/gray wheels, MIP, from $35 to $45.00

40-E, Bedford Horse Box w/2 Horses, reg, 1977, red w/beige box, gr windows, MIP, from $16 to $20.00

41-A, D-Type Jaguar, reg, 1957, gr w/41 decal, gray plastic wheels, MIP, from $40 to $50.00

41-B, D-Type Jaguar, reg, 1960, gr, blk plastic tires on red hubs, MIP, from $175 to......................................$200.00

41-C, Ford GT, reg, 1965, wht w/red wheels, #6 decal, MIP, from $100 to..$120.00

41-D, Ford GT, SF, 1970, wht or metallic orange, MIP, ea ...$15.00

41-E, Siva Spider, reg, 1972, red w/silver trim, MIP, from $15 to..$20.00

42-A, Bedford Evening News Van, red, 1957, yel-orange, metal wheels or gray or blk plastic wheels, MIP, ea from $40 to.$50.00

42-D, Iron Fairy Crane, SF, 1970, red w/lime gr boom, MIP, from $90 to..$100.00

42-D, Iron Fairy Crane, SF, 1970, red w/yel boom, MIP, from $60 to $75.00

42-F, Mercedes Benz Container Truck, reg, 1977, red w/beige container, OCL labels, MIP..............................$10.00

43-A, Hillman Minx Sedan, reg, 1958, turq w/cream roof, gray plastic wheels, MIP, from $30 to..............................$40.00

43-C, Pony Trailer w/Two Horses, reg, 1968, MIP, from $6 to $10.00

43-D, Pony Trailer w/Two Horses, SF, 1970, beige, from $6 to..$10.00

43-H, Peterbilt Conventional, reg, 1982, blk, MIP, from $2 to $5.00

43-K, Lincoln Town Car, reg, 1989, wht w/metal or plastic base, MIP, ea from $2 to...$5.00

44-A, Rolls Royce Silver Cloud, reg, 1958, metallic bl, metal wheels, MIP, from $30 to $40.00

44-B, Rolls Royce Silver Cloud, 1964, metallic tan, M, from $15 to $20.00

44-E, Boss Mustang, reg, 1972, yel, MIP, from $5 to $8.00

44-K, Ford Probe, red, 1995, blk w/bl & pk acents, MIP $3.00

45-A, Vauxhall Victor Sedan, reg, 1958, yel w/clear windows, gray plastic windows, MIP, from $30 to......................$40.00

45-A, Vauxhall Victor Sedan, reg, 1958, yel w/gr windows, silver plastic wheels, MIP, from $40 to...............................$50.00

45-B, Ford Corsair w/Boat & Roof Rack, reg, 1965, gray wheels, MIP, from $30 to..$40.00

45-D, BMW 3.0 CSL, reg, 1976, wht w/gr tampo, MIP, from $60 to $70.00

46-A, Morris Minor 1000, reg, 1958, dk bl w/gray plastic wheels, MIP, from $80 to...$100.00

46-A, Morris Minor 1000, reg, 1958, dk gr w/metal wheels, MIP, from $50 to..$60.00

46-B, Pickford Removal Van, reg, 1960, dk bl w/gray plastic wheels, MIP, from $60 to $75.00

46-C, Mercedes Benz 300SE, reg, 1968, gr or metallic bl, MIP, ea from $8 to..$12.00

46-D, Mercedes Benz 300SE, SF, 1970, metallic bl, MIP, from $60 to $75.00

46-G, Hot Chocolate Volkswagen Beetle, reg, 1982, blk w/metallic brn sides, MIP, from $4 to $6.00

47-A, Trojan 1-Ton Brooke Bond Tea Van, reg, 1958, red w/gray plastic wheels, MIP, from $40 to................................$50.00

47-B, Commer Ice Cream Canteen, reg, 1963, bl w/gray plastic wheels, MIP, from $150 to.....................................$175.00

47-B, Commer Ice Cream Canteen, reg, 1963, metallic bl w/blk plastic wheels, MIP, from $100 to $120.00

47-C, DAF Tipper Container Truck, reg, 1968, bl w/yel container, gray container cover, MIP, from $25 to..........$30.00

48-A, Meteor Sports Boat & Trailer, reg, 1958, tan deck, bl hull, silver plastic wheels, MIP, from $80 to.....................$100.00

48-B, Sports Boat & Trailer w/Outboard Motor, reg, 1961, gray wheels, MIP, from $60 to $75.00

49-A, M3 Army Halftrack Personnel Carrier, reg, 1958, gray plastic front wheels & rollers, MIP, from $90 to $100.00

49-A, M3 Army Halftrack Personnel Carrier, reg, 1958, metal front wheels & roller, MIP, from $40 to $50.00

49-B, Mercedes Benz Unimog, reg, 1967, tan w/turq chassis, MIP, from $10 to...$12.00

49-D, Chop Suey Motorcycle, reg, 1973, magenta w/blk handlebars, MIP, from $15 to...$20.00

49-D, Chop Suey Motorcycle, reg, 1973, magenta w/silver handlebars, MIP, from $275 to $325.00

49-J, BMW 850i, reg, 1993, metallic silver, MIP, from $2 to ...$5.00

50-A, Commer Pickup, reg, 1958, lt tan w/gray plastic wheels, MIP, from $40 to...$50.00

50-A, Commer Pickup, reg, 1958, red & wht w/silver plastic wheels, from $275 to $300.00

50-B, John Deere Tractor, reg, 1964, gray plastic tires, MIP, from $25 to...$30.00

50-C, Ford Kennel Truck, 1969, with four dogs and regular wheels, 2¾", MIB, from $6.00 to $9.00. (Photo courtesy Dana Johnson)

50-G, Harley-Davidson Motorcycle, reg, 1980, MIP, from $4 to...$6.00

50-I, Dodge Dakota Pickup, reg, 1989, bright red w/blk & wht stripes, MIP, from $2 to..$4.00

51-A, Albion Chieftain Flatbed Transporter, reg, 1958, metal or gray plastic wheels, MIP, ea from $30 to....................$40.00

51-A, Albion Chieftain Flatbed Transporter, reg, 1958, silver plastic wheels, MIP, from $60 to................................$80.00

51-B, John Deere Trailer w/3 Barrels, reg, 1964, blk plastic tires, MIP, from $20 to...$25.00

51-F, Combine Harvester, reg, 1978, dk gr, MIP, from $275 to..$325.00

51-J, Camaro IROC Z, reg, 1985, gr, MIP, from $6 to.........$8.00

51-K, Ford LTD Police, reg, 1988, purple w/Police PD-21 label, MIP, from $3 to...$5.00

52-A, Maserati 4CL T/1948 Racer, reg, 1958, red w/blk plastic tires on spoked wheels, MIP, from $100 to...............$125.00

52-B, BRM Racing Car, red, 1965, bl w/#3 decal, blk tires on plastic hubs, MIP, from $40 to....................................$50.00

52-E, BMW M1, reg, 1981, metallic gray w/#52 tampo, gr windows, opening hood, MIP, from $70 to.........................$80.00

53-A, Aston Martin DB2 Saloon, reg, 1958, metallic lt gr w/gray plastic wheels, MIP, from $30 to................................$40.00

53-A, Aston Martin DB2 Saloon, reg, 1958, metallic red w/gray plastic wheels, MIP, from $130 to $150.00

53-C, Ford Zodiac Mk IV Sedan, reg, 1968, metallic silver-bl, MIP, from $500 to...$600.00

53-G, Flareside Pickup, reg, 1982, yel w/blk interior, 8-spoke wheels, MIP, from $35 to..$40.00

54-A, Army Saracen Personnel Carrier, reg, 1958, blk plastic wheels, MIP, from $20 to..$35.00

54-F, Motor Home, reg, 1980, beige, MIP, from $4 to.........$8.00

55-A, DUKW Army Amphibian, reg, 1958, metal or gray plastic wheels, MIP, ea from $30 to......................................$45.00

55-B, Ford Fairlane Police Car, reg, 1963, lt bl w/silver plastic wheels, MIP, from $80 to.......................................$100.00

55-D, Mercury Parklane Police Car, reg, 1968, bl domelight, M...$10.00

55-F, Mercury Commuter Police Station Wagon, reg, 1971, amber roof light, MIP, from $45 to.............................$60.00

55-H, Ford Cortina 1600 GL, reg, 1979, metallic gr, doors open, MIP, from $4 to...$6.00

56-A, London Trolley Bus, reg, 1958, red rods, metal wheels, MIP, from $35 to...$45.00

56-B, Fiat 1500 w/Luggage on Roof, reg, 1965, red, MIP, from $80 to...$90.00

56-B, Fiat 1500 w/Luggage on Roof, reg, 1965, turq, MIP, from $8 to...$12.00

56-C, BMC 1800 Pininfarina, SF, 1970, metallic gold, w/ or w/o labels, MIP, ea from $15 to....................................$20.00

57-A, Wolseley 1500 Sedan, reg, 1958, pale gray w/silver grille, MIP, from $110 to...$120.00

57-A, Wolseley 1500 Sedan, reg, 1958, pale yel-gr w/gold grille, MIP, from $60 to...$80.00

57-C, Land Rover Fire Truck, reg, 1966, gray plastic wheels, MIP, from $180 to...$200.00

57-D, Land Rover Fire Truck, SF, 1970, MIB, from $25 to ..$40.00

58-A, British European Airways Coach, reg, 1958, silver plastic wheels, MIP, from $80 to...$100.00

58-B, Drott Excavator, reg, 1962, orange w/silver motor & base, blk rollers, MIP, from $35 to.....................................$45.00

58-B, Drott Excavator, reg, 1962, red w/silver motor & base, silver rollers, MIP, from $80 to....................................$100.00

58-H, Ruff Trek Holden Pickup, reg, 1983, wht w/#217 tampo, MIP, from $3 to...$5.00

59-A, Ford Thames Singer Van, reg, 1958, lt gr w/silver plastic wheels, MIP, from $80 to...$100.00

59-B, Ford Fairlane Fire Chief Car, reg, 1963, red w/silver plastic wheels, MIP, from $125 to.......................................$150.00

59-E, Mercury Parklane Fire Chief Car, reg, 1971, red w/purple windows, MIP, from $30 to.......................................$40.00

60-A, Morris J2 Builders Supply Pickup, reg, 1958, lt bl w/silver plastic wheels, red & blk decals, MIP, from $40 to $50.00

60-B, Leyland Site Office Truck, reg, 1966, MIP, from $15 to.$20.00

60-D, Lotus Super Seven, reg, 1971, yel, MIP, from $20 to...$25.00

60-F, Mustang Piston Popper, reg, 1982, yel w/red interior, no decals, MIP, from $8 to...$10.00

61-A, Ferret Scout Car, reg, 1959, olive gr w/blk plastic wheels, MIP, from $15 to...$25.00

61-C, Blue Shark, reg, 1971, scorpion label, MIP, from $20 to..$25.00

61-E, Peterbilt Wrecker, reg, 1982, bl w/amber windows, blk boom, no markings, MIP, from $80 to.....................$100.00

62-B, TV Service Van, reg, 1963, blk plastic wheels, Radio Rentals decals, MIP, from $40 to.................................$50.00

62-B, TV Service Van, reg, 1963, gray plastic wheels, Rentaset decals, MIP, from $125 to...$150.00

62-D, Mercury Cougar, SF, 1970, doors open, MIP, from $12 to **$15.00**

62-G, Corvette T-Roof, reg, 1980, blk w/opaque windows, gr & orange stripes, MIP, from $8 to **$10.00**

62-I, Rolls Royce Silver Cloud, reg, 1985, metallic silver-gray, MIP, from $6 to **$8.00**

63-B, Airport Foamite Crash Tender, reg, 1964, silver nozzle, MIP, from $5 to **$10.00**

63-E, BP Freeway Gas Tanker, reg, 1973, yel, MIP, from $30 to **$45.00**

63-I, Dunes Racer 4x4 Pickup, reg, 1984, MIP, from $4 to .**$6.00**

64-A, Scammell Breakdown Truck, reg, 1959, olive gr w/blk plastic wheels, gr or silver metal hook, MIP, ea from $30 to **$40.00**

64-C, MG 1100 w/Driver & Dog, SF, 1970, gr, MIP, from $125 to **$175.00**

64-F, Caterpillar Bulldozer, reg, 1979, yel w/blk blade, tan canopy, MIP, from $8 to...................................**$10.00**

65-A, 3.4 Litre Jaguar, reg, 1959, bl or metallic bl w/gray plastic wheels, MIP, ea from $30 to......................................**$40.00**

65-B, Jaguar 3.8 Litre Saloon, 1962, red with black wheels, 2⅝", MIB, from $20.00 to $30.00. (Photo courtesy Dana Johnson)

65-C, Class Combine Harvester, red wheels, 1967, M, from $6 to **$10.00**

65-D, Saab Sonnet, reg, 1973, wht, MIP, from $200 to ..**$250.00**

65-E, American Airlines Airport Coach, reg, 1977, metallic bl, no tab on base, MIP, from $20 to..............................**$25.00**

65-E, Lufthansa Airport Coach, reg, 1977, wht, MIP, from $25 to **$30.00**

65-I, Cadallic Allante, reg, 1988, metallic silver, MIP, from $2 to...**$5.00**

66-A, Citroen DS19, reg, 1959, yel w/gray plastic wheels, MIP, from $50 to..**$60.00**

66-B, Harley-Davidson Motorcycle & Sidecar, reg, 1962, metallic bronze w/blk tires, MIP, from $85 to.....................**$95.00**

66-D, Greyhound Bus, SF, 1970, MIP, from $15 to **$20.00**

66-E, Mazda RX-500, reg, 1971, orange w/amber windows, MIP, from $45 to..**$60.00**

66-I, Rolls Royce Silver Spirit, reg, 1988, metallic tan, MIP, from $2 to..**$4.00**

67-A, Saladin Armoured Car, reg, 1959, olive gr w/blk plastic wheels, MIP, from $30 to.............................**$40.00**

67-C, Volkswagen 1600TL, SF, 1970, red, MIP, from $30 to....**$40.00**

67-E, Datsun 260Z 2+2, reg, 1978, metallic purple, doors open, MIP, from $8 to..**$12.00**

67-H, Lamborghini Countach LP500S, reg, 1985, red w/logo on hood, gold wheels, MIP, from $10 to......................**$12.00**

68-B, Mercedes Benz Coach, reg, 1965, orange, MIP, from $8 to...**$12.00**

68-C, Porsche 910, SF, 1970, wht, MIP, from $20 to **$25.00**

68-D, Cosmobile, reg, 1975, metallic avocado & blk, amber windows, MIP, from $25 to..**$30.00**

68-E, Chevy Van, reg, 1979, wht w/bl windows, Adidas tampo, MIP, from $30 to..**$35.00**

68-F, Dodge Caravan, reg, 1984, burgundy w/blk stripes, England cast, MIP, from $16 to......................................**$20.00**

69-A, Nestle's Commer 30 CWT Van, reg, 1959, red w/gray plastic wheels, MIP, from $60 to..............................**$70.00**

69-B, Hatra Tractor Shovel, reg, 1965, orange w/red wheels & blk tires, MIP, from $12 to......................................**$16.00**

69-C, Rolls Royce Silver Shadow Convertible Coupe, 1969, metallic blue, SuperFast wheels only, 3", MIB, from $15.00 to $20.00. (Photo courtesy Dana Johnson)

69-C, Rolls Royce Silver Shadow Convertible Coupe, SF, 1969, metallic lime-gold, MIP, from $15 to........................**$20.00**

69-D, Turbo Fury, reg, 1973, #69 label, MIP, from $12 to....**$18.00**

69-E, Wells Fargo Armoured Truck, reg, 1978, red w/clear windows, MIP, from $25 to..**$35.00**

69-F, 1933 Willys Street Rod, reg, 1982, wht w/flame tampos, 313 on roof, MIP, from $3 to...................................**$5.00**

70-A, Ford Thames Estate Car, reg, 1959, yel & turq w/clear windows, gray plastic wheels, MIP, from $30 to **$40.00**

70-A, Ford Thames Estate Car, reg, 1959, yel & turq w/gr windows, blk plastic wheels, MIP, from $25 to.................**$35.00**

70-D, Dodge Dragster, reg, 1971, pk w/Wildcat or Rat Rod label, MIP, ea from $20 to **$25.00**

70-F, Ferrari 308 GTD, red, 1981, red, Data East/Secret Service tampos, MIP, from $60 to **$70.00**

70-G, Ford Skip Truck, reg, 1988, bl w/red metal skip, Preschool series, MIP, from $6 to......................................**$8.00**

71-B, Jeep Gladiator Pickup Truck, reg, 1964, gr interior, MIP, from $40 to..**$50.00**

71-C, Ford Esso Wreck Truck, reg, 1968, amber windows, MIP, from $60 to..**$75.00**

71-D, Ford Esso Heavy Wreck Truck, SF, 1970, bl, MIP, from $100 to **$120.00**

71-G, 1962 Corvette, reg, 1982, wht w/red accents, bl interior, MIP, from $8 to..**$10.00**

71-I, Porsche 944 Racer, reg, 1988, red w/944 Turbo on sides, MIP, from $2 to..**$4.00**

72-A, Fordson Power Major Farm Tractor, reg, 1959, bl w/blk front & rear tires on yel wheels, MIP, from $90 to...**$100.00**

72-A, Fordson Power Major Farm Tractor, reg, 1959, bl w/gray front wheels, gray tires on orange back wheels, MIP .**$50.00**

72-D, Hovercraft SRN6, reg, 1972, MIP, from $4 to..........**$6.00**

72-E, Maxi Taxi Mercury Capri, reg, 1973, MIP, from $8 to ..**$12.00**

72-I, Rescue Plane Transporter, reg, 1985, yel w/checkerboard pattern, MIP, from $6 to **$8.00**

73-A, RAF 10-Ton Pressure Refueling Tanker, 1959, blue-gray with gray plastic wheels, 2⅝", MIB, from $5.00 to $10.00. (Photo courtesy Dana Johnson)

73-B, Ferrari F1 Racer, reg, 1962, wht or gray driver, MIP, ea from $20 to..**$30.00**

73-C, Mercury Commuter Station Wagon, reg, 1968, chrome hubs, MIP, from $6 to **$10.00**

73-D, Mercury Commuter Station Wagon, SF, 1970, red, MIP, from $15 to..**$20.00**

73-F, Weasel Armored Vehicle, reg, 1974, olive drab, MIP, from $45 to **$50.00**

74-A, Mobile Canteen Refreshment Bar, reg, 1959, pk w/lt bl base & interior, gray wheels, MIP, from $400 to **$500.00**

74-A, Mobile Canteen Refreshment Bar, reg, 1959, silver w/blk plastic wheels, MIP, from $30 to..............................**$40.00**

74-A, Mobile Canteen Refreshment Bar, reg, 1959, wht w/bl base & interior, gray wheels, MIP, from $300 to **$350.00**

74-D, Toe Joe Wreck Truck, reg, 1972, metallic lime gr w/wht booms, blk hooks, MIP, from $65 to..........................**$80.00**

74-D, Toe Joe Wreck Truck, reg, 1972, yel w/gr booms, blk hooks, MIP, from $15 to **$20.00**

74-E, Mercury Cougar Villager Station Wagon, reg, 1978, army gr, MIP, from $275 to..**$325.00**

75-A, Ford Thunderbird, reg, 1960, cream & pk, blk plastic wheels, MIP, from $80 to..**$100.00**

75-A, Ford Thunderbird, reg, 1960, cream & pk, gray or silver plastic wheels, MIP, ea from $50 to **$60.00**

75-B, Ferrari Berlinetta, reg, 1965, metallic lt bl w/spoke wheels, MIP, from $60 to..**$80.00**

75-B, Ferrari Berlinetta, reg, 1965, red w/chrome hubs, MIP, from $500 to **$600.00**

75-D, Alfa Carabo, reg, 1971, metallic pk, no tampo, MIP, from $12 to **$18.00**

75-D, Alfa Carabo, reg, 1971, pk, no tampo, MIP, from $20 to...**$25.00**

75-E, Seasprite Helicopter, reg, 1977, dk gr or dk cream, MIP, ea from $275 to **$325.00**

75-F, MBTV News Helicopter, reg, 1982, wht w/blk base, w/pilot, MIP, from $4 to..**$6.00**

75-G, Ferrari Testarossa, SF, 1987, blk w/silver accents, MIP..**$5.00**

KING SIZE, SPEED KINGS, AND SUPER KINGS

K-1-A, Weatherhill Hydraulic Shovel, 1960, MIP, from $60 to **$75.00**

K-1-D, Kremer Porsche CK.5 Racer, 1989, MIP **$10.00**

K-2-A, Muir Hill Dumper, 1960, gray plastic wheels, MIP, from $35 to **$45.00**

K-2-B, KW Dump Cart, 1964, MIP, from $25 to **$40.00**

K-2-C, Scammel Heavy Wreck Truck, 1969, wht w/gr windows or gold w/amber windows, MIP, ea from $30 to **$40.00**

K-3-B, Hatra Tractor Shovel, 1965, MIP, from $25 to **$30.00**

K-3-D, Mod Tractor & Trailer, 1974, MIP, from $15 to **$20.00**

K-3-E, Heidelberger Zement Grain Transporter, 1980, gr, MIP, from $50 to..**$60.00**

K-4-B, GMC Tractor & Fruehauf Hopper Train, 1967, blk plastic tires, MIP, from $30 to......................................**$40.00**

K-5-A, Foden Tipper Truck, 1961, blk plastic tires on silver metal wheels, MIP, from $30 to **$40.00**

K-5-C, Muir Hill Tractor Trailer, 1972, 2-tone bl, MIP, from $35 to **$45.00**

K-6-C, GMC Cement Mixer, 1971, MIP **$15.00**

K-7-B, SD Refuse Truck, 1967, MIP, from $15 to **$20.00**

K-7-C, Racing Car Transporter, 1973, yel w/24-E Team Matchbox Formula 1 Racer in gr, MIP, from $55 to **$65.00**

K-8-A, Prime Mover w/Caterpillar Crawler, 1962, MIP, from $60 to **$75.00**

K-8-B, Guy Warrior Car Transporter, 1967, bl-gr w/orange trailer, gray plastic tires, orange wheels, MIP, from $30 to **$40.00**

K-8-C, Caterpillar Traxcavator, 1970, silver-gray, MIP, from $35 to **$45.00**

K-9-A, Diesel Road Roller, 1962, gray or red driver, MIP, ea from $30 to **$40.00**

K-9-C, Fire Tender, 1973, MIP **$15.00**

K-9-E, Ferrari F40 Racer, 1989, MIP **$10.00**

K-12-A, Heavy Breakdown Wreck Truck, 1963, 4¾", MIB, from $30.00 to $40.00. (Photo courtesy Dana Johnson)

K-10-B, Pipe Truck, 1967, MIP $25.00

K-10-C, Car Transporter, 1976, wild horse design, MIP, from $20 to $25.00

K-10-D, Bedford Courier Car Transporter, 1981, MIP, from $15 to $20.00

K-11-A, Fordson Tractor & Farm Trailer, 1963, metal wheels, MIP, from $30 to $40.00

K-11-D, Dodge Delivery Van, 1981, MIP, from $15 to $20.00

K-12-B, Scammell Crane Truck, 1970, silver-gray, MIP, from $35 to $45.00

K-12-C, Hercules Mobile Crane, 1975, yel, MIP, from $15 to $20.00

K-13-A, Foden Ready-Mix Concrete Truck, 1963, MIP, from $30 to $40.00

K-14-A, Taylor Jumbo Crane, 1964, MIP, from $20 to $25.00

K-14-C, Heavy Breakdown Truck, 1977, MIP $15.00

K-15-A, Merryweather Fire Engine, 1964, MIP, from $20 to .$25.00

K-15-B, Royal Wedding Londoner Bus, 1981, metallic silver, MIP, from $50 to $70.00

K-16-A, Dodge Tractor w/Twin Tippers, 1966, MIP, from $40 to $50.00

K-16-B, Quaker State Petrol Tanker, 1966, gr cab, MIP, from $75 to $100.00

K-17-A, Ford Tractor w/Dyson Low Loader & Case Tractor, 1966, MIP, from $30 to $40.00

K-18-A, Dodge Articulated Horse Box, 1966, MIP, from $25 to $35.00

K-18-B, Articulated Tipper Truck, 1974, metallic red cab, MIP, from $15 to $20.00

K-19-A, Scammell Tipper Truck, 1967, MIP, from $15 to.....$20.00

K-20-A, Tractor Transporter w/3 Tractors, 1968, MIP, from $40 to $50.00

K-20-C, Peterbilt Wreck Truck, 1979, wht, MIP, from $40 to..$50.00

K-21-A, Mercury Cougar, 1968, gold w/red interior, MIP, from $15 to $20.00

K-21-D, Ford Transcontinental Double Freighter, 1979, yel w/Continental decal, MIP, from $20 to......................$25.00

K-22-C, SRN6 Hovercraft, 1974, bl upper, wht lower, w/SRN6 & Seaspeed decals, MIP..................................$12.00

K-23-B, Scammell Crusader Low Loader w/Bulldozer, 1974, dk bl cab, Hoch & Tief label, MIP, from $40 to.............$50.00

K-24-A, Lamborghini Miura, 1969, MIP, from $15 to......$20.00

K-25-B, Digger & Plough, 1977, red, MIP, from $20 to....$25.00

K-26-A, Mercedes Benz Ambulance, 1971, MIP.............$15.00

K-26-B, McAlpine Cement Truck, 1980, red, MIP, from $15 to $20.00

K-27-A, Camping Cruiser, 1971, MIP..............................$15.00

K-27-B, Power Boat & Transporter, 1978, several different variations, MIP, ea $20.00

K-28-B, Hoch & Tief Skip Truck, 1978, MIP, from $30 to.....$35.00

K-29-B, Ford Delivery Van, 1978, turq cab w/75 Express decal, MIP, from $35 to $40.00

K-30-A, Mercedes C 111, 1972, w/battery compartment, MIP, from $120 to $150.00

K-31-B, Peterbilt Refrigerator Truck, 1978, wht w/Burger King logo, MIP, from $60 to $75.00

K-32-B, Farm Unimog & Livestock Trailer, 1978, MIP, from $15 to $20.00

K-33-A, Citroen SM, 1972, MIP....................................$15.00

K-34-B, Pallet Truck & Forklift, 1979, MIP, from $20 to $25.00

K-35-A, Lightning Custom Car, 1972, red w/Flame Out decal, MIP, from $60 to $75.00

K-36-B, Construction Transporter, 1978, MIP, from $15 to.....$20.00

K-37-A, Sandcat, 1973, orange or red, MIP, ea................$15.00

K-38-A, Gus's Gulper, 1973, MIP..................................$15.00

K-39-A, Milligan's Mill, 1973, MIP $15.00

K-40-A, Blaze Trailer Fire Chief's Car, 1973, MIP............$15.00

K-41-B, Brabham BT44B, 1977, MIP..............................$15.00

K-41-C, JCB Excavator, 1981, MIP, from $15 to $20.00

K-42-B, Caterpillar Traxcavator Road Ripper, 1979, MIP, from $12 to $18.00

K-43-B, Log Transporter, 1981, MIP, from $15 to.............$20.00

K-44-A, Bazooka Custom Street Rod, 1973, MIP............$15.00

K-45-A, Marauder Racer, 1973, MIP..............................$15.00

K-46-A, Race Pack Mercury Commuter & Thunderclap Racer, 1973, MIP, from $25 to $35.00

K-47-A, Easy Rider Motorcycle, 1973, w/wht driver, MIP, from $30 to $40.00

K-49-A, Ambulance, 1973, wht, MIP..............................$15.00

K-50-A, Street Rod, 1973, gr, MIP..................................$15.00

K-51-A, Barracuda Custom Racer, 1973, MIP................$15.00

K-52-A, Datsun 260Z Rally Car, 1974, MIP....................$15.00

K-53-A, Hot Fire Engine, 1975, MIP..............................$15.00

K-54-A, Javelin AMX, 1975, burgundy or red, MIP, ea....$15.00

K-55-A, Corvette Caper Cart, 1975, dk bl or bronze, MIP, ea..$15.00

K-56-A, Maserati Bora, 1975, metallic gold, MIP, from $40 to $50.00

K-57-A, Javelin Drag Racing Set, 1975, MIP, from $25 to.....$35.00

K-58-A, Corvette Power Boat Set, 1975, MIP......................$25.00

K-60-B, Ford Mustang Cobra, 1978, MIP, from $20 to......$25.00

K-62-A, Citroen SM Doctor's Car, 1977, MIP.................$15.00

K-63-A, Mercedes Benz Ambulance, 1977, MIP $15.00

K-65-A, Plymouth Trail Duster Rescue Vehicle, 1978, gr, MIP, from $40 to..$50.00

K-66-A, Jaguar XJ12 Police Set, 1978, MIP, from $15 to.....$20.00

K-69-A, Jaguar & Europa Caravan, 1890, MIP, from $30 to..$35.00

K-71-A Porsche Polizei, 1979, MIP, from $60 to $75.00

K-72-A, Brabham BT44B, 1980, bl-gr, MIP, from $15 to....$20.00

K-74-A, Volvo Estate Car, 1980, MIP..............................$15.00

K-75-A, Airport Rescue Fire Tender, 1980, MIP $15.00

K-77-A, Secours Routier Highway Rescue Vehicle, 1980, MIP, from $50 to..$60.00

K-78-A, Gran Fury Police Car, 1979, blk w/bl interior, MIP, from $25 to $30.00

K-81-A, Suzuki Motorcycle & Rider, 1981, MIP, from $12 to..$18.00

K-82-A, BMW Motorcycle & Rider, 1981, MIP, from $12 to ..$18.00

K-83-B, Harley-Davidson Chopper, 1994, MIP $10.00

K-86-A, Volkswagen Golf, 1981, yel, MIP, from $30 to....$35.00

K-88-A, Money Box Armored Car, 1981, wht w/Matchbox decal, MIP..$20.00

K-91-A, Motorcycle Racing Set, 1982, MIP, from $40 to....$50.00

K-98-A, Forestry Unimog & Trailer, 1979, MIP, from $40 to..$50.00

K-101-A, Racing Porsche, 1983, metallic beige, MIP, from $20 to $25.00

K-103-A, Peterbilt Tanker, 1983, metallic gray cab, MIP, from $30 to $40.00

K-104-A, Matra Rancho Rescue Set, 1983, MIP, from $15 to $20.00

K-108-A, Digger & Plough Transporter, 1984, MIP, from $20 to..$25.00

K-111-A, Peterbilt Refuse Truck, 1985, MIP $15.00

K-112-A, Fire Spotter Airplane Transporter, 1985, MIP, from $20 to $25.00

K-119-A, Fire Rescue Set, 1985, MIP, from $30 to..........$35.00

K-122-A, DAF Road Train, 1986, MIP, from $15 to.........$20.00

K-124-A, Mercedes Container Truck, 1986, metallic silver-gray, MIP, from $30 to......................................$40.00

K-129-A, Mercedes Power Launch Transporter, 1986, MIP, from $15 to...$20.00

K-130-A, Peterbilt Digger Transporter, 1986, MIP, from $20 to...$25.00

K-137-A, Road Construction Set, 1986, MIP, from $30 to..$40.00

K-138-A, Fire Rescue Set, 1986, MIP, from $20 to..........$25.00

K-145-A, Iveco Double Tipper, 1988, MIP, from $20 to...$25.00

K-146-A, Jaguar XJ6, 1988, dk gr, MIP $15.00

K-151-A, Leyland Skip Truck, 1988, MIP.........................$8.00

K-159-A, Porsche Racing Car Transporter, 1988, MIP, from $20 to...$25.00

K-161-A, Rolls Royce Silver Spirit, 1989, metallic red, MIP...$12.00

K-166-A, Road Construction Set, 1985, MIP, from $20 to..$25.00

K-168-A, Porsche 911 Carrera, 1989, metallic wht, MIP.$15.00

K-170-A, JCB 808 Excavator, 1989, MIP, from $20 to $25.00

K-173-A, Lamborghini Diablo, 1992, MIP $10.00

MODELS OF YESTERYEAR MATCHBOX

Y-1-A, 1926 Allchin Traction Machine, 1956, diagonal red-pnt treads, copper boiler door, MIP, from $75 to............$100.00

Y-1-A, 1926 Allchin Traction Machine, 1956, smooth unpnt treads, gold boiler door, MIP, from $500 to..............$600.00

Y-1-B, 1911 Ford Model T, 1965, red, MIP, from $20 to $25.00

Y-1-B, 1911 Ford Model T, 1965, wht, MIP, from $30 to $40.00

Y-1-C, 1936 Jaguar SS100, 1977, silver & bl, MIP $15.00

Y-2-A, 1911 B-Type London Bus, 1956, 8 windows over 4, MIP, from $65 to..$80.00

Y-2-B, 1911 Renault 2-Seater, 1963, silver-plated, MIP, from $50 to...$60.00

Y-2-C, 1914 Prince Henry Vauxhall, 1970, bl w/wht seats, MIP, from $20 to..$25.00

Y-2-C, 1914 Prince Henry Vauxhall, 1970, silver or gold, MIP, ea from $50 to..$60.00

Y-2-D, 1930 4.5 Litre Supercharged Bentley, 1984, purple, MIP, from $15 to..$20.00

Y-3-A, 1907 London E-Class Tram Car, 1956, w/Dewars decal, MIP, from $475 to......................................$500.00

Y-3-B, 1910 Benz Limousine, 1966, cream w/gr roof, gr seats & grille, high cast headlights, MIP, from $40 to............$50.00

Y-3-B, 1910 Benz Limousine, 1966, cream w/pale lime roof, gr seats & grille, MIP, from $125 to............................$150.00

Y-3-C, 1934 Riley MPH, 1974, metallic red w/12-spoke silver wheels, MIP, from $50 to.....................................$60.00

Y-3-D, 1912 Ford Model T Tanker, 1982, bl w/bl tank & Express Dairy decal, wht roof, red spoke wheels, MIP, from $30 to $35.00

Y-3-D, 1912 Ford Model T Tanker, 1982, blue with blue tank, white roof, gold spoked wheels, Express Dairy, MIB, from $15.00 to $20.00. (Photo courtesy Dana Johnson)

Y-3-D, 1912 Ford Model T Tanker, 1982, dk gr w/red tank, wht roof, gold spoked wheels, MIP, from $40 to................$50.00

Y-4-A, Sentinel Steam Wagon, 1956, unpnt metal wheels, MIP, from $50 to...$60.00

Y-4-C, 1909 Opel Coupe, 1966, wht w/textured tan roof, red seats, MIP, from $40 to $50.00

Y-4-D, 1930 Duesenberg Model J Town Car, 1976, metallic red w/blk roof, MIP, from $20 to................................$25.00

Y-5-A, 1929 LeMans Bentley, 1958, gray tonneau, MIP, from $150 to...$175.00

Y-5-B, 1919 4½ Litre S Bentley, 1962, gr, MIP, from $40 to $50.00

Y-5-C, 1907 Peugeot, 1969, bronze w/blk roof, MIP, from $125 to...$150.00

Y-5-C, 1907 Peugeot, 1969, yel w/blk roof, clear windows, MIP, from $60 to...$75.00

Y-5-D, 1927 Talbot Van, 1978, gr w/blk roof, gr spoked wheels, Lipton's decal, MIP, from $30 to..............................$40.00

Y-5-D, 1927 Talbot Van, 1978, yel w/blk roof, Greenwich Appeal decal, MIP, from $275 to............................$325.00

Y-5-E, 1929 Leyland Titan TD1 London Bus, 1989, maroon, w/Newcastle Brown Ale decal, MIP, from $15 to $20.00

Y-6-A, 1916 AEC Y-Type Lorry, 1958, dk gray w/metal wheels, MIP, from $90 to..$100.00

Y-6-B, 1923 Type-35 Bugatti, 1961, bl w/red dash & floor, blk tires, bl grille, MIP, from $75 to................................$85.00

Y-6-B, 1923 Type-35 Bugatti, 1961, red w/blk dash & floor, MIP, from $135 to $150.00

Y-6-C, 1913 Cadillac, 1967, metallic gold, 913 on base, MIP, from $50 to...$60.00

Y-6-D, 1920 Rolls Royce Fire Engine, 1977, red w/24-spoke gold wheels, blk seat, MIP, from $20 to............................$25.00

Y-7-A, 4-Ton Leyland Van, 1957, 3 lines of text, wht or cream roof, metal wheels, MIP, ea from $80 to...................$100.00

Y-7-B, 1913 Mercer Raceabout, 1961, gold-plated w/gold grille, MIP, from $225 to..$250.00

Y-7-C, 1912 Rolls Royce, 1968, metallic silver w/smooth red roof, MIP, from $30 to...$40.00

Y-8-B, Sunbeam Motorcycle & Milford Sidecar, 1963, bright gr sidecar seat, MIP, from $400 to $500.00

Y-8-C, 1914 Stutz, 1969, metallic red w/gold gas tank, MIP, from $60 to $75.00

Y-9-A, 1924 Fowler Big Lion Showman's Engine, 1958, MIP, from $80 to $110.00

Y-9-B, 1912 Simplex, 1968, pale gold w/blk roof, MIP, from $50 to $60.00

Y-9-D, 1936 Leyland Cub Hook & Ladder Truck, 1989, MIP, from $125 to $150.00

Y-10-A, 1908 Grand Prix Mercedes, 1958, cream, MIP, from $125 to...$150.00

Y-10-B, 1928 Mercedes Benz 36/220, 1963, wht, MIP, from $120 to...$140.00

Y-10-C, 1906 Rolls Royce Silver Ghost, 1969, lime gr, MIP, from $20 to $25.00

Y-11-B, 1912 Packard Landaulet, 1964, metallic red, M, from $25 to $35.00

Y-11-C, 1938 Lagonda Drophead Coupe, 1973, gold w/maroon chassis, MIP, from $50 to $60.00

Y-11-C, 1938 Lagonda Drophead Coupe, 1973, gold w/red chassis, MIP, from $400 to $500.00

Y-12-A, 1899 London Horse-Drawn Bus, 1959, beige driver & seats, MIP, from $65 to $75.00

Y-12-B, 1919 Thomas Flyabout, 1967, metallic bright bl w/yel seats & grille, MIP, from $900 to $1,000.00

Y-12-D, 1937 GMC Van, 1988, blk w/gray roof, Goblin decal, MIP, from $50 to $60.00

Y-13-C, 1918 Crossley, 1973, bl-gray w/tan roof & canopy, RAF decal, MIP, from $60 to..$75.00

Y-14-B, 1911 Maxwell Roadster, 1965, turq w/gold gas tank, MIP, from $40 to $50.00

Y-14-C, 1931 Stutz Bearcat, 1974, cream & red w/red wheels, MIP, from $30 to $40.00

Y-15-A, 1907 Rolls Royce Silver Ghost, 1960, silver-gr w/gray tires, MIP, from $50 to $65.00

Y-16-A, 1904 Spyker, 1961, yel w/blk tires, from $25 to...$35.00

Y-16-B, 1928 Mercedes Benz SS Coupe, 1972, lt gr w/emerald gr chassis, blk roof, MIP, from $175 to $225.00

Y-16-E, Scammell 100-Ton Truck w/Steam Locomotive, 1989, MIP, from $80 to $100.00

Y-17-A, 1938 Hispano Suiza, 1973, gr, MIP, from $20 to $25.00

Y-18-A, 1937 Cord 812, 1979, plum w/wht roof, chrome spoked wheels, MIP, from $30 to $40.00

Y-18-B, 1920 Atkinson Blue Circle Portland Cement Steam Wagon, yel, MIP, from $15 to...............................$20.00

Y-19-A, 1933 Auburn 851 Boattail Speedster, 1980, khaki & beige w/silver disk wheels, wht-wall tires, MIP, from $20 to...$30.00

Y-19-C, 1929 Morris 10 CWT Van, 1987, bl w/Michelin decal, MIP, from $15 to..$20.00

Y-20-A, 1937 Mercedes Benz 540K, 1981, metallic gray w/silver disk wheels, MIP, from $25 to.................................$30.00

Y-21-A, 1929 Ford Model A Woody Wagon, 1981, yel & brn, MIP, from $20 to $25.00

Y-22-A, 1930 Ford Model A Van, 1982, beige w/red roof, Toblerone decal, MIP, from $15 to $20.00

Y-23-A, 1922 AEC S-Type Omnibus, 1982, red w/dk brn interior, red wheels, Schweppes Tonic Water, MIP, from $20 to .$25.00

Y-24-A, 1927 Bugatti T44, 1983, blk w/blk interior, yel accents, MIP, from $20 to...$25.00

Y-25-A, 1910 Renault Type AG, 1983, gr w/gold spoked wheels, Perrier decal, MIP, from $15 to..................................$20.00

Y-26-A, 1918 Crossley Beer Lorry, 1984, wht w/maroon canopy, Gonzales Byass decal, MIP, from $15 to $20.00

Y-27-A, 1922 Foden Steam Lorry, 1985, bl w/tow hook, Pickfords decal, MIP, from $30 to.....................................$40.00

Y-28-A, 1907 Unic Taxi, 1984, maroon, bl or wht, MIP, ea ...$15.00

Y-30-A, 1920 Mack Model AC Truck, 1985, cream w/Artic Ice Cream decal, MIP, from $15 to...................................$20.00

Y-31-A, 1933 Morris Pantechicon Van, 1990, MIP, from $15 to...$20.00

Y-34-A, 1933 Cadillac 452 V-16, 1990, MIP, from $15 to....$20.00

Y-37-A, 1931 Garrett Steam Truck, 1990, MIP, from $15 to ...$20.00

Y-38-A, 1920 Rolls Royce Armored Car, 1990, MIP, from $25 to $30.00

Y-42-A, 1938 Albion 6-Wheeler, 1991, MIP, from $15 to ...$20.00

Y-45-A, 1930 Bugatti Royale, 1991, MIP, from $15 to......$20.00

Y-46-A, 1868 Merryweather Fire Engine, 1991, MIP, from $50 to $60.00

Y-48-A, 1931 Garrett Steam Wagon, 1996, MIP, from $50 to $60.00

Y-62-A, 1932 Ford Model AA 1½-Ton Truck, 1992, MIP, from $25 to $30.00

Y-64-A, 1938 Lincoln Zephyr, 1992, MIP, from $30 to.....$35.00

Y-65-A, 1928 Austin, 1928 BMW Dixi & 1928 Rosengart, 1992 Special Limited Edition, MIP, from $50 to................$60.00

SKYBUSTERS

SB-1-A, Federal Express Learjet, 1973, purple & wht, MIP, from $5 to $7.00

SB-1-A, US Air Force Learjet, 1973, wht, MIP, from $4 to $5.00

SB-2-A, Corsair A7D, 1973, khaki & wht w/brn & gr camouflage, MIP, from $6 to..$8.00

SB-3-A, Air France A300B Airbus, 1973, wht & gray, MIP, from $8 to $10.00

SB-4-A, Mirage F1, 1973, pk, MIP $6.00

SB-5-A, Starfighter F104, 1973, red or wht w/maple leaf labels, MIP, ea $10.00

SB-6-A, Mig 21, 1973, bl & wht, MIP.............................$10.00

SB-7-A, Junkers 87B, 1973, blk w/swastikas, MIP, from $80 to..$90.00

SB-8-A, Spitfire, 1973, metallic gr & gold, MIP.............$10.00

SB-9-A, Cessna 402, 1973, lt gr & wht, MIP...................$10.00

SB-10-A, South African Airways Boeing 747, 1973, wht, MIP..$15.00

SB-10-A, United States of America Boeing 747, 1973, wht & silver-gray, MIP $15.00

SB-11-A, Alpha Jet, 1973, bl & red, MIP.......................$12.00

SB-12-B, Pitts Special Biplane, 1980, dk gr & wht or bl & wht, MIP, ea $10.00

SB-13-A, Lufthansa Douglas DC-10, 1973, wht & silver-gray, MIP..$8.00

SB-13-A, UTA Douglas DC-10, 1973, wht, MIP, from $60 to ..$75.00

SB-14-A, Cessna 210, 1973, orange-yel & wht, MIP $10.00

SB-15-A, Phantom F4E, 1975, metallic red & wht or cherry red & wht, MIP, ea...$8.00

SB-16-A, Corsair F4U, 1975, metallic bl or orange, MIP, ea..$8.00

SB-17-A, Ram Rod, 1976, red, MIP..................................$10.00

SB-18-A, Wild Wind, 1976, lime gr & wht, MIP.............$10.00

SB-19-A, Piper Commanche, 1977, red & yel, MIP...........$8.00

SB-20-A, Coast Guard Helicopter, 1977, wht & lt bl, MIP..$8.00

SB-21-A, Lightning, 1977, olive or silver-gray, MIP, ea....$10.00

SB-23-A, Singapore Airlines SST Super Sonic Transport, 1979, wht, MIP, from $75 to..$100.00

SB-24-A, USAF F-16, 1979, wht & red, no side labels, MIP..$8.00

SB-25-A, Rescue Helicopter, 1979, wht, MIP $10.00

SB-25-A, Royal Air Force Rescue, 1979, dk bl, MIP $8.00

SB-26-A, Cessna 210 Float Plane, 1981, red & wht or blk & wht, MIP, ea $8.00

SB-26-B, USAF Lockheed F-117A Stealth, 1990, dk gray, MIP...$5.00

SB-27-A, Harrier Jet, 1981, wht & red, MIP $8.00

SB-28-A, Air Malta A300 Airbus, 1981, wht, MIP..........$18.00

SB-29-A, USAF Lockheed SR-71 Blackbird, 1989, blk, MIP..$5.00

SB-30-A, Grumman Navy F-14 Tom Cat, 1989, gray & wht, MIP..$5.00

SB-31-A, British Airways Boeing 747-400, 1990, lt gray & dk bl, MIP...$6.00

SB-32-A, Fairchild A10 Thunderbolt, 1990, dk gray w/gr cam- ouflage, MIP $5.00

SB-33-A, Bell Jet Ranger Helicopter, 1990, wht & bl, MIP...$5.00

SB-34-A, Lockheed A130/C-130 Hercules, 1990, wht w/USGC decal, MIP $5.00

SB-35-A, Mil M24 Hind-D Chopper, 1990, brn & gray or cam- ouflage khaki & army gr, MIP, ea................................$5.00

SB-36-A, USAF Lockheed F-117A Stealth, 1991, dk gray, MIP $5.00

SB-37-A, Royal Air Force Hawk, 1992, red, MIP..............$8.00

SB-38-A, Dan-Air BAE 146, 1992, wht, MIP....................$5.00

SB-39-A, Boeing Stearman Biplane, 1992, orange-yel w/Crunchie printed on underside of wings, MIP, from $25 to $30.00

SB-40-A, Brittania or KLM Boeing 737-300, 1992, wht & dk bl or lt bl & silver-gray, MIP, ea $5.00

Model Kits

While values for military kits seem to have leveled off and others may have actually gone down, this is certainly not the case with the Aurora monster and character kits which are continuing to increase in value.

Though model kits were popular with kids of the '50s who enjoyed the challenge of assembling a classic car or two or a Musketeer figure now and then, when the monster series hit in the early 1960s, sales shot through the ceiling. Made popular by all the monster movies of that decade, ghouls like Vampirella, Frankenstein, and the Wolfman were eagerly built up by kids everywhere. They could (if their parents didn't object too strongly) even construct an actual working guillotine. Aurora had other successful series of figure kits, too, based on characters from comic strips and TV shows as well as a line of sports stars.

But the vast majority of model kits were vehicles. They varied in complexity, some requiring much more dexterity on the part of the model builder than others, and they came in several scales, from 1/8 (which might be as large as 20" to 24") down to 1/43 (generally about 3" to 4"), but the most popular scale was 1/25 (usually between 6" to 8"). Some of the largest producers of vehicle kits were AMT, MPC, and IMC. Though production obviously waned during the late 1970s and early 1980s, with the intensity of today's collector market, companies like Ertl (who now is producing 1/25 scale vehicles using some of the old AMT dies) are proving that model kits still sell very well.

As a rule of thumb, assembled kits (built-ups) are priced at about 25% to 50% of the price range for a boxed kit, but this is not always true on the higher-priced kits. One mint in the box with the factory seal intact will often sell for up to 15% more than if the seal were broken, though depending on the kit, a sealed perfect box may add as much $100.00. Condition of the box is crucial. For more information, we recommend *Classic Plastic Model Kits* by Rick Polizzi (Collector Books); *Aurora History and Price Guide* by Bill Bruegman; and *Collectible Figure Kits of the '50s, '60s & '70s,* by Gordy Dutt.

Advisors: Mike and Kurt Fredericks (F4).

Other Sources: B10, J2, P4.

See also Plasticville.

Ace, Tales From the Crypt, Cryptkeeper #55300, 5", MIB.$4.00

Adams, Chuck Wagon, 1958, MIB.................................$40.00

Addar, Planet of the Apes, Cornelius, MIB (sealed), A, $90.00. (Photo courtesy John and Sheri Pavone)

Addar, Planet of the Apes, Dr Zira #105, 1974, 1/11, MIB (sealed)..$80.00

Addar, Super Scenes, Jaws, 1975, NM (VG+ box)...........$30.00

Addar, World Wildlife, Outlaw Mustang, 1975, MIB.......$35.00

AEF, Aliens, Bishop #AC-3, 1980s, 1/35, MIB $35.00
AEF, Aliens, Ferro #AM-11, 1980s, 1/35, MIB $26.00
AEF, Aliens, Sgt Apone #AM-5, 1980s, 1/35, MIB $26.00
AEF, Aliens, Warrior Alien #AX-3 (kneeling), 1980s, 1/35,
    MIB $35.00
Airfix, Apollo Saturn V #9170, 1/44, MIB (sealed) $30.00
Airfix, Coldstream Guardsman #205, 1960s, 1/12, MIB...$15.00
Airfix, Datsun 280-ZX Champion, 1980, M (EX+ sealed
    box) $33.00
Airfix, Famous Women of History, Anne Boleyn, MIB
    (sealed) $15.00
Airfix, James Bond 007 (You Only Live Twice), Little Nellie
    Autogyro, 1996, MIB...$25.00
Airfix, Lunar Module #3013, 1991, 1/72, MIB (sealed)....$10.00
Airfix, Mounted Bengal Lancer #7501, 1991, 1/12, MIB
    (sealed) $35.00
Airfix, Saturn 1B #6172, 1991, 1/144, MIB (sealed) $75.00
Airfix, Skeleton #3541, 1979, 1/6, MIB $14.00
Airfix, Wildlife Series, Robin #4830, 1979, 1/1, MIB
    (sealed) $30.00
Alabe, Neanderthal Man #2963, 1976, 1/8, MIB $40.00
Alternative Images, Dracula Prince, 1992, NM (plain wht
    box) $145.00
AMT, '74 Corvette, MIB..$40.00
AMT, BJ & the Bear, KW Aerodyne & Trailer #7705, 1982,
    1/32, MIB (sealed) $35.00
AMT, Denny McLain's Horse Hide Hauler, 1970, MIB ...$45.00
AMT, Farrah's Foxy Vette, 1977, MIB $45.00
AMT, Flintstones, Family Sedan #496, 1974, 6", MIB $75.00
AMT, Graveyard Ghoul Duo, Overtaker & Bodysnatcher, 1970,
    MIB...$125.00
AMT, Hang-Outs, Baseball #615, 1970s, MIB (sealed) $25.00
AMT, Interplanetary UFO #960, 1970s, 1/635, MIB (sealed) ..$130.00
AMT, John Greenwood's Championship GT Corvette, 1970s,
    MIB, from $50 to $65.00
AMT, Lola-70, 1960s, MIB (sealed), from $100 to.........$125.00
AMT, Man From UNCLE Car #912, 1967, 1/25, MIB...$220.00
AMT, Munster Koach, 1964, MIB $150.00
AMT, Novacaine Chevy Nova Funny Car, 1970s, MIB
    (sealed)..$125.00
AMT, Star Trek, Galileo 7 #959, 1974, 1/48, orig issue, MIB
    (sealed) $50.00
AMT, Star Trek, Mr Spock, 1967, MIB $135.00
AMT, Star Trek, USS Enterprise #921, 1967, orig issue, 1/635,
    MIB (sealed) $175.00
AMT, The CAT, 1967, MIB...$125.00
AMT, Vegas, '57 Thunderbird #3105, 1979, 1/25, MIB....$25.00
AMT, 69 Chevelle SS 396 Hardtop, MIB.........................$35.00
AMT/Ertl, Airwolf Helicopter, 1984, M (EX sealed box)..$25.00
AMT/Ertl, Batman (movie), Batmobile #6877, 1989, 1/25, MIB
    (sealed)..$14.00
AMT/Ertl, Batman (movie), Joker Goon Car, 1989, MIB
    (sealed) $16.00
AMT/Ertl, Batman Returns, Batmissile #6614, 1/25, MIB
    (sealed) $14.00
AMT/Ertl, Batmobile, 1989, MIB (sealed) $20.00
AMT/Ertl, Dick Tracy Coupe, 1990, MIB (sealed)...........$10.00
AMT/Ertl, Dodge Viper GTS Coupe #8055, 1994, 1/25, MIB..$8.00

AMT/Ertl, Knight Rider 2000, KITT 4000 #8084, 1991, 1/25,
    MIB (sealed) $16.00
AMT/Ertl, Rescue 911, Rescue Ambulance #6416, 1993, 1/25,
    MIB (sealed) $14.00
AMT/Ertl, Star Trek (TV), Kirk, 1994, 12", MIB (sealed) ..$20.00
AMT/Ertl, Star Trek III: The Search for Spock, USS Enterprise
    #6693, 1984, 1/535, MIB...$30.00
AMT/Ertl, Star Trek: Deep Space Nine, Defiant #8255, 1996,
    15½", MIB $15.00
AMT/Ertl, Star Trek: Generations, Klingon Bird of Prey, 1995,
    MIB $22.00
AMT/Ertl, Star Trek: The Next Generation, Ferengi/Klingon/Romu-
    lan #6858, 1989, MIB (sealed)....................................$20.00

**AMT/Ertl, Star Trek, U.S.S. Enterprise, Chrome Set, Special
edition, #6005, MIB, $30.00.**

AMT/Ertl, Star Wars, Han Solo #8785, 1995, MIB (sealed) $30.00
AMT/Ertl, Star Wars, TIE Fighter Flight Display, 1996, MIB...$20.00
Anubis, Star Trek (IV), Tholian Patrol Ship #9103, 1991, 7½",
    MIB $35.00
Aoshima, Batman (movie), Batmobile #618075, 1989, 1/32,
    MIB $40.00
Arii, Macross, Quilted-Queleual Ship #332, 1/2000, MIB..$30.00
Arii, Macross, Valkyrie VF-1J #318, 1/100, MIB $16.00
Arii, Southern Cross, ATAC-Andrzei Slawsky #603, 1/12,
    MIB $24.00
Arii, Southern Cross, ATAC-Bowie Emerson, MIB $25.00
Atlantic, Goldrake-Toei Animation, Actarus Figure Set #GK1,
    1978, MIB $15.00
Aurora, Addam's Family House, MIB $800.00
Aurora, Adventure Series, Spartacus #405, 1964, 1/8, MIB .$270.00
Aurora, Alfred E Neuman, 1969, assembled, EX $125.00
Aurora, American Buffalo, 1964, MIB (sealed) $100.00
Aurora, Astronaut #409, 1967, 1/12, MIB (yel logo) $100.00
Aurora, Batboat, 1968, MIB, from $400 to $500.00
Aurora, Batcycle, 1960s, MIB $500.00
Aurora, Batman, 1966, MIB, A.....................................$285.00
Aurora, Batmobile, 1966, MIB......................................$500.00
Aurora, Batplane, 1967, MIB $200.00
Aurora, Bighorn Sheep & Lynx, 1963, MIB $125.00
Aurora, Black Falcon Pirate Ship, 1972, MIB (sealed).....$50.00

Aurora, Bloodthirsty Pirates, Captain Kidd #464, 1965, 1/8, MIB $80.00

Aurora, Captain America #476, 1966, orig issue, 1/12, partially assembled $260.00

Aurora, Captain Kidd, MIB (sealed) $150.00

Aurora, Castle Creatures, Frog, 1966, MIB.....................$250.00

Aurora, Chinese Mandarin, MIB $40.00

Aurora, Comic Scenes, Batman, 1974, MIB $85.00

Aurora, Comic Scenes, Incredible Hulk #184, 1974, 1/12, MIB..$100.00

Aurora, Comic Scenes, Lone Ranger, 1974, MIB $50.00

Aurora, Comic Scenes, Spider-Man, assembled, NM.....$100.00

Aurora, Comic Scenes, Superman #185, 1974, 1/18, MIB..$90.00

Aurora, Creature From the Black Lagoon, assembled, M .$65.00

Aurora, Customizing Monster Kit, #2 Mad Dog/Vulture/Etc #464, 1963, 1/8, MIB...$290.00

Aurora, Dick Tracy, 1967, MIB $150.00

Aurora, Dr Jekyll as Mr Hyde, 1964, MIB......................$250.00

Aurora, Dracula, 1972, glow-in-the-dark, MIB..............$200.00

Aurora, Dracula's Dragster, assembled, M $100.00

Aurora, Famous Fighters, Mace TM Guided Missile #130, 1958, 1/48, MIB..$200.00

Aurora, Famous Fighters, Nike Hercules Missile, 1958, MIB..$300.00

Aurora, Famous Fighters, US Air Force Pilot, 1958, MIB.......$300.00

Aurora, Famous Fighters, Vikings #K6, 1958, 1/8, MIB .$350.00

Aurora, Forged Foil Cougar, 1969, MIB $65.00

Aurora, Forgotton Prisoner, 1972, glow-in-the-dark, MIB..$195.00

Aurora, Frankenstein, 1961, MIB $400.00

Aurora, Frankenstein #449 (no blk rope knot), 1972, 1/8, MIB $120.00

Aurora, Frightening Lightning Strikes, Dracula, MIB....$350.00

Aurora, Frightening Lightning Strikes, Frankenstein, 1969, MIB..$400.00

Aurora, Godzilla, 1969, glow-in-the-dark, MIB..............$200.00

Aurora, Great Moments in Sports, Johnny Unitas, 1965, MIB, from $175 to $225.00

Aurora, Great Presidents, George Washington, 1967, MIB ..$100.00

Aurora, Green Beret, MIB (sealed) $250.00

Aurora, Green Beret #413, 1966, 1/8, assembled.............$60.00

Aurora, Guillotine, 1964, orig issue, MIB......................$650.00

Aurora, Hercules & the Lion, assembled, NM................$110.00

Aurora, Hercules & the Lion, 1965, MIB........................$250.00

Aurora, Incredible Hulk, 1966, MIB...............................$250.00

Aurora, Invaders, UFO #813, 1968, orig issue, 1/72, MIB .$210.00

Aurora, Jesse James, assembled, NM $100.00

Aurora, King Kong, 1964, assembled, EX........................$75.00

Aurora, King Kong's Thronester, 1966, MIB $160.00

Aurora, Knights in Shining Armor, Sir Galahad, 1973, MIB..$50.00

Aurora, Knights in Shining Armor, Sir Kay, 1973, MIB...$50.00

Aurora, Knights in Shining Armor, Sir Percival, 1973, MIB $65.00

Aurora, Land of the Giants, Snake Scene, assembled, M ..$165.00

Aurora, Land of the Giants, Spaceship, 1968, MIB........$325.00

Aurora, Lost in Space, Diorama #MA 420, 1966, 1/32, MIB...$540.00

Aurora, Lunar Probe, 1960s, MIB $175.00

Aurora, Man From UNCLE, Napoleon Solo, MIB (sealed)..$350.00

Aurora, Mod Squad Station Wagon, 1969, MIB (sealed) $150.00

Aurora, Monster Scenes, Dr Deadly #631, 1971, 1/13, MIB....$75.00

Aurora, Monster Scenes, Dr Deadly's Daughter, 1971, MIB....$65.00

Aurora, Monster Scenes, Pain Parlor, 1971, MIB $65.00

Aurora, Monster Scenes, Vampirella, complete, unassembled, EX $125.00

Aurora, Monsters of the Movies, Dracula, 1975, MIB....$250.00

Aurora, Monsters of the Movies, Frankenstein, MIB (sealed) $225.00

Aurora, Godzilla, 1964, glow-in-the-dark, assembled, EX, $110.00. (Photo courtesy June Moon)

Aurora, Mummy, 1972, glow-in-the-dark, M (VG box), $100.00. (Photo courtesy Rick Polizzi)

Aurora, Mummy, 1972, glow-in-the-dark, MIB (sealed) .$135.00

Aurora, Mummy #427, 1963, orig issue, 1/8, MIB $250.00

Aurora, Munster's Living Room, 1964, assembled, EX ...**$400.00**

Aurora, Phantom of the Opera, 1972, glow-in-the-dark, MIB..............**$100.00**

Aurora, Phanton of the Opera, Canadian issue, MIB.....**$200.00**

Aurora, Prehistoric Scenes, Allosaurus #736, 1971, orig issue, MIB..............**$125.00**

Aurora, Prehistoric Scenes, Armoured Dinosaur, assembled, NM..............**$65.00**

Aurora, Prehistoric Scenes, Cave Bear, 1972, MIB (sealed) **$65.00**

Aurora, Prehistoric Scenes, Cro-Magnon Woman, 1971, MIB **$100.00**

Aurora, Prehistoric Scenes, Flying Reptile, complete, unassembled, M **$40.00**

Aurora, Prehistoric Scenes, Jungle Swamp, 1971, MIB..**$100.00**

Aurora, Prehistoric Scenes, Neanderthal Man, assembled, M **$40.00**

Aurora, Prehistoric Scenes, Neanderthal Man #729, 1971, orig issue, 1/12, MIB (sealed)..............**$80.00**

Aurora, Prehistoric Scenes, Sail Back Reptile, 1975, MIB..**$90.00**

Aurora, Prehistoric Scenes, Three-Horned Dinosaur #741, 1972, 1/13, MIB..............**$90.00**

Aurora, Prince Valiant, 1959, MIB **$200.00**

Aurora, Robin the Boy Wonder, 1966, MIB (sealed) **$100.00**

Aurora, Roman Bireme Warship, MIB..............**$50.00**

Aurora, Roman Gladiator With Trident, 1959, MIB, $125.00.
(Photo courtesy June Moon)

Aurora, Salem Witch, 1965, assembled, EX..............**$65.00**

Aurora, Scene Machines, Butterfly Catcher, MIB............**$40.00**

Aurora, Spider-Man, 1974, MIB (sealed)..............**$160.00**

Aurora, Tarzan, 1967, MIB..............**$165.00**

Aurora, Thoroughbred Race Horse, 1964, MIB (sealed) ..**$100.00**

Aurora, Tonto, 1967, MIB..............**$200.00**

Aurora, Tonto, 1974, MIB (sealed) **$50.00**

Aurora, UFO from the Invaders, MIB..............**$150.00**

Aurora, Voyage to the Bottom of the Sea, Seaview #707, 1966, M (NM box)..............**$325.00**

Aurora, Wacky Back-Wacker, 1965, MIB..............**$185.00**

Aurora, Whoozis?, Kitty, 1968, MIB..............**$65.00**

Aurora, Whoozis?, Snuffy #206, 1966, assembled, EX **$60.00**

Aurora, Witch, 1972, glow-in-the-dark, MIB..............**$100.00**

Aurora, Wolf Man, glow-in-the-dark, MIB..............**$50.00**

Aurora, Wolf Man #450, 1972, 1/8, MIB..............**$120.00**

Aurora, Wolf Man's Wagon, 1965, MIB, $250.00.
(Photo courtesy Rick Polizzi)

Aurora, Zorro, 1965, assembled, EX..............**$125.00**

Aurora, 12 O'Clock High, Focke-Wulf 190, 1965, MIB..**$175.00**

Aurora, 2001: A Space Oddyssey, Space Shuttle Orian #252, 1975, 1/144, MIB (sealed)..............**$170.00**

Bachmann, Animals of the World, Alaskan Timber Wolf, 1960s, MIB..............**$40.00**

Bachmann, Birds of the World, Barn Swallow, 1950s, MIB..**$30.00**

Bachmann, Birds of the World, Hooded Warbler #19013, 1990, 1/1, MIB..............**$20.00**

Bachmann, Birds of the World, Rose-Breasted Grosbeak, 1950s, MIB..............**$40.00**

Bachmann, Dogs of the World, German Shepherd, 1960s, MIB (sealed)..............**$35.00**

Bandai, Captain Harlock, Queen Esmerelda's Ship, 1980s, MIB..............**$30.00**

Bandai, Galaman figure, 1/350, NM (VG+ box)..............**$20.00**

Bandai, Gundam, Mobile Suit #11 #36199, 1980, 1/44, gr, MIB..............**$20.00**

Bandai, Kinggridah, 1990, MIB..............**$40.00**

Bandai, Prehistoric Animal Series, Stegosaurus #8332, 1973, 1/35, MIB..............**$65.00**

Bandai, Thunderbird #536188, 1984, MIB..............**$40.00**

Billiken, Batman (Type A or Type B), vinyl, MIB..........**$200.00**

Billiken, Creature From the Black Lagoon, MIB............**$185.00**

Billiken, Dracula, 1989, vinyl, MIB **$275.00**

Billiken, Frankenstein, MIB..............**$125.00**

Billiken, It Conquered the World, IT Alien, 1985, vinyl, MIB..............**$90.00**

Billiken, King Kong, MIB..............**$95.00**

Billiken, Phantom of the Opera, 1982, vinyl, 1/8, NMIB..**$175.00**

Billiken, Predator, 1991, vinyl, MIB..............**$80.00**

Billiken, Ultra Zone, Peguila, 1989, vinyl, MIB..............**$90.00**

Dark Horse, Frankenstein #22, 1991, 1/8, MIB..............**$130.00**

Dark Horse, Mummy, 1995, MIB $150.00

Dark Horse, Ray Harryhausen's King Kong, MIB $95.00

Dimensional Designs, IT the Terror From Space, 1991, NM (plain wht box)..$125.00

Dimensional Designs, Outer Limits, Man Never Born (Andro), resin, MIB $100.00

Dimensional Designs, Outer Limits, Nightmare (Ebonite Guard), resin, MIB..................................$80.00

Educational Products, Modern Man Skeleton #5400, 1966, 1/6, MIB $30.00

Entex, Battle of the Planets, Phoenix #8401, 1978, MIB (sealed) $125.00

Ertl, Blueprint Replica Corvette, 1:25 scale, M (VG box), $50.00.

Fujimi Mokei, Mad Police, Destroyer Car #1 or Falcon Car #4, 1980s, MIB, ea $50.00

Fundimensions, Six Million Dollar Man, Bionic Bust-Out, MIB..$25.00

FX, Tales From the Darkside, Gargoyle, resin, 17", MIB...$120.00

Garage Resin Kit, Star Trek: Next Generation, Duralyne Hypo Spray, MIB $25.00

Geometric Designs, Clash of the Titans, Medusa, vinyl or resin, 1994, 1/6, MIB...$60.00

Gerba, US Navy Vanguard Missile, 1950s, MIB.............$200.00

Halcyon, Alien Warrior w/Egg & Base, MIB $50.00

Hawk, Convair Manned Satellite, 1960, MIB.................$100.00

Hawk, Indian Totem Poles, Grave of Ske-Dans Totem #556, 1966, MIB $45.00

Hawk, Jupitor C/Explorer, 1966, MIB $50.00

Hawk, Silly Surfers, Hot Dogger Hangin' Ten #541, 1964, M (G-box)..$60.00

Hawk, Weird-Ohs, Daddy the Way Out Suburbanite, 1963, MIB..$100.00

Hawk, Weird-Ohs, Freddy Flameout the Way Out Jet Jockey, 1963, MIB $75.00

Hawk, Weird-Ohs, Huey's Hut Rod, 1969, MIB..............$50.00

Hawk, Wild Woodie (Surfer Car) #545, 1965, 1/25, MIB ..$30.00

Horizon, Batman, 1989, MIB...$80.00

Horizon, Bride of Frankenstein, 1988, MIB $75.00

Horizon, Creature From the Black Lagoon, 1988, MIB..$110.00

Horizon, DC Comics, Joker #56, 1993, 1/6, partially assembled..$30.00

Horizon, Dracula, 1988, MIB...$50.00

Horizon, Indiana Jones, Indiana #34, 1993, 1/6, MIB.......$60.00

Horizon, Invisible Man, 1988, MIB..................................$50.00

Horizon, Marvel Universe, Cable, 1994, MIB $40.00

Horizon, Marvel Universe, Dr Doom #17, 1991, MIB......$40.00

Horizon, Marvel Universe, Silver Surfer #8, 1989, MIB...$30.00

Horizon, Marvel Universe, Thor #25, 1993, 1/6, MIB......$50.00

Horizon, Mole People, 1988, MIB...................................$50.00

Horizon, Mummy, 1988, MIB...$60.00

Horizon, Phantom of the Opera, 1988, MIB....................$50.00

Horizon, Robocop, Robocop #10, 1989, MIB $60.00

Horizon, Terminator 2 Judgement Day, 1991, MIB..........$35.00

Horizon, Wolf-Man, MIB $60.00

Hubley, 1932 Chevy Coupe, MIB, $50.00.

Ideal, XP-600 Fix It Car of Tomorrow, 1953-55, partially assembled, M (NM box) $285.00

Imai, Armored Knights, Philipp Graf Von Hessen #1517, 1984, orig issue, 1/12, MIB $15.00

Imai, Captain Scarlet, Spectrum Pursuit Vehicle #1713, 1988, MIB $40.00

Imai, Orguss, Dark Phoenix #16, 1991, 1/6, MIB $40.00

Imai, Orguss, Dr Doom, 1991, MIB.................................$40.00

Imai, Orguss, Thor #25, 1993, 1/6, MIB..........................$50.00

ITC, Bumble Bee, 1950s, MIB...$65.00

ITC, Launcher w/Soviet BB-1 Missile #3812, 1960, 1/32, MIB $140.00

ITC, Marvel Metal Cocker Spaniel, Elephant, Rhinoceros or Tiger, MIB, ea.......................................$35.00

ITC, Scottish Terrier #3825, 1960, MIB $30.00

ITC, Stegosaurus Skeleton, 1950s, MIB...........................$100.00

ITC, Wire Haired Terrier, 1959, MIB...............................$30.00

Kaiyodo, Godzilla, 1991, 1/400, soft vinyl, NM (VG+ box) ..$45.00

KGB, Batman (1960s TV), Batgirl on Cycle, 1/19, MIB..**$50.00**

Life-Like, Aerial Missiles on Helicopter, 1970s, MIB **$50.00**

Life-Like, American Wildlife, Bald Eagle #9350, 1974, MIB **$14.00**

Life-Like, Cro-Magnon Man #383, 1973, M (VG+ sealed box)..**$28.00**

Life-Like, Moorish North African Rifle, MIB...................**$45.00**

Life-Like, Neanderthal Man, MIB (sealed).......................**$50.00**

Life-Like, Protoceratops, 1973, MIB **$30.00**

Life-Like, Tyrannosaurus, MIB (sealed) **$35.00**

Lindberg, Bad Wheels (Lindy Loonies), Bert's Bucket (Scuttle Bucket) #6422, 1971, MIB.......................................**$150.00**

Lindberg, Brain Buster, 1965, assembled, EX **$125.00**

Lindberg, Brontosaurus, MIB..**$15.00**

Lindberg, Flying Saucer, 1952, MIB.................................**$200.00**

Lindberg, Ford Model A Roadster Mind Blower, 1970, MIB (sealed)..**$25.00**

Lindberg, Lighthouse #331, 1969, w/light, 10", MIB........**$30.00**

Lindberg, Lindy Loonys, Big Wheeler or Road Hog, 1965, MIB, ea..**$75.00**

Lindberg, Lucky Loser, 1965, MIB, $20.00. (Photo courtesy June Moon)

Lindberg, SST Continental, 1958, MIB.......................**$175.00**

Lindberg, Star Probe, Space Base #1148, 1976, 1/350, MIB..**$40.00**

Lindberg, Wells Fargo Overland Stagecoach, 1960s, MIB ..**$50.00**

Lunar Models, Lost in Space, Chariot #SF009, 1/35, MIB..**$120.00**

Lunar Models, Pumpkinhead (movie), 1989, MIB **$145.00**

Lunar Models, Voyage to the Bottom of the Sea, Seaview (Aurora recast), 1990, 1/300, MIB **$80.00**

Max Factory, Nagira Ultra Q the Movie, NM (EX+ box)...**$65.00**

MOC, Strange Changing Time Machine, 1974, MIB.......**$75.00**

Monogram, Backdraft (movie), Fire Chief Car, 1991, MIB.....**$20.00**

Monogram, Battlestar Galactica, Cylon Basestar, 1978, MIB..**$75.00**

Monogram, Battlestar Gallactica, Cylon Raider #6026, 1979, 1/48, MIB (sealed) **$90.00**

Monogram, Buck Rogers, Starfighter #6030, 1979, 1/48, MIB..**$70.00**

Monogram, Buck Rogers Marauder, 1979, MIB (sealed) ..**$35.00**

Monogram, Dracula, 1991, MIB (sealed) **$30.00**

Monogram, Elvira Macabremobile, MIB (sealed) **$35.00**

Monogram, Ford Tri-Motor Anarctic, 1950s, MIB **$50.00**

Monogram, Ghost of the Red Baron, 1969, MIB............**$200.00**

Monogram, Godzilla, 1978, glow-in-the-dark, NM (EX box)...**$85.00**

Monogram, Godzilla, 1978, MIB (sealed) **$125.00**

Monogram, Green Hornet Dragster, 1960s, MIB **$55.00**

Monogram, Luminators, Dracula, MIB (sealed)................**$15.00**

Monogram, Luminators, Frankenstein, MIB (sealed) **$15.00**

Monogram, Luminators, King Kong, MIB.........................**$40.00**

Monogram, Luminators, Mummy, MIB.............................**$20.00**

Monogram, Luminators, Wolfman, MIB............................**$20.00**

Monogram, Miami Vice, Daytona Spyder #2737, 1986, 1/24, MIB (sealed) **$22.00**

Monogram, Mummy, 1983, MIB (sealed) **$30.00**

Monogram, Rambo, Chopper & Riverboat #6039, 1985, 1/48, MIB (sealed) **$30.00**

Monogram, S'cool Bus, 1970, assembled, EX **$40.00**

Monogram, Snoopy Is Joe Cool, 1970, MIB **$135.00**

Monogram, Snoopy Motorcycle, 1970, MIB...................**$100.00**

Monogram, Speed Shift Fred Flypogger, 1965, MIB, $175.00.
(Photo courtesy June Moon)

Monogram, Spiked Dinosaur #6042, 1979, 1/13, MIB (sealed) **$18.00**

Monogram, Steve Scott's Uncertain T, 1960s, NMIB **$125.00**

Monogram, Superman, 1978, MIB (sealed) **$35.00**

Monogram, Tijuana Taxi, 1960s, MIB...............................**$85.00**

Monogram, UFO, 1996, MIB (sealed) **$35.00**

Monogram, Wolf-Man, 1983, MIB (sealed)......................**$60.00**

Monogram, Wooly Mammoth #6075, 1/13, MIB (sealed) ..**$30.00**

Monogram, Young Astronauts, Mercury/Gemii Capsules #5909, 1987, 1/48, MIB (sealed) **$50.00**

MPC, '71 Road Runner, NMIB **$50.00**

MPC, Advanced Dungeons & Dragons, Ore War #2101, 1982, MIB (sealed) **$30.00**

MPC, Alien, 1979, MIB **$70.00**

MPC, AMT, '53 Ford Baja Patrol Pickup Truck, 1960s, MIB, from $40 to..**$50.00**

MPC, Beatle's Yellow Submarine, 1968, MIB (sealed) ...**$300.00**

MPC, Bionic Woman Bionic Repair, MIB (sealed) **$32.00**

MPC, Black Hole, Cygnus Spaceship, 1979, MIB (sealed) ..**$130.00**

MPC, Black Hole, Maximillian Robot #1982, 1979, 1/12, MIB (sealed)..**$65.00**

MPC, CB Freak, 1975, MIB **$50.00**

MPC, Dark Shadows Werewolf, MIB...............................**$200.00**

MPC, Disney's Haunted Mansion, Escape From the Crypt #5053, 1974, 1/12, MIB...**$180.00**

MPC, Dukes of Hazzard, Daisy's Jeep, 1980, MIB **$50.00**

MPC, Ed Schlarman's Air Lift Rattler Funny Car, 1960s, NMIB, from $135 to $150.00
MPC, Fonz & His Bike, 1976, MIB.....................................$50.00
MPC, Glo Heads, Ape Man #303, 1975, 1/3, MIB...........$60.00
MPC, Hardcastle & McCormick Coyote Super Sports Car, MIB (sealed)..$45.00
MPC, Hot Rodder Magazine's Tall T w/Stroker McGurk #102, 1964, MIB..$130.00
MPC, Ironside's Van, 1970, MIB.......................................$80.00
MPC, Magic Bubble Radar Mast Patrol Boat, 1950s, M (worn box) $55.00
MPC, Mummy Machine, 1970s, MIB (sealed) $50.00
MPC, Night Crawler, 1975, assembled, EX......................$50.00

MPC, Pirates of the Caribbean, Hoist High the Jolly Rogers, 1972, MIB...$65.00
MPC, Six Million Dollar Man, Evil Rider or Jaws of Doom, 1975, MIB, ea...$35.00
MPC, Six Million Dollar Man #602, 1975, 1/12, MIB $50.00
MPC, Star Wars, A-Wing Fighter #1973, 1983, 1/48, MIB (sealed)..$70.00
MPC, Star Wars, C-3PO, 1977, MIB (sealed) $35.00
MPC, Star Wars, R2-D2 #1912, 1978, 1/8, MIB..............$50.00
MPC, Star Wars, X-Wing Fighter, 1978, MIB..................$40.00
MPC, Star Wars Return of the Jedi, Jabba the Hutt Throne Room, 1983, MIB (sealed) $35.00
MPC, Strange Changing Mummy, #902, 1974, 1/12, MIB (sealed) $100.00
MPC, Sweat Hogs Dream Machine, 1976, MIB $50.00
MPC, TJ Hooker, Police Car, 1982, MIB.........................$30.00
MPC, 1970 Jeepster Safari Wagon, EX (EX box).............$40.00

MPC, Paul Revere, Mark Lindsay, and the Raiders Own Raiders Coach, #14, MIB (sealed), $300.00. (Photo courtesy Bojo)

MPC, '72 Corvette Sting Ray, MIB, $55.00. (Photo courtesy June Moon)

MPC, Pirates of the Caribbean, Condemned to Chains, MIB (sealed), A, $85.00. (Photo courtesy John and Sheri Pavone)

MPC, Pirates of the Caribbean, Dead Men Tell No Tales, 1972, MIB..$60.00
MPC, Pirates of the Caribbean, Ghost of Treasure Guard #5006, 1972, 1/12, MIB...$150.00

Multiple, Ripley's Believe It or Not, Torture Chair or Torture Wheel, 1966, MIB, ea $150.00
Nitto, Jerry Heavy Armored Fighting Suit #24110, 1980s, 1/20, MIB $60.00
Palmer, Animals of the World, White Tail Deer #25, 1950s, MIB $30.00
Palmer, Brontosaurus Skeleton, 1950s, MIB $60.00
Palmer, Happy Days Burger Buggy, 1974, MIB, from $50 to...$75.00
Paramount, Lord Mayor of London's Coach #2, 1960s, 1/30, MIB $25.00
Parks, Born Losers, Napoleon, MIB..................................$85.00
Precision, Royal Bengal Tiger Head, 1957, MIB $40.00
Pyro, Burmese Paddy Boat #318, 1960s, 1/45, MIB $20.00
Pyro, Classic Auburn Speedster, MIB................................$85.00
Pyro, Curler Super Surf Tricycle, 1970, MIB....................$40.00
Pyro, Der Baron & His Harley-Custom, 1970, MIB $75.00
Pyro, Ghost Rider, 1970, MIB $50.00
Pyro, Gladiator Show Cycle, 1970, MIB............................$50.00
Pyro, Indian Medicine Man #282, 1960s, 1/8, MIB..........$70.00
Pyro, Li'l Corporal, 1970, MIB $50.00
Pyro, Peacemaker 45, 1960, MIB (sealed)......................$100.00

Pyro, Rawhide, 1959, MIB, H8 ....**$250.00**
Pyro, Rawhide Cowpuncher, 1958, MIB **$60.00**
Pyro, Surf's Up! Surf Trailer Bicycle, 1970, MIB **$40.00**
Pyro, Texas Cowboy #284, 1960s, 1/8, MIB **$60.00**
Pyro, Western Figures, Deputy Sheriff, 1961, MIB **$35.00**
Remco, Flintstone's Motorized Paddy Wagon, 1961, MIB ..**$200.00**
Revell, '31 Ford Woody, 1964, MIB **$85.00**
Revell, Aerobee Hi Research Rocket #1814, 1958, 1/40,
    MIB **$90.00**
Revell, Apollo-Soyuz Link-up #1800, 1975, 1/96, MIB
    (sealed) **$80.00**
Revell, Astronaut in Space, 1968, MIB **$100.00**
Revell, Beatles, any member, 1964, MIB, ea, from $200 to ..**$250.00**
Revell, Bonanza, Ben, Hoss & Little Joe #1931, 1966, 1/7,
    MIB **$160.00**
Revell, Cat in the Hat, 1958, MIB.................................**$100.00**
Revell, Charlie's Angels Mobile Unit Van, 1977, MIB, from $40
    to **$50.00**
Revell, Coast Guard Cutter Campbell, 1956, EX (EX box) ...**$50.00**
Revell, Code Red, Emergency Van #6029, 1981, 1/32, MIB ..**$20.00**
Revell, Corporal Missile, 1958, MIB...............................**$100.00**
Revell, Douglas #DC-7 United, 1974, MIB (sealed) **$25.00**
Revell, Dr Suess Zoo, Gowdy the Dowdy Grackle, 1958,
    MIB **$85.00**
Revell, Dr Suess Zoo, Norval the Bashful Blinket, 1952,
    MIB **$85.00**
Revell, Eastern Airlines Golden Falcon, 1950s, MIB **$75.00**
Revell, Ed 'Big Daddy' Roth, Brother Ratfink on a Bike, 1964,
    MIB **$100.00**
Revell, Ed 'Big Daddy' Roth, Fink Eliminator #6196, 1990,
    MIB..**$60.00**
Revell, Ed 'Big Daddy' Roth, Superfink, 1964, MIB.......**$300.00**
Revell, Endangered Animals, California Condor #6462, 1991,
    15", MIB (sealed) **$25.00**
Revell, Evil Eye, 1980, glow-in-the-dark, MIB **$35.00**
Revell, F-89D Scorpion USAF Jet, 1950s, MIB...............**$75.00**
Revell, Flash Gordon & the Martian, 1965, MIB...........**$225.00**
Revell, Freaky Riders, Korporal Amerika or Shift Kicker, 1971,
    MIB, ea...**$65.00**
Revell, Grand Prix Lotus, 1960s, MIB (sealed), from $100
    to **$125.00**
Revell, Happy Days '29 Model Pickup, 1982, MIB...........**$30.00**
Revell, Happy Days '57 Chevy Nomad, 1982, MIB, from $25
    to..**$35.00**
Revell, Hardy Boys' Van, 1978, MIB, from $30 to **$40.00**
Revell, Historic PT-109, 1963, 1/72, EX (EX box) **$30.00**
Revell, History Makers, Nike Hercules #8613, 1982, 1/40, MIB
    (sealed)..**$35.00**
Revell, Hunt for Red October, F/A-18 Hornet, 1990, MIB
    (sealed)..**$15.00**
Revell, Jacques Cousteau, PBY Flying Boat #576, 1972, 1/72,
    MIB **$30.00**
Revell, John Travolta's Firebird Fever, 1979, MIB (sealed),
    J6 ....**$45.00**
Revell, Lacross Missile #1816, 1958, 1/40, MIB **$200.00**
Revell, Lockheed F-104 USAF Starfighter, 1950s, MIB...**$75.00**
Revell, Los Angeles Dodgers Electra, 1962, MIB............**$240.00**
Revell, McHale's Navy PT-73, 1965, MIB **$75.00**

Revell, Mercury/Gemini #1834, 1964, 1/48, MIB.............**$70.00**
Revell, Monsters of the Movies, Dracula, MIB (sealed) ...**$15.00**
Revell, Monsters of the Movies, Frankenstein, MIB
    (sealed) **$15.00**
Revell, Northrop Snark Missile #1801, 1957, 1/96, MIB..**$50.00**

**Revell, Outlaw, MIB, $100.00; Ed 'Big Daddy Roth,'
Beatnik Bandit, MIB, $150.00.** (Photo courtesy Martin and Carolyn Berens)

Revell, Phantom & the Voodoo Witch Doctor, 1965, MIB ..**$200.00**
Revell, Robotech, Nebo #1400, 1984, 1/72, MIB **$30.00**
Revell, Robotech, Trigon or VF-1S Battloid, 1985, MIB, ea..**$40.00**
Revell, Robotech, Vexar #1402, 1984, 1/72, MIB (sealed).....**$40.00**
Revell, Saint's Jaguar XJS, 1979, MIB (sealed) **$35.00**
Revell, Search Patrol 2-in-1 Kit #1140, 1984, 1/170, MIB ..**$25.00**
Revell, Space Pursuit, 1969, MIB...................................**$240.00**
Revell, Stingray (TV), Stingray Corvette Coupe #7377, 1987,
    1/25, MIB (sealed) **$30.00**
Revell, Teddy the Koala Bear, MIB **$40.00**
Revell, Unimog U 1300 L 2T Military, MIB.....................**$25.00**
Revell, VF-1A Fighter #1409, 1985, 1/100, MIB (sealed) .**$40.00**
Revell, X-17 Research Missile, 1957, MIB.......................**$65.00**
Screamin', Air Assault Martian #4030, 1995, 1/8, MIB ...**$50.00**
Screamin', Bettie Page — Jungle Fever, 1994, MIB..........**$85.00**
Screamin', Hellraiser (movies), Chatter Cenobite #800, 1991,
    1/4, MIB...**$50.00**
Screamin', London After Midnight Vampire, MIB...........**$75.00**
Screamin', Mars Attacks, No Place To Hide, assembled...**$50.00**
Screamin', Mars Attacks, Target Earth, 1/8, assembled **$30.00**
Screamin', Star Wars, C-3PO #3500, 1993, 1/4, MIB.......**$45.00**
Screamin', Suburban Commando, General Suitor Mutant, 1991,
    MIB **$55.00**
Screamin', Werewolf, MIB...**$50.00**

Strombecker, Disneyland Stagecoach #D28, 1950s, MIB ..**$210.00**

Strombecker, Walt Disney's Rocket to the Moon, 1956, MIB **$225.00**

Superior, Seeing Eye, 1959, MIB **$35.00**

Superior, Yankee Stadium, unassembled, complete, NM ..**$95.00**

Superior Plastics, Yankee Stadium, unassembled, complete, M **$100.00**

Testors, Davey the Cyclist #731, 1993, MIB (sealed) **$15.00**

Testors, Top Gun, A-4 Aggressor, 1987, MIB **$10.00**

Testors, Weird-Ohs, Beach Bunny Catching Rays #751, 1994, MIB (sealed) **$30.00**

Tomy, Lensman, Galactic Fighter Striker I #7201, 1/72, MIB...**$40.00**

Tomy, Lensman, Grappler & Shuttle Truck, 1984, MIB...**$40.00**

Toy Biz, Ghost Rider #48660, 1996, MIB.................**$30.00**

Toy Biz, Storm, 1996, MIB (sealed).................**$30.00**

Toy Biz, Thing #48652, 1996, MIB (sealed).................**$25.00**

Tsukuda, Flying Sub, Land of the Giants, M (G box), $95.00.
(Photo courtesy Tom Duncan)

Tsukuda, Ghostbusters, Stay Puft Man (sm), 1984, MIB ..**$40.00**

Tsukuda, Metaluna Mutant, MIB **$75.00**

Tsukuda, Mummy, MIB.................**$75.00**

Tsukuda, Wolf Man, MIB **$60.00**

Wave, Gargantuas Sandra vs Gaira, NM (EX box) **$110.00**

Whiting, Space: 1999, Mammoth Model, 1976, MIB **$50.00**

Movie Posters and Lobby Cards

This field is a natural extension of the interest in character collectibles, and one where there is a great deal of activity. There are tradepapers that deal exclusively with movie memorabilia, and some of the larger auction galleries hold cataloged sales on a regular basis. The hottest genre right now is the monster movies, but westerns and Disney films are close behind.

A Boy Named Charlie Brown, lobby cards, Cinema Center Films, 1969, 11x14", set of 6, EX **$50.00**

Ace Ventura, Pet Detective, 1994, 1-sheet, M.................**$40.00**

Aladdin, 1993, dbl-sided, 1-sheet, 27x41", M.................**$75.00**

Alice in Wonderland, WD, 1951, 1-sheet, linen-bk, 41x27", NM **$1,000.00**

Alice in Wonderland, 1980, 40x60", EX.................**$65.00**

Bambi, 1967, Italian, 4-sheet, 55x77", NM **$250.00**

Beatles — Hard Day's Night, lobby card, US version, 11x14", EX, B3.................**$225.00**

Beatles — Hard Days Night, half-sheet, 22x14", EX, B3 ..**$285.00**

Beatles — Help!, lobby cards, UK, 8x10", rare, set of 8, B3...**$600.00**

Beatles — Yellow Submarine, lobby card, UK, 8x10", VG, B3.................**$100.00**

Bringing Up Father, 1920s, 3-sheet, linen-bk, 72x48", rare, EX, A.................**$200.00**

Bug's Life, 1998, 1-sheet, M.................**$35.00**

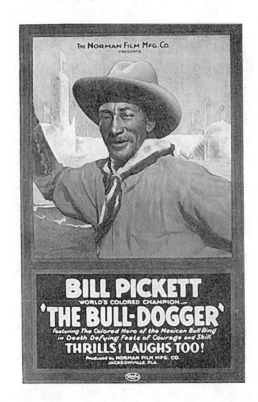

Bull-Dogger, 1923, 1-sheet, M, A, $2,200.00.

Chamber of Horrors, 1966, lobby card set, complete, EX+/NM, $50.00. (Photo courtesy John and Sheri Pavone)

Charlie Chaplin, The Immigrant, 1917, 40x27", EX ..$1,600.00
Creature Walks Among Us, window card, Universal, 1956,
    18x14", VG...$125.00
Donald Duck's Birthday, Spanish, 1965, 1-sheet, 27x41", EX...$95.00
Dracula's Daughter, 1936, window card, 13½x21½", VG ..$650.00
Escape From the Planet of the Apes, 1971, 76x43", EX .$250.00
Fantasia, 1970, 1-sheet, 27x41", heavy card stock, M $225.00
Flipper, Japan, 1960s, 20x14", EX, A7...............................$35.00

House of
Franken-
stein, 1944,
1-sheet, 41"
x 27", EX,
$2,750.00.

Forbidden
Planet, 1956,
1-sheet, 41"
x 27", M, A,
$4,000.00.

Hound of the Baskervilles, lobby card, 1959, 11x14", EX.$25.00
HR Pufnstuf, lobby card, 1970, 11x14", NM.....................$35.00
Hunchback of Notre Dame, 1996, 1-sheet, 27x41", M.....$55.00
James Bond, Dr No, 1967, 1-sheet, VG $775.00
Jungle Book, 1967, Spanish, 1-sheet, 27x41", VG.........$150.00
Lady & the Tramp, 1972, 2-sheet, 81x81", NM.............$240.00

Frank & Ollie, 1994, 1-sheet, 27x40", M $75.00
Godzilla, King of the Monsters, 1956, 35x14", EX $925.00
Goofy Movie, 1995, 1-sheet, 27x40", EX $40.00
Hopalong Cassidy Enters, 1930s, 33x48", EX $365.00

Rebel Without
a Cause, 1955,
1-sheet, on
linen, 41" x
27", M, A,
$1,500.00.

Horror House, 1970, lobby card set, complete, NM, $35.00.
(Photo courtesy John and Sheri Pavone)

Little Mermaid, 1989, 1-sheet, 27x41", NM $100.00

Meet the Mummy, 1955, trimmed window card, EX $195.00

Mr Magoo's Holiday Festival, 1960s, 1-sheet, 41x27", VG ..$40.00

Music Land, Disney, 1955, 1-sheet, 27x41", NM...........$250.00

New Adventures of Batman & Robin the Boy Wonder, 1949, 3-
    sheet, 81x41", NM, T2, from $2,000 to...............$3,000.00

Pinocchio, 1962, 1-sheet, 27x41", EX $40.00

Private Snuffy Smith, Monogram, 1942, 36x14", EX........$65.00

Rocketeer, 1991, dbl-sided, 1-sheet, 27x41", NM+ $50.00

Shadow Returns, lobby card, 11x14", NM, C10 ....$225.00

Shadows of Tombstone — Rex Allen, 1953, 41" x 27", VG, A, $100.00.

She Monster, 1958, half-sheet, 22x28", EX....................$435.00

Sleeping Beauty, 1970, 3-sheet, 41x81", M $95.00

Snow White, 1983, 1-sheet, 27x41", NM $45.00

Snow White & the Seven Dwarfs, lobby card, 1951 re-release,
    NM..$85.00

Spider-Man, Columbia, 1977, 1-sheet, 40x26", NM, T2, from
    $50 to $75.00

Star Wars, 1977, 40x60", EX $500.00

Superman, The Payoff, Columbia Serial, 1948, 1-sheet, 39x26",
    NM, T2, from $800 to.......................................$1,200.00

Superman Comes to Earth, lobby card, Columbia Serial, 1948,
    11x13", NM, T2, from $50 to...................................$75.00

Tales From the Crypt, Cinerama, 1972, 41x27", NM $50.00

Tarzan the Fearless, 1933, linen-bk, 41x27", NM $800.00

Toy Story, 1995, 1-sheet, 27x41", NM+ $40.00

Walt Disney's Wonderful Adventures of Pinocchio, lobby card,
    1945 re-release, 11x14", NM $65.00

Winnie the Pooh & Tigger Too, 1974, 1-sheet, 27x41", M ...$150.00

101 Dalmatians, 1961, 1-sheet, 27x41", VG+ $165.00

Musical Toys

Whether meant to soothe, entertain, or inspire, musical toys were part of our growing-up years. Some were as simple as a windup music box, others as elaborate as a lacquered French baby grand piano.

See also Character, TV, and Movie Collectibles; Disney; Rock 'n Roll; Western.

Accordion, Golden Piano Accordion, Emenee, missing song
    book, o/w complete, EX (VG box)............................$45.00

Church Piano, Reed, litho-graphed paper, 14" x 12", VG, A, $195.00.

Drum, litho tin w/Boy Scout scene, 8" dia, VG, A $75.00

Drum, stamped tin sides w/stars-&-stripes shield & colored stars,
    wood rims w/repeated design, 9" dia, VG, A $500.00

Farmer in the Dell Music Box, Mattel, litho tin, hand crank,
    10", not working, EX (EX box), A $100.00

Farmer in the Dell Musical Barn, Mattel, plastic figures rotate in
    & out of barn, silent, 9½x7", EX...............................$35.00

Fluta, Weiss, cb & metal clarinet-syle harmonica, 14", EX (VG
    box), A..$150.00

Hohnerette, Hohner, wood & metal accordion-style harmonica
    w/single horn, 11", VG (VG box), A......................$150.00

Koch's Zauberflote, cb & metal slide clarinet-style harmonica,
    EX, A $200.00

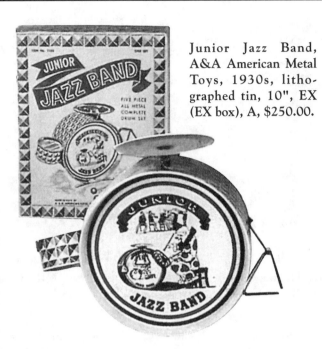

Junior Jazz Band, A&A American Metal Toys, 1930s, lithographed tin, 10", EX (EX box), A, $250.00.

Melody Player Roller Organ, litho tin w/hand-operated paper roller player, w/2 rolls, 6", EX, A $100.00
Music Box, Quartet Mandeville, 4 cloth-dressed compo & wood figures on paper-covered wood box, 14" L, EX, A ..$2,750.00
Musical Sail Way Ferris Wheel, Unique Mfg, metal w/plastic boats, 9¼x6½" dia, EXIB $320.00
Piano, Bliss, wood w/paper litho image of cherubs playing various instruments, 8 keys, 9½" L, G, A $75.00
Piano, unknown maker, wood w/children's items stenciled on front, 7 keys, EX $100.00
PlaRola Organ, litho tin & wood, 4", EX (EX box), A...$200.00
Rol Monica, harmonica mounted in Bakelite player housing, 5", VG (VG box), A $200.00
Showboat Band Set #50, Spec-Toy-Culars Inc, 1952, banjo-uke, clarinet, trombone, horn & paper baton, plastic, EXIB...$35.00

Tambourine, T. Cohn, lithographed tin, 8" diameter, NM, A, $100.00. (Photo courtesy Linda Baker)

Toyland Band Deluxe Drum Set, Ohio Art, litho tin, complete, 7½", MIB, A $100.00
Trumpet Call Harmonica, Hohner, wood & metal w/5 brass horns, 5", VG, A..$150.00
Tuneyville Player Piano, Tomy, 1978, plastic, battery-op, complete w/4 records, 8½", EX $30.00

Nodders

Nodders representing comic characters of the day were made in Germany in the 1930s. These were small doll-like figures approximately 3" to 4" tall, and the popular ones often came in boxed sets. But the lesser-known characters were sold separately, making them rarer and harder to find today. While the more common nodders go for $125.00 and under, The Old Timer, Widow Zander, and Ma and Pa Winkle often bring about $350.00 to $400.00 — Happy Hooligan even more, about $625.00. (We've listed the more valuable ones here; any German bisque nodder not listed is worth $125.00 or under.)

See also Character Bobbin' Heads; Political; Rock 'n Roll; Santa; Sporting Collectibles.

Uncle Bim, $125.00; Ching Chow, $125.00; Old Timer, $350.00.

Ambrose Potts, NM...$350.00
Auntie Blossom, NM..$150.00
Auntie Mamie, NM..$250.00
Avery, NM $200.00
Bill, NM..$200.00
Buttercup, NM...$250.00
Chubby Chaney, NM..$250.00
Corky, NM...$475.00

Dinty Moor, NM..$500.00
Dock, NM $200.00
Fanny Nebbs, NM..$250.00
Ferina, NM..$350.00
Grandpa Teen, NM..$350.00
Happy Hooligan, NM $625.00
Harold Teen, NM...$150.00
Josie, NM $425.00
Junior Nebbs, NM..$625.00
Lilacs, NM $425.00
Lillums, NM...$150.00
Little Annie Roonie, movable arms, NM $300.00
Little Egypt, NM..$350.00
Lord Plushbottom, NM......................................$150.00
Ma & Pa Winkle, NM, ea $350.00
Marjorie, NM...$425.00
Mary Ann Jackson, NM $250.00
Max, NM $200.00
Min Gump, NM..$150.00
Mr Bailey, NM...$150.00
Mr Bibb, NM $400.00
Mr Wicker, NM $250.00
Mushmouth, NM..$175.00
Mutt or Jeff, med or lg, NM, ea $250.00
Mutt or Jeff, sm, NM, ea $175.00
Nicodemus, NM...$350.00
Our Gang, 6-pc set, MIB...................................$1,200.00
Pat Finnegan, NM $400.00
Patsy, NM..$425.00
Pete the Dog, NM"...$250.00
Pop Jenks, NM $200.00
Rudy Nebbs, NM..$250.00
Scraps, NM $250.00
Uncle Willie, NM...$250.00
Widow Zander, NM..$400.00
Winnie Winkle, NM $150.00

Optical Toys

Compared to the bulky viewers of years ago, contrary to the usual course of advancement, optical toys of more recent years have tended to become more simplified in concept.

See also Character, TV, and Movie Collectibles; Disney; View-Master and Tru-View; Western.

Charlie Chaplin Ombro-Cinema, France, early 1900s, turn hdl for flickering blk & wht celluloid silhouettes, EX, A..$600.00
Comicscope viewer, Remington Morris, 1900s, comic strip viewer, w/3 comic strips, EX $45.00
Easy Show Motorized Movie Projector, Kenner, 1960s, battery-op, MIB...$110.00
El Torero, Franco, optical illusion trick, shows matador cutting off bull's head, 2⅛" dia, EX................................$20.00
Give a Show Projector #802, Kenner, 1963, w/kaleidoscope attatchment, 168 color slides, EXIB..................$95.00

Give-A-Show Projector, Kenner, 1960s, features Huckleberry Hound, Yogi Bear, Flintstones, and others, MIB, from $100.00 to $125.00. (Photo courtesy Martin and Carolyn Berens)

Give-A-Show Projector, Kenner, 1970s-present, red & bl plastic, battery-op, 9½", EX....................................$30.00
Give-A-Show Projector, Kenner, 1974, 16 film strips, EXIB...$45.00
Grapho-Scope, Federal Stamping & Engineering, 1934, camera lucida for drawing & copying, VG (orig box)............$75.00
Irwin Projector, Irwin, 1940s, w/projector & 1 film, NMIB ..$35.00
Kaleidoscope, Du-All Product, 1940s, camera shape, leatherette textured cb, glass interior items, VG+ $260.00
Mag-O-Flex Projector/Viewer, Walt Disney Prod, battery-op, VG (orig box) $60.00
Magic Lantern, brass & tin on wood base, orig chimney, 9", VG, A..$250.00

Magic Lantern, Ernst Plank, EX (EX 10" x 15" box), A, $130.00; Columbus Lantern, Germany, red-painted tin with decals, kerosene lamp base, 10", EX, A, $3,400.00; Magic Lantern, Ernst Plank, EX (EX 8" x 11" box), $200.00.

Magic Lantern, Gloria, Ernst Plank, tin w/glass chimney, brass lens holder, w/12 slides, 17", VG (worn wooden box), A $450.00
Magic Lantern, mk Luna, Made in Germany, metal w/decorated porcelain sides, mechanical kaleidoscope slide, 16", EX, A $1,600.00
Magnajector Model #MJ-100, Rainbow Crafts Inc, 1953, projects image onto paper, Bakelite, EX (orig box & instructions)...$30.00
Optical Illusions Science Kit, Remco, 1961, NM (orig can)...$25.00

Petits Metamorphisis, 1970 repro, 3 cards divided into 3 sections ea to make different figures, 2¾x4", EXIB $30.00

Praxinoscope Theater, candle illuminated, twenty image strips (seven not original, some repaired and incomplete), VG/EX (EX 10" x 10" x 5" wooden case), A, $1,150.00.

Real Sound Movie Projector, Kenner, 1968, comes w/3 movie reels, EX (orig box)....................................$210.00
See-Action Football, Kenner, 1973, NMIB $25.00
Show-N-Tell Phono Viewer, GE Model #A630B, 1967, w/6 records & film strips, NM (VG box).........................$90.00
Tantalizer the Optical Puzzler, Northern Signal Co, 1960s, game, EXIB...$25.00
Telstar Kaleidoscope, Green Monk Products, 1950s, litho tin, 5x2" dia, EX $35.00
Zoetrope, tin drum on brass & wood base, w/6 animated strips mounted to heavy paper, 17", EX, A.......................$850.00

Paper Dolls

Turn-of-the-century paper dolls are seldom found today and when they are, they're very expensive. Advertising companies used them to promote their products, and some were printed on the pages of leading ladies' magazines. By the late 1920s most paper dolls were being made in book form — the doll on the cover, the clothes on the inside pages. Because they were so inexpensive, paper dolls survived the Depression and went on to peak in the 1940s. Though the advent of television caused sales to decline, paper doll companies were able to hang on by making paper dolls representing Hollywood celebrities and TV stars. These are some of the most collectible today. Even celebrity dolls from more recent years like the Brady Bunch or the Waltons are popular. Remember, condition is very important; if they've been cut out, even when they're still in fine condition and have all their original accessories, they're worth only about half as much as an uncut book or box set. Our values are for mint and uncut dolls unless noted otherwise.

For more information, refer to *Price Guide to Lowe and Whitman Paper Dolls* and *Price Guide to Saalfield and Merrill Paper Dolls* by Mary Young, *Collecting Toys* by Richard O'Brien, and *Toys, Antique and Collectible,* by David Longest.

Advisor: Mary Young (Y2).

Adventures of Polly and Peter Perkin, Pictorial Review, July 1933, $16.00. (Photo courtesy Mary Young)

Airline Stewardess, Lowe #4913, 1957..............................$35.00
Annette, Whitman #2083, 1958.......................................$75.00
Annie Laurie, Lowe #1030, 1941 ....$65.00
Annie Oakley, Whitman #2056, 1955 ....$75.00
Archie Girls/Betty & Veronica, Lowe #2764, 1964..........$50.00
Archies, Whitman #1987, 1969, from $45 to $50.00
Army Nurse & Doctor, Merrill #3425, 1942, from $100 to..$125.00
Best Frields, Saalfield #2619, 1953 ....$35.00
Betty & Peggy, Platt & Munk #230B, 1937, from $25 to .$40.00
Betty Bo-Peep/Billy Boy Blue, Lowe #1043, 1942.............$75.00
Betty Grable, Merrill #1558, 1951, 8-pg version, from $175 to..$250.00
Betty Hutton & Her Girls, Whitman #2009, 1951, from $70 to..$100.00
Beverly Hillbillies, Whitman #1955, 1964......................$85.00
Big & Little Sister, Whitman #4411, 1962 ....$25.00
Blondie, Whitman #967, 1947 or 1948, 2 versions (circus cover or singer), ea from $75 to $125.00
Blue Bonnet, Merrill #3444, 1942, from $90 to..............$125.00
Bobbsey Twins Play Box, GP Putman's Sons #C2000, 1950...$60.00
Brady Bunch, Whitman #1976, 1973, from $50 to...........$60.00
Brenda Lee, Lowe #2785, 1961, from $50 to....................$75.00
Bride & Groom, Lowe #2493, 1959 ....$35.00

Buffy, Whitman #1985, 1969.....................................$35.00
Career Girls, Lowe #958, 1950 ....$35.00
Carol Lynley, Whitman #2089, 1960 ....$60.00
Charlie Chaplin & Paulette Goddard, Sallfield #2356, 1941, from $200 to $300.00
Charmin' Chatty Around the World Wardrobe, Whitman #1959, 1964 ....$50.00
Circus Paper Dolls, Saalfield #2610, 1952, from $35 to....$50.00
Claudette Colbert, Saalfield #2451, 1943, from $125 to...$200.00
Cyd Charisse, Whitman #2084, 1956 ....$115.00
Darling Dolls w/Wavy Hair, Saalfield #6194, 1957, from $25 to $40.00
Deanna Durbin, Merrill #4804, 1941, from $175 to.......$300.00

Debbie Reynolds, Whitman #1178, 1953 ....$125.00
Dolls of Other Lands, Whitman #2074, 1963, from $20 to..$25.00
Dolly Goes Around the World, Lowe #4264, 1955...........$12.00
Dress Alike Dolls, Whitman #2058, 1951, from $60 to..$100.00
Dude Ranch Turnabouts, Lowe #1026, 1943 ....$40.00
Elizabeth Taylor, Whitman #2057, 1957.................$150.00
Elly May, Watkins-Strathmore, #1819A, 1963 ....$50.00
Evelyn Rudie, Saalfield #4446, 1958, from $40 to $60.00
Family of Dolls, Whitman #4574, 1960 ....$40.00
Fashion Reviews, Lowe #1246, 1949 ....$45.00
Flintstones, Whitman #4796, 1962 ....$50.00
Flying Nun, Saalfield #1317, 1969 ....$75.00

Dolly Dingle, Pictorial Review, April 1933, $14.00.
(Photo courtesy Mary Young)

Foreign Dolls To Cut Out and Dress, Platt & Munk, #241, 1957, VG in 11" x 13" box (with small repairs), from $50.00 to $60.00. (Photo courtesy Marvelous Books)

Four Hi-Heel Standing Dolls, Saalfield #6128, boxed $35.00
Gabby Hayes/Tall Tales for Little Folks, Lowe #4171, 1954 ...$55.00
Gene Tierney, Whitman #992, 1947, from $125 to........$200.00
Gloria's Make-Up, Lowe #2585, 1952 ....$50.00
Golden Girl, Merrill #1543, 1953, from $75 to $100.00
Goldilocks & the Three Bears, Saalfield #2245, 1939, from $100 to $200.00
Good Neighbor, Saalfield #2487, 1944 ....$40.00
Grace Kelly, Whitman #2049, 1955..............................$125.00
Greer Garson, Merrill #4858, 1944, from $185 to $300.00
Gretchen, Whitman #4613, 1966 ....$15.00
Happiest Millionaire, Saalfield #4487, 1967, from $50 to...$75.00
Henry & Henrietta, Saalfield #2189, 1938 ....$25.00
Here Comes the Bride, Whitman #1189, 1952................$50.00
High School Dolls, Merrill #1551, 1948, from $75 to $100.00
Hollywood Personalities, Lowe #1049, 1941..................$400.00
I Love Lucy/Lucille Ball & Desi Arnez, Whitman #2101, 1953, EX $125.00
It's a Date, Whitman #1976, 1956, from $35 to..............$50.00
Jane Powell, Whitman #1185, 1951.............................$120.00
Jane Russell, Saalfield #4328, 1955 ....$95.00
Jane Withers, Whitman #977, 1936..............................$200.00

Donna Reed, Saalfield #4412, 1959, from $75.00 to $100.00. (Photo courtesy Mary Young)

I Love Lucy Packaway Kit, Whitman, #5624, 1953, EX, $125.00. (Photo courtesy Bill Bruegman)

Jill & Her Trunk Full of Clothes, Merrill #4828, 1943, from $35 to $50.00
Joanne Woodward, Saalfield #4436, 1958, from $75 to..$125.00
Johnny, Janey & Judy in Storybook Land, Merrill #1544, 1952, from $30 to..$40.00
Judy Garland, Whitman #999, 1940 ....$100.00

Julia, Saalfield #4435, 1968, from $50.00 to $75.00. (Photo courtesy Mary Young)

Julia, Saalfield #6055, 1969, from $50 to $75.00
June Allyson, Whitman #970, 1950................................$125.00
Junior Miss Dolls, Platt & Munk #229, 1942 ....$45.00
Laugh-In Party, Saalfield #6045, 1969, boxed, from $40 to...$65.00
Let's Play w/the Baby, Merrill #1550, 1948, from $40 to ..$65.00
Lindy-Lou 'N Cindy-Sue, Merrill #2564, 1954, from $65 to ..$90.00
Little Family & Their Little House, Merrill #1561, 1949, from $85 to..$125.00
Little Friends From History, Rand McNally #186, 1936...$40.00
Little Women, Saalfield #1345, 1963 ....$35.00
Magic Stay-On Doll, Whitman #4618, 1963 ....$20.00
Mary Hartline, Whitman #2104, 1952............................$75.00
Mickey & Minnie Steppin' Out, Whitman #1979, 1977..$25.00

Mommy & Me, Whitman #977, 1954, from $30 to..........$35.00
Mother & Daughter, Saalfield #1330, 1962 ....$35.00
Mouseketeers, Whitman #1974, 1963............................$60.00
Movie Starlets, Whitman #960, 1946 ....$125.00
Nanny & the Professor, Artcraft #5114, 1971, from $40 to ..$60.00
National Velvet, Whitman #1958, 1961 ....$50.00
Nurses, Whitman #1975, 1963 ....$40.00
One Hundred & One Dalmatians, Whitman #1993, 1960..$60.00
Partridge Family, Saalfield #5137, 1971 ....$50.00
Pat Crowley, Whitman #2050, 1955 ....$75.00
Patti Page, Lowe #2488, 1958..$75.00

Patty Duke, Whitman #1991, from $40.00 to $50.00. (Photo courtesy Greg Davis and Bill Morgan)

Patty Duke, Whitman #4775, 1965, boxed $50.00
Pebbles & Bamm-Bamm, Whitman, 1983, 1964 & 1966, ea ..$35.00
Penny's Party, Lowe #4207, 1952....................................$25.00
Pink Wedding, Merrill #1559, 8-pg book, 1952, from $50 to $75.00
Quiz Kids, Saalfield #2430, 1942, from $90 to................$175.00
Raggedy Ann & Andy, Whitman #4319, 1973, MIB $35.00
Roy Rogers & Dale Evans, Whitman #1950, 1956, EX ..$100.00
Sally, Sue & Sherry, Lowe #2785, 1969............................$10.00
Sally's Silver Skates, Merrill #1549, 1956 ....$50.00
Seven & Seventeen, Merrill #3441, 1945, from $100 to ..$140.00
Shari Lewis & Her Puppets, Saalfield #6060, 1960, boxed, from $50 to $65.00
Shirley Temple Dolls & Dresses Her Movie Wardrobe, Saalfield #1773, 1938, from $200 to $300.00
Skediddle Kiddles, Whitman #4722, 1969, boxed $35.00
Sleeping Beauty, Whitman #4723, 1958 ....$65.00
Slumber Party, Merrill #4854, 1943, from $65 to............$90.00

Snow White & the Seven Dwarfs, Whitman #970, 1938, bl background $200.00

Square Dance, Lowe #968, 1950 ....$25.00

Star Princess, Whitman #1839, 1979, from $10 to $15.00

Susan Dey as Laurie, Saalfield #6024, 1971-72 ....$50.00

Tammy & Her Family, Whitman #1997, 1964...................$60.00

Tender Love 'N Kisses, Whitman #1944-1, 1978.............$15.00

Tiny Chatty Twins, Whitman, #1985, 1963......................$35.00

Tom the Aviator/Dick the Sailor/Harry the Soldier, Lowe #1074, 1941, ea from $50 to $75.00

Toni Hair-Do Dress-Up Dolls, Lowe #1251, 1951.............$75.00

TV Tap Stars, Lowe #990, 1952 ....$30.00

Tyrone Power & Linda Darnell, Merrill #3438, 1941, from $185 to...$300.00

Vera Miles, Whitman #2986, 1957, from $80 to $125.00

Victory Paper Dolls, Saalfield #2445, 1943, from $85 to...$125.00

Virginia Weidler, Whitman #1016, 1942, from $60 to $80.00

Waltons, Whitman #1995, 1975, from $50 to $60.00

Wonderful World of Brothers Grimm, Saalfield #1336, 1963, from $35 to...$50.00

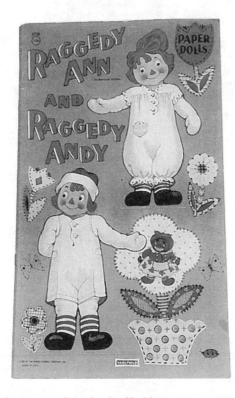

Raggedy Ann and Andy, Saalfield #2739, 1961, authorized edition, from $35.00 to $45.00. (Photo courtesy Kim Avery)

Paper-Lithographed Toys

Following the development of color lithography, early toy makers soon recognized the possibility of using this technology in their own field. Both here and abroad, by the 1880s toys ranging from soldiers to involved dioramas of entire villages were being produced of wood with colorful and well-detailed paper lithographed surfaces. Some of the best known manufacturers were Crandall, Bliss, Reed, and McLoughlin. This style of toy remained popular until well after the turn of the century.

Advisors: Mark and Lynda Suozzi (S24).

See Also Black Americana; Boats; Dollhouses; Games; Musical Toys; Pull Toys; Puzzles and Picture Blocks; Schoenhut.

ABC Blocks, Singer, set of 15, VG (VG box), A $575.00

Army & Navy Block Set, Westcott Bros, 1895, scenes of fighting ships, armies & officers, set of 12, rare, EX (EX box), A..$750.00

Around the World Trunk, Bliss, hinged lid, allover graphics, 10x6x4", EX, A...$165.00

Bagatelle, 1895, 2 clowns w/cup hats, 13" L, A $450.00

Block, 1980s, w/letter of alphabet & child, EX $65.00

Block Wagon, Western Express, Bliss, complete, 13" L, EX, A...$450.00

Brownie Blocks, McLoughlin Bros, 1891, set of 20, VG (VG box), A..$900.00

Brownie 10 Pins, McLoughlin, complete w/stands & balls, EX (EX 16x14" box), A $2,700.00

Buster Bown & Tige Target Game, Bliss, early 1900s, 10x24", VG, A $950.00

Cinderella Coach, Bliss, 26", EX, A............................$1,650.00

Flip Top, 1850, 4 dbl-sided sections depicting Napoleon III, 7", VG (in torn slip case), A..$725.00

Goblin Pins, Ives Blakeslee, 1875, 10 figures & heads, stand rpl, orig cannon, VG (VG box), A $1,200.00

Happiwork Fire Dept, Gibson Art, 1924, complete, NM (NM box), A..$350.00

Jackson Park Horse-Drawn Trolley, Bliss, original driver and conductor, 27" long, EX, A, $5,250.00.

Military Ten-Pins, Ives, complete, EX (worn box), A ...$3,500.00

Nesting Blocks, Crandall's Mammoth ABCs, set of 10, EX, A...$550.00

Nesting Blocks, 1936, w/Black Sambo & other characters, set of 5, EX+, H8..$350.00

Noah's Ark, Spear Co, animals peer from sides, contains various paper animals on tin bases, roof lifts off, 12" L, EX..$650.00

Noah's Ark Animals, Tuck, joined diecut prs, slightly embossed, 12 animals in decorated 10½x8" box, EX, A $450.00

Old Guard Soldiers, 10 on wooden base, w/wooden cannon that shoots ball (missing), EX (9x15" box, no lid), A..$1,100.00

Punch & Judy, Forbes, Boston, pull lever, Punch, Judy & policeman pop up into full view, EX, A $750.00

Nine-Pin and ABC Spelling Blocks, McLoughlin, EXIB, A, $750.00.

Puzzle Blocks, Germany, 1890s, set of twenty with different scenes of young ladies at play, 8" x 10" x 2", EX/VG, $350.00. (Photo courtesy Buffalo Bay Auction Company)

Puzzle Blocks, Germany, 1890s, set of 12 w/fairy tale on ea side, EX (worn box), A $300.00

Puzzle Blocks, Three Bears, Geo Rutledge & Sons, complete, VG (VG box), A $550.00

Puzzle Blocks, 12 cb/wood cubes in paper on wood 12x16x4" box, many circus themes, guide sheets, EX, A......$1,400.00

Soldier Shooting Set, 38 cb soldiers on wooden bases w/2 pistols & cannon, 6" soldiers, EX, A $550.00

Spelling Blocks, Emb Co, 1900, set of 18 w/various animals & letters, EX (VG box), A $300.00

Train, Bliss, B&M Railroad, w/loco & 3 gondolas, 23", VG, A...$1,700.00

Train, Bliss, Lincoln Park Railroad, loco & 3 cars w/6-pc puzzle, 21", VG, A $1,250.00

Train, Bliss, locomotive w/solid disk wheels, 3 cars, ea 10" L, EX, A...$4,950.00

Train, Bliss, New York Central Railroad, loco & 2 cars (1 w/7 blocks), 27", EX, A..$2,400.00

Trinity Chimes, turned columns, cathedral scenes in upright case, 8 chimes, 18", VG, A.......................................$175.00

United States & Canada Express, Bliss 1895, wagon containing blocks (half are missing), 17" L, EX, A $375.00

Pedal Cars and Other Wheeled Goods

Just like Daddy, all little boys (and girls as well) are thrilled and happy to drive a brand new shiny car. Today both generations search through flea markets and auto swap meets for cars, boats, fire engines, tractors, and trains that run not on gas but pedal power. Some of the largest manufacturers of wheeled goods were AMF (American Machine and Foundry Company), Murray, and Garton. Values depend to a very large extent on condition, and those that have been restored may sell for upwards of $1000.00, depending on year and model.

Advisor: Nate Stoller (S7).

Airplane, Murray - Otto Mfg Co, pressed steel, prop turns when plane is pedaled, EX, 45" long, A, $2,900.00. (Photo courtesy Noel Barrett Antiques and Auctions)

Austin Healy Convertible, metal with rubber tires, vinyl seats, original condition, G, A, $800.00. (Photo courtesy Noel Barrett Antiques and Auctions)

Air Pilot, Am National, orange w/gr wing & tail, 50", prof rstr $2,300.00

Allis Chalmers C Tractor & Cart, ca 1950s, tractor missing 1 pedal & hubcap, cart has dents & sm cracks, VG ..$1,500.00

Allis Chalmers CA, minor dents, needs rpt, VG.........$1,075.00

Atomic Missile, Murray, 1950s, wht plane-type vehicle w/bl & orange trim, chain drive, 2 levers, 44", rstr...........$2,500.00

Austin J40, England, 1950s, electric headlights, nickel-plated grille, bumpers & hood ornament, 61", VG, A $1,600.00

Biplane, wht & red sheet metal & wood w/gold accents, 52" L, prof rstr, A...$900.00

Black Beauty, Corcoran Mfg, 1930, pnt steel, raises up & down as it moves forward, 40" L, VG+ $2,700.00

BMC Special Race Car #8, rubber tires, 41", G...........$1,250.00

Boat, Murray, rear outboard motor , 47", prof rstr, A......$825.00

Bugatti Racer, 1920s, bl w/silver tires, hood opens, 48", prof rstr, A...$2,500.00

Buick, Lines Brothers, ca 1930, bl w/blk trim, red wheels, driver door opens, 38" L, EX...$1,025.00

Cadillac Continental, cream w/gold stripes, 40", EX orig...$1,400.00

Casey Jones Cannonball Express No 9, red & blk w/ yel lettering, 45", G orig, A $600.00

Casey Jones Train, missing smokestack, orig, VG $625.00

Caterpillar Bulldozer, red, 41", G orig, A......................$1,850.00

Caterpillar Diesel Tractor, New London Metal Products, 1950s, yel w/blk detail, rubber treads, rstr, S7, from $3,000 to ...$6,000.00

Champion Ball Roadster, Murray, prof rstr, from $900 to .$1,000.00

Champion Wrecker, Murray, cream w/red detail, airplane hood ornament, working boom, 46", prof rstr.................$1,200.00

Champion 610, Murray, bl w/wht detail, 36", G orig, A..$600.00

Earth Mover Dump Truck, Murray, 1961, M, restored, from $1,100.00 to $1,500.00. (Photo courtesy Nate Stoller)

Farmall 450, Eska, all orig w/VG decals, VG+ $825.00

FBI Radio Cruiser, 1950s, 37", EX orig...........................$700.00

Fire Chief, Murray Ace, Steelcraft, 1940s, red, all orig, VG+...$450.00

Fire Dept #1, AMF, needs rpt, 18x36" L, VG..................$450.00

Fire Engine, Murray, 'sad face' style, w/2 ladders, prof rstr, from $1,000 to...$1,500.00

Fire Fighter Unit No 508, AMF, red w/yel decals, 42", G orig $200.00

Fire Truck, AMF, ladder racks & wooden ladders, NM (new old stock), A..$1,300.00

Ford, Gaston, 1937, gr w/cream detail & interior, rstr, from $1,500 to...$1,800.00

Ford, Steelcraft, 1936, red w/cream detail, 36", prof rstr, A..$1,800.00

Ford Mustang, w/gear shift, red w/wht detail, VG orig.............$850.00

Hot-Rod #5, Garton, lime gr w/blk & maroon detail, 35", prof rstr, A..$900.00

International Harvester 400, red, all orig, VG...............$500.00

Jeepster, 1945, prof rstr $900.00

Chrysler Convertible, Steelcraft, 1941, hard to find, M, restored, from $2,225.00 to $2,500.00. (Photo courtesy Nate Stoller)

Dan Patch Racer, metal & wood w/bl spoke wheels, DP label on doors, 50", EX orig...$350.00

Dump Truck, Murray, jet flow drive, working dump body & tailgate, 48", VG/EX, A...$650.00

Dump Truck No 742, Murray Jet Flow, red & blk, 46", prof rstr, A...$850.00

Farmall, Eska, 1950s, all orig, needs rpt o/w EX.............$875.00

Farmall 400 Tractor, ESKA, cast aluminum, 38", prof rstr, A $500.00

Jet Flower No. 742 Dump Truck, Murray, push lever at back to dump, 46" long, M, restored, $850.00.

John Deere, Ertl #520, cast aluminum, rpt to top of hood, 38", EX, A $175.00

John Deere #130 Tractor & Wagon, rpt, EX...............$1,150.00

John Deere Tracor & Wagon, Ertl #520, 65" L, EX, A, from $400 to..$500.00
John Deere 60, Eska, 1954, rstr, EX, from $550 to..........$750.00
Kidillac, Garten, late, scarce, G, from $700 to $1,000.00
Lincoln Zephyr, Garton, ca 1937, cream w/orange trim & red pinstripe, cream wheels w/chrome hubs, 45", rstr.$4,000.00
Lincoln Zephyr, Steelcraft, 1940, 44", prof rstr, A.......$1,800.00
Lincoln Zephyr, 1930s, red w/wht detail, chrome bumper & hubcaps, 40", prof rstr, A $3,500.00
Mack Fire Truck, Steelcraft, 1939, prof rstr $2,000.00
Massey Ferguson Tractor #1100AP, Ertl, late 1970s, NRFB $450.00

Mobo Horse, England (?), ca 1930s – 50s, M, restored, from $850.00 to $1,200.00. (Photo courtesy Nate Stoller)

Mustang, AMF Junior, yel, missing 1 hubcap, EX...........$575.00
Mustang, Junior Toy Division AMF, plastic hubs, spoke wheels, detailed gauges on dash, 40", prof rstr, A $500.00
Mustang Convertible, Am Machine & Foundry, red w/cream detail, 39½", prof rstr, A...$500.00
Oliver Super 88, Eska, rpt, rpl pedals, rims & tires, EX...$1,400.00
Packard, Gendron, gr w/blk detail, chrome lights, windshield, steering wheel & luggage rack, prof rstr, from $4,000 to ...$5,000.00
Palge Car, Gendron, spoke wheels, 52", VG orig $12,500.00
Red Baron Plane, red canvas over wood w/radial engine design & machine guns, pressed steel fuselage, 60" L, prof rstr, A $925.00
Rickenbacker Fire Chief Car, Am National, 1920s, pressed steel w/wood chassis, red & yel pinstriping, 42", G $1,800.00
Roadster, maroon & silver, 38", prof rstr, A.................$1,000.00
Roamer, Am National, w/tonneau, gr w/yel & blk detail, red hubcaps, prof rstr, from $3,000 to $5,000.00
Sand & Gravel Dump Truck, Murray #7, 'sad face,' lift lever & back dumps, 49", EX prof rstr, A $1,200.00

Silver King, Toledo, detailed dash etc, EX, from $3,500 to...$4,500.00
Skipper, Murray, wht w/red & yel trim, missing front light, VG $635.00
Space Cruiser, Garton, 1953, 3-wheeled, extra wide seat, 48" L, VG+ $675.00
Spirit of St Louis, Am National, 1932, gray & red w/blk & yel trim, pneumatic tires w/red skokes, 36" wingspan, rstr........$4,500.00
Streamliner, Steelcraft, chrome-plated trim, tufted leather upholstery, 49", rstr, A..$2,500.00
Studebaker, 1950s, lt aqua bl, all orig, EX $725.00
Super-Sonic Jet, Murray, wht w/red & chrome detail, EX orig, from $800 to $1,200.00
Super-Sonic Jet, Murray, 1950s, needs rpt, G $635.00
US Mail Airplane, red sheet metal w/wood seat, blk rubber tires w/red wheels, 39", VG..$400.00
Volkswagen Convertible, red w/blk tires, plastic trim, 33", VG orig $350.00
White Tractor, Scale Models, cast aluminum w/plastic seat, 38", EX pnt & decals, A..$175.00
Woody Station Wagon, Steelcraft, 1941, prof rstr.......$2,300.00
3-Wheels Police Motorcycle, Evans, 1940s-50s, red, 24x36" L, EX $530.00

Trike, ca 1930s, M, restored, $1,800.00. (Photo courtesy Nate Stoller)

Wagons

Airflow Express, Mills Novelty, mk Phantom Patrol, dk gr & cream w/wooden wheels, 17", rstr, A $265.00
Streak Lite Express, blk & silver streamline wagon w/battery-op headlights, 32", prof rstr, A $650.00

Penny Toys

Penny toys were around as early as the late 1800s and as late as the 1920s. Many were made in Germany, but some were made in France as well. With few exceptions, they ranged in size from 5" on down; some had moving parts, and a few had clockwork mechanisms. Though many were unmarked, you'll sometimes find them signed 'Kellermann,' 'Meier,' 'Fischer,' or 'Distler,' or carrying an embossed company logo such as the 'dog and cart' emblem. They were made of lithographed tin with exquisite detailing — imagine an entire carousel less than 2½" tall. Because of a recent surge in collector interest, many have been crossing the auction block of some of the country's large galleries. Our values are prices realized at several of these auctions.

Advisors: Kerry and Judy Irvin (K5).

Airplane, Distler, red & yel 4-prop, w/pilot, orig pull string, EX $1,200.00
Ambulance, Fischer, yel w/red tires, 4", EX, A $325.00
Armored Tank Car, Distler, VG, A $175.00
Baby Carriage, gr, blk & cream w/spoke wheels, 3½", EX, A $250.00
Baby in Rolling Chair w/Nanny, Meier, 3¼", EX $385.00
Bellows Camera Mounted on Tripod, Meier, 5", EX.......$310.00
Boat, Germany, mk JD, ca 1920, litho tin, gr w/blk smokestack, 1½x5", EX...$145.00
Boy in Rocking Chair, mk Ges Gesch, boy holding ball in hand, 3x2¾", EX...$475.00
Boy on Sled, boy on stomach w/feet in the air, 3½", VG...$300.00
Boy on Sled, Meier, mc, 3", EX, A $425.00
Cat on Wheels, gray striped cat on gr platform w/4 wheels, 2½x3½", EX $105.00
Child in Stroller, Germany, ca 1910, 3", EX, A $300.00
Chinaman w/Parasol on Cart, 4 spoke wheels, 3", EX, A ..$300.00
Clown in Barrel, Stock & Co, clown's head & feet protruding from barrel, 3" L, VG...$250.00

Donkey-Drawn Cart w/Driver, 6", VG, A.......................$150.00
Double-Decker Bus, Fisher, mk General, clockwork, 4¾", EX $550.00
Field Kitchen Auto, Meier, w/driver, VG, A $275.00
Fire Ladder Truck, Meier, fireman on open bench seats w/ladders on platform bed, spoke wheels, 3½", EX..................$225.00
Fire Pumper Truck, Meier, w/driver, 3", EX, A...............$350.00
Fire Truck, Meier, ca 1910, spinning motor, 3⅛x2¼", NM ...$285.00
Garage w/2 Cars, Germany, mk CKO, bl garage w/red roof, 1 yel open car, 1 gr sedan, 3½" sq garage, 3¼" cars, EX ...$125.00
Girl in Cart Pulled by Goat, Meier, slight pnt loss, EX ..$195.00
Gnome on Easter Egg w/Rabbit on Wheeled Platform, Meier, EX $825.00
Goat on Platform, Meier, blk & wht w/red bell collar, silver-tone platform, 3", EX $300.00
Hen Pecking at Egg on Platform, 3", EX $250.00
Horse-Drawn Cab, Fischer, w/driver, mc w/red spoke wheels, 4", EX, A $225.00
Horse-Drawn Carriage, Meier, driver on open bench seat, single wht horse, spoke wheels, 5", EX $250.00

Horse-Drawn Military Wagon, Meier, yellow and black with red wheels, polychromed horses, 4½", EX, A, $800.00.

Horse-Drawn Postal Van, Meier, metallic gold, dapple gray horse, 5½", EX...$250.00
Japanese Battleship, w/6 flags, 4 spoke wheels, 4¼", VG ..$800.00

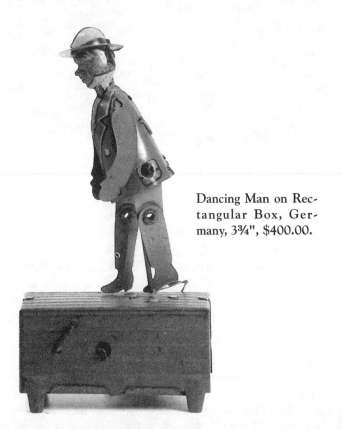

Dancing Man on Rectangular Box, Germany, 3¾", $400.00.

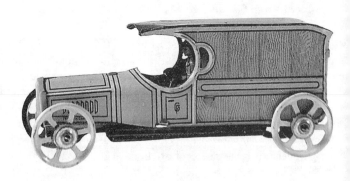

Limousine, 4", VG, $190.00. (Photo courtesy Continental Hobby House)

Man Feeding Dog, Germany, red rectangular base, EX...$650.00
Man Pushing Wheelbarrow, mc, 3", EX, A $175.00
Military Motorcycle w/Sidecar, w/2 figures, 4", G, A $150.00
Motorcycle, Spain, 1925, w/driver, 4", NM, A $225.00
Motorcycle w/Driver, Kellerman, 2", VG, A...................$500.00
Motorcycle w/Driver, Meier, 1910-20, gr motorcycle w/driver in orange & wht, 4⅜", EX $225.00

Oceanliner, Japan, 1930s, red & blk w/yel rnd windows, 2¾", VG $100.00
Porter Pushing Cart w/Trunk, Fischer, 3", EX $400.00
Race Car, Germany, w/driver, 'GF' on doors, 4¾", EX ...$250.00
Racer #14, Distler, wht w/bl trim, wht spoke wheels w/side spare, w/driver, 4", VG..$325.00
Sedan, Fisher, 4", VG $150.00
St Bernard on Wheels, Germany, 3¼x2¾", EX..............$385.00
Steam Engine, Distler, operating piston & wheel, 4", VG ..$350.00
Steamship, Germany, ca 1915, wht w/red & bl trim, 2 smoke stacks, EX $160.00
Touring Car, red, yel & cream, w/driver, 3", NM............$400.00
Touring Sedan, w/driver & 4 passengers, gr w/yel trim, 4½", VG+ $160.00
Tractor w/Driver, 4½", G, A.....................................$100.00
Train Set, Japan, prewar, w/loco, tender & 5 cars, 13", NM (G box), A..$250.00
Train Set, 5 pcs, 15", EX (worn box), A.......................$200.00
Trolley, Germany, gr & yel sides w/blk roof, 4⅜" L, EX..$260.00

Pez Dispensers

Pez was originally designed as a breath mint for smokers, but by the '50s kids were the target market, and the candies were packaged in the dispensers that we all know and love today. There is already more than three hundred variations to collect, and more arrive on the supermarket shelves every day. Though early on collectors seemed to prefer the dispensers without feet, that attitude has changed, and now it's the character head they concentrate on. Feet were added in 1987, so if you were to limit yourself to only 'feetless' dispensers, your collection would be far from complete. Some dispensers have variations in color and design that can influence their values. Don't buy any that are damaged, incomplete, or that have been tampered with in any way; those are nearly worthless. For more information refer to *A Pictorial Guide to Plastic Candy Dispensers Featuring Pez* by David Welch and *Collecting Toys* #6 by Richard O'Brien. Values are for mint-condition dispensers unless noted otherwise.

Advisor: Richard Belyski (B1).
Other Sources: B10, H4, P10.

Aardvark, w/ft $5.00
Angel, no ft $50.00
Arlene, w/ft, pk, from $3 to $5.00
Asterix Line, Asterix, Obelix, Roman or Getafix, ea from $4 to $6.00
Baloo, w/ft $20.00
Bambi, no ft..$50.00
Barney Bear, no ft...$40.00
Barney Bear, w/ft..$30.00
Baseball Glove, no ft $175.00
Batgirl, no ft, soft head $125.00
Batman, no ft $10.00
Batman, no ft, w/cape...$100.00
Batman, w/ft, bl or blk, ea, from $3 to $5.00
Betsy Ross, no ft...$150.00

Bouncer Beagle, w/ft $6.00
Boy, w/ft, brn hair $3.00
Bozo, no ft, diecut $200.00
Bubble Man, w/ft..$5.00
Bubble Man, w/ft, neon hat $6.00
Bugs Bunny, no ft $15.00
Bugs Bunny, w/ft, from $1 to $3.00
Bullwinkle, no ft $275.00
Bullwinkle, no ft $275.00
Candy Shooter, red & wht, w/candy & gun license, unused ...$125.00
Captain America, no ft...$100.00
Captain Hook, no ft...$85.00
Casper, no ft...$225.00
Charlie Brown, w/ft, from $1 to $3.00
Charlie Brown, w/ft & tongue....................................$20.00
Chicago Cubs 2000, Charlie Brown in pkg w/commerative card $50.00
Chick, w/ft, from $1 to...$3.00
Chick in Egg, no ft $25.00
Chick in Egg, no ft, w/hair $125.00
Chip, w/ft $80.00
Clown, w/ft, whistle head $6.00
Clown w/Collar, no ft $65.00
Cockatoo, no ft, bl face, red beak $60.00
Cool Cat, w/ft $65.00
Cow (A or B), no ft, bl, ea, from $80 to.......................$90.00
Creature From the Black Lagoon, no ft.......................$300.00
Crocodile, no ft $95.00
Crystal Hearts, eBay, limited edition, set of 4 ....$10.00
Daffy Duck, no ft...$15.00
Daffy Duck, w/ft, from $1 to $3.00
Dalmatian Pup, w/ft $50.00
Daniel Boone, no ft $200.00
Dino, w/ft, purple, from $1 to $3.00
Dinosaur, w/ft, 4 different, ea, from $1 to $3.00

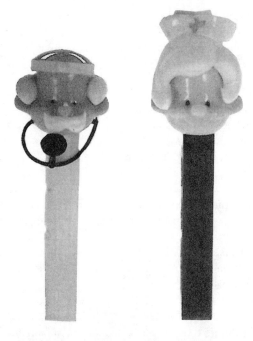

Doctor, $225.00; Nurse, blond hair, $175.00.

Donald Duck, no ft, diecut $175.00
Donald Duck, no ft, from $10 to $15.00
Donald Duck's Nephew, no ft $30.00
Donald Duck's Nephew, w/ft, gr, bl or red hat, ea $10.00
Donkey, w/ft, whistle head $6.00
Droopy Dog (A), no ft, plastic swivel ears $25.00
Droopy Dog (B), w/ft, pnt ears, MIP................................$6.00
Duck Tales, any character, w/ft, ea...................................$6.00
Dumbo, w/ft, bl head..$25.00
Eerie Spectres, Air Spirit, Diabolic or Zombie (no ft), ea ..$200.00
Fat-Ears Rabbit, no ft, pk head $20.00
Fat-Ears Rabbit, no ft, yel head $15.00
Fireman, no ft...$95.00
Fishman, no ft, gr..$185.00
Foghorn Leghorn, w/ft...$95.00
Football Player $175.00
Fozzie Bear, w/ft, from $1 to $3.00
Frankenstein, no ft..$300.00
Fred Flintstone, w/ft, from $1 to $3.00
Frog, w/ft, whistle head $40.00
Garfield, w/ft, orange w/gr hat, from $1 to $3.00
Garfield, w/ft, teeth, from $1 to $3.00
Garfield, w/ft, visor, from $1 to $3.00
Gargamel, w/ft...$5.00
Girl, w/ft, yel hair $3.00
Glow-in-the-Dark Ghost Set, set of 4, MOC.....................$15.00
Glowing Ghosts (heads glow in the dark), Polly Pumpkin, Naughty
     Neil, Happy Henry or Slimy Sid, ea from $4 to $6.00
Gonzo, w/ft, from $1 to $3.00
Goofy, no ft, ea...$10.00
Gorilla, no ft, blk head..$80.00
Green Hornet, 1960s, from $200 to $250.00
Gyro Gearloose, w/ft...$6.00
Henry Hawk, no ft $65.00
Hulk, no ft, dk gr..$60.00
Hulk, no ft, lt gr, remake $3.00
Indian, w/ft, whistle head $20.00
Indian Brave, no ft, reddish $150.00
Indian Chief, no ft, yel headdress...................................$100.00
Indian Maiden, no ft...$150.00
Inspector Clouseau, w/ft...$5.00
Jerry Mouse, w/ft, plastic face $15.00
Jerry Mouse, w/ft, pnt face $6.00
Jiminy Cricket, no ft...$200.00
Joker (Batman), no ft, soft head $175.00
Jungle Mission, interactive dispenser $10.00
Kermit the Frog, w/ft, red, from $1 to $3.00
Knight, no ft $300.00
Koala, w/ft, whistle head...$40.00
Krazy Animals, Blinky Bill, Lion, Hippo, Elephant or Gator, ea
     from $4 to...$6.00
Lamb, no ft...$15.00
Lamb, w/ft, from $1 to..$3.00
Lamb, w/ft, whistle head $20.00
Lazy Garfield, w/ft..$5.00
Li'l Bad Wolf, w/ft...$20.00
Lion w/Crown, no ft $100.00
Lion's Club Lion, minimum value...............................$2,000.00

Lucy, w/ft, from $1 to $3.00
Make-A-Face, works like Mr Potato Head, minimum value..$2,500.00
Mary Poppins, no ft $1,300.00
Merlin Mouse, w/ft...$20.00
Merry Melody Makers, rhino, donkey, panda, parrot, clown, tiger
     or penguin, w/ft, MOC, ea..$6.00
Mexican, no ft...$250.00
Mickey Mouse, no ft, removable nose or cast nose, ea from $10
     to $15.00
Mickey Mouse, w/ft, from $1 to $3.00
Mimic Monkey (monkey w/ball cap), no ft, several colors,
     ea $40.00
Miss Piggy, w/ft, ea from $1 to...$3.00
Miss Piggy, w/ft, eyelashes...$15.00
Monkey Sailor, no ft, w/wht cap......................................$50.00
Mowgli, w/ft..$15.00
Muscle Mouse (gray Jerry), w/ft, plastic nose $15.00
Nermal, w/ft, gray...$3.00
Nintendo, Mario, Yoshi, Koopa Trooper or Diddy Dong, ea from
     $4 to $6.00
Non-Glowing Ghosts, Naughty Neil, Happy Henry or Slimy
     Sid, ea...$2.00
Nurse, no ft, brn hair $175.00
Octopus, no ft, blk $85.00
Odie, w/ft..$5.00
Olive Oyl, no ft..$200.00
Panda, no ft, diecut eyes $20.00
Panda, w/ft, remake, from $1 to $3.00
Panda, w/ft, whistle head $6.00
Papa Smurf, w/ft, red $6.00
Parrot, w/ft, whistle head $6.00
Pebbles Flintstone, w/ft, from $1 to $3.00
Penguin, w/ft, whistle head $6.00
Penguin (Batman), no ft, soft head $175.00
Peter Pez (A), no ft..$65.00
Peter Pez (B & C), w/ft, from $1 to $3.00

Pirate, $50.00; Elephant, $80.00; Mr. Ugly, $45.00.

Pilgrim, no ft $150.00
Pink Panther, w/ft $5.00
Pinocchio, no ft $150.00
Pluto, no ft $10.00
Pluto, w/ft, from $1 to $3.00
Pokemon, non US; Pikachu, Mew, Psyduck, Kottins, Meowith,
    ea, from $5 to $10.00
Popeye (B), no ft $115.00
Popeye (C), no ft, w/removable pipe $110.00
Practical Pig (B), no ft $30.00
Psychedelic Eye, no ft $500.00
Psychedelic Eye, remake, blk or pk, MOC, ea $20.00
Psychedelic Flower, no ft $550.00
Pumpkin (A), no ft, from $10 to $15.00
Pumpkin (B), w/ft, from $1 to $3.00
Raven, no ft, yel beak $70.00
Rhino, w/ft, whistle head $6.00
Ringmaster, no ft $275.00
Road Runner, no ft $20.00
Road Runner, w/ft $15.00
Rooster, w/ft, whistle head $35.00
Rooster, w/ft, wht or yel head, ea $30.00
Rudolph, no ft $50.00
Santa Claus, w/ft, from $1 to $3.00

Policeman, $55.00; Stewardess, $175.00.

Santa Claus (A), no ft, steel pin $125.00
Santa Claus (B), no ft $125.00
Santa Claus (C), no ft, from $5 to $15.00
Santa Claus (C), w/ft, B1, from $1 to $3.00
Scrooge McDuck (A), no ft $35.00
Scrooge McDuck (B), w/ft $6.00
Sheik, no ft $55.00
Skull (A), no ft, from $5 to $10.00
Skull (B), w/ft, from $1 to $3.00
Smurf, w/ft $5.00
Smurfette, w/ft $5.00
Snoopy, w/ft, from $1 to $3.00
Snow White, no ft $175.00
Snowman (A), no ft $10.00
Snowman (B), w/ft, from $1 to $5.00
Space Trooper Robot, no ft, full body $325.00
Spaceman, no ft $200.00
Speedy Gonzales (A), w/ft $15.00
Speedy Gonzales (B), no ft, from $1 to $3.00
Spider-Man, no ft, from $10 to $15.00
Spider-Man, w/ft, from $1 to $3.00
Spike, w/ft, B1 ....$6.00
Star Wars, Darth Vader, C3PO, Storm Trooper or Chewbacca,
    ea from $1 to $3.00
Star Wars, Princess Leia, Luke Skywalker, Ewok or Boba Fett, ea
    from $1 to $3.00
Sylvester (A), w/ft, cream or wht whiskers, ea $5.00
Sylvester (B), w/ft, from $1 to $3.00
Teenage Mutant Ninja Turtles, w/ft, 8 variations, ea from $1
    to $3.00
Thor, no ft $300.00
Thumper, w/ft, no copyright $45.00
Tiger, w/ft, whistle head $6.00

Tom, $35.00.

Tinkerbell, no ft $275.00
Tom, w/ft, plastic face $15.00
Tom, w/ft, pnt face $6.00
Truck, many variations, ea, minimum value.......................$1.00
Tweety Bird, no ft...$10.00
Tweety Bird, w/ft, from $1 to $3.00
Tyke, w/ft...$15.00
Uncle Sam, no ft..$175.00
Valentine Heart, B1, from $1 to $3.00
Wal-Mart Smiley Pez, ea from $1 to $2.00
Whistle, w/ft, from $1 to $3.00
Wile E Coyote, w/ft...$60.00
Winnie the Pooh, A, w/ft $75.00
Winnie the Pooh; Pooh (B), Tigger, Eeore, Piglet, ea from $1
    to $2.00
Witch, 3-pc, no ft..$10.00
Wolfman, no ft...$300.00
Wonder Woman, no ft, soft head $185.00
Wonder Woman, w/ft, from $1 to $3.00
Woodstock, w/ft, from $1 to..$3.00
Woodstock, w/ft, pnt feathers $15.00
Yappy Dog, no ft, orange or gr, ea $65.00
Yosemite Sam, w/ft, from $1 to $3.00
Zorro, MIP, C10 ....$200.00

MISCELLANEOUS

Bank, truck #1, metal $200.00
Bank, truck #2, metal $40.00
Body Parts, fit over stem of dispenser & make it look like a per-
    son, many variations, ea......................................$1.00
Bracelet, pk...$5.00
Bubble Wand..$6.00
Clicker, US Zone Germany, 1950, litho tin, 3½", NM ..$300.00
Clicker, 1960s, metal, 2", EX, N2 ....$45.00

Coin Plate $15.00
Coloring Book, Safety #2, non-English, B1.........................$15.00
Power Pez, rnd mechanical dispenser, B1 ....$5.00
Puzzle, Ceaco, 550 pcs, MIB $30.00
Puzzle, Springbok/Hallmark, 500 pcs...............................$15.00
Refrigerator Magnet Set...$10.00
Snow Dome, bride & groom, 4½", M..................................$20.00
Snow Dome, ringmaster & elephant, M...............................$20.00
Tin, Pez Specials, stars & lines on checked background, gold col-
    ors, 2½x4½", rare, EX $225.00
Toy Car, Johnny Lightning Psychedelic Eye racer $20.00
Toy Car, Johnny Lightning Racing Dreams PEZ racer......$10.00
Watch, pk face w/yel band or yel face w/bl band, ea $10.00
Watch, Psychedelic Hand...$10.00
Yo-yo, 1950s, litho metal w/peppermint pkg, rare, NM ..$300.00

Pin-Back Buttons

Pin-back buttons produced up to the early 1920s were made with a celluloid covering. After that time, a large number of buttons were lithographed on tin; these are referred to as tin 'lithos.'

Character and toy-related buttons represent a popular collecting field. There are countless categories to base a collection on. Buttons were given out at stores and theatres, offered as premiums, attached to dolls, or received with a club membership.

In the late '40s and into the '50s, some cereal companies packed one in each box of their product. Quaker Puffed Oats offered a series of movie star pin-backs, but probably the best known are Kellogg's Pep Pins. There were eighty-six in all, so theoretically if you wanted the whole series as Kellogg hoped you would, you'd have to buy at least that many boxes of their cereal. Pep pins came in five sets, the first in 1945, three more in 1946, and the last in 1947. They were printed with full-color lithographs of comic characters licensed by King Features and Famous Artists — Maggie and Jiggs, the Winkles, and Dagwood and Blondie, for instance. Superman, the only D.C. Comics character, was included in each set. Most Pep pins range in value from $10.00 to $15.00 in NM/M condition, but some sell for much more.

Nearly all pin-backs are collectible. Be sure that you buy only buttons with well-centered designs, well-alligned colors, no fading or yellowing, no spots or stains, and no cracks, splits, or dents. In the listings that follow, sizes are approximate.

Advisors: Michael and Polly McQuillen (M11).

Other Source: C10.

See also Political; Premiums; Sporting Collectibles.

Banana Splits, 1972, colorful image on gr, M....................$40.00
Bartman Evenger of Evil, Button-Up, image & Watch-It Dude,
    6" dia, MOC, K1 ....$5.00
Batman, Creative, 1966, I'm a Batman Crime Fighter, 1½" dia,
    EX..$10.00
Batman, 1966, Join the Secret Society & colorful image of Bat-
    man & Robin, 3½" dia, MIP $25.00
Beatles, blk & wht group photo w/names in red, 3½" dia, NM,
    B3...$30.00

Beatles, flashes from full-figure photo to head shots w/names, 2½" dia, EX, B3 ....$30.00

Beatles, flashes from I Like the Beatles to head shots, red or bl, 2½" dia, NM, ea...$35.00

Beatles, I Love the Beatles, bl & red on wht, 3½" dia, NM, B3 ....$25.00

Beatles, Vari-vue, flashes from full-figures to I Love Ringo, I Love Paul or I Love John, 2½" dia, NM, ea $30.00

Beatles, We All Live in a Yellow Submarine, 1980s, yel, orange & blk on wht, 1¾" dia, NM, B3 ....$5.00

Beatles, Yeah, Yeah, Yeah, red, wht & bl, 3½" dia, EX, B3 ....$35.00

Bill Haley & His Comets Fan Club, 1950s, blk & wht photo on wht, 2" dia, EX $60.00

Bozo the Clown, 1960-61, 3" dia, EX, T2 ....$15.00

Breathless Mahoney, 1980s, image & lettering in red, M .$15.00

Captain America Official Member Super Hero Club, Button World, 1966, full-color image, 3" dia, NM, T2 ....$50.00

Dale Evans, 1950s, blk & wht photo on gr, 1½" dia, EX ..$40.00

Dick Tracy Secret Service Patrol Member, Quaker, 1939, EX, D11 ....$25.00

Elvis, Always Your Elvis & image on red, ⅞" dia, NM $25.00

Felix for President, 1¼" dia, EX, C10............................$25.00

Fonzie, 1970s, Fonz Is Cool & image, 3" dia, NM $8.00

Fox Grandpa Prize Badge, early 1900s, mc tin & celluloid, 1¼" dia, NM..$65.00

Green Hornet Society Official Member, Button World, 1966, flying insect logo, 3" dia, NM....................................$50.00

Hawkman Official Member Super Hero Club, Button World, 1966, full-color image, 3" dia, NM $30.00

Howdy Doody, New Color Comic — Sunday News, 2", $65.00.

Lone Ranger, multicolored, 1950s, $50.00. (Photo courtesy Lee Felbinger)

Mickey Mouse, Official Mickey Mouse Store, 1937, 1½" dia, NM..$50.00

Mickey Mouse Club, 1928-30, blk lettering, 1¼" dia, NM, A $125.00

Mickey Mouse Club, 1970s, w/logo, 1¼" dia, NM............$10.00

Mickey's Birthdayland, 1980s, 3" dia, NM $10.00

Mod Mickey, Beny-Albee, late 1960s, 3½" dia, NM $25.00

Monkees, 1967, cartoon image on wht, 1" dia, M............$10.00

Peanuts, Charlie Brown, 1970s, Go Fly a Kite & image, 2" dia, NM..$5.00

Peanuts, Curse You, Red Baron!, Ace Snoopy on his doghouse on bull's-eye design, 6" dia, M, from $15 to $20.00

Peanuts, It's the Great Pumpkin Charlie Brown, 1991, bl background, 6", NM..$20.00

Peanuts, Snoopy, 1970s, Born To Sleep & image of Snoopy asleep on doghouse, 2", NM $4.00

Hopalong Savings Club, red and black on white, 3", $45.00.

Howdy Doody's 40th Birthday, 1988, Fries Distribution Co surrounds image, 3½" dia, EX $25.00

Huckleberry Hound for President, 1960, yel background, 3" dia, EX...$25.00

Lion King, 1993, rectangular, 2⅛x3⅛", NM.....................$4.00

Peanuts, Snoopy & Peppermint Patty, 1970s, Just Call Me Sugar
    Lips, 2", NM..$5.00
Peanuts, Snoopy for President, Snoopy in top hat, red, wht & bl,
    3", M..$15.00
Peanuts, You're a Good Man Charlie Brown, 1960s, orange
    background, NM..$12.00

Peanuts, 1975, 4", $30.00. (Photo courtesy Andrea Podley & Derrick Bang)

Purple People Eater, NM, C10...$12.00
Raggedy Ann, Bobbs-Merrill, 1974, Start Each Day w/a Smile,
    3½" dia, EX...$15.00
Shaun Cassidy as Joe Hardy, Fun Time, 1978, photo image, 3"
    dia, NM..$6.00
Spooknik, NM, C10...$20.00
Starsky & Hutch, 1970s, several variations, NM, ea $15.00
Tarzan Signal Club, NM, C10..$110.00
Thor Official Member Super Hero Club, Button World, 1966,
    full color image, MIP, T2 ....$75.00
Universal Monsters, Creature From the Black Lagoon, Mummy,
    or Phantom of the Opera, NM, C10, ea.....................$25.00
Wonder Woman Sensation Comics, DC Comics, 1940s, full-color
    portrait w/yel border, 1" dia, rare, from $800 to $1,000.00

KELLOGG'S PEP PINS

BO Plenty, NM $30.00
Corky, NM $16.00
Dagwood, NM..$30.00
Dick Tracy, NM..$30.00
Fat Stuff, NM...$15.00
Felix the Cat, NM...$85.00
Flash Gordon, NM..$23.00
Flat Top, NM..$23.00
Goofy, NM $10.00
Gravel Gertie, NM $15.00
Harold Teen, NM..$15.00
Inspector, NM $12.50
Jiggs, NM..$25.00

Judy, NM $10.00
Kayo, NM $12.00
Little King, NM $15.00
Little Moose, NM $15.00
Maggie, NM $25.00
Mama De Stross, NM..$30.00
Mama Katzenjammer, NM...$25.00
Mamie, NM $15.00
Moon Mullins, NM $6.00
Olive Oyl, NM...$18.00

Orphan   Annie,
NM, $25.00

Pat Patton, NM...$10.00
Perry Winkle, NM $15.00
Phantom, NM $80.00
Pop Jenks, NM..$15.00
Popeye, NM $30.00
Rip Winkle, NM $20.00
Skeezix, NM..$15.00
Superman, NM..$45.00
Toots, NM $15.00

Uncle Walt, NM,
$20.00.

Uncle Willie, NM..$12.50
Winkle Twins, NM $50.00
Winnie Winkle, NM..$15.00

Plastic Figures

Plastic figures were made by many toy companies. They were first boxed with playsets, but in the early '50s, some became available individually. Marx was the first company to offer single figures (at 10¢ each), and even some cereal companies included one in boxes of their product. (Kellogg offered a series of sixteen 54mm Historic Warriors, and Nabisco had a line of ten dinosaurs in marbleized, primary colors.) Virtually every type of man and beast has been modeled in plastic; today some have become very collectible and expensive. There are a lot of factors you'll need to be aware of to be a wise buyer. For instance, Marx made cowboys during the mid-'60s in a flat finish, and these are much harder to find and more valuable than the later figures with a waxy finish. Marvel Super Heroes in the fluorescent hues are worth about half as much as the earlier, light gray issue. Because of limited space, it isn't possible to evaluate more than a representative few of these plastic figures in a general price guide, so if you'd like to learn more about them, we recommend *Geppert's Guide* by Tim Geppert. See the Clubs, Newsletters, and Other Publications section for information on how to order the *Plastic Figure & Playset Collector* magazine.

Note: All of the listings below are figures by Marx unless noted otherwise.

Advisors: Mike and Kurt Fredericks (F4); Bob Wilson, Phoenix Toy Soldier Co. (P11).

See also Playsets.

ACTION AND ADVENTURE

Alien, 35mm, NM...$5.00
Apollo Astronaut Explorers, orange, 54mm, set of 8 in 7 poses, NM...$35.00
Apollo Astronaut Moon Walking, lt bl, 6", EX...................$6.50
Apollo Astronaut w/American FLag, wht, 6", NM..........$14.50
Ben Hur, 54mm, set of 16, NM.......................................$70.00

Captain Video, Lido, 1950s, various poses and colors, 4", $25.00 each. (Photo courtesy June Moon)

Fox Hunt, fox running, 60mm, NM $10.00
Fox Hunt, hound sniffing, 60mm, NM..........................$10.00

Man From UNCLE, Alexander Waverly, steel bl, 6", NM, from $12 to $20.00
Man From UNCLE, Illya Kuryakin, steel bl, 6", NM, from $12 to $20.00
Man From UNCLE, Napoleon Solo, steel bl, 6", NM, from $12 to $20.00

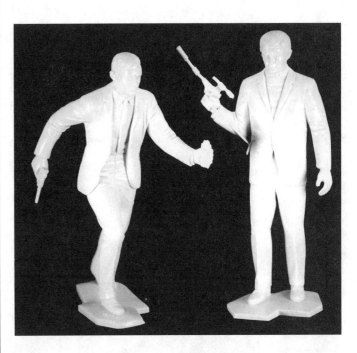

Man From UNCLE, Napoleon Solo and Illya Kuryakin, light gray, 6", NM, $25.00 each. (Watch for Mexican copies in near-exact gray plastic.) (Photo courtesy June Moon)

Royal Canadian Police, Dulcop, NM $5.00
Space Men, Premier, various poses & colors, 3", ea $5.00
Space Patrol, driver seated, tan or orange, 45mm, NM, ea ..$15.00
Spacemen, metallic bl or yel, 45mm, NM, ea.....................$5.00
Sports, bowler, boxer, figure skater, golfer, or runner, wht, 60mm, NM, ea, from $2.50 to..$3.50
Sports, hockey player, matt lt bl, 60mm, NM $12.50
Untouchables, 54mm, NM, ea..$15.00

ANIMALS

Champion Dogs, dachshund, reddish brn, 84mm, NM.......$6.50
Champion Dogs, English setter, brn, 84mm, NM $6.50
Champion Dogs, Scottish terrier, brn, 84mm, NM $6.50
Circus Animals, elephant w/howdah, NM.......................$10.00
Circus Animals, gorilla, NM..$3.00
Farm Stock, colt, 2nd issue, NM......................................$2.00
Farm Stock, cow standing, brn or gray, 60mm, NM, ea from $2 to $5.00
Farm Stock, horse standing, brn, 60mm, NM, from $2 to...$5.00
Farm Stock, hog, 2nd issue, NM.......................................$2.00
Ice-Age Animals, Megatherium (giant sloth), lt gr, NM..$20.00
Ice-Age Animals, Wooly Mammoth (elephant), rust brn, NM, from $10 to...$15.00
North American Wildlife, beaver, reddish brn, 60mm, NM ..$1.00
Prehistoric Dinosaurs, Brontosaurus, gray, NM, ea.............$8.00

Prehistoric Dinosaurs, Dimetrodon, marbled gray, NM, from $5 to $10.00
Prehistoric Dinosaurs, Parasaurolophus, brn, NM, from $5 to.$10.00
Prehistoric Dinosaurs, Plateosaurus, lt gr, NM, ea $5.00
Prehistoric Dinosaurs, Styracosaurus, tan, NM, from $10 to ..$14.00
Prehistoric Dinosaurs, Trachodon, marbled gray, NM, from $5 to $10.00
Prehistoric Dinosaurs, Tyrannosaurus Rex, brn, NM $12.50
Prize Livestock, Clydesdale, tan, 54mm, NM, ea, from $2 to $5.00
Ranch & Rodeo, bucking bronco, reddish brn, 60mm, NM, from $4 to $6.00
Ranch & Rodeo, Indian pony running, various colors, 54mm, EX $3.50
Ranch & Rodeo, longhorn steer halting, reddish brn, 60mm, NM, from $5 to..$10.00
Ranch & Rodeo, pack mule w/pack, dk gray, 60mm, NM ..$35.00
Wild Animals, alligator, red-brn, NM $3.50
Wild Animals, giraffe, beige, NM, from $5 to $10.00
Wild Animals, tiger, Ben Hur..$35.00

CAMPUS CUTIES AND AMERICAN BEAUTIES

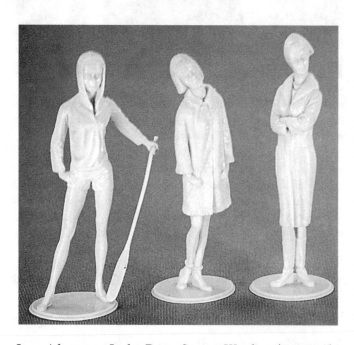

Lazy Afternoon, Lodge Party, Stormy Weather, $8.00 each.

American Beauties, ballerina, 1955, NM $20.00
Campus Cuties, Dinner for Two, M $8.00
Campus Cuties, On the Beach, M $8.00
Campus Cuties, Shoppin Anyone, M $8.00

COMIC, DISNEY, AND NURSERY CHARACTERS

Disney, Babes in Toyland Soldier w/bugle, 60mm, NM $25.00
Disneykid, Wendy, M, M8 ....$35.00
Disneykins, Bagheera, NM, M8..$45.00
Disneykins, Baloo, MIB, from $35 to $45.00
Disneykins, Captain Hook, NM..$14.50

Disneykins, Goofy, MIB, from $15 to...............................$20.00
Disneykins, Shere Khan, NM, M8 ....$60.00
Disneykins, Si, NM, M8 ....$75.00
Disneykins, Sleeping Beauty, NM, M8................................$45.00
Disneykins, Sonny, NM, M8...$60.00
Disneykins TV Scenes, Snow White, 1950s, MIB............$50.00
Fun on Wheels, Brer Rabbit, 1950s, MIB............................$25.00
Fun on Wheels, Olive Oyl, 1950s, 2", scarce, NMIB, A.$200.00
Fun on Wheels, Pluto, 1950s, MIB......................................$35.00
Rolykin, Donald Duck, NM, from $10 to............................$15.00
Rolykin, Pluto, NM, from $10 to...$15.00

Rolykins, Donald and friend, MOC, $25.00. (Photo courtesy Michael Stern)

NUTTY MADS

All Heart Hogan, pk w/cream swirl, NM, F5 ....$20.00
Bull Pen Boo Boo, dk gr, NM $30.00
Dippy the Deep Sea Diver, cobalt, 1st issue, EX, F5 ....$10.00
End Zone Football Player, dk gr, 1st issue, NM, from $15 to..$20.00
Lost Teepee, flourescent red, NM, F5, from $15 to $20.00
Manny the Wreckless Mariner, lime gr, NM, F5 ....$20.00
Manny the Wreckless Mariner, lt gr, 1st issue, NM, F5 ....$35.00
Rocko the Champ, lime gr, 1st issue, NM, from $15 to $20.00
Rocko the Champ, pk, NM $16.50
Roddy the Hotrod, chartreuse gr, 1st issue, NM, F5.........$35.00
Suburban Sidney, dk gr, 1st issue, NM, F5......................$32.00
The Thinker, dk gr, NM $35.00
Waldo the Weight Lifter, pk, 1st issue, NM, F5 ....$25.00

Lost Teepee, green, from $15.00 to $20.00.

WESTERN AND FRONTIER HEROES

Flint McCullough, cream, M, from $50 to $75.00
Rip Masters, cream, NM $18.00
Rip Masters, powder bl, NM...$28.00
Roy Rogers, mounted, 54mm, M $25.00
Tonto, cream, 54mm, M $15.00

Cowboys, from $4.00 to $6.00.

Plastic Toys

During the 1940s and into the 1960s, plastic was often the material of choice for consumer goods ranging from dinnerware and kitchenware items to jewelry and even high-heel shoes. Toy companies used brightly colored plastic to produce cars, dolls,

pull toys, banks, games, and thousands of other types of products. Of the more imaginative toys, those that have survived in good collectible condition are beginning to attract a considerable amount of interest, especially items made by major companies.

Army Caravan, Irwin, w/ambulance, wrecker, troop carrier & 4 figures, 22", MIP (sealed), A $165.00

Bump and Dump Truck, Saunders, MIB, $125.00.
(Photo courtesy John Turney)

Cargo Plane, Eldon, complete w/polyethylene plane, 3 armored vehicles & ramp, NM (NM Box), A.........................$200.00
Circus Train, Banner, 1950, tractor pulls merry-go-round, lion cage & calliope, M (NM box), P4...........................$150.00

Plasticar Streamline Automobiles, Irwin, MIB, $150.00.
(Photo courtesy John Turney)

Fix-It Tow Truck, Ideal, complete w/accessories, 8", NM (NM box), A..$175.00

International Stake Truck, Product Miniature Co Inc, 1950s, bl w/blk tires, 11½", NMIB, A $200.00

International Tractor Truck, Product Miniature Co Inc, 1950s, red & yel w/blk tires, 9", NMIB, A $165.00

Jeep & House Trailer, England, bl & yel jeep w/red tires, red & wht trailer, 15", NM (VG box), A $150.00

Sea & Air Combat Action Set, Thomas Toys, complete w/battleship, bomber w/bombs & submarine w/torpedos, NMIB, A $235.00

Service Station w/Cars, Ideal, 1950s, Auto Laundry & Lubritorium, complete w/4 cars, NM (NM box), A $200.00

Tractor Truck, Product Miniature Co Inc, 1950s, red & yel w/blk tires, 9", NMIB, A $165.00

Whizzer Fan, Irwin, wind-up, MIB, $95.00. (Photo courtesy John Turney)

Plasticville

From the 1940s through the 1960s, Bachmann Brothers produced plastic accessories for train layouts such as buildings, fences, trees, and animals. Buildings often included several smaller pieces — for instance, ladders, railings, windsocks, etc. — everything you could ever need to play out just about any scenario. Beware of reissues.

Advisor: Gary Mosholder, Gary's Trains (G1).

#AD-4 Airport Administration Building, EXIB.............$65.00

#AP-1 Airport Hanger, bl roof, EX (EX box)..................$25.00

#BL-2 Bridge & Pond, EX (EX box)..................................$8.00

#BN-1 Barn, wht sides, red roof, EX (EX box), G1..........$15.00

#C-18 Cathedral, EX (EX box) $35.00

#CC-8 Church, EX (EX box), G1 ....$12.00

#CS-5 5 & 10 Cent Store, EXIB $16.00

#DE-7 Diner, gray sides, yel roof & trim, VG (VG box), G1...$20.00

#DH-2 Hardware/Pharmacy $18.00

#FB-1 Frosty Bar, yel & wht, EXIB................................$18.00

#FH-4 Firehouse, EXIB..$16.00

#HS-6 Hospital, no furniture, VG (VG box), G1............$25.00

#HU-6, MIB, $150.00, EX, $75.00.

#LC-2 Log Cabin, EX, G1 ....$6.00

#LM-3 Freight Station Kit, gr roof, brn platform, G (orig box) $8.00

#MH-2 New England Rancher, wht sides, gray roof & bl trim, EX (EX box), G1 ....$20.00

#PD-3 Police Station, lt gray, EXIB...............................$18.00

#PF-4 Citizens, EXIB $15.00

#PH-1 Town Hall, red, EXIB..$40.00

#PO-1 Post Office, EXIB $18.00

#RH-1 Ranch House, bl sides, gray roof, wht trim, G (orig box)..$10.00

#RH-1 Ranch House, wht sides, med bl roof, EX, G1 ......$10.00

#RS-7 Suburban Station, EX, G1 ....$8.00

#SG-3 Signal Bridge, VG (VG box), G1 ....$10.00

#SW-2 Switch Tower, EXIB..$14.00

#V-10 Vehicle Set, VG (orig box)...................................$75.00

#0103 Littletown Colonial Mansion, missing door, EX, G1..$20.00

#0953 Lionel Figure Set, complete, VG (VG box), G1 ....$65.00

#1403 Signal Bridge, EX (EX box), G1 ....$10.00

#1406 Playground, salmon, yel & gr, MIB, G1................$25.00

#1407 Watchman's Shanty, EX, G1................................$8.00

#1600 Church, EX (EX box), G1 ....$15.00

#1603 Ranch, wht sides, bl roof & trim, EX (EX box), G1 ..$12.00

#1608 Schoolhouse, EX (EX box), G1 ....$16.00

#1616 Passenger Station, no signs, EX, G1 ....$10.00

#1620 Loading Platform, EX, G1....................................$10.00

#1622 Dairy Barn, red & gray, EX, G1 ....$10.00

#1700 Two-Story Colonial, red sides, gray roof & wht trim, EX (EX box), G1 ....$20.00

#1701 1½ Story Rancher, tan sides, brn roof & red trim, VG (VG box), G1 ....$20.00

#1800 Gas Station, lg, G (G box), G1 ....$25.00

#1803 Colonial Church, EX, G1 ....$18.00

#1852 Ranch, bl sides, gray roof & wht trim, EX (EX box), G1 ....$15.00

#1901 Union Station, EX (EX box), G1 ....$30.00
#1906 Factory, EX (EX box), G1 ....$25.00
#1907 Apartment Building, tan sides, red roof & brn trim, EX
   (EX box), G1 ....$55.00
#1921 Firehouse w/2 Fire Trucks, EXIB...........................$19.00
#5000-100 Storytown (3 Men in a Tub), EXIB...............$145.00

Playsets by Marx

Louis Marx is given credit for developing the modern-age playset and during the '50s and '60s produced hundreds of boxed sets, each with the buildings, figures, and accessories that when combined with a child's imagination could bring any scenario alive, from the days of Ben Hur to medieval battles, through the cowboy and Indian era, and on up to Cape Canaveral. Marx's prices were kept low by mass marketing (through retail giants such as Sears and Montgomery Wards) and overseas production. But on today's market, playsets are anything but low-priced; some mint-in-box examples sell for upwards of $1,000.00. Just remember that a set that shows wear or has even a few minor pieces missing quickly drops in value. The listings below are for complete examples unless noted otherwise.

Advisors: Bob Wilson, Phoenix Toy Soldier Co. (P11); Mike and Kurt Fredericks (F4).

Adventures of Robin Hood #4722, 1956, EX (EX box) .$450.00
Adventures of Robin Hood #4723, EX (EX box) $450.00
Alamo #3544, few pcs missing, NM (NM box), A $450.00
American Airport International Jetport, box only, Series 1000,
   EX...$35.00
Army Combat #4155, Sears Exclusive, 1964, MIB.........$450.00
Artic Explorer #3702, Series 2000, 1958, EX (VG box)..$750.00
Astro Jet Airport, 1961, NMIB $485.00

Battle of the Alamo, Sears/Heritage, 1972, EXIB, from $300.00 to $350.00. (Photo courtesy Bob Wilson)

Battle of the Blue & Gray #2646, EX+ (VG box) $400.00
Battle of the Blue & Gray #4746, Series 1000, 1958, EX (EX
   box)..$700.00
Battleground #4204, EX (EX box) $150.00
Battleground #4752, Series 2000, 1958, EX (EX box)....$350.00
Battleground #4756, few pcs missing, EX........................$125.00
Battleground Europe #5939, 1965, NM (NM box) $1,300.00
Ben-Hur #4702, Series 2000, 1959-62, NMIB, P11 ....$1,000.00
Big Top Circus #4310, NMIB, from $400 to $600.00
Boot Camp #4645, 1968, EX (EX metal case) $200.00
Bradley's Toy Town Post Office, VG (VG box) $100.00
Britains Sovereign Escort #7835, NMIB $125.00
Buddy L Roundup, unused, NMIB $450.00
Canadian Frontier Set #4610, NM (worn box), P11 ......$700.00
Cape Canaveral #4521, MIB, P11....................................$350.00
Cape Canaveral #4528, 1959-60, EX (EX box) $375.00
Cape Canaveral Missile Set #4526, few pcs missing, VG (VG
   box)..$200.00
Captain Gallant of the Foreign Legion #4730, 1956, EX (EX
   box), from $900 to $1,100.00
Captain Gallant of the Foreign Legion #4730, 1956, few pcs
   missing, NM (NM box), A $1,500.00
Captain Space Solar Port, box only, 1954, EX..................$60.00
Cattle Drive #3983, 1972, EX (EX box) $325.00
Civil War Centennial #5929, Marx/Sears, few pcs missing, VG
   (G box) $400.00
Construction Camp #4442, EX (EX box) $300.00
Construction Camp #4444, 1956, Montgomery Ward, EX (EX
   box)..$400.00
Construction Camp #4446, Series 1000, 1957, NM (NM box),
   F5 ....$350.00

Cowboy & Indian Camp #3849, EX (EX box) $375.00
Daktari #3717, 1967, EX (EX cartoon box) $750.00
Daniel Boone Wilderness Scout #2640, EX (EX box) $375.00
Davy Crockett at the Alamo #3544, 1955, VG (VG box) .$500.00
Desert Fox #417MO, Marx, EX (EX box).......................$450.00
Desert Patrol #4174, 1967, MIB...................................$400.00
Dow Service Center w/Sky-View Parking, NM $265.00
Farm Set #3930, Canadian, few pcs missing, EX (EX box) .$325.00
Fighting Knights Carry-All Set #4635, 1968, MIB, P11.$125.00
Fighting Marine Combat Unit #1172, NM (NM box)...$350.00
Flintstones #4672, 1961, orig issue, EX (EX box) $350.00

Fort Apache #3681, 1973, EX (EX box) $185.00
Fort Apache #3683, Marx/Sears, 1968-71, few pcs missing, (EX (VG box) $75.00
Fort Apache #5962, Marx/Sears Happi-Time, 1962-63, M (M Sears-Allstate box) $700.00
Fort Apache Stockade #3612, EX (EX box) $200.00
Fort Apache Stockade #3612, several pcs missing, VG (VG box) $115.00
Fort Apache Stockade #3615, few pcs missing, EX (EX box) ..$200.00
Fort Apache Stockade #3616, VG (VG box) $285.00
Fort Apache Stockade #3675, Series 5000, EX (VG box) ..$275.00

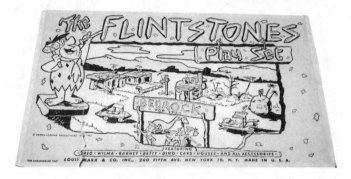

Flintstones, #5948, 1962, MIB, rare, $450.00. (Photo courtesy Bob Wilson)

Fort Apache #3632C, box only, EX...................................$50.00
Fort Apache #3647, 500 Series, EX (EX box).................$235.00
Fort Apache #3680, NM (EX box) $200.00

Masterbuilder Kit, Capitol of the United States, with thirty-five miniature presidents, MIB, from $75.00 to $125.00. (Photo courtesy Bob Wilson)

Fort Dearborn #3514, few pcs missing, EX (G box)........$200.00
Fort Dearborn #3514, 1955, EX (EX box)......................$300.00
Freight Terminal #5420, MIB................................$700.00
Galaxy Command #4206, Marx, EX (EX box) $100.00
Guid-A Traffic, PFPC #32, Sears, Marx, EX $100.00
Indian Warfare #4778, complete, Marx, EX (EX box) ...$800.00
Iwo Jima #4147, 1954, EX (worn box)......................$350.00
Jailside Western Town #4229, EX (EX box) $650.00
Jetport #4812, few pcs missing, EX (EX box)................$325.00
Jungle Set #3705, NM (NM box) $700.00
Knights & Vikings Carryall #4635, EX $125.00
Lone Ranger Rodeo #3696, 1952, MIB.......................$450.00
Medieval Castle #4700, MIB................................$850.00
Medieval Castle Fort #4709, ca 1950s, VG (VG box) ...$150.00
Modern Farm #3931, EX (EX box)............................$85.00
Prehistoric Dinousaur Set #4208, 1975-78, EX (EX box)..$100.00
Prehistoric Mountain #3414, few pcs missing, EX (worn
    box)...$125.00

Prehistoric Times, #3390, 1957, twenty-three dinosaurs, twelve cavemen, large (13" x 24") vaccuform base, with terrain and pool, MIB, $400.00. (Photo courtesy Bob Wilson)

Prince Valiant Castle Fort #4706, 1954-55, EX (G box) ..$375.00
Red River Gang, complete, 1978, box mk 'Red River Playset,'
    EX (VG box) $100.00
Rifleman Ranch #3998, Series 1000, 1961, EX (EX box),
    P11...$750.00
Rin Tin Tin at Fort Apache #3627, few pcs missing, EX (EX
    box)..$285.00
Rin Tin Tin at Fort Apache #3658, few pcs missing, EX (EX
    box)..$300.00
Robin Hood Castle Set #4718, 1956-1958, EX (EX box) ..$235.00
Robin Hood Castle Set #4719, 1956, EX (EX box)........$375.00
Roy Rogers & Trigger, 1950s, MIB, A.......................$650.00
Roy Rogers Mineral City #4258, EX (EX box) $250.00
Roy Rogers Rodeo #3690, few pcs missing, EX (EX box)..$275.00
Silver City Frontier Town #4220, 1955, few pcs missing, EX (EX
    box), from $300 to.................................$400.00
Sons of Liberty #79-59147, Marx/Sears Heritage, 1972-74, EX
    (EX box) $400.00
Star Station Seven #4115, 1978, MIB $125.00
Tom Corbett Space Academy #7010, EX (EX box), from $425
    to...$475.00
Tri-Level Farm Set #3948, EX (EX box) $350.00

Tri-Level Farm Set #3953, MIB.............................$600.00
Tricky Action Construction Set, MIB $150.00

U.S. Naval Base, #888, complete in EX box, $375.00.
(Photo courtesy Bob Wilson)

World of Dinosaurs #4130, EX (EX box) $100.00
Zorro #3753, NMIB......................................$1,100.00

Political

As far back as the nineteenth century, children's toys with a political message were on the market. One of the most familiar was the 'Tammany Bank' patented by J. & E. Stevens in 1873. The message was obvious — a coin placed in the man's hand was deposited in his pocket, representing the kickbacks William Tweed was suspected of pocketing when he was the head of Tammany Hall in New York during the 1860s.

Advisors: Michael and Polly McQuillen (M11).

Agnew, Spiro; Presidental semi-trailer, Winross, 1972, MIB....$35.00
Agnew, Spiro; The Spiro Agnew Jigsaw Puzzle, as Superman,
    1970s, NMIB..$25.00
Bush, George; doll, 1980s, 8", NMIB $30.00
Carter, Amy; rag doll, 1970s, 18", M (worn box).............$65.00
Carter, Jimmy; doll, 1970s, 8", NMIB.....................$50.00
Carter, Jimmy; Walking Peanut Toy, Japan, 1970s, plastic & tin,
    4½", MIB $25.00
Clinton/Gore, yo-yo, Humphrey, 1990s, NM................$10.00
Clout, American Political Game, Scofield, 1985, EXIB...$18.00
Eisenhower, Dwight D; figure, Excel, 1974, fully jtd, complete
    w/pistol & uniform, 9½", NM (G box)................$15.00
Kennedy, Jackie; doll, 1960s, 14", M.....................$450.00
Kennedy, John F; book, A Day in the Life of President Kennedy,
    Random House, 1964, hardcover, w/dust jacket, EX .$12.00
Kennedy, John F; jigsaw puzzle, Tuco, 1960s, 350 pcs, EX (VG
    box)...$12.50
Kennedy, John F; Lincoln Continental Parade Vehicle,
    Minichamp, 1/43 scale, MIB $55.00
Kennedy, John F; model kit, Aurora #851-149, 1965, unassem-
    bled, NM (EX box)...................................$105.00
MacArthur, General Douglas; bank, Save for Victory & portrait
    flanked by flags, glass & cb, 7", EX, A.............$55.00

MacArthur, General Douglas; puzzle, Forward America, Tuco, 320 pcs, EX (EX box), A1 ....$85.00

Mao/Nixon, ping-pong paddle set, 1970s, EX (orig pkg) ..$55.00

Mr President, board game, 3M, 1970s, EXIB......................$22.50

Nixon/Agnew, semi-trailer, Winross, 1972, Presidental Election on side of wht trailer, bl cab, EXIB.............................$35.00

Powell, Colin; doll, 1980s, 8", NMIB.............................$30.00

Presidents of the USA, Marx Toy Co, 1963, figures from G Washington to JF Kennedy, 1½" ea, NM (EX box)...$75.00

Reagan, Ronald; yo-yo, plastic, NM.................................$10.00

Reagan, Ronald; yo-yo, wht w/The White House & faux signature in blk, M...$15.00

Roosevelt, Eleanor; doll, 1980s, 14", MIB.......................$85.00

Roosevelt, Franklin D; puzzle, Forward America, Tuco, 320 pcs, EX (EX box), A1 ....$85.00

Roosevelt, Teddy; Rough Riders, Reed, 1900, panarama of fifteen 5½" soldiers (one missing) on scissor board, retains three of four original flags, EX (EX box), minimum value, $2,000.00.

Uncle Sam, doll, Dressel, jtd wood & compo w/bsk head, cloth outfit w/gray felt hat, 15", EX, A $1,500.00

Uncle Sam, Savings Bank & Clock, Uncle Sam holds clock beside bank, cb & wood, 7", NM, A $40.00

Washington, George & Martha; figures, Japan, prewar, celluloid, 7", NM, A $85.00

Washington, George; action figure, Fun-World, Collectors Series of Great Americans #1776-1, fully jtd, 7½", NRFB....$23.50

Washington, George; model kit, Air Fix, Collectors Series, mounted on horse, 54mm, M (EX box) $12.00

Washington, George; puzzle, Washington Pleading for Democracy, Perfect Picture Puzzle, 400 pcs, NMIB, A1 ....$35.00

Washington, George; toy soldier, Elastolin #7080, plastic, MIB...$27.50

Premiums

Those of us from the pre-boomer era remember waiting in anticipation for our silver bullet ring, secret membership kit, decoder pin, coloring book, or whatever other wonderful item we'd seen advertised in our favorite comic book or heard about on the Tom Mix show. Tom wasn't the only one to have these exciting premiums, though, just about any top character-oriented show from the '30s through the '40s made similar offers, and even through the '50s some were still being distributed. Often they could be had free for a cereal boxtop or an Ovaltine inner seal, and if any money was involved, it was usually only a dime. Not especially durable and often made in somewhat limited amounts, few have survived to the present. Today some of these are bringing fantastic prices, but the market at present is very volatile. Note: Those trademark/logo characters created to specifically represent a cereal product or company (for example Cap'n Crunch) are listed in the Cereal Boxes and Premiums category.

Condition is very important in assessing value; items in pristine condition bring premium prices.

Advisor: Bill Campbell (C10).

Other Sources: J5.

See also Advertising; Cereal Boxes and Premiums; Pinback Buttons.

Agent 007, ring, Seal, 1960s, from $35 to $50.00

Bart Simpson, figurine, Winchell's Donut Shop, 1993, Bart lying on donut, 1993, MIP..$12.00

Batman, ring, sterling silver w/batwing logo, MIB, C10 ...$85.00

Bazooka Joe, initial ring, 1950s, EX................................$250.00

Beatles, ring, plastic, w/photo inserts, 1964, set of 4, NM, from $50 to $60.00

Buck Rogers, badge, Chief Explorers, NM, C10 ....$400.00

Buck Rogers, badge, Solar Scouts, NM, C10 ....$100.00

Buck Rogers, badge, Space Explorer, w/whistle, NM, C10..$325.00

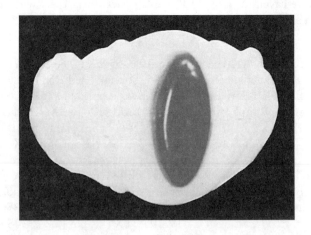

Buck Rogers, ring, Ring of Saturn, white plastic band with red stone, glows in the dark, EX, A, $400.00.

Buck Rogers, ring, Ring of Saturn, M, C10.....................$600.00

Buck Rogers, Space Ranger Kit, Sylvania TV, 1952, complete, EX (EX envelope)...$100.00

Buck Rogers, spaceship, Morton Salt, 1940, heavy paper w/rubber tip, complete, 3", NM (EX mailer), A $175.00

Buffalo Bill, ring, 1950s, VG..$45.00

Captain America, badge, Sentinels of Liberty, M, C10 ..$850.00

Captain Marvel, club membership card w/secret code on bk, EX, C10...$25.00

Captain Marvel, comic book, Billy's Big Game, Carnation giveaway, EX, C10...$50.00

Captain Marvel, Magic Whistle, NM, C10.....................$65.00

Captain Marvel, membership card, Captain Marvel Club, Fawcett Comics, 1940s, EX, T2....................................$30.00

Captain Marvel, shoulder patch, EX, C10 ....$85.00

Captain Midnight, code wheel, new issue, NM, C10 ....$20.00

Captain Midnight, decoder, 1942, w/photo, NM, C10...$225.00

Captain Midnight, decoder badge, 1948, EX, $150.00.
(Photo courtesy June Moon)

Captain Midnight, membership kit, 1957, complete w/decoder insert, NM, C10..$625.00

Captain Midnight, patch, cloth wings, M, C10.............$150.00

Captain Midnight, patch, Secret Squadron, 1955 or 1957, EX, C10, ea $35.00

Captain Midnight, ring, Flight Commander, EX, C10 ...$525.00

Charlie McCarthy, figure, diecut litho fold-up, eyes and mouth move, Chase & Sanborn, 18", NM (EX original mailer), A, $135.00.

Captain Midnight, ring, Sun God, 1947, gold-tone w/red plastic stone, EX, A $1,200.00

Captain Midnight, Secret Squadron membership card, 1955-56, EX, A $55.00

Captain Midnight, Skelly Oil Wings, w/weather indicator strip, NM, C10...$50.00

Captain Video, ring, Flying Saucer, w/papers, M, C10....$1,500.00

Captain Video, ring, Seal, M, C10.............................$550.00

Charlie McCarthy, ring, Chase & Sanborn, 1940s, brass, EX..$150.00

Clyde Beatty, Magic Moving Picture Eye, 1950s, MIP......$75.00

Dan Daring, book, Dan Daring's Book of Magic Tricks, M (EX mailer), C10...$50.00

Davy Adams, ring, Siren, rare, M, C10.........................$725.00

Davy Crockett, ring, Profile, gr or red enamel on brass, 1950s, NM, from $75 to..$100.00

Davy Crockett, ring, TV Flicker, M, C10 ....$150.00

Dick Tracy, pin-back button, Secret Service Patrol Member, Quaker, 1939, EX, D11...$25.00

Dick Tracy, ring, Post Cereal, MIP, C10...........................$30.00

Dick Tracy, ring, profile in circle, stars on sides, gold-tone, 1930s, from $200 to..$250.00

Ernie Keebler, ring, Keebler Cookies & Crackers, 1970, wht figure on red base, MIP..$15.00

Flash Gordon, ring, Post Cereal, MIP, C10 ....$85.00

Frank Buck, Sun Watch, EX, C10 ....$70.00

Frito Bandito, ring, Frito Lays, 1969, plastic, MIP............$15.00

Gabby Hayes, ring, Cannon, 1951, M, C10, from $300 to..$350.00

Gene Autry, Adventure Story Trail Map, Schafer's Bread, 1950s, EX $100.00

Gene Autry, ring, face, copper- or silver-tone, 1950s, from $100 to...$150.00

Green Hornet, flicker ring, plastic, 1960s, 12 in set, ea from $15 to...$20.00

Green Hornet, ring, Seal, 1947, gold-colored metal with glow-in-the-dark secret compartment, NM, from $850.00 to $950.00.

Have Gun Will Travel, ring, wht or blk top, 1960s, from $35 to...$50.00

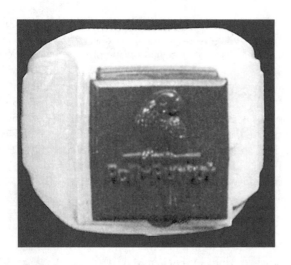

Howdy Doody, ring, Jack in the Box, 1950s, Howdy pops up when lid is lifted, yellow plastic, Poll Parrot embossed on red lid, NM, $800.00.

Hopalong Cassidy, ring, Bust, silver, NM, C10 ....$75.00
Jack Armstrong, Bomb Sight Kit, complete, MIB, C10..$525.00
Jack Armstrong, Junior Ace First Aid Kit, 1930s, litho tin, com-
    plete, NM..$300.00
Jack Armstrong, ring, Siren Whistle, Egyptian design, gold-tone,
    1940s, from $125 to $150.00
Jack Armstrong, Sound Effects Kit, 1940s, complete, MIB,
    C10 ....$300.00
Lone Ranger, deputy badge, w/secret compartment & code book,
    NM, C10..$175.00
Lone Ranger, National Defenders Stamp Album, complete
    w/stamps, EX (EX mailer), C10................................$55.00

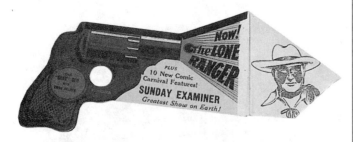

Lone Ranger, paper gun promoting comic strip, 1938, M, $150.00. (Photo courtesy Lee Felbinger)

Lone Ranger, ring, Filmstrip Saddle, 1950, M, C10........$265.00
Lone Ranger, ring, Flashlight, 1947, NM (VG mailer), C10..$175.00
Lone Ranger, ring, Weather, 1947, NM, C10 ....$225.00
Mary Marvel, badge, Club Member, w/cord, rare, NM, C10 .$450.00
Mickey Mouse Club, ring, emb face, plastic, 1960s, from $45
    to $75.00
Peter Paul, ring, Weather, w/paper, rare, NM, C10 ....$215.00
Phantom, ring, Post Cereal, NM, C10 ....$75.00
Quaker, ring, Jingle Bells, 1950s, M $30.00
Radio Orphan Annie, decoder, 1935, EX, C10................$60.00
Radio Orphan Annie, manual & badge, Secret Society, EX (EX
    mailer), C10...$75.00

Radio Orphan Annie, membership kit, 1945, decoder badge &
    code manual, complete, EX (EX mailer), C10.........$250.00
Radio Orphan Annie, ring, Post Cereal, MIP, C10...........$30.00
Radio Orphan Annie, ring, Silver Star, M.....................$200.00

Radio Orphan Annie, ring, Triple Mystery, silver metal band, top lifts off to reveal secret compartment with serial number, VG, A, $500.00 (M, $1,300.00).

Radio Orphan Annie, Talking Stationery, 1937, complete, rare,
    NM (NM mailer), A $150.00
Red Ryder, Lucky Coin, EX, C10 ....$15.00
Rin-Tin-Tin, Wondascope, Nabisco, 1950s, complete, NMIB,
    A...$75.00
Roger Wilco, ring, Flying Tiger, complete w/whistle, NM,
    C10..$325.00

Roger Wilco, ring, Flying Tiger Rescue, red plastic band with glow-in-the-dark box, metal piece for Morse Code, whistle, with user's leaflet, MIB, A, $360.00.

Roy Rogers, Lucky Coin, EX, C10...................................$25.00
Roy Rogers, pin, Roy Rogers Riders Club, Post Cereal, NM,
    C10 ....$65.00

Roy Rogers, ring, Branding Iron, complete w/cap, NM, C10..$225.00
Roy Rogers, ring, Microscope, EX $115.00
Roy Rogers, ring, Roy on Trigger, sterling silver, oval, NM, C10 ....$475.00
Sgt Preston, 10-in-1 Electric Trail-Kit, Quaker, complete, rare, EX $750.00
Shadow, ink blotter, Blue Coal, EX, C10 ....$135.00
Shadow, lapel stud, Shadow Club, NM, C10 ....$400.00
Shadow, ring, Blue Coal, 1941, scarce, NM, from $500 to..$600.00
Shadow, ring, Bust, MIB, C10 ....$200.00
Shadow, ring, Secret Agent, scarce, MIB, C10 ....$300.00
Sky King, Club Wings, Nabisco, 1959, NM, C10...........$125.00
Sky King, Detecto-Microscope, 1950s, complete, EX (EX box), A $250.00
Sky King, ring, Navajo Treasure, VG $75.00
Sky King, ring, Radar Signal, 1946, brass w/glow-in-the-dark top, NM, C10 ....$215.00
Sky King, ring, Teleblinker, M, C10..................................$255.00
Sky King, ring, TV, complete w/photos, M, C10 ....$285.00
Space Kidettes, hat, Hanna-Barbera, dtd 1978, cb, unbuilt, EX $15.00
Space Patrol, Cosmic Smoke Gun, complete, EX (EX mailer), C10 ....$400.00
Space Patrol, membership badge, EX, J6.........................$350.00
Space Patrol, ring, Hydrogen Ray Gun, 1950s, glow-in-the-dark, NM, C10...$375.00
Steve Canyon, membership card, 1959, EX $20.00
Straight Arrow, ring, Cave Nugget, w/photo, M, C10....$225.00
Straight Arrow, ring, Face, w/paperwork, NM, C10 ....$150.00
Superman, Krypton Rocket, National Comics, Kellogg's, 1956, plastic, complete, EX (G box), A.............................$225.00
Superman, ring, Crusader, 1940s, NM, C10 ....$250.00
Superman, ring, logo in center, Post Toasties, 1976, EX/NM, from $25 to...$35.00
Superman, ring, Pep Airplane, 1940s, blk, NM (NM mailer), C10 ....$475.00
Superman, ring, Secret Candy Compartment, Leader Novelty Candy, 1940s, complete, rare, NM $8,500.00
Superman, ring, Superman of America, 14k gold w/statue, M, C10 ....$500.00

Tarzan, stamp book, Cuba, 1930s – 40s, with 95 of the original 100 stamps, 7" x 9", EX, A, $500.00.

Tennessee Jed, ring, Magnet, extremely rare, NM, C10...$1,100.00
Terry & the Pirates, ring, Gold Ore Detector, EX+ $115.00
The Shadow, ring, movie premium, 1990s, M (orig mailer)..$30.00

Tom Corbett Space Cadet, patch, Kellogg's, 1951, red & bl fabric w/rocket logo, NM...$65.00
Tom Mix, arrowhead w/compass & magnifying glass, glow-in-the-dark, EX, C10...$75.00

Tom Mix, badge, Straight Shooter, 1937, gold, EX, $85.00.

Tom Mix, badge, Straight Shooter, 1937, silver, EX, C10..$95.00
Tom Mix, badge, Wrangler, NM, C10.............................$150.00
Tom Mix, compass, glow gun & arrowhead whistle, complete w/papers, M (worn mailer), C10 ....$225.00
Tom Mix, decoder badge, Six-Gun, NM, C10...............$165.00
Tom Mix, Golden Bullet Telescope & Birdcall, M, C10 ..$75.00
Tom Mix, medal & ribbon, Straight Shooters, MIB, C10 ....$125.00
Tom Mix, ring, Magic Picture, w/Tom & Tony photo, NM, C10 ....$300.00
Tom Mix, ring, Magnet, NM, C10..................................$125.00
Tom Mix, ring, Picture, NM, C10...................................$300.00
Tom Mix, ring, Siren, steel version, NM, C10...............$175.00
Tom Mix, ring, Whistle, NM $130.00
Tom Mix, siren badge, Sheriff of Dobie County, EX, C10...$60.00
Tom Mix, whistle, 1948, arrowhead shape, glow-in-the-dark, EX $35.00
Wizard of Oz, Toto, puppet, Proctor & Gamble Detergent, 1960s, EX $20.00
Wonder Woman, figure, Kraft Macaroni & Cheese, 7", EX..$13.00
Zorro, ring, gumball, blk plastic w/Zorro emb, EX $15.00
Zorro, ring, Logo, lg Z, 1960s, M $75.00

Pressed Steel

Many companies were involved in the manufacture of pressed steel automotive toys which were often faithfully modeled after actual vehicles in production at the time they were made. Because they were so sturdy, some from as early as the 1920s have survived to the present, and those that are still in good condition are bringing very respectable prices at toy auctions around the country. Some of the better-known manufacturers are listed in other sections.

Advisors: Kerry and Judy Irvin (K5).

See also Aeronautical; Buddy L; Keystone; Marx; Pedal Cars and Other Wheeled Goods; Structo; Tonka; Wyandotte.

CARS AND BUSSES

BMW Style Roadster, Distler, wind-up with forward and reverse action, 9½", EX, A, $200.00.

Brougham, Kingsbury, bl w/wht rubber tires & rear spare, electric headlights, 12", EX, A...$2,100.00

Brougham, Kingsbury, brn & red w/wht rubber tires, electric headlights, 12", EX, A...$2,400.00

Brougham, Kingsbury, gr w/orange stripe, tires mk Little Jim Playthings JC Penney, 12", EX, A........................$3,900.00

Bus, Kingsbury, dk bl w/orange stripe, wht rubber tires, 16", NM, A..$2,500.00

Bus, Kingsbury, dk bl w/orange stripe, wht rubber tires w/orange hubs, 16", G, A..$850.00

Bus, Kingsbury, gr w/red stripe, wht rubber tires w/red hubs, 16", rare, EX+, A...$2,000.00

Bus, Kingsbury, lt bl w/red stripe, wht rubber tires w/red hubs, 16", EX, A..$1,450.00

Cabriolet, Kingsbury, cream, bl & gr w/wht rubber tires, 14", rare, EX, A...$4,200.00

Chrysler Airflow, Cor Cor, 1934, bl w/chrome detail, 16½", prof rstr, A..$1,100.00

Chrysler Airflow Sedan, Cor Cor, 1930s, gr w/NP detail, electric headlights, 17", EX, A...$650.00

Chrysler Airflow Sedan, Kingsbury, 1934, gr w/wht rubber tires, electric headlights, 14", EX, A..............................$1,450.00

Chrysler Airflow Sedan, Kingsbury, 1935, gr w/blk rubber tires, 14", VG, A..$1,100.00

Chrysler Airflow Sedan, Kingsbury, 1936, bl w/wht rubber tires & metal spokes, electric headlights, 14", VG, A.....$850.00

Chrysler Airflow Sedan, Kingsbury, 1936, red w/wht rubber tires & metal spokes, electric headlights, 14", G, A........$250.00

Coupe, Kingsbury, 2-tone gr w/wht rubber tires, electric headlights, 12", VG+, A..$1,500.00

Flivver Center Door Sedan, Cowdery Toy Works, 1980s, blk w/aluminum wheels & red-pnt spokes, 11½", MIB, A..$650.00

Greyhound Limited Bus, Kingsbury, dk bl w/blk rubber tires, opening rear door, 18", VG, A...............................$475.00

Lincoln Sedan, Turner, 1920s, red w/cream stripe & roof, blk rubber tires w/red-pnt hubs, 27", VG, A...............$2,100.00

Lincoln Zephyr & Boat Trailer, Kingsbury, 1937, orange car & trailer w/gr boat, blk rubber tires, 24", VG, A.........$850.00

Lincoln Zephyr & Camper, Kingsbury, 1937, gr w/blk rubber tires, 23", VG, A..$500.00

New York Bus, Kingsbury, lt bl & cream w/wht rubber tires, 18", EX, A..$800.00

New York Bus, Kingsbury, red & cream w/blk rubber tires, 18", VG, A..$400.00

Packard Convertible, American National, nickeled windshield frame, 28", VG, A, $11,000.00.

Packard Coupe, Turner, red w/tan top, disk wheels, 26", VG, A..$850.00

Pierce Arrow Coupe, Girard, pk & maroon, battery-op lights (1 missing), 14", EX, A...$1,000.00

Roadster, Kingsbury, brn & red w/wht rubber tires, electric headlights, 12", VG, A...$925.00

Roadster, Kingsbury 300 Series, red, yel & bl w/wht rubber tires, 13", VG, A...$1,375.00

Roadster, Turner, red, inertia drive, 8", missing driver, EX, A..$100.00

Woody Station Wagon, Kingsbury, brn w/blk running boards, metal tires mk Little Jim Playthings..., 11", EX, A .$4,200.00

CONSTRUCTION

Cement Mixer, Doepke Mfg Co, yel w/blk Goodyear tires, 10", EX, A..$185.00

Road Grade, Ny-Lint, yel w/blk rubber tires, 19", EX (EX box), A...$250.00

FIREFIGHTING

Aerial Ladder Truck, Kingsbury, red w/wht rubber tires, NP ladders, 36", EX (VG box), A....................................$3,300.00

Aerial Ladder Truck, Kingsbury, red w/wht rubber tires, NP ladders, Little Jim decal on floor, 34", VG, A..........$2,600.00

Aerial Ladder Truck, Kingsbury, red w/yel ladder, blk rubber tires, CI driver, 23", EX, A.......................................$250.00

Aerial Ladder Truck, Kingsbury, red w/yel ladder, wht rubber tires, CI driver, 19", VG, A $400.00

American LaFrance Pumper Truck, Sturditoy, 1920s, red w/blk rubber tires, rpl hose & nozzle, 26", VG+, A $1,400.00

Fire Chief Car, Hoge, clockwork w/battery-op headlights, 14", VG, A $400.00

Fire Chief Car, Kingsbury, red w/disk wheels, CI driver, 10", EX, A $650.00

Fire Pumper, Turner, flywheel motor and bell, 21", VG, A, $300.00.

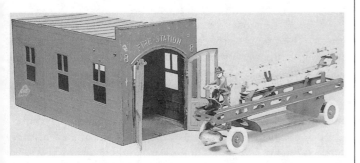

Ladder Truck and Fire Station, Kingsbury, clockwork truck, 18½" long, VG, A, $1,000.00.

Ladder Truck, Kingsbury, red w/yel ladders, blk rubber tires, 14", VG, A $200.00

Mack Fire Truck, Steelcraft, 1920s, mk City Fire Dept, 28", VG, A.........................$1,100.00

Pumper Truck, Kingsbury, red w/yel spoke wheels, CI driver, 9", EX, A $200.00

Pumper Truck, Kingsbury No 272, red w/wht rubber tires, gold boiler, 23", rare, VG, A $3,400.00

Water Tower Truck, Sturditoy, red w/blk rubber tires, 33", G, A.........................$850.00

White Aerial Ladder Truck, Kelmet, 1920s, red w/wht rubber tires, VG, A $1,100.00

TRUCKS AND VANS

American Railway Express Truck, Sturditoy, blk open cab w/gr screened-in body, 25", VG, A $850.00

Army Truck, Kingsbury, brn w/blk rubber tires & red hubs, orig canvas cover, 11", EX, A $925.00

Army Truck, Kingsbury, gr w/canvas cover, w/up, 14", EX, A $225.00

Artillery Truck, Kingsbury, gr w/blk rubber tires, complete w/wooden shells, 15", EX (VG box), A $275.00

Baggage Express Stake Truck, red & bl w/blk rubber tires, 12", G, A $125.00

Big Boy Tanker, Kelmet, 1920s, blk doorless cab, red chassis, wht rubber tires, 26½", rare, EX, A.........................$2,500.00

Coal Truck, Sturditoy, 1920s, red doorless cab, blk rubber tires w/red hubs, 25", prof rstr, A $1,200.00

Delivery Truck, Kingsbury, bl box-type w/blk rubber tires, 11", VG, A $285.00

Divco Groceries Truck, Kingsbury, orange w/blk rubber tires, 9", EX, A $850.00

Dump Truck, Kingsbury, bl & orange w/wht rubber tires, 10", G, A $150.00

Dump Truck, Kingsbury, gr w/disk wheels & red-pnt hubs, CI driver, 9", G, A $125.00

Dump Truck, Kingsbury, red & blk w/wht rubber tires, 14", G, A $1,000.00

Dump Truck, Steelcraft, gr & yel w/disk wheels, 24", rstr, A.......$100.00

Dump Truck, Turner, Deluxe series, 2-tone bl, 28", NMIB, A....$2,400.00

Dump Truck, Turner, 1930s, yel w/orange bed & gr chassis, tandem rear wheels, 26", VG, A $250.00

Express Tractor Trailer Truck, Kingsbury, yel & red w/blk rubber tires, 20", EX, A.........................$200.00

Lincoln Dump Truck, Turner, headlights, working dump body, all original, 31" long, G/VG paint, A, $1,200.00.

Mack Dump Truck, Steelcraft, gr open cab w/red dump bed & hubcaps, 23", G+, A $300.00

Motor Driven Truck, Kingsbury, stake-side body with decals, spring-driven motor, 24" long, G, A, $5,200.00.

Moving Van, Cor Cor, 1930s, blk & red w/aluminum disk wheels, open van body w/rear step, 24", EX, A........$900.00

Parcel Delivery Truck, Kingsbury, bl open cab w/screened-in body, wht rubber tires, 10", VG, A...........................$550.00

Son-ny US Army Artillery Truck, Dayton, olive gr, revolving cannon, 24", NM, A...$625.00

Stake Truck, Kingsbury, gray w/red-pnt disk wheels, CI driver, 11", VG, A..$200.00

Stake Truck, Kingsbury, orange w/blk rubber tires & gr-pnt hubs, 12", VG, A..$600.00

Stake Truck, Marklin, red & gr w/chrome parts, 16", NM, A..$1,300.00

Tanker Truck, Sturditoy, gr w/blk rubber tires & red-pnt hubs, 25", rare, VG, A..$1,700.00

Tanker Truck, Sturditoy, red w/blk rubber tires, 32", rstr, A..$1,750.00

Tow Truck, Tri-Ang, 1920s, red w/blk rubber tires, 20", VG, A $375.00

Uranium Hauler, Ny-Lint, mk USA 2700, gr w/yel detail, hydraulic dump trailer, 23", EX, A $350.00

US Army Truck, Turner, gr w/blk rubber tires, orig canvas cover, 24", VG, A..$200.00

US Mail Truck, Sturditoy, blk open cab w/gr screened-in body, 26", VG, A $1,100.00

White Clamshell Bucket Truck, Steelcraft, 26" long, VG, A, $2,600.00.

White Dump Truck, Kelmet, 1920s, blk doorless cab, red chassis, wht rubber tires, 26", EX, A..................................$1,300.00

White Dump Truck, Kelmet, 1920s, blk doorless cab w/red spoke wheels, 26", VG, A $2,100.00

Wrecker, Kingsbury, red w/blk rubber tires, 11", VG, A $500.00

Wrecker, Kingsbury, red w/wht rubber tires, CI driver, 13", G, A..$350.00

Wrecker, Kingsbury, red w/wht rubber tires, 12", EX, A..$2,800.00

MISCELLANEOUS

Erie Locomotive, rider, Steelcraft, blk & red, orig pull cord, 28", EX, A...$750.00

Railway Express Baggage Car, rider, Steelcraft, gr & red, 23", EX, A..$600.00

Promotional Vehicles

Miniature Model T Fords were made by Tootsietoy during the 1920s, and a few of these were handed out by Ford dealers to promote the new models. In 1932 Tootsietoy was contacted by Graham-Paige to produce a model of their car. These 4" Grahams were sold in boxes as sales promotions by car dealerships, and some were sold through the toy company's catalog. But it wasn't until after WWII that distribution of 1/25 scale promotional models and kits became commonplace. Early models were of cast metal, but during the 1950s, manufacturers turned to plastic. Not only was the material less costly to use, but it could be molded in the color desired, thereby saving the time and expense previously involved in painting the metal. Though the early plastic cars were prone to warp easily when exposed to heat, by the early '60s they had become more durable. Some were friction powered, and others battery-operated. Advertising extolling some of the model's features was often embossed on the underside. Among the toy manufacturers involved in making promotionals were National Products, Product Miniature, AMT, MPC, and Jo-Han. Interest in '50s and '60s models is intense, and the muscle cars from the '60s and early '70s are especially collectible. The more popularity the life-size model attained, the more popular the promotional is with collectors.

Check the model for damage, warping, and amateur alterations. The original box can increase the value by as much as 100%. Jo-Han has reissued some of their 1950s and 1960s Mopar and Cadillac models as well as Chrysler's Turbine Car. These are usually priced between $20.00 and $30.00.

Nothing controls values of promos more than color. Thus the difference between a blue and a black car can be substantial. Until the early '90s, black cars were always in limited distribution, and many companies did not make their cars in black. For this reason, though we always use abbreviations for colors in our descriptions, we have chosen to forego that practice and instead write the color designations out in full to avoid any possible confusion. If you'd like more information we recommend *The Little Ones Sell the Big Ones!*, by our advisor Larry Blodget; ordering information may be found in the Categories of Special Interest in the Directory under Promotional Vehicles.

Advisor: Larry Blodget (B2).

1950 Ford, four-door sedan with mirrored windows, windup mechanism, 7½", EX, $125.00.

Mercury Cyclone Pace Car, Cardinal Red, EX $350.00
1940s Ford Chicago Police Car, Ford on hubcaps by Master Caster Chicago, 7", VG......................................$135.00
1949 Ford Custom, Seamist Green, EX..........................$75.00
1949 Hudson Commodore, deep maroon/ruby red, EX ..$750.00
1949 Oldsmobile Futuramic, Seafoam Green, EX $475.00
1949 Pontiac Silver Streak, Mayan Gold, EX................$135.00
1953 Ford Sunliner w/Coronado Deck, Seafoam Green, EX......$195.00
1954 Mercury Monterey Sport Coupe, Bloomfield Green, EX...$350.00
1954 Pontiac Catalina, Winter White over Coral Red, EX........$175.00

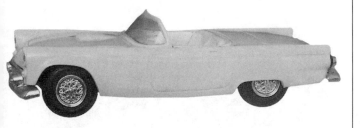

1955 Ford Thunderbird, mint green, 7¼", EX, $150.00.

1955 Ford Thunderbird, Raven Black, EX......................$350.00
1956 Chevrolet Belair, white over blue, bank, 8", EX $85.00
1956 Ford Thunderbird Convertible, coral w/cream interior, friction, NM..$200.00
1956 Plymouth Savoy, turquoise, 2-door sedan, EX........$225.00
1957 Ford Custom Sedan, gray & white, friction, rare color, EX...$350.00
1957 Ford Thunderbird, Thunderbird Bronze, EX..........$375.00
1958 Buick Roadmaster, Polar Mist, EX........................$135.00
1958 Ford Country Sedan Station Wagon, Gulfstream Blue/Colonial White, EX..$175.00

1959 Ford Thunderbird Convertible, 8", EX, $150.00.

1959 Volkswagen, coral, two-door, friction drive, no interior, EX, 7", $75.00.

1958 Ford Thunderbird, turquoise & white, friction, EX..$100.00
1958 Pontiac Bonneville, Patina White over Reefshell Pink, EX $150.00
1959 Ford Fairlane 500, dk green, friction, 8¼", EX........$85.00
1959 Oldsmobile 98, lt turquoise, plastic, EX $45.00
1960 Cheverolet Impala Convertible, Roman Red, EX .$160.00
1960 Chevrolet El Camino, pale green, EX, A $100.00
1960 Chevrolet Yellow Cab, 4-door sedan, EX...............$200.00
1960 Chrysler New Yorker, Polar White over Starlight Blue, EX $95.00
1960 Edsel Convertible, Sherwood Green, non-friction version, MIB..$550.00
1960 Ford F-100 Pickup, green w/white top, friction, NM, A $150.00
1960 Ford Galaxie Starliner, black & white, EX $175.00
1960 Ford Thunderbird, silver gray M (poor box) $55.00
1960 Mercury Park Lane, 2-door hardtop, 8" L, EX........$110.00
1961 Ford Country Squire, Mint Green w/wood trim, EX.....$300.00
1961 Ford F-100 Pickup, lt green w/white top, friction, EX...$150.00
1962 Chevrolet Corvette, Roman Red, EX $750.00
1962 Ford Thunderbird, lt blue, friction, 8", VG..............$50.00
1962 Ford Thunderbird Convertible, lt blue, friction, EX ..$200.00
1962 Imperial Crown, Oyster White, EX........................$375.00
1962 Mercury Meteor, Sultana White, EX......................$250.00
1963 Buick Riviera, Silver Cloud, EX............................$350.00
1963 Ford Galaxie, red, molded undercarriage, friction, VG .$45.00
1963 Ford Thunderbird Convertible, beige, friction, NM....$150.00
1963 Ford Thunderbird Convertible, metallic silver, EX (EX box)..$200.00
1963 Ford Thunderbird Convertible, silver, VG, A..........$50.00
1964 Cadillac DeVille Hardtop, red, Jo-Han, EX $155.00
1964 Chevrolet El Camino, Saddle Tan, EX...................$135.00
1964 Ford Fairlane Hardtop, Chantilly Beige, M (VG orig Ford mailing box)..$65.00
1964 Ford XL Convertible, cream, VG $75.00
1964 Mercury Parklane, Anniversary Silver, MIB..........$750.00
1965 Chevrolet Imapala Convertible, Evening Orchid, EX ..$375.00

1965 Ford Mustang Coupe, light blue, 7", EX, $65.00.

1965 Ford Mustang Coupe, red, EX..................................$75.00
1965 Ford Mustang Coupe, turquoise, 7", EX, A $65.00
1965 Ford Mustang Indianapolis 500 Pace Car, white, EX, car only $225.00
1965 Ford Mustang Indianapolis 500 Pace Car, white, EX, car on wood base..$350.00

1965 Ford Thunderbird Convertible, Vintage Burgundy, EX...**$350.00**

1965 Pontiac GTO, medium metallic green, NM (NM clear plastic case)..**$400.00**

1966 Chevy Custom 10 Pickup, medium red, VG, A.....**$275.00**

1966 Ford Mustang, built-in Philco radio, EX **$105.00**

1966 Ford Thunderbird, dk red, AMT, EX+ **$45.00**

1967 Ford Mustang Fastback, bright yellow, friction, NM, A .**$100.00**

1968 Chevy Camaro Rally Sport SS, cream, NM...........**$250.00**

1969 Chevrolet SS 427, blue, 8½", EX **$70.00**

1969 Corvette Convertible, red, hood mk 427, 9", NMIB, A .**$175.00**

1969 Dodge Coronet, olive green, NMIB......................**$450.00**

1970 Chevelle Hardtop, Desert Sand, EX......................**$150.00**

1970 Pontiac GTO, red, NM..**$95.00**

1972 Chevy Corvette Mille Migila Red w/454 insignias, MIB **$300.00**

1972 Chevy Corvette, Mille Miglia Red with 454 insignias, 7¼", NM, $250.00.

1972 Ford Mach I Mustang, metallic pewter, EX............**$350.00**

1973 Chevy Camaro Rally Sport 350, metallic orange, NM (VG box)..**$100.00**

1974 Chevy Corvette, metallic burnt orange, .454 engine, NM, A **$165.00**

1976 Chevy Monza 2+2, green, 7¼", NM **$15.00**

1992 Chevrolet Camaro Z28, Heritage Edition, bright red, 8", orig unused decal sheet, MIB.....................................**$32.00**

1993 Chevy Corvette, metallic burgundy, M **$25.00**

Pull and Push Toys

Pull and push toys from the 1800s often were made of cast iron with bells that were activated as they moved along on wheeled platforms or frames. Hide and cloth animals with glass or shoe-button eyes were also popular, and some were made of wood. **See also specific companies such as Fisher-Price.**

Action Andy Lawnmower, Ohio Art, head moves back & forth, VG **$45.00**

Airdale Terrier, lt brn w/blk accents, red collar, red frame w/metal wheels, EX...**$105.00**

Bear in Cart Pulled by Horse, Gong Bell, paper litho, red metal wheels, EX **$155.00**

Blimp, Los Angeles on side, early 1900s, pnt CI, gr & gold, orig wheels, 3½x11" L, VG **$610.00**

Cow on Platform, early 1900s, hide-covered cow w/glass eyes on wheeled platform, moos when head turns, 17½", EX, A **$400.00**

Daisy Bell Toy, little girl holding her doll on sled, CI w/heart-shaped spokes in wheels, 8½", VG, A **$2,900.00**

Dancing Puppies, lg puppy plays bells as heads move up & down, sm puppy spins around, EX **$135.00**

Dog on Platform, CI w/spoke wheels, 3", EX, A **$200.00**

Dog w/Basket on Platform, pnt tin w/CI spoke wheels, 6", VG, A **$275.00**

Drumming Dog Bell Toy, Gong Bell Mfg, VG+ **$75.00**

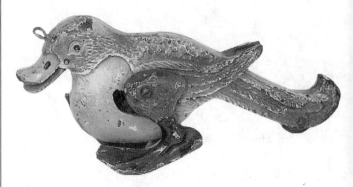

Duck, Hubley, cast iron with good original paint, waddles when pulled, mouth opens, 9½", A, $850.00.

Dutchy Dog, Gong Bell Mfg, EX (VG box)....................**$235.00**

Fireman Trix, Gong Bell Mfg #403, 1940s, paper litho on metal, wooden wheels, bell rings as it rolls along, 8x14x6", EX..**$535.00**

Fish, CI w/2 spoke wheels, mouth opens when pulled, 5", EX, A **$650.00**

Grasshopper, Hubley, CI & aluminum w/rubber tires, orig pull string, 9", EX, A **$500.00**

Horse, Germany, glass eyes, orig mane, tail & leather straps, 9½x9" L **$235.00**

Horse & Jockey Push Toy, Wilkins, horse & jockey w/2 spoke wheels, CI w/wood hdl, 30", VG, A.......................**$350.00**

Horse & Wagon, 2 wooden horses w/paper litho, legs move as if trotting, wooden wagen bed w/metal axles & wheels, EX **$115.00**

Horse on Platform, Am, pnt tin w/CI spoke wheels, 9", VG+, A **$450.00**

Horse on Platform, Germany, 1920s, blk velveteen w/wht fur mane, papier-mache saddle, wood platform w/tin wheels, EX, A **$200.00**

Horse-Drawn Ambulance Wagon, Germany, tin, w/2 figures & 2 dapple gray horses, 7", NM, A..................................**$150.00**

Horse-Drawn Cart, Fallows, red- & blk-pnt tin w/spoke wheels, single wht horse, 12", EX, A **$1,200.00**

Horse-Drawn City Car, yel- & red-pnt tin w/spoke wheels, single horse, 10", G, A...**$275.00**

Horse-Drawn Coal Wagon, Mason & Parker, CI & pressed steel w/spoke wheels, 23", VG, A..................................**$450.00**

Horse-Drawn Covered Wagon, Gibbs, wooden horse w/metal legs, metal cart w/CI spoke wheels, canvas cover, 14", EX, A **$350.00**

Horse-Drawn Covered Wagon, Gibbs, 2 wooden horses w/metal legs, metal cart w/spoke wheels, canvas cover, 19", EX, A...$300.00

Horse-Drawn Dairy Wagon, Borden's Farm Products, Rich's Dairy, pnt wood w/decals, 28", VG, A $300.00

Horse-Drawn Dairy Wagon, Sheffield Farms, wood, 21", EX, A...$650.00

Horse-Drawn Express Wagon, Fallows, red- & gr-pnt tin w/spoke wheels, single blk horse, 123", VG, A......................$350.00

Horse-Drawn Fire Pumper, Fallows, red- & blk-pnt tin w/spoke wheels, w/driver & single blk horse, 11", EX, A......$800.00

Horse-Drawn Milk Wagon, Am Milk Co, cloth-covered horse on wheeled platform, wooden cart w/8 tin milk cans, 31", EX, A $685.00

Horse-Drawn Plantation Wagon, Gibbs, 2 wooden horses w/metal legs, wooden cart w/CI spoke wheels, 19", EX, A..$200.00

Horse-Drawn Trolley, Althof Bergman, tin, 8", EX, D10...$850.00

Horse-Drawn US Mail Cart, Gibbs, wood w/metal legs, tin cart w/CI spoke wheels, 12", EX, A...............................$525.00

Horses & Cart, NN Hill Brass Co, 2 wooden horses pull wooden cart w/metal wheels, 6x15½" L, EX............................$65.00

Horses on Platform Bell Toy, Fallows, 1870s, spoke wheels, 8½", rare, EX, D10, from $3,000 to $5,000.00

Jockey on Horse, Fallows, ca 1880, painted tin, 9½" long, EX, $1,300.00 to $1,500.00. (Photo courtesy Dunbar Gallery)

King & Queen Coronation, Brio (Sweden), 2 figures in carriage pulled by 2 horses, 12½", EX......................................$70.00

Lady Riding Donkey Bell Toy, CI w/spoke wheels, 5", VG, A.$200.00

Mary & Lamb on Platform, Am, pnt tin w/CI spoke wheels, 7", rare, EX, A..$2,100.00

Monkey on Tricycle Bell Toy, Stevens, japanned CI, 8", EX, A..$2,100.00

Mule on Wheeled Platform Bell Toy, Gong Bell Mfg, CI w/ornate spoke wheels, mule pivots around & rings bell, 8", EX, A..$1,100.00

Milk Truck, Gong Bell Mfg., lithographed tin and wood, NMIB, $400.00. (Photo courtesy John Turney)

Omnibus, Merriam, ca 1870s, painted tin, 12" long, EX, from $5,000.00 to $6,500.00. (Photo courtesy Dunbar Gallery)

Old Dobbin, NN Hill Brass Co, head on horse bobs as it is pulled, chimes in rear wheels, EX...............................$65.00

Pony Cart, Gibbs, wood w/metal legs, metal cart w/CI spoke wheels, 13", VG, A...$225.00

Racing Skull, 1898, CI, w/8-man rowing team & coxswain, ornate red spoke wheels, 14½", prof rstr, A..........$3,800.00

Rooster Cart, Gibbs, wood w/metal legs & CI spoke wheels, 16", VG, A $825.00

Stagecoach & Horses (2), Northwestern Products, 1930s, tin w/hard plastic wheels, metal axles, 5½x11½", EX.....$95.00

Two-Faced Head on Cart, Gong Bell, rocks back & forth to ring bells, CI w/wooden hdl, EX......................................$185.00

Puppets

Though many collectible puppets and the smaller scale marionettes were made commercially, others were handmade and are today considered fine examples of folk art which sometimes sell for several hundred dollars. Some of the most collectible today are character-related puppets representing well-known television stars.

Advisors: Bill Bruegman (T2), finger puppets, hand puppets, and push-button puppets; Steven Meltzer (M9), marionettes and ventriloquist dolls.

See also Advertising; Black Americana; Political.

FINGER PUPPETS

Alf, Coleco, 1987, plush, M (EX box)...............................$14.00
Barney Rubble, Knickerbocker, 1972, MOC....................$15.00
Butterfly, Gymboree, soft plush fabric wings make crinkle sound
    when moved, EX...$15.00
Dick Tracy, mk Daily New Sync, 1961, EX.......................$25.00
Huckleberry Hound, hard plastic head w/cloth body, 9",
    EX $14.00
Monkees, Remco, 1970, vinyl w/cloth clothes, EX, ea $35.00
New Zoo Revue, any character, Rushton, 1970s, vinyl, NM, ea
    from $25 to...$30.00
Peanuts, Ideal/Determined, 1975, set of 6, MIB, from $30
    to $40.00
Popeye & Friends, Denmark Plastics, 1960s, Popeye, Olive Oyl,
    Sweet Pea, Whimpy & Brutus, MOC $18.00
Raggedy Ann, Bobbs-Merrill, 1977, MOC.......................$20.00

Three Stooges, 1960s, G, from $200.00 to $300.00 for the set.

HAND PUPPETS

Aliens (the movie), Medicon, 1995, soft rubber, 15", NM...$55.00
Alligator, Steiff, 1950s, multicolored mohair, M $360.00
Animal (Muppets), Fisher-Price #854, 1976-78, eyebrows move,
    mouth opens & closes, 25", EX $50.00
Babes in Toyland Toymaker, Gund, cloth & vinyl, MIB ..$50.00
Batman, Ideal, 1965, bl vinyl, MOC...............................$50.00
Bear, Steiff #6992/30, 1980-81, w/tag & button, 12", EX...$110.00
Chip & Dale Rescue Rangers, Helm Products, Disney, NM,
    pr...$60.00
Clang (HR Pufnstuf), Remco, 1970, vinyl body & head
    w/orange hair, 11", EX $50.00
Dick Tracy, Ideal, 1961, cloth & vinyl, complete w/record,
    NMIB, T2 ....$125.00

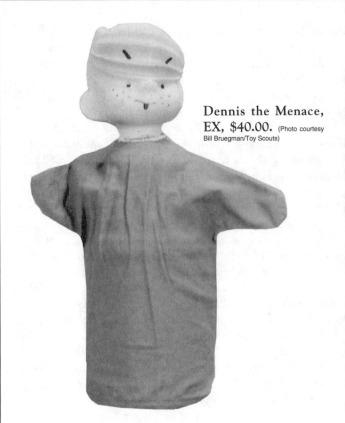

Dennis the Menace, EX, $40.00. (Photo courtesy Bill Bruegman/Toy Scouts)

Dopey, 1930s, cloth & compo, VG, M8 ....$75.00
Drool the Boglin, Mattel, 1987, glow-in-the-dark eyes, MIB...$70.00
Dumbo the Elephant, Gund, 1955, cloth & vinyl, 9", NM (EX
    box), A...$65.00
Flub-A-Dub, Zimmerman/Bob Smith, 1951, 7", EX (EX box),
    A..$150.00
Hemlock Holmes, Ideal, 1961, cloth & vinyl, NM, from $75
    to...$100.00

Mickey Mouse, Steiff, NM, $1,500.00. (Photo courtesy Dunbar Gallery)

Herman Munster, Kayro-Vue, 1964, compo head w/cloth body, EX...$65.00

Hucky Black Bird, Steiff, #6690/17, 1962-69, blk mohair, w/button, 6⅝", EX..$65.00

Jocko, Steiff #6991-30, all tags, 12", NM.......................$105.00

Joe Jitsu, Ideal, 1961, cloth & vinyl, 10", EX.................$30.00

Joe Jitsu (Dick Tracy), Ideal, 1960s, plastic head w/cloth body, w/sound effects record, NMIB.....................................$100.00

Knucklehead Smiff, Jerry Mahoney Club, 1966, MIB $190.00

Miss Piggy, Fisher-Price, EX, $35.00.
(Photo courtesy Linda Baker)

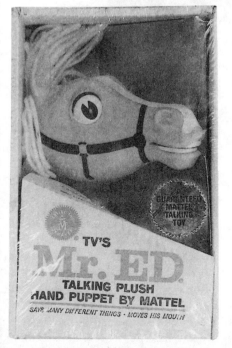

Mr. Ed, Mattel, 1962, pull-string talker, MIB, $150.00.
(Photo courtesy Bill Bruegman)

Miss Piggy, Fisher-Price, 1978, M (EX box) $45.00

Moe, Three Stooges, vinyl head w/cloth body, EX............$65.00

Monkees, Mattel, 1967, cloth & vinyl, MIB, T2 ....$300.00

Monkey, Norah Wellings (England), mohair w/glass eyes, 9", EX..$70.00

Morticia Addams, Ideal, 1965, cloth & vinyl, NM..........$65.00

Mortimer Snerd, 1950s, compo head, brn & wht checked body, EX..$95.00

Mr Bluster, Zimmerman/B Smith, 1951, 7", EX (EX box), A...$125.00

New Zoo Revue, any character, Rushton, 1970s, cloth & vinyl, NM, ea from $15 to $20.00

Olive Oyl, Gund, 1950s, cloth & vinyl, 10", M, T2, from $50 to..$60.00

Pinocchio, Gund, 1960s, cloth & plastic w/rubber boots, 11", EX, M8 ....$50.00

Pinocchio, WDP, VG, $45.00.

Raggedy Ann, unmk, 1960s?, cloth w/felt face & hands, 12", NM...$30.00

Raggedy Ann & Andy, Knickerbocker, 1973, cloth w/yarn hair, 10", MIP, ea...$25.00

Robin (Batman), Nat'l Periodicals, 1966, rubber head w/vinyl body, EX...$40.00

Rootie Kazootie, 1953, cloth & vinyl, 10", EX $30.00

Sgt Garcia (Zorro), cloth & rubber, EX, C10....................$35.00

Sherlock Holmes, Kersa (Germany), 1930s, magnifying glass in hand, button eyes, metal tag, 11½", EX...................$100.00

Smokey the Bear, Ideal, 1960s, cloth & vinyl, 10", EX.....$40.00

Tabby Cat, Steiff #0317/00, all tags, all orig, NM..........$185.00

Teddy Bear, Made in Czech, straw filled head, glass eyes, felt hands, 8", EX..$70.00

Teddy Snow Crop, 1950s, plush & rubber, 8", NM..........$50.00

Tinkerbelle, Gund, talker, cloth & vinyl, EX (EX box)....$75.00

Witchiepoo, Remco, 1971, cloth & vinyl, M $135.00

Woodstock, Determined, 1970s, velveteen w/yarn feathers, 6", NM, from $15 to...$20.00

Yoda (Empire Strikes Back), Kenner, 1980, MIB.............$42.00

MARIONETTES

Charlie Brown, Marimo Craft Ltd, 1980s, wood, 7", NM, from $65 to...$85.00

Charlie Brown, Pelham, late 1970s, 8", MIB, from $75 to .$100.00

Chinese Lady, Chinese Opera Puppet, 1940s, cvd clay head, silk embroidered costume, 18", NM..............................$160.00

Clarabelle the Clown, 1940-50, compo & wood, EX $190.00

Clippo, Virginia Austin, mfg by Curtis Crafts, 1938, w/instructions, EXIB..$90.00

Cowboy, Hazelle Special Talking Marionette #313, 1930s, 14", missing gun o/w NM (VG box)................................$105.00

Donald Duck, Pelham, in sailor uniform, EX (VG box).$105.00

Dopey (Snow White & the Seven Dwarfs), Peter Puppet Playthings, 1952, 15", NM $105.00

Dutch Boy, Hazelle #907, NM.......................................$90.00

Flub-a-Dub (Howdy Doody), 1950s, compo & wood, 4x13", EX $185.00

Frog, Pelham, 1950s, gr w/red jacket & tan pants, 12", EX ..$70.00

Horse, Hazelle, 1940s, soft vinyl head, paper-filled tan felt body, blk-pnt wooden hooves, 14x16", EX (VG box).......$110.00

Howdy Doody, Madame Alexander #15230, 8", NRFB....$80.00

Howdy Doody, Peter Puppet Playthings, 1950s, 16", EX...$100.00

Howdy Doody, Peter Puppet Playthings, 1950s, 16", EXIB..$175.00

Lion Tamer, cvd wood & compo w/cloth clothes, 25", VG...$75.00

Peppi or Sultan, Schmider Marionette Theater, Black Forest of Germany, early 1970s, cvd wood, 14", MIP, ea $90.00

Pinocchio, Pelham, 1962, 11½", EX $100.00

Princess Summerfall/Winterspring (Howdy Doody), Peter Puppet Playthings, 1950s, compo & wood w/cloth clothes, EXIB $140.00

Queen, Pelham Puppets, 1963, compo & wood w/fabric gown, MIB...$160.00

Raggedy Ann, Knickerbocker, complete, 12", NM.........$100.00

Raggedy Ann, Knickerbocker's Pushinettes, action controlled by paddle w/levers connected to strings, EXIB $275.00

Robin Hood, Hazelle's #809, 1960s, MIB......................$70.00

Snoopy, Marimo Craft Ltd, 1980s, wood, 6", NM, from $65 to...$85.00

Snoopy, Pelham, late 1970s, 8½", MIB, from $85 to.....$135.00

Snow White & the Seven Dwarfs, Madame Alexander, 1930s, compo w/cloth clothes, EX, ea $400.00

Teto the Clown, Hazelle #801, red & wht clown suit, EXIB..$80.00

Tomboy, Hazelle #804, 1938-39, EX (VG box) $105.00

Woodstock, Pelham, late 1970s, 8", MIB, from $50 to $75.00

John (of the Beatles), Mexico, ca 1960s, EX/NM, $250.00.
(Photo courtesy Barbara Crawford, Hollis Lamon, and Michael Stern)

PUSH-BUTTON PUPPETS

Atom Ant Tricky Trapeze, Kohner, 1962, EX $25.00

Bamm-Bamm, Kohner, 1960s, EX $25.00

Bronco Bill, Kohner #125, wooden, 6", EX......................$40.00

Bullwinkle, Imperial, 1972, EX $110.00

Cowboy on Horse, Kohner #3990, wht horse, cowboy w/gr shirt, red pants, blk hat & boots, blk base, 5", NM $65.00

Mickey Mouse and Donald Duck, Pelham, 1970s, Made in England, M (in blue box, numbered edition), $350.00 each.
(Photo courtesy Joel Cohen)

**Atom Aunt, Kohner,
1960s, EX, $25.00.**
(Photo courtesy June Moon)

**Mickey Mouse, Kohner,
1948, EX, $150.00.**
(Photo courtesy June Moon)

Elmo, Sony/Japan, 4", MOC, A7......................................$25.00
Elsie the Cow, Mespo, 6", EX $80.00
Fred Flintstone, Arco, 1975, 4", NM..................................$35.00
Happy the Dog, Kohner, 1950s, wooden, EX (VG box)...$40.00
Huckleberry Hound, Kohner, NM.......................................$45.00
I'm Robot, Kohner, 1960s, 4¾", NM...................................$60.00
Kermit the Frog, Sony/Japan, 4", MOC, A7 ....$25.00
Lone Ranger, Kohner, 1960s, M $70.00

Popeye, Kohner, 1950s, hard plastic, 4", NM....................$32.00
Pumpkin Man, Funworld, pumpkin head, gr body w/blk arms,
    legs & hat, pumpkin base, 3½", VG+ $15.00
Snoopy Flying Trapeze, Aviva/Hasbro, 1979, MIB............$15.00
Superman, Kohner, 1966, 4", NM, A.............................$125.00
Wilma Flintstone, Kohner, 1960s, NM, J6........................$35.00
Winnie the Pooh, Kohner, 1960s, EX+ $35.00
Winnie the Pooh, Toybox/Japan, M, A7.........................$20.00
Woodstock Flying Trapeze, Aviva/Hasbro, 1979, MIB, from $10
    to $15.00

VENTRILOQUIST DOLLS

Ventriloquist dolls have pull-strings from the back of the neck for mouth movement. Dummies have a hollow body, with the head mounted on a pole controlled through an opening in the back of the body. Charlie McCarthy was produced in doll or hand puppet form by Ideal, Juro, and Goldberger (currently). Jerry Mahoney was produced by Juro and later by Paul Winchell's own company. Vinyl-headed ventriloquist dolls are still being produced by Goldberger and include licensed versions of Charlie McCarthy, Mortimer Snerd, Bozo, Emmet Kelly, Laurel and Hardy, Howdy Doody, Danny O'Day, WC Fields, and Groucho.

Charlie McCarthy, Effanbee, 1930s, EX..........................$210.00
Emmet Kelly, Juro, 30", NM (w/trunk) $100.00
Jerry Mahoney, head mk Paul Winchell 1966, 22", MIB, M9 ...$350.00
Knucklehead Smiff, Juro, 1960s, vinyl head & hands, orig
    clothes & instruction booklet, 24", NM $360.00
McGruff the Crime Dog, Puppet Productions, 28", EX ..$125.00
Mickey Mouse, Horseman, 1973, NM..............................$70.00
Mortimer Snerd, Juro, 1968, 30½", EX............................$140.00

**Lucy, Ideal, EX,
$45.00.**

Olive Oyl, Kohner, 1950s, hard plastic, 4", EX $35.00
Pebbles, Kohner, 1960s, EX $25.00

Oliver Hardy, Goldberger/Eegee, 1983, 25", MIB $50.00

Pee-Wee Herman, Matchbox, 1988, 25", NM (NM box)..$150.00

Rodney Rabbit, Axtell, stuffed body, EX....................$245.00

Slappy, Bozo the Clown, Goldberger, 1986, 30", NRFB ...$60.00

Stan Laurel, Goldberger/Eegee, 1983, 25", MIB $50.00

Velvel, Juro, 1960s, NM $200.00

WC Fields, Play Pal, 33", NM (VG box) $80.00

Willie Talk, Horsman, stuffed cloth & vinyl w/cloth clothes, 22", EX, from $25 to $35.00

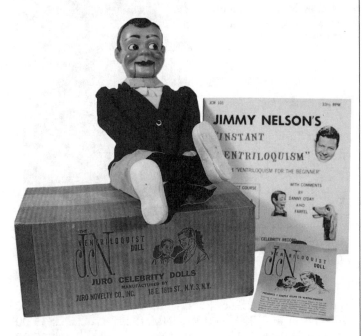

Jerry Mahoney, Jimmy Nelson, 1950s, with instruction sheet and LP record 'Instant Ventriloquism,' comments by Danny O'Day, MIB, $185.00. (Photo courtesy June Moon)

Puzzles

Jigsaw puzzles have been around almost as long as games. The first examples were handcrafted from wood, and they are extremely difficult to find. Most of the early examples featured moral subjects and offered insight into the social atmosphere of their time. By the 1890s jigsaw puzzles had become a major form of home entertainment. Cube puzzles or blocks were often made by the same companies as board games. Early examples display lithography of the finest quality. While all subjects are collectible, some (such as Santa blocks) often command prices higher than games of the same period.

Because TV and personality-related puzzles have become so popular, they're now regarded as a field all their own apart from character collectibles in general, and these are listed here as well, under the subtitle 'Character.'

Advisors: Bob Armstrong (A4), non-character related; Bill Bruegman (T2), character.

See also Advertising; Barbie; Black Americana; California Raisins; Paper-Lithographed Toys; Political.

After 50 Years, Rollo Purrington, 1930s, plywood, 345 angular-knob interlocking pcs, EX (EX box), A4 ....$125.00

All on a Summer's Day, Tuck/Zag-Zaw, 1930s, plywood, 350 ear-let interlocking pcs, EX (EX box), A4 ....$140.00

Ann Hathaway's Cottage, 1930s, plywood, 566 interlocking pcs, MIB, A4 ....$75.00

Autumn Reflections, early 1900s, wood, 255 push-to-fit pcs, color-line cut, EX (rpl box), A4 ....$100.00

Bearing the Brunt, FAO Schwarz, 1950s, plywood, 750 random interlocking pcs, EX (EX box), A4 ....$125.00

Bombs Away, Perfect Picture Puzzle, 375 pcs, NMIB, A1 ..$40.00

Boy Eating Apples (Untitled), 1930s, plywood, 135 pcs, EX (rpl box), A4...$25.00

Cathedral of Amiens, Parker Bros/Pastime, 1930-40, plywood, 363 curve-knob jagged-edge interlocking pcs, EX (EX box), A4 ....$175.00

Convent in Bruges, Parker Bros/Pastime, 1941, plywood, 202 bulb-knob jagged-edge pcs, color-line cut, EX (EX box), A4..$95.00

Coronation of Queen Elizabeth, Hayter/Victory, 1953, plywood, 300 rnd-knob strip-cut interlocking pcs, EX (EX box), A4..$50.00

Eiffel Tower, 1930s, plywood, 300 fantasy-knob interlocking pcs, EX (rpl box), A4...$65.00

Falls at Yellowstone, J Straus, 1950-60, plywood, 1,000 rnd-knob strip-cut interlocking pcs, EX (EX box), A4............$125.00

Fighters for Freedom, Whitman, 250 pcs, EX (EX box), A1..$35.00

Forest Rangers in Action, J Straus, 1940s, plywood, 200 rnd-knob semi-strip cut interlocking pcs, EX (EX box), A4 ....$25.00

Fox Hunters Meet, Parker Bros, 1930s-40s, plywood, 300 rnd-knob interlocking pcs, color-line cut, EX (EX box), A4 ....$125.00

Game Robber, Puzzle Port, 1930s-40s, plywood, 1,191 rnd-knob jagged-edge semi-interlocking pcs, EX (EX box), A4 ....$300.00

Grim Outlook, portrait of a Black Feet Chief, by Winold Reiss, approximately eight hundred pieces, shrink wrapped, original box, A, $690.00.

George Washington at Valley Forge, L Clift/Miloy, 1930s, plywood, 395 crescent-knob interlocking pcs, EX (EX box), A4..$120.00

Glamour of the East, Tuck/Jazz, 1910-20, plywood, 100 jagged-edge pcs, EX (EX box), A4...$30.00

Grand Canyon, J Straus, 1940-50, plywood, 250 rnd-knob interlocking pcs, EX (EX box), A4.................................$35.00

Hazy Hills, Parker Bros/Pastime, 1950s, plywood, 1,000 rnd-knob earlet interlocking pcs, color-line cut, EX (EX box), A4...$450.00

Here's to Another Success, Hayter/Victory/Popular, 1950s, plywood, 600 rnd-knob strip-cut interlocking pcs, EX (EX box)..$75.00

Hey Diddle Diddle, Madmar/Interlox, 1930s, plywood, 30 random-knob interlocking pcs, EX (EX box) $10.00

Home of Shakespeare's Mother, Tuco, 1930s, 200 crooked-line strip-cut pcs, EX (EX box), A4...................................$16.00

In the Valley, early 1900s, wood, 236 push-to-fit pcs, color-line cut, EX (rpl box), A4...$80.00

Interrupted Supper, Fuller Novelty, 1930s, plywood, 250 random-knob interlocking pcs, EX (EX box), A4...........$75.00

Land of the Sky Blue Water, J Straus, 1930s, plywood, 500 rnd-knob strip-cut interlocking pcs, EX (EX box), A4.....$60.00

Limit of Wind & Sail, F Bell, 1930s, plywood, 269 rnd-knob interlocking pcs, EX (EX box), A4.............................$65.00

Mother Goose, pressboard, 1910s, each 18-piece puzzle: 9" x 15¾", puzzle only, $10.00. (Photo courtesy Bob Armstrong)

Ludwig's Castle, Austria, 1930s, plywood, 144 curve-knob interlocking pcs, color-line cut, EX (EX box), A4.............$40.00

Market in Cairo, Parker Bros/Pastime, 1924, plywood, 496 curve-knob pcs, color-line cut, EX (EX box), A4....$225.00

Market Place in Spain, Parker Bros/Pastime, 1930s, plywood, 352 jagged-edge pcs, color-line cut, EX (EX box), A4......$175.00

Mary Ardens Cottage, Tuck/Zag-Zaw, 1930s, plywood, 200 earlet interlocking pcs, EX (EX box), A4..........................$85.00

Mount Holy Cross, Sat-Put, 1930s, plywood, 724 curve-knob interlocking pcs, EX (EX box), A4 ....$125.00

Mountain Splendor, Palatial, 1930s, cb, 300 sq-knob strip-cut interlocking pcs, EX (EX box), A4...$15.00

Natures Splendor, Galles, 1930s, plywood, 300 sq-knob interlocking pcs, EX (EX box), A4 ....$75.00

Old Forum & Senate in Rome, 1930s, plywood, 500 rnd-knob strip-cut interlocking pcs, EX (rpl box), A4 ....$50.00

Old Musicians, Parker Bros/Pastime, 1909, plywood, 163 push-to-fit pcs, color-line cut, EX (EX box), A4 ....$75.00

On the Riviera, J Straus, 1930s, plywood, 300 jagged-edge interlocking pcs, EX (EX box), A4 ....$80.00

Oven at Bar Harbor, Hayes/JMH Woodcraft, 1940s, plywood, 696 rnd-knob interlocking pcs, EX (EX box), A4 ...$175.00

Pharoah's Horses, Tuco, 1930s, cb, 357 crooked-line strip-cut pcs, EX (EX box), A4 ....$20.00

Poor Poet, Halfway House Curative, 1930s, plywood, 300 interlocking pcs, EX (EX box), A4 ....$85.00

Progress of Democracy, A Lowell, 1920-30, plywood, 171 angular push-to-fit pcs, EX (EX box), A4 ....$50.00

Progress of Democracy, Perfect Picture Puzzle, 375 pcs, NMIB, A1 ....$45.00

Purple Shadows, Hayter/Victory/Super-Cut, 1940-50, plywood, 600 rnd-knob pcs, color-line cut, EX (EX box), A4...$200.00

Quiet Retreat, Atlantic/Kingsbridge, 1950-60, plywood, 312 rnd-knob strip-cut interlocking pcs, EX (EX box), A4.......$30.00

Raking the Hay, Parker Bros, early 1900s, plywood, 230 curve-knob semi-interlocking pcs, color-line cut, EX (EX box), A4 ....$85.00

Ramsar Church, Germany, Ambassador, 1960-70, plywood, 400 rnd-knob strip-cut interlocking pcs, EX (EX box), A4 .$40.00

Ruins of Merchants Exchange, C Russell, 1976, plywood, 320 rnd-knob interlocking pcs, color-line cut, EX (EX box), A4 .$115.00

Safeguards of Liberty, Tuco, 320 pcs, EX (EX box), A1 ....$55.00

Saturday Afternoon, A Grinnell/Superior, 1909, plywood, 272 push-to-fit pcs, color-line cut, EX (EX box), A4........$75.00

Shepherd w/Flock (Untitled), Parker Bros, 1920s, plywood, 300 earlet interlocking pcs, color-line cut, EX (EX box), A4.....$100.00

Stay-At-Home, Milton Bradley/Mayfair, 1932, cb, 200 crooked-line strip-cut pcs, EX (EX box), A4............................$15.00

There Are Fish Dad, J Straus, 1950s, plywood, 250 rnd-knob strip-cut interlocking pcs, EX (EX box), A4 ....$50.00

Those Good Old Times, Tri-Ply, 1930s, plywood, 136 sq-knob interlocking pcs, EX (EX box), A4............................$40.00

Trail Herd, J Straus, 1950s, plywood, 250 rnd-knob strip-cut interlocking pcs, EX (EX box), A4............................$35.00

Trouble Bruin, J Straus, 1940-50, plywood, 750 rnd-knob strip-cut interlocking pcs, EX (EX box), A4 ....$125.00

United States Map, Parker Bros, 1915, plywood, 52 rnd-knob interlocking pcs, color-line cut, EX (rpl box), A4 .....$20.00

Untitled (loading freighter), 1940s, plywood, 140 pieces, puzzle only, 9¾" x 11", $16.00. (Photo courtesy Bob Armstrong)

Venice at Eventide, J Straus, 1930s, plywood, 200 jagged-edge interlocking pcs, EX (EX box), A4 ....$25.00

Washington Goes to Church, Hawkes, 1930s, plywood, 350 push-to-fit pcs, color-line cut, EX (EX envelope), A4 ....$120.00

Way-Up Forward, Madmar/Interlox, 1930s, plywood, 400 lg earlet interlocking pcs, EX (EX box), A4 ....$100.00

Wings in the Night, All American by Dell, 1942, 280 pcs, EX (EX box), A1 ....$40.00

Winter, Parker Bros, 1938, plywood, 509 rnd-knob interlocking pcs, color-line cut, EX (EX box), A4 ....$200.00

CHARACTER

Aquaman, jigsaw, Whitman, 1968, 100 pcs, MIB, T2 ......$50.00

Babes in Toyland, jigsaw, Whitman, 1961, 70 pcs, M (VG box), M8 ....$25.00

Banana Splits, fr-tray, Whitman, 1969, set of 4, MIB $50.00

Banana Splits, fr-tray, Whitman, 1969, 10x8", complete, EX, A7 ....$40.00

Batman, jigsaw, United Kingdom, 1966, Crashing the Barrier, complete, 15x10", EXIB $30.00

Batman, jigsaw, Whitman, 1966, 150 pcs, 14x18", NMIB ..$30.00

Batman w/Robin the Boy Wonder, jigsaw, APC, 1973, 81 pcs, EX (EX canister) $15.00

Beverly Hillbillies, jigsaw, Jaymer, complete, MIB, from $25 to $30.00

Bionic Woman, fr-tray, APC, 1976, complete, MIP, from $35 to $45.00

Bionic Woman, jigsaw, Whitman, 1976, complete, MIB, from $40 to $50.00

Brady Bunch, fr-tray, Whitman #4558, complete, EX.......$45.00

Captain America, fr-tray, 1966, complete, EX $25.00

Captain America, jigsaw, Whitman, 1976, complete, NMIB ..$30.00

Charlie's Angels, jigsaw, HG Toys, 1976, 150 pcs, MIB, from $25 to $30.00

Chatty Baby, fr-tray, Whitman, 1960s, MIP $30.00

Cinderella & the Prince at Midnight, jigsaw, Jaymar, 1950s, complete, VG (G box), M8 ....$20.00

Cloud Strife, jigsaw, Final Fantasy 7, Japan, 7x10⅛", M (sealed box) $35.00

Creatures of the Outer Limits, Milton Bradley, 1964, complete, 19x20½", EXIB $240.00

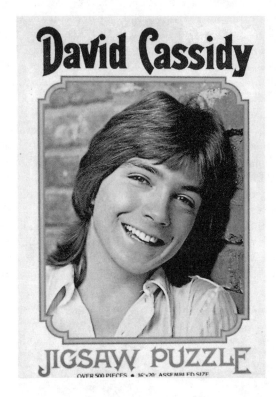

David Cassidy, APC, 1972, MIB, from $35.00 to $45.00.
(Photo courtesy Greg Davis and Bill Morgan)

Dick Tracy Big Little Book Picture Puzzles, Whitman, 1938, set of 2, NM (EX box), A $285.00

Disney World, jigsaw, Whitman/Western, 1970s, depicts Donald, Huey, Dewey & Louie in 20,000 Leagues Under the Sea, MIB $45.00

Donald Duck, jigsaw, Golden/Western, 1983, w/Daisy, Huey, Dewey & Louie in haunted house, 100 pcs, 14x18", MIB (sealed) $20.00

Donald Duck, jigsaw, Whitman, 1965, 100 pcs, 8½x11", M (sealed box) $40.00

Donald Duck, jigsaw, Whitman/Western, Donald, Uncle Scrooge, Huey, Dewey & Louie in money vault, MIB (sealed) $23.00

Donnie & Marie, jigsaw, Whitman, 1976, complete, MIB ..$35.00

Dracula, jigsaw, 1974, complete, EX (EX canister) $20.00

Eight Is Enough, jigsaw, APC, 1978, complete, MIB $25.00

Family Affair, fr-tray, Whitman, 1971, complete, MIP $35.00

Fantastic Four, jigsaw, Third Eye, 1971, 500 pcs, MIB, T2 ..$100.00

Farrah Fawcett, jigsaw, APC, 1977, 405 pcs, MIB, from $35 to $40.00

Flipper, jigsaw, Whitman, 1965, 100 pcs, MIB $25.00

Green Hornet, fr-tray, Whitman, 1966, set of 4, MIB, T2, from $100 to $125.00

H.R. Pufnstuf, Whitman #4507, 1970, frame tray, Whitchiepoo's boat, NM, from $25.00 to $35.00. (Photo courtesy Greg Davis and Bill Morgan)

James Bond, jigsaw, Thunderball, Bond's Battle, Milton Bradley, 1965, complete, EXIB.................................$45.00

Jonny Quest, jigsaw, Rescued, Milton Bradley, 1964, complete, 10x19", EXIB $80.00

Jonny Quest, jigsaw, Suprise Attack, Milton Bradley, 1964, complete, EXIB..$80.00

Josie & the Pussycats, HG Toys, 1976, complete, MIB.....$30.00

KISS, jigsaw, Casse-Tete, 1977, NMIB.............................$25.00

Lassie, fr-tray, Milton Bradley, 1959, w/puppies, complete, 14x10", EX $25.00

Lassie, fr-tray, Whitman, 1966, complete, NM $20.00

Lassie, fr-tray, Wrather, 1966, w/Forest Ranger, 8x10", EX...$15.00

Liddle Kiddles, fr-tray, Whitman, 1966, complete, M.......$55.00

Love Boat, jigsaw, HG Toys, 1978, 150 pcs, MIB..............$20.00

Ludwig Von Drake, jigsaw, Whitman Jr, 1962, 70 pcs, complete, EXIB...$60.00

Marvel Super Heroes, jigsaw, Milton Bradley, 1966, 100 pcs, MIB, T2 ....$125.00

Mary Poppins, fr-tray, Whitman #4436, 1964, 11½x14½", VG $18.00

Mighty Heroes, fr-tray, Whitman, 1967, complete, 14x11", M, T2...$50.00

Mork & Mindy, jigsaw, Milton Bradley, 1978, 250 pcs, MIB ...$15.00

Mr Magoo, fr-tray, Whitman, 1965, complete, NM..........$20.00

Munsters, jigsaw, Whitman, 1965, 100 pcs, EX (EX box)..$35.00

Nancy Drew, jigsaw, APC, 1970s, complete, NM (NM canister) $30.00

Patty Duke, jigsaw, Whitman Jr, 1963, 100 pcs, MIB, from $35 to $45.00

Peter Pan, jigsaw, Einson-Freeman, 1932, Every Week Puzzle Series #12, cb, 150 pcs, complete, 10½x14½", EX (G box) $38.00

Pinocchio, jigsaw, Jaymar, 300 pcs, complete, 14x22", VG (G box)..$38.00

Raggedy Ann, fr-tray, Milton Bradley, 1955, complete, 10x14", NM, from $25 to.....................................$35.00

Raggedy Ann & Andy, fr-tray, Whitman, 1976, complete, 11x8", MIP...$10.00

Raggedy Ann & Andy, jigsaw, Milton Bradley, 1989, 60 pcs, MIB...$15.00

Road Runner, fr-tray, 1966, complete, NM $20.00

Roger Ramjet, fr-tray, Whitman, 1966, complete, 14x11", M, T2..$75.00

Simpsons, jigsaw, Milton Bradley, 100 pcs, MIB (sealed), K1 ..$16.00

Six Million Dollar Man, fr-tray, APC, 1976, complete, MIP...$35.00

Six Million Dollar Man, jigsaw, APC #1536, from $8.00 to $12.00. (Photo courtesy Greg Davis and Bill Morgan)

Skippy, jigsaw, Consolidated Paper, 1933, set of 3, M (EX box), A $125.00

Snoopy, jigsaw, MB Games (Holland), 1989, Snoopy & Gang under a rainbow, 1,000 pcs, 27x20", EXIB $10.00

Snow White, Whitman, 1938, complete (VG box), $125.00.

Snoopy, jigsaw, Milton Bradley, 1989, Snoopy & Gang playing baseball, 1,000 pcs, complete, 27x20", EXIB $10.00

Snoopy, jigsaw, Virca (Italy), 1965, Snoopy plaing billiards w/Woodstock, 1,000 pcs, complete, 20x28", EX (VG box) $42.00

Snoopy's House, jigsaw, Milton Bradley, 1989, 1,000 pcs, complte, 26½x19½", EXIB $12.00

Space 1999, jigsaw, Hope (England), 80 pcs, 9¼x12½", EX (G box) $32.00

Spider-man, fr-tray, Playskiil, 1981, EX $18.00

Spider-Man, jigsaw, Whitman, 1982, 100 pcs, MIB (sealed)...$8.00

Spider-Man w/Thor, jigsaw, 4-G Toys, 1974, 75 pcs, MIB, T2...$50.00

Star Wars, jigsaw, Kenner, 1977, Victory Celebration, 500 pcs, M (sealed box) $25.00

Starsky & Hutch, jigsaw, HG Toys, 1976, complete, MIB, from $25 to $30.00

Street Hawk, jigsaw, Salters, 1984, 150 pcs, complete, EXIB...$35.00

Superman, fr-tray, Whitman, 1965, complete, EX $20.00

Superman Picture Puzzles, jigsaw, Saalfield/Superman Inc, 1939, set of 6, EX (EX box), A $1,000.00

Tammy & Pepper, jigsaw, Ideal, 100 pcs, VG (VG box)...$25.00

Thunderbirds, jigsaw, Whitman, 1968, complete, EX (EX box), A7 ....$25.00

Tiny Chatty Twins, fr-tray, Whitman, 1960s, MIP............$30.00

Tom & Jerry, fr-tray, 1965, complete, NM.........................$20.00

Uncle Scrooge, jigsaw, Western, 100 pcs lg pcs, 14x18", MIB (sealed)...$40.00

Underdog, fr-tray, Whitman #4522, 1965, MIB (sealed)..$23.00

Underdog, jigsaw, Whitman, 1975, 100 pcs, MIB, T2 ......$25.00

Woodsy Owl, jigsaw, Whitman, 1976, circular, 125 pcs, complete, 20" dia, EX (VG- box)..$25.00

Radios, Novelty

Many novelty radios are made to resemble a commercial product box or can, and with the crossover interest into the advertising field, some of the more collectible, even though of recent vintage, are often seen carrying very respectible price tags. Likenesses of famous personalities such as Elvis or characters like Charlie Tuna house transistors in cases made of plastic that scarcely hint at their actual function. Others represent items ranging from baseball caps to Cadillacs. To learn more about this subject, we recommend *Collector's Guide to Novelty Radios, Books I* and *II*, by Marty Bunis and Robert F. Breed.

Ballantine's Scotch, bottle shape, made in Hong Kong, 9", EX $25.00

Batman, 1973, bust figure, EX (EX box) $30.00

Boxing Kangaroo, cloth figural, official product of American Cup Defense in 1987, Korea, 11" H, NM $100.00

Bubble Yum, Soft 'N Juicy Bubble Gum, box shape, made in Hong Kong, 3½x4¾", NM..$50.00

Budweiser, can shape, complete w/battery that came in box, MIB $25.00

Bugs Bunny, Warner Bros/Looney Tunes, 1995, Bugs on set of headphone radios, AM/FM, with input jack for CD or cassette player, NM, $35.00.
(Photo courtesy Marty Bunis and Robert Breed)

Welcome Back Kotter, Whitman, 1977, frame tray, MIP, $12.50.

Chaparral Boats/Yamaha, Isis model 103 or model 39, ea ...$35.00

Cherry 7-Up, Popworks jukebox, M, from $50 to $75.00

Chicken & Egg, clock/radio, AM/FM, quartz, Japanese clock movement, 6⅛x9", NM...$60.00

Coco-Cola, Enjoy Coco-Cola Classic, Isis billboard style, AM/FM, NM $100.00

Cool Sounds, cooler bag w/AM/FM radio, distributed by Sunhill, 8x13", NM $25.00

Dockers, FM only, made in Taiwan, 3¼x2¼", NM..........$30.00

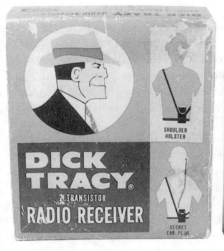

Dick Tracy, Japanese transistor distributed by America of Brooklyn, NY, #1000, NM, 4", from $100.00 to $125.00. (Photo courtesy Marty Bunis and Robert Breed)

Evil Knievel, tire shape, Montgomery Wards, 1974, battery-op, EX..$35.00

Ford 250 Camper, Philco-Ford model P-23, NM, from $300 to..$350.00

Girl w/Bird, girl holds bird in hand that moves as station pointer, Japan, 7½x7", NM $40.00

Heileman's Old Style Beer, can shape, NM......................$65.00

Heinz's Tomato Soup Can, Hong Kong, NM, from $40 to $60.00

Hershey's Syrup, bottle shape, battery-op, 4x8", MIB.......$40.00

Kellogg's Special K, AM/FM, made in China, NM...........$50.00

Kendall Dual Action Heavy Duty Motor Oil, sm profile can, NM..$35.00

Little Debbie Swiss Cake Rolls, Isis model 103, NM, from $25 to..$35.00

Malibu Rum, bottle shaped, AM/FM, 11", EX $20.00

MCI, Make Our Customers See Stars, Friends & Family, Isis model 39, NM...$30.00

McIlhenny Tabasco Brand Pepper Sauce, AM/FM, made in China, 2¾x5", NM...$75.00

Mountain Dew Can, Hong Kong, NM, from $35 to.........$50.00

Mr T, 1983, shows BA Baracus (Mr T) flexing his muscles, belt clip on back, battery-op, 4¼x5", NM.........................$30.00

Mug Root Beer, 1970s, can shape, MIB............................$25.00

National Adhesives, oil-drum shape, made by PRI/HKA of Hong Kong, NM $65.00

Nixon, likeness of Nixon in victory sign pose, NM $75.00

Pink Panther, stuffed cloth, 12", NM, from $25 to $35.00

Polaroid 600 Plus, film pack shape, 4x5", NM $30.00

Power Rangers, Micro Games of America, 6" x 5½", NM, $25.00. (Photo courtesy Marty Bunis and Robert Breed)

Pepsi, shirt-pocket style, $25.00. (Photo courtesy Marty Bunis and Robert Breed)

Poweready Batteries, older mold that used water reservoir covers, from $50.00 to $75.00. (Photo courtesy Marty Bunis and Robert Breed)

Radio Shack, rnd battery shape, AM, 4½x2½" dia, NM..**$20.00**
RADIO/Mountain Dew, Isis model 20, NM **$75.00**
Safety Kleen, parts-washing sink shape, PRI, NM **$50.00**
Scooby Do, 1972, brn head w/gr collar & red tongue hanging
    out of his mouth, NM...**$28.00**
Sears Best Easy Living Paint Can, Hong Kong, NM, from $35
    to...**$50.00**

**Smurf, Peyo, 1964, stereo series, radio: 5½" x 6", speakers: 5¼"
x 5", NM, from $50.00 to $75.00.** (Photo courtesy Marty Bunis and Robert Breed)

Snoopy, Determined, 1983, plush figure w/battery housed in zip-
    pered stomach, 8", MIB, from $35 to **$45.00**
Snoopy Doghouse, Determined, 1970s, plastic, 6x4", NMIB,
    from $50 to..**$60.00**
Snoopy Spaceship, Concept 2000/Determined, 1970s, AM, plas-
    tic, 6x8", MIB, from $125 to **$175.00**
Sosnick Hot Mustard, Russian Style, AM/FM, made in China,
    3x5", NM **$75.00**
Sunkist Orange Soda, AM/FM, NM **$40.00**
Thunderbirds, ITC Entertainment Group Ltd, 1992, NM, from
    $75 to..**$100.00**
Tune-A-Fish, AM/FM shower radio, Spectra, MIP...........**$20.00**
Watkins Baking Powder, can shape, battery-op, 5½", NM (VG
    box)..**$35.00**
Wrangler, resembles leather w/stitching around edges, 3½x4¾",
    NM...**$35.00**
Yogi Bear, Hanna-Barbera/Markson, NM, from $100 to...**$125.00**

Ramp Walkers

Ramp walkers date back to at least 1873 when Ives produced two versions of a cast-iron elephant walker. Wood and
composition ramp walkers were made in Czechoslovakia and the

U.S.A. from the 1930s through the 1950s. The most common
were made by John Wilson of Pennsylvania and were sold worldwide. These became known as 'Wilson Walkies.' Most are two-
legged and stand approximately 4½" tall. While some of the
Wilson Walkies were made of a composite material with wood
legs (for instance, Donald, Wimpy, Popeye, and Olive Oyl),
most are made with cardboard thread-cone bodies with wood
legs and head. The walkers made in Czechoslovakia are similar
but they are generally made of wood.

Plastic ramp walkers were primarily manufactured by the
Louis Marx Co. and were made from the early 1950s through the
mid-1960s. The majority were produced in Hong Kong, but
some were made in the United States and sold under the Marx
logo or by the Charmore Co., which was a subsidiary of the
Marx Co. Some walkers are still being produced today as fast-
food premiums.

The three common sizes are: (1) small, about 1½" x 2"; (2)
medium, about 2¾" x 3"; and (3) large, about 4"x 5". Most of
the small walkers are unpainted while the medium or large sizes
were either spray painted or painted by hand. Several of the
walking toys were sold with wooden plastic or colorful lithographed tin ramps.

Advisor: Randy Welch (W4).

Advertising

Captain Flint, Long John Silvers, 1989, w/plastic coin
    weight **$15.00**
Choo-Choo Cherry, Funny Face drink mix, w/plastic coin
    weight...**$60.00**
Flash Turtle, Long John Silvers, 1989, w/plastic coin weight...**$15.00**
Goofy Grape, Funny Face drink mix, w/plastic coin weight **$60.00**
Jolly Ollie Orange, Funny Face drink mix, w/plastic coin
    weight **$60.00**
Quinn Penguin, Long John Silvers, 1989, w/plastic coin
    weight **$15.00**
Root'n Toot'n Raspberry, Funny Face drink mix, w/plastic coin
    weight...**$60.00**
Sydney Dinosaur, Long John Silvers, 1989, yel & purple, w/plas-
    tic coin weight **$15.00**
Sylvia Dinosaur, Long John Silvers, 1989, lavender & pk,
    w/plastic coin weight **$15.00**

Czechoslovakian

Dog **$30.00**
Man w/Carved Wood Hat...**$45.00**
Monkey **$45.00**
Pig **$30.00**
Policeman...**$60.00**

Disney Characters

Unless another manufacturer is noted within the descriptions, all of the following Disney ramp walkers were made by the
Marx company.

Big Bad Wolf & Mason Pig..**$50.00**
Big Bad Wolf & Three Little Pigs **$150.00**

Donald Duck, pulling nephews in wagon $35.00
Donald Duck, pushing wheelbarrow, all plastic................$25.00
Donald Duck, pushing wheelbarrow, plastic w/metal legs, sm ...$25.00
Donald Duck & Goofy, riding go-cart $40.00

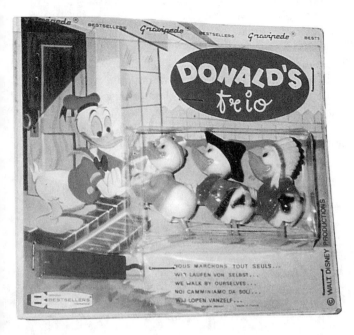

Donald's Trio, nephews as cowboy, Indian chief, the third carrying flowers, France, NMOC, $150.00. (Photo courtesy Randy Welch)

Fiddler & Fifer Pigs $50.00
Figaro the Cat, w/ball..$30.00
Goofy, riding hippo $45.00
Jiminy Cricket, w/cello $30.00
Mad Hatter w/March Hare $50.00

Mickey Mouse and Donald Duck riding alligator, $40.00.
(Photo courtesy Randy Welch)

Mickey Mouse, pushing lawn roller $35.00
Mickey Mouse & Minnie, plastic w/metal legs, sm $40.00
Mickey Mouse & Pluto, hunting $40.00
Minnie Mouse, pushing baby stroller $35.00

Pluto, plastic w/metal legs, sm $35.00

HANNA-BARBERA, KING FEATURES & OTHER CHARACTERS BY MARX

Astro, Hanna-Barbera $150.00

Astro and George Jetson, $75.00. (Photo courtesy Randy Welch)

Astro & Rosey, Hanna-Barbera $75.00
Bonnie Braids' Nursemaid, missing baby, EX $35.00
Chilly Willy, penguin on sled pulled by parent, Walter Lantz ...$25.00
Fred & Wilma on Dino, Hanna-Barbera $60.00
Fred Flintstone on Dino, Hanna-Barbera $75.00
Hap & Hop Soldiers $25.00
Little King & Guard, King Features $60.00
Pebbles on Dino, Hanna-Barbera $75.00
Popeye, Irwin, celluloid, lg..$60.00

Popeye and Wimpy, MIB, $85.00.

Popeye Pushing Spinach Can Wheelbarrow $30.00
Santa, w/gold sack...$45.00

Santa, w/wht sack $40.00
Santa, w/yel sack $40.00
Santa & Mrs Claus, faces on both sides $50.00
Santa & Snowman, faces on both sides $50.00
Spark Plug $200.00
Top Cat & Benny $65.00
Yogi Bear & Huckleberry Hound, Hanna-Barbera $50.00

MARX ANIMALS WITH RIDERS SERIES

Ankylosaurus w/Clown $40.00
Bison w/Native $40.00
Brontosaurus w/Monkey $40.00
Hippo w/Native $40.00
Lion w/Clown $40.00
Stegosaurus w/Black Caveman $40.00
Triceratops w/Native $40.00
Zebra w/Native $40.00

PLASTIC

Baby Walk-A-Way, lg $40.00
Baseball Player w/Bat & Ball $50.00
Bear $20.00
Boy & Girl Dancing $45.00
Bull $20.00
Bunnies Carrying Carrot $35.00
Bunny Pushing Cart $60.00
Camel w/2 Humps, head bobs $20.00
Chicks Carrying Easter Egg $35.00
Chinese Men w/Duck in Basket $30.00
Chipmunks Carrying Acorns $35.00
Chipmunks Marching Band w/Drum & Horn $35.00
Cow, w/metal legs, sm $20.00
Cowboy on Horse, w/metal legs, sm $30.00
Dachshund $20.00
Dairy Cow $20.00
Dog, Pluto look-alike w/metal legs, sm $20.00
Double Walking Doll, boy behind girl, lg $60.00
Duck $20.00
Dutch Boy & Girl $40.00
Elephant $20.00
Elephant, w/metal legs, sm $30.00
Farmer Pushing Wheelbarrow $30.00
Firemen $35.00
Frontiersman w/Dog $95.00
Goat $20.00
Horse, circus style $20.00
Horse, lg $30.00
Horse, yel w/rubber ears & string tail, lg $30.00
Horse w/English Rider, lg $50.00
Indian Woman Pulling Baby on Travois $95.00
Kangaroo w/Baby in Pouch $30.00
Mama Duck w/3 Ducklings $35.00
Marty's Market Lady Pushing Shopping Cart $65.00
Mexican Cowboy on Horse, w/metal legs, sm $30.00
Milking Cow, lg $40.00
Monkeys Carrying Bananas $60.00

Nursemaid Pushing Baby Stroller $20.00
Pig $20.00
Pigs, 2 carrying 1 in basket $40.00
Pumpkin Head Man & Woman, faces both sides $100.00
Reindeer $45.00
Sailors SS Shoreleave $25.00
Sheriff Facing Outlaw $65.00
Teeny Toddler, walking baby girl, Dolls Inc, lg $40.00
Tin Man Robot Pushing Cart $150.00
Walking Baby, in Canadian Mountie uniform, lg $50.00
Walking Baby, w/moving eyes & cloth dress, lg $40.00
Wiz Walker Milking Cow, Charmore, lg $40.00

WILSON

Pinocchio, $200.00; Elephant, $30.00; Donald Duck, $175.00. (Photo courtesy Randy Welch)

Eskimo $100.00
Indian Chief $70.00
Mammy $40.00
Nurse $30.00
Olive Oyl $175.00
Penguin $25.00
Pig $40.00
Popeye $200.00
Rabbit $75.00
Sailor $30.00
Santa Claus $90.00
Soldier $30.00
Wimpy $175.00

Records

Most of the records listed here are related to TV shows and movies, and all are specifically geared toward children. The more successful the show, the more collectible the record. But condition is critical as well, and unless the record is excellent or better, its value is lowered very dramatically. The presence of the original sleeve or cover is crucial to establishing collectibility.

Advisor: Peter Muldavin (M21) 45 rpm, 78 rpm, and Kiddie Picture Disks.

33⅓ RPM RECORDS

Adventures of Batman & Robin, Leo/MGM, 1966, EX (EX cover), T2 ....$30.00
Spidey Super Stories, Peter Pan, 1977, EX (EX cover), T2 ..$25.00
Uncle Wiggily, 1970, EX (EX cover), N2.........................$25.00
Wonder Woman, Batman & Superman Christmas, 1977, EX (EX cover)..$45.00

Wonder Woman, Peter Pan, 33⅓ rpm, 1977, EX (EX sleeve), $25.00. (Photo courtesy Bill Bruegman)

45 RPM RECORDS

Bing Crosby Sings Mother Goose, Golden, 1957, EX (EX sleeve), from $4 to $6.00
Flipper the Fabulous Dolphin, Golden, 1962, EX (EX sleeve), from $4 to...$6.00

Planet of the Apes Book and Record, Power Record Company, 45rpm, EX/EX+, set of four, $60.00. (Photo courtesy John and Sheri Pavone)

Popeye — Where There Is a Will, Peter Pan, 1962, EX (EX sleeve), from $10 to $12.00
Raggedy Ann & Andy at the Circus, Kid Stuff, 1980, complete w/booklet, NM (NM sleeve) $15.00
Raggedy Ann & Andy Book of Manners, Kid Stuff, 1980, complete w/booklet, NM (NM sleeve) $15.00
Raggedy Ann & Andy on a Journey Beneath the Enchanted Pond, Hallmark, complete w/booklet, EX (EX sleeve), from $30 to $35.00
Raggedy Ann & Andy Visit the Kingdom of Every Wish, Hallmark, complete w/booklet, EX (EX sleeve), from $30 to..$35.00
Wonder Woman Christmas Island, 1978, EX (EX sleeve), C10 ....$25.00

78 RPM PICTURE AND NON-PICTURE RECORDS

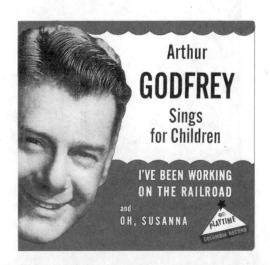

Arthur Godfrey Sings for Children, Playtime, Columbia Records, EX/NM, from $3.00 to $5.00. (Photo courtesy Peter Muldavin)

Adventures of Mighty Mouse, Rocking Horse, 1957, EX (EX cover), T2 ....$15.00

Bozo & His Rocket Ship, Capitol, 1947, EX (EX cover), from $15 to $20.00

The Churkendoose, Ray Bolger, Decca, ca 1946 (one of the all-time favorites from this era), EX (EX cover), from $10.00 to $15.00. (Photo courtesy Peter Muldavin)

Davy Crockett & the River Pirates, Golden, 1955, EX (EX cover), from $10 to $15.00

Flipper the Fabulous Dolphin, Golden, EX (EX cover), from $4 to $6.00

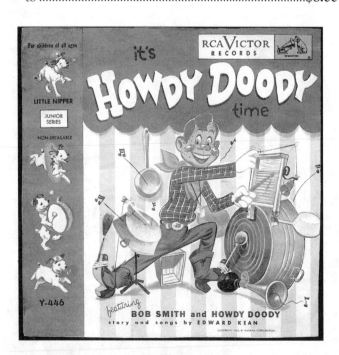

It's Howdy Doody Time, RCA Victor, 1951, EX (EX cover), from $50.00 to $60.00. (Photo courtesy Peter Muldavin)

Gabby Hayes 1001 Western Nights, RCA, 1950s, EX (VG cover) $35.00

Gulliver's Travels, Bluebird, 1939, extremely rare, EX (EX cover), from $150 to................................$200.00

Howdy Doody's Laughing Circus, RCA Victor, 1950, EX (EX cover), from $15 to................................$25.00

Little Engine That Could, RCA, 1949, EX (EX cover), from $15 to $20.00

The Lone Ranger, Decca, 1952, #6 in the series, EX (EX cover), from $30.00 to $40.00. (Photo courtesy Peter Muldavin)

Mickey & the Beanstalk, Capitol, 1948, complete w/booklet, EX (EX cover), from $20 to.............................$30.00

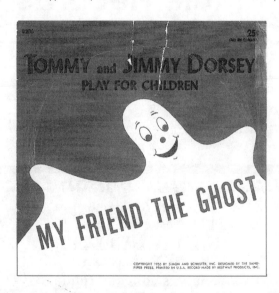

My Friend the Ghost, Tommy and Jimmy Dorsey Play for Children, Golden, 1955, EX (VG cover), from $8.00 to $12.00. (Photo courtesy Peter Muldavin)

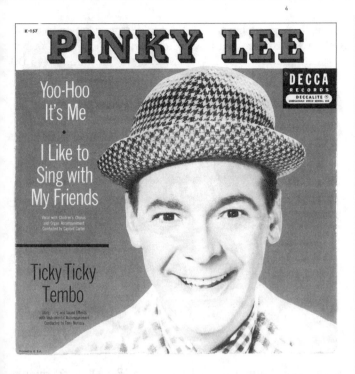

Pinky Lee, Decca Records, ca 1954, EX/NM, from $25.00 to $35.00. (Photo courtesy Peter Muldavin)

What Is a Boy, What Is a Girl, Jackie Gleason, Decca, 1954, EX/NM, from $8.00 to $15.00. (Photo courtesy Peter Muldavin)

KIDDIE PICTURE DISKS

Listed here is a representative sampling of kiddie picture disks that were produced through the 1940s. Most are 6" to 7" in diameter and are made of cardboard with plastic-laminated grooves. They are very colorful and seldom seen with original sleeves. Value ranges are for items in very good to near-mint condition. Ultimately, the value of any collectible is what a buyer is willing to pay, and prices tend to fluctuate. Our values are for records only (no sleeves except where noted). Unlike other records, the value of a picture disk is not diminished if there is no original sleeve.

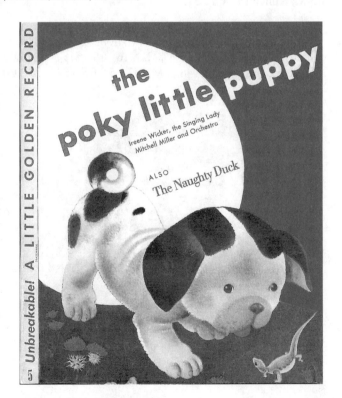

The Poky Little Puppy, Little Golden Records (from the first series, the largest kiddie record series ever made), ca 1948, EX (EX cover), from $7.00 to $12.00. (Photo courtesy Peter Muldavin)

Popeye the Sailor Man, Golden, 1957, EX (EX cover), from $8 to $12.00
Rusty in Orchestraville, Capitol, 1947, EX (EX cover), from $10 to $20.00
Simpsons Deep Deep Trouble, Geffen, M (M cover), K1 .$45.00

Bible Storytime, Standard Publishing, 78rpm, ca 1948, 7", EX/NM, from $5.00 to $10.00 each. (Photo courtesy Peter Muldavin)

A Birthday Song to You, Voco 35215, 1948, 5" sq, NM, M21, w/mailer envelope, from $40 to $45.00

A Birthday Song to You, Voco 35215, 1948, 5" sq, NM, no mailer envelope..$25.00

The Fox, Talking Book Corporation, 78rpm, 1917, very rare, 4", EX/NM, from $90.00 to $150.00. (Photo courtesy Peter Muldavin)

Gilbert & Sullivan series, Picture Tone Record Co., 78rpm, 1948, rare, 6½", EX/NM, from $30.00 to $40.00 each. (Photo courtesy Peter Muldavin)

Kitty Cat, Voco 'Pic Disc,' ca 1948, 7", EX/NM, from $4.00 to $8.00; 6" (rare size), EX/NM, from $15.00 to $25.00. (Photo courtesy Peter Muldavin)

Lionel Train Sound Effects, 1951, NM, M21, from $40 to...$60.00

Red Ryder, Record Guild of America, 1948, NM, from $35 to..$45.00

'Round and 'Round the Village, Voco 'Pic Disc,' 78rpm, ca 1948, 7", EX/NM, from $4.00 to $8.00; 6" (rare size), EX/NM, from $15.00 to $25.00. (Photo courtesy Peter Muldavin)

Rover the Strong Man, Voco, 1948, NM, from $30 to $40.00

Ten Little Indians, Voco, 1948, NM, M21, 16", from $15 to ...$25.00

Ten Little Indians, Voco, 1948, NM, M21, 7", from $4 to..$8.00

Terry and the Pirates, Record Guild of America, F501, ca 1949, 6½", EX/NM, from $35.00 to $45.00. (Photo courtesy Peter Muldavin)

Reynolds Banks

Reynolds Toys began production in 1964, at first making large copies of early tin toys for window displays, though some were sold to collectors as well. These toys included trains, horse-drawn vehicles, boats, a steam toy, and several sizes of Toonerville trolleys. In the early 1970s, they designed and produced six animated cap guns. Finding the market limited, by 1971 they had switched to a line of banks they call 'New Original Limited Numbered Editions (10 – 50) of Mechanical Penny Banks.' Still banks were added to their line in 1980 and figural bottle openers in 1988. Each bank design is original; no reproductions are produced. Reynolds's banks are in the White House and the Smithsonian as well as many of the country's major private collections. *The Penny Bank Book* by Andy and Susan Moore (Schiffer Publishing, 1984) shows and describes the first twelve still banks Reynolds produced. Values are given for mint-condition banks.

Advisor: Charlie Reynolds (R5).

MECHANICAL BANKS

Uncataloged, elephant (conversion), 1970, edition of 4.**$100.00**
1M, Train Man, 1971, edition of 30 ....**$350.00**
2M, Trolley, 1971, edition of 30 ....**$450.00**
3M, Drive-In, 1971, edition of 10 ....**$1,000.00**
4M, Pirate, 1972, edition of 10 ....**$725.00**
5M, Blackbeard, 1972, edition of 10 ....**$650.00**
6M, Frog & Fly, 1972, edition of 10 ....**$1,200.00**
7M, Toy Collector, 1972, unlimited edition **$650.00**
8M, Balancing Bank, 1972, edition of 10........................**$725.00**
9M, Save the Girl, 1972, edition of 10 ....**$2,000.00**
10M, Father Christmas, 1972, 1 made ea year at Christmas..**$850.00**
11M, Gump on a Stump, 1973, edition of 10 ....**$1,100.00**
12M, Trick Bank, 1973, edition of 10 ....**$1,000.00**
13M, Kid Savings, 1973, edition of 10.........................**$1,200.00**
14M, Christmas Tree, 1973, edition of 10......................**$725.00**
15M, Foxy Grandpa, 1974, edition of 10 ....**$975.00**
16M, Happy Hooligan, 1974, edition of 10 ....**$1,075.00**
17M, Chester's Fishing, 1974, edition of 10....................**$900.00**
18M, Gloomy Gus, 1874, edition of 10 ....**$2,800.00**
19M, Kids' Prank, 1974, edition of 10 ....**$1,100.00**
20M, Mary & Her Little Lamb, edition of 20 ....**$850.00**
21M, Spook, 1974, edition of 10 ....**$800.00**
22M, Decoy, 1974, edition of 10 ....**$600.00**
23M, Decoy Hen, 1974, edition of 10 ....**$600.00**
24M, Comedy Bank, 1974, edition of 10 ....**$975.00**
25M, Bozo, 1974, edition of 10 ....**$950.00**
26M, Reynolds Foundry, 1974, edition of 15 ....**$3,400.00**
27M, Toonerville, 1974, edition of 10 ....**$1,200.00**
28M, Bank of Reynolds Toys, 1974, edition of 10 ....**$425.00**
29M, Simple Simon, 1975, edition of 10 ....**$925.00**
30M, Humpty Dumpty, 1975, edition of 20.................**$1,250.00**
31M, Three Blind Mice, 1975, edition of 15 ....**$1,100.00**
32M, Clubhouse, 1975, edition of 10...........................**$1,100.00**
33M, Boat, 1975, edition of 10 ....**$1,500.00**
34M, St Nicholas, 1975, edition of 50 ....**$775.00**
35M, Forging America, 1976, edition of 13.................**$1,200.00**
36M, Suitcase, 1979, edition of 22 ....**$825.00**
37M, North Wind, 1980, edition of 23........................**$1,100.00**
39M, Quarter Century, 1982, edition of 25 ....**$4,000.00**
40M, Columbia, 1984, edition of 25 ....**$1,350.00**
41M, Whirligig, edition of 30 ....**$1,300.00**

42M, Miss Liberty, 1986, edition of 36 ....**$1,300.00**
42M, Miss Liberty on a Pedestal, 1986, edition of 4....**$1,600.00**
43M, Auto Giant, 1987, edition of 30.........................**$2,250.00**
45M, Campaign '88, 1988, edition of 50 ....**$3,000.00**
46M, Hollywood, 1989, edition of 35 ....**$825.00**
47M, Buffalos Revenge, 1990, edition of 35 ....**$900.00**
48M, Williamsburg, 1991, edition of 35........................**$850.00**
49M, Duel at the Dome, 1992, edition of 50...............**$1,000.00**
50M, '92 Vote, 1992, edition of 50 ....**$3,000.00**
51M, Oregon Trail, 1993, edition of 50 ....**$800.00**
52M, Norway (Lillehammer), 1994, edition of 50..........**$825.00**
53M, Shoe House, 1994, edition of 50...........................**$950.00**

54M, The J. & E. Stevens Company, 1995, edition of 50, $1,850.00. (Photo courtesy Charlie Reynolds)

56M, '96 Political Wish, 1996, edition of 50, $900.00.
(Photo courtesy Charlie Reynolds)

55M, Hyakutake (The Comet), 1996, edition of 50.......**$625.00**
58M, Uncle Louie, 1997, edition of 50 ....**$350.00**

59M, Friar's Favorite, 1997, edition of 50 .... **$1,100.00**
60M, Wall Street, 1998, edition of 98 .... **$750.00**
61M, De Bug (Y2K Bug), edition of 50 .... **$495.00**
82S, Little League Home Bank, edition of 50 .... **$145.00**
83S, Santa's Last Check, edition of 30 .... **$200.00**

STILL BANKS

01S, Amish Man, 1980, edition of 50 .... **$135.00**
02S, Santa, 1980, edition of 50 .... **$95.00**
03S, Deco Dog, 1981, edition of 50 .... **$85.00**
04S, Jelly Bean King, 1981, edition of 100 .... **$265.00**
05S, Hag, 1981, edition of 50 .... **$160.00**
06S, Snowman, 1981, edition of 50 .... **$110.00**
07S, Mark Twain, 1982, edition of 50 .... **$200.00**
08S, Santa, 1982, edition of 50 .... **$125.00**
09S, Anniversary, 1982, special edition **$200.00**
10S, Redskins Hog, 1983, edition of 50 .... **$125.00**
11S, Lock-Up Savings, 1983, edition of 50 .... **$55.00**
12S, Miniature Bank Building, 1983, edition of 50 .... **$195.00**
13S, Santa in Chimney, 1983, edition of 50 .... **$90.00**
14S, Santa w/Tree (bank & doorstop), 1983, edition of 25 .. **$325.00**
15S, Redskins NFC Champs, 1983, edition of 35 .... **$185.00**
16S, Chick, 1984, edition of 50 .... **$80.00**
17S, Ty-Up, 1984, edition of 35 .... **$225.00**
18S, Tiniest Elephant, 1984, edition of 50 .... **$110.00**
19S, Baltimore Town Crier, 1984, edition of 50 .... **$75.00**
20S, Father Christmas Comes to America, July 4th, 1984, edi-
    tion of 25 .... **$325.00**
21S, Campaign '84, edition of 100 .... **$250.00**
22S, Santa, 1984, edition of 50 .... **$100.00**
23S, Reagan '85, 1985, edition of 100 .... **$310.00**
24S, Columbus Ohio, 1985, edition of 50 .... **$60.00**
25S, Austrian Santa (bank & doorstop), 1985, edition of
    25 .... **$350.00**
26S, Halloween, 1985, edition of 50 .... **$210.00**
27S, 1893 Kriss Kringle, 1985, edition of 20 .... **$2,000.00**
27S, 1893 Kriss Kringle (w/tree & candle decorations), 1985,
    edition of 20 .... **$2,400.00**
28S, Santa Coming to a Child, 1985, edition of 50 .... **$165.00**
29S, Halley's Comet, 1986, edition of 50 .... **$190.00**
30S, 20th Anniversary, 1986, edition of 86 .... **$165.00**
31S, Father Christmas (bank & doorstop), gr, edition of 25 .. **$280.00**
32S, Santa & the Reindeer, 1986, edition of 50 .... **$185.00**
33S, Charlie O'Conner, 1987, edition of 50 .... **$90.00**
34S, Chocolate Rabbit, 1987, edition of 50 .... **$110.00**
35S, St Louis River Boat, 1987, edition of 60 .... **$75.00**
36S, German Santa (bank & doorstop), 1987, edition of 25 .. **$275.00**
37S, Graduation, 1987, special edition **$200.00**
38S, Old Stump Halloween, 1987, edition of 50 .... **$95.00**
39S, Santa in Race Car, 1987, edition of 100 .... **$130.00**
40S, Technology Education, edition of 88 .... **$65.00**
41S, Super Bowl XXII Redskins, 1988, edition of 50 .... **$90.00**
42S, Easter Rabbit, 1988, edition of 50 .... **$55.00**
43S, Florida Souvenir, 1988, edition of 75 .... **$90.00**
44S, Father Christmas w/Lantern (bank & doorstop), 1988, edi-
    tion of 35 .... **$260.00**
45S, Halloween Spook, 1988, edition of 50 .... **$90.00**

46S, NCRPBC (National Capitol Region Club), 1988, edition
    of 20 .... **$300.00**
47S, Santa on Polar Bear, 1988, edition of 75 .... **$110.00**
48S, Bush-Quayle, 1989, edition of 100 .... **$260.00**
49S, Shuffle Off to Buffalo, 1989, edition of 75 .... **$70.00**
50S, Pocket Pigs, 1989, edition of 75 .... **$125.00**
51S, Regal Santa (bank & doorstop), 1989, edition of 35 .. **$275.00**
52S, Tiniest Snowman, 1989, edition of 75 .... **$85.00**
53S, Santa on Motorcycle, 1989, edition of 75 .... **$150.00**
54S, Rabbit w/Mammy, 1990, edition of 75 .... **$225.00**
55S, Antique Row Sign Post, 1990, edition of 75 .... **$70.00**
56S, Duck w/Puppy & Bee, 1990, edition of 75 .... **$110.00**
57S, 1895 Santa w/Wreath, 1990, edition of 35 .... **$250.00**
58S, Santa on a Pig, 1990, edition of 75 .... **$140.00**
59S, St Louis Sally, 1991, edition of 55 .... **$85.00**

60S, Santa With Wassail Bowl, 1991, edition of 35, $250.00. (Photo courtesy Charlie Reynolds)

61S, Santa Express, 1991, edition of 55 .... **$125.00**
62S, Pig on Sled, 1992, edition of 55 .... **$85.00**
63S, Santa About to Leave, 1992, edition of 25 .... **$290.00**
64M, Decision 2000, Bush-Gore, edition of 50 .... **$595.00**
64S, Jack-O'-Lantern, 1992, edition of 60 .... **$80.00**
65S, Santa in Zeppelin, 1992, edition of 100 .... **$145.00**
66S, Clinton, 1993, edition of 100 .... **$310.00**
68S, Santa & the Bad Boy (Summer Santa), 1993, edition of
    50 .... **$225.00**
69S, Arkansas President, 1994, edition of 100 .... **$325.00**
70S, Santa & the Good Kids, 1994, edition of 35 .... **$260.00**
71S, Penny Santa, 1994, edition of 60 .... **$125.00**

67S, Windy City (Chicago Convention), 1993, edition of 60, $85.00. (Photo courtesy Charlie Reynolds)

72S, School Days, 1995, edition of 100 ....$110.00
73S, 1880 Snow Santa, 1995, edition of 50 ....$220.00
74S, Santa on Donkey, 1995, edition of 50.....................$110.00

75S, Dole '96 (SBCCA '96), 1996, edition of 100, $280.00. (Photo courtesy Charlie Reynolds)

83S, Santa's Last Check, edition of 30, $200.00. (Photo courtesy Charlie Reynolds)

77S, Foxy Grandpa & Egelhoff Safe, 1997, edition of 60..$200.00
78S, Halloween Witch, 1997, edition of 50 ....$95.00
79S, Christmas Time, 1997, edition of 50 ....$110.00
80S, Portland Chicks, 1998, edition of 20, pr................$155.00
81S, Old St Nicholas, 1998, edition of 20 ....$450.00
82S, Little League Home Bank, edition of 50 ....$145.00
84S, Presidential 2000 Campaign Bank, edition of 60 ...$150.00

Robots and Space Toys

Space is a genre that anyone who grew up in the '60s can relate to, but whether you're from that generation or not, chances are the fantastic robots, space vehicles, and rocket launchers from that era are fascinating to you as well. Some emitted beams of colored light and eerie sounds and suggested technology the secrets of which were still locked away in the future. To a collector, the stranger, the better. Some were made of lithographed tin, but even plastic toys (Atom Robot, for example) are high on the want list of many serious buyers. Condition is extremely important, both in general appearance and internal workings. Mint-in-box examples may be worth twice as much as one mint-no-box, since the package art was often just as awesome as the toy itself.

Because of the high prices these toys now command, many have been reproduced. Beware!

Advisor: Ed Janey (J2).

See also Marx; Guns, Miscellaneous.

Action Planet Robot, Yoshiya, advances w/sparks in face, litho tin w/plastic helmet, clockwork, 8½", EX, A...........$450.00
Answer Game Machine Robot, Anico, pnt tin w/10 plastic keys, battery-op, 15", NMIB, A.......................................$800.00

Answer Game Machine, Japan, lithographed tin, battery-operated, 15", EX (EX box), minimum value, $550.00.

Apollo 11 Space Rocket, TN, 1960s, several actions, tin & plastic, battery-op, 14", EX $165.00

Arrow Jet Spaceship #12, K, 1950s, litho tin, w/up, 6½", NM (NM box) $535.00

Astrobase, Ideal, 1960s, several actions, battery-op, complete w/car & 2 rockets, 21", EX $350.00

Astronaut, Rosko, bl litho tin w/clear helmet, battery-op, 13", NMIB, A $1,600.00

Atlas ICBM Missile Launcher, several actions, battery-op, MIB, L4...$475.00

Atom Robot, KO, bump-&-go action, litho tin, friction, 7", EX, A $200.00

Atom Robot, Yonezawa, bump-&-go action, litho tin, friction, NMIB, A...$750.00

Atom Rocket 15 Interplanetary Space Ship, Y, 1960s, several actions, tin & plastic, battery-op, 13½", EX............$225.00

Atomic Future Fire Truck, Japan, 1950s, advances w/several actions, litho tin, battery-op, 9½", EX (EX box).....$475.00

Atomic Reactor, litho tin, battery-op, NMIB, L4...........$500.00

Atomic Robot, Y, advances as upper body rotates, face changes expressions, litho tin, w/up, 6½", NM, A $525.00

Atomic Robot Man, Japan, advances w/swinging arms, litho tin, w/up, 5", NMIB, A $1,600.00

Atomic Robot Man, Japan, advances w/swinging arms, litho tin, w/up, 5", EX (worn box), A......................................$600.00

Atomic Rocket X-1800, MT, 1960s, 3 actions, litho tin, battery-op, 9", EX...$300.00

Atomic Spaceship XX-2, Japan, litho tin, friction, 12", EX (EX box), A...$200.00

Attacking Martian, SH, advances, stops & gun fires from chest, tin & plastic, battery-op, 10", NMIB, A $250.00

Billy Blastoff Space Scout, Eldon, 1968, battery-op, 4½", EX..$200.00

Chief Smoky/Mr. Chief, KO, 1950s, several actions, battery-operated, lithographed tin, scarce, 12", EX (EX box), A, $3,200.00. (Photo courtesy Skinner Auctions)

Captain Lazer, litho tin, battery-op, M, L4 ....$150.00

Chime Trooper Astronaut, Aoshin, advances as music chimes, litho tin, w/up, 9½", NMIB, A $2,400.00

Columbia Space Shuttle, litho tin, battery-op, MIB, L4...$375.00

Cragstan Astronaut, advances w/lights & sound, red or bl version, battery-op, 14", EX, A $800.00

Cragstan Astronaut, rare version w/little boy's head, litho tin, battery-op, 14", EX (VG box), A.........................$2,600.00

Cragstan Astronaut, Yonezawa, advances w/swinging arms & sound, litho tin, friction, 9½", NMIB, A..............$1,200.00

Blink-A-Gear Robot, Taiyo, battery-operated, black tin chest and head, colorful plastic gears, plastic legs and arms, emits lights and noise, 15", MIB, A, $2,100.00.

Cragstan Robot, Yonezawa, tinplate, silver-gray body, red arms and chest, plastic head with visible mechanism, battery-operated, 10½", NMIB, A, $1,800.00.

Cragstan Flying Saucer, litho tin, battery-op, MIB, L4...$475.00

Cragstan Flying Saucer, litho tin, battery-op, NM, L4 ...$325.00

Cragstan Great Astronaut, Alps, advances w/lighted screen in chest, red w/blk arms & feet, battery-op, 14", NM, A $1,100.00

Cragstan Missile Launcher, shoot rocket & hit ball, litho tin w/cb rocket scene, battery-op, NM (NM box), A ...$350.00

Cragstan Mr Robot, Y, 1960s, several actions, litho tin, battery-op, 10½", EX/NM.................$700.00

Cragstan Radical Robot, advances w/lights & sound, tin & plastic, battery-op, 12", rare, NMIB, A.......................$2,500.00

Cragstan Ranger Robot, 1960s, several actions, mostly plastic, battery-op, 10½", rare, NM, minimum value $1,000.00

Cragstan Satellite, 1950s, litho tin, battery-op, 8" dia, EX..$185.00

Cragstan Talking Robot, Yonezawa, advances w/swinging arms, several phrases, tin w/plastic ears, 11", NMIB, A.$1,400.00

Cragstan Talking Robot, Yonezawa, litho tin, battery-op, EX, L4.................................$875.00

Cragstan's Mr Robot, bump-&-go action w/lights & sound, wht w/red arms, 11", NM (worn box), A.....................$1,000.00

Dino-Robot, Horikawa, advances & head pops open to reveal monster head, tin & plastic, battery-op, 11", NMIB, A $1,500.00

Door Robot, Alps, advances w/spinning head & rotating color wheel in mouth, tin & plastic, remote control, 10", NM, A.................................$2,100.00

Dux Astroman, Germany, advances w/lighted gears in chest, plastic, remote control, 12", NMIB, A $1,700.00

Excavator Robot, SH, 1960s, several actions, plastic, battery-op, 10", EX.................................$200.00

Explorer Robot X-27, Yonezawa, metallic bl tin w/red arms & feet, friction, 10½", rare, NM, A $4,400.00

Explorer Spaceship, MT, 1950s, litho tin w/spaceman under clear plastic dome, friction, 8", NM $200.00

Fiat Abarth 750 Space Jet, litho tin, friction, EX, L4 .....$300.00

Fighting Robot, Horikawa, advances w/several actions, light on head, tin, battery-op, 11", NMIB, A.....................$1,100.00

Fighting Robot, Horikawa, several actions, tin w/plastic gears in chest, battery-op, 9", EX (EX box), A.....................$375.00

Fighting Spaceman, SH, advances, stops & gun fires from chest w/flashing lights, litho tin, battery-op, 11", EX, A ..$300.00

Flying Saucer w/Space Pilot, KO, bump-&-go action w/flashing lights & space sounds, tin, battery-op, 8" dia, NMIB, A.................................$350.00

Fork Lift Robot, Japan, several actions, litho tin & plastic, battery-op, 12", EX (EX box), A $800.00

Fulgur Virevolte (Spaceship), CHR/France, 1950s, bump-&-go action w/lights, plastic, battery-op, 11", EX (EX box), A $200.00

Gear Robot, SH, advances spinning chest gears & flashing lights, litho tin, battery-op, 11½", rare, NM (EX box), A $725.00

Guided Missile Launcher, litho tin, battery-op, NMIB, L4.................................$275.00

Inter Planet Space Captain, Naito Shoten, advances w/swinging arms, litho tin, w/up, 8", rare, NMIB, A $7,100.00

Interplanetary Rocket, Y, 1960s, several actions, litho tin, battery-op, 15", NM.................$200.00

Jupiter Robot, Yonezawa, 1950s, several actions, litho tin, battery-op, 13", extremely rare, NM, minimum value..........$2,000.00

Giant Sonic Robot, Modern Toys, lithographed tin, battery-operated, rare, 15", A, NM (EX box), $7,500.00.

Jupiter Rocket Launching Pad, TN, 1960s, several actions, litho tin, battery-op, 7", NM.................$375.00

King Ding Robot w/a Brain, litho tin, battery-op, EX, L4 ....$325.00

Krome Drome, Yonezawa, advances & grows w/sound, plastic w/metal head, battery-op, 10", NMIB, A $600.00

Laser 008, Daiya, litho tin & plastic, flywheel mechanism, 7", NM, A $500.00

Laughing Robot, Y, 1970s, 3 actions, mostly plastic, battery-op, 9½", EX.................................$125.00

Lavender Robot, MT, bump-&-go action w/swinging arms & blinking eyes, litho tin, battery-op, 15", rare, NM, A.........$3,500.00

Lost in Space Robot, Remco, 1966, plastic, all red version, 12", EX (EX box), T2.................$500.00

Lunar Bulldozer, TN, bump-&-go action w/lights & sound, litho tin & plastic, battery-op, 9½", NM (EX box), A.....$375.00

Lunar Captain, TN, several actions, litho tin & plastic, battery-op, 12", MIB, A $250.00

Lunar Hovercraft, TPS, battery-op, MIB, L4 ....$325.00

Lunar Traffic Control, Strauss, battery-op, complete, NMIB...$85.00

Machine Robot, SH, 1960s, advances w/several actions & visible gears in chest, tin, battery-op, 12", EX...............$500.00

Man From Mars, Irwin, advances w/gun, fluorescent orange plastic w/transparent gr helmet, w/up, 11", EX, A $100.00

Mars Explorer Astronaut, SH, 1960s, advances w/several actions, litho tin, battery-op, 10", NM $500.00

Mars King, SH, advances on wheels w/TV screen in chest, litho tin, battery-op, 9", VG, A $150.00

Martin the Martian (Krome Dome Robot), Yonezawa, 1960s, advances w/several actions, litho tin, battery-op, 10", rare, NM.................................$700.00

Mechanized Robot, Nomura, advances w/spinning pistons, blk w/red feet & arms, battery-op, 13", NMIB, A..........$750.00

Marvelous Mike Electromatic Tractor, Saunders Tool & Die, pressed steel tractor features robot at controls, battery-operated, 12¾", MIB, A, $275.00.

Mercury X-1 Space Saucer, Mego, bump-&-go action w/lights & sound, tin & plastic, battery-op, 8" dia, NM (EX box), A $175.00

Mighty Robot, N, advances w/sparks in chest, litho tin, w/up, 5½", EX, A $150.00

Mighty Robot, SY, advances w/lighted screen in chest, litho tin, w/up, 6", EX (EX box), A $175.00

Mighty 8 Robot w/Magic Color, MT, 1960s, several actions, litho tin, battery-op, 12", extremely rare, NM, minimum value $2,400.00

Mischievous Monkey, MT, monkey scoots up & down tree in front of doghouse, litho tin, MIB, L4 ....$500.00

Monorail Rocket Ship, Linemar, travels back & forth on cable, litho tin, battery-op, NMIB, A................................$300.00

Moon Astronaut, Daiya, 1950s, several actions, litho tin, battery-op, 9", rare, NM, from $1,000 to $1,500.00

Moon Car/Moon Space Ship, TN, lithographed tin, battery-operated, 13" long, EX+ (EX box), $1,750.00.

Moon Crawler X-12, battery-op, M, L4 ....$100.00

Moon Explorer, Japan, advances w/engine sound & spinning antenna, tin, crank action, 7½", EX-, A..................$300.00

Moon Man 001, Hong Kong, 1960s, yel plastic w/red trim, battery-op, 6", NM..$300.00

Moon Patrol, radio controlled, litho tin, MIB, L4 ....$575.00

Moon Patrol 11 Flying Saucer, Y, 1960s, several actions, litho tin & plastic, battery-op, 9" dia, EX..............................$200.00

Moon Rocket, Masudaya, advances w/lights & sound as astronaut spins at periscope, litho tin, battery-op, 10", NMIB, A..$250.00

Moon Rocket XM-12, Y, 1950s, 3 actions, litho tin, battery-op, 15", NM $425.00

Mr Atomic Robot, Cragstan, 1950s, 3 actions, litho tin, battery-op, 11", rare, NMIB, minimum value $5,000.00

Mr Mars Astronaut, SH, 1960s, advances w/several actions, litho tin, battery-op, 11½", NM $400.00

Mr Mercury, Marx, advances & bends over w/several other actions, tin, remote control, 13", NM, A.................$900.00

Mr Robot the Mechanical Brain, Alps, advances as hands light up, tin, clockwork w/battery-op hands, 8", NMIB, A $1,500.00

Mr Sandman the Robot, Wolverine, advances w/shovel, litho tin, 11½", NM, A $500.00

Mr Zerox, SH, advances, stops & guns fire from chest w/lights & sound, litho tin, battery-op, 9", rare, NM (EX box), A ..$900.00

Mystery Action Satellite, Cragstan, 1960s, 3 actions, battery-op, 9", EX..$165.00

NASA Astro Captain, Japan, 1960s, camera flashes on face shield, tin w/plastic arms, w/up, 7", EX $200.00

NASA X-324 Saucer, Spain, bump-&-go action w/sound, litho tin & plastic, w/up, 8" dia, NM (EX box), A...........$250.00

New Astronaut, SH, advances, stops & rotates as guns fire w/lights & sound, plastic, battery-op, 9½", NM (EX box), A $100.00

New Sky Robot, SH, 1960s, 3 actions, mostly plastic, battery-op, 9", EX..$125.00

New Space Explorer, SH, 1960s, advances w/several actions, litho tin, battery-op, 11½", NM...........................$250.00

New Space Station, SH, litho tin, battery-op, 11" dia, EX (EX box), A $1,000.00

Operation X-500 Playset, Deluxe Reading, 1960s, few pcs missing, NM (EX box) $450.00

Pete the Spaceman, Bandai, litho tin, battery-op, MIB, L4...$200.00

Piston Action Robot, Japan, advances w/lighted pistons in head, tin, battery-op, remote control, 12", NM (EX box), A......$1,900.00

Planet Explorer, MT, 1960s, advances w/sound, litho tin, battery-op, 9½", EX, A.....................................$165.00

Planet Explorer X-80, MT, 1960s, several actions, litho tin, battery-op, 8" dia, EX $185.00

Planet Robot, KO, advances w/flashing lights & spinning antenas, tin, remote control, 9", NM (EX box), A......$1,600.00

Planet Rover, J, 1960s, advances w/several actions, litho tin, battery-op, 6½", EX $275.00

Planet Y Space Station, TN, 1960s, 3 actions, litho tin, battery-op, EX $275.00

Radar Tractor w/Robot Driver, SH, 1960s, tin & plastic, battery-op, 7½" L, NM...$500.00

Radicon Robot, MT, several actions, litho tin, battery-op, 15", extremely rare, NM (NM box), A $9,500.00

Radicon Robot, MT, 1950s, several actions, litho tin, battery-op, 15", extremely rare, EX, minimum value $4,000.00

Planet Y Space Station, Nomura, lithographed tin, battery-operated, 8½" diameter, NMIB, A, $475.00.

Ratchet Robot, Nomura, advances w/sparks in chest, metallic bl w/blk hands & feet, w/up, 8", NMIB, A $1,500.00

Road Construction Roller w/Robby the Robot, Daiya, advances w/lighted pistons, tin, battery-op, 9", EX (EX box), A $4,400.00

Robby Space Patrol, TN, 1950s, bump-&-go w/flashing lights, litho tin, battery-op, 13", scarce, NM, minimum value $4,000.00

Robert the Robot, Ideal, silver plastic w/red arms, cable control, 14", EX, A...$100.00

Robot Bulldozer, KO, advances w/flashing lights & sound, tin, battery-op, remote control, 7", NM (EX box), A.$1,000.00

Robot Bulldozer, Marusan, advances as figure waves flag, litho tin, friction, 7", NM (NM box), A..........................$950.00

Robot Dog, Hong Kong, litho tin, battery-op, NM, L4 ..$175.00

Robot R-35, Linemar, advances w/lighted eyes, litho tin, battery-op, remote control, 7½", MIB, A $600.00

Robot R-35, Linemar, advances w/swinging arms & lighted eyes, litho tin, remote control, 7½", NM, A $350.00

Robot U-5, Daiya, blk w/red plastic arms & feet, battery-op, 8", NM, A $500.00

Robot 2500, Durham, 1970s, advances w/several actions, plastic, battery-op, 10½", EX..$125.00

Robotank R-1, Nomura, 1960s, litho tin, battery-op, 10", EX, A $250.00

Robotank-Z, TN, 1960s, several actions, litho tin, metallic violet, battery-op, 10", EX, A $300.00

Rocket Express, Linemar, 1950s, 2 futuristic trains travel track as saucer flies above, litho tin, w/up, rare, NMIB, A ..$1,375.00

Rocket Launching Pad, Y, rocket fires after several actions, litho tin, battery-op, 10", NM (VG box), A.....................$525.00

Rocket Racer #3, Japan, 1950s, advances w/sound, litho tin w/celluloid driver, friction, 6½", EX $100.00

Robotank-Z, Japan, metallic brown version, 10½", NMIB, A, $350.00; metallic violet version, NMIB, A, $500.00.

Rocket Racer #8, Yonezawa, 1950s, litho tin, friction, 11½", NM..$750.00

Rocket X-2, Modern Toys, 1950s, litho tin, friction, 7½", NM..$275.00

Rotate-O-Matic Super Astronaut, SH, advances w/lights & sound, litho tin, battery-op, 12", MIB.....................$225.00

Satellite Interceptor, litho tin, battery-op, NMIB, L4 ....$475.00

Sky Patrol, TN, bump-&-go w/blinking jet engines, litho tin, battery-op, 13", EX (EX box), A $875.00

Sky Patrol Flying Saucer, KO, 1950s, advances w/several actions, litho tin, battery-op, 7½" dia, EX............................$200.00

Smoking Spaceman, Linemar, advances & emits smoke from mouth, lighted eyes & pistons, tin, battery-op, 12", rare, NMIB $3,000.00

Smoking Spaceman, Linemar, advances w/swirling light on head & smoke, metallic gray version, battery-op, 12", NMIB, A $1,600.00

Solar X Space Rocket, TN, 1960s, advances w/several actions, litho tin, battery-op, 15½", NM..............................$300.00

Sonicon Rocket, MT, 1960s, litho tin, battery-op, 13", EX ...$200.00

Space Commander, TN, lithographed tin, battery-operated, 9" diameter, NMIB, A, $375.00; Space Surveyor X-12, MT, lithographed tin, battery-operated, 8" diameter, NMIB, $500.00.

Space Beetle No 2, Y, 1970s, 3 actions, mostly plastic, battery-op, 9", EX **$100.00**

Space Chariot, litho tin, battery-op, NM, L4 ....**$325.00**

Space Commando, Sonsco, advances w/several actions, litho tin, remote control, 7½", NMIB, A **$4,600.00**

Space Commando Megascope, 1950s, plastic, battery-op, NMIB **$100.00**

Space Conquerer Man of Tomorrow, Daiya, 1950s, litho tin, battery-op, 12", VG, A **$400.00**

Space Conquerer of Tomorrow, Daiya, advances, lifts gun & fires, litho tin, w/up, 11", NMIB, A **$1,900.00**

Space Conquerer X-70, Cragstan, 1950s, red version, advances & lifts machine gun, litho tin, battery-op, 12", rare, NMIB **$975.00**

Space Dog, Yoshiya, advances w/open & close mouth & flapping ears, tin, friction, 8½", NMIB, A **$750.00**

Space Exploration Train, KO, 1950s, litho tin, battery-op, 4 pcs, 21", rare, NM **$800.00**

Space Explorer, Horikawa, advances w/lighted TV screen in torso, litho tin, 11", EX, A **$200.00**

Space Explorer, Yoshiya, advances & chest opens to reveal TV screen, litho tin, battery-op, 12", EX, A **$800.00**

Space Explorer Ship X-07, MT, 1960s, advances & spins w/lights & sound, litho tin, battery-op, 8" dia, NM (NM box), A **$300.00**

Space Fighter, Horikawa, bl & red w/dbl doors & guns in torso, litho tin, 12", EX, A **$200.00**

Space Frontier Rocket, Japan, 1960s, several actions, litho tin, battery-op, 18", NM (EX box) **$165.00**

Space Frontier Rocket, litho tin, battery-op, MIB, L4....**$375.00**

Space Jeep, Daiya, 1950s, litho tin, friction, 7", NM......**$485.00**

Space Jet X-001, Bandai, bump-&-go action w/lights, sound & smoking engine, litho tin, battery-op, 10", rare, NM, L4 ....**$750.00**

Space Man, Cragstan, w/flashlight & rifle, litho tin, battery-op, remote control, 9", NMIB, A **$600.00**

Space Orbitestor, Asakusa, 1960s, 3 actions, tin & plastic, battery-op, 8", EX **$185.00**

Space Patrol Car, TN, advances w/light-up gun, litho tin w/full-figure astronaut, battery-op, 9½", NMIB, A.........**$1,200.00**

Space Patrol Rocket Lite, Ray-O-Vac, 1950s, battery-op, 12", NM (NM box)...**$475.00**

Space Pioneer Vehicle, MT, 1960s, 3 actions, litho tin, battery-op, 12", EX **$300.00**

Space Port, Superior, 1950, unused, complete, NM (NM box), A **$1,400.00**

Space Ranger Flying Saucer #3, litho tin, battery-op, MIB, L4 ....**$175.00**

Space Ranger X-36, Japan, litho tin, friction, 6½", NM (EX box), A **$650.00**

Space Robot Car X-09, MT, 1950s, several actions, litho tin, battery-op, 9½", rare, EX (EX box), minimum value ...**$3,000.00**

Space Robot Trooper, KO, 1950s, 3 actions, litho tin, battery-op, 7½", rare, NM, minimum value............................**$1,000.00**

Space Rocket, Automatic Toy, 1950, advances w/siren sound, litho tin, friction, 9", EX (G box), A **$175.00**

Space Rocket Patrol Ship, Courtland, 1950s, litho tin w/red plastic dome, friction, 7", NM.....................................**$150.00**

Space Satellite, W Germany, 1950s, spaceship & Sputnik rotate around globe, litho tin, lever action, NMIB, A.........**$225.00**

Space Scout S-17, Japan, advances as astronaut swivels & fires space cannon, tin & plastic, battery-op, 10", EX (EX box)..**$850.00**

Space Shooting Range, litho tin, clockwork, 15x10", EX (EX box), A **$400.00**

Space Shuttle Challenger, litho tin, battery-op, MIB, L4 ..**$475.00**

Space Survey X-09, MT, 1960s, advances w/several actions, litho tin, battery-op, 9", EX...**$300.00**

Space Whale Pioneer, KO, 1950s, litho tin, w/up, 9", NM ..**$525.00**

Spaceship DB-2, OK Toys, 1965, astronaut floats outside dome, plastic, battery-op, 7" dia, MIB **$100.00**

Spaceship Sparkler, unmk, 1950s, props spins as sparks fly, plastic, push plunger for action, 8", EX, A **$100.00**

Sparking Ratchet Robot, Nomura, metallic bl w/blk hands & feet, w/up, 8", EX (EX box), A.................................**$700.00**

Sparkling Mike the Robot, Ace, 1950s, litho tin, battery-op, 7½", extremely rare, NM, minimum value...........**$2,000.00**

Sparky Robot, Linemar, advances w/swinging arms & blinking eyes, tin, w/up, 8", EX (G box), A **$475.00**

Star Strider Robot, litho tin, battery-op, MIB, L4 ....**$225.00**

Steve Zodiac's Fireball XL5 Space City, MPC, 1964, complete, EX (EX box), from $650 to **$750.00**

Strange Explorer, DSK, 1960s, several actions, battery-op, 7½", MIB, L4..**$425.00**

Super Astronaut Robot, SH, 1960s, several actions, litho tin, battery-op, 11½", EX..**$225.00**

Super Moon Patroler, Japan, bump-&-go action w/flashing lights, tin, battery-op, 9", EX (EX box), A..............**$500.00**

Super Moon Patroller, litho tin, battery-op, MIB, L4.....**$675.00**

Super Space Capsule, SH, bump-&-go, doors open to reveal astronaut, tin & plastic, battery-op, 9½", NMIB, A..........**$400.00**

Super Space Commander Robot, Japan, 1960s, plastic, battery-op, 10", EX (EX box) **$75.00**

Swinging Baby Robot, baby on swing, litho tin, w/up, 6", NM, A **$200.00**

Swivel-O-Matic Astronaut, Horikawa, advances w/swiveling torso, tin, 11½", NMIB, A **$500.00**

Swivel-O-Matic Astronaut, Horikawa, metallic gr w/twin lasers in chest, 11½", EX (EX box), A..............................**$200.00**

Talking Robot, Yonezawa, several phrases, brn plastic w/missiles on head, 12", NMIB, A **$150.00**

Target Robot, Masudaya, advances w/lighted eyes & mouth, litho tin, 15", rare, NM, A **$6,300.00**

Television Spaceman, Alps, advances w/lighted TV screen in chest, tin & plastic, battery-op, 14", NMIB, A........**$925.00**

Titan the Tumbling Robot, litho tin, battery-op, MIB, L4 ...**$475.00**

Tulip Head Robot X-70, Nomura, advances w/rotating camera & screen, litho tin & plastic, 9", NMIB, A **$2,100.00**

Tulip Head Robot X-70, Nomura, head opens to reveal camera, litho tin w/plastic arms, battery-op, 12", EX (EX box), A.....**$1,800.00**

Turbo Jet Car, Ideal, 1950s, advances w/sound, litho tin & plastic, w/up, NM (NM box)...**$165.00**

Twirly Whirly Rocket Ride, Alps, spins w/bell sound, litho tin, battery-op, 13½", NMIB, from $700 to **$950.00**

UFO X-05, MT, bump-&-go action w/lights & sound, tin & plastic, battery-op, 7½" dia, NMIB, A....................**$100.00**

USA-NASA Apollo, MT, 1960s, several actions, litho tin, battery-op, EX (EX box)......................................**$350.00**

USAF Gemini X-5, MT, 1960s, several actions, litho tin & plastic, battery-op, 9", EX **$175.00**

Venus Boat #27, Japan, advances w/spinning prop & sound, litho tin, crank action, 6½", NM (EX box), A........**$135.00**

Video Robot, Horikawa, advances w/moon scene in chest, tin & plastic, battery-op, 9½", NMIB, A.........................**$600.00**

Video Robot, SH, 1960s, 3 actions, litho tin, battery-op, 10", EX..**$175.00**

Wheel-A-Gear Robot, Taiya, advances w/spinning gears in chest, litho tin, battery-op, 14", NMIB, from $1,600 to **$2,200.00**

Zoomer the Robot, TN, advances w/lighted eyes, tin, battery-op, 8", NM (NM box), A................................**$1,500.00**

Zoomer the Robot, TN, advances w/lighted eyes, tin, battery-op, 8", NM, A....................................**$725.00**

MISCELLANEOUS

Moon Bank, Japan, 1955, embossed composition, 'Save Now for Your Trip to the Moon' on base, NMIB, A, $125.00.

Piano, wood with lithographed astronauts, missiles, and planets, 4" x 5" x 8", EX, $100.00.

Film, It Came From Outer Space, Castle Films, 1950s, 8mm, EX (EX box) **$50.00**

Flashlight, Space Boy, EX, L4 ....**$85.00**

Game, Rockets Away Bagatelle, England, 12", NM (EX box), A..**$150.00**

Helmet, Buck Rogers style, aluminum w/1-way visor, 10", G+, A..**$150.00**

Helmet, Flash Gordon style, Orbit Productions, 1950, plastic, 12", NM (G box), A....................................**$625.00**

Lantern, Japan, light-up globe features solar system, 5½", NM, A..**$250.00**

Party Favors, Space Patrol, CA Reed, 1950s, complete, MIP .**$150.00**

Sand Toy, Mr Sandman the Robot, Wolverine, bucket shape w/sifter shoulders, funnel cap head, litho tin, 12", EX, A **$850.00**

Space Helmet With Radar Goggles, Banner, 1950s, plastic, NMIB, A, $400.00.

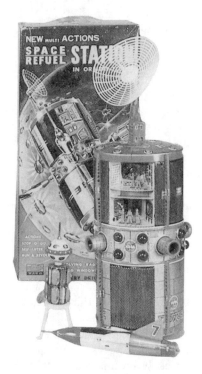

Space Refuel Station, Waco, lithographed tin, 15", EXIB, A, $2,700.00.

Yo-yo, 1960s, litho tin w/image of astronaut waving, tournament shape, MIP **$15.00**

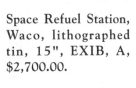

Zoo-M-Roo, pinball game, Northwest Prod, 1950, plastic, 7", NM (EX box), A..$75.00

Rock 'N Roll

From the '50s on, rock 'n roll music has been an enjoyable part of many of our lives, and the performers themselves have often been venerated as icons. Today some of the all-time great artists such as Elvis, the Beatles, KISS, and the Monkees, for instance, have fans that not only continue to appreciate their music but actively search for the ticket stubs, concert posters, photographs, and autographs of their favorites. More easily found, through, are the items that sold through retail stores at the height of their careers — dolls, games, toys, books, magazines, etc. In recent years, some of the larger auction galleries have sold personal items such as guitars, jewelry, costumes, automobiles, contracts, and other one-of-a-kind items that realized astronomical prices. If you're an Elvis or Beatles fan, we recommend *Elvis Collectibles* and *Best of Elvis Collectibles* by Rosalind Cranor (Overmountain Press); and *The Beatles, A Reference and Value Guide*, by Barbara Crawford, Hollis Lamon, and Michael Stern. For a more general guide try *Rock-n-Roll Treasures* by Joe Hilton and Greg Moore (Collector Books).

Advisors: Bob Gottuso, Bojo (B3), Beatles, KISS, Monkees; Rosalind Cranor (C15), Elvis.

See also Action Figures; Bubble Bath Containers; Character and Promotional Drinking Glasses; Coloring, Activity, and Paint Books; Dolls, Celebrity; Lunch Boxes; Model Kits; Paper Dolls; Pin-Back Buttons; Puppets.

Abba, annual, 1978, NM, A7...$25.00
Bay City Rollers, annual, 1977, NM, A7 ....$25.00
Beatles, balloon, wht & beige or pk, MIP (sealed), B3, ea $175.00
Beatles, banjo, Mastro, 22", EX (EX box)....................$3,000.00
Beatles, Beat Seat, features John Lennon on 1 side & group on the other, vinyl over foam, 14" dia, NM, B3 ....$1,750.00
Beatles, Beatle Twig, Beatle Twig Inc, complete, NMIP ...$275.00
Beatles, Beatlephones, Koss Electronics, EX (EX box) ..$2,000.00
Beatles, board game, Hullabaloo, 1965, VG (VG box) $75.00
Beatles, book, Apple to the Core, softcover, NM, B3.......$10.00
Beatles, book, Beatles Forever, Schaffner, 1978, hardcover, w/dust jacket, EX, B3 ....$18.00
Beatles, book, Help!, Random House, 1965, hardcover, EX, B3 ....$55.00
Beatles, book, Long & Winding Road, by Ted Greenwald, hardcover, w/dust jacket, NM, B3 ....$20.00
Beatles, book, True Story of the Beatles, Shepard, 1964, softcover, NM, B3...$10.00
Beatles, book, With the Beatles, by Dezo Hoffman, softcover, EX, B3 ....$18.00
Beatles, book, Yellow Submarine Gift Book, hardcover, EX...$90.00
Beatles, bracelet, blk & wht photo disk w/She Loves You on back, heavy link chain, MOC, B3............................$160.00
Beatles, brooch, blk & wht tin photo on gold metal guitar, 4", EX, B3 ....$125.00

Beatles, brooch, group photo set in plastic guitar, EX (EX card), B3 (beware of repro) $60.00
Beatles, carrier, Airflite, rectangular vinyl box w/group photo & facsimile signatures, 6x9", NM, B3 ....$1,400.00
Beatles, Cartoon Kit, Colorforms, 1966, complete, MIB ..$800.00
Beatles, chair, Yellow Submarine, inflatable vinyl, NM, B3 ...$50.00
Beatles, charms from gumball machine, record shape w/photo, ¾" dia, set of 4, EX, B3...$25.00
Beatles, coloring book, Saalfield, unused, EX, B3 ....$125.00
Beatles, decals, blk & orange on yel, unused, set of 11, B3...$90.00
Beatles, Disk-Go-Case, plastic w/group photo, bl, NM, B3, from $175 to...$225.00
Beatles, Disk-Go-Case, plastic w/group photo, brn, EX..$400.00
Beatles, dolls, cartoon style, inflatable vinyl, 13", set of 4, MIP, B3...$160.00

Beatles, dolls, Paul and Ringo, Remco/NEMS, facsimile signatures, movable heads, 5", NMIB, each $300.00.

Beatles, dolls, Remco, soft bodies, set of 4, NM.............$375.00
Beatles, figures, Swingers Music Set, NMOC.................$125.00

Beatles, Liquorice Records, Long Eating, NM, singles: from $70.00 to $75.00; group: $115.00.

Beatles, film, Live at Shea Stadium, 8mm, EX..................$30.00

Beatles, flasher rings, set of 4, EX $60.00

Beatles, guitar, Big Six by Selcol, rare, 6-string version, EX...$650.00

Beatles, guitar, Red Jet by Selcol, electric, 31", rare, NM .$1,500.00

Beatles, guitar strings, Hofner, NMIP..........................$80.00

Beatles, Hard Day's Night, 1964, 1st edition, softcover, G $10.00

Beatles, hummer, cb tube w/color photos, music notes & signatures, yel & red plastic tips, EX, B3 ....$185.00

Beatles, mobile, Sunshine Art Studios, cb w/pop-out figures, 14x9", M, B3 ....$175.00

Beatles, movie, Beatles Newsreel, 8mm, EX (EX box), B3..$50.00

Beatles, ornaments, hand-blown glass, 4 different, EX, ea...$200.00

Beatles, pencil case, wht vinyl w/blk photos in all-over design, zipper closure, 7", rare, NM, B3..........................$400.00

Beatles, Pencil-By-Number Colouring Set, Kitfix, 1964, complete, rare, MIB, from $2,000 to $2,500.00

Beatles, pennant, faces in circles w/names, wht on red w/bl trim, 29" (beware of repro), VG, B3 ....$120.00

Beatles, pennant, We Luv You Beatles in red on cream, George & Ringo inside hearts, VG+, B3 ....$200.00

Beatles, photo album, Sgt Pepper's Lonely Hearts Club Band, lg, EX $425.00

Beatles, Pop Stickles, Dal, MOC (sealed), B3..................$75.00

Beatles, Poster Put-Ons, Craftmaster, complete, unused, M (worn box), B3 ....$225.00

Beatles, poster put-ons, Yellow Submarine, unused, MIP...$225.00

Beatles, Punch-Out Portraits, Whitman, unused, complete, M, B3..$200.00

Beatles, purse, blk vinyl clutch-type w/wht printed photo & names, orig leather strap, rare, EX, B3 ....$400.00

Beatles, purse, John Lennon, Canadian issue, 1970s, colorful image of John on silky material w/gold metal clasp, VG, B3 ....$35.00

Beatles, purse, wht vinyl clutch-type w/blk printed busts & names, orig leather strap, EX, B3 ....$300.00

Beatles, record carrier, gr & wht cb w/wht plastic hdl, for 45 rpms, G+, B3 ....$250.00

Beatles, spatter toy, 16", rare, MIP, B3........................$300.00

Beatles, squirt gun, 1960s, yel plastic submarine, 6", EX, B3 ..$40.00

Beatles, sticker from gumball machine, gold & blk w/faces & names, clear plastic capsule, EX, B3 ....$25.00

Beatles, sunglasses, John Lennon, blk, gold or silver frame, EX, ea $5.00

Beatles, wig, Lowell, MIP (sealed) $125.00

Bee Gees, radio, Vanity Fair, 1979, 5½", NM, from $10 to $15.00

David Cassidy, annual, 1974, NM, A7 ....$30.00

David Cassidy, guitar, Carnival Toys, 1970s, MIB, from $75.00 to $100.00. (Photo courtesy Greg Davis/Bill Morgan)

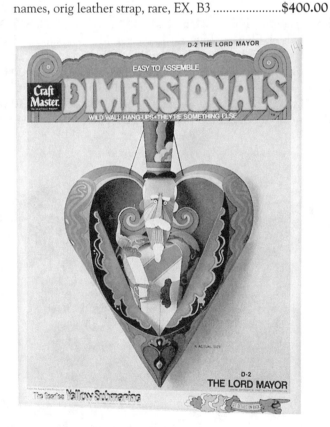

Beatles, Yellow Sumbarine Dimensionals Wall Hanging, Craft Master, MIB, $550.00. (Photo courtesy Greg Davis/Bill Morgan)

Dick Clark, Picture Patch, 1950s, MOC...........................$20.00

Donny & Marie Osmond, AM pocket radio, LJN, 1977, 5", NM, from $35 to...$45.00

Donny & Marie Osmond, Country & Rock Rhythm Set, Gordy, 1976, MOC, from $25 to...........................$30.00

Donny & Marie Osmond, iron-ons, 1970s, several different, ea from $10 to...$15.00

Donny & Marie Osmond, Microphone & Song Sheets, Gordy, 1976, MOC, from $25 to...........................$30.00

Donny & Marie, diary, Continental Plastics, 1977, M, from $8.00 to $12.00. (Photo courtesy Greg Davis/Bill Morgan)

Donny & Marie Osmond, Show Biz Wireless Microphone, LJN, 1977, MIP, from $50 to $75.00

Donny & Marie Osmond, Sing-Along AM Radio, LJN, 1977, wht plastic w/microphone attached to side, NM, from $75 to $100.00

Donny & Marie Osmond, tambourine, Lapin, 1977, 6" dia, M, from $30 to..$40.00

Elvis, autograph book, Elvis Presley Enterprises, 1956, EX, minimum value $500.00

Elvis, balloon toy, California Toytime, image of Elvis as boxer (Kid Galahad) on red balloon w/cb feet, 4", EX $65.00

Elvis, bracelet, Elvis Presley Enterprises, 1950s, dog tag, MOC (later repro by Box Car not on card), orig $150.00

Elvis, cigar box, Memphis Specialty Cigars Ltd, 1998, NM .$42.00

Elvis, cologne & teddy bear, Be My Teddy Bear, mk Elvis Presley Fragrances Inc, 7½", EX (EX plastic tube).................$50.00

Elvis, cookie jar, Elvis seated on Harley-Davidson in front of Harley water tower, Harley-Davidson, MIB.............$100.00

Elvis, cookie jar, Elvis sits in pk Cadillac playing guitar, Vandor Premier Limited Edition, 1997, MIB.......................$125.00

Elvis, cookie jar, Elvis TV, Vandor, M $45.00

Elvis, doll, Elvis in Concert, Starr, 1987, plays micro-cassettes (4), 17", MIB...$90.00

Elvis, doll, Hound Dog, Smile Toy Co, stuffed plush w/Elvis lettered on wht neck ribbon, NM, A $250.00

Elvis, fan club kit, 1956, w/button, membership card & letter, EX, from $300 to $400.00

Elvis, flasher ring, 1957, EX, minimum value $100.00

Elvis, guitar, Lapin, 1984, MOC (sealed) $75.00

Elvis, guitar, Selcol, 1959, UK, 32", EXIB........................$700.00

Elvis, lighter, 50 Years With Elvis, Zippo, 1987, EX.........$35.00

Elvis, music box, Elvis Presley Enterprises, solid maple, glass doors w/gold foil overlay, MIB.................................$36.00

Elvis, music box, Japan, wooden w/8 musical devices, ea plays different song, 4x6½x12", M....................................$70.00

Elvis, music box, Willitts, 1987, Elvis w/red Corvette, porcelain, musical, 6x9x14", M $42.00

Elvis, necklace, Elvis Presley Enterprises, 1956, Love Me Tender, NMOC, from $175 to...$225.00

Elvis, ornament, Carlton, 1995, musical, plays Blue Christmas, MIB $60.00

Elvis, ornament, Elvis Playing Guitar, Polonaise, hand-blown glass, MIB..$37.00

Elvis, plate, Aloha From Hawaii, Royal Orleans, 1983, 8¾", MIB $45.00

Elvis, plate, Elvis on Harley-Davidson, Delphi #926C, MIB..$80.00

Elvis, plate, Elvis Remembered, Hackett American, 1984, 10⅜", MIB $45.00

Elvis, plate, GI Blues, Delphi, NM $37.00

Elvis, poster, Elvis on Tour, 1972, 1-sheet, M....................$65.00

Elvis, purse, Elvis Presley Enterprises, 1956, bl foldover carryall w/Elvis playing guitar, 5x10", from $600 to $1,000.00

Elvis, scrapbook, Solid Gold Memories, Ballantine Books, 1977, EX..$30.00

Elvis, stein, Anheuser-Busch, '68 Comeback Special, 9¼", M...$40.00

Elvis, felt hat, 1950s, pictures all around sides, includes original picture tag, NM, $135.00. (Photo courtesy Tom Duncan)

KISS, pens (far right and far left), MOC, $80.00 each; pencils (center), set of four, MIP, $60.00. (Photo courtesy Bojo)

Elvis, stein, Gold & Platinium Records, Ceramarte #2591, 6⅝",
MIB $85.00
Grateful Dead, yo-yo, Hummingbird, 1980s, wood w/die-
stamped seal, tournament shape, NM $20.00
KISS, belt buckle, 1977, blk w/silver letters & border, M ...$30.00
KISS, book, The Dynasty Tour, M.....................................$70.00
KISS, chair, inflatable, M $80.00
KISS, costume, Gene Simmons, 1978, sm, EXIB............$160.00
KISS, key chain, Aucoin, 1977, 4 different, NM, ea $50.00
KISS, Kiss Army Membership Kit, 1978, M (orig KISS folder).$45.00
KISS, lighters, Zippo, set of 4 (ea member), MIB $90.00
KISS, puzzle, Paul Stanley, Milton Bradley, 1978, 200 pcs,
EXIB...$45.00
KISS, Rub 'N Play Magic Transfer Set, Colorforms, 1970s, com-
plete, EX (EX box) $120.00
KISS, sleeping bag, Aucoin Management, 1978, EX......$500.00
KISS, window blind shade, KISS Dynasty, Por View Screen Co,
35x64", MIP...$30.00
Marie Osmond, Hair Care Set, Gordy, 1976, MOC $25.00
Marie Osmond, Makeup Center, Mattel, 1976, complete, MIB,
from $50 to..$75.00
Monkees, book, Monkees Go Mod, 1967, softcover, EX ..$12.00
Monkees, book, Who's Got the Button, Whitman, 1968, hard-
cover, EX $20.00
Monkees, fan club kit, 1967, complete w/membership card, pho-
tos, magazine, etc, EX (EX folder), from $75 to.......$100.00
Monkees, puzzle, Fairchild, 1967, 340 pcs, NMIB $60.00
Osmonds, annual, 1976, NM, A7....................................$25.00
Paul McCartney & Wings, book, by Tony Jasper, hardcover,
w/dust jacket, EX, B3 ....$20.00
Rick Nelson, Picture Patch, 1950s, MOC........................$20.00
Three Dog Night, poster, 1970s, 22x14", EX $30.00

Roly Polys

Popular toys with children around the turn of the century,
roly polys were designed with a weighted base that caused the
toy to automatically right itself after being kicked or knocked
over. Their popularity faded to some extent, but they continued
to be produced until WWI and beyond. Most were made of
papier-mache, though some Japanese toy makers used celluloid
later on. Schoenhut made some that are especially collectible
today in a variety of sizes — up to almost a foot in height. They
represented clowns, animals, and children, as well as some well
known story book characters.

Baby, Schoenut, papier-mache, wht top w/ruffled collar, orange
base, 10", EX $650.00
Bear, papier-mache, hand-painted, red & orange suit w/bolo tie,
musical, 7", NM...$325.00
Black Clown, Germany, papier-mache, wht & red outfit, 5",
EX $400.00
Black Man, papier-mache, hand-painted, molded hands, 10",
EX $400.00
Boy Holding Suspenders, Schoenhut, papier-mache, wht shirt
w/red tie, bl hat, red lips, gold base, 6½", VG $165.00

**Boy on Ball, jointed arms, 13¾", EX, A, $2,200.00; Clown,
NOMA, composition, 7½", MIB, $225.00; Girl, Germany,
7", NMIB, $200.00; Clown With Bat, Japan, papier-mache,
6¼", MIB, $165.00.**

Boy Riding Horse, Germany, papier-mache, hand-painted, horse
atop pear-shaped base, 7½", EX $925.00
Buster Brown, Schoenhut, papier-mache, hand-painted, head wobbles when toy is moved, label on bottom, 9", EX........$850.00

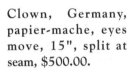 

**Clown, Germany,
papier-mache, eyes
move, 15", split at
seam, $500.00.**

Clown, Germany, papier-mache, hand-painted, pk vest under yel
jacket, 10", EX $400.00
Clown, mk Germany, compo, bl & yel outfit w/red hat & but-
tons, 6½", EX...$180.00
Clown, Schoenhut, papier-mache, hand painted, head wobbles
when moved side to side, 9", EX $700.00
Clown, Steiff, ca 1988, 11", NM......................................$175.00

Dog, papier-mache, hand-painted, yel & red suit, molded tie, musical, 6½", EX $165.00

Duck, Japan, prewar, celluloid, 3½", NM.........................$50.00

Foxy Grandpa, papier-mache, bl jacket & vest, red tie, 5¾", EX $500.00

Foxy Grandpa, Schoenhut, papier-mache, dk bl suit w/yel vest, 9½", EX, A $750.00

Girl, Germany, papier-mache, bl dress w/purple bow & hat, yel hair, 7", NMIB (box mk 7001), A............................$200.00

Girl, Schoenhut, musical, papier-mache, reddish hair w/rosy cheeks, yel dress, 9", EX.......................................$165.00

Happy Hooligan, papier-mache, orange shirt & hat, gr jacket, purple base, 5½", M...$150.00

Keystone Cop, German, papier-mache, med bl uniform & hat, brn mustache, dk rosy cheeks, 9¾", EX+, A............$500.00

Keystone Cop, papier-mache, bl suit & hat, mustache, 5½", M $385.00

Keystone Cop, papier-mache, med bl uniform & hat, blk trim, brn mustache & eyebrows, 5½", EX+ $385.00

Mother Goose, Schoenhut, papier-mache, pale bl outfit & hat, wht blouse w/ruffled collar, 8½", EX, A $950.00

Old Dixie Queen Tobacco Inspector, 6¾", VG $450.00

Rabbit, musical, papier-mache, wht head w/red & blk features, gr jacket, yel vest, bl & wht tie, red base, 8", EX+, A..$275.00

Rabbit, papier-mache, hand-painted, orange & gr suit w/wht ears, chimes, 8", M..$275.00

Rabbit, papier-mache, red coat w/orange shirt, glass eyes, 7½", EX $190.00

Rabbit w/Closed Umbrella, papier-mache, wht head w/glass eyes, yel jacket w/gray vest, orange bow tie & base, 10¾", A......$825.00

Sailor Girl, Schoenhut, papier-mache, smiling face w/reddish blond hair, bl & wht outfit w/blk trim, 7½", EX+ ...$825.00

Russian Toys

Many types of collectible toys continue to be made in Russia. Some are typical novelty windups such as walking turtles and pecking birds, but they have also made robots, wooden puzzles, and trains. In addition they've produced cars, trucks, and military vehicles that are exact copies of those once used in Russia and its Republics, formerly known as the Soviet Union. These replicas were made prior to June 1991 and are marked Made in the USSR/CCCP. They're constructed of metal and are very detailed, often with doors, hoods, and trunks that open.

Because of the terrific rate of inflation in Russia, production costs have risen to the point that some of these toys are no longer being made. Internet exposure has resulted in increasing interest and higher values.

Advisors: Natural Way (N1); David Riddle (R6).

REPLICAS OF CIVILIAN VEHICLES

Aeroflot (Russian Airline) Service Station Wagon, 1/43 scale, MIB, R6 ....$20.00

Belarus Farm Tractor, 1/43 scale, MIB..............................$20.00

Gorbi Limo, 1/43 scale, metal, MIB, R6............................$25.00

KamA3 Model #5320 Flat Bed Truck, cab tilts forward, 1/43 scale, MIB, R6...$35.00

KamA3 Model #53212 Oil Truck, 1/43 scale, MIB, R6....$40.00

KamA3 Model #53213 Airport Fire Truck, 1/43 scale, MIB, R6...$40.00

KamA3 Model #5410 Truck Cab, 1/43 scale, MIP, R6 .....$40.00

Lada #212 4x4, trunk, doors & hood open, 1/43 scale, MIB, R6..$20.00

Lada #2121 4x4 w/trailer, trunk, doors & hood open, 1/43 scale, MIB, R6 ....$20.00

Lada Auto Service Station Wagon, 1/43 scale, MIB.........$20.00

Lada Sedan, trunk & hood open, 1/43 scale, MIB, R6......$20.00

Lada Station Wagon, trunk & hood open, 1/43 scale, MIB, R6...$20.00

Moskvitch Medical Services Sedan, 1/43 scale, MIB, $20.00.
(Photo courtesy David Riddle)

Moskvitch Aeroflat (Soviet Airline) Station Wagon, hood opens, 1/43 scale, MIB, R6 ....$20.00

Moskvitch Auto Service Station Wagon, hood opens, 1/43 scale, R6..$20.00

Moskvitch Panel Station Wagon, hood opens, 1/43 scale, MIB, R6...$20.00

Moskvitch Sedan, hood opens, 1/43 scale, MIB, R6........$20.00

Moskvitch Slant-Back Sedan, 1/43 scale, MIB, R6 ....$20.00

Moskvitch Soviet Traffic Sedan, hood opens, 1/43 scale, MIB, R6...$20.00

Moskvitch Station Wagon, hood opens, 1/43 scale, MIB, R6 ....$20.00

Moskvitch Taxi Sedan, hood opens, 1/43 scale, MIB, R6 ...$20.00

OMO, 1937 Fire Truck, #1 in series of 6, 1/43 scale, MIB, R6...$40.00

OMO, 1937 Fire Truck, #2 in series of 6, 1/43 scale, MIB, R6...$40.00

RAF Ambulance Van, back & 3 doors open, 1/43 scale, MIB, R6...$25.00

RAF Traffic Police Van, 1/43 scale, MIB, R6....................$25.00

Volga Ambulance Station Wagon, back & 3 doors open, 1/43 scale, MIB, R6 ....$25.00

Volga Sedan, trunk, hood & doors open, 1/43 scale, MIB, R6 ....$25.00

Volga Taxi Sedan, trunk, hood & doors open, 1/43 scale, MIB, R6...$25.00

Volga Taxi Station Wagon, trunk, hood & doors open, 1/43 scale, MIB, R6 ....$25.00

Volga Traffic Police Sedan, 1/43 scale, MIB, $25.00.
(Photo courtesy David Riddle)

REPLICAS OF MILITARY VEHICLES

Armored Car, 1/43 scale, MIB, R6 ....$15.00
Armored Personnel Carrier, 1/43 scale, MIB, R6.............$15.00
Armored Troop Carrier, 1/86 scale, MIB, R6 ....$15.00
Cannon, 1/86 scale, MIB, R6 ....$15.00
Cannon (100mm), 1/43 scale, MIB, R6 ....$15.00
Cannon (76mm), 1/43 scale, MIB, R6 ....$15.00
Command Car, 1/86 scale, MIB, R6 ....$15.00
N-153 Biplane Fighter, 1/72 scale, MIB, R6......................$40.00
N-16 Fighter, 1/72 scale, MIB, R6 ....$40.00
Rocket Launcher Armored Truck, 1/86 scale, MIB, R6....$15.00
Self-Propelled Cannon, 1/86 scale, MIB, R6.....................$15.00
SU-100 Self-Propelled Cannon, 1/43 scale, MIB, R6.......$15.00

T 34-85 Tank, metal, rarest from the set of six, MIB, $25.00.
(Photo courtesy David Riddle)

Tank, battery-op, 1/72 scale, MIB, R6 ....$45.00
Tank, 1/86 scale, MIB, R6...$12.00
Troop Truck, 1/86 scale, MIB, R6 ....$15.00

MISCELLANEOUS

Bird, metal, w/up, MIB, N1..$5.00
Car on Garage Lift, MIB, N1 ....$8.00
Car Set, metal, 6-pc, MIB, N1..$12.00
Car Track, metal, w/up, MIB, N1 ....$30.00
Chicken, metal, MIB, N1 ....$5.00
Chicken Inside Egg, w/up, MIB, N1 ....$5.00
Doll, Maytryoshki, metal, w/up, MIB, N1 ....$18.00

Doll Set, Maytryoshki, wood, Lenin, Stalin, Khrushchev, Brezh-
    nez & Gorbachev, made in China, MIB, N1 ....$30.00
Hen, metal, w/up, MIB, N1 ....$8.00
Jet Fighter, plastic, bl, MIB, N1 ....$5.00
Monster Beetle, metal, MIB, N1...$8.00
Moon Buggy w/2 Cosmonauts, plastic & metal, w/up, MIB, N1 .$15.00
Parking Garage, metal, MIB, N1 ....$30.00
Rooster, metal, w/up, MIB, N1 ....$8.00
Tank, plastic, MIB, N1..$5.00
Train Track, metal, w/up, MIB, N1.....................................$30.00
WWII Soldiers w/Rifles, cast metal, set of 10, MIB, N1 ...$25.00

Sand Toys and Pails

In the Victorian era a sand toy was a boxed wooden or cardboard scene with a glass front and a mechanism involving a hopper and/or chute leading to a paddle, then to various rods and
levers attached to cardboard or tin figures or animals with
loosely jointed limbs at the front of the scene. When the sand
was poured, the mechanism was activated, and the figures went
through a series of movements. These were imported mostly
from Germany with a few coming from France and England.

By 1900, having seen the popularity of the European models, American companies were developing all sorts of sand toys,
including free-standing models. The Sand Toy Company of
Pittsburgh patented and made 'Sandy Andy' from 1909 onward.
The company was later bought by the Wolverine Supply &
Manufacturing Co. and continued to produce variations of the
toy until the 1970s.

Today if you mention sand toys, people think of pails,
spades, sifters, and molds, as the boxed scenes have all but disappeared due to their being quite fragile and not surviving use.

We have a rich heritage of lithographed tin pails with such
wonderful manufacturers as J. Chein & Co., T. Cohn Inc., Morton Converse, Kirchoff Patent Co., Marx Toy Co., Ohio Art
Co., etc, plus the small jobbing companies who neglected to sign
their wares. Sand pails have really come into their own and are
now recognized for their beautiful graphics and designs. For more
information we recommend *Pails by Comparison, Sand Pails and
Other Sand Toys, A Study and Price Guide*, by Carole and Richard
Smyth (our advisors for this category). They are S22 in the
Dealer and Collector Codes.

Dutch Mill, Mac Toys & Games, litho tin, 12", NM (worn box),
    A $300.00
Funnel Toy, T Cohn, features seesaw w/image of Popeye & Olive
    Oyl, litho tin, 9", VG, A $250.00
Pail, emb tin, Victorian, floral border around 2 scenes: children
    at the beach, 5½", EX, A $360.00
Pail, emb tin, Victorian, trellis & flowers w/Pied Piper, dog, &
    lambs, 6", F, A...$180.00
Pail, litho tin, Chein, kids on various carnival rides, 4", NM, A .$65.00
Pail, litho tin, Chein, Wonderful World of Disney, many charac-
    ters: Mickey Mouse, Snow White, Donald Duck, etc, 8", A,
    EX..$75.00
Pail, litho tin, Chein, 1966, Jungle Book, 6", M............$100.00

Funnel Toy, Shimer, 1899, painted cast iron, 12½", NM, $3,500.00.

Pail, litho tin, Happynak, Mickey Mouse & Donald Duck, 4", EX $125.00

Pail, litho tin, Happynak, 1930s, Mickey & Minnie fishing in rowboat, 8", EX...$200.00

Pail, litho tin, Keln US Zone Germany, 1940s, children planting garden, 4¼", EX, A...$235.00

Pail, litho tin, Ohio Art, duck, goat, mouse, & rabbit, all dressed up, 4¼", EX..$190.00

Pail, litho tin, Ohio Art, 1930s, fox, bear, squirrel, rabbit, all dressed up, rust on base, A $160.00

Pail, litho tin, Ohio Art, 1930s, Mickey & Minnie at Treasure Island, EX..$300.00

Pail, litho tin, Ohio Art, 1930s, Mickey & Minnie having picnic under umbrella, 5", NM....................................$350.00

Pail, litho tin, Ohio Art, 1930s, Mickey & Minnie on raft dressed as pirates, 8", NM.......................................$400.00

Pail, litho tin, Ohio Art, 1930s, Pluto pulling Mickey on roller skates, orig shovel, 4", NM..............................$350.00

Pail, litho tin, Ohio Art, 1930s, Snow White & the Seven Dwarfs, 10", NM..$800.00

Pail, litho tin, Ohio Art, 1950s, cowboys & Indians, EX.$100.00

Pail, litho tin, Ohio Art/WDE, 1930s, Mickey & Minnie in canoe, rare, M..$900.00

Pail, litho tin, Ohio Art/WDE, 1930s, Mickey's Garden, 8", M...$800.00

Pail, litho tin, Ohio Art/WDE, 1930s, Three Little Pigs, EX, from $200 to $300.00

Pail, litho tin, Ohio Art/WDE, 1938, Mickey & Donald golfing, 8", EX...$400.00

Pail, litho tin, Rose O'Neill Kewpies, ca 1937, at Kewpie Castle on the beach, dings & scratches, sm, A $685.00

Pail, litho tin, unsigned, 1950s, Mickey Mouse riding duck at seaside w/donkey, 5", EX, A $150.00

Pail, litho tin, Wolverine, Sandy Andy, EX, A.............$200.00

Pail, lithographed tin, Happynak, Mickey and Friends at Treasure Island, EX, $150.00; Mickey Mouse Beach Bag, EX, $100.00. (Photo courtesy David Longest)

Pail, litho tin, Happynak, Donald Duck riding a wave, 3", NM $125.00

Pail, litho tin, Happynak, Mickey, Minnie, Donald Duck, pirate scene, 4½", EX, A...$225.00

Pail, with sifter insert, nursery rhyme characters, EX, $175.00. (Photo courtesy Carole and Richard Smyth)

Sand Mill, pnt tin w/litho tin figure, crank operated, 8" L base, VG, A...$225.00

Shovel, litho tin, Ohio Art, 1930s, Donald & nephews on beach, EX, from $200 to..$275.00

Sifter, Ohio Art, litho tin w/various Disney characters playing, w/handle, 8" dia, NM $250.00

Sifter, Ohio Art, 1960s, Mickey & Minnie playing in the sand, 6" dia, VG...$200.00

Sifter, WDE, 1930s, litho tin w/Mickey playing banjo on the beach, VG...$200.00

Water Pump, litho tin, pictures fish & sailboats, EX, from $175 to...$225.00

Wheelbarrow Loader, litho tin, Wolverine, 1948, loader travels down ramps & dumps sand into tray, MIB..............$200.00

Windmill, litho tin, T Cohn, put sand in top & blades spin, flowers on rnd base, 9", MIB $150.00

Santa Claus

Christmas is a magical time for young children; visions of Santa and his sleigh are mirrored in their faces, and their eyes are wide with the wonder of the Santa fantasy. There are many who collect ornaments, bulbs, trees, etc., but the focus of our listings is Santa himself.

Among the more valuable Santas are the German-made papier-mache figures and candy containers, especially the larger examples and those wearing costumes in colors other than the traditional red.

See also Battery Operated; Books; Reynolds Toys; Windups, Friction, and Other Mechanicals; and other specific categories.

Bank, litho tin w/image of Santa & reindeer taking off, oval, 3", NM, A $125.00

Candy Container, bsk & compo, Santa w/2 dolls seated on tree stump, 3½", VG, A..................................$175.00

Candy Container, compo, gray coat w/wht fur trim, red hat, w/lantern, 8½", EX, A...........................$600.00

Candy Container, compo, standing in long robe, blk, pk, brn & wht, 8", EX, A..$125.00

Candy Container, compo, wht fur beard, red felt robe w/bl shoulders, basket on belt, holding feather tree, 21", EX, A.......................................$3,850.00

Candy Container, compo & cb, gray robe w/red & wht trim, w/sled & tree, 13", EX, A...............................$1,100.00

Candy Container, compo & papier-mache, wht beard, wht cloth robe w/wht trim & gold belt, w/bag & tree, 1950s, 9", G, A......................................$50.00

Candy Container, Germany, papier-mache, red coat & bl pants, blk boots, basket of toys on back, 18½", EX, A....$1,000.00

Candy Container, Germany, papier-mache, red robe & blk boots, arms folded across chest, w/tree, 7", G, A $300.00

Candy Container, papier-mache, red coat & bl pants, blk boots, w/tree, 19", EX, A.......................................$850.00

Candy Container, papier-mache & cb, wire arms, w/tree, 28", EX, A...$2,400.00

Candy Container, plastic, Santa in chimney, 6", 1950s, NM, A...$35.00

Crib Toy, Santa on swan holding lantern, celluloid, NM...$325.00

Crib Toy, Santa w/bag, celluloid, sm, NM.....................$100.00

Doll, Mattel, 1968, talker, stuffed cloth, NM...................$50.00

Doll, Steiff, 1970s, orig outfit & glasses, brass button & stock tag, 20½", rare, NM.......................................$585.00

Doll, stuffed cloth w/mask face, red cloth suit w/blk oilcloth boots & belt, 28", VG, A $125.00

Jack-in-the-Box, 1910, Santa in chimney box, 9½", EX...$350.00

Mask, Germany, papier-mache w/crepe hat & cloth beard, 12x8", NM, A......................................$175.00

Mask, Sloan & Woodard, 1904, cb, uncut, 14", rare, M.$100.00

Nodder, papier-mache and cardboard with glass eyes, fur beard, 45", EX, A, $600.00.
(Photo courtesy David Longest)

Nodder, Santa w/lantern, celluloid, 7", M, A $425.00

Nodder, Santa w/tree, cb & papier-mache w/red cloth robe, glass eyes, mica-flecked boots & base, 29", EX, A $1,900.00

Pull Toy, Santa on horse-drawn wagon, 2 leather hide-covered horses on wheeled platform, 36", VG $950.00

Rattle, Santa holding basket of fruit, celluloid, NM.......$150.00

Roly Poly, Germany, papier-mache, hand-pnt beard, suit, & bag over shoulder, 6", NM, A $300.00

Roly Poly, Schoenhut, compo, hand pnt, 6½", M, A $600.00

Roly Poly, Schoenhut, compo, hand pnt, 8", EX, A....$1,600.00

Santa in Basket, celluloid figure in wire mesh basket, 4", EX...$100.00

Santa in Truck w/House & Tree in Back, Japan, celluloid, 4", EX, A $75.00

Santa on Bench w/Lamb, cloth & compo w/bsk lamb, mica-flecked base, 4", EX, A $150.00

Santa on Sleigh, Germany, wood sleigh w/split log sides, compo figure w/cloth clothes, 12", VG, A......................$450.00

Santa Seated on Accordion, papier-mache head & hat w/wood body & accordion, cloth clothes, musical, 9", EX, A ...$1,000.00

Santa w/Tree & Basket of Toys, pulp, hand-pnt, 15", EX, A...$325.00

Sparkler, Japan, Santa appears in chimney as sparks show in window w/kids waving, tin, 5½", NM, A......................$175.00

Yo-yo, Festival, early 1980s, plastic w/Merry Christmas & image of Santa, MIP..$18.00

Yo-yo, 1980s, litho tin w/image of Santa kissing Mrs Claus, NM..$3.00

Roly Polys, papier-mache: Germany, fur beard, feather tree, 11", NM, A, $400.00; felt suit, fur beard, 10", EX, A, $375.00; Schoenhut, head wobbles when toy is moved, 9½", VG, A, $925.00.

Schoenhut

Albert Schoenhut & Co. was located in Philadelphia, Pennsylvania. From as early as 1872 they produced toys of many types including dolls, pianos and other musical instruments, games, and a good assortment of roly polys (which they called Rolly Dollys). Around the turn of the century, they designed a line they called the Humpty Dumpty Circus. It was made up of circus animals, ringmasters, acrobats, lion tamers, and the like, and the concept proved to be so successful that it continued in production until the company closed in 1935. During the nearly thirty-five years they were made, the figures were continually altered either in size or by construction methods, and these variations can greatly affect their values today. Besides the figures themselves, many accessories were produced to go along with the circus theme — tents, cages, tubs, ladders, and wagons, just to mention a few. Teddy Roosevelt's African hunting adventures inspired the company to design a line that included not only Teddy and the animals he was apt to encounter in Africa but native tribesmen as well. A third line featured comic characters of the day, all with the same type of jointed wood construction, many dressed in cotton and felt clothing. There were several, among them were Felix the Cat, Maggie and Jiggs, Barney Google and Spark Plug, and Happy Hooligan.

Several factors come into play when evaluating Schoenhut figures. Foremost is condition. Since most found on the market today show signs of heavy wear, anything above a very good rating commands a premium price. Missing parts and retouched paint sharply reduce a figure's value, though a well-done restoration is usually acceptable. The earlier examples had glass eyes; by 1920 eyes were painted on. Soon after that, the company began

to make their animals in a reduced size. While some of the earlier figures had bisque heads or carved wooden heads, by the '20s, pressed wood heads were the norm. Full-size examples with glass eyes and bisque or carved heads are generally more desirable and more valuable, though rarity must be considered as well.

During the 1950s, some of the figures and animals were produced by the Delvan Company, who had purchased the manufacturing rights.

For more information we recommend *Schoenhut Toy Price Guide* by Keith Kaonis and Andrew Yaffee. Mr. Kaonis is listed in the Directory under Schoenhut.

Consult the index for Schoenhut toys that may be listed in other categories.

Advisor: Keith and Donna Kaonis (K6).

See also Roly Polys; Santa.

HUMPTY DUMPTY CIRCUS ANIMALS

Humpty Dumpty Circus animals with glass eyes, ca. 1903 – 1914, are more desirable and can demand much higher prices than the later painted-eye versions. As a general rule, a glass-eye version is 30% to 40% more than a painted-eye version. (There are exceptions.) The following list suggests values for both glass eye and painted eye versions and reflects a low painted eye price to a high glass eye price.

There are other variations and nuances of certain figures: Bulldog — white with black spots or brindle (brown); open-and closed-mouth zebras and giraffes; ball necks and hemispherical necks on some animals such as the pig, leopard, and tiger, to name a few. These points can affect the price and should be judged individually.

Alligator, jointed, painted eyes, leather feet, 12" L, EX, from $300.00 to $400.00.

Arabian Camel, 1 hump, PE/GE, from $250 to $750.00
Bactrian Camel, 2 humps, PE/GE, from $200 to $1,200.00
Brown Bear, PE/GE, from $200 to $800.00
Buffalo, cloth mane, PE/GE, from $300 to......................$900.00
Buffalo, cvd mane, PE/GE, from $200 to $1,200.00
Bulldog, PE/GE, from $400 to $1,500.00
Burro (made to go w/chariot & clown), PE/GE, from $200 to $700.00
Cat, PE/GE, rare, from $600 to $3,000.00
Cow, PE/GE, from $300 to $1,200.00
Deer, PE/GE, from $300 to...$1,400.00
Donkey, PE/GE, from $75 to $300.00
Donkey w/Blanket, PE/GE, from $100 to......................$600.00

Donkey, glass eyes, shown in rare style I, EX, from $200.00 to $350.00.

Leopard, painted eyes, EX, from $400.00 to $600.00.

Elephant, PE/GE, from $75 to	$300.00
Elephant w/Blanket, PE/GE, from $200 to	$600.00
Gazelle, PE/GE, rare, from $500 to	$2,750.00
Giraffe, PE/GE, from $200 to	$900.00
Goat, PE/GE, from $150 to	$400.00
Goose, PE only, from $200 to	$600.00
Gorilla, PE only, from $1,500 to	$3,750.00
Hippo, PE/GE, from $250 to	$900.00
Horse, brn, saddle & stirrups, PE/GE, from $200 to	$500.00
Horse, wht, platform, PE/GE, from $190 to	$450.00
Hyena, PE/GE, rare, from $1,000 to	$6,000.00

Ostrich, PE/GE, from $250 to	$900.00
Pig, 5 versions, PE/GE, from $200 to	$800.00
Polar Bear, PE/GE, from $400 to	$2,000.00
Poodle, cloth mane, GE only, from $150 to	$450.00
Poodle, PE/GE, from $100 to	$300.00
Rabbit, PE/GE, rare, from $700 to	$3,500.00
Rhino, PE/GE, from $250 to	$800.00
Sea Lion, PE/GE, from $400 to	$1,500.00
Sheep (lamb) w/bell, PE/GE, from $200 to	$700.00
Tiger, PE/GE, from $250 to	$1,200.00
Wolf, PE/GE, rare, from $500 to	$5,000.00
Zebra, PE/GE, from $250 to	$1,200.00
Zebu, PE/GE, rare, from $600 to	$3,000.00

HUMPTY DUMPTY CIRCUS CLOWNS AND OTHER PERSONNEL

Clowns with two-part heads (a cast face applied to a wooden head) were made from 1903 to 1916 and are most desirable — condition is always important. There have been nine distinct styles in fourteen different costumes recorded. Only eight costume styles apply to the two-part headed clowns. The later clowns, ca. 1920, had one-part heads whose features were pressed, and the costumes were no longer tied at the wrists and ankles.

Note: Use the low end of the value range for items in only fair condition. Those in good to very good condition (having very minor scratches and wear, good original finish, no splits or chips, no excessive paint wear or cracked eyes and, of course, complete) may be evaluated by the high end.

Kangaroo, EX, from $1,000.00 to $1,800.00. (This is one of the most folky animals produced by Schoenhut; it has maintained this value for over a decade.) (Photo courtesy Keith and Donna Kaonis)

Black Dude, reduced size, from $100 to	$375.00
Black Dude, 1-part head, purple coat, from $250 to	$700.00
Black Dude, 2-part head, blk coat, from $400 to	$850.00
Black Dude, 2-part head, blk coat, from $400 to	$850.00
Chinese Acrobat, 1-part head, from $400 to	$800.00
Chinese Acrobat, 2-part head, rare, from $400 to	$1,300.00
Clown, early, G, from $150 to	$600.00
Clown, reduced size, from $75 to	$125.00
Gent Acrobat, bsk head, rare, from $300 to	$750.00
Gent Acrobat, 2-part head, very rare, from $600 to	$1,800.00

Lion, cloth mane, GE only, from $500 to	$1,000.00
Lion, cvd mane, PE/GE, from $250 to	$1,200.00
Lion, cvd mane, PE/GE, from $250 to	$1,200.00
Monkey, 1-part head, PE only, from $250 to	$600.00
Monkey, 2-part head, wht face, from $300 to	$900.00

Clown, leather ears, 9", from $250.00 to $400.00.

Hobo, reduced size, from $200 to $375.00
Hobo, 1-part head, from $200 to....................................$400.00
Hobo, 2-part head, curved-up toes, blk coat, from $500 to...$1,200.00
Hobo, 2-part head, facet toe ft, from $400 to.................$900.00
Lady Acrobat, bsk head, from $400 to $750.00
Lady Acrobat, 1-part head, from $200 to........................$400.00
Lady Rider, bsk head, from $250 to $500.00
Lady Rider, 1-part head, from $200 to............................$400.00

Ringmasters: Style I (two-part head, black coat), from $800.00 to $1,800.00; Style II (two-part head, red coat), from $700.00 to $1,600.00; Style IV, ca 1906 (bisque head), from $400.00 to $700.00. (Photo courtesy Keith and Donna Kaonis)

Lady Rider, 2-part head, very rare, from $700 to $1,800.00
Lion Tamer, bsk head, rare, from $500 to $1,000.00
Lion Tamer, 1-part head, from $400 to $750.00
Lion Tamer, 2-part head, early, very rare, from $700 to ..$1,500.00
Ringmaster, 1-part head, from $200 to............................$450.00

HUMPTY DUMPTY CIRCUS ACCESSORIES

There are many accessories: wagons, tents, ladders, chairs, pedestals, tight ropes, weights, and various other items.

Cage Wagon, rear door opens, contains lion with full mane, 12" x 12", VG, A, $1,000.00.

Circus #20/36, in original box (three clowns missing), overall EX, A, $3,000.00.

Circus Cage Wagon, 1920, red w/Schoenhut's...Greatest Show on Earth stenciled in yel, 10" & 12", EX, from $300 to.**$1,200.00**
Menagerie Tent, early, ca 1904, from $1,500 to...........**$2,500.00**
Menagerie Tent, later, 1914-20, from $1,200 to..........**$2,000.00**
Oval Litho Tent, 1926, from $4,000 to.....................**$10,000.00**
Sideshow Panels, 1926, pr, from $2,000 to **$5,000.00**

Schuco

A German company noted for both mechanical toys as well as the teddy bears and stuffed animals we've listed here, Schuco operated from the 1930s well into the 1950s. Items were either marked Germany or US Zone, Germany.

Advisor: Candace Gunther, Candelaine (G16).

See also Aeronautical; Battery-Operated; Character, TV, and Movie Collectibles; Diecast; Disney; Windups, Friction, and Other Mechanicals.

Bear, brn cinnamon ears, orig ribbon, 1950, 3½", NM...**$165.00**
Bear, cinnamon w/metal eyes, orig ribbon, 1950s, 3½", M...**$195.00**
Bear, orange w/metal eyes, shaved muzzle, 1950s, 3½", NM...**$275.00**
Bear, pale gold w/metal eyes, orig paper label, 1950s, 2½", NM.....................**$225.00**
Bear, tan, orig red ribbon, 1950s, 3½", NM **$150.00**
Bear, yel w/metal eyes, 1920s, 12", VG **$350.00**

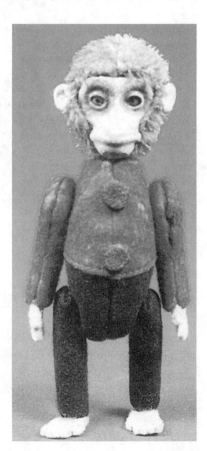

Bellboy Monkey perfume bottle, cork stopper, all original, EX, A, 4¾", $650.00.
(Photo courtesy Monsen and Baer)

Bigo-Bello Dog, orig clothes, 14", NM............................**$150.00**
Black Scottie, Noah's Ark, 1950s, 3", MIB.....................**$225.00**

Blackbird, Noah's Ark, 1950s, 3", MIB **$195.00**
Bottle Bear, pk, 3½", NM, minimum value **$1,000.00**
Dalmatian, Noah's Ark, 2½", rare, M **$375.00**
Duck Mascot, bl & wht striped outfit w/red shoes, 1950s, 3½", NMIB...**$125.00**
Elephant, Noah's Ark, mohair w/felt ears & blanket, fully jtd, 1950s, 2½", NM **$125.00**
Fox, Noah's Ark, 1950, 2½", MIB................................**$225.00**
Janus Bear, 2 faces (googly & bear), cinnamon, 1950s, 3½", M...**$750.00**
Janus Bear, 2 faces (googly & bear), tan, 1950s, 3½", EX...**$550.00**
Lion, Noah's Ark, 3½", EX **$95.00**
Monkey, cinnamon w/felt hands & feet, 2½", NM........**$150.00**
Orangutan, Noah's Ark, 1950, 3", rare, MIB **$295.00**
Owl, Noah's Ark, 1950, 3", M **$75.00**
Panda Bear, mohair w/blk metal bead eyes, 1950s, 2½", M..**$225.00**
Perfume Bear, bright gold, orig bottle, 1920-30, 5", NM...**$650.00**
Perfume Monkey, cinnamon w/felt hands & feet, 1930, 5", rpl bottle, VG..**$200.00**
Raccoon, Noah's Ark, 1950, 3½", M **$200.00**
Squirrel, Noah's Ark, 1950, 2½", M.............................**$150.00**
Teddy Bear, cream w/steel bead eyes, tan embroidered nose & mouth, fully jtd, 1920s, 2½", VG, A......................**$150.00**
Tiger, Noah's Ark, 1950, 3½", EX **$125.00**
Turtle, Noah's Ark, 1950, 3", NM...............................**$110.00**
Yes/No Baby Orangutan, 1948, orig FAO Schwarz tag, 8", rare, NMIB..**$700.00**
Yes/No Bear, blk w/glass eyes, 1950s, 5", rare, EX **$900.00**
Yes/No Bear, caramel w/glass eyes, 1950s, 5", NM..........**$450.00**
Yes/No Bear, chocolate brn w/glass eyes, orig yel ribbon, 1950s, 5", rare, NM...**$900.00**
Yes/No Bear on Wheels, 1920s, ginger mohair, steel fr, CI wheels, 11½", EX, A..**$375.00**
Yes/No Bellhop Monkey, 1920s, 13½", NM **$950.00**
Yes/No Bulldog, cream & brn mohair w/tricolor glass eyes, 1930s, 7", NM...**$1,200.00**
Yes/No Cat, 5", M **$650.00**
Yes/No Charlie Dog, cream & rust, red felt tongue, 1920-30, rare, NM **$550.00**
Yes/No Donkey, mohair w/felt ears, orig felt collar & ribbon, 1950, 5", NM...**$475.00**
Yes/No Elephant, mohair w/felt tusks & ears, cloth US Zone tag, 1948, 5", EX...**$400.00**
Yes/No Fox, tan & cream mohair w/faceted jewel eyes, metal glasses fit into head, fully jtd, 1920s, 13", NM **$1,200.00**
Yes/No Monkey, gray w/orig shirt, jacket & handkerchief, 1920s, 12½", rare, NM.......................................**$750.00**
Yes/No Monkey, limited edition replica of Tricky Monkey, mohair & felt w/glass eyes, 18", NM **$200.00**
Yes/No Panda, mohair w/glass eyes, 1950s, 3½", NM..**$1,000.00**
Yes/No Panda, orig pk bow, 1950s, 5", MIB **$900.00**
Yes/No Panda, orig red ribbon, 1948, 13", rare, NM ...**$1,200.00**
Yes/No Panda, 1940-50, 8", rare, EX **$850.00**
Yes/No Parrot, gr, yel & red mohair w/brn & blk glass eyes, 1926, 11" L, rare, NM...**$650.00**
Yes/No Rabbit, 5", NM **$650.00**
Yes/No Rooster, mohair w/felt beak, comb, waddle & tail, glass eyes, cloth clothes, 1950s, 12", NM **$350.00**

Yes/No Tricky Bear, golden mohair w/amber glass eyes, red plastic medallion, 1950, 8", NM..................................$950.00

Yes/No Tricky Bear, tan, orig red ribbon & US Zone tag, 1948, 13", M...$1,200.00

Yes/No Tricky Elephant, mohair w/felt ears & tusks, glass eyes, 1940-50, NM $425.00

Yes/No Tricky Monkey, orig ribbon, 1948, 10½", EX $300.00

Yes/No Tricky Monkey, orig ribbon & tag, 1948, 14", NM.....$450.00

Yes/No Tricky Orangutan, cinnamon w/glass eyes, 14", NM ..$950.00

Yes/No Tricky Orangutan, mohair & felt w/glass eyes, 1948, 8", NM...$375.00

Slot Cars

Slot cars first became popular in the early 1960s. Electric raceways set up in retail storefront windows were commonplace. Huge commercial tracks with eight and ten lanes were located in hobby store and raceways throughout the United States. Large corporations such as Aurora, Revell, Monogram, and Cox, many of which were already manufacturing toys and hobby items, jumped on the bandwagon to produce slot cars and race sets. By the end of the early 1970s, people were loosing interest in slot racing, and its popularity diminished. Today the same baby boomers that raced slot cars in earlier days are revitalizing the sport. The popularity of the Internet has stabilized the pricing of collectible slots. It can confirm prices of common items, while escalating the price of the 'rare' item to new levels. As the Internet grows in popularity, the accessibility of information on slots also grows. This should make the once hard-to-find slot cars more readily available for all to enjoy. Slot cars were generally well used, so finding vintage cars and race sets in like-new or mint condition is difficult. Slot cars replicating the 'muscle' cars from the '60s and '70s are extremely sought after, and clubs and organizations devoted to these collectibles are becoming more and more commonplace. Large toy companies such as Tomy and Tyco still produce some slots today, but not in the quality, quantity, or variety of years past.

Aurora produced several types of slots: Screachers (5700 and 5800 number series, valued at $5.00 to $20.00); the AC-powered Vibrators (1500 number series, valued at $20.00 to $150.00); DC-powered Thunderjets (1300 and 1400 number series, valued at $20.00 to $150.00); and the last-made AFX SP1000 (1900 number series, valued at $15.00 to $75.00).

Advisor: Gary Pollastro (P5).

COMPLETE SETS

AMT, Cobra Racing Set, NMIB $185.00

Atlas, Racing Set #1000, HO scale, G (G box)..............$100.00

Aurora, Home Raceway by Sears, #79N9513C, VG $195.00

Aurora, Jackie Stewart Oval 8, VG (VG box)..................$85.00

Aurora AFX, Jackie Stewart Challenger Raceway, NMIB ..$75.00

Aurora AFX, Jackie Stewart Day & Night Enduro, complete, EX (EX box) $75.00

Aurora AFX, Revamatic Slot Car Set, EX (EX box) $75.00

Aurora AFX, Ultra 5, complete, EX (EX box)..................$75.00

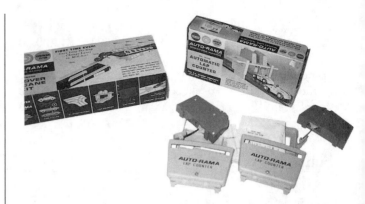

AC Gilbert, Fly Over Chicane Kit #19342, MIB, $40.00;
AC Gilbert Automatic Lap Counter #19339, MIB, $35.00.
(Photo courtesy Gary Pollastro)

Cox, Baja Bug Raceway, Super Scale, NMIB, P5............$150.00

Cox, Ontario 8, #3070, w/Eagle & McLaren, G (G box) .$75.00

Eldon, Challenge Cup Sport & Stock, 1/32 scale, complete, NMIB..$195.00

Eldon, Gold Cup Road Race, 1962, 1/32 scale, complete, EX (EX box) $150.00

Eldon, Raceway 24, 1/24 scale, VG (VG box), P5 ....$195.00

Eldon, Sky High Triple Road Race, w/Ferrari, Lotus, Stingray & Porsche, G (G box) $75.00

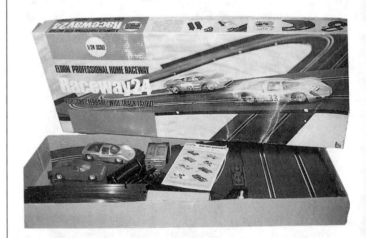

**Eldon Professional Home Raceway 24, 1/24 scale, MIB,
$195.00.** (Photo courtesy Gary Pollastro)

Gilbert Race Set #19041, VG (VG box), $95.00.
(Photo courtesy Gary Pollastro)

Ideal, Dukes of Hazzard Speed Jumper, 1981, includes General Lee and Sheriff's car, printed stunt jump bridge and town, track, controllers, power pack, and instructions, M (sealed box), $65.00. (Photo courtesy June Moon)

Ideal, Alcan Highway Torture Track, 1968, complete, MIB...**$50.00**

Ideal, Mini-Motorific Set, #4939-5, EX **$85.00**

Marx, Race & Road Cross-Over Trestles, complete, w/Corvette & Thunderbird, NMIB...**$195.00**

Remco, Mighty Mike Action Track, NMIB.....................**$75.00**

Revell, HiBank Raceway Set, #49-9503, w/Cougar GTE & Pontiac Firebird, EX (EX box).............................**$150.00**

Scaletrex, Electric Motor Racing Set, Officially Approved by Jim Clark, made in England, NMIB........................**$400.00**

Sears Allstate #49-9561, Strombecker, 'Competition 8' Road Race Set, VG **$125.00**

Strombecker, Competition 8 Road Racing Set, VG (VG Sears-Allstate box), P5...**$125.00**

Strombecker, Plymouth Barracuda, 1/32nd scale set **$250.00**

Strombecker, Road Race Set, from $125 to **$150.00**

Strombecker, Thunderbolt Monza, Montgomery Ward, VG (VG box)..**$150.00**

Strombecker, 4 Lane Mark IV Race Set, VG (VG box) ...**$250.00**

Tyco, Collector Edition #6994, Petty '92 STP Special #43 & Petty '70 Superbird #43, bl, twin pk..........................**$48.00**

Tyco, International Pro Racing Set, #930086, EX **$125.00**

SLOT CARS ONLY

Aurora, Ford Baja Bronco, #1909, red, EX.....................**$15.00**

Aurora, Ford Street Van, #1943, lt bl & brn, NM **$15.00**

Aurora, Javelin, red, wht & bl, NM **$30.00**

Aurora, Snowmobile, #1485-400, yel w/bl figure, MIB.....**$55.00**

Aurora AFX, '57 Chevy Nomad, orange w/bl pipes, EX...**$40.00**

Aurora AFX, Autoworld Beamer #5, wht w/bl stripes, NM ..**$12.00**

Aurora AFX, Autoworld McLaren XIR, #1752, bl & wht, EX **$14.00**

Aurora AFX, Aztec Dragster, #1963, red, EX..................**$20.00**

Aurora AFX, Blazer, #1917, blk, bl & wht, VG **$12.00**

Aurora AFX, Camaro Z-28, #1901, red, wht & bl, EX **$20.00**

Aurora AFX, Chevy Chevelle #29, red, wht & bl, EX **$30.00**

Aurora AFX, Datsun Baja Pickup, #1745, bl & blk, EX ...**$20.00**

Aurora AFX, Dodge Challenger, #1773, lime & bl, NM ..**$35.00**

Aurora AFX, Dodge Charger #11, red, wht & bl, EX **$25.00**

Aurora AFX, Dodge Daytona #7, orange, bl & silver, no lights, EX..**$50.00**

Aurora AFX, Dodge Fever Dragster, wht & yel, EX..........**$15.00**

Aurora AFX, Dodge Rescue Van, red, gold & wht, EX.....**$15.00**

Aurora AFX, Dodge Street Van, orange & red, MIB........**$40.00**

Aurora AFX, Dragster, from $15 to **$20.00**

Aurora AFX, Ferrari 512M, #1763, wht & bl, MIB **$25.00**

Aurora AFX, Firebird, #1965, blk & gold, EX **$15.00**

Aurora AFX, Ford Escort #46, blk, red & gr, EX..............**$25.00**

Aurora AFX, Ford Thunderbird Stock Car, NMIB...........**$25.00**

Aurora AFX, Javelin #5, bl & blk, EX...............................**$20.00**

Aurora AFX, Jeep CJ-7 Flamethrower, #1987, orange & red, NM..**$18.00**

Aurora AFX, Magnatraction, from $15 to **$20.00**

Aurora AFX, Mario Andretti NGK Indy Car, blk, M.......**$35.00**

Aurora AFX, Matador GT, red & butterscotch, NM........**$25.00**

Aurora AFX, Matador Stock Car #5, #1930, orange, blk & red, EX..**$18.00**

Aurora AFX, Matador Taxi, wht, EX **$20.00**

Aurora AFX, Peace Tank, gr, EX **$15.00**

Aurora AFX, Peterbilt Lighted Rig, #1156, red & yel, EX ..**$20.00**

Aurora AFX, Plymouth Roadrunner #43, #1762, bl & wht, EX..**$20.00**

Aurora AFX, Plymouth Roadrunner Stock Car, #1762, bl & wht, EX **$30.00**

Aurora AFX, Pontiac Firebird, blk & gold, EX **$25.00**

Aurora AFX, Pontiac Firebird #9, wht, bl & blk, EX........**$25.00**

Aurora AFX, Porsche 510-K, #1786, gold, chrome & orange stripe, EX..**$16.00**

Aurora AFX, Porsche 917, wht & bl, MIB........................**$40.00**

Aurora AFX, Rallye Ford Escort, #1737, gr & bl, EX **$15.00**

Aurora AFX, Roarin' Rolls Golden Ghost, #1781, yel & bl or wht & blk, EX, ea..**$18.00**

Aurora AFX, Shadow Cam Racer, blk, EX........................**$20.00**

Aurora AFX, Speed Beamer #11, red, wht & bl, NM.......**$15.00**

Aurora AFX, Turbo Turn On, #1755, orange, yel & purple, EX **$15.00**

Aurora AFX, Ultra Shadow #5, #3007, type A, wht, red, orange & yel, M...**$25.00**

Aurora AFX, Vega Van Gasser, #1754, yel & red, EX **$15.00**

Aurora AFX, Volkswagen Bug, lime w/bl tanks, EX **$30.00**

Aurora AFX, 1929 Model A Woodie, yel & brn, M.........**$15.00**

Aurora Cigarbox, Dino Ferrari, red, EX **$20.00**

Aurora Cigarbox, Ford GT, wht w/bl stripe, NM..............**$20.00**

Aurora G-Plus, Amrac Can Am, yel & blk w/wht stripe, EX ..**$15.00**

Aurora G-Plus, Capri, wht w/gr & bl stripe, EX................**$15.00**

Aurora G-Plus, Corvette, #1954, orange, red & silver, EX...**$12.00**

Aurora G-Plus, Indy Valvoline, blk, VG **$12.00**

Aurora G-Plus, Lotus F1, #1783, blk & gold, EX **$20.00**

Aurora G-Plus, NASCAR Camaro, #76, wht, orange & gold, EX **$12.00**

Aurora G-Plus, Rallye Ford Escort, #1737, gr & bl, EX **$15.00**

Aurora T-Jet, Hot Rod Coupe, #1554-298, gr, VG **$50.00**

Aurora T-Jet, Volkswagon, #1404, wht w/Flower Power, EX ...**$30.00**

Aurora Thunderjet, '63 Corvette, #1356, yel, EX.............**$50.00**

Aurora Thunderjet, '73 Duster, EX $30.00
Aurora Thunderjet, Alfa Romeo Type 33, #1409, yel, EX ..$25.00
Aurora Thunderjet, AMX #5, red, wht & bl, EX.............$25.00
Aurora Thunderjet, Batmobile, EX $150.00
Aurora Thunderjet, Chaparral 2F#7, #1410, lime & bl, EX $25.00
Aurora Thunderjet, Cheetah, #1403, gr, EX....................$35.00
Aurora Thunderjet, Cobra, #1375, yel w/blk stripe, VG ..$30.00
Aurora Thunderjet, Cobra GT, yel & blk, EX $30.00
Aurora Thunderjet, Cougar, #1389, wht, EX....................$40.00
Aurora Thunderjet, Dino Ferrari #3, red, wht & gr, EX ...$30.00
Aurora Thunderjet, Dune Buggy, wht w/red striped roof, EX $30.00
Aurora Thunderjet, Dune Buggy Roadster, #1398, bl & blk, EX $35.00
Aurora Thunderjet, Ferrari 250, red & wht, EX $50.00
Aurora Thunderjet, Ford 'J,' #1382, wht & bl, VG...........$35.00
Aurora Thunderjet, Ford GT 40, #1374, red w/blk stripe, EX...$25.00
Aurora Thunderjet, Ford Lola GT, #1378, dk gr w/wht stripe, VG $30.00
Aurora Thunderjet, Hot Rod Coupe, #1554-298, gr, VG (VG box), P5...$50.00
Aurora Thunderjet, Hot Rod Coupe, red, VG..................$25.00
Aurora Thunderjet, Hot Rod Roadster, tan, NM.............$35.00
Aurora Thunderjet, International Tow Truck, wht & blk w/red stripe, NM..$100.00
Aurora Thunderjet, Jaguar, red, VG................................$30.00
Aurora Thunderjet, Lola GT, #1378, turq & wht w/bl stripe, VG $25.00
Aurora Thunderjet, Mangusta Mongoose, #1400, yel, EX ..$45.00
Aurora Thunderjet, McLaren Elva Flamethrower, #1400, yel, EX $20.00
Aurora Thunderjet, Porsche 904, #1376, bl w/wht stripe, EX...$30.00
Aurora Thunderjet, Sand Van Dune Buggy, #1483, pk & wht, EX $25.00
Aurora Ultra-5 AFX, #3007, Shadow Type A, wht w/yel & orange, NMIB $25.00
Aurora Vibrator, Hot Rod Coupe, #1554, bl, VG.............$50.00
Aurora Vibrator, Hot Rod Roadster, #1533, bl, yel or gr, EX, ea...$75.00
Aurora Vibrator, Mercedes, #1542, yel, EX.....................$50.00
Aurora Vibrator, Mercedes 300SL, #1542, wht, EX, P5....$60.00
Aurora Vibrator, Van Body Trailer, #1586, gray, G...........$20.00
Bauer, BMW 501 Police, #4303, gr, MIB $65.00
Cox, Javelin, superscale road race car.................................$50.00
Hot Rod Coupe, #1554-298, yel, EX, P5...........................$50.00
Monogram, Cooper Ford w/Tiger 100 Motor, SR-3204-598, red, 1/32 scale, VG..$80.00
Palmer Toys, Sting Ray Corvette, MOC...........................$95.00
Revell, Model Race, Carroll Shelby's Cobra Ford, #R3100-600, w/SP 500 motor, 1/32 scale...$80.00
Screecher, Cuda Funny Car, wht, red & orange, EX.........$20.00
Strombecker, Jaguar SKE, #9220-595, red, MIB $50.00
Strombecker, Pontiac Bonneville, EX $40.00
TCR, Jam Car, yel & blk, EX $15.00
TCR, Mack Truck, EX $15.00
TCR, Maintenance Van, red & wht, EX...........................$15.00
TCR, Mercury Stock Car, purple & chrome, VG $15.00

Tomy, Camaro GT #88 Auto Tech, M, from $10.00 to $20.00.

Tomy, Thunderbird #11 (Bill Elliot sgn), red & wht, EX..$25.00
Tyco, '57 Chevy, red & orange w/yel stripes, EX.............$20.00
Tyco, '57 Chevy Pro Stock, red, orange & yel w/gray bumpers, EX...$20.00
Tyco, '79 Covette, silver, bl & orange, EX $30.00
Tyco, '83 Corvette Challenge #33, silver & yel, EX $25.00
Tyco, '97 Corvette, yel, EX...$15.00
Tyco, A-Team Van, blk & red, EX...................................$20.00
Tyco, Bandit Pickup, blk & red, EX................................$12.00
Tyco, Blackbird Firebird, #6914, blk & gold, EX $12.00
Tyco, Camaro Funny Car, silver, gr, & blk, EX $40.00
Tyco, Caterpillar #96, blk & yel, EX................................$20.00
Tyco, Chaparral 2G #66, #8504, VG................................$14.00
Tyco, Corvette, glow-in-the-dark, any color, EX, ea.........$10.00
Tyco, Corvette #12, wht & red w/bl stripes, EX...............$12.00
Tyco, Corvette Curvehanger, chrome w/flames, EX $15.00
Tyco, Firebird, #6914, cream & red, VG $12.00
Tyco, Firebird Turbo #12, blk & gold, EX $10.00
Tyco, Funny Mustang, orange w/yel flames, EX $25.00
Tyco, GM Aerocoupe #43, bl & flourescent red, EX $65.00
Tyco, Highway Patrol #56, blk & wht, w/sound, EX.........$16.00
Tyco, Lamborghini, red, VG..$12.00
Tyco, Lamborghini, silver, EX...$20.00
Tyco, Lighted Porsche #2, silver w/red nose, EX $20.00
Tyco, Lighted Super American, #8525, red, wht, & bl, EX..$20.00
Tyco, Lola 260, #8514, red, wht, & bl, EX.......................$14.00
Tyco, Military Police #45, wht & bl, EX $30.00
Tyco, Mustang #1, orange w/yel flames, EX $20.00
Tyco, Oldsmobile #88, yel & bl, EX................................$25.00
Tyco, Pinto Funny Car Goodyear, red & yel, EX $20.00
Tyco, Porsche Carrera, #8527, yel & blk, EX $25.00
Tyco, Porsche 908, red, wht & bl, EX...............................$20.00
Tyco, Pro #8833, Superbird, candy apple red, VG $45.00
Tyco, Silverstreak Pickup, silver w/pk & orange stripes, EX..$15.00
Tyco, Silverstreak Racing Vette, #8556, silver & pk w/orange stripe, VG...$15.00
Tyco, Thunderbird #15, red & yel, VG $10.00
Tyco, Turbo Firebird, blk & gold, NM.............................$12.00

Tyco, Turbo Hopper #27, red, EX $12.00
Tyco, Valvoline Thunderbird #6, bl & wht, EX $20.00
Tyco, Volvo 850 #3, wht & bl, EX...........................$20.00
Tyco, VW Bug, gold & red, EX...............................$40.00
Tyco, 1940 Ford Coupe, #8534, blk w/flames, NM $20.00
Tyco US1, Peterbilt Cab, red & wht, EX $20.00

ACCESSORIES

AMT Service Parts Kit, #2000, VG $100.00
AMT Steering Wheel Controller, #TH-300, 1/24 scale, EX ..$20.00
Aurora AFX Carrying Case, blk, 2-level, EX $15.00
Aurora AFX Pit Kit, G $15.00

Aurora AFX Accessories: Speed Steer Breakout Wall #6056, MIB, $18.00; Speed Steer Intersection (shown lower right)/Overpass #6055, MIB, $20.00. (Photo courtesy Gary Pollastro)

Aurora AFX 45 OHM Hand Controller w/Brakes, EX (EX box)...$15.00
Aurora Model Motoring, 1969, color, EX $30.00
Aurora Model Motoring Auto Starter, #1507, EX (EX box)..$15.00
Aurora Model Motoring Hill Track, 9", EX $10.00
Aurora Model Motoring in HO Scale Layout & Service Manual, 1961, VG $10.00
Aurora Model Motoring Loop the Loop Track Set, #1504, EX (EX box) $20.00
Aurora Model Motoring Monza Banked Curve, #1467, EX (EX box) $20.00
Aurora Model Motoring Steering Wheel Controller, EX .$10.00
Aurora Model Motoring Y Turn-Off Track w/Switch, EX...$20.00
Aurora Model Motoring 4-Way Stop Track, 9", EX..........$15.00
Aurora Speedline Finish Set, 1968, MOC $25.00
Aurora Speedline Slingslot Starter, 1968, MOC $25.00
Aurora Thunderjet Carrying Case, butterscotch, VG $15.00
Aurora Thunderjet Country Bridge Roadway, EX (EX box).....$20.00
Aurora Thunderjet Speed Control Steering Wheel Stile, EX...$20.00
Aurora Thunderjet Transformer, VG $20.00

Autorama Grand Stand #19340, M (NM box), $25.00.
(Photo courtesy Gary Pollastro)

Books, 'Here Is Your Hobby Slot Car Racing' & 'Complete Book of Model Raceways & Roadways,' VG, ea $50.00
Catalog, Aurora 1971, AFX, color, VG......................$20.00
Eldon Curve Track, MOC $10.00
Eldon Power Track, MOC $10.00
Gilbert Autorama Fly Over Chicane Kit, #19342, MIB ...$40.00
Gilbert Autorama Lap Counter, #19339, MIB.................$40.00
Monogram Lane Change Track, MIB...........................$20.00
Monogram Tapered Chicane Track, MIB.......................$20.00
Strombecker, lap counter, NIB $25.00
Strombecker Grandstand, #9399, EX $25.00
Strombecker Scale Lap Counter, 1/32 scale, MIB............$25.00
Thunderjet Hop Up Kit, lift kit, from $15 to $20.00
Tyco Stick Shift 4-Speed Controller, EX....................$10.00
Tyco Trigger Controller, orange, EX $8.00

Smith-Miller

Smith-Miller (Los Angeles, California) made toy trucks from 1944 until 1955. During that time they used four basic cab designs, and most of their trucks sold for about $15.00 each. Over the past several years, these toys have become very popular, especially the Mack trucks which today sell at premium prices. The company made a few other types of toys as well, such as the train toy box and the 'Long, Long Trailer.'

Bank of America Truck, gr w/blk rubber tires, opening rear doors, w/padlock & keys, 14", EX, A $400.00

Bekins Van & Storage Company Tractor-Trailer, wht w/red & blk decals, EX $1,100.00

Bell Telephone System Truck, 2-tone gr w/wht lettering, orig canvas cover, 19", NM, A $2,000.00

Blue Diamond Dump Truck, wht w/bl detail & blk rubber tires, hydraulic dump, 19", VG, A $475.00

Dump Truck, red, 12", prof rstr, A $400.00

Dump Truck, 1954, red w/blk rubber tires, 12", NM, A..$450.00

Emergency Towing Service, #802, 1940s-50s, wht cab w/red wrecker bed, EX $675.00

Fruehauf Machinery Hauler, orange, 26", EX.................$410.00

GMC Searchlight Truck, Hollywood Film-Ad, wht cab w/red bed, red trailer for light, EX.....................................$900.00

GMC Super Cargo Tractor Trailer, silver cab, red bed w/wooden deck, VG $275.00

GMC Texaco Oil Tanker Truck, long frame truck w/metal tank on wooden base, EX...$325.00

GMC Wrecker, 1949, wht cab w/red chassis, wrecker boom, & bumper, missing spare tire o/w EX...........................$240.00

Gulf B Model Mack Tanker, contemporary, 19", NM, A, $500.00.

Hennis 14 Wheel Tractor Trailer, red cab, silver trailer w/yel letters, 1950s, 32" L, EX $2,280.00

Hollywood Film-Ad Truck, wht cab w/red bed, EX $450.00

Long, Long Trailer, 1950s Lincoln Capri & House Trailer, 39¼" L, NM $1,400.00

Mack Bell Telephone System, gr w/wooden bed, w/canvas for bed, EX...$425.00

Mack Lumber Truck, mk Mackinac Logging Works on doors, complete w/lumber & chains, 35", NMIB, A $1,200.00

MIC Aerial Ladder Truck, mk LAFD, 1950s, red w/silver bumper, grille, ladder, & running boards, 23½", NM...............$900.00

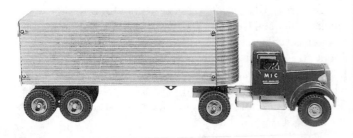

MIC, cast model with polished aluminum body, bulldog hood ornament, 28", EX, A, from $700.00 to $1,100.00.

MIC Dump Truck, yel, hydraulic dump w/lift-up tailgate, 17", prof rstr, A...$600.00

MIC Fruehauf Semi-Trailer, red cab w/silver trailer, EX $1,100.00

MIC Liftgate Truck, red cab, red bed w/silver lift gate, wooden stakes, hydraulic lift, EX................................$780.00

MIC Tow Truck, wht w/silver bumper, grille, & boom, EX $610.00

Mobilgas Tanker Semi-Trailer, red w/blk rubber wheels, EX $575.00

PIE (Pacific Intermountain Express) 18 Wheeler, 1950s, red, silver, & blk, 24½", EXIB $950.00

Red Diamond Dump Truck, silver w/red fenders & frame, rstr, M $975.00

Searchlight Truck & Trailer, mk Hollywood Film-Ad, red & wht, battery-op searchlight, 27", EX, A...............$1,000.00

Semi Tractor Trailer w/Flat Bed, 1950s, gr cab w/bl flat bed, 3 orig cb logs, 24", EX $1,400.00

Silver Streak, #509E, Fruehauf decal, NMIB..............$1,200.00

Sparkeeta Truck, 1940s, gr cab w/gr wooden bed, VG+ $1,025.00

Tow Truck, wht GMC cab w/red boom, blk rubber tires, 14", EX, A $250.00

Triton Oil Cab Over Truck, polished aluminum body, wooden floor, 14", VG/EX, A, $300.00.

US Army Personnel Carrier, 19", professionally restored, A, $500.00.

US Army Truck, dk gr, front bumper damage & 1 missing headlight o/w VG+ $350.00

Snow Domes

Snow domes are water-filled paperweights that come in several different styles. The earliest type was made in two pieces and consisted of a glass globe on a separate base. First made in the middle of the nineteenth century, they were revived during the '30s and '40s by companies in America, Italy, and Germany. Similar weights are now being imported into the country from the Orient. The most common snow dome on today's market are the plastic half-moon shapes made as souvenirs or Christmas toys, a style that originated in West Germany during the 1950s. Other shapes were made as well, including round and square bottles, short and tall rectangles, cubes, and other simple shapes.

During the 1970s, figural plastic snow domes were especially popular. There are two types — large animate shapes themselves containing the snow scene, or dome shapes that have figures draped over the top. Today's collectors buy them all, old or new.

Advisor: Nancy McMichael (M18).

ADVERTISING

Air Canada, wht & red jumbo jet flying over city skyline, EX $15.00
American Express Vacations, Collect a World of Memories, graphic of wht plane in bl sky, wht ftd dome, M $60.00
Days Inn, Catch Some Rays at Days, w/2 Flintstones characters, sm oval plastic dome, M $10.00
Michelin Man, Mr Bib in mountains, European issue, MIB..$30.00
New York Times, 1987, bear & bull on seesaw, caption reads One Constant in an Ever-Changing Market, EX, minimum value..$100.00
Newsweek, 1990, No One Covers the World Like Newsweek, name floats around on red bars, globe in background, plastic, M...$70.00
Texaco, tanker truck against cityscape in rnd dome, trapezoid base w/dealer advertising, EX $65.00

CHARACTER

Bambi TV, 1959, Bambi scene inside a TV, EX.................$25.00
Barbar the Elephant, plastic dome on wht ftd base, M $15.00
Bugs Bunny, wood w/glass dome, plays Singing in the Rain, MIB...$85.00
Clarabelle, Kurt Alder, 1988, wooden base, 1988, M $15.00
Creature From the Black Lagoon, figural, MIB.................$15.00
Donald Duck, dressed for skiing, glass globe on rnd wooden base, M...$10.00
Donald Duck as Santa, M..$15.00
Dragons, 1 dragon in dome w/2nd dragon hanging onto Medievel town base, MIB..$25.00
Elmer Fudd w/Beehive, mk Oops! on base, EX $10.00
Flintstones, Hanna-Barbera, 1975, Fred, Pebbles, Bamm-Bamm & Dino in front of Bedrock City sign, M $25.00
Flintstones, Hanna-Barbera, 1975, Fred, Pebbles, Bamm-Bamm & Dino against bl ground, plastic dome on ftd base, NM ..$95.00
Goofy, Kurt Alder, 1988, wooden base, M $15.00

Happy Face, Germany, yel w/legs & arms in tall dome w/glitter, rnd blk base, EX...$15.00
Lone Ranger Round-Up, Driss, 1940s, lassoing cow in glass dome on rnd base, NM $75.00
Mice Tea Party, San Francisco Music Box Co, musical, plays Tea for Two, rnd dome on teapot-shaped base, 6", EX $30.00
Mickey & Donald, Walt Disney, playing on seesaw, M.....$25.00
Mickey Mouse, as Santa climbing into chimney, musical, M...$22.00
Mickey Mouse, Bully, 1977, blk & wht striding Mickey in dome, EX...$18.00
Mickey Mouse w/Playing Cards, Monogram Products/WDP, yel base, EX..$25.00
Paul Bunyon & Blue Ox, plastic dome on wht ftd base, M ..$15.00
Pluto, Kurt Alder, 1988, wooden base, M $15.00

Red Riding Hood and the Wolf, Germany, from $10.00 to $12.00. (Photo courtesy Helene Guarnaccia)

Snoopy, Willits, 1966, on yel doghouse, M $20.00
Wizard of Oz, red base, M $15.00
Yosemite Sam, plays Home on the Range, glass dome on wooden base, MIB $50.00

FIGURES

Cat Playing Drum, drum is water compartment, M $12.00
Elephant, realistic detail, seated atop dome w/2 elephants inside against gr trees w/dk bl ground, wht oval base, M......$18.00
Salty Seaman & Captain, standing behind rnd dome w/sailing ship inside, German, M $45.00

HOLIDAYS AND SPECIAL OCCASIONS

Birth Announcement, boy & girl babies on seesaw w/stork in middle of plastic dome, ftd base, M $8.00
Birthday, boy & girl holding up cake on platform mk Happy Birthday against bl ground in plastic dome on wht ftd base, EX..$8.00

Birthday, Happy Birthday! lettered on side of 3-tiered cake w/red candles, plastic dome, wht rnd ftd base, M...................$8.00

Champion, gold figure inside of trophy, M...........................$8.00

Christmas, figural bear in Santa hat & gr neck ribbon, no plaque, M $12.00

Christmas, figural dog w/gift (water compartment), M.....$12.00

Christmas, figural Santa on lamppost, M $12.00

Christmas, Santa & snowman on seesaw, plastic dome on ftd base, M $25.00

Christmas, tree in glass dome, mk Made in USA, 4", NM..$45.00

Easter, rabbit w/Easter eggs standing next to pine tree, Austrian glass dome, new, M $10.00

Graduation, figural graduation cap cocked atop dome w/Congratulations lettered inside, M....................................$8.00

Halloween, Halloween Happy!, Hallmark, haunted house, NM, H9 ....$12.00

Halloween, haunted house on dome atop tall rnd base, Marcel Schurman/San Francisco, M..$8.00

Halloween, Trick or Treat!, Hallmark, haunted house & skeleton, NM, H9 ....$12.00

New Year, Let's Celebrate, champagne bottle & wht gloves in top hat next to 2 glasses in dome on rnd base, M.........$8.00

Snowmen, various scenes in globes, from $15.00 to $20.00.
(Photo courtesy Helene Guarnaccia)

SOUVENIR AND COMMEMORATIVES

Alaska, polar bear bending over stream, sm oval plastic dome, M..$6.00

Berlin Bledt Doch Berlin (Berlin Will Always Be Berlin), mc city scene, sm oval plastic dome, M..............................$8.00

Cancun, Cozumel Mexico, fish on string in lg plastic dome, M..$8.00

Cancun, Mexico, 2 pk dolphins in lg dome, M $6.00

Cape Cod, 2 sailboats in sm oval plastic dome, old, M $7.00

Cooper Union (NYC Building), detailed replica, clear all around, broad blk base w/gold decal, rnd, lg, M $18.00

Florida, salt & pepper shakers, 2 different views in pk & bl plastic TVs, M, pr $20.00

Gillette Castle State Park, CT, castle inside dome on 3-legged base, M...$10.00

Holiday World, Santa Claus IN, Santa waving against name on bl background, plastic dome, M..................................$12.00

Jerusalem, from $15.00 to $18.00. (Photo courtesy Helene Guarnaccia)

Lake George, sailboat on lake scene, lg plastic dome, M $6.00

Lake Tahoe, sailboats against pine trees on shoreline, NM..$10.00

Mount Rushmore, Black Hills SD, plastic dome, M $12.00

Ozarks, log cabin scene w/figure & deer on seesaw, minimum value...$8.00

San Juan Capistrano, bottle shape, M $10.00

Sears Tower Chicago, lg blk letters in flat bullet-shaped dome, M $1.00

Six Flags Over Georgia, calendar dome, M $15.00

St Thomas Virgin Islands, parrot inside on sm oval plastic dome, M..$10.00

USS Constitution, open-work ship inside plastic dome, old, M $12.00

Soldiers and Accessories

'Dimestore soldiers' were made from the 1920s until sometime in the 1960s. Some of the better-known companies who made these small-scale figures and accessories were Barclay, Manoil, and American Metal Toys, also known as Jones (hollow cast lead); Gray Iron (cast iron); and Auburn (rubber). They're about 3" to 3½" high. They were sold in Woolworth's and Kresge's 5 & 10 Stores (most for just five cents), hence the name 'Dimestore.' Marx made tin soldiers for use in target gun games; these sell for about $8.00 to $20.00. Condition is most important as these soldiers saw a lot of action. They're most often found with much of the paint worn off and with some serious 'battle wounds' such as missing arms or legs. Nearly two thousand different figures were made by the major manufacturers, plus a number of others by minor makers such as Tommy Toy and All-Nu.

Another very popular line of toy soldiers has been made by Britains of England since 1893. They are smaller and usually more detailed than 'Dimestores,' and variants number in the thousands. Serious collectors should refer to *Collecting American Made Toy Soldiers* for 'Dimestore' soldiers, and *Collecting Foreign-*

Made Toy Soldiers for Britains and others not made in America. Both books are by Richard O'Brien (1997).

You'll notice that in addition to the soldiers, many of our descriptions and values are for the vehicles, cannons, animals, and cowboys and Indians made and sold by the same manufacturers. Note: Percentages in the description lines refer to the amount of original paint remaining, a most important evaluation factor.

Advisors: Sally and Stan Alekna (A1).

See also Dinky; Plastic Figures.

American Metal, fox, brn or gray, scarce, 99%, A1, ea.....**$25.00**
American Metal, knight w/pennant, scarce, 98%, A1......**$95.00**
American Metal, soldier, antiaircraft gunner, khaki, scarce, 96%, A1 ....**$100.00**
American Metal, soldier, machine gunner, prone, khaki, scarce, 95%, A1..**$125.00**
Auburn Rubber, collie, 95%, A1 ....**$18.00**
Auburn Rubber, goose, scarce, 95%, A1 ....**$18.00**
Auburn Rubber, guard officer, yel w/red trim, scarce, 99%, A1..**$40.00**
Auburn Rubber, Marmon-Harrington tank, 4½", 93%, A1.**$25.00**
Auburn Rubber, officer on horse, scarce, 98%, A1 ....**$50.00**
Auburn Rubber, soldier, charging w/tommy gun, 97%, A1 ..**$25.00**
Auburn Rubber, soldier, machine gunner, 99%, A1 ....**$20.00**
Auburn Rubber, soldier, marching, port arms, bl, 97%, A1..**$16.00**
Auburn Rubber, soldier, marching, port arms, khaki, 98%, A1..**$20.00**
Auburn Rubber, trench mortar, scarce, 96%, A1 ....**$45.00**
Auburn Rubber, US infantry officer, khaki, 95%, A1.......**$15.00**
Barclay, aircraft carrier, scarce, 98%, A1....................**$100.00**
Barclay, ambulance, w/sm red cross, 1930s, 96%, A1........**$45.00**
Barclay, aviator, 98%, A1 ....**$30.00**
Barclay, boy, 98%, A1 ....**$15.00**
Barclay, boy skater, various colors, 97%, A1, ea...............**$16.00**
Barclay, bride & groom, HO scale, scarce, 98%, A1, ea ...**$20.00**
Barclay, cannon, silver w/red spoke wheels, NM, A1 ....**$40.00**
Barclay, cavalryman on gray horse, 1930, 95%, A1 ....**$32.00**

Barclay, conductor, 97%, A1 ....**$15.00**
Barclay, cop on motorcycle, scarce, 94%, A1 ....**$50.00**
Barclay, cow grazing, 98%, A1 ....**$16.00**
Barclay, cowboy w/2 pistols, 94%, A1 ....**$20.00**
Barclay, cowboy wearing mask on horse w/lasso, scarce, 99%, A1..**$60.00**
Barclay, detective in bl suit, scarce, 97%, A1 ....**$170.00**
Barclay, doctor in wht, 85%, A1................................**$15.00**
Barclay, engineer, HO scale, 99%, A1..........................**$12.00**
Barclay, field cannon, closed hitch, sm, 97%, A1 ....**$18.00**
Barclay, girl, 96%, A1 ....**$15.00**
Barclay, horse standing, 97%, A1 ....**$15.00**
Barclay, Indian chief w/tomahawk & shield, 97%, A1 .....**$22.00**
Barclay, Indian w/hatchet & shield, 97%, A1................**$15.00**
Barclay, knight w/shield, 97%, A1................................**$20.00**
Barclay, knight w/sword across chest, 98%, A1................**$40.00**
Barclay, mailman, 99%, A1 ....**$20.00**
Barclay, man on sled, 97%, A1 ....**$25.00**
Barclay, marine, bl cap, long stride, tin helmet, 98%, A1 ...**$36.00**
Barclay, marine w/sword, long stride, tin helmet, 95%, A1..**$38.00**
Barclay, minister walking, scarce, 97%, A1 ....**$75.00**
Barclay, officer on motorcycle, scarce, 98%, A1 ....**$70.00**
Barclay, officer w/bugle on rearing horse, movable arm, scarce, 96%, A1 ....**$75.00**
Barclay, officer w/sword, long stride, tin helmet, 94%, A1...**$25.00**
Barclay, officer w/sword on gray horse, movable arm, scarce, 99%, A1 ....**$75.00**
Barclay, oiler, HO scale, 98%, A1 ....**$10.00**
Barclay, oxen-drawn wagon, 1849 on canvas cover, scarce, 93%, A1 ....**$85.00**
Barclay, parachute jumper, 98%, A1 ....**$35.00**
Barclay, policeman, HO scale, 98%, A1..........................**$10.00**

Barclay, fireman, 98%, $20.00.

Barclay, soldier at searchlight, smooth lens variation, scarce, M, $350.00. (Photo courtesy Sally and Stan Alekna)

Barclay, porter w/whisk broom, 98%, A1 ....$25.00

Barclay, ram, 99%, A1 ....$18.00

Barclay, reindeer, extremely rare, minimum value, A1 ...$125.00

Barclay, sailor in bl bell bottoms, long stride, 95%, A1 ....$25.00

Barclay, Santa on sled, 99%, A1.................................$50.00

Barclay, sentry, 97%, A1..$30.00

Barclay, shoeshine boy, scarce, 94%, A1 ....$35.00

Barclay, soldier, bomb thrower, gr, 95%, A1.....................$25.00

Barclay, soldier, charging, khaki, 99%, A1......................$20.00

Barclay, soldier, charging w/gas mask & rifle, 98%, A1 ....$30.00

Barclay, soldier, charging w/machine gun, tin helmet, 96%, A1 ....$25.00

Barclay, soldier, flame thrower, gr, 98%, A1....................$22.00

Barclay, soldier, kneeling at anti-tank gun, 98%, A1 ....$32.00

Barclay, soldier, kneeling w/rifle, gr, scarce, 99%, A1 ....$28.00

Barclay, soldier, machine gunner lying flat, 95%, A1 ....$25.00

Barclay, soldier, marching, shoulder arms, long stride, tin helmet, 95%, A1 ....$20.00

Barclay, soldier, marching w/slung rifle, 98%, A1 ....$40.00

Barclay, soldier, on crutches, gr, scarce, 98%, A1.............$48.00

Barclay, soldier, peeling potatoes, 96%, A1 ....$28.00

Barclay, soldier, port arms, tin helmet, 99%, A1 ....$30.00

Barclay, soldier, sharpshooter standing & firing, long stride, tin helmet, 97%, A1..$25.00

Barclay, soldier, standing & firing, gr, 99%, A1 ....$22.00

Barclay, soldier, telephone operator, 94%, A1..................$25.00

Barclay, soldiers, 2 on raft, scarce, 95%, A1 ....$90.00

Barclay, surgeon w/soldier, scarce, 94%, A1 ....$110.00

Barclay, tractor, red w/blk metal wheels, 97%, A1 ....$45.00

Barclay, transport set w/2 cars, 1960s, 97%, A1 ....$50.00

Barclay, US Army fuel truck, 1968, scarce, 99%, A1........$25.00

Barclay, US Army plane, silver, 95%, A1.........................$30.00

Barclay, US Mail tractor trailer, 1960, NM, A1 ....$30.00

Barclay, woman in red, HO scale, 98%, A1 ....$10.00

Britains, #33 16th Queen's Lancers, 5-pc, EX, A.............$185.00

Britains, #37 Coldstream Guards Band, 21-pc, EX, A.......$400.00

Britains, #47 Skinner's Horse of the Indian Army, EX (EX box), A $200.00

Britains, #66 Duke of Connaught's Lancers, 5-pc, G, A......$150.00

Britains, #114 Queen's Own Cameroon Highlanders, EX (EX box), A $200.00

Britains, #115 Egyptian Calvary, ca 1960, 4-pc, EX, A...$100.00

Britains, #137 Royal Army Medical Corps, 1901-05, 24-pc, EX, A $450.00

Britains: #194, Machine Gun Section, M (NM Whisstock box), A, $150.00; #124, Irish Guards, M (NM Whisstock box), A, $265.00.

Britains, #196 Greek Evzones, 8-pc, VG, A $75.00

Britains, #429 Scots Guards & Life Light Guards, 13-pc, VG (worn World's Armies box), A................................$450.00

Britains, #1260 British Infantry, 9-pc, EX, A..................$150.00

Britains, #226 Bersagliere (Whisstock box), $125.00; Britains, #169 West Point Cadets, 1925, rare, MIB, A, $200.00.

Courtenay, King Henry V, full gold armor, movable right arm, VG, A, $250.00.

Britains, #1424 Bodyguard of the Emperor of Abyssinia, complete, EX (EX Armies of the World box), A............$450.00

Britains, #1448 Staff Car w/Driver & General, EX, A....$225.00

Britains, #1720 Band of the Royal Scots Greys, 7-pc, EX, A ..$425.00

Britains, #2080 Royal Navy, 10-pc, EX, A $150.00

Britains, #2185 Bahamas Police Band, complete, extremely rare, NM, A..$2,300.00

Britains, #6 Middlesex Regiment, dtd 1905, 8-pc, G, A.$200.00

Courtenay, Alain, Lord of Montendre, extremely rare, NM, A...$1,200.00

Grey Iron, aviator, orange harness, prewar, scarce, 93%, A1..$85.00

Grey Iron, Black man digging, prewar, scarce, 98%, A1 ...$35.00

Grey Iron, boy in brn traveling suit, postwar, 99%, A1 ....$18.00

Grey Iron, boy w/life preserver, prewar, scarce, 95%, A1..$65.00

Grey Iron, cadet, right shoulder arms, prewar, 94%, A1 ...$30.00

Grey Iron, calf, prewar, 97%, A1 ....$15.00

Grey Iron, colonial officer in red tunic, rare, postwar, 98%, A1 ....$30.00

Grey Iron, colonial officer mounted, prewar, 96%, A1 .....$48.00

Grey Iron, conductor, prewar, 98%, A1 ....$15.00

Grey Iron, cow, copper brn & yel, prewar, 97%, A1 ....$15.00

Grey Iron, cowboy, prewar, 98%, A1.................................$25.00

Grey Iron, doctor in wht w/red cross, prewar, scarce, 95%, A1 ....$40.00

Grey Iron, engineer, prewar, 99%, A1 ....$16.00

Grey Iron, Ethiopian chief, prewar, scarce, 94%, A1 ....$65.00

Grey Iron, farmer, prewar, 94%, A1 ....$15.00

Grey Iron, garage man in gr, postwar, scarce, 98%, A1 .....$25.00

Grey Iron, girl, prewar, 94%, A1 ....$15.00

Grey Iron, holdup man in blk, prewar, 99%, A1 ....$40.00

Grey Iron, holdup man in gray, postwar, scarce, 95%, A1...$38.00

Grey Iron, horse, dk brn & tan, prewar, 97%, A1 ....$15.00

Grey Iron, Indian chief w/knife, prewar, 98%, A1 ....$32.00

Grey Iron, Italian officer, prewar, scarce, 96%, A1 ....$255.00

Grey Iron, knight in armor, prewar, 98%, A1 ....$38.00

Grey Iron, legion drum major, prewar, 97%, A1 ....$28.00

Grey Iron, mailman, prewar, 98%, A1 ....$15.00

Grey Iron, man in traveling suit, postwar, 99%, A1 ....$18.00

Grey Iron, man w/watering can, prewar, 95%, A1 ....$15.00

Grey Iron, milkman in tan outfit, prewar, scarce, 98%, A1...$25.00

Grey Iron, Mohawk Indian w/raised tomahawk & knife, prewar, scarce, 96%, A1 ....$115.00

Grey Iron, nurse, prewar, 92%, A1 ....$25.00

Grey Iron, old man & woman sitting on bench, prewar, 98%, A1..$40.00

Grey Iron, pig, prewar, 97%, A1 ....$15.00

Grey Iron, pirate w/sword, gr, prewar, 97%, A1 ....$35.00

Grey Iron, porter, prewar, 99%, A1 ....$20.00

Grey Iron, Royal Canadian mounted police, standing at port arms, prewar, 99%, A1..$38.00

Grey Iron, sailor in wht, prewar, 92%, A1 ....$18.00

Grey Iron, ski trooper, prewar, scarce, 97%, A1 ....$85.00

Grey Iron, soldier, machine gunner seated, prewar, 93%, A1 ..$25.00

Grey Iron, soldier, on crutches, prewar, scarce, 96%, A1..$70.00

Grey Iron, soldier, on stretcher, prewar, scarce, 97%, A1 .$45.00

Grey Iron, soldier, rifleman at attention, postwar, 95%, A1..$15.00

Grey Iron, soldier, US machine gunner, postwar, 96%, A1...$18.00

Grey Iron, soldier, US machine gunner, prewar, 97%, A1 ..$20.00

Grey Iron, soldier, US machine gunner lying down, prewar, 97%, A1 ....$24.00

Grey Iron, stretcher bearer, prewar, scarce, 95%, A1 ....$45.00

Grey Iron, US doughboy, bomber crawling, postwar, 97%, A1 ....$28.00

Grey Iron, US doughboy, bomber crawling, prewar, 98%, A1 ....$32.00

Grey Iron, US doughboy, grenade thrower, prewar, scarce, 98%, A1 ....$55.00

Grey Iron, US doughboy, sentry, prewar, 97%, A1 ....$30.00

Grey Iron, US doughboy, w/range finder, prewar, scarce, 95%, A1 ....$90.00

Grey Iron, US infantry, port arms, prewar, 99%, A1........$25.00

Grey Iron, US navy officer in wht, prewar, 92%, A1 ....$20.00

Grey Iron, woman w/basket, prewar, 96%, A1 ....$15.00

HB Toys, Indian mounted on horse, scarce, 94%, A1.......$40.00

HB Toys, Indian w/knife, scarce, 98%, A1 ....$28.00

Jones, 1775 British marine firing musket, 54mm, scarce, 94%, A1 ....$25.00

Jones, 1814 Scot Highlander, 54mm, scarce, 99%, A1 .....$30.00

Jones, 1921 British Guardsman, scarce, 97%, A1 ....$20.00

Manoil, antiaircraft gun w/range finder, 95%, A1 ....$28.00

Manoil, bench, 96%, A1 ....$14.00

Manoil, bull, 98%, A1 ....$25.00

Manoil, cadet, hollow base, scarce, 65%, A1 ....$35.00

Manoil, cannon, gray w/wooden wheels, 97%, A1 ....$25.00

Manoil, colt, brn, maroon or tan, scarce, 99%, A1, ea $30.00

Manoil, convertible, red w/lg tail fin, scarce, 97%, A1.....$90.00

Manoil, cowboy #18, gray suit, red gun, blue vest, EX, $20.00.

Manoil, doctor in wht w/red cross, 94%, A1....................$28.00

Manoil, ensign, hollow base, scarce, 90%, A1 ....$75.00

Manoil, farmer at water pump, 95%, A1 ....$25.00

Manoil, fire pumper, red, 99%, A1 ....$45.00

Manoil, girl in sleeveless dress, 94%, A1 ....$12.00
Manoil, lineman on pole, scarce, 97%, A1 ....$120.00
Manoil, man & woman on park bench, 97%, A1 ....$38.00
Manoil, man w/barrel of apples, scarce, 97%, A1 ....$70.00
Manoil, marine, hollow base, scarce, 92%, A1 ....$85.00
Manoil, nurse, 96%, A1..$28.00
Manoil, officer, hollow base, scarce, 94%, A1....................$80.00
Manoil, oil tanker, red, 95%, A1 ....$40.00
Manoil, parachutist landing, yel harness, 96%, A1...........$55.00
Manoil, policeman, 96%, A1..$28.00
Manoil, road scraper, plastic, scarce, 98%, A1 ....$25.00
Manoil, scarecrow in top hat, 95%, A1............................$25.00
Manoil, sedan, bl, scarce, 98%, A1 ....$65.00
Manoil, shepherd w/flute, scarce, 90%, A1 ....$55.00
Manoil, soldier, antiaircraft gunner, compo, scarce, 95%, A1 ..$75.00
Manoil, soldier, digging trench, scarce, 99%, A1 ....$70.00
Manoil, soldier, flag bearer, hollow base, scarce, 94%, A1 ..$95.00
Manoil, soldier, lying down wounded, 95%, A1 ....$25.00
Manoil, soldier, marching w/pack & slung rifle, 97%, A1...$30.00
Manoil, soldier, sniper kneeling w/rifle, 99%, A1 ....$30.00
Manoil, soldier, standing & firing rifle, 96%, A1 ....$28.00
Manoil, soldier, standing wounded, 97%, A1....................$32.00
Manoil, soldier, w/barrel of apples, scarce, 96%, A1 ....$80.00
Manoil, soldier, w/camera, scarce, 95%, A1 ....$80.00
Manoil, soup kitchen, sm, 99%, A1 ....$26.00
Manoil, tow truck, 2-pc, scarce, 98%, A1 ....$90.00
Manoil, tractor, plain front, 99%, A1...............................$28.00
Marx, Sikh Indian, VG, A1...$8.00
Marx, US cavalry soldier mounted on horse, VG, A1 ......$10.00
Marx, US infantry captain w/binoculars, EX, A1 ....$10.00
Marx, US infantry colonel, EX, A1...................................$14.00
Marx, US infantry doughboy, EX, A1 ....$10.00
Marx, US infantry private at attention, NM, A1 ....$10.00
Marx, US infantry private marching, EX, A1 ....$10.00
Marx, US infantry sergeant, VG, A1 ....$12.00
Miller Plaster, chick w/bobbing head, scarce, 99%, A1 ....$30.00
Miller Plaster, horse, sm, 98%, A1 ....$10.00
Miller Plaster, soldier, marching w/M-1 rifle, 99%, A1.....$40.00
Miller Plaster, soldier, w/sentry dog & rifle, scarce, 98%, A1 ..$125.00
Miller Plaster, soldier, w/stretcher, 98%, A1 ....$45.00
Molded Products, aviator, sq harness, 97%, A1 ....$16.00
Molded Products, cow, blk & wht, scarce, 99%, A1 ....$15.00
Molded Products, horse, blk & wht, scarce, 95%, A1.......$10.00
Molded Products, marine in bl, 93%, A1 ....$15.00
Molded Products, officer on horse, WWII helmet, scarce, 98%,
    A1 ....$25.00
Molded Products, soldier, at antiaircraft gun, WWI helmet,
    96%, A1..$15.00
Molded Products, soldier, flag bearer, WWII helmet, 98%,
    A1 ....$20.00
Molded Products, soldier, prone w/machine gun, WWII helmet,
    95%, A1..$14.00
Molded Products, soldier, w/parachute, 99%, A1..............$18.00
Playwod Plastics, soldier, machine gunner, prone, 97%, A1...$20.00
Playwod Plastics, soldier, machine gunner, seated, 95%, A1..$18.00
Playwod Plastics, soldier, w/gas mask & flare gun, 95%, A1..$15.00
Playwod Plastics, stretcher bearer, 97%, A1.....................$25.00
Solido, howitzer, 4-wheeled, short barrel, 6", NM, A1 .....$25.00

Solido, UNIC missile launcher, 7½", NM, A1 ....$45.00
Soljertoy, officer in lt bl tunic on gray horse, scarce, 98%, A1 ..$48.00
Soljertoy, sailor in bl, scarce, 97%, A1 ....$25.00
Soljertoy, soldier, marching, left shoulder arms, scarce, 98%,
    A1 ....$20.00

Sporting Collectibles

Baseball — the great American Pastime — has given us hundreds of real-life sports heroes plus a great amount of collectible memorabilia. Baseball gloves, bats, game-worn uniforms, ephemera of many types, even games and character watches are among the many items being sought out today. And there are fans of basketball, football, and hockey that are just as avid in their collecting.

As you can see, many of our listings describe Kenner's Starting Lineup figures. These small plastic likenesses of famous sports greats were first produced in 1988. New they can be purchased for $5.00 to $8.00 (though some may go a little higher), but they have wonderful potential to appreciate. As the sports' stars fluctuate in popularity, so do their Starting Lineup figures. Some may occasionally sell for several hundred dollars, but on the average most from 1988 run from $25.00 to $50.00. Football and basketball series have been made as well, and in 1993 Kenner added hockey. If you're going to collect them, be critical of the condition of the packaging.

Bobbin' head dolls made of papier-mache were manufactured in Japan during the 1960s until about 1972 and were sold at ball parks, stadiums, and through the mail for about $2.98. They were about 7" high or so, hand painted and then varnished. Some of them represent sports teams and their mascots. Depending on scarcity and condition, they'll run from as low as $35.00 up to $100.00, though there are some that sell for $300.00 or so. A few were modeled in the likeness of a particular sports star; these are rare and when they can be found sell in the $500.00 to $1,500.00 range. Base colors indicate when the doll was made. During 1961 and 1962, white bases were used; today these are very scarce. Green bases are from 1962 until 1966, and gold bases were used from 1967 until 1972. Mascot-heads are favored by collectors, and football figures are becoming very collectible as well. Our advisor has prepared a *Bobbin' Head Guide*, with a rarity scale and current values. See Dealer Codes for his address.

Advisors: Tim Hunter (H13); James Watson (W8) Hartland Figures.

See also Cereal Boxes and Premiums; Character and Promotional Drinking Glasses; Character Clocks and Watches; Dolls, Celebrity; Games; Pin-Back Buttons and other specific categories.

Arkansas Razorbacks, bank, wht metal, 5", M $30.00
Babe Ruth, scorer, 1930s, photo on front w/game scene on
    reverse, celluloid, 1¾" dia, NM, A $150.00
Brooklyn Dodgers, doll, 1955-56, stuffed cloth & vinyl, ...World
    Champions stamped on chest, 13", rare, EX, A.......$350.00
California Angels, yo-yo, 1960s, wood w/sticker seal, miniature,
    NM $5.00

Chicago Cubs, pin-back button, 1930s-40s, blk & wht w/bear image, 1¼" dia, NM, A $40.00

Cincinnati Reds, yo-yo, 1960s, plastic w/paper insert seal, tournament shape w/view lens, NM $20.00

Cleveland Indians, bank, Gibbs, 1950, 7", EX, A...........$200.00

Cleveland Indians, pennant, 1954, felt, red w/wht graphics & lettering, EX, A..$65.00

Connie Mack, bank, baseball shape w/signature, litho tin, 4", M $275.00

Detroit Tigers, doll, stuffed cloth, 12", EX, from $35 to....$45.00

Detroit Tigers, pin-back button, 1930s-40s, Souvenir of... & tiger image, 1¼" dia, NM, A $40.00

Don Drysdale, figure, Salvino, 1989, NMIB, A $75.00

Gill Hodges, game, Gill Hodges' Pennant Fever, Research Games, 1970, EX (EX box) $55.00

Hank Aaron, autographed baseball bat, Louisville Slugger model 125, NM, A $100.00

Harlem Globetrotters, game, Official Globetrotter Basketball, Meljak, 1950s, EX (EX box)................................$100.00

Hulk Hogan, yo-yo, Spectra Star, Hulk Rules, plastic w/imprint seal, MIP..$5.00

Jerry Rice, trading card, Topps, 1986, NM, A $55.00

Joe Montana, autographed football, Wilson NFL model, NM, A $75.00

Joe Namath, trading card, Topps, 1966, EX, A $75.00

Los Angeles Dodgers, card game, Ed-U Cards, 1964, EX (EX box)...$50.00

Mark McGwire, trading card, Topps, 1985, NM, A........$100.00

Michael Jordon, autographed baseball, Wilson, NMIB, A..$225.00

Michigan Wolverines, bank, wht metal, 5", M $45.00

Mike Tyson, doll, 1980s, 9", MIP......................................$40.00

Minnesota Golden Gophers, bank, wht metal, 6", M.....$110.00

New York Mets, card game, Ed-U Cards, 1961, EX (EX box) $45.00

New York Yankees, game, Challenge the Yankees, Hasbro, 1964, complete, NMIB...$175.00

Notre Dame Fighting Irish, bank, wht metal, 6", M $155.00

OJ Simpson, game, See Action Football, Kenner, 1974, complete, EX (EX box)..$85.00

Philadelphia Eagles, pennant, 1960s, NM, A...................$55.00

Philadelphia Phillies, yo-yo, 1980s, plastic w/paper sticker seal, MIP...$5.00

Pittsburgh Pirates, pennant, 1950s, felt, EX, A $50.00

Roger Maris, wiffle bat, 1960s, EX...................................$65.00

San Diego Padres, yo-yo, 1980, plastic w/paper sticker, NM ...$3.00

Sandy Koufax, figure, Salvino, 1989, NMIB, A..............$100.00

Walter Payton trading card, Topps, 1976, #148, NM, A, $85.00; Michael Jordan trading card, Fleer, 1986 – 87, #57, NM/M, A, $875.00.

BOBBIN' HEAD DOLLS

Atlanta Braves, team mascot, 1967-72, gold base...........$135.00

Atlanta Falcons, 1967, rnd gold base, NM........................$75.00

Baltimore Bullets, Little Dribblers, NM $200.00

Baltimore Colts, 1966-68, realistic face, rnd gold base, NM..$250.00

Baltimore Orioles, team mascot, 1961-62, wht base, rare, NM, minimum value..$450.00

Boston Braves, Minor League Hockey, bl base, NM $350.00

Boston Patriots, Type IV, lg shoulder pads, NM, from $300 to..$400.00

Boston Patriots, 1960s, wht helmet version, NMIB..........$95.00

Buffalo Bills, Japan, 1965, w/ear pads, NM $360.00

Chicago Bears, Black player, 1962, gold base.................$350.00

Chicago Bears, 1965, NM..$70.00

Chicago Bears, 1967, rnd gold base, NM $100.00

Chicago Bulls, Little Dribbler, 1969, gold base, EX $75.00

Chicago Cubs, 1960s, wht base, NM..............................$225.00

Chicago White Sox, 1960s, gr base, NM $130.00

Cincinnati Reds, 1960s, mascot, NM..............................$160.00

Cleveland Indians, team mascot, 1961-62, sq wht base, rare ..$500.00

Dale Earnhardt, in sunglasses holding helmet, Sports Accessories & Memorabilia, M..$80.00

Dallas Cowboys, team mascot, 1962-66, bl base, minimum value $180.00

Detroit Lions, 1968, '00' on back of jersey, NM................$60.00

Green Bay Packers, 1967, gold base, NM.......................$150.00

Hershey Bears, Minor League Hockey, 1962, NM..........$325.00

Houston Oilers, 1966-67, rnd gold base, NM...................$55.00

Kansas City Chiefs, 1968, rnd gold base, NM, from $50 to.$75.00

Kansas State Wildcats, rnd gr base, NM...........................$50.00

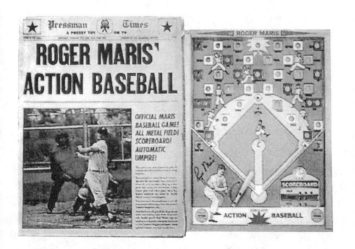

Roger Maris' Action Baseball Game, lithographed tin, replaced marbles, NM (EX box), A, $135.00.

Kansas State Wildcats, round gold base, no toes up, from $50.00 to $100.00.
(Photo courtesy Tim Hunter)

Los Angeles Dodgers, Black player, 1962-66, gr base, NM ..$1,200.00
Los Angeles Lakers, 1962, NM.......................................$225.00
LSU Tigers, rare, NM $820.00
Mickey Mantle, 1961-62, scarce, NM.............................$600.00
Minnesota Vikings, sq gold base, NM, from $100 to $150.00
New York Jets, 1968, rnd gold base, EX...........................$95.00
New York Mets, 1960-61, sq bl base, NM $200.00
New York Mets, 1960-61, sq bl base, VG+ $100.00

NFL, Black player, 1962, rare series, beware of fakes, from $350.00 to $500.00. (Photo courtesy Tim Hunter)

Notre Dame Fighting Irish, 1960s, rnd gr base, gold helmet, NM...$80.00
Philadelphia Eagles, 1961-62, 1960 Champions emb on gr base, scarce, NM..$135.00
Roger Maris, 1961-62, sq wht base, NM, from $375 to ..$435.00
San Francisco 49ers, 1960s, gr base, NM $175.00
Seattle Sonics, 1967, yel uniform, NM $225.00
St Louis Cardinals, team mascot, 1961-62, wht base, NM, minimum value $500.00
St Louis Cardinals, 1961, NM......................................$110.00
Washington Redskins, 1960s, Type 2, toes-up version, gold base, EX $460.00
Washington Redskins, 1961-62, lt face, rnd maroon base..$175.00
Willie Mayes, 1962, dk face version, M $375.00

HARTLAND FIGURES

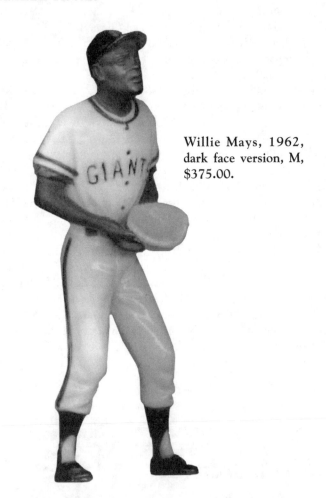

Willie Mays, 1962, dark face version, M, $375.00.

Babe Ruth, 1960s, NM, from $125 to $175.00
Batboy, 25th Anniversary, NM.......................................$50.00
Dick Groat, 1960s, w/bat, NM, minimum value.............$800.00
Dick Groat, 25th Anniversary, M (NM box)....................$45.00
Don Drysdale, 1960s, EX $410.00
Duke Snyder, 1960s, EX+ $360.00
Eddie Matthews, 1960s, NM $150.00
Ernie Banks, 1960s, EX...$260.00
Ernie Banks, 25th Anniversary, MIB..............................$40.00
Hank Aaron, 1960s, EX...$190.00

Hank Aaron, 25th Anniversary, M (NM box)..................$45.00
Harmon Killebrew, NM, from $400 to $500.00
Harmon Killebrew, 1960s, EX $290.00
Harmon Killebrew, 25th Anniversary, M (NM box) $45.00
Little Leaguer, 4", EX, from $50 to $75.00
Lou Gehrig, 1960s, NMIB...$200.00
Luis Aparicio, 1960s, NM, from $250 to $300.00
Luis Aparicio, 25th Anniversary, MIB $32.00
Mickey Mantle, 1960s, MIB..$535.00
Mickey Mantle, 1960s, NM..$350.00
Mickey Mantle, 25th Anniversary, M (NM box) $55.00
Nellie Fox, 1960s, EX, from $150 to $200.00
Rocky Colavito, 1960s, NM, from $600 to $700.00
Rocky Colavito, 1960s, rpl bat o/w NM.........................$425.00
Roger Maris, 1960s, NM..$390.00
Roger Maris, 25th Anniversary, M (NM box) $55.00
Stan Musial, 1960s, NM $235.00
Ted Williams, 1960s, EX..$305.00
Ted Williams, 25th Anniversary, M (NM box)..................$50.00
Washington Redskins, 1960s, EX $310.00
Willie Mays, NM, from $225 to $250.00
Willie Mays, 25th Anniversary, M (NM box)....................$45.00
Yogi Berra, no mask, NM...$160.00
Yogi Berra, w/mask, NM, from $175 to $250.00
Yogi Berra, w/mask, 25th Anniversary, M (NM box) $37.00

KENNER STARTING LINEUP FIGURES

Barry Bonds, 1989, MIP..$50.00
Bernie Kosar, 1988, MIP..$30.00
Brett Favre, 1995, MIP $35.00
Charles Barkley, 1995, MIP $15.00
Clyde Drexler, 1991, MIP...$20.00
Dale Earnhardt, 1998, MIP..$22.00
Danny Ainge, 1988, MIP..$75.00
Dominique Wilkins, 1988, MIP......................................$45.00
Doug Flutie, Heisman, 1997, MIP $15.00
Frank Reich, 1996, MIP..$15.00
Grant Hill, Backboard Kings, 1997, MIP $20.00
Jeff George, 1991, 1st edition, MIP $25.00
Jeff Hornacek, 1988, MIP...$65.00
Jerry Rice, 1989, MIP...$20.00
Jim Everett, 1990, MIP...$10.00
Jim Kelly, 1988, MIP...$150.00
Joey Browner, 1988, MIP..$50.00
John Stockton, 1990, MIP..$35.00
Julius Erving, Legends, 1989, MIP.................................$40.00
Ken Davis, 1988, MIP...$90.00
Larry Bird, Slam Dunk, 1988-89, MIP (red) $165.00
Magic Johnson, 1988, MIP...$50.00
Mark Messier, 1993, MIP...$50.00
Michael Jordan, 1993, NMIP $40.00
Mike Singletary, 1990, MIP..$25.00
Muggsy Bogues, 1995, MIP $10.00
Ozzie Smith, 1989, MIP...$50.00
Pete Rose, 1988, EXIP $35.00
Reggie White, 1989, MIP $65.00
Roger Clemens, 1989, MIP...$35.00

Scottie Pippen, 1988, MIP...$145.00
Steve Young, 1989, MIP..$275.00
Steve Yzerman, 1998, MIP..$18.00
Terry Bradshaw, 1989, Legends Collection, NMIP $35.00
Tim Brown, 1990, MIP..$65.00
Troy Aikman, 1998, MIP...$15.00
Wilt Chamberlain, MIP...$40.00

Michael Jordan, 1988, MIP, $140.00.

Star Trek

The Star Trek concept was introduced to the public in the mid-1960s via a TV series which continued for many years in syndication. The impact it had on American culture has spanned two generations of loyal fans through its animated TV cartoon series (1977), six major motion pictures, Fox network's 1987 TV show, 'Star Trek, The Next Generation,' and two other television series, 'Deep Space 9,' and 'Voyager.' As a result of its success, vast amounts of merchandise (both licensed and unlicensed) has been marketed in a wide variety of items including jewelry, clothing, calendars, collector plates, comics, costumes, games, greeting and gum cards, party goods, magazines, model kits, posters, puzzles, records and tapes, school supplies, and toys. Packaging is very important; an item mint and in its original box is generally worth 75% to 100% more than one rated excellent.

See also Character and Promotional Drinking Glasses; Comic Books; Fast-Food Collectibles; Halloween Costumes; Lunch Boxes; Model Kits.

FIGURES

Mego, 1974, Alien, orange & wht gown, 8", EX..............$48.00
Mego, 1974, Captain Kirk, 8", M (NM card)..................$35.00

Mego, 1974, Klingon, 8", MOC $35.00

Mego, 1974-76, Spock, 1st series, 8", EX.........................$22.00

Mego, 1974-76, Uhura, 8", M..$35.00

Mego, 1979, Motion Picture, Captain Kirk, 12", M (NM box)...$50.00

Mego, 1979, Motion Picture, Decker, 12", MIB, from $150 to...$200.00

Playmates, Borg, STNG, 9", M (NM box) $35.00

Playmates, Borg Queen, Warp Factor Series 5, 5", MOC .$25.00

Playmates, Captain Janeway, Voyager Series, 5", M (VG card) $42.00

Playmates, Captain Picard, Masterpiece Edition, 1997, 12", MIB $25.00

Playmates, Commander Chakotay, Voyager Series, 5", MOC $25.00

Playmates, Counselor Troi, STNG, 12", MIB $40.00

Playmates, Deanna Troi, 12", MIB $30.00

Playmates, Gorn, 12", MIB..$30.00

Playmates, Harry Kim, Star Trek Voyager, Collector Series, 9", MIB $50.00

Playmates, Intendant Kira, Warp Factor Series 4, 5", MOC..$25.00

Playmates, Kang the Klingon, Warp Factor Series 4, 5", MOC..$25.00

Playmates, Klingon Warrior, 9", MOC.............................$25.00

Playmates, Lt B'elanna Torres, STNG, 5", MOC $25.00

Playmates, Lt Tuvok, Voyager Series, 5", MOC...............$35.00

Playmates, McCoy, 12", MIB..$30.00

Playmates, Romulan Commander, STNG, 9", MIB..........$23.00

Playmates, Seven of Nine, Collectors Edition, 9", MIB....$48.00

Playmates, Sulu, 12", MIB $30.00

Playmates, Trelane, Squire of Gothos episode, 9", MIB....$25.00

Playmates, Vina, Original Star Trek Series, M (EX card)....$35.00

MISCELLANEOUS

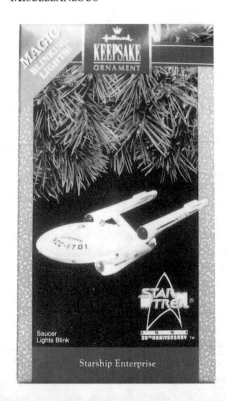

Ornament, Hallmark Keepsake, Starship Enterprise, 1991, MIB, from $175.00 to $225.00. (Photo courtesy Martin and Carolyn Berens)

China Set, Original Series, cup, saucer & plate, Pfaltzgraff, Limited Edition of 5,000, MIB..$75.00

Electronic D'K Tahg Knife, Klingon, Playmates, M..........$15.00

Game, Star Trek, Ideal, 1965, complete, EX (EX box) $75.00

Game, Star Trek Marble Maze, Hasbro, 1967, EX (EX box) ..$85.00

Game, Super Phaser Target, Mego, 1970s, MIB................$75.00

Inter-Space Communicator, Lone Star, 1974, plastic, MIB, A...$100.00

Phaser, Classic Star Trek, Playmates, 1994, M (NM box) $75.00

Phaser Ray Gun, 1976, MOC..$35.00

Pinball Game, AHI, 1976, Captain Kirk or Mr Spock, MIB, ea...$65.00

Playset, Electronic Bridge, STNG, Playmates, MIB..........$60.00

Pocket Watch, Klingon Bird of Prey, Franklin Mint, sterling silver & 24k gold, MIB, from $100 to.........................$125.00

Star Trekulator, Mego, 1976, rare, MIB............................$85.00

Starfleet Medical Tricorder, Playmates, MIB....................$70.00

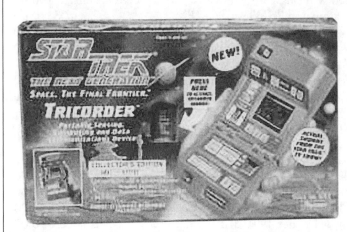

Tricorder, Playmates, Next Generation, MIB, $25.00.

Vehicle, Ferengi Fighter, STNG, Galoob, 1989, MIB.......$60.00

Vehicle, Galileo Shuttlecraft, Playmates, MIB $35.00

Vehicle, USS Enterprise NCC-1701-E First Contact, Playmates, 1996, NMIB, from $50.00 to $60.00.

Vehicle, Klingon Attack Cruiser, STNG, Playmates, 1993, MIB..**$65.00**

Vehicle, Romulan Warbird, Playmates, 1993, MIB..........**$35.00**

Vehicle, Space Ship Set, 1976, MIB (sealed)....................**$30.00**

Vehicle, Transwarping Starship Enterprise, Playmates, MIB..**$70.00**

Vehicle, USS Defiant, Playmates, MIB............................**$95.00**

Vehicle, USS Voyager NCC-74656, Playmates, Collectors Edition, MIB **$175.00**

Yo-yo, Deep Space 9, Commander Benjamin Sisko photo, plastic w/sculpted rim, NM **$5.00**

Yo-yo, Motion Picture, 1979, glitter plastic w/metal string slot axle, tournament shape, MIP **$30.00**

Star Wars

The original 'Star Wars' movie was a phenomenal box office hit of the late 1970s. A sequel called 'Empire Strikes Back' (1980) and a third hit called 'Return of the Jedi' (1983) did just as well. In 1998, a new trilogy began with 'Star Wars Episode 1.' As a result, an enormous amount of related merchandise was released — most of which was made by the Kenner Company. Palitoy of London supplied England and other overseas countries with Kenner's products and also made some toys that were never distributed in America. Until 1980 the logo of the 20th Century Fox studios (under whom the toys were licensed) appeared on each item; just before the second movie, 'Star Wars' creator, George Lucas, regained control of the merchandise rights, and items inspired by the last two films can be identified by his own Lucasfilm logo. Since 1987 Lucasfilm, Ltd., has operated shops in conjunction with the Star Tours at Disneyland theme parks.

The first action figures to be introduced were Luke Skywalker, Princess Leia, R2-D2, and Chewbacca. Because of delays in production that prevented Kenner from getting them on the market in time for Christmas, the company issued 'early bird' certificates so that they could be ordered by mail when they became available. In all, more than ninety action figures were designed. 'Power of the Force' figures (the 1985 series) are steadily climbing in value. A collector coin was included on each 'Power of the Force' card.

Original packaging is very important in assessing a toy's worth. As each movie was released, packaging was updated, making approximate dating relatively simple. A figure on an original 'Star Wars' card is worth more than the same character on an 'Empire Strikes Back' card, etc.; and the same 'Star Wars' figure valued at $50.00 in mint-on-card condition might be worth as little as $5.00 'loose.'

Especially prized are the original 12-back Star Wars cards (meaning twelve figures were shown on the back). Second issue cards showed eight more, and so on. Unpunched cards tend to be valued at about 15% to 20% more than punched cards, and naturally if the proof of purchase has been removed, the value of the card is less. (These could be mailed in to receive newly introduced figures before they appeared on the market.) A figure in a factory (Kenner) bag is valued at $2.00 to $3.00 more than

it is worth loose, and an original backing card adds about $1.00 to $2.00. In our listings, you'll find many of these variations noted. These have been included for the information of potential buyers; remember, pricing is not a science — it hinges on many factors.

For more information we recommend *Everything You Need To Know About Collecting Star Wars Collectibles*, by our advisor Brian Semling (Beckett) (See Directory, Star Wars).

Advisor: Brian's Toys (S8).

Other Sources: B3, B10, D4, D9, J2, S8. (Unless noted otherwise, listings for the figures were provided by S8.)

See also Character and Promotional Drinking Glasses; Fast-Food Collectibles; Halloween Costumes; Lunch Boxes; Model Kits.

Key:	ESB — Empire Strikes Back
	POTF — Power of the Force
	ROTJ — Return of the Jedi
	SW — Star Wars
	* — proof of purchase removed

FIGURES

A-Wing Pilot, POTF, complete, NM, from $65 to............**$75.00**

A-Wing Pilot, POTF, M (NM card)................................**$100.00**

A-Wing Pilot, Tri-logo, M (NM card) **$120.00**

Admiral Ackbar, ROTJ, complete, NM **$8.00**

Admiral Ackbar, ROTJ, M (VG card)............................**$35.00**

Amanaman, POTF, M (EX card) **$250.00**

Amanaman, Tri-logo, M (EX card) **$175.00**

Anakin Skywalker, Tri-logo, M (EX card) **$110.00**

AT-AT Commander, ESB, M (NM card)........................**$100.00**

AT-AT Commander, ROTJ, M (VG+ card) **$40.00**

Back of a 12-back Star Wars card.
(Photo courtesy June Moon)

AT-AT Commander, Tri-logo, M (EX+ card) $65.00
AT-AT Driver, ESB, M (EX card) $100.00
AT-AT Driver, Tri-logo, M (NM card)..........................$125.00
AT-ST Driver, POTF, 1995-present, MOC (gr w/slide)....$60.00
AT-ST Driver, ROTJ, complete, NM, from $10 to $15.00

B-Wing Pilot, POTF, MOC (unpunched), $150.00.
(Photo courtesy Martin and Carolyn Berens)

B-Wing Pilot, ROTJ, M (NM card) $40.00
Barada, POTF, M (NM card)...$125.00
Barada, Tri-logo, M (VG+ card)......................................$75.00
Ben Obi-Wan Kenobi, ESB, M (NM card).....................$120.00
Ben Obi-Wan Kenobi, POTF, 1995-present, long saber, MOC (red) $25.00
Ben Obi-Wan Kenobi, POTF, 1995-present, MOC (gr) $8.00
Ben Obi-Wan Kenobi, POTF, 1995-present, w/blast helmet, 12", MIB $25.00
Ben Obi-Wan Kenobi, ROTJ, M (NM card).................$100.00
Ben Obi-Wan Kenobi, SW, M (NM unpunched card) (12-back)...$800.00
Ben Obi-Wan Kenobi, SW, M (VG+ card) (12-back) ...$295.00
Ben Obi-Wan Kenobi, SW, w/saber tip, NM, from $14 to...$18.00
Ben Obi-Wan Kenobi, SW, 12", MIB (sealed), from $600 to $700.00
Ben Obi-Wan Kenobi, Tri-logo, M (NM card)..............$125.00
Bespin Security Guard (Black or Caucasian), ROTJ, M (VG card) (65-back)..$30.00
Bespin Security Guard (Black), ESB, complete, NM........$12.00
Bespin Security Guard (Black), ESB, M (NM card) $60.00

Bespin Security Guard (White), ESB, M (EX+ card).......$65.00
Bib Fortuna, ROTJ, M (NM card), from $50 to..............$75.00
Biker Scout, ROTJ, M (NM card).....................................$65.00
Biker Scout, Tri-logo, M (NM+ card) $65.00
Boba Fett, ESB, M (NM unpunched card) $550.00
Boba Fett, POTF, 1995-present, MOC (gr).....................$15.00
Boba Fett, POTF, 1995-present, 12", MIB.......................$75.00
Boba Fett, ROTJ, desert scene, M (EX card) $325.00
Boba Fett, ROTJ, desert scene, M (G card) $150.00
Boba Fett, ROTJ, Palitoy (space scene), M (NM+ card)..$495.00
Boba Fett, SW, complete, EX, from $15 to.......................$20.00
Boba Fett, SW, complete, NM...$75.00
Boba Fett, SW, M (EX card) (20/21-back) $1,195.00
Boba Fett, SW, 12", MIB...$400.00
Boba Fett, Tri-logo, M (EX+ card) $950.00
Boss Nass, Episode I/Wave 3, MOC.................................$12.00
Bossk, ESB, M (NM Canadian card) $175.00
Bossk, ESB, M (NM card)..$140.00
C-3PO, ESB, removable limbs, M (NM+ card)..............$175.00
C-3PO, POTF, M (EX card) $70.00
C-3PO, POTF, removable limbs, M (NM card)...............$120.00
C-3PO, SW, M (NM card) (12-back)...............................$375.00
C-3PO, SW, M (VG card) (12-back)................................$175.00
C-3PO, SW, 12", M (VG sealed box) $250.00
C-3PO, SW, 12", MIB (sealed) $600.00
Captain Piet, POTF, 1995-present, MOC (gr w/slide)......$20.00
Captain Tarpuls, Episode I/Wave 4, MOC.......................$15.00
Chancellor Valcrum, Episode I/Wave 3, MOC.................$10.00
Chewbacca, ESB, M (VG card)..$55.00
Chewbacca, POTF, 1995-present, MOC (gr)....................$12.00
Chewbacca, ROTJ, Endor photo, M (NM card)...............$90.00
Chewbacca, SW, complete, NM...$10.00
Chewbacca, SW, M (NM card) (12-back).......................$360.00
Chewbacca, SW, 12", M (VG box) $250.00
Chewbacca, Tri-logo, M (EX+ card) $90.00
Chief Chirpa, ROTJ, M (NM card), S8 ....$45.00
Chief Chirpa, Tri-logo, M (NM+ card)............................$65.00
Clone Emperor, POTF, 1995-present, MOC....................$30.00
Cloud Car Pilot, ESB, M (EX card), from $65 to............$75.00
Darth Vader, ESB, M (EX+ card) $175.00
Darth Vader, POTF, M (EX card)...................................$125.00
Darth Vader, POTF, 1995-present, long saber, MOC (red)...$20.00
Darth Vader, POTF, 1995-present, removable helmet, MOC (gr w/slide)...$15.00
Darth Vader, POTF, 1995-present, short saber in long tray, MOC (red) $60.00
Darth Vader, POTF, 1995-present, 12", MIB $45.00
Darth Vader, ROTJ, M (NM Canadian card).................$120.00
Darth Vader, SW, complete, NM, from $12 to.................$15.00
Darth Vader, SW, M (NM card) (12-back).....................$695.00
Darth Vader, SW, M (VG card) (12-back) $350.00
Darth Vader, SW, 12", MIB..$325.00
Death Squad Commander, SW, M (EX+ card) (12-back)..$275.00
Death Squad Commander, SW, M (M unpunched card) (20/21-back) $300.00
Death Squad Commander, SW, M (NM card) (20/21-back)....$160.00
Death Squad Commander, SW, M (NM+ card) (20/21-back).$225.00
Death Star Droid, ESB, M (EX+ card)............................$120.00

Death Star Droid, ESB, M (NM unpunched card) (45-back)..$150.00
Death Star Droid, ROTJ, M (EX+ card) $75.00
Death Star Droid, SW, M (NM card) (20/21-back) $295.00
Death Star Droid, Tri-logo, M (EX+ card)....................$175.00
Death Star Gunner, POTF, 1995-present, MOC (red) $15.00
Death Star Monster, POTF, complete, NM.................$30.00
Dengar, ESB, N (NM card) $110.00
Dengar, ROTJ, M (NM card) $75.00
Dengar, ROTJ, M (VG card) $25.00
Dengar, Tri-logo, M (EX+ card) $60.00
Destroyer Droid, Episode I/Wave 9, MOC $15.00
Emperor, ROTJ, M (NM Canadian card) $75.00
Emperor, Tri-logo, M (EX+ card) $50.00
Emperor's Royal Guard, ROTJ, M (NM card) $75.00
EV-9D9, POTF, complete, NM...................................$85.00
FX-7, ESB, complete, NM $8.00
FX-7, ESB, M (EX Canadian card)...............................$65.00
FX-7, ESB, MOC* $100.00
Gammorrean Guard, POTF, M (NM card) $495.00
Gammorrean Guard, ROTJ, M (NM card) $40.00
Garindan, POTF, 1995-present, MOC (gr w/slide).........$40.00
General Madine, ROTJ, complete, NM.......................$10.00
General Madine, ROTJ, M (EX card) $35.00
General Madine, ROTJ, M (NM card) $70.00
Greedo, ESB, M (NM card) $120.00
Greedo, POTF, 1995-present, 12", MOC $35.00
Greedo, ROTJ, M (NM card)..$75.00
Greedo, SW, M (NM 20/21-back card)......................$350.00
Hammerhead, ESB, M (NM+ card) $150.00
Hammerhead, SW, M (EX card) (20/21-back) $175.00
Hammerhead, SW, M (NM card) (20/21-back) $295.00

Han Solo, SW, MOC (12-back, unpunched), from $850.00 to $900.00. (Photo courtesy June Moon)

Han Solo, ESB, Bespin outfit, M (NM card) $200.00
Han Solo, ESB, Hoth gear, M (NM card) $130.00
Han Solo, ESB, M (NM card) $260.00
Han Solo, POTF, Carbonite Chamber, NM...................$100.00
Han Solo, ROTJ, M (EX card)....................................$150.00
Han Solo, ROTJ, trench coat, NM (NM card)..............$65.00
Han Solo, SW, lg head, complete, NM $20.00
Han Solo, SW, 12", M (NM sealed box)......................$895.00
Han Solo, SW, 12", M (VG+ box)..............................$395.00
Han Solo, Tri-logo, Carbonite chamber outfit, M (NM+ card) $250.00
Han Solo, Tri-logo, Hoth gear, M (VG+ card) $50.00
Han Solo, Tri-logo, M (NM card)...............................$225.00
IG-88, ESB, M (NM card)..$200.00
IG-88, ESB, 12", EX...$950.00
IG-88, Tri-logo, M (EX card) $240.00
Imperial Commander, ESB, M (NM+ Canadian card)...$100.00
Imperial Commander, ROTJ, M (EX card) $40.00

Imperial Dignitary, POTF, M (EX+ card), $120.00.
(Photo courtesy June Moon)

Imperial Dignitary, Tri-logo, M (EX+ card) $80.00
Imperial Gunner, POTF, complete, NM, from $55 to.......$65.00
Imperial Gunner, POTF, M (EX+ card) $120.00
Imperial Gunner, POTF, M (VG+ card) $80.00
Imperial Gunner, Tri-logo, M (EX+ card)......................$100.00
Ishi, POTF, 1995-present, MOC (gr w/slide) $20.00
Jann Tosh, Droids, complete, NM $40.00
Jar Jar Binks, Episode I/Wave 9, swimming, MOC $25.00
Jawa, ESB, M (VG+ card) $60.00
Jawa, POTF, M (NM card) $135.00
Jawa, SW, M (NM card) (12-back)................................$295.00
Jawa, SW, M (NM+ card) (20/21-back) $225.00

Jawa, SW, 12", M (EX box) $250.00
Jawa, SW, 12", M (NM sealed box), from $375 to..........$450.00
Klaatu, ROTJ, M (NM card) $35.00
Klaatu, ROTJ, Skiff Guard outfit, NM.....................$10.00
Kyle Katarn, POTF, 1995-present, MOC.......................$20.00
Lando Calrissian, ESB, M (NM card) $100.00
Lando Calrissian, ROTJ, Skiff Guard outfit, NM $10.00
Lando Calrissian, Tri-logo, M (EX+ card) $100.00
Lando Skiff, Tri-logo, M (VG card) $20.00
Lobot, ESB, M (EX card)...$60.00
Lobot, POTF, 1995-present, MOC (gr w/slide)...................$8.00
Lobot, ROTJ, M (G card)..$20.00
Lobot, Tri-logo, M (NM+ card) $125.00
Logray, ROTJ, complete, NM......................................$10.00
Luke Skywalker, ESB, Bespin outfit, complete, NM $20.00
Luke Skywalker, ESB, blond hair, M (NM card) $250.00
Luke Skywalker, ESB, brn hair, M (NM Canadian card)...$275.00
Luke Skywalker, ESB, Hoth gear, M (NM+ card) $175.00
Luke Skywalker, POTF, battle poncho, NM.....................$70.00
Luke Skywalker, POTF, Stormtrooper outfit, EX $100.00
Luke Skywalker, POTF, Stormtrooper outfit, MOC
  (unpunched) $450.00
Luke Skywalker, POTF, X-Wing Pilot outfit, M (NM card) ...$175.00
Luke Skywalker, POTF, 1995-present, Jedi Knight outfit, MOC
  (gr) $15.00
Luke Skywalker, POTF, 1995-present, X-Wing Pilot outfit, short
  saber in long tray, MOC (red) $20.00
Luke Skywalker, POTF, 1995-present, 12", MIB...............$25.00
Luke Skywalker, ROTJ, Jedi Knight outfit, bl saber, M (EX+
  card)...$175.00
Luke Skywalker, ROTJ, Jedi Knight outfit, bl saber, NM .$50.00
Luke Skywalker, ROTJ, Jedi Knight outfit, gr saber, NM .$25.00
Luke Skywalker, ROTJ, Jedi Knight outfit, M (NM Canadian
  card) $135.00
Luke Skywalker, ROTJ, X-Wing pilot outfit, M (EX+ card) ..$60.00
Luke Skywalker, SW, M (EX+ card) (20/21-back) $375.00
Luke Skywalker, SW, M (NM card) (12-back) $795.00
Luke Skywalker, SW, M (VG+ card) (12-back) $325.00
Luke Skywalker, SW, X-Wing Pilot outfit, M (NM+ card)
  (20/21-back) $350.00
Luke Skywalker, SW, 12", M (NM sealed box)...............$650.00
Luke Skywalker, Tri-logo, Imperial Stormtrooper outfit, M (EX+
  card) $295.00
Luke Skywalker, Tri-logo, Jedi Knight outfit, M (NM card)......$125.00
Luke Skywalker, Tri-logo, Stormtrooper outfit, M (NM card) ..$300.00
Lumat, POTF, complete, NM $35.00
Lumat, ROTJ, M (EX card) $50.00
Lumat, Tri-logo, M (VG+ card) $60.00
Nien Numb, ROTJ, NM (NM card) $50.00
Nikto, ROTJ, complete, NM..................................$18.00
Nikto, ROTJ, M (NM+ Canadian card) $50.00
Paploo, POTF, complete, NM..................................$30.00
Paploo, ROTJ, NM (NM card) $60.00
Pit Droid, Episode I/Wave 9, 2-pack, MOC...................$15.00
Power Droid, ESB, M (NM card) $125.00
Power Droid, SW, complete, NM $10.00
Power Droid, SW, M (EX card) (20/21-back) $175.00
Power Droid, SW, M (NM+ card) (20/21-back)............$295.00

Princess Leia Organa, ESB, Bespin outfit, M (NM card, looking
  photo) $170.00
Princess Leia Organa, ESB, Bespin outfit, M (VG card) ..$95.00
Princess Leia Organa, ESB, crewneck, complete, NM......$20.00
Princess Leia Organa, ESB, Hoth gear, complete, NM $20.00
Princess Leia Organa, ESB, Hoth gear, M (NM+ card)..$180.00
Princess Leia Organa, ESB, M (NM+ card) $260.00
Princess Leia Organa, ESB, turtleneck, complete, NM.....$35.00
Princess Leia Organa, POTF, combat poncho, M (VG card)...$55.00
Princess Leia Organa, POTF, 1995-present, Boushh Disguise,
  MOC (gr)..$20.00
Princess Leia Organa, POTF, 1995-present, 12", MIB $25.00
Princess Leia Organa, ROTJ, Bespin Chamber outfit, M (EX
  card) $75.00
Princess Leia Organa, ROTJ, Boushh Disguise, M (EX+
  card) $65.00
Princess Leia Organa, ROTJ, combat poncho, M (NM+ Cana-
  dian card) $60.00
Princess Leia Organa, ROTJ, Hoth gear, M (NM+ card) ..$175.00
Princess Leia Organa, ROTJ, turtleneck, M (NM card) .$100.00
Princess Leia Organa, SW, M (NM 12-back card)..........$550.00
Princess Leia Organa, SW, M (VG card) (12-back) $295.00

Princess Leia Organa, SW, 12", M (VG+ box), $200.00.
(Photo courtesy Linda Baker)

Princess Leia Organa, SW, 12", MIB (sealed)................$325.00
Princess Leia Organa, Tri-logo, Boushh disguise, M (NM+
  card)..$200.00
Prune Face, ROTJ, NM (NM card).................................$40.00
Queen Amidala, Episode I/Wave 9, battle fatigues,
  MOC $18.00
Qui-Gon Jinn, Episode I/Wave 6, MOC........................$15.00
Qui-Gon Jinn, Episode I/Wave 9, Jedi Master, MOC.......$18.00

Rancor Keeper, POTF, 1995-present, MOC (gr w/slide) ..$12.00
Rancor Keeper, ROTJ, complete, NM $12.00
Rancor Keeper, Tri-logo, M (NM card)..........................$40.00
Rebel Commander, ESB, M (NM Canadian card) $75.00
Rebel Commander, Tri-logo, M (NM card) $100.00
Rebel Commando, ROTJ, complete, NM, from $8 to $12.00
Rebel Commando, ROTJ, M (NM card) $30.00
Rebel Soldier, ESB, M (NM card) $75.00
Ree-Yees, POTF, 1995-present, MOC (gr w/slide)...........$25.00
Ree-Yees, ROTJ, M (NM card) $40.00
Romba, POTF, complete, NM $45.00
R2-D2, Episode I/Wave 5, MOC...................................$20.00
R2-D2, ESB, M (NM card) $125.00
R2-D2, ESB, w/sensorscope, M (NM card).....................$125.00
R2-D2, POTF, w/pop-up light saber, M (EX card) $85.00
R2-D2, POTF, 1995-present, MOC (gr) $20.00
R2-D2, ROTJ, w/sensorscope, M (NM Canadian card) ...$75.00
R2-D2, SW, complete, EX $12.00
R2-D2, SW, M (EX card) (12-back) $210.00
R2-D2, SW, M (NM card) (12-back)..............................$450.00
R2-D2, SW, M (NM card) (20/21-back) $260.00
R2-D2, SW, 12", M (EX+ sealed box)............................$350.00
R5-D4, POTF, 1995-present, MOC (red) $15.00
R5-D4, SW, complete, NM $12.00
R5-D4, SW, M (EX+ card) (20/21-back) $175.00
R5-D4, SW, M (NM+ card) (20/21-back) $395.00
Sand People, ESB, M (EX card) $125.00

Sand People, SW, M (NM card) (12-back) $350.00
Sand People, SW, pk legs, M (EX card) (20/21-back) $140.00
Sandtrooper, POTF, 1995-present, MOC (red) $20.00
Sio Bibble, Episode I/Wave 9, MOC............................$20.00
Snaggletooth, ESB, M (NM card)................................$130.00
Snaggletooth, ROTJ, Palitoy, M (EX+ card) $60.00
Snaggletooth, SW, M (NM+ card) (20/21-back) $395.00
Squid Head, ROTJ, M (EX card) $35.00
Star Destroyer Commander, ROTJ, M (EX card) $35.00
Stormtrooper, ESB, Hoth gear, complete, NM................$12.00
Stormtrooper, ESB, Hoth gear, M (NM+ card) $150.00
Stormtrooper, POTF, 1995-present, 12", MIB..............$40.00
Stormtrooper, ROTJ, M (NM+ card) $100.00
Stormtrooper, SW, M (NM card) (12-back) $450.00
Stormtrooper, SW, 12", M (EX+ sealed box)................$550.00
Stormtrooper, SW, 12", M (VG box) $230.00
Stromtrooper, ESB, M (NM card)...............................$140.00
Taun Taun, ESB, M (EX box).....................................$50.00
Teebo, POTF, M (EX card) $135.00
Teebo, ROTJ, complete, NM......................................$12.00
Teebo, ROTJ, M (NM+ Canadian card) $50.00
TIE Fighter Pilot, ESB, complete, NM.........................$12.00
TIE Fighter Pilot, POTF, 1995-present, 12", MIB...........$35.00
TIE Fighter Pilot, ROTJ, M (EX card) $55.00
Tusken Raider, POTF, 1995-present, MOC (red) $15.00
Tusken Raider, POTF, 1995-present, w/gun, 12", MIB $30.00
Tusken Raider, ROTJ, M (G card) $80.00
Tusken Raider, Tri-logo, M (NM card) $125.00
Ugnaught, ESB, bl or purple smock, complete, NM, ea from $10
 to $15.00
Ugnaught, ESB, M (NM card) $90.00
Ugnaught, ROTJ, M (NM card) $110.00
Ugnaught, Tri-logo, M (NM card) $125.00
Walrus Man, ESB, M (EX card) $100.00
Walrus Man, SW, M (EX card) (20/21 back).................$280.00
Walrus Man, SW, M (NM card) (20/21-back) $350.00
Warok, POTF, complete, NM......................................$60.00
Weequay, ROTJ, M (NM card) $45.00
Wicket W Warrick, ROTJ, complete, NM $20.00
Wicket W Warrick, ROTJ, M (NM Canadian card)........$65.00
Yak Face, POTF, complete, EX, from $150 to $175.00
Yak Face, POTF, 1995-present, MOC (gr) $8.00
Yak Face, Tri-logo, M (EX+ card) $495.00
Yoda, Episode I/Wave 5, MOC....................................$20.00
Yoda, ESB, brn or orange snake, complete, NM, ea from $30
 to $35.00
Yoda, ESB, orange snake, M (EX+ card)........................$175.00
Yoda, POTF, M (G card) $375.00
Yoda, POTF, 1995-present, w/hologram, MOC (red) $40.00
Zuckuss, ESB, NM (NM Canadian card)........................$150.00
Zuckuss, POTF, 1995-present, MOC (gr w/slide) $25.00
Zuckuss, ROTJ, M (EX+ card) $75.00
2-1B, ESB, complete, NM $10.00
2-1B, Tri-logo, M (NM+ card) $100.00
4-Lom, ESB, NM (NM card)......................................$350.00
4-Lom, POTF, 1995-present, MOC (gr)........................$10.00
8D8, ROTJ, M (NM card)...$40.00
8D8, Tri-logo, M (NM+ card) $125.00

**Sand People, SW, MOC (12-back, unpunched),
from $400.00 to $500.00.** (Photo courtesy June Moon)

PLAYSETS AND ACCESSORIES

Bespin Control Room, Micro Collection, MIB................$75.00
Bespin Freeze Chamber, Micro Collection, MIB.............$90.00
Bespin Gantry, Micro Collection, MIB...........................$75.00
Bespin World, Micro Collection, M (EX box)...............$150.00
Biker Scout Laser Pistol, MIB (sealed)...........................$85.00
Bop Bag, Darth Vader, MIB...$125.00
Cantina Adventure Set, Sears, MIB.............................$225.00
Cloud City, Canadian, M (EX box)...............................$500.00
Cloud City, ESB, M (EX box).......................................$275.00
Cloud City, ESB, MIB (sealed)......................................$500.00
Creature Cantina, EX (EX box).....................................$100.00
Creature Cantina, NMIB (sealed)..................................$325.00
Dagobah, ESB, Yoda, training kit sticker, MIB.............$250.00
Death Star Compactor, Palitoy, M (EX box).................$600.00
Death Star Compactor, SW, Micro Collection, M (EX box)...$150.00
Death Star Compactor, SW, Micro Collection, M (NM sealed box)..$250.00
Death Star Escape, Micro Collection, M (EX box).........$50.00

Death Star Space Station, SW, M (EX sealed box), $475.00.
(Photo courtesy Linda Baker)

Death Star World, Micro Collection, MIB.....................$225.00
Droid Factory, MIB...$100.00
Endor Chase, POTF, MIB..$235.00
Ewok Assult Catapult, ROTJ, MIB (sealed)...................$50.00
Ewok Family Hut, MIB...$50.00
Ewok Fire Cart, M (NM box)..$40.00
Ewok Village, ROTJ, M (NM box)...................................$75.00

Ewok Village, ROTJ, MIB (sealed).................................$175.00
Force Lightsaver, ROTJ, gr, w/sleeve, NM.....................$100.00
Gun Turret & Probot, ESB, Kenner, M (EX Canadian box)...$125.00
Hoth Generator Attack, Micro Collection, MIB (sealed)..$100.00
Hoth Ice Planet, M (VG box)..$100.00
Hoth Ice Planet, MIB (sealed).......................................$375.00
Hoth Ion Cannon, Micro Collection, M (VG+ box).......$75.00
Hoth Rescue, POTF, MIB...$250.00
Hoth Turret Defense, Micro Collection, MIB (sealed), from $60 to..$75.00
Hoth Wampa Cave, Micro Collection, M (EX box).........$60.00
Hoth World, Micro Collection, MIB...............................$190.00
Imperial Attack Base, ESB, Meccano, complete, EX......$100.00
Imperial Attack Base, M (decals applied) (EX+ Canadian box)..$85.00
Jabba the Hutt, ROTJ, M (EX sealed box)....................$100.00

Jabba the Hutt Dungeon, ROTJ, MIB (sealed), $250.00.
(Photo courtesy Manion's Auction Gallery)

Jabba's Dungeon, POTF, M (NM sealed box).................$350.00
Land of the Jawas, M (NM sealed box)..........................$450.00
Patrol Dewback, MIB (sealed)..$125.00
Radar Laser Cannon, ESB, MIB......................................$25.00
Rebel Command Center, ESB, M (EX box)....................$250.00
Sy Snootles & the Rebo Band, ROTJ, silver microphone, M (NM sealed box)..$225.00
Sy Snootles & the Rebo Band, Tri-logo, M (EX box)....$140.00
Tripod Laser Cannon, ESB, M (NM sealed box).............$35.00
Tripod Laser Cannon, ROTJ, M (EX box).......................$20.00
Turret & Probot, ESB, MIB (sealed)..............................$250.00
Vehicle Maintenance Energizer, ESB, MIB (sealed)........$35.00
Vehicle Maintenance Energizer, ROTJ, M (NM sealed box)..$25.00

VEHICLES

A-Wing Fighter, POTF, 1995-present, MIB.....................$25.00

AT-AT, ESB, MIB...$300.00
AT-AT, POTF, 1995-present, MIB (sealed)......................$75.00
AT-AT, ROTJ, M (NM box), from $275 to $325.00
ATL Interceptor, MIB..$135.00
B-Wing Fighter, ROTJ, MIB (sealed) $350.00
B-Wing Fighter, ROTJ, NM (NM box) $225.00
Boba Fett's Slave I, POTF, 1995-present, MIB (gr or purple)...$35.00
Darth Vader's Star Destroyer, ESB, M (EX box) $125.00
Darth Vader's TIE Fighter, POTF, 1995-present, MIB $20.00
Darth Vader's TIE Fighter, SW, diecast, M........................$60.00
Darth Vader's TIE Fighter, SW, diecast, M (NM unpunched
    card) $140.00
Darth Vader's TIE Fighter, SW, MIB..............................$125.00
Desert Sail Skiff, ROTJ, MIB $40.00
Endor Forest Ranger, ROTJ, M (EX sealed box)...............$25.00
Endor Forest Ranger, Tri-logo, MIB (sealed)....................$65.00
Ewok Battle Wagon, POTF, MIB $235.00
Ewok Combat Glider, ROTJ, MIB $40.00
Imperial Cruiser, ESB, M (EX box) $100.00
Imperial Cruiser, SW, diecast, MIB (sealed) $235.00

Imperial Cruiser, ESB, MIB (sealed), from $190.00 to
$225.00.

Imperial TIE Fighter, SW, diecast, MOC, from $75 to ...$100.00
Imperial Troop Transporter, ESB, w/sound, MIB, from $400
    to $450.00
Jawa Sandcrawler, SW, complete, NM..........................$350.00
Jawa Sandcrawler, SW, MIB (sealed), from $1,500 to ...$1,800.00
Land Speeder, SW, Sonic Controlled, VG (VG box).....$300.00
Landspeeder, SW, MIB $145.00
Landspeeder, SW, Sonic Controlled, M (G+ box) $395.00
Millenium Falcon, ESB, diecast, MIB $175.00
Millenium Falcon, ROTJ, MIB, from $250 to $275.00
Millenium Falcon, SW, diecast, M (EX card) $175.00
Millenium Falcon, SW, M (EX box) $695.00
Millennium Falcon, POTF, 1995-present, MIB...............$40.00
Millennium Falcon, ROTJ, M (EX+ box) $295.00
Rebel Transport, M (EX box) $175.00
Scout Walker, ESB, MIB..$85.00
Scout Walker, ROTJ, M (EX box) $85.00
Scout Walker, Tri-logo, MIB $100.00
Slave I, ESB, M (NM sealed box) $250.00
Slave I, ROTJ, Palitoy, M (EX sealed box) $250.00
Snowspeeder, ESB, EX (worn box)...................................$45.00
Snowspeeder, ESB, M (NM pk box) $100.00
Speeder Bike, ROTJ, M (NM box) $40.00
Speeder Bike, Tri-logo, MIB $75.00
Star Destroyer, POTF, 1995-present, electronic, MIB.......$25.00
Tatooine Skiff, M (EX box) $425.00
TIE Fighter, ESB, M (NM box)......................................$500.00
TIE Fighter, SW, diecast, MOC $150.00
TIE Fighter (Battle Damaged), ROTJ, M (EX box)..........$75.00
TIE Interceptor, ROTJ, M (EX box) $100.00
TIE Interceptor, ROTJ, MIB (sealed) $225.00
Twin Pod Cloud Car, ESB, diecast, MOC......................$200.00
Twin Pod Cloud Car, ESB, MIB.....................................$250.00
X-Wing Fighter, M (EX Canadian box) $225.00
X-Wing Fighter, Tri-logo, MIB......................................$235.00
X-Wing Fighter (Battle Damaged), ESB, M (EX box)....$125.00
X-Wing Fighter (Battle Damaged), ESB, M (VG+ box) ..$65.00
X-Wing Fighter (Battle Damaged), ROTJ, M (VG+ box)..$65.00
Y-Wing Fighter, ESB, diecast, MIB (sealed)...................$200.00
Y-Wing Fighter, ROTJ, MIB (sealed).............................$325.00
Y-Wing Fighter, SW, diecast, M (EX box) $200.00

MISCELLANEOUS

Bank, Chewbacca (kneeling), Sigma, M...........................$75.00
Bank, C3-PO, Roman Ceramics, M $75.00
Bank, R2-D2, Roman Ceramics, M.................................$200.00
Bank, Yoda, SW, Sigma, M...$150.00
Book, Empire Strikes Back, pop-up, M.............................$15.00
Book, Return of the Jedi, Ballantine, 1983, 1st edition, soft-
    cover, EX $10.00
Book & Cassette, Return of the Jedi, EX...........................$8.00
Bookends, Darth Vader/Chewbacca, Sigma, ceramic $100.00
Bop Bag, Jawa, MIB..$200.00
Card Game, Return of the Jedi, Parker Bros, 1983, MIB
    (sealed) $10.00
Case, Darth Vader, EX $15.00
Chewbacca Bandolier Strap, ROTJ, EX (worn box).........$25.00

Imperial Shuttle, ROTJ, NRFB, $400.00.
(Photo courtesy Manion's Auction Gallery)

Chewbacca Bandolier Strap, ROTJ, MIB $40.00
Color 'N Clean Machine, Craftmaster, M.....................$50.00
Coloring Book, ESB, Luke, Bespin outfit, Kenner, M.......$10.00

Cookie Jar, C-3PO, Roman Ceramics, 1977, gold-glazed ceramic, from $350.00 to $400.00. (Photo courtesy June Moon)

Costume, Yoda, Ben Cooper, w/mask, NM $75.00
Display, any character, diecut cb standups, life-sz, EX, F1, ea...$30.00
Doll, Chewbacca, Kenner, 1978-79, synthetic fur w/plastic eyes
& nose, 20", EX $25.00
Doll, Paploo, Ewok, ROTJ, plush, MIB..........................$135.00
Doll, R2-D2, Kenner, 1978-79, stuffed cloth, w/speaker, 10",
EX $25.00
Game, Destroy Death Star, VG......................................$20.00
Game, Escape From Death Star, Kenner, 1977, complete, NM
(EX box) $25.00
Game, Laser Battle, SW, M (EX box) $75.00
Give-A-Show Projector, ESB, Kenner, complete, NM.....$75.00
Hand Puppet, Yoda, ESB, MIB......................................$75.00
Headset Radio, Luke Skywalker, SW, MIB.....................$550.00
Ice Skates, Darth Vader & Royal Guards, ROTJ, MIB.....$45.00
Laser Pistol, SW, Kenner, 1978-83, plastic, battery-op, 18½",
EX $40.00
Laser Rifle, ESB, Kenner, 1980, plastic, battery-op, 18½",
EX $75.00
Laser Rifle Carrying Case, ROTJ, M $80.00
Magnets, ROTJ, set of 4, MOC, B5 ....$25.00
Mask (Don Post), Boba Fett, hard plastic, EX, F1 ....$100.00
Mask (Don Post), Chewbacca, hard plastic, EX, F1.........$80.00

Mask (Don Post), Darth Vader, hard plastic, EX, F1 ....$65.00
Mask (Don Post), Emperor's Royal Guard, hard plastic, EX,
F1...$75.00
Movie Viewer, SW, Kenner, 1978-79, plastic w/snap-in cartridge,
7", EX $35.00
Mug, Biker Scout, Sigma, ceramic, MIB $30.00
Mug, Darth Vader, Sigma, ceramic, M $15.00
Paint Kit, Craftmaster, Luke Skywalker or Han Solo, MOC,
ea $15.00
Pencil Tray, C-3PO, Sigma, ceramic, MIB $50.00
Pillow, Jabba the Hutt, plush, M.....................................$50.00
Playdoh Adventure Modeling Set, SW, Palitoy, MIB.....$200.00
Playmat, SW, Recticel Sutcliffe, UK, NM $125.00
Poster Set, Craftmaster, 1979, w/2 posters, MIB (sealed) .$30.00
Presto Magix Transfer Set, ROTJ, Battle on Endor, NRFB..$15.00
Presto Magix Transfer Set, Wicket, set of 120, MIB, B5 ...$28.00
Puppet, Yoda, Kenner, 1981, hollow vinyl, 10", EX $25.00
Radio Watch, Lucasfilm/Bradley, 1982, R2-D2 & C-3PO on
face, MIB...$50.00
Record, Ewoks Joins the Fight, 45 rpm, w/booklet, M
(sealed) $10.00
Record, ROTJ, dialogue & music from orig motion picture, 33
3/3 rpm, 1983, EX $15.00
Sew 'N Show Cards, Wicket & Friends, MIB $18.00
Sit 'N Spin, Ewoks, MIB..$80.00
Speaker Phone, Darth Vader, MIB, P12........................$145.00
Talking Telephone, Ewoks, MIB....................................$50.00
Tankard, Ben Obi-Wan Kenobi, CA Originals, ceramic, M ..$90.00
Yo-yo, Darth Vader, Dairy Queen promo, Humphrey, 1970s, rare,
NM $25.00
Yo-yo, Stormtrooper, Spectra Star, sculpted plastic, MIP....$5.00
3-D Poster Art Set, 1978, complete, MIP $30.00

Steam Powered

During the early part of the twentieth century until about 1930, though not employed to any great extent, live steam power was used to activate toys such as large boats, novelty toys, and model engines.

See also Boats; Trains.

Accessory, butter churn, Marklin, model #4206, 1902, red & sil-
ver w/silver pin-striping, 7", VG, A $925.00
Accessory, elevator, Doll, pnt tin w/compo figures, 16", EX,
A $1,700.00
Accessory, Ferris wheel, Falk, red w/gold highlights, 6 dbl-seat
chairs w/figures, 12", rstr, A $500.00
Accessory, Ferris wheel, pnt tin, 6 gondolas w/2 figures in ea,
19", EX, A $2,100.00
Accessory, fodder cutter, Marklin, 1902, mk Futterschneidmas
chine, gr & red, 9" L, rare, EX, A...........................$900.00
Accessory, power station, Doll & Co, tin, tall red chimney,
revolving base causes chimney sweep to enter door, 7x9",
EX $325.00
Accessory, seed sorter, Marklin, model #4207, 1902, mk Trieur,
gr & yel, repro tin base, 8" L, VG, A $350.00

Accessory, threshing machine, Bing, pnt tin: yel w/red highlights & gr cranks, red funnel, 9" L, G, A $150.00

Accessory, threshing machine, Marklin, model #4201, 1902-05, yel & red w/gr pin-striping, 11", rare, EX, A $8,200.00

Accessory, threshing machine, Marklin, pnt tin: gr w/red trim, wood rollers under rear cap, 3 conveyor rails, 8" L, EX.............$465.00

Accessory, turnip cutter, Marklin, model #4204, 1902, gr & red w/yel pin-striping, 5", rare, VG, A $350.00

Accessory, walking beam pump, Ernst Plank, litho tin, wind-mill & roof-covered beam pump, bl w/rel & red, 10½", M, A $300.00

Accessory, wheat sifter, Bing, pnt tin: red & yel, stenciled: Wheat Sifter, on bl base, 5½" L, VG, A $685.00

Accessory, winnowing machine, Marklin, model #4202, 1902, red, internal fan & mechanical sifter, 6" L, rare, EX, A..$500.00

Beam Engine, Buckman, 1880s, blk, orange, & bl w/brass boiler, 6x5" base, EX, A..$700.00

Beam Engine, J&E Stevens, 1870s, inscr Frisbees Pat'd..., gr, red, & gold w/gold & red winged shield logo, 8", EX, A.....$1,375.00

Kaleidoscope, early, glass-faced w/brass fr, on wood base, 7½", MIB, A..$850.00

Meteor Mill Engine, Ernst Plank, 1902, EP maker's plate on simulated brick firebox, tinplate tile on wood base, EX, A .$400.00

Mill Engine, Doll, 1925-30, bl & blk w/red & bl pinstriping, flyball governor, 12x11" base, EX, A............................$575.00

Mill Engine w/Dynamo, Marklin, model #4149/5/91, 1920s, gr & gray w/silver & bl pin-striping, 13x10" base, EX (EX box), A $1,100.00

Organ Grinder, Germany, litho tin figure cranks lg wheel of box organ which plays as it revolves, 5½", EX, A $800.00

Pillar Engine, Ernst Plank, 1895-1900, blk boiler w/brass highlights, 6" sq wood base, EX, A..................................$600.00

Pillar Engine, Weeden, model #17, 1920, gray & maroon, oscillating cylinder w/reversing lever & governor, 9", VG, A..$250.00

Steam Engine, Doll Co, horizontal boiler w/dual flywheel, much nickel detail, level glass tube, CI base, 11½", M, A...$650.00

Steam Engine, GC&C, horizontal boiler w/top-mtd CI bracket supporting nickeled flywheel & levers, CI base, 9", M, A..$575.00

Steam Engine, Weeden, tin horizontal boiler, 1-cylinder, nickeled valves/whistle, CI support, no-view valve, EX, A.......$250.00

Steam Engine, Weeden, 1-cylinder, nickeled base & working parts, gun bl boiler & stack, 8" L, EX, A..................$850.00

Carousel, Germany, hand-painted tin, hand crank, live steam attachment, 15", EX, A, $1,100.00.

Carousel, w/airplane, zeppelin & hot-air balloon, pnt tin, beveled base, 32", prof rstr, A $32,000.00

Hercules Engine & Machine Tool Set, Ernst Plank, 1902, vertical pillar-type engine w/fly-ball governor, EX (G box), A..$850.00

Steam Plant, Fleischmann (Germany), brass boiler, cast-iron flywheel with nickeled gears and pull rods, on enameled green base, 14" x 14", MIB, A, $385.00.

Steam Plant w/Dynamo, Doll, 1925-30, bl & blk w/red pin-striping, DC trademark on cylinder, 13x8" base, EX, A .$500.00

Tricycle, yel-pnt tin w/copper boiler, spoke wheels, tailgate opens for dbl wick burner, 11", VG, A $2,900.00

Walking Beam Engine, Ernst Plank, 1885-90, cut brass engine, EP maker's plate on boiler, 11x5" ftd wood base, EX, A................$1,400.00

Workshop, Marklin, model #4281, 1906-07, CI tools on gr & yel litho tile base, 23x10", rare, VG, A $4,400.00

Steiff

Margaret Steiff made the first of her felt toys in 1880, stuffing them with lamb's wool. Later followed toys of velvet, plush, and wool, and in addition to the lamb's wool stuffing, she used felt scraps, excelsior, and kapok as well. In 1897 and 1898 her trademark was a paper label printed with an elephant; from 1900 to 1905 her toys carried a circular tag with an elephant logo that was different than the one she had previously used. The most famous 'button in ear' trademark was registered on December 20, 1904. The button with an elephant (extremely rare) and the blank button (which is also rare) were used in 1904 and 1905. The button with Steiff and the underscored or trailing 'F' was used until 1948, and the raised script button is from the 1950s.

Steiff Teddy bears, perhaps the favorite of collectors everywhere, are characterized by their long thin arms with curved wrists and paws that extend below their hips. Buyer beware: The Steiff company is now making many replicas of their old bears. For more information about Steiff's buttons, chest tags, and stock tags as well as the inspirational life of Margaret Steiff and the fascinating history of Steiff toys, we recommend *Button in Ear Book* and *The Steiff Book of Teddy Bears*, both by Jurgen and Marianne Cieslik; *Teddy Bear Treasury* by Ken Yenke; *Teddy Bears and Steiff Animals, 1st, 2nd,* and *3rd Series* by Margaret Fox Mandel; *4th Teddy Bear and Friends Price Guide* by Linda Mullins; *Collectible German Animals Value Guide* by Dee Hockenberry; and *Steiff Sortiment 1947 – 1995* by Gunther Pefiffer. (This book is in German; however, the reader can discern the size of the item, year of production, and price estimation.) See also Clubs, Newsletters, and Other Publications (for Cynthia's Country Store).

Advisors: Cynthia's Country Store, Cynthia Brintnall (C14); Candelaine (G16).

See also Character, TV, and Movie Collectibles; Disney.

Baby Chick, spotted Dralon w/felt comb, plastic feet & beak, all ID, 1971, 4", NM $85.00

Baby Duck, yel mohair w/brn airbrushed markings, orange felt beak & feet, all ID, 1959-61, 5½", EX $195.00

Bazi Dog, mohair, plastic eyes, orig bl collar, chest tag, 1960s, 4", NM................$110.00

Bear, beige mohair w/blk bead eyes, ear button, 1905, 3½", EX, A $800.00

Bear, blond mohair, FF underscored button, orig collar & tie, 1908, 18", NM................$6,000.00

Bear, blond mohair, FF underscored button, 1913, 13", NM..$2,500.00

Bear, curly wht mohair, glass eyes, raised script button & stock tag, 1920s, 10" L, NM $2,300.00

Bear, ginger mohair w/glass eyes, fully jtd, no ID, 1910, 5", VG, A $375.00

Bear, gold mohair, glass eyes, orig bl ribbon, raised script button, 1950s, 13", NM................$500.00

Bear, gold mohair, glass eyes, side squeaker, FF underscored button, 1920s, 5", EX $975.00

Bear, gold mohair, shoe-button eyes, FF underscored button, pre-1910, 20", NM................$8,000.00

Bear, gold mohair w/felt pads, glass eyes, all ID, 1950, 6", EX................$225.00

Bear, lt brn curly mohair, shoe-button eyes, no ID, 1917, 30", rare, VG $15,000.00

Bear, Margaret Strong, cream, orig button & tag, 1984-86, 9", NM................$125.00

Bear, pre-1910, FF button, replaced nose and pads, 27", from $9,500.00 to $11,500.00. (Photo courtesy Cynthia's Country Store)

Bear, wht mohair, clear glass eyes, FF underscored button & US Zone tag, w/growler, 1947, 17", EX $1,800.00

Bear, wht mohair, glass eyes, orig bl ribbon, raised script button, 1950s, 6", EX................$500.00

Bear, yel mohair w/blk steel eyes, fully jtd, ear button, 1905, 5", EX, A $1,100.00

Bendy Bear, dk brn, all ID, 1984, 3½", M $45.00

Bendy Panda, mohair, all ID, 1960s, 3", NM $325.00

Bengal Tiger, mohair, glass eyes, raised script button & chest tag, 1959-61, 5½", rare, M $450.00

Bessy Cow, mohair w/felt horns & udders, glass eyes, orig collar & bell, no ID, 1950s, 9", NM $145.00

Biggie Beagle, mohair, plastic eyes, orig red collar, all ID, 1960s, 7½", M................$185.00

Bison, mohair w/felt horns, all ID, 1950, 8", M $225.00

Boar, blk w/brn face, all ID, 1950s, 11", M.....................$175.00

Bully Dog, blk & cream mohair w/velvet face, glass eyes, FF underscored button, 1920s, 4", EX $600.00

Camel, mohair & felt, all ID, 1950, 5¾", NM................$135.00

Clownie Clown, orig outfit, chest tag, 5", M $100.00

Clownie Clown, orig outfit & chest tag, 16", EX, from $200 to...$400.00

Cocker Spaniel, blk & wht w/freckles, glass eyes, jtd head, no ID, 1930s, 13", EX, A $200.00

Cockie Dog, seated, blk & wht, orig collar, no ID, 4½", EX...$85.00

Coco Monkey, gray mohair w/wht fringe around face & ears, glass eyes, orig red leather collar, all ID, 5½", NM ..$150.00

Collie, laying down, all ID, 1960, 9", M..........................$225.00

Cosy Koala, all ID, 1970, 5", M......................................$65.00

Crabby Lobster, felt w/vivid airbrushing, glass eyes, all ID, 4½", M...$350.00

Dally Dog, mohair, glass eyes, swivel head, orig red collar, raised script button, 6½", NM....................................$150.00

Deer (Buck), beige mohair w/blk glass eyes, FF underscored button, 10", VG...$250.00

Diggy Badger, mohair w/glass eyes, 6", EX........................$100.00

Dinosarus Stegosauras, mohair with glass eyes, original tag and raised button, 13", minimum value, $1,250.00.

Dog on Wheels, tan & brn velveteen, blk glass eyes, CI spoke wheels, 1910, 6" L, rare, EX....................................$950.00

Eric Bat, mohair, with tag, 1960s, rare, EX, minimum value, $675.00.

Donkey, velvet w/rope tail & leather harness, raised script button & stock tag, 1959-67, 4½", M $165.00

Donkey on Wheels, gray wool flannel, shoe-button eyes, FF button, w/saddle & blanket, 9½", rare, M $1,500.00

Dormili Rabbit, tan & wht, all ID, 1986-88, 7", M...........$65.00

Elephant, ride-on, gray mohair w/glass eyes, red & yel felt blanket & red leather harness, steel fr, 24½", EX, A $450.00

Elephant, w/anniversary blanket, all ID, 1959-67, 2½", M $145.00

Floppy Beagle, sleeping, mohair, orig ribbon, chest tag, 8", NM $125.00

Floppy Hens, mohair & felt, all ID, 1958, 8" & 7", rare, pr...$300.00

Floppy Kitty, sleeping, tan w/blk stripes, orig ribbon & chest tag, 8", EX...$100.00

Fox, standing, mohair w/glass eyes, raised script button, 5", EX...$80.00

Froggy Frog, seated, velvet w/glass eyes, all ID, 1968, 3", NM...$135.00

Froggy Frog, swimming, mohair, chest tag, 1960s, 10", NM...$125.00

Giraffe, velvet, all ID, 1959-67, 6", M............................$145.00

Gogo Chinchilla, Dralon & felt, all ID, 5½", M $200.00

Halloween Cat, blk mohair, plastic eyes, orig ribbon, raised script button, 9½", NM...$175.00

Halloween Cat, blk velvet & mohair, glass eyes, chest tag, raised script button & remnant stock tag, 1950s, 4", EX ...$165.00

Hedgehog, incised button & stock tag, 1966-67, 2¼", NM ..$35.00

Hide-A-Gift Rabbit, all ID, 1950, 5½", M, from $175 to ...$185.00

Hoppy Rabbit, mohair, glass eyes, orig ribbon & bell, all ID, 1968, 9", NM..$200.00

Hoppy Rabbit, mohair, plastic eyes, orig ribbon & bell, all ID, 1968, 7½", NM...$165.00

Jackie Bear, raised script button & remnant stock tag, 1950s, 9½", rare, EX $900.00

Jolanthe Pig, mohair w/felt ears, incised button, 1960, 5", NM $125.00

Jumbo Elephant, mohair w/red felt bib, all ID, 1968, 9", M $385.00

Kangaroo, turq velveteen w/blk glass bead eyes, no ID, pre-1910, 6", rare, EX..$600.00

Koala Bear, fully jtd, all ID, 1955-58, 9", M....................$700.00

Koala Bear, jtd head, all ID, 1959-61, 4½", M...............$425.00

Lamb (from Mary Had a Little Lamb), all ID, 1986, 5", M ..$75.00

Leo Lion, seated, incised button, 1960, 5", NM................$85.00

Lioness, mohair w/glass eyes, fully jtd, raised script button & stock tag, 1951-57, 6", rare, M $250.00

Lora Parrot, mohair & felt, incised button & stock tag, 1968, 9", EX...$150.00

Manni Rabbit, mohair, glass eyes, w/squeaker, orig ribbon & bell, no ID, 1950s, 16", NM $950.00

Max & Moritz, all ID, 1950s, 3½", rare, MIP $385.00

Maxi Mole, mohair, all ID, 1965, 4", M........................$135.00

Molly Dog, wht mohair w/red-brn tipping, glass eyes, orig ribbon & bell, all ID, 1950s, 7", M $225.00

Molly Dog, wht mohair w/red-brn tipping, glass eyes, swivel head, all ID, 1958, 10", rare, EX................................$450.00

Moosy Moose, all ID, 1963-64, 4½", rare, M.................$425.00

Nagy Beaver, mohair w/felt hands & feet, glass eyes, all ID, 1958, 3¾", M..$100.00

Nagy Beaver, mohair w/felt hands & feet, glass eyes, all ID, 1958, 7", M...$165.00

Nelly Snail, velveteen & vinyl, all ID, 1962, 6", EX, A.$200.00

Niki Rabbit, mohair, glass eyes, fully jtd, orig ribbon, raised script button & stock tag, 7", M................................$400.00

Original Teddy, caramel, all ID, 1950s, 6", M $400.00

Original Teddy, caramel mohair, fully jtd, chest tag, 3½", M..$325.00

Original Teddy, caramel mohair, glass eyes, orig button & tag, 38", M, from $1,000 to $2,000.00

Original Teddy, gold mohair, glass eyes, orig bl ribbon, chest tag & raised script button, 8", M....................................$565.00

Original Teddy, gold mohair, blk bead eyes, fully jtd, chest tag, 1950s, 3½", EX...$265.00

Original Teddy, tan mohair, glass eyes, fully jtd, chest tag, 3½", NM...$375.00

Orsi Bear, caramel mohair, amber glass eyes, raised script button & chest tag, 1956, 8½", NM $850.00

Peggy Penguin, chest tag, 1959, 5", NM $100.00

Peky Dog, plush & felt, chest tag, 1950, 3", EX $75.00

Pieps Mouse, wht mohair, all ID, M $100.00

Pony, mohair, glass eyes, orig red leather saddle & plastic reins, chest tag, 1950s, 5", NM $125.00

Raccy Raccoon, mohair, glass eyes, stock tag, 6", EX $100.00

Renny Reindeer, chest tag, 1950s, 4½", M $185.00

Siamy Cat, wht mohair w/brn tipping, glass eyes, no ID, 1950s, 5", rare, NM...$300.00

Skunk, mohair & velvet, glass eyes, chest tag, 1962-63, 4¼", M..$250.00

Snucki Ram, tan mohair w/blk face & feet, orig chest tag, 1950s, 6", NM..$125.00

Teddy Bear, dk brn mohair, glass eyes, orig collar & bell, chest tag & raised script button, 1948, rare, 9", EX.......$1,100.00

Tessie Schnauzer, gray mohair, glass, eyes, orig red collar, chest tag, 4½", NM...$150.00

Tysus Dinosaur, all ID, 1980s, 7½", MIB.......................$125.00

Woolie Baby Duck, metal feet, raised script button & stock tag, 1950s, 1½", M...$55.00

Woolie Bird, raised script button & stock tag, 1949, 2", NM...$50.00

Woolie Fish, gr & yel, raised script button & stock tag, 1968, 1½", NM..$35.00

Woolie Frog, incised button & stock tag, 1960s, 2½", NM..$35.00

Woolie Mouse, wht, no ID, 1960, 1½", M $35.00

Woolie Skunk, raised script button, 1950s, 1½", NM $150.00

Woolly Teddy, tan mohair, shoe-button eyes, FF underscored button, pre-1920, 7", EX..$900.00

Yuku Gazelle, all ID, 1962-63, 7½", rare, NM $325.00

Zotty Bear, caramel mohair, plastic eyes, orig red ribbon, chest tag, 6½", M..$250.00

Store Display Ferris Wheel, NM, A, $3,000.00.
(Photo courtesy Jeff Bubb Auctions)

Spidy Spider, mohair, script button on leg, 7" (top of head to bottom of torso), scarce, paper tag missing, from $700.00 to $1,000.00. (Photo courtesy McMaster's Doll Auctions)

Squirrel, puppet, mohair w/felt hands & feet, glass eyes, 8½", NM..$75.00

St Bernard on Wheels, long pile wht mohair w/red-brn tulip ears, amber glass eyes, FF underscored button, 10" L, M.$1,200.00

Teddy Baby, tan, all ID, 1985-86, 15", M......................$250.00

Strauss

Imaginative, high-quality, tin windup toys were made by Ferdinand Strauss (New York, later New Jersey) from the onset of World War I until the 1940s. For about fifteen years prior to his becoming a toy maker, he was a distributor of toys he imported from Germany. Though hard to find in good working order, his toys are highly prized by today's collectors, and when

ound in even very good to excellent condition, many are in the
500.00 and up range.

Advisor: Scott Smiles (S10).

Air Devil, 1926, w/pilot, 8½", EX, from $500 to **$600.00**

Big Show Circus Truck, trainer raises whip as lion rears up, 11",
VG **$900.00**

Big Show Circus Wagon, lion and tamer inside, seated driver,
" long, VG, $850.00.

oob McNutt, man in red polka-dot pants & blk jacket, flat rnd
hat, 9", VG **$625.00**

Bus De Luxe, 1920s, with original driver, 13" long, VG, A,
750.00.

Dandy Jim Clown Dancer, 1921, does jig & plays cymbals atop
circus tent, 10", EX **$600.00**

Emergency Town Car #74, w/driver, red, gray & bl w/disk
wheels, 11½", VG **$1,200.00**

Flying Airship, 1930s, aluminum w/brass prop, 10", NMIB, from
$850 to **$900.00**

Graf Zeppelin Jr #2, aluminum w/brass propeller, 10", EX (EX
box), from $600 to **$750.00**

Ham & Sam, 1921, Black banjo player beside piano player, MIB..**$1,200.00**

Ham & Sam, 1921, Black banjo player beside piano player, 5½",
EX **$950.00**

Inter-State Bus, brown with yellow trim, 10" long, VG (poor box), A, $1,100.00.

Inter-State Bus, dbl-decker bus w/rear stairway, brn w/yel detail,
10", VG, from $900 to **$950.00**

Jackie the Hornpipe Dancer, boat advances as sailor dances on
deck, 9", EX (EX box) **$900.00**

Jazzbo Jim, 1920s, figure plays banjo & dances atop roof, 10",
NM (EX box), A **$925.00**

Jazzbo Jim, 1920s, figure plays banjo & dances atop roof, 10",
VG (worn box) **$600.00**

Jenny the Balky Mule, 1925, advances w/crazy action as farmer
bounces in seat, 9½", EX (EX box), from $500 to ..**$600.00**

Jitney Bus, w/driver, gr & yel w/disk wheels, 9", EX **$1,200.00**

Jolly Pals, 1920, bulldog pulls monkey in cart, EX..........**$475.00**

Kraka Jack Irish Mail Car, w/driver, 5", EX, A................**$600.00**

Leaping Lena Car, 1930, w/driver, blk w/wht lettering, 8", EX,
from $400 to **$500.00**

Parcel Post Delivery Truck, orange & yel w/blk roof & fenders,
11", NM...**$1,300.00**

Red Cap Porter, Black man pushes travel trunk w/dog inside,
6½", G **$450.00**

Red Flash Racer #31, w/driver, red & yel, 9½", scarce, EX, from
$850 to...**$900.00**

Rollo-Chair, litho tin, NMIB...**$1,500.00**

Santee Claus in Sleigh, 1923, 11", NM, A **$1,400.00**

Santee Claus in Sleigh, 1923, 11", NM (NM box) **$1,700.00**

Sparko, clown sharpens knife, 5", EX (EX box), A, $300.00.

Standard Oil Truck #73, w/driver, yel & gr w/red detail, 10½", NM...$650.00

Thrifty Tom's Jigger Bank, Black man dances on base, 10", EX, A...$2,100.00

Timber Truck, w/driver, litho tin w/C-style cab, missing stake pins & timber, 18½", EX.................................$650.00

Tip Top Dump Truck, w/driver, red & yel, 10", NM....$1,100.00

Tip Top Porter, 1925, Black man pushes 2-wheeled cart, 6½", EX (EX box)...$450.00

Tip Top Porter, 1925, Black man pushes 2-wheeled cart, 6½", VG...$250.00

Tombo the Alabama Coon Jigger, Black man dances atop base, litho tin, 10½", EX...$500.00

Trackless Trolley, red & yel, 14", VG.............................$175.00

Travelchiks, 1925, railroad car advances as chickens peck for food on top, 7½", NMIB, from $400 to...................$450.00

Trikauto What's It, #53, travels with crazy action, clown driver, NM (G box), A, $600.00.

Trikauto, 1920s, full-figure chauffeur, moves in erratic directions, Strauss name and logo on rear, 7" Long, EX , A, $450.00.

Water Sprinkler Truck #72, bl & yel w/red bumper & sprinkler bar, 10½", VG...$1,100.00

Yell-O-Taxi, w/driver, orange & blk w/disk wheels, rear spare, 7½", EX...$750.00

Structo

Pressed steel vehicles were made by Structo (Illinois) as early as 1920. They continued in business well into the 1960s, producing several army toys, trucks of all types, and firefighting and construction equipment.

Advisors: Kerry and Judy Irvin (K5).

Aerial Ladder Truck, mk SFD, red w/silver ladder, 35" L, EX ..$110.00

Airlines Traffic Control Truck, ride-on, wht w/blk lettering, 10x10x25½", EX...$105.00

Auto Transport Carrier, silver w/yel trailer, complete w/5 vehicles & loading ramp, EX.................................$155.00

Bearcat Racer, gr w/CI spoke wheels, 12", EX, A...........$825.00

Bearcat Roadster, 15" long, VG, A, $800.00.

Caterpillar Tractor, 12" long, EX, A, $650.00.

Caterpillar Tractor, 1921, red & gr, 9" L, VG.................$210.00

Communications Center Truck, complete, 20" L, EX $110.00

Deluxe Dumper & Sandloader, yel cab w/red bed, yel elevator w/red trough, EX...$85.00

Dump Truck, gr cab w/red dump bed, 23" L, VG...........$280.00

Dump Truck, red open cab w/blk rubber tires, battery-op headlights, 18", VG, A...$200.00

Farm Stake truck w/Horse Trailer, dk sea gr w/yel interior, wht
stakes on bed, EX..$130.00

Fire Truck, ca 1930s – '40s, 18" long, EX, $750.00.
(Photo courtesy Dunbar Gallery)

Freight Hauler, #935, bl truck w/silver trailer, EXIB.......$140.00

Hydraulic Dump Truck, #425, 1950s-60s, dk bl w/orange bed,
w/Pow-r-r-r Motor Sound, 13½", NMIB...................$160.00

Hydraulic Dump Truck, gr & orange w/blk rubber tires, 21", NM
(EX box), A $350.00

IGA Foodliners Tractor Trailer, bl cab w/wht trailer, 24" L,
EX $365.00

Livestock Trucking, 1960s, gr, EX $110.00

Machinery Hauler w/Steam Shovel, orange truck w/bl shovel,
EX $155.00

Mobil Communications Center Truck, No 270, bl w/2 telegraph
units, aerial cable & catalog, 19½", NMIB, A..........$350.00

Mobile Crane, yel w/blk lettering, EX..............................$85.00

North American Van Lines Tractor Trailer, red cab w/wht trailer
w/red lettering, 8x21", EX $90.00

Package Delivery Truck, wht cab w/orange bed, 12" L, NM $120.00

Studebaker Wrecker, 1930s, wht w/bl cab & boom, 21" L, VG...$200.00

Tank, WWI style, gr & red, clockwork, 12", VG, A.......$325.00

Truck Set No 725, complete, EX (worn box), A $300.00

Wrecker, #251, wht w/red removable top, fold-down windshield,
NMIB...$210.00

Wrecker, red w/wht tow hook, 24 Hour Service decal on sides,
15", NM, A $150.00

56 Gas Tanker, red cab w/yel tank, 13", EX.....................$80.00

Teddy Bears

The history of old teddy bears goes way back to about 1902
– 1903. Today's collectors often find it difficult to determine
exactly what company produced many of these early bears, but
fortunately for them, there are many excellent books now available that contain a wealth of information on those early makers.

Interest in teddy bears has been increasing at a fast pace,
and there are more and more collectors entering the market.
This has lead to an escalation in the values of the early bears.
Because most teddies were cherished childhood toys and were

usually very well loved, many that survive are well worn, so an
early bear in mint condition can be very valuable.

We would like to direct your attention to the books on the
market that are the most helpful on the detailed history and
identification of teddies. *Teddy Bear Treasury* by Ken Yenke;
Teddy Bears & Steiff Animals, 1st, 2nd, and *3rd Series,* by Margaret Fox Mandel; *A Collector's History of the Teddy Bear* by Patricia Schoonmaker; *Teddy Bears Past and Present* (*Volumes I and II*)
and *American Teddy Bear Encyclopedia* by Linda Mullins; *Teddy
Bears — A Complete Guide to History, Collecting, and Care,* by
Sue Pearson and Dottie Ayers; *Teddy Bear Encyclopedia* and *Ultimate Teddy Bear Book* by Pauline Cockrill; and *Big Bear Book* by
Dee Hockenberry. The reader can easily see that a wealth of
information exists and that it is impossible in a short column
such as this to give any kind of a definitive background. If you
intend to be a knowledgeable teddy bear collector, it is essential
that you spend time in study. Many of these books will be available at your local library or through dealers who specialize in
bears.

Advisor: Cynthia's Country Store, Cynthia Brintnall (C14).
See also Schuco; Steiff.

**28", golden mohair, glass eyes, fully jointed, excelsior stuff-
ing, American, 1907 – 09, VG, A, $6,300.00; 38", golden
mohair, glass eyes, excelsior stuffing, Ideal (possibly made as
window display), minor fur loss, fine moth damage on pads,
early twentieth century, from $7,000.00 to $9,000.00.**

9", wht mohair w/glass eyes, pearl cotton nose & mouth, fully
jtd, w/squeaker, unknown maker, 1940s, EX............$175.00

12", gold mohair w/shiny button eyes, excelsior stuffed, fully jtd,
Ideal, ca 1910, VG...$750.00

13", brn & wht cotton plush w/yel plastic heart-shaped eyes, not
jtd, Am, 1950, VG...$20.00

13", cream mohair w/blk shoe-button eyes, brn embroidered
nose, mouth & claws, fully jtd, Ideal, 1915, VG, A.$250.00

15", brn mohair w/shoe-button eyes, excelsior & kapok stuffing,
fully jtd, unknown maker, 1915, VG........................$375.00

15", gold mohair w/glass eyes, excelsior stuffing, fully jtd,
unknown maker, 1930s, EX.....................................$350.00

16", tan mohair w/amber glass eyes, excelsior & kapok stuffing,
fully jtd, w/squeaker, Chiltern, 1947, NM $325.00

17", yel mohair w/glass eyes, orig cotton romper, fully jtd, Ideal, 1920s, VG, A $225.00

18", copper mohair w/glass eyes, bl neck ribbon, excelsior stuffed, fully jtd, Bing, 1920s, M $8,000.00

18", tan mohair w/shoe-button eyes, excelsior stuffed, fully jtd, Ideal, 1903, EX $5,500.00

19", gold mohair w/glass eyes, excelsior stuffing w/beige felt pads, fully jtd, 1920s-30s, VG, A......................................$300.00

21", tan mohair w/glass eyes, fully jtd, orig pk ribbon, Am, 1908, NM, minimum value $450.00

22", brn curly mohair w/shoe-button eyes, web embroidered feet, fully jtd, Merrythought, 1890, EX $950.00

24", champagne mohair w/resin eyes, fully jtd, G, A......$250.00

24", frosted mohair w/rpl shoe-button eyes, excelsior stuffed, fully jtd, w/growler, Bing, 1920, NM....................$7,000.00

26", brn mohair w/amber glass eyes, excelsior stuffed head, kapok body, no jtd, Chiltern, 1960, VG $175.00

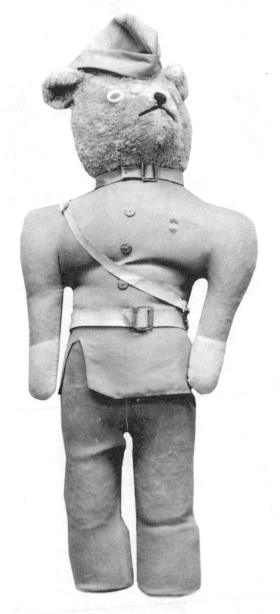

30", Teddy the Ace WWI Sweetheart, EX, from $1,200.00 to $1,600.00. (Photo courtesy Dunbar Gallery)

Tekno

The Tekno company was formed in Denmark during the late 1920s. The toy vehicles they made were of the highest quality, fully able to compete with the German-made Marklin toys then dominating the market. The earliest Tekno vehicles were made of tinplate, and though some were not marked at all, others were stamped with a number. The factory continued to expand until WWII broke out and restrictions made further building impossible. In 1940 the government prohibited the use of tinplate for toy production, and the company began instead to manufacture diecast vehicles in a smaller (1/43) scale. These were exported worldwide in great volume. Collectors regard them as the finest diecasts ever made. Due to climbing production costs and the resulting increases in retail prices that inevitably hurt their sales, the company closed in 1972. Tekno dies were purchased by Mercury Kirk Joal who used them to produce toys identical to the originals except for the mark.

#356A, Porsche, from $150.00 to $175.00.
(Photo courtesy Continental Hobby House)

#127, Mercedes 180, MIB..$235.00

#410, Firestone VW Truck, red & wht, NM....................$165.00

#410, Philips VW Van Taxi, MIB $195.00

#425/#542, Volvo F89 6 Wheel Rigid Covered Truck & Drawbar Trailer, ASG logos, NM (EX boxes)...........................$75.00

#442, Vespa Scooter De Luxe 125, NMIB $110.00

#488, Ambulance Aircraft, 8" wingspan, NM $200.00

#724, Opel Kadette, cream w/red interior, MIB................$95.00

#731-32, Mercedes 220 Ambulance, EX $95.00

#810, Volvo Amazon Police Car, M (G box, 1 end flap missing)..$155.00

#812, Cooper Norton #1, silver, NM $135.00

#828, VW 1500, MIB $105.00

#829, Lincoln Continental, silver w/red interior, MIB $80.00

#834R, 1966 Ford Mustang Rally, M (EX box) $75.00

#851, Scania CR76 City Bus Air France, NM (G window box).$70.00

#950, Mercedes 0302 Coach Arkereizen Bus, M (EX box) ..$65.00

Telephones

Novelty phones representing a well-known advertising or cartoon character are proving to be the focus of a lot of collector activity — the more recognizable the character the better. Telephones modeled after a product container are collectible too, and with the intense interest currently being shown in anything advertising related, competition is sometimes stiff and values are rising.

Advisor: Bill Bruegman (T2).

Alvin (Alvin & the Chipmunks), 1984, MIB..................$50.00
Bart Simpson, Columbia, 1990s, 3-D figure, eyes flash as phone rings, M, K1 ....$30.00
Batmobile, Columbia, 1990, MIB, from $25 to.................$35.00
Beavis & Butthead, EX (EX box) $18.00
Care Bears, purple, intercom system only, 1983, MIB.......$50.00

Garfield, eyes open when receiver is lifted, EX, $40.00.

Crest Toothpaste's Gelman, EX, $30.00.

Dale Earnhardt, #3 Goodwrench car, headlights flash when phone rings, 9x3½", MIB $60.00
Flintstones, gray body w/red horn-shaped handset, 5-hole dial, early 1960s, EX $80.00
Ghostbusters, wht ghost inside red circle, receiver across center, Remco, 1987, EX $20.00
Jeff Gordon, race car style, Columbia Tel-Com, MIB.......$25.00
John Force's Castrol GTX Funny Car, Columbia Tel-Com, 9x3½", EX...$35.00
Opus the Penguin, receiver locks into back, Tyco, 1987, 14", EX $60.00
Power Rangers, NM $25.00

Raid Bug, from $90.00 to $100.00. (Photo courtesy Martin and Carolyn Berens)

Roy Rogers, 1950s, plastic wall-type, 9x9", EX, A7 ....$50.00
R2-D2 (Star Wars), top spins when phone rings, 12" $35.00
Snoopy & Woodstock, American Telecommunications Corp, Disney, hi/low volume switch underneath, 1976, EX..$65.00
Spiderman, REC Sound, 1994, M (EX box) $30.00
Star Trek Enterprise, 1993, NM.......................................$25.00

Tonka

Since the mid-'40s, the Tonka Company (Minnesota) has produced an extensive variety of high-quality painted metal trucks, heavy equipment, tractors, and vans.

Our values are for items with the original paint. A repainted item is worth much less.

AAA Wrecker, wht, w/tow boom & emergency light, prof rstr, 12", A..$200.00

Ace Stores Delivery Truck, 1954, M.....................$600.00

Airport Service Set, complete, EX (EX box), A.............$650.00

Allied Van Lines Tractor Trailer, orange w/blk rubber tires, 1960s, 24", VG, A...$200.00

Allied Van Lines Truck, #1089, 1962, 16", NMIB, A.....$150.00

Army Jeep, mk GR 2-2431, gr, 11", EX, A......................$150.00

Big Mike State Highway Dept Dump Truck w/V Plow, orange, 1958, EX...$500.00

Builders Supply Fleet, #0875-5, lumber truck w/lumber, interchangable bed & step-side pickup, 1955, NM (VG box)................$2,000.00

Car Carrier, #3990, complete, MIB.......................$675.00

Cement Truck, red w/wht rotating drum on bk, blk rubber tires, NM...$145.00

COE Allied Van Lines Truck, G.....................................$125.00

COE Low Boy & Shovel, M..$200.00

Construction Set, #822, complete, MIB.....................$100.00

Dragline Crane, yel w/blk bucket, 1959, NM (EX box).$500.00

Dump Truck, #406, red cab w/gr bed, 1963, MIB...........$300.00

Fire Department Set, w/hook & ladder truck, ambulance van, pumper, chief van & rescue truck, MIB...................$125.00

Fire Jeep, #425, 1963-64, M...$300.00

Fire Truck #5, red, w/grab bar, threaded hose fittings & hydrant, 1957, NM...$425.00

Frederick & Nelson Delivery Truck, gr w/opening doors, 23", VG, A..$500.00

Golf Club Tractor, orange w/blk seat, steering wheel & tires, 12", EX, A..$135.00

Hydraulic Dump Truck No 2480, bl w/wht cab roof, 14", EX (EX box), A..$125.00

Jeep Dispatcher, #200, turq, NM (NM box)................$150.00

Marshall Field & Co Delivery Truck, gr Ford-style w/opening rear doors, 23", VG, A..$400.00

MFD Aerial Ladder Truck, #700, mk No 5 on doors, 1954, NM...$400.00

Mobile Clam Truck, 24", VG, A................................$250.00

Outdoor Living Set #2142, complete w/camper truck, farm truck, jeep & boat, NM (VG box), A...................$1,000.00

Parcel Delivery Van, red w/wht lettering, 1950s, EX......$600.00

Pick-up Truck, #50, Mini-Tonka series, 9", NMIB, A.......$75.00

Pickup Truck & Utility Trailer, bl, 20", VG, A..............$200.00

Ramp Hoist & Loader, #2992, complete, MIB...............$350.00

Road Grader, orange w/blk rubber tires, bl plastic light on top, VG, A...$85.00

Ser-Vi-Car, wht w/red seat & decal, 9", EX, A...............$75.00

Stake Truck w/Tandem Platform, #30, 1959, M............$375.00

Standard Wrecker, 1961, rare, NM.............................$600.00

State Hi-Way Dept Dump Truck, orange w/blk rubber tires, 18", VG, A...$100.00

State Hi-Way Dept Hydraulic Dump Truck, dk gr w/blk rubber tires, working, 16", soiled/pnt chips overall, A.........$85.00

State Hi-Way Dept Hydraulic Land Rover, #42, 1959, rare, MIB..$1,300.00

State Hi-Way Dept Steam Shovel, orange w/yel decals, blk rubber tires, 1950s, 28", EX, A.................................$500.00

State Hi-Way Dump Truck, red w/blk rubber tires, 13", minor pnt chips, o/w VG, A......................................$135.00

Steam Shovel, orange & bl, 1950s, 20", G-, A...............$50.00

Steel Carrier, orange with green bed, black rubber tires, 24", EX, A, $150.00.

Jeep Surrey, pink with fringed striped top, 10½", EX, A, $125.00.

Jet Delivery Truck, wht & lt turq, 1962, NM..................$265.00

Livestock Truck, red w/blk rubber tires, 1950s, 24", EX+, A...$275.00

Loader, #3920, yel, 1972, NM (VG box).........................$95.00

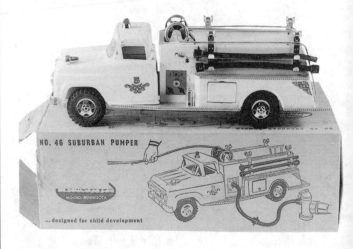

Suburban Pumper #46, white with black rubber tires, MIB, $425.00. (Photo courtesy Continental Hobby House)

tock Rack Truck w/Animals, 1957, 16", complete, EX ...**$350.00**
uburban Fire Pumper #46, 1960s, 18", EX (EX box), A..**$350.00**
FD Aerial Ladder Truck, red w/NP hydraulic ladders, 1950s,
    33", VG, A...**$200.00**
hunderbird Express Semi, #37, 1960, MIB **$600.00**
onka Farms Stake Truck w/Horse Trailer, #35, 1959, NM **$350.00**
onka Toy Transport Van, #140, 1949, EX **$275.00**
roop Carrier, #380, 1964, 14", NM **$200.00**
Vilson Semi, red cab w/yel trailer, 1953, rare, EX.......**$1,000.00**
Vrecker, #250, 1953, EX...**$250.00**

Toothbrush Holders

Figural ceramic toothbrush holders have become very popu-
ar collectibles, especially those modeled after well-known car-
oon characters. Disney's Mickey Mouse, Donald Duck, and the
hree Little Pigs are among the most desirable, and some of the
arder-to-find examples in mint condition sell for upwards of
200.00. Many were made in Japan before WWII. Because the
aint was not fired on, it is often beginning to flake off. Be sure
o consider the condition of the paint as well as the bisque when
valuating your holdings. For more information we recommend
ictorial Guide to Toothbrush Holders by Marilyn Cooper. Plate
umbers in the following listings refer to Marilyn's book.

Advisor: Marilyn Cooper (C9).

ndy Gump & Min, Japan, bsk, plate #221, 4", from $85 to..**$100.00**
nnie Oakley, Japan, plate #11, 5¾", from $100 to.......**$145.00**
aby Deer, mk Brush Teeth Daily, Japan, plate #12, 4", from
    $110 to...**$140.00**
ear w/Scarf & Hat, Japan, plate #16, 5½", from $80 to..**$95.00**
ig Bird, Taiwan (RCC), plate #263, 4½", from $80 to ...**$90.00**
onzo w/Sidetray, Germany, plate #23, 5⅝", from $135 to ..**$150.00**
oy in Top Hat, Japan, plate #29, 5½", from $75 to.........**$95.00**
oy w/Violin, Japan (Goldcastle), plate #30, 5½" **$80.00**
andlestick Maker, Japan (Goldcastle), plate #150, 5", from $70
    to **$85.00**
at (Calico), Japan, plate #37, 5½", from $90 to...........**$110.00**
at on Pedestal, Japan (Diamond T), plate, #225, 6", from $150
    to **$175.00**
ircus Elephant, Japan, plate #56, from $85 to **$100.00**
lown Holding Mask, Japan, plate #62, 5½", from $110 to ..**$150.00**
lown Juggling, Japan, plate #60, 5", from $75 to **$90.00**

Calico dogs, Japan, from $55.00 to $70.00.
(Photo courtesy Carol Bess White)

Dachshund, Japan, plate #71, 5¼", from $80 to **$120.00**
Doctor w/Satchel, Japan, plate #206, 5¾" **$90.00**
Dog w/Basket, Japan, plate #72, from $90 to **$100.00**
Donald Duck, WDE, bsk, plate #83, 5", from $250 to **$300.00**
Dutch Boy & Girl Kissing, Japan, plate #88, 6", from $55 to...**$65.00**
Flapper, plate #230, 4¼", from $110 to **$130.00**
Indian Chief, Japan, plate #115, 4½", from $225 to.......**$275.00**
Little Orphan Annie & Sandy Seated on Couch, Japan, plate
    #267, 3¾", from $110 to...**$135.00**
Little Red Riding Hood, Germany (DRGM), plate #210, 5½",
    from $200 to **$225.00**
Mary Poppins, Japan, plate #119, 6"...............................**$150.00**
Mickey Mouse, Donald Duck & Minnie, Japan/WDE, plate
    #121, 4½", from $300 to...**$375.00**
Old King Cole, Japan, plate #125, 5¼", from $85 to......**$100.00**
Old Mother Hubbard, Germany, plate #3, 6", from $350 to ...**$410.00**
Pinocchio & Figaro, Shafford, plate #242, 5", from $500 to....**$525.00**
Pluto, Japan, plate #133, 4½", from $300 to...................**$350.00**
Skippy, plate #245, jtd arms, 5⅝" **$100.00**
Three Bears w/Bowls, Japan (KIM USUI), plate #248, 4", from
    $90 to...**$125.00**
Tom, Tom the Piper's Son, Japan, plate #154, 5¾", from $95
    to **$125.00**
Traffic Cop, Germany, Don't Forget the Teeth, plate #243, 5",
    from $350 to **$375.00**

Tootsietoys

The first diecast Tootsietoys were made by the Samuel
Dowst Company in 1906 when they reproduced the Model T
Ford in miniature. Dowst merged with Cosmo Manufacturing in

1926 to form the Dowst Manufacturing Company and continued to turn out replicas of the full-scale vehicles in actual use at the time. After another merger in 1961, the company became known as the Stombecker Corporation. Over the years, many types of wheels and hubs were utilized, varying in both style and material. The last all-metal car was made in 1969; recent Tootsietoys mix plastic components with the metal and have soft plastic wheels. Early prewar mint-in-box toys are scarce and command high prices on today's market.

For more information, we recommend *Collector's Guide to Tootsietoys, 2nd Edition,* by David Richter (Collector Books).

Advisors: Kerry and Judy Irvin (K5).

American Railway Express, #4670, 1929-32, yel cab w/gr trailer, 4", EX, from $85 to $125.00

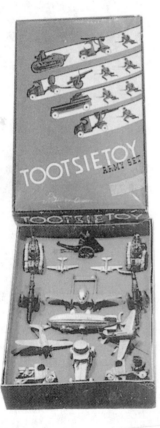

Army Set #5220, complete, EX (EX box), A, $500.00. (Photo courtesy New England Auction Gallery)

Auto Transport Hauler, #190, 1930s, w/3 cars, 8⅜" L, VG+...$135.00
Autogyro Airplane, #4659, tan, VG+ $95.00
Bild-A-Truck Set, #7600, complete, VG (VG box), A ..$150.00
Boat Transport Tractor Trailer w/Boats, 1969, maroon cab w/yel trailer, wht & bl boats (2), MIP.................................$70.00
Box Van, #1010, 1940s, red, NM.................................$70.00
Buck Rogers 25th Century Battle Cruiser, #1031, yel & red, 5", MIB, A..$650.00
Buck Rogers 25th Century Destroyer, #1032, 1937, wht & bl, 5", MIB, from $400 to.......................................$500.00
Car & Boat w/Trailer, Tee-Nee, bl car w/yel trailer, brn & wht boat, EX (VG box) $70.00
Coast to Coast Van, 1947, red & silver, 9", NM (G box), A ..$125.00
Doodlebug, #716, 1935, gr, EX $195.00
Federal Grocery Van, #4630, 1924-29, NM $130.00

Federal Milk Truck, #4634, complete, EX.....................$130.00
Fire Department, #5211, complete, NM (NM box), A ..$600.00
Fire Department, #5211, EX (VG+ box) $260.00
Ford Coupe, #0112, 1935, NM $60.00
Graham Commercial Tire & Supply Company Van, 1935, rare EX $270.00
Graham 5-Wheeled Coupe, #514, red, 4", EX...............$135.00

Graham Six-Wheel Town Car #0616, blue and black, M $150.00. (Photo courtesy David E. Richter)

Greyhound Scenicruiser, 7", EX (G box), A...................$175.00
HO Sport Set, #4110, NMIB.....................................$120.00
IH Army Military Missile Launcher Semi, olive drab, NM..$235.00
Interchangeable Truck Set, 1940s, complete, EX (EX box) A $300.00
International K11 Sinclair Oil Truck, 1949, 6", NM......$110.00
Land & Air Set, #3198, 8 pcs, VG (G box)..................$105.00
LeSalle Sedan, gr, all orig, 4", EX $170.00
Lincoln Zephyr, #6015, lime gr, windup (missing key), 4" EX $440.00
Logging Truck, #569, red cab, complete w/logs, 9" L, MIB...$160.00
Logging Truck, #569, red, complete w/6 logs, 9", NM (G box) A $135.00
Long Distance Hauling Mack, #0803, complete, NM $190.00
Mack A&P Truck, #4670, 1929-32, red, 4", VG $110.00
Mack Anti-Aircraft Gun Truck, #4643, EX $80.00
Mack Contractor Set, truck & 3 side-tipping trailers, gr truck body w/orange trailers, 4-pc set 12¼", EX $175.00
Mack Express Semi-Trailer w/Stake Bed, 1935-41, orange, 5½" EX..$75.00
Mack Long Distance Hauling Semi-Trailer, #803, EX....$130.00
Mack Railway Express Truck, #810, 1932, Wrigley's Chewin Gum decal, EX...$145.00
Mack US Mail Airmail Service Truck, #4645, 1940s, EX...$115.00
Mercedes Benz 300SL Gull-wing, #995, 1956-58, gr (rare color) 7", EX..$270.00
Mercedes Benz 300SL Gull-wing, #995, 1956-58, red, EX (E box), A...$150.00
Mercedes Benz 300SL Gull-wing, #995, 1956-58, red, 7" EX..$80.00
Metro Parcel Service Truck, lt bl, EX..........................$165.00
Model A Ford US Mail Truck, 1930s, gr w/yel trim, blk USA Mail lettering, EX...$70.00
Motors Set, #7200, complete, MIB, A $875.00
Navy Jet, 1970s, red, NM $12.0

Oil Tanker, 1947, red, 9", EX (EX box), A $125.00
Overland Buslines, #4680, EX $60.00
P-39 Fighter, 1940s-50s, silver w/red wings, 5¼" wingspan, 4½"
    L, EX $210.00
Road Construction Assortment, #6000, complete, NM (EX
    box), A...$400.00
Road Roller, 1930s, red & blk, 3", EX.............................$175.00
Rocket Launcher, #3925, dk gr Army truck w/red, wht & bl
    rocket, EX (G box)...$175.00
Rol-ezy Vehicle Set, complete, NM (NM box), A $450.00
Safari Hunt, #1463, 1968, MIB $95.00

Set #5149, nine vehicles with insert, NM (NM box), A,
$350.00; Set #4600, prewar, rare items with box insert, M
(NM box), A, $675.00.

Shell Oil Tanker, #1009, 1938, 6", NM $175.00
Smitty Delivery Wagon, motorcycle w/sidecar, 1933, 3" L,
    EX..$200.00
Sunoco Oil Tanker, #669, red, 9" L, MIB......................$150.00

Texaco Oil Truck, #1008, 1939 – 1941, EX, $60.00.
(Photo courtesy David E. Richter)

Township School Bus, 1960s, yellow and black with silver
grille, HO series, scarce, NM, $40.00. (Photo courtesy David E. Richter)

Tri-Motor Plane, red w/silver props, 5¼" wingspan, 3⅝" L,
    EX..$140.00

Truck w/Lowboy Trailer, red, 11" L, EX..........................$110.00
Woody Car, #1045, 1940s, brn & yel, EX $180.00
1949 Shell Oil Tanker, yel, 6", VG...................................$65.00

Tops and Other Spinning Toys

Tops are among the oldest toys in human history. Homer in
The Iliad, Plato in the *Republic*, and Virgil in *The Aeneid* mention
tops. They are found in nearly all cultures, ancient and modern.

There are seven major categories: 1) the twirler — spun by
the twisting action of fingers upon the axis. Examples are Teeto-
tums, Dreidels, advertising spinners, and Tippe Tops. 2) the supported top — started with a string while the top is supported
upright. These include 'recuperative,' having a string that automatically rewinds (Namurs); 'seperative,' with a top that
detaches from the launcher; 'spring launched,' which is spun
using a wound spring; 'pump' or 'helix,' whereby a twisted rod is
pumped to spin the top; and 'flywheel-' or 'inertia wheel-pow-
ered.' 3) the peg top — spun by winding a string around the peg
of the top which is then thrown. 4) the whip top — which is
kept spinning by the use of a whip. 5) the yo-yo or return top. 6)
the gyroscope. 7) the Diavuolo or Diabolo.

Advisor: Bruce Middleton (M20).

**See also Character, TV, and Movie Collectibles; Chein,
Miscellaneous; Political; Yo-yos.**

Early supported wooden top, from $50.00 to $75.00.
(Photo courtesy Bruce Middleton)

Air Powered, Cracker Jack, Dowsy, Chicago, red, wht & bl, M ..$16.00
Air Powered, Poll Parrot Shoes, yel, NM $16.00
Aladdin Ball & Top, early 1900s, helix rod powered, EX (EX
    box), M20 ....$550.00
Archimeds Flying Top Mars (advertised as New Boomerang),
    Lehman, 5 blades propel on swivel bar, 8½", EX.....$200.00
Autogyro Horse Race, Britains, lead & wire, flywheel mecha-
    nism, w/4 jockeys on horses, 11" L, EX.................$1,000.00

Circus Horse & Rider, lead w/wire & tin, horse & female rider on rods attached to base, 7", VG............................$375.00

Competition Award Patches, top shape, 1st, 2nd, & 3rd, M, ea...$50.00

Dancing Couple, Ives, japanned & polychromed CI, w/arms entwined, she in lead bell-shaped skirt, 3½", EX.....$135.00

Disk, maroon & red wood flat-top w/natural wood holder, 3½" dia, EX..$45.00

Disk, red & natural wood w/gr stripes, w/hdl, 4" dia, EX ..$75.00

Game, Big Top, Marx, plastic, battery-op, MIB $35.00

Game, Brownie Kick-In, MH Miller, litho tin w/Brownies, top kicks ball into indentions for score, VG (G box) $50.00

Game, Double Diablos, Parker Bros, 1930s, EX (EX box)...$60.00

Game, Voyage Around the World Gyro-Aero, France, complete, EX (EX box) $500.00

Gyro-Cycle Top, British, boy rides circular track, EX (EX box) $600.00

Hummer, German, litho tin, clown-head knob w/wooden hat, 8", VG...$575.00

Hummer, inverted wood beehive-shape w/mc stripes, 2½" dia, VG $415.00

Hummer, wht celluloid ball w/mc stripes, 7", EX............$415.00

Merry-Go-Round, 2 figures spiral down rod, tin & wood, 12", EX $200.00

Namur, wooden ball w/brass string housing, EX................$20.00

Peg Top, Duncan Chicago Twister, #329, wood, MIP.......$20.00

Peg Top, Duncan Tournament, #349, wood, MIP.............$20.00

Peg Top, Duncan Twin Spin, #310, wood, MIP $20.00

Peg Top, Duncan Whistler, #320, MIP..............................$20.00

Peg Top, Helix Rod Launcher, advertises Kinney Shoes, VG...$15.00

Recuperative, natural wood w/pnt stripes, wood string housing, EX, from $75 to $100.00

Recuperative, wood, 6-sided string housing over ovoid body, G $85.00

Spinner, Alemite Motor Oil, Bakelite, Keep Your Car Running Like a Top, NM...$25.00

Spinner, Brown-Bilt Shoes, Buster Brown, blk & red letters on yel background w/red trim, EX $45.00

Spinner, Cracker Jack, M, from $45 to $75.00

Spinner, man w/mug of beer, Hven Betaler on hat, litho tin, spin to see who pays, NM..$85.00

Spinner, Nolde's American Made Breads & Cakes, red & wht, NM...$30.00

Spinner, OTC Trenton Oyster Crackers, bl letters on wht, M...$50.00

Spinner, Robin Hood Shoes, M, from $45 to....................$75.00

Spinner, shaped like a pointing spaniel, Heads I Win, Tails You Lose, NM $25.00

Spinner, Tastykake Cakes & Pies, M, from $45 to...........$75.00

Spinner, Tip Top Bread, plastic, NM................................$10.00

Supported, pressed board disk w/graphics of boy shooting a toy gun, M $60.00

Supported, Rainbow, Seneca, pnt metal w/4 tooth disks inside lg disk rotating around shaft, changes color, NM..........$65.00

Supported Top, Winner Spinner, Bakelite, NMOC, M20 ....$50.00

Tip Tray, Canada Dry, dimple in center to spin on, G $20.00

Tip Tray, SS Pierce, Wine & Spirits Merchants..., dimple in center to spin on, M $60.00

Trading Cards

Modern collector cards are really just an extension of a hobby that began well before the turn of the century. Advertising cards put out by the food and tobacco companies of that era sometimes featured cute children, their pets, stage stars, battle scenes, presidential candidates, and so forth. Collectors gathered them up and pasted them in scrapbooks.

In the twentieth century, candy and bubble gum companies came to the forefront. The cards they issue with their products carry the likenesses of sports figures, fictional heroes, TV and movie stars, Disney characters, Barbie dolls, and country singers!

Distinguishing a collectible trading card from other cards may be a bit confusing. Remember, trading cards are released in only two ways: 1) in a wax or foil pack, generally in multiples of twelve — twenty-four, thirty-six, or forty-eight; or 2) as a premium with another product. The only exception to this rule are sets issued as limited editions, with each set individually numbered. Cards issued as factory sets are not trading cards and have no collector value unless they cross over into another collecting area, for example, the Tuff Stuff Norma Jean (Marilyn Monroe) series. In general, from 1980 to the present, wrappers tend to fall into the 50¢ to $2.00 range, though there are some exceptions. For more information we recommend *Collector's Guide to Trading Cards* by Robert Reed.

Advisors: Mark and Val Macaluso (M1).

Ratchet Ballerina, Marx, NM, from $125.00 to $150.00.
(Photo courtesy Bruce Middleton)

Charlie's Angels, Topps, 1977, set of 66 w/11 stickers $50.00

Happy Days, Topps, 1976, 1st series, set of 44 w/11 stickers, from $40 to $50.00
Marvel Super Heroes, Donruss, 1966, set of 66..............$125.00
Marvel Super Heroes, Philadelphia Gum Corp, 1966, set of 55 stickers $400.00
Mod Squad, Topps, 1968, set of 55..................................$150.00
Partridge Family, Topps, 1971, 1st series, set of 55 ....$75.00
Simpsons, Topps, 1990, set of 88 w/22 stickers $20.00
Six Million Dollar Man, Donruss, 1975, set of 66 stickers ..$75.00
Starsky & Hutch, Monty Gum, 1970s, set of 72, from $250 to...$300.00
Superman, Topps, 1966, set of 66..................................$300.00
Zorro, Topps, 1958, set of 39 ....$160.00

Trains

Some of the earliest trains (from ca 1860) were made of tin or cast iron, smaller versions of the full-scale steam-powered trains that transversed America from the east to the west. Most were made to simply be pushed or pulled along, though some had clockwork motors. Electric trains were produced as early as the late nineteenth century. Three of the largest manufacturers were Lionel, Ives, and American Flyer.

Lionel trains have been made since 1900. Until 1915 they produced only standard gauge models (measuring 2½" between the rails). The smaller O gauge (1¼") they introduced at that time proved to be highly successful, and the company grew until by 1955 it had become the largest producer of toys in the world. Until discontinued in 1940, standard gauge trains were produced on a limited scale, but O and 027 gauge models dominated the market. Production dwindled and nearly stopped in the mid-1960s, but the company was purchased by General Mills in 1969, and they continue to produce a very limited number of trains today.

The Ives company had been a major producer of toys since 1896. They were the first to initiate manufacture of the O gauge train and at first used only clockwork motors to propel them. Their first electric trains (in both O and #1 gauge) were made in 1910, but because electricity was not yet a common commodity in many areas, clockwork production continued for several years. By 1920, #1 gauge was phased out in favor of standard gauge. The company continued to prosper until the late 1920s when it floundered and was bought jointly by American Flyer and Lionel. American Flyer soon turned their interest over to Lionel, who continued to make Ives trains until 1933.

The American Flyer company had produced trains for several years, but it wasn't until it was bought by AC Gilbert in 1937 that it became successful enough to be considered a competitor of Lionel. They're best noted for their conversion from the standard (wide gauge) three-rail system to the two-rail S gauge (⅞") and the high-quality locomotives, passenger, and freight cars they produced in the 1950s. Interest in toy trains waned during the space-age decade of the 1960s. As a result, sales declined, and in 1966 the company was purchased by Lionel. Today both American Flyer and Lionel trains are being made from the original dies by Lionel Trains Inc., privately owned.

For more information we recommend *Collecting Toy Trains, An Identification and Value Guide*, by Richard O'Brien.

Advisor: Gary Mosholder (G1).

See also Buddy L (for that company's Outdoor Railroad); **Cast Iron, Trains; Paper-Lithographed Toys**.

American Flyer

Accessory, #102 passenger station, VG (VG box), A.....$500.00
Accessory, #104 Kenilworth station, EX (EX box), A.......$425.00

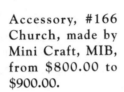

Accessory, #166 Church, made by Mini Craft, MIB, from $800.00 to $900.00.

Accessory, #581 girder bridge, NMIB, A.........................$100.00
Accessory, #585 tool shed, VG (VG box), A..................$150.00
Accessory, #586E wayside station, VG (VG box), A........$150.00
Accessory, #596 water tank, VG (VG box), A $300.00
Accessory, #755 talking station, VG (VG box) $250.00
Accessory, #779 oil drum loader, VG (VG box), A.......$300.00
Accessory, #2020 water tank, VG (VG box), A $375.00
Accessory, #2116 crossing signal, VG (VG box), A $400.00
Accessory, #23750 trestle bridge, EX (VG box), A $175.00
Car, #484 10th Anniversary caboose, NM......................$100.00
Car, #615 auto unloader/Manoil, EX.............................$100.00
Car, #631 T&P gondola, gr, EX $40.00
Car, #632 Lehigh hopper, gray, EX $40.00
Car, #633 boxcar, red, EX $50.00
Car, #640 hopper, gray, EX..$40.00
Car, #751 lumber loader, VG (worn box) $175.00
Car, #779 oil drum loader, NMIB..................................$150.00
Car, #815 auto unloader/Manoil, EX..............................$100.00
Car, #905 log car, M..$70.00

Car, #907 wrecker caboose, M $75.00
Car, #909 steel girder, EX..$65.00
Car, #4006 hopper, red, EX (EX box).............................$450.00
Car, #4011 caboose, red & brn, VG (VG box).................$275.00
Car, #24039 Rio Grande Cookie boxcar, EX $175.00
Car, #24309 Gulf tank car, EX..$75.00
Car, #24603 caboose, EX $45.00

Car, AF Lines Air Service, yellow on blue platform, brass railing, MIB, A, $2,000.00.

Loco, #1201, VG, A $175.00
Loco, #3115, bl, G, A..$200.00
Loco & Tender, #312, VG, A...$125.00
Loco & Tender, #325AC, steam powered, G, A.............$200.00
Loco & Tender, #332, steam powered, G, A..................$375.00

Set, 0-4-0 #4678 locomotive and three passenger coaches: #4040, #4041, and #4042; red with brass trim and inner and outer boxes, M, A, $2,000.00.

Set, #1090 Empire Express, w/loco & 3 cars, VG, A $300.00
Set, #1090 Nationwide Lines, w/loco & 3 cars, EX, A ...$1,100.00
Set, #20767 The Eagle, complete, NM (EX box), A..$4,675.00
Set, Golden State, w/loco, tender & 3 cars, VG, A........$275.00
Set, Little Hiawatha, w/loco, tender & 4 cars, VG, A....$300.00
Set, Potomac, w/loco & 3 cars, EX, A............................$450.00
Set, Statesman, w/loco, tender & 2 cars, bright orange w/brass trim, complete, EX (EX boxes), A $2,100.00

LIONEL MODERN ERA 1970 – 96

Accessory, #2127 horn shack, diesel, EX, G1 ....$25.00
Accessory, #2316 gantry crane, remote control, MIB, G1 ....$125.00
Accessory, #3360 burro crane, MIB, A.............................$100.00
Accessory, #4060 transformer, EX, G1 ....$40.00
Accessory, #4250 transformer, 50 watts, EX, G1 ....$25.00
Accessory, #12723 microwave tower, EX (EX box), G1 ...$20.00
Accessory, #12862 oil drum loader, EX (EX box), G1 ......$95.00
Accessory, #12937 Norfolk intermodal crane, EX (EX box), G1 ....$185.00
Car, #52 fire car, MIB, A $75.00
Car, #397 coal loader, EX (EX box), A $50.00
Car, #782 Lionel Railroader club car, M, G1 ....$35.00
Car, #784 Lionel Railroader club car, MIB, G1..................$55.00
Car, #5721 Soo Line reefer, EX (EX box), G1 ....$20.00
Car, #5739 B&O tool car, EX (EX box), G1 ....$30.00
Car, #6104 Southern quad hopper w/load, EX (EX box), G1 ..$45.00
Car, #6123 Pennsylvania covered hopper, MIB, A $45.00
Car, #6138 B&O hopper, EX (EX box), G1 ....$25.00
Car, #6307 Pennsylvania tank car, MIB, A $50.00
Car, #6449 Wendy's Hamburgers caboose, MIB, A............$25.00
Car, #6530 Fire & Safety training car, NMIB, A $40.00
Car, #6800 flat car w/airplane, MIB, A $200.00
Car, #6908 Pennsylvania caboose, MIB, A $50.00
Car, #7404 Jersey Central boxcar, NM (NM box), G1 .....$45.00
Car, #7518 Carson City mint car, MIB, G1 ....$35.00
Car, #7904 giraffe car, NMIB, A.......................................$35.00
Car, #8469 Canadian Pacific F-3 B, MIB, A....................$165.00
Car, #8474 Denver & Rio Grande F-3 B, NM, A $50.00
Car, #8912 LCAC Canadian Southern club car, VG (VG box), G1 ....$125.00
Car, #9054 JC Penney boxcar, M, G1 ....$12.00
Car, #9157 flat car w/construction crane kit, NMIB, A....$35.00
Car, #9158 flat car w/steam shovel, NMIB, A...................$35.00
Car, #9160 Illinois Central N5C caboose, EX, G1 ....$25.00
Car, #9162 Pennsylvania caboose, porthole-type, EX, G1 ....$30.00
Car, #9193 Budweiser vat carrier, NMIB, A......................$50.00
Car, #9226 Delaware & Hudson flat car, EX (EX box), G1 .....$35.00
Car, #9229 Express Mail boxcar, MIB, G1 ....$30.00
Car, #9232 Allis-Chalmers flat car, EX, G1 ....$25.00
Car, #9307 Erie animated gondola, MIB, G1 ....$50.00
Car, #9338 Pennsylvania Power & Light hopper, EX (EX box), G1 ....$100.00
Car, #9349 San Francisco mint car, MIB, G1 ....$115.00
Car, #9742 Minneapolis & St Louis freight car, MIB, A $50.00
Car, #9785 Conrail boxcar, EX (EX box), G1 ....$25.00
Car, #9864 TCA Seattle club car, M, G1............................$22.00
Car, #9867 Hershey billboard reefer, NMIB, A.................$35.00
Car, #9877 Gerber Baby Food reefer, NMIB, A $35.00
Car, #16235 Railway Express Agency reefer, EX (EX box), G1 ....$25.00
Car, #16322 Sealand Trailers flat car, EX (EX box), G1 ...$75.00
Car, #16323 Lionel Lines flat car w/trailers, MIB, G1 ......$25.00
Car, #16324 Pennsylvania Railroad depressed flat car w/reels, EX (EX box), G1 ....$18.00
Car, #16368 MKT liquid oxygen flat car, EX (EX box), G1 ..$25.00

Car, #16371 Burl North I-Beam flat car w/load, EX (EX box), G1 ....$40.00

Car, #16515 Lionel Lines Railscope caboose, EX (EX box), G1 ....$25.00

Car, #16640 Rutland boxcar, w/diesel rail sounds, MIB, G1 ..$125.00

Car, #16800 Lionel Railroader club car, MIB, G1 ....$55.00

Car, #16803 Lionel Railroader searchlight car, MIB, G1 ..$35.00

Car, #16933 flat car w/autos, MIB, G1 ....$30.00

Car, #16983 Pennsylvania Railroad F-9 well car, EX (EX box), G1 ....$25.00

Car, #17225 Pennsylvania Central boxcar, EX (EX box), G1..$30.00

Car, #17306 Pacific Fruit Express reefer, EX (EX box), G1 ..$30.00

Car, #17403 Chessie gondola w/coil covers, EX (EX box), G1 ..$35.00

Car, #17405 Reading gondola w/coil covers, EX (EX box), G1 ....$25.00

Car, #17518 Pennsylvania flat car w/2 Mack trucks, EX (EX box), G1..$35.00

Car, #17605 Reading caboose, MIB, G1 ....$30.00

Car, #17881 TTOS Phelps Dodge club car, MIB, G1 ....$30.00

Car, #17900 Santa Fe unibody tank car, MIB, G1 ....$40.00

Car, #17901 Chevron unibody tank car, EX (EX box), G1..$28.00

Car, #17906 SCM unibody tank car, EX (EX box), G1 ....$28.00

Car, #18401 handcar, orange, diesel, MIB, G1..................$40.00

Car, #19203 Detroit-Toledo boxcar, MIB, G1...................$20.00

Car, #19246 Disney boxcar, MIB, G1.................................$45.00

Car, #19303 Lionel Lines quad hopper, MIB, G1 ....$25.00

Car, #19311 Southern Pacific covered hopper, MIB, G1..$25.00

Car, #19404 Western Maryland caboose, w/smoke, MIB, A ..$50.00

Car, #19411 NKP flat car w/Sears trailer, EX (EX box), G1 ...$45.00

Car, #19419 Charlotte mint car, M, G1 ....$28.00

Car, #19506 Thomas Newcomer boxcar, MIB, G1 ....$20.00

Car, #19508 Leonardo DeVinci boxcar, MIB, G1 ....$20.00

Car, #19602 Johnsons tank car, MIB, G1 ....$33.00

Car, #19656 Milwaukee Road bunk car, MIB, G1 ....$25.00

Car, #19703 caboose, MIB, A..$35.00

Car, #19939 1995 Christmas boxcar, MIB, G1 ....$40.00

Car, #19940 Lionel Railroader vat car, MIB, G1 ....$25.00

Car, #19945 Christmas boxcar, 1996, MIB, G1 ....$35.00

Car, #52010 TTOS Weyerhauser club car, MIB, G1 ....$55.00

Loco, #624 Chesapeake & Ohio switcher, diesel, MIB, A $135.00

Loco, #8056 Chicago Northwestern, MIB, A $125.00

Loco, #8062 Burlington dummy unit, chrome, NMIB, A $100.00

Loco, #8154 Alaska SW-1 switcher, MIB, A $100.00

Loco, #8209 dockside switcher, NMIB, A.........................$35.00

Loco, #8369 GP-20 Eerie Lackawanna, diesel, MIB, A $100.00

Loco, #8380 flat top, diesel, orange & bl, MIB, A $75.00

Loco, #8477 New York Central GP-9, diesel, NMIB, A $100.00

Loco, #8602 Pennsylvania 4-4-2, steam, MIB, G1............$65.00

Loco, #8655 Boston & Maine GP-9 dummy unit, MIB, A ...$75.00

Loco, #8659 Virginian GE E-33, electric, MIB, A.........$100.00

Loco, #8687 Jersey Central Fairbanks Morse, diesel, MIB, A.$125.00

Loco, #8951 Southern Pacific Fairbanks Morse, diesel, MIB, A $200.00

Loco, #18302 Great Northern, electric, NMIB, A $150.00

Loco, #18303 Amtrak GG1, diesel, MIB, G1 ....$375.00

Loco, #18501 Western Maryland NW-2 switcher, diesel, NMIB, A $125.00

Loco, #18818 Lionel Railroad Club GP-38, diesel, MIB, A ..$100.00

Loco, #33000 GP-9 railscope, diesel, MIB, G1 ....$185.00

Locomotive (#1-390-E) and Tender (#13100), standard gauge, with paperwork, MIB, A, $650.00. (Photo courtesy Stout Auctions)

Loco & Tender, #8101 4-6-4 Hudson, MIB, A $200.00

Loco & Tender, #8210 Joshua Lionel Cowen, MIB, A $200.00

Loco & Tender, #8309 Southern Railroad Mikado, Series No 4, MIB, A..$200.00

Loco & Tender, #8603 Chesapeake & Ohio, MIB, A $100.00

Loco & Tender, #8702 Southern Crescent Ltd, steam, MIB, A..$200.00

Loco & Tender, #8801 Blue Comet, MIB, A $200.00

Loco & Tender, #18011 & #17608 Chessie T1 w/cab, steam, MIB, G1 ....$900.00

Set, #1463 Coca-Cola Special, w/loco, tender & 5 cars, MIB, A..$500.00

Set, #1632 SSS Santa Fe Work Train, MIB, G1 ....$275.00

Locomotive (1-384-E) #2-4-0 and Tender (#13101), standard gauge, with paperwork, MIB, A, $625.00. (Photo courtesy Stout Auctions)

Set, #8003 2-8-4 Chessie Steam Special, NM (NM boxes),
A..$600.00
Set, #8152 Maple Leaf Limited, MIB, A.....................$200.00
Set, #8266 Norfolk & Western Continental Limited, diesel,
NMIB, A...$200.00
Set, #8300 Cannonball Express, EX (EX box), A...........$100.00
Set, #8458 Erie Lackawanna Limited, MIB, A $300.00
Set, #8585 Burlington Northern Limited, NMIB, A $300.00
Set, #8603 Mid-Atlantic Limited, MIB, A $200.00
Set, #8851 New Haven F-3A-A, MIB, A $200.00
Set, #8962 Redding Lines Quaker City Limited, EX (EX box),
A $150.00
Set, #11744 New Yorker, MIB (sealed), A.....................$425.00
Set, #12033 Southern Express, MIB, A..........................$100.00
Set, #16360 Norfolk & Western Maxi-Stack flat car set, EX (EX
box), G1..$65.00
Set, #18200 Conrail Limited, MIB, A..........................$250.00

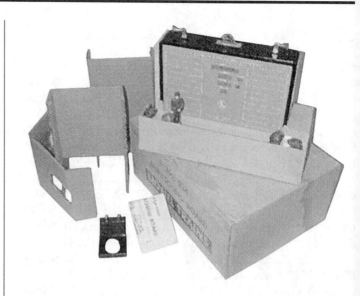

Accessory, #334 Dispatching Board, with all inserts, instruction street and controller, NM (original box with water stains), A, $475.00. (Photo courtesy Stout Auctions)

Accessory, #362 barrel loader, EX (EX box), G1 ....$125.00
Accessory, #375 motorized turntable, NM (NM box), A....$150.00
Accessory, #397 coal elevator, NM (NM box), A $250.00
Accessory, #445 switch tower, EX (EX box), G1 ....$75.00

Set, Midnight Flyer, #1960, ca 1979 – 81, MIB (sealed),
$95.00. (Photo courtesy June Moon)

Set, Norfolk & Western Powhatan Arrow, w/loco, tender & 8
cars, NM (EX boxes), A.......................................$1,100.00

LIONEL POSTWAR

Accessory, #30 water tower, EX (G box), A....................$135.00
Accessory, #69 bell signal, EX, G1 ....$35.00
Accessory, #79 lighting set, EX (EX box), A $125.00
Accessory, #115 passenger station, cream w/orange detail, VG,
A $525.00
Accessory, #118 whistling newsstand, EX (EX box), G1.....$120.00
Accessory, #150 telegraph pole set, EX (EX box), A $125.00
Accessory, #161 mail pick-up, EX (EX box), G1 ....$45.00
Accessory, #175 rocket launcher & rocket, NM, A........$500.00
Accessory, #195 floodlight tower, EX (EX box), A.........$125.00
Accessory, #197 rotating radar antenna, EX (EX box), A....$250.00
Accessory, #282 operating gantry crane, NM, A $325.00
Accessory, #313 bascule bridge, VG, A..........................$350.00
Accessory, #313 drawbridge, silver w/gr base, EX, A $250.00
Accessory, #314 girder bridge, EX (EX box), G1 ....$35.00
Accessory, #342 culvert loader w/drums, EX (EX box), A....$275.00
Accessory, #345 culvert unloader, VG, A $300.00
Accessory, #350 engine transfer table, NM (NM box), A....$400.00
Accessory, #352 ice depot w/car, NM (NM box), A.......$250.00

Accessory, #455 Derrick, unusual red top, complete operating packet and inserts, MIB, A, $650.00. (Photo courtesy Stout Auctions)

Accessory, #456 coal ramp set, EX (EX box), A $375.00
Accessory, #494 rotating beacon, EX (EX box), A $100.00

Accessory, #494 rotating beacon, red, VG, G1 ....$35.00

Accessory, #957 farm building & animal set, MIB, A.....$275.00

Accessory, #959 barn set, MIB, A $100.00

Accessory, #968 TV transmitter set, EX, A....................$100.00

Accessory, #981 freight yard set, EX (EX box), A..........$200.00

Accessory, #1015 transformer, 45 watts, EX, G1 ....$15.00

Accessory, #1025 transformer, 45 watts, EX, G1 ....$15.00

Accessory, #1033 transformer, 90 watts, w/whistle, EX (EX box), G1 ....$55.00

Accessory, #1034 transformer, 75 watts, EX, G1 ....$45.00

Accessory, #1044 transformer, 90 watts, w/whistle, EX (EX box)..$45.00

Accessory, #1045 operating watchman, NMIB, A..........$275.00

Accessory, #1053 transformer, 60 watts, w/whistle, EX, G1 .$35.00

Accessory, #3360 burro crane, EX (EX box), A $250.00

Accessory, #350-50 transfer table extension, NMIB, A..$150.00

Accessory, KW transformer, 190 watts, EX (EX box), G1...$145.00

Accessory, LW transformer, 125 watts, EX, G1 ....$85.00

Accessory, ZW-174 transformer, 275 watts, NMIB, A $325.00

Car, #44 US Army launcher, EX (EX box), A $625.00

Car, #50 gang car, NM (NM box), A $125.00

Car, #51 Navy yard switcher, VG (VG box), A..............$100.00

Car, #54 ballast tamper, EX (EX box), A $350.00

Car, #55 tie-jector, NM (NM box), A $350.00

Car, #58 Great Northern snowplow, gr & wht, NMIB, A.........$500.00

Car, #624 Chesapeake & Ohio switcher, diesel, NMIB, A......$150.00

Car, #1877 flat car w/horses & fence, NMIB, A $125.00

Car, #2346 GP-9 Boston & Maine road switcher, NMIB, A..$400.00

Car, #2414 Santa Fe pullman, NM (G box), A $125.00

Car, #2435 Elizabeth pullman, EX (VG box), A $225.00

Car, #2436 Mooseheart observation, unrun, MIB, A $400.00

Car, #2530 baggage car, EX (EX box), A $650.00

Car, #2532 vista dome car, EX (VG box), A $175.00

Car, #3356 horse car & corral, NMIB, A $200.00

Car, #3376 Bronx Zoo, gr w/yel lettering, EX+, A..........$125.00

Car, #3419 flat car w/helicopter, NMIB, A $135.00

Car, #3435 aquarium car, MIB, A $325.00

Car, #3444, gondola, animated, with original instruction sheet, M (unrun) (NM box), A, $150.00. (Photo courtesy Stout Auctions)

Car, #3451 log dump flat car, EX, G1 ....$40.00

Car, #3459 dump car, aluminum bin, VG (G box), A....$325.00

Car, #3462 milk car, w/cans & platform, EX, G1 ....$45.00

Car, #3470 target launcher, lt bl version, NM (NM box), A $850.00

Car, #3474 Western Pacific boxcar, VG, G1.....................$35.00

Car, #3530 generator, MIB, A $350.00

Car, #3562-1 gondola w/figure, EX, A............................$200.00

Car, #3650 searchlight extension car, lt gray, NMIB, A....$150.00

Car, #3665 Minuteman missile launcher, NMIB, A $275.00

Car, #3830 flat car w/submarine, EX (EX box), G1 ....$125.00

Car, #3854 merchandise car, VG, A $450.00

Car, #3927 track cleaning car, MIB, A...........................$150.00

Car, #4452 Pennsylvania Railroad gondola, EX (EX box), A..$500.00

Car, #4457 Pennsylvania Railroad caboose, VG (VG box), A $425.00

Car, #6014 Airex boxcar, red, VG, G1 ....$35.00

Car, #6017 Boston & Maine caboose, NM (EX box), A.........$325.00

Car, #6027 Alaska Railroad caboose, EX, G1 ....$75.00

Car, #6162-60 Alaska Railroad gondola, yel, EX, G1 ....$60.00

Car, #6262 flat car w/wheels, rare red version, EX, A.....$850.00

Car, #6315 Gulf tank car, NM, A...................................$225.00

Car, #6405 flat car w/trailer, NM (NM box), A..............$300.00

Car, #6407 flat car w/rocket, red, wht & bl, NM, A........$675.00

Car, #6416 boat loader, NMIB, A $225.00

Car, #6417 Pennsylvania Railroad caboose, NMIB, A $85.00

Car, #6418 machinery car, NMIB, A $150.00

Car, #6434 poultry car, EX (EX box), A $175.00

Car, #6437 Pennsylvania caboose, porthole-type, EX, G1 ....$40.00

Car, #6445 Fort Knox Gold Reserve transport car, NMIB, A..$225.00

Car, #6446-60 Lehigh Valley hopper, NM (EX box), A ...$250.00

Car, #6457 caboose, red, VG, G1 ....$30.00

Car, #6460 crane car, NMIB, A......................................$125.00

Car, #6464 Missouri Pacific boxcar, NMIB, A................$150.00

Car, #6464-300 Rutland boxcar, EX (EX box), A...........$300.00

Car, #6464-375 Central of Georgia boxcar, NM (NM box), A $150.00

Car, #6464-400 B&O boxcar, VG (EX box), A..............$175.00

Car, #6464-425 New Haven boxcar, NM (VG box), A....$200.00

Car, #6464-510 Pacemaker Freight Service NYC boxcar, EX, A $650.00

Car, #6464-515 M-K-T Katy boxcar, EX, A....................$600.00

Car, #6464-700 Santa Fe boxcar, EX (EX box), A..........$200.00

Car, #6464-825 Alaska boxcar, VG, A............................$400.00

Car, #6464-900 NYC boxcar, NM (EX box), A $265.00

Car, #6475 Heinz 57 vat car, NMIB, A..........................$135.00

Car, #6800, flatcar with airplane, EX (G box), A, $145.00.
(Photo courtesy Stout Auctions)

Car, #6501 transport car w/jet motor boat, MIB, A........$200.00
Car, #6520 searchlight, maroon generator, EX, G1..........$55.00
Car, #6544 missile firing flatcar, VG, A $150.00
Car, #6544 missile launcher, EX (EX box), G1 ....$150.00
Car, #6801 flat car w/boat, EX (EX box), A..................$175.00
Car, #6823 flat car w/missiles, NM (EX box), A.............$275.00
Car, #6824 USMC work caboose, VG, A $300.00
Loco, #44 US Army launcher, G, G1............................$125.00
Loco, #53 Rio Grande snowplow, G, G1.......................$125.00
Loco, #205A Missouri Pacific, diesel, VG, G1.................$95.00
Loco, #231A Rock Island, diesel, VG, G1.....................$90.00
Loco, #550 Wabash, EX (EX box), A...........................$265.00
Loco, #614 Alaska Railroad NW-2, EX, G1 ....$175.00
Loco, #621 Jersey Central NW-2, VG (VG box), G1 ....$135.00
Loco, #628 Northern Pacific, center cab, VG, A $200.00
Loco, #736 Lionel Lines 2046W, w/smoke, whistle & light, NM,
    G1 ....$400.00
Loco, #1066 Union Pacific, diesel, VG, G1....................$65.00
Loco, #2322 Virginian FM, diesel, EX (VG box), A ...$1,200.00

Accessory, #8 traffic and crossing signal, G (dirty, no signs of deterioration) (VG+ box), A, $350.00.

Locomotive, #2329 Virginian, G (very dirty), A, $350.00.
(Photo courtesy Stout Auctions)

Loco, #2338 Milwaukee Road GP-9, VG, A $350.00
Loco, #2346 Boston & Maine GP-9 road switcher, diesel, NMIB,
    A...$400.00
Loco, #2350 New Haven, diesel, VG (VG box), A........$175.00
Tender, #2046-50 Pennsylvania Railroad, VG (worn box),
    A $150.00
Tender, #6026, w/whistle, EX, G1 ....$45.00
Tender, #6466, w/whistle, EX, G1 ....$45.00

Accessory, #437 switch tower, G, A, $500.00.
(Photo courtesy Stout Auctions)

LIONEL PREWAR

Accessory, #79 crossing signal, all silver version, VG (G box),
    A $475.00
Accessory, #81 controlling rheostat, EX, A $125.00
Accessory, #89 flagpole, EX (EX box), A...................$575.00
Accessory, #119 tunnel, metal, EX+, A $275.00
Accessory, #137 train station, EX (worn box), A $500.00
Accessory, #313 drawbridge, VG, A............................$250.00
Accessory, #911 country estate, NM, A.......................$800.00
Accessory, #912 suburban home, VG, A........................$625.00
Car, #214 boxcar, yel w/orange roof, EX (EX box), A.......$525.00
Car, #2672 caboose, brn, EX, G1.................................$25.00

Accessory, #438 signal tower, cream and white with a red roof on silver structure, roof slightly faded, G, A, $475.00. (Photo courtesy Stout Auctions)

Car, #2813, stock car, yellow with maroon roof, nickel trim and plates, EX (VG+ box), A, $475.00.

Set, #33 loco w/3 cars, gr, G, A $600.00
Set, #256 loco w/3 cars, orange, G, A $950.00
Set, Blue Comet, w/loco, tender & 3 cars, VG, A.......$1,400.00
Set, Blue Streak, w/loco, tender & 3 cars, VG, A $3,000.00

MISCELLANEOUS

Bing, accessory, railroad station, emb litho tin, 8x15", EX, A $800.00
Bing, loco, mk Phoenix, maroon- & gr-pnt tin w/red pin-striping, steam powered, 8", EX, A $1,100.00
Bing, loco, mk Uranus, maroon-pnt tin w/gold pin-striping, steam powered, 10", EX, A....................................$1,100.00
Bing, set, loco & tender w/2 cars, litho tin, clockwork, VG, A $750.00
Bing, set, Miniature Table Railway, litho tin, w/loco, 3 passenger cars & 16 pcs of track, NMIB, A..............................$600.00

Bing Train Station, embossed lithographed tin, 10" x 15", EX-, A, $1,000.00.

Carette, loco & tender, steam powered, gr w/brass boiler, emb coal compartment on tender, 11", VG, A...............$450.00
Converse, car, mk Live Stock 1910, red-pnt wood w/yel trim, VG, A $75.00
Cor-Cor, set, w/loco, tender & passenger car, blk & red, 54", EX, A $1,100.00
Doll, loco, model #201/1, maroon- & blk-pnt tin w/yel pin-striping, DC nameplate on firebox, steam powered, 7", EX, A ..$550.00
Elektoy, set, Pennsylvania Railroad, w/loco, tender & 3 cars, EX, A..$1,500.00
Fallows, loco, mk Boss, pnt & stenciled tin w/CI wheels, clockwork, 8", G, A..$250.00
Fallows, loco, mk Nero, pnt & stenciled tin w/CI wheels, clockwork, 10", VG, A..$725.00
Gunthermann, loco & tender, mk 999, litho tin, clockwork, 11", G, A $200.00
Hafner, set, Union Pacific Railway, litho tin, 24", VG, A..$200.00
Ives, car, #129 Saratoga pullman, 2-tone gr, EX, A...........$75.00
Ives, loco, mk America, pnt & stenciled tin w/CI wheels, clockwork, 12", G, A..$600.00
Ives, set, Blue Vagabond, w/loco, tender & 3 cars, CI, G, A $225.00

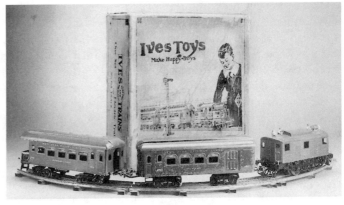

Ives, set #690, locomotive (#3235) 0-4-0, electric; buffet car (#171) and observation cars (#173), in green for NYC & HR, with track and original box, VG/EX, A, $400.00.

Marklin, loco, #1030 New York Central, electric, VG, A $750.00
Marklin, set, w/loco, tender, 3 cars & track, pnt & litho tin, EX (VG box), A $850.00
Marx, set, #4305, electric, NMIB..................................$200.00
Schoenner, loco, brn-pnt tin w/gold pin-striping, spoke wheels, steam powered, 12", VG, A $2,500.00
Schoenner, loco, steam powered, blk & gr w/red spoke wheels, NP boiler, 8", rpt, A..$385.00
Schoenner, loco & tender, tin w/brass boiler, spoke wheels, steam powered, 12", VG, A $1,200.00
Voltamp, caboose, N&M, pnt tin, 10", VG, A $400.00
Williams, loco & tender, #5601 Norfolk & Western 4-8-4, MIB, A..$400.00
Williams, loco & tender, #6100 Pennsylvania 2-8-2 Mikado, MIB, A..$225.00

Transformers

Made by the Hasbro Company, Transformers were introduced in the United States in 1984. Originally there were twenty-eight figures — eighteen cars known as Autobots and ten Decepticons, evil robots capable of becoming such things as a jet or a handgun. Eventually the line was expanded to more than two hundred different models. Some were remakes of earlier Japanese robots that had been produced by Takara in the 1970s. (These can be identified through color differences and in the case of the Diaclone series, the absence of the small driver or pilot figures.)

The story of the Transformers and their epic adventures were told through several different comic books and animated series as well as a highly successful movie. Their popularity was reflected internationally and eventually made its way back to Japan. There the American Transformer animated series was translated into Japanese and soon inspired several parallel series of the toys which were again produced by Takara. These new Transformers were sold in the U.S. until the line was discontinued in 1990.

A few years ago, Hasbro announced their plans to reintroduce the line with Transformers: Generation 2. Transformers once again had their own comic book, and the old animated series was brought back in a revamped format. So far, several new Transformers as well as recolored versions of the older ones have been released by Hasbro, and the size of the series continues to grow. Sustained interest in them has spawned a number of fan clubs with chapters worldwide.

Because Transformers came in a number of sizes, you'll find a wide range of pricing. Our values are for Transformers that are mint in mint or nearly mint original boxes. One that has been used is worth much less — about 25% to 75%, depending on whether it has all its parts (weapons, instruction book, tech specks, etc.) and what its condition is — whether decals are well applied or if it is worn. A loose Transformer complete and in near-mint condition is worth only about half as much as one mint in the box.

Advisor: David Kolodny-Nagy (K2).

SERIES 1, 1984

Autobot Car, #TF1035, Hound, jeep, MIB, $235.00.

Autobot Car, #TF1023, Sunstreak, yel Countach $135.00
Autobot Car, #TF1025, Bluestreak, bl Datsun Z $350.00
Autobot Car, #TF1025, Bluestreak, silver Datsun $135.00
Autobot Car, #TF1027, Jazz, Porsche....................$175.00
Autobot Car, #TF1029, Ratchet, ambulance..................$120.00
Autobot Car, #TF1031, Trailbreaker, camper $235.00
Autobot Car, #TF1033, red Countach $235.00
Autobot Car, #TF1037, Mirage, Indy car.................$235.00
Autobot Car, #TF1039, Prowl, police car $400.00
Autobot Car, #TF1041, Wheeljack, Mazzerati $335.00
Autobot Car, #TF1055, Camshaft, silver car, mail-in.......$40.00
Autobot Car, #TF1057, Downshift, wht car, mail-in........$40.00
Autobot Car, #TF1059, Overdrive, red car, mail-in $100.00
Autobot Car, #TF1061, Powerdasher #1, jet, mail-in.......$20.00
Autobot Car, #TF1063, Powerdasher #2, car, mail-in.......$20.00
Autobot Car, #TF1063, Powerdasher #3, drill, mail-in.....$40.00
Autobot Commander, #TF1053, Optimus Primus w/Roller, tractor-trailer...$200.00
Case, #TF-1069, Collector's Showcase...........................$15.00
Case, #TF1069, Collector's Case $15.00
Case, #TF1071, Collector's Case, red, 3-D version $25.00
Cassette, #TF1017, Ravage & Rumble...........................$30.00
Cassette, #TF1019, Frenzy & Lazerbreak $30.00
Decepticon Communicator, #TF1049, Soundwave & Buzzsaw, tape player & gold condor $150.00

Decepticon Jet, #TR1043, Starcream, gray jet, MIB, $150.00.

Decepticon Jet, #TF1045, Thundercracker, bl jet...........$230.00
Decepticon Jet, #TF1047, Skywarp, blk jet.....................$225.00
Decepticon Leader, #TF1051, Megatron, Walther P-38 ...$400.00
Minicar, #TF1000, Bumblejumper (Bumblebee card)......$40.00
Minicar, #TF1000, Bumblejumper (Cliffjumper card)......$50.00
Minicar, #TF1003, Bumblebee, red VW Bug $25.00
Minicar, #TF1005, Cliffjumper, gr race car $35.00
Minicar, #TF1007, Cliffjumper, yel race car....................$35.00
Minicar, #TF1009, Huffer, orange semi cab $35.00

Minicar, #TF1011, Windcharger, red Firebird...................$35.00
Minicar, #TF1013, Brawn, gr jeep $35.00
Minicar, #TF1015, Gears, bl truck $35.00
Minicar, #TF1102, Bumblebee, yel w/minispy $40.00
Watch, #TF1067, Time Warrior, transforming watch w/Autobot
    insignia, mail-in $80.00

SERIES 2, 1985

Autobot Air Guardian, #TF1201, Jetfire F-14 jet...........$160.00
Autobot Car, #TF1163, Skids, Le Car.....................$135.00
Autobot Car, #TF1165, Red Alert, fire Chief.................$135.00
Autobot Car, #TF1167, Grapple, crane $135.00
Autobot Car, #TF1169, Hoist, tow truck.......................$150.00
Autobot Car, #TF1171, Smokescreen, red, wht & bl Datsun
    S...$150.00
Autobot Car, #TF1173, Inferno, fire engine $150.00
Autobot Car, #TF1175, Tracks, Corvette $160.00
Autobot Car, #TF1175, Tracks, Corvette, red $400.00
Autobot Communicator, #TF1199, Blaster, radio/tape player...$145.00
Autobot Scientist, #TF1197, Perceptor, microscope $60.00
Constructicon, #TF1127, Bonecrusher (1), bulldozer.......$60.00
Constructicon, #TF1129, Scavenger (2), steam shovel..$125.00
Constructicon, #TF1131, Scrapper (3), front-end loader.$50.00
Constructicon, #TF1133, Hook (4), crane.......................$50.00
Constructicon, #TF1135, Long Haul (5), dump truck......$50.00
Constructicon, #TF1137, Mixmaster (6), cement mixer..$50.00
Constructicon, #TF1139, Devastator, construction gift set.$300.00
Decepticon Jet, #TF1187, Ramjet................................$110.00
Decepticon Jet, #TF1189, Dirge.....................................$110.00
Decepticon Jet, #TF1191, Thrust, maroon jet $120.00
Decepticon Military Operations Commander #TF1203, Shock-
    wave, lazer gun..$200.00
Deluxe Insecticon, #TF1155, Chop Chop, beetle.............$90.00
Deluxe Insecticon, #TF1159, Beno, bee............................$90.00
Deluxe Insecticon, #TF1161, Ransack, grasshopper.......$125.00

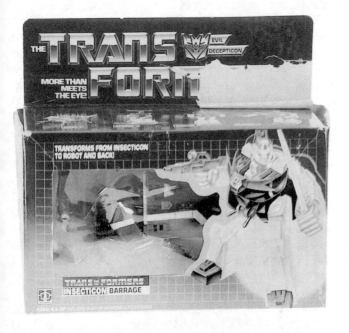

Deluxe Insecticon, #TF1157, Barrage, MIB, $125.00.

Deluxe Vehicle, #TF1193, Whirl, lt bl helicopter $70.00
Deluxe Vehicle, #TF1195, Roadster, off-road vehicle.......$60.00
Dinobot, #TF1177, Grimlock, Tyannosaurus..................$250.00
Dinobot, #TF1179, Slag, Triceratops $135.00
Dinobot, #TF1181, Sludge, Brontosaurus $175.00
Dinobot, #TF1183, Snarl, Stegosaurus.........................$175.00
Insecticon, #TF1141, Kickback, grasshopper $50.00
Insecticon, #TF1143, Shrapnel, beetle.............................$50.00
Insecticon, #TF1145, Bombshell, boll weevil $50.00
Jumpstarter, #TF1147, Twin Twist, drill tank.................$50.00
Jumpstarter, #TF1149, Topspin.......................................$45.00
Minicar, #TF01001, Bumblebee, yel VW Bug..................$50.00
Minicar, #TF1101, Bumblebee, yel VW Bug.....................$45.00
Minicar, #TF1103, Bumblebee, red VW Bug $45.00
Minicar, #TF1104, Bumblebee, red w/minispy $30.00
Minicar, #TF1105, Cliffhanger, red race car $45.00
Minicar, #TF1106, Cliffjumper, red w/minispy $50.00
Minicar, #TF1107, Cliffhanger, yel race car $45.00
Minicar, #TF1108, Cliffhanger, yel w/minispy $50.00
Minicar, #TF1109, Huffer, orange semi cab $45.00
Minicar, #TF1110, Huffer, w/minispy.............................$50.00
Minicar, #TF1111, Windcharger, red Firebird...................$45.00
Minicar, #TF1112, Windcharger, w/minispy $50.00
Minicar, #TF1113, Brawn, gr jeep, MIP.........................$40.00
Minicar, #TF1115, Gears, bl truck $35.00
Minicar, #TF1116, Gears, w/minispy..............................$35.00
Minicar, #TF1117, Seaspray, hovercraft $25.00
Minicar, #TF1119, Powerglide, plane.............................$25.00
Minicar, #TF1121, Warpath, tank...................................$30.00
Minicar, #TF1123, Beachcomber, dune buggy $30.00
Minicar, #TF1125, Cosmos, spaceship $30.00
Motorized Autobot Defense Base, #TF1205, Omega Supreme,
    rocket launcher base $300.00
Triple Charger, #TF1151, Blitzwing, tank/plane $80.00
Triple Charger, #TF1153, Astrotrain, shuttle/train...........$80.00
Watch, #TF1207, Autoceptor, Kronoform, watch car $25.00
Watch, #TF1211, Listen 'N Fun, w/tape & yel Cliffjumper .$35.00
Watch, TF1209, Deceptor, Kronoform, watch jet.............$25.00

SERIES 3, 1986

Aerialbot, #TF1263, Air Raid (1), F-14 jet.......................$25.00
Aerialbot, #TF1265, Skydive (2), F-15 jet........................$25.00
Aerialbot, #TF1267, Fireflight (3), Phantom jet $25.00
Aerialbot, #TF1271, Silverbot (5), Concorde $50.00
Aerialbot, #TF1273, Superion, gift set............................$275.00
Autobot Car, #TF1333, Blurr, futuristic car $90.00
Autobot Car, #TF1335, Kup, pickup truck $100.00
Autobot Car, #TF1337, Hot Rod, red race car $375.00
Autobot City Commander, #TF1365, Ultra Magnus, car car-
    rier $135.00
Autobot City Commander, #TF1367, Reflector, Spectro,
    Viewfinder & Spyglass into camera, mail-in............$225.00
Autobot City Commander, #TF1369, STARS Control Center,
    action cb, mail-in $225.00
Battlecharger, #TF1311, Runamuck, Corvette $35.00
Battlecharger, #TF1313, Runabout, Trans Am $30.00
Cassette, #TF1315, Ratbat & Frenzy, bat & bl robot........$60.00

Cassette, #TF1317, Rewind & Steeljaw, gold weapons, blk robot & lion..$60.00

Cassette, #TF1318, Rewing & Steeljaw, silver weapons, blk robot & lion..$65.00

Cassette, #TF1319, Ramhorn & Eject, gold weapons, rhino & gray robot..$65.00

Cassette, #TF1320, Ramhorn & Eject, gold weapons, rhino & gray robot..$65.00

Combaticon, #TF1287, Brawl (1), tank........................$35.00

Combaticon, #TF1289, Swindle (2), jeep.......................$40.00

Combaticon, #TF1293, Vortex (4), helicopter.................$35.00

Combaticon, #TF1295, Onslaught (5), missile transport .$40.00

Combaticon, #TF1297, Bruticus, gift set......................$450.00

Combaticon, Blast Off (3), shuttle..............................$30.00

Decepticon City Commander, #TF1363, Galvatron.....$225.00

Heroes, #TF1131, Rodimus Prime, futuristic RV...........$150.00

Heroes, #TF1329, Wreck-Car, futuristic motorcycle.....$125.00

Jet, #TF1353, Scourge, hovercraft..............................$125.00

Jet, #TF1355, Cyclonus Space Jet...............................$175.00

Minicar, #TF1252, Wheelie, futuristic car.....................$35.00

Minicar, #TF1253, Outback, brn jeep...........................$35.00

Minicar, #TF1255, Tailgate, wht Firebird......................$35.00

Minicar, #TF1257, Hubcap, yel race car.......................$35.00

Minicar, #TF1259, Pipes, bl semi cab..........................$35.00

Minicar, #TF1261, Swerve, red truck...........................$35.00

Motorized Autobot Space Shuttle Robot, #TF1359, Sky Lynz shuttle...$135.00

Motorized Decepticon City/Battle Station, #TF1357, Trypticon, dinosaur w/Brunt, robot tank & Full Tilt...............$225.00

Predacon, #TF1339, Razorclaw (1), lion.......................$70.00

Predacon, #TF1341, Rampage (2), tiger.........................$70.00

Predacon, #TF1343, Divebomb (3), vulture....................$70.00

Predacon, #TF1345, Tantrum (4), bull..........................$70.00

Predacon, #TF1347, Headstrong (5), rhino.....................$70.00

Predacon, #TF1351, Gnaw, futuristic shark....................$70.00

Stuncticon, #TF1277, Breakdown (2), Countach.............$30.00

Stunticon, #TF1275, Dead End (1), Porsche...................$30.00

Stunticon, #TF1279, Wildrider (3), Ferrari....................$30.00

Stunticon, #TF1281, Drag Strip (4), Indy car.................$30.00

Stunticon, #TF1283, Motormaster (5), tractor-trailer......$75.00

Stunticon, #TF1285, Menasor, gift set.........................$450.00

Triple Charger, #TF1321, Springer, armored car/helicopter......$150.00

Triple Charger, #TF1323, Sandstorm, dune buggy/helicopter ..$100.00

Triple Charger, #TF1325, Broadside, aircraft carrier/plane.......$100.00

Triple Charger, #TF1327, Octane, tanker truck/jumbo jet..........$85.00

SERIES 4, 1987

Cassette, #TF1441, Slugfest & Overkill, Stegasaurus & Tyrannosaurus...$25.00

Clone, #TF1443, Pounce & Wingspan, puma & eagle.....$45.00

Clone, #TF1445, Fastlane & Cloudraker, dragster & spaceship...$65.00

Double Spy, #TF1441, Punch-Counterpunch, Fiero.........$75.00

Duocon, #TF1437, Battletrap, jeep/helicopter..............$50.00

Duocon, #TF1439, Flywheels, jet/tank.........................$25.00

Headmaster Autobot, #TF1477, Chromedome w/Stylor, futuristic car..$200.00

Headmaster Autobot, #TF1479, Hardhead w/Duros, tank..$120.00

Headmaster Autobot, #TF1481, Highbrow w/Gort, helicopter $120.00

Headmaster Autobot, #TF1483, Brainstorm w/Arcana, jet .$75.00

Headmaster Base, #TF1497, Scorponok w/Lord Zarak & Fasttrack, scorpion, mini-tank.................................$225.00

Headmaster Base, #TF1499, Fortress Maximus w/Cerebros & Spike, Gasket, Grommet, battle station/city...........$800.00

Headmaster Decepticon, #TF1485, Skullrunner w/Grax, alligator...$70.00

Headmaster Decepticon, #TF1487, Mindwipe w/Vorath, bat.....$70.00

Headmaster Decepticon, #TF1489, Weirdwolf w/Monzo, wolf...$80.00

Headmaster Horrorcon, #TF1491, Apeface w/Spasma, jet/ape.$100.00

Headmaster Horrorcon, #TF1493, Snapdragon w/Krunk, jet/dinosaur...$100.00

Monsterbot, #TF1461, Grotusque, tiger........................$50.00

Monsterbot, #TF1463, Doublecross, 2-headed dragon......$40.00

Monsterbot, #TF1465, Repugnus, insect........................$90.00

Sixchanger, #TF1495, Sixshot, starfighter jet, winged wolf, lazer pistol, armored carrier, tank................................$75.00

Targetmaster Autobot, #TF1449, Pointblank w/Peacemaker, race car & gun...$30.00

Targetmaster Autobot, #TF1451, Sureshot w/Spoilsport, off-road buggy & gun...$30.00

Targetmaster Autobot, #TF1453, Crosshairs w/Pinpointer, truck & gun...$30.00

Targetmaster Autobot, #TF1455, Hot Rod & Firebolt, race car & gun...$150.00

Targetmaster Autobot, #TF1457, Kup & Recoil, pickup truck & gun...$60.00

Targetmaster Autobot, #TF1459, Blurr w/Haywire, futuristic car & gun...$90.00

Targetmaster Decepticon, #TF1469, Misfire w/Aimless, spaceship & gun...$60.00

Targetmaster Decepticon, #TF1475, Scourge w/Fracas, hovercraft & gun...$125.00

Targetmaster Deception, #TF1471, Slugslinger w/Caliburst, twin jet & gun...$50.00

Technobot, #TF1425, Afterburner (1), motorcycle..........$20.00

Technobot, #TF1426, Afterburner, w/decoy....................$30.00

Technobot, #TF1427, Nosecone (2), drill tank...............$25.00

Technobot, #TF1428, Nosecone, w/decoy......................$30.00

Technobot, #TF1429, State (3), fighter plane................$20.00

Technobot, #TF1430, State, w/decoy............................$30.00

Technobot, #TF1431, Lightspeed (4), race car..............$20.00

Technobot, #TF1432, Lightspeed, w/decoy....................$25.00

Technobot, #TF1433, Scattershot (5), spaceship............$40.00

Terrecon, #TF1413, Rippersnapper (1), lizard...............$10.00

Terrocon, #TF1414, Rippersnapper, w/decoy..................$15.00

Terrocon, #TF1415, Sinnertwin (2), 2-headed dog..........$10.00

Terrocon, #TF1416, Sinnertwin, w/decoy.......................$15.00

Terrocon, #TF1417, Cutthroat (3), vulture....................$10.00

Terrocon, #TF1418, Cutthroat, w/decoy........................$15.00

Terrocon, #TF1419, Blot (4), monster..........................$10.00

Terrocon, #TF1420, Blot, w/decoy...............................$15.00

Terrocon, #TF1421, Hun-grr (5), 2-headed dragon..........$30.00

Throttlebot, #TF1403, Freeway, Corvette......................$15.00

Throttlebot, #TF1404, Freeway, w/decoy......................$20.00

Throttlebot, #TF1401, Goldbug, VW bug, MIB, $15.00.

Throttlebot, #TF1405, Chase, Ferrari $12.00
Throttlebot, #TF1406, Chase, w/decoy...........................$18.00
Throttlebot, #TF1407, Wideload, dump truck.................$15.00
Throttlebot, #TF1408, Wideload, w/decoy $20.00
Throttlebot, #TF1409, Rollbar, jeep $15.00
Throttlebot, #TF1410, Rollbar, w/decoy $20.00
Throttlebot, #TF1411, Searchlight, race car....................$15.00
Throttlebot, #TF1412, Searchlight, w/decoy $20.00

SERIES 5, 1988

Cassette, #TF1539, Squawkalk & Beastbox, hawk & gorilla .$15.00
Cassette, TF1541, Grand Slam & Raindance, tank & jet...$15.00
Firecon, #TF1507, Cindersaur, dinosaur $10.00
Firecon, #TF1509, Flamefeather, monster bird $10.00
Firecon, #TF1561, Sparkstalker, monster..........................$10.00
Headmaster Autobot, #TF1555, Horsehead w/Lug, fire
  engine..$30.00
Headmaster Autobot, #TF1557, Siren w/Quig, fire chief
  car...$25.00
Headmaster Autobot, #TF1559, Nightbeat w/Muzzle, race
  car $25.00
Headmaster Decepticon, #TF1561, Horri-Bull w/Kreb, bull ..$40.00
Headmaster Decepticon, #TF1563, Fangry w/Brisko, winged
  wolf...$40.00
Headmaster Decepticon, #TF1565, Squeezeplay w/Lokos,
  crab...$40.00
Powermaster Autobot, #TF1567, Getaway w/Rev, Mr2....$50.00
Powermaster Autobot, #TF1569, Joyride w/Hotwire, off-road
  buggy $70.00
Powermaster Autobot, #TF2571, Slapdash w/Lube, Indy car ..$70.00
Powermaster Autobot Leader, #TF1617, Optimus Prime w/HiQ,
  tractor trailer, minimum value $200.00
Powermaster Decepticon, #TF1573, Darkwing w/Throttle, dk
  gray jet..$60.00
Powermaster Decepticon, #TF1575, Dreadwing w/Hi-Test, lt
  gray jet..$60.00
Powermaster Mercenary, #TF1613, Doubledealer w/Knok
  (robot) & Skar (bat), missile launcher........................$75.00

Pretender, #TF1577, Landmine, race car w/shell $60.00
Pretender, #TF1579, Cloudburst, jet w/shell....................$60.00
Pretender, #TF1581, Waverider, submarine w/shell..........$40.00
Pretender, #TF1583, Skullgrin, tank w/shell....................$40.00
Pretender, #TF1585, Bomb-burst, spaceship w/shell.........$60.00
Pretender, #TF1587, Submarauder, submarine w/shell $60.00
Pretender, #TF1589, Groundbreaker, race car w/shell $40.00
Pretender, #TF1591, Sky High, jet w/shell.......................$40.00
Pretender, #TF1593, Splashdown, sea skimmer w/shell....$40.00
Pretender, #TF1595, Iguanus, motorcycle w/shell.............$40.00
Pretender, #TF1599, Finback, sea skimmer w/shell...........$25.00
Pretender Beast, #TF1601, Chainclaw, bear shell.............$30.00
Pretender Beast, #TF1603, Catilla, sabertooth tiger w/shell..$30.00
Pretender Beast, #TF1605, Carnivac, wolf w/shell $30.00
Pretender Beast, #TF1607, Snarler, boar w/shell..............$30.00
Pretender Vehicle, #TF1609, Gunrunner, red jet w/vehicle
  shell..$40.00
Pretender Vehicle, #TF1611, Roadgrabber, purple jet w/vehicle
  shell..$40.00
Seacon, #TF1513, Overbite (1), shark..............................$15.00
Seacon, #TF1515, Seawing (2), manta ray $15.00
Seacon, #TF1517, Nautilator (3), lobster $15.00
Seacon, #TF1519, Skalor (4), fish....................................$15.00
Seacon, #TF1521, Tenakil (5), squid $15.00
Seacon, #TF1523, Snaptrap (6), turtle.............................$35.00
Seacon, #TF1525, Piracon, gift set, minimum value $200.00
Sparkbot, #TF1501, Fizzle, off-road buggy.....................$10.00
Sparkbot, #TF1503, Sizzle, funny car $10.00
Sparkbot, #TF1505, Guzzle, tank $10.00
Targetmaster Autobot, #TF1543, Scoop w/Tracer & Holepunch,
  front-end loader & 2 guns $25.00
Targetmaster Autobot, #TF1545, Landfill w/Flintlock &
  Silencer, dump truck & 2 guns $25.00

Triggercon, #TF1537, Crankcase, jeep, MOC, $15.00.

Targetmaster Autobot, #TF1547, Quickmix w/Boomer & Ricochet, cement mixer & 2 guns $25.00

Targetmaster Decepticon, #TF1549, Quaker w/Tiptop & Heater, tank & 2 guns $50.00

Targetmaster Decepticon, #TF1551, Spinster & Singe & Hairsplitter, helicopter & 2 guns $50.00

Targetmaster Decepticon, #TF1553, Needlenose w/Sunbeam & Zigzag, jet & 2 guns..$50.00

Tiggerbot, #TF1527, Backstreet, race car $15.00

Tiggerbot, #TF1529, Override, motorcycle $15.00

Triggercon, #TF1533, Ruckus, dune buggy....................$15.00

Triggercon, #TF1535, Windsweeper, B-1 bomber $15.00

SERIES 6, 1989

Legends, K-Mart Exclusive, #TF1727, Bumblebee, VW big...$35.00

Legends, K-Mart Exclusive, #TF1729, Jazz Porsche $35.00

Legends, K-Mart Exclusive, #TF1731, Grimlock, dinosaur..$35.00

Legends, K-Mart Exclusive, #TF1733, Starscream, jet......$40.00

Mega Pretender, #TF1717, Vroom, dragster w/shell $35.00

Mega Pretender, #TF1719, Thunderwing, jet w/shell $35.00

Mega Pretender, #TF1721, Crossblades, helicopter w/shell...$35.00

Micromaster Base, #TF1679, Skyhopper & Micromaster, helicopter & F-15...$50.00

Micromaster Base, #TF1681, Groundshaker & Micromaster, self-propelled cannon & stealth fighter $35.00

Micromaster Base, #TF1735, Skystalker, Space Shuttle Base & Micromaster Porsche $55.00

Micromaster Base, #TF1737, Countdown, Rocket Base & Micromaster Lunar Boxer...$50.00

Micromaster Patrol, #TF1651, Off-Road Series, 4 different, ea..$25.00

Micromaster Patrol, #TF1657, Sports Car Patrol Series, 4 different, ea...$25.00

Micromaster Patrol, #TF1661, Battle Patrol Series, 4 different, ea..$30.00

Micromaster Station, #TF1671, Greasepit, pickup w/gas station..$20.00

Micromaster Station, #TF1675, Ironworks, semi w/construction site..$20.00

Micromaster Transport, #TF1663, Overload, car carrier...$20.00

Micromaster Transport, #TF1665, Flattop, aircraft carrier ..$20.00

Micromaster Transport, #TF1667, Roughstuff, military transport $20.00

Pretender, #TF1697, Pincher, scorpion w/shell.................$35.00

Pretender, #TF1699, Longtooth, hovercraft w/shell $35.00

Pretender, #TF1701, Stranglehold, rhino w/shell $35.00

Pretender, #TF1705, Bludgeon, tank w/shell $125.00

Pretender, #TF1707, Doubleheader, twin jet w/shell $45.00

Pretender Classic, #TF1709, Bumblebee, VW Bug w/shell ..$50.00

Pretender Classic, #TF1711, Grimlock, dinosaur w/shell .$50.00

Pretender Classic, #TF1713, Starscream, jet w/shell..........$50.00

Pretender Classic, #TF1715, Jazz, Porsche w/shell $40.00

Pretender Monster, #TF1683, Icepick (1) $12.00

Pretender Monster, #TF1683, Wildfly (3).........................$12.00

Ultra Pretender, #TF1725, Roadblock, tank w/figure & vehicle...$40.00

Ultra Pretender, #TF1727, Skyhammer, race car w/figure & vehicle...$40.00

SERIES 7, 1990

Action Master, #TF1781, Soundwave: Soundwave (bat), Wingthing...$15.00

Action Master, #TF1785, Grimlock: Grimlock, Anti-Tank Cannon (tank gun)..$15.00

Action Master, #TF1789, Rad: Rad, Lionizer (lion) $15.00

Action Master, #TF1793, Devastator: Devastor, Scorpulator (scorpion)..$25.00

Action Master, #TF1799, Blaster: Blaster, Flight-Pack (jet pack)..$25.00

Action Master, #TF1805, Shockwave: Shockwave, Fistfight (mini-robot)...$25.00

Action Master, #TF1809, Inferno: Inferno, Hydro-Pack (water laser backpack) $25.00

Action Master, #TF1817, Prowl: Prowl, Turbo Cycle $60.00

Action Master, #TF1821, Over-Run: Over-Run, Attack Copter..$40.00

Action Master, #TF1825, Wheeljack: Wheeljack, Turbo Racer..$70.00

Action Master, #TF1829, Gutcruncher: Stratotronic Jet .$50.00

Action Master, #TF1833, Optimus Prime: Optimus Prime, Armored Convoy..$100.00

Action Master, #TF1873, Skyfall: Skyfall, Top-Heavy Rhino $30.00

Micromaster Combiner, #TF1763, Battle Squad: Meltdown, Half-Track, Direct Hit, Power Punch, Fireshot & Vanguish $25.00

Micromaster Combiner, #TF1767, Metro Squad: Wheel Blaze, Road Runner, Oiler, Slide, Power Run & Strikedown $25.00

Micromaster Combiner, #TF1771, Tanker Truck: Tanker Truck, Pipeline & Gusher $30.00

Micromaster Combiner, #TF1775, Missile Launcher: Missile Launcher, Retro Surge $25.00

Micromaster Combiner, #TF1777, Anti-Aircraft Base, Anti-Aircraft Base, Blackout & Spaceshot...............................$25.00

Micromaster Patrol, #TF1751, Race Track Patrol: Barricade, Roller Force, Ground Hog Motorhead $10.00

Micromaster Patrol, #TF1755, Air Patrol: Thread Bolt, Eagle Eye, Sky High & Blaze Master..................................$10.00

Micromaster Patrol, #TF1759, Hot Rod Patrol, Big Daddy, Trip-Up, Greaser & Hubs $10.00

Micromaster Patrol, #TF1761, Military Patrol: Bombshock, Tracer, Dropshot & Growl...$10.00

BEAST WARS

Maximal, Airrazor, loose, M $25.00

Maximal, Blackarachnia, 1996, MOC $85.00

Maximal, Cheetor, MOC $18.00

Maximal, Depth Charge, MIB $20.00

Maximal, Optimus Primal (Gorilla), MIB $110.00

Maximal, Polar Claw, 1995, MIB $45.00

Maximal, Rattrap, MOC..$100.00

Predacon, Dinobot, 1995, MOC $110.00
Predacon, Inferno, 1996, MIB $25.00
Predacon, Megatron (Dragon), Transmetal II, MIB..........$20.00

Predacon, Megatron (T-Rex), MIB, $110.00.

Decepticon, Mixmaster, MOC, $15.00.

Predacon, Scorponok, dk purple/bl, MIB (Japanese) $85.00
Predacon, Shokaract, BotCon 2000 exclusive (convention),
    MIB $70.00
Predacon, Terrorsaur, MOC..$90.00
Predacon, Tripredacus, w/instructions, loose, M $60.00
Predacon, Waspinator, rare, MOC $110.00

GENERATION 2, SERIES 1, 1992 – 93

Autobot Car, #TF1863, Jazz, Porsche $35.00
Autobot Car, #TF1867, Inferno, fire truck.......................$25.00
Autobot Leader, #TF1879, Optimus Prime w/Roller, tractor-
    trailer w/electronic sound-effect box $35.00
Autobot Minicar, #TF1881, Bumble, metallic VW bug ...$30.00
Autobot Minicar, #TF1883, Hubcap, metallic..................$20.00
Autobot Minicar, TF1887, Seaspray, metallic hovercraft .$15.00
Autobot Obliterator (Europe only), Spark.......................$45.00
Color Change Transformer, #TF1905, Deluge $20.00
Color Change Transformer, #TF1911, Gobots.................$20.00
Constructicon (orange version), #TF1851, Bonecrusher (1),
    bulldozer $7.00
Constructicon (orange version), #TF1855, Scrapper (3), fron-
    tend loader $7.00
Constructicon (orange version), #TF1859, Long Haul (5), dump
    truck $7.00
Constructicon (yel version), #TF1851, Bonecrusher (1), bull-
    dozer $6.00
Constructicon (yel version), #TF1855, Scrapper (3), front-en
    loader...$6.00
Constructicon (yel version), #TF1859, Long Haul (5), dump
    truck $6.00
Decepticon Abliterator (Europe only), Colossus $45.00

Decepticon Jet, #TF1875, Starscream, gray jet w/electronic light
    & sound-effect box $30.00
Decepticon Leader, #TF1913, Megatron, gr tank w/electronic
    sound-effect treads $45.00
Dinobot, #TF1869, Grimlock, bl Tyrannosaurus $25.00
Dinobot, #TF1870, Grimlock, turq Tyrannosaurus...........$40.00
Dinobot, #TF1873, Snarl, orig gray Stegosaurus $35.00
Dinobot, #TF1873, Snarl, red Stegosaurus......................$25.00
Small Autobot Car, #TF1899, Skram...............................$15.00
Small Autobot Car, #TF1903, Turbofire $15.00
Small Decepticon Jet, #TF1889, Afterburner $15.00
Small Decepticon Jet, #TF1891, Eagle Eye $15.00
Small Decepticon Jet, #TF1895, Windrazor.....................$15.00
Small Decpeticon Jet, #TF1893, Terradive $15.00

GENERATION 2, SERIES 2, 1994

Aerialbot, #TF1915, Skydive (1), F-15 ....$15.00
Aerialbot, #TF1919, Firefight (3), Phantom......................$7.00
Aerialbot, #TF1923, Silverbot (5), Concorde $25.00
Combaticon, #TF1927, Brawl (1), tank $7.00
Combaticon, #TF1931, Blast Off (3), shuttle $7.00
Combaticon, #TF1935, Onslaught (5), missile transport .$18.00
Heroes, #TF1953, Autobot Hero Optimus Prime $20.00
Heroes, #TF1953, Autobot Hero Optimus Prime, M (Japanese
    box)...$35.00
Heroes, #TF1955, Decepticon Hero Megatron $20.00
Laser Rod Transformer, #TF1937, Electro......................$15.00

Laser Rod Transformer, #TF1937, Electro, M (Japanese box)...$20.00
Laser Rod Transformer, #TF1941, Jolt..............................$15.00
Laser Rod Transformer, #TF1941, Jolt, M (Japanese box)...$20.00
Rotor Force, #TF1945, Leadfoot..................................$7.00
Rotor Force, #TF1947, Manta Ray $7.00
Rotor Force, #TF1951, Ransack $7.00
Stunticon, BotCon '94 Exclusive, #TF1925, Breakdown (2),
    Countach $100.00
Watch, #TF1957, Superion $12.00
Watch, #TF1961, Ultra Magnus..................................$12.00
Watch, #TF1965, Scorpia..$12.00

Bootleg/Unlicensed Transformers

Action Master Blue Streak w/Action Master Optimus Prime's
    Vehicle, K2 ....$30.00
Action Master Jazz, gray & purple or gray & ultramarine bl, K2,
    ea $5.00
Action Master Rad, orange & purple, K2.........................$5.00
Blitzwing, plastic, K2..$6.00
Dai-Atlas (Dai-Atris), same as orig Japanese toy except for
    recolored stickers, battery-op, K2 ....$25.00
Dino King, oversized version from Victory series, K2 ....$25.00
Generation 3 Inferno, plastic, yel arms & legs, K2.............$6.00
Gumball Transformer Models, Japanese, set of 4, very rare, MIP,
    K2 ....$30.00
G2 Combaticon Blast-Off, giant size, K2 ....$10.00
Mini Max, sm version of Fortress Maximus, spike forms head, 7",
    K2 ....$15.00
Power Master Decepticon Jet, different colors than orig, K2..$15.00
Sky Garry, remake of robot from Star Convoy series, no micro-
    masters or shuttles, K2 ....$10.00
Star Saber, Brainmaster from Japanese Victory series, no com-
    ponets to form super robot, K2 ....$15.00
Superion, lg firearm, gold helmet, 13", K2 ....$25.00
Transformer Landross, Japanese remake, K2 ....$15.00

Trolls

The first trolls to come to the United States were modeled after a 1952 design by Marti and Helena Kuuskoski of Tampere, Finland. The first trolls to be mass produced in America were molded from wood carvings made by Thomas Dam of Denmark. As the demand for these trolls increased, several US manufacturers were licensed to produce them. The most noteworthy of these were Uneeda Doll Company's Wishnik line and Inga Scandia House True Trolls. Thomas Dam continued to import his Dam Things line. Today trolls are enjoying a renaissance as baby boomers try to recapture their childhood. As a result, values are rising.

The troll craze from the '60s spawned many items other than dolls such as wall plaques, salt and pepper shakers, pins, squirt guns, rings, clay trolls, lamps, Halloween costumes, animals, lawn ornaments, coat racks, notebooks, folders, and even a car.

In the '70s, '80s, and '90s, new trolls were produced. While these trolls are collectible, the avid troll collector still prefers those produced in the '60s. Remember, trolls must be in mint condition to receive top dollar.

For more information, we recommend *Collector's Guide to Trolls* by Pat Peterson.

Advisor: Pat Peterson (P1).

A+ Teacher, #18436, Russ/China, 4½" $8.00
Astronaut, Dam, 1964, 11", EX....................................$125.00
Ballerina, bright red hair, gr eyes, MIP $55.00
Blue Troll w/Frogs, mk Made in Hong Kong, wht hair, amber
    eyes, 3", NM..$20.00
Boy in raincoat, bank, Dam, 1964, 12", from $115 to $155.00
Bride-Nik, Uneeda Wishnik, 1980s, reissue, orig gown & veil,
    red hair, amber eyes, 6", NM $20.00
Cave Girl, leopard-skin outfit, Dam, 3", from $20 to........$25.00
Caveman, leopard-skin outfit, Dam, 1964, 12", from $115 to..$155.00
Cheerleader, Dam, 1964, pnt-on clothes, several variations, 2½",
    NM, ea $20.00
Chuck-O-Luck Santa Claus, gr pnt-on clothing, molded wht
    beard, pk hair, EX $45.00

Clown (often referred to as Emmet Kelly's 'Willie the Clown'), Dam Things, painted-on clothes, 1965, 5¼", from $175.00 to $250.00. (Photo courtesy Roger Inouye)

Cook-Nik, Uneeda Wishnik, bendable, orig outfit, bl hair, brn
    eyes, 5", EX $20.00
Cowboy, Wishnik, red hat, red print shirt & bl pants, 3½"..$15.00
Cowgirl, bank, Creative Mfg, molded outfit, 1978, 8½"...$30.00
Doll-Faced Troll, Uneeda Wishnik, red & wht petal-shaped
    dress, red hair, pnt eyes, 7", NM................................$20.00

Donkey, Dam, 1964, blond hair, amber eyes, 3", NM $35.00
Fire Chief, Treasure Trolls, bl hair & eyes, 4", M $12.00
Girl, bank, Dam, various outfits, hair & eye color, 7" $30.00
Girl w/Accordion, Norwegian, Nyform, pnt-on clothes, brn hair,
    amber eyes, 6", NM..$50.00
Goo Goo Baby, Russ Trolls, 1990s, 9" $13.00
Good-Luck-Nik, Uneeda Wishnik, 1970s, M (orig tube).$30.00
Grandpa Claus, Dam, 1977, orig outfit, wht hair, brn eyes, 1",
    EX, from $100 to $125.00
Here Comes the Judge, Uneda (sic)/Wishnik, 6", from $45
    to...$50.00

Hippies, Thos. Dam, made in Denmark, 1977, 7" (to top of head), from $50.00 to $70.00 each.

Horned Troll, Norwegian, gray rabbit fur glued to body w/red
    plastic heart necklace, w/suction cup, 4", NM...........$40.00
Hula-Nik, Uneeda Wishnik, purple rooted skirt, orange hair
    (faded), yel eyes, 5", EX $30.00
Hunt-nik, w/rifle, Totsy/Wishnik, from $20 to.................$25.00
Iggy-Normous, Dam, 1964-65, wht sailor-style suit w/blk tie,
    blond hair, amber eyes, 12", EX, from $150 to.........$175.00
Indian Girl, Dam, headband w/feather, felt outfit, 7", from $45
    to $50.00
Koko Monkey, Norfin's Ark/Dam, 2½" $4.00
Lion, Dam, 1960s, wht mane & tail, amber eyes, 5", NM, from
    $125 to...$150.00
Love Bug, Regal, yel rooted hair, bl-pnt eyes, bl wings, purple
    dress & bow, 4", MIB, from $75 to $150.00
Lucky Shnook, nodder, Japan, 4½", from $30 to $40.00
Luv-You Nik, Uneeda Wishnik, 1980s, reissue, orig outfit, red
    hair, amber eyes, 5", MM $20.00
Miss America, unmk, wht satin & net gown, pearl tiara, wht
    hair, amber eyes, 3", EX $25.00
Neanderthal Man, Bijou Toy Inc, 1963, 7½"....................$35.00
No Good-Nik, Uneeda Wishnik, 1980s, 5".......................$15.00
Norfin Boy, Dam, 1979, purple pants & bl shirt, orange hair,
    amber eyes, fully jtd, 18", NM $65.00
Norfin Exercise Girl, Dam, 1977, bl outfit, wht hair, amber eyes,
    9¾", NM..$35.00

Norfin Girl, Dam, 1979, purple dress w/wht leotards & hair bow,
    orange hair, amber eyes, fully jtd, 18", NM...............$65.00
Norfin Sea P'Troll, Dam, 1977, bl & wht sailor suit, blk hair, brn
    eyes, 9¾", NM $35.00
Norfin Turtle, Dam, 1984, amber eyes, 4", NM $50.00
Nursenik, Uneeda Wishnik, 1970s, 6", MOC....................$50.00
Pik-nik, Uneeda Wishnik, 1970s, bendable, 5", MOC.....$40.00
Poppa-He-Nik, Uneeda Wishnik, felt outfit, 5", from $20
    to...$23.00
Robin Hood, Russ Storybook series, red hair, brn eyes, complete
    w/bow & arrow, 4½", NM $15.00
Rock'N Troller, Magical World of Trolls by Largo, 4 different, 3",
    M, ea $12.00
Seal, Norfin Pets/Dam, 1984, 6½"....................................$50.00
Shekter, smiling monkey in lacy diaper, USA, 1966, 3", from
    $30 to $40.00
Short Order Cook, Russ China, #18582, 4½" $8.00
Sock-It-To-Me, Uneeda Wishnik, orig outfit, wht hair, amber
    eyes, 6", NM...$50.00
Tartan Girl, Dam, 1964, orig outfit w/matching ribbons in blk
    hair, amber eyes, 12", M, from $145 to $165.00
Uglie Elephant, Made in Japan, bl-pnt body, blk rabbit fur hair,
    amber eyes, 3½", NM $25.00

Uglie Lion, Made in Japan, amber inset eyes, painted lips, 3", from $20.00 to $25.00.

Viking, John Miessen, molded helmet & boots, felt tunic &
    cape, 7", from $50 to...$80.00
Viking, Norwegian, gray felt tunic w/gr cloak, brn rabbit fur hair
    & beard, bl eyes, 7", NM $80.00
Wizard, Treasure Trolls, lt purple hair, bl eyes, 4", M........$15.00

Viking, Dam Things, silver sword, horned helmet, and felt tunic, 5½", minimum value, $100.00.

MISCELLANEOUS

Carrying Case, Ideal, w/molded waterfall, M	$25.00
Outfit, any style, MIP, ea	$15.00
Pillow, Treasure Trolls Surf Patrol, 14x14", NM	$10.00
Pin, Patsy O'Troll, Russ, 3", MOC	$5.00
Playhouse, Wishnik Mini Trolls, Ideal, 1960s, EX	$25.00
Ring, several variations, EX, ea	$3.00
Stik-Shack, vinyl, EX	$30.00
Troll Party, Marx, rare, MIB	$50.00
Troll Village, EX (EX box)	$175.00
Valentine Kit, Mello Smello, complete, MIB	$8.00
Wristwatch, Treasure Trolls, several variations, MOC, ea	$5.00

View-Master and Tru-Vue

View-Master, the invention of William Gruber, was introduced to the public at the 1939 – 1940 New York World's Fair and the Golden Gate Exposition in California. Since then, View-Master reels, packets, and viewers have been produced by five different companies — the original Sawyers Company, G.A.F (1966), View-Master International (1981), Ideal Toys, and Tyco Toys (the present owners). Because none of the non-cartoon single reels and three-reel packets have been made since 1980, these have become collectors' items. Also highly sought after are the three-reel sets featuring popular TV and cartoon characters. The market is divided between those who simply col-

lect View-Master as a field all its own and collectors of character-related memorabilia who will often pay much higher prices for reels about Barbie, Batman, The Addams Family, etc. Our values tend to follow the more conservative approach.

The first single reels were dark blue with a gold sticker and came in attractive gold-colored envelopes. They appeared to have handwritten letters. These were followed by tan reels with a blue circular stamp. Because these were produced for the most part after 1945 and paper supplies were short during WWII, they came in a variety of front and back color combinations, tan with blue, tan with white, and some were marbleized. Since print runs were low during the war, these early singles are much more desirable than the printed white ones that were produced by the millions from 1946 until 1957. Three-reel packets, many containing story books, were introduced in 1955, and single reels were phased out. Nearly all viewers are very common and have little value except for the very early ones, such as the Model A and Model B. Blue and brown versions of the Model B are especially rare. Another desirable viewer, unique in that it is the only focusing model ever made, is the Model D. For more information we recommend *View-Master Single Reels, Volume I*, by Roger Nazeley. Unless noted otherwise, values are for reels complete with cover and book.

Advisor: Roger Nazeley (N4).

Other Sources: C1.

Six Million Dollar Man, GAF, 1974: BB-559-4 E, one reel on card from Belgium, from $25.00 to $30.00; AVB-559, US talking version in box, from $30.00 to $40.00; B-559 US reels in envelope, from $15.00 to $20.00. (Photo courtesy Greg Davis and Bill Morgan)

SINGLE REELS

A Team, #4426, 1983, sealed	$15.00
Buffalo Bill Jr, #965b	$5.00
Chilly Willy, #823	$4.00
Day at the Circus II, #702	$4.00
Goldilocks & the Three Bears, FT-6, w/book	$5.00
Historic Philadelphia, #351	$4.00
Huckleberry Hound-Project Green Thumb, B-5123	$3.00
Jack & the Beanstalk, FT-3	$4.00
KISS, #002305	$8.00
Land of the Giants, B-4942	$4.00
Little Black Sambo, FT-8, w/book	$12.00

Mary Poppins, B-3762 ....$3.00
Mickey's Trailer, #3-54 ....$3.00
Mother Goose Nursery Rhymes, B-4103 ....$3.00
National Parks, RP-2105 ....$3.00
Performing Elephants — St Louis Zoo, #925 ....$4.00
Quick Draw McGraw, #5341 ....$3.00
Roy Rogers — The Holdup, #946 ....$5.00
Scooby Doo — That's Snow Ghost, #1016 ....$3.00
Seven Ancient Wonders of the World, B-9011 ....$4.00
Snow White & the Seven Dwarfs, FT-4, w/book $5.00
Strange Animals of Africa & North America, B-6153 ......$4.00
Tarzan Rescues Cheetah, #975, w/book $7.00
Tom & Jerry — Cat Trapper, #810 ....$4.00
Welcome Back, Kotter, #002056 ....$4.00
Winnie the Pooh, B-3622 ....$3.00
Your United Nations, #420a-c, no cover, w/book $18.00

THREE-REEL SETS

ABC Circus, B-411 ....$18.00
Alice in Wonderland, B-360 ....$15.00
American Indian, B-725 ....$15.00
Apollo Moon Landing, B-663 ....$15.00
Archies, B-574, sealed $38.00
Aristocats, B-365, no cover $8.00
Bambi, B-400 ....$14.00
Batman, B-492 ....$25.00
Big Blue Marble, B-587, sealed $26.00
Big Easter Story, B-880, slight wear $14.00
Black Hole, K-35, sealed $28.00
Bugs Bunny-Big Top Bunny, B-549, sealed $22.00
Carlsbad Caverns Tour #1, A-376 ....$15.00
Casper the Friendly Ghost, B-533, sealed $20.00

Children's Zoo, B-617, sealed $18.00
Cinderella, B-318 ....$12.00
Conquest of Space, B-681 ....$18.00
Daktari, B-498, sealed $45.00
Dennis the Menace, B-539, sealed $22.00
Fat Albert, B-554 ....$8.00
Flintstones, B-514 ....$22.00
Godzilla, J-23, sealed $23.00
Goldilocks & the Three Bears, B-317 ....$18.00
Lassie Rides the Flumes, B-489 ....$15.00
Little Drummer Boy, B-871, sealed $18.00
Little Red Riding Hood, B-310, sealed $22.00
Marineland in Florida, A-964 ....$14.00
Mickey Mouse, B-528 ....$15.00
Million Dollar Duck, B-506, sealed $30.00
Muppet Movie, K-27, sealed $24.00
Niagara Falls, A-655 ....$15.00
Niagara Falls — Canadian Side, A-656 ....$12.00

Partridge Family, B-592, Male Chauvinist, GFA, 1973, MIP, from $35.00 to $45.00. (Photo courtesy Greg Davis and Bill Morgan)

Peanuts, B-536 ....$15.00
Pink Panther, J-12 ....$16.00
Pinocchio, B-315 ....$16.00
Popeye, B-516 ....$12.00
Prehistoric Animals, B-619 ....$22.00
Puss-in-Boots, B-320 ....$12.00
Return From Witch Mountain, J-25, sealed $20.00
Robin Hood, B-342, sealed $25.00
Romper Room, K-20, sealed $18.00
Rookies, B-452, sealed $26.00
Run Joe Run, B-594 ....$16.00
Search — NBC TV Series, B-591, sealed $33.00
Shaggy DA, B-368, sealed $20.00

Kung Fu, B-598 GAF, 1974, MIP, from $20.00 to $25.00.
(Photo courtesy Greg Davis and Bill Morgan)

Sleeping Beauty, B-308 ....$15.00
Snoopy & the Red Baron, B-544, sealed $20.00
Spiderman vs Dr Octopus, K-31 ....$12.00
Star Trek — Mr Spock's Time Trek, B-555 ....$30.00
Treasure Island, B-432, sealed $33.00
War Between The States, B-790 ....$15.00
Washington, A-270 ....$15.00
Winnie the Pooh & the Blustery Day, K-37, sealed $22.00
Wonders of the Deep, WDPX $18.00
Yellowstone National Park, A-306 ....$15.00
123 Farm, B-412 ....$20.00
20,000 Leagues Under the Sea, B-370 ....$35.00

TALKING VIEW-MASTER

Bambi, AVB-400, slight wear on cover $12.00
Bugs Bunny, AVB-531, no book $10.00
Casper's Ghostland, ABV-545, no book $10.00
Flintstones, AVB-514, slight wear on cover $18.00
Flipper, AVB-485, slight wear on cover $18.00
Jack & the Beanstalk, AVB-314 ....$15.00
Mark Twain's Tom Sawyer, AVB-340 ....$15.00
Mickey Mouse-Clock Cleaners, AVB-551 ....$14.00
Peter Pan, AVB-372, no book $12.00
Scooby Doo — Snow Ghost, AVB-533 ....$17.00
Snow White & the Seven Dwarfs, AVB-300, sealed $20.00
Superman, AVB-584 ....$16.00

MISCELLANEOUS

Alice in Wonderland, FT-20c, book only $3.00
Bonanza, book only $6.00
Casper viewer & reels, 1995, MIB $12.00
Jurassic Park Gift Set, viewer & 3 reels, MIB (unopened) ..$12.00
Mary Poppins, B-376, book only $4.00
Mickey Mouse View-master Viewer, 1989 ....$5.00
Roy Rogers — Adventure Roundup, B-475, book only $5.00
Talking View-master (viewer only), EX $26.00
View-master 100 Deluxe Projector, NMIB $12.00
Welcome Back, Kotter, J-19, book only $5.00

Western

No friend was ever more true, no brother more faithful, no acquaintance more real to us than our favorite cowboys of radio, TV, and the silver screen. They were upright, strictly moral, extrememly polite, and tireless in their pursuit of law and order in the American West. How unfortunate that such role models are practically extinct nowadays.

This is an area of strong collector interest right now, and prices are escalating. For more information and some wonderful pictures, we recommend *Character Toys and Collectibles, First* and *Second Series*, by David Longest and *Guide to Cowboy Character Collectibles* by Ted Hake. Other publications include *The Lone Ranger* by Lee Felbinger; *The W.F. Cody Buffalo Bill Collector's Guide* by James W. Wojtowicz; and *Roy Rogers and Dale Evans*

Toys & Memorabilia by P. Allan Coyle. With the exception of Hake's, all are published by Collector Books.

Advisors: Donna and Ron Donnelly (D7).

See also Advertising Signs, Ads, and Displays; Books; Cereal Boxes; Character and Promotional Drinking Glasses; Character Clocks and Watches; Coloring, Activity, and Paint Books; Guns; Lunch Boxes; Premiums; Puzzles and Picture Blocks; Windups, Friction, and Other Mechanicals.

Annie Oakley, outfit, Pla-master, 1950, red blouse & fringed skirt w/silkscreen of Annie on pockets, NMIB $200.00
Bat Masterson, Indian Fighter playset, Multiple, complete, NM (NM box) $200.00
Bat Masterson, wallet, Croyder, 1950s, NMIB, A $75.00
Bonanza, Foto Fantastiks Coloring Set, Eberhard Faber, 1965, complete, M (EX box), A $100.00
Cheyenne, cowboy gloves, fringed w/name & image of horse head, unused, M $50.00

Buffalo Bill Jr, belt and buckle, aluminum and plastic, Flying A Productions, 1950s, EX, $45.00. (Photo courtesy June Moon)

Corporal Rusty (Rin-Tin-Tin), outfit, Iskin/Screen Gems, 1955, with gun and holster, EX (EX box), A, $225.00.

Dale Evans, outfit, Yankeeboy, w/skirt, vest, blouse & holster, EX (EX box) $265.00

Daniel Boone, Fess Parker Inflatable Indian Canoe, Multiple, 1965, NMIP $55.00

Daniel Boone, Fess Parker Super Slate, Saalfield, 1964, cb w/lift-up erasable film sheet, unused, NM..........................$50.00

Daniel Boone, figure, Am Tradition, 1964, plastic w/soft vinyl head & coonskin cap, 5", NM, from $75 to.............$100.00

Daniel Boone, Woodland Whistle, Autolite, 1964, NMIB..$65.00

Davy Crockett, Auto-Magic Picture Gun, Stephens, 1950s, complete w/film, EX (EX box), A $125.00

Davy Crockett, bank, plaster figure, VG........................$125.00

Davy Crockett, bank, 1950s, bust figure w/rifle, copper-tinted metal, 5", NM (EX box) $125.00

Davy Crockett, Camera Ensemble, Herbert-George, complete w/camera, flash attachment & bulbs, scarce, NM (EX box) $400.00

Davy Crockett, Dart Gun Target Set, Knickerbocker, 1950s, complete, NRFB..$75.00

Davy Crockett, doll, Fortune Toy/WDP, compo w/cloth clothes & coonskin hat, open/close eyes, 8", NMIB, A $175.00

Davy Crockett, doll, unmarked, 1950s, stuffed cloth with hand-painted vinyl face, name on chest, 27", EX, A, $150.00.

Davy Crockett, flashlight, 1950s, litho tin w/red plastic top, 3", EX...$30.00

Davy Crockett, night light, 1950s, head figure, 1950s, EX..$50.00

Davy Crockett, Pistol & Knife, Multiple, blk plastic blunderbuss-type gun & knife emb w/name, NMOC, A........$65.00

Davy Crockett, ring, 1960s, from gumball machine, M....$15.00

Davy Crockett, slide-tile puzzle, Roalex, 1950s, blk & wht plastic w/image of Davy & friends, NMOC $50.00

Davy Crockett, Thunderbird Moccasin Kit, Blaine, 1950s, complete, NM (EX box), A $175.00

Davy Crockett, tool kit, Liberty Steel, 1955, litho tin chest, complete w/tools & manual, M...............................$450.00

Davy Crockett, TV tray, WDP, 1955, litho tin w/image of Davy fighting Indian, 12x17", EX.....................................$100.00

Davy Crockett, Wagon Train, Marx, 1950s, horse-drawn coach w/3 units, plastic, 14", EX (EX box), A....................$425.00

Davy Crockett, wallet, 1955, brn vinyl w/faux fur on Davy's hat, NM, from $75 to..$100.00

Davy Crockett, Yo-Yo, Fli-Back, 1950s, wood w/gold leaf stamp, tournament shape, NM...$90.00

Gabby Hayes, hat, wool, EX $135.00

Gabby Hayes, Sheriff Set, John Henry, 1950, w/handcuffs & badge, MOC, from $100 to $125.00

Gabby Hayes, Target Set, complete, EX (EX box)..........$300.00

Gene Autry, drum set, 3-pc set w/cb figure seated on lg drum, NMIB..$900.00

Gene Autry, guitar, plastic, 31", EX, A $150.00

Gene Autry, Official Ranch Outfit, Leslie-Henry, 1940s, brown suede vest and chaps, red felt trim, NM (VG box), $265.00.

Gene Autry, stencil book, Stencil Art, 1950, unused, NM, A...$75.00

Gunsmoke, outfit, Matt Dillon, Seneca, 1958, complete, EX (EX box)..$125.00

Have Gun Will Travel, Paladin playset, Multiple, 1960, complete, EX (VG box), A $250.00

Hopalong Cassidy, Bar 20 Ranch Horn, Perlin Products, 1950s, plastic w/rubber honker at ea end, EX (VG box), A .$250.00

Hopalong Cassidy, chaps, 1950s, blk suede w/image of Hoppy, VG $85.00

Hopalong Cassidy, dinnerware set, three-piece, $225.00.

Hopalong Cassidy, dominoes, Milton Bradley, 1950, complete, EX (EX box), from $75 to $100.00

Hopalong Cassidy, drum, Rubbertone/Wm Boyd, 1950, 2 different images of Hoppy on drum tops, 5" dia, EX $225.00

Hopalong Cassidy, outfit, J Bard, 1950, blk pants w/red detail, blk & wht shirt w/red vinyl fringe, EX, A................$200.00

Hopalong Cassidy, outfit, Sun Valley, w/blk shirt & pants, red neckerchief w/metal holder, leather boots, NM, A .$450.00

Hopalong Cassidy, Picture Gun & Theatre, battery-op, MIB, L4..$350.00

Lone Ranger, doll, composition, with Bond Bread Safety Club Sheriff's Badge, cast-iron gun and holster, original store tag marked Dollcraft Novelty Co., 15", EX+ (missing hat), A, $750.00.

Hopalong Cassidy, sparkler, 1950, plastic bust figure w/metal plunger, 3½", EX, A $275.00

Hopalong Cassidy, Switch-A-Buckle Belt, complete, NMOC...$225.00

Legend of the Lone Ranger, playset, HG Toys, 1978, MIB (sealed)...$50.00

Lone Ranger, Action Arcade, 1975, NMIB, from $100 to..$125.00

Lone Ranger, beanie, 1940, felt, wht image & lettering on blk w/red trim, NM, from $75 to...................................$100.00

Lone Ranger, crayons, 1953, complete, NM (NM tin box), from $75 to..$100.00

Lone Ranger, doll, Dollcraft/TLR, pnt compo, standing w/guns-drawn, wearing chaps & felt mask, 10", NMIB........$650.00

Lone Ranger, doll, Mego, 1972, talker, stuffed cloth, 24", MIB, L6...$65.00

Lone Ranger, First Aid Kit, American White Cross Inc, 1938, complete, EX..$65.00

Lone Ranger, First Aid Kit, 1938, complete in 4x4" tin container, EX, A..$100.00

Lone Ranger, harmonica, 1947, silverplated, NMIB, from $75 to...$125.00

Lone Ranger, horseshoe, Gardner Games, 1950, rubber, complete, NMIB, from $175 to.......................................$195.00

Lone Ranger, magic slate, Whitman, 1978, cb w/lift-up erasable film sheet, EX, from $55 to.................................$75.00

Lone Ranger, movie viewer, Lone Ranger Rides Again, 1940, lg, NMIB, from $200 to...$250.00

Pla-master Play Suits, child's range rider outfit, includes chaps, shirt, vest, handkerchief, metal gun with holster, 1950s, MIB, $135.00. (Photo courtesy June Moon)

Lone Ranger, Mysterious Prospector Playset, Gabriel, 1976, complete, scarce, NM (NM box) $100.00

Lone Ranger, outfit, TLR Inc, 1930s, complete w/chaps & vest, rare, VG (worn box), A................................$250.00

Lone Ranger, pencil box, 1940, bl w/emb gold image & lettering, NM, A $100.00

Lone Ranger, Picture Printing Set, 1938, complete, NMIB, from $200 to...$225.00

Lone Ranger, playset, Legend of the Lone Ranger Western Frontier, HG Toys, 1981, complete, NMIB $75.00

Lone Ranger, Punch-Out Set, 1947, complete, NMIB, from $175 to...$250.00

Lone Ranger, telescope, 1946, NMIB, from $150 to.......$200.00

Lone Ranger Movie Viewer, Acme Plastics, 1940, Bakelite viewer w/5 movies, EXIB..............................$165.00

Lone Ranger Rides Again, Prairie Wagon, 4-in-1, Gabriel, MIB, from $45 to...$55.00

Maverick, TV Eras-O-Picture Book, Hasbro, 1959, MIB (sealed) $100.00

Range Ryder, chair, 1956, wood folding-type w/image on blk fabric bk, wht fringe on bottom, 24", scarce, EX, T2 ......$75.00

Red Ryder, Junior Braces, Slesinger, 1950, complete, rare, NM (EX box), A..$225.00

Rifleman, outfit, Pla-master, 1959, flannel & corduroy w/felt hat, complete, NM (NM box)................................$200.00

Rin-Tin-Tin, Magic Picture Set, Transogram, 1956, complete, NMIB $65.00

Rin-Tin-Tin, outfit, Corporal Rusty 101st Cavalry, Pla-master, 1955, complete, scarce, EX (EX box)..................$150.00

Roy Rogers, Archery Set, Ben Pearson, 1950s, complete w/bow, quill & arrows, scarce, EX (worn box) $275.00

Roy Rogers, bandanna, 1950s, brn, red & bl litho on tan, EX $55.00

Roy Rogers, bank, Almar Metal Arts, 1950s, 3-D cowboy boot atop horseshoe-shaped base, copper luster, 5", EX ...$125.00

Roy Rogers, bank, Ohio Art, litho tin w/colorful image of Roy & Trigger, 8", MIP, A.....................................$250.00

Roy Rogers, Burn-Rite Wood Burning Set, Rapaport Bros, complete, NM (EX box), A $175.00

Roy Rogers, Crayon Set, Standard Toykraft, 1950s, complete, VG (VG box) $75.00

Roy Rogers, Fix-It Chuck Wagon & Jeep, Ideal, plastic, complete, NM (EX box), A $250.00

Roy Rogers, flashlight, Bantam, 1974, red & wht plastic, complete w/Trail Guide pamphlet, 3", NM $165.00

Roy Rogers, horseshoe set, NMIB $145.00

Roy Rogers, Modeling Clay Set, Standard Toykraft, complete, NM (NM box) $125.00

Roy Rogers, movie, Silver Fox Hunt, Hollywood Film Ent, 1950s, 8mm, VG+ $60.00

Roy Rogers, outfit, Merit Playsuits, 1950s, complete, NMIB ..$350.00

Roy Rogers, outfit, Yankeeboy, 1950s, tan pants, vest & folding cloth hat, EX (G box) $275.00

Roy Rogers, phonograph, RCA Victor, 1950s, plastic & metal, rare, VG+..$295.00

Roy Rogers, pull toy, NN Hill Brass Co, wood, image of Roy on Trigger, w/bell, 9", NM $275.00

Roy Rogers, Quick Shooter Hat, Ideal, MIB..................$385.00

Roy Rogers, riding horse, Reliable Toy, Canada, plush Trigger with molded plastic face, 26" long, EX+, A, $400.00.

Roy Rogers, slippers, blk & wht, M (VG+ box w/mc paper label)...$165.00

Roy Rogers, tattoo transfers, Fawcett, EX (EX envelope), A $85.00

Roy Rogers, telescope, Herbert George, 1950s, blk w/no markings, NM (VG box), A $225.00

Roy Rogers & Dale Evans, Colorforms Dress-Up Kit, 1950s, complete, EX (EX box) $150.00

Roy Rogers & Trigger, bank, litho tin & plastic w/image of Roy & Trigger in horseshoe, rectangular, 8", EX, A........$125.00

Roy Rogers Riders, harmonica, 1955, 4", NMOC............$95.00

Straight Arrow, powder horn, 1950s, rare, NM $100.00

Texas Ranger, bank, litho tin & plastic w/image of Texas Ranger in horseshoe, rectangular, 8", EX...........................$75.00

Tom Mix, belt, 1930s, wht plastic w/red checkerboard & cowboy design, brass buckle w/secret compartment, EX.......$125.00

Tom Mix, spurs, glow-in-the-dark, MIB, C10.................$150.00

Wild Bill Hickok, Bunkhouse Kit, Vornado Air Circulators, 1950s, NM (NM envelope) $65.00

Wyatt Earp, outfit, Yankeeboy, 1950s, complete, VG (VG box), A $125.00

Zorro, cape, Carnival Creations, NMOC.........................$65.00

Zorro, movie, Zorro's Suicide Express, United Artists, 1971, MIB (sealed)...$30.00

Zorro, Pencil Craft By Numbers, Hassenfeld Bros/WDP, complete, EX (EX box)...$75.00

Zorro, pinwheel, WDP, 1950s, plastic w/wood hdl, metal bell rings w/movement, 18", scarce, EX, from $75 to $100.00

Zorro, ring, silver & blk, EX $15.00

Zorro, wallet, brn or wht vinyl w/Zorro & horse, EX, ea...$75.00

Zorro, 3-D Cut-Outs, Aldon Industries, 1950s, litho plastic, complete, NMIP, from $75 to.................................$100.00

Windups, Friction, and Other Mechanicals

Windup toys represent a fun and exciting field of collecting — our fascination with them stems from their simplistic but exciting actions and brightly colored lithography, and especially the comic character or personality-related examples are greatly in demand by collectors today. Though most were made through the years of the '30s through the '50s, they carry their own weight against much earlier toys and are considered very worthwhile investments. Various types of mechanisms were used — some are key wound while others depend on lever action to tighten the mainspring and release the action of the toy. Tin and celluloid were used in their production, and although it is sometimes possible to repair a tin windup, experts advise against investing in a celluloid toy whose mechanism is not working, since the material is usually too fragile to withstand the repair.

Many of the boxes that these toys came in are almost as attractive as the toys themselves and can add considerably to their value.

Advisors: Richard Trautwein (T3); Scott Smiles (S10).

See also Aeronautical; Automobiles and Other Replica Vehicles; Boats; Chein; Lehmann; Marx; Robots and Space Toys; Strauss.

AMERICAN

Acrobatic Monkeys, Wyandotte, 10", EX, from $350.00 to $425.00.

Action Ski Jumper, Wolverine, skier somersaults down ski jump, litho tin, 26" ramp, MIB..............................$350.00
Airport, Ohio Art, ca 1950, 2 planes circle terminal, litho tin, 9", NM (EX box) $250.00
America Locomotive, Ives, pnt & stenciled tin w/CI spoke wheels, clockwork, 12", VG, A $600.00
Artie the Clown, Unique Art, clown drives comical car w/several action, litho tin , 9½", EX $500.00
Auto Speedway, Automatic Toy Co, 1930s, NM (VG box)...$225.00
Bombo the Monkey, Unique Art, monkey swings in tree, litho tin, 10", EX (G- box), A.............................$150.00
Bombo the Monkey, Unique Art, monkey swings in tree, litho tin, 10", EX (VG box), A.............................$200.00
Boss Locomotive, Fallows, pnt & stenciled tin w/CI spoke wheels, clockwork, 8", G, A $250.00
Boy & Girl on Seesaw, Gibbs, pnt tin, 14", EX, A $200.00
Boy on Tricycle, Stevens & Brown, tin & compo figure w/cloth clothes, CI tricycle w/spoke wheels, 11", VG, A..$1,350.00
Boy on Velocipede, Stevens & Brown, compo figure w/cloth outfit, tin 3-wheeler, 11", NM..............................$2,300.00

Capitol Hill Racer, Unique Art, car travels back & forth from station house through bridge, litho tin, 17", EX (G box)..$175.00
Carousel, Wyandotte, w/swans & airplanes, spins w/music, litho tin, 4½" dia, VG, A....................................$275.00
Casey the Cop, Unique Art, advances w/swinging arms, litho tin, 9", EX (EX box) $900.00
Charlie Chaplin, att Unique Art (smiliar to 1 made by Gunthermann), litho tin, 8", VG+.........................$650.00
Charlie Chaplin String Rider, AC Gilbert, litho tin w/counterweight, 8", EX, A................................$300.00
Coast Guard Seaplane, Ohio Art, litho tin, 10", EX, A .$200.00
Commando Joe, Ohio Art, soldier realistically crawls w/rifle, litho tin, 8", MIB......................................$200.00
Crane, Wolverine, rotating boom & sky hook, litho tin, 17", VG $100.00
Crawling Baby, Irwin, compo w/cloth clothes, 6", EX (EX box), A..$100.00
Cuzner Trotter, Ives, Pat March 7, 1871, red-pnt tin w/blk spoke wheels, full-figure driver & wht horse, 11½", EX, A...$2,500.00
Dancing Cinderella & Prince, Irwin, 1950, figures perform waltz, plastic, 5", M (EX box)....................$200.00
Dancing Dutch Boy, Lindstrom, vibrates around, litho tin, EX (EX box) $275.00
Dancing Monkey, Ives, 1895, monkey dances on wooden base, 9", EX, A $850.00
Dandy Andy Rooster, Wolverine, rooster plucks worm from tree trunk as baby chick looks on, wheeled base, tin, 10", NMIB..$600.00
Dandy Jim the Jolly Clown Dancer, Unique Art, clown dances & plays cymbals atop roof, litho tin, 9½", G+, A....$700.00
Dandy Jim the Jolly Clown Dancer, Unique Art, 1922, clown w/cymbals does the jig atop circus tent, tin, 10", rare, NMIB $1,000.00
Daredevil Motor Cop, Unique Art, advances, tumbles & rights itself, litho tin, 9½", NM (EX box) $1,300.00

Dump Truck #352, Wyandotte, MIB, from $140.00 to $175.00. (Photo courtesy Jeff Bub Auctions)

Donald Duck & Pluto Handcar, Lionel, Donald pumps cart w/Pluto in doghouse, litho tin & compo, 10", VG, A.$700.00
Drum Major, Wolverine, advances & plays drum, litho tin, 13½", EX, A $275.00
Easter Bunny Motorcycle, Wyandotte, bunny advances on motorcycle w/sidecar, litho tin, 9½", G, A $200.00

Easter Greetings Truck, Courtland, litho tin, 8½", VG, A...$225.00
Electricar, Kingston Prod, red-pnt tin w/blk rubber tires, 14½", EX (VG box), A $500.00
Emergency Auto Service Wrecker, Wyandotte, litho tin & plastic, 15", VG, A $150.00

Felix the Cat Dancing Toy, Pat Sullivan, Made in USA, very rare, EX+ (EX box), A, $1,650.00.

GI Joe and His K-9 Pups, Unique Art, EX, S10, from $250.00 to $300.00. (Photo courtesy Scott Smiles)

Finnegan Porter, Unique Art, porter standing on front of baggage car, litho tin, 14", NMIB, A $350.00

Fire Engine w/Fire Fightin' Firemen, Nosco, plastic, friction, 8", NMIB, A...$100.00

Flasho the Mechanical Grinder, Girard, 1925, litho tin, 4½", EX $150.00

Flying Circus, Unique Art, plane & clown circle elephant, litho tin, 11", NM (G box)...$1,500.00

GI Joe & His Jouncing Jeep, Unique Art, advances w/crazy action as figure bounces in seat, litho tin, 7", EX, A $200.00

GI Joe & His Jouncing Jeep, Unique Art, 1941, litho tin, NM..$250.00

Giant Ride Ferris Wheel, Ohio Art, litho tin w/plastic seats, 17", G, A $175.00

Giant Ride Ferris Wheel, Ohio Art, 17", VG, S10, $225.00 (EX, $275.00). (Photo courtesy Scott Smiles)

Girl String Rider, AC Gilbert, litho tin w/counterweight, 6", EX, A $150.00

Grocery Truck, Kingsbury, w/driver, gr-pnt tin w/wht rubber tires, 8", EX, A...$400.00

Gurdy the Goose, Unique Art, advances w/moving head, litho tin, 9", G, A...$75.00

Hee-Haw, Unique Art, donkey pulls farmer in cart & kicks, litho tin, 10½", G..$200.00

Hobo on Unicycle String Rider, AC Gilbert, litho tin w/counterweight, 8", rare, EX, A $600.00

Hobo Train, Unique Art, dog tugs on man's pants atop train, litho tin, 8", EX $350.00

Hoky & Poky, Wyandotte, 2 clowns work handlebars on handcar, litho tin, 6", NM (EX box)..............................$400.00

Hott & Tott, Unique Art, Black banjo player standing beside piano player, litho tin, 9", EX (G box) $1,250.00

Howdy Doody Cart, Nylint, Howdy works handlebars, litho tin, 9", NM, A...$425.00

Humphrey Mobile, Wyandotte, 1950, figure pedals trike w/attached shack, litho tin, 8½", EX $450.00

Humphrey Mobile, Wyandotte, 1950, figure pedals trike w/attached shack, litho tin, 8½", NMIB, A............$750.00

Jackie Gleason Bus, Wolverine, 1955, litho tin, 13", EX (EX box) $1,000.00

Jazzbo Jim, Unique Art, Black man plays banjo & dances atop roof, litho tin, 9½", G, A $450.00

Jet Roller Coaster, Wolverine, litho tin, 21", G, A.........$225.00

Johnny Clown, Lindstrom, litho tin, 8", VG, A $275.00

Kid Special, B&R, man on scooter travels in zig-zag pattern, litho tin, pull-string action, 6½", rare, VG (G- box)..........$275.00

Kiddie-Go-Round, Unique Art, 4 horses & boats w/figures circle w/bell sound, litho tin & plastic, 10", VG $250.00

Kiddy Cyclist, Unique Art, boy pedals tricycle w/bell sound, litho tin, 9", VG, A...$275.00

Kiddy Cyclist, Unique Art, litho tin, 9", EX, A.............$375.00

Li'l Abner's Dogpatch Band, Unique Art, 8" x 9", EX, A, from $575.00 to $625.00. (Photo courtesy McMasters Doll Auctions)

Li'l Abner & His Dogpatch Band, Unique Art, figures surround piano, several actions, litho tin, 9", NM (NM box), A..$1,000.00

Lincoln Tunnel, Unique Art, vehicles enter & exit tunnels, litho tin, 24", G, A $250.00

Little Red Hen, Baldwin, turn crank & she cackles & lays eggs, litho tin, 5", NM (EX box).....................................$200.00

Loop-A-Loop, Wolverine, track shakes as cars go through loop, litho tin, 19" track, NM $450.00

Man on the Flying Trapeze, Wyandotte, figure tumbles & spins on highbar, litho tin, 9", NM (EX box), A $250.00

Merry-Go-Round, Mattel, circus animals circle candy-stripe pole w/music, tin & plastic, crank action, 7", NM (EX box), A $150.00

Merry-Go-Round, Wolverine, w/5 horses & 4 airplanes, litho tin & plastic, 12", EX...$300.00

Merry-Go-Round, Wyandotte, w/swans & airplanes, spins & plays music, litho tin, 5", NM (EX box), A $350.00

Mickey Mouse Handcar, Lionel, Mickey & Minnie work handle-bars, tin w/compo figures, 9", G, A $500.00

Mickey Mouse Handcar, Lionel, Mickey & Minnie work handle-bar, metal w/compo figures, 9", EX (EX box), A ..$1,100.00

Monkey Shines, Emporium Specialties, monkey climbs coconut tree, litho tin, 18", EX (EX box) $250.00

Moto-Fix Towcar, litho tin w/blk rubber tires, 16", G, A...$125.00

Music Box Carousel, Mattel, 1953, horses & riders move up & down as they spin, litho tin & plastic, 9", NM (NM box), A...$150.00

Mystery Car, Wolverine, silver-pnt tin, push-down action, 13", EX (worn box), A...$375.00

Nero Locomotive, Fallows, pnt & stenciled tin w/CI spoke wheels, clockwork, 10", VG, A $725.00

O-Look the Juggler, Irwin, 1930s, rocks back & forth while balancing balls & flags, mixed materials, 14", NMIB...$275.00

Over & Under, Wolverine, race car travels track & automatically comes to the top, litho tin, 2½" car, EX (EX box) $300.00

Overland Trail Bus, Girard, 1921, 14", rare, prof rstr, NM (EX box), A $1,100.00

Peter Rabbit Chick-Mobile, Lionel, figure pumps handcar, hand-pnt compo, 9", VG $400.00

Police Car, Lupor, 1950, litho tin, 7", EX (EX box), A ..$150.00

Police Motorcycle, Unique Art, litho tin, 8½", G, A.....$325.00

Policeman String Rider, AC Gilbert, litho tin w/counterweight, 8", EX, A $350.00

Preacher at Pulpit, Ives, Black preacher behind pulpit, wood w/compo figure, 10", EX..................................$3,000.00

Racing Car, Irwin, 1950s, red & yel plastic, 12½", scarce, MIB...$200.00

Red Ranger Ride 'Em Cowboy, Wyandotte, horse & rider on rocking base, litho tin, 7", EX $300.00

Red Ranger Ride 'Em Cowboy, Wyandotte, horse & rider on rocking base, litho tin, 7", NM (G box) $300.00

Rocking R Ranch, Courtland, girl & boy rock back & forth on seesaw, 17", NM, A..$150.00

Rodeo Joe, Unique Art, advances w/crazy action as figure bounces, litho tin, 9", EX $225.00

Roosevelt Bear String Rider, AC Gilbert, litho tin w/counter-weight, 6", EX, A..$300.00

Sail Away Carousel, Unique Art, 1940s, 3 sailboats w/children circle tower, litho tin, 9½", EX $200.00

Saloon Car, Chad Valley, red w/litho driver & passenger, 9", EX, A...$450.00

Santa Handcar, Lionel, Santa pumps handcar w/Mickey Mouse in bag on his back, compo, 9", G, A $850.00

See-Saw Circus, Lewco, 9", VG, $150.00 (EX, $200.00; MIB, $250.00). (Photo courtesy Scott Smiles)

Sky Ranger, Unique Art, airplane & zeppelin circle control tower, litho tin, 10", VG $300.00

Sulky Racer, Wilverine, plastic, 9", EX (EX box) $150.00

Sunbeam Racer, Kingsbury, w/driver, red w/blk rubber tires, 18", EX, A $2,700.00

Talking Fire Chief's Control Car, Irwin, turn crank on roof for action, plastic, 9", NM (EX box) $150.00

Toonerville Trolley, Fontaine Fox, 1922, litho tin w/figure standing on platform, 7", EX $1,000.00

Touring Car, Dayton Friction, red-pnt sheet metal w/gold spoke wheels, 12", VG, A...$475.00

Trolley Car #784, Kingsbury, orange, 14", EX, A...........$250.00

Tunnel, Unique Art, vehicles enter & exit tunnels, litho tin, 24", G...$200.00

Uncle Sam String Rider, AC Gilbert, litho tin w/counterweight, 8", EX, A $400.00

Union Station, Automatic Toy, train navigates track through station, litho tin, 20", EX, A $150.00

Unique Artie, Unique Art, advances in erratic pattern as clown bounces in seat, litho tin, 7", EX, A........................$375.00

US Mail Cart, Unique Art, litho tin w/figure on front platform, 13½", NM...$275.00

US Mail Truck, AC Gilbert, yel & blk w/red spoke wheels, 8", VG, A $300.00

Woman Churning Butter, Ives, wood & tin figure w/cloth clothes on wooden box, 9", NM $4,500.00

Wonder Cyclist, Unique Art, boy pedals tricycle w/bell sound, litho tin, 7½", EX (worn box)..................................$450.00

Zilotone, Wolverine, figure plays zilotone, litho tin, includes 3 record disks, 8", VG, A..$700.00

ENGLISH

Clown on Motorcycle, Mettoy, litho tin, 7½", EX, from $700 to .$1,000.00

Double-Decker Bus, Minic, mk Bovril, emb enameled tin, 7", NMIB, A...$350.00

Dump Truck, Tri-ang Minic, silver & gr, 5½", VG, A....$125.00

Happy Dan the Eccentric Milkman, 1950s, advances & circles, litho tin, 4", EX (EX box), A $200.00

London Transport Bus, Tri-ang Minic, red & cream, friction, 5", EX (EX box) $300.00

Mary Had a Little Lamb, Wells, advances w/lamb behind her, plastic, 4½", NMIB, A $125.00

Midget Racer, Tri-ang, gr-pnt pressed steel w/wht rubber tires, scarce, VG, A...$1,300.00

Minic Dairies Tractor Trailer, Tri-ang Minic, red & wht w/blk rubber tires, 7", EX (worn box), A $100.00

Musical Car, Tri-ang Minic, advances & plays music, purple plastic, NMIB, from $150 to $200.00

Petrol Tank Lorry, Minic, emb enameled tin, 5½", NMIB, A $300.00

Police Motorcycle, Mettoy, litho tin, 7½", VG, A $200.00

Racer #3, Tri-ang Minic, gr w/red detail & wht rubber tires, 5½", EX (worn box) $150.00

Southern Railway Delivery Truck, Tri-ang Minic, gr w/Tri-ang Tricycles decal, 5½", EX....................................$100.00

Steam Tractor, Tri-ang Minic, gr, 4", EX (EX box).........$100.00

Big Chief Riding Motorcycle, Mettoy, tin litho with plastic head, 7½", NM (EX box), from $1,100.00 to $1,300.00.

FRENCH

Advocate, Martin, man raises arm & turns behind podium, pnt tin w/cloth clothes, 9", EX, A $1,000.00

Auto Transport, Martin, ca 1920, truck w/driver pulls 2-wheeled wagon, 10½", EX (EX box)...................................$1,500.00

Barrel Man, Martin, man rolls 2 barrels, hand-pnt tin w/cloth clothes, 7", VG, A...$1,300.00

Bimbo Clown Car, litho tin, 4½", EX, A.......................$100.00

Boy Twirling Balls, no cap, pnt tin, 8½", EX $500.00

Boy Twirling Balls, w/cap, pnt tin, 10", EX $900.00

Cable Car Ride, 2 cable cars travel track, tin, 30", G, A ..$200.00

Chevrolet Dump Truck, Vebe, 1938, red-pnt tin w/Hutchins tires, working headlights, 12", G+, A $300.00

Father Francis' Pigs, Martin, figure advances w/2 pigs, hand-pnt tin w/cloth clothes, 7½", VG..............................$1,000.00

Fisherman, Martin, pnt tin w/cloth clothes, 7", EX.....$1,800.00

Gai Violinist (Gay Violinist), Martin, figure plays violin, hand-pnt tin cloth clothes, 7½", EX, A.........................$1,200.00

Jose Carioca, shifts body side-to-side, 8", NM (NM box), A...$500.00

Lady w/Fan, dances around as torso moves, pnt tin, 7", VG....$850.00

Maximum Load 1L Dump Truck, Martin, w/driver, litho tin w/side dump action, 8½", VG, from $250 to $375.00

Miracle Car, travels in sq pattern, stops, doors open & man appears, hood opens to reveal engine, tin, 5½", NMIB, A...$200.00

Motorcycle w/Sidecar, JML, w/driver, litho tin, 12", EX, A...$850.00

Motorcycle w/Sidecar, JML, w/driver, litho tin, 6½", EX...$325.00

Super Racer #42, Gem, 1950s, litho tin w/full-figure driver, blk rubber tires, NM, A...$1,000.00

Voisin Saloon Car, Bing, forward & reverse action, clockwork w/battery-op spotlight, 14½", EX.........................$1,300.00

GERMAN

Acrobat, Gunthermann, Black man performs acrobatics, litho tin, 6", NM, SA...$1,300.00

Acrobat Bear, Schuco, 1950s, does somersaults, yel mohair w/glass eyes, 5", EX (VG box) $500.00

Aeromobie, 1950s, converts from car to airplane, red- & silver-pnt tin, 8", EX (EX box)...$700.00

Airplane Go Round, Distler, 2 airplanes circle tower, litho tin w/celluloid props, 7", NM (G box), A $275.00

Antonio the Organ Grinder, litho tin, 6", EX (worn box), A...$2,400.00

Army Tank, Marklin, litho tin w/rubber treads, 6½", EX, A...$225.00

Balloon Vendor w/Mickey Mouse, 1930s, several actions, litho tin, 7", NM, from $750 to..$900.00

Banjo Player, Gunthermann, Black man plays banjo, hand-pnt tin, 8", G..$1,200.00

Bee & Flower Sparkler, Arnold, bee jumps around flower petals w/sparking action, litho tin, 4½", NM.....................$175.00

Bella Scooter w/Driver, Tipp, litho tin w/compo head, friction, 8", NM...$825.00

Black Dancer, man vibrates around, tin & compo w/cloth clothes, 9", EX, A $400.00

Boston Store Delivery Truck, Bing, mk 195 on doors, litho tin w/spoke wheels, 8", VG, A...................................$1,400.00

British Soldier on Morotcycle, Arnold, advances w/sparking headlight, 7", VG $400.00

Candy Bear on Tricycle, advances w/sm bear on handlebars & 1 attached to rod on bk, litho tin, 8½", EX, A........$1,900.00

Carousel, 3 boats w/figures circle tower, musical, litho tin, 11", VG, A...$500.00

Champion, Goso, 2 boxers (Black/wht) fighting, articulated figures, litho tin, great action, 9" base, VG, rare $1,000.00

Charlie Chaplin, Schuco, wobbles & spins cane, metal w/cloth clothes, 6½", NM, A $950.00

Charlie Chaplin, 1925, push plunger & figure plays cymbals, flat litho tin, 5½", rare, NM, A..................$1,100.00

Chicken w/Egg Cart, Gunthermann, litho tin, 10", G, A..$125.00

Clown Artist, seated clown draws picture on easel, litho tin, 5x5", EX, A $1,200.00

Clown Car, advances w/crazy action, litho tin, 6", VG, A..$300.00

Clown on Cart, G&K, advances w/crazy action, litho tin, 4½", VG $400.00

Clown on Three-Wheeled Cycle, Fischer, clown pedals & performs wheelies, litho tin, 8", NM.........................$2,500.00

Clown Pushing Clown in Hoop, Gunthermann, pnt tin, 6", rstr, A.....................................$500.00

Clown w/Umbrella Walking Dog, mk Made in Germany, advances in erratic pattern, litho tin, 4", EX $375.00

Coney Island Carnival Ride, Technofix, vacuform plastic and tin, with two windup cars, 14" x 20", NM (EX box), from $275.00 to $325.00.

Curvo 1000 Motorcycle, Schuco, w/driver, litho tin, 5", NMIB..$550.00

Cycle-Car Traffic Delivery, Hoge, w/driver, opening rear door, litho tin, 10", EX, A.......................$2,700.00

Donald Duck, Schuco, 1935, vibrates around as mouth opens & closes, litho tin w/felt jacket, 6", VG, from $350 to .$375.00

Donald Duck on Rocket, advances w/engine sound, litho tin, friction, 7", EX, A.........................$300.00

Double-Decker Bus, Gunthermann, litho tin, 12", EX, A $1,500.00

Duck, Kohler, 1950s, quacks & flaps wings, litho tin, NM $75.00

Easter Rabbit on Cart, picks up egg as cart advances, litho tin, friction, 8", EX, A.........................$200.00

Elf on Snail, advances as elf's arms go up & down, litho tin, 10", EX, A $575.00

Famous Juggler, clown juggles 3 sets of rings, tin w/celluloid face & plastic hands, cloth clothes, 9", EX (EX box)......$275.00

Ferrari Racer #21, red w/blk plastic seats, friction, 6", NMOC $75.00

Fire Chief Car, Hoge, 1930s, red & blk, electric headlights & siren, 14", EX, A....................$600.00

Flying Aero Car, B&S/US Zone, advances as wings & propellor emerge, metal, 8", EX (EX box) $750.00

Ford Model T Roadster, Bing, litho tin w/spoke wheels & rear spare, simulated soft top, missing driver, 6½", EX, A ..$350.00

Ford Sedan, Bing, w/driver, litho tin w/spoke wheels, 6", VG, A $200.00

Ford Touring Car, Bing, litho tin w/spoke wheels, 6", EX, A ...$300.00

Frog, Gunthermann, frog hops around & does flips, litho tin w/glass eyes, 4", EX, A....................$125.00

Gama 520, 1950s, mouse travels in & out of cage, litho tin, 3½", MIB................................$125.00

Happy Clown, US Zone, 1948, eyes roll, head moves up and down, 6", NM, from $250.00 to $300.00. (Photo courtesy Dunbar Gallery)

Hi-Way Henry, Fischer, comical auto w/laundry hanging on roof, litho tin, 10", EX....................$3,000.00

Hobo, Gama/US Zone, waddles side to side, litho tin 7", NM..$200.00

Horse & Silky, 1940s, litho tin w/compo figure, 6½" L, EX, A..$125.00

Howdy Doody Acrobat, Arnold, Howdy performs on highbar, litho tin w/cloth clothes, 15", VG...........$250.00

Hurdy Gurdy, figure plays organ as monkey dances atop, litho tin, 7½", VG, A.......................$800.00

Indian Motorcycle, litho tin w/full-figure driver, friction, 6", NM, from $125 to...................$225.00

Jiggs Jazz Car, Nifty, 1924, litho tin, 6", VG $1,200.00

K-342 Motorcycle w/Sidecar, CKO, advances as figure in sidecar shoots machine gun, litho tin, 4", EX, A $350.00

Limousine, Bing, w/chauffer, red w/blk top, spoke wheels, opening doors, 8", VG, A..............$1,250.00

Limousine, Gunthermann, w/driver, pnt tin w/beveled glass window in passenger compartment, 17", EX, A $1,000.00

Mac Motorcycle, Arnold, litho tin w/full-figure driver, 7½", VG, A $550.00

Mac 700 Motorcycle, Arnold, rider mounts & dismounts, blk version, 8", EX $750.00

Mac 700 Motorcycle, Arnold, rider mounts & dismounts, red & silver version, 8", NM $1,000.00

Magic Shunting Train, loco & boxcar navigate track, litho tin, 17" platform, VG (VG box), A $100.00

Main Street Trolley, Nifty, litho tin, 9", VG, A $350.00

Mickey Mouse Jazz Drummer, Nifty, Mickey plays drum, litho tin, M (EX box)...$6,500.00

Mighty Midget, Distler, forward & reverse action, red-pnt tin, 3", NMIB, A $85.00

Military Motorcycle, Kellerman, litho tin w/full-figure driver & passenger, 6", NM (EX box mk Socius) $1,100.00

Military Motorcycle, litho tin w/full-figure driver, 5½", VG, A $225.00

Military Motorcycle w/Sidecar, Tipp, litho tin w/compo figure in cloth clothes, 4½", NM $1,800.00

Military Motorcycle w/Sidecar, Tipp, litho tin w/3 soldiers, 8½", EX, A $3,000.00

Mirakomat 1012 Motorcycle, Schuco, w/driver, litho tin, 5", NMIB, A...$600.00

Monkey in Open Auto, advances as monkey tips hat, litho tin, 6", EX, A $800.00

Moto-Cross, Huki, 2 motorcycles circle & jump over ramp, tin, 16", NMIB $500.00

Motodrill 1006, Schuco, motorcyle advances in circles, stops & spins, litho tin, 5", NM (G box), A $450.00

Motorcycle, Schuco, litho tin w/full-figure driver, 5", G, A...$200.00

Motorcycle #2 w/Driver, Technofix, litho tin, 7", G, A .$250.00

Motorcycle w/Sidecar, Tipp, mk TCO-59, litho tin w/full-figure driver, 7", VG, A $1,000.00

Motorcycle w/Sidecar, Tipp, young couple w/mother-in-law in sidecar, litho tin, electric headlights, 8½", NM, A.........$2,400.00

Mouse Wagon, Schuco, 1932, mouse tumbles & pulls 2-wheeled cart w/mouse, litho tin & plush, 7", EX $750.00

Musical Baby Television, screen shows cartoon western scene, litho tin, NMIB, A $250.00

Nifty-Truk (sic), w/driver & automatic dump, 9½", VG, A ..$450.00

Nursemaid w/Baby, Gunthermann, figure walks w/baby in front of her, pnt tin w/wire legs & lead feet, 6", EX $2,700.00

Open Roadster, Gundka, litho tin w/lady driver, 5½", EX, A $650.00

Performing Circle Elephant, holds beam w/ball & balances revolving whirligig on nose, 7½", NMIB...............$350.00

Performing Poodle, Gunthermann, rocks back & forth while moving front paws, pnt tin, 8", EX..........................$700.00

Police Motorcycle, Gunthermann, 1920s, litho tin w/full-figure driver, 6½", EX, A...$2,700.00

Police Motorcycle, Tipp, advances w/sound & working headlight, litho tin, friction, 11", EX $475.00

Porter w/Cart, Stock, figure pushes 2-wheeled cart w/suitcase, litho tin, 6½", EX, A $750.00

Puss 'N Boots, cat advances w/purse & cane, litho tin w/plastic boots, 5", NM $400.00

Red Cross Ambulance, litho tin camouflage design w/canvas sides, clockwork w/electric headlights, 11", EX, A ..$850.00

Motorcycle With Driver, Arnold US Zone, 7½", NMIB, $850.00 to $950.00. (Photo courtesy Dunbar Gallery)

Motorcycle w/Driver, Schuco, litho tin, 5", VG, A $200.00

Motorcycle w/Sidecar, Distler, w/driver & child passenger, litho tin w/spoke wheels, 7½", EX, A............................$2,500.00

Motorcycle w/Sidecar, Huki, w/driver, litho tin, 6", EX, A ..$300.00

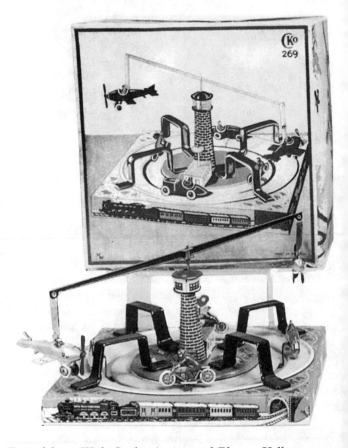

Roundabout With Cycle, Autos, and Planes, Kellerman, two racing cycles, two auto racers and two airplanes, 8" x 8", NMIB, from $5,500.00 to $6,500.00.

Ruck-Ruck Auto, Geppert & Kelch, 3-wheeled vehicle w/driver, litho tin, 6", EX, A $700.00

Santa Claus, Arnold, advances w/sack & pocket full of toys, litho tin, 4", EX $350.00

Sedan, Bing, w/lady driver, blk w/spoked wheels, 8½", G, A ...$350.00

Silver Racer #5 w/Sidecar, Tipp, w/driver & rider standing in sidecar, litho tin, 7½", EX, A................................$1,000.00

Skeeter-Bug Bumper Car, Lindstrom, w/2 figures, tin, 9", VG, A $250.00

Slugger Champions, US Zone, boxers in ring, litho tin, 3½" sq ring, NM (EX box), A...$350.00

Somersault Clown, jumps rope while somersaulting, celluloid w/cloth clothes, 6", MIB...$175.00

Sports Car, Kellerman, w/driver, red-pnt tin w/celluloid windshield, 8", NMIB, from $700 to $825.00

Stork w/Babies, 1950s, mother stork on rod glides around nest of babies, litho tin, lever action, 15", NM (NM box), A.$350.00

Strassenbaukasten, Tippco, complete w/tracks, gas pump island, 2 cars & bus, EX (G box), A $300.00

Teddy Bear on Scooter, Schuco, 1920s-30s, mohair teddy bear on tin scooter, friction, 6", NM, from $1,000 to...$1,300.00

Three Little Pigs, Schuco, 4½", prewar version, felt over tin, M (G box), from $1,100.00 to $1,200.00 for the set.

Toonerville Trolley, Fischer, 1922, advances in erratic motion w/figure on platform, litho tin, 5", NM....................$800.00

Topsy Turvy Tom Car, Ri N Co, litho tin, 10", NMIB....$2,800.00

Touring Car, Bing, w/driver, litho tin w/spoke wheels, 5", VG, A...$300.00

Touring Car, Bing, 1915, w/driver, gray w/yel-pnt spoke wheels, 12½", VG, A $1,600.00

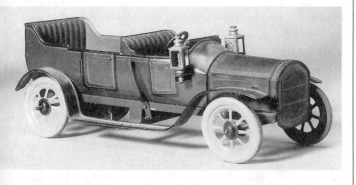

Touring Car, Bing, green with black and yellow lining, red button seats and black wings, orange and gray wheels, 12½", (EX, lacking chauffeur), A, $1,600.00.

Touring Car, Tipp, w/driver, litho tin, 9", EX, A............$500.00

Touring Cyclone Cycle, Grepport & Kelch, w/driver, litho tin w/spoke wheels, 6½", NM...$825.00

Touring Motorcycle w/Gondola Sidecar, Distler, w/chauffer & little boy passenger, litho tin, 6", very rare, EX, A $5,500.00

Town Car, Fischer, w/driver, litho tin w/spoke wheels, 7", VG, A $600.00

Town Car, Fischer, w/driver, litho tin w/wht rubber tires & red hubs, 8", G, A $400.00

Town Car, Gunthermann, w/driver, litho tin w/roof rack & spoke wheels, 7", VG, A...$500.00

Tractor, Bing, litho tin w/full-figure driver, spoke wheels, 7", VG, A $700.00

Trick Motorcycle, Technofix, advances, tips over, rights itself, litho tin, 7", NMIB...$600.00

Troop Carrier, Tipp, litho tin w/7 compo soldiers, 12", EX, A $475.00

Uncle Wiggily Car, Distler, advances w/crazy action, full-figure driver, litho tin, 9½", EX $3,500.00

Vis-A-Vis, Gunthermann, tin w/full-figure driver, wht rubber tires w/gr spokes, 11", EX, A.............................$9,300.00

Volkswagen Convertible, Huki, yel tin w/plastic seats, friction, 6", NMOC $75.00

Yello Taxi, mk Lenox 2300, Karl Bub, w/driver, blk & yel, 11", NM $3,100.00

Yellow Taxi, Bing, w/driver, orange & blk w/disk wheels, 8½", EX, A...$1,500.00

Zeppelin Go-Round, zeppelin w/figure standing in observation basket circles tower, 17", EX $7,700.00

JAPANESE

Accordion Bear, plays accordion & sways, plush & tin w/cloth clothes, 6", NM (VG box) $100.00

Aerial Ladder Fire Engine, K, 1950s, litho tin, friction, complete w/4 figures, 11", NM (EX box).................................$150.00

African Drummer, Trademark, Made in Japan, 6", NM, A, $160.00.

Airplane G-Round, prewar, 6 airplanes w/figures circle base w/sound, tin & celluloid, 14", rare, EX, from $500 to.**$700.00**

Airport Limousine, KKK, 1960s, advances w/sound, bl & wht, friction, 6", NMIB **$100.00**

Ali & His Flying Carpet, KO, 1950s, several actions, litho tin, NM, from $165 to...**$190.00**

Amphibious Boat Silver Queen, Yonezawa, advances w/siren, litho tin w/molded driver, 11", EX (VG box), from $110 to...**$130.00**

Animal Scooter w/Rabbit, Haji, litho tin, NM (VG box), from $100 to..**$125.00**

Army Combat Carrier, litho tin, friction, complete w/8 plastic & tin vehicles, 19", MIB, A..**$175.00**

Atom Racer #27, Yonezawa, litho tin, friction, 16", rare, NM, A **$1,400.00**

Atom Racer #153, Yonezawa, litho tin, friction, 16", rare, EX **$1,000.00**

Auto Cycle, Occupied Japan, full-figure driver, advances w/sound, tin, 5", NM (G box), A..............................**$325.00**

Auto Racer, Linemar, 3 stock cars take off in front of grandstand, litho tin, NM (EX box), A, from $225 to **$250.00**

Avenue Coach Bus, Y, 1950s, litho tin w/curtained windows, friction, 15", NM **$185.00**

Babes in Toyland Soldier, Linemar, 1961, litho tin, 6", EX....**$260.00**

Baby Carriage, prewar, celluloid, umbrella spins as girl walks, NM (EX box), from $350.00 to $400.00.

Banjo Player, Linemar, vibrates around & plays banjo, head nods, litho tin, 5", NM **$200.00**

Barney on Dino (Flintstone Pals on Dino), Linemar, advances & Dino growls, litho tin & celluloid, 8½", NMIB.......**$675.00**

Batmobile, ASC, advances w/sound, litho tin, friction, 11", rare, NM (EX box), A **$1,200.00**

Batmobile, 1960s, futuristic style w/Batman & Robin lithoed in windows, license plate mk 2001, tin, 4", scarce, EX **$1,100.00**

Beach Jeep, Cragstan, litho tin, friction, 7", NM (NM box), A.**$95.00**

Bellhop, Occupied Japan, boy advances w/suitcase, celluloid, 4", VG, A..**$125.00**

Bestmaid Marionette Theatre, CK, prewar, clown & ballerina perform on moving stage, tin w/celluloid figures, 11", NMIB..**$850.00**

Big Joe Chef, Yonezawa, advances w/plate of food, litho tin, 7", MIB..**$150.00**

Black Boy on Tricycle, travels in circular motion as bell rings, litho tin w/celluloid figure, 4", NM, A.....................**$240.00**

Black Porter, Occupied Japan, advances as head moves, celluloid, 3½", NM, A, from $150 to...........................**$200.00**

Blacksmith, Occupied Japan, man swings hammer & hits anvil w/bell sound, litho tin, 6", rare, VG (G box), A **$300.00**

Blacksmith Teddy, TN, bear sits on stump & hammers horseshoe, litho tin & plush, 6", EX (EX box) **$200.00**

Blacksmith Teddy, TN, several actions, plush & tin, 6", MIB, A, from $200 to **$230.00**

Bonzo the Educated & Barking Dog, set number, ask question & he barks & nods, litho tin, 5", NM (G box) **$150.00**

Boy on Sled, prewar, advances & spins, tin, 6½", EX, A, from $225 to...**$245.00**

Boy on Tricycle, pedals tricycle w/bell sound, tin w/celluloid figure, 5½", VG, A **$140.00**

Boy on Tricycle, prewar, pedals trike w/ringing bell, litho tin & celluloid, 7½", EX..**$575.00**

Bozo the Juggling Clown, TPS, several actions, litho tin, 6", EX (VG box), A **$400.00**

Brave Indian, K, horse & rider advance in realistic motion, litho tin, 5", rare, NM (EX box), A **$225.00**

Bulldog, 1950s, advances & shakes shoe in mouth, litho tin, 4", NM (NM box)..**$150.00**

Bunny Cycle, Alps, peddles tricycle w/ringing bell, tin & celluloid, 6", EX (EX box), A.......................................**$275.00**

Bunny Cycle, Japan, 1950s, pedals tricycle as ears rise & bell rings, tin, 5", rare, NM (EX box), A **$300.00**

Calypso Joe the Drummer, Linemar, native plays bongo drum & rocks back & forth, 6", NM (EX box), A.................**$300.00**

Calypso Joe the Drummer, TS, native rocks back & forth while playing drum, litho tin, 6", NM (NM box).............**$350.00**

Casper the Ghost, Linemar, hops around, litho tin, 5", EX, A **$265.00**

Champion Race Car #8, ATC, w/driver, litho tin, friction, 8½", EX (EX box) **$150.00**

Champion Racer #98, Sanyo, w/driver, litho tin, friction, 18", NM, A..**$1,200.00**

Cheery Cook, SNK, waddles around w/plate of food, celluloid, 5", NM (EX box), A...**$125.00**

Chico the Cha Cha Monkey, Alps, plays maracas & sways, mixed material, 9", MIB **$100.00**

Child Indian, Y, advances w/shield & spear, tin & vinyl w/cloth clothes, 7", MIB, A, from $50 to **$80.00**

Cigars & Cigarette Vendor, advances w/box of cigars & cigarettes, tin w/cloth clothes, 8½", not working, G, A..............**$225.00**

Circus Cart, prewar, horse pulls bear & whirligig toy on platform, celluloid, 7½", NM, from $250 to **$260.00**

Circus Clown, TN, shuffles around w/sign & ringing bell, litho tin & celluloid, 5", NM (EX box), A.....................**$200.00**

Circus Clown Cycle, Haji, litho tin w/vinyl-headed figure, friction, 5", EX (EX box) $150.00

Circus Clown on Mule, CK, prewar, vibrates as clown balances block on head, litho tin & celluloid, 8½", EX, A....$275.00

Circus Elephant, M, advances on ball w/several actions, litho tin, 6½", NM (EX box), A.......................................$300.00

Circus Elephant Whirligig, prewar, elephant stands on ball w/spinning umbrella, celluloid, 7½", EX, A $125.00

Circus Merry-Go-Round, Sonsco, elephant holds clown on spinning umbrella, seals peak through base, celluloid, 9", MIB, A $750.00

Circus Monkey, TN, travels on rope to reach bananas, tin, plush & celluloid, 8", NMIB, A, from $100 to $135.00

Clarabelle the Clown, Linemar, waddles back & forth on hands, litho tin, 5", EX $300.00

Clown Juggler, Linemar, swivels & spins arms while balancing plate of fruit on his nose, 8½", NM, from $450 to...$550.00

Clown on Donkey, Occupied Japan, celluloid, 4½", NM (EX box)..$250.00

Clown on Motorcycle, clown performs acrobats on motorcycle, litho tin, 6½", VG, A................................$250.00

Cock Fighting, litho tin, 6", EX (EX box), A $110.00

Comical Clara, TPS, 1950s, 5½", NMIB, from $300.00 to $375.00.

Cock Fighting, Made in Japan, tin, 3⅜" x 2½", EX (EX box), from $125.00 to $140.00.

Coffin Bank, place coin in coffin & skeleton raises his head & arm comes out, tin, 6½", MIB, A $75.00

College Bear, MT, advances w/swinging arms, plush over tin w/celluloid hands, 6½', MIB $200.00

Comet Racer #7, w/driver, litho tin, friction, 7½", VG, A...$200.00

Condor Motorcycle, litho tin w/full-figure driver, friction, 11½", G, A..$1,000.00

Continental Trailways Bus, litho tin, friction, 14", NM, A..$150.00

Crawling Baby, Occupied Japan, crawls w/realistic movement, celluloid w/cloth dress, 5", NM (G box), A $50.00

Crazy Clown Car, Yonezawa, advances w/crazy action as driver's head spins, litho tin w/plastic wheels, 7", NMIB, A ..$100.00

Cycling Quacky, K, duck peddles tricycle & quacks, litho tin, 6", EX (EX box), A $175.00

Dachshund, advances in realistic motion w/bone in mouth, plush over tin, 7", EX (VG box)................................$75.00

Dancing Sam, S&E, figure dances atop revolving stage w/plink plunk music, litho tin, 9", MIB, A $150.00

Dancing Sam, S&E, figure dances atop revolving stage w/plink plunk music, litho tin, 9", EX (EX box)....................$130.00

Deep Sea Diver, CK, prewar, squeeze bulb for swimming action, celluloid, 4½", MIB, A $200.00

Disney Airplane, Linemar, litho tin, friction, 6" W, rare, EX (VG box) $950.00

Disney Character Carousel, Linemar/WDP, 1960s, litho tin, NM..$1,800.00

Donald Cyclist, MT, prewar, tin & celluloid w/cloth clothes, EX (EX box), A..$3,200.00

Donald Duck, Borgfeldt, 1936, celluloid, 5", NM (EX box), A..$1,700.00

Donald Duck & Nephews, Donald pulls nephews on attached rod, plastic, 11", NM $175.00

Donald Duck & Pluto, prewar, Pluto pulls Donald in cart, tin w/celluloid figures, 9", NM (EX box), A $2,300.00

Donald Duck Boxers, Occupied Japan, 2 figures face ea other on wheeled platforms, celluloid, NM........................$1,500.00

Donald Duck Driver, Linemar, celluloid figure in tin convertible, friction, 5", NM (EX box), A $975.00

Donald Duck Drummer, Linemar, advances & plays drum, litho tin, VG..$400.00

Donald Duck in Rocking Chair, Linemar, litho tin & celluloid, EX (EX box mk Walt Disney's Rocking Chair)....$1,100.00

Donald Duck on Motorcycle, Linemar, 1960s, litho tin, friction, 3", NM..$450.00

Donald Duck on Rocking Horse, Japan, prewar, Donald's legs swing as horse rocks, tin & celluloid, 4½", NM, A .$3,000.00

Donald Duck on Trapeze, Borgfeldt, celluloid & tin, NMIB..$1,200.00

Donald Duck Waddler, Occupied Japan, advances w/nodding head, litho tin & plush, 5½", EX (EX box) $500.00

Donkey w/Rider, mk Occupied Japan, celluloid, 5", NMIB...$200.00

Drummer Boy, advances & plays drum, litho tin w/celluloid head, 7½", EX, A..$200.00

Drummer Boy, prewar, stands on base & plays drum, celluloid & wood, 12", EX (EX box) $250.00

Duck Family, mother & 2 ducklings on wheeled cart w/umbrella spinning above, celluloid, 7", NM (EX box)............$150.00

Easter on Parade, Occupied Japan, rabbit pulls ducklings on sled, tin & celluloid, 8", NMIB, A $200.00

Egg Laying Duck, Occupied Japan, waddles along & lays 6 eggs, litho tin, 5", EX (EX box) $150.00

Elephant on Barrel, Occupied Japan, elephant pushes barrel around w/spinning carousel above, celluloid, 8", MIB, from $200 to..$250.00

Farmer on Cart Pulled by Horse, 1950s, VG, from $125.00 to $150.00. (Photo courtesy Scott Smiles)

Fast Freight Continental Express Truck, 1950s, litho tin, friction, 14", NM $175.00

Fifer Pig (Three Little Pigs), Linemar, litho tin, 4½", NM, A $175.00

Fire Department Boat 207, KO, bump-&-go action, litho tin w/full-figure driver, 7½", EX.....................................$100.00

Fisherman, prewar, waddles back & forth w/nodding head, celluloid, 8", NM...$350.00

Fishing Boy, Linemar, boy gets line caught on No Fishing sign, litho tin, 6", NM (EX box), A, from $200 to...........$240.00

Flapping Lovebirds, advances w/flapping wings & moving tail, litho tin, 6", EX (EX box) $100.00

Flintstone Turnover Tank, Linemar, 1961, litho tin, 4", MIB...$925.00

Flying-Fish Speedboat, Asahi Toy, mk F-55, litho tin, 12", EX..$375.00

Football Player, Occupied Japan, w/Notre Dame ribbon & pin, advances & spins, celluloid, M, A..........................$240.00

Ford 60 Dump Truck, S&E, litho tin, friction, 15½", NM (NM box)..$250.00

Fred Flintstone on Dino (Flintstone Pals on Dino), Linemar, litho tin, 8", EX (EX box) $500.00

Frosty Bar Ice Cream Truck, 1950, advances w/ringing bell, litho tin, friction, 7½", NM $175.00

G-Men Car, MT, advances w/siren sound, tin, friction, 6", NM (EX box), A $175.00

Gay 90s Cyclist, TPS, man peddles tricycle w/ringing bell, litho tin w/cloth clothes, 7", NM (EX box), A.................$350.00

Gentleman Frog, Occupied Japan, waddles back & forth w/cane & cigarette, tin & celluloid, 4", EX (EX box), A $275.00

Gerry the Juggler, Toyland, moves hands as balls on wire spin in front of him, tin w/cloth clothes, 6½", NMIB, A $175.00

Giraffe, Occupied Japan, hops around, litho tin, 8", rare, NM (EX box) $240.00

Girl Pushing Baby Carriage, prewar, pushes carriage w/spinning umbrella, celluloid, 8", NM (EX box).....................$400.00

Goofy Unicyclist, Linemar, advances, stops, & turns, litho tin, 9", NMIB, from $1,500 to $1,800.00

Grasshopper, TN, advances w/realistic movement, litho tin, 6", MIB, A..$100.00

Great Mickey the Magician, Linemar/WDP, several actions, litho tin w/cloth cape, NM $1,600.00

Greyhound Bus, litho tin, friction, 6", NM (EX box), A..$235.00

Greyhound Lines Red Ribbon Bus, Marusan, 1950s, tin w/passengers lithoed in windows, friction, 12½", M $750.00

Greyhound Super Cruiser, 1950s, litho tin w/bi-level top, friction, 11", EX $150.00

Groolies Car, Yonezawa, litho tin w/Dracula, Frankenstein, & Wolf Man in windows, 4½", NM (EX box), A........$175.00

Happy Hippo, TPS, native rider dangles bananas in front of hippo, litho tin, 6", NM (NM box).........................$500.00

Happy Life, Alps, girl sits on beach w/spinning umbrella & several other actions, tin & celluloid, 9½", NMIB, A..$475.00

Happy-Go-Lucky Magician, TN, lifts hat & different objects appear, litho tin, 9", EX (EX box) $650.00

Harley-Davidson Motorcycle, Occupied Japan, 1940s, litho tin w/full-figure driver, friction, EX $350.00

Harley-Davidson Motorcycle, TN, litho tin & plastic, 9", NM (NM box mk Auto Cycle)......................................$550.00

Harley-Davidson Motorcycle, TN, 1950s, litho tin, friction, 8", NM, from $350 to..$400.00

Hawaiian Dance, Occupied Japan, girl performs hula, tin & celluloid w/grass skirt, 6½", NM (EX box), A.............$150.00

Hawaiian Dance, prewar, girl performs hula dance, celluloid w/silk grass skirt, 9", EX (EX box), A.......................$175.00

Henry & His Brother, prewar, Henry pulls brother behind him on wheeled platform, celluloid, 7", NM, from $1,000 to .$1,500.00

Henry on Trapeze, Bordfeldt, prewar, figure performs on trapeze, tin w/celluloid figure, 5", NM (EX box), A $950.00

Highway Patrol Car, Ichiko, advances as driver raises & lowers his gun, litho tin, friction, 8", EX (EX box).............$125.00

Horse Van, 1950s, litho tin, friction, 7½", NM $120.00

Ice Cream Vender, Occupied Japan, tin & celluloid, 4", MIB, A $250.00

Ice Cream Vendor Truck, KO, mystery action, litho tin, friction, 7", EX (EX box)...$350.00

Indian on Horse, celluloid, 8", NMIB, A $275.00

Japanese Monster w/Baby, 1960s, vinyl, friction, 5", rare, NMIB, A $150.00

Jet Boat J-105, litho tin, friction, 11", EX $175.00

Jet Racer, Marusan, 1955, advances w/sound, litho tin, friction, 8½", NM (EX box), A......................................$500.00

Jet Racer Y53, Yonezawa, w/driver, litho tin, friction, 11", NM (NM box) $750.00

Jiminy Cricket, Linemar/WDP, 1960s, advances w/umbrella, litho tin, EX..$400.00

Jolly Snake, advances & wiggles as head turns side to side, litho tin, 6", EX (EX box) $175.00

Jumbo the Elephant w/Safari Hunter Standing in Howdah, advances & rocks, litho tin, 4", NM.....................$1,000.00

Jumpy Rudolph, Asahi Toy, 1950s, cable action, 6", EX ...$150.00

Kennel Frolics, TN, dog chases rabbit around kennel, litho tin w/celluloid figures, 3", NM (EX box), A..................$300.00

King Merry, CK, balls revolve around 2 parrots in cage, celluloid, 12", EX (EX box)...$200.00

Lady Bug & Tortoise w/Babies, TPS, flips over to reveal lady bug & tortoise, litho tin, 7", EX (EX box) $250.00

Lazy Bones the Sleepy Pup, 1960s, several actions, plush & tin, 11", NM (NM box) $125.00

Lion Teaser, Occupied Japan, lion advances as monkey on his back dangles bone before him, celluloid, 6", NMIB .$350.00

Little Miss Automatic Ironer, MT, 1950s, litho tin, 4", NMIB, A...$75.00

Livestock Truck, TN, 1950s, litho tin, friction, 10", NMIB...$125.00

Lucky Jeep, TN, advances w/sound, litho tin, friction, 8", MIB, A..$100.00

Lucky Santa Dancer, prewar, waddles back & forth w/ball & bag of toys, celluloid w/cloth outfit, 6½", rare, NMIB, A......$300.00

Lucky Sledge, Occupied Japan, boy advances & spins on sled, celluloid, 5", rare, M (G box), A..............................$300.00

Ludwig Von Drake on Go Cart, Linemar, 1960s, litho tin, NM $450.00

Machine Gunner, prewar, Japanese soldier moves machine gun & barrel vibrates, celluloid, tin & wood, 10", EX, A......$675.00

Magic Action Locomotive, advances in erratic pattern, litho tin, friction, 5", EX (EX box) $75.00

Magic Circus, TPS, monkey & seal perform on carousel-type platform, litho tin & plastic, 6", EX (EX box), from $150 to..$180.00

Magic Whale, whale gobbles up attached fish, litho tin, 6½", EX (EX box) $200.00

Mama Kangaroo & Playful Baby, TPS, baby jumps in & out of mother's pouch, litho tin, 6", NM (EX box), A.......$300.00

Merry Tourist Land, airplane circles above base, litho tin, 6x6", EX, A $200.00

Messerschmitt Car, Bandai, blk-pnt tin w/blk rubber tires, friction, 8", NM (EX box), A, from $525 to $650.00

Mickey, see also Great Mickey

Mickey & Minnie Acrobats, Borgfeldt, figures perform on trapeze, tin w/celluloid figures, 13", VG..................$400.00

Mickey Cyclist, Linemar, 5", EX (EX box), from $1,100.00 to $1,200.00. (Photo courtesy Dunbar Gallery)

Mickey Mouse, Borgfeldt, 1934, celluloid, NM (EX box) $7,500.00

Mickey Mouse & Pluto, prewar, Pluto pulls Mickey in cart, tin w/celluloid figures, 9", NM (EX box), A $3,000.00

Mickey Mouse & Pluto, prewar, Pluto pulls Mickey in 3-wheeled cart, celluloid, 5", rare, NM, A $1,700.00

Mickey Mouse Acrobat, Gym-Toys by Linemar, Mickey performs on high bar, tin & celluloid, 9½", EX (EX box).........$700.00

Mickey Mouse Crazy Car, Occupied Japan, forward & reverse action, tin w/celluloid figure, 5", rare, NMIB.......$2,100.00

Mickey Mouse on Horse, Occupied Japan, celluloid, EX..$2,100.00

Mickey Mouse on Pluto, Occupied Japan, celluloid, EX...$3,000.00

Mickey Mouse Unicyclist, Linemar, advances in erratic pattern, litho tin w/cloth pants, 6", EX (EX box) $1,200.00

Mickey Mouse Whirligig, Borgfeldt, prewar, Mickey spins on ball as umbrella spins above him, celluloid, 9", rare, NMIB $3,000.00

Mickey's Delivery Cart, Linemar/WDP, Pluto pedals cart, litho tin & celluloid, friction, NM....................................$600.00

Ludwig Von Drake, Linemar, 1950s, NM, A, $500.00 (VG, $350.00). (Photo courtesy Jeff Bubb)

Military Motorcycle, advances w/sparking machine gun, litho tin camouflage w/full-figure driver, 5½", VG, A......$250.00

Minnie Mouse & Pluto, prewar, Pluto pulls Minnie in cart, tin w/celluloid figures, 9", NM (EX box), A $2,800.00

Miss Cat, Occupied Japan, lifts ball & moves head, celluloid, 4½", MIB, A...$225.00

Monkey & Bee, MT, monkey tries to shake bee off of his tail, celluloid, 4", NM (EX box), A, from $200 to $250.00

Monkey Banana Vender, Yonezawa, advances w/cart, litho tin, 8½", MIB, A $100.00

Monkey Batter, litho tin, 7", NM (EX box), A...............$350.00

Monkey Cycle, Bandai, advances w/ringing bell, litho tin, 5", NMIB...$350.00

Monkey Playing Banjo, Occupied Japan, monkey sits on stump & plays banjo, celluloid, 7½", VG, A.....................$175.00

Mother & Baby Carriage, figure pushes carriage, litho tin, 6½", NM (EX box), A $200.00

Motor-Cycle (sic) Cable Rider, Modern Toys, litho tin, 3½", NMIB...$350.00

Mounted Calvary Man w/Cannon, TPS, litho tin w/rubber sword, 5", NMIB...$250.00

Mr Butts the Cigarette Boy, Alps, bends over w/case of cigarettes, litho tin w/cloth clothes, 9", NMIB $300.00

Mr Nice Guy, prewar, butterfly moves back & forth on man's head as facial expressions change, celluloid, 9", EX...........$1,000.00

Mr Tortoise, 1960s, litho tin, NMIB $75.00

Musical Squirrel, advances & plays cymbals, 8", MIB $150.00

Mystery Police cycle, KO, litho tin, friction, 6", NMIB .$450.00

New Car w/Boat Trailer, Daiya, pnt tin, friction, NMIB...$300.00

Ninkimono Clown, MT, prewar, sways back & forth while balancing balls & flags on his forehead, celluloid, 12", NMIB..$700.00

North American Van Lines Truck, Y, litho tin, friction, 13", NM (EX box), A $150.00

Old Jalopy, Linemar, litho tin, friction, 5", VG, A $100.00

Oscar the Seal, TPS, advances w/spinning attachment on nose, litho tin, 7", EX (EX box) $200.00

Pango-Pango African Dancer, TPS, litho tin, NM (NM box) $300.00

PD Auto Cycle, TYO, w/driver, litho tin, friction, 7", NM (EX box), A...$450.00

Peacock, Alps, advances & tail fans out, litho tin, 6", EX $150.00

Peter Pan's Crocodile, Klimax Series, advances in circular motion as mouth opens & closes, litho tin, 7", rare, NMIB, A..$300.00

Pheasant Hunt Set, OKP, shoot w/up pheasant w/dart gun, NM (EX box), A $150.00

Pinky Racer, AAA, monkey driver leans forward as car advances & spins, litho tin, 5½", EX (EX box), A..................$125.00

Pinocchio, Borgfeldt, compo, 10½", NM.......................$450.00

Pluto on Motorcycle, Linemar, 1960s, litho tin, friction, 3", NM $350.00

Pluto Pulling Cart, Linemar/WDP, 1960s, litho tin, friction, NM $450.00

Pluto Riding Unicycle, Linemar/WDP, litho tin, EX......$750.00

Police Car No 1, litho tin, friction, 4", EX (EX box)........$75.00

Police Motorcycle, Linemar, litho tin, 4½", EX, A $100.00

Police Motorcycle, mk Police Dept, litho tin, friction, 6½", G, A $175.00

Popeye on Tricycle, Linemar, litho tin w/cloth pants, 6½", VG, A $500.00

Popeye on Unicycle, litho tin w/cloth pants, 5½", VG, A $600.00

Popeye Turnover Tank, Linemar, Popeye forces tank to turn over, litho tin, 4", NM (EX box), A.......................$850.00

Popeye Turnover Tank, Linemar, Popeye forces tank to turn over, litho tin, 4", G, A.......................................$325.00

Postal Saving Truck Bank, SSS, litho tin, friction, 7", EX, A $150.00

Power Mower, litho tin, friction, 6", NMIB...................$150.00

Prehistoric Animal, Linemar, dinosaur advances & growls, litho tin, 8", NM (EX box), A...$275.00

Puzzle Car, Occupied Japan, advances to edge of table & turns around, gr-pnt tin, 6", EX (EX box), A....................$100.00

Queen Pop Pop Boat, litho tin, 4", EX (EX box) $50.00

Rabbit Pulling Chicks on Sled, Daihachi, prewar, advances w/ringing bell, celluloid, 7", NM (EX box mk Easter Toy), A $165.00

Railroad Handcar, 2 figures work handlebars, litho tin, 6", EX, A $150.00

Reading Bunny, Alps, bunny flips pgs in book, tin & plush w/cloth outfit, 7", MIB, A $175.00

Ride 'Em Cowboy, Wyandotte, 7", A, NMIB, from $275.00 to $350.00.

Roaring Lion, Alps, vibrates around & roars, plush over tin, 7" MIB, A $100.00

Rocket Shooting Navy Fighter, Y, 1950s, fires rockets, litho tin friction, 14", NM (EX box), A.................................$400.00

Roly Poly Circus Clown, SK, advances & spins in hoop w/bell sound, litho tin w/cloth clothes, 6" dia, M (EX box), A $225.00

Runner Boat, Daiya, advances w/spinning prop & engine noise, litho tin, 11", NM (EX box), A................................$200.00

Sailor w/Boat, Japan, prewar, balances boat on head w/ringing bells, celluloid & wood w/cloth clothes, 13", NMIB, A...$1,800.00

Santa Claus, MT, waddles around w/bag of toys, celluloid, 4", NM (EX box), A $200.00

Santa Claus, Occupied Japan, advances, rings bell & nods head, celluloid, 5", NM, A $240.00

Santa Claus, TN, shakes bell & holds Merry Christmas sign, litho tin & celluloid, 5", EX (EX box), A $85.00

Santa Claus Christmas Eve, prewar, advances on sleigh w/ringing bell, tin & celluloid, 6½", NM (G box), A $200.00

Santa on Skis, litho tin, 5½", VG, A $225.00

School Bus System #15, 1960s, litho tin, friction, 11", NM..$90.00

Sea Bear B-313, Bandai, litho tin, friction, 9½", EX $200.00

Sea Dart B-264, BC, litho tin, w/driver, 10", EX $150.00

Sea Elizabeth U-35, 1950s, litho tin, 8½", EX (EX box)...$125.00

Shingun, MT, prewar, kneeling soldier lowers & raises rifle, head turns, celluloid, 10", NM (EX box), A $1,300.00

Singing Bird in Cage, celluloid, 7", EX (EX box) $100.00

Ski Boy, TT, advances on skis, litho tin w/celluloid head, friction, 4", NM, A $150.00

Snoopy All-American Express, Aviva, 1975, wood, MIB, from $125 to...$150.00

Snow Blower, Linemar, 1950s, litho tin, friction, 5½", EX (EX box)..$100.00

Sparkling Destroyer K-55, TN, litho tin, friction, 9", NMIB $75.00

Sports Car, TN, 1950s, tin w/see-through gr plastic top, friction, 8", NM (EX box) $200.00

Stock Car #15, 1960s, litho tin, friction, 12½", EX........$150.00

Strolling Duck, Occupied Japan, wings flap & beak moves, celluloid, MIB..$230.00

Super Racer #42, litho tin, friction, 18½", EX $1,200.00

Superman Turnover Tank, Linemar, Superman forces tank to turn over, litho tin, 4", NM, A..............................$400.00

Swift Cruiser, MT, 1950s, advances w/spinning prop, litho tin, 11", EX (EX box), A..$200.00

Taxi Cab, Sanyo, 1960s, advances w/sound, litho tin, friction, 6", NMIB $100.00

Three Little Pigs, see Fifer Pig

Toddling Baby, Occupied Japan, waddles back & forth w/bottle, celluloid, 4½", MIB, A..$100.00

Tortoise, MT, litho tin, 5", NM (EX box), A $55.00

Toto Clown Acrobat, clown does acrobats on high car, celluloid, 12", EX (EX box) $200.00

Tractor w/Cargo Trailer, red-pnt tin, friction, 16", NM (EX box), A $125.00

Traveling Boy, Alps, advances w/suitcase, litho tin & celluloid, 4½", NMIB...$175.00

Trick Seal, Alps, balances ball & spins, celluloid, 6", MIB, A $95.00

Trumpet Player, Linemar, vibrates around & plays trumpet, head nods, litho tin, 5", NM $350.00

Tumbling Popeye, Linemar, litho tin, 4½", NM, A........$700.00

Venus Motorcycle, no driver, litho tin, friction, 9", G, A $200.00

Waiter, TPS, litho tin w/rayon trousers & apron, 6½", EX, A, from $200 to $235.00

Walking Baby, Occupied Japan, advances in waddling motion, celluloid, 6½", EX (EX box), A....................................$75.00

Walking Bear, Occupied Japan, plush over tin, 5", NMIB, A $50.00

Western Ranger, K, horse advances in realistic motion, litho tin, 5", NM (EX box), A $170.00

World Circus Truck, M, advances as clown & seal perform on top, litho tin, friction, 9", NM (EX box), A $300.00

SPANISH

Bears on Motorcycle, Rico, mk RSA, big bear driver w/2 sm bear passengers, litho tin, 9", EX, A $1,600.00

Bugatti I-907, Paya, 1986, w/driver, tin, 1 of 5,000 made, 19", NM, from $175 to..$250.00

Charlie Chaplin, 1950s, figure in famous pose w/valise labeled Juguetes Roman, plastic, 6½", EX $200.00

Donald Duck, Guerrero, WDP, Donald drives tank around base w/WWII litho, tin w/plastic figure, 10" base, NMIB, A ..$150.00

Donald Duck Walking Car, advances as Donald's head bobs, litho tin w/celluloid figure, 5½", MIB.....................$300.00

Goofy Walking Car, advances as Goofy's head bobs, litho tin w/celluloid figure, 5½", MIB $500.00

Louie Walking Car, advances as Louie's head bobs, litho tin w/celluloid figure, 5½", MIB $250.00

Vaquero Mareado (Spanish version of Rodeo Joe), Rico, crazy action, litho tin, 5", rare, NM (NM box) $500.00

Sweeping Mammy, Lindstrom, 8", EX (VG box), from $225.00 to $275.00.

Wyandotte

Though the Wyandotte Company (Michigan) produced toys of all types, included here are only the heavy-gauge pressed-steel cars, trucks, and other vehicles they made through the 1930s and 1940s.

See also Aeronautical; Boats; Character, TV, and Movie Collectibles; Guns; Windups, Friction, and Other Mechanicals.

American Airlines, yel w/red & blk trim, 10", NM **$155.00**
Car Carrier, red & bl, complete w/4 vehicles, battery-op headlights, 23", EX, A...**$550.00**
Circus Truck & Trailer, red cab w/yel cage on bed & matching trailer (tail gate missing), VG (G- box)...................**$650.00**
Construction Engineering Dump, 1940s, working side action dump, 20", EX+, A **$225.00**
Convertible, 1930s, Art Deco style, gr, 10", VG, A........**$300.00**
Cord Roadster, yel w/gr top, blk rubber tires w/red hubs, friction, 13", VG, A...**$425.00**

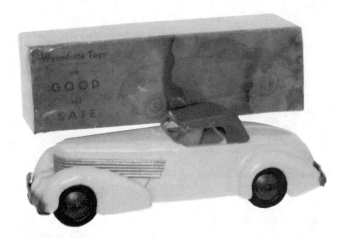

Cord, Roadster, 1937, yellow and red with gold and nickel-plated highlights, 13" L, EX- (VG box), A, $1,100.00.

Cord w/Trailer, rpl front & rear bumpers, broken trailer hitch, G pnt, 24", A **$275.00**
Coupe, red w/blk running boards, wht rubber tires, 8", EX (worn box), A...**$800.00**
Crane Truck, gr w/yel crane, lever action, 24", NM (EX box), A..**$200.00**
Dump Truck, orange with embossed tires, spring-loaded dump, 9", NM, A...**$300.00**
Dump Truck, red w/orange bed, yel wooden wheels, orig decal, 15", EX, A **$1,000.00**
Express Truck, 1940s, red w/yel stake bed, complete w/baggage cart, 22", G, A **$250.00**
Flash Strat-O-Wagon, red, wht & bl, bright colors, NM (VG box)..**$165.00**
Greyvan Lines Semi-Trailer, red cab w/silver trailer w/red decals, 24", VG+ **$245.00**

Delivery Truck, 1940s, red and yellow, opening rear door, black rubber tires, 18", G, A, $200.00.

High Wing Passenger Monoplane, blk w/orange wing (18" wingspan), orig, 12½" L, EX **$215.00**
Humphrey Mobile, 1940s, complete & orig, 9x8", NM..**$480.00**

LaSalle and Trailer, tires replaced, otherwise all original with VG paint, 24", A, $475.00.

Metropolitan Dept of Public Service Garbage Truck, NM **$525.00**
Minitown Parcel Service, wht & bright orig colors, 12", NM...**$175.00**
Speedster, 1930s, gr, complete & orig, 10", NM **$400.00**
Stake Truck, red & gr w/blk rubber tires, battery-op headlights, 15", G, A...**$200.00**
Tanker, 1930s, red w/silver grille/headlights & bumper, blk rubber tires, EX **$180.00**
Woody Roadster Convertible, 1940s, red & yel, retractable top & opening trunk, 12½", VG, A **$250.00**
Wrecker Car, bl & red w/gr chassis & yel disk wheels, 14", VG, A **$150.00**

Yo-yos

Yo-yos are starting to attract toy collectors, especially those with special features such as Hasbro's 'Glow-Action' and Duncan's 'Whistler.' For more information we recommend *Lucky's Collectors Guide to 20th Century Yo-Yos, History and Values*, written by our advisor Lucky J. Meisenheimer, M.D. He is listed under (M3) in the Coded Dealers and Collectors section.

See also Advertising, Character, TV, and Movie Collectibles, Disney; Fast Food; Political; Santa Claus.

Alox Flying Disk, wood w/decal seal, tournament shape, NM..**$25.00**
Alox Flying Disk, wood w/3 rhinestones, tournament shape, NM...**$45.00**
Cheerio Champion, 1950s, wood w/plastic medallion seal, tournament shape, NM **$200.00**
Cheerio Pee-Wee, 1950s, wood w/die-stamped seal, NM .**$110.00**

Cheerio Rainbow Pro Model, 1950s, wood w/die-stamped seal, tournament shape, NM..............$85.00

Cheerio Whistler, 1950s, wood w/die-stamped seal, butterfly shape, NM..............$100.00

Cheerio 55 Beginner, 1950s, wood w/die-stamped seal, tournament shape, NM..............$50.00

Cheerio 99 Official Tournament, 1930s, wood w/foil-sticker seal, no maple leaf, NM..............$150.00

Chemtoy Mark V, 1970s, plastic w/imprint seal, tournament shape, MIP..............$10.00

Chico Olympic Tournament, 1950s-60s, wood w/foil-sticker seal, tournament shape, MIP..............$110.00

Chico Superb Junior, 1950s-60s, wood w/gold-leaf stamped seal, 3-pc, NM..............$45.00

Chico Superb Standard, 1950s-60s, wood w/gold-leaf stamped seal, tournament shape, NM..............$45.00

Dell Big D Astronaut, 1960s, plastic, no seal, satellite shape, MIP..............$30.00

Dell Big D Royal, 1960s, plastic w/hot-stamped seal, tournament shape, MIP..............$30.00

Dell Big D Sleeper King, 1960s, plastic w/hot-stamped seal, 4 stars, tournament shape, NM..............$8.00

Dell Big D Trickster, 1960s, plastic w/hot-stamped seal, 3 stars, tournament shape, NM..............$8.00

Dell Big D Trickster, 1960s, plastic w/hot-stamped seal, 4 stars, tournament shape, MIP..............$15.00

Duncan Butterfly, early 1960s, wood w/gold-leaf stamped seal, NM..............$30.00

Duncan Chief, 1959, wood w/foil-sticker seal, tournament shape, 3-pc, NM..............$275.00

Duncan Colorama, 1960s, plastic w/paper-insert seal, tournament shape w/view lens, MIP..............$75.00

Duncan Genuine Beginner, 1930s-40s, wood w/gold-leaf stamped seal, tournament shape, NM..............$30.00

Duncan Genuine Jewel, 1930s, wood w/die-stamped seal, 9 jewels, NM..............$800.00

Duncan Glow, 1960s, plastic w/orange hot-stamped seal, sunrise design, tournament shape, MIP..............$30.00

Duncan Glow, 1970s, plastic w/orange hot-stamped seal, 8-ray distant star, tournament shape, NM..............$6.00

Duncan Imperial, 1960s, marbleized plastic w/hot-stamped seal, MIP..............$35.00

Duncan Imperial Jr, 1960s, plastic w/paper-insert seal of Mr Yo-Yo w/bees, tournament shape w/metal string slot, NM..............$20.00

Duncan Jewel, 1950s-60s, wood w/die-stamped seal, 4 jewels, gold finish, tournament shape, MIP..............$200.00

Duncan Jewel, 1960s, wood w/gold-leaf stamped seal, 4 jewels & crossed flag, tournament shape, MIP..............$95.00

Duncan Jumbo Executive, 1950s, wood w/brass seal, tournament shape, MIP..............$70.00

Duncan Litening, 1950s, wood w/paper-sticker seal, tournament shape, rare, MIP..............$1,000.00

Duncan O-Boy, 1929, wood w/gold-leaf stamped seal, tournament shape, NM..............$300.00

Duncan Rainbow, 1956, wood w/silver foil-sticker seal, tournament shape, NM..............$175.00

Duncan Special 44, wood w/gold-leaf stamped seal, tournament shape, 3-pc, NM..............$40.00

Duncan Tournament Genuine Deluxe, 1950s, plastic w/hot-stamped seal, NM $60.00

Duncan Tournament 77, 1950s, wood w/decal seal, NM..$110.00

Duncan Trickster, 1960s, plastic w/hot-stamped seal, tournament shape, MIP $40.00

Duncan Whistler, early 1930s, litho tin, tournament shape, NM $155.00

Festival Little Zapper, 1970s, wood w/foil-sticker seal, tournament shape, 3-pc, MIP..............$15.00

Festival Screamer, 1960s-70s, tin w/paper-sticker seal, tournament shape, MIP...............$55.00

Fli-Back Orbit-A-Way, 1970s, plastic w/aluminum axle, tournament shape, NM $15.00

Fli-Back 65, 1960s, wood w/gold-leaf stamped seal, tournament shape, 3-pc, NM............$45.00

Flores Beginner, 1930s, wood w/decal seal, ball shape, miniature, NM..........................$400.00

Flores Original Tournament, 1950s, wood w/gold-leaf stamped seal, NM..........................$200.00

Franklin Mint Litening, 1994, wood w/engraved metal seal, tournament shape, 3-pc, NM $250.00

Jewel Tournament Filipino Spinning Top Company, 1950s, decal seal, tournament shape, one-piece, $50.00. (Photo courtesy Lucky J. Meisenheimer)

Hi-Ker 55 Famous, 1950s, wood w/die-stamped seal, NM .$110.00

Ka-Yo Musical, 1930s, litho tin, tournament shape, NM...$150.00

Kohner Bros Spinmaster, 1950s, wood w/foil-sticker seal, tournament shape, NM $75.00

Kusan Twin Whirler, 1960s, marbleized plastic w/falcon, molded seal, MIP $35.00

Master Craft Tournament, 1950s, wood w/gold-leaf stamped seal, NM..........................$75.00

Nadson Twirler Top, 1960s, wood w/ink-stamped seal, 4 jewels, tournament shape, MIP $85.00

Royal Butterfly, 1960s, wood w/gold-leaf stamped seal, 5-point crown w/chevron, NM $150.00

Royal Champion Filipino, 1950s, wood w/decal seal, 5-point crown, tournament shape, NM....................$50.00

Royal Crownless Champion, 1950s, plastic w/hot-stamped seal, tournament shape, NM........................$45.00

Royal Jewel Champion Super Deluxe, 1940s-50s, wood w/decal seal, 4 jewels, tournament shape, NM.............$150.00

Royal 500, 1950s-60s, wood w/die-stamped seal, 5-point crown w/chevron, NM........................$35.00

Sock-It Space Whirler, 1960s, wood w/paper-sticker seal, butterfly shape, NM........................$25.00

Tom Kuhn Champion, 1970s, wood w/die-stamped seal, tournament shape, NM $60.00

Toy Tinkers Spalding Toy-O-Ball, 1950s, plastic baseball shape w/imprint seal, NM........................$25.00

Whirl-King Tournament, 1960s, wood w/die-stamped seal, 1g crown, NM........................$10.00

Woodcraft Twirler, 1950s, wood w/paper-sticker seal, tournament shape, NM $35.00

World's Fair 1939, wood w/decal seal, tournament shape, 3-pc NM........................$60.00

World's Fair 1982, plastic w/imprint seal, tournament shape NM........................$10.00

Yomega Twin Trik, 1990s, plastic w/paper-insert seal, flywheel shape, MIP $12.00

Fred Flintstone, 1970s, plastic sculpted head, $12.00.
(Photo courtesy Lucky J. Meisenheimer)

Goody Champion, 1950s-60s, wood w/pnt seal, 3 jewels, tournament shape, NM........................$200.00

Goody Joy-O-Top, 1950s-60s, wood w/pnt seal, tournament shape, NM $120.00

Goody Rainbow, 1950s-60s, wood w/pnt seal, 7 jewels, tournament shape, NM........................$1,000.00

Goody Winner, 1950s-60s, wood w/pnt seal, tournament shape, NM........................$125.00

Hasbro Glow Action, 1960s, plastic, no seal, tournament shape, MIP........................$18.00

Hi-Ker Spin Master, 1950s, wood w/sparkle pnt finish, gold-leaf stamped seal, tournament shape, MIP..............$110.00

Dealer and Collector Codes

Most of our description lines contain a letter/number code just before the suggested price. They correspond with the names of the following collectors and dealers who sent us their current selling list to be included in this edition. If you're interested in buying an item you find listed, don't hesitate to call or write them. We only ask that you consider the differences in time zones and try to call at a convenient time. If you're corresponding, please send a self-addressed, stamped envelope for their reply. Because our data was entered several months ago, many of the coded items will have already sold, but our dealers tell us that they are often able to restock some of the same merchandise over and over. Some said that they had connections with other dealers around the country and might be able to locate a particular toy for you. But please bear in mind that because they may have had to pay more to restock their shelves, they may also have to charge a little more than the price quoted in their original sales list. We must stress that these people are not appraisers, so please do not ask them to price your toys.

If you have lists of toys for sale that you would like for us to use in the next edition, please send them to us at as soon as possible. We will process incoming lists as they arrive and because our space is limited, the earlier you send it, the better. Please do not ask us to include you in our Categories of Special Interest unless you contribute useable information. Not only are we limited on available space, it isn't fair to those who do. If you would like to advertise with us but cannot contribute listings, display ads are available (see page 481 for rates). We will hold a previously assigned dealer code over for you who are our contributors/advisors from year to year as long as we know you are interested in keeping it, but if we haven't heard from you by February 1, we will reassign that code to someone else. Because the post office prefers your complete 9-digit zip code, please send us that information for our files.

Direct your correspondence to: **Huxford Enterprises, Inc., 1202 7th St., Covington, IN 47932**

(A1)
Stan and Sally Alekna
732 Aspen Lane
Lebanon, PA 17042-9073
717-228-2361; fax 717-228-2362

(A4)
Bob Armstrong
15 Monadnock Rd.
Worcester, MA 01609
508-799-0644
e-mail: RAAHNA@oldpuzzles.com
www.oldpuzzles.com

(A5)
Geneva Addy
Winterset, IA 50273

(A7)
Tatonka Toys
Matt and Lisa Adams
8155 Brooks Dr.
Jacksonville, FL 32244
904-389-9534
e-mail: mattradams@earthlink.net

(B1)
Richard Belyski
P.O. Box 14956
Surfside Beach, SC 29587
e-mail: peznews@juno.com
www.pezcollectorsnews.com

(B2)
Larry Blodget
Box 753
Rancho Mirage, CA 92270
760-674-9469
e-mail: BestInFords@aol.com

(B3)
Bojo
Bob Gottuso
P.O. Box 1403
Cranberry Twp., PA 16066-0403
Phone or fax 724-776-0621
e-mail: bojo@zbzoom.net

(B5)
Martin and Carolyn Berens
Collection Connection
P.O. Box 18552
Fairfield, OH 45018
Phone or fax 513-851-9217

(B6)
Jim Buskirk
3009 Oleander Ave.
San Marcos, CA 92069
760-599-1054

(B8)
Stanley A. and Robert S. Block
P.O. Box 51
Trumbull, CT 06611
203-261-3223 or
203-775-0138
www.pages.prodigy.com/marbles/mcc.
html; Prodigy:BWVR62A

(B10)
Ditto Enterprises
Tom Bremer
P.O. Box 49
Newark, NY 14513
Phone or fax 315-331-7688
e-mail: Dittoent@aol.com
http://members.aol.com/DITTO
ENT/catalogpage.index.html

(C1)
Casey's Collectible Corner
HCR Box 31, Rt. 3
N Blenheim, NY 12131
607-588-6464
e-mail: CASEYSCC@aol.com
www.csmonline.com/caseys

(C2)
Mark E. Chase
Collector Glass News
P.O. Box 308
Slippery Rock, PA 16057
724-946-2838
fax 724-946-9012
e-mail: mark@glassnews.com
www.glassnews.com

(C3)
Ken Clee
Box 11412
Philadelphia, PA 19111
215-722-1979
e-mail: waxntoys@aol.com
http://members.aol.com/waxntoys/
main/kidsmeal.htm

(C6)
Cotswold Collectibles
P.O. Box 716
Freeland, WA 98249
877-404-5637 (toll free)
fax 360-331-5344
www.elitebrigade.com

(C9)
Marilyn Cooper
8408 Lofland Dr.
Houston, TX 77055-4811
713-465-7773
Summer: P.O. Box 755
Douglas, MI 49406
616-857-4202
Author of *The Pictorial Guide to
Toothbrush Holders*

(C10)
Bill Campbell
1221 Littlebrook Lane
Birmingham, AL 35235
205-853-8227
fax 205-853-9951
e-mail: acamp10720@aol.com

(C12)
Joel J. Cohen
Cohen Books and Collectibles
P.O. Box 810310
Boca Raton, FL 33481-0310
561-487-7888
fax 561-487-3117
e-mail: disneyana@disneycohen.com
www.disneycohen.com

(C13)
Brad Cassity
2391 Hunters Trail
Myrtle Beach, SC 29579
843-236-8697

(C14)
Cynthia's Country Store
12794 W Forest Hill Blvd., #15A
West Palm Beach, FL 33414
561-793-0554
fax 561-795-4222 (24 hours)
e-mail: cynbears@aol.com
www.cynthiascountrystore.com

(C15)
Rosalind Cranor
P.O. Box 859
Blacksburg, VA 24063

(D2)
Marl Davidson (Marl & B Inc.)
10301 Braden Run
Bradenton, FL 34202
941-751-6275; fax 941-751-5463
www.marlbe.com

(D3)
Larry DeAngelo
516 King Arthur Dr.
Virginia Beach, VA 23464
757-424-1691

(D4)
John DeCicco
57 Bay View Dr.
Shrewsbury, MA 01545
508-852-0005
e-mail: jctoygift@aol.com
www.Johns-Toys.com

(D7)
Ron and Donna Donnelly
Saturday Heroes
6302 Championship Dr.
Tuscaloosa, AL 35405

(D8)
George Downes
Box 572
Nutley, NJ 07110
201-935-3388
e-mail: gad@advanix.net
www.advanix.net/~gad

(D9)
Gordy Dutt
P.O. Box 201
Sharon Center, OH 44274-0201
330-239-1657 or fax 330-239-2991

(D10)
Dunbar's Gallery
Leila and Howard Dunbar
76 Haven St.
Milford, MA 01757
508-634-8697; fax 508-473-5711
e-mail: dunbars@mediaone.net

(D11)
Larry Doucet
2351 Sultana Dr.
Yorktown Heights, NY 10598
914-245-1320

(F1)
Anthony Balasco
P.O. Box 19482
Johnston, RI 02919
401-946-5720; fax 401-942-7980
e-mail: figinc@aol.com
www.ewtech.com/figures

(F3)
Paul Fink's Fun and Games
P.O. Box 488
59 S Kent Rd.
Kent, CT 06757
860-927-4001
e-mail: PAUL@gamesandpuzzles.com
www.gamesandpuzzles.com

(F4)
Mike and Kurt Fredericks
145 Bayline Cir.
Folsom, CA 95630-8077
916-985-7986

(F5)
Fun House Toy Co.
G.F. Ridenour
P.O. Box 444
Warrendale, PA 15086
724-935-1392 (fax capable)
e-mail: info@funhousetoy.com
www.funhousetoy.com

(F7)
Finisher's Touch Antiques
Steve Fisch, proprietor
8 Old Route 9
Wappingers Falls, NY 12590-4033
845-298-8882; fax 845-298-8945

(F9)
Donald Friedman
560 W Grand Ave.
Chicago, IL 60610; 312-226-4741
e-mail: dfried4142@aol.com

(G1)
Gary's Trains
186 Pine Springs Camp Road
Boswell, PA 15531
814-629-9277
gtrains@floodcity.net

(G16)
Candelaine (Candace Gunther)
1435 Wellington Ave.
Pasadena, CA 91103-2320
626-796-4568; fax 626-796-7172
e-mail: Candelaine@aol.com

(H1)
Bill Hamburg
Happy Memories Collectibles
P.O. Box 536
Woodland Hills, CA 91367
818-346-1269
fax 818-346-0215
e-mail: WHamburg@aol.com

(H3)
George Hardy
1670 Hawkwood Ct.
Charlottesville, VA 22901
804-295-4863; fax 804-295-4898
e-mail: georgeh@comet.net
www.comet.net/personal/georgeh/

(H4)
Jerry and Joan Harnish
110 Main St.
Bellville, OH 44813
Phone 419-886-4782 after 10:00 AM
Eastern time
e-mail: jharnish@neo.rr.com

(H6)
Phil Helley
Old Kilbourne Antiques
629 Indiana Ave.
Wisconsin Dells, WI 53965
608-254-8770

(H7)
Jacquie and Bob Henry
Antique Treasures and Toys
Box 17
Walworth, NY 14568-0017
315-986-1424
e-mail: jhenry@rochester.rr.com
www.cyberattic.com/dealer/toysndolls

(H8)
Homestead Collectibles
Art and Judy Turner
P.O. Box 173
Mill Hall, PA 17751
570-726-3597
e-mail: jturner@cub.kcnet.org

(H9)
Pamela E. Apkarian-Russell, The
Halloween Queen
C.J. Russell & The Halloween
Queen Antiques
P.O. Box 499
Winchester, NH 03470
603-239-8875
e-mail: halloweenqueen@cheshire.net

(H11)
N.F. Huber, the SNO-PEA Trader
Norman Huber, Buyer
931 Emerson St.
Thousand Oaks, CA 91362-2447
805-497-0119

(H13)
Tim Hunter
4301 W. Hidden Valley Dr.
Reno, NV 89502
702-856-4357 or fax 702-856-4354
e-mail: thunter885@aol.com

(I1)
Sharon Iranpour
24 San Rafael Dr.
Rochester, NY 14618-3702
716-381-9467; fax: 716-383-9248
e-mail: watcher1@rochester.rr.com

(I2)
Terri Ivers
Terri's Toys and Nostalgia
114 Whitworth Ave.
Ponca City, OK 74601
580-762-8697 or 580-762-5174
e-mail: toylady@cableone.net

(I3)
Dan Iannotti
212 W. Hickory Grove Rd.
Bloomfield Hills, MI 48302-1127S
248-335-5042
e-mail: modernbanks@prodigy.net

(J2)
Character Company
Ed Janey
P.O. Box 15699
Fernandina Beach, FL 32035-3112
e-mail: edjaney@aol.com

(J3)
Dana Johnson
P.O. Box 1824
Bend, OR 97709-1824
503-382-7176
e-mail: mailto:toynutz@earthlink.net
www.toynutz.com

(J5)
Just Kids Nostalgia
310 New York Avenue
Huntington, NY 11743
516-423-8449; fax 516-423-4326
e-mail: justkids25@aol.com

(J6)
June Moon
1486 Miner Street
Des Plaines, IL 60016
847-294-0018
e-mail: junmoonstr@aol.com
www.junemooncollectibles.com

(K1)
K-3 Inc.
Simpson Mania
2335 NW Thurman
Portland, OR 97210

(K2)
David Kolodny-Nagy
Toy Hell
P.O. Box 75271
Los Angeles, CA 90075
e-mail: toyhell@yahoo.com
www.angelfire.com/ca2/redpear

(K4)
Debby and Marty Krim
P.O. Box 2273
W Peabody, MA 01960
978-535-3140 or fax 978-535-7522

(K5)
Kerry and Judy's Toys
1414 S. Twelfth St.
Murray, KY 42071
270-759-3456
e-mail: kjtoys@apex.com

(K6)
Keith and Donna Kaonis
P.O. box 344
Centerport, NY 11721
Daytime: 631-261-4100
Evenings: 631-351-0982
fax 631-261-9684

(L1)
Jean-Claude H. Lanau
740 Thicket Ln.
Houston, TX 77079
281-497-6034 (after 7:00 pm, CST)
e-mail: jchl@houston.rr.com

(L4)
Tom Lastrapes
P.O. Box 2444
Pinellas Park, FL 33782
727-545-2586
e-mail: tomlas@ij.net

(L6)
Kathy Lewis
Whirlwind Unlimited (formerly
   Chatty Cathy's Haven)
187 N Marcello Ave
Thousand Oaks, CA 91360
805-499-8101

(L7)
Terry and Joyce Losonsky
7506 Summer Leave Ln.
Columbia, MD 21046-2455
401-381-3358

(M1)
Mark and Val Macaluso
3603 Newark Rd.
Marion, NY 14505
315-926-4349
fax 315-926-4853

(M2)
John McKenna
Colorado Springs, CO 80905

(M3)
Lucky J. Meisenheimer, M.D.
7300 Sandlake Commons Blvd.,
Suite 105
Orlando, FL 32819
407-352-2444
fax 407-363-2869
e-mail: LuckyJ@MSN.com
www.yo-yos.net

(M5)
Mike's General Store
52 St. Annes Rd.
Winnipeg, Manitoba, Canada R2M-2Y3
204-255-3463
fax 204-253-9975

(M7)
Judith A. Mosholder
186 Pine Springs Camp Road
Boswell, PA 15531
814-629-9277
e-mail: jlytwins@floodcity.net

(M8)
The Mouse Man Ink
P.O. Box 3195
Wakefield, MA 01880
781-246-3876
e-mail: mouse_man@msn.com
www.mouseman.com

(M9)
Steven Meltzer
1255 2nd St.
Santa Monica, CA 90401
310-656-0483
www.puppetmagic.com

(M10)
Gary Metz
P.O. Box 1430
Salem, VA 24153

(M11)
Michael and Polly McQuillen
McQuillen's Collectibles
P.O. Box 50022
Indianapolis, IN 46250-0022
317-845-1721
e-mail: michael@politicalparade.com
www.politicalparade.com

(M12)
Helen L. McCale
Holly Hobbie Collector
1006 Ruby Ave.
Butler, MO 64730-2500

M15)
Marcia's Fantasy
Marcia Fanta
4275 S. 33rd St. SE
Tappen, ND 58487-9411
701-327-4441
e-mail: tofantas@bektel.com

M18)
Nancy McMichael
P.O. Box 53262
Washington DC 20009

M19)
Model Auto
P.O. Box 79253
Houston, TX 77279
Phone or fax 713-468-4461 (phone
  evenings; fax anytime)

M20)
Bruce Middleton
5 Lloyd Rd.
Newburgh, NY 12550
845-564-2556

M21)
Peter Muldavin
73 W 78th St., Apt. 5-F
New York, NY 10024
212-362-9606
kiddie78s@aol.com

N1)
Natural Way/dba Russian Toy Co.
322½ Massachusetts
P.O. Box 842
Lawrence, KS 66044
785-865-5466

N2)
Norman's Olde & New Store
Philip Norman
126 W Main St.
Washington, NC 27889-4944
252-946-3448

N3)
Neil's Wheels, Inc.
Box 354
Old Bethpage, NY 11804-0354
516-293-9659
fax 516-420-0483
www.neilswheels.com

N4)
Roger Nazeley
4921 Castor Ave.
Philadelphia, PA 19124
215-743-8999
e-mail: vmreelguy2@aol.com (will
  answer all messages)

P1)
Pat Peterson
1105 6th Ave. SE
Hampton, IA 50441

P2)
Dawn Diaz
20460 Samual Dr.
Saugus, CA 91350-3812
661-263-8697
e-mail: jdnm01@telocity.com

P4)
Plymouth Rock Toy Co. Inc.
Box 1202
Plymouth, MA 02362-1202
508-746-2842 or 508-830-1880
  (noon to 11 PM EDT)
fax 508-830-0364
e-mail: plyrocktoy@aol.com

P5)
Gary Pollastro
5047 84th Ave. SE
Mercer Island, WA 98040
206-232-3199

P6)
Judy Posner
P.O. Box 2194
Englewood, FL 34295
e-mail: judyandjef@aol.com
www.judyposner.com

P8)
Diane Patalano
P.O. Box 144
Saddle River, NJ 07458
201-327-2499

P10)
Bill and Pat Poe
220 Dominica Circle E
Niceville, FL 32578-4085
850-897-4163
fax 850-897-2606
e-mail: McPoes@aol.com or
Patpoe toys@aol.com

P11)
The Phoenix Toy Soldier Co.
Bob Wilson
8912 E. Pinnacle Peak Rd.
PMB 552
Scottsdale, AZ 85255
480-699-5005
toll free: 1-877-269-6074
fax 480-699-7628
e-mail: bob@phoenixtoysoldier.com
www.phoenixtoysoldier.com

P12)
Michael Paquin, That Toy Guy
72 Penn Blvd.
E Lansdowne, PA 19050
610-394-8697 (10 am – 10 pm EST);
fax 610-259-8626 (24 hr)
e-mail: Mike@thattoyguy.com
www.thattoyguy.com

R3)
Jim Rash
135 Alder Ave.
Egg Harbor Twp., NJ 08234-9302
609-646-4125 (evenings)

R4)
Robert Reeves
107 Brandon St.
Union, SC 29379-1707

(R5)
Reynolds Toys
Charlie Reynolds
2836 Monroe St.
Falls Church, VA 22042
703-533-1322
e-mail: reynoldstoys@erols.com

(R6)
David E. Riddle
1930 East Indianhead Drive
Tallahassee, FL 32301
850-877-7207
e-mail: derkoftally@webtv.net

(S5)
Son's a Poppin' Ranch
John Rammacher
1610 Park Ave.
Orange City, FL 32763-8869
386-775-2891
www.bitstorm.net/sap
e-mail: sap@bitstorm.net

(S6)
Bill Stillman
P.O. Box 167
Hummelstown, PA 17036
717-566-5538

(S7)
Nate Stoller
960 Reynolds Ave.
Ripon, CA 95366
209-599-5933
www.maytagclub.com
e-mail: multimotor@aol.com

(S8)
Brian's Toys
W730 Hwy. 35; P.O. Box 95
Fountain City, WI 54629
www.brianstoys.com
e-mail: sales@brianstoys.com

(S10)
Scott Smiles
157 Yacht Club Way, Apt. #112
Hypoluxo, FL 33462-6048
561-582-6016
e-mail: ssmiles@msn.com

(S14)
Cindy Sabulis
P.O. Box 642
Shelton, CT 06484
203-926-0176
e-mail: toys4two@snet.net
www.dollsntoys.com

(S18)
The Silver Bullet
Terry and Kay Klepey
P.O. Box 553
Forks, WA 98331
360-327-3726
e-mail: slvrbllt@olypen.com

(S19)
Craig Stifter
218 S. Adams St.
Hinsdale, IL 60521
630-789-5780

(S22)
Carole & Richard Smyth
Carole Smyth Antiques
P.O. Box 2068
Huntington, NY 11743

(S24)
Mark and Lynda Suozzi
P.O. Box 102
Ashfield, MA 01330
Phone or fax 413-628-3241 (9am to 5pm)
e-mail: marklyn@valinet.com
www.marklynantiques.com

(S25)
Steve Stevenson
11117 NE 164th Pl.
Bothell, WA 98011-4003
425-488-2603
fax 425-488-2841

(T2)
Toy Scouts, Inc.
Bill Bruegman
137 Casterton Ave.
Akron, OH 44303
330-836-0668
fax 330-869-8668
e-mail: toyscouts@toyscouts.com
www.toyscouts.com

(T3)
Richard Trautwein
Toys N Such
437 Dawson St.
Sault Ste. Marie, MI 49783
906-635-0356
e-mail: rtraut@up.net

(T5)
Bob and Marcie Tubbs
424 Redding Rd.
Fairfield, CT 06430

(T6)
TV Collector
Diane and Steve Albert
6704 Fruit Flower Avenue
Las Vegas, NV 89130
702-369-4106

(V2)
Marci Van Ausdall
P.O. Box 719
McCloud, CA 96057
530-964-2468
e-mail: dreams707@aol.com

(W1)
Dan Wells Antique Toys
P.O. Box 7
Goshen, KY 40026-0007

(W4)
Randy Welch
27965 Peach Orchard Rd.
Easton, MD 21601-8203
410-822-5441

(W7)
Larry White
108 Central St.
Rowley, MA 01969-1317
978-948-8187
e-mail: larrydw@erols.com

(W8)
James Watson
5 Gilmore St.
Whitehall, NY 12887
518-499-0643 or fax 518-499-1772

(Y1)
Henri Yunes
971 Main St., Apt. 2
Hackensack, NJ 07601
201-488-2236

(Y2)
Mary Young
Box 9244
Dayton, OH 45409
937-298-4838

Categories of Special Interest

If you would like to be included in this section, send us a list of your 'for sale' merchandise. These listings are complimentary to those who participate in the preparation of this guide by doing so. Please understand that the people who are listed here want to buy and sell. They are not appraisers. Read the paragraph under the title *Dealer and Collector Codes* for more information. If you have no catalogs or lists but would like to advertise with us, see the display ad rate sheet on 481.

Action Figures
Also GI Joe, Star Wars and Super Heroes
John DiCicco
7 Bay View Dr.
Shrewsbury, MA 01545
508-852-0005
24-hour fax 508-852-0066
e-mail: jctoygift@aol.com
www.Johns-Toys.com

Captain Action, Star Wars, Secret Wars, and other character-related Western, TV, movie, comic, or paperback tie-ins
George Downes
Box 572
Nutley, NJ 07110
201-935-3388
e-mail: gad@advanix.net
www.advanix.net/~gad

Figures
Anthony Balasco
P.O. Box 19482
Johnston, RI 02919
401-946-5720
fax: 401-942-7980
e-mail: figinc.@aol.com
wtech.com/figures

GI Joe, Captain Action and other character-related TV, advertising, Marx and Mego figures; send $2 for sales catalog
Jerry and Joan Harnish
110 Main St.
Bellville, OH 44813
Phone 419-886-4782 after 10:00 AM
e-mail: jharnish@neo.rr.com

Advertising
M&M Toppers
Ken Clee
P.O. Box 11412
Phil., PA 19111; 215-722-1979
e-mail: waxntoys@aol.com
members.aol.com/waxntoys/main/
    kidsmeal.htm

Also Halloween, Toys, coin-operated machines, motorcycle memorablilia; Buying and selling
Dunbar's Gallery
Leila and Howard Dunbar
76 Haven St.
Milford, MA 01757
508-634-8697 or 508-473-5711
e-mail: dunbars@mediaone.net

Gary Metz
263 Key Lakewood Dr.
Moneta, VA 24121
540-721-2091
fax 504-721-1782

Also general line
Mike's General Store
52 St. Annes Rd.
Winnipeg, Manitoba, Canada R2M 2Y3
204-255-3463
fax 204-253-9975

Advertising figures, novelty radios, Barbies, promotional watches, character toys, and more
Michael Paquin, That Toy Guy
72 Penn Blvd.
E Lansdowne, PA 19050
610-394-8697 (10 am – 10 pm EST)
or fax 610-259-8626 (24 hrs)
e-mail: Mike@thattoyguy.com
www.thattoyguy.com

Coca-Cola, Pepsi-Cola, and soda pop toys
Craig Stifter
218 S. Adams St.
Hinsdale, Il 60521
630-789-5780

Advertising Wristwatches
Sharon Iranpour (editor of newsletter)
24 San Rafael Dr.
Rochester, NY 14618-3702
716-381-9467
fax: 716-383-9248
e-mail: watcher1@rochester.rr.com

Automobilia
Especially model kits, promotional model cars, books and literature
Model Auto
P.O. Box 79253
Houston, TX 77279
Phone or fax 713-468-4461 (phone evenings; fax anytime)

Banks
Ertl; sales lists available
Homestead Collectibles
Art and Judy Turner
P.O. Box 173
Mill Hall, PA 17751
570-726-3597
e-mail: jturner@cub.kcnet.org

Modern mechanical banks: Reynolds, Sandman Designs, James Capron, Book of Knowledge, Richards, Wilton; Sales lists available
Dan Iannotti
212 W. Hickory Grove Rd.
Bloomfield Hills, MI 48302-1127S
248-335-5042
e-mail: modernbanks@prodigy.net

Also children's sadirons, Black Americana dolls and memorabilia
Diane Patalano
Country Girls Appraisal and Liquidation Service
P.O. Box 144
Saddle River, NJ 07458
201-327-2499

Penny banks (limited editions): new, original, mechanical, still or figural; also bottle openers
Reynolds Toys
Charlie Reynolds
2836 Monroe St.
Falls Church, VA 22042-2007
703-533-1322
e-mail: reynoldstoys@erols.com

Antique tin and iron mechanical penny banks; no reproductions or limited editions; cast-iron architectural bank buildings in Victorian form. Buy and sell, list available upon request
Mark and Lynda Suozzi
P.O. Box 102
Ashfield, MA 01330
Phone/fax 413-628-3241 (9 am – 5 pm). Mail order and shows only
e-mail: marklyn@valinet.com
www.marklynantiques.com

Specializing in still banks, safe banks, and antique safes
Larry Egelhoff
4175 Millersville Rd.
Indianapolis, IN 46205
317-846-7228

Barbie and Friends
Wanted: Mackies as well as vintage Barbies; buying and selling ca 1959 dolls to present issues
Marl Davidson (Marl & B Inc)
10301 Braden Run
Bradenton, FL 34202
941-751-6275
fax 941-751-5463
www.marlbe.com

Battery-Operated
Tom Lastrapes
P.O. Box 2444
Pinellas Park, FL 33782
727-545-2586
e-mail: tomlas@ij.net

Beatles Memorabilia
Buying and selling old and new memorabiia; 1 piece or collection
Bojo
P.O. Box 1403
Cranberry Township, PA 16066
Phone or fax: 724-776-0621
bojo@zbzoom.net

Specializing in Little Golden Books and look-alikes
Steve Santi
19626 Ricardo Ave.
Hayward, CA 94541
510-481-2586
Author of *Collecting Little Golden Books, Volumes I and II*; Also publishes newsletter, *Poky Gazette*, primarily for Little Golden Book collectors

Breyer
Author of book, order direct
Felicia Browell
123 Hooks Lane
Cannonsburg, PA 15317
e-mail: fbrowell@nauticom.net

Bubble Bath Containers
Including foreign issues; also character collectibles, character bobbin' head nodders, and Dr. Dolittle; write for information or send SASE for Bubble Bath Bulletin
Tatonka Toys
Matt and Lisa Adams
8155 Brooks Dr.
Jacksonville, FL 32244
904-389-9534
e-mail: mattradams@earthlink.net

Building Blocks and Construction Toys
Anchor Stone Building Blocks by Richter
George Hardy
1670 Hawkwood Ct.
Charlottesville, VA 22901
804-295-4863
fax 804-295-4898
email: georgeh@comet.net
www.comet.net/personal/georgeh/

California Raisins

Ken Clee
Box 11412
Philadelphia, PA 19111-0412
215-722-1979
e-mail: waxntoys@aol.com
members.aol.com/waxntoys/main/
kidsmeal.htm

California Raisins (PVC); buying collections, old store stock, and closeouts
Larry DeAngelo
516 King Arthur Dr.
Virginia Beach, VA 23464
757-424-1691

Candy Containers

Also toys
Jeff Bradfield
Jeff's Antiques
90 Main St.
Dayton, VA 22821
540-879-9961

Also Tonka, Smith-Miller, Shafford black cats, German nodders
Doug Dezso
864 Patterson Ave.
Maywood, NJ 07607
201-488-1311

Cast Iron

Pre-war, large-scale cast-iron toys and early American tinplate toys
John McKenna
801 W Cucharres
Colorado Springs, CO 80905
719-520-9125

Victorian bell toys, horse-drawn wagons, fire toys, carriages, penny banks, pull toys, animated coin-operated machines. Buy and sell, list available upon request, mail order and shows only
Mark and Lynda Suozzi
P.O. Box 102
Ashfield, MA 01330
Phone/fax 413-628-3241 (9 am – 5 pm)
e-mail: marklyn@valinet.com
www.marklynantiques.com

Character and Promotional Glasses

Especially fast-foods and sports glasses; publisher of Collector Glass News
Mark Chase
P.O. Box 308
Slippery Rock, PA 16057
724-946-2838
fax 724-946-9012
e-mail: mark@glassnews.com
www.glassnews.com

Character Clocks and Watches

Also radio premiums and decoders, P-38 airplane-related items from World War II, Captain Marvel and Hoppy items, Lone Ranger books with jackets, selected old comic books, toys and cap guns; buys and sells Hoppy and Roy items
Bill Campbell
Kirschner Medical Corp.
1221 Littlebrook Ln.
Birmingham, AL 35235
205-853-8227
fax 205-853-9951
e-mail: acamp10720@aol.com

Character Collectibles

Dolls, rock 'n roll personalities (especially the Beatles), related character items and miscellaneous toys
Bojo
Bob Gottuso
P.O. Box 1403
Cranberry Twp., PA 16066
Phone or fax 724-776-0621
bojo@zbzoom.net

1940s – '60s character items such as super heroes, TV and cartoon items, games, playsets, lunch boxes, model kits, comic books and premium rings
Bill Bruegman
Toy Scouts, Inc.
137 Casterton Ave.
Akron, OH 44303
330-836-0668
fax 330-869-8668
e-mail: toyscouts@toyscouts.com
www.toyscouts.com

TV, radio, and comic collectibles; sports and non-sports cards; silver and golden age comics
Casey's Collectible Corner
HCR Box 31, Rt. 3
N Blenheim, NY 12131
607-588-6464
e-mail: CASEYSCC@aol.com
www.csmonline.com/caseys

Disney, books, animation art
Cohen Books and Collectibles
Joel J. Cohen
P.O. Box 810310
Boca Raton, FL 33481
561-487-7888
fax 561-487-3117
e-mail: disneyana@disneycohen.com
www.disneycohen.com

Early Disney, Gone with the Wind, Western heroes, premiums, and other related collectibles
Ron and Donna Donnelly
Saturday Heroes
6302 Championship Dr.
Tuscaloosa, AL 35405

Dick Tracy collectibles; free appraisals of DT items with SASE and photo or detailed description
Larry Doucet
2351 Sultana Dr.
Yorktown Heights, NY 10598
914-245-1320

Snoopy/Peanuts classics, new and old
N.F. Huber, The SNO-PEA Trader
931 Emerson St.
Thousand Oaks, CA 91362-2447
805-497-0119

Any and all, also Hartland figures
Terri Ivers
Terri's Toys & Nostalgia
114 Whitworth Ave.
Ponca City, OK 74601
580-762-8697 or 580-762-5174
e-mail: toylady@cableone.net

Action figures, die-cast, Strawberry Shortcake, Nightmare Before Christmas, Star Wars, TV & Movie Character Toys

June Moon
1486 Miner Street
Des Plaines, IL 60016
847-294-0018
Open T – Th 12 – 5; F & S 12 – 4
e-mail: junmoonstr@aol.com
www.junemooncollectibles.com

TV, Western, Space, Beatles; auction as well as set-price catalogs available

Just Kids Nostalgia
310 New York Ave.
Huntington, NY 11743
516-423-8449
fax 516-423-4326
e-mail: justkids25@aol.com

Especially bendy figures and the Simpsons

K-3 Inc.
Simpson Mania
2335 NW Thurman
Portland, OR 97210

Auction house with consignments welcomed; specializing in western Hartlands, airplanes, boats, cars, trucks, robots, windups, battery-ops, dolls, character items, and playset figures

Kerry and Judy's Toys
1414 S. 12th St.
Murray, KY 42071
502-759-3456
e-mail: kjtoys@apex.com

Especially Disney; send $8 for annual subscription (6 issues) for sale catalogs

The Mouse Man Ink
P.O. Box 3195
Wakefield, MA 01880
781-246-3876
e-mail: mouse_man@msn.com
www.mouseman.com

Especially pottery, china, ceramics, salt and pepper shakers, cookie jars, tea sets and children's china; with special interest in Black Americana and Disneyana; illustrated sale lists available

Judy Posner
P.O. Box 2194
Englewood, FL 34295
e-mail: judyandjef@aol.com
www.judyposner.com

Lone Ranger collector, buy and sell; publisher of Silver Bullet Newsletter (see Clubs, Newsletters, and Other Publications)

The Silver Bullet
Terry and Kay Klepey
P.O. Box 553
Forks, WA 98331
360-327-3726
e-mail: slvrbllt@olypen.com

Wizard of Oz memorabilia; always buying Oz

Bill Stillman
P.O. Box 167
Hummelstown, PA 17036
717-566-5538

Especially tinplate toys and cars, battery-op toys and toy trains

Richard Trautwein
Toys N Such
437 Dawson St.
Sault Ste. Marie, MI 49783
906-635-0356
e-mail: rtraut@up.com

TV, movie, rock 'n roll, comic character, commercials, radio, theater, etc., memorabilia of all kinds; Send $4 for sale catalog. We are not interested in buying items. All inquiries must include SASE for reply unless ordering catalog.

TV Collector
Diane and Steve Albert
6704 Fruit Flower Ave.
Las Vegas, NV 89130
702-369-4106

Especially ceramic figures, Garfield, Muppets, Kliban, Snoopy, Ziggy, Smurfs, Raggedy Ann, Strawberry Shortcake, Care Bears, Monsters, Enesco, Holt Howard, etc.; lists available

Adrienne Warren
1032 Feather Bed Lane
Edison, NJ 08820
732-381-1616 (EST)
e-mail: adrienne.w@worldnet.att.net

Chinese Tin Toys

Also buying and selling antiques, old toys and collectibles; custom refinishing and quality repairing

Finisher's Touch Antiques
Steve Fisch, proprietor
8 Old Route 9
Wappingers Falls, NY 12590-4033
845-298-8882
fax 845-298-8945

Cracker Jack

Author of Cracker Jack Toys and Cracker Jack, The Unauthorized Guide to Advertising Collectibles

Larry White
108 Central St.
Rowley, MA 01969-1317
978-948-8187
e-mail: larrydw@erols.com

Dakins

Jim Rash
135 Alder Ave.
Egg Harbor Twp., NJ 08234-9302

Diecast

Diecast and other automotive toys; editor of magazine

Mr. Dana Johnson, publisher
Toy Car Collector magazine
c/o Dana Johnson Enterprises
P.O. Box 1824
Bend, OR 97709-1824 USA
541-318-7176
e-mail: mailto:toynutz@earthlink.net
www.toynutz.com

especially Dinky; also obsolete French,
German, Italian, and English-made
vehicles
Jean-Claude Lanau
40 Thicket Ln.
Houston, TX 77079
281-497-6034
e-mail: jchl@houston.rr.com

Matchbox of all types including Dinky,
Commando, Convoys, Harley-
Davidson, Indy/Formula 1, and
Looney Tunes; also Corgi, Hartoy,
Hot Wheels, Tomica, and Tyco slot
cars
Neil's Wheels, Inc.
Box 354
Old Bethpage, NY 11804
516-293-9659
fax 516-420-0483
www.neilswheels.com

Ertl, banks, farm, trucks, and construction
Son's a Poppin' Ranch
John Rammacher
610 Park Ave.
Orange City, FL 32763-8869
386-775-2891
e-mail: sap@bitstorm.net
www.bitstorm.net/sap

All types; also action figures such as GI
Joe, Johnny West, Matt Mason, and
others
Robert Reeves
07 Brandon St.
Union, SC 29379-1707

especially Soviet-made toys (marked
USSR or CCCP)
David E. Riddle
930 E. Indianhead Dr.
Tallahassee, FL 32301
850-877-7207
e-mail: derkoftally@webtv.net

Hot Wheels
Steve Stevenson
11117 NE 164th Pl.
Bothell, WA 98011-4003
425-488-2603
fax 425-488-2841

Hot Wheels, Matchbox, and all obsolete
toy cars, trucks, and airplanes
Dan Wells Antiques Toys
P.O. Box 7
Goshen, KY 40026-0007
e-mail: dwatcatDan@aol.com

Dolls
Strawberry Shortcake dolls, accessories
and related items
Geneva Addy
Winterset, IA 50273

Chatty Cathy and Mattel
Kathy Lewis
Whirlwind Unlimited (formerly
Chatty Cathy's Haven)
187 N Marcello Ave.
Thousand Oaks, CA 91360
805-499-8101
e-mail: cadrm99@gte.net
Author of book: Chatty Cathy Dolls,
An Identification and Value Guide

Ad dolls, Barbies, and other Mattel
dolls, premiums, character memorabilia, modern dolls, related items
Marcia Fanta
Marcia's Fantasy
4275 33rd St. SE
Tappen, ND 58487-9411
701-327-4441
e-mail: tofantas@bektel.com

Holly Hobbie dolls and collectibles
Helen L. McCale
1006 Ruby Ave.
Butler, MO 64730-2500

Liddle Kiddles and other small dolls from
the late '60s and early '70s
Dawn Diaz
20460 Samual Dr.
Saugus, CA 91350-3812
661-263-TOYS
e-mail: jdnm01@telocity.com

Dolls from the 1960s – 70s, including
Liddle Kiddles, Barbie, Tammy,
Tressy, etc.
Cindy Sabulis
P.O. Box 642
Shelton, CT 06484
203-926-0176
www.dollsntoys.com
e-mail: toys4two@snet.net
Author of Collector's Guide to Dolls of
the 1960s and 1970s (Collector
Books); co-author of The Collector's
Guide to Tammy, the Ideal Teen (Col-
lector Books)

Betsy McCall
Marci Van Ausdall
P.O. Box 719
McCloud, CA 96057
530-964-2468
e-mail: dreams707@aol.com

Celebrity and character dolls
Henri Yunes
971 Main St., Apt. 2
Hackensack, NJ 07601
201-488-2236

Dollhouse Furniture
Renwal, Ideal, Marx, etc.
Judith A. Mosholder
186 Pine Springs Camp Road
Boswell, PA 15531
814-629-9277
e-mail: jlytwins@floodcity.net

Dollhouses

Tin and fiberboard dollhouses and plastic furniture from all eras
Bob and Marcie Tubbs
424 Redding Rd.
Fairfield, CT 06430

Elvis Presley Collectibles
Rosalind Cranor
P.O. Box 859
Blacksburg, VA 24063
Author of books: *Elvis Collectibles, Best of Elvis Collectibles*

All restaurants and California Raisins
Ken Clee
Box 11412
Philadelphia, PA 19111-0412
215-722-1979
e-mail: waxntoys@aol.com
members.aol.com/waxntoys/main/ kidsmeal.htm

McDonald's
Terry and Joyce Losonsky
7506 Summer Leave Lane
Columbia, MD 21046-2455
410-381-3358
Authors of *Illustrated Collector's Guide to McDonald's® Happy Meals® Boxes, Premiums, and Promotionals* ($9 plus $2 postage), *McDonald's® Happy Meal® Toys in the USA* and *McDonald's® Happy Meal® Toys Around the World* (both full color, $24.95 each plus $3 postage), and *Illustrated Collector's Guide to McDonald's® McCAPS®* ($4 plus $2 postage)

Source for catalog: McDonald's Collectibles and Other Fast-Food Toys and Memorabilia
Bill and Pat Poe
220 Dominica Circle E
Niceville, FL 32578-4085
850-897-4163
fax 850-897-2606
e-mail: McPoes@aol.com or Patpoe toys@aol.com
Send for lists of items for sale (Beanies, TBB's, Raisins, Smurfs, PEZ, Fast Food Toys, Cartoon Glasses, M&M Items, McDonald Lapel Pins, and much more); send one LSASE for each list except the M&M and McDonald Pins — they each require a SASE with 3 stamps; See Clubs, Newsletters, and Other Publications for information on McDonald's club

Fisher-Price
Brad Cassity
2391 Hunters Trail
Myrtle Beach, SC 29579
843-236-8697
Author of *Fisher-Price Toys*

Games
Victorian, cartoon, comic, TV, and nostalgic themes
Paul Fink's Fun & Games
P.O. Box 488
59 S Kent Rd.
Kent, CT 06757
860-927-4001
e-mail: PAUL@gamesandpuzzles.com
gamesandpuzzles.com

GI Joe
Also diecast and Star Wars
Cotswold Collectibles
P.O. Box 716
Freeland, WA 98249
877-404-5637 (toll free)
fax 360-331-5344
www.elitebrigade.com

Guns
Pre-WWII American spring-air BB guns, all Red Ryder BB guns, cap guns with emphasis on Western six shooters; especially wanted are pre WWII cast iron six-guns
Jim Buskirk
3009 Oleander Ave.
San Marcos, CA 92069
760-599-1054

Specializing in cap guns
Happy Memories Collectibles
Bill Hamburg
P.O. Box 536
Woodland Hills, CA 91367
818-346-1269
fax 818-346-0215
e-mail: WHamburg@aol.com

Also model kits, toy soldiers and character toys and watches; character watch service available; space ray guns major interest
Plymouth Rock Toy Co., Inc.
P.O. Box 1202
Plymouth, MA 02362-1202
508-746-2842 or 508-830-1880
(noon to 11 pm EDT)
fax 508-830-0364
e-mail: plymouthrocktoy@aol.com

Specializing in Western Hartlands
Kerry and Judy's Toys
1414 S. Twelfth St.
Murray, KY 42071
502-759-3456
e-mail: kjtoys@apex.com

Specializing in Hartland Sports Figures
James Watson
25 Gilmore St.
Whitehall, NY 12887
518-499-0643
fax 518-499-1772

Halloween Collectibles
Also postcards, author of books
Pamela E. Apkarian-Russell
C.J. Russell and The Halloween
Queen Antiques
P.O. Box 499
Winchester, NH 03470
603-239-8875
e-mail: halloweenqueen@cheshire.net
*The Tastes & Smells of Halloween, a
Trick or Treat Trader Publication
cookbook — Bogie book for collec-
tors, regularly $25.00, order from the
author at $20.00 plus shipping*

Norman's Olde and New Store
Philip Norman
126 W Main St.
Washington, NC 27889-4944
252-946-3448

*Also characters such as cowboys, TV
shows, cartoons, and more*
Terri's Toys
Terri Ivers
114 Whitworth Ave.
Ponca City, OK 74601
580-762-8697 or
580-762-5174
e-mail: toylady@cableone.net

Marbles
*Block's Box is the longest continu-
ously running absentee marble auction service in the country; catalogs issued*
Stanley A. & Robert S. Block
P.O. Box 51
Trumbull, CT 06611
203-261-3223 or 203-926-8448
www.pages.prodigy.com/marbles/mcc.
html; Prodigy: BWVR62A

Marionettes and Puppets
Steven Meltzer
1255 2nd St.
Santa Monica, CA 90401
310-656-0483
www.puppetmagic.com

Marx
*Figures, playsets, and character toy;
send three 32¢ stamps for extensive
sales lists*
G.F. Ridenour
Fun House Toy Co.
P.O. Box 444
Warrendale, PA 15086
724-935-1392 (fax capable)
e-mail: info@funhousetoy.com
www.funhousetoy.com

*Plastic figures and parts from playsets;
Also figures from about 100 other old
manufacturers*
Phoenix Toy Soldier Co.
Bob Wilson
8912 E. Pinnacle Peak Rd.
PMB 552
Scottsdale, AZ 85255
877-269-6074
fax 480-699-7628
e-mail: bob@phoenixtoysoldier.com
www.phoenixtoysoldier.com

Model Kits
*Specializing in figures and science fic-
tion; especially figure-related model
kits*
Gordy Dutt
P.O. Box 201
Sharon Center, OH 44274-0201
330-239-1657
fax 330-239-2991

*Character, space, monster, Western,
radio, and cereal premiums and toys;
GI Joe, Captain Action, tin toys, and
windups*
Character Company
Ed Janey
P.O. Box 15699
Fernandina Beach, FL 32035-3112
e-mail: edjaney@aol.com

Non-Sport Trading Cards
*Send $1 for our 40-page catalog of non-
sport cards ca 1970 to date; dealers
send large SASE for our 10-page
wholesale and closeout list*
Mark and Val Macaluso
3603 Newark Rd.
Marion, NY 14505
315-926-4349
fax 315-926-4853

Paper Dolls
Author of books
Mary Young
Box 9244
Dayton, OH 45409
937-298-4838

*Antique McLoughlin games, Bliss and
Reed boats, toy wagons, Ten Pin sets,
cube blocks, puzzles, and Victorian
doll houses. Buy and sell; lists available upon request. Mail order and
shows only*
Mark and Linda Suozzi
P.O. Box 102
Ashfield, MA 01330
Phone or fax 413-628-3241
(9am to 5pm)
e-mail: marklyn@valinet.com
www.marklynantiques.com

Pedal Cars
Also specializing in Maytag collectibles
Nate Stoller
960 Reynolds Ave.
Ripon, CA 95366
510-481-2586
www.maytagclub.com
e-mail: multimotor@aol.com

Pez Candy Dispensers
Richard Belyski
P.O. Box 14956
Surfside Beach, SC 29587
e-mail: peznews@juno.com
www.pezcollectorsnews.com

Plastic Figures

Also Dakins, cartoon and advertising figures, and character squeeze toys
Jim Rash
135 Alder Ave.
Egg Harbor Twp., NJ 08234-9302
609-649-4125

Playsets

Also GI Joe, Star Trek and dinosaurs
Mike and Kurt Fredericks
145 Bayline Circle
Folsom, CA 95630-8077
916-985-7986

Political Toys

Michael and Polly McQuillen
McQuillen's Collectibles
P.O. Box 11141
Indianapolis, IN 46201
317-845-1721
e-mail: michael@politicalparade.com
www.politicalparade.com

Promotional Vehicles

'50s and '60s models (especially Ford); also F&F Post Cereal cars
Larry Blodget
Tech-Art Publications
Box 753
Rancho Mirage, CA 92270
760-674-9469
e-mail: BestInFords@aol.com
Author of two books: *Free Inside! Scale Model Car!* (contains history of cereal premiums and identifies the more than 200 Detroit-made scale model cars offered in cereal packages between 1949 and 1969, 70 pgs, softbound, $24+$2 postage); *The Little Ones Sell the Big Ones* (reprints of original advertisements for scale model American postwar cars, dealer's displays, coin banks, order forms, and much more, 103 pgs, softbound, $24+$2 postage)

Puzzles

Wood jigsaw type, from before 1950
Bob Armstrong
15 Monadnock Rd.
Worcester, MA 01609
508-799-0644
e-mail: RAAHNA@oldpuzzles.com
www.oldpuzzles.com

Specializing in advertising puzzles
Donald Friedman
660 W Grand Ave
Chicago, IL 60610
312-226-4741
e-mail: dfried4142@aol.com

Ramp Walkers

Specializing in ramp-walking figures, also mechanical sparklers and other plunger-type toys
Randy Welch
Raven'tiques
27965 Peach Orchard Rd.
Easton, MD 21601-8203
410-822-5441

Records

78 rpm children's records and picture disks; buys, sells, and trades records as well as makes cassette recordings for a small fee
Peter Muldavin
173 W 78th St., Apt. 5-F
New York, NY 10024
212-362-9606
kiddie78s@aol.com
members.aol.com/kiddie78s/

Russian and East European Toys

Wooden Matrioskha dolls, toys of tin, plastic, diecast metal; military theme and windups
Natural Way/DBA Russian Toy Co.
822½ Massachusetts
P.O. Box 842
Lawrence, KS 66044
785-865-5466

Specializing in Russian toys
David E. Riddle
1930 E. Indianhead Dr.
Tallahassee, FL 32301
850-877-7207
e-mail: derkoftally@webtv.net

Sand Toys

Authors of book; send $25 plus $3 for postage for a signed copy. New York residents please add 8¼% sales tax.
Carole and Richard Smyth
Carole Smyth Antiques
P.O. Box 2068
Huntington, NY 11743

Schoenhut

Keith and Donna Kaonis
P.O. Box 344
Centerport, NY 11721-0344
Daytime: 613-261-4100
Evenings: 631-351-0982
fax 631-261-9864

Specializing in slots and model racing from the '60s – '70s; especially complete race sets in original boxes
Gary Pollastro
5047 84th Ave. SE
Mercer Island, WA, 98040
206-232-3199

Snow Domes

Broad assortment from states, cities, tourist attractions, novelties, also glass domes; list available
Nancy McMichael
P.O. Box 53262
Washington DC 20009
Editor of *Snow Biz*, newsletter, see Clubs, Newsletters, and Other Publications

Soldiers

Barclay, Manoil, Grey Iron, other Dimestores, and accessories; also Syroco figures
Stan and Sally Alekna
732 Aspen Lane
Lebanon, PA 17042-9073
717-228-2361
fax 717-228-2362

Sports Bobbin' Head Dolls

Tim Hunter
1301 W. Hidden Valley Dr.
Reno, NV 89502
702-856-4357
fax 702-856-4354
e-mail: thunter885@aol.com

Star Wars

Also GI Joe, Transformers, Indiana Jones
Brian's Toys
W730 Hwy. 35; P.O. Box 95
Fountain City, WI 54629
608-687-7572; fax: 608-687-7573
www.brianstoys.com
e-mail: sales@brianstoys.com
Author of *Everything You Need To Know About Collecting Star Wars Collectibles*, 256 pgs, ISBN 1-887432-56-5 (Beckett). Watch for ads in Toy Shop; See also Clubs, Newsletters, and Other Publications

Also vehicles, model kits, GI Joes, games, ad figures, View-Master, nonsports cards, Star Trek, advertising, antiques, fine art, and much more (see their display ad for more information)
June Moon
Jim and Nancy Frugoli
1486 Miner St.
Des Planes, IL 60016
847-294-0018
e-mail: junmoonstr@aol.com
www.junemooncollectibles.com

Steiff

Also Schucos and children's things
Candelaine (Candice Gunther)
1435 Wellington Ave
Pasadena, CA 91103-2320
626-796-4568; fax 626-796-7172
e-mail: Candelaine@aol.com.

Especially Steiff, R John Wright, and other collectible bears
Cynthia's Country Store
12794 W Forest Hill Blvd, #15A
West Palm Beach, FL 33414
561-793-0554; fax 561-795-4222
e-mail: cynbears@aol.com
www.cynthiascountrystore.com

Tonka

Also candy containers and German nodders
Doug Dezso
864 Patterson Ave.
Maywood, NJ 07607
201-488-1311

Toothbrush Holders

Also Pez
Marilyn Cooper
8408 Lofland Dr.
Houston, TX 77055-4811
713-465-7773
Summer: P.O. Box 755
Douglas, MI 49406

Tops and Other Spinning Toys

Yo-yos, advertising spinners, gyroscopes, spinning games, Victorian figural tops; any unique spinning toy. Buy, sell, trade
Bruce Middleton
5 Lloyd Rd.
Newburgh, NY 12550
845-564-2556

Trains

Lionel, American Flyer, and Plasticville
Gary's Trains
186 Pine Springs Camp Road
Boswell, PA 15531
814-629-9277
e-mail: gtrains@floodcity.net

Trains of all types; holds cataloged auctions, seeking quality collections for consignment
Greg Stout, Stout Auctions
11 West Third Street
Williamsport, IN 47993-1119
765-764-6901; fax 765-764-1516
www.stoutauctions.com
e-mail: stoutauctions@hotmail.com

Toy mall; general line (toys on 2nd floor)

Bo-Jo's Antique Mall
3400 Summer Avenue
Memphis, TN 38122
901-323-2050

Transformers

Also Star Wars, GI Joe, Indiana Jones, Masters of the Universe
Brian's Toys
W730 Hwy 35; P.O. Box 95
Fountain City, WI 54629
608-687-7572
www.brianstoys.com

Specializing in Transformers, Robotech, Shogun Warriors, Gadaikins, and any other robot; want to buy these MIP — also selling
David Kolodny-Nagy
Toy Hell
P.O. Box 75271
Los Angeles, CA 90075
e-mail: toyhell@yahoo.com
www.angelfire.com/ca2/redpear
For copy of BotCon Transformer Comic Book, *Comic Smorgasbord Special*, send $3 + $1.50 for single issues, $2.50 each for 10 or more + $2

Trolls

Pat Peterson
1105 6th Ave. SE
Hampton, IA 50441

View-Master

*Also games, slot cars, Pez, lunch boxes,
  Halloween costumes, dolls, premiums, TV Guides, Mad magazines*

Ditto Enterprises
Tom Bremer
P.O. Box 49
Newark, NY 14513
Phone or fax 315-331-7688
e-mail: Dittoent@aol.com
members.aol.com/DITTOENT/
  catalogpage.index.html

Roger Nazeley
4921 Castor Ave.
Philadelphia, PA 19124
215-743-8999
fax 215-288-8030
e-mail: vmreelguy2@aol.com

Windups

*Especially German and Japan tin toys,
  Cracker Jack, toothbrush holders,
  radio premiums, pencil sharpeners,
  dexterity games and comic strip toys*

Phil Helley
Old Kilbourne Antiques
629 Indiana Ave.
Wisconsin Dells, WI 53965
608-254-8770

*Pressed steel toys, cast-iron drawn toys,
  soldiers, fire department toys, dolls,
  doll accessories, tin windups, toy cars,
  motorcycles, and airplanes*

Jacquie and Bob Henry
Antique Treasures, Toys and Dolls
Box 17
Walworth, NY 14568-0017
315-986-1424
e-mail: jhenry@rochester.rr.com
www.cyberattic.com/dealer/toysndolls

*Also friction and battery operated; fast-
  food toys, displays*

Antique Toy Information Service
Send: SASE, good photos (35mm
preferred) and $9.95 per toy to:
Scott Smiles
157 Yacht Club Way, Apt. #112
Hypoluxo, FL 33462-6048
561-582-6016
e-mail: ssmiles@msn.com

Yo-yos

Lucky J. Meisenheimer, M.D.
7300 Sand Lake Commons Blvd.
Suite 105
Orlando, FL 32819
407-352-2444
fax 407-363-2869
e-mail: LuckyJ@MSN.com
www.yo-yos.net
Author of book, *Lucky's Collectors
Guide to 20th Century Yo-Yos*. To
order call 1-877-969-6728. Cost is
$29.95 + $3.20 postage.

Clubs, Newsletters, and Other Publications

There are hundreds of clubs, newsletters, and magazines available to toy collectors today. Listed here are some devoted to specific areas of interest. You can obtain a copy of many newsletters simply by requesting a sample.

We will list other organizations and publications upon request. Please send your information to us by June 1.

Antique Advertising Association of
  America
P.O. Box 1121
Morton Grove, IL 60053
e-mail: aaa@aol.com
Publishes *Past Times* newsletter; sub-
scription $35

*Antique & Collectors Reproduction
  News*
Mark Chervenka
Antiques Coast to Coast
P.O. Box 12130
Des Moines, IA 50312-9403
515-274-5886 or (subscriptions only)
800-277-5531. Monthly newsletter
showing differences between old
originals and new reproductions; sub-
scription: $32 per year (US); $41
(Canada); $59 (all other foreign)

Antique Doll Collector Magazine
Keith and Donna Kaonis, Managing
  Publishers
P.O. Box 344
Centerport, NY 11721
Daytime: 631-261-4100
Evenings: 631-351-0982
fax 631-261-9684

Antique Trader Weekly
Nancy Crowley, Editor
P.O. Box 1050
Dubuque, IA 52004
Subscription $37 (52 issues) per year;
toll free for subscriptions only: 800-334-7165

Assoc. of Game and Puzzle Collectors
PMB 321; 197M Boston Post Road W.
Marlborough, MA 01752
e-mail: membership@agpc.org
www.agca.com

The Autograph Review Newsletter
Jeffrey Morey
305 Carlton Rd.
Syracuse, NY 13207
315-474-3516
e-mail: jmorey@twcny.rr.com
Subscription: $14.95 (six issues) per
year, 20 words free classified advertisement; Free review copy available

Barbie Bazaar (magazine)
5711 Eighth Ave.
Kenosha, WI 53140
262-658-1004
fax 262-658-0433
www.barbiebazaar.com
6 issues, bimonthly, $23.95 US;
$38.95 Canada; $58.95 Foreign

Betsy McCall Fan Club
P.O. Box 719
McCloud, CA 96057
e-mail: dreams@psln.com
Quarterly subscription rate: $16 per year

Beyond the Rainbow Collector's Exchange
P.O. Box 31672
St. Louis, MO 63131

Big Little Times
Big Little Book Collectors Club of
  America
Larry Lowery
P.O. Box 1242
Danville, CA 94526
925-837-2086

Bobbing Head Doll Newsletter and
  Price Guide
Tim Hunter
4301 W. Hidden Valley Dr.
Reno, NV 89502
e-mail: thunter885@aol.com

Bojo
P.O. Box 1403
Cranberry Township, PA 16066-0403
724-776-0621 (9 am to 9 pm EST)
e-mail: bojo@zbzoom.net
Issues fixed-price catalog containing
Beatles and rock 'n roll memorabilia

Buckeye Marble Collectors Club
Wally Westlake
209 Crocus Court
Newark, OH 43055

Candy Container Collectors of
  America
The Candy Gram newsletter
Joyce L. Doyle
P.O. Box 426
North Reading, MA 01864-0426
Send for application

Candy Container Collectors of
  America
119 N. Mars
Witchita, KS 67212
Or contact: Jeff Bradfield
90 Main St., Dayton, VA 22821

Cast Iron Toy Collectors of America
Paul McGinnis
1340 Market St.
Long Beach, CA 90805

Cat Collectors Club & Newsletter
4505 Harding Pike Apt 163
Nashville, TN 37205-2128
Write for subscription information

Cat Talk
Karen Shanks, Publisher/Editor
P.O. Box 150784
Nashville, TN 37215-0784
615-297-7403
e-mail: musiccitykitty@yahoo.com
www.CatCollectors.com

The Cereal Car Trader, F&F
Larry Blodget
Box 753
Rancho Mirage, CA 92270
760-674-9469
e-mail: BestInFords@aol.com

Collector Glass News
P.O. Box 308
Slippery Rock, PA 16057
724-946-2838 or fax 724-946-9012
e-mail: mark@glassnews.com
www.glassnews.com
6 issues per year focusing on character glasses, $15 per year

Collector's Life
The world's foremost publication for
  Steiff enthusiasts
Beth Savino
P.O. Box 798
Holland, OH 43528
419-473-9801 or
toll free 1-800-862-TOYS
fax 419-473-3947
www.toystorenet.com

*Cookie Jarrin' With Joyce: The Cookie
  Jar Newsletter*
1501 Maple Ridge Rd.
Walterboro, SC 29488

Cynthia's Country Store
Wellington Mall #15A
12794 West Forest Hill Blvd.
West Palm Beach, FL 33414
fax or phone 407-793-0554
e-mail: cynbears@aol.com
www.cynthiascountrystore.com
Specializing in Steiff new, discontinued and antique. Publishes quarterly Steiff and bear-related newsletter and limited edition yearly price guide. $15 per year for both. Call or fax for information or if you have any questions. Also specializes in pieces by R. John Wright, other bear manufacturers, toy soldiers and some old toys; many Steiff color catalogs and books available

Dionne Quint Collectors
(*Quint News*)
Jimmy Rodolfos
P.O. Box 2527
Woburn, MA 01888
781-933-2219

Doll Castle News Magazine
P.O. Box 247
Washington, NJ 07882
908-689-7042
fax 908-689-6320
Subscription: $19.95 per year or $37.95 for 2 years; issued 6 times a year, serves general interests of doll and miniature collectors as well as dollmaking

Doll News
United Federation of Doll Clubs
P.O. Box 14146
Parkville, MO 64152

Dollhouse Toys 'N Us
Bob and Geraldine Scott, authors/editors of *Dollhouse and Miniatures* newsletter
Membership includes:
5 issues per year, participation in articles for the newsletter, annual get-together, regional get-togethers, online club bulletin board and website.
For more information contact:
Geraldine@Collector.org or
BobScott@WriteMe.com
BobScott.com/Club

Dunbar's Gallery
76 Haven St.
Milford, MA 01757
508-634-8697 or
508-473-5711
e-mail: dunbars@mediaone.net.
Specializing in quality advertising, Halloween, toys, coin-operated machines; motorcycle memorabilia. Buying and selling; holds cataloged auctions

Edsel Archives Digest, Edsel
Larry Blodget
www.FinestInFords.com

Fiend Magazine
PO Box 20181
Tallahassee, FL 32316-0181
fiendmagazine.com
Runs collector's columns and tracks collectible yo-yo prices. To order call 1-888-284-8548. Subscription rate is $16/year for 4 issues.

The Fisher-Price Collector's Club
This club issues a quarterly newsletter packed with information and ads for toys. For more information write to:
Fisher-Price Club,
C/o Jeanne Kennedy
1442 N. Ogden
Mesa, AZ 85205

Game Times
Gene Autry Star Telegram
Gene Autry Museum
P.O. Box 67
Gene Autry, OK 73436

Hello Again, Old-Time Radio Show Collector
Jay A. Hickerson
P.O. Box 4321
Hamden, CT 06514
203-248-2887
fax 203-281-1322
Sample copy upon request with SASE

Hobby News
J.L.C. Publications
Box 258
Ozone Park, NY 11416

Hopalong Cassidy Fan Club
Laura Bates
6310 Friendship Dr.
New Concord, OH 43762
614-826-4850
e-mail: LBates1250@cs.com
Subscription: $20 (USA) or $25 (overseas); includes quarterly newsletter and information on annual Cambridge, Ohio, festival

Ideal Doll & Toy Collectors Club
P.O. Box 623
Lexington, MA 02420
e-mail: jizenres@aol.com

International Wizard of Oz Club Inc.
P.O. Box 95
Kinderhook, IL 62345

John's Collectible Toys and Gifts Catalog
John DeCicco
57 Bay View Dr.
Shrewsbury, MA 01545
www.Johns-Toys.com
$1.00 per issue. To order call toll free 1-800-505-Toys

Marble Mania
Marble Collectors Society of America
Stanley Block
P.O. Box 222
Trumbull, CT 06611
203-261-3223

Marl & B Catalog
Marl Davidson
10301 Braden Run
Bradenton, FL 34202
941-751-6275
fax 941-751-5463
www.marlbe.com
Subscription: US $25/year; Canada
$30/year; foreign $40/year; sample
copy US $7.95/foreign $12.95.
Released 4 times a year

McDonald's Collectors Club
PMB 200
1153 S. Lee Street
Des Plains, IL 60016-6503
www.mcdclub.com

McDonald's Collector Club
Joyce Terry Losonsky
7506 Summer Leave Ln.
Columbia, MD 21046-2455
401-381-3358
Authors of *Illustrated Collector's Guide
to McDonald's® Happy Meal® Boxes,
Premiums, & Promotions©* ($9 plus $2
postage), and *Illustrated Collector's
Guide to McDonald's Mccaps* ($3 plus
$2), both available from the authors

Florida Sunshine Chapter, McDonald's Collector's Club
Bill and Pat Poe, founders and current chapter officers (president and treasurer)
220 Dominica Circle E.
Niceville, FL 32578-4085
850-897-4163
fax 580-897-2606
e-mail: McPoes@aol.com or Patpoe toys@aol.com
Club membership: $15 for individual; $20 family/couple; $7 junior; out of state $15; International $20. Annual show in February of each year in central Florida area. *The Sunshine Express* newsletter published monthly

Model and Toy Collector Magazine
Toy Scouts, Inc.
137 Casterton Ave.
Akron, OH 44303
330-836-0668
fax 330-869-8668
e-mail: toyscouts@toyscouts.com
www.toyscouts.com

Modern Doll Collectors' Inc.
Earl Meisinger
11 S 767 Book Rd.
Naperville, IL 60564

National Fantasy Fan Club
(for Disney collectors)
Dept. AC, Box 19212
Irvine, CA 92623
714-731-4705; www.nfcc.org
Membership: $24 per year ($30 Canada, $40 all other countries) includes newsletters, free ads, chapters, conventions, etc.

Paper Collectors' Marketplace
470 Main St., P.O. Box 128
Scandinavia, WI 54977
715-467-2379
Subscription: $19.95 (12 issues) per year in USA; Canada and Mexico add $15 per year

Paper Doll News
Emma Terry
P.O. Box 807
Vivian, LA 71082
Published quarterly, $12 per year (4 issues), half year, $6; sample and illustrated list, $3

Pez Collector's News
Richard & Marianne Belyski, Editors
P.O. Box 14956
Surfside Beach, SC 29587
e-mail: peznews@juno.com
www.pezcollectorsnews.com

Plastic Figure & Playset Collector magazine
5894 Lakeview Ct. E
Onalaska, WI 54650

The Prehistoric Times
Mike and Kurt Fredericks
145 Bayline Circle
Folsom, CA 95630
916-985-7986
For collectors of dinosaur toys; 6 issues (1 yr), $28

The Premium Watch Watch Newsletter
Sharon Iranpour, Editor
24 San Rafael Dr.
Rochester, NY 14618-3702
716-381-9467
fax: 716-383-9248
e-mail: watcher1@rochester.rr.com
Only newsletter on advertising watches; $15 per year/bimonthly. Details on latest watch offers, news, free ads for subscribers. Send LSASE for sample copy.

The Prize Insider Newsletter for
Cracker Jack collectors
Theresa Richter
5469 South Dorchester
Chicago, IL 60615
773-241-6361
e-mail: waddytmr@aol.com

The Promo Car Collector
Larry Blodget
www.FinestInFords.com

The Puppet Collector's Newsletter
Steven Meltzer
1255 2nd St.
Santa Monica, CA 90401
310-656-0483
www.puppetmagic.com

Record Collectors Monthly
P.O. Box 75
Mendham, NJ 07945;
201-543-9520
e-mail: dgmennie@netscape.net
No new issues are being published; back issues are available for $2 each postpaid (discounts on bulk purchases). For further information, e-mail the publisher or send a 34-cent stamp with your written inquiry.

The Replica
Craig Purcell, Editor
Hwys 136 & 20
Dyersville, IA 52040
319-875-2000
Marketing tool that previews upcoming diecast releases and articles of interest to collectors; included are Wm Britain pewter figures, Ertl diecast automotive replicas, and John Deere kits (Pre-School)

Roy Rogers-Dale Evans Collectors Assn.
Nancy Horsley
P.O. Box 1166
Portsmouth, OH 45662

Schoenhut Collectors Club
For membership information:
Patricia J. Girbach
1003 W Huron St.
Ann Arbor, MI 48103-4217
e-mail: aawestie@provide.net

Shirley Temple Collectors Convention, Inc.
Marge Meisinger
11 S 767 Book Rd.
Naperville, IL 60564

The Silver Bullet
Terry and Kay Klepey
P.O. Box 553
Forks, WA 98331
360-327-3726
e-mail: slvrbllt@olypen.com
Subscription $20 per year, sample issue $5; back issues available; operating since 1988

Snow Biz
c/o Nancy McMichael
P.O. Box 53262
Washington, DC 20009
Newsletter published three times a year (subscription $10 per year) and collector's club, annual meeting/swap meet

Star Wars on-line newsletter
Host: Brian's Toys
groups.yahoo.com/brianstoys
To sign up for newsletter, go to sign-up field on www.brians toys.com

Still Bank Collectors Club of America
Larry Egelhoff
4175 Millersville Rd.
Indianapolis, IN 46205
317-846-7228

The Sno-Pea Trader catalog/price guide
Send $3 to:
N.F. Huber
931 Emerson St.
Thousand Oaks, CA 91362-2447
805-497-0119
Subscriptions available $12/year — refundable with purchase

Toy Car Collector Magazine
Dana Johnson, publisher
c/o Dana Johnson Enterprises
P.O. Box 1824
Bend, OR 97709-1824
541-318-7176
e-mail: mailto:toynutz@earthlink.net
www.toynutz.com

Toy Collector Club of America (for SpecCast toys)
P.O. Box 368
Dyersville, IA 52040
800-452-3303

Toy Gun Collectors of America Newsletter
Jim Buskirk, Editor and Publisher
3009 Oleander Ave.
San Marcos, CA 92069
760-599-1054
Published quarterly, covers cap guns, spring air BB guns, and other toy guns. Dues: $17 per year; SASE for information

Toy Shop
700 E State St.
Iola, WI 54990-0001

Toychest
Antique Toy Collectors of America, Inc.
2 Wall St., 13th Floor
New York, NY 10005
212-238-8803

Train Collectors Association
National Headquarters News; Directory of Information newsletters (both limited to members only)
Train Collectors Quarterly, 48-pg magazine (offered to the public as well as members)
John V. Luppino, Operations Manager
P.O. Box 248; 300 Paradise Lane
Strasburg, PA 17579-0248
717-687-8623 (business office)
fax: 717-687-0742
e-mail:toytrain@traincollectors.org;
www.traincollectors.org
Also National Toy Train Museum (open daily: May 1 – Oct 31 and weekends in April, Nov, and Dec. Museum houses Toy Train Reference Library open Tues to Sat all year); 717-687-8976

The Trick or Treat Trader
CJ Russell and the Halloween Queen Antiques
P.O. Box 499
4 Lawrence St. and Rt. 10
Winchester, NH, 03470
e-mail: halloweenqueen@cheshire.net
Subscription is $15 a year for 4 issues or $4 for a sample

The TV Collector
Diane L. Albert
6704 Fruit Flower Ave.
Las Vegas, NV 89130
702-369-4106
Send $4 for sample copy

View-Master Reel Collector
Roger Nazeley
4921 Castor Ave.
Philadelphia, PA 19124; 215-743-8999
e-mail: vmreelguy2@ad.com

Western & Serials Club
527 S. Front St.
Mankato, MN 56001-3718
Phone/fax 507-344-0255
e-mail: keitzer@mctcnet.net
www.angelfire.com/biz2/norman kietzerpubs/

The Working Class Hero (Beatles newsletter)
3311 Niagara St.
Pittsburgh, PA 15213-4223
Published 3 times per year; send SASE for information

Yo-Yo Times
P.O. Box 1519-SCT
Herndon, VA 22070

DON'T MISS YOUR CHANCE
TO REACH THOUSANDS OF TOY COLLECTORS

TO RESERVE YOUR AD SPACE FOR THE NEXT EDITION
PLEASE CONTACT HUXFORD ENTERPRISES *IMMEDIATELY*

RATES
(Ad Size)

FULL PAGE	**7½" wide x 9¾" tall – $750.00**
HALF PAGE	**7½" wide x 4½" tall – $400.00**
QUARTER PAGE	**3½" wide x 4½" tall – $250.00**
EIGHTH PAGE	**3½" wide x 2¼" tall – $150.00**
(or business card)	

*NOTE: The above rates are for **camera ready copy only** – Add $50.00 if we are to compose your ad. These prices are net – no agency discounts allowed. Payment in full must accompany your ad copy.*

All advertising accepted under the following conditions:

1. *The Publisher will furnish advertising space in sizes and at rates as set forth in this rate sheet upon full payment in advance of its annual advertising deadline as set forth herein.*

2. Submission of Copy. *The publisher shall have the right to omit any advertisement when the space allotted to Advertiser in a particular issue has been filled. In addition, the Publisher reserves the right to limit the amount of space the Advertiser may use in any one edition.*

3. Content and Design. *Publisher reserves the right to censor, reject, alter, or refuse any advertising copy at its sole discretion or disapprove any advertising copy in accordance with any rule the Publisher may now have, or may adopt in the future, concerning the acceptance of advertising matter, but no intentional change in advertising copy will be made without the prior consent of the Advertiser.*

4. Publisher's Liability for Deletions. *Publisher's liability for failure of the Publisher to insert any advertisement in their books shall be limited to a refund of the consideration paid for the insertion of the advertisement or, at Advertiser's option, to such deleted advertisement being inserted in the next edition.*

5. Copyright and Trademark Permission. *Any Advertiser using copyrighted material or trademarks or trade names of others in its advertising copy shall obtain the prior written permission of the owners thereof which must be submitted to the Publisher with the advertising copy. Where this has not been done, advertising will not be accepted.*

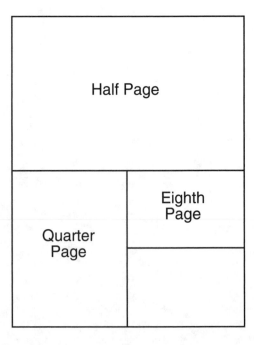

Make checks payable to:

**HUXFORD ENTERPRISES
1202 7th St.
Covington, IN 47932**

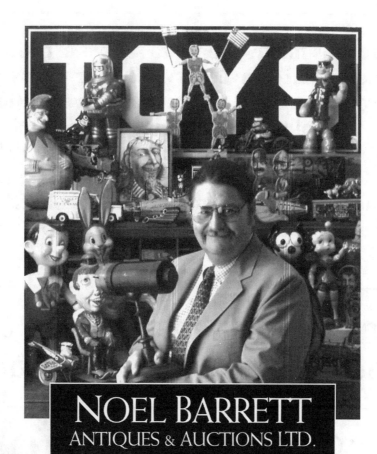

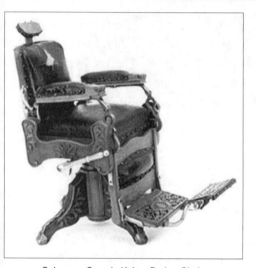

Index to Advertisers

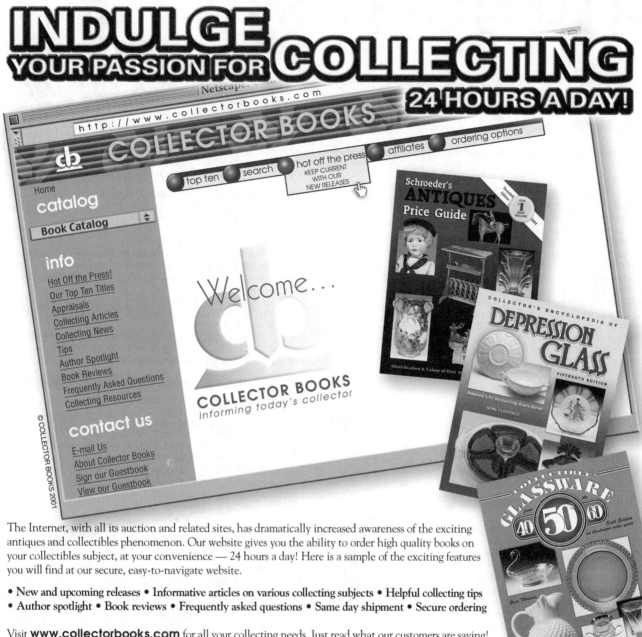

COLLECTOR BOOKS

Informing Today's Collector

For over two decades we have been keeping collectors informed on trends and values in all fields of antiques and collectibles.

DOLLS, FIGURES & TEDDY BEARS

4707	A Decade of **Barbie Dolls** & Collectibles, 1981–1991, Summers	$19.95
4631	**Barbie Doll** Boom, 1986–1995, Augustyniak	$18.95
2079	**Barbie Doll** Fashion, Volume I, Eames	$24.95
4846	**Barbie Doll** Fashion, Volume II, Eames	$24.95
3957	**Barbie** Exclusives, Rana	$18.95
4632	**Barbie** Exclusives, Book II, Rana	$18.95
5672	The **Barbie Doll** Years, 4th Ed., Olds	$19.95
3810	**Chatty Cathy** Dolls, Lewis	$15.95
5352	Collector's Ency. of **Barbie** Doll Exclusives & More, 2nd Ed.,Augustyniak	$24.95
2211	Collector's Encyclopedia of **Madame Alexander** Dolls, Smith	$24.95
4863	Collector's Encyclopedia of **Vogue Dolls**, Izen/Stover	$29.95
5821	**Doll Values**, Antique to Modern, 5th Ed., Moyer	$12.95
5829	**Madame Alexander** Collector's Dolls Price Guide #26, Crowsey	$12.95
5833	**Modern Collectible Dolls**, Volume V, Moyer	$24.95
5689	**Nippon Dolls** & Playthings, Van Patten/Lau	$29.95
5365	**Peanuts Collectibles**, Podley/Bang	$24.95
5253	Story of **Barbie**, 2nd Ed., Westenhouser	$24.95
5277	**Talking Toys** of the 20th Century, Lewis	$15.95
1513	**Teddy Bears & Steiff** Animals, Mandel	$9.95
1817	**Teddy Bears & Steiff** Animals, 2nd Series, Mandel	$19.95
2084	**Teddy Bears, Annalee's & Steiff** Animals, 3rd Series, Mandel	$19.95
5371	**Teddy Bear** Treasury, Yenke	$19.95
1808	Wonder of **Barbie**, Manos	$9.95
1430	World of **Barbie** Dolls, Manos	$9.95
4880	World of **Raggedy Ann** Collectibles, Avery	$24.95

TOYS, MARBLES & CHRISTMAS COLLECTIBLES

2333	Antique & Collectible **Marbles**, 3rd Ed., Grist	$9.95
5353	**Breyer Animal** Collector's Guide, 2nd Ed., Browell	$19.95
4976	**Christmas Ornaments**, Lights & Decorations, Johnson	$24.95
4737	**Christmas Ornaments**, Lights & Decorations, Vol. II, Johnson	$24.95
4739	**Christmas Ornaments**, Lights & Decorations, Vol. III, Johnson	$24.95
4559	Collectible **Action Figures**, 2nd Ed., Manos	$17.95
2338	Collector's Encyclopedia of **Disneyana**, Longest, Stern	$24.95
5038	Collector's Guide to **Diecast Toys** & Scale Models, 2nd Ed., Johnson	$19.95
4651	Collector's Guide to **Tinker Toys**, Strange	$18.95
4566	Collector's Guide to **Tootsietoys**, 2nd Ed., Richter	$19.95
5169	Collector's Guide to **TV Toys** & Memorabilia, 2nd Ed., Davis/Morgan	$24.95
5360	**Fisher-Price Toys**, Cassity	$19.95
4720	The Golden Age of **Automotive Toys**, 1925–1941, Hutchison/Johnson	$24.95
5593	Grist's Big Book of **Marbles**, 2nd Ed.	$24.95
3970	Grist's Machine-Made & Contemporary **Marbles**, 2nd Ed.	$9.95
5267	**Matchbox Toys**, 1947 to 1998, 3rd Ed., Johnson	$19.95
5830	**McDonald's** Collectibles, 2nd Edition, Henriques/DuVall	$24.95
5673	Modern **Candy Containers** & Novelties, Brush/Miller	$19.95
1540	Modern **Toys** 1930–1980, Baker	$19.95
3888	**Motorcycle Toys**, Antique & Contemporary, Gentry/Downs	$18.95
5693	**Schroeder's Collectible Toys**, Antique to Modern Price Guide, 7th Ed.	$17.95

FURNITURE

1457	American **Oak** Furniture, McNerney	$9.95
3716	American **Oak** Furniture, Book II, McNerney	$12.95
1118	Antique **Oak** Furniture, Hill	$7.95
2271	Collector's Encyclopedia of **American** Furniture, Vol. II, Swedberg	$24.95
3720	Collector's Encyclopedia of **American** Furniture, Vol. III, Swedberg	$24.95
5359	Early **American** Furniture, Obbard	$12.95
1755	Furniture of the **Depression Era**, Swedberg	$19.95
3906	**Heywood-Wakefield** Modern Furniture, Rouland	$18.95
1885	**Victorian** Furniture, Our American Heritage, McNerney	$9.95
3829	**Victorian** Furniture, Our American Heritage, Book II, McNerney	$9.95

JEWELRY, HATPINS, WATCHES & PURSES

1712	Antique & Collectible **Thimbles** & Accessories, Mathis	$19.9
1748	Antique **Purses**, Revised Second Ed., Holiner	$19.9
1278	Art Nouveau & Art Deco **Jewelry**, Baker	$9.9
4850	Collectible **Costume Jewelry**, Simonds	$24.9
5675	Collectible **Silver Jewelry**, Rezazadeh	$24.9
3722	Collector's Ency. of **Compacts**, Carryalls & Face Powder Boxes, Mueller	$24.9
4940	**Costume Jewelry**, A Practical Handbook & Value Guide, Rezazadeh	$24.9
1716	Fifty Years of Collectible **Fashion Jewelry**, 1925–1975, Baker	$19.9
1424	**Hatpins** & Hatpin Holders, Baker	$9.9
5695	**Ladies' Vintage Accessories**, Bruton	$24.9
1181	100 Years of Collectible **Jewelry**, 1850–1950, Baker	$9.9
4729	**Sewing Tools** & Trinkets, Thompson	$24.9
5620	Unsigned Beauties of **Costume Jewelry**, Brown	$24.9
4878	Vintage & Contemporary **Purse Accessories**, Gerson	$24.9
5696	Vintage & Vogue Ladies' **Compacts**, 2nd Edition, Gerson	$29.9

INDIANS, GUNS, KNIVES, TOOLS, PRIMITIVES

1868	Antique **Tools**, Our American Heritage, McNerney	$9.9
5616	Big Book of **Pocket Knives**, Stewart	$19.9
4943	Field Guide to Flint **Arrowheads** & Knives of the North American Indian	$9.9
2279	**Indian Artifacts** of the Midwest, Book I, Hothem	$14.9
3885	**Indian Artifacts** of the Midwest, Book II, Hothem	$16.9
4870	**Indian Artifacts** of the Midwest, Book III, Hothem	$18.9
5685	**Indian Artifacts** of the Midwest, Book IV, Hothem	$19.9
5687	**Modern Guns**, Identification & Values, 13th Ed., Quertermous	$14.9
2164	**Primitives**, Our American Heritage, McNerney	$9.9
1759	**Primitives**, Our American Heritage, 2nd Series, McNerney	$14.9
4730	Standard **Knife** Collector's Guide, 3rd Ed., Ritchie & Stewart	$12.9

PAPER COLLECTIBLES & BOOKS

4633	**Big Little Books**, Jacobs	$18.9
4710	Collector's Guide to **Children's Books**, 1850 to 1950, Volume I, Jones	$18.9
5153	Collector's Guide to **Children's Books**, 1850 to 1950, Volume II, Jones	$19.9
5596	Collector's Guide to **Children's Books**, 1950 to 1975, Volume III, Jones	$19.9
1441	Collector's Guide to **Post Cards**, Wood	$9.9
2081	Guide to Collecting **Cookbooks**, Allen	$14.9
5825	Huxford's **Old Book** Value Guide, 13th Ed.	$19.9
2080	Price Guide to **Cookbooks** & Recipe Leaflets, Dickinson	$9.9
3973	**Sheet Music** Reference & Price Guide, 2nd Ed., Pafik & Guiheen	$19.9
4654	**Victorian Trade Cards**, Historical Reference & Value Guide, Cheadle	$19.9
4733	**Whitman Juvenile Books**, Brown	$17.9

GLASSWARE

5602	Anchor Hocking's **Fire-King** & More, 2nd Ed.	$24.9
4561	Collectible **Drinking Glasses**, Chase & Kelly	$17.9
5823	Collectible **Glass Shoes**, 2nd Edition, Wheatley	$24.9
5357	Coll. **Glassware** from the 40s, 50s & 60s, 5th Ed., Florence	$19.9
1810	Collector's Encyclopedia of **American Art Glass**, Shuman	$29.9
5358	Collector's Encyclopedia of **Depression Glass**, 14th Ed., Florence	$19.9
1961	Collector's Encyclopedia of **Fry Glassware**, Fry Glass Society	$24.9
1664	Collector's Encyclopedia of **Heisey Glass**, 1925–1938, Bredehoft	$24.9
3905	Collector's Encyclopedia of **Milk Glass**, Newbound	$24.9
4936	Collector's Guide to **Candy Containers**, Dezso/Poirier	$19.9
4564	**Crackle Glass**, Weitman	$19.9
4941	**Crackle Glass**, Book II, Weitman	$19.9
4714	**Czechoslovakian Glass** and Collectibles, Book II, Barta/Rose	$16.9
5528	Early American **Pattern Glass**, Metz	$17.9
5682	**Elegant Glassware** of the Depression Era, 9th Ed., Florence	$19.9
5614	Field Guide to **Pattern Glass**, McCain	$17.9
3981	Evers' Standard **Cut Glass** Value Guide	$12.9
4659	**Fenton** Art Glass, 1907–1939, Whitmyer	$24.9
5615	Florence's **Glassware Pattern Identification** Guide, Vol. II	$19.9

COLLECTOR BOOKS
Informing Today's Collector

719	**Fostoria**, Etched, Carved & Cut Designs, Vol. II, Kerr	$24.95
883	**Fostoria Stemware**, The Crystal for America, Long/Seate	$24.95
261	**Fostoria Tableware**, 1924 – 1943, Long/Seate	$24.95
361	**Fostoria Tableware**, 1944 – 1986, Long/Seate	$24.95
604	**Fostoria**, Useful & Ornamental, Long/Seate	$29.95
644	**Imperial Carnival Glass**, Burns	$18.95
827	**Kitchen Glassware** of the Depression Years, 6th Ed., Florence	$24.95
600	Much More Early American **Pattern Glass**, Metz	$17.95
690	Pocket Guide to **Depression Glass**, 12th Ed., Florence	$9.95
594	Standard Encyclopedia of **Carnival Glass**, 7th Ed., Edwards/Carwile	$29.95
595	Standard **Carnival Glass** Price Guide, 12th Ed., Edwards/Carwile	$9.95
272	Standard Encyclopedia of **Opalescent Glass**, 3rd Ed., Edwards/Carwile	$24.95
617	Standard Encyclopedia of **Pressed Glass**, 2nd Ed., Edwards/Carwile	$29.95
731	**Stemware Identification**, Featuring Cordials with Values, Florence	$24.95
732	**Very Rare Glassware** of the Depression Years, 5th Series, Florence	$24.95
656	**Westmoreland Glass**, Wilson	$24.95

POTTERY

927	**ABC Plates & Mugs**, Lindsay	$24.95
929	**American Art Pottery**, Sigafoose	$24.95
630	**American Limoges**, Limoges	$24.95
312	**Blue & White Stoneware**, McNerney	$9.95
958	So. Potteries **Blue Ridge Dinnerware**, 3rd Ed., Newbound	$14.95
959	**Blue Willow**, 2nd Ed., Gaston	$14.95
851	Collectible **Cups & Saucers**, Harran	$18.95
373	Collector's Encyclopedia of **American Dinnerware**, Cunningham	$24.95
931	Collector's Encyclopedia of **Bauer Pottery**, Chipman	$24.95
932	Collector's Encyclopedia of **Blue Ridge Dinnerware**, Vol. II, Newbound	$24.95
658	Collector's Encyclopedia of **Brush-McCoy Pottery**, Huxford	$24.95
034	Collector's Encyclopedia of **California Pottery**, 2nd Ed., Chipman	$24.95
133	Collector's Encyclopedia of **Cookie Jars**, Roerig	$24.95
723	Collector's Encyclopedia of **Cookie Jars**, Book II, Roerig	$24.95
939	Collector's Encyclopedia of **Cookie Jars**, Book III, Roerig	$24.95
748	Collector's Encyclopedia of **Fiesta**, 9th Ed., Huxford	$24.95
718	Collector's Encyclopedia of **Figural Planters & Vases**, Newbound	$19.95
961	Collector's Encyclopedia of **Early Noritake**, Alden	$24.95
439	Collector's Encyclopedia of **Flow Blue China**, Gaston	$19.95
312	Collector's Encyclopedia of **Flow Blue China**, 2nd Ed., Gaston	$24.95
431	Collector's Encyclopedia of **Homer Laughlin China**, Jasper	$24.95
276	Collector's Encyclopedia of **Hull Pottery**, Roberts	$19.95
962	Collector's Encyclopedia of **Lefton China**, DeLozier	$19.95
855	Collector's Encyclopedia of **Lefton China**, Book II, DeLozier	$19.95
609	Collector's Encyclopedia of **Limoges Porcelain**, 3rd Ed., Gaston	$29.95
334	Collector's Encyclopedia of **Majolica Pottery**, Katz-Marks	$19.95
358	Collector's Encyclopedia of **McCoy Pottery**, Huxford	$19.95
677	Collector's Encyclopedia of **Niloak**, 2nd Edition, Gifford	$29.95
837	Collector's Encyclopedia of **Nippon Porcelain**, Van Patten	$24.95
665	Collector's Ency. of **Nippon Porcelain**, 3rd Series, Van Patten	$24.95
712	Collector's Ency. of **Nippon Porcelain**, 4th Series, Van Patten	$24.95
053	Collector's Ency. of **Nippon Porcelain**, 5th Series, Van Patten	$24.95
678	Collector's Ency. of **Nippon Porcelain**, 6th Series, Van Patten	$29.95
447	Collector's Encyclopedia of **Noritake**, Van Patten	$19.95
038	Collector's Encyclopedia of **Occupied Japan**, 2nd Series, Florence	$14.95
951	Collector's Encyclopedia of **Old Ivory China**, Hillman	$24.95
564	Collector's Encyclopedia of **Pickard China**, Reed	$29.95
877	Collector's Encyclopedia of **R.S. Prussia**, 4th Series, Gaston	$24.95
679	Collector's Encyclopedia of **Red Wing Art Pottery**, Dollen	$24.95
618	Collector's Encyclopedia of **Rosemeade Pottery**, Dommel	$24.95
841	Collector's Encyclopedia of **Roseville Pottery**, Revised, Huxford/Nickel	$24.95
842	Collector's Encyclopedia of **Roseville Pottery**, 2nd Series, Huxford/Nickel	$24.95
713	Collector's Encyclopedia of **Salt Glaze Stoneware**, Taylor/Lowrance	$24.95
314	Collector's Encyclopedia of **Van Briggle Art Pottery**, Sasicki	$24.95
563	Collector's Encyclopedia of **Wall Pockets**, Newbound	$19.95
11	Collector's Encyclopedia of **Weller Pottery**, Huxford	$29.95
680	Collector's Guide to **Feather Edge Ware**, McAllister	$19.95
876	Collector's Guide to **Lu-Ray Pastels**, Meehan	$18.95

3814	Collector's Guide to **Made in Japan Ceramics**, White	$18.95
4646	Collector's Guide to **Made in Japan Ceramics**, Book II, White	$18.95
2339	Collector's Guide to **Shawnee Pottery**, Vanderbilt	$19.95
1425	**Cookie Jars**, Westfall	$9.95
3440	**Cookie Jars**, Book II, Westfall	$19.95
4924	Figural & Novelty **Salt & Pepper Shakers**, 2nd Series, Davern	$24.95
2379	Lehner's Ency. of **U.S. Marks** on Pottery, Porcelain & China	$24.95
4722	**McCoy Pottery**, Collector's Reference & Value Guide, Hanson/Nissen	$19.95
5691	**Post86 Fiesta**, Identification & Value Guide, Racheter	$19.95
1670	**Red Wing Collectibles**, DePasquale	$9.95
1440	**Red Wing Stoneware**, DePasquale	$9.95
1632	**Salt & Pepper Shakers**, Guarnaccia	$9.95
5091	**Salt & Pepper Shakers** II, Guarnaccia	$18.95
3443	**Salt & Pepper Shakers** IV, Guarnaccia	$18.95
3738	**Shawnee Pottery**, Mangus	$24.95
4629	Turn of the Century **American Dinnerware**, 1880s–1920s, Jasper	$24.95
3327	**Watt Pottery** – Identification & Value Guide, Morris	$19.95

OTHER COLLECTIBLES

5838	Advertising **Thermometers**, Merritt	$16.95
4704	Antique & Collectible **Buttons**, Wisniewski	$19.95
2269	Antique **Brass & Copper** Collectibles, Gaston	$16.95
1880	Antique **Iron**, McNerney	$9.95
3872	Antique **Tins**, Dodge	$24.95
4845	Antique **Typewriters & Office Collectibles**, Rehr	$19.95
5607	Antiquing and Collecting on the **Internet**, Parry	$12.95
1128	**Bottle** Pricing Guide, 3rd Ed., Cleveland	$7.95
3718	Collectible **Aluminum**, Grist	$16.95
4560	Collectible **Cats**, An Identification & Value Guide, Book II, Fyke	$19.95
5060	Collectible **Souvenir Spoons**, Bednersh	$19.95
5676	Collectible **Souvenir Spoons**, Book II, Bednersh	$29.95
5666	Collector's Encyclopedia of **Granite Ware**, Book 2, Greguire	$29.95
5836	Collector's Guide to **Antique Radios**, 5th Ed., Bunis	$19.95
5608	Collector's Gde. to Buying, Selling & Trading on the **Internet**, 2nd Ed., Hix	$12.95
4637	Collector's Guide to **Cigarette Lighters**, Book II, Flanagan	$17.95
3966	Collector's Guide to **Inkwells**, Identification & Values, Badders	$18.95
4947	Collector's Guide to **Inkwells**, Book II, Badders	$19.95
5681	Collector's Guide to **Lunchboxes**, White	$19.95
5621	Collector's Guide to **Online Auctions**, Hix	$12.95
4862	Collector's Guide to **Toasters** & Accessories, Greguire	$19.95
4652	Collector's Guide to **Transistor Radios**, 2nd Ed., Bunis	$16.95
4864	Collector's Guide to **Wallace Nutting Pictures**, Ivankovich	$18.95
1629	**Doorstops**, Identification & Values, Bertoia	$9.95
5683	**Fishing Lure** Collectibles, 2nd Ed., Murphy/Edmisten	$29.95
5259	**Flea Market Trader**, 12th Ed., Huxford	$9.95
4945	**G-Men and FBI Toys** and Collectibles, Whitworth	$18.95
5605	**Garage Sale & Flea Market Annual**, 8th Ed.	$19.95
3819	**General Store** Collectibles, Wilson	$24.95
5159	Huxford's Collectible **Advertising**, 4th Ed.	$24.95
2216	**Kitchen Antiques**, 1790–1940, McNerney	$14.95
5686	**Lighting Fixtures** of the Depression Era, Book I, Thomas	$24.95
4950	The **Lone Ranger**, Collector's Reference & Value Guide, Felbinger	$18.95
2026	**Railroad** Collectibles, 4th Ed., Baker	$14.95
5619	**Roy Rogers and Dale Evans** Toys & Memorabilia, Coyle	$24.95
5692	**Schroeder's Antiques Price Guide**, 19th Ed., Huxford	$14.95
5007	**Silverplated Flatware**, Revised 4th Edition, Hagan	$18.95
5694	Summers' Guide to **Coca-Cola**, 3rd Ed.	$24.95
5356	Summers' Pocket Guide to **Coca-Cola**, 2nd Ed.	$9.95
3892	**Toy & Miniature Sewing Machines**, Thomas	$18.95
4876	**Toy & Miniature Sewing Machines**, Book II, Thomas	$24.95
5144	Value Guide to **Advertising Memorabilia**, 2nd Ed., Summers	$19.95
3977	Value Guide to **Gas Station Memorabilia**, Summers & Priddy	$24.95
4877	Vintage **Bar Ware**, Visakay	$24.95
4935	The **W.F. Cody Buffalo Bill** Collector's Guide with Values	$24.95
5281	**Wanted to Buy**, 7th Edition	$9.95

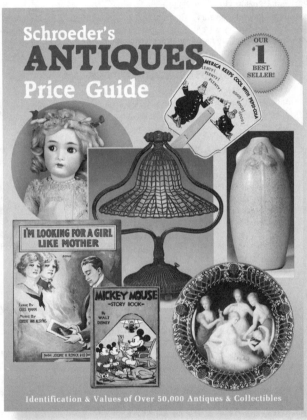